# *The Blue*

# Washington, D.C.

Candyce H. Stapen, Ph.D.

BLUE GUIDE

A&C Black • London
W. W. Norton • New York

First edition 2000

Published by A & C Black (Publishers) Limited
35 Bedford Row, London WC1R 4JH

A CIP catalogue record of this book is available from the British Library.

ISBN 0-7136-3875-3

Published in the United States of America by
W. W. Norton & Company, Inc.
500 Fifth Avenue, New York, NY 10110

Printed in the United States of America

The text and display type of this book are composed in Photina
Composition by Allentown Digital Services Division of R.R. Donnelley & Sons Company.
Manufacturing by the Haddon Craftsmen, Inc.

The author and the publishers have done their best to ensure the accuracy of all the information in *Washington, D.C.*, however, they can accept no responsibility for any loss, injury, or inconvenience sustained by any traveler as a result of information or advice contained in the guide.

Library of Congress Cataloging-in-Publication Data

Stapen, Candyce H.
     Washington, D.C. / Candyce H. Stapen.
         p. cm. — (Blue guide)
     Includes index.
     **ISBN 0-393-31997-0 (pbk.)**
     1. Washington (D.C.)—Tours. 2. Washington Region—Tours. 3. Washington
(D.C.)—Guidebooks. 4. Washington Region—Guidebooks. I. Title. II. Series.
     F192.3 .S73 2000
     917.5304'41—dc21                                                   99-047973

W. W. Norton & Company, Inc., 500 Fifth Avenue, New York, N.Y. 10110
www.wwnorton.com

W. W. Norton & Company Ltd., 10 Coptic Street, London WC1A 1PU

1 2 3 4 5 6 7 8 9 0

# *Contents*

**Introduction**  11

**Practical Information**

**Background Information**

## Washington, D.C.: The Guide

# Acknowledgments

I want to acknowledge those research assistants and writers who have helped me with this project. I thank Karen Jensen, Maureen Rehg, Jennifer Pokorny, and Neil Weston. Special praise goes to Robert Moll for writing several walks. Diane Ney has my sincerest appreciation for sticking with me through this long project. Her writing and research have contributed much to this book. The Historical Society of Washington, D.C., has served as a valuable resource. I am grateful for the assistance of Gail Redmann, Library Director, and Barbara Franco, Executive Director. I appreciate the hard work of Tabitha Griffin, my editor, and of Don Rifkin, my copy editor.

# Acknowledgments

# Dedication

To Iva Ashner (1943–1998), a wonderful editor, whose encouragement and patience were critical to this project. I will always appreciate the faith she had in me.

# Introduction

Washington is one of the few capitals of the world that wasn't a city first, and that has made all the difference. Built to embody the new country's aspirations, Washington is a graceful city, combining grand, neoclassical government buildings with monuments, memorials, museums, the National Mall, and many neighborhoods.

Our capital is currently undergoing an extraordinary resurgence, heralded by the art galleries along 7th St, the MCI Sports Center, a new convention center, and the proposed Corcoran Gallery of Art addition to be designed by Frank Gehry. But downtown revitalization is only part of D.C.'s renaissance. Its residential areas are experiencing a revival, too—not the usual gentrification, where those who have less are moved out to make way for those who have more, but a true grass-roots movement to bring back the city's sense of community.

I feel a part of this city, having lived here for more than 20 years. Each evening near dusk I walk my dogs past the pre–World War II brick colonials of my northwest D.C. neighborhood. When I turn the corner at the top of the hill, I know I'll see the gray, thick trunk and sprawling branches of what is reputed to be the oldest oak, at nearly 250 years, in the District of Columbia.

At this transitional hour, when the day has not quite shifted from car pools to houses with lit kitchens and rows of kids in upstairs bedrooms puzzling out their fractions, I keep my eyes on that tree. I like to picture George Washington astride his horse here. I envision the Father of Our Country as a young man, gangly like the high school seniors who walk by this corner on their way home from basketball practice. The tree is a stripling feathered with buds, and the land is green and seems full of promise.

Did George ever ride here? No one can be certain. But as this is among the city's highest hills, and George was an ambitious surveyor who assisted in 1749 in laying out Alexandria, Virginia, just across the river, it is most likely that he came to what is now upper-northwest D.C. to scan the possibilities of an area he may never then have imagined to bear his name.

This connection with history and legend is what I like most about living in D.C. To the throngs of visitors, the District of Columbia, with its Federal landscape of Capitol, White House, and Supreme Court, is a place representative of our nation's precepts. But for its 554,000 residents, the District takes shape as a series of neighborhoods whose sites help pin faces to the legendary personalities, whose buildings keep our country's art and artifacts handy, and whose important symbols comprise the background for our daily chores.

In the District even the unassuming brownstones tell a tale. On my way to my local research facility, for example, the Library of Congress—itself a structure of grand proportions and mission—I pass the Sewall-Belmont House, a home that in 1913 became the headquarters for the National Woman's Party. Here Alice Paul and other leaders created strategies for suffrage, planning marches that resulted in their imprisonment in the Occoquan workhouse in nearby Lorton, Virginia. In Chinatown, while waiting for some good take-out food, I stand near a building whose plaque announces it as the former Suratt Boarding House, where

John Wilkes Booth and his co-conspirators plotted Abraham Lincoln's assassination. In Georgetown, just downstairs from where I get my hair cut, Pierre L'Enfant, more than 200 years ago, met with the Republic's leaders to dream the new capital's grand design.

For me, as for many Washingtonians, the city's history is part of the excitement of living here. Sometimes on my evening walks I imagine George Washington, an aged statesman retired to Mount Vernon, in his nearby riverfront home, sipping his after-dinner port in pure delight as he thinks about the proud, new capital and the country's future.

Most of the sites in this book can be seen in the neighborhood walks. Other sites, equally interesting but not practical to reach on foot, are presented in Walks 33, 34, and 35.

The designation *DL* means a building is protected as a designated landmark from destruction or major alteration. The designation *M* on a map indicates a Metro subway stop. Area codes are given for all non-District telephone numbers. The area code for the District of Columbia is 202. URL addresses of Web sites sometimes extend over two lines of text but should be read as a single unit.

# Practical Information

## Getting to Washington, D.C.

### By air

Washington, D.C. is served by three major airports. Two of the airports, **Ronald Reagan Washington National Airport** and **Dulles International Airport** (Web: www.metwashairports.com), are located in suburban Virginia.

**Ronald Reagan Washington National Airport (DCA)** is the closest to downtown. The drive is approximately 4.5 miles or 15 minutes in nonrush hour traffic. The centerpiece of the redevelopment plan is the new 35-gate terminal building that opened in July 1997. The new terminal is connected by moving sidewalks with the airport's Metro station and a new parking garage. Over the next four to five years, Terminal A (built in 1941) is going to be restored to its 1941 look. Also, an underground walkway is going to be built from Terminal A to the parking facilities. The airlines serving Ronald Reagan Washington National Airport include: **Domestic:** American, America West, Air Canada, Continental, Delta, Delta Shuttle, Midway, Midwest Express, Northwest, TWA, United, USAirways, USAirways Shuttle. **International:** None. **Commuter:** American Eagle, TWA Express, USAirways Express.

A **taxi** ride from Ronald Reagan Washington National Airport to downtown—whether by D.C., Maryland, or Virginia cabs—should cost approximately $12. D.C. cabs do not have meters. Instead, fares are based on a mileage system that uses zones. From Reagan National Airport to the Maryland suburbs, a taxi ride should be about $20; from the airport to the Virginia suburbs, the fare should be approximately $15. A zone map should be posted in the cab, and you can obtain one from the dispatcher. Ask the cab dispatcher for a fare estimate before you enter the cab.

**SuperShuttle** operates door-to-door **van** service from National Airport; $8 per person, children under 3 are free. For information, ☎ 584-2222 or (800) 258-3826.

There is a **Metro subway** station at the airport, which is served by both the Blue and Yellow Lines to and from downtown. Fares to downtown Washington begin at $1.55 during rush hour and $1.10 during nonrush hour. (See "Subway" section below.) For information, ☎ 637-7000 or 638-3780 (TTY).

**Metrobus** provides service to the airport from those suburban areas not served by Metrorail subway. Information: ☎ 637-7000 or 638-3780.

**Washington Dulles International Airport (IAD)** is approximately 26 miles from downtown Washington, D.C. Without rush hour traffic, the drive is about 40 minutes. In rush hour, the drive can be significantly longer. The airport opened a $34.5 million international arrivals building in early 1991. The main terminal doubled in size in 1996, and in 1998 the first permanent midfield concourse (Concourse C) opened. The airlines serving Washington Dulles International Airport include: **Domestic:** AirTran Airways, American, America West, ComAir, Continental, Delta, MetroJet, Northwest, Sun Country, TWA, United, USAirways. **International:** Aeroflot, Air France Canada, All Nippon Airways, Austrian,

British Airways, Ethiopian, Korean Air, Lufthansa, Northwest/KLM Royal Dutch, Saudi Arabian, Spanair, TACA, United, Virgin Atlantic. **Commuter:** American Eagle, Colgan Air, Continental Express, United Express, US Airways Express.

For taxi service, **Washington Flyer** cabs travel downtown for a fare of approximately $45. For information, ☎ (888) WASH-FLY or (703) 685-1400. SuperShuttle also operates from Dulles; ☎ (800) BLUE-VAN; Web: www.supershuttle.com. Washington Flyer vans operate every half hour (20 and 50 minutes past the hour) from the airport and the **Convention Center** downtown at 11th and New York Ave N.W. Fare: $16; $26 round-trip. Children under 6 are free. Information: ☎ (888) WASH-FLY (927-4359) or (703) 685-1400.

Washington Flyer also operates direct bus service every half hour to the West Falls Church Metro station (Orange Line) in Falls Church, Virginia. Fare: $8; $14 round-trip. Information: ☎ (703) 685-1400 or (202) 637-7000.

There is no city bus service available to or from IAD.

**Baltimore/Washington International Airport (BWI)** (Web: www.bwiairport.com) is approximately 28 miles from downtown Washington, D.C., or about a 50-minute drive in nonrush hour traffic. Served by all major airlines with 600 flights a day, BWI completed renovations to its main terminal and added more parking areas in 1990. In Dec 1997, the International Pier opened, doubling BWI's international capacity. The airlines servicing BWI are: **Domestic:** American, America West, Continental, Delta, Frontier, MetroJet, Northwest, ProAir, Southwest, TWA, USAirways. **International:** Air Aruba, Air Jamaica, Air Ontario, British Airways, El Al Israel Airlines, Icelandair, LB Ltd, USAirways, World, American Transit, ATI, North American. **Commuter:** Atlantic Coast, Continental Express, Eagle, TransStates, USAirways Express.

Maryland taxis charge about $60 to take you from BWI to downtown D.C.

SuperShuttle operates door-to-door van service from BWI to Prince George's County, Montgomery County, Northern Virginia, and downtown Washington. For information, ☎ 584-2222 or (800) 258-3826.

There is no subway or city bus service available to D.C. BWI is served by an **Amtrak** train station used daily by Amtrak and **Maryland Rail Commuter (MARC)** trains from Washington's Union Station. Amtrak information ☎ (800) 872-7245; MARC ☎ (800) 325-7245.

**For ground transportation between National and Dulles Airports,** the 25-mile drive takes about 45 minutes. Virginia taxis charge approximately $45. Washington Flyer vans operate hourly nonstop. Fare is $16; $26 round-trip. Children under 6 are free. Information: ☎ (888) WASH-FLY (927-4359) or (703) 685-1400.

Metro's Blue Line operates between National Airport and the Pentagon; Metro's Orange Line operates between the Pentagon and West Falls Church station. The Washington Flyer bus operates between West Falls Church Metro station and Dulles Airport.

For complete information on airport bus service to and from National and Dulles Airports, ☎ (703) 685-1400; for service to and from BWI, call The Airport Connection ☎ (301) 352-2400 or (800) 284-6066. Door-to-door service is available between 4 A.M. and 10 P.M.; $35 for one person, $42 total for two, $47 for three.

### By rail

Many trains arrive daily at **Union Station,** 50 Massachusetts Ave N.E. Amtrak, the national railway passenger system, offers more than 50 trains daily to major east coast cities. These connections join more than 500 cities in the U.S. and Canada to Washington. Union Station on Capitol Hill is splendidly renovated and contains eateries, restaurants, shops, parking facilities, and movie theaters. Taxis are readily available, and a Metrorail (subway) stop is located here too. Amtrak also offers **Metroliner** and **Metroliner Express** service between Washington, D.C., and New York City. For Amtrak train information and reservations, ☎ 484-7540 or (800) USA-RAIL. Web: www.amtrak.com.

When calling Amtrak, ask about discounted fares. For information about travel packages that can include accommodations and car rental, call Great American Vacations ☎ (800) 321-8684. Another rail option is the Maryland Rail Commuter, or MARC, which operates trains between Baltimore's Penn Station and Washington's Union Station, a route that includes a stop at BWI every hour, Mon–Fri. For MARC information, ☎ (800) 325-RAIL.

### By bus:

**Greyhound** buses, which connect the city to most other parts of the U.S., arrive in the District at the 1st and L Sts terminal, 1005 1st St N.E., about four blocks from Union Station. Other Greyhound stops include Silver Spring in Maryland, and Springfield, Arlington, Rosslyn, and Fairfax in Virginia. For information and schedules, ☎ 289-5154 or (800) 231-2222. Web: www.greyhound.com.

### By car

Eventually all roads lead to Washington, D.C., which is easily accessible by car. Most major routes leading to the city intersect with the **Capital Beltway,** I-495, which circles the city. From the north, US 1, I-95, and the Baltimore–Washington Pkwy lead toward the city. From the northwest, I-270, which links the area with transcontinental I-70, leads into the Beltway. US 29 and US 50 also connect with the Beltway.

From the south, via Alexandria and Arlington, Virginia, take US 1 and I-395. From the southwest, take I-66. Be aware that high-occupancy vehicle (HOV) restrictions apply during rush hours on I-66. Mon through Fri traffic heading east (downtown) is restricted from 6:30 A.M. to 9 A.M. in all lanes to vehicles with two or more people. Similar restrictions apply outbound (west) from the District from 3:30 to 6:30 P.M.

During rush hours roads are congested. Outside of rush hour, traffic generally flows. If your plans are confined to the traditional tourist areas, such as the Mall, Capitol Hill, downtown, the memorials, Arlington, and Alexandria, then renting a car is not necessary. Metro subways and buses as well as tourmobiles and cabs make sightseeing easy. Parking is limited on the District's streets, and parking garages charge between $10 and $15 for all-day parking. Most hotels offer parking, which may or may not be included in the room package.

**Car rentals** are available at the airports, and many rental companies have offices downtown. Call the rental company's toll-free number for information, and check the yellow pages of the phone directory. Some area rental companies include: **Avis** ☎ (800) 331-1212, **Budget** ☎ (800) 358-2335, **Dollar** ☎ (800) 800-4000, **Hertz** ☎ (800) 654-3131, and **National** ☎ (800) 227-7368.

# Getting around Washington, D.C.

### Streets

Whatever your mode of transportation, it is important to understand the logic of Washington's streets. The city is divided into four distinct sections: northeast (**N.E.**), southeast (**S.E.**), northwest (**N.W.**), and southwest (**S.W.**). Numbered streets run north and south, and lettered streets run east and west.

At the Capitol Building, N. Capitol, S. Capitol, and E. Capitol Sts, as well as the Mall, split D.C. into its respective quadrants. Street addresses become higher the farther away the location is from the Capitol. Addresses indicate the block location and the cross street. As an example, for Ford's Theatre—511 10th St N.W.—use the 5 in the address to count to the 5th letter in the alphabet, E. The theater is located on 10th St N.W. between E and F Sts. This works most of the time as long as it is remembered that there are no J, X, or Z streets. Note also that I St is sometimes written as "Eye" St to avoid confusion with 1st St. To find the cross street for lettered streets, simply look at the first digits of the address. For example, the Hard Rock Cafe, 999 E St N.W., is located at 9th and E Sts N.W. The Canterbury Hotel, 1733 N St N.W., is located at 17th and N Sts N.W. Diagonal avenues cut across this grid of streets. These avenues generally radiate from circles and are named after states. For example, at Scott Circle, Massachusetts Ave and Rhode Island Ave converge.

As the city grew, a second and a third set of lettered streets were created. The second set uses two-syllable, alphabetical names (Calvert, Porter, etc.). The third set uses three-syllable names (Davenport, Fessenden, Quesada, etc.). Before heading out, always know a destination's full address, including whether the location is N.W., N.E., S.E., or S.W.

### Walking

Walking is the best way to see any city, especially Washington, D.C. As in any urban area, use common sense and caution. But generally, the main tourist areas—the Mall, Capitol Hill, etc.—are safe for walking. At night, keep to well-lit, busy streets and the main tourist areas. When in doubt, ask the desk manager at your hotel about the safety of walking or simply opt to take a cab. Do not walk in parks at night, including Rock Creek Park and along the C&O Canal, as the paths are obviously less well-lit and sparsely populated.

### Taxis and car service

There are more than 9,000 taxicabs in Washington and the fares are very reasonable. The city works on a zone system for taxi rates. Zones begin in the central city and spread outward. By law, basic rates must be posted in the cab. Travel within Zone 1, which includes the Capitol, the White House, and many Smithsonian museums, costs $4 for a single passenger. Generally, there is a $1.50 charge for each additional passenger in the party and a $1 surcharge during morning (7–9:30 A.M.) and evening (4–6:30 P.M.) rush hours. The basic price for going into a second zone is $5.50; a third zone, $6.90; a fourth zone, $8.25; a fifth zone, $9.25; etc.

Taxi companies include **Diamond**, ☎ 387-6200, and **Yellow Cab**, ☎ 544-1212. Several companies offer cars and limousines for hire. **Red Top Executive**

**Sedans,** 1200 N. Hudson St, Arlington, ☎ (703) 522-3300 or (800) 296-3300, can arrange for an executive car, which is, as the company says, more than a taxi but less than a limousine. This service, usually in a Lincoln Continental or similar car, is a convenience for many business travelers, especially women who like knowing they will be met by a courteous driver. Payment can be made with credit card or cash: $35 per hour plus 15 percent gratuity.

### Subway

Washington's subway system is not only clean, but also safe, especially during the day and early evening hours. This is a system that locals use and tourists should too. Almost all hotels and motels in the area offer shuttle service to the nearest Metro station. Metro is divided into five lines. The **Orange Line** travels from New Carrollton, Maryland, to Vienna, Virginia. The **Blue Line** runs from Addison Rd, Maryland, to Franconia-Springfield, Virginia. The Blue Line also stops at National Airport, as does the **Yellow Line,** which runs from Huntington, Virginia, to Mt. Vernon Square in the District. The **Green Line** currently runs from U St–Cardozo to Anacostia, and also from Fort Totten to Greenbelt, Maryland. To access this small portion of the Green Line to Greenbelt, you must take the Red Line to the Fort Totten stop and transfer trains. The **Red Line** extends from Shady Grove, Maryland, to Glenmont, Maryland.

To locate a Metro station, look for a tall brown column with a large *M* on it. The colored stripes underneath the M indicate which lines are served by that station. For example, orange and blue stripes inform the traveler that trains on the Orange and Blue Lines stop at that station. Obtain the color-coded Metro map, *All About the Metro System,* at the station (ask the station manager at the kiosk), or pick one up at the **Visitors Center,** 1212 New York Ave N.W., ☎ (202) 789-7000. These maps aid in understanding the fare system and finding the right stations.

Once inside the station, head for the system map and find the station you are currently at and the Metro stop nearest your desired destination. Trains are named for their end terminals, so check which terminal you will be traveling toward on the system map. For example, to get from the University of the District of Columbia, Van Ness campus, to the shops at Union Station, you would board the Red Line train at Van Ness and take a Metro headed toward Glenmont (the end terminal), but you would get off at the Union Station stop. To make it easier, posts beside each track list the stations where the train stops. Make sure you read the color and destination of a train before boarding, especially on multitrain tracks. For example, the Blue and Orange Lines run together for many stops, but if you're trying to go to Reagan National Airport, the Blue Line will take you there but the Orange Line will not. (The Yellow Line also stops at Reagan National.)

Several stations allow **transfers** between lines. At Metro Center, you can transfer among Red, Blue, and Orange Lines. Gallery Place Chinatown has Red, Yellow, and Green Lines. The Stadium-Armory has Orange and Blue Lines. L'Enfant Plaza has access to Blue, Orange, Green, and Yellow Lines. Rosslyn has Orange and Blue Lines. King Street has the Blue and Yellow Lines as does the Pentagon stop.

Trains operate approximately every 10–15 minutes weekdays from 5:30 A.M. to midnight, and weekends from 8 A.M. to midnight. During rush hours, 5:30–9:30 A.M. and 3–7 P.M., trains operate every six minutes.

**Farecards** are needed both *to enter* and *to exit* the Metro system, so don't throw away your farecard once you've boarded your train. Once you've figured out your route and stop, look up the stop on the nearby fare chart so you'll know the exact one-way cost from the station you are at to your desired destination. Keep in mind what time you'll be traveling (during rush hour, weekdays from 5:30 to 9:30 A.M. and from 3 to 7 P.M., fares increase). Then go to the **farecard vending machine** to purchase your fare. Each person needs their own farecard, except for up to two children under 5, who may travel free with an adult. It's easiest to purchase round-trip fare, but **Addfare machines** are located near exits. Farecard machines take bills ($1, $5, and sometimes $10 and $20) and coins. After inserting money, select the dollar value you want, then press button 3—"Take Farecard"— to receive your card and your change. Each time the card is used, the fare amount is deducted. Cards may be used several times until the fare amount is depleted, and cards may also be traded in for a new one with space for additional rides if the remaining fare is $7 or less. Farecards can be bought for as little as $1.10, the minimum nonrush hour fare, or as much as $100. To save money when you buy Farecards, purchase in large amounts. With farecards over $20, you get a 10 percent bonus fare. Keep in mind that farecard machines give change only up to $4.95 and that they give coin change, not bills. Leftover value on a farecard can not be reimbursed by Metro, but farecards never expire and can be used on any future trips to D.C.

Transfers are not issued from Metrobuses to Metrorail, but you may obtain a transfer from the Metrorail to a Metrobus for 25 cents on regular Metrobus routes, and $1.15 on express bus routes (in Maryland C11, N7, P13, P17, P19, and W13; in Virginia 11Y, 17A, 17B, 17G, 17H, 17K, 17L, 17M, 18E, 18G, 18H, 18P, 29E, 29G, 29H, 29X). The transfer is good for full fare within the District, and partial fare in other locations. Remember to obtain these transfers when you *enter* the subway station, not at the exit destination. A transfer machine is generally located near the escalator on the mezzanine level.

One-day **railpasses** can be purchased for $5 and allow unlimited same-day travel weekdays after 9:30 A.M. However, the availability of these passes isn't good. They can be purchased at the sales outlet at **Metro Center,** open daily from 8 A.M. to 6 P.M., and at some downtown hotels. If you're planning a longer stay, you might want to purchase a longer pass. A **Weekly Short Trip pass** is $17.50 and allows unlimited rides that cost $1.75 or less. A **Weekly FAST pass** costs $25 and allows unlimited rides for seven consecutive days. The **28-day FAST pass** allows unlimited rides for 28 consecutive days for $100. All of these passes are available at the Metro Center sales office and many are available at area supermarkets.

Bicycles are allowed on Metro trains weekdays 10 A.M.–2 P.M. (only two per car; after 7 P.M., four per car) and all day on Saturdays, Sundays, and holidays except July 4th (four per car). Guidelines for bicycles on trains are posted in stations. For more information, ☎ 962-1116. Many stations have bicycle lockers to rent for 6 months ($45) or 12 months ($70). For information, ☎ 962-1116.

For **Metro Information,** ☎ 637-7000, weekdays 6 A.M.–10:30 P.M., weekends 8 A.M.–10:30 P.M., or 638-3780 (TTY). Web: www.wmata.com. For customer assistance, ☎ 637-1328, weekdays 8:30–4. For Lost and Found, ☎ 962-1195, 9:30–4; to see items, hours are 11–3. For Metro ID cards for people with disabilities, ☎ 962-1245, weekdays 7:30–3:30, or 628-8973 (TTY). For Transit Police, ☎ 962-2121. To learn about reduced fares for senior citizens, ☎ 637-7000; for disabled persons ☎ 962-1245.

Metro also has a handy *Guide to the Nation's Capital,* which lists the nearest Metrorail stations to monuments, museums, shopping areas, and theaters. ☎ 637-1328.

## Bus

For areas not served by Metrorail, **Metrobuses** are inexpensive and easily available. Red, white, and blue signs at street corners indicate bus stops. Fares for buses in the District, Maryland, and Virginia are $1.10 for regular routes and $2 for express routes (Maryland: C11, N7, P13, P17, P19, W13; Virginia: 11Y, 17A, 17B, 17G, 17H, 17K, 17L, 17M, 18E, 18G, 18H, 18P, 29E, 29G, 29H, 29X). Seniors (65 and older) ride for 50 cents. Up to two children under 5 may travel free with a paying adult. In Maryland, Metrobus covers all of Prince George's County and a lot of Montgomery County; in Virginia, Metrobus covers Arlington County, part of Alexandria County, and two-thirds of Fairfax County.

There are no transfers from buses to subways, but you can transfer from bus to bus by getting a free transfer pass from the driver as soon as you board. A **Regional One Day Pass** for $2.50 is available for unlimited bus rides regionwide. A **Metrobus Weekly Pass** is $10 and a **Metrobus 28-Day Pass** is $40. A **Weekly Bus/Rail Short Trip** pass costs $20 and allows unlimited rides on regular and express buses; it covers Metrorail rides costing up to $1.75 during rush hour on weekdays and is also valid for any trip at other times. A **Weekly Bus/Rail FAST Pass** for $30 allows unlimited rides on regular and express buses and Metrorail. The bus routing system is complex. The best way to find out about buses is to call Metrorail/Metrobus information for routes and schedules, ☎ 637-7000 or 637-3780 (TTY). Web: www.wmata.com.

Washington welcomes **physically challenged travelers** and has made great efforts to make the city accessible. Most hotels, museums, restaurants, shopping malls, and public transportation can accommodate the special needs of any visitor. For information on the National Capital Park's special services, ☎ 619-7222 or 619-7083 (TTY). For information on the White House, ☎ 456-2200 or 456-6213 (TTY). For information on the Smithsonian Museums' services, ☎ 357-2700 or 357-1729 (TTY). For information on Metro, ☎ 962-1245. For information on Tourmobile Sightseeing trams, ☎ 554-7020.

Washington welcomes **international travelers.** Currency exchange is available at many banks; American Express locations are throughout the city, ☎ (800) 528-4800 or (800) 221-9950 (TTY); Thomas Cook is at 1800 K St N.W., ☎ 872-1233, and at Union Station, ☎ 371-9220. The **Washington Visitors Information Center,** 1212 New York Ave N.W., ☎ 789-7000, offers free maps and information in a variety of languages. Travelers Aid offers 24-hour assistance at Ronald Reagan Washington National, Dulles International, and Baltimore-Washington airports, as well as at Union Station. The International Visitors Information Service, ☎ 939-5544, offers a 24-hour "language bank" service for visitors needing help with translations. Call the Convention and Visitors Bureau (☎ 789-7000) for a complete list of multilingual tours. The Smithsonian Museums (☎ 357-1300) also provide information in a variety of languages. Many museums also offer multilingual tours.

# Hotels

Washington, D.C., offers a wide range of accommodations for a variety of budgets. Visitors can choose from luxury hotel chains such as the Four Seasons and the Inter-Continental as well as select from a range of moderate lodgings. Some of the District's best lodging buys are the **weekend hTCSotel packages.** These special room rates reduce prices as much as 30–50 percent. Always ask for these packages when booking weekend accommodations. Hotels that frequently run weekend packages include: Hyatt Regency Washington–Capitol Hill, Loews L'Enfant Plaza, Embassy Suites, Hotel Washington, Washington Hilton, Four Seasons, and Hyatt Regency Bethesda.

For reduced rates every night of the week, call **Capitol Reservations,** ☎ (800) VISIT-DC, or ☎ (800) 847-4832. Web: www.hotelsdc.com. This reservation service, at 1730 Rhode Island Ave N.W., advertises discounts of approximately 30 percent at 70 area hotels, all in safe neighborhoods.

In addition to looking for weekend packages, and trying Capitol Reservations, families should consider staying at one of the area's **all-suite** properties. These include Embassy Suites Hotel–Downtown, Carlyle Suites, New Hampshire Suites, Savoy Suites, and Embassy Suites Chevy Chase Pavilion. These often provide kitchenettes, microwaves, and refrigerators for breakfast and snacks, plus extra space for added convenience. Also, families should consider booking a downtown hotel that has easy access to a Metro subway stop. This not only makes touring easier, but also allows quick stops back at the hotel. If your children are young, and they like to swim, book a property with an indoor pool. A family swim is a great way to relax at the end of a busy tourist day.

Besides checking the special packages and romantic rooms at the Willard, the Four Seasons, and other luxury properties, the Washington area has three upscale **inns.** The **Morrison-Clark Inn,** 1015 L St N.W., ☎ 898-1200, has the patina of fine wood and old money. The inn offers classic, country, and Victorian rooms (these are the nicest) as well as a romantic candlelit dining room that features good food. In Alexandria the **Morrison House,** 116 S. Alfred St, ☎ (703) 838-8000), creates a gracious inn atmosphere and also serves good food. In Fairfax, the **Bailiwick Inn,** 4023 Chain Bridge Rd, ☎ (703) 691-2266, which also has a restaurant, offers 19C decor, afternoon tea, and around Halloween a murder-mystery weekend.

Three area agencies book **bed-and-breakfast** accommodations. Both **Bed and Breakfast League/Sweet Dreams,** PO Box 9490, Washington, DC 20016, ☎ 363-7767, in the $80–150 range, and **Bed 'n' Breakfast, Ltd.,** PO Box 12011, Washington, DC 20005, ☎ 328-3510, Web: www.bnbaccom.com, ranging from budget to deluxe, offer rooms in private homes and apartments in the District and adjacent suburbs. Another find is **Alexandria and Arlington Bed & Breakfast Network,** PO Box 25319, Arlington, VA 22202-9319, ☎ (703) 255-1933 or (888) 549-3415. This reservation service offers rooms in 18C and 19C townhouses in historic Alexandria. Most of these homes are graced with original moldings, carved mantels, and fine antiques, as well as gracious hosts. Some come with private courtyards and gardens. Rates range from $79 to 325 and include a continental-plus breakfast at the least. Children are welcome; ask about age limits and additional pricing. Virginia offers a toll-free bed-and-breakfast reservation number: ☎ (800) 934-9184 or (202) 872-0523. Reservations can also be made in person at the **Virginia Tourism Office,** 1629 K St N.W.

In addition the **Kalorama Guest House,** 1854 Mintwood Place N.W., Washington, DC 20009, ☎ 667-6369, and also at 2700 Cathedral Ave N.W., Washington, DC 20008, ☎ 328-0860, offers lodging in six houses. Founder Roberta Piecznik calls these four properties on Mintwood Place in the heart of Adams Morgan and the two on Cathedral Ave, a quieter residential section, "the grandmother's house you wish you had." The rooms are furnished with a combination of antiques and flea market finds. No children under 5.

The following agencies make **reservations** at Washington hotels. Ask if discounts are available. **Capitol Reservations,** 1730 Rhode Island Ave N.W., 20036, ☎ 452-1270 or (800) VISIT-DC. **Washington DC Accommodations,** 2201 Wisconsin Ave N.W., 20007, ☎ 289-2220 or (800) 554-2220. Web: www.dcaccommodations.com. It's also wise to check out national services such as **Hotel Reservations Network,** ☎ (800) 964-6835, Web: www.hotel discount.com, and **Expedia.com,** Web: www.expedia.com.

For the **hearing-impaired,** the **Phoenix Park Hotel,** Capitol Hill, ☎ (800) 824-5419 or (202) 638-6900, offers some rooms with closed-captioned television monitors, a flashing light, a vibrating alarm situated under the pillow that signals someone is at the door, and a TTY telephone and answering machine.

For more information, contact the **Washington, D.C., Convention and Visitors Bureau,** 1212 New York Ave N.W., ☎ 789-7000, for an accommodations brochure and for a list of seasonal hotel packages. You should also visit the official Washington, D.C., tourism Web site at www.washington.org.

The following, instead of a complete list of properties, includes the best bets in lodging in a variety of price ranges. Rates are based on a single room, midweek, and exclusive of packages. Be sure to ask about special package rates and weekend rates, which often offer up to a 30 percent rate reduction. Expensive hotels charge over $185. Moderate hotels charge between $126 and $184. Budget hotels charge $125 or less.

## Capitol Hill

### Expensive
**Hotel George,** 15 E St N.W., 20001, ☎ 347-4200 or (800) 576-8331. Metro: Union Station.
**Hyatt Regency Washington–Capitol Hill** 400 New Jersey Ave N.W., 20001, ☎ 737-1234 or (800) 233-1234. Metro: Union Station.
**Phoenix Park Hotel,** 520 N. Capitol St N.W., 20001, ☎ 638-6900 or (800) 824-5419. Metro: Union Station.
**Washington Court Hotel on Capitol Hill,** 525 New Jersey Ave N.W., 20001, ☎ 628-2100. Metro: Union Station.

### Moderate
**Capitol Hill Suites,** 200 C St S.E., 20003, ☎ 543-6000 or (800) 424-9165. Metro: Capitol South Station.

### Budget
**Best Western Downtown Capitol Hill,** 724 3rd St N.W., 20001, ☎ 842-4466 or (800) 242-4831.
Web: www.bestwestern.com. Metro: Union Station.

## Chinatown/Convention Center

### Expensive

**Grand Hyatt Washington**, 1000 H St N.W., 20001, ☎ 582-1234 or (800) 233-1234. Metro: Metro Center.

**Henley Park Hotel**, 926 Massachusetts Ave N.W., 20001, ☎ 638-5200 or (800) 222-8474. Metro: Metro Center or Gallery Place.

**Marriott at Metro Center**, 775 12th St N.W., 20005, ☎ 737-2200. Metro: Metro Center.

**Renaissance Washington, D.C.**, 999 9th St N.W., 20001, ☎ 898-9000 or (800) 468-3571. Metro: Gallery Place/Chinatown.

### Moderate

**Courtyard by Marriott**, 900 F St N.W., 20004, ☎ 638-4600 or (800) 321-2211.
Web: www.marriott.com. Metro: Gallery Place/Chinatown.

**Red Roof Inn Downtown D.C.**, 500 H St N.W., 20001, ☎ 289-5959. Metro: Gallery Place/Chinatown.

### Budget

**Premier Convention Center Hotel**, 1201 K St N.W., 20005, ☎ 842-1020 or (800) 562-3350. Metro: McPherson Square.

## Downtown

### Expensive

**Capital Hilton**, 1001 16th St N.W., 20036, ☎ 393-1000 or (800) 445-8667.
Web: www.capital.hilton.com. Metro: McPherson Square.

**Crowne Plaza Washington, D.C.**, 16th and Massachusetts Ave N.W., 20036, ☎ 682-0111 or (800) 2-CROWNE. Metro: McPherson Square.

**Embassy Suites–Downtown**, 1250 22nd St N.W., 20037, ☎ 857-3388 or (800) EMBASSY.
Web: www.embassysuites.com. Metro: Dupont Circle or Foggy Bottom.

**Governors House Hotel**, 1615 Rhode Island Ave N.W., 20036, ☎ 296-2100 or (800) 821-4367. Metro: Farragut North.

**Hay-Adams Hotel**, 16th and H Sts N.W., 20006, ☎ 638-6600 or (800) 424-5054. Metro: Farragut West or McPherson Square.

**Hotel Washington**, 15th St and Pennsylvania Ave N.W., 20004, ☎ 638-5900 or (800) 424-9540. Metro: Metro Center.

**The Jefferson**, 1200 16th St N.W., 20036, ☎ 347-2200 or (800) 368-5966. Metro: Farragut North.

**JW Marriott Hotel**, 1331 Pennsylvania Ave N.W., 20004, ☎ 393-2000 or (800) 228-9290.
Web: www.marriott.com. Metro: Metro Center.

**Loews L'Enfant Plaza Hotel**, 480 L'Enfant Place S.W., 20024-2197, ☎ 484-1000 or (800) 23-LOEWS.
Web: www.loewshotels.com. Metro: L'Enfant Plaza.

**The Madison**, 15th and M Sts N.W., 20005, ☎ 862-1600 or (800) 424-8577. Metro: McPherson Square or Farragut North.

**Morrison-Clark Inn,** 1015 L St N.W., 20001, ☎ 898-1200 or (800) 332-7898. Metro: Metro Center.
**St. Regis Hotel,** 923 16th St N.W., 20006, ☎ 638-2626 or (800) 325-3535. Metro: McPherson Square or Farragut North.
**Stouffer Mayflower,** 1127 Connecticut Ave N.W., 20036, ☎ 347-3000 or (800) 468-3571. Metro: Farragut North.
**Willard Inter-Continental,** 1401 Pennsylvania Ave N.W., 20004, ☎ 628-9100 or (800) 327-0200. Metro: Metro Center.
**Wyndham Washington,** 1400 M St N.W., 20005, ☎ 429-1700. Metro: McPherson Square.

## Dupont Circle/Embassy Area

**Expensive**
**Canterbury Hotel,** 1733 N St N.W., 20036, ☎ 393-3000 or (800) 424-2950. Metro: Dupont Circle.
**Carlyle Suites Hotel,** 1731 New Hampshire Ave N.W., 20009, ☎ 234-3200 or (800) 964-5377. Metro: Dupont Circle.
**Doubletree Hotel Park Terrace on Embassy Row,** 1515 Rhode Island Ave N.W., 20005, ☎ 232-7000 or (800) 222-8733. Metro: Dupont Circle.
**Embassy Square, a Summerfield Suites Hotel,** 2000 N St N.W., 20036, ☎ 659-9000 or (800) 424-2999.
Web: www.staydc.com. Metro: Dupont Circle.
**Hilton Washington & Towers,** 1919 Connecticut Ave N.W., 20009, ☎ 483-3000 or (800) DC-HILTON.
Web: www.washington-hilton.com. Metro: Dupont Circle [but the walk is long].
**Hotel Sofitel Washington,** 1914 Connecticut Ave N.W., 20009. ☎ 797-2000 or (800) 424-2464. Metro: Dupont Circle.
**Quality Suites Downtown,** 1315 16th St N.W., 20036, ☎ 232-8000 or (800) 368-5689.
Web: www.qualitysuite.com. Metro: Dupont Circle.
**Westin Fairfax, Washington, D.C.,** 2100 Massachusetts Ave N.W., 20008, ☎ 293-2100.
Web: www.westin.com. Metro: Dupont Circle.

**Moderate**
**Clarion Hampshire Hotel,** 1310 New Hampshire Ave N.W., 20036, ☎ 296-7600 or (800) 368-5691. Metro: Dupont Circle.
**Doyle Normandy Inn,** 2118 Wyoming Ave N.W., 20008, ☎ 483-1350 or (800) 424-3729. Metro: Dupont Circle.
**Holiday Inn Central, Washington, D.C.,** 1501 Rhode Island Ave N.W., 20036, ☎ 483-2000 or (800) 248-0016. Metro: McPherson Square
**Washington Courtyard by Marriott,** 1900 Connecticut Ave N.W., 20009, ☎ 332-9300 or (800) 842-4211. Metro: Dupont Circle
**Windsor Inn,** 1842 16th St N.W., 20036, ☎ 667-0300. Metro: Dupont Circle

## Foggy Bottom and West End

### Luxury

**Swissôtel Washington—the Watergate**, 2650 Virginia Ave N.W., 20037, ☎ 965-2300.
Web: www.swissotel.com. Metro: Foggy Bottom.

### Expensive

**Park Hyatt Washington**, 1201 24th St N.W., 20037, ☎ 789-1234 or (800) 233-1234.
Web: www.hyatt.com. Metro: Foggy Bottom.

**Radisson Barcelo**, 2121 P St N.W., 20034, ☎ 293-3100 or (800) 333-3333. Metro: Dupont Circle.

**Washington Marriott**, 1221 22nd St N.W., 20037, ☎ 872-1500.
Web: www.marriott.com. Metro: Foggy Bottom or Dupont Circle.

**Washington Monarch Hotel**, 2401 M St N.W., 20037, ☎ 429-2400 or (877) 222-2266.
Web: www.washingtonmonarch.com. Metro: Foggy Bottom or Dupont Circle.

### Moderate

**Best Western New Hampshire Suites Hotel**, 1121 New Hampshire Ave N.W., 20037, ☎ 457-0565 or (800) 762-3777. Metro: Foggy Bottom.

**Doubletree Guest Suites New Hampshire Ave**, 801 New Hampshire Ave N.W., 20037, ☎ 785-2000 or (800) 222-TREE.
Web: www.doubletreehotels.com. Metro: Foggy Bottom.

**Doubletree Guest Suites Pennsylvania Ave**, 2500 Pennsylvania Ave N.W., 20037, ☎ 333-8060 or (800) 222-TREE.
Web: www.doubletreehotels.com. Metro: Foggy Bottom.

**Hotel Lombardy**, 2019 I St N.W., 20006, ☎ 828-2600 or (800) 424-5486. Metro: Foggy Bottom.

**Wyndham Bristol Hotel**, 2430 Pennsylvania Ave N.W., 20037, ☎ 955-6400 or (800) WYNDHAM.
Web: www.wyndham.com. Metro: Foggy Bottom.

### Moderate

**State Plaza Hotel**, 2117 E St N.W., 20037, ☎ 861-8200 or (800) 424-2859. Metro: Foggy Bottom.

## Georgetown

### Luxury

**Four Seasons Hotel**, 2800 Pennsylvania Ave N.W., 20007, ☎ 342-0444.
Web: www.fourseasons.com. Metro: Foggy Bottom.

### Expensive

**Georgetown Dutch Inn**, 1075 Thomas Jefferson St N.W., 20007, ☎ 337-0900 or (800) 388-2410. Metro: Foggy Bottom [but a long walk].

**Georgetown Inn**, 1310 Wisconsin Ave N.W., 20007, ☎ 333-8900. Metro: Foggy Bottom [but a long walk].

**Latham Hotel,** 3000 M St N.W., 20007, ☎ 726-5000. Metro: Foggy Bottom [but a long walk].

**Moderate**
**Georgetown Suites–30th St,** 1111 30th St N.W., 20007, ☎ 298-7800 or (800) 388-2410. Metro: Foggy Bottom.
**Holiday Inn Georgetown,** 2101 Wisconsin Ave N.W., 20007, ☎ 333-8900. Metro: Foggy Bottom [but a long walk].

## Upper Northwest

**Expensive**
**Embassy Suites Washington, D.C., Uptown at the Chevy Chase Pavilion,** 4300 Military Rd N.W., 20015, ☎ 362-9300 or (800) EMBASSY.
Web: www.embassysuites.com. Metro: Friendship Heights.
**Marriott Wardman Park,** 2660 Woodley Rd N.W., 20008, ☎ 328-2000 or (800) 228-9290.
Web: www.marriott.com. Metro: Woodley Park/Zoo.
**Omni Shoreham,** 2500 Calvert St N.W., 20008, ☎ 234-0700. Metro: Woodley Park/Zoo.

**Moderate**
**Days Inn Connecticut Ave,** 4400 Connecticut Ave N.W., 20008, ☎ 244-5600 or (800) 952-3060.
Web: www.daysinn-washingtondc.com. Metro: Van Ness/UDC.
**Kalorama Guest House at Kalorama Park,** 1854 Mintwood Place N.W., 20009, ☎ 667-6369.
Web: www.washingtonpost.com/yp/kgh. Metro: Woodley Park/Zoo.
**Kalorama Guest House at Woodley Park,** 2700 Cathedral Ave N.W., 20008, ☎ 328-0860.
Web: www.washingtonpost.com/yp/kgh. Metro: Woodley Park/Zoo.
**Savoy Suites,** 2505 Wisconsin Ave N.W., 20007, ☎ 337-9700 or (800) 523-5377. Metro: Shuttle service at certain times to a Metro station.

## Washington Waterfront

**Moderate**
**Channel Inn Hotel,** 650 Water St S.W. 20024, ☎ 554-2400 or (800) 368-5668. Metro: Waterfront.

## Maryland

**Moderate**
**American Inn of Bethesda,** 8130 Wisconsin Ave, Bethesda, 20814, ☎ (301) 656-9300 or (800) 323-7081.
Web: www.american-inn.com. Metro: Bethesda.
**Bethesda Marriott,** 5151 Pooks Hill Rd, Bethesda, 20814, ☎ (301) 897-9400 or (800) 228-9290.
Web: www.marriott.com. Metro: Medical Center.

**Holiday Inn Bethesda,** 8120 Wisconsin Ave, Bethesda, 20814, ☎ (301) 652-2000 or (800) HOLIDAY. Metro: Bethesda.

**Holiday Inn Chevy Chase,** 5520 Wisconsin Ave, Bethesda, 20815, ☎ (301) 656-1500 or (800) HOLIDAY. Metro: Friendship Heights.

**Hyatt Regency Bethesda,** One Bethesda Metro Center, Bethesda, 20814, ☎ (301) 657-1234 or (800) 233-1234. Metro: Bethesda.

**Residence Inn by Marriott Bethesda,** 7335 Wisconsin Ave, Bethesda, 20814, ☎ (301) 718-0200. Metro: Bethesda

## Virginia

### Expensive

**Crystal Gateway Marriott,** 1700 Jefferson Davis Hwy, Arlington, 22202, ☎ (703) 920-3230 or (800) 228-9290.
Web: www.marriott.com. Metro: Crystal City.

**Holiday Inn Select Old Town Alexandria** 480 King St, Alexandria, 22314, ☎ (703) 549-6080 or (800) 368-5047.
Web: www.hiselect.com. Metro: King St.

**Hyatt Arlington,** 1325 Wilson Blvd, Arlington, 22209, ☎ (703) 525-1234 or (800) 223-1234.
Web: www.hyatt.com. Metro: Rosslyn.

**Hyatt Regency Crystal City,** 2799 Jefferson Davis Hwy, Arlington, 22202, ☎ (703) 418-1234 or (800) 223-1234.
Web: www.hyatt.com. Metro: Crystal City.

**Key Bridge Marriott,** 1401 Lee Hwy, Arlington, 22209, ☎ (703) 524-6400 or (800) 327-9789.
Web: www.marriott.com. Metro: Rosslyn.

**Morrison House,** 116 S. Alfred St, Alexandria, 22314, ☎ (703) 838-8000 or (800) 367-0800. Metro: King St.

**Ritz-Carlton, Pentagon City,** 1250 S. Hayes St, Arlington, 22202, ☎ (703) 415-5000 or (800) 241-2333. Metro: Pentagon City.

**Ritz-Carlton Tysons Corner,** 1700 Tysons Blvd, McLean, 22102, ☎ (703) 506-4300 or (800) 241-3333. Metro: none.

### Moderate

**Americana Hotel,** 1900 Jefferson Davis Hwy, Arlington, 22202, ☎ (703) 979-3772 or (800) 548-6261. Metro: Crystal City.

**Bailiwick Inn,** 4023 Chain Bridge Rd, Fairfax, 22030, ☎ (703) 691-2266. Metro: Vienna via local shuttle bus.

**Crystal City Marriott,** 1999 Jefferson Davis Hwy, Arlington, 22202, ☎ (703) 413-5500 or (800) 228-9290.
Web: www.marriott.com. Metro: Crystal City.

**Old Town Holiday Inn,** 480 King St, Alexandria, 22314, ☎ (703) 549-6080. Metro: King St.

## Other Accommodations

### Campgrounds

**Capitol KOA Campground,** 768 Cecil Ave, Millersville, MD 21108, ☎ (410) 923-2771 or (800) KOA-0248.

Web: www.koakampgrounds.com. This campground is a 5-minute drive to commuter trains serving Union Station on the hour and half hour, a 20-minute drive to the New Carrollton Metro, and 40 minutes by car to Convention Center. Free daily shuttle to commuter trains. Camp reservation office opens in January; camp opens in March.

**Cherry Hill Park,** 9800 Cherry Hill Rd, College Park, MD 20740-1210, ☎ (301) 937-7116 or (800) 801-6449.
Web: www.rvamerica.com. This is the closest RV park to Washington, D.C., located at I-95/Capital Beltway Interchange. Metrobus and Grayline tour buses pick up at bus depot inside campground. There are 400 tent and RV camping sites.

**Hostel**
**Hostelling International–Washington, D.C.,** 1009 11th St N.W., 20001, ☎ 737-2333. Metro: Metro Center. These inexpensive dormitory-style rooms offer separate quarters for men and women. If space allows, families may be able to have their own room. The maximum stay is six days.

# Restaurants
These brief descriptions of restaurants are a compilation of personal recommendations, newspaper and magazine reviews, and restaurant surveys. At an *inexpensive* restaurant the cost of a three-course meal, excluding wine, tax, and tip is less than $25 per person. At a *moderate* restaurant, the cost is $26–45. At an *expensive* restaurant the cost is $46–75, and at a *very expensive* restaurant the cost is more than $75 per person. Always call ahead to ascertain credit card and reservation policies, wheelchair accessibility, hours of operation, and if children are truly welcome.

Virtually any of the restaurants on the "Best Bargains" list would be good bets for **families.** Many offer kids' menus, and some accommodate children by serving half-portions; ask if these are available. In addition, consider ordering an appetizer as an entrée for a child. Here's a quick list of some of Washington's family-friendly restaurants: America, Armand's Chicago Pizzeria, Austin Grill, Cactus Cantina, Chadwick's, Cheesecake Factory, Foong Lin, Georgetown Bagelry, Hard Rock Cafe, Houston's, Krupin's, Pizzeria Paradiso, Rio Grande Cafe, Sequoia, South Austin Grill, Tortilla Coast, the Union Station Food Court, and Uno's Pizzeria.

Here's a quick list of some of the Washington area's most **popular** restaurants, not all of which are expensive. Favorites include: Austin Grill, Aux Beaux Champs, Bice, Bombay Club, Cactus Cantina, Café Atlantico, Cheesecake Factory, D.C. Coast, Galileo, Georgia Brown's, I Matti, I Ricchi, Kinkead's, La Chaumiere, L'Auberge Chez Francois, the Mark, McCormick & Schmick's Seafood Restaurant, New Heights, Morton's of Chicago, Morton's-Tysons, Nora, Obelisk, The Palm, Prime Rib, Red Hot & Blue, Red Sage, 701 Pennsylvania Avenue, Twenty-One Federal, and Vidalia.

Several services **deliver** food from a range of restaurants to your hotel door. **A La Carte Express,** ☎ 232-8646, delivers from 90 restaurants to locations in Capitol Hill, Adams Morgan, Dupont Circle, downtown, Georgetown, and Glover Park. Delivery fees, which range up to $5, vary depending on the size of the order. The **Butlers** ☎ 686-7337 (Web: www.butlersdc.com) delivers food from 25 restaurants to zip codes 20015, 20016, 20008, 20815 and upper 20007. The delivery fee is around $5. **Takeout Taxi,** ☎ 986-0111, (301) 571-0111, or (703) 435-3663, delivers food from over 150 restaurants throughout the city, as well as Maryland and Virginia suburbs. There is a $4.99 delivery fee.

Like any big city, Washington, D.C., comes with its coterie of **take-out** places. Some restaurants, which also offer on-site dining, are good places to call for some take-out food when all you want to do is relax in your hotel room. For pizza, call Pizzeria Paradiso, which offers a variety of pies, and Maggie's New York Pizzeria, which as the name suggests, features New York–style thin-crust pizza. Armand's, at several locations, offers Chicago-style thick-crust pies as well as deliveries through Armand's Express Delivery. In Bethesda, Il Forno features traditional pizza. For Chinese food in Bethesda, try Foong Lin. See the listings that follow.

For **bagels,** try Bethesda Bagels, 4819 Bethesda Ave, ☎ (301) 652-8990, which has inexpensive bagels and bagel sandwiches to go, as well as Chesapeake Bagel Bakery (Capitol Hill and upper northwest locations), and Whatsa Bagel (upper northwest).

Marvelous Market doesn't feature on-site dining or delivery, but its breads are among the area's best. Marvelous Market offers sandwiches at lunch, as well as some cheese, pies, and fresh pastas to cook. Come here to pick up some picnic fare, or a "marvelous" snack to take back to your hotel room.

Some **Marvelous Market** locations are: In the District: 1510 19th St N.W., ☎ 332-3690; 5035 Connecticut Ave N.W., ☎ 686-4040. In Maryland: 15 Wisconsin Circle, Chevy Chase, ☎ (301) 652-0080; 4832 Bethesda Ave, Bethesda, ☎ (301) 986-0555. In Virginia: 9889 Georgetown Pike, Great Falls, ☎ (703) 759-5666.

## In the District

### Adams Morgan
**Ben's Chili Bowl,** 1213 U St N.W., ☎ 667-0909. A neighborhood staple with the best chili dogs in town. Inexpensive.

**Cities,** 2424 18th St N.W., ☎ 328-7194. Walk past the bar to the restaurant. The menu and the decor reflect a different city every few months. Moderate.

**Grill from Ipanema,** 1858 Columbia Road N.W., ☎ 986-0757. At this Brazilian restaurant critics favor the *feijoada,* a cassoulet of black beans, sausage, beef, and pork. Moderate.

**I Matti,** 2436 18th St N.W., ☎ 462-8844. Great pizza and pasta as well as hearty soups at this Italian restaurant. Moderate.

**Meskerem,** 2434 18th St N.W., ☎ 462-4100. This is a popular place for those who like Ethiopian food. Inexpensive.

**Perry's,** 1811 Columbia Rd N.W., ☎ 234-6218. The progressive music is as important here as the sushi and Japanese specialties. In summer, dine on the rooftop. Moderate.

**Polly's Cafe,** 1342 U St N.W., ☎ 265-8385. A cozy hangout complete with jukebox and fireplace. Moderate.

**Red Sea,** 2463 18th St N.W., ☎ 483-5000. Ethiopian fare, with one of the city's best vegetarian menus. Moderate.

**Roxanne & Peyote,** 2319 18th St N.W., ☎ 462-8330. Southwestern fare on three levels. Inexpensive.

**Tom Tom,** 2333 18th St N.W., ☎ 588-1300. Pizza, tapas, salads, grilled entrées, and desserts a specialty. Moderate.

### Capitol Hill

**America,** Union Station, 50 Massachusetts Ave N.E., ☎ 682-9555. This ambitious menu of American fare has something for everyone. Moderate.

**Armand's Chicago Pizzeria,** 226 Massachusetts Ave N.E., ☎ 547-6600. A branch of a popular chain, this casual eatery offers thick-crust pizza and a salad bar. Inexpensive.

**Bistro Bis,** Hotel George, 15 E St. N.W., ☎ 661-2200. This French bistro–style restaurant in one of Washington's newer hotels has the same owners as Vidalia, one of Washington's most popular restaurants. Items combine French cuisine with a hearty touch of the American south. Moderate.

**Bullfeathers,** 410 1st St S.E., ☎ 543-5005. This Capitol Hill pub has good hamburgers and a full menu of entrées. Moderate.

**Chesapeake Bagel Bakery,** 215 Pennsylvania Ave S.E., ☎ 546-0994. Good bagels and bagel sandwiches are available here. Several locations throughout the D.C. area. Inexpensive.

**Dirksen Senate Office Building South Buffet Room,** 1st and C Sts N.E., ☎ 224-4249. Open for lunch only, Mon–Fri, this restaurant lets you rub elbows with congressional staffers. Closes at 2:30 P.M. Inexpensive.

**La Brasserie,** 239 Massachusetts Ave N.E., ☎ 546-9154. Located in adjoining townhouses, this restaurant serves good French fare and is the place to spot Hill staffers and lobbyists. Expensive.

**La Colline,** 4000 N. Capitol St N.W., ☎ 737-0400. This bistro-style restaurant has earned a reputation as a good value for French cuisine. Expensive unless you get a pre-theater fixed-price menu.

**Library of Congress Cafeteria,** James Madison Memorial Building, 101 Independence Ave S.E., 6th floor, ☎ 707-8300. Open for breakfast and lunch and light fare until 3:30 P.M., this cafeteria has an array of choices and a good view. Inexpensive.

**Monocle,** 107 D St N.E., ☎ 546-4488. At this long-time Capitol Hill restaurant it's easy to spot senators at lunch. May be exciting to some tourists, but the food is often only adequate. Moderate.

**Refectory,** the Capitol, 1st floor, Constitution Ave and 1st St N.E., ☎ 224-4870. Located on the Senate side, stop here for breakfast and snacks. Inexpensive.

**Supreme Court Cafeteria,** 1st St N.E., between E. Capitol St and Maryland Ave, ☎ 479-3246. Try the soups and sandwiches for convenient snacks Mon–Fri. Closed to the public 12–1:15. Main cafeteria open until 2; snack bar until 3:15. Inexpensive.

**Tortilla Coast,** 201 Massachusetts Ave N.E., ☎ 546-6768. This Tex-Mex eatery is popular with congressional staffers. Inexpensive.

**Union Station Food Court,** 50 Massachusetts Ave N.E., ☎ 371-9441. This may be the most fun and the least expensive place for the family to eat while exploring Capitol Hill; the eateries here offer a wide variety of food. But be advised: When it's full, the noise level is off the charts. Inexpensive.

## Chinatown/Convention Center/MCI Center

**BET on Jazz Restaurant,** 730 11th St N.W., ☎ 393-0975. Owned by Black Entertainment Television, this themed eatery has jazz videos, memorabilia, and music. Moderate.

**Cafe Atlantico,** 405 8th St N.W., ☎ 393-0812. The Caribbean-inspired cooking is good here, especially the shrimp-and-potato croquettes and other seafood items. Moderate.

**Cafe Mozart,** 1331 H St N.W. ☎ 347-5732. The restaurant serves Wiener schnitzel, beef goulash, pork roast, and a long list of desserts. Make sandwiches yourself at the deli or buy from the carry-out. Moderate.

**China Inn,** 631 H St N.W., ☎ 842-0909. This neighborhood restaurant has been serving Chinese food for more than 55 years. Inexpensive.

**Coco Loco,** 810 7th St N.W., ☎ 289-2626. From the tapas menu order several appetizer portions of Mexican cuisine or order steaks, lamb, chicken, and pork dishes from the dinner menu, which has items typical of a Brazilian steakhouse. Moderate.

**District Chophouse and Brewery,** 509 7th St N.W., ☎ 347-3434. Steaks, seafood, and chops are served in a brew-pub atmosphere. Moderate.

**Fadó,** 808 7th St N.W., ☎ 789-0066. The pub food and the bar built in Dublin make this an authentic Irish pub. Moderate.

**Full Kee,** 509 H St N.W., ☎ 371-2233. A good assortment of Cantonese-style roasted meats. Moderate.

**Hunan Chinatown,** 624 H St N.W., ☎ 783-5858. Critics recommend the tea-smoked duck and Szechuan-style lobster. A good Chinatown choice. Inexpensive.

**Jaleo's,** 480 7th St, N.W., ☎ 628-7949. The Spanish-influenced tapas are great, as is the paella. Expensive.

**Li Ho,** 501 H St N.W., ☎ 289-2059. Good food served simply. Moderate.

**The Mark,** 401 7th St N.W., ☎ 783-3133. Noted Washington chef Alison Swope, formerly of New Heights, continues her tradition of unusual combinations. Try the smoked trout ravioli or the miso-glazed Norwegian salmon. Expensive.

**Morrison-Clark Inn,** Massachusetts Ave and 11th St N.W., ☎ 898-1200 or (800) 332-7898. This inn offers a candlelit, cozy dining room with good American and Continental cuisine. Expensive.

**Tony Cheng's Mongolian Restaurant,** 619 H St N.W., ☎ 842-8669. Try the all-you-can-eat barbecue at this Mongolian restaurant. Inexpensive.

**Velocity Grill,** MCI Center, 7th & H St N.W., ☎ 347-7780. A sports restaurant with a glass wall overlooking the Wizards' practice court. Moderate.

## Downtown

**Benkay Japanese Restaurant,** 727 15th St N.W., ☎ 737-1515. Specializes in sushi and karaoke. Moderate.

**Bertolini's,** 801 Pennsylvania Ave N.W., ☎ 638-2140. This restaurant is known for its pastas, grilled fish, and huge desserts. Expensive.

**Bice,** 601 Pennsylvania Ave N.W., (entrance on Indiana Ave, between 6th and 7th Sts), ☎ 638-2428. This handsome restaurant serves classic Italian cuisine. Expensive.

**Bacchus,** 1827 Jefferson Place N.W., ☎ 785-0734. If you can't decide what to have at this Lebanese restaurant, try the assortment of appetizers. Moderate.

**Bombay Club,** 815 Connecticut Ave N.W., ☎ 659-3727. At this upscale Indian restaurant, a favorite of the Clintons, try the tandoori prawns and the lamb roganjosh. Moderate.

**Chesapeake Bagel Bakery,** 1636 Connecticut Ave N.W., ☎ 328-7985. See "Capitol Hill" listing. Inexpensive.

**Coeur de Lion,** 926 Massachusetts Ave N.W., ☎ 414-0500. This romantic dining room features New American food with a French accent. Expensive.

**D.C. Coast,** 1401 K St N.W., ☎ 216-5988. This popular restaurant is a two-story, Art Deco–inspired space. It is noisy and busy, but the "tricoastal American cuisine"—east, west, and southern—is terrific. The seafood is especially noteworthy (try the crabcakes), but meat and even vegetarian dishes are also available. Expensive.

**Food Court at the Old Post Office Pavilion,** 1100 Pennsylvania Ave N.W., ☎ 289-4224. For cheap eats on the go when sightseeing on Pennsylvania Avenue, sample the food from the numerous eateries. Inexpensive.

**Food Hall at the Shops at National Place,** 1331 Pennsylvania Ave N.W., ☎ 783-9090. An assortment of fast-food places. Inexpensive.

**Galileo,** 1110 21st St N.W., ☎ 293-7191. This stylish restaurant serves creative Italian cuisine prepared by an internationally recognized chef. Expensive.

**Georgia Brown's,** 950 15th St N.W., ☎ 393-4499. A popular, noisy restaurant, Georgia Brown's dishes up large portions of innovative Southern cuisine. Classics include the she-crab soup, fried chicken, and shrimp and grits. Expensive.

**Hard Rock Cafe,** 999 E St N.W., ☎ 737-ROCK. The burgers, fries, and salads come with rock 'n' roll memorabilia. Inexpensive.

**Hay-Adams Hotel, The Lafayette,** 1 Lafayette Square, 16th and H Sts N.W., ☎ 638-6600. Serves American and Continental fare for dinner. Expensive.

**I Ricchi,** 1220 19th St N.W., ☎ 835-0459. This Italian restaurant offers traditional Tuscan cuisine. Expensive.

**Jefferson Restaurant,** Jefferson Hotel, 1200 16th St N.W., ☎ 347-2200. This small, romantic restaurant serves "New Virginia" cuisine in an elegant but understated setting. Expensive.

**Legal Sea Foods,** 2020 K St N.W., ☎ 496-1111. This local version of the popular Boston chain serves good seafood. The restaurant is very busy for midweek lunch as D.C.'s lawyers and lobbyists dine here (and elsewhere). Moderate.

**McCormick & Schmick's Seafood Restaurant,** 1652 K St N.W., ☎ 861-2233. There is an extensive seafood menu.

**Morton's of Chicago,** 1050 Connecticut Ave N.W., ☎ 955-5997. One of D.C.'s top steakhouses. Regulars come back for the porterhouse. Very expensive.

**Occidental Grill,** 1475 Pennsylvania Ave N.W., ☎ 783-1475. This lunch spot, popular with businesspeople, is noted for its swordfish sandwich and black bean soup. Moderate.

**Old Ebbitt Grill,** 675 15th St N.W., F and G Sts, ☎ 347-4801. The upscale pub atmosphere of brass and wood is pleasing. Kids like the hamburgers, and adults like the pastas. Moderate.

**Oodles Noodles,** 1120 19th St N.W., ☎ 293-3138. This Pan-Asian restaurant offers a variety of noodle dishes and noodle soups. The food is good and the price is right. Inexpensive.

**The Palm,** 1225 19th St N.W., ☎ 293-9091. This well-known dining spot is famous for steaks and lobsters. Expensive.

**Planet Hollywood,** 1101 Pennsylvania Ave N.W., ☎ 783-7827. Dine among Hollywood paraphernalia at this tribute to the stars. Moderate.

**Prime Rib,** 2020 K St N.W., ☎ 466-8811. This classy lunch spot serves up steaks and a 1940s Manhattan superclub ambience. Expensive.

**Red Sage,** 605 14th St N.W., ☎ 638-4444. Stylish restaurant with trendy Southwestern food. Expensive.

**Sam & Harry's,** 1200 19th St N.W., ☎ 296-4333. Porterhouse, crabcake, and lobster are good choices at this popular steakhouse. Expensive.

**701 Pennsylvania Avenue,** 701 Pennsylvania Ave N.W., ☎ 393-0701. The international cuisine served here has received rave reviews, as has the lounge for its many varieties of vodka and fine caviar. Expensive.

**Sichuan Pavilion,** 1820 K St N.W., ☎ 466-7790. An expert Chinese chef prepares the food at this upscale restaurant. Expensive.

**Skyroom Terrace,** Hotel Washington, 15th St and Pennsylvania Ave N.W., call the hotel at ☎ 638-5900. From May to Oct, this terrace café offers light fare and good views. Inexpensive.

**Taberna del Albardero,** 1776 I St N.W., entrance on 18th St between I and H Sts, ☎ 429-2200. The lobster paella is a favorite at this Spanish restaurant. Expensive.

**Le Tarbouche,** 1801 K St N.W., ☎ 331-5551. This Middle Eastern restaurant also has a variety of vegetarian entrées. Moderate.

**Twenty-One Federal,** 1736 L St N.W., ☎ 331-9771. The chef is a top modern American cook who uses fresh ingredients and imaginative touches. Try the wild rice soup with chicken. Expensive.

**Vidalia,** 1990 M St N.W., ☎ 659-1990. Some of the specialties of this restaurant's updated southern American cooking are the lemon chess pie, roasted onion soup with spoon bread, and beef brisket braised in local apple cider. Expensive.

**Willard Room,** Willard Hotel, 1401 Pennsylvania Ave N.W., ☎ 637-7440. The dining room has the gracious feel of wood and brass, plus good food and attentive service. Expensive.

### Dupont Circle

**BeDuCi,** 2100 P St N.W., ☎ 223-3824. Mediterranean cuisine with southern European and North African influences. Moderate.

**Buffalo Billiards,** 1330 19th St N.W. ☎ 331-7665. Western decor and flavorful entrées. Inexpensive.

**Chesapeake Bagel Bakery,** 1636 Connecticut Ave N.W., ☎ 328-7985. See "Capitol Hill" listing. Inexpensive.

**I Ricchi,** 1220 19th St N.W., ☎ 835-0459. The pasta and fish are especially good choices at this decade-old, D.C. favorite, Italian restaurant. Expensive.

**Iron Gate,** 1734 N St N.W., ☎ 737-1370. The Mediterranean food comes with a romantic inn atmosphere. Moderate.

**Jockey Club,** Westin Fairfax Hotel, 2100 Massachusetts Ave N.W., ☎ 835-2100. Washington insiders and lobbyists have been dining here for years. Expensive.

**Kramerbooks & Afterwords Cafe,** 1517 Connecticut Ave N.W., ☎ 387-1462. Go here for a sandwich or a snack to accompany your book browsing. Inexpensive.

**Nora,** 2132 Florida Ave N.W., ☎ 462-5143. Fresh ingredients and imaginative cooking have made the New American cuisine popular at this pretty and unpretentious place. Moderate.

**Obelisk,** 2029 P St N.W., ☎ 872-1180. Authentic Italian cuisine with a fixed-price menu. Expensive.

**Pizzeria Paradiso,** 2029 P St N.W., ☎ 223-1245. This restaurant serves great pizza with great crust. Inexpensive.

**Raku,** 1900 Q St N.W., ☎ 265-7258. Good Asian-style cuisine, including tempura, sushi, and grilled dishes. Also located in Bethesda. Moderate.

**Sala Thai,** 2016 P St N.W., ☎ 872-1144. A colorful café serving Thai food. Moderate.

**Straits of Malaya,** 1836 18th St N.W., ☎ 483-1483. When the weather is nice, sit on the roof deck and sample Malaysian and Singaporean dishes. Moderate.

### Foggy Bottom/Georgetown/West End

**Aquarelle,** Watergate Hotel, 2650 Virginia Ave N.W., ☎ 298-4455. This French restaurant has a menu that changes with the seasons. Expensive.

**Asia Nora,** 2213 M St N.W., ☎ 797-4860. This intimate Nouvelle Asian restaurant presents mostly seafood. Expensive.

**Au Pied de Cochon,** 1335 Wisconsin Ave N.W., ☎ 333-5440. This café is open 24 hours. The menu has omelets, salads, quiche, and crepes. Moderate.

**Aux Beaux Champs,** Four Seasons Hotel, 2800 Pennsylvania Ave N.W., ☎ 342-0444. Fine French cuisine. Expensive.

**Bistro Francais,** 3128 M St N.W., ☎ 338-3830. Good bets at this French bistro are the daily specials and the onion soup. Moderate.

**Chadwick's,** 3205 K St N.W., ☎ 333-2565. Kids get balloons and a children's menu. The salads and burgers are generally good, as are the daily specials. Several locations. Inexpensive.

**Clyde's,** 3236 M St N.W., ☎ 333-9180. A long-standing tradition in Georgetown, Clyde's is known for its pub food. Moderate.

**Colonnade,** Washington Monarch Hotel, 24th and M Sts N.W., ☎ 457-5000. This restaurant offers a pretty setting in a courtyard plus good American food. Moderate.

**Dean & DeLuca Café,** 3276 M St N.W., ☎ 342-2500. This upscale food market also serves soups, salads, and sandwiches to go or to eat in, café style. Inexpensive.

**Enriqueta's,** 2811 M St N.W., ☎ 338-7772. A popular Georgetown spot serving Mexican food. Moderate.

**Filomena's,** 1063 Wisconsin Ave N.W., ☎ 338-8800. The best choices at this lively and noisy restaurant are the pastas. The vegetable herb bread is terrific. Moderate.

**Georgetown Bagelry,** 3245 M St N.W., ☎ 965-1011. Good bagel sandwiches. Inexpensive.

**Houston's,** 1065 Wisconsin Ave N.W., ☎ 338-7760. Known for their ribs and chicken, Houston's has long lines. Inexpensive.

**Japan Inn,** 1715 Wisconsin Ave N.W., ☎ 337-3400. Choose group dining and watch the cooks put on a show, or choose the privacy of the tatami rooms. Moderate.

**Kinkead's,** 2000 Pennsylvania Ave N.W., ☎ 296-7700. Chef Bob Kinkead's seafood-oriented menu is innovative. The signature dish is the pepita-crusted salmon. Expensive.

**La Chaumiere,** 2813 M St N.W., ☎ 338-1784. This is an old-fashioned French country restaurant in the heart of Georgetown. Noted for couscous, venison, and fresh seafood. Expensive.

**Martin's Tavern,** 1264 Wisconsin Ave N.W., ☎ 333-7370. A neighborhood pub and restaurant that welcomes visitors. Moderate.

**Miss Saigon,** 3057 M St N.W., ☎ 333-5545. A big bowl of soup here is a meal all by itself. Inexpensive.

**Morton's of Chicago,** 3251 Prospect St N.W., ☎ 342-6258. Rated as one of the top steakhouses in the area. Signature dishes include the porterhouse and the prime rib. Very expensive.

**Sea Catch,** Canal Square, 1054 31st St N.W., ☎ 337-8855. This is a good choice for seafood in Georgetown. Expensive.

**Sequoia Restaurant,** 3000 K St N.W., ☎ 944-4200. The lengthy menu offers eclectic fare, including sandwiches, pastas, and grilled seafood, but the food can be mediocre. On weekends the bar is mobbed with twenty-somethings in search of other twenty-somethings. A great view of the Potomac River. Moderate.

**1789,** 1226 36th St N.W., ☎ 965-1789. Dine upstairs in a nicely appointed Georgetown townhouse on Modern American cuisine. Expensive. Downstairs is an inexpensive burger restaurant.

**The Tombs,** 1226 36th St N.W., ☎ 337-6668. Local college students, especially from neighboring Georgetown University, and 20-somethings gather at this popular pub to see and be seen. The food includes burgers, chili, and sandwiches. Inexpensive.

**Uno's Pizzeria & Bar,** 3211 M St N.W., ☎ 965-6333. Known for its pizza. Inexpensive.

**Zed's Ethiopian Cuisine,** 3318 M St N.W., ☎ 333-4710. Ethiopian cuisine. The signature dish is broiled short ribs. Inexpensive.

### Mall Area

**Air and Space Museum Flight Line Cafeteria,** Independence Ave at 6th St S.W., ☎ 357-2700. Buffet station offers pizza, sandwiches, and hot entrées. Come early because this is a popular spot. Inexpensive.

**Air and Space Museum Wright Place Restaurant,** upstairs from the Flight Line Cafeteria, Independence Ave at 4th St S.W., ☎ 371-8777. This Air and Space alternative offers burgers and chicken sandwiches. Reservations are suggested 11:30–3:00. Inexpensive.

**Hirshhorn Museum's Full Circle Plaza Cafe,** south side of the Mall at Independence Ave and 8th St S.W., ☎ 357-2700. The outdoor café serves salads and sandwiches. Open Memorial Day to Labor Day. Inexpensive.

**National Gallery of Art Cascade Cafe,** between the two wings of the National Gallery, 3rd and 7th Sts N.W., ☎ 737-4215. A view of an interior waterfall brightens this space, and the buffet choices are acceptable. Kids like the view. Inexpensive.

**National Gallery of Art Garden Cafe,** West Building, 6th St and Constitution Ave N.W., ☎ 357-2700. This restaurant has a fountain for atmosphere and a light lunch fare. Moderate.

**National Gallery of Art Terrace Cafe,** East Building, 4th St and Constitution Ave N.W., ☎ 357-2700. For a quieter atmosphere than the downstairs buffet, try this restaurant's salads and sandwiches. Moderate.

**National Museum of American History,** Cafeteria Carousel, Constitution Ave

N.W. at 14th St, ☎ 357-2700. Convenience is the most marketable item here as the fare tends to hot dogs and hamburgers. Inexpensive.

**National Museum of American History,** Palm Court (Victorian Ice Cream Parlor), 14th St and Constitution Ave N.W., ☎ 357-1832. Take the kids here for ice cream from 11 to 4. Inexpensive.

**National Museum of Natural History Cafeteria,** 10th St and Constitution Ave N.W., ☎ 357-2700. Burgers, hot dogs, and chicken sandwiches are among the average standards here. Inexpensive.

### Upper Northwest—Cleveland Park, Woodley Park, Chevy Chase, etc.

**American City Diner,** 5532 Connecticut Ave N.W., ☎ 244-1949. This 24-hour diner serves omelets all the time. The French toast is good and kids even like the meatloaf, but the place can be noisy and items vary in quality. Inexpensive.

**Ardeo,** 3311 Connecticut Ave N.W., ☎ 244-6750. D.C. restaurateur Ashok Bajaj, noted for the Bombay Club, 701, and the Oval Room, has opened this neighborhood restaurant in Cleveland Park. The Art Deco–inspired setting establishes a nice tone and the food is very good. Moderate.

**Armand's Chicago Pizzeria,** 4231 Wisconsin Ave N.W., ☎ 686-9450, and 4400 Massachusetts Ave N.W., ☎ 966-4800. This popular, inexpensive eatery offers a salad bar and thick-crust pizza. The pizza can be delivered via **Armand's Express** ☎ 363-5500.

**Austin Grill,** 2404 Wisconsin Ave N.W., ☎ 337-8080. The Tex-Mex cuisine here is not only good, it's cheap. Inexpensive.

**Busara,** 2340 Wisconsin Ave N.W., ☎ 337-2340. This top-rated Thai restaurant near Georgetown has a dramatic decor and good food. Moderate.

**Cactus Cantina,** 3300 Wisconsin Ave N.W., ☎ 686-7222. The Tex-Mex cuisine here includes fajitos, spare ribs, and barbecued quail, as well as tacos and enchiladas. Inexpensive.

**Chadwick's,** 5257 Wisconsin Ave N.W., ☎ 362-8040. See "Foggy Bottom/Georgetown/West End" listing. Inexpensive.

**Cheesecake Factory,** 5345 Wisconsin Ave N.W., ☎ 364-0500. The wait can be long, so come early to this popular restaurant that serves a variety of pastas, sandwiches, and salads in huge portions, plus a good Sun brunch. Save room for the cheesecake, of course. Moderate.

**Dancing Crab,** 4611 Wisconsin Ave N.W., ☎ 244-1882. Come to this neighborhood eatery for buckets of steamers and Maryland crabs served on paper tablecloths. Moderate.

**Krupins,** 4620 Wisconsin Ave N.W., ☎ 686-1989. Stop by this New York–style deli for an overstuffed sandwich. Inexpensive.

**Lebanese Taverna,** 2641 Connecticut Ave N.W., ☎ 265-8681. A casual and friendly Lebanese restaurant. Try the rotisserie chicken wrapped in thin bread. Moderate.

**Maggiano's Little Italy,** 5333 Wisconsin Ave N.W., ☎ 966-5500. At this friendly Italian restaurant the portions are huge and designed for sharing. Moderate.

**New Heights,** 2317 Calvert St N.W., ☎ 234-4110. *Gourmet* magazine called this restaurant serving New American cuisine (traditional dishes mixed with ingredients from Asia, India, South America, and other locales) one of Washington's top 20 restaurants.

**Saigon Gourmet,** 2635 Connecticut Ave N.W., ☎ 265-1360. This is one of the leading Vietnamese restaurants in the area. Inexpensive.

**Whatsa Bagel,** 3513 Connecticut Ave N.W., ☎ 966-8990. Order fresh bagels to go or sit and munch at one of the few tables. Inexpensive.

## In Maryland

**Andalucia,** 12300 Wilkins Ave, Rockville, ☎ (301) 770-1880. The southern Spanish cuisine here is good. Try the red snapper with mushrooms. Expensive.

**Armand's Chicago Pizzeria,** 1909 Seminary Rd, Silver Spring, ☎ (301) 588-3400. Express Delivery, 190 Halpine Rd, Rockville, ☎ (301) 231-5000, or 18208 Contour Rd, Gaithersburg, ☎ (301) 990-2500. See "In the District—Capitol Hill" listing. Inexpensive.

**Austin Grill,** 7278 Woodmont Ave, ☎ (301) 656-1366. The Tex-Mex food is inexpensive, the atmosphere lively, but the quality of the entrées varies. Inexpensive.

**Bacchus Bethesda,** 7945 Norfolk Ave, Bethesda, ☎ (301) 657-1722. See "In the District—Downtown" listing. Moderate.

**Bethesda Bagels,** 4819 Bethesda Ave, Bethesda, ☎ (301) 652-8990. A take-out place worth knowing for its bagels and bagel sandwiches. Inexpensive.

**Bethesda Crab House,** 4958 Bethesda Ave, Bethesda, ☎ (301) 652-3382. Come here to taste Maryland's traditional hard-shell crabs. Inexpensive.

**Cottonwood Café,** 4844 Cordell Ave, ☎ (301) 656-4844. The paella and the duck are good bets at this upmarket Southwestern restaurant. Moderate.

**Crisfield Seafood Restaurant,** 8012 Georgia Ave, Silver Spring, ☎ (301) 589-1306, and **Crisfield Seafood Restaurant at Lee Plaza,** 8606 Colesville Rd, Silver Spring, ☎ (301) 588-1572. Whether you're dining at the original Georgia Ave location, with its plain decor, or at the newer branch on Colesville Road, you'll find out why the seafood here has been a Maryland tradition. Try the flounder stuffed with crab or the grilled fish. Moderate.

**Crisp & Juicy,** 3800 International Drive Ave, Silver Spring, ☎ (301) 598-3333, and 1331-G Rockville Pike, Rockville, ☎ (301) 251-8833. The Peruvian-style grilled chicken is a hit. Another location in Virginia. Inexpensive.

**Faryab,** 4917 Cordell Ave, ☎ (301) 951-3484. Some of the specialties of this Afghanistan restaurant are sautéed pumpkin, boulani (ravioli stuffed with scallions), and chicken kebab. Moderate.

**Foong Lin,** 7710 Norfolk Ave, ☎ (301) 656-3427. This neighborhood restaurant has a variety of good dishes and quick service—sometimes a little too quick. Moderate.

**Joe's Restaurant,** 1488-C Rockville Pike, Rockville, ☎ (301) 881-5518. The Thai food here is good. Inexpensive.

**Good Fortune,** 2646 University Blvd West, Wheaton, ☎ (301) 929-8818. This Cantonese restaurant offers more than 200 dishes. Inexpensive.

**Hard Times Cafe,** 1117 Nelson St, Rockville, ☎ (301) 294-9720. Choose either the Texas- or the Cincinnati-style chili. Inexpensive.

**Houston's,** 12256 Rockville Pike, Rockville, ☎ (301) 468-3535, and 7715 Woodmont Ave, Bethesda, ☎ (301) 656-9755. See "In the District—Foggy Bottom/Georgetown/West End" listing. Moderate.

**Il Forno,** 4926 Cordell Ave, Bethesda, ☎ (301) 652-7757. The pizza is noteworthy. If the weather's good, enjoy sitting outside. Moderate.

**Louisiana Express Co.,** 4921 Bethesda Ave, Rockville, ☎ (301) 652-6945. This small, informal cafeteria serves New Orleans–style food. Good bets include the gumbos and the jambalaya. Inexpensive.

**Maharaja,** 8825 Greenbelt Rd, Greenbelt, ☎ (301) 552-1600. This small restaurant serves good tandoori chicken and lamb biryani. Inexpensive.

**Matuba,** 4918 Cordell Ave, Bethesda, ☎ (301) 652-7449. Sushi and tempura are among the popular choices at this Japanese restaurant. Inexpensive.

**Old Angler's Inn,** 10801 MacArthur Blvd, Potomac, ☎ (301) 299-9097. Near Great Falls Park, this restaurant appeals with a varied menu. Try the smoked cod ravioli or braised Maryland guinea fowl. Expensive.

**Persepolis,** 7130 Wisconsin Ave, Bethesda, ☎ (301) 656-9339. A Persian restaurant with unbeatable kebabs and an all-you-can-eat lunch buffet. Moderate.

**Oodles Noodles,** 4907 Cordell Ave, Bethesda ☎ (301) 986-8833. This Pan-Asian restaurant offers a variety of noodle dishes and noodle soups. The tables are close together and the service a bit too quick, but the food is good. Lots of families eat here. Inexpensive.

**Pho 75,** 1510 University Blvd, East Lanley Park, ☎ (301) 434-7844. Delicious soup and side dishes at bargain prices. Inexpensive.

**Raku, An Asian Diner,** 7240 Woodmont Ave ☎ (301) 718-8680. Good Asian-style cuisine, including tempura, sushi, and grilled dishes. Also in D.C.'s Dupont Circle area. Moderate.

**Red Hot & Blue,** 677 Main St, Laurel, ☎ (301) 953-1943, and 200 Old Mill Bottom Rd, Annapolis, ☎ (410) 626-7427. Several locations in Virginia. Ribs—Memphis-style, smoked over hickory wood—bring the crowds. Inexpensive.

**Rio Grande Cafe,** 4919 Fairmont Ave, Bethesda, ☎ (301) 656-2981. The Tex-Mex nachos, enchiladas, and tacos are hits at this popular and noisy eatery. No reservations are allowed; the wait can be long, so arrive early. Moderate.

**Sam Woo,** 1054 Rockville Pike, Rockville, ☎ (301) 424-0495 or 0496. Best bets at this Korean restaurant include fish fillet and egg dumplings. Moderate.

**Tastee Diner,** 7731 Woodmont Ave, Bethesda, ☎ (301) 652-3970. A classic community eatery, open 24 hours a day. Also at 118 Washington Blvd, Laurel, ☎ (301) 953-7567, and 8516 Georgia Ave, Silver Spring, ☎ (301) 589-8171. Inexpensive.

**Thyme Square Café,** 4735 Bethesda Ave, Bethesda, ☎ (301) 657-9077. The restaurant uses organic food and healthy ingredients in its eclectic menu. Along with chicken and fish dishes, there are salads and several vegetarian dishes. Moderate.

**Tragara,** 4935 Cordell Ave, Bethesda, ☎ (301) 951-4935. This attractive Italian restaurant can be erratic. The pastas and the veal are generally good. Expensive.

## In Virginia

**Amphora,** 377 Maple Ave W., Vienna, ☎ (703) 938-7877, and 1151 Elden St, Herndon, ☎ (703) 925-0900. A 24-hour-a-day diner and restaurant serving a wide variety of American food with some Greek. Moderate.

**Armand's Chicago Pizzeria,** 111 King St, Old Town, ☎ (703) 683-0313, and 4716 King St, Skyline, ☎ (703) 578-3303. See "In the District—Upper Northwest" listing. Inexpensive.

**Atami,** 3155 Wilson Blvd, Arlington, ☎ (703) 522-4787. The sushi is popular at this restaurant, which serves Japanese and Vietnamese foods. Critics also recommend the spring rolls and lemongrass chicken. Inexpensive.

**Atlacatl and Pupuseria,** 2716 North Washington Blvd, Arlington, ☎ (703) 524-9032, and **Atlacatl II,** 4701 Columbia Pike, Arlington, ☎ (703) 920-3680. This Salvadoran restaurant is known for its fried yucca, tamales, fillet of pork, and fish dishes. Inexpensive.

**Bistro Bistro,** 4021 S. 28th St, Arlington, ☎ (703) 379-0300; 1811 Library St, Reston, ☎ (703) 834-6300; and 4301 N. Fairfax Dr, Arlington, ☎ (703) 522-1800. A friendly and unpretentious place that has a seasonally changing menu. Try the oyster stew. Moderate.

**Blue Print Grill,** 600 Franklin St, Alexandria, ☎ (703) 739-0404. Their Creole-inspired dishes include Chesapeake oysters in cornmeal. Expensive.

**Cajun Bangkok,** 907 King St, Alexandria, ☎ (703) 836-0038. The unlikely combination of Cajun and Thai food works here. Critics recommend the pecan-crushed catfish. Inexpensive.

**Calvert Grille,** 3106 Mount Vernon Ave, Alexandria, ☎ (703) 838-8425. Specialties at this neighborhood restaurant include barbecued ribs, crab cakes, and grilled chicken. Inexpensive.

**Carnegie Delicatessen & Restaurant,** Embassy Suites Hotel, 8517 Leesburg Pike, Vienna, ☎ (703) 790-5001. This is a New York–style deli with oversized corn beef and pastrami sandwiches. Inexpensive.

**Chadwick's,** 203 S. Strand, Old Town, ☎ (703) 836-4442. Several locations. See "In the District—Foggy Bottom/Georgetown/West End" listing. Inexpensive.

**Chesapeake Seafood and Crab House,** 3607 Wilson Blvd, Arlington, ☎ (703) 528-8888. Vietnamese-style seafood. Inexpensive.

**Crisp & Juicy,** 4540 Lee Hwy, Arlington, ☎ (703) 243-4222. The Peruvian-style grilled chicken is a hit. Inexpensive.

**Faccia Luna,** 2909 Wilson Blvd, Clarendon, ☎ (703) 276-3090. See "In the District—Upper Northwest" listing. Inexpensive.

**Food Factory,** 4221 N. Fairfax Dr, Ballston, ☎ (703) 527-2279. This no-frills restaurant serves simple but good Pakistani food. Inexpensive.

**Generous George's,** 3006 Duke St, Alexandria, ☎ (703) 370-4303; 6937 Telegraph Rd, Hayfield, ☎ (703) 719-5600; and 6131 Backlick Rd, Springfield, ☎ (703) 451-7111. The portions of pizza and pasta are oversize and good. Inexpensive.

**The Grill,** Ritz-Carlton Pentagon City Hotel, 1250 S. Hayes St, Arlington, ☎ (703) 415-5000. This popular dining spot is known for its contemporary and innovative French and American cuisine.

**Hard Times Cafe,** 1404 King St, Alexandria, ☎ (703) 683-5340, and 3028 Wilson Blvd, Clarendon, ☎ (703) 528-2233. See "In Maryland" listing. Inexpensive.

**Inn at Little Washington,** Middle and Main Sts, Washington, ☎ (703) 675-3800. Chef Patrick O'Connell labels his cuisine New American, a style that uses the freshest ingredients. The inn offers gracious and exceptional dining. Book months ahead. It's worth the one-hour drive from the District. Very expensive.

**Kazan,** 6813 Redmond Dr, McLean, ☎ (703) 734-1960. This is a good-value Turkish restaurant. Moderate.

**L'Auberge Chez François,** 332 Springvale Rd, Great Falls, ☎ (703) 759-3800.

A cheery French restaurant with the atmosphere of a country inn plus good food. Expensive.

**La Bergerie,** 218 N. Lee St, Alexandria, ☎ (703) 683-1007. Excellent Basque cuisine. Try the duck and don't miss the desserts. Expensive.

**Le Gaulois Cafe,** 1106 King St, Alexandria, ☎ (703) 739-9494. This pleasant restaurant serves well-priced French family fare. Moderate.

**Le Refuge,** 127 N. Washington St, Alexandria, ☎ (703) 548-4661. Cassoulet, bouillabaisse, and leg of lamb are good choices at this country French restaurant. Moderate.

**Lite-N-Fair,** 1018 King St, Alexandria, ☎ (703) 549-3717. The reason people line up at this small restaurant is the tasty food, including the chocolate mousse. Inexpensive.

**Matuba Japanese Restaurant,** 2915 Columbia Pike, Arlington, ☎ (703) 521-2811. Sushi and tempura are among the popular choices at this Japanese restaurant. Inexpensive.

**Morton's-Tysons,** Fairfax Square, 8075 Leesburg Pike, Vienna, ☎ (703) 883-0800. One of the top-rated steakhouses in the D.C. area. Very expensive.

**Pasha Cafe,** 3815 Lee Hwy, Arlington, ☎ (703) 528-2126. A variety of Egyptian foods. Inexpensive.

**Peking Gourmet Inn,** 6029-33 Leesburg Pike, Baileys Crossroads, ☎ (703) 671-8088. Specializing in Peking duck, this Chinese restaurant was a favorite of President Bush. Moderate.

**Pines of Italy,** 237 N. Glebe Rd, Arlington, ☎ (703) 524-4969. The pasta and the osso buco are good choices at this Italian restaurant. Inexpensive.

**Red Hot & Blue,** 1600 Wilson Blvd, Arlington, ☎ (703) 276-7427, and 8637 Sudley Rd, Manassas, ☎ (703) 330-4847. Several locations. See "In Maryland" listing. Inexpensive.

**The Restaurant,** Ritz-Carlton Tysons, 1700 Tysons Blvd, McLean, ☎ (703) 506-4300. The good-quality American food here includes a moderately priced Friday night seafood buffet that is worth a try. Expensive.

**Rio Grande Cafe,** 4301 N. Fairfax Dr, Arlington, ☎ (703) 528-3131, and Reston Town Center, 1827 Library St, Reston ☎ (703) 904-0703. Several Locations. See "In Maryland" listing. Moderate.

**RT's Restaurant,** 3804 Mount Vernon Ave, Alexandria, ☎ (703) 684-6010. Creative seafood prepared with Cajun and Italian influences. Moderate.

**Savio's,** 514A S. Van Dorn St, Alexandria, ☎ (703) 212-9651. The seafood and pastas are especially good here. Inexpensive.

**South Austin Grill,** 801 King St, Alexandria, ☎ (703) 684-8969. Affordable Tex-Mex cuisine. Go for the chili. Inexpensive.

**Tachibana Japanese Restaurant,** 6715 Lowell Ave, McLean, ☎ (703) 847-1771. The sushi here is excellent, and so are the tempura dishes. Inexpensive.

**Union Street Public House,** 121 S. Union St, Alexandria, ☎ (703) 548-1785. This pub serves Virginia-native beer, good burgers, and gumbo. Moderate.

## Best Bargains

**Inexpensive Restaurants in the District of Columbia**
**Aditi,** 3299 M St N.W., ☎ 625-6825. Indian.
**Armand's Chicago Pizzeria,** 4231 Wisconsin Ave N.W., ☎ 686-9450. Pizza.

**Austin Grill,** 2404 Wisconsin Ave N.W., ☎ 337-8080. Tex-Mex.

**Ben's Chili Bowl,** 1213 U St N.W., ☎ 667-0909. American.

**Cactus Cantina,** 3300 Wisconsin Ave N.W., ☎ 686-7222. Tex-Mex.

**Chadwick's,** 3205 K St N.W., ☎ 333-2565, and 5257 Wisconsin Ave N.W., ☎ 362-8040.

**Chesapeake Bagel Bakery,** 215 Pennsylvania Ave S.E., ☎ 546-0994; 1636 Connecticut Ave N.W., ☎ 328-7985. Bagels and bagel sandwiches.

**China Inn,** 631 H St N.W., ☎ 842-0909. Chinese.

**Faccia Luna,** 2400 Wisconsin Ave N.W., ☎ 337-3132. Pizza.

**Food Court at the Old Post Office Pavilion,** 1100 Pennsylvania Ave N.W., ☎ 289-4224. American and ethnic.

**Food Hall at the Shops at National Place,** 1331 Pennsylvania Ave N.W., ☎ 783-9090. American and ethnic.

**Georgetown Bagelry,** 3245 M St N.W., ☎ 965-1011. Bagels.

**Georgetown Cafe,** 1523 Wisconsin Ave N.W., ☎ 333-0215. American.

**Hard Rock Cafe,** 999 E St N.W., ☎ 737-ROCK. American.

**Houston's,** 1065 Wisconsin Ave N.W., ☎ 338-7760; 7715 Woodmont Ave, Bethesda, ☎ (301) 656-9755; and 12256 Rockville Pike, Rockville, ☎ (301) 468-3535. Ribs and Chicken.

**Hunan Chinatown,** 624 H St N.W., ☎ 783-5858. Chinese.

**Kramerbooks & Afterwords Cafe,** 1517 Connecticut Ave N.W., ☎ 387-1462. American.

**Lebanese Taverna,** 2641 Connecticut Ave N.W., ☎ 265-8681. Lebanese.

**Library of Congress Cafeteria,** James Madison Memorial Building, 101 Independence Ave S.E., 6th floor, ☎ 554-4114. American.

**Madurai,** 3318 M St N.W., ☎ 333-0997. Indian.

**Meskerem,** 2434 18th St N.W., ☎ 462-4100. Ethiopian.

**Pizzeria Paradiso,** 2029 P Street N.W., ☎ 223-1245. Pizza.

**Polly's Cafe,** 1342 U St N.W., ☎ 265-8385. American.

**Saigon Gourmet,** 2635 Connecticut Ave N.W., ☎ 265-1360. Vietnamese.

**Sfuzzi,** Union Station, 50 Massachusetts Ave N.W., ☎ 842-4141. Italian.

**Sky Terrace,** Hotel Washington, 15th St and Pennsylvania Ave N.W., ☎ 638-5900. American.

**Tom Tom,** 2333 18th St N.W., ☎ 588-1300. Mediterranean.

**Tony Cheng's Mongolian Restaurant,** 619 H St N.W., ☎ 842-8669. Mongolian/Chinese.

**Union Station Food Court,** 50 Massachusetts Ave N.E. ☎ 371-9441. Variety of eateries.

**Uno's Pizzeria & Bar,** 3211 M St N.W., ☎ 965-6333. Pizza.

**Whatsa Bagel,** 3513 Connecticut Ave N.W., ☎ 966-8990. Bagels.

**Zed's Ethiopian Cuisine,** 3318 M St N.W., ☎ 333-4710. Ethiopian.

### Inexpensive Restaurants in Maryland

**Bethesda Crab House,** 4958 Bethesda Ave, Bethesda, ☎ (301) 652-3382. Seafood.

**Hard Times Cafe,** 1117 Nelson St, Rockville, ☎ (301) 294-9720. Chili.

**Houston's,** 7715 Woodmont Ave, Bethesda, ☎ (301) 656-9755, and 12256 Rockville Pike, Rockville, ☎ (301) 468-3535. Ribs and Chicken.

**Joe's Restaurant,** 1488-C Rockville Pike, Rockville, ☎ (301) 881-5518. Thai.

**Louisiana Express Co.,** 4921 Bethesda Ave, Rockville, ☎ (301) 652-6945. New Orleans.

**Maharaja,** 8825 Greenbelt Rd, Greenbelt, ☎ (301) 552-1600. Indian.

**Matuba,** 4918 Cordell Ave, Bethesda, ☎ (301) 652-7449. Japanese.

**Pho 75,** 1510 University Blvd, East Langley Park, ☎ (301) 434-7844.

**Red Hot & Blue,** 677 Main St, Laurel, ☎ (301) 953-1943, and 200 Old Bottom Rd, Annapolis, ☎ (410) 626-7427. Ribs, Memphis-style.

**Rio Grande Cafe,** 4919 Fairmont Ave, Bethesda, ☎ (301) 656-2981. Tex-Mex.

**Sam Woo,** 1054 Rockville Pike, Rockville, ☎ (301) 424-0495 or 0496. Korean.

**Tastee Diner,** 7731 Woodmont Ave, Bethesda, ☎ (301) 652-3970. American.

### Inexpensive Restaurants in Virginia

**Armand's Chicago Pizzeria,** 111 King St, Old Town, ☎ (703) 683-0313, and 4716 King St, Skyline, ☎ (703) 578-3303. Pizza.

**Atami,** 3155 Wilson Blvd, Arlington, ☎ (703) 522-4787. Japanese, Vietnamese.

**Atlacatl and Pupuseria,** 4701 Columbia Pike, Arlington, ☎ (703) 524-9032. Salvadoran.

**Atlacatl II,** 2602 Columbia Pike, Arlington, ☎ (703) 920-3680. Salvadoran.

**Cajun Bangkok,** 907 King St, Alexandria, ☎ (703) 836-0038. Cajun-Thai.

**Calvert Grille,** 3106 Mount Vernon Ave, Alexandria, ☎ (703) 838-8425. American.

**Carnegie Delicatessen and Restaurant,** Embassy Suites Hotel, 8517 Leesburg Pike, Vienna, ☎ (703) 790-5001. New York–style deli.

**Chadwick's,** 203 S. Strand St, Old Town, ☎ (703) 836-4442.

**Chesapeake Seafood and Crab House,** 3607 Wilson Boulevard, Arlington, ☎ (703) 528-8888. Seafood.

**Crisp & Juicy,** 4540 Lee Hwy, Arlington, ☎ (703) 243-4222. Chicken.

**Food Factory,** 4221 N. Fairfax Drive, Ballston, ☎ (703) 527-2279. Pakistani.

**Generous George's,** 3006 Duke St, Alexandria, ☎ (703) 370-4303; 6937 Telegraph Rd, Hayfield, ☎ (703) 719-5600; and 6131 Backlick Rd, Springfield, ☎ (703) 451-7111. Pizza and pasta.

**Hard Times Cafe,** 1117 Nelson St, Rockville, ☎ (301) 294-9720; 1404 King St, Alexandria, ☎ (703) 683-5340; and 3028 Wilson Blvd, Clarendon, ☎ (703) 528-2233. Chili.

**Pasha Cafe,** 3815 Lee Hwy, Arlington, ☎ (703) 528-2126. Egyptian.

**Pines of Italy,** 237 N. Glebe Rd, Arlington, ☎ (703) 524-4969. Italian.

**Red Hot & Blue,** 1600 Wilson Blvd, Arlington, ☎ (703) 276-7427, and 8637 Sudley Rd, Manassas, ☎ (703) 330-4847. Memphis-style ribs.

**Rio Grande Cafe,** 4301 N. Fairfax Dr, Arlington, ☎ (703) 528-3131, and Reston Town Center, 1827 Library St, Reston, ☎ (703) 904-0703. Tex-Mex.

**Savio's,** 514A S. Van Dorn St, Alexandria, ☎ (703) 212-9651. Italian.

**South Austin Grill,** 801 King St, Alexandria, ☎ (703) 684-8969. Tex-Mex.

**Tachibana,** 4050 Lee Hwy, Arlington, ☎ (703) 528-1122. Japanese.

**Union Street Public House,** 121 S. Union St, Alexandria, ☎ (703) 548-1785. American.

## Brunch

**Amphora,** 377 Maple Ave W., Vienna, VA, ☎ (703) 938-7877, and 1151 Elden St, Herndon, VA, ☎ (703) 925-0900.

**Bombay Palace,** 1835 K St N.W., ☎ 331-0111.
**Cactus Cantina,** 3300 Wisconsin Ave N.W., ☎ 686-7222.
**Chadwick's,** 3205 K St N.W., ☎ 333-2565; 5257 Wisconsin Ave N.W., ☎ 362-8040; and 203 S. Strand St, Old Town, VA, ☎ (703) 836-4442.
**Cheesecake Factory,** 5345 Wisconsin Ave N.W., ☎ 364-0500.
**Cities,** 2424 18th St N.W., ☎ 328-7194.
**Clyde's,** 3236 M St N.W., ☎ 333-9180.
**Coeur de Lion,** Henley Park Hotel, 926 Massachusetts Ave N.W., ☎ 638-5200.
**Foong Lin,** 7710 Norfolk Ave, Bethesda, ☎ (301) 656-3427.
**Madurai,** 3318 M St N.W., ☎ 333-0997.
**Old Ebbitt Grill,** 675 15th St N.W., ☎ 347-4801.
**Rio Grande Cafe,** 4919 Fairmont Ave, Bethesda, ☎ (301) 656-2981.
**Roxanne & Peyote Cafe,** 2319 18th St N.W., ☎ 462-8330.
**Sichuan Pavilion,** 1820 K St N.W., ☎ 466-7790.
**Tom Tom,** 2333 18th St N.W., ☎ 588-1300.
**Willard Room,** Willard Hotel, 1401 Pennsylvania Ave N.W., ☎ 637-7440.

## Late Night

**America,** Union Station, 50 Massachusetts Ave N.E., ☎ 682-9555.
**American City Diner,** 5532 Connecticut Ave N.W., ☎ 244-1949.
**Chadwick's,** several locations. See "Brunch" listing.
**Clyde's,** 3236 M St N.W., ☎ 333-9180.
**Hard Rock Cafe,** 999 E St N.W., ☎ 737-ROCK.
**Kramerbooks & Afterwords Cafe,** 1517 Connecticut Ave N.W., ☎ 387-1462.
**Meserkem,** 2434 18th St N.W., ☎ 462-4100.
**Old Ebbitt Grill,** 675 15th St N.W., ☎ 347-4801.
**Perry's,** 1811 Columbia Rd N.W., ☎ 234-6218.
**Polly's Cafe,** 1342 U St N.W., ☎ 265-8385.
**Sequoia,** 3000 K St N.W., ☎ 944-4200.

## Pre-theater/Early Dining

**Cafe Atlantico,** 405 8th St N.W., ☎ 393-0812.
**Clyde's,** 3236 M St N.W., ☎ 333-9180.
**Galileo,** 1110 21st St N.W., ☎ 293-7191.
**La Chaumiere,** 2813 M St N.W., ☎ 338-1784.
**La Colline,** 400 N. Capitol St N.W. ☎ 737-0400.
**McCormick & Schmick's,** 1652 K St N.W., ☎ 861-2233.
**Old Ebbitt Grill,** 675 15th St N.W., ☎ 347-4801.
**701 Pennsylvania Avenue,** 701 Pennsylvania Ave N.W., ☎ 393-0701.
**1789,** 1226 36th St N.W., ☎ 965-1789.
**Twenty-One Federal,** 1736 L St N.W., ☎ 331-9771.

# Shopping

Washington, D.C., is a shopper's city. Besides souvenir T-shirts, boxer shorts with capital sites, "snowballs" that sprinkle miniature replicas of the Washington Monument, and other capital keepsakes, the District and the surrounding areas offer some good shopping opportunities. There are several malls, some more upscale than others, as well as some discount malls. In addition, the D.C. area boasts some unique shops, including craft galleries that feature handmade furniture, ceramics, jewelry, glass objects, and clothing.

For those who cannot get enough of politics, several stores sell **political memorabilia,** including buttons and posters. The perfect Washington present can be wrapped in sheets of uncut crisp $1 bills, authentic legal tender, from the Bureau of Engraving and Printing.

Kids adore **astronaut ice cream,** a freeze-dried, foil-wrapped chocolate, vanilla, and strawberry treat. Purchase this looks-like-Styrofoam-but-tastes-almost-like-ice-cream creation at the National Air and Space Museum gift shop, as well as other mall stores, area toy stores, and the Discovery Channel Store at the MCI Center ☎ 639-0908.

For **gourmet food** from Maryland and Virginia, browse the **Sutton Place Gourmet** Bethesda shop, ☎ (301) 564-3100, or the D.C store, ☎ 363-5800, to ship a personalized gift basket.

**Cookbooks** are another interesting capital keepsake. For kitchen aficionados, recipes of the rich and powerful prove interesting. Browse the Smithsonian gift shops for books such as *The White House Family Cookbook* by Henry Haller, executive White House chef for five presidents—Johnson, Nixon, Ford, Carter, and Reagan. Take home insider tips such as Jimmy Carter's secrets for sweet and sour pork, LBJ's recipe for chili con queso, and directions for Reagan's hamburger soup. Available at the **National Museum of American History** shop, ☎ 357-1527.

Just like any other city, the District has its allotment of **kitschy souvenirs,** which are especially popular with **kids.** The best place for spending allowance money is at the mall museums. Not only do kids delight in the red, white, and blue pencils, stickers, key chains, and coloring books, but these shops also have an array of interesting books, tapes, and educational toys. Always allow time to browse these stores.

Two favorite gift shops are the ones at the National Air and Space Museum and the National Museum of American History. The shelves at the **National Air and Space Museum** shop, ☎ 357-1387, bulge with picture books and histories of aviation from hot-air balloons to rockets, including *The Smithsonian's Book of Flight,* by Walter J. Boyne. Pick up the *Kids' Smithsonian Experience,* a coloring book of notable sites in D.C. The **National Museum of American History,** ☎ 357-1527, is one of the largest museum shops, with a vast array of books, posters, educational kits, and lots more.

There is no shortage of politically inspired **T-shirts** or tops featuring city sites. Check the supply available from sidewalk vendors and the museum shops, especially the National Museum of American History, for a variety from proper pointillist renditions of the Smithsonian Castle to tops based on exhibitions.

The following is a selected list of malls and museum shops. If Metro stops are not listed, then the store is not within a convenient walk to a Metrorail. The Washington, D.C., Convention and Visitors Bureau, ☎ 789-7000, Web: www.washington.org, publishes a *Dining and Shopping Guide.*

## Shopping Malls and Centers in the District

### Capitol Hill
**Union Station,** 50 Massachusetts Ave N.E., ☎ 371-9441. Metro: Union Station. Once the most elegant railroad station in the U.S., this 1908 Beaux-Arts building

has been renovated to serve as a train and Metro station but also a shopping mall with more than 120 retail stores, cafes, restaurants, and movie theatres.

Those hooked on politics should browse **Political Americana,** ☎ 547-1685, a shop that sells "authentic but newly printed" posters and vintage buttons from past political campaigns. **Made In America,** ☎ 842-0540, has reproduction presidential dessert plates as well as craft items. **Appalachian Spring,** ☎ 682-0505, also has handcrafted, functional items. Clothing stores include the **White House,** ☎ 289-1639, which features all-white clothing; **Victoria's Secret,** ☎ 682-0686, for lingerie; and **Ann Taylor,** ☎ 371-8010.

Children should not miss the **Great Train Store,** ☎ 371-2881, which has model trains and train-related items, and the **Food Court,** which offers an array of inexpensive eateries.

### Downtown

**The Pavilion at the Old Post Office,** 1100 Pennsylvania Ave N.W., ☎ 289-4224. Metro: Federal Triangle. This renovated 1899 post office features a central atrium ringed with corridors. The stage on the main level frequently offers free performances of jazz, classical music, and dancing. The facility has scores of shops, restaurants, and eateries. Many of the shops, like **Condor Imports,** ☎ 289-7971, with its Latin American and African crafts, offer items not seen at most shopping malls. Take the elevator to the tower observation deck for a great city view. Besides stores, various vendors offer inexpensive items.

For children and families, eateries abound, offering a range of ethnic food, plus **Ben & Jerry's,** ☎ 842-5882, has ice cream. The Old Post Office Pavilion is a good place to take a touring break and enjoy some entertainment and an inexpensive meal.

**The Shops at National Place,** 1331 Pennsylvania Ave N.W., ☎ 662-1250 or 662-7005. Metro: Metro Center. **B. Dalton Bookseller,** ☎ 393-1468, offers a variety of paperback and hardcover books. The food hall features eateries for inexpensive sit-down dining. **August Max,** ☎ 347-0108; **Casual Corner,** ☎ 737-9280; and **Filene's Basement,** ☎ 638-4110, offer fashion variety. **Fifth Avenue Nails,** ☎ 639-9558, is a relaxing stop for hands and feet, and **Fire and Ice,** ☎ 783-3669, offers traditional and craft jewelry. **Washington Kids,** ☎ 737-5151, a speciality store for children, opened in Dec 1998.

**MCI Center: Discovery Channel Store,** 6th and F Sts N.W.; ☎ (202) 639-0908; Web: www.discovery.com. Metro: Gallery Place/Chinatown. Interactive educational experiences mix with nifty shopping in this four-level store, with dinosaurs, fossils, and gems on the first floor, famous shipwrecks and ocean life on the mezzanine, a giant ant colony and travel books on the second floor, a World War II bomber cockpit and space technology on the third floor, and the Discovery Channel Theater with its "high-definition theater experience" on the fourth floor. Everything here is either fun or for sale or both.

### Georgetown

**Georgetown Park Mall,** 3222 M St N.W., ☎ 298-5577. Metro: Foggy Bottom, or Rosslyn and walk across Key Bridge. This shopping center, with more than 100 shops, creates a Victorian ambience with fountains, wrought-iron railings, skylights, and lots of potted palms. Shops include **Platypus,** ☎ 338-7680, for upscale gifts and housewares; **Polo/Ralph Lauren,** ☎ 965-0905, for pricey sports clothes; **The Sharper Image,** ☎ 337-9361, for novelty electronics; **Ann Taylor,** ☎ 338-5290, and **Talbots,** ☎ 338-3510, for upscale women's clothing, and **Crabtree & Evelyn,** ☎ 342-1934, for fine soaps and cosmetics.

**Benetton Kids,** ☎ 333-4140, features all the colors of Benetton's rainbow for ages 6 months to 12 years. **FAO Schwarz,** ☎ 965-7000, offers unique toys that children love, including six-ft rocking horses, child-size cars, and Madame Alexander dolls. It also allows children to play with display toys.

Adjacent to the mall is **Dean & DeLuca,** ☎ 342-2500, an upscale food market that also has soups, pasta salads, and sandwiches and an enclosed seating area. On the first floor of the mall is a small food court and seating area.

### Upper Northwest

**Chevy Chase Pavilion,** 5345 Wisconsin Ave N.W., ☎ 686-5335. Metro: Friendship Heights. This glitzy mall across the street from Mazza Gallerie has the **Embassy Suites** hotel, and the popular restaurant **Cheesecake Factory,** ☎ 895-1701, as well as about 40 shops. Chain stores include **Victoria's Secret,** ☎ 686-9165; **The Limited,** ☎ 686-7513; and **The Limited Too,** ☎ 686-7666. **Sam Goody,** ☎ 364-1957, has the usual collection of tapes, CDs, and videos. Also try **Hold Everything,** ☎ 363-7840, and **Pottery Barn,** ☎ 244-9330, for interesting household items, and **Gazelle,** ☎ 686-5656, for unusual crafts, jewelry, and clothes. The Metro level has an eatery with a handful of choices.

**Mazza Gallerie,** 5300 Wisconsin Ave N.W., ☎ 966-6114. Metro: Friendship Heights. This upscale mall is in the process of getting a much-needed $30 million facelift. There's new ownership, and new stores are being added. A final list of tenants hasn't been announced; for the time being several of the present merchants remain. The mall anchors remain **Neiman Marcus,** ☎ 966-9700, and **Record Town,** 537-6653, which carries pop, rock, classical, country, jazz, and children's CDs, along with tapes, compact discs, and posters. **Krön Chocolatier,** ☎ 966-4946, has great chocolate, including truffles and chocolate-covered strawberries. Gift boxes are available. **Villeroy and Boch,** ☎ 364-5180, sells china made by the company. **Saks Men's Shop** plans on opening a store here. For many Washingtonians, the most interesting addition to this mall is **General Cinema** (see "Movie Theaters" for description).

Across the street from the Gallerie are **Borders,** ☎ 686-8270, a chain bookstore; **Linens 'N Things,** ☎ 244-9025, which sells household items, framing supplies, and, yes, linens; and **Roche-Bobois,** ☎ 686-5667, an upscale store that sells contemporary French furniture.

Two blocks north of Mazza Gallerie, just across the border into Maryland, are several upscale women's stores, including **Saks Fifth Avenue,** ☎ (301) 657-9000, **Saks-Jandel,** ☎ (301) 652-2550, and **Saint Laurent Rive Gauche,** ☎ (301) 656-8868, plus **Gap** and **Gap Kids,** ☎ (301) 907-1656, and **Banana Republic,** ☎ (301) 907-7740.

## Shopping Malls in Maryland

**City Place,** 8661 Colesville Rd, Silver Spring, ☎ (301) 589-1091. Metro: Silver Spring. This off-price shopping mall features about 40 shops and is anchored by **Nordstrom Rack,** ☎ (301) 608-8118, and **Marshall's,** ☎ (301) 495-9566. As with any off-price mall, the shopping here is hit or miss. **Ross,** ☎ (301) 588-7993, may appeal to children.

**Montgomery Mall,** 7101 Democracy Blvd, Bethesda, ☎ (301) 469-6000. This shopping center is anchored by **Nordstrom,** ☎ (301) 365-4111, the mall's big draw; **Hecht's,** ☎ (301) 469-6800; **Sears,** ☎ (301) 469-4000; and **JC Penney,** ☎ (301) 365-5588. Popular chain stores include **Ann Taylor,** ☎ (301) 365-0771; **Banana Republic,** ☎ (301) 365-5507; **J. Crew,** ☎ (301) 365-2000; **Armani Exchange,** ☎ (301) 365-9095; **Guess,** ☎ (301) 365-3490; and **Abercrombie & Fitch,** ☎ (301) 469-9688.

Teens like **Georgetown Leather Design,** ☎ (301) 469-8840. Kids will flock to the **Disney Store,** ☎ (301) 365-2727; **GapKids,** ☎ (301) 365-5504; **Kids Foot Locker,** ☎ (301) 365-0004; **The Limited Too,** ☎ (301) 469-0992; and **Abercrombie Kids,** ☎ (301) 365-6521.

**White Flint Mall,** 11301 Rockville Pike, North Bethesda, ☎ (301) 468-5777. Metro: White Flint. Anchored by **Bloomingdale's,** ☎ (301) 984-4600, and **Lord & Taylor,** ☎ (301) 770-9000, this mall has many specialty shops, movie theaters, and an eatery. **Borders,** ☎ (301) 816-1067, offers a comprehensive collection of books, including an excellent children's department.

## Shopping Malls in Virginia

**The Fashion Center at Pentagon City,** 1100 South Hayes St at Army-Navy Dr and I-395, ☎ (703) 415-2400. Metro: Pentagon City. This mall offers more than 140 shops and is anchored by **Macy's,** ☎ (703) 418-4488, and **Nordstrom,** ☎ (703) 415-1121. Popular chain and specialty stores include **Crate & Barrel,** ☎ (703) 418-1010, and **The Limited,** ☎ (703) 418-4973.

**Tysons Corner Center,** 1961 Chain Bridge Rd, ☎ (703) 893-9400. Metro: West Falls Church. A rush hour bus (6:40–8:40 A.M., 4:20–6:40 P.M.) runs from here every 20 minutes; fare 75 cents. Among the draws are **Nordstrom,** ☎ (703) 761-1121, and **Lord & Taylor,** ☎ (703) 506-1156, as well as more than 200 shops, including **Ann Taylor,** ☎ (703) 893-0777, the **Disney Store,** ☎ (703) 448-8314, and **Britches,** ☎ (703) 893-2083.

**Tysons Galleria,** 2001 International Dr, McLean, ☎ (703) 827-7700. Metro: West Falls Church. A rush hour bus (6:40–8:40 A.M., 4:20–6:40 P.M.) runs from here every 20 minutes; fare 75 cents. Across from Tysons Corner, Tysons Galleria is an upscale mall adjacent to the **Ritz-Carlton** hotel. It is anchored by **Saks Fifth Avenue,** ☎ (703) 761-0700; **Macy's,** ☎ (703) 556-0000; and **Neiman Marcus,** ☎ (703) 761-1600. The mall features many trendy boutiques, and chain fashion stores like **J. Crew,** ☎ (703) 734-9555.

**Potomac Mills,** exit 156 off I-95, Dale City, ☎ (800) VA-MILLS or (800) 826-4557. This extensive mall, with more than 200 stores, is an off-price shopper's heaven, located about 30 miles south of the District. Van shuttle service is available from the D.C. area with pickups between 8:30 and 10 A.M. at five Metro stations: Dupont Circle and Metro Center in the District; Rosslyn, Crystal City, and Pentagon City in Virginia. One pick-up Mon, Wed, Thurs, Fri, and three on Sat. The van departs from Potomac Mills at 5 P.M. Call ☎ (703) 551-1050 for prices and hours.

A sample of the designer and department store clearance centers includes **Calvin Klein,** ☎ (703) 494-6292; **Carter's,** ☎ (703) 494-2157; **Eddie Bauer,** ☎ (703) 490-3855; **Georgetown Leather Design,** ☎ (703) 497-0521; and **Nordstrom Rack,** ☎ (703) 490-1440. **Daffy's,** ☎ (703) 494-3636, offers men's and women's clothing.

## Museum Shops

**Arts and Industries Building,** 900 Jefferson Dr S.W., ☎ 357-1367. Metro: Smithsonian. Good finds here include silk scarves with love stamps, wooden toys, and marbles.

**Bureau of Engraving and Printing,** 14th and C Sts S.W., ☎ 874-3019. Metro: Smithsonian. Their sheets of uncut currency make memorable wrapping paper, and kids like the bags of shredded currency. The shop also sells reproductions of presidential portraits and prints of speeches such as the Gettysburg Address.

**Corcoran Gallery of Art,** 500 17th St N.W., ☎ 639-1790. Metro: Farragut West or Farragut North. Besides art books, note cards, and posters, the shop offers lunchboxes featuring the Corcoran Building and socks with the Mona Lisa on them.

**Hirschhorn Museum and Sculpture Garden,** Independence Ave at 7th St S.W., ☎ 357-1429. Metro: L'Enfant Plaza, Smithsonian exit. Come here for modern art books, puzzles, kaleidoscopes, and jewelry.

**Indian Crafts Shop,** Department of the Interior Building, 18th and C Sts N.W., ☎ 208-4056. Metro: Farragut West. This shop has handmade jewelry, weavings, and carvings from Alaska and the Southwest.

**John F. Kennedy Center for the Performing Arts,** 2700 F St N.W., ☎ 416-8346. Metro: Foggy Bottom. The lobby stores feature T-shirts sporting celebrity photos, alarm clocks, books, posters, and miniature musical instruments.

**Library of Congress,** 101 Independence Ave S.E., ☎ 707-0204. Metro: Capitol South. The shop has note cards, tote bags, and T-shirts with a literary theme.

**National Air and Space Museum,** Independence Ave and 7th St S.W., ☎ 357-1387. Metro: L'Enfant Plaza, Smithsonian exit. The museum shop on the ground floor has astronaut ice cream, food trays for the kids, rocket kits, and all manner of space and science toys.

**National Archives,** Constitution Ave and 8th St N.W., ☎ 501-5245. Metro: Archives. Come here for replicas of famous documents.

**National Building Museum,** 401 F St N.W., ☎ 272-7706. Metro: Judiciary Square. Buy architecture-related toys, books, and T-shirts.

**National Gallery of Art,** 6th St and Constitution Ave N.W., ☎ 737-4215. Metro: Archives/Navy Memorial or Judiciary Square. This store features reproduction art posters, calendars, and stylish gift wrap by artists, as well as coffee-table art books.

**National Museum of African Art,** 950 Independence Ave S.W., ☎ 786-2147. Metro: Smithsonian. Good finds include scarves, sashes, ties in kente cloth, beaded bags, wooden bowls, and wall hangings, as well as tapes of African music.

**National Museum of American Art** ☎ 357-1545; **National Portrait Gallery,** 8th and G Sts N.W., ☎ 357-1447. Metro: Gallery Place, 9th St exit. Good buys include scarves, picture frames, and pins.

**National Museum of American History,** 14th St and Constitution Ave N.W., ☎ 357-1527. Metro: Smithsonian or Federal Triangle. One of the largest of the Mall gift shops, this one has almost everything, from CDs and tapes of famous jazz artists to coloring books, chemistry sets, funky pencils, and posters.

**National Museum of Women in the Arts,** 1250 New York Ave N.W., ☎ 783-7994. Metro: Metro Center. Come here for calendars, cards, pins and bookmarks.

**National Zoo,** 3001 Connecticut Ave N.W., ☎ 673-4657. Metro: Woodley Park/National Zoo. Books, mugs, T-shirts, and stuffed animals, as well as animal mobiles that especially delight kids.

**Renwick Gallery,** 17th St and Pennsylvania Ave N.W., ☎ 357-1445. Metro: Farragut West, 17th St exit. Pins, earrings, glassware, and ceramics can often be found here.

**Arthur M. Sackler Gallery,** 1050 Independence Ave S.W., ☎ 357-4880. Metro: Smithsonian. Phrasebooks, batiks, origami kits, and Asian dolls entice buyers here.

## Sightseeing Services

The Washington, D.C., Convention and Visitors Association offers a wide assortment of informational pamphlets for tourists, including a guide that lists tour companies. Copies are distributed at the **Visitors Information Center,** 1212 New York Ave N.W., open Mon–Sat 9–5, ☎ 789-7000, Web: www.washington.org.

### General Tours

Two well-known trolley tours that stop at major attractions are Old Town Trolley Tours and the Tourmobile. The **Old Town Trolley** makes stops throughout Washington along its 135-minute narrated tour. After leaving the trolley, visitors can reboard for another stop at any of the 19 stops along the route. The trolley runs every 30 minutes 7 days a week, 9–4. ☎ 832-9800.

    **Tourmobile Sightseeing, Inc.** offers a year-round narrated tour that stops at 18 sites, including the White House, Washington Monument, Smithsonian Museums, Arlington National Cemetery, and Mount Vernon. Riders are allowed to reboard and ride to another stop on their route. ☎ 554-5100.

### Specialized Tours

#### Black History

**Capitol Entertainment Services, Inc.** provides three different tour packages in which Capitol Hill, the Mall, and black history sites are covered. Student groups receive discounts. Often these tours are for groups only, but sometimes individuals or families can join an already existing group. ☎ 636-9203.

#### Humorous

**Scandal Tours of Washington** serves up an irreverent look at the sites of D.C.'s past and current scandals. The guides enact such characters as Clinton, Monica Lewinsky, or whoever is in today's scandal news. The coach tour lasts 75 minutes and is hosted by the local comedy group Gross National Product. Tours depart Sat at 1:00 P.M. from the Old Post Office Building. Call ahead for reservations, ☎ 783-7212. In summer the tours accept individuals; otherwise, the company is booked with groups.

#### Helicopter

**Heloair,** ☎ (800) 782-1585, offers helicopter tours over the city. Individuals can join Heloair when it does traffic reports (6:30–8 A.M., 4:40–6 P.M.) for $90, or rent a helicopter to see the city from wayyyy up, for $590 per hour for three, $1,100 per hour for five.

## Multilingual

For bilingual (Japanese/English) guides, as well as bus/sedan charters and hotel arrangements, contact **Ana Hallo Tours (USA), Inc.,** ☎ 223-8610. Ana Hallo is a subsidiary of All Nippon Airways.

**Japan Travelers Service, Inc.** has guided Japanese tourists in D.C. for over 20 years, offering sightseeing tours via sedan, minivan, and coach, with Japanese-speaking guides. ☎ 223-9172.

**American Tours International** caters to incentive services for both group and individual travel, providing multilingual guides as well as hotel and transportation arrangements throughout Washington and the rest of the United States. ☎ 842-2588.

## Special Interest

**The Guide Service of Washington, Inc.** offers tours to individuals and groups who are interested in D.C.'s architecture and history. Multilingual licensed tour guides are available. Call the 24-hour phone line for half- or full-day tours. ☎ 628-2842.

For groups interested in either art, architecture, or history, **The National Fine Arts Associates** offers customized (and some behind-the-scenes) tours with professional guides in their respective fields. Tour packages include lunch, dinner, or receptions, if requested. ☎ 966-3800.

Customized tours for groups or individuals interested in museums, art galleries, historic sites, and embassies are offered by **WashingtonInc.** The duration of the tour is left to the visitor's discretion. Reserve in advance, ☎ 828-7000.

The **Discovery Channel Store** offers an hour-and-a-half-long "Discover Historic Downtown Washington" tour, Sat at 1:30 and Sun at 11:30. ☎ 639-0908.

## Unusual

**The Ghost Tour,** which includes folklore, myths, and other stories during a six-block walk to an 18C graveyard, takes place close to Halloween in Alexandria, Virginia. ☎ (703) 838-4200. Another ghost tour, called **The Leesburg Hauntings,** is held in Leesburg, Virginia, by the Loudon Museum, ☎ (703) 777-0099, for four nights in October. In Harpers Ferry, West Virginia, there's a one-hour tour on Fri, Sat, and Sun nights, May–Nov. ☎ (304) 725-8019.

In April, May, Sept, and Oct, the **Surratt Society** holds day-long bus tours of John Wilkes Booth's escape route. No children under 12 admitted. ☎ (301) 868-1121.

## Walking

**A Tour De Force: Guided Tours of Washington** provides customized tours, led by local author, historian, and lecturer Jeanne Fogle, a fourth-generation Washingtonian, to any size group. Along with typical sites, Fogle's tours feature many accurate anecdotes about D.C.'s personalities. These tours are highly recommended. Make reservations in advance. ☎ (703) 525-2948. Some of Fogle's walking tours can also be booked through the Smithsonian Resident Associates Program.

**Smithsonian Resident Association Program** offers two-hour walking tours through D.C.'s historical and cultural neighborhoods, and often behind-doors tours of institutions and museums. Tours are held on Sat and Sun throughout the year. Call for upcoming tour announcements. ☎ 357-3030.

**Capital Entertainment Services** offers tours dealing with Washington's African American history for groups of 30 or more. Individuals and families are welcome to join scheduled groups. ☎ 636-9203.

## Additional tours

**All About Town, Inc.** offers "glass-top" coach tours of Washington and Georgetown and regular coach tours for Arlington and Mount Vernon every day of the year except Christmas and New Year's Day. Call the 24-hour phone line for full-, half-day, and evening tours, and for information about convention transportation and bus charters. ☎ 393-3696.

**Atlantic Kayak,** ☎ (800) 297-0066 or (703) 838-9072, Web: www. atlantickayak.com, offers two-and-a-half-hour kayak trips on the Potomac River. On some routes you'll pass by Fort Washington and Mount Vernon, George Washington's plantation. The Georgetown trip takes paddlers under Key and Memorial Bridges, then around Roosevelt Island. For Halloween take a haunted river tour and on the Fourth of July try a fireworks outing.

**Bike the Sites, Inc.** offers a bicycle tour covering eight miles and 55 landmarks in three hours. Bicycles, helmets, water, and snacks provided. ☎ 966-8662.

**C&O Canal Barge Rides** harks back to the days when supply barges traveled the canal regularly. Tours depart from the C&O Visitors Center across from the Foundry on Thomas Jefferson St in Georgetown. ☎ (301) 739-4200.

**Capitol River Cruises** takes visitors on a 50-minute narrated tour of Washington from the river, departing daily from Georgetown's Harbour Place every hour on the hour. ☎ (303) 460-7447.

**DC Ducks: The Boats on Wheels** offers a narrated 90-minute tour on rebuilt World War II amphibious vessels, departing regularly from Union Station April–Nov 10 A.M.–3 P.M. ☎ 832-9040. Cruise tours on the Potomac River are offered by the *Spirit of Washington,* ☎ 554-8000, the *Odyssey,* ☎ 488-6010, and the **Potomac Riverboat Company,** ☎ (703) 548-9000, which offers tours of Old Town Alexandria's historic waterfront, trips to George Washington's Mount Vernon, and ferry service between Georgetown and Old Town Alexandria.

**Georgetown Walking Tours** bring the romance, history, and mystery of this port city alive. ☎ (301) 588-8999. Tours of other area historic neighborhoods, such as Adams Morgan and Old Town Alexandria, are also available. ☎ (301) 294-9514.

**Capital Helicopters** offers helicopter tours above Washington from Ronald Reagan Washington National Airport, and complimentary ground transportation is also available. ☎ (703) 417-2150.

**Photo Safari** takes camera buffs to some of Washington's most photogenic sites, along with professional photographer E. David Luria, who offers personalized instruction and written tips. ☎ 537-0937.

**Old Town Trolley** offers transportation between 19 stops around the city, 9 A.M.–4 P.M. Its two-and-a-half-hour "Washington After Hours" tour takes in the major monuments by moonlight. ☎ 832-9800.

**Guide Service of Washington** provides an expert guide to ride along in the car. ☎ 628-2842.

Specializing in school and adult groups, the **Washington Insider Tours** offers tour packages including hotel accommodations, guide service, and transportation. ☎ 659-4404.

**The Black History National Recreation Trail** is a self-guided walking tour highlighting several black history sites throughout Washington, D.C., including the Metropolitan A.M.E. Church, Frederick Douglass's home, Howard University, and more. Informational pamphlets are distributed at each of the trail's sites. For a pamphlet and more information call the National Park Service, ☎ 619-7222.

**Gray Line/American Sightseeing Road Tours** offers nine tour routes of Washington and the surrounding area, treating all the important sites on morning and afternoon air-conditioned bus tours varying in length from three to nine hours. Pickup is free. Multilingual services are available. For more information, call ☎ (301) 386-8300.

**VIP Tours** are available at no charge for the **White House,** the **Capitol,** the **Federal Bureau of Investigation Building,** the **John F. Kennedy Center,** and the **Bureau of Engraving and Printing Building.** Tickets are available to visitors by contacting their senator or congressman months in advance, specifying the number of tickets required and acceptable dates. Do this as far ahead as possible, as tickets available to each congressional office are limited.

# Theater

Theater is a major part of Washington's nightlife. The play's the thing in a variety of venues. (For a comprehensive list of addresses and Web sites, see "Theaters.") The city's stages host pre- and post-Broadway hits with all the latest production razzle dazzle, Shakespearean plays set in intimate theaters, classic dramas staged in the round, satiric works and dramas by unknown playwrights, plus a full course of dinner theaters in the suburbs. **The John F. Kennedy Center for the Performing Arts,** a multitheater complex, offers the most diverse program with six theaters. **The Eisenhower Theater, Opera House, Concert Hall, Terrace Theater, Theater Lab,** and the **American Film Institute**—all part of the Kennedy Center—host Broadway productions, ballet, opera, concerts, drama, and classic films. The Kennedy Center also offers a reduced-rate ticket policy for senior citizens, students, and children, along with free Open House events. Every day of the year at 6 P.M. in the Grand Foyer, hour-long free performances by artists from all disciplines (pop, jazz, dance, storytelling, mime, classical music) are presented on the **Millennium Stage.** Call ☎ 467-4600 or (800) 444-1324.

The **Shakespeare Theatre** at the Lansburgh presents three Shakespearean productions and one non-Shakespearean production a year, all of them staged in an intimate but comfortable 500-seat theater. This is the place to introduce your pre-teen to the Bard. The theater offers 50 percent student and senior citizen discount for tickets purchased one hour before showtime. Call ☎ 547-1122. The **Folger Shakespeare Library** presents readings from Shakespeare's plays in its Elizabethan Theatre as well as performances of Renaissance music by the Folger Consort. Call ☎ 544-7077.

**Ford's Theatre** offers family-oriented musicals and dramas, with Charles Dickens's *A Christmas Carol* a standard Christmas treat. Although the theater remains dark in July and Aug, the *Lincoln Museum* is open year-round. Call ahead concerning student and family discounts, ☎ 347-4833. And in the historic 14th and U Sts section of northwest Washington, the restored **Lincoln Theatre** offers musicals and performances reflecting the African American experience.

The **National Theatre,** a tradition in D.C. since 1835, puts on Broadway hits in its 1,100-seat house on Pennsylvania Ave. Call ☎ 628-6161 for schedule of current performances. On Mon nights in summer, the National features a free Summer Cinema Series in the **Helen Hayes Gallery.** For children ages 4 and older, the National Theater offers free one-hour skits on Sat mornings during fall and winter; call ☎ 783-3372. For adults, the National Theater offers a one-hour skit program on Mon evenings; call ☎ 783-3372. The renovated **Warner Theatre** offers a variety of plays and performances; call ☎ 783-4000.

Across town along the Southwest waterfront, **Arena Stage** ( ☎ 488-3300) offers classic and contemporary plays on its main stages, as well as cabaret and one-man shows in the **Old Vat Room.** Student discounts are available for tickets purchased the same week.

Smaller theaters, which present works by local playwrights as well as contemporary plays, sometimes with an irreverent edge, include the Source Theatre Company, GALA, Scena Theatre, Studio, Olney, Woolly Mammoth Theatre Company, Signature Theatre, American Showcase Theatre, Washington Stage Guild, Horizon, and the Roundhouse Theatre.

In addition to debuting works by Washington-area playwrights and presenting modern dramas, the **Source Theatre Company,** established in 1976, is noted for its summer festival of new plays. **GALA Hispanic Theatre** (☎ 234-7174) and **Teatro de la Luna** (☎ 548-3092), Washington's Latin American and Spanish theaters, offer classics in Spanish and English. **Le Neon** performs original works in both English and French; call ☎ (703) 243-6366. The **Washington Jewish Theatre,** in Rockville, offers plays by Jewish playwrights or those that deal with Jewish themes; call ☎ (301) 230-3775.

The **Scena Theatre** performs in several different locales around town, including the National Museum for Women in the Arts and the Woolly Mammoth Theatre. For contemporary theater that is occasionally offbeat but generally well acted, try the **Woolly Mammoth Theatre Company.** For those on a budget, the company offers pay-what-you-can previews. Other stages include the **American Showcase Theatre,** which currently operates out of a storefront, and the **Washington Stage Guild** (☎ 529-2084), which offers rarely performed classics.

One of the best theater bargains in town is the **Kennedy Center's Millennium Stage**—it's free! Hour-long performances ranging from blue grass to classical to folk to tap to jazz are given daily at 6 P.M. on the main floor of the Kennedy Center. ☎ 467-4600.

The area's universities offer some good theatrical productions at reasonable prices. The **American University Department of Performing Arts** stages student productions ranging from classical to contemporary and experimental theater throughout the school year. **Hartke Theatre,** part of the Catholic University Drama Department, is well known for its professional productions. The group stages classical, musical, and experimental theater from Oct through April. The students have shared the lights with such special guests as Helen Hayes and Mercedes McCambridge. Graduates of the drama department include Susan Sarandon, Jon Voight, Laurence Luckinbill, and Henry Gibson.

**George Washington University's Lisner Auditorium** hosts plays, ballet, and concerts. **Theater of the First Amendment,** associated with the George Mason University's Institute of the Arts, is a production group of professionals and students who perform at the Center for the Arts Concert Hall. The center offers dance, theater, performance art, and music on its three stages: the Concert Hall, the Harris Theater, and the Black Box Theater Space. **Tawes Theater,** at the University of Maryland in College Park, offers musicals and drama, as well as special programming; call ☎ (301) 405-2201.

## For Children and Families

### In the District

**Arthur M. Sackler Gallery** offers a year-round program of storytelling and craft sessions for kids ages 4 and up accompanied by an adult. ☎ 357-1300.

**Discovery Theater** at the Smithsonian, Arts and Industries Building, 900 Jefferson Dr S.W., offers year-round plays geared to preschoolers through high school students throughout the year. These shows are popular, so reservations are recommended. ☎ 357-1500.

**Ford's Theatre.** See listing under "Theaters."

**The John F. Kennedy Center for the Performing Arts** offers the Imagination Celebration, children's entertainment throughout the year. There are plays, dance for preschoolers and elementary school kids, and puppet shows. ☎ 416-8830. The Kennedy Center also stages puppet and theatrical adaptations of popular children's books on weekends in the **Terrace Theater** and **Theater Lab.**

The **National Museum of African Art** performs dramatized folktales on Tues at 10:30 A.M. throughout the year. Also the museum holds storytelling hours during July and Aug. ☎ 357-1300.

The **National Theatre** offers free one-hour skits for children ages 4 and older on Sat mornings. ☎ 628-6161.

The **Rock Creek Nature Center and Planetarium** in Rock Creek Park, open Wed–Sun 9–5, offers free planetarium and nature shows—one for children ages 4–7 and another for those 7 and older. Tickets are available 30 minutes before showtime. ☎ 426-6829. Also in Rock Creek Park is the **Discovery Creek Museum,** ☎ 364-3111, with inventive programs concerning environmental issues geared to young children. All through the summer the **D.C. Department of Recreation** sponsors plays and puppet shows at various city locations. Call Activities Services, ☎ 673-7663, or Dial-an-Event, ☎ 673-7671.

**Shakespeare at Carter Barron Amphitheatre.** If funding is available, this free summer program traditionally begins in June and runs for two to three weeks in the 4,000 seat amphitheater. Showtime is 7:30 P.M. Tues through Sun. Tickets are available for pickup on a first-come, first-served basis at the following locations: The Shakespeare Theatre at the Lansburgh, the *Washington Post* Building, and the Carter Barron box office. During the day there may also be storytelling backstage tours, workshops, student productions, and adaptations of Shakespeare's plays. ☎ 547-1122.

The **Shakespeare Theatre** at the Lansburgh, a quality Shakespearean company geared to adults, offers a great opportunity to introduce your older children and teens to Shakespeare's plays, especially the comedies.

### In Maryland

**Adventure Theater** is full of energy, music, and, every so often, puppets. The theater performs year-round at Glen Echo Park in Maryland on weekends only. ☎ (301) 320-5331.

**Bethesda Academy of Performing Arts,** White Flint Shopping Center, offers selected performances for families. ☎ (301) 320-2550.

**Burn Brae Dinner Theater,** Burtonsville, stages musicals that frequently appeal to adults as well as to children. At times there are also special matinees just for kids. ☎ (301) 384-5800 or (800) 777-2238.

**Jewish Community Center,** Rockville, often has weekend children's concerts, plays, and programs. ☎ (301) 881-0100.

**Publick Playhouse,** Landover, offers Sat matinee performances of plays and storytellers. ☎ (301) 277-1710

### In Virginia

**Alden Theater,** McLean Community Center, 1234 Ingleside Ave, McLean, is known for its McClean Kids Series, a hodgepodge of children's entertainment including music, plays, puppetry, mime, and dance, performed on weekends during the school year. ☎ (703) 790-9223.

**Children's Theater of Arlington,** Gunston Arts Center. Arlington's community theater group stages plays for children and by children. ☎ (703) 548-1154.

**Mount Vernon Children's Theater,** Heritage Presbyterian Church, Alexandria, offers family-oriented productions in March and Nov. ☎ (703) 360-9546 or (703) 360-0686.

**Wolf Trap's "Theater in the Woods"** is a popular summer series for kids set outdoors in Vienna. In addition, if in town don't miss Wolf Trap's **International Children's Festival,** held during Labor Day weekend. With activities for children of all ages and a farm park setting with numerous stages, this yearly event is a special treat. Puppets, ethnic dance troupes, storytellers, mimes, jugglers, singers, and children's plays are just some of the special events. ☎ (703) 255-1860 or (703) 255-1824.

## Theater Listings

Comprehensive listings of Washington's theater scene are found in The *Washington Post,* the *Washington Times,* the *City Paper,* the *Washingtonian Magazine, This Week in the Nation's Capital,* and *Where* magazine.

## Tickets

When checking on prices, ask for weekend or holiday price packages. Half-price, same-day tickets are available through **TICKETplace,** ☎ TIC-KETS or 842-5387. Tickets may be paid for with cash or a major credit card. A 10 percent service fee is charged. TICKETplace is located in the Old Post Office Building at 1100 Pennsylvania Ave N.W. TICKETplace is open Tues–Sat 11–6. Tickets for Sun and Mon shows are available on Sat.

TicketMaster sells tickets by phone; payment can be made with credit card. ☎ (202) 432-SEAT, 10–9 daily. Ask for the nearest TicketMaster center. **Top Centre Ticket** is a ticket broker offering seats for sporting events, concerts, and plays. These tickets often come with a hefty surcharge. Top Centre Ticket—open Mon 9–5, Tues–Fri 9–6, and Sat 10–4—does have a D.C. outlet at 2000 Pennsylvania Ave N.W., ☎ 452-9040. Other ticket brokers outside of Washington, D.C., include: **Ticket Connection,** 8121 Georgia Ave, Suite 101, Silver Spring, MD, ☎ (301) 587-6850 or (800) 666-6TIX; **Ticket Finders,** 6801 Kenilworth Ave, Riverdale, MD, ☎ (301) 513-0300; **Stagefront Tickets,** 416 Maine St, Laurel, MD, ☎ (301) 953-1163; **Ticket Outlet,** 701 W. Broad St, Falls Church, VA, ☎ (703) 538-4044. All of these services offer Federal Express delivery at an added cost. Otherwise the services are within driving distance for pickup. Be certain to understand the arrangements for picking up these tickets before ordering.

## Theaters

Here is a convenient list of area theaters. If no Metro stop is listed, then the theater is not situated near a subway. The Washington, D.C., area Metro offers a free *Guide to the Nation's Capital,* which lists the subway and bus stops convenient to area theaters. Call ☎ 637-7000 to receive a copy, or stop by a Metro sales office. In D.C. the sales offices include: Metro Center, 12th and F Sts N.W., and the Metro Headquarters, Jackson Graham Building, 600 Fifth St N.W.

### In the District
**American University Department of Performing Arts: The Experimental Theatre, Kay Spiritual Life Center, McDonald Recital Hall;** 4400 Massachusetts Ave N.W., ☎ 885-2787. Metro: Tenleytown.
**Arena Stage,** 6th St and Maine Ave S.W., ☎ 488-3300, Web: www.arenastage.org. Metro: Waterfront.
**Carter Barron Amphitheatre,** 16th St and Colorado Ave N.W., ☎ 426-0486.
**Discovery Theater,** Arts and Industry Building, the Smithsonian, 900 Jefferson Dr S.W., ☎ 357-1500, Web: www.si.edu. Metro: Smithsonian.
**Ford's Theatre,** 511 10th St S.E., ☎ 347-4833, Web: www.fordstheatre.org. Metro: Metro Center or Archives.
**GALA Hispanic Theatre,** 1625 Park Rd N.W., ☎ 234-7174. Metro: Cleveland Park or Dupont Circle.
**Hartke Theatre,** Harewood Rd N.E., at 4th St and Michigan Ave, ☎ 319-4000. Metro: Brookland.
**John F. Kennedy Center for the Performing Arts: Eisenhower, Opera House, Millennium Stage, Concert Hall, Terrace, Theater Lab, AFI;** New Hampshire Ave at Rock Creek Pky N.W., ☎ 467-4600 or (800) 444-1324, Web: www.kennedy-center.org. Metro: Foggy Bottom.
**Lincoln Theatre,** 1215 U St N.W., ☎ 328-6000. Metro: U St/Cardoza.
**Lisner Auditorium,** George Washington University, 21st and H Sts N.W., ☎ 994-1500, Web: gwu.edu/~lisner. Metro: Foggy Bottom.
**National Theatre,** 1321 Pennsylvania Ave N.W., ☎ 628-6161, Web: www.nationaltheatre.org. Metro: Foggy Bottom.
**Scena Theater,** 1019 7th St N.W., ☎ (703) 684-7990. Metro: Gallery Place/Chinatown.
**Shakespeare Theatre,** 450 7th St N.W., ☎ 547-1122, Web: www.shakespearedc.org. Metro: Gallery Place/Chinatown.
**Source Theatre,** 1835 14th St N.W., ☎ 462-1073. Metro: U St/Cardoza.
**Studio Theatre,** 1333 P St N.W., ☎ 332-3300. Metro: Dupont Circle or McPherson Square.

**Warner Theatre,** 1299 Pennsylvania Ave N.W., ☎ 783-4000, Web: www. warnertheatre.com. Metro: Metro Center or Federal Triangle.

**Washington Stage Guild,** for information ☎ 529-2084.

**Woolly Mammoth,** 1401 Church St N.W., ☎ 393-3939. Metro: Dupont Circle. (This location is expected to change in August 2000 to an as yet unannounced site.)

### In Maryland

**Adventure Theater,** 7300 MacArthur Blvd, Glen Echo, ☎ (301) 320-5331. Metro: Friendship Heights or Bethesda, then Ride-On bus #29 to Glen Echo.

**Olney Theater,** 2001 Sandy Spring Rd, Olney, ☎ (301) 924-3400.

**Round House Theatre,** 2210 Bushey Dr, Silver Spring, ☎ (301) 933-1644. Metro: Wheaton.

**Tawes Theater,** University of Maryland, College Park, ☎ (301) 405-2201. Metro: College Park/U of Md.

**Washington Jewish Theater,** Jewish Community Center, 6125 Montrose Rd, Rockville, ☎ (301) 230-3775. Metro: White Flint or Twinbrook.

### In Virginia

**Alden Theater,** McClean Community Center, 1234 Ingleside Ave, McClean, ☎ (703) 790-9223. Metro: West Falls Church.

**American Showcase Theater,** 1822 Duke St, Alexandria, ☎ (703) 548-9044. Metro: King St

**Center for the Arts: Concert Hall, Harris Theater, Black Box Theater Space;** Institute of the Arts, George Mason University, 4400 University Dr, Fairfax, ☎ (703) 993-8888. Metro: Vienna.

**Children's Theater of Arlington,** Gunston Arts Center, 2700 S. Lang St, Arlington, ☎ (703) 548-1154.

**Horizon Theater,** 4350 N. Fairfax Dr, Arlington, ☎ (703) 243-8550.

**Mount Vernon Children's Theater,** Heritage Presbyterian Church, 8503 Fort Hunt Rd, Alexandria, ☎ (703) 360-9546. Metro: Huntington.

**Signature Theatre,** 3806 S. Four Mile Run Dr, Arlington, ☎ (703) 820-9771.

**Wolf Trap Farm Park for the Performing Arts,** 1624 Trap Rd, Vienna, ☎ (703) 255-1868, Web: www.wolf-trap.org. Metro: West Falls Church (shuttle bus).

### Dinner Theaters

**Burn Brae Dinner Theatre,** US Rte 29 & Blackburn Rd, Burtonsville, MD, ☎ (301) 384-5800.

**Lazy Susan Dinner Theatre,** Rt 1 and Furnace Rd, Woodbridge, VA, ☎ (703) 494-6311.

**Toby's Dinner Theatre,** South Entrance Rd (next to Merriweather Post Pavilion), Columbia, MD, ☎ (301) 596-6161.

**West End Dinner Theatre,** 4615 Duke St, Alexandria, VA, ☎ (703) 370-2500. Metro: King St.

# Music and Dance

A variety of choral groups, symphonies, opera companies, and other musical groups perform in and around the Washington area. Surprisingly good places to hear free concerts are Washington's galleries, both public and private. The following is a listing of concert locales, clubs, museums, galleries, and other venues as well as a list of choral, symphonic, and musical groups.

## Choral Groups

### In the District

**Cathedral Choral Society,** ☎ 537-8980. This 200-voice symphonic chorus-in-residence of the National Cathedral, Wisconsin and Massachusetts Ave N.W., has been singing at the cathedral for more than 50 years.

**Choral Arts Society,** ☎ 244-3669. Performs at the Kennedy Center, New Hampshire Ave and Rock Creek Pkwy N.W., and other locations.

**Gay Men's Chorus,** New York Ave Presbyterian Church, 13th St and New York Ave N.W., ☎ 338-SING. Performs holiday, spring, and summer concerts. The group rehearses on Sun 6:30–9:45 P.M.

**Master Chorale of Washington and the Washington Chamber Singers,** ☎ 364-4321. This 150-voice group performs several times a season in the Kennedy Center and at other locations around town.

**Society for the Preservation and Encouragement of Barber Shop Quartet Singing in America** (SPEBSQSA). This is exactly what it sounds like. They rehearse at St. Paul's Lutheran Church, 36th St and Connecticut Ave N.W., Mon 7:30 P.M. ☎ 966-8788 or (301) 946-4820. Concerts at various locations.

### In Maryland

**Concert Society at Maryland,** ☎ (301) 405-7847. The group generally performs at three locales: the Conference Center of the University of Maryland College Park, the Washington National Cathedral, and the National Presbyterian Church.

## Concerts

### In the District

**Corcoran Gallery of Art Musical Evenings Series,** 500 17th St N.W., ☎ 639-1700 ext 246, Office of Special Events. The Corcoran's prized musical possessions, two stringed instruments, have been played in concerts. These instruments, one of which is a violin originally crafted for King Louis XIV of France, were fashioned by Nicolo Amati, the famed teacher of Stradivari. The popular concerts are offered in the Frances and Armand Hammer Auditorium Oct–May Fri at 8 P.M., but often the musical evenings are sold as a series, so few individual tickets are available. Receptions are held after each concert. Call for a listing.

**DAR Constitution Hall,** 18th and D Sts N.W., ☎ 638-2661. Hosts pop, jazz, and rap artists among others.

**Dumbarton Concert Series,** 3133 Dumbarton St N.W. (Georgetown), ☎ 965-2000. From Oct through April the Dumbarton Concert Series offers a variety of music and entertainment, including jazz, chamber, Christmas, and Renaissance music. Performances begin at 8 P.M. A preconcert buffet is offered at 6:30. Season subscriptions and individual tickets are available. Students with a valid ID receive discounted admission; kids under 12 enter for free.

**Folger Consort,** located at the Folger Shakespeare Library, 201 E. Capital St S.E.,

☎ 544-7077, Web: www.folger.edu. The ensemble-in-residence performs baroque, Renaissance, and medieval productions. Preconcert discussions and lectures are offered on Sun.

**Kennedy Center Terrace Concerts,** John F. Kennedy Center for the Performing Arts, New Hampshire Ave and Rock Creek Pkwy N.W., ☎ 467-4600 or (800) 444-1324, Web: www.kennedy-center.org. Pianists, cellists, singers, opera singers, quartets, ensembles, chamber groups, family concerts, violinists, jazz musicians, and the Young Concert Artists Series are offered throughout the year. Concerts start at 7:30.

**MCI Center,** 325 7th St N.W., ☎ 628-3200, Web: www.mcicenter.com. Megastars fill the arena; generally rock and country concerts are held here.

**National Symphony Orchestra,** John F. Kennedy Center, Concert Hall, is located off of New Hampshire Ave and Rock Creek Pkwy N.W., ☎ 467-4600 or (800) 444-1324. Performances are held in the Kennedy Center Concert Hall Nov–May. Performance Plus concerts include lectures, demonstrations, free chamber recitals, and/or receptions.

**The Phillips Collection,** 1600 21st St N.W., ☎ 387-2151, Web: www. phillipscollection.org. This weekly classical concert series runs Labor Day through the end of May, Sun afternoons at 5. The entrance fee is equivalent to admission to the museum; senior citizens and students (with ID) received discounted admission, children under 18 enter for free. Seating is on a first-come basis.

**Robert F. Kennedy Memorial Stadium,** 2001 E. Capitol St S.E., ☎ 547-9077. Major concerts are held in this 55,000-seat stadium. Past performers who have packed the place are Guns N'Roses, U2, Michael Jackson, Bob Dylan, and the Rolling Stones.

**Smithsonian Resident Associate Program,** ☎ 357-3030, Web: www.si.edu. This program sponsors concerts throughout the city and offers a variety of musical performances in Smithsonian buildings. Members receive a discount.

**Washington Symphony,** DAR Constitution Hall, 18th and D Sts N.W., ☎ 857-0970. This volunteer symphony offers 2,700 free balcony seats to "needy and homeless music lovers." Performances are at 7:30 P.M., often followed by open receptions for the audiences and musicians.

**Washington National Cathedral's Summer Festival of Music,** ☎ 537-6200. A varied summer concert series, with most performances beginning at 7:30 P.M.

**Washington Performing Arts Society,** 2000 L St N.W., ☎ 833-9800. This organization sponsors various concerts and offers tickets to events at the Lisner Auditorium, Dance Place, Warner Theatre, Constitution Hall, the Kennedy Center, and other venues. Subscriptions and individual tickets are available.

### In Maryland

**Baltimore Arena,** 201 W. Baltimore St, ☎ (410) 347-2020. This venue doubles as a sports arena and concert hall. The Beatles played here in the '60s. Circuses and other traveling extravaganzas stop here as well.

**Manchester String Quartet** performs chamber music Sat nights at 7:30 from Nov through May at the Holton Arms School, James Whittier Lewis Performing Arts Center, 7303 River Rd, Bethesda, ☎ (301) 365-5300.

**National Chamber Orchestra,** plays in the F. Scott Fitzgerald Theatre in the

Rockville Civic Center, 603 Edmonston Dr, Rockville, Fri and Sat nights at 8:30 from Oct through April. ☎ (301) 762-8580.

**USAir Arena,** 1 Harry Truman Dr, exit 15E or 17E off the Capital Beltway, Landover, ☎ (301) 622-3865. Hosts up to 19,000 spectators eager for sports and for concerts, which are usually rock and pop, but even Pavarotti has performed here.

## Free Concerts

There are scores of free musical events, but tourists must know when and where. In addition to the following listing, check the events listed under "For Children and Families"; many of these are free as well.

### In the District

The **American University Department of Performing Arts,** 4400 Massachusetts Ave N.W., ☎ 885-2787, offers two free concerts of choral and orchestral programs each spring and fall. Performances are held on campus at one of three locations, the Experimental Theatre, the Kay Spiritual Life Center, or the McDonald Recital Hall in the Kreeger Building.

**Arthur M. Sackler Gallery,** 1050 Independence Ave S.W., ☎ 357-4880, sponsors monthly free concerts, usually of Asian music.

The **Canadian Embassy,** 501 Pennsylvania Ave. N.W., ☎ 682-7797, sponsors musical events (jazz, classical) at various venues around the city throughout the year.

**Corcoran Gallery,** 500 17th St N.W., ☎ 638-3211, offers free year-round jazz and classical concerts, Wed 12:30, the Frances and Armand Hammer Auditorium.

**Downtown Noon Hour Concerts.** Local performers provide lunchtime entertainment Tues at McPherson Square (15th and I Sts N.W.) and Thurs at Franklin Park (13th and I Sts N.W.) from the end of June through Aug. ☎ 619-7222.

The **Library of Congress,** First and Independence Sts S.E., ☎ 707-5502, has sponsored a free chamber music series since 1925 that has played host to such luminaries as the Juilliard String Quartet and the Beaux Arts Trio. Currently, performances are being held at the Coolidge Auditorium in the Jefferson Building of the Library. Tickets are free, but reservations are required.

**Military Band Summer Concert Series.** Hear the best military bands every evening of the summer from Memorial Day through Labor Day. All concerts are held outdoors and begin at 8. Call for the schedule and location: Army Band, ☎ (703) 696-3718; Marine Band, ☎ 433-4011; Navy Band, ☎ 433-2525; Air Force Band, ☎ 767-5658.

**GW's Mount Vernon College,** 2100 Foxhall Rd N.W., ☎ 625-4655, sponsors "In Series," musical events offering classics and new works, throughout the year.

**"Music Under the Stars" Wednesday Evening Concerts.** From the end of June through Aug, the **Sylvan Theatre** opens its stage to the smooth sounds of "big band." The concerts are held from 7 to 9 every Wed night on the grounds of the Washington Monument—except when the monument is under repair, as has been the case for much of 1999.

**National Building Museum,** 401 F St N.W., ☎ 272-2448, offers its midday "Music in the Great Hall" program, featuring jazz and classical concerts, on selected weekdays each month; starting time is 12:15.

**National Gallery Orchestra, ☎** 842-6941. Weekly classical concerts are held in the National Gallery of Art, West Garden Court of the West Building, Sun 7 P.M. from Oct through June. Seating is on a first-come basis. Arrive early (doors open at 6 P.M.), as this is a popular program.

**National Independence Day Celebration, ☎** 619-7222. The National Symphony Orchestra performs on the west steps of the Capitol Building, 8 P.M. on July 4th. Fireworks follow to end the day's festivities. Arrive early for a good spot; locals often bring picnic dinners.

**U.S. Army Band Anniversary Concert, ☎** (703) 696-3399. The band celebrates its anniversary every March with a free concert of musical and choral selections at the Kennedy Center.

**U.S. Navy Band Holiday Concerts** at DAR Constitution Hall 18th and D Sts N.W., ☎ 433-2525. Traditionally held around the weekend of Dec 20th on a Sat and a Sun evening, the band performs special holiday music. The concerts are free, but reservations must be made in advance by sending a self-addressed, stamped envelope to Holiday Tickets, U.S. Navy Band, Building 105, Washington Navy Yard, Washington, DC 20374.

**U.S. Navy Birthday Concert, ☎** 433-2525. This Navy Band concert is held annually at the Kennedy Center's Concert Hall in mid-Oct. Same procedure as above for free tickets.

### In Maryland

**Mormon Choir of Washington, ☎** (301) 942-0103. The 90-voice choir includes members from congregations of the Church of Jesus Christ of Latter-Day Saints in D.C., Baltimore, and West Virginia. Concert locations vary.

### In Virginia

**Carillon Saturday Evening Recitals, ☎** (703) 289-2530. From May through Aug recitals are held at the Netherlands Carillon on the grounds of the Iwo Jima Memorial in Arlington. Concerts begin at 2 P.M. May and Sept, and at 6:00 P.M. June, July, and Aug.

**U.S. Army Band Concert Series, ☎** (703) 696-3399. The band performs Tues and Thurs Jan through April, and Oct and Nov. This series, which features soloists and ensembles, takes place at Bruckner Hall at Fort Myer in Arlington at 8 P.M.

## Concerts for Children and Families

Check the listings under theater and concerts, as many of the regularly scheduled performances at the Kennedy Center, the Warner Theatre, the Lisner, DAR Constitution Hall, the USAirways Arena, and other traditional locations will delight children.

### In the District

**D.C. Youth Orchestra, ☎** 723-1612. Since 1960 this youth orchestra of students ages 5 to 19 has performed for the president and other dignitaries.

**National Symphony Orchestra,** John F. Kennedy Center, Concert Hall, New Hampshire Ave and Rock Creek Pkwy N.W., ☎ 416-8830. Ticketed performances with an admission fee are held in the Kennedy Center's Concert Hall from Nov through May. The symphony offers "Meet the Orchestra," an informative musical program that comes complete with an instrument "petting zoo." From Oct through May, the orchestra has a variety of programs for young people. Call for information.

### In Maryland
**Jewish Community Center of Greater Washington,** 6125 Montrose Rd, Rockville, ☎ (301) 881-0100, sponsors concerts, plays, and programs for children. Call the box office, ☎ (301) 230-3775.

### In Virginia
**Fairfax Choral Society,** 4028 Hummer Rd, Annandale, ☎ (703) 642-0862. This choral group features a 65-voice youth choir and an 80-voice adult chorus. The group performs at various locations in the D.C. area.
**Opera Theater of Northern Virginia,** ☎ (703) 528-1433 in January offers a one-act opera geared for families and children. The Opera Theater of Northern Virginia usually performs at an Arlington community center. Call for location addresses.

## Dance

### In the District
**African Heritage Dancers and Drummers,** 4018 Minnesota Ave N.E., ☎ 399-5252, perform on a home stage as well as throughout the area. The group, which celebrated its 40th anniversary in 1998, specializes in traditional West African dance and drumming. Along with performing, the group offers open dance classes for children Sat mornings in the fall from 10 A.M. to noon.
**Dance Place,** 3225 8th St N.E., ☎ 269-1600. Presents various dance companies each weekend offering modern dance, performance art, and dance festivals, including an annual African dance festival, and a hip-hop festival in Oct. Children and student discounts are available with a valid ID. Dance classes are offered during the week.
**Everyday Theater,** Randall School at 65 I St S.W., ☎ 554-3893. This is a dance group whose performers interpret Afrocentric music and history through the medium of dance. The group is made up of talented dancers ages 16–24. The group performs approximately 60 shows per year, mostly at colleges, high schools, and prisons.
**John F. Kennedy Center for the Performing Arts,** New Hampshire Ave and Rock Creek Pkwy N.W., ☎ 467-4600 or 416-8524 (TTY). The Kennedy Center offers ballet and a variety of dance performances. The Joffrey Ballet, the Washington Ballet, and the Dance Theater of Harlem have performed at the Kennedy Center. Check the main information number for performances.

Through the facility's **Performance Plus** series, theatergoers can do special things, such as meeting the performers and attending open rehearsals, master classes, and receptions. Performance Plus tickets are available as a series or for individual events. ☎ 416-8811 or 416-8822 (TTY). For example, the "Elements of Ballet" is a series in which the public may attend rehearsals and discussions with artistic directors. An introduction to Latin dance is also offered. "Dance America" is another popular series that offers contemporary dance performances along with postperformance discussions.
The **Washington Ballet** performs at the Kennedy Center, New Hampshire Ave

and Rock Creek Pkwy N.W., and sometimes at other locations. Call Kennedy Center information, ☎ 467-4600. For the Washington Ballet office, 3515 Wisconsin Ave N.W., call ☎ 362-3606. This group offers several productions a year. A celebrated Christmas treat is the company's performance of *The Nutcracker*, which may be held elsewhere than the Kennedy Center. Discounted tickets are available to veterans, senior citizens, students (with valid ID), and children.

**Washington Performing Arts Society,** 2000 L St N.W., ☎ 833-9800. The society organizes and sponsors a large number of diverse dance groups and productions.

### In Virginia
**Center for the Arts, George Mason University,** 4400 University Dr, Fairfax, ☎ (703) 993-8888. This center not only hosts student dance productions but also hosts national and international dance groups and productions. Student and senior-citizen discounts are available.

**Reston Community Center,** 2310 Colts Neck Rd, Reston, ☎ (703) 476-4500, rents its stage to the **Conservatory Ballet, Dance Theatre Expressions,** and other dance groups. The community center also offers dance classes for children ages 3 and up throughout the year. Reduced ticket rates are offered for children under 18 and senior citizens.

## Dance for Children and Families

### In the District
In addition to performances at the John F. Kennedy Center and Lisner Auditorium, families should check the events at the area's embassies (see "Embassy Entertainment"), and also consider these options:

**Capitol Ballet Company,** 1200 Delafield Place N.W., ☎ 882-4039 is a student group from the Jones-Haywood School of Ballet, who perform in D.C. at various locales.

### In Maryland
**Maryland Youth Ballet,** 7702 Woodmont Ave, Bethesda, ☎ (301) 652-2232, is a student ballet company that has launched many professional dancers. Each Christmas they perform *The Nutcracker.*

**Metropolitan Ballet Theater,** 10076 Darnestown Rd, Rockville, ☎ (301) 762-1757, performs *The Nutcracker* annually as well as other seasonal performances.

### In Virginia
**Kintz-Mejia Ballet Company,** 1524 Springfield Rd, McLean, ☎ (703) 506-1039, performs at the Center for the Arts, George Mason University.

**Reston Community Center,** 2310 Colts Neck Rd, Reston, ☎ (703) 476-4500, offers dance classes for children ages 3 and older, and rents space to various dance companies.

## Embassy Entertainment
A well-kept secret in Washington, D.C., is that the city's embassies and cultural institutes offer locals and tourists an interesting array of entertainment choices, including concerts, art shows, lectures, and films, often in elegant settings. Most

events are **free** and **open to the public.** Here is a list of some popular favorites. Always call first to determine the proper ticket protocol and the specific offerings.

**Australian Embassy,** 1601 Massachusetts Ave N.W., ☎ 797-3000. Features temporary art exhibits. Open to the public Mon–Fri, 9–5.

**Austrian Embassy,** 3524 International Ct N.W., ☎ 895-6700. Offers concerts, movies, art exhibitions, and lectures.

The **Brazilian-American Cultural Institute,** 4103 Connecticut Ave N.W., open 9–9 weekdays, ☎ 362-8334, while not an embassy, is devoted to Brazilian culture, offering films (usually subtitled), lectures, music recitals, art exhibitions, and video screenings.

The **Canadian Embassy,** 501 Pennsylvania Ave N.W., ☎ 682-1740, offers several items of interest. The Embassy Gallery (open 10–5 Mon–Fri) hosts free art exhibits year-round. Jazz and blues concerts are sponsored by the embassy at various venues around the city. The Embassy Library opens its doors to the public by appointment only, 10:30–4 weekdays. To arrange a visit, ☎ 682-1740, 8–10:30 A.M. weekdays.

The **French Embassy,** *(La Maison Française),* 4101 Reservoir Rd N.W., ☎ 944-6000, across from the Georgetown University Hospital, offers French films (usually with subtitles), art exhibitions, music, and theater (some productions are in French, others in English, some are bilingual). Call ☎ 944-6000 for a current listing. Fees apply to all events, and student discounts are available for the film series. Tell the gate attendant that you are attending an embassy function and you may be able to use one of the 200 parking spaces.

The **Embassy of Indonesia,** 2020 Massachusetts Ave N.W., ☎ 775-5200, offers Indonesian arts and crafts shows, as well as lectures that are open to the public during office hours.

**Japan Information & Culture Center,** 1155 21st St N.W. (in the lower level of Lafayette Center), ☎ 238-6949, has an exhibition gallery that is open to the public 9–5 weekdays. Videos and 16 mm films can be checked out with a cash deposit of $25. At times, the center hosts free cultural and educational video screenings about Japan, as well as a series of Japanese films. Call ☎ 238-6900 for recorded information.

**Mexican Cultural Institute,** 2829 16th St N.W., ☎ 728-1628, Tues–Sat 11–5, features an art gallery highlighting Mexican artists.

**Royal Embassy of Saudi Arabia,** 601 New Hampshire Ave N.W., ☎ 342-3800, can accommodate groups of ten or more people to view a 20-minute informational slide show on Saudi Arabia and its culture, followed by a discussion session. Appointments for viewing can be made for weekdays and evenings.

**Swiss Embassy,** 2900 Cathedral Ave N.W., ☎ 745-7900, offers free concerts, films, lectures, and exhibitions during the year.

## Opera

### In the District

GW's **Mount Vernon College,** 2100 Foxhall Rd N.W., ☎ 625-4655, features experimental opera in the Hand Chapel throughout the year. Discounted ticket prices are available for students, senior citizens, artists, and children under 16.

**Summer Opera Theatre Company,** Hartke Theatre, Catholic University, Harewood Rd N.E., at 4th St and Michigan Ave N.E., ☎ 526-1669, is an independent professional company that performs two fully staged operas during June and July. **Washington Opera,** the Kennedy Center, New Hampshire Ave N.W. and Rock Creek Pkwy, ☎ (800) 87-OPERA, performs seven works from Nov through March.

### In Virginia
**Opera Theater of Northern Virginia,** ☎ (703) 528-1433, offers performances of English opera three times per season. Christmas brings a unique one-act opera geared for families and children. It usually performs at an Arlington community center. Call for location addresses.

## Movie Theaters
D.C. offers a variety of movie theaters, including commercial theaters with 70 mm screens, multiscreen theaters located in shopping centers, and repertory cinemas. Standouts offering something different include the Kennedy Center's **AFI Theater,** with its classics and documentaries; the **Cineplex Odeon Uptown,** an old-fashioned big screen movie theater complete with a balcony; the **National Air and Space Museum,** which has IMAX screens five stories high; and for a different experience, the **Arlington Cinema 'n' Draft House,** ☎ (703) 486-2345, serves beer, second-run movies, and encourages clapping, commentary, hissing, and booing.

General Cinema, in the Mazza Gallerie at 5300 Wisconsin Ave N.W., ☎ 537-9553, is a seven-screen multiplex with two Club Cinema movie theaters. These have oversize leather seats with extra-wide armrests, big enough for holding the salads, sandwiches, or alcoholic drinks you can purchase at the theater's small bar/eatery. Tickets cost $12.50 each. You can reserve tickets by phone for all movies.

For complete listings of the area's nearby movie theaters and show times, check the Style and Weekend sections of the *Washington Post* and the listings in *City Paper* and the *Washington Times*.

# Amusements

## Spectator Sports
The Washington area offers football, basketball, hockey, as well as horse racing. For baseball, Washingtonians go to Baltimore's stadium at Camden Yards.

The **Washington Redskins** are Washington's National Football League (NFL) team and an area obsession during good years and bad. In 1997, the late Jack Kent Cooke opened the 80,000-seat Jack Kent Cooke Stadium in Raljon, Maryland ("Raljon" for Cooke's two sons, Ralph and John), which was actually part of Landover. Unfortunately, the new stadium has the same problem as the old stadium—most of the seats are held by season ticket holders. In 1999, a group of investors, led by Daniel Snyder, bought the team for just under $800 million. Snyder went back to using "Landover" and sold the stadium's naming rights for 27 years to Federal Express for more than $200 million. So now the Redskins play at FedEx Field. Obtaining seats is difficult, but you can call ☎ (301) 276-6050.

The **Washington Wizards** (Washington's NBA basketball team), the **Washington Mystics** (WNBA [women's] basketball), and the **Washington Capitals** (NHL hockey) all play at the MCI Center, 7th & F Sts N.W., ☎ 628-3200.

The **Baltimore Orioles** are Washingtonians' adopted favorites. The "O's" play in Oriole Park at Camden Yards, 333 W. Camden St, Baltimore, about a one-hour drive away. The stadium, which debuted to raves in 1992, mixes an old-time ballpark feel with modern amenities. For tickets and game times call ☎ 296-2473 or (410) 685-9800.

## Participant Sports

### Bicycling

Bicycling opens up the city to visitors. Pedal by Embassy Row and admire the mansions on Massachusetts Ave, turn down Connecticut Ave into the heart of the business district, glide along Pennsylvania Ave past the White House, and gear up for the many Mall attractions, all without the hassles of looking for parking.

For a scenic and green city tour follow the marked bike path from the Lincoln Memorial through Rock Creek Park, which has more than 15 miles of paved biking and jogging paths. On Sat and Sun Beach Dr between Military and Broad Branch Rds N.W. closes to traffic from 7 to 7. This attracts many bikers, roller skaters, and weekend strollers. Listening to the babbling creek while sitting in the sun on one of the boulders lining the banks is a favorite and free weekend delight for many Washingtonians.

The **C&O (Chesapeake and Ohio) Canal tow path** runs parallel to the eastern shore of the Potomac River from Georgetown in Washington, D.C., to Cumberland, Maryland. About 15 miles northwest of Washington, on the Maryland side of the river, is the **C&O Canal National Historical Park,** which the locals call Great Falls, Maryland. Here is the Great Falls Tavern, which is now the Visitor Center and has a permanent exhibit about the canal. There's also room for picnics and hiking. Here also are canal boat rides, just like those offered along the canal in Georgetown, and a boardwalk system that leads to an island from which one can view the river. Across the river on the Virginia side is **Great Falls Park.** This is also open for public recreation, but there is no Visitor Center nor boat rides. But some feel this is the more scenic of the two views of the river (Maryland and Virginia views). Both sides are open to the public sunrise until dark year-round. The phone number for the Maryland side is ☎ (301) 299-3613; for the Virginia side, ☎ (703) 285-2966.

The **Mount Vernon Trail** stretches for 18.5 miles along the Potomac River from Memorial Bridge to George Washington's historic estate. Scenic stops along the way include **Theodore Roosevelt Island,** the **Lyndon Baines Johnson Memorial Grove** in Alexandria, and the **Jones Point Lighthouse.**

Commercial **bike rental** shops include:
**Fletcher's Boat House,** 4940 Canal Rd N.W., ☎ 244-0461.
**Thompson's Boat Center,** 2900 Virginia Ave N.W., ☎ 333-4861.
**Big Wheel Bikes** has three locations: Georgetown, 1034 33rd St N.W., ☎ 337-0254; Old Town, 2 Prince St, Alexandria, ☎ (703) 739-2300; and Bethesda, 6917 Arlington Rd, ☎ (301) 652-0192. Big Wheel Bikes rents traditional ten-speeds and mountain bikes by the hour or by the day. Helmet rentals are optional and cost an additional fee. All bicycles must be returned to the same store from which they were rented. Children's bikes are available.
**Bike the Sites, Inc.,** ☎ 966-8662, Web: www.bikethesites.com, offers pedal-

by guided tours of the city's attractions. The one-hour Early Bird Fun Ride costs $25 per person, and the three-hour Capital Sites Ride covers many attractions in an eight-mile loop for $35. Children 8 or older are welcome.

**Saddles Bike Rentals,** a company based in Seattle and San Francisco, has leased space at 1001 Pennsylvania Ave N.W. (no phone as of press time). They plan to rent bikes that feature a computerized mapping system, so riders will know exactly where they are along a route.

For information about the **C&O Canal National Historical Park**'s trails, call the Office of the Superintendent, Sharpsburg, Maryland, ☎ (301) 739-4200. For the Georgetown to Seneca section call ☎ (301) 299-3613. For the **Mount Vernon Trail** call the Superintendent of the George Washington Memorial Parkway, ☎ (703) 289-2500.

The **Washington Area Bicyclist Association (WAVA),** 733 15th St N.W., offers information and maps on biking in D.C. and the surrounding area. ☎ 628-2500. The **Potomac Pedalers Touring Club** offers free guided bike tours on weekends. Write PO Box 23601, Washington, D.C. 20026. ☎ 363-TOUR.

## Boating

The National Park Service operates three boat rental facilities. All are concessions and remain open seasonally, sunrise to sunset.

**Fletcher's Boat House,** 4940 Canal Rd N.W., ☎ 244-0461. Fletcher's offers wooden rowboats, canoes, and bicycle rentals to the public from March to mid-Nov. Both Fletcher's canoes and rowboats may be used on the C&O Canal and the Potomac River. Besides offering a large area with 30–40 grills and tables for picnicking, Fletcher's also sells fishing bait, tackle, and licenses, as well as light lunches and snacks. To find Fletcher's Boat House drive, bike, jog, or walk two miles west of the Key Bridge and look for the old stone building nestled along the banks of the canal. Call ahead to check on weather conditions, hours of operation, and fees.

**Jack's Boats,** in Georgetown, 3500 K St N.W., ☎ 337-9642, offers canoe, kayak, and rowboat rentals from April until early Nov, weather permitting. While Jack's Boats encourages picnicking, there are only three picnic tables. The facility remains open 8–8 daily.

**Swain's Lock Boat House,** 10700 Swain's Lock Rd, Potomac, Maryland, ☎ (301) 299-9006, offers canoe, kayak, and rowboat rentals for use on the C&O Canal only from March to Nov. Swain's also rents three-speeds and mountain bikes. Canoe lessons are offered every Thurs night during the summer. Swain's has 15 picnic tables and grills, as well as snacks. Swain's also rents bicycles, including tandem bikes.

**Thompson's Boat Center,** 2900 Virginia Ave N.W., ☎ 333-4861, is located at the intersection of Rock Creek Pkwy and Virginia Ave N.W. Thompson's Boat Center provides a broader range of boats for a wider breadth of water. Resting on the shores of the Potomac River, Thompson's Boat Center offers canoes, rowboats, and kayaks, and for the more serious boater, sunfish sailboats, and rowing sculls. Complete novices are welcome. Thompson's offers five-day rowing scull instructional sessions Mon–Fri. The 75-minute lessons are offered three times a day from mid-May through early Oct. A reservation must be made in person to secure a spot in an instructional group. Thompson's does not have fishing licenses, tackle, or equipment for sale or rent. Thompson's has more than 20 regattas throughout the year, including the Schwepps International Regatta and the George Washington University Invitational Regatta.

## Golf

Golf is available from sunrise to sunset every day of the year at the city's three public golf courses (Web: www.golfdc.com). With no reservations for tee times taken, and no lockers, simply show up in your golfing attire and plan to wait for at least a little while. Senior-citizen rates apply at all three locations.

**East Potomac Park Golf Course,** in the East Potomac Park, Ohio Dr S.W., at Haines Point, ☎ 554-7660, is geared for the whole family. Located near the Jefferson Memorial, this facility has an 18-hole course, a driving range, and a miniature golf course. Adults' and children's golf equipment are available for rent.

**Langston Golf Course,** 26th St and Benning Rd N.E., ☎ 397-8638. Use the driving range to warm up before attacking the lengthy 6,340-yard course, which Langston dubs "the capital test in golf."

**Rock Creek Golf Course,** in Rock Creek Park, at 16th and Rittenhouse Sts N.W., ☎ 882-7332, features a tricky 15th hole, rated among the top ten most difficult in D.C. Beware of the narrow and difficult back nine. To avoid long waits, play after 2 on weekends.

## Horseback Riding

**Meadowbrook Stables,** 8200 Meadowbrook Stables, Chevy Chase, Maryland, ☎ (301) 589-9026, is a no-nonsense riding facility offering lessons, many of which are booked by locals. One-time lessons are not available; riders must sign up for a series. Call ahead to ascertain openings. Hours of operation vary seasonally. Meadowbrook holds three WBTA shows per year—in May, July, and Oct—and all are free to the public.

The horse trails in Rock Creek Park provide miles of paths. The **Rock Creek Park Horse Center,** 5100 Glover Rd N.W., ☎ 362-0117, offers lessons, barn tours, pony rides, and guided trail rides. Since the facility is a public barn, visitors are welcome.

## Ice Skating

Rinks include the **National Sculpture Garden Ice Rink,** on the Mall at 7th St and Constitution Ave N.W., ☎ 737-4215, and the **Pershing Park Rink,** 14th St and Pennsylvania Ave N.W., ☎ 737-6938. The skating seasons at these facilities run from about the middle of Nov until March, weather permitting. Call ahead about rental and ice time fees. The **Fort Dupont Ice Arena,** 3779 Ely Place S.E., ☎ 584-5007, is an indoor rink.

If the weather proves especially cold, skating options double when the C&O Canal and the Reflecting Pool, located between the Lincoln Memorial and the Washington Monument, freeze over. Before heading down to the canal and the pool, check with the park service for information about ice conditions, ☎ 619-7222.

Just outside the Washington area, in suburban Virginia and Maryland, four other rinks offer public skating time. The **Bethesda Metro Center,** at the intersection of Wisconsin Ave and E. West Hwy, has a small outdoor rink situated adjacent to the Hyatt Regency Hotel. ☎ (301) 656-0588. **Cabin John Ice Rink,**

10610 Westlake Dr, also in Bethesda, ☎ (301) 365-0585, has two covered out-door rinks and a snack bar. In Virginia the **Fairfax Ice Arena** is open year-round at 3779 Pickett Rd, ☎ (703) 323-1132. Skate rentals are available.

## Swimming
Some of the better-equipped public pools include:
**Capital East Natatorium,** indoor pool, 635 North Carolina Ave S.E., ☎ 724-4495.
**East Potomac Park,** outdoor pool, ☎ 727-3285.
**Georgetown Pool,** outdoor pool, 34th and Volta Sts N.W., ☎ 282-2366.
**Wilson High School**'s indoor pool, Nebraska Ave and Chesapeake St N.W., ☎ 282-2216.
All of these pools offer free hours to the public (including non-District residents). For exact times call ahead. For more information on public pools, call ☎ 576-6436 or 673-7660.

## Tennis
The **East Potomac Tennis Center,** 1090 Ohio Dr S.W., at Haines Point. ☎ 554-5962, offers 15 courts, of which 3 are lit at night. Courts may be reserved, but rackets are not provided. Call to reserve instruction time. The center is especially busy from 4 P.M. to midnight during the week and any time during weekends.

The **Rock Creek Tennis Center,** known also as the **William H. G. FitzGerald Tennis Center,** 16th and Kennedy Sts N.W., across from the Carter Barron Amphitheatre, ☎ 722-5949, offers 15 clay- and 10 hard-surface courts. From Sept through April five courts are enclosed for indoor play. To reserve instructional sessions, call ☎ 722-5949. Reservations for court time and lessons may be phoned in up to one week in advance. Racket rentals are available.

In addition to these facilities, the **D.C. Department of Recreation** offers 135 tennis courts at 44 different locations throughout the city. For night play, 25 courts are lit. Court time is free and available on a walk-on basis. For the locations of these courts, call the Sports Office, ☎ 645-3944 or 645-3940. For additional help, call Customer Service, ☎ 673-7647.

To watch some world-class tennis, purchase tickets to the Nations Bank Classic in July and the Womens' Tennis Association (WTA) Champions Challenge in Sept.

# Woodland Walks, Hikes, and Trails
**Black History National Recreation Trail.** Dedicated during Black History Month, Feb 1988, the Black History National Recreation Trail was the idea of a 17-year-old Eagle Scout, Willard Andre Hutt. The trail was designed as a grouping of historical points and areas of Black history made accessible by either driving, biking, or walking. There is no specific route to follow. The trail incorporates sites and attractions from slavery days to the New Deal. Stops along the way include: Mt. Zion Cemetery and Female Union Band Cemetery, behind 2515-2531 Q St N.W., in Georgetown; the Metropolitan A.M.E. Church, 1518 M St N.W., Downtown; Lincoln Park, featuring statues devoted to Mary McLeod Bethune and Abraham Lincoln, E. Capitol St between 11th and 13th Sts and North Carolina and Massachusetts Aves, Capitol Hill; Frederick Douglass National Historic Site, 1411 W St SE, Anacostia; Howard University, 2400 6th St N.W., LeDroit Park; and the Mary McLeod Bethune Council House National Historic Site, 1318

Vermont Ave N.W., Logan Circle. Informative brochures, highlighting the histories of all stops along the trail are available at every Black History National Recreation Trail site. ☎ 619-7222.

**C&O Canal.** For a short time this canal bolstered the Georgetown and Washington area as a commercial hub for tobacco and raw materials, but because of the advent of the railroad the canal lost financial support. The canal remained a working waterway until 1924 when a devastating flood rendered it useless.

Claimed as a national monument in 1961, then named a national historical park in 1971, the C&O Canal remains a technological treasure: Its system of lift locks raise the canal's waters from near sea level to 605 ft above sea level at Cumberland, Maryland, 184.5 miles upstream.

The towpath offers a scenic and soothing backdrop for walks and bike rides. A favorite place to start is Great Falls in Potomac, Maryland. The falls, not high but powerful, draw crowds, but the trails, especially farther away from the park's Visitor Center, are peaceful. A snack bar offers light fare for the hungry traveler.

For children and families, there are mule-drawn **barge trips** narrated by costumed interpreters on the C&O Canal from mid-April to mid-Oct. The 90-minute trips originate at Georgetown for the *Georgetown* barge, ☎ 653-5844, and at the Visitor Center in the park at Great Falls, Maryland, for the *Canal Clipper* barge, ☎ (301) 299-3613. In Georgetown sign on at the C&O Visitor Center, ☎ 653-5844, which is across from the Foundry, 1055 Thomas Jefferson St N.W.

**Dumbarton Oaks Park.** Dumbarton Oaks, in Upper Georgetown at the intersection of Lover's Lane and R St N.W., is part of a chain of parks that lead to Rock Creek Park. The 27 acres of woods and foot paths are characteristic of this natural park, untouched by the hands of man. Phone the Rock Creek Park Office of the Superintendent, ☎ 426-6829.

**Rock Creek Park.** Rock Creek Park is a wonderful oasis in the heart of the city. The park has miles of wooded trails, paths for horseback riding and bicycling, and numerous picnic facilities. Contact the park headquarters, 5000 Glover Rd N.W., ☎ 282-1063. For specific information on activities, refer to other parts of the outdoor section.

For children and families, the **Nature Center and Planetarium,** 5200 Glover Rd N.W., ☎ 426-6829, offers guided nature walks and environmental programs (a wheelchair-accessible, self-guided nature trail is nearby), animal demonstrations, films, puppet shows, and other activities for children. The Planetarium shows the film *The Night Sky* Wed at 4 P.M. and has regular children's programs Sat and Sun at 1 and 4 P.M. **Peirce Mill,** at Beach Dr and Tilden St N.W., ☎ 426-6908, is a former 19C gristmill located in a scenic spot on the creek bank. Tours of the mill are on Sat, and programs include interpretive talks, corn-shelling demonstrations, and storytelling. Adjacent to the mill is the **Rock Creek Gallery,** also known as the **Art Barn.** This former carriage house serves as a gallery for local artists, as well as a center for art activities for children. ☎ 426-6829 for a schedule.

**Discovery Creek Children's Museum** at Glen Echo Park, 7300 MacArthur Blvd N.W., ☎ 364-3111, is committed to helping children experience and appreciate the natural environment of the Washington area. Weekdays are reserved for school groups and summer camps, but on weekends there are hands-on programs geared to different age groups available both days. Call for a schedule. The museum's schoolhouse, 4954 MacArthur Blvd N.W., is reserved for school groups.

**Theodore Roosevelt Island.** This nature preserve located between Theodore Roosevelt Bridge and Key Bridge at Turkey Run Park along the George Washington Memorial Pkwy in McLean, Virginia, ☎ (703) 289-2530, serves as a city oasis. In addition to a memorial to Teddy Roosevelt, the island offers 2.5 miles of trails, taking the visitor through three different terrains—swamp, marsh, and upland forest.

**Tidal Basin and West and East Potomac Parks.** West and East Potomac Parks are divided by the Tidal Basin. Each spring the cherry trees blossom near the Jefferson Memorial at Haines Point, attracting thousands of visitors. In warm weather paddle boats can be rented. ☎ 619-7222.

## Specialized Museums and Attractions

The following section provides a listing of museums and attractions by interest. For a listing of current special events at museums at attractions, check the Fri edition of the *Washington Post*'s Weekend Guide, the *City Paper,* and the Thurs edition of the *Washington Times*.

**African American Art and Culture:** Anacostia Neighborhood Museum, Bethune Museum and Archives, Black History National Recreational Trail, Frederick Douglass Home, National Museum of African Art, National Museum of American Art, National Museum of American History, National Portrait Gallery.

**American Indian:** Interior Department Museum, National Museum of American Art, National Museum of Natural History, National Museum of the American Indian Cultural Resources Center (in Suitland, Maryland), National Museum of the American Indian (opens in 2002), National Portrait Gallery.

**Antiques and Decorative Arts:** Anderson House, Arlington House, Arthur M. Sackler Gallery, Arts and Industries Building, Corcoran Gallery of Art, DAR Museum, Decatur House, Diplomatic Reception Rooms at the State Department, Dumbarton House and Dumbarton Oaks, Freer Gallery of Art, Hillwood, Historical Society of Washington, D.C., Mount Vernon, National Gallery of Art, National Museum of American History, The Octagon, Old Executive Building, Renwick Gallery, Sewall-Belmont House, Treasury Building, Tudor Place, White House.

**Architecture:** National Building Museum, The Octagon.

**Art: Ancient and Textiles:** Dumbarton Oaks, National Gallery of Art, National Museum of of Natural History, Textile Museum.

**Art: 17C and 18C:** Corcoran Gallery of Art, Decatur House, Diplomatic Reception Rooms at the State Department, Dumbarton House, National Gallery of Art, National Museum of American Art, National Museum of Women in the Arts, National Portrait Gallery, White House.

**Art: 19C and 20C:** Arlington House, Corcoran Gallery of Art, Decatur House, Diplomatic Reception Rooms at the State Department, Dumbarton House, Ford's Theatre, Hirshhorn Museum and Sculpture Garden, National Gallery of Art, National Museum of American Art, National Museum of Women in the Arts, National Portrait Gallery, Phillips Collection.

**Art: Asian:** Anderson House, Arthur M. Sackler Gallery, Freer Gallery, National Gallery of Art, National Museum of Natural History.

**Art: Folk:** Art Museum of the Americas, Capital Children's Museum, National Gallery of Art, National Museum of American Art.

**Art: Latin American and Hispanic:** Art Museum of the Americas, Dumbarton Oaks, Organization of American States, Fondo del Sol.

**Bible:** Library of Congress (contains a copy of the Gutenberg Bible on display).

**Cemeteries: Historic:** Arlington National Cemetery, Congressional Cemetery, Civil War Cemetery at St. Elizabeth's Hospital (by special permission), Oak Hill Cemetery, Rock Creek Cemetery.

**Children:** Bureau of Engraving and Printing, Capital Children's Museum, the Capitol, Ford's Theatre, Interior Department Museum, John F. Kennedy Center for the Performing Arts, National Air and Space Museum, National Aquarium, National Gallery of Art, National Geographic Society's Explorers Hall, National Museum of African Art, National Museum of American History, National Museum of Natural History, National Postal Museum, National Zoological Park, Navy Memorial Museum, Paul E. Garber Facility, Smithsonian Carousel, U.S. Holocaust Memorial Museum, Washington Dolls' House and Toy Museum, Washington Navy Yard (includes Navy Museum and Marine Corps Museum), White House.

**Churches and Places of Worship:** Adas Israel Synagogue, All Souls' Unitarian Church, Franciscan Monastery and Gardens, Grace Episcopal Church, Metropolitan A.M.E. Church, Mt. Zion United Methodist Church, National Shrine of the Immaculate Conception, St. John's Episcopal Church, St. Matthew's Cathedral, St. Sophia Cathedral, Scottish Rite Temple, Temple of the Church of Jesus Christ of Latter-Day Saints, Washington National Cathedral.

**Civil War, D.C.:** Civil War Cemetery at St. Elizabeth's Hospital (by special permission), Emancipation Monument, Ford's Theatre, Fort Lesley J. McNair, Lincoln Memorial, Marine Corps Museum, National Archives, National Museum of American Art, National Museum of Health and Medicine, National Portrait Gallery, Navy Memorial Museum, Navy Museum, Petersen House, Renwick Gallery.

**Civil War, Md.:** Antietam National Battlefield, Army Ordnance Museum—Aberdeen Proving Grounds, Barbara Fritchie House and Museum, Boonsboro Museum of History, Fort McHenry National Monument and Historic Shrine, Monocacy Battlefield, U.S. Naval Academy Museum.

**Civil War, Va.:** Arlington House, Fredericksburg Area Museum and Cultural Center, Fredericksburg and Spotsylvania National Military Park, Lee's Boyhood Home, Manassas Museum, Manassas National Battlefield Park, Pamplin Historical Park and the National Museum of the Civil War Soldier.

**Gardens:** Capitol Building, Carlyle House, Constitution Gardens, Dumbarton House and Dumbarton Oaks, Enid A. Haupt Garden, Folger Shakespeare Library, Franciscan Monastery, Hillwood Museum and Gardens, Kenilworth Aquatic Gardens, Lee-Fendall House, Malcolm X Park, Mount Vernon, Old Stone House, Organization of American States, Tudor Place, U.S. Botanic Gardens, U.S. National Arboretum, Washington National Cathedral, Woodlawn Plantation.

**Historic Homes and Period Rooms:** Anderson House, Arlington House, Bethune Museum and Archives, Carlyle House, Clara Barton House, Daughters of the American Revolution, Decatur House, Dumbarton House, Dumbarton Oaks, Hillwood Museum and Gardens, Historical Society of Washington, D.C., Lee-Fendall House, Mount Vernon, The Octagon, Peterson House, Robert E. Lee Boyhood Home, Sewall-Belmont House, Tudor Place, White House, Woodlawn Plantation, Woodrow Wilson House.

**Jewelry:** Corcoran, Dumbarton Oaks, Freer Gallery, Museum of American Art, Museum of Women in the Arts, National Museum of African Art, National Museum of Natural History, Renwick Gallery.

**Judaica:** B'nai B'rith Klutznick Museum, Jewish Historical Society, National Museum of African Art, National Museum of American History, National Museum of American Jewish Military History, U.S. Holocaust Memorial Museum.

**Libraries and Research Facilities:** Anderson House, Dumbarton Oaks, Folger Shakespeare Library, Hillwood Museum and Gardens, Historical Society of Washington, D.C., James Monroe Museum and Memorial Library, Library of Congress, Martin Luther King, Jr., Library, National Institute of Health, National Library of Medicine, National Museum of Health and Medicine, National Postal Museum, Performing Arts Library at the Kennedy Center, U.S. Holocaust Memorial Museum.

**Medical:** Armed Forces Medical Museum, National Institute of Health, National Museum of American History, National Museum of Health and Medicine.

**Military:** Armed Forces Medical Museum, Anderson House, Armed Forces Medical Museum, Firearms Museum/National Rifle Association, Marine Corps Museum, National Museum of American History, National Museum of American Jewish Military History, National Museum of Health and Medicine, Navy Museum, U.S. Holocaust Museum, U.S. Navy Memorial Museum.

**Photography:** Corcoran Gallery of Art, Historical Society of Washington, D.C., Jewish Historical Society, Library of Congress, National Archives, National Gallery of Art, National Geographic Society, National Museum of American Art, U.S. Holocaust Museum.

**Sculpture:** Corcoran Gallery of Art, Hirshhorn Museum and Sculpture Garden, National Air and Space Museum, National Gallery of Art, National Museum of African Art, National Museum of American Art, National Portrait Gallery. In addition, tour the various monuments and memorials in town.

**Television:** Library of Congress, Museum of American History, Newseum.

**Textiles:** Anderson House, Dumbarton Oaks, National Museum of African Art, Textile Museum.

**Theater:** Performing Arts Library at the Kennedy Center.

**Toys:** Daughters of the American Revolution, Dumbarton House, National Museum of American History, Washington Dolls' House and Toy Museum.

**Transportation:** Marine Corps Museum, National Air and Space Museum, National Museum of American History, Navy Museum, Paul E. Garber Facility,

**Washingtoniana:** Historical Society of Washington, D.C., Jewish Historical Society, Martin Luther King, Jr., Library's Washingtoniana Collection.

## Annual Events

For additional information, call the Washington, D.C., Convention and Visitors Association (WCVA), ☎ 789-7000, Web: www.washington.org.

### January
**Martin Luther King, Jr.'s Birthday** (Jan 15). Commemorated with a variety of activities.
**Washington Antique Show.** Dealers meet annually at an area hotel.
**Inauguration** celebration every four years.

### February
**Chinese New Year.** Fireworks and special holiday menus at the restaurants in the Chinatown district.

**Black History Month.** Special month-long activities, events, lectures, and films to honor the contributions of African Americans.

**Lincoln's Birthday Celebration.** Feb 12 at the Lincoln Memorial.

**Washington's Birthday Celebration.** Feb 22 at the Washington Monument and Mount Vernon.

**Frederick Douglass's Birthday Celebration.** Feb 14 at the Frederick Douglass House in Anacostia.

### March

**Annual International Washington Flower and Garden Show.** Floral arrangements at the Washington Convention Center.

**St. Patrick's Day Parade.** Bands and a parade down Constitution Ave N.W.

**Smithsonian Kite Festival.** Kite flyers of all ages compete for prizes and trophies at the Washington Monument.

### April

**White House Easter Egg Roll** (sometimes in March, depending when Easter falls). Children 10 and under accompanied by parents roll Easter eggs on the White House lawn.

**Cherry Blossom Festival/Parade** (end of March/beginning of April). Week-long celebration that concludes with the annual Cherry Blossom Parade.

**Georgetown House Tour.** Private homes open for public touring.

**White House Spring Garden Tour.** The Presidential Mansion's gardens open to the public.

**Smithsonian Crafts Show.** Juried craft show of the nation's best artisans.

**Shakespeare's Birthday Celebration Open House.** Folger Shakespeare Library.

**Jefferson's Birthday Celebration.** April 13 at the Jefferson Memorial.

### May

**Asian Pacific Heritage Month.** Celebrations and exhibitions at the Smithsonian.

**Goodwill Industries Guild Embassy Tour.** Some of Washington's embassies open to the public.

**Malcolm X Day.** Speakers, music, and food honor this leader at Anacostia Park in Southeast Washington.

**Georgetown Garden Tour.** Many of the gardens of private homes open to the public.

**Memorial Day Ceremony.** A traditional wreath-laying ceremony at Arlington National Cemetery.

**D.C. International Film Festival.** Dozens of foreign, national, and local films debut.

### All Summer Long
### Military Band Summer Concert Series.

Mon: U.S. Navy Band—U.S. Capitol/west side.

Tues: U.S. Army Band—Sylvan Theater on the Washington Monument Grounds. U.S. Air Force Band—U.S. Capitol/west side.

Wed: U.S. Marine Band—U.S. Capitol/west side.

Thurs: U.S. Navy Band—U.S. Capitol/west side.

Fri: U.S. Army Band—U.S. Capitol/west side. U.S. Air Force Band—Sylvan Theater.

Sun: U.S. Marine Band—Sylvan Theater.

**Navy Summer Ceremony Series.** Wed evenings at Washington Navy Yard waterfront. Watch a multimedia presentation showcasing the history and character of the U.S. Navy.

**U.S. Navy Memorial Summer Concert Series.** Thurs and Sat evenings. Hear military bands play at the U.S. Navy Memorial on Pennsylvania Ave N.W.

**Marine Corps Sunset Parades.** Tues evenings. The U.S. Marine Band, the Bugle Corps, and the Silent Drill team perform at the Iwo Jima Memorial in Arlington.

**Polo matches.** Every Sat afternoon on the field at the Lincoln Memorial.

## June

**Smithsonian Festival of American Folklife** (June into July). Craftspeople, musicians, and dancers representing different ethnic groups perform and demonstrate crafts, native dances, and music on the Mall.

**Mostly Mozart Annual Music Festival.** John F. Kennedy Center for the Performing Arts hosts the works of Wolfgang Amadeus Mozart.

**Annual National Capital Barbecue Battle.** Pennsylvania Ave N.W., between 9th and 14th Sts. Attractions include the world's largest traveling grill.

**Dupont-Kalorama Museum Walk Day.** Special events at the area's museums and historic houses.

## July

**Independence Day Celebration** (July 4). The National Symphony Orchestra plays on the steps of the U.S. Capitol and a grand display of fireworks lights the Mall.

**Latin American Festival.** Washington's Latino community in the Adams Morgan and Mt. Pleasant area host a week-long festival.

**Virginia Scottish Games.** One of the largest festivals in the country, held in Alexandria on the grounds of the Episcopal High School.

## August

**1812 Overture.** The U.S. Army Band plays on the Washington Monument Grounds.

**Lollipop Concert.** Music and Disney characters presented by the U.S. Navy Band at the Jefferson Memorial.

**Maryland State Farm Fair.**

## September

**International Children's Festival.** Labor Day weekend. Wolf Trap Farm in Vienna, Virginia, hosts a variety of puppet shows, plays, and dances for children.

**National Symphony Orchestra's Labor Day Concert.** On the West Lawn of the Capitol.

**Annual Kennedy Center Open House.** Celebrates the arts with free concerts and performances.

**Black Family Reunion.** A weekend-long celebration of the black family, featuring headline performers, exhibits, food, workshops, and family activities.

**Annual National Frisbee Festival.** Join the fun of the largest noncompetitive frisbee festival, which features world-class frisbee champions and disk-catching dogs. On the Mall, near the National Air and Space Museum.
**Washington Cathedral Open House.** Watch demonstrations of stone cutting and flower arranging.

### October
**Annual "Taste of D.C." Festival.** Sample food from a variety of D.C.'s restaurants. Enjoy entertainment and, for the kids, a special children's area.
**Decorator's Showcase.** Tour a Washington-area residence turned into a showcase home for visitors.
**White House Fall Garden and House Tour.** See the White House gardens, including the famous Rose Garden and the South Lawn.
**Marine Corps Marathon.** A 26-mile course past some of the Washington area's most impressive monuments.

### November
**Washington Craft Show.** Juried show of contemporary American artists.
**Veteran's Day.** There is a wreath-laying at the Tomb of the Unknowns in Arlington National Cemetery.

### December
**Annual Poinsettia Show.** U.S. Botanic Gardens.
**U.S. Capitol Tree Lighting.** A tree is lit on the eve of the Pageant of Peace.
**Pageant of Peace.** The lighting of the National Christmas Tree, usually performed by the president, begins a two-week holiday celebration.
**Lighting of the Menorah.** Lafayette Park.
**Seasonal Band Concerts.** Military bands perform free holiday concerts at either Wolf Trap Farm Park for the Performing Arts or DAR Constitution Hall.
**White House Candlelight Tours.** The presidential mansion is adorned with yuletide decorations for special evening tours between Christmas and New Year's.
**Kennedy Center Holiday Festival.** Performances and concerts all month.
**Washington National Cathedral Christmas Celebration and Services.**
**First Night, Washington, D.C.** A family-oriented New Year's Eve celebration.

## Annual Events for Children and Families
(See list above.)

### January
Martin Luther King, Jr.'s Birthday (Jan 15).

### February
Black History Month. For information on special lectures and exhibits, call the Smithsonian Institution, ☎ 357-2700, and the Martin Luther King, Jr., Memorial Library, ☎ 727-0321.

### March
Smithsonian Kite Festival.
White House Easter Egg Roll (late March/early April).
St. Patrick's Day Parade.

### April
Cherry Blossom Festival/Parade (end of March/beginning of April).
White House Spring Garden Tour.
Shakespeare's Birthday Celebration Open House.

### June
Festival of American Folklife.
Annual National Capital Barbecue Battle.
Summer concerts.

### July
Independence Day Celebration (July 4). Evening fireworks above the Mall.
Latin American Festival.
Summer concerts.

### August
Lollipop Concert. Music and Disney characters presented by the U.S. Navy Band at the Jefferson Memorial.
County and state fairs.
Summer concerts.

### September
International Children's Festival at Wolf Trap Farm in Vienna, Virginia. Labor Day weekend events.
Black Family Reunion.
Annual National Frisbee Festival.

### October
Annual "Taste of D.C." Festival.
White House Garden Tour.

### December
U.S. Capitol Tree Lighting.
Lighting of the Menorah.
White House Candlelight Tours of the Christmas decorations.
Ford's Theatre offers a musical version of Dickens's *A Christmas Carol.*
First Night, Washington, D.C.

### Fall through Spring
From fall through spring, the **Kennedy Center's Imagination Celebration** hosts plays, puppet shows, and dance theater geared for children. When the **National Symphony Orchestra** presents a "petting," kids can try a tuba, finger a flute, bang the drums, and test out other symphonic instruments before the symphony's child-friendly performance.

## Useful Addresses and Phone Numbers
The **Washington Convention and Visitors Association (WCVA)** (Web: www.washington.org) lists the following useful information in their *Visitor's Guide.*

### Events and Information
For brochures and information when in town, stop by the WCVA Visitor Information Center, 1212 New York Ave N.W., Suite 600, Washington, DC 20005, ☎ 789-7000.

### Emergency Information
**Police/Fire/Ambulance,** ☎ 911.
**Police** (non-emergency), ☎ 727-1010.
**Metro Transit Police,** ☎ 962-2121.
**Medical Referral Service** (24-hour), ☎ (800) 362-8677.
**Dental Referral Service,** ☎ 547-7613.
**CVS Pharmacy** (24-hour) Dupont Circle, ☎ 628-0720.

### Helpful Information
**American Automobile Association,** ☎ (703) 222-5000 or (800) 763-9900.
**Currency Exchange: Thomas Cook Currency Services, Inc.,** ☎ 879-6000.
**TICKETplace,** (half-price theater tickets day of show), ☎ 842-5387.
**Time,** ☎ 844-2525.
**Travelers Aid Society,** ☎ 546-3120.
**Weather,** ☎ 936-1212.

### Lost or Stolen Traveler's Checks
**American Express,** ☎ (800) 221-7282.
**First National City Bank,** ☎ (212) 373-1000.
**VISA/CitiCorp** ☎ (800) 541-8882.

### Metrorail/Metrobus Information
**Schedules, Routes** for D.C., Maryland, Virginia, ☎ 637-7000, Web: www.wmata.com.

### National Capital Park Information
**Information,** ☎ 619-7222, Web: www.nps.gov/ncro.
**Dial-A-Park** (24-hour daily activities recording), ☎ 619-PARK.

### Smithsonian
**Smithsonian Dial-A-Museum** (recorded information on daily events), ☎ 357-2020, Web: www.si.edu.
**Smithsonian Dial-A-Phenomenon** (weekly recorded announcements on short-lived natural phenomena), ☎ 357-2000, Web: www.si.edu.
**Smithsonian Visitor Information and Associates' Reception Center,** ☎ 357-2700, Web: www.si.edu.

# Washington, D.C., and Physically Challenged Travelers
For physically challenged travelers, Washington, D.C., is an accessible city. Most museums, hotels, restaurants, and shopping malls have ramps or are otherwise accessible for travelers in wheelchairs.

## Getting around Town
The best way for a physically challenged traveler to get around town is to ride **Metrorail,** Washington's modern and safe subway system. Each metro station is

equipped with an elevator (complete with Braille number plates). To aid visually impaired travelers, the train drivers announce destinations and stops. To aid hearing-impaired travelers, the Metrorail system warns of an approaching train with lights that flash along the edge of the platform. Travelers who have a disabled ID receive reduced fares. For information, call ☎ 962-0128, 962-6464, or 638-3780 (TTY). Web: www.wmta.com.

For a comprehensive overview of Washington, physically challenged sight-seers—and all sightseers—should consider a ride on a **Tourmobile** tram. Regular Tourmobile trams are accessible to physically impaired tourists. Tourmobile also operates a special air-conditioned van for immobile travelers, complete with a wheelchair lift. Reservations must be made at least 24 hours in advance. For more information, call ☎ 554-5100.

For **taxicabs,** ask ahead if the company offers transportation services for people in wheelchairs. **Jones Transportation Services, Inc.,** 1342 S. Capitol St S.E., provides van transfers that accommodate individuals in wheelchairs. Call ☎ 554-2301 at least one day in advance. If traveling from the District into Montgomery County, Maryland, **Barwood Cab,** 4900 Nicholson Lane, Kensington, also offers its "Taxi Plus" service. Call ☎ (301) 984-1900 at least two days in advance.

## Attractions for Physically Challenged Travelers
Here is a brief summary of services available to tourists with special needs. To request special tours or services, always call as far in advance as possible. Every attraction listing in the *Blue Guide* includes information on wheelchair accessibility.

For special guided tours of the **Capitol Building,** contact the **Congressional Special Services Office,** ☎ 224-4048 or 224-4049 (TTY). The office provides wheelchair loans, tours in sign language, escorts for the visually impaired, and tactile tours.

The **Bureau of Engraving and Printing** offers sign language tours if scheduled in advance. ☎ 874-3019.

To schedule a sign language tour of the **Library of Congress,** call ☎ 707-6362.

**Monuments:** To schedule a sign language tour of the **FDR Memorial, Jefferson Memorial, Korean Memorial, Lincoln Memorial, Vietnam Memorial,** and the **Washington Monument,** call the Ranger station for the Mall, ☎ 426-6841.

For a sign language interpreter for a tour of the **National Archives,** call ☎ 501-5205 or 501-5404 (TTY) at least two weeks in advance.

The **National Capital Park Service,** which operates the Jefferson, Washington, and Lincoln Monuments, as well as many other attractions, offers large-print information brochures. Sign language interpreters are available at some park sites. For complete information on the Park Department's special services for physically disabled visitors, call ☎ 619-7222 or 619-7083 (TTY).

The **National Zoo**'s *Zoo Guide for Disabled Visitors,* outlines the park's physically challenged accessibility. To receive a copy of the publication, write to FONZ, National Zoological Park, Washington, DC 20008, or call ☎ 673-4717 or 673-4823 (TTY).

The **Pentagon** has wheelchairs for its daily tours. Request a sign language interpreter two weeks in advance. ☎ (703) 545-6700.

All of the **Smithsonian Institution Museums** are accessible to wheelchairs. By advance request, the Smithsonian offers sign language interpreters or "touch tour" leaders if requested at least two weeks in advance. The Smithsonian also publishes large-print, Braille, and cassette materials for several of its museums.

To receive copies of a Smithsonian publication explaining special resources for disabled travelers, *Smithsonian Access,* call ☎ 357-2700 or 357-1729 (TTY), or write to: Visitor Information Associates Reception Center, Smithsonian Institution, Washington, DC 20560.

The **White House** has a special entrance on Pennsylvania Ave reserved for visitors arriving in wheelchairs. No admission ticket is required. For more information, ☎ 456-2322 or 456-6213 (TTY).

## Resources for Physically Challenged Travelers

The **Washington Visitor Information Center,** 1212 New York Ave N.W., offers free maps, brochures, and information. The center also maintains reference copies *(not for distribution)* of tactile atlases of Washington, D.C., and Maryland, the Smithsonian's disabled visitors guide, and a large-print attractions guide for visually impaired people. The center is open from 9 to 5 Mon through Sat and is accessible to all disabled visitors. ☎ 789-7000. Web: www.washington.org.

The **Columbia Lighthouse for the Blind,** 1421 P St N.W., a nonprofit organization, offers free tactile maps of the Metro system. ☎ 462-2900.

## Helpful TTY Numbers and Web Sites for Hearing-Impaired Travelers

(E=Eastern, C=Central, M=Mountain, P=Pacific time)

### Airlines
**American Airlines,** ☎ (800) 543-1586, 7 days/week 9 A.M.–12 A.M. (E). Web: www.aa.com.
**Continental Airlines,** ☎ (800) 343-9195, 7 days/week 24 hours/day. Web: www.flycontinental.com.
**Delta,** ☎ (800) 343-9195, 7 days/week 24 hours/day. Web: www.delta airlines.com
**Northwest Airlines,** ☎ (800) 328-2298 or (800) 692-2105, 7 days/week 5 A.M.–12:30 A.M. (C). Web: www.nwa.com.
**TWA,** ☎ (800) 421-8488, (800) 421-8480, or (800) 252-0622 in CA, 7 days/week 5 A.M.–9 P.M. (P). Web: www.twa.com.
**United Airlines,** ☎ (800) 323-0170 or (800) 942-8819 in IL, 7 days/week 24 hours/day. Web: www.ual.com.
**USAir,** ☎ (800) 245-2966, 7 days/week 6:30 A.M.–10:30 P.M. (E). Web: www.usairways.com.

### Buses
**Greyhound Lines, Inc.,** ☎ (800) 345-3109, 7 days/week 24 hours/day. Web: www.greyhound.com.

### Trains
**Amtrak** ☎ (800) 523-3109, Mon–Fri 8:30 A.M.–8 P.M. (E). Web: www. amtrak.com.

**Car Rentals**
**Avis,** ☎ (800) 331-2323, 7 days/week 6 A.M.–11:30 P.M. (C). Web: www.avis.com.
**Budget,** ☎ (800) 826-5510, Mon–Fri 8 A.M.–8:30 P.M. (C). Web: www.budget.com.
**Hertz,** ☎ (800) 654-2280, Mon–Fri 8 A.M.–5 P.M. (C). Web: www.hertz.com.
**National Car Rental,** ☎ (800) 328-6323, 7 days/week 5 A.M.–12 A.M. (C). Web: www.nationalcar.com.

**Hotels and Motels**
**Best Western International,** ☎ (800) 528-2222, 7 days/week 8 A.M.–5 P.M. (C). Web: www.bestwestern.com.
**Days Inn of America,** ☎ (800) 222-3297 or (800) 325-3297 in GA, 7 days/week 8:30 A.M.–5:30 A.M. (E). Web: www.daysinn.com.
**Hilton Hotels,** ☎ (800) 368-1133, 7 days/week 24 hours/day. Web: www.hilton.com.
**Holiday Inns,** ☎ (800) 238-5544, 7 days/week 6 A.M.–12 A.M. (C). Web: www.basshotels.com.
**Howard Johnson Motels,** ☎ (800) 654-8442, Mon–Fri 5 A.M.–2 A.M. (C). Web: www.hojo.com.
**Hyatt Hotels,** ☎ (800) 228-9548, 7 days/week 6 A.M.–2 A.M. (C). Web: www.hyatt.com.
**Marriott Hotels,** ☎ (800) 228-7014, 7 days/week 6 A.M.–2 A.M. (C). Web: www.marriott.com.
**Quality Inns International,** ☎ (800) 228-3323, 7 days/week 24 hours/day. Web: www.hotelchoice.com.
**Ramada Inns,** ☎ (800) 228-3232, 7 days/week 4 A.M.–1 P.M. (P). Web: www.ramada.com.
**Sheraton Hotels,** ☎ (800) 325-1717, 7 days/week 24 hours/day. Web: www.sheraton.com.

## Shopping for Physically Challenged Travelers

The newer shopping malls in town also welcome disabled visitors. The **Shops at National Place** are equipped with a wheelchair ramp, as well as elevators and escalators. Wheelchairs may be obtained at the security offices on each floor by calling ahead, ☎ 662-1250. The **Pavilion at the Old Post Office,** ☎ 289-4224, a collection of eateries, cafes, and gift shops, has a wheelchair ramp and elevators, as does **Georgetown Park,** an expansive mall in the heart of Georgetown. **Union Station** is also fully accessible, including Amtrak facilities and its shops and restaurants.

## Theater for Physically Challenged Travelers

Many of the larger theaters in town offer special listening systems for the hearing-impaired. The **John F. Kennedy Center for the Performing Arts** has infrared listening systems in all of its six main theaters. Simply borrow a set of headphones before the performance, sit anywhere, and adjust the volume to your preference. For blind patrons, the Kennedy Center offers audio descriptions of some shows performed in the Opera House, Eisenhower, and Terrace Theaters. Sign language interpreters can accompany hearing-impaired visitors on their tours. All of the

Kennedy Center's individual stages are accessible for patrons utilizing wheelchairs. Also available are Braille and large-print versions of *Stagebill*. For further information and to request an accommodation, ☎ 416-8727.

At the **National Theatre,** in the heart of downtown Washington, once a month the main house performance is narrated for visually impaired theatergoers. The National Theatre is one of the only theaters in the country maintaining a permanent booth near the mezzanine staffed by a narrator who describes the show scene by scene. To obtain earphones for the narration or to secure infrared headsets for hearing-impaired patrons, see an usher before the performances. The National Theatre also offers a limited number of half-price tickets for physically challenged patrons on Tues and Wed evenings and for Sun matinees. ☎ 628-6161 or 783-3370. These are designated performances, so call in advance.

## Transportation for Physically Challenged Travelers

### Buses
**Greyhound/Trailways** charges a disabled person and his or her companion a single fare. ☎ (800) 752-4841. Web: www.greyhound.com.

### Trains
**Access Amtrak,** 60 Massachusetts Ave N.E., Washington, DC 20002, ☎ (800) USA-RAIL, Web: www.amtrak.com, provides information on the accessibility of Amtrak stations and trains on the northeast corridor (Richmond to Boston). Write to receive a free brochure. Some, but not all trains, offer special seats, and some, but not all stations, offer special assistance for the physically challenged. Call at least 24 hours in advance for reservations. Physically challenged customers receive discounted fares on regularly priced tickets.

# Washington, D.C., Area's Most Popular Attractions (1998)

(Rankings are based on visitor counts provided by each attraction listed. Note that numerous attractions were unable to provide visitor counts and that attractions vary in their hours and days of operation and thus vary in the number of visitors they can physically accommodate. The White House, for example, is only open two hours a day, five days per week, but a Smithsonian museum is open daily.)

1. Smithsonian National Air and Space Museum
2. Union Station
3. Smithsonian National Museum of Natural History
4. National Gallery of Art
5. Smithsonian National Museum of American History
6. Arlington National Cemetery
7. National Zoo
8. U.S. Holocaust Memorial Museum
9. Smithsonian Castle Building
10. Vietnam Veterans Memorial
11. Lincoln Memorial

12. White House
13. Smithsonian Arts and Industries Building
14. Mount Vernon
15. Library of Congress
16. U.S. Capitol (tours only)
17. Jefferson Memorial
18. Washington National Cathedral
19. Washington Monument
20. Hirshhorn Museum and Sculpture Garden
21. U.S. Supreme Court
22. National Portrait Gallery/National Museum of American Art
23. National Postal Museum
24. National Geographic Explorers Hall
25. Bureau of Engraving and Printing
26. Newseum
27. National Aquarium
28. Corcoran Gallery of Art
29. Navy Museum
30. Freer Gallery of Art
31. National Museum of African Art
32. National Building Museum
33. Capital Children's Museum
34. Arthur M. Sackler Gallery
35. Phillips Collection
36. Renwick Gallery
37. National Museum of Women in the Arts
38. Anacostia Museum
39. Textile Museum
40. Woodrow Wilson House
41. Decatur House

# Nearby City/County Visitor Bureaus

**Maryland**
**Montgomery County, Maryland, Conference and Visitors Bureau,** 12900 Middlebrook Rd, Suite 1400, Germantown, MD 20874 ☎ (301) 428-9702 or (800) 925-0880.
**Frederick County Tourism Council,** 19 E. Church St, Frederick, MD 21701, ☎ (301) 663-8687.
**Prince George's County, Maryland, Conference and Visitors Bureau,** 9200 Basil Ct, Suite 101, Largo, MD 20774, ☎ (301) 967-8687 or (888) 925-8300.

**Virginia**
**Alexandria Convention and Visitors Bureau,** 221 King St, Alexandria, VA 22314, ☎ (703) 838-4200 or (800) 388-9119, Web: www.funside.com.
**Arlington Convention and Visitors Service,** 2100 Clarendon Blvd, Suite 318, Arlington, VA 22201, ☎ (703) 228-3988 or (800) 296-7996, Web: www.co.arlington.va.us.

**Fairfax County Tourism and Convention Bureau,** 8300 Boone Blvd, Suite 450, Tysons Corner, VA 22182, ☎ (703) 790-3329, Web: www.visitfairfax.org.
**Fredericksburg Office of Economic Development and Tourism,** 706 Caroline St, Fredericksburg, VA 22401, ☎ (540) 372-1216 or (800) 260-3646, Web: www.fredericksburgva.com.
**Prince William County Tourism Information Services,** 10530 Linden Lake Plaza, Suite 105, Manassas, VA 20109, ☎ (703) 392-0330 or (800) 334-9876.

# Embassies

The diplomatic list, a Department of State publication that contains a listing of embassy personnel, is available from the U.S. Government Printing Office, Washington, DC 20402, ☎ 512-1800.

**Albania**—Embassy of the Republic of Albania, 1511 K St N.W., Suite 1010, 20005, ☎ 223-4942, fax 628-7342.

**Algeria**—Embassy of the Democratic and Popular Republic of Algeria, 2118 Kalorama Rd N.W., 20008, ☎ 265-2800, fax 667-2174. National holiday: Anniversary of the Revolution, Nov 1.

**Angola**—Embassy of the Republic of Angola, 1615 M St N.W., 20036, ☎ 785-1156, fax 822-9049. National holiday: Day of Independence, Nov 11.

**Antigua and Barbuda**—Embassy of Antigua and Barbuda, 3400 International Dr N.W., Suite 4M, 20008, ☎ 362-5211, 5166, or 5122, fax 362-5225. National holiday: Day of Independence, Nov 1.

**Argentina**—Embassy of the Argentine Republic, 1600 New Hampshire Ave N.W., 20009, ☎ 939-6400 to 6403, fax 332-3171. National holiday: National Day, May 25.

**Armenia**—Embassy of the Republic of Armenia, 2225 R St N.W., 20008, ☎ 319-1976, fax 319-2982. National holiday: Day of Independence, May 28.

**Australia**—Embassy of Australia, 1601 Massachusetts Ave N.W., 20036, ☎ 797-3000, fax 797-3168. National holiday: Australia Day, Jan 26.

**Austria**—Embassy of Austria, 3524 International Ct N.W., 20008, ☎ 895-6700, fax 895-6750. National holiday: Passing of the Neutrality Law, Oct 26.

**Azerbaijan**—Embassy of the Republic of Azerbaijan, Suite 700, 927 15th St N.W., 20005, ☎ 842-0001, fax 842-0004. National holiday: Republic Day, May 28.

**Bahamas**—Embassy of The Commonwealth of the Bahamas, 2220 Massachusetts Ave N.W., 20008, ☎ 319-2660, fax 319-2668. National holiday: National Day, July 10.

**Bahrain**—Embassy of the State of Bahrain, 3502 International Dr N.W., 20008, ☎ 342-0741 or 0742, fax 362-2192. National holiday: Independence Day, Dec 16.

**Bangladesh**—Embassy of the People's Republic of Bangladesh, 2201 Wisconsin Ave N.W., 20007, ☎ 342-8372 to 8376, fax 333-4971. National holiday: Independence Day, March 26.

**Barbados**—Embassy of Barbados, 2144 Wyoming Ave N.W., 20008, ☎ 939-9200 to 9202; ambassador's office: ☎ 939-9218 or 9219; fax 332-7469. National holiday: Independence Day, Nov 30.

**Belarus**—Embassy of the Republic of Belarus, 1619 New Hampshire Ave N.W., 20009, ☎ 986-1604, fax 986-1805. National holiday: National Day of Celebration, July 3.

**Belgium**—Embassy of Belgium, 3330 Garfield St N.W., 20008, ☎ 333-6900; economics: ☎ 625-7567; fax 333-3079. National holiday: National Day, July 21.

**Belize**—Embassy of Belize, 2535 Massachusetts Ave N.W., 20008, ☎ 332-9639, fax 332-6888.

**Benin**—Embassy of the Republic of Benin, 2737 Cathedral Ave N.W., 20008, ☎ 232-6656 to 6658, fax 265-1996. National holiday: National Day, Aug 1.

**Bolivia**—Embassy of Bolivia, 3014 Massachusetts Ave N.W., 20008, ☎ 483-4410 to 4412, fax 328-3712.

**Botswana**—Embassy of the Republic of Botswana, 1531 New Hampshire Ave N.W., 20008, ☎ 244-4990 or 4991, fax 244-4164. National holiday: Independence Day, Sept 30.

**Brazil**—Brazilian Embassy, 3006 Massachusetts Ave N.W., 20008, ☎ 238-2700, fax 238-2827. National holiday: Independence Day, Sept 7.

**Brunei**—Embassy of the State of Brunei Darussalam, Watergate, 2600 Virginia Ave N.W., Suite 300, 3rd floor, 20037, ☎ 342-0159, fax 342-0158. National holiday: Feb 23.

**Bulgaria**—Embassy of the Republic of Bulgaria, 1621 22nd St N.W., 20008, ☎ 387-7969, fax 234-7973. National holiday: Independence Day, March 3.

**Burkina Faso**—Embassy of Burkina Faso, 2340 Massachusetts Ave N.W., 20008, ☎ 332-5577 or 6895, fax 667-1882. National holiday: Anniversary of the Revolution, Aug 4.

**Burma** (see **Myanmar**).

**Burundi**—Embassy of the Republic of Burundi, 2233 Wisconsin Ave N.W., Suite 212, 20007, ☎ 342-2574, fax 342-2578. National holiday: Independence Day, July 1.

**Cameroon**—Embassy of the Republic of Cameroon, 2349 Massachusetts Ave N.W., 20008, ☎ 265-8790 to 8794, fax 387-3826. National holiday: Independence Day, May 20.

**Canada**—Embassy of Canada, 501 Pennsylvania Ave N.W., 20001, ☎ 682-1740, fax 682-7726. National holiday: Independence Day, July 1.

**Cape Verde**—Embassy of the Republic of Cape Verde, 3415 Massachusetts Ave N.W., 20007, ☎ 965-6820, fax 965-1207. National holiday: Independence Day, July 5.

**Central African Republic**—Embassy of Central African Republic, 1618 22nd St N.W., 20008, ☎ 483-7800 and 7801, fax 332-9893. National holiday: Independence Day, Dec 1.

**Chad**—Embassy of the Republic of Chad, 2002 R St N.W., 20009, ☎ 462-4009, fax 265-1937. National holiday: Independence Day, Aug 11.

**Chile**—Embassy of Chile, 1732 Massachusetts Ave N.W., 20036, ☎ 785-1746, fax 887-5579. National holiday: Independence Day, Sept 18.

**China**—Embassy of the People's Republic of China, 2300 Connecticut Ave N.W., 20008, ☎ 328-2500 to 2502, fax 328-2582. National holiday: National Day, Oct 1.

**Colombia**—Embassy of Colombia, 2118 Leroy Place N.W., 20008, ☎ 387-8338, fax 387-0176. National holiday: Independence Day, July 20.

**Congo, Republic of**—Embassy of the Republic of Congo, 4891 Colorado Ave N.W., 20011, ☎ 726-5500 or 5501, fax 726-1860. National holiday: Congolese National Day, Aug 15.

**Congo** (formerly **Zaire**)—Embassy of the Democratic Republic of Congo, 1800 New Hampshire Ave N.W., 20009, ☎ 234-7690 or 7691, fax 237-0748.

**Costa Rica**—Embassy of Costa Rica, 1825 Connecticut Ave N.W., Suite 211, 20009, ☎ 234-2945 to 2947, fax 234-8653. National holiday: Independence Day, Sept 15.

**Côte d'Ivoire**—Embassy of the Republic of Côte d'Ivoire, 2424 Massachusetts Ave N.W., 20008, annex: 2412 Massachusetts Ave N.W., 20008; ☎ 797-0300, fax 265-2454. National holiday: Day of Independence, Dec 7.

**Croatia**—Embassy of the Republic of Croatia, 2343 Massachusetts Ave N.W., 20008, ☎ 588-5899, fax 588-8936.

**Cyprus**—Embassy of the Republic of Cyprus, 2211 R St N.W., 20008, ☎ 462-5772, fax 483-6710. National holiday: Independence Day, Oct 1.

**Czechoslovakia**—Embassy of the Czech Republic, 3900 Linnean Ave N.W., 20008, ☎ 274-9100, fax 966-8540. National holidays: National Liberation Day, May 9, and Founding of the Republic, Oct 28.

**Denmark**—Royal Danish Embassy, 3200 Whitehaven St N.W., 20008, ☎ 234-4300, fax 328-1470. National holiday: Birthday of the Queen, April 16.

**Djibouti**—Embassy of the Republic of Djibouti, 1156 15th St N.W., Suite 515, 20005, ☎ 331-0270, fax 331-0302. National holiday: Day of Independence June 27.

**Dominican Republic**—Embassy of the Dominican Republic, 1715 22nd St N.W., 20008, ☎ 332-6280, fax 265-8057. National holiday: Independence Day, Feb 27.

**Ecuador**—Embassy of Ecuador, 2535 15th St N.W., 20009, ☎ 234-7200, fax 265-6385. National holiday: Independence Day, Aug 10.

**Egypt**—Embassy of the Arab Republic of Egypt, 2310 Decatur Place N.W., 20008, ☎ 895-5400; consular section: ☎ 234-3903; fax 244-4319. National holiday: Anniversary of the Revolution, July 23.

**El Salvador**—Embassy of El Salvador, 2308 California St N.W., 20008, ☎ 265-9671 or 9672, fax 234-3834. National holiday: Independence Day, Sept 15.

**Eritrea**—Embassy of the State of Eritrea, 1708 New Hampshire Ave N.W., 20009, ☎ 319-1991, fax: 319-1304. National holiday: Independence Day, May 24.

**Estonia**—Embassy of Estonia, 2131 Massachusetts Ave N.W., 20008, ☎ 588-0101, fax 588-0108. National holiday: Independence Day, Feb 24.

**Ethiopia**—Embassy of Ethiopia, 2134 Kalorama Rd N.W., Suite 1000, 20008, ☎ 234-2281 or 2282, fax 483-8407. National holiday: National Revolution Day, Sept 12.

**Fiji**—Embassy of the Republic of Fiji, 2233 Wisconsin Ave N.W., Suite 240, 20007, ☎ 337-8320, fax 337-1996. National holiday: Independence Day, Oct 10.

**Finland**—Embassy of Finland, 3216 New Mexico Ave N.W., 20016, ☎ 363-2430, fax 363-8233. National holiday: Independence Day, Dec 6.

**France**—Embassy of France, 4101 Reservoir Rd N.W., 20007, ☎ 944-6000, fax 944-6040. National holiday: Bastille Day, July 14.

**Gabon**—Embassy of the Gabonese Republic, 2034 20th St N.W., 20009, ☎ 797-1000, fax 332-0668. National holiday: Day of Independence, Aug 17.

**Gambia, The**—Embassy of The Gambia, 1155 15th St N.W., Suite 1000, 20005, ☎ 785-1399, 1379, or 1425, fax 785-1430. National holiday: Independence Day, Feb 18.

**Georgia**—Embassy of the Republic of Georgia, 1615 New Hampshire Ave N.W., Suite 300, 20009, ☎ 387-2390, fax 393-4537. National holiday: Constitution Day, Sept 3.

**Germany, Federal Republic of**—Embassy of the Federal Republic of Germany, 4645 Reservoir Rd N.W., 20007, ☎ 298-4000, fax 298-4249. National holiday: Reunification of Germany Day, Oct 3.

**Ghana**—Embassy of Ghana, 3512 International Dr N.W., 20008, ☎ 686-4520, fax 686-4527. National holiday: Independence Day, March 6.

**Great Britain** (see **United Kingdom of Great Britain and Northern Ireland**).

**Greece**—Embassy of Greece, 2221 Massachusetts Ave N.W., 20008, ☎ 939-5800, fax 939-5824. National holiday: Independence Day, March 25.

**Grenada**—Embassy of Grenada, 1701 New Hampshire Ave N.W., 20009, ☎ 265-2561, fax 265-2468. National holiday: Independence Day, Feb 7.

**Guatemala**—Embassy of Guatemala, 2220 R St N.W., 20008, ☎ 745-4952 to 4954, fax 745-1908. National holiday: Independence Day, Sept 15.

**Guinea**—Embassy of the Republic of Guinea, 2112 Leroy Place N.W., 20008, ☎ 483-9420, fax 483-8688. National holiday: Independence Day, Oct 2.

**Guinea-Bissau**—Embassy of the Republic of Guinea-Bissau, 918 16th St N.W., Mezzanine Suite, 20006, ☎ 872-4222, fax 872-4226. National holiday: Independence Day, Sept 24.

**Guyana**—Embassy of Guyana, 2490 Tracy Place N.W., 20008, ☎ 265-6900 to 6903, fax 232-1297. National holiday: Republic Day, Feb 23.

**Haiti**—Embassy of the Republic of Haiti, 2311 Massachusetts Ave N.W., 20008, ☎ 332-4090 to 4092, fax 745-7215. National holiday: Independence Day, Jan 1.

The **Holy See**—Apostolic Nunciature, 3339 Massachusetts Ave N.W., 20008, ☎ 333-7121, fax 327-4036. National holiday: Anniversary of installation of most recent pope, (currently) Oct 22.

**Honduras**—Embassy of Honduras, 3007 Tilden St N.W., 20008, ☎ 966-7702, 2604, 5008, or 4596, fax 966-9751. National holiday: Independence Day, Sept 15.

**Hungary**—Embassy of the Republic of Hungary, 3910 Shoemaker St N.W., 20008, ☎ 362-6730, fax 966-8135. National holiday: Statehood Day, Aug 20.

**Iceland**—Embassy of Iceland, 2022 Connecticut Ave N.W., 20008, ☎ 265-6653 to 6655, fax 265-6656. National holiday: Anniversary of the Establishment of the Republic, June 17.

**India**—Embassy of India, 2107 Massachussetts Ave N.W., 20008, ☎ 939-7000, fax 265-4351. National holiday: Anniversary of the Proclamation of the Republic, Jan 26.

**Indonesia**—Embassy of the Republic of Indonesia, 2020 Massachussetts Ave N.W., 20036, ☎ 775-5200, fax 775-5365. National holiday: Independence Day, Aug 17.

**Ireland**—Embassy of Ireland, 2234 Massachusetts Ave N.W., 20008, ☎ 462-3939, fax 232-5993. National holiday: St. Patrick's Day, March 17.

**Israel**—Embassy of Israel, 3514 International Dr N.W., 20008, ☎ 364-5500, fax 364-5610. National holiday: Independence Day, May 7.

**Italy**—Embassy of Italy, 1601 Fuller St N.W., 20009, ☎ 328-5500, fax 328-5593. National holiday: Anniversary of the Republic, June 2.

**Ivory Coast** (see **Côte d'Ivoire**).

**Jamaica**—Embassy of Jamaica, 1850 K St N.W., Suite 355, 20006, ☎ 452-0660, fax 452-0081. National holidays: Emancipation Day, Aug 3; Independence Day, Aug 6.

**Japan**—Embassy of Japan, 2520 Massachusetts Ave N.W., 20008, ☎ 238-6700, fax 328-2187. Information center: 1155 21st St N.W., 20036, ☎ 238-6900, fax 822-6524. National holiday: Birthday of His Majesty the Emperor, Dec 23.

**Jordan**—Embassy of the Hashemite Kingdom of Jordan, 3504 International Dr N.W., 20008, ☎ 966-2664, fax 966-3110. National holiday: Independence Day, May 25.

**Kazakhstan**—Embassy of the Republic of Kazakhstan, 1401 16th St N.W., 20036, ☎ 232-5488, fax 232-5845. National holiday: Independence Day, uiOct 25.

**Kenya**—Embassy of the Republic of Kenya, 2249 R St N.W., 20008, ☎ 387-6101, fax 462-3829. National holiday: Independence Day, Dec 12.

**Korea**—Embassy of Korea, 2450 Massachusetts Ave N.W., 20008, ☎ 939-5600, fax 387-0413, National holiday: Independence Day, Aug 15.

**Kuwait**—Embassy of the State of Kuwait, 2940 Tilden St N.W., 20008, ☎ 966-0702, fax 966-0517. National holiday: National Day of Kuwait, Feb 25.

**Kyrgyzstan**—Embassy of the Kyrgyz Republic, 1732 Wisconsin Ave N.W., 20007, ☎ 338-5141, fax 338-5139. National holiday: Independence Day, Aug 31.

**Laos**—Embassy of the Lao People's Democratic Republic, 2222 S St N.W., 20008, ☎ 332-6416 or 6417, fax 332-4923. National holiday: National Day, Dec 2.

**Latvia**—Embassy of Latvia, 4325 17th St N.W., 20011, ☎ 726-8213 or 8214, fax 726-6785. National holiday: Independence Day, Nov 18.

**Lebanon**—Embassy of Lebanon, 2560 28th St N.W., 20008, ☎ 939-6300, fax 939-6324. National holiday: Independence Day, Nov 22.

**Lesotho**—Embassy of the Kingdom of Lesotho, 2511 Massachusetts Ave N.W., 20008, ☎ 797-5533 to 5536, fax 234-6815. National holiday: Independence Day, Oct 4.

**Liberia**—Embassy of the Republic of Liberia, 5303 Colorado Ave N.W., 20011, ☎ 723-0437, fax 723-0436. National holiday: Independence Day, July 26.

**Lithuania**—Embassy of the Republic of Lithuania, 2622 16th St N.W., 20009, ☎ 234-5860 or 2639, fax 328-0466. National holiday: Independence Day, Feb 16.

**Luxembourg**—Embassy of Luxembourg, 2200 Massachusetts Ave N.W., 20008, ☎ 265-4171, fax 328-8270. National holiday: National Day, June 23.

**Madagascar**—Embassy of the Democratic Republic of Madagascar, 2374 Massachusetts Ave N.W., 20008, ☎ 265-5525 or 5526, fax 265-3034. National holiday: Independence Day, June 26.

**Malawi**—Embassy of Malawi, 2408 Massachusetts Ave N.W., 20008, ☎ 797-1007, fax 265-0976. National holiday: Independence Day, July 6.

**Malaysia**—Embassy of Malaysia, 2401 Massachusetts Ave N.W., 20008; Annexes: 2407 California St N.W., 20008; and 1900 24th St N.W., 20008; ☎ 328-2700, fax 483-7661. National holiday: National Day, Aug 31.

**Mali**—Embassy of the Republic of Mali, 2130 R St N.W., 20008, ☎ 332-2249 or 939-8950, fax 333-6603. National holiday: Anniversary of the Proclamation of the Republic, Sept 22.

**Malta**—Embassy of Malta, 2017 Connecticut Ave N.W., 20008, ☎ 462-3611 or 3612, fax 387-5470. National holiday: Independence Day, Sept 21.

**Marshall Islands**—Embassy of the Republic of the Marshall Islands, 2433 Massachusetts Ave N.W., 20008, ☎ 234-5414, fax 232-3236. National holiday: Independence Day, Oct 21.

**Mauritania**—Embassy of the Islamic Republic of Mauritania, 2129 Leroy Place N.W., 20008, ☎ 232-5700, fax 319-2633. National holiday: Independence Day, Nov. 28.

**Mauritius**—Embassy of Mauritius, 4301 Connecticut Ave N.W., Suite 441, 20008, ☎ 244-1491 or 1492, fax 966-0983. National holiday: Independence Day, March 12.

**Mexico**—Embassy of Mexico, 1911 Pennsylvania Ave N.W., 20006; annex: 2829 16th St N.W., 20009; ☎ 728-1600, fax 728-1615. National Holiday: Independence Day, Sept 16.

**Micronesia**—Embassy of the Federated States of Micronesia, 1725 N St N.W., 20036, ☎ 223-4383, fax 223-4391. National holiday: National Day, Nov 3.

**Moldova**—Embassy of the Republic of Moldova, 2101 S St N.W., 20008, ☎ 667-1130 or 1131 or 1137, fax 667-1204.

**Mongolia**—Embassy of Mongolia, 2833 M St N.W., 20007, ☎ 333-7117, fax 298-9227. National holiday: Anniversary of the Mongolian People's Revolution, July 11, 12, and 13.

**Morocco**—Embassy of the Kingdom of Morocco, 1601 21st St N.W., 20009, ☎ 462-7979 to 7982, fax 265-0161. National holiday: National Day, March 3.

**Mozambique**—Embassy of the Republic of Mozambique, 1990 M St N.W., Suite 570, 20036, ☎ 293-7146, fax 835-0245. National Holiday: Independence Day, June 25.

**Myanmar**—Embassy of the Union of Myanmar, 2300 S St N.W., 20008, ☎ 332-9044 or 9045, fax 332-9046. National holiday: Independence Day, Jan 4.

**Namibia**—Embassy of the Republic of Namibia, 1605 New Hampshire Ave N.W., 20009, ☎ 986-0540, fax 986-0443. National holiday: Independence Day, March 21.

**Nepal**—Royal Nepalese Embassy, 2131 Leroy Place N.W., 20008, ☎ 667-4550, fax 667-5534. National holiday: Birthday of His Majesty the King, Dec 28.

**Netherlands**—Embassy of the Netherlands, 4200 Linnean Ave N.W., 20008, ☎ 244-5300, after 6 P.M. 244-5304, fax 362-3430. National holiday: April 30, Queen's Day.

**New Zealand**—Embassy of New Zealand, 37 Observatory Circle N.W., 20008, ☎ 328-4800, fax 667-5227. National holidays: Waitangi Day, Feb 6; Independence Day, July 5.

**Nicaragua**—Embassy of Nicaragua, 1627 New Hampshire Ave N.W., 20009, ☎ 939-6570. National holiday: Independence Day, Sept 15.

**Niger**—Embassy of the Republic of Niger, 2204 R St N.W., 20008, ☎ 483-4224 to 4227. National holiday: Republic Day, Dec 18.

**Nigeria**—Embassy of the Federal Republic of Nigeria, 2201 M St N.W., ☎ 822-1500. National holiday: Independence Day, Oct 1.

**Norway**—Royal Norwegian Embassy, 2720 34th St N.W., 20008, ☎ 333-6000, fax 337-0870. National holiday: Constitution Day, May 17.

**Oman**—Embassy of the Sultanate of Oman, 2342 Massachusetts Ave N.W.,

20008, ☎ 387-1980 to 1982, fax 945-4933. National holiday: National Day, Nov 18.

**Pakistan**—Embassy of Pakistan, 2315 Massachusetts Ave N.W., 20008, ☎ 939-6200; annex: 2201 R St N.W., 20008; ☎ 939-6205, fax 387-0484. National holiday: Pakistan Day, March 23.

**Panama**—Embassy of the Republic of Panama, 2862 McGill Terrace N.W., 20008, ☎ 483-1407, fax 483-8413. National holiday: Independence Day, Nov 3.

**Papua New Guinea**—Embassy of Papua New Guinea, 1615 New Hampshire Ave N.W., 3rd Floor, 20009, ☎ 745-3680, fax 745-3679. National holiday: Independence Day, Sept 16.

**Paraguay**—Embassy of Paraguay, 2400 Massachusetts Ave N.W., 20008, ☎ 483-6960 to 6962, fax: 234-4508. National holiday: Independence Day, May 15.

**Peru**—Embassy of Peru, 1700 Massachusetts Ave N.W., 20036, ☎ 833-9860 to 9869, fax 659-8124. National holiday: Independence Day, July 28.

**Philippines**—Embassy of the Philippines, 1617 Massachusetts Ave N.W., 20036, ☎ 483-1414, fax 328-7614. National holiday: Independence Day, June 12.

**Poland**—Embassy of the Republic of Poland, 2640 16th St N.W., 20009, ☎ 234-3800 to 3802, fax 328-6271. National holiday: Constitution Day, May 3.

**Portugal**—Embassy of Portugal, 2125 Kalorama Rd N.W. (entrance through private drive), 20008, ☎ 328-8610, fax 462-3726. National holiday: Day of Portugal, June 10.

**Qatar**—Embassy of the State of Qatar, 4200 Wisconsin Ave N.W., 20016, ☎ 274-1600, fax 237-0061. National holiday: Independence Day, Sept 3.

**Romania**—Embassy of Romania, 1607 23rd St N.W., 20008, ☎ 232-4747, fax 232-4748. National holiday: National Day of Romania, Dec 1.

**Russia**—Embassy of the Russian Federation, 2650 Wisconsin Ave N.W., 20007, ☎ 298-5700, fax 298-5735. National holiday: The Great October Socialist Revolution, Nov 7 and 8.

**Rwanda**—Embassy of the Republic of Rwanda, 1714 New Hampshire Ave N.W., 20009, ☎ 232-2882, fax 232-4544. National holiday: Independence Day, July 1.

**Saint Kitts and Nevis**—Embassy of Saint Kitts and Nevis, 2100 M St N.W., Suite 608, 20037, ☎ 833-3550, fax 833-3553. National holiday: Independence Day, Sept 19.

**Saint Lucia**—Embassy of Saint Lucia, 2100 M St N.W., Suite 309, 20037, ☎ 463-7378 or 7379 fax 887-5746. National holiday: Independence Day, Feb 22.

**Saint Vincent and the Grenadines**—Embassy of Saint Vincent and the Grenadines, 3216 New Mexico Ave N.W., 20016, ☎ 364-6730, fax 364-6736. National holiday: Independence Day, Oct 27.

**Saudi Arabia**—Royal Embassy of Saudi Arabia, 601 New Hampshire Ave N.W., 20037, ☎ 342-3800, fax 944-5983. National holiday: Unification of the Kingdom, Sept 23.

**Senegal**—Embassy of the Republic of Senegal, 2112 Wyoming Ave N.W., 20008, ☎ 234-0540 or 0541. National holiday: Independence Day, April 4.

**Sierra Leone**—Embassy of Sierra Leone, 1701 19th St N.W., 20009, ☎ 939-9261, fax 483-1793. National holiday: Republic Day, April 27.

**Singapore**—Embassy of the Republic of Singapore, 1824 R St N.W., 20009; annex: 3501 International Drive N.W., 20008; ☎ 537-3100, fax 537-0876. National holiday: National Day, Aug 9.

**Slovak Republic**—Embassy of the Slovak Republic, 2201 Wisconsin Ave N.W., 20007, ☎ 965-5160, fax 965-5166. National holiday: Constitution Day, Sept 3.

**South Africa**—Embassy of South Africa, 3051 Massachusetts Ave N.W., 20008, ☎ 232-4400, fax 265-1607. Annex: 3201 New Mexico Ave N.W., 20016, ☎ 966-1650. National holiday: Republic Day, May 31.

**Spain**—Embassy of Spain, 2375 Pennsylvania Ave N.W., 20037, ☎ 452-0100 or 728-2340, fax 833-5670. National holiday: Columbus Day, Oct 12.

**Sri Lanka**—Embassy of the Democratic Socialist Republic of Sri Lanka, 2148 Wyoming Ave N.W., 20008, ☎ 483-4025 to 4028, fax 232-7181. National holiday: Independence and National Day, Feb 4.

**Sudan**—Embassy of the Republic of the Sudan, 2210 Massachusetts Ave N.W., 20008, ☎ 338-8565 to 8570, fax 667-2406. National holiday: Independence Day, Jan 1.

**Suriname**—Embassy of the Republic of Suriname, 4301 Connecticut Ave N.W., Suite 108, 20008, ☎ 244-7488 or 7490 to 7492, fax 244-5878. National holiday: Independence Day, Nov 25.

**Swaziland**—Embassy of the Kingdom of Swaziland, 3400 International Dr N.W., 20008, ☎ 362-6683 or 6685, fax 244-8059. National holiday: Sept 6.

**Sweden**—Embassy of Sweden, 600 New Hampshire Ave N.W., Suites 1200 and 715, 20037, ☎ 944-5600, fax 342-1319. National holiday: National Day, June 6.

**Switzerland**—Embassy of Switzerland, 2900 Cathedral Ave N.W., 20008, ☎ 745-7900, fax 387-2564. National holiday: Anniversary of the Founding of the Swiss Confederation, Aug 1.

**Syria**—Embassy of the Syrian Arab Republic, 2215 Wyoming Ave N.W., 20008, ☎ 232-6313, fax 234-9548. National holiday: National Day, April 17.

**Tanzania**—Embassy of the United Republic of Tanzania, 2139 R St N.W., 20008, ☎ 939-6125, fax 797-7408. National holiday: Union Day, April 26.

**Thailand**—Royal Thai Embassy, 1024 Wisconsin Ave N.W., 20007, ☎ 944-3600, fax 944-3611. National holiday: Birthday of His Majesty the King, Dec 5.

**Togo**—Embassy of the Republic of Togo, 2208 Massachusetts Ave N.W., 20008, ☎ 234-4212 or 4213, fax 232-3190. National holiday: National Day, Jan 13.

**Trinidad and Tobago**—Embassy of the Republic of Trinidad and Tobago, 1708 Massachusetts Ave N.W., 20036, ☎ 467-6490, fax 785-3130. National holiday: Independence Day, Aug 31.

**Tunisia**—Embassy of Tunisia, 1515 Massachusetts Ave N.W., 20005, ☎ 862-1850, fax 862-1858. National holiday: National Day, March 20.

**Turkey**—Embassy of the Republic of Turkey, 1714 Massachusetts Ave N.W., 20036, ☎ 659-8200, fax 659-0744. National holiday: Anniversary of the Declaration of the Republic, Oct 29.

**Turkmenistan**—Embassy of the Republic of Turkmenistan, 2207 Massachusetts Ave N.W., 20036, ☎ 588-1500, fax 588-0697.

**Uganda**—Embassy of the Republic of Uganda, 5909 16th St N.W., 20011;

annex: 5911 16th St N.W., 20011; ☎ 726-7100 to 7102 or 726-0416, fax 726-1727. National holiday: Independence Day, Oct 9.

**Ukraine**—Embassy of Ukraine, 2001 L St N.W., Suite 200, 20036, ☎ 452-0939, fax 955-3995. National holiday: Independence Day, Aug 24.

**United Arab Emirates**—Embassy of the United Arab Emirates, 1255 22nd St N.W., Suite 700, 20037, ☎ 955-7999, fax 337-7029. National holiday: National Day, Dec 2.

**United Kingdom of Great Britain and Northern Ireland**—British Embassy, 3100 Massachusetts Ave N.W., 20008, ☎ 462-1340, fax 898-4255. National holiday: Celebration of the Birthday of the Monarch, in June.

**Uruguay**—Embassy of Uruguay, 1918 F St N.W., 20006, ☎ 331-1313 to 1316, fax 331-8142. National holiday: Independence Day, Aug 25.

**Venezuela**—Embassy of the Republic of Venezuela, 1099 30th St N.W., 20007; annex: 2437 California St N.W., 20008; ☎ 342-2214. National holiday: Independence Day, July 5.

**Western Samoa**—Embassy of Western Samoa, 1155 15th St N.W., Suite 510, 20005, ☎ 833-1743, fax 833-1746. National holiday: Independence Day, June 1.

**Yemen**—Embassy of the Republic of Yemen, 2600 Virginia Ave N.W., Suite 705, 20037, ☎ 965-4760 or 4761, fax 337-2017. National holiday: National Day, May 22.

**Yugoslavia**—Embassy of the Socialist Federal Republic of Yugoslavia, 2410 California St N.W., 20008, ☎ 462-6566, fax 797-9663. National holiday: Proclamation of the Socialist Federal Republic of Yugoslavia, Nov 29.

**Zambia**—Embassy of the Republic of Zambia, 2419 Massachusetts Ave N.W., 20008, ☎ 265-9717 to 9721, fax 332-0826. National holiday: Independence Day, Oct 24.

**Zimbabwe**—Embassy of the Republic of Zimbabwe, 1608 New Hampshire Ave N.W., 20009, ☎ 332-7100, fax 483-9326. National holiday: Independence Day, April 18.

**Delegation of the Commission of the European Communities,** 2100 M St N.W., 7th Floor, 20037, ☎ 862-9500, fax 429-1766. Official holiday: Europe Day, May 9.

### Countries with Which Diplomatic Relations Have Been Severed

After each country, in parentheses, is the name of the country's protecting power in the United States.

**Cuba** (Switzerland)—Cuban Interests Section, Embassy of Switzerland, 2630 and 2639 16th St N.W., 20009, ☎ 797-8518, 8520, 8609, or 8610, fax 797-8521.

**Iran** (Algeria)—Iranian Interests Section, Embassy of the Democratic and Popular Republic of Algeria, 2209 Wisconsin Ave N.W., 20007, ☎ 965-4990.

**Iraq** (Algeria)—Iraqi Interests Section, Embassy of the Democratic and Popular Republic of Algeria, 1801 P St N.W., 20036, ☎ 483-7500, fax 462-5066.

# Background Information

## Chronology

**A note on terms:** In 1791 the District of Columbia was a ten-mile-square area through which the Potomac River ran. The District included the city of Washington, the area where the federal buildings were planned, plus the cities of Georgetown and Alexandria, which were self-governing municipalities ceded to the District from Maryland and Virginia, respectively. In 1801, Congress divided the District along the Potomac into two counties. In Alexandria County, Virginia law applied, and in Washington County, Maryland law prevailed.

In 1846, Alexandria County, including the city of Alexandria, was retroceded to Virginia. In 1871, Congress abolished the county of Washington as well as the municipal corporations of Georgetown and Washington, and replaced them with one municipal corporation officially called the District of Columbia. In 1895, Georgetown lost the remainder of its status as a separate entity but remained a District neighborhood.

The documented use of the term *District of Columbia* dates to 1793 when it appeared in an act of the Maryland legislature. In November 1800 President John Adams referred to the "District of Columbia" when he invoked Congress to assume jurisdiction over the area.

| | |
|---|---|
| 1608 | Captain John Smith discovers the mouth of the Potomac River and reaches the little falls above the Anacostia River. |
| 1663–1686 | Lord Baltimore issues patents of land that later would encompass the District of Columbia. |
| 1749 | Alexandria established. |
| 1751 | Georgetown established. |
| 1771 | Foggy Bottom (called Hamburgh by its developer) established. |
| 1776 | The American colonies declare their independence. |
| 1783 | Peace of Paris ends the Revolutionary War. |
| 1787 | Article I, Section 8, of the Constitution provides for a seat of federal government and gives Congress power over that district. |
| 1788 | Maryland and Virginia offer the federal government any territory in those states, not exceeding ten square miles, for the seat of its government. |
| 1789 | Georgetown University, the city's first institute of higher learning, is founded. George Washington inaugurated as first president of the United States in New York City, the nation's temporary capital. |
| 1790 | Northern factions led by Alexander Hamilton and Southern factions led by Thomas Jefferson reach a compromise. The Federal City is located on the banks of the Potomac River. President Washington signs the bill authorizing him to select the actual site for the city. |
| 1791 | Washington chooses a ten-mile-square area along the Potomac that includes Georgetown and Alexandria. The area where federal buildings are to be located is named the city of Washington. Washington appoints Major Pierre Charles L'Enfant chief architect and engineer of the city. Andrew Ellicott, whose unofficial title is "geographer general |

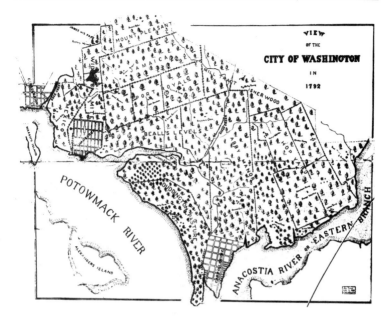

*City of Washington in 1792. Courtesy of the Washingtoniana Division, D.C. Public Library.*

of the United States," and Benjamin Banneker, an African American almanac publisher and mathematician, are appointed to survey the site. A three-day sale of lots in Washington results in a disappointing 35 out of a potential 10,000 being sold.

1792    Washington dismisses L'Enfant because of hostilities between L'Enfant and the city's commissioners. Banneker reconstructs the city plans from memory. James Hoban wins a local competition for the Executive Mansion (the White House) and construction on the president's residence begins.

1793    George Washington lays the cornerstone of the Capitol. The construction crew consists of 90 slaves. The first census taken in the Federal City shows that the population is 820.

1794    Stephen Hallet discharged by the city commissioners as assistant superintendent of the construction of the Capitol because he has laid the foundation of the building in a square, corresponding to his own plan, rather than in a circle, as indicated by Dr. William Thornton's approved plan.

1796    Pennsylvania Ave is laid out.

1798    Construction begins on the first of the executive office buildings, the Treasury Building, located east of and parallel with the south front of the President's House, which is still under construction.

1799    George Washington dies at Mount Vernon. The first Navy Yard in the U.S. is begun at the 7th St wharf.

1800 Washington has 3,244 inhabitants—623 of them black slaves. There are 109 brick houses and 263 wooden ones. In May, two-horse carriages begin to operate between Georgetown and Capitol Hill, the first reported public transportation in the city. In Aug, Washington's first theater opens. Called the United States Theatre, it closes a month later because of poor attendance. In Oct, the Library of Congress is founded, with a collection of 243 books. On Nov 1, President John Adams arrives to take up residence in a partially completed President's House. On Nov 11, citizens of the District of Columbia who are white, male, and over the age of 21 vote in the presidential election, the last in which Washington's citizens will be allowed to participate until 1964. On Nov 13, Abigail Adams arrives to join her husband at the President's House. On Nov 17, Congress attempts to hold its first meeting in Washington, but neither house can muster a quorum. On Nov 18, the House has a quorum; Nov 21, the Senate manages one; and on Nov 22, President Adams addresses a joint session of Congress. In Dec, the District of Columbia officially becomes the seat of government of the United States of America. Congress passes an act denying District residents a vote in national elections or representation in Congress.

1801 In Jan, the first book is published in Washington. Called *Washington Repository*, it's a combination almanac and guidebook. In late Jan, a fire breaks out in the auditor's room of the Treasury office and a Republican newspaper charges it's a Federalist plot to cover up misconduct. A branch of the Bank of the United States opens in Washington. The Supreme Court meets for the first time on Feb 2.

1802 The municipal charter granted by Congress allows free, white, taxpaying, male Washingtonians, 25 years or older, to elect a city council of 12 men. The city's mayor is to be appointed by the president. Robert Brent is appointed by President Thomas Jefferson as the first mayor for what was supposed to be a one-year term. Brent will serve until 1812.

1805 Thomas Jefferson rides his horse from the President's House to the Capitol along Pennsylvania Ave, initiating the custom of the inaugural parade. Congress defeats a resolution to free slaves upon maturity in the District. The city's school board adopts the first comprehensive plan for public education in Washington. No provisions are made for the education of African Americans.

1806 The Navy Yard is the city's biggest employer, with 175 workmen earning $1.81 per day.

1807 Three former slaves establish Washington's first black school. The first teacher is white.

1808 Washington's first so-called black code is adopted. Slaves have a 10 P.M. curfew. The owner of any lawbreaking slave is fined, but if the owner has the slave whipped, the owner's fine is remitted.

1809 The first bridge connecting the city with its "suburbs" is built—a bridge from Maryland Ave in the city to Alexandria.

1811 The mayor doubles the city's police force, from one to two.

1812 On June 16, war begins between Great Britain and the United States.

1814 On Aug 24, Washington is captured by the British, who burn the President's House and the Capitol, as well as many other public buildings. In Dec, the Peace of Ghent ends the War of 1812.

1815    The Washington Canal opens.

1817    President and Mrs. James Monroe move back into the repaired President's House, now called the Executive Mansion.

1819    The Capitol reopens after repairs.

1820    The population of the District of Columbia is 22,614 whites, 4,048 free blacks, and 6,377 slaves. The first independent black church, the African Methodist Episcopal Church, is founded. On May 15, an amendment to the city's charter grants the city the right to elect its mayor.

1821    Columbian College, later to become George Washington University, is founded by Baptists.

1825    Pierre Charles L'Enfant dies and is buried in an unmarked grave in Prince George's County, Maryland.

1826    The Washington Society for the Abolition of Slavery in the District of Columbia is created.

1827    The city council passes a harsher black code, in response to whites alarmed at the growing black population. Free blacks and so-called mulattoes (those of mixed black and white blood) are now included in the restrictions that have previously only applied to slaves.

1828    Congress bars African Americans from the Capitol unless there on business. Congress receives more than 1,000 petitions to end slavery in the District. On July 4th, President John Quincy Adams turns over the first spadeful of earth for the C&O Canal.

1832    Pennsylvania Ave is paved, and indoor plumbing is installed in the Capitol.

1833    The city passes a law denying shop licenses for free blacks, and an even harsher black code is adopted.

1835    From Aug 28 to Sept 5, angry whites, frightened by abolitionist writings and lectures, attack black homes, businesses, churches, and schools. This riot later is known as the Snow Storm because the violence centers on the Epicurean Eating House, a popular restaurant owned and operated by an African American, Beverly Snow. On Sept 26, the Washington National Monument Society is formed to solicit contributions from private citizens to build a monument to George Washington.

1836    The Smithsonian Institution is born, when Englishman James Smithson donates his estate for the establishment of a center in Washington for the "diffusion of knowledge."

1840    The city completes the renovation of the Washington Canal.

1842    Congress establishes a night police force in Washington.

1843    The city government makes Washington schools free for all white students.

1844    The city is shocked when the "Peacemaker," an experimental gun, explodes aboard the USS *Princeton,* killing the secretaries of state and war, as well as several other prominent Washingtonians. The National Observatory opens on a hill in Foggy Bottom. The first public message to be transmitted over Samuel F. B. Morse's electric telegraph, from Washington to Baltimore, is "What hath God wrought!"

1846    Alexandria city and the county of Alexandria are reannexed to Virginia. The District of Columbia shrinks by a third. Congress refuses to give Georgetown back to Maryland.

1848    The slaves of some of Washington's most prominent families attempt to escape aboard the schooner *Pearl*. Their ship is overtaken about 140 miles from Washington. The captain of the ship is sent to prison, but pardoned four years later. The 77 slaves are returned to their owners. A new city charter authorized by Congress allows free, white, male property owners in the District to elect a mayor, aldermen, common councilmen, and other city offices.

1849    The Washington Gas Company's first gas works supply gas to the East Room of the White House.

1850    African Americans comprise 26 percent of Washington's population. Congress abolishes slave trading in the District of Columbia.

1851    The Washington Canal has fallen into such disrepair that Washingtonians look upon it as a sewer. The Library of Congress, located in the Capitol Building, is destroyed by fire.

1853    Anthony Bowen, a former slave, establishes a YMCA for black males in Washington.

1855    Lack of money stops construction of the Washington Monument.

1856    Washington's small Jewish population forms the city's first Hebrew congregation.

1857    The *Dred Scott* decision by the Supreme Court holds that no slave or descendant of a slave is a citizen of the United States and that slaves are property under the meaning of the Fifth Amendment to the Constitution. The Castle, the Smithsonian's first building, opens.

1860    In Dec, South Carolina secedes from the United States, followed by the rest of the Southern states over the next four months.

1861    In March, Abraham Lincoln is inaugurated president, and the Confederated States of America adopt a constitution. In April, Confederate troops fire on Fort Sumter, South Carolina, and the Civil War begins.

1862    Slavery is abolished in the District of Columbia. Owners are compensated $300 per slave, the black code is repealed, and black children are admitted to the public schools. Alexander Robey "Boss" Shepherd is elected president of the 60th Council of the city of Washington.

1863    On Jan 1, President Lincoln issues the Emancipation Proclamation declaring all slaves in the areas still in rebellion "then, thenceforth, and forever free." Thousands of African Americans flock to Washington following the proclamation. Eight hundred black Washingtonians enlist in the Union forces, forming the First U.S. Colored Troops Unit. The 19½ ft statue *Freedom* is hoisted into place atop the Capitol dome. The city establishes regular garbage pickup. Ford's Theatre is built.

1864    Freedman's Bank opens to serve the financial needs of Washington's freed slaves. Arlington National Cemetery is dedicated on the land that was formerly the home of Robert E. Lee, leader of the Confederate forces.

1865    On April 9, Lee surrenders to Ulysses S. Grant at Appomattox Courthouse, Virginia. On April 14, John Wilkes Booth assassinates President Lincoln at Ford's Theatre. The next morning, Lincoln dies in a house across the street. In Dec, the states complete ratification of the Thirteenth Amendment to the Constitution, abolishing slavery.

1866    Washington's African American population grows by 12 percent, as blacks own 20 percent of the city's private real estate. Congress passes an act allowing black men to vote in District elections. Congress also passes the Civil Rights Act of 1866 conferring citizenship on African Americans and granting the same civil rights to everyone born in the United States, except Native Americans and women, who are not given the right to vote.

1867    Howard University is established to provide higher education for African Americans.

1869    Washington passes its first civil rights law, and the owner of a public place is fined for refusing to admit black customers.

1870    Frederick Douglass moves to Washington.

1871    With the District Territorial Act, Congress ends municipal government in the city and replaces it with a presidential-appointed governor, council, board of public works, and a nonvoting delegate to Congress. The corporations of Georgetown and Washington are abolished. The entire District corporation is named the District of Columbia. Alexander "Boss" Shepherd is appointed head of the Board of Public Works. Four hundred appointive jobs are created to take over the duties of 160 District and city officials. The Corcoran Gallery of Art opens.

1872    More than 1,000 citizens petition the House of Representatives, charging the Board of Public Works and other city officials with mismanagement. After a four-month investigation, Congress concludes the charges are well founded.

1873    "Boss" Shepherd is appointed governor of the District of Columbia by President Ulysses S. Grant. Shepherd begins a massive city improvement program that leaves Washington $16 million in debt. After failure of the banking house of Jay Cooke, the financial panic of 1873 hits the city.

1874    Congress abolishes the governorship and replaces it with three commissioners appointed by the resident. The city loses its nonvoting delegate to Congress and will not be allowed another until 1972.

1875    Blanche Kelso Bruce becomes the first elected African American senator to serve a full term when he replaces the first African American senator, Hiram Revels, who was appointed midterm to fill Mississippi senator Jefferson Davis's vacated seat.

1877    Frederick Douglass is appointed the first black marshall of the District of Columbia by President Rutherford B. Hayes. Congress approves $200,000 to finish the Washington Monument, provided the private society formed for this purpose cedes the land and monument to the federal government. The *Washington Post* newspaper is founded.

1878    Congress creates yet another form of government for the District of Columbia, with two commissioners in charge.

1882    The *Washington Bee*, one of the most important African American newspapers of its time, begins publication under a masthead that reads "Honey for Our Friends, and Stings for Our Enemies."

| | |
|---|---|
| 1884 | The Washington Monument is completed. |
| 1885 | Mary Church Terrell becomes the first African American to sit on a school board anywhere in the U.S. when she is appointed to the D.C. School Board. |
| 1887 | Almost 2,500 new buildings go up in Washington. Land is selling for 48 cents a square ft. |
| 1888 | Washington has its first electric streetcar. |
| 1892 | The White House gets electricity. |
| 1895 | Congress abolishes Georgetown as a legal entity when it officially merges with the District. |
| 1897 | The Library of Congress moves into its new $6 million building, the largest library in the world. |
| 1898 | The Spanish-American War begins and the Potomac is mined to prevent Spanish ships from attacking Washington. |
| 1899 | The Treaty of Paris ends the Spanish-American War. The Height of Buildings Act limits private buildings in Washington to 14 stories. |
| 1900 | The city's population is 278,718, of which 90,000 are African Americans. The Capitol gets electricity. |
| 1901 | The McMillan Committee is formed to oversee the beautification of the city. Its plans for a park system, the Mall, and memorials are adopted. |
| 1902 | The Washington Symphony Orchestra gives its first performance, conducted by Reginald de Koven at the new National Theatre. |
| 1903 | The District Public Library is built with money donated by Andrew Carnegie. Commissioners authorize a study of the government of the District of Columbia. |
| 1906 | African Americans in the city protest Washington's Jim Crow laws. The District Building opens. |
| 1907 | Union Station is completed. President Theodore Roosevelt lays the cornerstone for Washington National Cathedral. Carrie Nation is arrested for disturbing the peace at a wholesale liquor store on Pennsylvania Ave. She gives her occupation as "Servant of the Lord." |
| 1912 | The NAACP opens a Washington branch that soon becomes one of the nation's largest. First Lady Helen Taft plants the first cherry tree that is part of Japan's gift to Washington at the Tidal Basin. The tree doesn't bloom for four years. |
| 1913 | Segregationist rules are passed for the federal departments in Washington. Alice Paul leads the "Great Suffrage Parade" down Pennsylvania Ave. |
| 1914 | Congress closes the city's houses of prostitution. Illegal houses continue to thrive. |
| 1916 | Tourism is the city's biggest industry, after government and real estate. |
| 1917 | The United States enters World War I. |
| 1918 | The first D.C.–New York City airmail flight is attempted. The plane breaks down and is forced to land near Waldorf, Maryland. The mail is taken by truck to Philadelphia and from there flown to New York. In October, the "Spanish Influenza" epidemic hits Washington, with 25,000 cases and over 1,500 deaths. World War I ends on the 11th day of the 11th month at the 11th hour. |
| 1919 | An all-black platoon is established in the city fire department. In 25 |

American cities, including Washington, D.C., there are five days of rioting when tensions between black and white soldiers returning from World War I erupt. Federal troops restore order. Prohibition is passed by Congress.

1920    The *Washington Bee* ceases publication.

1921    The Lincoln Theatre opens and becomes the center of Washington's "black Broadway." Margaret Gorman, a student at Washington's Western High School, becomes the first Miss America, in Atlantic City, New Jersey.

1922    Lincoln Memorial is dedicated. Black participants are segregated from whites by a dirt road and a rope enclosure. The roof of the Knickerbocker Theatre at the corner of 18th St and Columbia Rd N.W. collapses under the weight of a 28-inch snowfall. Ninety-eight people are killed, 136 injured.

1923    Following years of diminishing use, the C&O Canal is closed to commercial traffic.

1924    The Washington Senators baseball team wins the World Series.

1925    The American Beauty rose is designated the official flower of the District of Columbia. The first traffic light in Washington is installed at the intersection of 18th St and New Hampshire Ave. The poet Vachel Lindsay gives a reading of his poetry at the Wardman Park Hotel (now the Sheraton-Washington Hotel). During dinner, a 23-year-old busboy at the hotel named Langston Hughes gives Lindsay three of his poems to read. Lindsay includes Hughes's poems in his reading and tells his audience he has discovered a new poet. In July, 25,000 Ku Klux Klan members march in front of the White House.

1926    Congress approves the Public Buildings Act, and plans are begun for the Federal Triangle.

1929    The Capitol gets air-conditioning. The first woman juror to serve in the D.C. police court, Emma Eiseman, is elected foreman. On Oct 24, the stock market crash begins with 13 million shares changing hands. In two months, the stock market loses $30 billion in market value, marking the beginning of the Great Depression.

1932    In May, 17,000 World War I veterans descend on Washington demanding their bonus payments for their service in the war. Discouraged by inaction on the part of Congress, by July only 2,000 are left, and these veterans are dispersed with tanks, calvary, and fixed bayonets by federal troops under Douglas MacArthur and Dwight Eisenhower.

1933    Prohibition repealed.

1935    The Supreme Court Building is dedicated. The Washington Transit System combines all streetcar and bus companies in the city.

1937    The Washington Redskins play their first game, in Griffith Stadium. They beat the New York Giants by a score of 13 to 3. The Federal Writers Project publishes a tourbook of Washington.

1938    Congress adopts the present flag of the District of Columbia, which is an adaptation of George Washington's family coat of arms. There are 9,717 African Americans working for the federal government, but 90 percent of these are in custodial positions.

1939    Marion Anderson is denied permission to sing at the DAR Constitution

Hall because of her race. First Lady Eleanor Roosevelt arranges for her to sing at the Lincoln Memorial, and a crowd of 75,000 assembles to hear her on April 9. Black protestors picket *Gone With The Wind* outside the Lincoln Theatre.

1941    National Airport opens. The National Gallery opens. The Japanese attack Pearl Harbor and the United States enters World War II.

1942    Because of wartime rationing of gasoline, tires, and cars, many Washingtonians bicycle to work.

1943    The Washington Citizen's Committee on Race Relations is formed. The Pentagon is completed. The Jefferson Memorial is dedicated.

1945    World War II ends with the surrender of Japan.

1949    Catholic schools in Washington are integrated.

1950    Public swimming pools in the city are integrated.

1951    The song "Washington" by future Disney mouseketeer Jimmy Dodd is designated the official song of the District of Columbia.

1952    Picketed for 16 weeks, G.C. Murphy's downtown stores seat African Americans at the stores' lunch counters. The government of the District of Columbia is reorganized by President Truman's Reorganization Plan No. 5. The president states that he strongly believes the citizens of D.C. are entitled to home rule.

1953    Racial discrimination in Washington restaurants, movie houses, and theaters is outlawed. Allyn Cox finishes frescoes in the Capitol Rotunda started in 1877 by Constantino Brumidi.

1954    The Supreme Court case of *Brown v. Board of Education* leads to school desegregation, including the desegregation of public schools in Washington.

1955    Congress authorizes the citizens of D.C. to vote in political party elections. For the first time in 82 years, Washingtonians can vote for delegates to presidential conventions and for party officers. In the first party election the following year, voter participation is estimated at 3 percent of the eligible voters.

1958    The District Bar Association approves admission of African Americans on its seventh vote.

1959    Construction of the Capital Beltway is begun to alleviate traffic problems.

1960    The Scarlet Oak is adopted as the official tree of Washington.

1961    "Our Nation's Capital," by Lieutenant Anthony A. Mitchell, is adopted as the official march of the District of Columbia. The Twenty-third Amendment is ratified, allowing District residents to vote for president and vice president of the United States.

1963    Dulles Airport opens. In Aug, more than 200,000 people from all over the United States come to the grounds of the Lincoln Memorial for the "March on Washington for Jobs and Freedom." Martin Luther King, Jr., delivers his "I Have a Dream" speech. In Nov, President John F. Kennedy is assassinated in Dallas, Texas. Congress approves President Lyndon Johnson's Reorganization Plan for the District of Columbia that calls for the replacement of the panel of commissioners with a mayor and biracial council appointed by the president. Walter E. Washington is appointed the city's first black mayor.

1964 The home of Frederick Douglass becomes the Museum of African Art, the first museum to promote African artistic heritage.

1967 The wood thrush is adopted as the official bird of the city of Washington.

1968 In April, Dr. Martin Luther King, Jr., is assassinated in Memphis, Tennessee. Rioting erupts in Washington, primarily in the downtown area of the city. The rioting lasts for three days. Twelve people are killed, 1200 are injured, and property damage is estimated at $24 million.

1969 On Nov 15, 250,000 peace demonstrators march in front of the White House protesting the U.S. presence in Vietnam. Construction begins on the Metrorail system.

1970 Congress creates a commission to study the government of the District of Columbia.

1971 Washingtonians elect their first nonvoting delegate to Congress since 1875. The John F. Kennedy Center for the Performing Arts opens.

1972 Burglars are apprehended inside the Democratic Committee headquarters in the Watergate Office Building. The Martin Luther King, Jr., Memorial Library is dedicated. The Washington Senators baseball team is sold and moves to Texas. Washington will remain without a baseball team into the next millennium.

1973 The District of Columbia Self-Government and Governmental Reorganization Act of 1973 provides for Home Rule, with an elected mayor and city council.

1974 President Richard M. Nixon resigns. Walter Washington is elected by the citizens of Washington in the first election under Home Rule.

1975 The J. Edgar Hoover FBI Building opens.

1976 Metrorail opens in time for the Bicentennial celebrations.

1977 Hanafi Muslims take hostages at the District Building. Councilperson Marion Barry is wounded.

1978 Marion Barry is elected mayor of the District of Columbia. He will be in office for the next 12 years.

1979 Farmers' Tractorcade descends on the Mall.

1982 The Vietnam Memorial is dedicated. Washington Convention Center opens.

1985 A statue of Martin Luther King, Jr., is dedicated at the Washington National Cathedral.

1986 Martin Luther King Day is celebrated for the first time as a national holiday.

1990 Jesse Jackson becomes Washington's first shadow senator, a nonvoting office. Eleanor Holmes Norton is elected as the District's nonvoting delegate to the U.S. House of Representatives. (Later, Norton wins the right to vote in committee.) Marion Barry is arrested in a downtown hotel room and charged with possession of cocaine. A deadlocked jury finds him guilty on one of 13 charges and he serves six months in prison. Washington National Cathedral, begun in 1907, is completed.

1992 Marion Barry is elected to the D.C. City Council.

1993 U.S. Holocaust Memorial Museum opens. National Postal Museum opens. Vietnam Women's Memorial is dedicated.

1994 Marion Barry is elected mayor of the District of Columbia.

1995    The District of Columbia Financial Responsibility and Management Assistance Authority, also called the Control Board, is signed into law by President Bill Clinton on April 17. The law, in effect, guts the power of the mayor and the city council. Korean War Veterans Memorial is dedicated.

1996    The Washington Redskins play their last football game in RFK Stadium.

1997    The Federal Triangle Complex is completed with the construction of the Ronald Reagan Building. Washington National Airport opens a brand new terminal building. The Washington Redskins football team kicks off at the new Jack Kent Cooke Stadium, Raljon, Maryland, near Landover. The MCI Center, a $200 million, 20,000 seat sports/entertainment center debuts downtown. Franklin Delano Roosevelt Memorial opens. The Newseum, an interactive museum for news, opens. Women in Military Service for America Memorial opens.

1998    Anthony Williams is elected mayor of Washington, D.C. His term begins in Jan 1999. Washington National Airport is renamed Ronald Reagan Washington National Airport.

1999    A partnership led by David M. Snyder buys the Washington Redskins for an estimated $800 million. In Nov the Washington Redskins football team agrees to rename their Landover stadium FedEx Field. The delivery-services company pays more than $200 million for a 27-year lease on the naming rights. The new name will likely first appear in 2000.

2002    National Museum of the American Indian is scheduled to open on the Mall.

2003    A new Washington Convention Center is scheduled to open. Across the street from the convention center, a new City Museum will also open. The National Air and Space Museum's Dulles Center, housing more than 280 air- and spacecraft is scheduled to open.

# Glossary of Architectural Terms

ABACUS: The flat slab on the top of the capital of a column.

ANTHEMION: Stylized honeysuckle form, used in classical and Greek revival architecture.

ARCADED GALLERY: Covered passageway with openings through a series of arches supported by columns.

ARCHITRAVE: The lowest part of an entablature; in classical architecture it rested directly on a column and usually supported a frieze and cornice.

BALUSTRADE: A railing supported by a series of small posts or balusters.

BARREL VAULT: A vault in the form of a very deep arch.

CAPITAL: The topmost, or crowning, feature of a column.

CLERESTORY: Part of an interior raised above adjacent rooftops, usually windowed to allow light into the central part of the building. Typically used in Gothic churches, where the nave is built higher than the aisles, allowing windowed clerestory walls above the aisles.

COFFER: Recessed ceiling ornamentation, usually square or polygonal.

COLONNETTE: Small column, used for decorative purposes.

CONSOLE: Ornamental bracket, sometimes of stone, to support cornices, balconies, or other elements.

COPING: The protective cap or cover on top of a wall.

CORBEL: Block or bracket projecting from a wall to support timbers, girders, or masonry.

CORINTHIAN COLUMN: Having a capital decorated with stylized acanthus leaves and small scrolls, or volutes.

CORNICE: A prominent, continuous, horizontal projection surmounting a wall.

CRENELATIONS: Battlements, the toothed ramparts of a medieval fortification designed to protect a shooter or archer.

CRESTING: Decorative coping or ornamental ridge to give a building an interesting skyline.

DENTIL: One of an ornamental band of small, rectangular, toothlike blocks.

DORIC COLUMN: Having a plain capital.

ENTABLATURE: The upper section of a classical order, resting on the capitals and including the architrave, frieze, and cornice.

FRIEZE: The middle division of an entablature, between the architrave and the cornice. Horizontal ornamental band, often in relief.

GABLE ROOF: Double-sloping, or pitched, roof.

GAMBREL ROOF: A gabled roof with two pitches, the upper-half gentler, the lower-half steeper.

IMPOST: A bracketed piece of masonry projecting from a wall to support an arch or part of a roofing structure.

IONIC COLUMN: Having a capital decorated with prominent scrolls, or volutes.

KEYSTONE: Central wedge-shaped stone of an arch.

LINTEL: A beam supporting weight over a window or door opening.

LUNETTE: Area of wall enframed by a vault or arch, often penetrated by a window.

MACHICOLATION: A projecting gallery on top of a castle wall, supported by corbeled arches with an opening through which boiling liquids or missiles can be dropped on attackers.

MANSARD ROOF: Steep, attic, urban roof, which allowed an added story on a building.

MODILLION: A carved scroll of a bracket, placed horizontally.

MULLION: Slender, vertical, usually nonstructural bars or piers forming a division between doors, screens, or panes of windows.

NARTHEX: Originally the open porch of a church; now any kind of vestibule to the nave.

OCULUS: Eye or eyelike. A round window.

ORIEL: A high, projecting bay window, supported by corbels, or brackets.

PARAPET: The low wall along the edge of a roof or balcony.

PEDIMENT: The triangular, gabled end of a temple roof-front. In classical architecture, supported by the colonnade and often decorated with sculpture.

PERISTYLE: The series of columns surrounding a building or courtyard.

PIER: A vertical supporting structure, the portion of a wall between windows.

PILASTER: Attached, rectangular column used decoratively.

QUOIN: Cornerstone of a building.

REREDOS: A background for an altar, often carved.

SPANDREL: The flat space between two arches and the surrounding rectangular framework. Also, the material between the head of one floor's windows and the sill of the next.

TIE-ROD: A tensile member used to hold together parts of a building that tend to separate.

TRUSS: Rigid framework made of small triangular elements and designed to span an opening.

TYMPANUM: The sculptured pediment, or triangular end crest, of a Greek or Roman temple. Later, the arched space over Romanesque or Gothic doors, often filled with sculpture.

VAULT: An arched masonry ceiling.

ZIGGURAT: Terraced pyramids used as holy places by the ancient Assyrians and Babylonians.

# Further Reading

Alexander, John. *Ghosts. Washington's Most Famous Ghost Stories.* Arlington, Va.: Washington Book Trading Company, 1988. Whether fact or legend, these tales of ghostly sightings and doings prove entertaining.

Altshuler, David. *The Jews of Washington, D.C.: A Communal History Anthology.* Chappaqua, NY: Jewish Historical Society of Greater Washington and Rossel Books, 1985. A collection of articles and studies on Jewish issues in Washington taken from *The Record,* the Jewish Historical Society's official publication.

Anderson, Cherrie, and Kathleen Sinclair Wood. *Cleveland Park: A Guide to Architectural Styles and Building Types.* Washington, D.C.: Cleveland Park Historical Society, 1988. This study discusses the history and types of architecture in Cleveland Park.

Arnebeck, Bob. *Through A Fiery Trial: Building Washington 1790–1800.* Lanham, Md.: Madison Books, 1991. This detailed history of the beginnings of the Federal City describes the attending politics and personalities.

Ashworth, Marjorie. *Glory Road: Pennsylvania Avenue Past and Present.* McLean, Va.: Link Publishers, 1986. Offers useful details about this avenue.

Bergheim, Laura. *The Washington Historical Atlas.* Rockville, Md.: Woodbine House, 1992. The book's subtitle—*Who Did What When and Where in the Nation's Capital*—describes this mix of historical fact and folklore.

Bigler, Philip. *Washington in Focus: The Photo History of the Nation's Capital.* Arlington, Va.: Vandemere Press, 1988. Although his essays are brief, the author provides good background on selected sites and incidents in Washington, D.C., as well as many early photographs.

Blumenson, John J. G. *Identifying American Architecture.* Nashville, Tenn.: American Association for State and Local History, 1986. This is a guide to types of architectural styles in the U.S.

Borchert, James. *Alley Life in Washington: Family, Community, Religion, and Folklife in the City, 1850–1970.* Urbana and Chicago: University of Illinois Press, 1982. This book presents a thoughtful study of alley life.

Bowling, Kenneth R. *Creating the Federal City, 1774–1800: Potomac Fever.* Washington, D.C.: American Institute of Architects Press, 1988. The author provides a detailed history of the politics, finances, and problems of the Federal City's first six years.

Commission of Fine Arts. *Massachusetts Avenue Architecture, Vol. 1.* Washington, D.C.: Commission of Fine Arts, 1973. A useful guide to the architectural history of the important buildings along this street.

———. *Massachusetts Avenue Architecture, Vol. 2.* Edited by James Jennings, Jr., Sue A. Kohler, and Jeffrey R. Carson. Washington, D.C.: Commission of Fine Arts, 1975. This second volume covers buildings not included in the first volume, providing a detailed architectural history of the important buildings along this street.

———. *Sixteenth Street Architecture, Vol. 1.* Edited by Sue A. Kohler and Jeffrey R. Carson. Washington, D.C.: Commission of Fine Arts, 1978. A detailed guide to the noted buildings along this main street.

———. *Sixteenth Street Architecture, Vol. 2.* Edited by Sue A. Kohler and Jeffrey R. Carson. Washington, D.C.: Commission of Fine Arts, 1988. A detailed guide to the noted buildings along this main street that were not included in the first volume.

Cooling, Benjamin Franklin, III. *Symbol, Sword, and Shield: Defending Washington During the Civil War.* Shippensburg, Pa.: White Mane Publishing Company, 1991. Besides text, the author employs photographs, charts, and maps to cover the four-year battle to defend the capital.

Cooling, Benjamin Franklin, III, and Walton H. Owen II. *Mr. Lincoln's Forts: A Guide to the Civil War Defenses of Washington.* Shippensburg, Pa.: White Mane Publishing Company, 1988. Those interested in the Civil War will want to read this detailed history of the city's fortifications.

Cox, Warren J. *A Guide to the Architecture of Washington, D.C.* New York: McGraw-Hill, 1974. This guide has brief descriptions of buildings, along with selected architectural information.

Davis, Deerin, Stephen Dorsey, and Ralph Cole Hall. *Georgetown Houses of the Federal Period, 1780–1830.* New York: Bonanza Books, 1944. Brief descriptions accompanying black-and-white photographs of historic houses help the reader understand Georgetown architecture.

D.C. Department of Housing and Community Development. *LeDroit Park Conserved.* Washington, D.C.: D.C. Department of Housing and Community Development, 1979. Provides a history of LeDroit Park.

D.C. History Curriculum Project. *City of Magnificent Intentions: A History of the District of Columbia.* Washington, D.C.: Intac, 1983. This basic text designed for school children details the District's history from its beginning through 1946.

Eberlein, Harold Donaldson, and Cortlandt Van Dyke Hubbard. *Historic Houses of Georgetown and Washington City.* Richmond, Va.: Dietz Press, 1958. After a brief overview this book describes the history and architecture of specific houses, providing both exterior and interior photographs.

Enyart, Byron. *A Mile of Glory: Pennsylvania Avenue from the Capitol to the White House.* New York: Vantage Press, 1976. This brief account of Pennsylvania Ave offers some anecdotal information.

Evelyn, Douglas E., and Paul Dickson. *On This Spot: Pinpointing the Past in Washington, D.C.* Washington, D.C.: Farragut Publishing Company, 1992. Although somewhat confusing to follow, this guide offers historical tidbits about past and current sites.

Ewing, Charles. *Yesterday's Washington, D.C.* Miami, Fla.: E.A. Seemann Publishing, 1976. A "photographic story" of Washington from its early beginnings to the 1950s.

Ewing, Heather. "The Architecture of the National Zoological Park," in *New Worlds, New Animals: From Menagerie to Zoological Park in the Nineteenth Century*, edited by R. J. Hoage and William A. Deiss (Baltimore: Johns Hopkins Press, 1996). Written by a high school student, this work offers a detailed history of some of the zoo's buildings, particularly those embellished with carvings paid for by the WPA.

Fitzpatrick, Sandra, and Maria R. Goodwin. *The Guide to Black Washington: Places and Events of Historical and Cultural Significance in the Nation's Capital.* New York: Hippocrene Books, 1990. This carefully researched guide presents quick bits of information on black history throughout the District.

Fogle, Jeanne. *Two Hundred Years: Stories of the Nation's Capital.* Arlington, Va.: Vandamere Press, 1991. Packed with facts, this entertaining narrative presents the District's history by emphasizing various personalities. Fogle is thoroughly familiar with the city's history, as she is the operator of the tour company A Tour de Force.

Frary, I. T. *They Built the Capitol.* Richmond, Va.: Garrett and Massie, 1940. A detailed account of the politics and priorities of the artisans, architects, and statesmen who were involved in building the Capitol.

Goode, James M. *Best Addresses: A Century of Washington's Distinguished Apartment Houses.* Washington, D.C.: Smithsonian Institution Press, 1988. This illustrated guidebook offers detailed information about some of the city's noted apartment buildings.

―――. *The Outdoor Sculpture of Washington, D.C.: A Comprehensive Historical Guide.* Washington, D.C.: Smithsonian Institution Press, 1974. The definitive sourcebook for details concerning the city's outdoor sculpture through the early 1970s.

Goodrum, Charles A., and Helen W. Dalrymple. *Guide to the Library of Congress.* Washington, D.C.: Library of Congress, 1988. Produced by the Library, this guide offers basic information about services and architecture.

Green, Constance McLaughlin. *Washington: Village and Capital, 1800–1878.* Vol. 1 of *Washington.* Princeton, N.J.: Princeton University Press, 1962. This detailed history of life in the capital provides much useful information. Included is a valuable list of critical sources.

―――. *Washington: Capital City, 1879–1950.* Vol. 2 of *Washington.* Princeton, N.J.: Princeton University Press, 1962. This second volume continues the detailed and scholarly history of Washington, D.C.

Highsmith, Carol M., and Ted Landphair. *Embassies of Washington.* Washington, D.C.: Preservation Press, 1992. The photographs and descriptions get the reader "inside" some of the city's embassies.

―――. *Pennsylvania Avenue: America's Main Street.* Washington, D.C.: American Institute of Architects Press, 1988. A collection of old and new photos, interviews, anecdotes, and history concerning the development of Pennsylvania Ave.

―――. *Union Station: A Decorative History of Washington's Grand Terminal.* Washington, D.C.: Chelsea Publishing, 1988. The photographs and text detail the building of the station.

Hilton, Suzanne. *A Capital City, 1790–1814.* New York: Atheneum, 1992. Provides a detailed account of the city's first 24 years and insights into various key individuals.

Hoage. R. J., and William A. Deiss, eds. *New Worlds, New Animals: From Menagerie to Zoological Park in the Nineteenth Century.* Baltimore: Johns Hopkins University Press, 1996. The editors trace the development of certain key zoos in Europe, Australia, India, and America and the movement toward establishing zoos as scientific parks.

Holt, Thomas, Cassandra Smith-Parker, and Rosalyn Terborg Penn. *A Special Mission: The Story of Freedmen's Hospital, 1862–1962.* Washington, D.C.: Howard University Academic Affairs Division, 1975. Presents the early history of this important hospital.

Hutchinson, Louise Daniel. *The Anacostia Story, 1608–1930.* Washington, D.C.: Smithsonian Institution Press, 1977. A detailed account of this sometimes forgotten part of the city.

Junior League of Washington. *The City of Washington: An Illustrated History.* Edited by Thomas Froncek. New York: Alfred A. Knopf, 1985. This valuable book combines many illustrations and photographs with brief but informative text.

Kousoulas, Claudia, and George W. Kousoulas. *Contemporary Architecture in Washington, D.C.* New York: The Preservation Press/John Wiley and Sons, 1995. A description and history of modern architecture in the District.

Lee, Richard M. *Mr. Lincoln's City: An Illustrated Guide to the Civil War Sites of Washington.* McLean, Va.: EPM Publications, 1981. The facts, quotes, and illustrations present a lively account of the city during the Civil War.

Lesko, Kathleen M. Valerie Babb, and Carroll R. Gibbs. *Black Georgetown Remembered.* Washington, D.C.: Georgetown University Press, 1991. An informative history of Georgetown's black residents.

Lewis, David L. *District of Columbia: A History.* New York: W. W. Norton & Company, 1976. An entertaining history of the city.

Longstreth, Richard, ed. *The Mall in Washington, 1791–1991.* Hanover, N.H., and London: National Gallery of Art, Washington, 1991. A detailed history of the Mall, accompanied by illustrations and photographs.

Mann-Kenney, Louise. *Rosedale: the Eighteenth-Century Country Estate of General Uriah Forrest.* Washington, D.C.: Youth for Understanding International Exchange/Queene Ferry Coonley Foundation, Inc./Uriah Forrest Descendants, 1989. This work provides a history of this early Washington-area estate.

Maroon, Fred J. *Maroon on Georgetown.* Charlottesville, Va.: Thomasson, Grant & Howell. The photographs in this book of Georgetown and its historic houses are lovely.

Melder, Keith. *City of Magnificent Intentions: A History of Washington, District of Columbia.* 2d Ed. Washington, D.C., and Silver Spring, Md.: Intac, 1997. Originally published in 1983 as a textbook for the District's ninth-grade public school students, this revised edition added material that makes the book an easy-to-read and reliable compendium of facts about the District.

Miller, Hope Ridings. *Great Houses of Washington, D.C.* New York: Clarkson N. Potter, 1969. This guide offers details on some of the city's elaborate mansions.

Mitchell, Mary. *Chronicles of Georgetown Life, 1865–1900.* Cabin John, Md.: Seven Locks Press, 1986. Presents some of the interesting personalities of that period.

Moore, David, and William A. Hill. *Cleveland Park.* 1904. Reprint, Washington, D.C.: Columbia Historical Society, 1982. Details the development and the architecture of the Cleveland Park neighborhood.

*Notes on Hillwood: A Guidebook.* Washington, D.C.: Hillwood, 1996. Describes the history, collections, and gardens of Hillwood.

Page, Jake. *From Back-lot Menagerie to Nascent BioPark in Only a Hundred Years.* Washington, D.C.: Smithsonian Press, 1989.

Peter, Grace Dunlop, and Joyce D. Southwick. *Cleveland Park: An Early Residential Neighborhood of the Nation's Capital.* Washington, D.C.: Cleveland Park Community Library Committee, 1958.

Peters, James Edward. *Arlington National Cemetery: Shrine to America's Heroes.* Kensington, Md.: Woodbine House, 1986. This book provides profiles of scores of soldiers, and patriots buried at Arlington.

Pottker, Jan. *Celebrity Washington.* Potomac, Md.: Writer's Cramp Books, 1995. This slim guide pinpoints the homes of Washington's famous and infamous.

Reed, Robert. *Old Washington, D.C., in Early Photographs, 1846–1932.* New York: Dover Publications, Inc. 1980. This "picture book" conveys a true sense of early Washington.

Robertson, James I., Jr. *Civil War Sites in Virginia: A Tour Guide.* Charlottesville, Va.: University Press of Virginia, 1987. Provides a quick list and brief information on Civil War sites that points history buffs in the right direction.

Ross, Betty. *Washington D.C. Museums: A Ross Guide: Museums, Historic Houses, Art Galleries, and Other Special Places.* 3d ed. Washington D.C.: Americana Press, 1992. A comprehensive guide to the District's museums with extensive descriptions of the collections.

Schlessinger, Ken. "A New Deal for the Zoo." *Zoogoer* (Nov/Dec 1989), pages 9–13. The article describes some changes in the philosophy of the National Zoological Park.

Scott, Pamela, and Antoinette Lee. *The Buildings of the District of Columbia.* New York: Oxford Press, 1993. This is a comprehensive architectural guide to the city's buildings, including a brief history of its neighborhoods.

Seale, William. *The President's House.* 2 vols. Washington, D.C.: White House Historical Association, 1986. The definitive history of the White House and its occupants.

Small, Herbert. *The Library of Congress: Its Architecture and Decoration.* New York: W. W. Norton & Company, 1982. The definitive text on the Library's decorative details.

Smith, Kathryn Schneider, ed. *Washington at Home: An Illustrated History of Neighborhoods in the Nation's Capital.* Northridge, Calif.: Windsor Publications, 1988. Its illustrations and historical essays on various city neighborhoods make this a valuable text.

Smithsonian Books. *Washington, D.C.: A Smithsonian Book of the Nation's Capital.* Washington, D.C.: Smithsonian Books, 1992. Various essays cover different aspects of the capital.

Templeman, Eleanor Lee. *The Blair-Lee House.* McLean, Va.: EPM Publications, 1980. A history of the president's guest house written by one of the home's descendants. This book, however, was written before the house underwent renovations.

Weeks, Christopher. *AIA Guide to the Architecture of Washington, D.C.* Baltimore and London: Johns Hopkins University Press, 1994. This is a comprehensive guide to the District's buildings.

White House Historical Association. *The White House: An Historic Guide.* Washington, D.C.: White House Historical Association, 1987. This illustrated guide offers photographs and much information about the building's furnishings.

Whitehill, Walter Muir. *Dumbarton Oaks: The History of a Georgetown House and Garden, 1800–1966.* Cambridge, Mass.: Belknap Press of Harvard University, 1967. Presents the early history of Dumbarton Oaks.

Wiencek, Henry. *The Smithsonian Guide to Historic America: Virginia and the Capital Region.* New York: Stewart, Tabori & Chang, 1989. This basic guide offers brief bits of information.

Wirz, Hans, and Richard Striner. *Washington Deco: Art Deco Design in the Nation's Capital.* Washington, D.C.: Smithsonian Institution Press, 1984. Washington does have Art Deco buildings, and a selection of these are described and listed in this book.

Worth, Fred L. *Strange and Fascinating Facts about Washington, D.C.* New York: Bell Publishing Company, 1988. The author serves up unusual information and historical tidbits.

*Washington, D.C.: City and Capital.* Federal Writers' Project of the WPA. New York: Hastings House, 1942. This early guide offers insight into the development of the city and its institutions.

*The WPA Guide to Washington, D.C.* New York: Pantheon Books, 1983. This later reprint is an abridged version of the WPA's *Washington, D.C.: City and Capital.*

Yochelson, Ellis L. *The Natural Museum of Natural History: Seventy-Five Years in the Natural History Building.* Washington, D.C.: Smithsonian Institution Press, 1990. An informative text, this book presents the development and changes in this museum up to 1990.

# THE GUIDE

## 1 · Capitol Hill North and East

Metro: Red Line to Union Station.
Bus: 80, 96, D1, D3, D4, D6, D8, X2, or X8.

### Capitol Hill

Capitol Hill encompasses the streets surrounding the Capitol, Union Station, and the areas to the east, reaching as far south as the Navy Yard on the banks of the Anacostia River. Although replete with massive federal buildings, including the Capitol Building itself, the Hill is a vibrant neighborhood with many historical connections.

#### History

Major Pierre L'Enfant described the site he choose for the nation's Capitol, then called Jenkin's Hill, as "a pedestal awaiting a monument." Descendants of the Rozier-Young-Carroll family dominated the area for nearly 100 years and farmed the land. In 1791, the year construction of the Capitol began, Daniel Carroll of Duddington owned most of the land. Carroll began building the neighborhood's first mansion, which he named Duddington, not far from the proposed Capitol site in 1791. L'Enfant, a perfectionist who didn't want to deviate from his plan, ordered the constructed parts of Duddington demolished as it lay in the projected path of New Jersey Ave. When Carroll refused to comply, L'Enfant destroyed Duddington himself, a controversial act that eventually contributed to his dismissal. Carroll rebuilt the imposing Georgian-style house south of the Capitol between 1st and 2nd Sts on the present Duddington Place S.E. The manor has since been razed.

Another homeowner in Capitol Hill's early days was British merchant William Mayne Duncanson, who built the Maples mansion in 1795, six blocks south of where the Capitol would be built, at what is now 619 D St S.E. Duncanson, who like Carroll expected to be living the high life in the city's center, became another casualty of Capitol Hill. Several bad real estate investments left him bankrupt, and he was forced to sell the Maples. The elegant home was converted to a social services center in 1937 and renamed the Friendship House.

Capitol Hill attracted other investors. Duddington and George Walker, a Scottish merchant from Philadelphia, and others purchased lots hoping to increase their fortunes by selling parcels. Capitol Hill, however, developed slowly and inconsistently. Compared to the established port community of Georgetown, Capitol Hill had little to offer. Landowners had overestimated the value of their property, and many buyers began to settle in less expensive, swampy sections, east of Georgetown on Pennsylvania Ave, in the area now called Foggy Bottom.

This wasn't the way it was supposed to happen. In fact, the financing of the Capitol and other public buildings might be considered the first in a very long line of well-intentioned government programs that didn't quite work out as planned.

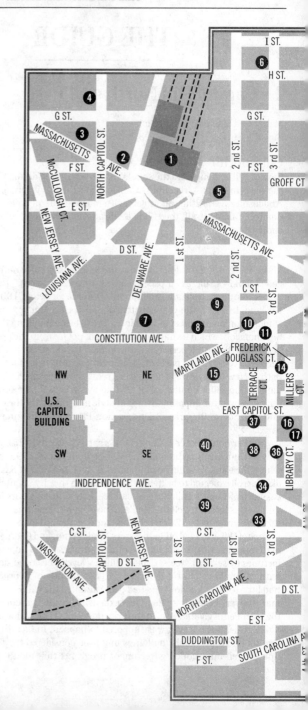

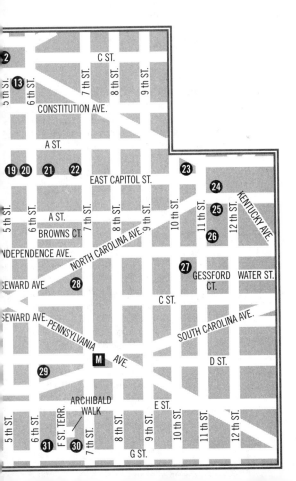

1 Union Station
2 National Postal Museum
3 National Guard Memorial
4 Government Printing Office
5 Thurgood Marshall Federal Judiciary Building
6 Capital Children's Museum
7 Russell Senate Office Building
8 Dirksen Senate Office Building
9 Hart Senate Office Building
10 Sewall-Belmont House
11 Veterans of Foreign Wars Building
12 Stanton Square
13 George Peabody School
14 Home of Frederick Douglass
15 Supreme Court Building
16 325–327 E. Capitol St.
17 326 A St S.E.
18 408 A St S.E.
19 S. W. Tullock House
20 Sarah McC. Spofford House
21 616 E. Capitol St N.E.
22 638–642 E. Capitol St N.E.
23 D. T. and Eugenia E. Donohoe House
24 Lincoln Park
25 Sladen's Walk
26 Philadelphia Row
27 200–208 10th St S.E.
28 Eastern Market
29 The Maples
30 636 G St S.E.
31 Christ Episcopal Church of Washington
32 Ebenezer United Methodist Church
33 Theodore Mayer Row
34 Mayer's Bock
35 120 4th St S.E.
36 St. Mark's Episcopal Church
37 Folger Shakespeare Library
38 John Adams Building (Library of Congress)
39 James Madison Memorial Building (Library of Congress)
40 Thomas Jefferson Building (Library of Congress)

The original plan was that the government would pay nothing for those plots of land specified on L'Enfant's plan of the city as public building sites, "reservations," and streets. Half of the remaining land would revert to the original owners, and the U.S. government would pay £25 Maryland currency (about $67) an acre for the rest. Sale of the lots, it was speculated, would easily cover the cost of erecting public buildings like the Capitol and the White House.

The sale didn't. The first auction, held in Sept 1791, netted merely $2,000, and subsequent auctions produced much the same results. The birthing of the capital city was a more arduous process than anticipated.

But that didn't discourage those who came to work. And many of those who came settled on Capitol Hill. The first residents of Capitol Hill were laborers involved in the construction of the Capitol. Many came from Virginia, including native and recently immigrated whites, and free and enslaved blacks. Other recruits eventually came from northern states and Europe. The workers lived on the grounds of the Capitol in wooden barracks and in nearby makeshift houses. Construction foremen and master craftsmen built larger two-story framed homes. Capitol Hill was becoming an interesting mix of laborers and gentry.

To stimulate growth in the neighborhood, George Washington built two townhouses on N. Capitol St. Other fine homes were built by a group of British men who had prospered as merchants in East India. They hoped to create a Washington–East India trading post on the Anacostia River, then called the Eastern Branch (of the Potomac River). These wealthy British merchants built several mansions in the area, some constructed by Thomas Law, but the trade route never fully materialized.

Thomas Law also funded the construction of Tiber Creek Canal from 1810 to 1815. Created in order to transport building materials, the canal ran from the Capitol to the Potomac. Poorly built, unclean, and foul-smelling, the Tiber Creek Canal added an unpleasant stench to the area. As a result, Law took some blame for the lack of investors in the neighborhood. In the 1870s, as one of several city improvements, Boss Shepherd filled in Tiber Creek.

Since the executive office buildings were clustered around the White House rather than the Capitol, the city's future development seemed to be heading westward, away from Capitol Hill. Many major landowners felt betrayed. Daniel Carroll summed up the price of investing in the Hill when he wrote in 1837 that, "after nearly half a century the result is now fully known: the unfortunate proprietors are generally brought to ruin and some have scarcely enough to buy daily food for their families."

After the Capitol workers, the next major wave of Hill residents were employees at the U.S. Navy Yard constructed in 1799 on Anacostia's west bank. Strategically located two miles above the river's junction with the Potomac, the Navy Yard offered a hidden enclave from which U.S. warships could attack boats coming up the Potomac.

In 1800 when the nation's capital moved from Philadelphia to Washington, Capitol Hill remained relatively undeveloped. Congressmen and Vice President Thomas Jefferson lodged in boarding houses and taverns in the area surrounding the Capitol. Gradually a scattered crescent of houses formed southeast of the Capitol arching toward the Navy Yard.

In 1807 Benjamin Latrobe, architect of the Capitol and St. John's Church on Lafayette Square, constructed the Christ Episcopal Church on 620 G St S.E. The oldest church in the original city limits, the facility's first service was in 1794 in Daniel Carroll's tobacco barn. Several presidents were parishioners of the church, including James Madison and John Quincy Adams. By 1810 a community had developed, including shops, artisans, a farmer's market, several churches, and a school for white children.

In Aug 1814 the British invaded the new Federal City, torching many of the government's buildings, including the Capitol and White House. The Navy Yard was also burned during the occupation. During the attack, the commander of the U.S. Navy set fire to the ships docked there, as well as those being built, to keep them out of British hands.

In the days immediately following the near destruction of the city, there was great concern among the residents that Congress might now vote to move the capital back to Philadelphia or New York. Congress met in session at what was then the Post Office and Patent Office Building (see Walk 13: "Judiciary Square/ Chinatown Area"). Several cities offered their services as a capital, including that small town up the road called Georgetown, which promised to board congressmen at $10 a week instead of the $16 charged by Washington hotels.

The South balked at a more northern capital, and politics of every sort were joined in the argument. In the end, money was the determining factor: Washington bankers volunteered a $500,000 loan to the government to rebuild. Congress agreed to the deal and reconstruction began anew. A temporary "Brick Capitol" was constructed on the site of the present Supreme Court Building, and Congress met there until 1819 when they reoccupied the reconstructed Capitol.

Through the mid-1800s, the Hill's population grew steadily, mirroring the expanding federal government. Diverse groups of new residents, including blacks and immigrants from Germany, Ireland, and southern Europe, many of whom participated in the 1850s Capitol extension, necessitated the construction of additional churches.

With the Civil War, Capitol Hill was transformed. The Union Army occupied all public buildings as well as many private residences. Mary Clemmer Ames, a resident of Washington, describes the city during the conflict: "Capitol Hill was dreary, desolate and dirty, stretched away into an uninhabited desert. Arid hill and sodden plain showed alike the horrid trail of war. Forts bristled above every hilltop. Soldiers were entrenched at every gate-way."

But war brought prosperity as well. Horse-drawn streetcar lines came in 1862, including one which linked the Navy Yard with the Capitol and the White House. Speculators began building row houses, expanding the Capitol Hill neighborhood in anticipation of a population boom.

In 1873, Adolph Cluss constructed Eastern Market. Centrally located between the Capitol and the Navy Yard, at 7th St and North Carolina Ave, Eastern Market stimulated growth in the neighborhood as did expanding federal government. As public transportation improved, the neighborhood, previously clustered within walking distance of the Navy Yard and the Capitol, expanded.

Many developers saw the profit in building town houses targeted at the middle class. Between 1875 and 1895 Charles Gessford, a developer specializing in "formula" row houses, built more houses than anyone previously had in the neighborhood. Middle-class residents moved into newly built two- and three-story single-family homes.

The neighborhood attracted many black leaders after the Civil War. In May 1865 the first black public school was opened in a row house. In 1872, Frederick Douglass arrived to serve as editor of the *New National Era*, buying a house at 316 A St, N.E. This building later served as the Museum of African Art from 1964 until 1988, after which the museum moved to its current location on the Mall.

By 1898 the Navy Yard, still the city's largest employer, had established itself as the world's largest ordinance producer and engineering research center. In need of unskilled workers, it drew many immigrants, including Jews from eastern Europe. A large Jewish community established itself in Southwest Washington near the yard.

During this period the federal government grew substantially. In the first part of the 20C many old private homes in the neighborhood were razed to create space for congressional office buildings, the Library of Congress, and the Supreme Court. Casualties included most of the original boarding houses and taverns frequented by government employees, as well as Daniel Carroll's and Thomas Law's residences. Federal buildings now occupy the large avenues and side streets around the Capitol, which were originally lined with town houses.

Capitol Hill continued to grow during the first part of the 20C. After World War II, some people realized the importance of preserving the old buildings. This gentrification, with its increase in taxes and property values, gradually pushed working-class whites and blacks out of homes on the streets immediately surrounding the Capitol.

During the 1960s the preservationist trend intensified. Young families and single professionals gradually restored the townhouses between the Capitol and Lincoln Park, which is 11 blocks east. Hill residents helped block federal proposals during the 1970s that included turning E. Capitol St into a strip of federal office buildings and dividing the area with a highway. In 1976, the area nearest to the Capitol, comprising more than 8,000 primary buildings, received historic district status.

*Capitol Hill (northeastern side), 1863. Courtesy of the Historical Society of Washington, D.C.*

### Washington Notes

Even though Jenkin's Hill was renamed Capitol Hill, several pockets of the area went by other names. For many years after the Civil War, the area south of the Capitol was known as Bloody Hill, because of the field hospital that had once been located there. Another area, now known as Garfield Park, was referred to as Bloody Field, due to the scary amount of violence in the area.

## Union Station

Massachusetts and Delaware Aves N.E. ☎ 371-9441. Open 24 hours daily. Retail shops open Mon–Sat 10–9; Sun 12–6. More than 25 restaurants, 130 retail shops, a nine-theater movie complex. Amtrak ticketing, baggage handling. Foreign currency exchange. Restrooms, telephones, ATM. Wheelchair accessible. Wheelchairs available.

Union Station (1908; Daniel H. Burnham; 1988 restoration, Harry Weese & Associates, Benjamin Thompson & Associates; DL) began operation in 1907, a time when railroads dominated America's political and economic horizons. Automobile travel, shipping, and the invention of the airplane contributed to the railroad's steady decline. Union Station gradually fell into disrepair. In the 1980s a movement was begun to restore this splendid Beaux-Arts building. After a massive renovation, the building stands as a beautiful monument to the glory days of the railroad, and the structure is also a functioning, modern station complete with a shopping arcade and restaurants.

**Highlights:** Charles W. Elliot's intricate allegorical statues above the main entrance and the large Main Hall.

**History**

One of the goals of the McMillan Commission and the City Beautiful Movement in the early 1900s was to remove the train depots and railroad tracks from the Mall. The commission, of which Daniel H. Burnham was a member, advised Congress to consolidate the Baltimore and Pennsylvania and Baltimore & Ohio (B&O) railroads (which served points north and west) and relocate the Baltimore & Pennsylvania Railroad Station (then located where the National Gallery of Art's West Building stands today). The McMillan Commission recommended building the new station on the site where the B&O station stood near the Capitol at the intersection of Washington's grand avenues. In 1903 Congress appointed Daniel H. Burnham as the principal architect and Frederick Law Olmsted, Jr., as the landscape architect.

Burnham drafted a Beaux-Arts design modeled after Rome's Baths of Caraculla and the Arch of Constantine. The cornerstone for the building was laid in 1905. The station, which cost $25 million to build, opened on Oct 27, 1907, when the B&O's Pittsburgh Express pulled into the station at 6:50 A.M. By today's standards, the station offered some unique features: Turkish baths, a bowling alley, a mortuary, and an ice house. Construction was completed in 1908.

Union Station has been the site of many significant events in Washington and U.S. history. In 1909, President Taft became the first president to use the station's Presidential Suite, which became the greeting point for foreign dignitaries, including King George VI and Queen Elizabeth of England. On Jan 23, 1911, financier J. P. Morgan was a passenger on a train that broke a railroad speed record when it made the trip from New York to Union Station in three hours and 55½ minutes—more than an hour faster than the previous record. During World War I, Union Station served as a mobilization center. In 1945, the private train car carrying President Franklin Delano Roosevelt's casket arrived at Union Station.

On Jan 15, 1953, the Pennsylvania Railroad's *Federal Express,* en route from Boston with 16 cars of passengers coming to the Capitol for Dwight Eisenhower's inauguration, lost its brakes and crashed into the station's main concourse. The floor collapsed underneath the train. Although no deaths resulted, the station suffered millions of dollars in damage.

One attempt to revive the station involved building a National Visitors Center. The center opened July 4, 1976, featuring a bookstore, a hall of flags, multilingual information kiosks, and an automated slide show orienting visitors to the Capitol. Few tourists visited the center. Deemed a failure, it closed in 1978. During the late 1970s and early 1980s, the station deteriorated further. The roof leaked, and after a section caved in, mushrooms grew in many of the decrepit offices. Rail passengers, however, continued to use the station.

In 1981, Congress enacted the Union Station Redevelopment Act to restore the station as a national landmark. Under the aegis of Elizabeth Dole and the Department of Transportation, the Union Station Redevelopment Corporation was created. It raised $160 million from various sources. The restoration began on Aug 13, 1986. On Sept 29, 1988, the station reopened. A presidential nod to the restoration was made in 1989, when President Bush's inaugural ball was held in the Grand Concourse.

## Exterior

Burnham fashioned the main entrance at the south side of the building, a triple-arched portico, after the Arch of Constantine. Allegorical Grecian figures atop the

Ionic columns of the portico depict Prometheus for fire, Thales for electricity, Themis for freedom or justice, Apollo for imagination or inspiration, Ceres for agriculture, and Archimedes for mechanics. The figures in the center focus on creativity, whereas the figures to the right and left sides address the operation of the railroads. Each statue weighs 25 tons and stands 18 ft tall. The subjects, like the inscriptions on the frieze above the arches, were chosen by Charles W. Elliot, former president of Harvard University.

The **Columbus Fountain** (1908; Lorado Taft) graces the plaza south of Union Station. The fountain contains an Old World/New World sculpture of Christopher Columbus. The dedication ceremony, in 1912, attracted thousands of Knights of Columbus from across the country.

## Interior

**Main Hall, or Head House.** This 120 ft long and 220 ft wide hall has a barrel-vaulted, coffered ceiling 96 ft high. The gold leafing, replaced during restoration, amounted to more than 70 pounds. Thirty-six plaster figures of Roman legionnaires stand around the ledge of the balcony. Louis Saint-Gaudens's original figures were nude. Controversial, these figures were retrofitted with shields concealing their pelvic area so as not to embarrass lady travelers. The freestanding fountains in the Main Hall each weigh approximately ten tons.

To the right of the main entrance is the **East Hall.** As you enter the East Hall from the Main Hall, notice the large clock over the entrance. The Roman numerals are all correct, except for the number *IV,* produced as *IIII.* The restorers did not change this feature, although they replaced the original workings with quartz fittings. The East Hall has ten kiosks and six galleries that complement its historical elements and architectural design. The columns surrounding the hall are made of scagiola, an imitation ornamental marble comprising a mixture of gypsum, glue, and paint. During construction this style saved money, but restoring the columns cost more than the price of replacing them with real marble. Pompeiian-style traceries (detailed stencils) featuring fish, griffins, fruit, and geometric shapes, decorate the walls and ceiling.

During the restoration, the workers carved three levels of commercial space into the open-air **concourse.** The area houses 130 stores, a food court, and a movie theater complex with nine screens.

The gray, antique gates in the **train concourse** are part of the original structure. Near the baggage claim area is a bust honoring A. Philip Randolph (1990; Ed Dwight). The AFL-CIO commissioned the piece, which was placed here in memory of the founding leader of the Brotherhood of Sleeping Car Porters, a group which rallies for the rights of these employees. A plaque in the corridor between the train concourse and the Main Hall honors Amtrak employees who were killed on the job.

Exit the station through the west side doors closest to the street-level Metro entrance. Directly across from these doors and 1st St N.E., at the junction of N. Capitol St and Massachusetts Ave, stands the old City Post Office, which houses the National Postal Museum.

## *National Postal Museum*

2 Massachusetts Ave at 1st St N.W. ☎ 357-2700 or 357-1729 (TTY). Information recording in Spanish: ☎ 633-9126. Web: www.si.edu/postal. Open daily

10–5:30. Closed Christmas Day. Admission: free. One-hour tours Mon–Fri 11, 1, 2; Sat–Sun 11, 1. Tours for the sight- or hearing-impaired should be arranged two weeks in advance. ☎ 357-2991 or 633-9849 (TTY). Restrooms, telephones. Wheelchairs available. Museum shop. Handheld photography with flash permitted.

The National Postal Museum, a Smithsonian museum, maintains the world's most comprehensive collection of stamps and philatelic materials and chronicles the history of the U.S. postal system. The museum is housed in the former City Post Office (1914; Graham and Burnham; 1992 renovation, Shalom Baranes Associates; DL), which at one time was Washington's main post office. After extensive renovation, the building reopened in 1993 as Postal Square. In addition to the museum and an active post office, the building features the Capitol City Brewing Company.

**Highlights:** More than 55,000 stamps are displayed throughout the museum at any given time. Also exhibited are early vehicles used in transporting mail such as planes, stagecoaches, and mail trucks. The museum has more than 40 interactive exhibits that make learning about the postal system fun. The hands-on Discovery Center for children is open the third Sun of each month from 1 to 3 P.M. Activities for ages 4 and older include designing stamps and learning about mail delivery vehicles. Ages 8 and older solve the mystery of how criminals alter money orders, and ages 12 and older match the portraits of the notable people displayed on stamps with interesting trivia.

### History

In 1903 Daniel H. Burnham, a member of the McMillan Commission, was asked to design a structure to complement his neighboring building, Union Station. He and Postmaster General Frank Hitchcock worked together on the plan. With the Public Buildings Act in June 1910, Congress authorized the acquisition of the site west of Union Station. At the time, the city's main post office, built in 1899, was located on Pennsylvania Ave N.W. With the growth of the city and government, it was no longer large enough to handle the volume of mail.

Foundations for the new structure were laid in 1912. Construction was completed in 1914. With the advent of parcel post and the boom of mail during World War I, an addition was needed. In 1931 Graham, Anderson, Probst, and White created the plans. The building served as the capital's central post office from 1914 until 1986. The National Postal Museum opened on the lower level of the City Post Office in 1993 as a joint effort between the Smithsonian Institution and the U.S. Postal Service.

The Smithsonian's collection began in 1886 with the donation of a sheet of ten-cent Confederate stamps.

## Exterior

The City Post Office is characterized by its classical appearance. Inscribed on the east and west façades above the Ionic colonnade are inscriptions celebrating the mail carrier selected by Charles W. Eliot, former president of Harvard University. The structure was designed by Daniel H. Burnham to complement his neighboring building, Union Station. The museum's exterior is faced with white granite from Bethel, Vermont.

## Interior

Enter the building from the east side, directly across from Union Station. When the building functioned as a post office, the Grand Main Hallway served as the public area. Administrative offices were located on the second and third floors. The three basement levels feature large open spaces that were used to sort and process U.S. mail.

Walk to the center of the **Grand Main Hallway** on the ground level. To the right is the information desk and the escalator that transports visitors downstairs into the museum's 90 ft high atrium, in which early mail planes are suspended. At the foot of the escalators are two museum shops. A stamp store is on the left; a museum shop is on the right.

The museum features six exhibit galleries: Binding the Nation, Customers and Communities, Moving the Mail, The Art of Cards and Letters, Artistic License: The Duck Stamp Story, and Stamps and Stories. Among the dozens of hands-on and interactive activities, visitors can address, meter, and send postcards, sort mail, assemble a stamp collection, and sit in a stagecoach. A 90-minute film shown continuously in the museum's theater features interviews with postal workers who offer stories about their jobs.

The escalators lead visitors into the Main Hall, the gallery where Moving the Mail is located. To begin the history of the postal service chronologically, walk through the Main Hall to the gallery along the north wall, Binding the Nation.

**Binding the Nation** traces the history of U.S. mail services from its infancy around 1673, when mail was carried between New York and Boston on Indian trails, through the colonial period, when Ben Franklin, who was instrumental in establishing mail service, ran a post office for the British government, to the turn of the 20C. Visitors walk through the gallery, a re-created forest with faux trees, rocks, and piped-in woodland sounds. The first postal clerks of 1673 rode through the woods to deliver the mail. Proceed through the forest and turn right. This exhibit depicts how leaflets, which were nailed to posts around cities to disseminate news, evolved into newspapers, often with "Post" in their titles.

Turn left. The next section, **The Expanding Nation,** details how the territorial and population expansion of the country affected the mail service and how mail was sent to to frontier towns. Visitors can climb into a life-size stagecoach to relive what it was like to travel with the mail in the 19C—an unpleasant experience since coaches were bumpy and crowded. To the right of the stagecoach a video dramatizes a first-person account of a Pony Express rider. Period artifacts include a saddle, spittoon, and quilt. The interactive exhibit **Create-A-Route** underscores how postal routes were established in the 1800s. The four stories it dramatizes encourage players to create a postal route. Exit the gallery and proceed into the Main Hall. Turn left and enter **Customers and Communities.**

The faux-cobblestone floor suggests a 19C city. To the right is an actual mail wagon. Period artifacts include a pneumatic mail tube and historic mailboxes. Walk south to the life-size model of an early-20C post office. A video explains all of the services a post office offers: selling of products such as stamps and money orders, distribution of tax forms and selective service materials, and shipping services. Walk south.

The next section displays several quirky folk-art mailboxes. Turn right and enter the highly interactive exhibit, **What's in the Mail for You!** Holographs, videos, and multimedia computer kiosks address direct mail marketing and discuss the historic significance of catalogs from L.L. Bean, Tiffany, and Burpee. Touch screens enable visitors to develop a direct mail profile of themselves like the ones employed by catalog companies. At the end of the gallery a machine spits out souvenir envelopes addressed with the visitor's profile. Turn left and enter the main hall.

> ### Washington Notes
> Among the strangest packages ever mailed was May Pierstroff, a 4 year old, on Feb 19, 1914. At 48 pounds she was just under the parcel-post limit of 50 pounds. Her parents wanted her to visit her grandparents, but no one wanted to pay the train fare from Grangeville to Lewiston, Idaho. Since there were no regulations then about mailing people, her parents attached 53 cents postage to a tag around May's coat and sent her off. She traveled in the train's mail compartment and was delivered to her grandparents. When postal officials heard about her journey, they created rules that forbade the mailing of people.

Planes, trains, automobiles, and other means of transporting mail is the focus of **Moving the Mail.** The exhibit discusses the birth and proliferation of airmail and the employment of private, contractual mail carriers who travel by motorcycle and other nontraditional modes. Three historic airmail planes hang overhead. The Wiseman-Cooke was the first plane to make an official mail-delivery mission for the U.S. Postal Service. During the 1920s the De Havilland was the workhorse of the postal service. The Stinson Reliant was used to make mail drops and pick up shipments "on the fly" from communities without airfields. Along the south wall are colorful postboxes from countries such as Japan, Sweden, Germany, and Canada. A 1931 Ford Model A is on display, as is a 1950s Mailster. At the east end of the main hall is a re-created railcar used to transport mail. Nearby videos discuss robberies and other themes related to moving the mail by train. In a case outside the rail car is Owney, a mounted dog. This stray was adopted by a post office in New York and quickly became the mascot of the entire service. He traveled with mail around the world. At many of the stops a postmaster medallion was added to his collar. At the computer kiosks visitors can address and meter postcards. Walk to the gallery located in the northwest corner of the main hall.

The **Art of Cards and Letters** shows the importance of communication through mail. Actual letters of soldiers writing home, greeting cards, and postcards are displayed as social and historical documents. The writings capsulate the ideas of an era. There is also an exhibit called **Undercover: Evolution of the American Envelope.** It discusses the history of envelopes and exhibits early machines that folded, gummed, and embossed envelopes. A kiosk to the left enables visitors to create and mail custom-made Hallmark greeting cards. Exit into the main hall and walk south. Enter the gallery immediately to the west.

**Artistic License: The Duck Stamp Story** traces the history of the Federal Duck Stamp Program and examines its significance in preserving wetlands and maintaining migrating bird populations. Mallards and other migratory birds hang from the ceiling. The walls are decorated with murals depicting wetlands. Life-size figures are dressed as hunters and birders. Cases display decades of migratory bird stamps. A video explains how the annual design competitions are held and enables visitors to appreciate the artistic effort put into creating the stamps. Enter the next gallery through from the southwest.

The beauty and practicality of stamps is shown in **Stamps and Stories.** A video addresses the history and evolution of stamps. To the right is another video that demonstrates the printing process. Interactive exhibits, on the left, teach visitors to look at stamps as a collector, identifying them by type and condition. The museum displays more than 55,000 stamps at any given time. Hanging on the wall to the right are poster-size sheets that display thousands of stamps by theme and specialization, such as transportation and Olympic stamps. Walk through a vaultlike doorway to view rare stamps as well as hundreds of stamps from countries around the world.

Exit from the vault and walk through Moving the Mail to the escalators. Proceed south down the corridor and between the escalators. A life-size statue of Benjamin Franklin is at the center of the hall. Franklin was postmaster of colonial North America from 1755 to 1774. Inscribed in gold leaf on the walls to the right and left are quotations from various postmaster generals chosen by Charles Eliot. An active post office is at the south end of this corridor.

Recent exhibits include **Posted Aboard the RMS *TITANIC*** (Sept 1999–indefinitely), the story of five seapost clerks who perished aboard the ill-fated ship, with artifacts such as the keys to *Titanic*'s mailbags and a gold pocket watch found on the body of one of the five clerks.

Exit the Postal Museum onto Massachusetts Ave. Walk west and cross N. Capitol St. On the northwest corner is the National Guard Memorial.

## National Guard Memorial
The National Guard Memorial (1991; Alex Jeffries), 1 Massachusetts Ave N.W. (the northwest corner of Massachusetts Ave and N. Capitol St), ☎ 789-0031, home of the National Guard Association, was established in 1878 to provide the National Guard with representation before Congress.

### Interior
As visitors enter the memorial, through the rotunda, they see a bronze statue depicting a Minuteman (Evangelos Frudakis), symbolizing the colonial roots of the National Guard.

To the right, hanging above the reception desk, is the National Guard All-States Needlepoint Quilt. The idea for the quilt was initiated by Mrs. Ellen Frettered in 1989. The spouse of each state's general was responsible for a panel that reflected the National Guard heritage in that state or territory. The 56 ten-by-ten-inch panels were stitched together by Joan Price in the order the states were admitted to the Union.

Behind the Minuteman is a staircase leading down to the **Medal of Honor Gallery.** At the top of the stairs are two bronze six-pounder cannons cast by Revere Copper Works c. 1790–1810 for the Massachusetts militia. The cannons feature the state emblem of the Indian Massasoit.

Two panoplies decorate the walls flanking the staircase. The panoply on the right combines four flags from each of the combatants in the War of Independence. In the upper corner is an early-American color carried by independent companies from Westmoreland County, Pennsylvania—an ancestor of the 109th

Field Artillery Battalion, part of the 28th Infantry Division. The orange-and-green flag is the regimental color of the Touraine Infantry Regiment of the Royal Army of France. The yellow flag, with the British Union Jack in the upper corner, is a regimental color of the English 9th Regiment. The flag with the standing lion is based on the regimental color of the Hessian Infantry Regiment, one of the three regiments captured by American troops in Trenton, New Jersey. The drum is from the 43rd British Regiment, a regiment that fought in Lexington and Concord, Massachusetts.

The panoply to the left features flags and soldier's items from the Civil War. There are two flags representing each side. One is from the National U.S. Color of the 2nd Wisconsin Volunteer Regiment, a unit which fought as part of the "Iron Brigade." There is also the flag of the 5th Battery, Washington, Light Artillery, a group from the Confederate Army in Tennessee. Also displayed is the regimental color of the 6th Massachusetts Regiment, one of the oldest units of American military dating to 1636. The Army of Northern Virginia's battle flag comes from a unit of Baltimore men who sided with the Southern cause and fought with General Thomas "Stonewall" Jackson. The drum is from the 1st Regiment of Grey Reserves of Philadelphia.

Beneath the panoplies, at the foot of the staircase, are display cases. Against the left wall is a case containing models of aircraft used by the Air National Guard as well as handcarved wooden figures of the Air National Guardsmen in historical uniforms. The case on the right side displays the Vanvilet Collection. This collection of handcarved wooden figures was begun in 1960 by M. S. Vanvilet. There are 53 figures (the 50 U.S. States plus D.C., Puerto Rico, and the U.S. Virgin Islands) representing uniformed militia from each state's early history. In the back row are figures from the 13 original states shown as they would have been dressed for the War of Independence.

Proceed to the Medal of Honor Gallery opposite the cases. The Medal of Honor was created by Congress in December 1861 and approved by President Lincoln. The Medal of Honor Gallery, a tiny, round room at the entrance to the Hall of States, honors National Guard members who have been awarded the Medal of Honor since 1898. There are several dioramas depicting some of the members' acts of courage and also a state-by-state Honor Roll of National Guard recipients. At the center of the room is a case displaying the four versions of the Army Medal of Honor (1862–96, 1896–1904, 1904–44, 1944–present) and the Air Force Medal of Honor.

Continue through the Medal of Honor Gallery to the **Walsh-Reckord Hall of States.** This is a conference and reception room dedicated Sept 1991 in memory of two National Guard heroes, Major General Ellard Walsh from Minnesota and Lieutenant General Milton Reckord from Maryland. Hanging from the dark-wood walls are flags from every U.S. state and territory.

**Diversion:**

To see the **Government Printing Office (GPO)** (1861; architect unknown; additions 1901, 1928, 1937, and 1940), 710 N. Capitol St N.W., walk north on N. Capitol St. The GPO, established by Congress in 1860, has grown to become the largest printer in the world. The main building of this multibuilding complex spanning a city block, features 33 acres of floor space. The GPO provides the three branches of government (legislative, executive, and judicial) with copies of bills and laws, regulations and budgets, and rulings and decisions. The GPO also publishes informative pamphlets and other materials for the general public.

Although the GPO is not open to the public, the retail bookstore is open weekdays 8–4. It sells government-written and-published books, pamphlets, and manuals about military history, transportation, agriculture, social services, and government-related topics such as Congressional directories.

From the National Guard Memorial, walk east to Massachusetts Ave. The **Thurgood Marshall Federal Judiciary Building** (1989–92; Edward Larrabee Barnes Associates) is the glass and white-granite structure on the east side of Union Station and Columbus Circle. It houses the U.S. Court's administrative offices as well as offices of retired Supreme Court Justices. Only the glassed-in lobby, notable for its interior tree, is open to the public.

**Diversion:**
If traveling with children, visit the Capital Children's Museum. From the Thurgood Marshall Federal Judiciary Building, continue east on Massachusetts Ave. Turn left at 3rd St and walk north three blocks.

## Capital Children's Museum
800 3rd St N.E. ☎ 675-4120. Web: www.ccm.org. 10–5; 10–6 between Easter and Labor Day. Closed New Year's Day, Thanksgiving, and Christmas Day. Admission: $6 per person; $4 for senior citizens; children under 2, free. Half-price admission on Sun before noon. Tours at 10, 11:30, and 2. Reservations requested. Wheelchair accessible.

ScienTERRific Sundays feature classes where kids can learn about fingerprinting, gears, the solar system, fireworks, and other science-related themes. Classes for children 7 and younger are at 11 and 2. Classes for children 8 and older are at 12 and 3–4. ☎ 675-4120. Other events honor ethnic heritage months.

In Dec/Jan of each year, the museum hosts the top entries in the PBS-TV children's art festival.

The Capital Children's Museum (1876) examines urban life through hands-on activities and exhibits and also attempts to educate visitors about the diversity of this country's cultures. It operates on the twin principles that learning begins with active exploration and exchange with others *and* that learning can be fun.

**Highlights:** CMA Chemical Science Center, Mexico, Japanese Tatami Room.

### History
The group of buildings that the museum occupies served as a convent and nursing home of Little Sisters of the Poor. In the 1970s educator Ann White Lewin developed the idea for the museum. After receiving a $1.7 million grant from the Department of Housing and Urban Development, the museum opened in 1977 at Lovejoy Elementary School and relocated to this three-acre site in 1979.

In 1984 the museum became a member of the National Learning Center, an organization that creates new educational structures, methods, and materials. A second major boost of support came from International Telephone and Telegraph (ITT). The company underwrote an exhibit area called Communications. Other funding or donations were provided by the Mexican government and the Washington, D.C., Fire Department.

## Exterior

While this cluster of red brick buildings looks drab from the street, follow the curving stone path in the parking lot to the main entrance on the south side of the courtyard. Leading into the main entrance of the museum is the **Nek Chand Fantasy Garden.** Chand, an Indian folk artist, created these murals and several hundred colorful life-size and miniature figures of men, women, children, and animals from discarded objects such as bicycle parts, fabric scraps, and broken jewelry. The robed figures, some with shimmery turbans and others with colorful, flowing caftans, herd sheep, move donkeys, scatter ducks. Tiled policemen stand guard outside the main doors. The garden was modeled after a 12-acre rock garden in Chandigarh, India.

At the west side of the courtyard is a giant, multicolored **Cootie,** a buglike figure from a children's game.

## Interior

**First floor.** Enter the lobby, pay admission, and proceed south to the hallway. Turn left and walk east. Make the second left. In the hallway on the right is the Invisible Harp. This hands-on instrument enables kids to make music and create sound effects with the push of a button. Temporary art exhibits, such as displays of poster contest entries, and the auditorium are located on the first floor. Also displayed here are architectural models created by Metropolitan-area school students, an ongoing collaborative project of the museum and area schools. Turn right and proceed to the elevator. Go up to the third floor. Permanent exhibits are located on the second and third floors.

**Third floor.** Exit the elevator and turn left into the **Japanese Tatami Room.** (Note: By the beginning of 2000, the Tatami Room should have been moved to the other end of the building, around the corner from the City Room, and will have been expanded in that single space to include another room representative of the day-to-day life of a Japanese child.) Designed to introduce children to the customs, culture, and lifestyle of Japan, the room features a 12 ft by 15 ft tatami room, a Japanese dining room, built with such traditional materials as rice paper and reeds. Children cross the reed mat floor and sit on floor cushions at a table. In the 20–25-minute presentation kids learn about typical Japanese foods and how to use chopsticks. Outside the tatami structure, a 28-minute video entitled *My Day* shows children what a day in the life of an 11-year-old school boy is like. Objects that Japanese children carry to school in their backpacks—a pencil case, lunch box, and books—are displayed on a nearby table. Children are encouraged to try on Japanese school uniforms. Above the table is a Koi wind sock, which is traditionally flown around Japan on May 5, Children's Day. Visitors are taught to say simple phrases in Japanese. Signboards on the walls show characters from the written language. Also on the walls are kimonos and photographs of city and domestic life. To the left of the entrance is a *pachinko*, or pinball machine. The exhibit also includes a re-created (but nonmoving) Japanese Bullet Train, one of the fastest trains in the world.

Cross the hallway and enter the **Bubbles Room.** Several types of hands-on bubble machines are scattered around the room. The main attraction is the life-size bubble machine. Visitors stand in the middle of a circular base, reach down and pull a circular shower curtain rod above their head to envelope themselves in a bubble. The wall mirror lets visitors see themselves inside the bubble.

Exit the room and turn right. On the right is the **Metamorphomaze.** This life-size labyrinth fills the entire room. Adjacent to Metamorphomaze, a full-size Metro subway car, where kids can design their own Metro station, opened in 1999.

Return to the hall and turn right. Walk to the adjoining hallway and turn right. Proceed along the hallway to **Animation: The World of Chuck Jones.** Images of famous cartoon characters like Bugs Bunny, Tom and Jerry, Betty Boop, Mickey Mouse, and Felix the Cat line the hallway walls. Activities in the gallery teach children about cartoon history, how cartoons are created from a storyboard through inking and cells, to video. Kids can draw their own storyboards. Through the use of blue-screen technology kids can also star in their own cartoon and then watch it on a nearby screen. The **Acme Sound Company** exhibit lets kids make sound effects commonly heard in cartoons: honks, clicks, and doorbells. The **Animation Lab** shows how cartoons are translated from cells to video. Workshops should be arranged in advance. ☎ 675-4149. In **Mouse Pad,** the country's first public access computer classroom, kids can study desktop publishing, web page design, and computer graphics.

Return to the main hallway; walk to the east end to **Changing Environments.** Pass through the archway. On the right is a room-size model of the imaginary H.B. Drezwell clothing factory. Kids can see the steps of creating garments including weaving, dyeing, sewing, and stocking inventory. On the left of the main hallway is **The Importance of Looking at Ourselves.** Fun-house mirrors distort one's image. Diagrams of facial structures accompanied by mirrors teach visitors that everyone is slightly different and special.

Return to the main hallway and proceed east. On the right is the **Puppet Playroom.** Two stained glass windows depict characters from *Alice in Wonderland.* A stage in the corner is used for puppet productions. In a case are ornately decorated marionettes.

Exit the room and continue east to the **City Room.** Just inside the entrance, to the left, is the front section of a Metro bus. Kids can sit in the driver's seat and pretend to drive. The walls have murals of Washington, D.C., cityscapes as well as actual license plates and street signs. These rooms have city items such as mailboxes, newspaper vending machines, phone booths, and parking meters. Kids can try on a postal service uniform, a doctor's lab coat, a telephone repairman's helmet, or fire helmets, and also slide down a firehouse's brass pole.

To exit, retrace the steps back to the main hall. On the right is **Simple Machines,** a collection of assorted puzzles. Proceed down the stairs to the second floor.

**Second floor. Mexico!,** the museum's inaugural exhibit, introduces kids to the culture of our nearest southern neighbor by tasting its food, hearing its music, making Mexican crafts, and wearing its traditional garb. Complete with Mexican music and a tile fountain, this gallery re-creates a Mexican city plaza. Murals depict building façades. Turn right and enter the **Yucatan Peninsula Room.** On the south wall is a giant sandbox meant to resemble a beach. The north wall has model ruins kids can climb. Proceed through the room and turn right into the **Provincial Kitchen.** Brass vessels and clay pots hang on the walls. In the kitchen kids can taste Mexican hot chocolate. To the right in the life-size *Miscelanea* (corner store), kids can stand behind the counter and pretend to be a clerk.

Continue through the Provincial Kitchen. To the right is a log cabin similar to the houses in the mountains of Mexico. Walk through the main hallway. On the right is the **Storyteller Theatre**, which has videos and hosts special presentations.

Walk north, cross the main hallway, and enter the **Ice Age Cave,** where displays help visitors understand how ideas were transferred from one person to another in prehistoric times. From here walk east to the **CMA Chemical Science Center,** where chemistry comes alive in hands-on experiments to expose children to the wonders of science. Here they can actually feel the kind of atomic-level collisions that result in chemical reactions and see demonstrations that produce colorful fireworks, flowers that shatter like glass, and bananas strong enough to drive a nail. Children are also given the opportunity to participate in supervised chemical experiments.

To skip the Children's Museum and continue with this walk, proceed south from the Federal Judiciary Building on 2nd St. At D St, turn right and walk two blocks to Delaware Ave. Walk south one block on Delaware Ave to the entrance of the Russell Senate Office Building (1905–8; Carrère and Hastings).

## Russell Senate Office Building

1st and C Sts, N.E. ☎ 224-3121. Open weekdays 9–5. Closed New Year's Day, Thanksgiving, Christmas Day, and weekends. Building not open for public tours. For a special appointment with your state congressperson, contact his/her office prior to your visit. Restrooms, telephones. Wheelchair accessible at 1st St and Delaware Ave.

**Highlights:** The Beaux-Arts design—an eclectic late-19C–early-20C style incorporating Roman, Rennaissance, and baroque elements—and the entrance's rotunda make this building interesting. The Caucus Room (not open to the public) is an impressive space and has been the scene of many important political hearings.

### History

In 1891 the Senate purchased the Maltby Building, a five-story commercial building on the corner of New Jersey and Constitution Aves (then called B St N.). For nearly two decades, the building, renamed the Senate Annex, was used by senators for offices. The structural integrity of the building was questioned as early as 1904, and in 1905 the building was razed.

In 1904 when members of the House of Representatives voted to erect a building for their offices (the Cannon Building), the Senate also decided to build new offices. Ever mindful of status, the architects situated the Senate and the Cannon buildings in the same relationship to the Capitol.

The cornerstone was laid on July 31, 1906, using the same trowel as employed in the ceremony for the House building. The 61st Congress occupied the building in March 1909. The new structure allotted space for a dining room, barber shop, bathing room, and the Senate Exercise Room—a popular facility during the 1920s.

Twenty years later the Architect of the Capitol, David Lynn, constructed a fourth side to the building on the 1st St side and added 2 committee rooms and 28 suites. At this time, they also decided to enhance the C St façade of the building.

The building was originally known as the Senate Office Building. It was renamed the Richard Brevard Russell Senate Office Building in 1972 to honor the

Georgia senator (1897–1971) respected for his intelligence, independence, loyalty, and expertise in national defense.

## Exterior

The U-shaped Beaux-Arts design employs repetitive arches and colonnades on the façade facing Constitution Ave. The exterior and public space use white marble from Vermont. The courtyard walls use Indiana limestone. The terraces on Constitution and Delaware Aves were completed with gray granite from New York, and the C and 1st Sts fronts are Georgia marble.

## Interior

Enter the Russell Building on the ground floor at the Delaware and Independence Aves entrance. If you have secured an appointment and permission, proceed through the metal detector and walk east to the elevator bank. Go up two floors to the second floor. Across from the elevator bank is a bronze bust of Henry "Scoop" Jackson, a senator and representative from Washington who served in the Senate from 1953 to 1983. It was dedicated in Nov 1987. Walk to the end of the hallway. Turn left and proceed to the end of this hall and into the **rotunda.** The ornate entablature and coffered dome is supported by 18 Corinthian columns. A statue of Richard B. Russell (1996; Frederick Hart) is displayed in the rotunda.

Return into the hallway and turn left to the staircase. Climb the stairs to the third floor, or use the elevators at the other end of the hall.

At the top of the stairs turn right. The gallery of the rotunda is on the right. On the left is the **Caucus Room,** Room 325. It has marble walls and floors. The ceiling is adorned with gilded rosette windows, rows of acanthus leaves, and a Greek key motif. Still in use is the original mahogany furniture created in 1910 by the Francis Bacon Company of Boston. The building has hosted important senatorial hearings and discussions such as those concerning the Teapot Dome scandal (1923–24), the attack on Pearl Harbor (1941), the Kefauver Crime Committee (1950–51), the U.S. Army vs. Senator Joseph McCarthy (1954), conduct during the Vietnam War (1966), Watergate (1973–74), the Iran-Contra affair (1987), and Clarence Thomas's appointment to the Supreme Court (1991).

> ### Washington Notes
> When the building was known as the Senate Office Building, staff and senators reputedly joked that "When giving constituents your Washington address, do not fail to spell out in full 'Senate Office Building.' If you give him the abbreviation S.O.B., he will not know whether you are calling him one, or expect him to call you one."

Exit the Russell Senate Office Building from the rotunda. Turn east on Constitution Ave. Turn left at 1st St and walk north to C St. Turn right and enter the Dirksen Senate Office Building (1947–58; Eggers and Higgins) at 1st and C Sts, the second of the three Senate office buildings built on the north side of the Capitol.

# Dirksen Senate Office Building

1st and C Sts N.E. ☎ 224-3121. Open weekdays 9–5. Closed New Year's Day, Thanksgiving, Christmas Day, and weekends. Building not open for public tours.

For an appointment with your congressperson, contact his/her office. Restrooms, telephones. Wheelchair accessible.

### History

In the 1930s and 1940s the rapid growth of senatorial staffs and committees prompted a need for additional office space. Congress authorized the Architect of the Capitol, David Lynn, to solicit plans for a new building in July 1947. Lynn contracted Otto R. Eggers and David Paul Higgins, the successors to the firm of John Russell Pope, to design a building that would complement its neoclassical neighbors. On land acquired and cleared during 1948 and 1949, the architects drafted a seven-story structure that would house 12 committee suites and 45 other suites.

Though the Senate approved the architectural plans in 1949, construction was delayed until 1954. Due to inflation during the five-year wait, the cost of the building ballooned. To come in on budget, a proposed wing was eliminated.

Ground was broken on Jan 26, 1955, in a ceremony attended by Vice President Richard M. Nixon and Chief Justice Earl Warren. By Oct 15, 1958, staff members began occupying the building.

In 1979 the 92nd Congress named the building after Illinois senator and Minority Leader Everett McKinley Dirksen, who served from 1951 to 1969.

## Exterior

On 1st St, the main elevation contains a pilastered central bay with entablature and pediment. The saying "The Senate Is the Voice of Our Union of States" is inscribed on the pediment. Otto R. Eggers designed the doors at the south and north entrances. Symbols representing equality and liberty and the American eagle appear in the center of the doors, with five figures on the spandrels of the door depicting shipping, farming, mining, and lumbering. The building is faced with Danby marble from Vermont.

## Interior

Unlike the two other Senate office buildings, the Dirksen does not feature any rooms or pieces of art worthy of note to the casual visitor.

Proceed east along C St to the entrance of the Hart Senate Office Building (1973–82; John Carl Warnecke and Associates), the most recent and modern of the three Senate office buildings, which boasts a number of innovations.

## *Hart Senate Office Building*

2nd and C Sts N.E. ☎ 224-3121. Open weekdays 9–5. Closed New Year's Day, Thanksgiving, Christmas Day, and weekends. Not open for public tours. Visitors can view the Alexander Calder sculpture in the atrium weekdays 7 A.M.–6 P.M. For an appointment with your congressperson, contact his/her office. Restrooms, telephones. Wheelchair accessible.

**Highlights:** The Hart's interior features the sculpture *Mountains and Clouds* (1976; Alexander Calder).

### History

Like the two other Senate buildings, construction of the Hart came in response to a lack of office space. Excavation began in Dec 1975, but construction was not completed until 1986. During this period the construction costs jumped by 76 percent, and $24 million dollars worth of space had to be excluded from the design. In Aug 1976 the Senate passed a resolution naming the building the Philip M. Hart Senate Office Building, in honor of the senator from Michigan.

## Exterior

The building design introduced some "firsts" into the Capitol Hill office scene. The design is free of classical ornamentation; a nine-story atrium is employed to light the offices and conserve energy; moving partitions allow Senators flexibility in arranging their space.

## Interior

Enter at the C St entrance and proceed south to the **atrium.** Alexander Calder's (1898–1976) *Mountains and Clouds* was installed in Nov 1986 and dedicated in May 1987. It was the artist's last work. The piece incorporates both mobile and stable elements and is constructed of matte black aluminum. The 70 ft work depicts clouds floating over mountains.

From the atrium, turn east and exit the Hart Senate Office Building onto 2nd St. Turn right and walk south to the corner. To the right is the Sewall-Belmont House.

## *Sewall-Belmont House*

144 Constitution Ave N.E. ☎ 546-3989. Open Tues–Fri 10–3; Sat 12–4. Closed Sun and Mon. House and garden tours Tues–Fri 11, 12, 1, 2; Sat 12, 1, 2, 3. Admission: free. Gift shop. Not wheelchair accessible.

The Sewall-Belmont House (1800; Robert Sewall; DL) is one of the oldest homes on Capitol Hill and was declared a National Historic Site in 1974. Today, the ground floor of the house serves as the headquarters for the **National Woman's Party (NWP),** an organization founded by Alice Paul in 1913. The main and second floors display a historical collection of paintings, sculpture, and furniture commemorating women such as Alice Paul, Elizabeth Cady Stanton, and Lucretia Mott, who inspired and lead the suffrage movement.

**Highlights:** Among the noteworthy art objects are five busts of suffrage leaders sculpted by Adelaide Johnson. The Florence Bayard Hilles Library was established in 1943 and contains volumes relating to women's history. The NWP labels this facility the oldest feminist library in the U.S.

### History

This site was part of a parcel granted from King Charles II to the second Lord Baltimore in 1632. During the next 160 years the land exchanged hands several times. Eventually it was inherited by Daniel Carroll, a man who owned all of southeast and southwest Washington as well as much of Jenkin's Hill (now Capitol Hill). In 1799 Robert Sewall purchased this plot on Capitol Hill from Carroll. A year later he built a house, incorporating an existing carriage house that dated to 1680.

> ### *Washington Notes*
> In 1801 Albert Gallatin, secretary of the Treasury under Presidents Jefferson and Madison, rented the house; he lived here until 1813. From this

home, while serving President Jefferson, Gallatin negotiated a $15 million deal known as the Louisiana Purchase, and later he negotiated the Treaty of Ghent.

During the War of 1812, when the British invaded the new capital city in 1814, this house was one of few sites of local resistance. Several of U.S. Commodore Joshua Barney's men, hidden in the garden, fired shots at the British soldiers, killing one man and the horse General Robert Ross, leader of the British troops, was riding. Embarrassed and indignant, Ross ordered his troops to torch the house. A plaque outside the house commemorates the U.S. soldiers' actions. Historians credit this exchange with prompting the angered British to torch the White House and the Capitol Building.

Sewall rebuilt the house before his death in 1822. The property stayed in the family for 123 years and was passed from generation to generation. In 1921 Porter H. Dale, a senator from Vermont, purchased the house and subsequently restored it to its 19C charm.

In 1929, the National Woman's Party purchased the property for their new headquarters, adding Alva Belmont's name to the house. Alva E. Belmont had provided the funds for the previous NWP headquarters on Capitol Hill, called the Old Brick Capitol, which was taken by the U.S. government in order to construct the Supreme Court Building. Alva Belmont, before her marriage to the wealthy Oliver Hazard Perry Belmont, was married to William K. Vanderbilt. Since 1929 the NWP has owned and occupied the Sewall-Belmont House. During the 1950s there was talk of razing the Sewall-Belmont House to build a parking lot. President Eisenhower, recognizing the house's historical significance, stepped in and vetoed the plans.

## Exterior

The exterior has undergone significant changes over almost three centuries. Consequently, the stately four-story brick style blends Federal architectural features with other architectural elements. The fan light above the main door is a notable detail.

## Interior

**Main floor.** Inside, the house exudes the well-bred élan of decorative colors, Oriental rugs, and period furniture. Set up as a house museum, the rooms with their well-appointed 18C and 19C pieces must have been furnished by women of affluent social standing. Appropriately enough, the setting, perhaps incidentally, reminds us that most of the 19C suffrage leaders left the comfort of such rooms to endure protest marches, ridicule, and jail terms so that women would eventually be given their right to vote.

Portraits and busts of many important women leaders are displayed in the **Hall of Statues.** Among the most notable works are busts of women leaders by Adelaide Johnson, the self-proclaimed sculptor of the suffrage movement. Johnson's Susan B. Anthony looks careworn but formidable, her hair in a tight bun, her chin set at a determined angle. Nearby, the bust of Elizabeth Cady Stanton, former president of the National American Woman Suffrage Association and cofounder of the International Council of Women, looks larger than life. Lucretia Mott, conveyer with Stanton of the first Equal Rights Convention in 1848, appears with her bonnet tied resolutely under her chin. In the sculpture of Alice Paul (Avard Fairbanks), founder of the NWP and proponent of the Equal Rights Amendment in 1923, the subject sports both a chic fur draped around her shoulders and the revolutionary jail door necklace, a symbol she gave to women imprisoned in the Occoquan workhouse in Lorton, Virginia, for their suffrage activism. At the end of the hall, the ivory and marble statue of Joan d'Arc (Madame Prosper d'Epiney), stands guard. Belmont donated the statue as a reminder of the ardor of women who fight for a cause.

The portraits are of noteworthy suffragists (many of whom spent time in jail because of their activism), such as Florence Bayard Hilles, former head of the National Woman's Party; Anna Kelton Wiley, editor of *Equal Rights* and national chair of the NWP; Elizabeth Seldon Rogers, chair of the Advisory Committee of the NWP during the suffrage movement; and Inez Milholland Boissevain, depicted in her characteristic flowing white gown astride her white horse, carrying a banner proclaiming "Forward Into Light," a stance she took at the head of a suffrage procession during President Wilson's inauguration in 1913. Copies of this vintage suffrage poster are for sale in the small museum gift shop. Because Boissevain collapsed from exhaustion during one of her campaigns, and then died of pneumonia, the painting is inscribed "who died for the freedom of women."

The **Living Room** has a bust of Dr. Caroline Brown (Adelaide Johnson), the first woman to receive a medical degree west of the Alleghenies. It also features portraits of Helen Hunt West, a former NWP chairperson in Florida and editor of *Equal Rights*, and Elizabeth L. Chittick, who worked to obtain National Historic Landmark status for the house, as well as congressional funds for its further restoration. The room also displays Alva Belmont's furniture.

In the **Alice Paul Office** the rolltop desk belonged to Susan B. Anthony, as did the framed white handkerchief with its carefully embroidered *S*. The two other desks belonged to Henry Clay and Alva Paul. The spool-turned-chair belonged to Elizabeth Cady Stanton. The chair was presented to her at the 1848 Seneca Falls convention. The trowel, now hanging above Anthony's desk, was used to clear off her grave in Rochester, New York. The trowel was later presented to Charlotte L. Pierce, who was, at the time of the gift, the last living person to have attended the Seneca Falls convention and the only woman participant who lived long enough to cast a vote. Pierce later presented the trowel to the NWP.

The **Florance Bayard Hilles Library** was rededicated in September 1998. Many of the volumes have been restored to their original condition. The library is open by appointment only.

Continue east on Constitution's north side across 2nd St N.E. to the intersection of 2nd St and Constitution and Maryland Aves N.E., and the Veterans of Foreign Wars Building.

## Veterans of Foreign Wars Building
200 Maryland Ave N.E. ☎ 543-2239. Tours available for veterans. Wheelchair accessible.

**Veterans of Foreign Wars (VFW)** encompasses several organizations that monitor the legislation and disbursement of benefits for veterans in this country. These services include the National Veterans Service, National Security and Foreign Affairs Department, and the Special Assistant for Employment. Although the organization's national headquarters is in Kansas City, Missouri, this building in Washington plays a crucial role as the organization's lobbying headquarters and also as a memorial to those soldiers who have sacrificed their lives for the nation.

### History

James E. Van Zandt, onetime commander in chief of the VFW, suggested the idea for a Washington building and memorial in the 1930s, but property costs and bad luck intervened to delay the project for over 20 years.

The first site chosen became the Soviet Embassy when the VFW could not raise the purchase price. Later, the organization turned over another site north of the Capitol to the federal government so additional Senate offices could be built.

In 1953, at the 54th National Encampment in Milwaukee, former commander in chief Clyde A. Lewis presented a resolution proposing that the long-awaited building serve not only as a Washington office, but as a memorial to soldiers lost in battle. The resolution stated that the VFW had "no suitable memorial to honor our honored dead." The building would also lift the $21,000-a-year burden of renting offices in the District. The 200 Maryland Ave N.E. site was purchased in 1954.

Funding for the building came through donations and dues from within the organization. Still, things did not go as smoothly as planned. Dues had to be increased several times to meet costs. In 1956, the District government threatened the undeveloped property with condemnation.

Construction finally began in June 1958. Vice President Nixon dedicated the cornerstone in 1959, and President Dwight Eisenhower gave an opening dedication speech on Feb 8, 1960. The final cost was $2 million.

## Exterior

The **VFW/Auxiliary Monument** was a collaborative effort by the VFW and the Ladies Auxiliary as a Bicentennial gift to the nation. It was dedicated on July 31, 1976, and is called *The Torch of Freedom* (1976; Felix de Weldon). Four panels on each side of the pyramid statue depict America's battles for freedom. The scenes include: the Spanish-American War, "Remember the *Maine*"; The Korean War, "Land of Morning Calm—Prelude to the Storm"; Civil War—Appomattox, "Thought May the Minds of Men Divide, Love Makes the Heart of Nations One"; Civil War, Union; American Revolution—Battle of Yorktown, "These Are the Times That Try Men's Souls"; American Revolution, Spirit of '76; World War II—Pacific, "Uncommon Valor Was Common Virtue"; Vietnam War, "The Missing Will Never Be Forgotten, Their Glory Will Live Forever"; World War II—Atlantic, "Victory, However Long and Hard the Road May Be, For Without Victory There Is No Survival"; World War I, "Lafayette, We Are Here"; War of 1812, "Oh, Say Can You See . . . Our Flag Was Still There"; Civil War, Confederacy.

## Interior

The **chapel** is at the west side of the main lobby. It features five stained glass windows representing the five branches of the armed services: army, navy, marines, coast guard, and air force. The seal of each branch is depicted above a life-size soldier, sailor, or airman created with green, gray, and blue pieces of glass. Sitting on the floor before the windows is a three-ft-wide Cross of Malta emblem and the

Eternal Light. President Eisenhower switched on the red bulb of the light for the first time during the dedication. Display cases around the lobby contain awards, medals, the Ladies Auxiliary Book of memories, and a scroll representing the original Congressional Charter.

This walk continues to the Supreme Court.

**Diversion:**
The diversions are Stanton Square, three blocks northeast of the VFW, the George Peabody School (1879–80; Office of the Building Inspector), the first home of Frederick Douglass, and some of the alleys that are part of D.C.'s history.

**Stanton Square**—bordered by Massachusetts and Maryland Aves, and C and D Sts N.E.—is named for Edwin M. Stanton, President Lincoln's secretary of war. Standing in the center of the park is a bronze equestrian **Statue of Nathanael Greene** (1876; Henry Kirk Brown). Greene was a Continental Army revolutionary who joined the Rhode Island militia in 1774 as a private, but earned major general honors within a year. Among his accomplishments: leading the successful Rhode Island and Carolina campaigns, convicting a British spy, and fighting in all the mid-Atlantic battles. The Greene statue was placed here in 1876 as a result of the imminent Peabody School construction. During the late 19C educators placed monuments of military heroes near schools to instill patriotism.

The **Peabody School,** 5th and C Sts N.E., currently a public school, was named for George Peabody, a clerk in a Georgetown dry goods store who volunteered time and donated money to local schools and libraries. The D.C. school superintendent at the time had planned to name the school for Major Pierre Charles L'Enfant. Neighbors overruled, claiming that the school's children would be mocked for going to an "infant school." A stone had already been engraved with "L'Enfant," so the stone was turned around and engraved with Peabody's name. This red brick structure was one of the largest elementary schools the Office of the Building Inspector ever designed.

To see the first Washington **Home of Frederick Douglass,** freed slave and famed orator, walk south on 5th St two blocks and cross Constitution Ave. At A St turn right and proceed to 316 A St N.E. Douglass moved here in 1872 to become editor of the *New Era* newspaper. In 1877 Douglass moved across the Anacostia River to a sprawling estate he named Cedar Hill. From 1964 to 1987 Douglass's first home housed the Museum of African Art.

> ### *Washington Notes: Alleys and Alley Life*
> To the west of 316 A St is **Frederick Douglass Alley.** Directly across A St is **Miller's Alley.** The townhouses lining the middle-class neighborhoods of Capitol Hill and many other parts of the city conceal alleys, such as this pair, which once housed many of Washington's working poor and its black population.
>
> Forced to live in the city's back alleys by financial, spatial, and racial constraints, Washington's poor developed neighborhoods within neighborhoods from which they emerged daily to work as unskilled laborers in factories, in the homes of the affluent, or as government employees. Though in the mid-

19C many reform efforts aimed at abolishing these often cramped and unsanitary enclaves, many alleys survived into the 1970s.

These communities, with names such as Grease Alley, Cabbage Alley, Blood Alley, and Tin Pan Alley, began in Washington before the city's post–Civil War expansion. A survey of the city directory in 1858 reveals 349 families living in at least 49 alley communities. Lack of affordable housing and adequate transportation systems helped create alley life because unskilled laborers needed inexpensive housing convenient to their workplaces. In 1858, the majority of alley residents in D.C. were poor whites.

From the 1850s to the decades immediately following the Civil War, Washington's population more than doubled, expanding from around 40,000 inhabitants in the early 1850s to more than 110,000 in 1870. Blacks accounted for more than half of the new arrivals, and alley populations increased dramatically. In 1871, the city directory listed 1,500 households in 118 alleys. Blacks accounted for 83 percent of alley dwellers. By 1873, there were 500 alley settlements. This change not only represented the larger number of black migrants, but stiffening segregationist and racist attitudes in the city itself. White alley dwellers eventually achieved a certain upward mobility denied their black counterparts, who were excluded from many economic pursuits. By 1897, the Federal City contained an estimated 17,244 alley residents—16,046 of whom were black. These numbers are probably low estimates, as many alley areas were considered by the authorities unsafe to enter. Many of the streets throughout Capitol Hill (and the rest of the District) that have "Court" in their names were at one time alley settlements.

Dwellings varied substantially over the years. In the mid-1800s, shacks and makeshift shelters appeared. Structures previously erected for other purposes, such as storage or working space, were sometimes rented to workers. Overcrowding was commonplace. By the 1870s, developers realized the potential market for small permanent structures and began building small, wooden row houses. Though simple, these usually featured ovens and fireplaces, and occasionally had some decoration, like shutters or woodworking, on their façade. These houses tended to be about 12 ft wide and 30 ft long, with a small backyard.

During the 1880s and 1890s brick structures became the norm. These small but solid houses featured relatively elaborate brick decor. Construction of these ceased in 1892 when Congress banned further alley construction.

There were a number of attempts to end alley settlements because of their poor living conditions and the prevalence of crime and disease. The alleys were generally paved with cobblestones and had no drainage systems. Since many were used as garbage dumps by homeowners, the filth and stench of the alleys, particularly in summer months, could be unbearable. President Woodrow Wilson's first wife made a deathbed plea to forbid alley residences in the capital. After her death, Wilson pushed such legislation through, but the law was rarely enforced. Reforms failed largely because inexpensive housing was scarce.

The use of trolleys and automobiles had the biggest impact on the eradication of alleys. These new modes of transportation enabled the middle and upper-middle classes to relocate to suburban neighborhoods. As the affluent classes moved away from the city, owning or renting houses in town became much more affordable.

Historical preservationist movements in the 1950s led to the rehabilitation of many alley dwellings, and ironically, as the area gentrified over the next three decades, professionals began to see former alley residences as desirable addresses.

From the VFW, walk east on Maryland Ave. The visitor's entrance to the Supreme Court Building is on the south side of the street about one block from the VFW.

## Supreme Court Building

1st and E. Capitol Sts N.E. ☎ 479-3211. Web: www.law.cornell.edu. Open weekdays 9–4:30. Closed weekends and holidays. Rotating exhibits and a 20-minute film about the Court are located on the ground floor.

Lectures in the courtroom are given every hour on the half hour, 9:30–3:30. When the Court is hearing oral arguments (10–12 P.M. and 1–3 from the first Mon in Oct to the last Mon in Apr), presentations begin at 11:30. Court proceedings are open to the public, but seating is limited. Two lines form at the west plaza. One line is for those who wish to attend the entire argument; the other is for those who want to be in the courtroom for just a few minutes. Seating lines for the former begin at 9:30 and 12:30; lines for the latter begin at 10 and 1. No public sessions Thurs–Fri. Visitors use a booklet to guide themselves around the ground floor.

Restrooms, telephones. Cafeteria open 7:30–10:30 and 11:30–2:00. Closed 12–12:15 and 1–1:15. Snack bar open 10:30–3:30. Gift shop open 9:30–4:25. Wheelchairs available. FM and infrared listening systems available in courtroom. No cameras, radios, pagers, recording devices, hats, books and periodicals, briefcases, or luggage in courtroom while in session. Checkroom and coin-operated lockers available. Remain silent in courtroom. Infants and small children are not recommended.

The Supreme Court Building (1929–35; Cass Gilbert) houses the judicial branch of the federal government, which is the highest tribunal in the country. The Court interprets the Constitution, and is limited to ruling on related cases.

**Highlights:** This neoclassical giant features ornately decorated pediments over its east and west entrances. The courtroom boasts a marble colonnade and a number of detailed, sculpted marble panels.

### History

The Constitution, ratified in 1788, called for a "Supreme Court" to serve as the last interpreter of the law and to hold in check the legislative and executive branches of the federal government. The Court may also overturn unconstitutional legislation that has been passed by Congress. (The first exercise of this power was in 1803 with the *Marbury v. Madison* decision.)

The Judiciary Act of 1789 divided the country into 13 judicial districts. These were organized into three circuits: eastern, middle, and southern. The Supreme Court, the highest tribunal, was to be seated in the nation's capital. At the time, the Court was comprised of a chief justice and five associate justices. Except for a brief period during the 19C, justices had to "ride circuit"; in other words, they held

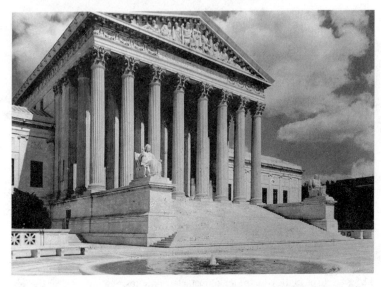

*U.S. Supreme Court. Courtesy of the Washington, D.C., Convention & Visitors Association.*

court twice a year in each of the judicial districts. This occurred for the Court's first 101 years. The Court's first decision was handed down in 1792.

Justices are appointed by the president, with Senate approval, and, barring voluntary retirement or congressional impeachment, serve for life. The number of justices fluctuated six times in the Court's first century, but the Judiciary Act of 1869 increased the number of justices from six to nine. (On average, a new justice joins the Court every 22 months.)

The Court has convened in a number of buildings in various cities. The first meetings were held in the Royal Exchange Building in Manhattan. Philadelphia's Independence Hall, and later, City Hall, housed the Court until 1800, when the capital moved to the Federal City in Washington. In Washington the Supreme Court moved into the basement of the Capitol Building.

When the British occupied Washington in 1814, they used Court documents as kindling for the fire that damaged the Capitol and much of the city. A group of prominent citizens and businessmen formed the Capitol Hotel Company, an investment company, and constructed the temporary Old Brick Capitol on the site of a former hotel and tavern. The Old Brick Capitol stood on the site of the future Supreme Court Building. Congress and the Court convened in the Old Brick Capitol from Dec 1815 to late 1819, when they returned to the unfinished new Capitol. The Old Capitol Building then became, in succession, a private school, a boarding house, a Civil War federal prison, and a home to a women's rights organization, before Congress appropriated the land for the Supreme Court Building.

The Court met in several rooms in the present Capitol, the most significant being the Old Supreme Court Chamber, which it occupied from 1819 to 1860. The room, a vault beneath the ground level of the Capitol Building, later became the Law Library of the Congress. In 1860, the Court moved upstairs to the Old Senate Chamber, where it remained for the next 75 years.

The present Supreme Court Building owes its existence primarily to the efforts of William Howard Taft, the only person to serve the United States both as a president and a chief justice of the Court. Upon his appointment as chief justice in 1921, he committed himself to building the court a permanent home. In 1928, Congress appropriated $9,740,000 for construction.

The building was designed in a classical style by architect Cass Gilbert. Taft died in 1930, two years before the construction began. Chief Justice Charles Evans Hughes laid the cornerstone on Oct 13, 1932. Cass Gilbert died in 1934, a year before the building's completion. Associate architects Cass Gilbert, Jr., and John R. Rockart finished the construction. The building was completed under budget in 1935. The remaining $94,000 was returned to the Treasury.

### Washington Notes

The Supreme Court Building is one of the largest marble structures in the world, and a prime example of the academic classicism that dominated federal architecture in the 1930s. Its size, solemnity, and grandeur have been targets of criticism since its completion.

Upon its opening, Justice Stone remarked that the justices "ought to ride over on elephants." He added that he found the structure "almost bombastically pretentious . . . wholly inappropriate for a quiet group of old boys such as the Supreme Court." Another justice, whose identity remains a mystery, worried that the justices would look like "nine black beetles in the temple of Karnak."

## Exterior

The Supreme Court Building resembles a Greek temple. This white marble building is comprised of a central section and two flanking wings. These wings are longer and higher than the rest of the building, leading from an embellished front portico (west side) to a similar, less ornate design element on the east side. Roughly $3 million of imported and domestic marble were used. The exterior walls are of Vermont marble—24,700 blocks in all—varying in weight from 200 pounds to 63 tons. The roof features white tile bordered by a white marble terrace and balustrade. The inner courtyards are white Georgia marble. Above the basement level, the entrance halls and corridors are Alabama marble. The courthouse measures 385 ft from front to back and 304 ft from side to side.

A short staircase, bordered by candelabra, leads to a 100 ft wide, oval **plaza.** The candelabra feature carved panels depicting Justice holding a sword and scales, and the three Fates weaving the Thread of Life. The lampposts also feature ram's heads on the top of the base and lion's feet at the bottom to symbolize strength. Flagpoles with sculptured bronze bases stand at either end of the plaza. The bas-relief sculptures feature eight tiers of designs such as a shield and rinceau; cherubs holding symbols of Justice, including scales of Justice, a sword (symbolizing the strength of Justice), a mask and torch (ability to uncover truth), a book (education and learning), a pen and mace (legislation and power of law); and the four elements: air, earth, water, and fire. An eagle is perched atop each pole.

In the center of the plaza, a great staircase rises toward the **front portico,** flanked near the summit by two huge white marble cheek blocks weighing 45 tons each. Both bear allegorical statues by James E. Fraser. To the west is the female figure of *Contemplation of Justice.* In her right hand she holds a model of the figure of Justice. Her left hand rests on a book of laws. The other, male figure represents *The Guardian, or Authority, of Law.* All of the building's sculptures, except for these two statues, were completed on the premises. These statues were installed on Nov 25, 1935.

Above the steps, Corinthian columns support a **pediment bearing nine sculptures** by Robert Aitken. The three center figures are Liberty Enthroned, guarded by Order and Authority. The scales of Justice lie across Liberty's lap. On either side are figures representing council, research past, and research present. Aitken sculpted his figures to resemble people who had been instrumental in the creation of law and the Supreme Court. On the north side are a young Chief Justice Taft (portrayed as a student at Yale and representing research present), Secretary of State Elihu Root, and Court architect Cass Gilbert. To the south are Chief Justice Hughes, the pediment's sculptor Robert Aitken, and Chief Justice Marshall as a young man, representing research past. The frieze in the pediment declares, "Equal Justice under Law."

The **bronze doors** at the top of the steps were designed by John Donnely, Jr. They were modeled after the Columbus doors on the east side of the Capitol Building. Each weighs 13,000 pounds, and together they depict the evolution of the legal system from ancient times to the 20C. The doors stand 17 ft high, measure 9½ ft across, and bear four bas-relief panels. The scenes depict such events as the trial scene from the shield of Achilles; a Roman praetor publishing an edict; Julian and a pupil; Justinian publishing the Corpus Juris; King John sealing the Magna Carta; the chancellor publishing the first Statute of Westminster; Lord Coke barring King James from sitting as judge; and Chief Justice Marshall and Justice Story.

The **pediment on the east side of the building** bears sculptures by Herman A. MacNeil and explores the contributions of Eastern and Mediterranean civilizations to the development of the law. These lawgivers are Moses, the central figure bearing the tablets of Hebraic law; Confucius, to the north, and Solon, codifier of Greek law, to the south. These central figures are flanked by symbolic groups representing means of enforcing the law, tempering justice with mercy, settlement of disputes between states, and maritime and other functions of the Supreme Court. Aesop's tortoise and hare appear at the ends of the sculpture group, representing the slow but sure progress of the law. The architrave is inscribed with the words "Justice the Guardian of Liberty."

## Interior
**Ground floor.** Enter the Supreme Court Building through the entrance on the north side. Walk south along the corridor, passing the cafeteria and snack bar, to the east end of the **Lower Great Hall.** A statue of John Marshall (1883; William Wetmore Story) is located here. This piece stood on the west lawn of the Capitol until 1981, when it was moved inside the Court Building. Behind the statue are cases displaying models of the current courtroom and the Old Supreme Court Chamber in the Capitol.

From the Marshall statue, turn right into the Lower Great Hall, which features changing exhibits. The permanent exhibit at the west end of the hall discusses the history of the Court, the construction of the building, the allegorical artwork found on the exterior of the building, and displays models of the lavish interior rooms, including the offices of the justices. The gift shop is located on the east side of the hall. Restrooms flank the gift shop.

Return to the Lower Great Hall. After the exhibit about the construction of the Court, turn left. On the right is a staircase to the first floor.

**First floor.** The staircase leads into the **Great Hall,** a beamed and coffered passage lined with Doric columns leading to the courtroom. Busts of former justices are set in niches on marble pedestals along the corridor. Two oak doors at the corridor's east lead into the courtroom.

The **courtroom** measures 82 by 91 ft and has a 44 ft high ceiling. The room is bordered by 24 Ionic columns from Old Convent Quarry Siena marble from Liguria, Italy. The four walls and their adorning friezes are constructed of Ivory Vein marble from Alicante, Spain. Italian and African marble border the floor.

The **four marble panels** on the walls are the work of Adolph A. Weinman. Above the justices' bench (**east wall**), the two seated figures at the center symbolize the majesty of the law and power of government; the group on the far left of the same panel represents the safeguard of the liberties and rights of the people in their pursuit of happiness. To the far right on this panel is the defense of human rights, suggested by figures armed with a hammer and sword, and protection of innocence, depicted by a woman hugging a young boy and girl.

The **south wall** illustrates a procession of lawgivers: Menes (holding the ankh, an Egyptian symbol for life), Hammurabi (wearing a sword and quiver over his toga), Moses (carrying the two stone tablets of the Ten Commandments), Solomon (wearing a crown and pondering an issue with his chin resting on his fist), Lycurgus (holds a helmet and scroll), Solon (holds a scroll), Draco (looks stern), Confucius (the only one not depicted with a profile image), and Octavian (dressed in Roman battle garb with a spear and sword). The allegorical figures at either end represent history (left) and fame (right). The winged figure between Moses and Solomon is Authority. Between Solon and Draco is the winged Light of Wisdom.

The panel on the **north wall** features the lawgivers Napoleon (holding a staff and wearing an intricate gown), John Marshall (cloaked in a Supreme Court gown and holding a book of laws), Sir William Blackstone (wearing an English wig and judicial robe), Hugo Grotius (holding a book of laws), St. Louis (Louis IX) (wearing a crown and holding a sword), King John (holding a scroll representing early English constitutional law and wearing chain-mail armor), Charlemagne (wearing a crown and holding a sword vertically), Mohammed (wearing a shroud and holding an open book), and Justinian (holds a staff and crown). These characters are flanked by winged figures representing liberty, peace, and philosophy. At the center is Equity and Rights of Man.

The **west wall**'s panel depicts Justice (holding a balance) and the winged female figure of Divine Inspiration in the center. They are flanked by Wisdom (a male with an owl on his shoulder) and Truth (a female holding a mirror and rose). To the far left, the struggle of good over evil portrays the powers of good—security, harmony, peace, charity, and defense of virtue—protecting a child while listening to a harpist, with one figure holding a dove. The far right represents the powers of evil—corruption (two figures wrestling a serpent), slander (two cloaked figures whispering), deceit (a masked figure), and despotic power (a figure suited in armor).

The windows were installed on the north and south walls to prevent sunlight from streaming into the faces of the justices or the counsel addressing the bench. The justices are seated by seniority, as is customary in American courts. The chief justice is seated in the middle and the associate justices flank this seat alternating to the right and left. Counsel sits at the desk behind the chief justice. The marshall of the Court sits to the right of the justices. This person is responsible for maintenance and security of the Court. At the desk to the left is the clerk of the Court who administers the Court's calendars and supervises admission of attorneys to the Supreme Court bar. The red benches along the north side of the courtroom are reserved for the press. Guests of the Court are seated on the red benches to the south. The black chairs before both benches are for Court officials and visiting dignitaries. The justices have been wearing black robes since 1800. As per tradition, each day that the Court is in session, white quills are placed on counsel tables.

Exit the courtroom and walk west through the Great Hall. At the first doorway, turn left and proceed down the steps to the right. At the foot of the staircase, turn right. Walk through the Lower Great Hall and return to the John Marshall statue. To the right at the end of the hall is the **theater.** Also to the right is a viewing area for one of the Supreme Court's spiral staircases. Walk toward the theater. Turn left into the first hallway. Immediately on the left is the **staircase.** Closed to public traffic, the staircase is one of the building's two cantilevered Alabama marble staircases. The only others like them in the world are in the Paris Opera and the Vatican. Each is five stories tall and completely supported by the 136 overlapping steps that extend into the wall.

The three other floors are inaccessible to the public.

To see a sampling of historic Capitol Hill structures and the residences of famous Washingtonians exit the Supreme Court Building and walk east on Maryland Ave to Constitution Ave N.E. Follow Constitution Ave to 4th St. Turn right and walk south on 4th St to E. Capitol St. On the south side of E. Capitol St are two houses (c. 1880; August C. Schoenborn), **325–327 E. Capitol St,** worth noting. These three-story Italianate houses were designed by a draftsman who worked with Thomas U. Walter on the 1850s and 1860s Capitol Building extensions.

Walk one more block south on 4th St. At A St turn right to **326 A St S.E.** (1850). Constantino Brumidi, an Italian immigrant who devoted 25 years to painting the interior of the Capitol, including the *Apotheosis of Washington* on the Capitol Rotunda, lived in this house. Turn back and walk east to **408 A St S.E.** (1892; Nicholas T. Haller). Known as the **Mary L. Hill House,** it was built at a cost of $8,500 for John H. Nolan. Note the pressed copper walls, mosaic detailing, and carved oak posts in the recessed entry.

Continue east to 5th St and turn left. Cross E. Capitol St, turn right, and walk to **506 E. Capitol St N.E.** This is the **S. W. Tullock House** (1887; attributed to William Sheets). Builder T. J. Holmes added this unique façade to an existing house, an "improvement" that cost $4,000. Also note the arched stained glass windows. Next door is the **Sarah McC. Spofford House** (1896; William Yost and Bros.), **508 E. Capitol St N.E.** The façade of the house was revamped in a classical style, including the addition of the bay window, as Victorian-period design elements became less fashionable.

Proceed east on E. Capitol St to **616 E. Capitol St N.E.** (c. 1885; Appleton P. Clark, Jr.). This house has been described as the "purest example of the Queen

Anne style on Capitol Hill"—Queen Anne is a catchall label for buildings incorporating various styles and eclectic design elements. This three-story house features a square bay that projects out from the basement all the way up to the roof. The red brickwork is highlighted with corbeled, or protruding, bricks and molded ornamental terra-cotta. Clarke had worked with Alfred B. Mullett, architect of the Old Executive Office Building, for three years before striking out with his own office in 1886.

Continue east to **638–642 E. Capitol St N.E.** (1890; Charles Gessford). This four-house row is Queen Anne in style and has similar features to 616 E. Capitol, such as a protruding bay, corbeled brick, and terra-cotta detailing. Gessford was a prolific architect and builder on Capitol Hill.

Walk east nearly four blocks to **1014 E. Capitol St N.E.** (1889; Edwin H. Fowler). This house is known as the **D. T. and Eugenia E. Donohoe House.** The white limestone building is in the Richardsonian Romanesque style, a genre that combines such Romanesque elements as columns with rounded archways, a favorite detail of famed architect H. H. Richardson.

Continue east and cross 11th St to Lincoln Park (Hilliard Robinson), E. Capitol St, between 11th and 12th Sts N.E.

## Lincoln Park
**Highlights:** At the west end of this seven-acre park is the Emancipation Monument.

> ### Washington Notes
> Though part of L'Enfant's original 1791 plan, this plot remained nameless until 1867, when it became the first site in the country dedicated to the memory of President Lincoln. Until then the area was used as a neighborhood dump, and during the Civil War it housed the Lincoln Hospital.

## Grounds
On the park's east side stands the **Emancipation Monument** (1876; Thomas Ball), a life-size bronze statue of President Lincoln standing over a slave, urging him to rise to freedom. Beside the slave figure is a frayed whip, a whipping post, chains, and other symbols of bondage. The head of the slave was based on a photograph of David Archer, the last person to be recaptured under the Fugitive Slave Act. Former slaves raised $17,000 and commissioned the monument. Frederick Douglass was the keynote speaker at the 1876 dedication.

The **Mary McLeod Bethune Monument** (1974; Robert Berks) at the east end of the park honors Bethune, the 15th child born to a family of freed slaves in 1875 on a cotton plantation near Mayesville, South Carolina. She grew up to become a great educator and founder of the National Council of Negro Women in 1935, an organization that worked to improve the living and working conditions of African American families. This organization sponsored the monument's construction. Bethune served as president of the Cookman Institute of Jacksonville, Florida, for 30 years until her retirement in 1947. She was the only African American woman advisor to Franklin D. Roosevelt, acting as director of the Division of Negro Affairs of the National Youth Administration during the Depression.

The monument depicts Bethune handing a copy of her legacy to an 11-year-old boy and an 8-year-old girl. In her right hand she holds the cane presented to her by Franklin Roosevelt. Bethune's own words, her "Last Will and Testament," are inscribed on the base: "I leave you love. I leave you hope. I leave you the challenge of developing confidence in one another. I leave you a thirst for education. I leave a respect for the use of power. I leave you faith. I leave you racial dignity. I leave you a desire to live harmoniously with your fellow man. I leave you, finally, a responsibility to our young people."

The monument was the first in the capital dedicated to an African American, as well as the first dedicated to an American woman in a public park.

### Washington Notes

Charlotte Scott, a freed woman from Virginia who is credited with conceiving the idea for a moment to freed slaves, donated the first five dollars. These dollars were her first earnings as a free woman.

Exit Lincoln Park on 11th St S.E., cross North Carolina Ave, and proceed south. One block south is **Sladen's Walk,** a cobblestone alley stretching from 11th to 12th St S.E. There is a small swatch of grass to the left of the alley called Sladen's Park. Continue south on 11th St to **132–144 11th St S.E.** (1865–67; Charles Gessford). This span, called **Philadelphia Row,** is known as one of the longest unbroken blocks of row houses in the capital. Gessford is said to have given these houses plain façades so they might be reminiscent of the Federal-style townhouses in his homesick wife's native city of Philadelphia. Another way Gessford made them different from neighboring residences was by building them lower to the ground—only five steps separate the double front doors from the sidewalk. The row was nearly demolished in the 1960s to make way for a highway, but public outcry prevented this from happening.

Walk one block south to Independence Ave S.E. Turn right and walk one block to 10th St. Turn left and proceed to **200–208 10th St S.E.** (1891; Charles Gessford). These five two-and-one-half story red brick houses are known as **George W. Gessford Row.** Gessford spent $10,000 on this Queen Anne–style row as a speculative venture. These houses represent typical 19C middle-class housing. A high basement level afforded more privacy and kept out street noise for the first-floor living room set in the projecting, square bay; it also let natural light into the basement.

Return to Independence Ave and turn left. Walk west three blocks to 7th St and turn left. Before the advent of supermarkets, Washingtonians purchased meat, fish, produce, baked goods, and sundry goods from purveyors who set up stalls at markets that dotted the city, such as Eastern Market (1873; Adolph Cluss; 1908, Snowden Ashford; DL).

## Eastern Market

7th St and North Carolina Ave S.E. ☎ 546-2698. Open Tues–Sat 7:30–6; Sun 9–4. Closed Mon. The city's famed flea market, outside the building, is open Sat–Sun 7–6 year-round.

### History

A farmer's market has been located on this site since 1802. This building was constructed in two major phases. The South Hall, the market's original structure, built in 1873, was designed by Adolph Cluss, a German architect known for his Marxist politics. Cluss also designed or oversaw construction of nearly all D.C. public buildings erected between 1862 and 1876. The North and Center Halls, constructed by Snowden Ashford, the building inspector and later municipal architect for the District of Columbia, in 1908. In 1991 the market was placed on the National Register of Historic Places.

Originally, 85 stalls selling flowers, meat, baked goods, and produce filled the three halls. Rent for a stall was $3.75 per month. By 1960, however, changing shopping habits and the advent of the large supermarket had reduced the market's usefulness, and only two retail tenants occupied the building. In 1963, 15 fish merchants who were forced to leave the Central City Fish Market made the Eastern Market their new home, and the market enjoyed a revival.

The Eastern Market has endured many changes in tenants and use since, and today most of its space is occupied. Unfortunately, the physical structure of the building requires serious renovation. Though the Capitol Hill neighborhood remains firmly committed to maintaining the market's existence, debate over the nature of its rehabilitation has, to this point, delayed any substantial renovation.

Plans to renovate the Eastern Market first got under way around 1970, when the federal and District governments both provided $250,000 to repair the brick building's exterior. Later in the same decade, the U.S. Department of Commerce allocated $1 million to repair the roof. Since then relatively little has been done to renovate the structure.

## Exterior
This warehouse-like red brick structure features bull's-eye and round-arched windows and a tile roof. A cast-iron shed runs the length of the 7th St exterior.

## Interior
Various purveyors, such as Union Meat Co., Thos. Calomiris and Sons, Bowers Fancy Dairy, and Capitol Hill Poultry have established stalls at this indoor/outdoor emporium. Customers can buy a variety of fresh food items.

## *The Maples*
Continue south on 7th St, crossing Pennsylvania Ave. Turn right at D St. and walk to **619 D St S.E.**, one of the oldest houses still standing on Capitol Hill. It was once known as the Maples (1795–96; William Lovering).

### History
This house was constructed for Captain William Mayne Duncanson, an entrepreneur who invested heavily in the speculative real estate market of the new capital. When demand for property was lower than anticipated, Duncanson was forced to declare bankruptcy in 1809. During the War of 1812 the British used the house as a field hospital. Francis Scott Key bought the house in 1815 but quickly sold it. In the 1840s Major A. A. Nicholson and his wife, a high-society couple, lived here. Their marriage crumbled as the major doted on their neighbor Daniel Carroll's daughter Sallie. Faced with depression and heartache, Mrs. Nicholson killed herself in the house and the major married his mistress. Senator John Clayton purchased the Maples in 1856 and soon added a ballroom. He hired Capitol muralist Constantino Brumidi to decorate the room with frescoes, which

were destroyed when the addition was later razed. The house was expanded in 1871 to 21 rooms. In 1936 Friendship House, the city's oldest settlement house (a social services organization), purchased the property and hired Horace W. Peaslee to renovate it. Lovering had designed the house to be entered through the South Carolina Ave façade, but Peaslee relocated the main entrance to D St.

Return to 7th St and turn right. Walk south, cross E St, and turn right onto G St. Proceed west to **636 G St S.E.** (1844). John Philip Sousa, leader of the U.S. Marine Band from 1880 to 1892, was born in this house on Nov 6, 1854. According to legend, Sousa was actually born John Philip So, but added the *usa* as a tribute to his country.

## Christ Episcopal Church of Washington

Continue west on G St to Christ Episcopal Church of Washington (1805–7, Benjamin Latrobe and Robert Alexander; 1824, 1849, architects unknown; 1877–78, William Hoffman; 1953–54, Horace W. Peaslee; 1966, additional architects; DL), 620 G St S.E. This Episcopal church is the one of the oldest churches in Washington—Washington Parish was created in 1794 by an act of the Maryland Assembly—and is the mother church of the Episcopal parishes within the original boundaries of the Federal City.

### History

The congregation was founded on May 25, 1795, and met in David Carroll's tobacco barn on New Jersey Ave near D St. In 1806 William Prout, a wealthy landowner, donated land on which the parish built a new church. The cornerstone of the two-story structure was laid on Aug 3, 1806. Benjamin Henry Latrobe had been given credit for the original section of Gothic revival structure, but later evidence determined it was the work of Robert Alexander—a member of the vestry and Latrobe's chief contractor for the Washington Navy Yard project. This part of the church is sandwiched between the 1824 expansion to the north and the 1849 narthex and bell tower addition to the south. Other renovations were made in 1877–78, 1891, and 1921, but Horace W. Peaslee restored the church to Alexander's original intentions in 1954–55. Many servicemen from the Navy Yard and the Marine Barracks attended church here at one time, and it was affectionately known as "the new church in the Navy Yard."

In addition to the first commodore of the Navy Yard, several commandants of the Marine Corps, U.S. Marine Band leader John Philip Sousa, and Presidents Jefferson, Madison, and John Quincy Adams attended the church's services. In March 1812 Christ Church received the deed to Congressional Cemetery, the graveyard where many congressmen, city officials, and planners are buried.

## Ebenezer United Methodist Church

Continue west for nearly three blocks on G St. Turn right onto 4th St and walk three blocks north to D St. Standing on the northeast corner is Ebenezer United Methodist Church (1897; Crump and Palmer), 400 D St S.E.

### History

In 1807, the members of the Methodist Episcopal Church relocated from a structure on S. Capitol and N Sts into Daniel Carroll's barn in 1807. (The Christ Church congregation had recently moved out of the barn and into their newly completed church at 620 G St S.E.) Methodist Episcopal Church moved again in 1811 to a newly built church on 4th St between South Carolina Ave and G St. At one point the church was named Ebenezer, though it was later changed to Fourth Street Methodist Church. The black members of this integrated congregation quickly outgrew the gallery section assigned to them and established their own church—Little Ebenezer. The congregation purchased a lot on the corner of 4th and D Sts from William and Rachel Prout in 1838 and built a small frame building.

### Washington Notes

In 1864 Little Ebenezer became the first publicly funded school for blacks. The school was popular in the community and many government workers volunteered to teach classes.

To house the growing congregation a larger building was constructed on this site in 1870 but was severly damaged by a storm. The cornerstone for the current church was laid on May 18, 1897. Note the large rose window above the D St entrance. On the 4th St side of the church is a model of Little Ebenezer.

Walk north on 4th St and cross North Carolina Ave. Turn left onto C St. Walk one block, then turn right on 3rd St. On the west side of the street is **Theodore Mayer Row** (1887; John Granville Meyers), **217–223 3rd St S.E.** These four houses were constructed for $2,500 each. The use of brick, which was abundant and inexpensive at the time, coupled with such Victorian styling as wide, square bays and narrow windows are telltales of speculative housing. Continue north to Pennsylvania Ave. To see **Mayer's Block** (1887; John Granville Meyers), a row of three Queen Anne–style buildings built for $15,000 to house shops at the street level and families above, turn left and proceed west on Pennsylvania Ave to **221–225 Pennsylvania Ave S.E.**

Or, cross Pennsylvania Ave and turn right on Independence Ave. Walk one block to 4th St. Just north of Independence Ave, on the E. side at **120 4th St. S.E.,** is a three-story Italianate house (c. 1867; architect unknown; 1958–68 restoration, C. Dudley Brown). From 1880 to 1888 Filippo Costaggini lived in this house. Costaggini was a painter who, after Constantin Brumidi, worked on the friezes and frescoes in the Capital Rotunda.

Continue north and turn left on A St. On the southeast corner of of A and 3rd Sts is **St. Mark's Episcopal Church** (1888–89; T. Buckler Ghequier; 1894, addition; 1926, addition, Delos Smith; 1930, addition; 1965 renovations, Kent Cooper & Associates; DL). The red brick church exhibits a marriage of Victorican and Romanesque revival styles and features heavy oak doors with wrought-iron hinges, molded terra-cotta belts enriching the brickwork, and a Louis Comfort Tiffany stained glass window (1888–89) in the clerestory. This window is a reproduction of the central section of Gustave Doré's *Christ Leaving the Praetorium.* The other windows were created by the New York studio of Mayer of Munich. The tower is 103 ft tall; the arched belfry is open. The church began as a mission of Christ Church but became a separate parish in 1869. From 1896 to 1902 it served as the Episcopal cathedral for the Diocese of Washington. President Lyndon Johnson and other Washington power brokers have attended services here.

Turn right and walk north on 2nd St. To the left is the Folger Shakespeare Library.

## Folger Shakespeare Library

201 E. Capitol St S.E. ☎ General information: 544-4600; theater box office: 544-7077. Web: www.folger.edu. Open Mon–Sat 10–4. Closed federal holidays. Admission: free. Folger Reading Room and Architecture tours Mon–Fri 11; Sat 11 and 1. Garden tours every third Sat April–Oct 10 and 11. Group tours by appointment; ☎ 675-0365. Wheelchair accessible at south entrance. Museum shop open Mon–Sat 10–4. Special events include musical concerts by in-residence Folger Consort, lectures, early music ensemble, children's programs, monthly poetry readings, PEN/Faulkner fiction readings, and Shakespeare's Birthday Open House (Sun closest to April 23). For special events, ☎ 544-7077. Folger Reading Room and research facilities accessible only by prior arrangement.

The Folger (1928–32; Paul Cret; 1985, Hartman-Cox) houses the world's largest collection of early Shakespearean works as well as other rare Renaissance books and manuscripts. The Folger Library is devoted to the preservation and celebration of English Renaissance culture. Although the library's main function is as a research institution for the academic community and the collection is accessible primarily to scholars, the Folger Shakespeare Library offers many exhibits, concerts, lectures, performances, festivals, and literary readings for the general public.

**Highlights:** The Folger presents performances of Elizabethan music and plays. The Great Hall features rotating exhibits from the library's collection of Renaissance books, paintings, prints, manuscripts, musical instruments, and costumes. The Reading Room, accessible only by prior arrangement, houses the library's extensive collection and serves as a research center. The interior of the Elizabethan Theatre is a small, roofed replica of the Globe Theatre, the playhouse where Shakespeare's works were originally performed.

### History

The Folger Shakespeare Library is the result of Henry Clay Folger and wife Emily Jordon's inspiration. In 1879, after hearing a speech delivered by Ralph Waldo Emerson while studying at Amherst College, Folger purchased his first set of Shakespeare's plays. The young scholar went on to receive a law degree from Columbia but pursued business. He clerked for Charles Pratt, a partner of John D. Rockefeller. This led to employment with Standard Oil Company. He eventually became chairman of the board.

According to legend, Folger bought his first copy of the Fourth Folio at Bang's Auction House in New York. His $107.50 bid was more than he could afford, so he arranged to pay it in four installments. In 1885 he married Emily Jordan, a schoolteacher with an interest in literature. As a wedding gift, Folger gave his bride a reduced facsimile of the 1623 First Folio edition of Shakespeare's works.

As Folger climbed the corporate ladder and his wealth increased, so did his collection of rare Shakespearean and Renaissance works. In the following years, Folger acquired hundreds of other priceless works. By 1930, the Folgers owned 79 of the approximately 250 First Folios known to exist. The Folgers traveled to England frequently on buying trips to supplement the collection. The Folgers acquired the collection's rarest book, the only surviving quarto of *Titus Andronicus*, for

$10,000 in 1905. As the collection grew, the Folgers had their books and other holdings cataloged, packed, and stored in fireproof warehouses.

To give their 7,000-volume collection a proper home, the Folgers built the Folger Shakespeare Library. Emily Folger had lived in Washington during the Civil War, and fond memories of those years coupled with the proximity to the Library of Congress brought the couple to Washington. Over the course of nine years Folger purchased 14 parcels of land due east of the Library of Congress. Architect Paul Phillipe Cret, designer of the Organization of American States building, designed the Folger Shakespeare Library with Alexander Trowbridge, a consulting architect. Henry Clay Folger died in 1930, two weeks after the cornerstone of the building was laid. The building was dedicated in 1932 on April 23, the date accepted as Shakespeare's birthday, with President Herbert Hoover in attendance. Emily Folger died in 1936, after years of active participation and support.

The library's first director, Joseph Quincy Adams, broadened the scope and focus of the Folger Library. He acquired the extensive collection of Sir Leicester Harmsworth. This 9,000-volume collection included rare books printed in England between 1475 and 1640. The next director, Louis B. Wright, enhanced the collection with background material published in England and Europe before 1800, along with modern critical commentaries.

The library's collection of 250,000 volumes, 50,000 manuscripts, theatrical prints, drawings, Shakespearean playbills, and costumes makes the Folger Shakespeare Library one of the primary sources for English Renaissance studies. Throughout the years directors have added to the library's renowned collection. To date, the Folger Shakespeare Library owns 79 copies of Shakespeare's 1623 First Folio, 57 copies of the 1632 Second Folio, 23 copies of the Third Folio, 37 copies of the 1685 Fourth Folio, and 208 quarto copies of plays and poems published before 1640. In addition to the Shakespeare collection, the library also has valuable books and materials from Europe in the 16C, 17C, and 18C.

## Exterior

The exterior has been described as neoclassical as well as Art Deco and is constructed of white Georgia marble. The façade features a variety of embellishments. Nine bas-relief sculptures (1932; John Gregory) adorn the **north façade** (E. Capitol St Side) directly below the windows of the Great Hall. Entitled *Scenes from Shakespeare,* these six-ft-square panels depict scenes from Shakespeare's tragedies, comedies, and historical plays. The first relief (left to right) illustrates Bottom and Titania from *A Midsummer Night's Dream.* The next is a scene from *Romeo and Juliet,* when the couple is parting after their wedding ceremony. Juliet's nurse is there as her chaperone. The third panel recreates a climactic scene from *The Merchant of Venice.* The characters (left to right) are Shylock, a judge, Portia, Bassanio, and Antonio. The group watches as Shylock wields a knife and demands a "pound of flesh" from Antonio. The fourth panel depicts a scene from *Macbeth.* Macbeth (right) looks on as the three witches chant incantations over a boiling cauldron. The center relief, from *Julius Caesar,* shows Brutus and his comrades inspecting the dead body of Julius Caesar. The sixth scene depicts the heath scene from *King Lear.* The emotionally distraught Lear shouts in the storm and is observed by the Fool and the Earl of Kent. A relief for *Richard III* depicts the title character with his two nephews, Edward V and brother Richard. On either side are the Archbishop of Canterbury and the Duke of Buckingham. The eighth relief shows

Prince Hamlet, his mother Queen Gertrude, and the ghost of his father. The final relief represents a scene from *Henry IV*. Price Hal, later Henry V, stands to the left. Falstaff occupies the center, with Bardolph at the far right.

Other bas-relief panels also adorn the façade. Greek masks of Comedy and Tragedy (1932; John Gregory) are located on the west and north façades. Also at the two entrances on E. Capitol St, two sculptures of the winged horse Pegasus decorate the plaza.

An Elizabethan Garden graces the east side of the library. It features herbs and flowers grown in Shakespeare's period.

The *Puck Fountain* (1932; Brenda Putnam) is located at the west side of the library. The four-ft-high statue depicts Puck, the impish fairy from *A Midsummer Night's Dream*. The figure kneels on his left knee, with his hands raised looking off into the distance. His spry facial expression is one of mock horror. One of Puck's noted statements is inscribed on the pedestal: "What fools these mortals be."

## Interior

The visitors' entrance is at the northeast end of the library. Once inside, the information desk and box office are immediately on the left. At the south end of this foyer is the **Elizabethan Theatre.** This half-timbered reproduction of a 16C Elizabethan theater allows modern-day patrons to experience drama somewhat as people did in Shakespeare's time. The theater features a rectangular stage supported by carved oak columns. In keeping with the habit of Shakespeare's time, there are no curtains. Scenery is moved into place in view of the audience. A curtain, painted the color of the sky, suggests an open-air venue; Shakespeare's plays were performed in an open-air theater.

On the ceiling above the stage is Shakespeare's famous quote: "All the world's a stage and all their men and women merely players." Leaded glass Juliet windows also hark to the Elizabethan era. Shakespearean plays as well as works by contemporary playwrights are staged here. The library's in-residence ensemble also hosts concerts.

Just west of the theater's entrance is a staircase. Restrooms, a cloakroom, and water fountains are located downstairs. From the foyer turn west and proceed into the Great Hall.

The Tudor-style **Great Hall** has floor-to-ceiling oak paneling on the walls. The strapwork (a pattern of beams and plaster that appears like a honeycomb) ceiling bears Shakespeare's coat of arms, fleur-de-lis, and the Tudor rose—motifs that are continued throughout the library. A bust of Folger is placed at the center of the south wall. At the west end wall of the gallery is the shield and eagle of the United States. Inset in the tile floor are the Greek masks for Comedy and Tragedy. At the opposite end of the hall, the coat of arms of Queen Elizabeth, who reigned during Shakespeare's time, is mounted above the doorway. A tiled floor connects the two ends, in theory connecting the United States to the spirit of Shakespeare and England. Temporary exhibitions of priceless artifacts from the library's collections are displayed here. To reach the Folger museum shop, continue west through the Great Hall. Pass the researcher's entrance. The shop is located just west of that entrance. From this foyer turn left.

The entrance to the **Folger Reading Room** is on the left side of this hallway. Note: Permission to visit the Folger Reading Room must be arranged in advance.

At one end of the room sits a bust of Shakespeare, a replica of a piece by Geraert Janssen; the original is in Trinity Church, the church in Stratford-upon-Avon where the Bard's body rests. Behind the bust, Frank O. Salisbury's portraits of the Folgers in their honorary academic robes from Amherst can be seen. The Folgers' ashes rest here behind a memorial plaque. The stained glass window at the other end of the room illustrates Shakespeare's descriptions from *As You Like It* (Nicola D'Ascenzo) about the seven stages of man from infancy to old age.

Exit the Folger onto E. Capitol St. Walk west to 2nd St S.E. and turn left. Walk one block to the entrance of the Library of Congress–John Adams Building.

# Library of Congress

The Library of Congress was created in 1800 to assist congressmen in the preparation of debates and drafting of legislation. First located in the basement of the Capitol, the Library today is composed of three buildings—named for Thomas Jefferson, John Adams, and James Madison—and houses a collection of more than 115 million items in 460 languages, including archaic languages. The Library features more than 17 million books in its catalogs. More than 9 million of these items are monographs, bound newspapers, pamphlets, technical reports, books printed in large type or raised letters, or books printed before 1501. More than 88 million items in the special collections consist of record albums, radio and television broadcasts and other audio materials, manuscripts, maps, microforms, and other visual materials. It is said that the Library collects a new item every five seconds of each workday.

Today the Library's resources are also available to the executive and judicial branches of government, as well as the general public. Library facilities are open to researchers, including students, older than 18. In Fiscal Year 98 the Library responded to reference inquiries from 548,763 readers who visited the Library in person, plus 560,000 research assignments for Congress. The general public can use the materials in the Library but may not take any materials out.

The Library also comprises the U.S. Copyright Office, which administers copyright law, and the Congressional Research Service, which researches and compiles data for members of Congress. Through the National Library Service for the Blind and Physically Handicapped, the Library produces magazines and books in Braille and large type that are distributed through regional libraries.

### History

An Act of Congress on April 24, 1800, signed by President John Adams, authorized the creation of a library as a reference facility for members of Congress. Previously, Congress had been supplied with books by the Philadelphia Library Company (the federal government was then based in Philadelphia). However, with the government relocating to the new Federal City, Congress decided to develop a governmental library. With $5,000 the first books were ordered from England. The initial collection of 740 volumes and 3 maps arrived in 11 hair trunks and a map case. The new collection included books on law, political science, and history, as well as maps.

The Capitol housed this collection in the office of the secretary of the Senate until 1814. On Aug 24, 1814, British troops invaded the Federal City and torched the Capitol, using the Library's 3,000 books as kindling. It is said the British did this in retaliation for the previous year's burning by Americans of Parliament in what is today called Toronto. The Library's collection went up in smoke.

Thomas Jefferson, retired at this point, needed money and believed in the Library. He offered Congress his private book collection, considered one of the finest in the U.S., at his cost for the books—on the condition that the Library take all of them. After much debate, Congress in Jan 1815 agreed to Jefferson's price of $23,950 for 6,487 volumes. By the following May, ten wagons carting the collection from Jefferson's home at Monticello had arrived and been unpacked. The Library, along with Congress, was located in the Old Brick Capitol (where the Supreme Court stands today) while the Capitol was being rebuilt.

Two more fires in the 1800s destroyed much of the Library's resources. In 1825, a small blaze burned some duplicate volumes. But on Christmas Eve, 1851, a serious fire destroyed more than 35,000 volumes, about two-thirds of the Library's holdings, including the collection purchased from Jefferson—which was then referred to as Mr. Jefferson's Library. Congress quickly appropriated a sum of money to replace the books and construct a multigalleried series of rooms in the west front of the Capitol Building to house the collection.

A few years later, Joseph Henry, the secretary of the Smithsonian, decided the institution's mission was to perform scientific research, and transferred the Smithsonian's collection of 40,000 volumes to the Library. The government decided that the Smithsonian was responsible for preserving artifacts, the National Archives kept governmental documents, and the Library of Congress held books, maps, and images. But the most significant turn in the Library's history occurred with the naming of Ainsworth Rand Spofford as Librarian of Congress.

In 1864 President Lincoln appointed Spofford, who served from 1864 to 1897. Spofford told Congress and the president that he could greatly increase the Library's collection without spending any money. His master stroke was advocating a change in copyright procedures. In 1870 Spofford convinced Congress to pass a law in which the Library would receive two free copies of every book, map, chart, dramatic or musical composition, engraving, cut, print, or photograph submitted for copyright. Within the first 25 years of this copyright law, the Library received 371,636 books, 257,153 magazines, 289,617 musical scores, 73,817 photographs, 95,249 prints, and 48,048 maps. Additional legislation provided the Library with free copies of the *Congressional Record* and all American statutes. As a result, the Library's collection increased dramatically. In fact, the Library quickly outgrew its three-story space and Spofford used the Capitol's hallways, attic, and cellars for additional stack space. Spofford realized that the Library of Congress had become too large for the Capitol building to house and he approached Congress for additional space in 1871.

In 1873 Spofford won the lobby for more space. Congress appropriated funds to construct a new building to house the nation's growing collection. Congress announced a design competition for the building and received 28 designs. Eventually, an Italian Renaissance–style façade, submitted by Washington architects John L. Smithmeyer and Paul J. Pelz, was chosen. Their design was based, in part, on the British Museum, the Bibliotheque Nationale, and Charles Garnier's Paris Opera House, which had been completed in 1875 and was one of the most acclaimed buildings in the 19C.

However, the Joint Committee soon decided that it did not want the Italian design and announced a second contest. This contest yielded another 41 designs, including classic Greek architecture, Victorian Gothic, French, German, Romanesque, and Modern Renaissance. Finally in 1885, after much debate, the Joint Committee agreed to a modified version of Smithmeyer and Pelz's original 1873 design. In 1896 Congress authorized the purchase of land east of the Capitol for the new structure.

The design was changed drastically between 1873 and 1885 from a functional institution to a public showplace. The architects decided to create a "Temple of the Arts" as a tribute to art and literature, and as testimony to American culture. Ground breaking took place in 1886, but an argument between the contractors and the architects brought construction to a standstill in Aug 1887. Six months passed, during which Smithmeyer conducted 615 tests on cement. Congress, fed up with the delays, fired him in 1888 and appointed General Thomas Lincoln Casey, chief of the Army Engineers. Casey had been involved with the construction of the Executive Office Building and was responsible for the eventual completion of the Washington Monument. Casey appointed Bernard Richard Green, a civil engineer, as superintendent and engineer for the project. Casey also appointed his son, Edward Pearce Casey, in 1892, to oversee the interior work and advise on the decoration. Green and the junior Casey approved each piece of ornamentation in the building.

The structure honors the "American Renaissance" with murals, mosaics, marble pillars, and sculptures by 50 American artists. The crowning glory of this building is the Main Reading Room's dome, which is 125 ft high and 100 ft wide. The first Library of Congress building was completed in 1897, ahead of schedule and $150,000 under the original budget appropriation of $6.5 million.

The collection was moved into the new building during the summer of 1897. The Library was opened to the public on Nov 1, 1897. In the first 11 months of 1888, half a million visitors toured the Jefferson Building.

John Russell Young, the first librarian in the Jefferson Building, skillfully organized the collection. As a former journalist Young had no prior experience in library management, but he devised programs and organized the Library's collection so that it was more useful and accessible. After two years, Young was succeeded by Herbert Putnam, former head of the Boston Public Library. Putnam remained at the post for 40 years.

Putnam made access to the collection even more efficient by cataloging resources on index cards. He also raised money for the Library by selling card sets to other libraries. He designed the first programs for the blind and loaned Braille books as well as books on phonograph and playback machines, in effect creating the "talking books" concept.

In 1912, Putnam, along with members of Congress, created a legislative reference bureau to prepare indexes, digests, and compilations of law for Congress. The Legislative Reference Service went into effect in 1914, and became the forerunner of the Congressional Research Service.

By the 1930s the Library had again outgrown its space. In 1939 the Art Deco John Adams Building, then known as the Annex, opened. In 1965 the Library petitioned for more space. The James Madison Memorial Building opened in 1980.

## *John Adams Building*

2nd St between Independence Ave and E. Capitol St S.E. ☎ Visitor Information (recording): 707-8000 or 707-9779; Visitor Services: 707-9956 (TTY). Web:

www.loc.gov. Open Mon–Sat 8:30–5. Closed Sun, federal holidays. Admission: free. Restrooms, telephones. Wheelchair accessible.

The John Adams Building (1935–39; Person and Wilson), the second Library of Congress building, has offices, storage space, and reading rooms. Murals in the two fifth-floor reading rooms may be of interest.

### History

In the late 1920s Putnam ran out of space in the Jefferson Building. In 1930, Congress authorized a plan for a second building and construction began on the "Annex" in 1935. The building's main functions are storage of the Library's holdings—it can hold twice as many books as the Jefferson Building—and office space for the cataloging specialists. By design, it features only two public reading rooms. The building was opened in 1939.

## Exterior

The building is faced with white Georgia marble. Adorning the bronze **entrance doors** are bas-relief sculptures by Lee Lawrie. The center doors on the west entrance feature six figures thought to have added to language and world communication. These are: Hermes, messenger of the gods; Odin, the war god who created the Viking-Germanic runic alphabet; Ogma, the god who created the Gaelic alphabet; Itzama, the Mayan god; Quetzalcoatl, the legendary god of the Aztecs; and Sequoya, creator of the Cherokee alphabet.

The other doors on the west entrance depict the history of the written word through legendary heroes: Thoth, an Egyptian god; Ts'ang Chieh, China's patron of writing; Nabu Sumero, an Akkadian god; Brahma, the Indian god; Cadmus, the prince who introduced writing to the Greeks; and Tahmurath, the ancient hero of the Persians.

The single door at the Independence Ave entrance is affixed with two figures. A man representing physical labor stands beneath the seal of the United States. A woman holding a book, in the center of laurel leaves, symbolizes intellectual labor.

## Interior

Enter the building through the bronze doors on the west side. In the lobby is the elevator bank. Take an elevator to the fifth floor. Proceed east along the corridor to the **Thomas Jefferson Reading Room.** Running the length of the walls in this room are impressive, 72 ft long murals painted by Ezra Winter. These murals feature Chaucer's Canterbury pilgrims. Winter painted the pilgrims as they were introduced in the *Canterbury Tales.* The piece begins on the west wall with the Miller. Chaucer rides with his back to the room. He is preceded by the Doctor of Physics and is shown turning to speak with the Lawyer. A quotation from the text explaining the pilgrimage is inscribed in the lunette on the north wall. A scene from the Prologue of the Franklin's Tale is depicted in the lunette on the south wall.

Return to the corridor and turn left. Walk south to the **South Reading Room.** Winter also painted the murals in this room. They were dedicated to Thomas Jefferson by Attorney General Francis Biddle on Dec 15, 1941, the sesquicentennial anniversary of the adoption of the Bill of Rights. Although separate, the four panels form a frieze which surrounds the room. The theme reflects Jefferson's thoughts on freedom, labor, the living generation, education, and democratic government. Quotations from Jefferson's writings about democracy, freedom, and government are inscribed on the paintings and the scenes depicted illustrate Jefferson's beliefs on each issue. At the north end, a portrait of Jefferson with Monticello in the background was painted in a lunette above the information desk. The frieze begins on the east wall.

Continue south along 2nd St. Cross Independence Ave and the plaza on the south side of the street to the entrance of the Library of Congress–James Madison Memorial Building.

# James Madison Memorial Building

Independence Ave between 1st and 2nd Sts S.E. ☎ Visitor Information (recording): 707-8000 or 707-9779; Visitor Services: 707-9956 (TTY). Web: www.loc.gov. Open Mon–Fri 8:30 A.M.–9:30 P.M.; Sat 8:30 A.M.–6 P.M. Closed Sun, federal holidays. Admission: free.

National Digital Library Visitors' Center. ☎ 707-4159. Open by appointment Mon–Fri 8:30–5. Library cafeteria located on the sixth floor. Open Mon–Fri 12:30–3. Snack bar located on ground floor. James Madison Sales Shop located in the lobby, open Mon–Sat 9:30–5. Restrooms, telephones. Wheelchair accessible.

The James Madison Memorial Building (1966–80; DeWitt, Poor and Shelton) is the largest library building in the world. It houses a Visitors' Information center, a number of reading rooms, and the Library of Congress's head offices. It also provides office space for the staffs of the Congressional Research Systems, Processing, and Copyright offices. The Madison Memorial Hall, Madison Foyer, and Current Events Corridor display rotating exhibits.

### History

By 1965, the Library of Congress had outgrown the Thomas Jefferson Building and the "Annex." Many of its staff and books were scattered around the metropolitan D.C. area. Congress authorized construction of a new building. The House of Representatives suggested that the building stand as a memorial to James Madison, fourth president of the U.S. and author of the Constitution, since there were no memorials honoring him in the District. The building was dedicated on April 24, 1980. When it opened, the Madison Building doubled the Library of Congress's space.

## Exterior

The façade is white marble and has an austere, modern design. A sculpture (Frank Eliscu) above the Independence Ave entrance illustrates a cascade of falling books.

## Interior

**First floor.** Enter the building through the Independence Ave side. To the left is **James Madison Memorial Hall.** It features marble columns and teak walls inscribed in gold with quotations of Madison's regarding government and democracy. A statue of James Madison (Walter Hancock) seated and marking a page of a closed text is at the end of the hall. At the entrance of the hall are two cases containing changing exhibits. Some of the items displayed are recent acquisitions while others are treasures from the collection of "America's Memory," the nickname for the Library of Congress. Across the lobby from Memorial Hall is the gift shop.

Just beyond the lobby is the **Madison Foyer.** Temporary exhibitions concerning current and historical events are displayed here. The **National Digital Library Visitors' Center** is in the room south of the Madison Foyer. The Library of Congress has undertaken an effort to digitalize its collection so access can be gained by people around the world via the Internet or CD-ROMs. So far 111 million items are accessible online. Multimedia demonstrations teach visitors how to use the Digital Library.

Return to the Madison Foyer and turn left. Take an elevator to the fourth floor.

**Fourth floor.** Proceed to the gallery at the end of the hall where the elevators are located. In the hallway outside the **U.S. Copyright Office** is an exhibit of original items that were submitted for copyrighting. Among the displays are the first Bert and Ernie puppets, Ken and Barbie dolls, an ad for Coke, baseball cards, and a copy of the "I Have a Dream" speech by Martin Luther King, Jr.

Take an elevator to the sixth floor.

**Sixth floor.** Walk to the gallery at the east end of the hall. The famous **Coronelli Globes** (1692–93) are exhibited in the hallway outside the cafeteria. Father Vincenzo Maria Coronelli (1650–1718) was an Italian scholar and geographer. He gained fame in 1683 when he created a set of globes for Louis XIV of France.

The cafeteria serves up great views and moderately priced fare. (Note: Credit cards are not accepted.) ☎ 707-8300.

Walk west along Independence Ave to 1st St. Turn right and cross Independence Ave. Walk to the Library of Congress–Thomas Jefferson Building (1871–75; John L. Smithmeyer and Paul Pelz; DL).

## Thomas Jefferson Building

1st St and Independence Ave S.E. ☎ Visitor Information (recording): 707-8000 or 707-9779; Visitor Services: 707-9956 (TTY). Web: www.loc.gov. Open Mon–Sat 10 A.M.–5:30 P.M. Closed Dec 25 and New Year's Day. The Main Reading Room in the Jefferson Building is open to researchers only. Tours are available Mon–Sat 11:30, 1, 2:30, and 4. Free, same-day tickets are available at Visitors' Center on ground floor of Jefferson Building. Some tours offer a sign language interpreter. Tour group size is limited and free tickets are necessary and available at the Visitor Information Desk in the lobby. Call the Visitor Services Office during the week for more information. ☎ 707-9779. Tickets for the American Treasures, a rotating exhibition of rare and significant items from the Library's collection, are free, but required. They are available on a first-come, first-served basis at the Visitor Information Desk on the ground floor. They may also be ordered for a nominal processing fee through Ticketmaster. ☎ (800) 551-SEAT. For information, ☎ 707-3834 or 707-6200 (TTY). A 12-minute orientation film runs continuously from 10–5:15 in the Visitors' Center. The Library also sponsors concerts, lectures, exhibits, and symposiums. Restrooms, telephones. Gift shop open Mon–Sat 9:30–5.

**Highlights:** An $81.5 million renovation of the interior of the Thomas Jefferson Building was completed in 1997. The Main Reading Room has been restored to its 19C splendor. A Gutenberg Bible, one of three surviving examples printed on vellum, is permanently displayed in this building, as is the 15C manuscript Bible of Mainz. The American Treasures exhibition displays a rotating collection of documents and artifacts from American history that includes books, maps, photographs, and recordings. The Bob Hope Gallery of Entertainment, which opened in May 2000, includes radio recordings and television and movie clips of a variety of famous performers as well as interactive stations where visitors can hear jokes told by Bob Hope.

### Washington Notes

On a site from 1st St to the center of the Library of Congress's Thomas Jefferson Building, there once stood a block called Carroll Row, named after its builder, Daniel Carroll. There were a half dozen houses on the block as well as the Carroll Hotel, where the inaugural ball for James Madison was held. This block was used as the British headquarters during the War of 1812 when British soldiers torched the Capitol and White House. During the Civil War political prisoners were jailed here, and the block became known as Carroll Prison. Abraham Lincoln, while a member of Congress, lived along this block in Anna G. Sprigg's boarding house.

## Exterior

The Thomas Jefferson Building is formidable in size and in decoration. The exterior granite walls were quarried in Concord, New Hampshire. Without the basement, the original floor space measured 326,195 ft, or almost eight acres. The structure has 2,165 windows. From north to south, the Library stretches 470 ft long, and from west to east it is 340 ft deep. The golden **Torch of Learning** capping the dome of the Main Reading Room rises to a height of 195 ft. The copper dome, located in the central portion of the building, originally was gilded with 23-karat gold leaf, though over the past 100 years the decoration has vanished.

As an "American Renaissance" structure, the Jefferson Building showcases the work of 50 American sculptors and painters. Even though each artist worked independently under separate contracts, their differing styles blend harmoniously. Spofford determined the symbols and allegories to be illustrated. Casey and Green instructed the artists what figures and scenes to create and where their pieces ought to be placed.

*The Fountain in the Court of Neptune* (Roland Hinton Perry), is located on the west side of the building between the two staircases on the street level of 1st St. The fountain represents the court of Neptune, who is seated in the center. Albert Weinert sculpted the two Nereids (daughters of Nereus), who are mounted on seahorses and flank Neptune. Also on either side of Neptune are Tritons, (Greek demigods with the lower body of a fish), who are blowing conch shells. Jets of water spew from the shells, as well as sea turtles, frogs, and a serpent located in the semicircular pool.

Look up to the **main entrance pavilion,** the exterior's most ornate façade. At 140 ft, it runs almost a third of the length of the structure. The long flight of steps leading to the three main entrance arches are made of granite quarried in Troy, New Hampshire. The posts at the foot of the steps support elaborate, electrified bronze candelabra. Three female figures sculpted in high-relief granite by Bela Lyon Pratt represent literature, science, and art, and adorn the triangular spaces flanking the entrance arches. Above Pratt's figures are nine granite busts of eminent men of literature—Demosthenes, Emerson, Irving, Goethe, Macaulay, Hawthorne, Scott, Dante, and Benjamin Franklin (positioned in the center)—above the main library windows visible behind the arches. Herbert

*Thomas Jefferson Building (Library of Congress). Courtesy of the Washington, D.C., Convention & Visitors Association.*

Adams, Fredrick Wellington Ruckstull, and Jonathon Scott Hartley sculpted these busts.

Adorning the 33 keystones of the second-story center and corner pavilion windows are thirty-three **male ethnological heads.** Sculptors William Boyd and Henry J. Ellicott, aided by a team of researchers from the Department of Ethnology in the National Museum of Natural History, created one of the most scientifically accurate series of ethnological models ever made. Beginning at the left side, the series of ethnicities includes: Russian Slav, Blond European, Brunette European, Modern Greek, Persian, Circassian, Hindu, Hungarian, Jew, Arab, Turk, Modern Egyptian, Abyssnian, Malay, Polynesian, Australian, Negrito, Zulu, Papuan, Sudan Negro, Akka, Fuegian, Botocudo, Pueblo Indian, Esquimaux, Plains Indian, Samoyede, Korean, Japanese, Ainu, Burmese, Tibetan, and Chinese.

Within the arches of the main pavilion the entrance to the Library is marked with three **bronze doors,** each about 14 ft high, 7½ ft wide, and weighing 3½ tons. The doors represent the evolution of the written word. *Tradition,* by Olin Levi Warner adorns the left side; *The Art of Printing,* by Frederick MacMonnies, decorates the central door; and *Writing,* begun by Warner and finished after his death by Herbert Adams, stands on the right.

## Interior

To enter the building, climb the first set of steps to the right of the Neptune fountain. Turn right into the plaza and walk toward the building. Cross the driveway and turn left. Proceed under the main set of steps that lead to the second floor. The visitor's entrance is to the right, under the steps.

Turn right in the foyer and walk past the water fountains. Turn left and walk through the metal detector. Turn left and walk to the information desk on the right. Continue down the corridor past the information desk. **The Visitor Orientation Theater** presents a 15-minute film about the Library of Congress. Farther down the corridor is the **George and Ira Gershwin Room,** containing rotating objects from the Library's Gershwin collection. The exhibition at press time features George Gershwin's piano and desk, Ira's typing table, and musical manuscripts, photos, and drawings from *Funny Face, Porgy and Bess,* and other Gershwin hits.

At the end of the corridor is the **Bob Hope Gallery of American Entertainment,** which opened in May 2000. This permanent exhibition presents a history of American entertainment from vaudeville through movies and television. Along with items from the Bob Hope Collection, including a special section devoted to Bob Hope's USO shows, the exhibit features material from the Library's film and television collection, the largest such collection in the world. At the interactive Joke File and Dial-a-Joke stations, visitors can select a topic and hear a joke told by Bob Hope from the comedian's more than 88,000 pages of jokes.

Exit the Bob Hope Gallery, walk back down the corridor past the visitor information desk, and turn right. Turn left and walk to the stairs. Climb this staircase to the first floor.

**First floor.** At the head of the stairs, turn right and walk west toward the front of the building. This hallway is known as the **South Corridor.** It features **murals by Henry Oliver Walker.** The mosaic and murals honor poetry. American poets are named in the ceiling on the north end and European poets are listed in the south end. Classic poets are honored with medallions in the center. Illustrated in the semicircular paintings are lines from poems by Tennyson, Keats, Wordsworth, Emerson, Milton, and Shakespeare. Lyric Poetry, surrounded by her attributes— Pathos, Truth, Devotion, Passion, Beauty, and Mirth—is painted in the mural on the east wall.

At the end of the corridor, turn right. The interior of the Jefferson Building is a spectacular, colorful, and heavily ornamented space with more than 100 murals and countless sculptures. It was designed so that as visitors venture closer to the Main Reading Room, the artwork becomes more dramatic and elaborate.

If visitors were able to enter the Library through the main doors on the left, they would be greeted by two statues on the right representing Minerva, the Roman goddess of wisdom and war. One figure holds a sword and torch, the second bears a scroll and globe. The Minerva motif is also repeated throughout the Great Hall, especially on both sides of the light sconces.

Turn right and walk into the **Great Hall,** which is made of gleaming white Italian marble and soars 75 ft at its center. Different types of marble blend with sculptures, mosaics, and murals to create a dramatic spectacle of color and texture. The brown marble in the floor comes from Tennessee; the red and gray marble sections of the floor were quarried in France. The floor is decorated by **brass plaques** that replicate the zodiac. At the center is a brass sunburst marking the points of a compass.

Flanking the hall are two **grand staircases** on either side of the room, leading to the colonnade on the second floor. Both are decorated with a comical series of babies, or putti. The work *Cascade of Marble Babies* (Philip Martiny) runs the length of both staircase railings. Each baby represents a 19C vocation or pursuit. On the lower end of the left staircase are four figures. A baby holding a spade and rake represents gardening. The next three babies portray a butterfly collector, a student reading, and a printer. The two larger babies flanking the globe are symbols of Asia and Europe, each pointing to their respective continents on the globe. In a niche directly below is a bust of Thomas Jefferson, a copy of one created by Jean-Antoine Houdon, a French sculptor. Continuing up the staircase, the babies represent music, a doctor, an electrician (holding a telephone), and an astronomer peering through a telescope. The three figures across the top of the landing represent the arts: painting, architecture, and sculpture.

Along the right staircase, from the lower end, the babies represent a mechanic, a hunter, a vinter (dressed like Bacchus, the Roman god of wine), and a farmer. On either side of this globe are figures representing Africa and America. In the niche below is a bust of George Washington, a copy of anther work by Houdon. Completing the staircase are a fisherman, soldier, chemist (blowing glass), and cook. Capping the staircase landing are figures honoring literature with Greek masks of Comedy and Tragedy and a scroll of poetry. At the base of both staircases are bronze figures holding the torch of learning.

Among the decorations in the north and east corridors of the Great Hall are marble bays and vaulted mosaic ceilings. Walk behind the left staircase to the **North Corridor.** It is decorated with themes of education and family. The names listed in the mosaic are the names of famous educators. The murals, entitled *The Family*, were painted by Charles Sprague Pearce. Along the side walls, the semicircular paintings represent recreation, study, labor, and religion. Below the group portrait are the names of the Librarians of Congress and the dates of their terms.

Walk east to the end of the hallway and turn right into the **East Corridor.** At the north end of the East Corridor is a case containing the **Gutenberg Bible,** one of three perfect vellum copies. The bible was purchased in 1930 for $1.5 million. At the other end of the corridor is a case containing a copy of the hand-printed 15C manuscript **Bible of Mainz.**

This is perhaps the most impressive hallway. On the ceiling between the archways are **circular mosaic medallions** that symbolize professions: music, painting, sculpture, poetry, natural science, mathematics, astronomy, engineering, natural philosophy, and architecture. Beneath each medallion are the names of two Americans who have distinguished themselves in those fields. The three professions of medicine, law, and theology are marked with medallions across the center of the ceiling. They were placed in the center because they were considered the most learned professions. The names of several authors are inscribed on the ceiling, including Longfellow, Tennyson, Gibbon, Cooper, Scott, Hugo, Cervantes, Dante, Homer, Milton, Bacon, Aristotle, Goethe, Shakespeare, Moliere, Moses, and Herodotus. John White Alexander created the series of murals titled *The Evolution of the Book* in this corridor. The series spins its tale beginning from the South wall with *The Cairn.* It illustrates a prehistoric man piling stones. This is followed by *Oral Tradition* (a cloaked figure animatedly relates a story) and *Egyptian Hieroglyphics* (a female watches as a man hammers into stone). On the north wall are three titled *Picture Writing* (a man paints on an animal skin), *The Manuscript Book* (monks copying texts), and *The Printing Press* (printers reviewing a freshly printed sheet).

Continue east to the entrance of the **Main Reading Room**—open only to researchers. Another series of allegorical paintings (Elihu Vedder) surround the entrance. They were painted in the semicircular areas created by the vaulted ceilings.

*Library of Congress (Main Reading Room). Photo credit: Michael Dersin. Courtesy of the Library of Congress.*

Above the Main Reading Room doors is *The Government,* which illustrates the results of good and bad government. At the center a figure holds a plaque inscribed with a quote from Lincoln: "A government of the people, by the people, for the people." To the left is *Corrupt Legislation,* which demonstrates fraud with a sliding scale. Next is *Anarchy.* On the other side of the central mural is good government. The first, *Good Administration,* is illustrated with an honest scale and a man dropping his ballot in a box. The second, *Peace and Prosperity,* shows citizens planting a tree and painting a vase.

Return to the Great Hall through the three arches. Once in the hall, turn around and look above the arches. Framing the center arch are two figures, *The Students*. The younger man pores through a book while the older man contemplates the knowledge he has acquired.

Walk to the right staircase and proceed to the second floor.

**Second floor.** At the top of the stairs turn left. Portraits of women are painted on the ceilings and walls to symbolize aspects of civilization. In the corners of the room are two portraits of females who represent various virtues such as justice, fortitude, and providence. Charles Eliot, former president of Harvard University, chose the quotations which are above each doorway and window on this floor. Printers' marks are illustrated above each arch, round window, and round painting.

Turn left and walk into the **North Corridor.** The ceiling paintings, *The Five Senses* (Robert Reid), are the circular wall paintings: *Wisdom*, *Understanding*, *Knowledge*, and *Philosophy*. George W. Maynard painted the virtues *Fortitude*, *Justice*, *Industry*, and *Concordia*. Look up to the ceiling and note the American and British printers' marks in the mosaic.

Walk to the end of the hallway and turn left. The **West Corridor** is decorated with a series of paintings by Walter Shirlaw, *The Sciences*, and German printers' marks. The round paintings, in the center of the ceiling, were done by William B. Van Ingen. They are titled *The Arts*.

At the end of the hallway turn left. The ceiling paintings in the **South Corridor**, *The Three Graces* (Husbandry, Music, and Beauty), were painted by Frank W. Benson. The wall paintings, *The Four Seasons*, were completed by George R. Barse. Maynard painted the virtues *Prudence*, *Justice*, *Patriotism*, and *Courage* here as well. The printers' marks are French.

To the right is the **American Treasures** exhibition. Admission is free, though there is a nominal fee for use of the optional audio wand. Selections from rarest and most significant items of the Library's collection are displayed on a rotating basis. The 240-item exhibition is divided into three sections as Thomas Jefferson had organized items in his own library. They are Memory (history), Reason (philosophy, law, science, and geography), and Imagination (architecture, music, literature, and leisure arts). Among the artifacts that have been displayed in the Memory area are the contents of Abraham Lincoln's pockets on the night he was assassinated, a hand-corrected copy of Walt Whitman's poem "O Captain! My Captain!" and Maya Lin's original design for the Vietnam Veterans Memorial. Displayed in the area labeled Reason has been Thomas Jefferson's 1803 instructions to Lewis and Clark, and Samuel F. B. Morse's first telegraph message from 1844. Pierre L'Enfant's 1791 plan for Washington, D.C., and the first Walt Disney comic book have been a part of the Imagination section.

Walk to the east end of the South Corridor. Turn left into the **East Corridor.** The ceiling painting is *Literature* (George R. Barse, Jr.). The printers' marks in the ceiling mosaic are Spanish and Italian. The round paintings show the three Fates in the *Life of Man* (William A. Mackay).

On the right side of the East Corridor is a staircase that leads to the gallery of the **Main Reading Room.** At the top of the staircase is a mosaic depicting Minerva. Her shield and helmet rest on the ground, but she holds her spear to illustrate she is prepared. It is pointed downward, however, to indicate a peaceful defensiveness. In her left hand, Minerva holds a scroll which lists the departments of learning. An owl, Minerva's symbol, and a statue of Victory surround Minerva.

Climb the stairs to the **Main Reading Room Gallery.** A 1991 renovation returned the room to its original 19C glory. Certain modifications were made to accommodate modern life. Telecommunications cables were wired to add computer terminals and permit the use of laptop computers.

A decorated **dome ceiling,** 100 ft wide and 125 ft high at the collar, with elaborately ornamented panels, dominates the room. The collar around the base of the dome was designed and painted by Edwin Howland Blashfield. The design depicts 12 seated figures, each ten ft tall, representing countries or epochs that have made a significant contribution to man. The scenes represent: Egypt for written records, Judea for religion, Greece for philosophy, Rome for administration, Islam for physics, Middle Ages for modern languages, Italy for the fine arts, Germany for painting, Spain for discovery, England for literature, France for emancipation, and the U.S. for science. Edwin Blashfield's circular painting, *The Progress of Civilization,* at the top of the dome, depicts a female figure who represents human understanding. She is shown lifting her veil and looking upward toward future achievements. A cherub at her feet is holding a book for the female's review.

Around the sides of the Main Reading Room, eight piers, constructed of Algerian red marble, support eight arches. These divide the room into eight bays, or alcoves. The alcoves and the arches that cover them split the room into eight sections, which serve as ribs for the impressive dome. The alcoves have semicircular **stained glass windows.** In the middle of each window is the seal of the U.S., plus 6 seals of the states or territories, representing the lower 48 states. From the most eastern window, the seals are in the order in which the states signed the Constitution and then in the order in which they were admitted to the Union.

A column carved from brown Tennessee marble fronts each of the piers. Each column supports a symbolic statue, 11 ft tall, depicting characteristics of civilized life and thought: religion, commerce, history, art, philosophy, poetry, law, and science. Inscriptions on the tablets of winged figures above each statue describe the idea that each statue represents.

There are 16 **bronze statues** of portrait figures along the balustrade of the galleries. Each symbolizes one of eight characteristics historically associated with the person. Moses and St. Paul represent religion. Christopher Columbus and Robert Fulton depict commerce. Herodotus and Edward Gibbon are for history. Michelangelo and Ludwig van Beethoven stand for art. Plato and Francis Bacon represent philosophy. Homer and William Shakespeare are for poetry. Solon and James Kent stand for law. Isaac Newton and Joseph Henry represent science.

Many consider the **clock** above the main entrance to the Reading Room to be the most beautiful piece of art in the Library. It was created by John Flanagan. The marble clock sits in front of a mosaic depicting the signs of the zodiac in bronze. The dial of the clock measures 4 ft in diameter, with hands encrusted in semiprecious stones. In its center is a gilt sunburst. In high-relief bronze, a life-size statue of Father Time, with his scythe, stands above the clock face. Bronze statues of maidens with children stand on either side, representing the seasons.

Three other reading rooms are located on this floor: African and Middle Eastern, Asian, and European. Visitors need prior permission to view them.

To begin Walk 2, exit the Library of Congress via the 1st St exit. Walk north for one block to E. Capitol St and turn left into the United States Capitol Building.

# 2 · Capitol Hill West

Metro: Red Line to Union Station or Blue/Orange Line to Capitol South.
Bus: 32, 34, 35, 36, or 98.

## U.S. Capitol Building

1st St bet. Independence and Constitution Aves N.E. ☎ 225-6827, recorded information on visiting the Capitol. Web: www.aoc.gov, www.senate.gov, or www.house.gov. Open March 1–Aug 3 9 A.M.–8 P.M.; Sept 1–Feb 28 9–4:30. Closed New Year's Day, Thanksgiving, and Christmas Day. Accommodations for those with special needs, such as sign language and oral communication, arranged by calling the Congressional Special Services Office. ☎ 224-4048.

Passes to view Congress in session must be obtained from the office of your representative or senator, and generally, these VIP passes should be requested about six months in advance. Nonresidents of the U.S. may obtain a pass by asking at the information desk.

Coffee shop and cafeteria open 7:30–3:30. Restrooms, telephones, gift shop. Photography not permitted on third floor. Wheelchair accessible.

After more than 200 years of building and remodeling, the U.S. Capitol Building (begun 1793; William Thornton, Benjamin Henry Latrobe, Charles Bulfinch, Thomas U. Walter, Frederick Law Olmsted) still stands as a symbol of the American people.

During the busier spring, summer, and autumn months, tours meet near the fountain in the center of the park on the east side of the Capitol. Guides escort visitors through the Columbus Doors at the east front and into the **Rotunda.** In the winter months, tours meet in the Rotunda. Once inside the Rotunda area look for the guides; they wear red vests or blazers. Guides lead groups around the Rotunda, to National Statuary Hall, and into the Crypt where the tour ends. The Capitol houses the legislative branch of the government: the House of Representatives and the Senate. Originally, the Supreme Court and the Library of Congress were located here also.

**Highlights:** The following highlights can be seen on a self-guided tour of the Capitol: the Old Supreme Court Chamber, the Old Senate Chamber, the Rotunda, the National Statuary Hall, the first floor House Corridors, the Crypt, the Brumidi Corridors, the House Chamber, and the Senate Chamber. A free brochure outlines these sites.

### History

Once the location of the Federal City was decided, there was still debate about where to put the Capitol Building and what it should look like. According to Major L'Enfant's master plan for the city, the Capitol was to be placed on Jenkin's Hill, an area now known as Capitol Hill. Situated at the fork of the Anacostia and the Potomac Rivers, the hill was described by L'Enfant as "a pedestal waiting for a monument." Not all were in agreement. Thomas Jefferson was in favor of the Funkstown or Hamburgh neighborhoods west of the White House, now called Foggy Bottom. A site in Alexandria, then part of the Federal City, was also proposed.

The government expected L'Enfant to design the Capitol and oversee construc-

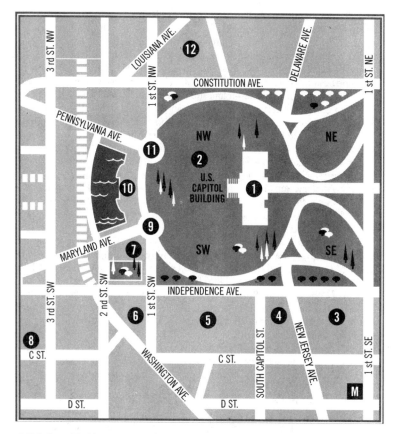

1 U.S. Capitol Building
2 Capitol Grounds
3 Cannon House Office Building
4 Longworth House Office Building
5 Rayburn House Office Building
6 Frederic Auguste Bartholdi Park

7 U.S. Botanic Garden Conservatory
8 Voice of America
9 President James A. Garfield Monument
10 Ulysses S. Grant Memorial
11 Peace Monument
12 Robert A. Taft Memorial

tion. However, the obstinate Frenchman refused to draft his plans for the building, claiming his plans were "in his head." This lack of cooperation, along with several other political gaffes, such as dismantling a wealthy citizen's house that stood in the way of one of L'Enfant's grand avenues (see "Capitol Hill: History"), contributed to L'Enfant's dismissal in 1792.

In 1792 President George Washington and Secretary of State Thomas Jefferson solicited designs for the Capitol. Although 16 plans were submitted, they all lacked exceptional qualities. Washington and Jefferson were contacted three months after the competition's deadline by William Thornton, an amateur architect living in the British Virgin Islands. He sought an extension to the deadline. The two agreed to let Thornton submit a plan five months late. His neoclassical design, featuring a central low-domed building with two adjacent wings, one each for the House of Representatives and the Senate, was accepted on April 5, 1793. For his winning design, Thornton received a $500 prize and a plot of land.

President George Washington laid the cornerstone of the Capitol on Sept 18, 1793, in a Masonic ceremony. Construction proceeded slowly. Concerned that Thornton was an amateur architect, Washington and Jefferson hired professional builder Stephen Hallet, the first runner-up in the design contest, to oversee construction. Because Hallet repeatedly altered Thornton's design without approval, Hallet was fired and replaced by James Hoban, architect of the White House. Hoban oversaw the first stage of construction. One of the initial problems Hoban faced was that few qualified laborers lived in the sparse, new city. Funding was also limited. Money for the construction of the Capitol Building was to come from the sale of lots in the city, but parcel prices were high and the undeveloped, swamp-like geography was not attractive to newcomers.

Initial construction concentrated on the Senate and House wings. By 1800 enough of the north wing was complete for Congress, the Supreme Court, the Library of Congress, and the city courts to occupy the building. President John Adams, who had recently moved into the White House, addressed the first joint session of Congress in the Federal City on Nov 22, 1800. The Supreme Court held its first session in Feb 1801. Jefferson hired Benjamin Henry Latrobe, a professional architect, to supervise the completion of the House's south wing. In 1807 the south wing was sufficiently complete to be occupied by the members of the House. The two wings, initially separate, were eventually attached by a wooden walkway, which crossed over a vacant yard where the Rotunda is today.

There was much rivalry and ill-will among the different architects and planners.

### Washington Notes

William Thornton, who was angry at Latrobe for altering Thornton's design of the Capitol, drafted a poem about Latrobe. "This Dutchman in taste, this monument builder / This planner of grand steps and wall / This falling arch-maker, this blunder-proof gilder / Himself an architect calls." Latrobe sued Thornton and won—the court ordered Thornton to pay Latrobe a penny.

Latrobe next began renovating the north wing, which was in disrepair. He initiated the colonnaded central section as described in Thornton's plans, although, in the midst of this project, British troops marched into the city. The soldiers, under orders from Admiral Sir Bruce Cockburn, torched the city on Aug 24, 1814, during the War of 1812. The White House, Capitol, and many other public buildings were left in ruins. The roofs of both Capitol wings lay in ashes. The windows had been blown out. The walls were smoke-stained.

A debate arose as to whether the Federal City should remain on this site in a damp city, infested with mosquitoes and often stinking from sewerlike canals. Although one-third of Congress was in favor of moving, the majority voted to rebuild. After meeting for one session in Blodgett's Hotel, Congress moved to the "Brick Capitol," a temporary building erected at the site of Tunnicliffe's Tavern (the present location of the Supreme Court).

*U.S. Capitol after the fire in 1814. Courtesy of the Washingtoniana Division, D.C. Public Library.*

When Latrobe began rebuilding the Capitol in 1815, he added low domes over the north and south wings, which can be seen today immediately to the left and right of the central dome. His contribution, which included redesigning the south wing's interior to make it semicircular, ended in Nov 1817 when he resigned after a dispute with the commissioner of Public Buildings.

Soon after, Boston architect Charles Bulfinch was appointed. Bulfinch oversaw the construction of the central dome, creating a link between the two wings. Unlike Thornton's original plan for a low stone vault, Bulfinch designed a more prominent, 55 ft high dome built of copper-leafed wood, based on the dome he created for the Massachusetts State House in the 1790s. By Dec 1819 Congress reconvened in its permanent home.

Bulfinch had barely finished his work when construction again became necessary. The country and Congress expanded significantly in the early 1800s, and both legislative houses had become crowded. In 1850 Congress appropriated $100,000 for the creation of two new wings to expand the House and Senate. Another contest was held and several suitable designs were submitted. Congress debated two plans and the final decision had to be made by President Millard Fillmore. He chose a design by Thomas U. Walter, an architect from Philadelphia.

President Fillmore laid the cornerstone in the northeast corner of the House wing on July 4, 1851. Within months Walter and the builder, Montgomery Meigs, were at odds. Walter convinced Congress to dismiss Meigs and work continued. The House side was completed in 1857 and the Senate side finished in 1859. In addition to the new wings, Walter decided to replace Bulfinch's wooden dome with a larger, more proportionate one to balance the building. Congress agreed to Walter's fireproof, cast-iron dome in 1855. The old one was removed in 1856. The new dome was constructed from nearly nine tons of cast iron. When the plaster model for *Freedom*, the statue by Thomas Crawford for the top of the dome, arrived, it was three ft taller than stated in the plan. The dome had to be adjusted to hold the extra weight. In a ceremony on Dec 2, 1863, *Freedom* was placed atop the dome. She was placed facing east because the Capitol's ceremonial grounds were on the east side of the building. (Every president through Jimmy Carter was inaugurated on the east steps. Although neither side of the Capitol is considered the front today, Thornton considered the east side to be the front when he designed the building. Originally, developers believed that settlement of the Federal City would progress eastward toward the Eastern Branch of the Potomac River [now called the Anacostia River] rather than westward as it did.)

### Washington Notes

Walter's improvements also included the installation of marble bathtubs in the basement for use by congressmen during long sessions. Although these bathtubs have since been removed, a ghost story still circulates about President Grant's vice president, Henry Wilson. Wilson, called unexpectedly from his bath on a cold day, caught a cold and died within a week. It is said his ghost can be seen wrapped in a towel in the old bathing area.

In 1874, not long after the addition's completion, Congress commissioned Frederick Law Olmsted, a well-known landscape architect, to beautify the Capitol's surrounding grounds, which had been cluttered with marble blocks for years during construction (see "Capitol Grounds"). Olmsted created a large plaza on the east side of the building, and built marble stairways and terraces on the south, north, and west sides.

The next major construction work on the Capitol didn't occur until 1949. With an appropriation of more than $5 million from Congress, the roofs of the Senate and House wings were rebuilt using concrete and steel and were covered with copper, as were the Senate and House Chambers.

In 1956, once again in need of space, Congress appropriated funds for an addition to the Capitol. In 1958–62, the east front of the building was extended 32½ feet. Its present marble façade is a reconstruction of the sandstone original. Many of the original columns have been relocated to the National Arboretum. At this time much of the building was repaired and cleaned. Congress acquired new furnishings for the interior, and a subway terminal was built under the Senate and House wing steps. The total bill for the project came to $24 million.

The Capitol's most recent architectural improvement, the restoration of its west central front, was completed in 1988. The project entailed strengthening and renovating the original façade, damaged over the years by material defects, building construction, and fire.

### Washington Notes

In 1835, Richard Lawrence attempted to assassinate President Andrew Jackson. As Jackson was leaving the Capitol by the eastern portico, Lawrence fired a pistol at him twice but missed. At his trial Lawrence claimed he was avenging the death of his father. He defended himself by declaring that he was the king of England and, therefore, above American law. He lost the case and was sentenced to an insane asylum.

## Exterior

The building is faced with sandstone from Virginia and marble from Massachusetts and Georgia quarries. Approach the building from the east. Walk to the south, or House, wing of the Capitol. Adorning the southeast front portico is *The Apotheosis of Democracy* (1916; Paul Waylard Bartlett, designer). The Piccirilli brothers carved the work from Georgia white marble. The pediment was unveiled on Aug 2, 1916. At the center, an armed Peace, represented by a woman wearing a long mantle, a breastplate, and a coat of mail, is protecting the young figure Genius. Agriculture and industry are represented on either side. Depictions of farmers and livestock and factory workers and tradesmen symbolize the wealth of the nation. The working model of this piece, donated to the government in 1963 by Bartlett's stepdaughter, Mrs. Armistead Peter III, is displayed on the platform of the Capitol-Rayburn subway in the Capitol's basement.

At the top of the stairs leading into the House wing are the **House Doors** (1855–57; Thomas Crawford). (These are not accessible by the public, but can be seen from the bottom of the stairs.) William H. Rinehart executed the models from 1863 to 1867, based on Crawford's design, but the model was not cast until 1904. The doors were installed in 1905. The 15 by 8 ft bronze doors depict great scenes from the Revolutionary War. Three panels on the left portray events during the war, including *The Massacre at Wyoming, Pennsylvania, July 3, 1778; The Battle of Lexington, April 19, 1775;* and *Presentation of the Flag and Medal to General Nathanael Greene.* The medallion below depicts *The Death of General Richard Montgomery, December 31, 1775.* The right panels show events related to the war: *Public Reading of the Declaration of Independence at Philadelphia; Treaty of Peace at Paris between the United States and Great Britain, September 3, 1783;* and *Washington's Farewell to His Officers, New York, December 4, 1783.* The right medallion shows *Benjamin Franklin in His Studio.* Walk north to the center portion of the east façade.

The **Center Portico** features *The Genius of America* (1828; Luigi Persico). America is represented by a woman armed with a spear and a shield, who has an American eagle at her side. On either side stand Hope and Justice—Hope with an anchor and Justice with scales. Together the three suggest that America can hope for success as long as justice is practiced.

Beneath the portico, at the top of the stairs, are the **Columbus Doors,** also known as the Rotunda Doors and the Rogers Doors (1858; Randolph Rogers). Cast from bronze, they weigh 20,000 pounds. The tympanum and eight door panels depict important events and individuals in the life and voyages of Christopher Columbus. Above the doors is a bust of Columbus, decorated with oak leaves indicating his rise to glory. Beneath the bust is a lunette portraying Columbus's first landing in the New World. The border around the lunette contains symbols of conquest, navigation, arts and sciences, history, agriculture, and commerce. The four figures represent America, Europe, Africa, and Asia and signify the world's acknowledgment of his achievement. The sequence of the panels begins on the bottom of the left door and proceeds clockwise. The first scene, *Columbus Before the Council of Salamanca,* is from 1487. It depicts Columbus's unsuccessful effort to convince King Ferndinand's council of a new trade route to India. The next scene, *Columbus' Departure from the Convent of La Rábida (1492),* shows Columbus mounted on a mule departing from the convent run by Friar Juan Perez, confessor to Queen Isabella. The third, *Audience at the Court of Ferdinand and*

*Isabella,* shows Columbus explaining his new route to the attentive Isabella and Ferdinand. In the fourth panel, *Departure of Columbus from Palos (1492),* Columbus is entrusting his son Diego to monks before leaving on his journeys. The fifth and sixth panels, *Landing of Columbus in the New World (1492)* and *Columbus' First Encounter with the Indians (1492),* illustrate Columbus claiming San Salvador for Spain and Columbus disapproving as one of his sailors carries off an Indian girl on his shoulders. The last two panels show Columbus's tragic end. *Columbus in Chains (1500)* depicts Columbus returning to Spain in 1500 as a prisoner. The final panel, *Death of Columbus (1506),* at the bottom of the right door, depicts the explorer on his deathbed surrounded by priests and his family.

Between the panels are the heads of historians and authors whose books on Columbus's voyage inspired the scenes on these doors. The authors include Washington Irving and William Hickling Prescott. The doors were designed at the request of Captain Montgomery C. Meigs. Meigs, at the time, was the supervising engineer of the Capitol Extensions. The doors, cast in 1860 at a foundry in Munich, Germany, by Ferdinand von Miller, were installed in 1863 at the entrance to the new House wing from Statuary Hall. In 1961 the doors were moved to their present location after the extension of the east front of the Capitol.

Before entering the Capitol through the street-level door to the north of the central staircase, walk north to the Senate wing. On the **Northeast Portico** is *The Progress of Civilization* (1863; Thomas Crawford). America, attended by an eagle, stands on a rock; the sun rises at her feet, and she holds a laurel wreath, a symbol of victory. Her left hand extends toward a pioneer. An athletic woodsman represents the pioneers. Native Americans are represented by a warrior with his family and also by a mother, a child, and a grave, illustrating despair and grief over the white man's triumph. Various fields of human endeavor are represented on America's right by a diversity of individuals. A vigilant soldier in Revolutionary dress stands next to a merchant seated on packaged export goods with his hand on a globe. Next are two young boys. A teacher sits behind them, instructing a youth. Finally, a mechanic rests on a cogwheel. The corn at his feet, a direct contrast to the grave, symbolizes fertility, and behind it is an anchor symbolizing hope.

The doors beneath the portico, at the top of the stairs leading to the Senate wing, are known as the **Senate Doors** (1868; Thomas Crawford). (These are not accessible by the public, but can be seen from the bottom of the stairs.) Like the set on the House wing, these doors feature panels depicting events during and after the Revolutionary War. Designed by Thomas Crawford, the doors were finished by William H. Rinehart after Crawford's death. The three left panels focus on events during the life of George Washington: *Laying of the Cornerstone of the United States Capitol, 1793; Inauguration of George Washington as First President, 1789;* and *Ovation of George Washington at Trenton, New Jersey, 1789.* The right panels portray great episodes in the War of Independence: *Battle of Bunker Hill and Death of General Joseph Warren, 1775; Battle of Monmouth and Rebuke of General Charles Lee, 1778;* and *Battle of Yorktown and Gallantry of Alexander Hamilton of New York, 1781.* The bottom medallions present allegorical scenes. To the left, an American farmer protects his family in combat from a Hessian soldier. The right side shows Peace, Agriculture, Maternity, Infancy, Childhood, Youth, and Manhood gathered around a plow.

Return to the plaza to the east of the Capitol and look at the **Dome.** The **statue of *Freedom*** stands atop a pedestal on the Capitol's dome. *Freedom* is in bronze,

19½ ft tall and weighs 14,985 pounds. In her left hand she holds a shield with 13 stripes and a laurel wreath of victory. Her right hand rests on the hilt of a sword. The brooch securing her fringed draperies reads "U.S." The crest of her helmet is an eagle's head, feathers, and talons, which refer to the costumes of Native Americans. Stars encircle the brim of the helmet. Originally Crawford had designed the statue to be topped by a Phrygian cap, an emblem of freed slaves in ancient Greece and symbolic of the liberty cap worn during the French Revolution. Amid the heated debate over slavery at the time, Southern loyalist (and Secretary of War) Jefferson Davis strongly objected to the symbolism and it was replaced by the present helmet. *Freedom*'s pedestal is a globe inscribed with the Latin phrase "E. Pluribus Unum."

### *Washington Notes*

Thomas Crawford completed a plaster model of *Freedom* in Feb 1857. He died suddenly in Oct 1857 before shipping the model from his studio in Italy. After being packed into six crates, the model was shipped on a small sailing vessel in 1858. The ship began to leak and sought repairs in Gilbraltar. After storms caused additional leaking, the ship stopped again in Bermuda. Three of the crates arrived in New York in Dec 1858. The remaining sections arrived in March 1859.

*Freedom* was cast in five sections by Clark Mills in 1860, though work ceased temporarily during the Civil War. *Freedom* was completed in 1862. On Dec 2, 1863, *Freedom* was hoisted onto the dome. She was removed for six months for restoration in 1993. The plaster model is displayed in the basement rotunda of the Russell Senate Office Building.

The **American flag** above the east central front of the Capitol flies 24 hours per day, 7 days per week. This tradition began during World War I. The flags over the Senate and House wings fly only when Congress is in session.

### *Washington Notes*

From poles on the west side of the Capitol, workmen hoist and lower American flags year-round. The flags, which fly for one minute, are available for sale to constituents who request them through their congressperson or senator.

## Interior

The **Rotunda** is a circular room on the second floor that is 96 ft in diameter and 180 ft tall. Its walls are sandstone. The room, at the center of the Capitol, connects the House and Senate wings. The Rotunda, which was part of Thornton's original proposal, is based on the Roman Pantheon. Due to several delays caused by funding issues and the British invasion, the room wasn't completed until 1824.

Congress commissioned John Trumbull in 1817 to paint the four Revolutionary War paintings adorning the west side of the Rotunda. The paintings depict events from the war and are titled *Declaration of Independence in Congress, Surrender of General Burgoyne at Saratoga, Surrender of Lord Cornwallis at Yorktown,* and *General George Washington Resigning His Commission to Congress as Commander in Chief of the Army.* The four were installed by 1824. Four other paintings in the Rotunda illustrate the discovery and colonization of America: *Landing of Columbus* by John Vanderlyn, *Discovery of the Mississippi by Desoto* by William Powell, *Bap-*

*tism of Pocahontas* by John Chapman, and *Embarkation of the Pilgrims* by Robert Weir. These paintings were in place by 1855.

Above the paintings, wreath panels frame the busts of explorers John Cabot, Christopher Columbus, Sir Walter Raleigh, and Rene Robert Cavelier Sieur de La Salle. Reliefs of episodes in American history crown the Rotunda's four entrances: *Conflict of Daniel Boone and the Indians and Landing of the Pilgrims* by Enrico Causici, *Preservation of Captain Smith by Pocahontas* by Antonio Capellano, and *William Penn's Treaty with the Indians* by Nicholas Gevelot.

From 1865 to 1866, Constantino Brumidi painted the fresco in the canopy of the dome, *The Apotheosis of Washington.* Washington is shown ascending into heaven, with female figures representing Liberty and Victory/Fame beside him. Thirteen young women symbolizing the original 13 states complete the circle. Six scenes around the group depict war (armed Freedom and an eagle defeating Tyranny and Kingly Power), the arts and sciences (Minerva, the goddess of wisdom, teaching Benjamin Franklin, Robert Fulton, and Samuel F. B. Morse), marine (Neptune wielding his trident and Venus holding the transatlantic cable, which was being laid down during the time Brumidi was painting the fresco), commerce (Mercury offering a bag of money to Robert Morris, financier of the American Revolution), mechanics (Vulcan forging a cannon and steam engine), and agriculture (Ceres atop the McCormick reaper, flanked by America wearing her liberty cap and Flora picking flowers).

Along the base of the Rotunda, a **frescoed frieze** depicts 400 years of American history from Columbus to the Wright Brothers. The work was begun in 1877 by Constantino Brumidi, and after Brumidi's death in 1880, Filippo Costaggini was commissioned to continue the work from Brumidi's sketches. The last depiction Costaggini painted was the discovery of gold in California. When completed in 1889, a gap of 31 ft remained, as was Brumidi's intent. In 1953 Allyn Cox completed the work with depictions of the Civil War, the Spanish-American War, and the "Birth of Aviation."

Near the east entrance to the Rotunda is a case containing a gold panel replicating text of the Magna Carta, a gift from the British government in 1976. The statues and busts around the room are primarily of presidents. A bust of George Washington was sculpted by P. J. David d'Angers. The statue of Washington is a copy of one by French artist Jean-Antoine Houdon. The marble statue of Lincoln is by Vinnie Ream. Other statues in the Rotunda are of James Garfield, Andrew Jackson, and Thomas Jefferson. There are also representations of Alexander Hamilton, the Women's Suffrage Movement, the Marquis de Lafayette, and a bust of Dr. Martin Luther King, Jr. Recent donations to National Statuary Hall are first displayed in the Rotunda for six months.

### Washington Notes

The country honors many distinguished citizens and leaders upon their death by displaying their coffins in the Rotunda, a tradition termed *lying in state.* This enables citizens to pay their final respects. Among the famous Americans who have laid in state here are: Henry Clay, July 1, 1852; Abraham Lincoln, April 19–21, 1865; Thaddeus Stevens, Aug 13–14, 1868; James Garfield, Sept 21–23, 1881; William McKinley, Sept 17, 1901; Major Pierre Charles L'Enfant, April 28, 1909 (reinterment; originally buried in 1825); Admiral George Dewey, Jan 20, 1917; William Howard

Taft, March 11, 1930; General John Joseph Pershing, July 18–19, 1948; John Fitzgerald Kennedy, November 24–25, 1963; General Douglas MacArthur, April 8–9, 1964; Herbert Clark Hoover, Oct 23–25, 1964; Dwight David Eisenhower, March 30–31, 1969; J. Edgar Hoover, May 3–4, 1972; Lyndon Baines Johnson, Jan 24–25, 1973; and Hubert Horatio Humphrey, Jan 14–15, 1978. The unknown soldiers of World Wars I and II, the Korean War, and the Vietnam War have also been so honored.

Pass through the south doorway of the Rotunda, through the foyer, and into **National Statuary Hall.** The room is also known as the Old Hall of the House since the House of Representatives met here for 50 years, from 1807 until 1857. Benjamin Latrobe designed the semicircular room, one of America's first Greek revival structures completed in 1807, and began restoration after the British fire in 1814. Charles Bulfinch completed the work in 1819. The walls are painted plaster, though the gallery walls and pilasters are sandstone. The columns are Breccia marble quarried from the banks of the Potomac River. The carved Corinthian capitals came from Carrara, Italy. The black marble for the floor was purchased specifically for this room, but the white marble was culled from scrap from the Capitol extension project.

Only two of the artworks shown in the room were here when the House occupied the hall. Above the doorway leading to the Rotunda is Carlo Franzoni's *Car of History*. It was one of the first classical statues made in the U.S. Clio, the muse of history, records the events in the chamber from the chariot of Time. The chariot's wheel holds a clock by Simon Willard. *Liberty and the Eagle*, by Enrice Causici, was placed in a niche above an area once occupied by the Speaker's platform. A sandstone relief eagle by Giuseppe Valaperta appears beneath this work in the frieze of the entablature.

Bronze disks mark the floor where desks of House members who were later elected presidents were once situated.

The Marquis de Lafayette became the first foreign citizen to address Congress in this room in 1824. Several presidents, including James Madison, James Monroe, John Quincy Adams, Millard Filmore, and Andrew Jackson were inaugurated in Statuary Hall as well.

The echoes bouncing around the room made business difficult for the members of the House. A new hall was authorized in 1850 and the House moved into its present chamber in the new wing in 1857.

After debating whether to offer the space to the overcrowded Library of Congress, the House designated the room as a National Statuary Hall on July 2, 1864. Each state was invited to submit two bronze or marble statues of prominent, deceased citizens to be displayed in the room. The first statue was displayed in 1870. In 1933 the hall was extremely overcrowded with 65 statues, some lined up three deep. Today, the collection of 96 statues extends beyond this room, although the hall houses 38 statues. Due to overcrowding the House developed some guidelines. Statues representing 10 of the 13 original colonies were moved to the central hall of the east front extension on the first floor of the Capitol. Others are exhibited in the Hall of Columns and the corridors connecting the House and Senate wings.

Return through the north doorway and follow the staircase in the foyer to the right down to the first floor. Displayed at the foot of the stairs are **bronze doors** created by Louis Amateis in 1910. On the transom is the *Apotheosis of America*, the door consisting of 8 panels, 28 medallions, and 18 statuettes that tell the story of the intellectual and physical progress of the country. The doors were loaned to the Corcoran Gallery of Art and displayed there for four years before being sent to the Smithsonian Institution's Museum of Natural History, which exhibited them from 1914 to 1967. In 1967 the doors were returned to the Capitol.

Turn left and walk west. The entrance to the **Crypt** is on the right. The Crypt is located directly below the Rotunda.

The Crypt contains sculpture, artifacts, and exhibits about the building's history. Also displayed are three models of early designs for the Capitol. The star in the center of the room marks the exact center point of Washington, D.C. Originally, the chamber below was meant to be George and Martha Washington's last resting place. However, construction was completed long after their deaths and the family refused to exhume the bodies from the Mount Vernon estate. The catafalque used to support the coffins of President Lincoln and other dignitaries while their bodies lay in state in the Rotunda is now stored in this space.

Many official tours end in the Crypt. To visit the Senate wing walk through the north door. Once in the oval-shaped room, turn right and proceed down the steps. Latrobe's famous **"Corncob"** columns and capitals stand just outside of the Old Supreme Court Robing Room. During the reconstruction of the north wing in 1809, Latrobe wanted to add high-vaulted ceilings and curved walls. In order to accommodate the weight of the vaulted ceilings, he had to erect six sandstone columns on new foundations. His design for the columns elsewhere in the building utilized the American elements of corncobs and tobacco leaves instead of the traditional acanthus leaves used in Greek and Roman columns. "These capitals obtained me more applause from the members of Congress than all the works of magnitude or difficulty that surrounded them," Latrobe remarked. The columns, constructed of sandstone from Aquia Creek, Virginia, stand nearly nine ft tall. Bundled ears of corn, with the husks folded back to show the kernels, form the capitals. The columns resemble cornstalks, and a rope carving strings them together. Though Latrobe designed the columns, Guiseppe Franzoni carved them.

Turn left and walk north into the **Robing Room.** Displayed in this anteroom are a bust and robes of Roger B. Taney, chief justice from 1836 to 1864 and author of the *Dred Scott* decision. Continue north and enter the **Old Supreme Court Chamber.** Originally in part of the space used as the Senate Chamber, this room was remodeled for the Supreme Court in 1810, which met here until 1860. Today, the Chambers contain the marble busts of the first four Supreme Court justices. From south to north, they are John Marshall, John Rutledge, John Jay, and Oliver Ellsworth. Annoyed with lawyers arriving late for court proceedings, Taney ordered the clock above the west fireplace in 1837. It was purposely set five minutes fast. Above the clock is a plaster relief carved by Carlo Franzoni in 1817, depicting a seated Justice holding scales in her left hand and the hilt of a sword in her right. Unlike many depictions, this Justice wears no blindfold. To her left, Young Nation, portrayed as a winged youth, holds the Constitution up to the rays of the rising sun. To Justice's right is an eagle perched upon law books. In 1976, this room was restored to its original appearance for the Bicentennial. Some of the furnishings are original. There are nine mahogany desks for the Supreme Court justices. Four are believed to be the original desks purchased for the Court in late 1819. Five of the chairs are original. The chairs, chosen by the justices themselves, reflect the varied tastes of the men who served in the room.

This chamber was used as a law library when the Court relocated directly upstairs to the Old Senate Chamber.

Exit the chamber through the doorway at the left. From the oval-shaped room turn right and walk north. Enter the new Senate wing constructed from 1851 to 1867. A restaurant is on the right side of the hall. Continue north, passing the souvenir shop and the appointment desk. This hallway intersects with the **Brumudi Corridors.**

The Brumidi Corridors are a series of five hallways—**Main, West, Inner, North,** and **Patent**—on the first floor of the Senate wing. The corridors are named for the artist Constantino Brumidi, who designed the murals painted in the vaulted ceilings. The murals were primarily completed from 1857 to 1859, though some were added as late as 1878. The scheme is based on Raphael's *Loggia* in the Vatican, but Brumidi focused on U.S. flora and fauna, history and technology. The walls display plants and animals of America, including birds, chipmunks, squirrels, and many types of flowers. Colorful Minton-tiled floors cover the first floor of the Senate wing. They were installed under Montgomery C. Meigs in 1856. The colors are created by imbedding colored clay in the tile. These tiles came from England, and tiles of this type also adorn the House of Parliament.

Walking north from the Old Supreme Court Chamber along the Main Corridor, turn left at the first perpendicular hallway. This is the Inner Corridor. Walk west to the **West Corridor.** The **lunettes,** or **semicircular murals,** over the committee rooms reflect the functions of the committees that met there during the time Brumidi painted the pieces. For example, *Columbus and the Indian Maiden* and *Bartolome de Las Casas, the Apostle of the Indians* were painted above the doorways of Rooms S-132 and 133, which once held the Senate Committee on Indian Affairs. Above room S-128, occupied by the Military Affairs committee during Brumidi's era, is *Bellona, the Roman Goddess of War.* At the end of the corridor, the 12 signs of the zodiac are set on the ceiling in a blue background. Along the walls in this corridor are monochrome profile portraits of the signers of the Declaration of Independence—including John Hancock, John Jay, and Robert Morris—as well as 40 American birds.

Walk north and turn right into the **North Corridor.** Brumidi painted portraits of Revolutionary War leaders (including Benjamin Franklin), small American animals (such as squirrels and chipmunks), and modern inventions. At the west end of the corridor, Brumidi painted *The Cession of Louisiana* above the door to Room S-124, which once housed the Committee on Territories. The work depicts the meeting of Robert Livingston, James Monroe, and the Marquis Barbe-Marbois in 1803.

The north entrance to the corridor is decorated with portraits of Andrew Jackson, Henry Clay, and Daniel Webster, among others. At the east end of the North Corridor Brumidi painted *The Signing of the First Treaty of Peace with Great Britain, 1782* over Room S-118. This room was originally occupied by the Senate Committee on Foreign Relations. This corridor also features works by later artists. An unknown artist added the Wright Brothers' plane and Charles Lindbergh's *Spirit of St. Louis* in the early 1930s. Charles Schmidt's depiction of the space shuttle *Challenger* and its crew, painted in 1987, appears here, as does Allyn Cox's *First Landing on the Moon, 1969.* Brumidi designed the ornate bronze railings for the stairways at each end of the corridor, and Edmond Baudin sculpted these intricate pieces, whose decorative pattern includes deer, eagles, and cherubs.

Walk east along the North Corridor to the **Patent Corridor.** This hallway features Brumidi's frescoed lunettes of John Fitch, Benjamin Franklin, and Robert Fulton.

To see the Old Senate Chamber and the Senate Gallery return to the Main Corridor and walk south. At the oval-shaped room, turn left and climb the stairs to the second floor.

Proceed west and enter the second floor oval-shaped room. Walk north and turn right into the **Old Senate Chamber.** The Senate used this room from 1810 to 1859. Like ancient amphitheaters, the two-story Old Senate Chamber is semi-circular and has a half-dome ceiling. A series of eight Ionic columns along the east wall support a gallery. Their design was based on the columns of the Erechtheion in Athens and are comprised of marble quarried from the banks of the Potomac River. Above this gallery hangs a "porthole" portrait of George Washington (1823; Rembrandt Peale), purchased for the chamber in 1832, the centennial of Washington's birth. The larger "Ladies' Gallery," located against the west wall, is supported with 12 steel columns topped with Corinthian capitals. (Originally, the columns were of cast iron.) On a raised platform at the center of the east wall of the room is an ornate table, the desk of the vice president, who serves as the president of the Senate. The secretary of the Senate and the chief clerk sat at the desk one tier below the vice president. The mahogany desks and chairs in the room are reproductions of an 1819 design by Thomas Constantine, a New York cabinet-maker. The original desks are still in use in the current Senate Chamber. When the Senate relocated to its current chamber in 1859, this room was quickly claimed by the Supreme Court. The Court met in this room for 75 years before moving to its own building east of the Capitol in 1935.

Exit the Old Senate Chamber and walk south to the Rotunda. Turn left and walk to the east door of the Rotunda. Turn left and walk north. An elevator will be on the right. Proceed to the third floor. Exit the elevator and turn left. At the hallway, turn right and walk north. Once inside the Senate wing, turn left. The entrance to the **Senate Gallery** is on the right.

The Senate Chamber was completed in 1859 and renovated in 1949–50. The ceiling contains the **Seal of the United States,** cut in glass and outlined with bronze. The niches in the gallery contain 20 busts of vice presidents. The senators still use the original mahogany desks from 1819; any additional desks are replicas. Traditionally, Republicans sit to the left of the president of the Senate (the vice president of the United States) and the Democrats sit to the right, according to seniority.

Walk south through the main corridor across the Capitol to the House wing. Once in the House wing, turn right. The entrance to the **House Chamber** is on the left. The House Chamber was first occupied in 1857, but underwent extensive renovation in 1949–50. An understated decor replaced the ornate decorations from the past. The ceiling is decorated by the seals of 50 states, 4 territories, and the District of Columbia. Also on the ceiling is a carved glass eagle outlined in bronze. In a sculptural relief above the gallery doors are portraits of lawgivers. Paintings of George Washington and General Lafayette hang to the left and right of the rostrum. The mace, the symbol of authority of the House, can be seen on the Speaker's right when the House is in session. Traditionally, as in the Senate Chamber, Republicans sit on the Speaker's left, whereas Democrats sit to the right.

Exit the House Chamber Gallery and walk east to the staircase. Descend to the first floor. This staircase opens into the **Hall of Capitols.** This corridor has been termed the Hall of Capitols because it features paintings of 16 different buildings that housed the Continental and U.S. Congresses from 1754 to 1865. Portraits of the nine men who served as Architect of the Capitol, 1793–1974, are in the groined vaults of the ceilings. In the ceilings' barrel vaults are eight historic events that occurred during the first 65 years of the Capitol.

Walk south and make the first right into **Great Experimentation Hall.** The 16 murals, by Allyn Cox, chronicle the legislative milestones of three centuries of American history, from the signing of the Mayflower Compact in 1629 to the enactment of women's suffrage in 1920. Painted in the ceiling are 16 medallion portraits in chronological order, and appropriate quotes appear above the 16 doorways.

Proceed north to the **Hall of Columns.** This hall has 28 columns with capitals of tobacco leaves, flowers, and thistles, variations of Latrobe's "corncob" capitals. Statues from the National Statuary Collection are also displayed in this corridor. Turn right and walk north. Just before reaching the Crypt, turn right. At the first hallway, turn left. Restrooms and a gift shop are located in this corridor.

## Chronology of the Capitol

| | |
|---|---|
| 1790 | Congress passes the "Residence Act," which states that the federal government will relocate and settle along the banks of the Potomac River by 1800. |
| 1791 | Pierre L'Enfant develops a plan for the new Federal City. George Washington and L'Enfant determine the site for the Capitol Building. |
| 1792 | L'Enfant dismissed for insubordination. Competition begins for Capitol design; 16 proposals are submitted. Thornton enters after the deadline. |
| 1793 | Thornton awarded the prize for best design. Washington lays the cornerstone. |
| 1800 | Congress moves from Philadelphia. The Capitol's north wing is completed. |
| 1801 | The Supreme Court meets for the first time in the Capitol. |
| 1803 | Latrobe appointed chief architect by Jefferson. |
| 1807 | House moves into the south wing. |
| 1808 | Latrobe begins reconstruction of the north wing. |
| 1810 | The Senate moves into the north wing. The Supreme Court's quarters are constructed beneath the Senate Chambers. |
| 1814 | The Capitol is torched by British troops. |
| 1815–1817 | Restoration of the Capitol begins under Latrobe, but he resigns after a dispute regarding his authority. |
| 1818 | President Monroe chooses Charles Bulfinch to complete the restoration. Building of the center of the Capitol begins. |
| 1819 | The Supreme Court, the Senate, and the House begin meeting in the reconstructed building. |
| 1824 | The Rotunda is first used in a ceremonial capacity for Lafayette's visit. |
| 1829 | The Capitol Building, including landscape, is completed. |
| 1850 | Five architects split the prize from a competition to extend the Capitol. |
| 1851 | Thomas U. Walter appointed "Architect of Capitol Extensions" by President Filmore. Construction commences. A fire destroys the Library of Congress, which has been housed in the Capitol. |

| 1855 | Congress decides to replace Bulfinch's copper dome with a larger, cast-iron dome designed by Walter. Brumidi paints the first fresco in the Capitol. |
| 1857 | First session of the House in its new wing. |
| 1859 | Senate's first session in its new wing. |
| 1860 | The Supreme Court moves into the former Senate Chamber. |
| 1861 | Due to the Civil War, work on the Capitol is temporarily suspended. The building is used as a barracks, hospital, and bakery. Work on its dome continues under orders from President Lincoln. |
| 1863 | The statue **Freedom** is placed atop the dome. |
| 1864 | The Old Hall of the House is designated as National Statuary Hall. |
| 1866 | Brumidi's *Apotheosis of Washington* is unveiled. |
| 1870 | Exteriors of extensions are finished. |
| 1874 | Frederick Law Olmsted begins designing the Capitol grounds. |
| 1884–1892 | Construction of the Olmsted terrace. |
| 1885 | Electric lighting installed in portions of the building on a trial basis. |
| 1890–1900 | Electric lighting placed throughout the building and its grounds. |
| 1894 | Modern plumbing installed throughout the building. |
| 1897 | The Library of Congress moves to the Thomas Jefferson Building. |
| 1902 | Old House and Senate wing roofs are rebuilt and fireproofed. |
| 1935 | The Supreme Court moves into its own building. |
| 1949–1951 | The House and Senate chambers are redesigned. |
| 1958–1962 | An extension to the east front adds 32.5 ft. A subway terminal is created under the Senate steps. |
| 1975–1976 | The Old Senate and Supreme Court Chambers are restored for the Bicentennial. Restoration of National Statuary Hall begins. |
| 1983–1988 | The west front is restored. |
| 1991–1993 | The west terrace is restored. |
| 1993 | The statue of *Freedom* is restored. |
| 1996 | The House's monumental stairs are restored. |

## Capitol Grounds

The Capitol is set on nearly 274 acres, 60 of which is a park area known as the Capitol Grounds. These gently landscaped areas also exhibit functional sculpture of historical significance.

### History

The land around the Capitol was originally a wooded area with clusters of shrub oak and nearby tributaries. According to early European settlers, the Manahoacs and the Monacans, Algonquin subtribes, had settlements here. There are also accounts that tribal council meetings were held around the hill where the Capitol was erected.

In the 1790s the federal government purchased the land, then known as Jenkin's Hill, from John Carroll of Duddington. With seemingly endless construction on the Capitol Building, the grounds were often muddy and cluttered with construction materials. By 1825, however, the area had been organized into rectangular plots of grass surrounded by trees, flowers, and stone walkways. This design proved exceptionally difficult and expensive to maintain. By the 1850s, when Thomas U. Walter began the extensions of the Capitol, most of the vegetation had died or been removed, and the grounds were muddy and littered with construction materials.

Frederick Law Olmsted, designer of New York City's Central Park, was commissioned in 1874 to develop a plan for the grounds. Olmsted based his design on his belief that the grounds surrounding the building were "part of the Capitol, but in all respects subsidiary to the central structure." Accordingly, his modifications to the grounds stressed simplicity and clear sight lines unimpeded by large clusters of trees, sculpture, or features of landscape. Olmsted had the ground elevation reduced in many areas; nearly 30,000 cubic yards of earth were removed. Unlike the earlier organized plan of rectangular plots and orderly walkways, Olmsted carried out a less-structured plan of large, open lawns; winding, shaded walks; and the construction of marble terraces on the north, west, and south sides of the Capitol.

By 1878, Olmsted established organized roads and walkways and planted more than 7,000 trees and plants. Many of the trees that have since been planted have historic or memorial associations and many have plaques. For example, more than 30 states have made a donation of their state tree. Others have been planted in memory of past congressmen or prominent citizens.

Olmsted also installed gas and water services and furnished the grounds with electrical lighting systems, including the red granite and bronze lamps lining the east plaza. Also near the east front are two waiting stations where people waited for horse-drawn trolleys.

Two round, brick towers were constructed on the west side of the House and Senate wings. These serve as air shafts and provide ventilation through underground ducts to the Capitol. At the north end of the grounds, nestled in vines and shrubbery, a red brick and terra-cotta grotto was built. Olmsted designed the Summer House, as it is called, as a retreat for congressmen, stating it was a "cool retreat during hot summer." The small, hexagonal structure with stone seats has a red tile roof, iron-grated windows, an ornamental fountain, and three drinking fountains and is shaded by trees.

Construction began on the terraces in 1882 and was complete within ten years. Olmsted retired in 1885, although he continued to supervise the grounds' improvement until 1889.

Walk Southeast from the Capitol Grounds to Independence Ave. Cross Independence Ave and proceed to the Cannon House Office Building at the corner of 1st St and Independence Ave.

## Cannon House Office Building

1st St and Independence Ave S.E., 20515. General Capitol Information ☎ 224-3121. Open Mon–Fri 9–5. Closed weekends, New Year's Day, Thanksgiving, and Christmas Day. Limited access. For an appointment with your state representative, contact his/her office prior to your visit. Restrooms, telephones. Wheelchair accessible.

This Beaux-Arts building (1905–8; Carrère and Hastings) is the oldest congressional office building, aside from the U.S. Capitol Building.

**Highlights:** The rotunda.

### History

As the nation continued to admit states into the Union, the number of representatives increased and Congress began outgrowing the Capitol. Additional office space was needed. In March 1901, the Sundry Civil Appropriation Act commissioned the Architect of the Capitol to develop plans for office facilities adjacent to the Capitol. In 1903, a similar appropriation authorized a site and the construction of the buildings.

On July 18, 1903, excavation of the sites began. A year later the famous New York architecture firm Carrère and Hastings was hired. They were given the task of designing two structures, one for the House and another for the Senate. Thomas Hastings oversaw the completion of the Cannon Building, while John Carrère worked on the Senate Office Building.

The cornerstone for the Cannon House Office Building, named for Illinois congressman "Uncle" Joe Cannon (1836–1926), was laid on April 14, 1906. The building was designed as a hollow square that would admit light into the interior offices.

The 60th Congress occupied the building on Dec 12, 1907. The 379 offices boasted many luxuries (for that era), such as a forced-air ventilation system, steam heat, individual lavatories with hot and cold running water, telephones, and electricity on many circuits. By 1913, the House needed more office space; 51 rooms were added to the building by raising the roof and constructing a fifth floor.

Plans for remodeling the building began in 1924, along with the construction of another House building, the Longworth. The remodeling project, completed between Aug and Nov of 1932, added 171 two-room suites, 14 three-room suites, 10 single rooms, and 23 committee rooms. In the following years the building was modernized with elevators, air-conditioning, and a parking garage.

## Exterior

The classical design of the building features a colonnade of 34 Doric columns. The Independence and New Jersey Ave fronts are faced with marble from South Dover, New York; the C and 1st St elevations with marble from Georgia; and the court fronts with marble from Bedford, Indiana.

## Interior

Enter the building at the New Jersey and Independence Aves entrance and proceed into the rotunda. The rotunda has a marble arcade in which 18 Corinthian columns support an ornately decorated entablature and dome. The glass oculus of the dome fills the room with natural light.

The Cannon Building is connected to the Capitol, like its sister House and Senate buildings, by a subway in its basement. The subway may be used by the public, although congressman have priority when Congress is in session. The Longworth Office Building is connected to the building via a basement corridor.

Cross New Jersey Ave S.E. to the Longworth House Office Building, which is immediately west of the Cannon Building.

# Longworth House Office Building

Independence and New Jersey Aves S.E., 20515. General Capitol Information ☎ 224-3121. Open Mon–Fri 9–5. Closed weekends, New Year's Day, Thanksgiving, and Christmas Day. Limited access. For an appointment with your state representative, call his/her office prior to your visit. House Gift Shop open Mon–Fri 9:30–4. Restrooms, telephones. Wheelchair accessible.

The Longworth House Office Building (1929–33; Allied Architects of Washington), like the Cannon and Rayburn Office Buildings, was built to alleviate crowding in House offices.

**Highlights:** The building offers a no-frills example of utilitarian governmental construction. A basement-level gift shop sells clothing, golf balls, Christmas tree ornaments, and pens emblazoned with the Capitol and House emblems.

### History

The second of the three House office buildings erected, the Longworth Building was planned in 1925 as an effort to alleviate the shortage of space in the Cannon Building. Congress appropriated $2,500 for the Architect of the Capitol, David Lynn, to use for design research. Lynn investigated the possibility of constructing an addition to the Cannon Building with the original architects, Carrère and Hastings. The famous architects wanted to build on the Cannon's courtyard, but the plan never received serious consideration.

A local firm, Allied Architects of Washington, submitted a proposal for the new House building. The architects—Frank Upman, Gilbert LaCoste Rodier, Nathan C. Wyeth, and Louis Justemente—created two plans for a building, one of which was selected in 1929.

That same year, the Architect of the Capitol hired Allied Architects as consultants. A cornerstone was laid on Jan 10, 1929, and the building was dedicated in honor of Nicholas Longworth (1869–1931), a congressman from Ohio and Speaker of the House from 1925 to 1931. Construction ended in Dec 1930. The building was fully occupied by April 20, 1933.

### Washington Notes

The Varnum Hotel was torn down in 1929 to make way for the Longworth Office Building. The hotel, previously known as Conrad and McMunn's Boarding House, had been a complex of three five-story town houses for boarders. Among its famous residents was Thomas Jefferson, who lived in the house from 1800 to 1801 while serving as vice president to John Adams and for a fortnight shortly after his own inauguration as president. Other buildings in the blocks that were razed to build the Longworth included the offices of the Coast and Geodetic Survey, an agency that surveyed the nation's coastal waters.

## Interior

The Longworth Building offers little of interest to the casual tourist apart from the elegant marbled foyers and the opportunity to spot a member of Washington's elite.

Walk west on Independence Ave across S. Capitol St into the Southwest quadrant of Washington. The visitor entrance of the Rayburn House Office Building is on the south side of Independence Ave.

## Rayburn House Office Building

Independence Ave and S. Capitol St S.W., 20512. General Capitol Information ☎ 224-3121. Open Mon–Fri 9–5. Closed weekends, New Year's Day, Thanksgiving, and Christmas Day. Limited access. For an appointment with your state representative, contact his/her office prior to your visit. Restrooms, telephones. Wheelchair accessible.

The **Rayburn House Office Building** (1962–65; Harbeson, Hough, Livingston, and Larson) supplies office space for the various staffs of the House.

### History

The Second Supplemental Appropriation Act of 1955 authorized the construction of an additional building for the House of Representatives at a cost of $135,279,000. A subway from the center of the Independence Ave upper-garage level connects the Rayburn Building to the southwest corner of the Capitol. The Rayburn is also connected by an underground corridor to the Longworth House Office Building.

The cornerstone for the nine-story building was laid on May 24, 1962, by Speaker of the House John W. McCormack. The ceremony featured an address from John F. Kennedy. House staffs fully occupied the building on April 2, 1965. The building is named for Sam Rayburn (1882–1961), a congressman from Texas who served as Speaker of the House from 1940 to 1946, 1949 to 1952, and 1955 to 1961.

### Exterior

The Independence Ave entrance is marked by two statues that face each other. At the west end is the seated *Majesty of Law*. Law is represented by a seated male holding a book of laws in his left hand and a scabbard in his right. The *Spirit of Justice* is at the east side of the staircase. Justice is a seated female who holds a vessel in her right hand. Her left arm caresses the shoulder of a child. The east and west façades are adorned with nine-ft-tall Greek rhytons, wine cups shaped like a ram's head.

### Interior

The building has 9 hearing rooms and more than 170 offices. In the lobby of the Independence Ave entrance is a statue of Speaker Rayburn (1965; Felix de Weldon).

Walk west on Independence Ave S.W. to 1st St S.W. The entrance to the Frederic Auguste Bartholdi Park of the United States Botanic Garden is on the southwest corner of this intersection.

## Frederic Auguste Bartholdi Park

Independence Ave between 1st St and Washington State Ave S.W. ☎ 225-8333. Open daily. Visitors tour the park on their own. Markers placed in the garden identify the plants and trees.

Frederic Auguste Bartholdi Park, a two-acre extension of the U.S. Botanic Garden (its conservatory is north, across Independence Ave), is a pleasant oasis. At the park's center is the magnificent Bartholdi Fountain (1876; Frederic Auguste Bartholdi). In the surrounding beds are nine themed gardens.

## Grounds

Enter the park at the 1st St and Independence Ave side. At the center of the park is the **Bartholdi Fountain.** Frederic Auguste Bartholdi, who is best remembered for his design of the Statue of Liberty, created the fountain for the International Centennial Exposition of 1876 in Philadelphia. Illuminated with gas lights (since replaced with electric globes) and spitting jets of water, the fountain was a novelty to Victorian Americans and was prominently displayed at the exposition. Like many of the exhibits at the exposition, the United States acquired the fountain. However, unlike other exhibits that were donated to the new Smithsonian Institution by foreign exhibitors unwilling to pay for their removal, the government bought the fountain, 30 ft tall and weighing 40 tons, from Bartholdi for $6,000 in 1877. Made of cast iron, constructed in three identical sections, the fountain was painted black to resemble bronze. Aquatic monsters at the base support three female Nereids (sea nymphs), who hold the fountain's basin above their heads. The work progresses upward to three Tritons. A bronze crown caps the piece. Bartholdi combined flowing water and lighting as allegories for the elements of water and light. He named the piece *Fountain of Light and Water.* It was the first statue in Washington to incorporate both sound and light. Originally, it was placed on the grounds of the U.S. Botanic Garden (USBG), then in the middle of the Mall. In 1932 it was moved to its current location. For its 100th anniversary in 1986, the fountain was restored.

Follow the path west, parallel to Independence Ave. On the north side are the **Independence Ave Beds.** The displays in these beds are seasonal, often annuals. Among the flowers that bloom here are red ambassador cannas and purple petunias. Several species of geranium are planted in the shade of the English yew.

At the Washington State Ave entrance is the **Entrance Garden.** There are assorted perennials, biennials, and annuals. Dotting the beds are gray, dwarf conifers. Turn left and follow the path south parallel to Washington State Ave.

Four seasons of foliage bloom at various times in the **All-Seasons Garden.** Some of the plants here are witch hazels, butterfly bush, heavenly bamboo, and ornamental grasses. The **Touch and Smell Garden** is a hands-on garden. Its plants, mostly herbs such as exotic sages like Spanish, blue, and pineapple-scented, appeal to many senses. The Botanic Garden encourages visitors to handle the plants, hence the garden's name.

Next is the **Daisy Garden.** The **Trial Garden** is used by All America Selections (AAS) to test plants not yet commercially available.

The small stone house, built in 1933, originally served as the garden director's residence. Today, the USBG administrative offices are located there. The beds on either side of the building are known as the **Cottage Garden,** and are designed to provide shade. A mixture of annuals, perennials, and biennials are displayed here, including ferns and rhododendrons.

Proceed behind the house and turn left. The **Botanical Bedding Garden** is comprised of tropical plants that can survive a moderate climate. Gardens such as this were popular in Victorian America. At the center is a **Chinese jujube tree.** The brown fruit, which tastes like a date or fig, was used to make jujube candies. Only perennials were planted in the Island Perennial Beds. This was done to demonstrate the shape and color varieties of perennials.

Exit Bartholdi Park, and continue west on Washington Ave S.W. to its juncture with Independence Ave S.W. Continue west to 3rd St S.W. and turn north across Independence to Maryland Ave S.W., then turn east, or right, to the entrance of the United States Botanic Garden Conservatory.

## U.S. Botanic Garden

The U.S. Botanic Garden is closed for renovation until the fall of 2000, and information regarding hours of operation, tours, and flower shows when it reopens is unknown at this time. Prior to the renovation, the following information was current.

Maryland Ave at 1st St S.W. ☎ 225-8333. Web: www.nationalgarden.org. Open daily 9–5. Summer hours 9 A.M.–8 P.M. Admission: free. Guided tours Mon–Fri at 10 and 2, approximately 40 minutes. Reservations necessary. Call one week in advance. ☎ 226-4082. The Botanic Garden sponsors four annual shows: Chrysanthemums in Nov, Poinsettias in Dec, a Spring Flower Show March–April, and a Summer Terrace Display from mid-May–early Oct. Temporary shows are displayed regularly. A series of free, hour-long horticultural seminars are open to the public. ☎ 226-4082. Restrooms, telephones, gift shop, café. Wheelchair accessible.

The U.S. Botanic Garden is the oldest botanic garden in North America. It houses a vast collection of exotic plants and flowers, including tropical species, rare hybrids, and varieties from the Americas, as well as other parts of the world.

**Highlights:** The renovated conservatory and Palm House. The new National Garden, a three-acre site adjacent to and an extension of the U.S. Botanic Garden.

### History

Several statesmen, including George Washington, Thomas Jefferson, and James Madison, proposed the idea for a national botanic garden in the late 18C. In 1796, Washington wrote a letter to the Federal City's commissioners requesting a plot for the construction of such a garden. In 1820, Congress established the Botanic Garden as a part of the Columbia Institute for the Promotion of Arts and Science. It was chartered "to collect, cultivate, and grow various vegetable products of this and other countries for exhibition and display."

The Columbia Institute dissolved seven years later and interest in the garden waned. The idea was revived in 1842 when Admiral Charles Wilkes returned from his 1838–42 expedition to the South Pacific with dozens of plant specimens. These were donated to the Botanic Garden. A greenhouse was constructed in 1842 behind the old Patent Office at the corner of 7th and G Sts N.W.

To permit an extension to the old Patent Office, the Botanic Garden was relocated to its current site at the east end of the Mall in 1849. The Joint Committee on the Library of Congress was awarded jurisdiction of the garden a few years later (this power was transferred to the Architect of the Capitol in 1934). In 1931 the architectural firm of Bennett, Parsons & Frost was hired to design the conservatory. The building was opened in 1933.

Today's USBG contains more than 12,000 plants in its permanent collection. The USBG grows, records, and displays plant life for study and exchange with other institutions. The majority of the collection is comprised of hybrids, primarily from the tropical Americas, although other continents are represented as well. The USBG's present focus is to preserve rare and endangered plants, and to increase its collection of historical hybrids and outstanding new hybrids.

Future plans for the conservatory include a New and Old World Desert Exhibit, an Epiphyte House with orchids and bromeliads, an Asian Garden in the west courtyard, and a Garden of Pompeii in the east courtyard. The National Garden, which opened in 1999, is an educational center located west of the conservatory.

> ### Washington Notes
> The USBG is responsible for caring for and preserving any confiscated protected plants that are illegally imported into the United States.

## Exterior

The United States Botanic Garden Conservatory (1931; Bennett, Parsons & Frost) was designed to resemble 17C French greenhouses. Arches topped with gargoyles line the north façade. The south façade reveals the functionality of the building: glass roofs and a glass-enclosed rotunda. During warmer months café seating is offered on the east terrace, another great little urban oasis.

The renovation (Daniel, Mann, Johnson, Mendenhall, Washington, D.C.; Rodney Robinson Landscape Architects, Wilmington, Delaware, associate architects), whose total cost will be around $33.5 million, will add new connecting houses between the gardens and an addition to the rear of the building that will create a south entry from Independence Ave. The **Palm House** will be restored in its original Art Deco style.

## Interior

The entire interior of the conservatory is being redesigned. The renovation will completely replace the glazing, interior floors, doors, and lighting. Exhibits in the west half of the conservatory will focus on the importance of plants to people. Themes within the greenhouses will emphasize plant conservation and endangered species, plant discoveries, orchids, and tropical medicinal plants. Case exhibits will examine the influence plants have had in the development of civilization, the therapeutic quality of plants, and how plants are represented in the arts. Exhibits in the east half of the building will focus on the ecology and evolutionary biology of plants. Greenhouse themes will include representation of primitive plants in a reconstructed Jurassic landscape (complete with dinosaur footprints), an oasis, and plants of the desert. The Palm House will be recreated as a jungle, representing the reclaiming of an abandoned plantation by the surrounding tropical rain forest. The **Subtropical House** will become an expanded exhibit of economic plants focusing attention on how the diversity of plants supports the vast majority of humanity's food supply, and fiber, cosmetic, and industrial products.

The **National Garden** focuses on the relationship between human beings and nature and emphasizes the importance of responsible environmental practices, with the use of composted fertilizers and natural pesticides. Separate entities focus on particular themes. (The garden titles may be changed when the renovation is complete.) The **Water Garden** is dedicated to all American first ladies in recognition of their contributions to the country. The **Rose Garden,** honoring the national flower, consists of two octagonal parterres featuring over 200 varieties of historical and modern roses. The **Showcase Garden** features an extensive display of the diversity of plants and flowers native to the mid-Atlantic region. Visitors are able to see plans for bog, stream, pond, and woodland habitats. Pathways through the National Garden lead to the **Senator John Heinz Environmental Learning Center,** an indoor/outdoor facility for the study of horticulture, botany, and the environmental sciences. The center, with its lecture hall, classroom, library, and outdoor amphitheater, features lectures, workshops, and demonstrations for adults and children. The **Butterfly Garden** features scented and nectar-producing plants that attract adult butterflies and complement the butterfly-larvae host plants found in the Showcase Garden. The **Garden Pergolas** feature arbors and trellises of ornamental plantings and provide views across the Rose Garden and Lawn Terrace from the north and south walls of the National Garden.

**Diversion:**
To see the Voice of America, walk southwest to 3rd St. Turn left and cross Independence Ave. Continue one block south on 3rd St. Turn right at C St and walk to the entrance of the **Wilber J. Cohen Building** (1939–41; Office of the Supervising Architect), where the Voice of America is headquartered.

## Voice of America

330 Independence Ave S.W. ☎ 619-3919. Web: www.voa.gov. Closed weekends, federal holidays. Guided tours begin at C St entrance Mon–Fri 10:30, 1:30, 2:30. Reservations preferred. No self-guided tours or admittance unless accompanied by an employee. Restrooms, telephones. Wheelchair accessible—entrance at C St.

Voice of America (VOA), the broadcasting service of the United States Information Agency, transmits newscasts, feature stories, and English-language lessons via radio and television airwaves to an international audience. Recent financial cutbacks by Congress have threatened the organization's existence. For now it will continue to broadcast, though programming may be cut back.

### History

In the 1930s several attempts were made by New York congressman Emmanuel Celler and other legislators to create a U.S. radio station that would counter German propaganda programs. Bills introduced in 1937, 1938, and 1939 never received enough support to pass. In 1941, however, the U.S. Coordinator for Inter-America Affairs (CIAA) leased private radio transmitters to broadcast programs to Latin America. That same year President Franklin Delano Roosevelt established the Foreign Information Service (FIS) and named his speechwriter Robert Sherwood as its director.

Sherwood assembled a staff of journalists in New York City to broadcast the American government's views. By December 1941 FIS had made its first broadcast to Asia. The first FIS broadcast to Europe occurred on Feb 24, 1942—79 days after the U.S. entered World War II. The 15-minute program was sent across the continent from a BBC transmitter and opened with the words "Here speaks the voice of America." The Office of War Information (OWI) assumed responsibility for VOA's programming in June 1942. At the end of World War II Voice of America was broadcasting to 23 countries in 41 languages.

After the war, Congress considered eliminating VOA. Led by Arthur McMahon, a professor at Columbia University, a committee of private citizens advised the federal government that the U.S. "could not be indifferent to the ways in which our society is portrayed in other countries." On Dec 31, 1945, oversight of VOA was transferred to the Department of State. Reluctantly, Congress appropriated funds for continued broadcasting.

With the emergence of the Cold War and accompanying hostile international broadcasting by the Soviet Union, the Smith-Mundt Act was passed in 1948 ensuring future funding for VOA and other projects.

The U.S. Information Agency (USIA) was established in 1953 to promote international informational and cultural exchange programs. Responsibility for the VOA was transferred to the infant USIA. In 1976 President Gerald Ford signed into law the VOA charter, which had been written in 1960. The organization's mission is to provide accurate, objective, and comprehensive programing.

After more than 55 years on the air, the VOA broadcasts in 52 languages 24 hours daily, 365 days a year.

## Interior

Tours begin in the C St lobby. After a brief lecture about Voice of America, its history, mission, and future and a five-minute video showing writers, editors, and producers creating various programs, visitors are guided into the corridors, where the broadcaster's 45 radio and 2 TV studios, as well as its newsroom, are located.

One hallway on the ground floor is decorated with a set of murals, *The Meaning of Social Security* (1942; Ben Shahn). Shahn was one of several artists hired in 1940 by the Section of Fine Arts of the Public Buildings Administration of the Federal Works Agency, an organization that charged artists with beautifying newly constructed federal buildings.

Shahn based these murals on three themes from Franklin Delano Roosevelt's June 8, 1934, address to Congress regarding his goals for society: decent homes, productive work, and a safeguard against misfortune. On the west wall is *Work, Family, Social Security.* Though the colors are somber, the message is upbeat. At the center is a gathered family, conveying a sense of community. To the left is the theme of work: various public works projects are illustrated to demonstrate a sense of accomplishment and public benefit. Security, the theme on the right, shows homes being built and fields harvested.

On the east wall is *Child Labor, Unemployment, Old Age.* This mural portrays the ills the New Deal was meant to alleviate. A line of men—sitting, standing, and waiting—conveys unemployment. To the left, a young girl opens a door to reveal boys working in a factory; a crippled boy hobbles from a mine entrance. These images illustrate child labor. To the right, the insecurity of dependents is portrayed an older woman clutching her crutches and a mother cradling her baby.

To skip Voice of America and continue, walk northeast on Maryland Ave to its intersection with 1st St S.W. Cross this intersection to the **President James A. Garfield Monument** (1887; John Quincy Adams Ward). The veterans of the Army of the Cumberland erected this statue in honor of the assassinated James Garfield (1831–1881), 20th president of the U.S. At the top of the granite monument is a nine-ft statue of Garfield. The figure faces west, down the path of Maryland Ave. The three allegorical figures seated around the base of the statue represent Garfield's career as a statesman, student, and soldier. As statesman, Garfield holds his inaugural address, which is inscribed with the phrase "Law Justice Prosperity." Garfield as student studies a book; Garfield as soldier draws his dagger from its scabbard.

Walk northeast across Maryland Ave to the **Ulysses S. Grant Memorial** (1922; Henry Merwin Shrady, sculptor; Edward Pearce Casey, architect) and **Union Square** (1976; Skidmore, Owings and Merrill), Maryland Ave and 1st St N.W. Union Square honors the Union soldiers of the Civil War and their final field commander, Ulysses S. Grant. The statuary that dominates this site is one of the most elaborate and impressive sculpture groups in the city. It includes the second largest equestrian statue in the world (Rome's Victor Emmanuel statue is the largest).

### History

The Society of the Army of Tennessee, Grant's first major command, proposed the idea of a memorial honoring Ulysses S. Grant (1822–1886) in 1895. In 1901, Congress passed the Hepburn Act, providing $250,000 for the sculpture as well as authorizing the formation of a commission to select a sculptor. A public competition in 1902 led to the selection of a design by Henry Merwin Shrady (1871–1922), a virtually unknown artist from New York City.

The selection caused an uproar among more established artists who believed the commission, the largest ever offered up to that time by Congress, should go to a more renowned sculptor. Shrady, in fact, had taught himself to sculpt. Although Shrady's mounted statue of Washington was selected for the Williamsburg Bridge Plaza in Brooklyn, Shrady had never executed a work of the magnitude required for Grant's statue.

Shrady prepared meticulously for the task. The commandant at West Point had cadets reenact artillery and cavalry drills for Shrady. The secretary of war provided him with authentic uniforms, and Shrady studied the anatomy of both living and dead horses. He also joined the New York National Guard for four years. The work went slowly, requiring Shrady to request several extensions.

Twenty-one years passed before Shrady completed the commission. The monument was dedicated April 27, 1922, the centennial of Grant's birthday. Vice President Calvin Coolidge and General John Pershing gave the addresses, and Grant's granddaughter and great-granddaughter unveiled the mounted figure of U. S. Grant. Physically exhausted by the project, Shrady had died two weeks earlier.

> ### Washington Notes
> The monument was originally intended for the Ellipse, but President Roosevelt argued that it would block the White House's view of the Potomac. The committee then choose the area at the east end of the Mall. Many Washingtonians protested, as this location would necessitate the removal of three large trees. The superintendent of the Botanic Garden, who was also concerned about the trees, took the case to court but lost. The foundations for the monument were laid in 1909.

The Ulysses S. Grant Memorial features a center equestrian statue of General Grant flanked by two wings of sculpture groups: *Cavalry* and *Artillery.* These figures are all based on a marble terrace 252 ft in width and 71 ft in depth. The statue is 17 ft and 2 inches tall and weighs 10,700 pounds. "Grant" is inscribed on the pedestal.

Grant's figure sits slack in the saddle of his horse, Cincinnatus, contemplating a battle in the distance. His uniform, a battered hat and a capelike overcoat, is a simple one, but what Grant favored during the campaign. Through Grant's relaxed composure, Shrady hoped to capture Grant's unshakable nerve. Cincinnatus, on the other hand, has an alert, tense stance and his nostrils are flaring as if he has caught an odor of gunpowder and smoke from a nearby battle.

On either side of the pedestal are bas-relief panels, *Infantry*, which depict troops marching into battle. Shrady designed these before his death, and Edmund Amateis and Sherry Fry executed the pieces from Shrady's sketches. The panels were installed after the 1922 dedication. Four lions, reclining atop smaller pedestals, surround the main pedestal and were placed around the memorial when the base was laid.

*Cavalry* occupies the area north of the Grant statue. Seven charging horseman of a color guard depict the tension and fury of battle. The officer rides the lead horse and, with his sword, summons those in his command into the fight. To the rear, a bugler, chest expanded, prepares to sound the charge. Another rider and his horse have fallen, and to his rear, a comrade reaches with his arm toward him. Shrady used his own face as the model for the fallen soldier. The other soldiers' faces were modeled from a group of Shrady's friends.

*Artillery* stands to the south of the Grant equestrian statue and, like *Cavalry*, captures the dynamic, frenzied nature of battle. The work shows a caisson with three men being pulled through muddy terrain by three horses. On one of the horses, the artilleryman carrying the guidon signals a hard right turn. Two horses have begun to halt for the turn, but a third, whose harness has snapped, continues forward. The three soldiers on the caisson struggle to maintain their balance and their fear is tangible. At the south end of this piece is a bronze plaque naming the West Point cadets from the class of 1908 who served as Shrady's models.

The six-acre pool west of the memorial is known as the Capitol Reflecting Pool and sits above a tunnel for I-395.

Proceed north on 1st St to the **Peace Monument** (1877; Franklin Simmons, sculptor; Edward Clark, architect), 1st St and Pennsylvania Ave N.W. This marble memorial, originally christened the Navy Monument, and in line with the Capitol's west façade, was sculpted in Rome by Simmons from a drawing by Admiral David Porter. The work honors the seamen who died during the Civil War.

Standing at the top of the monument are two allegorical female figures representing history and America. History holds a scroll listing the sailors killed in the war, while America weeps on History's shoulder over the loss of her heroes. The inscription on the scroll held by History reads, "They died that their country might live."

Halfway up the pedestal's west side, Victory holds a laurel wreath and an oak branch over the infant figures of Neptune, god of the seas, and Mars, god of war. Standing on the east side, facing the Capitol, is a female figure depicting peace. Two cherubs are at her feet and she holds an olive branch. Nearby a dove rests on a sheaf of wheat, symbols of peace and agriculture. To the right is a horn, the allegorical symbol of plenty.

At the foot of the 40 ft sculpture is a large basin; fountain jets project from each side.

**Diversion:**
To see the **Robert A. Taft Memorial** (1959; Douglas W. Orr), 1st St and Constitution Ave N.W., continue north on 1st St. Cross Constitution Ave. Follow the sidewalk on the north side of Constitution Ave east to the memorial.

The Robert A. Taft Memorial is the only monument honoring a senator in Washington, D.C. It is located in a grassy, parklike area and honors the Ohio senator, who was respected for his honesty, integrity, and firm belief in free government. Taft was also such a staunch advocate of the GOP that he became known on "the Hill" as Mr. Republican.

The memorial, constructed with funds solicited by subscription from every state, was dedicated on April 14, 1959, six years after Taft's death.

At the center of a concrete and paving stone apron is a 100 ft high tower built with Tennessee marble. In the upper part of the tower is a **carillon** that rings every 15 minutes. The bells are also sounded during presidential inaugural ceremonies, a tradition that began with the inauguration of President Reagan. The largest of the 27 bells, called a bourdon bell, weighs seven tons. The bells were cast in the Paccard Bell Foundry in France. At the base of the tower is a ten-ft-tall statue of Taft (1958; Wheeler Williams). Inscribed on the west face of the tower, above the statue, is a tribute to Taft. A moat with jets of water skirts the tower.

Walk 3 details the Congressional Cemetery and Walk 4 covers the Washington Navy Yard and other less-visited areas of Capitol Hill. To get to the beginning of Walk 3 and the beginning of Walk 4, it is necessary to drive or take a taxi cab. The distances are too far to walk and the areas traversed are sometimes the scene of crimes.

To continue to Walk 5, head west along Pennsylvania Ave to the National Gallery of Art.

# 3 · Congressional Cemetery and Environs

Metro: Blue/Orange Line to Potomac Ave or Stadium Armory.
Bus: 96, B2, or D2.

## *Congressional Cemetery*

1801 E St S.E. ☎ 543-0539. Web: www.geocities.com/Heartland/Meadows/4633. Open daily during daylight hours. Admission: free. Cemetery office open Sat 8–4. Brochures are sometimes available. Visitors tour on their own. Note: We suggest visiting Congressional Cemetery on Sat when the grounds and office are generally manned by volunteers and foot traffic is heavier. Though occasional dogwalkers traipse through during the week, the cemetery has been the victim of vandals and thievery.

The Congressional Cemetery (DL) sits on a 32½-acre plot and has more than 60,000 graves. Established on April 4, 1807, the cemetery is the oldest in the District of Columbia and the first national cemetery created in the United States.

Although the site is maintained, finding specific graves and monuments may be difficult as the grounds are densely populated with markers of similar heights and appearance. Where dates and the names of monument sculptors are missing from the following descriptions, this information is unknown.

**Highlights:** The cemetery is notable for its many fine examples of 19C funereal art. The cemetery also is important because it contains the graves of many prominent citizens, including Apache Chief Taza; Civil War photographer Mathew Brady; Belva Lockwood, the first woman to run for president and receive votes; Robert Mills, architect of the Washington Monument; conductor and composer John Philip Sousa; FBI Director J. Edgar Hoover; and more than 80 congressmen whose grave sites are marked by cenotaphs designed by Benjamin Latrobe. In June 1997 the National Trust for Historic Preservation added Congressional Cemetery to its list of America's 11 Most Endangered Historic Places.

### History

Capitol Hill residents established Congressional Cemetery. Plots in the original 4½-acre cemetery sold for $2. William Swinton, a renowned stonecutter from Philadelphia recruited by Benjamin Latrobe to do work for the Capitol, became the first interment. He was buried on April 11, 1807. On July 19, 1807, Senator Uriah Tracy of Connecticut was the first legislator interred in the cemetery.

Responsibility for the cemetery was transferred to Christ Church, Washington Parish, in 1812. Shortly thereafter, the cemetery was renamed Washington Parish Burial Grounds. In 1816, the vestry set aside 100 burial sites for members of Congress. The vestry later extended burial privileges to the families of congressional members and other dignitaries. Eventually, the government owned 924 burial sites to be used for members of Congress and officials who died in office. As the government's use of the cemetery increased, it became known as Congressional Cemetery.

The Public Vault was added in 1835 to provide a temporary resting place for a deceased until a grave site could be prepared or transportation arranged. In 1839 the House of Representatives adopted a resolution calling for the erection of cenotaphs, grave markers for a deceased buried in another site. The cenotaphs were used to honor congressional members who died in office as of 1807. Benjamin Latrobe designed the markers, which resemble cubes crowned with stout, inverted cones. By 1877 construction of cenotaphs was determined to be too costly. Representative George Hoar from Massachusetts (later a senator) announced in a speech that being buried beneath one of them would add a new terror to death. As a result, the 1839 resolution was repealed. Since then, few congressional members have been interred in the cemetery.

From the 1820s through the 1870s, Congress periodically raised money for improvements to the grounds. A brick wall was added, as was the Keeper's House and receiving vaults. A series of annexations in 1875 increased the cemetery's acreage to its present size.

During the 1950s, a decline in membership at Christ Church and a lack of federal funding left the cemetery in disrepair. This continued until 1976 when a nondenominational group formed the Congressional Cemetery Association. Although this group restored the Chapel and landscaped the grounds, the state of the cemetery has declined.

**Washington Notes**

Congressional Cemetery was the site of a Washington political scandal during the 19C. Occasionally, Mrs. Daniel Sickles would meet Attorney General Philip Barton Key II for trysts among the gravestones. When Sickles's husband learned of her unfaithfulness, he followed Key through Lafayette Park and murdered him on the steps of a ritzy social club. (See Walk 9: "The White House and Lafayette Square.")

## Grounds

Unlike most national cemeteries, which primarily inter military personnel, Congressional Cemetery holds a more diverse population. For instance, as a result of the high infant mortality rate during the 19C, many of the neighborhood's children were buried here.

From the entry gate proceed south along the paved road. Halfway to the chapel, on the left, is a field of **Cenotaphs.** Designed by Benjamin Latrobe, Architect of the Capitol, these monuments memorialize members of Congress who died in office from 1807 to 1877, such as Henry Clay and John Quincy Adams. While some mark actual graves, most serve as memorials. Other cenotaphs honor prominent citizens who did not serve in Congress. The cenotaphs' design varies. Latrobe's original models were more ornate than the simpler style Congress eventually authorized. Each of these four-sided sandstone monuments stands about 4½ ft tall.

South of the cenotaphs, a few rows east from the road, is a monument honoring **Major General Alexander Macomb,** (1841; sculptor unknown), a hero of the War of 1812 and a commanding general of the U.S. Army. This 14 ft tall neoclassical work is one of the most notable pre–Civil War monuments. The marble base is decorated with patterns of laurel leaves symbolizing victory and carvings of a butterfly and snake, as well as an hourglass above a scythe and wings, symbolizing the passage of time. The base supports four pairs of lion paws holding aloft an obelisk wrapped in the American flag. A Roman officer's helmet crowns the piece.

Continue south on the paved road to the **Chapel.** The chapel was built in 1903 and has been restored to its original condition. The interior is simply furnished with wooden pews and a modest altar. Flanking the altar are square wooden doors to temporary vaults built into the wall.

Exit the Chapel and follow the paved road heading east. At the first crosspath, turn left and walk north. A series of arched vaults, half-buried in berms, are primarily privately owned. However, the **Public Vault** was built with congressional money in 1835. It was used to hold the remains of officials prior to the digging of their grave site or before transportation to their home states. Among those temporarily interred here were Presidents William Henry Harrison, John Quincy Adams, and Zachary Taylor, and First Ladies Dolley Madison and Louisa Adams.

Continue north until reaching the brick crosspath. Turn right and walk east. Walk about 100 ft, pass the grave marker adorned with a praying angel on the right, and turn south. Six graves in, on the right, is the grave site of **Robert Mills,** who designed several important Washington buildings, including the Old Treasury, the Old Post Office, the Patent Office, and the Washington Monument. For more than 80 years his grave remained unmarked, until the American Institute of Architects placed a marker here in 1936.

Return to the path and walk ten ft, then turn north onto the grassy path. Past the field of cenotaphs is a newer cenotaph on the right. It marks the burial site of

Choctaw Indian chief **Push-ma-ta-ha.** He came to Washington to claim a debt the U.S. government owed his tribe. When Push-ma-ta-ha died from an illness in Washington in 1825, his friend President Andrew Jackson led the mile-long funeral procession. (The debt to the Choctaws was not paid until 1888.) Push-ma-ta-ha's last words, "let the big guns boom over me," are inscribed on his marker. To fulfill his wish, Jackson had Push-ma-ta-ha buried with a full military funeral. The current stone, narrower and slightly taller than the other cenotaphs around it, replaced the original marker, which had suffered weather damage.

Directly south, facing the Push-ma-ta-ha cenotaph, are the graves of architects **George Hadfield** and **William Thornton.** Hadfield worked on the Capitol and designed the Lee Mansion and the Old City Hall, now the District Courthouse. Thornton conceived and executed the original design of the Capitol Building and was a prominent figure in Washington social circles.

From Push-ma-ta-ha's marker, continue north along the path until reaching the cemetery's perimeter fence. Walk three rows east, then three markers south to the **Elbridge Gerry Monument** (1823; W. Frazee and John Frazee). This neoclassical piece, erected by Congress in 1823, honors Elbridge Gerry (1744–1814), a Massachusetts native who signed the Declaration of Independence. His memorial, a marble pyramid-shaped base capped by an urn and flame, stands 12 ft high.

> ### Washington Notes
>
> As a close friend of Samuel Adams, John Adams, John Hancock, and other Revolutionary War figures, Gerry participated in the First Continental Congress. Gerry also traveled to France as a member of the 1787 XYZ mission to prevent war with that country. Later, as governor of Massachusetts, he oversaw the passing of a redistricting bill that aided his own Republican Party. The term *gerrymander* traces its origins to this episode, as one of the redrawn districts looked like a salamander. Gerry, who was also vice president under Madison, died halfway through his term in 1814.

Return to the grassy footpath west of the Push-ma-ta-ha and Gerry monuments, and proceed south, away from the cemetery wall. Turn east on the crosspath. At the paved road, turn right and walk south.

Along the right side of this path, where the bench sits, is the fenced-in grave site of **J. Edgar Hoover,** first director of the Federal Bureau of Investigation. Continue south along the road to the grave of **Clyde Tolson,** Hoover's longtime companion and FBI associate.

Five sites to the left of Tolson lies **Leonard Matlovich,** a decorated veteran of the Vietnam War who was discharged for being a homosexual. His stone, decorated with pink triangles, a symbol of gay pride, is inscribed with the words "When I was in the military they gave me a medal for killing two men, and a discharge for loving one." Matlovich died in 1988, a casualty of AIDS.

Backtrack past the Hoover site to the crosspath. Turn right and walk east toward the brick cemetery wall. Three rows from the wall, turn right and walk south 20 ft along the grassy path. The marker for **Taza,** the son of the Apache chief Cochise, is adorned with a bust. Lured to Washington in 1876 by an unscrupulous Indian agent, the impoverished Taza was forced to perform dances and participate in sideshows to earn money to return home. Before he could escape he caught pneumonia and died. The government buried him with the honors befitting a chief. The bust was added by the American Indian Society of Washington.

Continue south to the paved road and head west toward the chapel. Walk 20 yards past the crossroad. Turn left into the field of graves and walk 30 yards south to find the grave of **Anne Royall** (1769–1854), a feisty reporter whom members of Congress would cross the street to avoid. Once, she was sentenced to be dunked in the Potomac for her outspokenness in court. Though the conviction was eventually overturned, legend has it that she invited her detractors to meet her at the river, stripped, and dove in.

From Royall's plot walk south to the grassy footpath. Turn left and walk west to the slate crosspath. On the rise of ground just above the row of vaults, is the **Lieutenant John T. McLaughlin Monument** (1847; Struthers). This unusual monument, carved by Struthers of Philadelphia, breaks from the military motifs of the time by not including carvings of crossed swords, anchors, and Roman helmets. The erect cannon atop stone balls was carved from a single piece of marble and placed on a pedestal with the inscription: "Sacred to the memory of John T. McLaughlin, a Lieutenant in the Navy of the United States, died July 6, 1847, AG. 35 years."

Head north and return to the paved road. At the paved road, turn left and walk west, toward the chapel. On the left of the road, in the southeast area immediately adjacent to the chapel, are the resting places of **Joseph Gales, Jr.,** and **General Archibald Henderson.** Gales founded the *National Intelligencer,* a politically and socially powerful newspaper, and served for a time as mayor of D.C. Four markers south of Gales rests Henderson, the longest serving commandant of the Marine Corps (1820–59). The **Andrew Coyle Monument,** dated 1855, the only truly Gothic piece in the cemetery with its tall, chapel-like spire representing a Scottish cathedral, is a few ft south, on the right side of the path.

Return to the paved road and walk around the chapel. Head west along the road, away from the chapel. Thirty yards down the path, on the left, lies **John Philip Sousa,** a Washington native and famous conductor and composer for the U.S. Marine Corps Band. On the path's right is the grave site of **Herbert Clark,** one of Sousa's musicians.

Continue west along the road until reaching the brick perimeter wall. Follow the wall north to the **Arsenal Monument** (1867; Lot Flannery). This monument pays tribute to 21 women killed in an explosion at the Washington Arsenal in 1864, during the Civil War. President Lincoln led a procession of 2,000 mourners to the cemetery for the dedication ceremonies.

Follow the wall south, crossing the road. About 20 ft south of the road is the burial site of **Marion Kahlert** (1905; sculptor unknown). Struck down at age 10 in 1904, Kahlert was Washington's first auto fatality. Her marker was once adorned with an image of her in Victorian clothing. Unfortunately, the statuette has been vandalized.

Continue south along the brick wall. At the paved road, turn left and walk east. At the first crosspath, walk south. Midway along the path, on the left side, about three rows deep, is the site of **Belva Lockwood.** She was one of the first women to be nominated for the presidency (1884) and a longtime fighter for equal rights. Although women could not vote, she received 4,000 male votes. Lockwood also battled successfully to allow women to argue as attorneys before the Supreme Court and she assisted the Cherokee people in their suit against the U.S. for encroachment on Cherokee land. In 1906 the Cherokee were awarded almost $5 million.

Return to the chapel and head north on the road. The grave of **Adelaide Johnson** is on the left, 30 ft from the chapel. Johnson was a sculptor and feminist whose work stands in the Capitol. She is known for her sculptures of Susan B. Anthony and Elizabeth Cady Stanton. At her wedding in 1896, a woman minister performed the ceremony and her husband took her last name. Just behind her is the unusual grave marker of **Sally Wood Nixon,** a member of the Daughters of the American Revolution. Her large stone is in the shape of a china cabinet. Her ashes rest inside the cabinet.

Continue north along the road. At the first crosspath, turn left and walk west 11 rows deep. Turn left to the site of **Mathew Brady,** renowned for his Civil War photographs.

Return to the road and walk north. Walk behind the keeper's house. To the right of the building is the grave site of **Captain Thomas Tingey,** a founder of the cemetery and commandant of the Washington Navy Yard.

### Diversion:

To visit the District of Columbia Armory, exit Congressional Cemetery and cross E St to Potomac Ave. Follow Potomac Ave S.E. two blocks until reaching 19th St. Walk north six blocks to E. Capitol St. Turn right and walk east to the entrance of the **District of Columbia Armory,** 2001 E. Capitol St S.E.

The armory is headquarters for the District of Columbia National Guard. After 75 years without a permanent home, construction began on the armory in 1940 and was completed in 1947. On Jan 19, 1960, the armory hosted President John F. Kennedy's inaugural ball. The building is only open to the public when the 13,000-square-ft Armory Hall hosts concerts, sporting events, or trade shows.

### Diversion:

To see **Robert F. Kennedy Memorial Stadium** (1961; McCloskey & Co.), continue east along E. Capitol St. to 2400 E. Capitol St S.E. Congress authorized construction of D.C. Stadium on Sept 7, 1957, to replace Griffith Stadium. Groundbreaking ceremonies were held on Oct 7, 1961. The stadium was renamed in 1968 to honor the slain attorney general. The Washington Senators played here until 1972, when they moved to Arlington, Texas, and became the Texas Rangers. Until the 1997 season, the 55,750-seat RFK remained home to the Washington Redskins. The team then relocated to Jack Kent Cooke Stadium in Raljon, Maryland, near Landover. RFK Stadium continues to host concerts and the D.C. United, Washington's professional soccer team.

To the southwest of the main gate is a red granite monument honoring George Preston Marshall, founder of the Redskins. Set on the grass facing the main gate is a bronze bust of Robert Francis Kennedy (Robert Berks). North of the bust is a white marble monument honoring Clark Calvin "Old Fox" Griffith. Griffith played for the Senators and later purchased the team. He was also one of the founders of baseball's American League and served as the first manager of the Chicago White Sox.

Walk west on E. Capitol St until 19th St. Turn left and walk south to the entrance of the Stadium/Armory Metro station.

# 4 · Washington Navy Yard and Environs

Metro: Green Line to Navy Yard.
Bus: 54, 52, V4, V6, 92, or 94.

## Washington Navy Yard

8th and M Sts S.E. ☎ 433-2218. Web: www.navy.mil. Admission: free. Photo identification required for entry. Food facilities open Mon–Fri 5:30 A.M.–5 P.M.; Sat 9–3; food facilities include McDonald's in Building No. 184, Subway and Dunkin' Donuts in Building No. 200, and the buffet-style Officer's Club, Building No. 101. Wheelchair accessible.

From its establishment in 1799 through World War II, the Washington Navy Yard (1799–1800; Benjamin Latrobe, William Lovering, and others; DL; construction has continued intermittently—the newest buildings will be completed in 2001) has served as one of the capital's main employers. Originally a shipbuilding facility, the yard's emphasis shifted in the 1850s to ordnance production. In 1961 the yard switched to administrative and historical functions.

**Highlights:** The Washington Navy Yard houses several public attractions, including the Marine Corps Historical Center, the Navy Museum, and the USS *Barry*, a decommissioned destroyer. There are several other historic structures on the 115-acre grounds.

### History

In 1799 Benjamin Stoddard, first secretary of the navy, authorized the construction of the Washington Navy Yard. The site, along the Anacostia River, then known as the Eastern Branch of the Potomac River, had already been earmarked by George Washington and Pierre L'Enfant for government use. Envisioning a bustling military and commercial port around which the city of Washington would develop, the men chose the location for its deep waters close to the city. Plans for the yard included shipbuilding facilities as well as merchants' warehouses and wharves.

In 1803, President Jefferson asked Benjamin Latrobe, Architect of the Capitol, to formulate a long-range architectural plan for the yard. The yard became a thriving shipbuilding station and an important employer.

> ### Washington Notes
>
> In 1806, production boomed with the order of 50 gunboats. One hundred and seventy-five new men were hired, some of whom were paid a wage of $1.81 per day, considered a good fee at that time. When the first commandant of the Navy Yard, Captain Thomas Tingey, discovered that the men were taking breaks at local whiskey sellers, Tingey, annoyed that the men were wasting time at "grog shops," bought 100-barrel lots of whiskey and provided alcohol on the premises.

The Navy Yard continued to expand. In 1814, during the War of 1812, the British occupied Washington. Captain Thomas Tingey was ordered to burn down the facilities before they could be captured by the British. After the war, the rebuilt yard resumed ship construction, but it never became a bustling commercial and

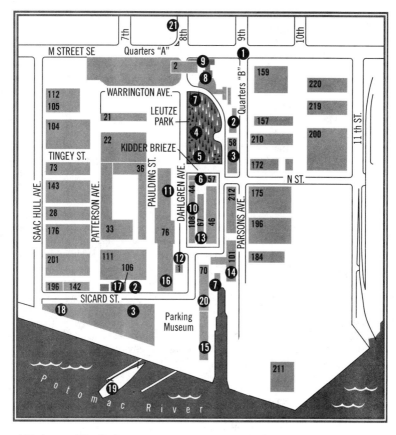

1 Washington Navy Yard
2 Second Officer's House
3 Marine Corps Historical Center
4 Leutze Park
5 USS *Enterprise* anchor
6 Optical Tower
7 USS *Mitscher* bell
8 Tingey House
9 Latrobe Gate
10 Dudley Knox Center for Naval History
11 Breech Mechanism Shop Annex
12 Commandant's Office
13 Navy Art Gallery
14 Navy War College
15 Experimental Model Basin
16 Navy Museum
17 Chapel
18 Willard Park
19 USS *Barry*
20 Cold War Museum
21 Marine Barracks

military port. Silting often plagued the port, and the newer ship designs required harbors deeper than the Anacostia River.

In the 1850s, the yard's primary function shifted from building ships to ordnance production. By 1860, the Navy Department decided that "In view of the great inconvenience attending the building and equipping of ships at a point so distant from the sea, the Yard would be limited to manufacturing anchors, cables, gears, and steam engines." Even so, the Navy Yard provided 1,700 jobs. In the 1860s the yard was renamed the Naval Gun Factory.

By World War I, the yard's importance as a military port had diminished, but its significance as a production center had grown. The yard designed and manufactured Naval Railway Batteries and 16-inch guns.

> ### Washington Notes
> In 1863, during the Civil War, a new foundry opened. When Navy Yard Commandant John A. Dahlgren's son, Ulric, lost a leg while pursuing Lee's troops at Gettysburg, he had the limb entombed in one of the walls. Today, a plaque memorializing the leg can be seen inside the building.

During both world wars the yard's functions centered on designing and testing modern weapons. The first airplane catapult, technology used on aircraft carriers, was successfully tested in the yard on Nov 12, 1912. In 1961 weapons production ceased, and the Navy Yard took on its present duties as a supply and administrative center. Two years later, the navy opened the Navy Museum to educate the public on the service's history and mission. The yard expanded its community education program in the 1970s with the establishment of the Marine Corps Historical Center in the former Marine Corps Barracks. The USS *Barry* was added to the public attractions in 1984.

## Grounds
Enter the Washington Navy Yard through the gate at M St S.E. and 9th Ave. Walk south along Parsons Ave. The first building on the right is the **Second Officer's House** (1801; Lovering and Dyer), also known as Quarters B. This two-and-a-half–story brick house, the oldest building in the yard, was constructed for the second officer. The structure encompasses parts of a farmhouse that stood on the property when the government purchased the land in 1799. Additions have significantly changed the building's original appearance. The building, which is not open to the public, serves as the home of the commandant of the Naval District of Washington.

Continue south along Parsons Ave. On the right is the Marine Corps Historical Center, Building No. 58. Turn right at N St and make a right at the driveway. Walk north to the entrance of the center.

## *Marine Corps Historical Center*
Building No. 58. ☎ 433-3840. Open daily Mon, Wed–Sat 10–4; Sun and federal holidays 12–5. In summer, open Fri evenings until 8. Closed on Tues, Thanksgiving, Christmas Day, and New Year's Day. Historical Center Office open Mon–Fri 8–4:30. Closed on federal holidays. Group tours available with prior arrangement. ☎ 433-0780. Visitor passes required to visit portions of the center other than the museum. Passes available at the security section inside the staff entrance or at the information desk near the front entrance. Parking spaces available in front of the museum. Wheelchair accessible; wheelchairs available. Museum shop. Restrooms. Food and beverages not allowed on the premises. No smoking permitted.

The Marine Corps Historical Center houses the library, research, archives, and museum of the United States Marine Corps. The museum, located on the first floor, details the role of the Marine Corps in American history from the Revolution to the present day. Exhibits display weapons, uniforms, maps, photographs, and art.

**Highlights:** The Time Tunnel, a comprehensive chronological history of the Marine Corps, and the two American flags raised on Mt. Suribachi, Iwo Jima, in Feb 1945.

### History
The Historical Center occupies the site of the pre-1814 "Old Stores Building," once a distribution center for canvas, twine, rope, navigational equipment, and paint. The Stores Building was burned by Captain Thomas Tingey in anticipation of the British attack on Washington. Although the dates of reconstruction are uncertain, an 1896 public works drawing of the Naval Yard shows a building labeled "Rigging and Sail Lofts, Storage, Offices, etc." In the 1920s and 1930s, the building was used as the yard's public works and personnel offices. The three-story brick building served as the Marine Barracks from 1941 to 1975. After establishment of the Marine Corps Historical Foundation in 1979, the navy converted the building to serve as an historical center.

## Interior
**First floor.** Enter the Historical Center and proceed up the stairs to the right. A carved mahogany plaque bearing an eagle guarding a trophy of arms hangs on the wall to the left. The emblem is a representation of the stamped brass plate that was attached to marine shakos—square military hats with a blunt bill and topped by a plume—from 1804 until 1819.

Walk past the reception desk and enter the exhibit galleries. Hanging on the wall in the corner are portraits of commandants of the Marine Corps. Turn left to view the landing guns from the 19C and the flags raised over Iwo Jima. (Two flags were raised at Iwo Jima. The first was too small to be seen by the ships offshore, so a second, larger flag was raised. The latter event is the one depicted in the famous photograph taken by Joe Rosenthal.) Turn left again and enter the **Time Tunnel,** which describes more than 200 years of Marine Corps history through 20 exhibit cases. The cases, to the left, display artifacts such as weapons, uniforms, artworks, and flags. Panels on the right describe the commandant and other officers. The following are exhibits in the Time Tunnel:

**Marines in the Revolution, 1775–1783** explains why the Second Continental Congress established two battalions of marines (to defend against British troops in Halifax, Nova Scotia). The exhibit displays muskets, swords, uniforms, and a 1779 recruitment poster with the famous line "a few good men." Within a decade after the Marine Corps was created by Congress on July 11, 1798, as a separate branch of the military, there were 37 officers and 1,294 enlisted men.

**Second War of Independence, 1812–1815** features the Chapeau Bras, or "cocked" hats worn by officers during the War of 1812, as well as swords, muskets, and a powder horn.

**The Age of Archibald Henderson** displays a brass swivel gun, a cutlass, a samurai sword presented to an officer during an expedition to Japan in 1854, and a scrimshaw ladle. Henderson was commandant of the Marine Corps from 1820 to 1859.

**Mexican War, 1846–1848** displays a uniform sash, musket charges, a military drum, and campaign diagrams. The marines fought in California and Mexico and raised a flag atop the Mexican National Palace on Sept 14, 1847.

**Civil War, 1859–1865** features a Union Ketchum grenade, muskets, a bugle, and officer and enlisted-men uniforms. After the marines captured abolitionist John Brown (1800–1859) on Oct 16, 1859, nearly one-third of the members of the Union Marines switched sides and joined the Confederate Army.

**Sail to Steam, 1865–1899** contains an enlisted man's overcoat and cape, a white dress helmet, and a .45 caliber rifle. The exhibit discusses the marine landings in Panama, the Bering Sea, Samoa, and other locations.

**Spanish-American War, 1898–1899** details the U.S. effort to help Cuba gain independence from Spain. A machete, a sketch by Rufus Zogabaum depicting Admiral Dewey on the bridge of the *Olympia* during the Battle at Manila Bay, a 6 mm Colt machine gun, bayonets, and shells of the first shot fired at the Battle of Santiago and the last shot fired at the Battle of Manila Bay are displayed.

**Marines in the Far East, 1899–1941** discusses the deployment of Marine Corps personnel in the Far East through World War II. Featured are a bronze Spanish lantaka captured from Philippine "insurrectors," a canteen and mess kit, a Medal of Honor, and a campaign hat worn by marines stationed in China from 1898 to 1904.

**Marines in the Caribbean, 1899–1934** displays a tropical uniform, pistols, and machine guns. Landings in Nicaragua, Panama, and Caribbean islands like Cuba and Haiti prepped the Marine Corps for jungle and guerrilla tactics.

**World War I, 1917–1918** features a watercolor by John T. McCoy of marines flying DeHavillands, a German hand grenade, and German body armor. The marines served in France on land and in the air. Women were permitted to join the Marine Corps during the war.

**Preparing for Amphibious War, 1898–1941** shows an officer's summer uniform, a field heliograph and telephone, and a model of an LCM (6)—a mechanized landing craft.

**World War II: Defense and Counterattack, 1941–1944** has a "shortsnorter" (a souvenir dollar bill signed by others that was used to buy a drink, or a "snort"), a chain of American and foreign currency bills, a siren, flight clothing, and the bugle used on Dec 7, 1941, to call marines to arms after the Japanese attack on Pearl Harbor.

**World War II: Drive to Victory, 1943–1945** contains K rations, a radio, various weapons, a Japanese flag, and a samurai sword. The marines fought on Tarawa, Guam, Saipan, and Tinian in some of the most intense battles in the Pacific.

**Vertical Envelopment, 1946–1965** features a rescue sling and retrieving hook, a model of an amphibious assault ship (LPH), and models of Marine Corps helicopters.

**Korean War, 1950–1953** exhibits a Chinese machine gun, a cold weather uniform, strategy maps, and the U.S. flag raised over Wolmi-Do Island, a strategic part of the Inchon landing.

**Force in Readiness, 1954–1965** has weapons developed after World War II, including a pressurized suit and helmet worn by air crews who flew at high altitudes, machine guns, a grenade launcher, and the 1954 executive order signed by President Eisenhower authorizing the Marine Corps seal. The exhibit also discusses the Marine Corps's humanitarian and contingency roles.

**Vietnam War, 1965–1971** shows antipersonnel devices and assault rifles. Marines were the first troops dispatched to Vietnam.

**Contingency Operations, 1972–1976** explores the peacetime activity of the Marine Corps, displaying uniforms and guns, as well as the bell from the SS *Mayaguez*, a U.S. container ship sailing for Sea-Land Service and boarded in May 1975 by the Khmer Rouge.

**21st Century Force-in-Readiness** addresses the modern roles of the Marine Corps and its use of technology, such as laptop computers and antichemical warfare devices.

Proceed to the right, past the **World War II posters.** To the right is a **Special Exhibits Gallery.** To the left is **Marines in Miniature, 1800–1918.** This gallery features models, such as one of the USS *Constitution,* and dioramas of battles, including the 1800 capture of the privateer ship *Sandwich* and the marines at Bladensburg in 1814. Proceed through this gallery and exit into another special exhibitions gallery. Continue through this gallery. On the left is the **museum shop,** which sells miniatures, memorabilia, and books on Marine Corps history.

The museum houses a **military music collection** and an extensive **art collection.** Since 1972, reserves, retirees, and active Marines, along with civilians, have produced works for the art exhibit. The pieces include paintings, drawings, sketches, sculpture, woodblock and silkscreen prints, and cartoons, representing the Vietnam War, World War II, Korea, and World War I. The museum also displays portraits from the early nineteenth century.

Located on the third floor, the **Historical Library** serves researchers of Marine Corps history. The collection contains more than 30,000 titles, including fiction, biographies, academic dissertations, journals, and Marine Corps newspapers dating back to the 1930s. The library also maintains a basic set of reference books and encyclopedias and is part of an interlibrary loan system. This library can be accessed only by appointment; ☎ 433-2218.

Exit the Marine Corps Historical Center and walk west to **Leutze Park,** used as the parade ground for formal affairs and named after Rear Admiral Eugene H. C. Leutze, commandant of the Naval Yard from 1905 to 1910. Surrounding the perimeter of Leutze Park are 17C, 18C, and 19C bronze cannons and howitzers manufactured for Spain, France, Italy, and the U.S. Many are battle trophies from the Barbary War and the Spanish-American War.

Continue West along Kidder Breeze. At the south end of the park is the anchor from the USS *Enterprise* (CV-6), an aircraft carrier that saw action in the South Pacific during World War II. At Dahlgren Ave turn right and walk north. From the west side of the park look east and spot the **Optical Tower,** Building No. 57 (1918–19; architect unknown), standing above the Second Officer's House. The tower was used to calibrate optical equipment manufactured in the Naval Yard. Sightings were taken on the U.S. Capitol, Washington Monument, and the Masonic Temple in Alexandria. Continue north along Dahlgren Ave.

Displayed in the northwest corner of the park is the bell from the USS *Mitscher* (DDG-35), a frigate that was converted from a frigate to a guided missile destroyer. The ship, named after Admiral Marc Andrew Mitscher, served in the U.S. Pacific fleet during World War II. To the north of Leutze Park is the **Tingey House** (1804; Lovering and Dyer), also known as Quarters A. Since 1977 it has served as a residence for the chief of Naval Operations. Not open to the public, this neo-classical two-story, white-washed brick house, although altered through additions, is among the yard's oldest structures. The building features intricate brickwork and interesting decorative touches, such as the glazed fanlight transom above the front door and arched lintels and keystones. The wisteria vine growing around the building started as a planting brought back from a mission to Japan in 1860. Commandant Tingey lived in the house until his death in 1829. This was the only building that Tingey did not torch during the War of 1812.

To the left of the Tingey House is the **Latrobe Gate** (1804; Benjamin Latrobe), Building No. 7. Latrobe, who designed the brick-and-stucco gate at the request of Thomas Jefferson, built it as a one-story, double-gated entrance, 40 ft in depth with guard posts on either side. Over the years, two additional stories have been added. During 1880–81, the original guard posts were removed, and the navy constructed Victorian-style guard houses on either side. The Latrobe Gate is the terminus for the 8th St axis, tying the Navy Yard to L'Enfant's city plan. The gate is the oldest continuously manned marine sentry post in the U.S.

Walk south along Dahlgren Ave and cross Kidder Breeze. On the southeast corner is the **Dudley Knox Center for Naval History,** Building Nos. 57 (first floor, 1866; extension, 1899), 44 (1890), and 108 (1902). This three-building complex was named after Dudley Knox (1877–1960), an officer appointed in 1921 to oversee the Naval Records and Library. Building No. 57, erected as a warehouse, later housed the offices of the Naval Ordnance School from the 1920s through World War II. Building No. 44 was also used for ordnance activities. Building No. 108 was constructed for ordnance activities and currently houses the Navy Department Library, one of the largest naval book collections.

Across the street is the **Breech Mechanism Shop Annex** (1917).

Continue along Dahlgren Ave until the corner. Directly across the street is the **Commandant's Office** (1837–38), Building No. 1, which is not open to the public. Also known as the Middledorf Building, this two-story brick structure was built to house the offices of the commandant of the yard. In 1947 it served as a post office and communications center. It is believed that President Lincoln visited Commandant John Dahlgren in this building during the Civil War.

Turn left and walk to the Navy Art Gallery.

## Navy Art Gallery
Building No. 67. ☎ 433-3815. Open Wed–Fri 9–4; Sat–Sun 10–4. Closed Mon–Tues. Admission: free. Visitors see attractions on their own. Restrooms. Wheelchair accessible. Two temporary exhibits, changed every three or four months, are displayed.

### History
The Navy Department Library began collecting naval art during the 19C to complement its book collection. Established in 1841, the Naval Combat Art Program was combined with the Combat Art Collection in 1986 to create the collection of the Navy Art Branch, charged with "collect[ing] and exhibit[ing] works of art depicting the history of the Navy and the activities of men and women in naval service." The collection maintains more than 10,000 pieces by 500 artists such

as Standish Backus, Thomas Hart Benton, Paul Cadmus, Reginald Marsh, and Henry Reuterdahl. Paintings, drawings, prints, and sculpture depict naval ships, personnel, and battle scenes, particularly of World War II, the Korean War, the Vietnam War, and the Persian Gulf War.

Exit the Navy Art Gallery and cross Sicard St. Located in Building No. 101 is the Navy War College and the Officer's Club, which is open to the public for lunch. To the left is the **Experimental Model Basin** (1897–98; David Watson Taylor), Building No. 70. To measure the effects of water on the hulls of ships, Naval Constructor Taylor designed and constructed this building with a basin in it. Scale ship models were towed the length of the 470 ft basin while photographs were taken and scientific data recorded. In 1939 when the basin became inadequate, it was replaced by the **David Taylor Model Basin,** built in 1939 in Carderock, Maryland. The Experimental Model Basin was filled and the building was used for storage. In 1931–34, Taylor constructed the navy's first wind tunnel, which no longer exists, adjacent to the basin. It was capable of generating a velocity of 6,000 ft per minute. The small building between Building Nos. 101 and 70 housed the Marine Railway (1822–23; Commodore John Rodgers), the first in the country. The railway hauled ships out of the water for repairs. The tracks have been removed and the building is closed to the public.

Walk south along Sicard St and turn right at the corner. At the south end of the Breech Mechanism Shop is the Navy Museum.

## Navy Museum

9th and M Sts S.E. ☎ 433-4882. Open Sept–May Mon–Fri 9–4. Open June–Aug Mon–Fri 9–5. Weekends and holidays 10–5. Closed Thanksgiving Day, Christmas Eve, Christmas Day, New Year's Day. Admission: free. Free parking available. Handouts are available to assist visitors touring on their own. Guided tours available. Wheelchair accessible. Photography permitted. Pilot House Museum Shop open Mon–Fri 9–5; Sat–Sun 10–4. Restrooms.

Special events include an annual Fall Festival, musical performances, demonstrations, lectures, and exhibit openings. There are several hands-on exhibits and activities geared for children, including the submarine room, a mock NASA space capsule, and the hull of an underwater research vessel. A scavenger hunt booklet guiding children around the museum is available at the information desk.

Established in 1961 the museum displays, collects, and preserves historical naval artifacts and artwork in order to educate and inspire navy personnel and the general public. The museum collection contains more than 5,000 artifacts. At press time the museum was closed for renovation and scheduled to reopen in late summer 2000. The plan is to retain the same exhibits, but the order of them and the specific items exhibited may vary from the description that follows.

### History

The museum is housed in the former Breech Mechanism Shop, which was constructed between 1887 and 1899 to produce ordnance missile components and electronic equipment. The south portico was added in 1899. The museum, established in 1961 at the suggestion of Chief of Naval Operations Admiral Arleigh Burke, opened in 1963.

## Exterior

Flanking the Navy Museum entrance is a six-ton starboard anchor from the USS *Anzio* CVHE-57, originally named the USS *Coral,* and an anchor from the steam sloop of war USS *Hartford.* The latter was built in Boston in 1858 and was Admiral Farragut's flagship in the Battles of New Orleans and Mobile Bay.

## Interior

The museum, one large room with separate galleries created by tall partitions, traces the history of the navy from the Revolution to the present. Exhibits on the right are arranged chronologically, while those on the left are thematic. The World War II section is the most extensive exhibit and contains six films. Other exhibits focus on peacetime endeavors such as polar exploration, space flight, and diplomacy.

To the right of the entrance is the **Pilot House Museum Shop,** a semicircular oak room designed as a replica of a cruiser bridge constructed 1904–7 at the Brooklyn Navy Yard. To the left of the entrance is **Dive, Dive: The U.S. Navy Submarine Force.** Multimedia exhibits enable visitors to explore buoyancy, steering, propulsion, and sonar. There is a model of the USS *Patrick Henry,* a submarine from the skipjack class, and a model of the Los Angeles class. Artifacts include a ship control panel and helm, a submarine battery, and a control panel of a diesel sub. Visitors can walk in to a mock control room with a working periscope. Hanging from the gallery's ceiling are colorful World War II battle flags of the submarines *Flying Fish, Balao, Spot,* and *Gurnard.*

Proceed to **American Revolution,** the gallery to the left of the museum shop. This exhibit pays tribute to the U.S.-French alliance during the Revolution. Artifacts include a sword presented to Commodore Hazelwood by the Continental Congress on Nov 4, 1777, and the forefoot of a galley used by General Benedict Arnold on Lake Champlain in the Battle at Valcour Island. Models include the *Rattlesnake,* a 1781 privateer ship, and the *Bonhomme Richard,* a 1760s design later used for the French Duc de Duras. A diorama details John Paul Jones's encounter with the English HMS *Serapis,* the battle in which he declared, "I have not yet begun to fight."

Walk north to **Forgotten Wars of the 19C.** This gallery discusses the Quasi-War with France (1798–1801), primarily fought in the West Indies, and the Barbary War (1801–5)—the U.S. Navy was established in 1798 to protect against Barbary pirate attacks. Among the artifacts are a 1785 letter from John Paul Jones informing John Jay, minister of foreign affairs, that Algeria had declared war on the U.S. and a cat-o'-nine-tails, a type of whip employed on 19C ships for flogging sailors. Oil paintings depict scenes from the Barbary War. From the War of 1812 are ship models made from bone by French sailors imprisoned during the Napoleanic Wars and a door from the USS *Constitution.* Preserved in the case is the dress uniform of Captain Thomas Tingey, first commandant of the Washington Navy Yard.

The **Civil War, Mexican War, and Spanish-American War** gallery exhibits a model of the USS *Monitor* and artifacts such as a cannon, shells, and helm from the *Hartford,* a flagship of the Gulf Squadron (1861–65).

**World War I: 1917–1918** discusses antisubmarine warfare and naval aviation. Featured are a 5-inch, 51 caliber gun and antisubmarine warfare items, including a moored contact mine mark, a case of uniforms, and a wooden propeller from an H-16 flying boat. A 14-minute film shows original footage of massive railway battery guns being fired in France in 1918.

An archway leads to **In Harm's Way: The U.S. Navy in World War II**, which chronicles the navy's role in the war from the attack on Pearl Harbor in 1941 to the Japanese surrender in 1945. The exhibit has three sections: the Atlantic Theater, the Pacific Theater, and the Home Front. **The Pacific Theater,** on the west side of the museum, traces navy campaigns in the Marshall and Mariana Islands, as well as in Okinawa and the Home Islands. The **Atlantic Theater**'s 20 exhibits detail threats from German subs and describe antisubmarine warfare, convoys, operations, and the invasion of southern France. A twin-mount 5-inch, 38 caliber gun used for surface and aircraft targets dominates the floor. Guns such as this one were on navy destroyers, but were added to battleships, cruisers, and carriers in 1939. Visitors can sit in the seat of a 3-inch, 50 caliber Dual Purpose Gun, the principal antiaircraft gun found on large warships. The bridge from the USS *Fletcher* (DD-445), a destroyer, is recreated, and an F4U Corsair, a gull-winged carrier plane nicknamed Big Hog, hangs from the ceiling. The living room in the **Home Front** section on the west side re-creates a wartime living room, complete with a "V for Victory" trash bin, a war bond booth, a Seabee (the construction battalion of the navy) helmet, and a chart explaining the semaphore alphabet.

**Undersea Explorations,** located in the northeast corner of the museum, addresses naval diving and exploration and features *Alvin* and *Trieste*. *Trieste*, a 1960 bathyscaphe that descended 35,800 ft, or 7 miles, to the murky depths, was designed by Swiss physicist Auguste Piccard and funded by the Italian city Trieste. The U.S. Navy employed *Trieste* for oceanographic research. An early underwater camera, diving helmets, and armored suits are also exhibited. Visitors can climb into a pressure sphere, a pressurized cabin that enabled humans to make deepwater descents. Between this gallery and the west galleries is a model of the USS *Forrestal*, a carrier used in Vietnam.

Proceed to the west side of the building. In the northwest corner is **Space.** The highlight of this small exhibit is the *Apollo 16* space suit worn by Captain John Young. Another case contains a Project Mercury training manual.

Russian, Chinese, and U.S. assault rifles are displayed in **Blue Sky–Brown Water: The United States Navy and the Vietnam Conflict.** There are two models of North Vietnamese POW camps, uniforms, and artifacts from camps.

The **British Exhibit** gallery, focusing on the relationship between the U.S. and British Navies and how the U.S. Navy adopted many British policies, primarily consists of handcolored prints of both country's ships, as well as sextants and charts. One case discusses the significance of rum in the British Navy.

The tools in **Navigation** include such early ones as sextants, octants, meteorological charts, magnetic needles, and a Fresnel lens. For weary visitors, there is a bench from the presidential yacht *Sequoia*.

**Polar Exploration** looks at navy expeditions to the Arctic and Antarctic. Time lines trace various explorations such as Charles Wilkes's Antarctic trek (1839–40) and Robert Scott's and Adolphus Greely's expeditions to the Antarctic and Arctic, respectively. The hut that Admiral Richard Byrd lived in for seven months during his trip to the Antarctic (1933–35) and cans of powdered food from Captain Robert Scott's 1910 Antarctic expedition are part of the exhibit.

**Medals and Awards,** located to the left of Polar Exploration, displays cases of military commendations plus a small collection of ships in bottles.

**Gun Deck,** which is to the left of Medals and Awards, is a walk-through re-creation of the gun deck from the *Constitution,* affectionately known as Old Iron-sides. The *Constitution* was designed to be powerful enough to attack larger enemy ships, fast enough to chase other frigates, and tough enough to sustain enemy fire. Her hull was constructed with strong oak framing and planking that ranged from two to three ft thick. She was dubbed Old Ironsides during an 1812 battle when a cannonball fired from *Guerrière* bounced off her side; U.S. sailors declared, "Huz-zah! her sides are made of iron!"

In the center of the museum is the fully rigged fighting top from the *Constitution.* The 3½-ton platform supports shrouds of the top mast and provides a look-out point.

The next gallery is used for temporary exhibitions.

Exit the Navy Museum and turn right. Walk west along Sicard St. The large build-ing on the right, originally the **Forge Shop** (1801), serves as offices for the U.S. Naval Criminal Investigative Service. Continue west to the **chapel** (1901; archi-tect unknown), Building No. 106. This small, one-story brick building was con-structed as the pneumatic power plant for the neighboring Forge Shop. In 1972–73 volunteers from the Navy's Self-Help Program converted the building into a chapel. Catholic and Protestant services are held.

Cross Sicard St and enter **Willard Park.** The park, named for Rear Admiral Arthur Lee Willard, commandant of the yard from 1917 to 1919 and 1927 to 1930, is the outdoor extension of the Navy Museum. It displays more than 60 19C and 20C artifacts. At the west end are U.S. and European turn-of-the-century naval ordnance and artifacts salvaged from the USS *Maine,* which was sunk on the eve of the Spanish-American War. To the east are naval landing guns and German and American deck guns. Among the World War II artifacts are a propeller from the battleship *South Dakota,* the Navy's first radar antenna, and armor plates from Japanese and American warships. A Regulus missile, a Sparrowhawk launcher, and a titanium pressure sphere from the bathyscaphe *Alvin* are also displayed.

Walk south through Willard Park to the water. Turn east to the entrance of Pier 2, where the USS *Barry* (DD-933) is moored.

## USS Barry *(DD-933)*

Pier 2. ☎ 433-3377. Open year-round seven days a week 10–3:30. Admission: free. Guided tours (30–45 minutes). No public facilities. Not wheelchair accessible.

### History

The USS *Barry* is named for Commodore John Barry, a Revolutionary War naval hero and the navy's first commissioned officer. The ship, the third destroyer of the Forrest Sherman class, was launched on Oct 1, 1955, from Bath Iron Works in Maine. Commissioned on Sept 7, 1956, in Boston, the ship's first captain was Commander Isaac C. Kidd, Jr. Though originally 418 ft long, the ship was ex-panded to 424 ft in order to accommodate sonar. The *Barry* has facilities for 22 of-ficers and 315 men.

The USS *Barry* served in several training missions and goodwill tours and par-ticipated in the Cuba quarantine during the Cuban Missile Crisis in Oct 1962. During two tours in the Vietnam War (1965 and 1967), she earned two battle stars for a shore bombardment of the Mekong Delta and for her support of Operation Double Eagle, an amphibious landing near Quang Ngi on Jan 28, 1966—the largest such landing since Inchon in Korea. In 1966, the *Barry* became the first ship to carry and employ the MK 86 Mod O Gun Fire Control System, marking the first time a digital computer fired a conventional gun. In 1967, the ship underwent antisubmarine warfare modernization. After 26 years of service, she was decommissioned on Nov 5, 1982, and has been permanently moored as a "visit ship" at the Washington Navy Yard since 1984.

## Exterior/Interior

Active-duty naval personnel meet visitors at the gate and take them to the end of Pier 2, where a propeller from the USS *Barry* is displayed. Visitors board the after gangway or "brow," stepping onto the missile deck. The large device in the center of the deck is an **ASROC (antisubmarine rocket) launcher,** used to fire homing torpedoes at submarines. At the rear of this deck the ship received supplies hoisted down from helicopters.

Descend the ladder to the fantail, or lower end of the ship. Highlights include the **five-inch, 54 caliber gun,** two **torpedo decoys,** and a **variable depth sonar.** The gun, and its counterpart on the forecastle, shot 70-pound projectiles to a range of almost 13 miles. More than 3,000 such rounds were fired from the *Barry* during the Vietnam War. The torpedo decoys, which produced noises similar to that of a ship, were towed behind the USS *Barry* to confuse early passive acoustic homing torpedoes.

Enter the ship through a watertight door on the starboard (right) side. Through the door immediately to the left and down is the **berthing area** for 63 sailors. Continue through the port (left) break (outside passageway). Turn right and enter the hatch. The **wardroom galley** is on the left. This kitchen prepared meals for the officers, who ate in the wardroom just past the galley. Walk five ft and turn right.

The room on the left is the **post office.** Next to that is the **infirmary.** Although no doctor was assigned, an independent duty chief corpsman served onboard. On the left, past the infirmary, is the **personnel office,** where crew records were kept. Continue down the passageway and enter the **galley** and **mess decks.**

Daily cooking duties began at 0400 (4 A.M.) on routine days. However, when the ship was on alert, food was prepared 24 hours per day. As the largest indoor common room on the ship, the mess deck was used for eating, entertainment, and religious ceremonies. The picnic-style tables could be removed to accommodate large numbers of wounded or sick crew members. To the left of the galley is the **ship store,** where the crew purchased cigarettes, toiletries, and other incidentals.

Exit the mess deck at the starboard (right) door and climb the ladder to the 02 level. To the left is the **motor whaleboat.** This 26 ft. boat was used to retrieve crew members who had fallen overboard, to rescue downed pilots, and also to shuttle crew to shore. A similar boat on the port side is the **captain's gig,** used to transport the commanding officer.

Walk toward the bow of the ship. To the right is the **torpedo tube mount.** Three short-range homing torpedoes could be shot out using compressed air. Also on this deck are two 50 caliber machine gun mounts used for defense against small craft.

Climb up to the 03 level and enter the **bridge.** In addition to the ship's wheel and EOT (engine-order telegraph), the bridge contains the captain's chair, which is mounted in the center on the starboard side. The USS *Barry* had a top speed in excess of 34 knots.

Proceed down the steep ladder. The **commodore's cabin** is at the foot of the ladder. The *Barry* often served as the lead ship in a destroyer squadron, so usually a commodore would be onboard. Turn left. **Radio central** and the **crypotolog-ical vault** are on the right. Access to these spaces was tightly controlled. Through this room is the **electronic shop**, where technicians fixed faulty equipment.

Exit the electronic shop and turn right. Proceed into the **junior officer's state-room,** furnished with bunk beds for two officers and a stowaway desk. A head (bathroom) connects this stateroom with another identical one.

Exit through the hatch on the right and descend down onto the main deck and walk forward to the **forecastle** (pronounced "foke'sel") where the forward five-inch gun mount is located. Anchors and ground tackle are also located here. The port anchor weighs 2,500 pounds. The centerline anchor weighs 7,000 pounds. Depart the ship via the forward brow.

Walk east to the south end of the Experimental Model Basin and the **Cold War Museum.** The Cold War Museum, Building No. 70 (formerly the Navy Museum Annex), is scheduled to open in April 2000 with an exhibit on the Korean War that will explore the navy's role in that conflict. Among the highlights of the exhibit will be a Korean War–vintage landing craft and naval uniforms worn during the war.

Walk west along Sicard St to Dahlgren Ave. Turn right at the intersection. At the next corner, turn left. Continue walking north. At N St, turn right. Walk to Parsons Ave and turn left. Exit the Washington Navy Yard onto M St. Cross M St and turn left. Walk one block to 8th St and turn right. Walk three blocks under the overpass for Rt 395 to the entrance of the Marine Barracks.

## Marine Barracks

8th and I Sts S.E. ☎ 433-4173. Open to the public upon request for guided tour (45 minutes) or reservations for Friday Evening Parades. Admission: free.

Friday Evening Parades are held every Fri at 9 (must be seated by 8) May–Aug. Parades include performances by "The President's Own" United States Marine Band, "The Commandant's Own," the United States Drum and Bugle Corps, and the Marine Corps Silent Drill Platoon. Reservations must be made in writing at least three weeks in advance. Requests should be addressed to: Adjutant, Marine Barracks, 8th and I Sts S.E., Washington, D.C. 20390. Requests should include the name of every member in the party, return address, and telephone number. Alternate parade dates should also be suggested. Parade information ☎ 433-6060.

### History

In March 1801 President Thomas Jefferson and Lieutenant Colonel Commandant William Ward Burrows rode horseback through the city looking for a suitable location for barracks for the capital's marines and for a home for the commandant. They chose Square 927 because of its proximity to the Washington Navy Yard and because it is within marching distance of the Capitol. Construction began within a few months. The Marine Barracks is the oldest post of the Marine Corps. Every commandant of the Marine Corps has resided on the base since 1806.

The 19C barracks were laid out in a quadrangle. Areas to the south and east were used for offices, maintenance facilities, and living spaces for troops. Officers quarters were to the west. In 1806, the Commandant's House was erected on the north side; it is the only original building still standing. The current complex was built between 1900 and 1906 in a Romanesque style.

Since 1801 the barracks have housed the United States Marine Band. This group was created by an act of Congress signed by President John Adams on July 11, 1798, and charged with providing music for the president of the United States and the commandant of the Marine Corps. Three years later the Marine Band played for the inauguration of Thomas Jefferson, who dubbed the band The President's Own. The Marine Band has played at every presidential inauguration since then. John Philip Sousa took over leadership of the band in Oct 1892 and remained at this post for 12 years.

The base also served as the headquarters of the Marine Corps until 1901. Marines based at the barracks man ceremonies, provide presidential support—including serving at Camp David—and are engaged in light infantry training. Marines from the base have served in the War of 1812, the Indian Wars of 1826–37, the War with Mexico, the Civil War, the Spanish-American War, and the Persian Gulf War.

### Grounds

The Marine Barracks (1801; 1902–6; George Hadfield, Hornblower & Marshall; DL) include the Commandant's House, Center House Mess, and the John Philip Sousa Band Hall, all of which can be viewed during the Friday Evening Parade.

The **Commandant's House** (1806; 1891; George Hadfield, Hornblower & Marshall; DL) was designed in the Georgian-Federalist style. Originally there were four large rooms. The kitchen was in the basement and servants lived in the attic. With the renovations that began in 1836, the house grew to 30 rooms.

The British spared the house in their 1814 torching of Washington. One explanation is that Admiral Cockburn and General Ross, commanders of the British troops, intended to use the house as their headquarters while in Washington. A second theory is that General Ross was so impressed with the marines fighting the Battle of Bladensburg that he spared the house and barracks out of soldierly respect.

# 5 · National Mall: National Gallery of Art and National Air and Space Museum

Metro: Red Line to Judiciary Square, Yellow/Green Line to Archives–Navy Memorial, or Blue/Orange Line to Smithsonian.
Bus: Stops located on 4th and 7th Sts. Use 13A, 13B, 13M, 32–36, 54, 70, P2, P6, or V8.

## National Mall

Officially, the National Mall stretches about 1.3 miles from 3rd St N.W. and the Capitol grounds to 14th St N.W. Constitution Ave forms the northern border of the Mall and Independence Ave the southern. Many of the Smithsonian Institution's museums line the Mall.

The Washington Monument grounds, the next open green space, is technically not part of the Mall; neither is West Potomac Park, the open green area that encompasses Constitution Gardens (17th–23rd Sts south of Constitution Ave to the Reflecting Pool) and the grassy area south of Independence Ave to the Jefferson Memorial. However, many visitors and locals refer to the entire open area from 3rd Street to the Lincoln Memorial, a distance of three miles from the Capitol grounds to the Lincoln Memorial, as "the Mall." (For more information, see Walk 10: "Monuments and Memorials.")

In addition to serving as a park, the Mall—the official and the larger region—hosts concerts, rallies, political demonstrations, cultural festivals, and fairs.

### History

The Mall did not always appear as it does now—a wide expanse of greenery, trees, and monuments. For a long time the Mall was a marshy lowland, cut through by creeks and crisscrossed with railroad tracks. The National Mall was part of Major Pierre Charles L'Enfant's 1791 plan for the Federal City. He envisioned the area as a grand boulevard, 400 ft wide and extending west of the Capitol to the site where the Washington Monument has been erected.

The Mall's topography was different in L'Enfant's era than now. The Tiber Creek Canal and the Potomac River, which ran along present-day Constitution Ave, 17th St, and Maine Ave, turned the Mall into boggy lowlands. Developing the Mall was a slow and frequently interrupted process. In the early 1800s a massive development project filled part of the Mall with dirt to raise it from a height of 8 ft to an elevation of 22 ft. In another attempt to improve the Mall's condition, Congress granted groups the authority to design gardens on small patches of the Mall. In 1820 the Columbian Institute, Washington's first major intellectual society, created two small ponds, one with an island, on a five-acre, fenced-in area at the Mall's east end. In 1848 ground was broken for the Washington Monument, and in 1847 construction began on the Smithsonian Castle.

In 1850 Andrew Jackson Downing, a New York horticulturist, was commissioned to landscape the Mall. His design called for a beautification program of winding carriage paths, Victorian gardens, and groves of American evergreens. In 1852 Downing died at the age of 37 in a steamboat accident. Although his plans weren't implemented, they influenced the later development of the Mall.

During the Civil War, regiments of the Army of the Potomac set up camp on the Mall. Temporary wooden structures served as offices, and the Armory Square Hospital, located where the National Air and Space Museum stands today, stretched across the Mall. Cattle that were used to feed soldiers grazed on the land near the Washington Monument.

After the Civil War, railroad traffic on the Mall increased. The Baltimore and Potomac Railroad Station was built between 1873 and 1878 on the site where the National Gallery of Art, West Building, stands today. Tracks also led to the armory building (no longer serving as a hospital) and were used in 1876 to transport Centennial exhibitions from Philadelphia to their new home in Washington.

As part of his crusade to transform Washington into a modern city, Governor Alexander "Boss" Shepherd wanted to beautify the Mall. To Shepherd, this meant removing the railroad tracks on the Mall. To avoid lengthy negotiations with the

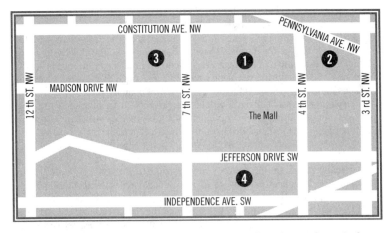

1 National Gallery of Art, West Building   3 National Gallery of Art Sculpture Garden
2 National Gallery of Art, East Building   4 National Air and Space Museum

railroad, Shepherd ordered his workers to disassemble the tracks at night. Even though long stretches of the tracks remained in the morning, one of the railroad's presidents, impressed by Shepherd's nerve, offered him a job. Shepherd refused, however, and continued his progress toward improving Washington. Shepherd paved streets, laid sewers, installed gaslights, and filled in Tiber Creek Canal, also known as Washington City Canal. Canals became obsolete with the development of the railroads since trains transported goods faster and cheaper.

During the 1880s the National Zoo was located on the Mall on the site of the present Enid Haupt Garden. Taxidermists from the Smithsonian mounted animal specimens and displayed "live models," including a small herd of buffalo. This popular tourist attraction moved to its present location near Rock Creek Park in 1889.

After a severe flood in Feb 1882, the Army Corps of Engineers dredged the area just west of the Washington Monument, creating a 739-acre area named West Potomac Park, which is officially not part of the Mall. During the late 1800s the U.S. Fish Commission used ponds created by the Potomac River to propagate European carp. These fish ponds, at the corner of present-day 17th St and Constitution Ave, were a popular attraction.

Despite Shepherd's efforts, the Mall remained unsightly at the turn of the 20C. In 1901 Senator James McMillan from Michigan assembled a distinguished group of landscape architects, including Daniel H. Burnham, Charles F. McKim, and Frederick Law Olmsted, Jr., to improve Washington's image. Deciding to follow L'Enfant's original plan, McMillan's group envisioned the Mall as a formal rectangular space lined with rows of elm trees on either side of a grassy center. They also planned to extend the Mall to the Potomac River, build a bridge from Arlington Cemetery to a proposed memorial honoring Abraham Lincoln, create a reflecting pool, and raze the Baltimore and Potomac Railroad Station.

Over the next three decades many of the McMillan Plan's ideas were implemented. The first step involved removing the remaining railroad tracks from the

Mall. In return for relocating their tracks to a section of Washington northeast of the Mall, the railroads received Union Station as a gift. The Lincoln Memorial was constructed between 1911 and 1922. The Freer Gallery of Art opened in 1923. In 1933 Secretary of the Interior Harold Ickes implemented the Mall Development Plan for landscaping and roadway construction. The federally financed program provided 350 jobs during the Depression. In 1937 the Reflecting Pool was constructed, and in 1938 the Jefferson Memorial was completed.

The world wars set back the beautification projects. To accommodate the growing government during World War I, temporary, barracklike structures—referred to as tempos—were constructed to house offices on the Mall and in West Potomac Park. More were added during World War II. These eyesores remained until 1969, when they were razed.

Two committees, the Fine Arts Commission and the National Capital Planning Commission, have been established to oversee development of the Mall. In order to maintain the sense of open space, a building restraint has been created. Since the 1960s five new Smithsonian buildings and the National Gallery of Art's East Building have been erected. West Potomac Park has become more developed, and in 1982, the Vietnam Veterans Memorial was constructed, as was Constitution Gardens. In 1995, the Korean War Veterans Memorial was dedicated. In 1999, construction began on the Smithsonian's newest museum, the National Museum of the American Indian, scheduled for completion in 2002.

## National Gallery of Art, West Building

On the National Mall between 4th and 6th Sts N.W. ☎ 737-4215 or 842-6176 (TTY) Mon–Fri 9–5. Web: www.nga.gov. Open Mon–Sat 10–5; Sun 11–6. Closed Christmas Day and New Year's Day. Admission: free. Introductory tours Mon–Fri 11:30; Sat 10:30 and 12:30; Sun 12:30 and 4:30. Foreign language tours Tues, Thurs, and Sat at 12. Sign language tours available with three weeks advance notice; ☎ 842-6247. Audio and digital tour–system rentals on main floor. For Gallery-Wide Calendar of Events, Film Calendar, or Concert Schedule, check at the art information desks at the main entrances or the Micro Gallery, or ☎ 842-6662 (Calendar of Events), ☎ 842-6799 (Film Calendar), or ☎ 842-6941 (Concert Schedule).

Restrooms, telephones, and the Garden Café are located on the ground floor, West Building. The Garden Café is open Mon–Sat 11:30–3; Sun 12–6:30. For reservations, ☎ 216-2494. Cascade Buffet, concourse level, open Mon–Sat 10–3; Sun 11–4:30. Cascade Café, concourse level, open Mon–Sat 10–4:30; Sun 11–5:30; ATM on premises. Well-stocked Gallery shops located on ground floor in the West Building and on the concourse level. Micro Gallery, an art information computer center, located on main floor.

All galleries and exhibitions are wheelchair accessible. Laminated guides to individual works provided in galleries. Strollers and wheelchairs are available. Easels provided for artists with permission to copy works.

National Gallery of Art, West Building (1941; John Russell Pope; 1983, ground floor remodeling, Keyes Condon Florance Architects). With an act of Congress, the National Gallery was established in 1937. Andrew Mellon's collection of 126 paintings and sculptures and the John Russell Pope–designed building to house them was reported to be the largest gift ever from an individual to a government. Hundreds of other individuals have since donated their works of art to the mu-

*National Mall. Courtesy of the Washington, D.C., Convention & Visitors Association.*

seum. The National Gallery's collections include more than 100,000 works of American and western European art from the Middle Ages to the 20C.

**Highlights:** The Gallery has one of the most comprehensive collections of Italian painting and sculpture in the United States, including Leonardo da Vinci's *Ginevra de' Benci*, the master's only painting in the Western Hemisphere. The museum also has an extensive collection of French impressionist works by Degas, Manet, Monet, Renoir, and others; as well as postimpressionist paintings by Cézanne and Van Gogh.

### History

The National Gallery of Art exists because of Andrew W. Mellon's passion for art and his belief that the nation's capital, unlike New York, Boston, and major European cities, did not have a great museum to display old master paintings. The Smithsonian had exhibited art since its opening in 1856, but never in a building dedicated solely to art. In the early 20C, the Smithsonian's Department of Fine Arts, then referred to as the National Gallery of Art, was housed in what is now the National Museum of Natural History. The staff hoped to acquire its own building, but efforts to do so in 1924 and 1939 both failed.

Andrew W. Mellon, a Pittsburgh financier, arrived in Washington in 1921. He served as secretary of the Treasury to three presidents and was later named ambassador to Great Britain. Before leaving for London to serve as ambassador, Mellon became the first person reputed to pay more than $1 million for a painting. The work was Raphael's *Alba Madonna*. Through brokers M. Knoedler and Company, Mellon purchased $6 million worth of masterpieces from the Soviet government, which was seeking hard currency to purchase tractors and other equipment for industrial development. Mellon's purchase accounted for one-third of Soviet exports to the United States in 1931.

Mellon left his position as ambassador in 1933, returning to his home in Pittsburgh and to Washington, where he lived in the McCormick Building, 1785 Massachusetts Ave. (Today, the building houses the National Trust for Historic Preservation.) In Washington, art dealer Lord Joseph Duveen, of Millbank, leased the apartment below Mellon's and installed works of art there so that Mellon could study them as much as he wished. Ultimately, Mellon purchased 24 of the paintings and 18 works of sculpture. Mellon paid $21 million—the largest transaction in the art world at that time. It was so large, in fact, Mellon had to pay Duveen in securities because he was short on cash. In order to safeguard the artwork, Mellon stored the pieces at the Corcoran Gallery.

When Mellon proposed building a public gallery for his collection he selected John Russell Pope as the architect. Pope was one of America's most prominent architects. He had graduated from Columbia College, the precursor of Columbia University, and traveled to Greece and Italy to study during the late 19C. Prior to his work with Mellon, Pope had designed residences, museums, university campuses, churches, and monuments. Other Pope buildings in Washington are Constitution Hall and the Jefferson Memorial. The site Mellon chose was an awkward trapezoidal shape on the north side of the Mall, south of Constitution Ave, between 3rd and 7th Sts. After attempting several designs, Pope ultimately suggested that the National Gallery be built on a rectangular portion of the plot between 4th and 7th Sts. (The area left vacant, 3rd to 4th Sts, is where the I. M. Pei–designed East Building now stands.)

Pope's design included a domed rotunda at the center of the building, with wide sculpture halls on either side. At the end of each hall Pope planned an interior garden court. Barrel-vaulted ceilings with skylights would provide natural light to the halls and garden courts. This natural lighting would be supplemented with concealed floodlights.

In Jan 1937 the United States Commission of the Fine Arts gave general approval to Pope's design, allowing plans to proceed. In April, however, the commission raised concerns about the Gallery's dome because they feared it would lead to a trend of domed buildings on the Mall. Pope tried to adjust his designs, but told the commission in June that "the National Gallery without an elevating central motif . . . will not hold its own with the National Museum." He vowed that "this building would not go on the lot unless it has a proper elevation." Reluctantly, the commission gave Pope the approval he wanted.

At Pope's suggestion, Mellon selected a pale pink marble from Tennessee for the building's exterior. The amount of marble needed for the façade was enormous, too large a quantity to be found in any one shade. To solve this problem, marble was selected in a narrow range of tones. The marble was laid so that the darkest shades would be on the lower levels and the lighter shades above. The difference is particularly noticeable when the structure is wet.

Mellon and Pope both died in Aug 1937, within 24 hours of each other. Although the plan for the façade had already been finalized, the layout and decoration of the interior were left to Otto Eggers, Pope's chief designer.

Construction began early in the summer of 1937 and continued for three and a half years, with Andrew's son Paul presiding over the project. The museum was dedicated on March 17, 1941, and opened to the public the next day. Like his father, Paul Mellon was a generous patron to the National Gallery of Art. By the time of his death in 1999, Paul Mellon had contributed more than 900 works of art to the collection. In his will, he donated more than 100 pictures, among them works by Winslow Homer, Georges Seurat, Edouard Manet, and Pierre Bonnard, plus a 73-piece collection that included a set of Edgar Degas waxes, as well as $75 million in cash.

### Washington Notes

The Baltimore and Potomac (B&P) Railroad Station, also known as the Sixth Street Depot, a Victorian Gothic structure built 1873–78, stood on the site where the National Gallery of Art's West Building is located today. The terminal served southbound trains and complemented the Baltimore and Ohio Railroad terminal at New Jersey Ave and C St N.W., which was used by trains heading north and west.

On July 2, 1881, President James A. Garfield was on his way to catch a train to his 25th reunion at Williams College when he was shot twice by Charles Guiteau, a civil-service employee. Aspiring to a bureaucratic post, Guiteau had pestered White House staff members for an appointment. Denied or ignored, Guiteau chose to seek revenge on Garfield. One bullet hit the president in the back; the second grazed his arm.

Thinking salt air would help his recovery, doctors recommended that Garfield retreat to his family's summerhouse in Elberon, New Jersey. He died there two months later on Sept 19, 1881. The B&P Station was draped in black bunting, and a silver star was installed in the floor and a plaque on the wall to mark the spot where Garfield was shot. Guiteau was hanged on June 29, 1882. The B&P Station was razed in 1904.

## Exterior

One of the largest marble structures in the world, the West Building was one of Pope's last designs. The museum is faced with Tennessee pink marble. Porticoes with Ionic columns are found on the south and north sides of the museum. Across Constitution Ave, on the north side of the West Building, is the **Andrew W. Mellon Memorial Fountain** (1952; Sidney Waugh, sculptor; Otto R. Eggers, architect). Water from three tiers of bronze basins flows into a granite pool. At the base of the pool are the signs of the zodiac in high relief.

## Interior

Visitors entering from the Mall first notice the **Art Information Room and Micro Gallery** on the left. This room contains an impressive multimedia computer system, the most comprehensive found in any American art museum. At its 13 kiosks, visitors are provided a wealth of information about 1,700 works of art in the Gallery's permanent collection. Touch-screen, color monitors provide information about artists, works of art, a time line of cultural events, and an illustrated dictionary and verbal pronunciations of art terms and proper names. The system also enables visitors to develop customized tours of the collection, including a map indicating the location of specific works. The information provided here is also available on CD-ROM, for sale in the Gallery shops.

From the foyer just inside the Mall entrance, walk north to the **rotunda.** At the center of the rotunda is *Mercury* (1749–1819; attributed to Francesco Righetti), a sculpture of the Roman messenger to the gods.

To the left of the Rotunda is the West Sculpture Hall; the East Sculpture Hall is to the right. At the end of each Sculpture Hall is a Garden Court. With lush plants surrounding a fountain and natural light from skylights above, the court is a relaxing place to pause.

The galleries are numbered sequentially and display the collection chronologically. Standing at the end of the West Sculpture Hall near the rotunda, Gallery 1 is on the right. The numbers continue consecutively around the Garden Court and back to the rotunda. The galleries are color coded on the National Gallery map to specify the periods and area of art exhibited. For example, Galleries 1–15, marked in yellow on the map, contain 13C–15C Italian art.

Note: Because of ongoing renovations to the galleries and additions to the collections, some paintings may have been moved to locations in the museum other than the sites listed here.

**Galleries 1–15: 13C–15C Italian.** Proceed west into the **West Sculpture Hall.** Enter the second gallery on the right, Gallery 4. Notice the *tondo*, or circular painting, upon entering this gallery. Painted during the early Italian Renaissance, *The Adoration of the Magi* (c. 1445) tells the story of three kings presenting their gifts to the newly born Christ at a time when very few people other than clergy and aristocrats could read. Scholars believe that two artists created this painting. Fra Angelico is considered the author of the Virgin and Child, whereas Fra Filippo Lippi most likely painted the other characters and the background.

Also in this gallery is *The Youthful David* (c. 1450; Andrea del Castagno). It is notable for its beauty, medium, and message. Castagno demonstrates his understanding of human anatomy by rendering muscle structure and veins. Scholars believe that David symbolizes Florence, a city trying to emerge on Italy's political stage. The medium is a leather shield used in ceremonial parades, and it is the only example of a painted shield that can be attributed to a master.

Walk through the left doorway and into Gallery 5. Turn left and enter Gallery 6. *Ginevra de' Benci* (c. 1474; Leonardo da Vinci) is the only painting by da Vinci in the Western Hemisphere. The subject is the daughter of a wealthy Florentine family who wed at age 16. It was customary in this period to have portraits painted for such occasions. However, while some scholars speculate that this was an engagement gift for Ginevra, others believe that Bernardo Bembo, the Venetian ambassador to Florence from 1474 to 1476 and 1478 to 1480, was the patron.

Exit Gallery 6 through the south doorway. Turn right in Gallery 7 and enter Gallery 8. Proceed through the north doorway and enter Gallery 9. *Giuliano de' Medici* (c. 1475–78; Andrea del Verrocchio) and *Lorenzo de' Medici* (1478–1521; Andrea del Verrocchio) are terra-cotta busts that commemorate these brothers of the Renaissance family who dominated Florence. Verrocchio had been a favorite artist of the Medicis.

Walk through the west doorway, continue walking west through Gallery 10, and enter Gallery 11. This gallery contains a bust called *A Little Boy* (c. 1455–60; Desiderio da Settignano). Da Settignano was considered one of the best marble carvers of the mid-15C.

**Galleries 16–28: 16C Italian.** From Gallery 12, proceed north into Gallery 17. Giovanni Bellini's and Titian's *The Feast of the Gods* (1514–29) was begun by Bellini and completed by Titian. Bellini was commissioned by Duke Alfonso to paint the first in a series of canvases with bacchanalian themes for the study of his palace. Perhaps to make Bellini's painting blend thematically and stylistically with his own pieces, Titian painted over the trees, adding the mountain landscape in their place. The painting typifies the style of the Venetian High Renaissance.

Walk west through Gallery 18 to Gallery 19. Turn left and proceed south into Gallery 20. *The Alba Madonna* (c. 1510; Raphael) hangs here. This piece demonstrates Raphael's style of complex composition (in this case, a pyramid within a circle) using his favorite subject of Madonna and Child. Considered a "Madonna of Humility" because the Virgin is seated on the ground rather than a throne or cushion, the work incorporates the High Renaissance ideals of beauty, order, and harmony. Raphael was 27 years old when he painted this work.

Walk east into Gallery 21. This gallery contains the bronze *Empire Triumphant over Avarice* (c. 1610; Adriaen de Vries.) De Vries, a major sculptor during the late Renaissance, created two intertwined females. This piece was previously thought to represent "Virtue Overcoming Vice," though it is now accepted as an allegory for the Holy Roman Emperor Rudolf II, who was attempting to win a war against the Turks and collect money from the lands he ruled in order to continue his battles.

Turn right and enter Gallery 22. Turn right and walk through Galleries 23 and 24. Turn left and enter Gallery 26. This gallery contains the fresco series the *Story of Cephalus and Procris* (c. 1520–22; Bernardino Luini). These frescoes, originally from the Milanese residence of the Rabia family, are reconstructed in the original sequence.

**Galleries 29–34, 36, 37: 17C–18C Italian, Spanish, and French.** Georges de La Tour's *The Repentant Magdalene* (c. 1640) is an excellent example of 17C French painting and demonstrates the influence of Caravaggio's tenebrism in France. The detailed painting shows Mary Magdalene in darkness, strategically lighted by a single candle, with her hand on a skull. A mirror reflection of the skull implies the transience of life.

Southern baroque painting is exemplified by Orazio Gentileschi's lyrical portrait *The Lute Player* (c. 1612–20), which employs chiaroscuro, an Italian term meaning "bright-dark." This refers to the use of light and shade to create the effect of volume or space. Gentileschi's trademark skill of conveying cloth textures is also evident in this work. Bartolomé Esteban Murillo's delightfully flirtatious *Two Women in a Window* (1655–60) is also featured.

Also displayed in these galleries are 18C Italian paintings, such as *The Campo di s.s. Giovanni e Paolo, Venice* (1743–47) by Bernardo Bellotto; *The Square of Saint Mark's, Venice* (1742–44); and *Entrance to the Grand Canal from the Molo, Venice* (1742–44) by Canaletto, who was principally known for his views of Venice and England. Here he combines observation and detail with soft atmosphere to create a poetic Venetian scene. His paintings were popular with English tourists visiting Venice. Also shown here is Giovanni Paolo Panini's *Interior of Saint Peter's, Rome* (1746–54), with its extraordinary detail and use of light.

The section of 17C Spanish art features one of Spain's most famous painters, the artist known as El Greco (born Domenikos Theotokopoulos in Crete); his painting *Laocoön* (c. 1610) is the only surviving mythological painting El Greco created.

**Galleries 35, 35A, 38–41A: 15C–16C Netherlandish and German.** Among the Netherlandish painters (1400–1530) represented is Jan Van Eyck, who originated a minutely realistic style of painting using surface effects and natural light, as in *The Annunciation* (oil on canvas transferred from panel; c. 1434–36).

Highlights include Netherlandish, German, and French painters (1485–1570), among them Hieronymus Bosch (*Death and the Miser,* c. 1485–99) and Albrecht Dürer, one of the greatest German artists of the Renaissance. Displayed here are two of Dürer's paintings exhibited back to back on one panel. On one side is *Madonna and Child* (c. 1496–97), which illustrates the influence of Venetian painters, particularly Bellini, on Dürer. Like Bellini's treatment of the same subject, Dürer's version renders the Virgin in a pyramid-like shape and Christ as athletic. (Look for the coat of arms in the lower left corner, which identifies the patron of the painting as a wealthy Nuremberg merchant.) On the other side is *Lot and His Daughters* (c. 1496–99), another example of Dürer's technical brilliance.

These galleries feature 16C and 17C Dutch and Flemish painters, such as Frans Hals, whose *Portrait of an Elderly Lady* (1633) demonstrates Hals' firm, broad brush strokes and use of boldly contrasting dark and light.

**Galleries 42–51: 17C Dutch and Flemish.** In *Woman Holding a Balance* (c. 1664), Johannes Vermeer weaves a parallel between the balance the woman is using and the painting on the wall behind her, *The Last Judgment,* an allegory encouraging a life of temperance and moderation. Jan Steen, one of the 17C Dutch painters shown here, was known for painting large, complex scenes of families and merrymakers, such as *The Dancing Couple* (1663).

When Rembrandt van Rijn died a pauper in 1669, he was buried in an unmarked, rented grave. Today his artistry is treasured. Several of his portraits are featured here, including his *Self-Portrait* (1659), along with *The Apostle Paul* (c. 1657) and *The Mill* (1645–48), in which Rembrandt portrays the drama of a man-made structure harnessing the power of nature.

Sir Peter Paul Rubens is known for his use of bold color, curvaceous lines, and dynamic energy, which are evident in *The Assumption of the Virgin* (c. 1626). Rubens was one of the innovators of the baroque style and an artist whose work was coveted in the 17C. Rubens's work can also be recognized by its striking colors and compositions. In *Daniel in the Lions' Den* (c. 1613–15), he depicts the biblical story of Daniel, tossed into a lions' den after refusing to worship a pagan god. Rubens's work was in such demand that he had a workshop of artists who helped paint the canvases to which he signed his name. However, in a letter to the English lord who was interested in purchasing this painting, Rubens insisted the work was "original, entirely by my hand." One of Rubens's favorite students was Sir Anthony Van Dyck, and displayed here is Van Dyck's portrait of Rubens's wife, Isabella Brant (1621).

**Galleries 52–57: 18C and early-19C French.** For a glimpse of Napoleon, stroll through this gallery and see Jacques-Louis David's *Napoleon in His Study* (1812). Napoleon is wearing a uniform reserved for special occasions. The background of a burned-out candle and the late hour on the clock imply that Napoleon has spent a hard night at work. Other symbolism includes the sword on the chair, which refers to Napoleon's military prowess. David worked on this painting as Napoleon embarked on his fateful Russian campaign.

In *A Young Girl Reading* (c. 1776), Jean-Honoré Fragonard uses thick strokes and saturated paint to define the textures of the girl's skirt. Jean-Antoine Houdon, one of the leading sculptors of his day, created busts of Benjamin Franklin, George Washington, and Voltaire. But two of his more tender portraits of children, *Louise Brongniart* (1777) and *Alexandre Brongniart* (1777), are shown here.

In Jean Baptiste Siméon Chardin's *Soap Bubbles* (c. 1733–34) the artist uses the activities of everyday life to carry philosophical purpose and meaning. In the 17C, bubbles were an allegory for the transience of life; this boy would have been regarded as wasting his time. Contrast this with *Soap Bubbles* (1764; Charles Amédée Philippe Vanloo), whose lighthearted characters with their sentimental expressions seem less judgmental about wasting time, unlike the boy in Jean-Siméon Chardin's *House of Cards* (1735), who seems very serious about his play.

These galleries also contain Spanish art, including the work of Francisco de Goya. *The Marquesa de Pontejos* (c. 1786) presents Goya's portraiture skills. The subject, María Ana de Pontejos y Sandoval, belonged to one of the wealthiest families in Spain. This portrait was probably painted for the Marquesa's first marriage.

**Galleries 58, 59, 61, 63: British.** *Watson and the Shark* (1778; John Singleton Copley) is a dramatic work depicting a brutal shark attack in 1749 on a young man, Brook Watson, who later became the Lord Mayor of London. The painting was a great success at the Royal Academy in 1778 because its grisly subject was such a novelty. John Constable's gift for creating a comfortable, intimate mood is evident in *Salisbury Cathedral from Lower Marsh Close* (1820). Also featured here are John Singleton Copley's *The Death of the Earl of Chatham* (1779) and Thomas Gainsborough's *Mountain Landscape with Bridge* (1783–84).

**Galleries 60A, 60B, 62, 64–71: American.** These galleries are ordered chronologically, beginning with paintings by 18C American artists such as Gilbert Stuart and Edward Savage. Included are Stuart's *The Skater* (1782) and Savage's *The Washington Family* (c. 1789–96). In the painting by Savage, the Washingtons probably sat for this portrait while in New York. According to Savage's notes, Washington's uniform and the papers under his arm refer to his "Military Character" and "Presidentship."

Highlights of **American Landscapes, 1830–70,** include works by Thomas Cole, a founder of the Hudson River School who profoundly influenced American landscape painting. Shown in this gallery is Cole's *Italian Coast Scene with Ruined Towers* (1838), which employs contrasts of dark and light as seen in the clouds reflected in the water and the white sheep against the dark towers.

The remaining American galleries feature artists of the late 19C and early 20C. Another member of the Hudson River School, Jasper Francis Cropsey, known for his autumn landscapes, is represented here by *Autumn—On the Hudson River* (1860). George Caleb Bingham was one of the earliest portrayers of the American West, as shown in *The Jolly Flatboatmen* (1846). In *The Biglin Brothers Racing* (c. 1873), Thomas Eakins evocatively captures men in midaction. Childe Hassam's *Oyster Sloop, Cos Cob* (1902) shows his use of bright colors and broad brushwork. Maurice Prendergast's love of bright pigments is well represented by his *Salem Cove* (1916). George Bellows's *Both Members of This Club* (1909) was inspired by the illegal fights he attended at Tom Sharkey's Athletic Club in New York. Here Bellows depicts the excitement and passion of a boxing match. Bellows chose a close-up view, skillfully using light and dark along with heavy textures to create an energetic mood. Also here are several paintings by Winslow Homer, including *Autumn* (1877) and *Right and Left* (c. 1909). Homer began to focus on the power and beauty of the sea when he moved to Prouts Neck, Maine, in 1883. The two ducks in *Right and Left* are the targets of a gun held by the hunter in the boat. Homer places the viewer in the line of fire. To get the correct perspective, Homer asked a friend to row offshore and fire blank cartridges at him. In *The White Girl (Symphony in White, No. 1)* (1862) James McNeill Whistler portrays his mistress, Joanna Hiffernan. The jury at the Paris Salon in 1863 refused to show this painting; however, it was received with a tremendous success at the controversial Salon des Refusés.

**Galleries 72–79: special exhibitions.** These galleries are designated for the housing of special traveling exhibitions.

**Galleries 52–56, 80–93: 19C French.** The National Gallery owns two of Claude Monet's paintings of the Rouen Cathedral. *Rouen Cathedral, West Façade* (1894) is painted with many layers of paint to create varied color and contrasts of light. *The Japanese Footbridge* is one of a series of paintings representing his water gardens at Giverny.

In 1846, Baudelaire encouraged artists to portray the "Heroism of Modern Life." Edouard Manet's *The Old Musician* (1862) depicts urban characters who lived near Manet's studio in a slumlike area that was being razed to broaden the boulevards of Napoleon's renovated Paris. Manet's use of a limited range of color and shallow background creates a feeling of immediacy in *The Dead Toreador* (c. 1864). Children love walking slowly past the picture, which creates the impression the toreador is changing position.

Industrial Paris was a popular subject for 19C avant-garde artists. Originally titled *Railroad*, Edouard Manet's *The Railway* (c. 1873) makes the viewer part of the picture by truncating the image's edges, much the way a camera does. The work is also notable for portraying an unposed slice of life.

Pierre Auguste Renoir's *A Girl With a Watering Can* (1876) is one of the most popular paintings in the museum. For Renoir, this canvas was important for commercial reasons. Renoir was in financial trouble after the disastrous reception of the first impressionist group exhibition, which he organized. This painting, of an unidentified girl but probably a neighbor whom Renoir chose for her appearance, was an attempt to demonstrate the artist's portraiture skills so he could solicit commissions.

Paul Cézanne's *The Artist's Father* (1866) is an emotionally charged piece that illustrates Cézanne's turbulent relationship with his father. Cézanne employed the violent palette-knife technique to create this expressive work. Paul Gauguin created numerous canvases in 1888 and 1889. One of them is *Self-Portrait* (1889), which was painted on a cupboard door in an inn in the Breton hamlet of Le Pouldu. Also here are two well-known paintings by Vincent Van Gogh: *Roses* (1890) and *Self-Portrait* (1889).

Return to the rotunda and take either of the two marble staircases to the ground floor. The east portion of the ground floor contains the West Building Gallery Shop and the stairs, elevator, and escalators leading to the concourse level and the East Building.

At the foot of the stairs proceed south. Under the rotunda is the Garden Café.

Proceed from the central galleries to the West Building Gallery Shop and from there to the escalators to the East Building. On the landing by the escalators, note the hallucinatory, surrealist *The Sacrament of the Last Supper* (1955) by Salvador Dalí.

## National Gallery of Art, East Building

On the National Mall between 3rd and 4th Sts N.W. ☎ 737-4215 or 842-6176 (TTY) Mon–Fri. Web: www.nga.gov. Open Mon–Sat 10–5; Sun 11–6. Closed Christmas Day and New Year's Day. Admission: free. Tours Mon–Fri at 10:30 and 1:30; Sat and Sun at 11:30, 1:30, and 3:30. Foreign language tours Tues, Thurs, and Sat at 2. Sign language tours available with three weeks advance notice; ☎ 842-6247. For film schedule, check at art information desk (ground level) or ☎ 842-6799. For concert information, check at the art information desk (ground level) or ☎ 842-6941.

Restrooms, telephones, ATM. Cascade Buffet, concourse level, open Mon–Sat 10–3; Sun 11–3. Cascade Café, concourse level, open Mon–Sat 10–4:30; Sun 10–5:30. Well-stocked Gallery shops.

All galleries and exhibitions are wheelchair accessible. Strollers and wheelchairs are available. Easels provided for artists with permission to copy works.

The National Gallery of Art, East Building (1978; I. M. Pei and Partners; Dan Kiley, landscape architect) was constructed in response to the changing needs of the National Galley of Art.

**Highlights.** Works by Pablo Picasso, Alexander Calder, Georgia O'Keeffe, Jackson Pollock, and Roy Lichtenstein.

### History

When the National Gallery opened in 1941 with only 5 of the 130 galleries filled, few imagined that it would run out of wall space in less than 30 years. In fact, the museum was initially so bare that its guards fashioned a basketball court in one of the vast galleries.

When Andrew W. Mellon established the National Gallery of Art (see "National Gallery of Art, West Building: History"), he stipulated that "future acquisitions [of the National Gallery of Art] . . . shall be limited to objects of the highest standard of quality, so that the collection shall not be marred by the introduction of art that is not of the best of its type." This was initially interpreted to mean only those artists whose work posterity had judged superior would be included in the collection. The Gallery, however, later pursued works by contemporary artists as well.

To house its growing collection, the Gallery looked to expand on the site Mellon had reserved through Congress in 1937 for that purpose. Paul Mellon and Alisa Mellon Bruce, children of Andrew W. Mellon, and the Andrew W. Mellon Foundation donated the necessary funding to expand the museum their father had founded. The East Building was placed on a trapezoidal piece of land set aside by Congress when it originally established the National Gallery of Art. The new building needed to fit this space and also complement the classical style of the West Building.

The architect, I. M. Pei, chose to divide the plot into two triangles. The larger is an isosceles triangle whose base faces the West Building while its exposed side parallels Pennsylvania Ave. The second is a right triangle whose base faces the Capitol and whose exposed side faces the Mall. The apex of the triangle creates a sharp angle (19½ degrees) at the building's southwest corner. A glass-paneled roof covers the airy triangular atrium created by the triangles. Even though the Tennessee quarries that supplied the marble for the exterior of the West Building had been closed for years, they were reopened to supply the marble for the East Building. In harmony with Pope's classic West Building, the East Building, which opened in 1978, is considered to be one of Pei's most successful designs.

> ### Washington Notes
> In 1932, abandoned shanties cluttered the site where the National Gallery's East Building was later built. More than 20,000 unemployed veterans of World War I had come to Washington to lobby for the early distribution of a cash bonus approved by Congress in 1924.

## Exterior

The plaza between the East Building and West Building contains **seven glass tetrahedrons** that serve as skylights for the concourse level below. The fountain in the plaza flows down a waterfall that is visible from the concourse level. Pei designed the building as two distinct triangles forming a trapezoid. The isosceles triangle is for exhibition galleries and public spaces, the right triangle for museum offices and the Center for Advanced Study in the Visual Arts. Sculptures are displayed on the apron of grass surrounding the East Building.

## Interior

Enter the East Building from 4th St, the west side of the building. Immediately to the right is the coat check room. Continuing east is the information desk. This level also features two exhibition galleries. The large atrium serves to welcome visitors; it is also used to accommodate lines of people waiting to enter special exhibits and to welcome visitors.

When the East Building was under construction in the 1970s, Alexander Calder (1898–1976) was asked to create a large mobile sculpture to complement the atrium's space. In the early 1930s, when Calder began experimenting with mobiles, they were motorized. However, his later designs are carefully balanced so that the sculptures move freely with air currents. Calder's red, blue, and black mobile *Untitled* (1976) has been on view in the East Building since it opened in 1978.

The East Building houses the National Gallery's 20C art and a changing series of special exhibitions. Works are exhibited in a constant state of flux, often being rotated and relocated throughout the year. Check with the information desk or the Micro Gallery, West Building, to discover whether a specific work is on view and its current location.

**Ground level.** The gallery to the left of the entrance is used for semipermanent exhibitions such as **Small French Paintings,** a small collection of 19C French impressionist and postimpressionist works. Among the highlights are *The Sisters* (1869; Morisot), *The Artist's Studio* (1855–60; Jean Baptiste-Camille Corot), and still lifes by Edouard Manet (1832–1883) and Auguste Renoir (1841–1919). Other featured artists include Edouard Vuillard (1868–1940), Pierre Bonnard (1867–1947), and Georges Seurat (1859–1891).

The second gallery, east of the information desk to the north side of the atrium, focuses on **American Modernist Paintings,** a collection of works by American artists such as Georgia O'Keeffe (1887–1986), Edward Hopper (1882–1967) and

Marsden Hartley (1877–1943). The rear gallery also serves as an observation deck for the Alexander Calder mobiles and sculptures displayed on the concourse level.

The tapestry *Woman* (1977), after Joan Miró (1893–1983), woven by Josep Royo (b. 1945) is hung along the south wall of the ground floor.

Marble staircases along the south wall lead down to the concourse level and up to the mezzanine.

**Concourse level.** A corridor equipped with two moving walkways connects the East Building with the West Building on the concourse level. Also located on this level is a museum shop, the Cascade Buffet and Cascade Café, and two auditoriums used for lectures and films.

The gallery space displays a permanent exhibition of **Twentieth-Century Art** created after World War II by artists such as Barnett Newman (1905–1970), Jackson Pollock (1912–1956), and Mark Rothko (1903–1970). Newman is known for the abstract paintings he began creating in the 1940s. They feature fields of color occasionally interrupted by vertical or horizontal stripes of another color. Look for *Achilles* (1952), a brown canvas cut by a broad swatch of brilliant red. Pollock made art by tacking canvases to his studio floor. Circling the canvas, Pollock would fling, drip, and splash additional colors onto the piece. An example of Pollock's unique technique is *Number 1 (Lavender Mist)* (1950). Mark Rothko sought "simple expression of the complex thought" by vertically stacking colorful rectangles of paint atop one another. Look for his painting *Untitled* (1953), a pink rectangle hovering above a black rectangle. Robert Rauschenberg bridged abstract expressionism and pop art and for a period worked closely with Jasper Johns. From 1984 to 1991, he coordinated ROCI (Rauschenberg Overseas Culture Interchange), a project devoted to bringing together ideas and artistic techniques from different countries. In *Narcissus/ROCI USA (Wax Fire Works)* (1990) he uses a screen-printing process to transfer photographic images onto stainless steel.

German artist Sigmar Polke's trademark is the use of political, philosophical, and historical subject matter, but his *Hope Is: Wanting to Pull Clouds* (1992) seems too whimsical for such postmodern concerns.

**Mezzanine.** The mezzanine is composed of extensive galleries, primarily used for temporary exhibitions. At the top of the stairs turn right and walk north. Turn left and walk southwest to the staircase. Proceed to the upper level.

**Upper level.** The spacious galleries on this level display paintings and sculpture from the National Gallery's 20C collection and temporary exhibitions. At the top of the stairs turn right. Walk north (the atrium is on the right). On the west wall are rotating pieces from the museum's collection, including large wall-reliefs by Frank Stella. Continue walking north into the gallery containing art from the first half of the 20C.

The first room in this suite of galleries is primarily filled with works by Pablo Picasso (1881–1973). *Family of Saltimbanques* (c. 1904–5; Picasso) is thought to be an autobiographical statement on the ostracism felt by both itinerant circus performers (saltimbanques) and avant-garde painters. Another Picasso, *Nude Woman* (1910), may owe its unusual form to the fact that it may be one of 11 intended works for a private library in New York. The faceted forms and muted colors are typical features of analytic cubism.

Walk through the south doorway to the next room. Works by Henri Matisse (1869–1954) are displayed here, including *Lorette with Turban, Yellow Jacket*

(1917). Set in his apartment in Nice, *The Pianist and Checker Players* (1924) depicts one of Matisse's favorite models, Henriette Darricarère, and her two brothers. It has been suggested that this is a surrogate family portrait, with Darricarère representing Matisse's daughter and the brothers filling in for the artist's sons. The apartment is identifiably Matisse's, as his drawings are pinned to a wall and violins (Matisse was also a musician) hang on the armoire.

Continue south into the next room, which displays mostly surrealistic pieces. With *Bird in Space* (1925), Constantin Brancusi (1876–1957) fulfilled his desire to convey the essence of flight through sculptural form. The streamlined shape evolved from a previous depiction of *Maiastra*, his representation of a mythic creature in Romanian folklore. Piet Mondrian, a Dutch artist, believed that his abstract or "neoplastic" images expressed the universal harmonies that preside in nature. His compositions evolved into a series of black lines intersecting at right angles to delineate rectangles painted in white or gray and primary colors. In *Diamond Painting in Red, Yellow and Blue* (c. 1921–25) those rectangles are sliced by the edge of the canvas, which Mondrian configured as a lozenge shape. Other pieces to look for in this room are *The Look of Amber* (1929; Yves Tanguy) and *La Condition Humaine* (1933; Rene Magritte).

A staircase on the east wall of this room leads to the tower level.

**Tower level.** Only one gallery is located on the tower level. It houses a spectacular group of paper cutouts by the French artist Henri Matisse. Late in his life, Matisse created collages using paper cutouts. *Large Composition with Masks* (1953) is the largest of these works, and was designed to be a full-scale study for a ceramic mural. The Tower Gallery is open Mon–Sat 10–2 and Sun 11–3.

## National Gallery of Art Sculpture Garden

Bounded by Constitution Ave and Madison Dr N.W. on the north and south, and by 7th and 9th Sts N.W. on the east and west. ☎ 737-4215. Web: www.nga.gov. Open Mon–Sat 10–5; Sun 11–6. Closed Christmas Day and New Year's Day. Admission: free. The pavilion offers year-round café service with indoor and outdoor seating, and the National Gallery offers lectures, films, and walking tours. Information guides are available at the 7th St entrance and at the Information Desks in the Gallery, East and West.

A gift to the nation from the Morris and Gwendolyn Cafritz Foundation, this 6.1 acre sculpture garden (1999; Laurie D. Olin, landscape architect, Olin Partnership, Philadelphia, in association with National Gallery of Art staff) was designed to provide what the Gallery calls "flexible spaces" to accommodate its growing collection of 20C sculpture. But the sculpture gallery also provides a beautiful and intimate oasis for tourists and Washingtonians alike—a place to experience lush greenery, flowing water in the summer, an ice-skating rink in the winter, and art year-round.

**Highlights:** The fountain offers an urban oasis in summer, and in winter the fountain area is converted into an ice-skating rink. Noted works include Alexander Calder's *Cheval Rouge*, Joan Miro's *Personnage Gothique, Oiseau-Eclair,* and Mark di Suvero's *Aurora.*

### History

In 1966 an agreement signed by Paul Mellon, then president of the National Gallery, and Secretary of the Interior Stewart Udall determined that the site would be developed into a sculpture garden under the joint auspices of the National Park Service and the National Gallery. While the National Park Service would pay for construction and maintenance, the National Gallery of Art would contribute sculptures. In 1969 the garden debuted as a circular pool skirted by two stands of topiary-trimmed linden trees, but there were no sculptures. In 1974 a skating rink was added.

In 1988 a steel pavilion, designed by Charles Bassett of Skidmore, Owings and Merrill, San Francisco, with a snack shop, skate rentals in winter, and restrooms opened. In 1991, the National Park Service transferred control of the park to the National Gallery. With funds provided by The Morris and Gwendolyn Cafritz Foundation, the Gallery contracted landscape architect Laurie Olin of the Olin Partnership, Philadelphia, to create a design for the garden. The completed plan, inspired in part by Andrew Jackson Downing's 1851 proposals for the National Mall, provides a setting primarily for 20C art. The sculpture garden opened in spring 1999.

Use the 7th St entrance. Turn south to *Thinker on a Rock* (1997; Barry Flanagan), an irreverent homage to Rodin's *The Thinker* in lapin form. Continue south to *Four-Sided Pyramid* (1997; Sol LeWitt), made of concrete blocks and mortar, and *Chair Transformation Number 20B* (1996), one of Lucas Samaras's series of works realized in a variety of materials, including wood, wire mesh and mirrored glass. (This one's made of patinated bronze.)

Turn west (facing the Hirshshorn Sculpture Garden across the Mall) and walk around the inner circle path to David Smith's *Cubi XXVI* (1965), part of a series created by the painter in 1960 and made of steel, which the artist said reflects the "power, structure, movement, progress, suspension, brutality" of this century. Continue west to *House I* (1996–98; Roy Lichtenstein), a fabricated and aluminum piece by an artist known more for his pop paintings and comic strips.

Walking north, on the left is Alexander Calder's dramatic *Cheval Rouge (Red Horse)* (1974), a stabile as appealing as the mobiles displayed in the National Gallery, East; on the right is *Cluster of Four Cubes* (1992; George Rickey), massive cubes of stainless steel, each precisely weighted and balanced, engineered to turn effortlessly in the lightest breeze.

At the south end of the pavilion is the whimsical *Typewriter Eraser, Scale X* (1999; Claes Oldenburg and Coosje van Bruggen), a stainless steel and fiberglass paean to Oldenburg's favorite office supply when he was a child. Across from this is Louise Bourgeois's *Spider* (1996–97), bronze cast with silver nitrate patina and one of a series of spider sculptures by the artist for whom the spider carries associations of a maternal figure.

To the north (facing Constitution Ave) is *Personnage Gothique, Oiseau-Eclair (Gothic Personage, Bird-Flash)* (1974; Joan Miro), a surrealist bronze that is one of Miro's largest sculptures.

Turn east to Isamu Noguchi's *Great Rock of Inner Seeking* (1974), made of the material the artist most favored—stone—which he called "the most flexible and meaning-impregnated material. When I tap it, I get an echo of that which we are. Then, the whole universe has resonance." Across from this is *Aurora* (1992–93; Mark di Suvero), eight tons of steel over three diagonal supports. The piece takes its name from a poem about New York City by Federico García Lorca.

A few steps beyond, on the left, is *Six-Part Seating* (conceived, 1985; fabricated,

1998) by Scott Burton, whose art has been described as "sculpture in love with furniture."

Turn south again to complete the inner square. On the right is Joel Shapiro's *Untitled* (1989), which was constructed from plywood sheets, then cast in bronze while retaining the wood grain pattern. Across from this is *Stele II* (1973; Ellsworth Kelly), which is loosely based on a French kilometer marker observed by Kelly during his years in Paris after World War II.

Continue south to the 7th St entrance and then west to the inner pathway surrounding the fountain/ice rink. A few steps to the left is Tony Smith's *Moondog* (model, 1964; Fabricated, 1998–99). The title comes from two sources identified by the artist: One was the name of a blind poet and folk musician who lived in New York, and the other was the Joan Miró painting *Dog Barking at the Moon.*

A few steps to the right is *Puellae* (1992; Magdalena Abakanowicz). Each of the 30 bronzes is a unique cast made from a burlap mold that Abakanowicz individually worked during the casting process.

Take time to enjoy the variety of plants and bushes, including American Elm, Horse Chestnut, Kentucky Coffee Tree, Littleleaf Linden, American Holly, Star Magnolia, and Sawtooth Oak.

Walk east to 4th St. Turn right and walk south across the Mall. Cross Jefferson Dr and proceed to Independence Ave.

The new building going up at 4th St and Independence Ave S.W., to the east of the National Air and Space Museum, will house the **National Museum of the American Indian.** It is scheduled for completion in 2002. The museum's current home, the George Gustav Heye Center of the National Museum of the American Indian in New York City, will remain open. The Heye Center features the George Gustav Heye Collection, a comprehensive assortment of Indian cultural material assembled over a 54-year period by Heye in his travels throughout North and South America. In 1922 Heye founded the Heye Foundation's Museum of the American Indian in New York. He was its director until his death in 1957.

The Smithsonian Institution acquired the collection and in 1994 opened the Heye Center in the Alexander Hamilton U.S. Customs House in New York (Web: www.si.edu), where about 10 percent of the collection is displayed. The new facility on the Mall will feature additional material from the Heye Collection.

Turn right at Independence Ave and walk west. The entrance to the Smithsonian Institution's National Air and Space Museum is on the right.

## Smithsonian Institution

The Smithsonian museums on the Mall are open daily 10–5:30. ☎ 357-2700 or 357-1729 (TTY). For recorded information, ☎ 357-2020 (English); 633-9126 (Spanish). Admission: free, unless noted otherwise.

### History

In 1846, the United States established the Smithsonian Institution with funds inherited by James Smithson, a noted English scientist who discovered a type of zinc ore. Despite his generous gift, Smithson spent his entire life in Europe and never visited the United States. Smithson was born in France in 1765 as James Lewis Macie. He was the illegitimate son of Hugh Smithson, first duke of Northumberland, and Elizabeth Hungerford Keate Macie, a descendant of Henry VII. When Smithson was 50, after his mother's death, he changed his name to Smithson.

Smithson died on June 27, 1829, in Genoa, Italy. His was interred in an English cemetery at San Benigno. In Smithson's will, a nephew was named to inherit the entire estate, except for a small sum bequeathed to a loyal servant. However, the will specified that if the nephew died without an heir, then all of the money should be transferred to the United States government "to found in Washington, under the name of the Smithsonian Institution, an establishment for the increase and diffusion of knowledge." The nephew died in 1835 without heirs.

In a prophetic statement, Smithson wrote that the name Smithson "shall live in the memory of man when the titles of the Northumberlands and Percys are extinct and forgotten." The reality is that we may never learn Smithson's intention, but for more than 150 years his name has been recognized around the world.

On July 1, 1836, Congress accepted the inheritance and pledged to carry out Smithson's wishes. In 1838, the U.S. received Smithson's estate—105 bags of gold sovereigns valued at $508,318.46, a huge fortune. The U.S. Congress debated how to spend the inheritance for ten years. Possibilities included a library, a laboratory, a school, and an experimental farm. In Aug 1846, Congress passed an act that established the Smithsonian Institution as a "multifaceted organization involved in the research and dispersal of academic buildings." On May 1, 1847, the cornerstone was laid for the first building, which was completed in 1855.

The Smithsonian Institution reaches much farther than the Mall. Currently, there are 16 museums, galleries, and the National Zoological Park. Most are situated on or near the Mall: the Freer Gallery of Art and Arthur M. Sackler Gallery; the National Museum of African Art; Hirshhorn Museum and Sculpture Garden; National Air and Space Museum; National Museum of American History; National Museum of Natural History; Arts and Industries Building; National Portrait Gallery; National Museum of American Art; and the Renwick Gallery. National Zoological Park, Anacostia Museum, and the National Postal Museum are located in other parts of the capital. The Paul E. Garber Preservation, Restoration, and Storage Facility, which houses part of the National Air and Space Museum's collection, is located in nearby Suitland, Maryland. The Cooper-Hewitt, National Design Museum and the National Museum of the American Indian are in New York City. (The National Museum of the American Indian will open a new site on the Mall in 2002.) The Smithsonian also has research facilities in eight states and Panama.

The Smithsonian Institution holds more than 140 million artifacts, specimens, works of art, and objects and is the world's largest museum complex.

### *Washington Notes*

In 1904, the Smithsonian Institution learned that the authorities in Genoa planned to demolish the cemetery containing Smithson's tomb. The Smithsonian immediately sent Alexander Graham Bell to retrieve the tomb and bring it to the United States. The tomb is now located adjacent to the north foyer in the Smithsonian Institution building, also called the Castle. While renovating the chamber, the Department of Physical Anthropology took the opportunity to examine the skeleton. It was determined that Smithson was five ft six inches tall, smoked a pipe, had an extra vertebra, was an avid fencer, and died of natural causes.

## National Air and Space Museum

Independence Ave between 4th and 7th Sts S.W. ☎ 357-2700 or 357-1729 (TTY). Web: www.nasm.edu. Open daily 10–5:30. Closed Christmas Day. Extended summer hours determined annually. Admission: free. Tours daily at 10:15 and 1; inquire at the information desk in Gallery 108. Interactive tours in several languages available for rental; inquire at tour desk in Gallery 100. Theater, planetarium, and tour reservations available for groups of 25 or more. Activities must be scheduled three to eight weeks in advance. Write: Tour Scheduler, NASM, Washington, DC 20560; or ☎ 357-1400. Admission to Albert Einstein Planetarium and Langley Theater: $4.50 for adults; $3.25 for ages 2 to 21 and senior citizens. Planetarium showtimes: every 40 minutes, 11–5:40. Langley Theater showtimes: 11 daily during museum hours; evenings after museum closes Mon–Thurs 5:45; Fri–Sun 5:30 and 7. Tickets available two weeks in advance. Two dining facilities on first floor at east end. The Wright Place Restaurant is sitdown–style, serving fancy sandwiches and light entrées. The Flight Line Cafeteria offers hot and cold sandwiches and salads. Three shops on first floor. Telephones, lost and found, ATM. Restrooms on both floors. Tours for mentally retarded, visually, physically, and hearing-impaired available upon request; reserve in advance. Materials in Braille, large print, or recorded form are available in limited quantities. All galleries are wheelchair accessible. Free wheelchair rental in Gallery 108.

The National Air and Space Museum (1972–76; Hellmuth, Obata & Kassabaum) opened to the public on July 1, 1976, as part of the United States' Bicentennial celebration. Its 8–10 million visitors annually have made it the most popular museum in Washington, D.C., and one of the most popular in the world. The touchable moon rock (inside the door on the Mall side), the aircraft hanging from the ceiling, and the video stations that relate the history of flight make it a favorite with children and teens.

In 2003, the museum plans to open an annex called the **Dulles Center,** located near Dulles Airport in Fairfax, Virginia. Current designs call for a facility three times the size of the museum on the Mall, with two levels of aircraft suspended from an atrium, an IMAX theater, and a restoration shop where visitors can observe work being done on vintage planes.

**Highlights:** Three major exhibits are the Milestones of Flight, the Space Race, and Air Transportation. These exhibits include such artifacts as the Wright brothers' 1903 Flyer, the *Spirit of St. Louis*, a moon rock to touch, the Skylab Orbital Workshop, and early planes such as the Pitcairn Mailwing. The Einstein Planetarium and the IMAX films in the Langley Theater are also popular.

### History

The Smithsonian Institution began exploring the realm of air and flight long before the National Air and Space Museum was conceived. In 1857, the Smithsonian used balloons to collect weather reports for the *Washington Evening Star.* Three years later, Thaddeus S. C. Lowe worked with the Smithsonian on a balloon project that resulted in President Lincoln's use of balloons for military observations during the Civil War. The institution's aeronautical collection began in 1876 when the Smithsonian acquired a group of kites from the Chinese Imperial Commission.

In the late 19C, the Smithsonian Institution's aeronautics program grew under the auspices of Samuel Pierpont Langley, who eventually was named third secretary of the Smithsonian. Langley was interested in aerodomes—unmanned, steam-driven, heavier-than-air craft. In 1890, the Smithsonian Astrophysical Observatory was established. Langley succeeded in launching *Aerodome No. 5* over the Potomac on May 6, 1896. It stayed in the air for one and a half minutes.

On Dec 17, 1903, the Wright brothers made the first manned, powered, and controlled heavier-than-air craft flight near Kitty Hawk, North Carolina. After petitioning Congress for three years, Secretary of the Smithsonian Charles D. Walcott, Alexander Graham Bell, Ernest W. Roberts, and others succeeded in 1915 in having Congress create the National Advisory Committee for Aeronautics (NASA's forerunner).

Congress established the National Air Museum as a bureau of the Smithsonian in 1946. Two years later, the Smithsonian acquired the Wright 1903 Flyer. Although Congress authorized a new aviation museum in 1958, construction did not begin until 1972, when funds were appropriated. S. Dillon Ripley, eighth secretary of the Smithsonian and the museum's first director, as well as Michael Collins, pilot of the *Apollo 11* mission, oversaw the construction of the National Air and Space Museum. In 1966 the legislation establishing the museum was amended to include space flight.

**Silver Hill Museum,** in Suitland, Maryland, the museum's preservation, restoration, and storage facility, opened to the public in 1977. In 1980 it was renamed the Paul E. Garber Preservation, Restoration, and Storage Facility, in honor of the museum's Historian Emeritus and Ramsey Fellow. Garber acquired much of the Air and Space Museum's collection. Free tours of this facility are Mon–Fri at 10; Sat–Sun 10 and 1. Reservations are required, ☎ (202) 357-1400 or 357-1505 (TTY) (see Walk 34: "Additional Sites of Interest in D.C. and Surrounding Areas of Maryland and Virginia").

### *Washington Notes*

The Washington Armory (also known as the Columbian Armory) stood on the site that became the NASM. The armory, constructed in 1855, served numerous functions during its 108 years. It had been designed to store weapons for the D.C. militia and to be a depository for military trophies from the American Revolution and other wars. However, during the Civil War the facility became the main building of the Armory Square Hospital, a collection of wooden wards stretching across the Mall from 5th to 7th Sts. Abandoned at the end of the war, the armory building remained vacant until 1878 when it was used to store exhibits from the 1876 Centennial Exposition in Philadelphia. In 1881 the Smithsonian's Arts and Industries Building was completed and the Centennial's exhibits were moved there. The armory's next tenant was the U.S. Fish Commission's labs, offices, and fish hatchery, which was a popular city attraction. Later uses for the armory included serving as a motion picture studio, office building, and paint shop for government buildings. In 1964, the building was razed to make way for the National Air and Space Museum.

## Exterior

The granite-and-glass structure is faced with Tennessee pink cedar marble, which complements the neoclassical style of the National Gallery of Art's West Building across the Mall. Three sculptures adorn the NASM's exterior. *Continuum* (1976; Charles O. Perry), a bronze, ribbonlike design, is displayed at the Independence Ave entrance. *Ad Astra* (1976; Richard Lippold), a painted stainless steel sculpture, is near the Jefferson Dr entrance. A Bicentennial gift from the Venezuelan government, *Delta Solar* (1976; Alejandro Otero) is above the reflecting pool on 7th St. This sculpture's stainless steel sails move in the breeze. Nearby, five japonica trees, planted in 1978, commemorate the cooperation in space programs between the United States and the former Soviet Union.

## Interior

**Note:** The Air and Space Museum is in the process of replacing all its glass walls and skylights in order to better protect its artifacts from light damage. During the renovation, which is being done in 11 phases and is scheduled for completion in July 2001, several exhibits will be closed and some popular items, including the airplanes suspended in the atrium, will be relocated or temporarily removed. For this reason, the exhibits described below may have been moved. Information on where particular exhibits currently are located can be obtained at the information desk or by using one of the kiosks inside the Independence Ave entrance.

To find out the latest gallery closings (and reopenings), check the Web site at www.nasm.edu. As of press time, the following galleries were temporarily closed: Jet Aviation (Gallery 106), Looking at Earth (Gallery 110), Apollo to the Moon (Gallery 210), and Space Race (Gallery 114). The dates for reopening these galleries were not known, but they could be available at any time. All the descriptions of exhibits that follow were written before any of them closed for renovation; when the galleries reopen they may contain different items.

**First floor galleries.** Entering from Independence Ave brings visitors into the **South Lobby,** Gallery 108. Straight ahead is an information desk where docent tours begin, and to the left are several computer kiosks providing information about the museum's exhibits, as well as information about particular subjects, such as African American and Hispanic participation in America's space program or airplanes used in World War I. Hanging from the ceiling above the desk is the sleek Voyager, the first aircraft to fly around the world without stopping or refueling. The two murals are Eric Sloane's *Earth Flight Environment* and Robert T. McCall's *The Space Mural—A Cosmic View.* Proceed north into Gallery 100, **Milestones of Flight.** Interactive audio tours can be rented at a desk in this gallery.

This two-story gallery features some of the United States's historical aviation treasures. On the first floor level is the Mercury *Friendship 7,* which made the first U.S. manned orbital flight in 1962. In July 1969 the first craft ever to land on the Moon, the *Apollo 11* command module *Columbia,* carried astronauts Neil Armstrong, Edwin Aldrin, and Michael Collins. On the upper level, in Gallery 210, the **moon rock** on display—a basaltic mineral more than 4 billion years old—was retrieved by the *Apollo 17* astronauts in Dec 1972.

Other highlights on the upper level include the Wright brothers' 1903 Flyer that Orville Wright flew in Kitty Hawk, North Carolina, on Dec 17, 1903. It is composed of wood and fabric bound together by steel wire. On May 20, 1927, Charles Lindbergh took off from Roosevelt Field, Long Island, in the *Spirit of St. Louis.* Within 33½ hours he had become the first person to fly solo across the Atlantic Ocean. *Pioneer 10* is a prototype of an unmanned craft designed to fly past Jupiter and Saturn. The final design was launched in 1972.

Walk west to Gallery 101, the first gallery on the right, for a display case of United States Air Force airplane models. Tucked beneath the escalator is a booth where visitors can have their names pressed into military dogtags for $4.95 each.

Continue east to Gallery 102, **Air Transportation.** This exhibit traces the progression of the air transportation of cargo, people, and mail. On display is one of the first Pitcairn Mailwings ever built. It flew between New York and Atlanta— with stops in Philadelphia, Baltimore, Washington, and Richmond. Pitcairn later evolved into Eastern Airlines. American Airways, the precursor to American Airlines, used the Ford Tri-Motor that is displayed for transcontinental flights during the 1930s. The amphibious Grumman G-21 (the Grumman Goose Amphibian), first flown in May 1937, was designed to shuttle wealthy passengers, but was later used as a commercial airlines workhorse. The heaviest plane to hang from the museum's ceiling is the 17,500-pound Douglas DC-3. Visitors can walk through a 1953 American Airlines Douglas DC-7, the first airliner to provide nonstop transcontinental service. At the bottom of the display's exit ramp is a series of placards relating the history of air traffic control. There is also a collection of airline personnel uniforms.

Walk west to the northwest corner of the museum (Gallery 103—closed during the renovation) and turn south. Gallery 104 is usually reserved for special exhibits.

Continue south and enter Gallery 105. **The Golden Age of Flight** documents the history of aviation between World War I and World War II, from 1919 through 1939. This was a revolutionary era for flight. Interactive video exhibits explain such technological advances as air- and liquid-cooled engines and aerodynamics. Peacetime activities by the military, such as polar exploration and attempts to break air flight records, are covered too. Trophies grace the entrance of the gallery. The Mackay Trophy, established in 1911, is awarded annually to personnel within the U.S. Air Force for meritorious flights. The Thompson Trophy was first awarded in 1930 to promote the development of faster, safer, and more maneuverable aircraft. Planes on display include the Northrop Gamma *Polar Star,* which made the first trans-Antarctic flight in 1935; the Beechcraft C17L Staggerwing, popular during the 1930s for private and commercial transportation; and the Curtiss Robin *Ole Miss,* which set a world record for sustained flight (approximately 27 days).

Exit Gallery 105 and turn right. Proceed east. Gallery 106, **Jet Aviation,** is on the right. At its entrance is a display of military jet crewman's equipment, including flightsuits and helmets. This gallery details jet evolution from military vehicle to commercial service. The evolution exhibit has 27 planes dating from 1939 to 1972, including the McDonnell FH-1 Phantom, an aircraft-carrier plane; a 1942 Messerschmitt Me 262, the first jet fighter used in combat; and a 1944 Lockheed XP-80, the first U.S.-operated fighter jet. At the interactive kiosks visitors can design jet aircraft. A small theater features a Sid Caesar and Imogene Coca comedy routine televised in the 1950s called "Shrieking Through the Sound Barrier." Exit through a jet engine cover.

The next gallery to the east, Gallery 107, is modeled after a 1913 indoor aeronautical trade exhibition. **Early Flight,** which explores the initial concepts about flight and planes, has such early planes as the Wright 1909 Military Flyer, the world's first military airplane; the 1912 Ecker Flying Boat, important for its pioneering step in seaplane design; and the 1894 Lilienthal hang glider made from cotton, wood, and twine. There's also a fine exhibit on early women pilots in America.

Continue east through Gallery 108. On the right is the Independence Ave entrance. On the left is Gallery 100, Milestones of Flight. The next gallery on the right is Gallery 109.

Formerly Flight Testing, Gallery 109 reopened as **How Things Fly** on Sept 20, 1996, as part of the museum's 20th anniversary. The exhibit presents the science that underlies aviation and space through numerous hands-on activities and interactive displays. These include a visitor-operated wind tunnel and a scale that determines how much visitors might weigh on other planets. Visitors can also climb into the cockpit and work the controls of a Cessna 150, a small passenger plane. Activities especially geared toward children, such as paper airplane contests, are scheduled throughout the day.

Exit the gallery and turn right. The next gallery on the right is Gallery 110, **Looking at Earth.** This area illustrates the development of aerial photography from early kite and balloon observations to advanced spacecraft and satellite technology. On display are a Lockheed U-2, a high-altitude U.S. reconnaissance plane flown in surveillance operations over Cuba, China, Vietnam, and the Middle East during the Cold War; and a deHavilland DH-4, an American plane used for mapping and surveying during World War I.

Gallery 111 houses the museum shop. Proceed north. On the right, Gallery 112 features two exhibits. **Stars,** in the southeast corner of the museum, discusses stars and their symbolic use in various cultures. The exhibit explores the known universe from ancient times to the present. On display is a model of the largest astronomical instrument in orbit, the Hubble Space Telescope, which was launched by the space shuttle *Discovery* in April 1990. Also displayed is a model of Stonehenge, the monolithic circle of rocks that early Britons probably used to monitor the passage of the seasons, as well as other astronomical instruments. In **Lunar Exploration Vehicles,** visitors view sophisticated machines such as the Apollo Lunar Module and unmanned space probes, including the Lunar Orbiter, Surveyor, and Ranger. Corridors flanking this gallery lead into the restaurants, the Flight Line Cafeteria and the Wright Place Restaurant.

Proceed north into Gallery 113, **Rocketry and Space Flight,** which traces the history of flight from the 13C to the present. Rocket engines, space suits, and early concepts of space flight are displayed. The flume from 18C Congreve rockets, like the one exhibited, is what Francis Scott Key described as "red glare" in the "Star-Spangled Banner." Cutaways show the interior workings of an RL-10 engine, the first hydrogen/oxygen engine to be flown in space.

Walk west to Gallery 114, **Space Race,** which exhibits the technology of space launch vehicles and manned spacecraft. On display are items from the 1975 Apollo-Soyuz Test Project—the first international manned space mission—as well as a model of the space shuttle *Columbia.* The gallery also features the Skylab Orbital Workshop, which visitors enter from the second floor. *Skylab 1* was "home" to three-person crews who lived in space for up to three months. A walk through the 198,000-pound craft reveals how the astronauts conducted experiments, ate, slept, and showered. Visitors see the trash airlock, the Waste Management Compartment, a collapsible shower, the Wardroom where astronauts ate, and the Experiment Room, which has a bicycle ergometer and other scientific equipment.

Exit the gallery and walk west. On the right is the **Langley Theater,** Gallery 115, which features IMAX films about flight. The films are projected onto a five-story screen.

To the left is an escalator to the second floor, and beneath the escalator is a theater gift shop, where films shown in the Langley can be bought.

**Second floor galleries.** Overhead is the Douglas Skyrocket. On Nov 20, 1953, A. Scott Crossfield piloted this plane at Mach 2, twice the speed of sound. The upper-half of the Skylab exhibit is visible from the second floor of the NASM. At the top of the escalator turn right and walk west toward the upper-level area of Gallery 100. Of particular interest is the dull-orange BELL X-1 *Glamorous Glennis.* Piloted by Captain Chuck Yeager on Oct 14, 1947, it became the first plane to fly faster than the speed of sound. A replica of *Sputnik 1,* the 1957 Soviet satellite that was the first artificial object to orbit Earth, also hangs here.

Continue walking west. On the right is the **Albert Einstein Planetarium,** Gallery 201. Approximately 9,000 stars as well as the Sun, Moon, and five planets are projected onto the 70 ft dome of the planetarium. Daily at 3, the planetarium offers a free informal presentation about the current night sky. The planetarium also shows a special film several times daily. Check at the visitors desk for times and cancellations. A shop is across the hall.

On the way to Gallery 203 walk past the top half of **Air Transportation** for a closer view of the hanging aircraft.

**Sea-Air Operations** simulates the interior of an aircraft-carrier hanger for the fictitious USS *Smithsonian.* The exhibit, which traces the development of flight over water and World War II carrier warfare in the Pacific Ocean, houses a Boeing F4B-4, a carrier plane used during the 1930s; the Douglas Dauntless dive bomber, a carrier plane used in the June 1942 Battle of Midway; the Grumman F4F Wildcat, used in the early days of World War II over Wakefield Island; and several other naval aircraft.

Outside the Sea-Air Operations gallery is a glass-enclosed model of the USS *Enterprise* built by Stephen Henninger over a 12-year period, working at a rate of about 1,000 hours per year.

Proceed to the southwest corner of the museum to Gallery 205, **World War II Aviation.** Here, aircraft and flightsuits from five countries are featured. Planes on display include the Messerschmitt Bf. 109G-6, a German fighter used against American bombers; a Macchi C.202 Folgore, an Italian fighter plane used over Africa, Italy, and the Soviet Union; the Mitsubishi A6M5 Zero, used in every major Japanese campaign; and the North American P-51 Mustang used by the Allies in every theater. The mural by Keith Ferris, *Fortresses Under Fire,* depicts the Eighth Air Force under attack over Germany.

Gallery 206 follows the explosive impact of aviation during World War I. Entitled **Legend, Memory, and the Great War in the Air,** the exhibit illustrates the influence of strategic bombing and includes a replica of a German aircraft factory, a red Pfalz D.XII (used more by Hollywood than as a German fighter plane), and a French observation balloon basket. Other planes include the Fokker D. VII, Germany's best World War I fighter plane, and the SPAD XIII, a French fighter plane used by the U.S. as well. "Hollywood Knights of the Sky" features clips from films such as *Dawn Patrol* and *Hell's Angels,* early depictions of daredevil pilots in war and peace.

At the entrance to Gallery 207, **Exploring the Planets,** is Tools of Planetary Exploration. It describes the five Surveyor spacecraft launched to the Moon between June 2, 1966, and Jan 10, 1968. These missions measured the Moon's thermal and geologic qualities. The *Surveyor 3* television camera landed on the Moon April 20, 1967, and was retrieved by the *Apollo 12* crew on Nov 24, 1969. Other exhibits detail Mars explorations and display tools used for space missions. A model of the Voyager spacecraft and a meteorite found in Antarctica believed to have fallen from Mars are displayed.

Continue east to Gallery 208, **Pioneers of Flight,** which highlights famous first flights and aircraft. Exhibits include Charles and Anne Lindbergh's Lockheed Sirius *Tingmissartoq*, the plane used to map airline routes during the 1930s, and Amelia Earhart's 5B Vega, the plane she flew to cross the Atlantic Ocean in 1932. **Blackwings** examines the role of African Americans in aviation.

In Gallery 209, **Exploring New Worlds in Space** addresses the many aspects of space that must be overcome before long-distance travel and settlement on other planets can occur. Three films are shown in the gallery's small theater: *Other Worlds, Spacefaring,* and *Contact!* A space garden depicts what astronauts could grow for food. A 3,000-square-ft simulated Martian landscape features redrock, ceiling-high formations suggestive of Mars and videos about the Red Planet.

Across from the top of Space Race is Gallery 210, **Apollo to the Moon.** Visitors experience the triumph through the 1960s and 1970s of manned airflight, including Project Mercury and the Apollo Moon landings. To the right of the entrance are lunar rocks collected during Apollo missions 15, 16, and 17. To the left is the *Apollo 11* command module hatch. The exhibit also displays artifacts such as *Gemini 7,* which carried astronauts Frank Borman and James Lovell, Jr., into orbit in Dec 1965; and the *Skylab 4* command module, used to shuttle astronauts Gerald P. Carr, Edward G. Gibson, and William R. Pugue to the Skylab Orbital Workshop. Situated on a re-created moonscape is an *Apollo 17* spacesuit, tools such as an Apollo lunar surface drill used to collect geologic specimens, and a lunar roving vehicle. The gallery also has a lunar module cockpit, a Saturn 5 F-1 engine, astronaut tools, equipment, and space food. The east wall is decorated with a time line illustrating the events of the July 16–24, 1969, *Apollo 11* trip to the Moon and its return to Earth.

To the right, in the southeast corner, Gallery 211 houses a small exhibit entitled **Flight in the Arts,** which displays space-themed artists' works.

In the northeast corner is Gallery 213, **Beyond the Limits: Flight Enters the Computer Age.** The exhibits in this gallery examine how computers have changed and advanced the aerospace industry. Among the highlights are the HiMAT, a robotic airplane in which a computer, not a pilot, controls the plane; a Minuteman III ICBM Guidance and Control System, the brains of a U.S. intercontinental ballistic missile; a theater featuring films about flight simulation; and the X29, an innovative jet with wings angled forward rather than backward.

The closest Metro station is L'Enfant Plaza (Green/Yellow Line). The 13A, 13B, 13M, 32, 34, 35, 36, 52, 70, V6, and V8 buses stop along Independence Ave.

To continue with Walk 6, exit the National Air and Space Museum onto Independence Ave N.W. Walk west on Independence Ave N.W. for one block, crossing 7th St, to the entrance to the Hirshhorn Museum.

# 6 . National Mall: Hirshhorn Museum and Other Sites

Metro: Blue/Orange Line to Smithsonian, or Yellow/Green Line to L'Enfant Plaza. Take Maryland Ave exit.
Bus: Stops located on Independence Ave. Use 13A, 13B, 13M, 32–36, 52, 70, V6, or V8.

## *Hirshhorn Museum and Sculpture Garden*

Independence Ave at 7th St S.W. ☎ 357-2700; 357-3091 for recorded information; 357-3235 (TTY). Web: www.si.edu/hirshhorn. Building open daily 10–5:30. Plaza open daily 7:30–5:30. Sculpture garden open daily 7:30 A.M. until dusk. Extended summer hours determined annually. Closed Christmas Day. Admission: free. Tours begin at the information desk on the lower level Mon–Fri at 10:30 and 12; Sat–Sun at 12 and 2. Tours of special exhibits vary; check for times at the information desk. Sculpture garden tours May and Oct only (weather permitting) 12:15. Tours for groups, in foreign languages and sign language, and tours for the visually impaired available by appointment; ☎ 357-3235. Wheelchair accessible. Wheelchairs available. Museum shop on plaza level. Full Circle, a self-service outdoor café in the sculpture garden, open daily during summer months. Hours and dates determined annually. Video introduction to collection, in Orientation Theater, shown several times daily. Except during summer months, films about art and artists are shown on Thurs at 12 and Sat at 1; independent films are shown Thurs–Fri at 8. Telephones, restrooms, checkroom. Flash photography and tripods are prohibited.

1999 marked the 25th anniversary of the Hirshhorn Museum and Sculpture Garden (1974; Gordon Bunshaft of Skidmore, Owings & Merrill), a Smithsonian showcase for modern and contemporary art. American, European, and other international artists are represented. The collection starts with modernism's early-19C beginnings and sweeps through developments such as cubism, realism, surrealism, abstraction, and pop. The museum is also endowed to acquire current contemporary artwork.

The collection of sculptures, primarily displayed outdoors in the sculpture garden and plaza surrounding the building, is considered one of the most comprehensive in the world. On display is a range of sculptures from mid-19C bronzes to mixed-media pieces by contemporary artists.

**Highlights:** Works from the permanent collection are periodically rotated and temporary exhibitions complement the collection. However, some works to look for are Joseph Cornell's *The Medici Princess,* Alberto Giacometti's *The Nose,* and Joan Mitchell's *Girolata.* Walk through the sculpture garden, which includes Auguste Rodin's *Monument to the Burghers of Calais,* Alexander Calder's *Stabile-Mobile,* and the geometric abstractions of David Smith. (Smith's *Cubi XII,* in the sculpture garden, is from the same generation as Smith's *Cluster of Four Cubes* on the southeast side of the National Gallery of Art, East Building.) Children visiting the museum should ask for the kid-friendly folder of cards that details facts about a piece and the artist.

### History

Joseph Hirshhorn (1899–1981), the 12th of 13 children in his family, passed through Ellis Island at the age of 6 as a Latvian immigrant with his brothers and sisters and their widowed mother. He dropped out of school at 13 to sell newspapers and help support his family. By the time he was 17, Hirshhorn established himself as a security broker. In ten months, he gambled $225 into $168,000. Just weeks before the stock market crashed in 1929, Hirshhorn sold his holdings for $4 million. He was 28.

With the American economy in severe depression, Hirshhorn set his sights north, to Canada. He placed a full-page advertisement in a Canadian newspaper: "My name is Opportunity and I am paging Canada." Less than 20 years later, Hirshhorn controlled the largest uranium mines ever discovered.

Hirshhorn always had an active interest in art. As a young man, he acquired two Dürer drawings. However, he was never represented by dealers or brokers and had the tendency to buy impulsively. While many collectors focus on specific styles or artists, Hirshhorn's collection blanketed the post–World War II New York art scene. One art critic wrote, "[Hirshhorn's] method of buying, like panning for gold, results in a large amount of dross for every few nuggets." By 1957, his collection filled two offices and a storage facility. In need of a curator for his massive—and growing—collection, Hirshhorn hired Abram Lerner. Lerner served as founding director of the Hirshhorn Museum before retiring in 1984.

Hirshhorn felt that his collection should belong to the public, and nearly a dozen museums around the globe expressed interest. But in May 1966 President Lyndon Johnson announced that Hirshhorn had donated his collection to the United States. (Congress debated the creation of a national museum of modern art as early as 1938. However, the idea was tabled as the nation struggled through the tail end of the Depression, followed by the country's participation in World War II.) The collection included 4,000 paintings and 2,000 sculptures, then twice the collection size of New York's Museum of Modern Art.

Acclaimed architect Gordon Bunshaft was asked to design a building for the approximately 6,000-piece collection. S. Dillon Ripley, secretary of the Smithsonian from 1964 to 1984, commented at the dedication that if the Hirshhorn Museum building "were not controversial in almost every way, it would hardly qualify as a place to house contemporary art." The doughnut-shaped museum opened to the public in Oct 1974 under the auspices of the Smithsonian.

When Hirshhorn passed away in 1981, he left another 6,000 works to the museum. The sculpture garden reopened that year, after renovations by landscape architect Lester Collins. From 1991 to 1992, the Hirshhorn's outdoor space underwent another renovation when its 2.7-acre outdoor plaza was redeveloped by landscape architect James Urban.

Today, the museum's collection consists of more than 12,500 works of art.

### Washington Notes

The Hirshhorn Museum and Sculpture Garden is on the former site of the Army Medical Museum. From 1887 to 1968, the Army Medical Museum contained one of Washington's most gruesome, yet popular, attractions. Its collection consisted of more than 25,000 specimens of body parts, including some disfigured by diseases and wounds. As the exhibit was previously housed at Ford's Theatre—which had closed its doors after President Lin-

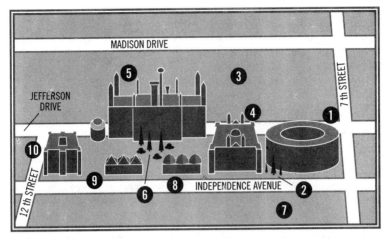

1 Hirshhorn Museum and Sculpture Garden
2 Mary Livingston Ripley
 Garden
3 Carousel
4 Arts and Industries Building

5 Smithsonian Castle
6 Enid A. Haupt Garden
7 Earth Day Park
8 National Museum of African Art
9 Arthur M. Sackler Gallery
10 Freer Gallery of Art

coln's assassination there—it was only fitting that it displayed the bullet removed from Lincoln's brain and the surgical instrument which removed it.
The gunshot-altered vertebrae of James Garfield, the next president to be
assassinated, was also exhibited.

One of the more bizarre tales relates to the specimen of General Daniel
Sickles's leg. This Union general donated the leg he lost at the Battle of Gettysburg, and the cannonball that removed it, to the museum. As the legend
is told, Sickle visited his leg annually, on the anniversary of its amputation,
and drank a toast to it.

The medical collection was relocated to Walter Reed Army Medical Hospital in northwest Washington. Walter Reed, who worked in the Army Medical Museum in the 1890s, is credited with discoveries that led to the end of
yellow fever.

## Exterior

The Hirshhorn Museum building is a three-story cylinder, 231 ft in diameter,
that encircles an open courtyard. It is supported by four 14 ft high concrete piers.
The surrounding lobby is partially lighted by sunlight streaming through floor-to-
ceiling windows. The only break in the solid-surfaced, concrete exterior wall is a
third-floor panoramic window from the Abram Lerner Balcony Room.

North of the museum, across Jefferson Dr, is the **sculpture garden.** The garden features works by Rodin, Miró, Calder, and Matisse. It can be accessed from either the Mall or Jefferson Dr.

On the Jefferson Dr Mall side of the museum is *Are Years What? (for Marianne*

*Moore)* (1967; Mark di Suvero). The 40 ft high compostion of red I-beams of painted steel and cable is considered one of di Suvero's greatest works. The ten-ton piece is a physical interpretation of a short poem by the American poet Marianne Moore (1887–1972). At the entrance to the sculpture garden is *Two-Piece Reclining Figure: Points* (1969–70; Henry Moore). Turn west and proceed down the staircase. At the foot of the stairs is *The Prophet* (1933, cast 1954–68; Pablo Gargallo). This bronze sculpture depicts a cloaked man raising his right arm and holding a staff in his left hand. His mouth is gaping open. Turn right and walk north. David Smith's *Cubi XII* (1963) is a burnished steel sculpture of precariously stacked cubes.

Another nearby sculpture by Smith is *Voltri XV* (1962). In 1962 Smith was invited to create sculptures for a music festival in Spoleto, Italy. Smith set up his studio in an abandoned steel factory in Volti, near Genoa. He created 27 sculptures in 30 days from the factory's scrap steel. This piece was created in New York, after Smith returned to the United States in the summer of 1962 with scrap metal from the factory. This work is meant to resemble a sun or a moon and clouds drifting in the sky.

Continue to the end of the path and turn west. Immediately to the left, flush with the garden wall, is *Resting* (1965; Paul Suttman). Continue west to the courtyard. Turn left. In the southeast corner of the courtyard is *Pregnant Woman (first state)* (1950, cast 1951–53; Pablo Picasso). At the center of the courtyard is Joan Miró's bronze work *Lunar Bird* (1944–46, enlarged cast 1966–67). Return to the entrance of the courtyard and proceed east. On the right is *Human Lunar Spectral* (1950, enlarged 1957; Jean Arp). Proceed east to the Mall entrance of the garden. At the foot of the stairs is *Horse and Rider* (1952–53; Marino Marini), noted for its feeling of movement. Continue east. On the right is *Young Girl on a Chair* (1955; Giacomo Manzu) and Willem de Kooning's abstract bronze figure *Clamdigger* (1972).

Enter the **east courtyard** and proceed to the northeast corner. The torso of the fighter is Emile-Antoine Bourdelle's *The Great Warrior of Montauban* (1898, cast 1956). Bourdelle was a studio assistant of Auguste Rodin's for 15 years and learned Rodin's technique of creating independent works from sections of his larger compositions. Bourdelle derived this piece from the *Monument to the Defenders of Tarn-and-Garonne in the War of 1870*, a piece commissioned by his Mantauban hometown.

At the center of the courtyard is Rodin's *Monument to the Burghers of Calais* (1884–99, cast 1953–59). Rodin was commissioned in 1884 by the town council of Calais in Normandy to design a monument to commemorate the end of a siege in 1346–47. The English agreed to spare the townspeople if six prominent citizens (burghers) would serve as permanent hostages. This piece depicts the burghers, faces revealing their agony, proceeding from their homes to the clutches of their captors.

Proceed along the path south of the courtyard. To the east note *Action in Chains: Monument to Louis-Auguste Blanqui* (1905–6, cast 1969) by Aristide Maillol and Giacomo Manzu's *Large Standing Cardinal* (1954). Proceed west down the ramp into the **main courtyard.** At the north end of the courtyard is the Jacob and Charlotte Lehrman Foundation Pool. Walk to the southeast corner to see Raymond Mason's *Falling Man* (1962), a series of three bronze torsos emulating the act of falling. In the southwest corner is the bizarre *Man Pushing Door* (1966; Jean Ipousteguy).

In the northwest corner is the voluptuous *Standing Woman (Heroic Woman)* (1932, cast 1981; Gaston Lachaise). Most of Lachaise's pieces are female nudes. He attributes his inspiration to his wife, Isabel Dutaud Nagle, to whom many of his sculptures paid homage. Rebelling against the popular Art Deco style of fashionably slender women, Lachaise created a full-bodied woman with roundish features. His goal was to portray Woman as "the incarnation of spiritual strength, emotional and physical nourishment, and maternal and sexual love."

Climb the stairs at the west end of the courtyard. Turn left and climb the stairs up to Jefferson Dr. Cross the road and proceed to the museum building.

An apron of walkways, known as the **plaza,** skirts the Hirshhorn Museum building. Many large, contemporary sculptures are displayed here. At the Jefferson Dr entrance to the plaza is the abstract form *Gymnast III* (1984–85; William Tucker). Proceed through the plaza in a clockwise direction. On the northeast lawn is the aluminum and stainless steel *Needle Tower* (1968; Kenneth Snelson). Opposite this sculpture, in an alcove against the northeast side of the museum building, is a bronze rabbit called *The Drummer* (1989–90; Barry Flanagan). East of the museum is *Throwback* (1976–79; Tony Smith), an asymmetrical composition of tetrahedrons and other geometric shapes.

Continue clockwise to the Independence Ave entrance of the plaza, where *Two Discs* (1965; Alexander Calder) is positioned. On the southwest lawn is *Conversation Piece* (1994–95; Juan Muñoz). This group of sculptures depicts human figures who, rather than having legs, balance themselves on balls. Proceed north to the sculpture of rubber stamps, *Subcommittee* (1991; Tony Cragg). *Spatial Concept: Nature* (1959–60; Lucio Fontana) is a collection of bronze balls scattered around a magnolia tree in the northwest corner of the plaza. To the southeast, in an alcove against the museum building, is *Post-Balzac* (1991; Judith Shea), an empty cloak standing on a pedestal. Return to the Independence Ave side of the building and enter the museum.

## Interior

**Plaza level.** Enter from Independence Ave into the main lobby. The museum shop, information desk, and escalators are located on this level. Take the escalator down to the lower level.

**Lower level.** At press time, the **Orientation Theater** was closed, but it is expected to open again. The theater features a 13-minute video, "Introduction to Modern Art at the Hirshhorn Museum and Sculpture Garden." Restrooms and a checkroom are also located on this level.

**The Collection Reviewed: Contemporary Art,** a permanent exhibit with rotating pieces, is on the floor's north side. This gallery contains artwork from the 1960s to the present and features styles such as neodada, pop art, and minimalism by artists such as Warhol, Murray, Polke, Johns, and Christo. Look for *Dictionary for Building: Closet under Stairs* (1985; Siah Armajani), a three-dimensional funhouselike sculpture fashioned with brightly painted wood and rope. Also note Sol LeWitt's *13/11* (1985), which looks like an erector-set creation painted white. Hanging on the east wall is *Marilyn Monroe* (1962; Andy Warhol). *Fisherman* (1968; Paul Thek), is a sculpture depicting a life-size man covered with fish and tangled in rope in the branches of a tree.

Return to the escalator and proceed to the second floor.

**Second floor.** Two walkways circle the second and third floors, creating an outer loop (or *ambulatory*, which is a circular walkway), and an inner loop, or inner ambulatory, of exhibits. Visitors arriving via escalator enter the outer loop, a series of galleries presenting four major special exhibitions of modern or contemporary art each year. The inner loop houses selections of contemporary art and small pieces tracing sculpture's evolution through the 19C into the cubist era.

At the top of the escalator is a gallery frequently used for special temporary exhibitions, as is the gallery west of the escalator bank. Between these two galleries, on the north side of the floor, is an exhibit of continuously rotated objects from the permanent collection. Typically, the pieces are grouped by theme, style, or subject.

The inner loop is used to display small sculptures from the permanent collection. Some pieces to look for are *Theseus Slaying the Centaur Bianor* (1850; Antoine-Louis Bayre), *Mask of the Man with a Broken Nose* (1864; Auguste Rodin), *Ratapoil* (1850, cast 1925; Honoré Daumier), a series of bronze dancers created in the 1880s by Edgar Degas, and *Fame* (1893, cast 1896; Louis-Ernest Barrias). Also look for *Third Architectural Model for "The Gates of Hell"* (1880; Auguste Rodin), *Head of a Jester* (1905, cast 1907–39; Pablo Picasso), *Madame Renoir* (1916; Pierre Auguste Renoir and Richard Guino), and a series of busts and nudes by Henri Matisse, including *Head of Jeanette I–V* (1910–13, cast c. 1948–50).

Take the escalator to the third floor.

**Third floor.** In the escalator bank are a series of pieces including Larry Rivers's *The Greatest Homosexual* (1964)—an oil, collage, pencil, and canvas montage portrait of Napoleon—and Roy Lichtenstein's (1967) oil and acrylic *Modern Painting with Clef.*

On this floor, which opened in Feb 1999, is **The Hirshhorn Collection at 25,** a combination of "old favorites," works not exhibited in recent years, and a diverse selection of new acquisitions, all representing modern and contemporary art. Among the artists featured are Francis Bacon, Constantin Brancusi, Dan Flavin, Alberto Giacometti, Edward Hopper, Robert Irwin, Yves Klein, Isamu Noguchi, Claes Oldenburg, Gerhard Richter, David Alfaro Siqueiros, and Andy Warhol. When visiting this exhibit, be sure to take advantage of one of the best views of the Mall, from the Abram Lerner Room.

Exit the Hirshhorn Museum and walk south to Independence Ave. Turn right and walk west one block. When the concrete wall cordoning off the Hirshhorn Museum's property ends, turn right. A brick path winds from Independence Ave to Jefferson Dr through the **Mary Livingston Ripley Garden,** between the Hirshhorn Museum and Sculpture Garden and the Arts and Industries Building. The garden was created in 1988 by the Smithsonian Institution's Women's Committee to honor Mary Livingston Ripley, the organization's founder and wife of the eighth secretary of the Smithsonian Institution. The walkways were designed by architect Hugh Newell Jacobsen. In season more than 200 varieties of perennials, shrubs, and trees carpet the garden's wide beds. At the north end of the garden is a 19C, Renaissance-style fountain. Atop the cast-iron sculpture is a figure of a boy and a fish. The sculptor is unknown.

At Jefferson Dr, turn left and walk west to the entrance of the Arts and Industries Building.

## *Arts and Industries Building*

900 Jefferson Dr S.W. ☎ 357-2700 or 357-1729 (TTY). Web: www.si.edu/ai. Open daily 10–5:30. Closed Christmas Day. Information desk staffed daily 10–4. Admission: free. Call for accessibility information for disabled visitors. Wheelchairs available. Museum shop. Discovery Theater for children. Performances Mon–Sat Sept–July. ☎ 357-1500 (voice and TTY) for showtimes and reservations. Restrooms.

The Arts and Industries Building (AIB) (1879–81; Cluss & Schulze, with Montgomery C. Meigs; 1897–1903 modifications, Hornblower & Marshall; 1976 restoration, Hugh Newell Jacobsen; DL) is the second oldest building on the Mall. Formerly known as the National Museum, it first housed exhibits donated to the U.S. government at the close of the 1876 Centennial Exposition in Philadelphia. Currently, the Building's four galleries display changing exhibits from present and future Smithsonian museums.

**Highlights:** The exhibit Speak to My Heart: Communities of Faith and Contemporary African American Life; in the rotunda, a working fountain surrounded by seasonal plants and geometric stencils in rich Victorian colors; the Discovery Theater for children.

### History

The United States National Museum (USNM), under the auspices of the Smithsonian, was established in 1858 to maintain a collection of models from the U.S. Patent Office. The USNM subsequently became the recipient of any piece of Americana donated to the U.S. government. (The Smithsonian was dubbed the Nation's Attic for this reason.)

At the close of the 1876 Centennial Exposition in Philadelphia, 38 of 41 foreign exhibitors and several governments donated their exhibits to the U.S. government rather than incur the cost of shipping them home. Congress turned the bequest over to the Smithsonian, despite complaints from Joseph Henry, the Smithsonian's first secretary. Henry insisted the Smithsonian's primary mission was that of a research institution, not a depository.

As trainloads of exhibits—42 freight cars in all—arrived in Washington, Congress recognized the Smithsonian's need for an additional building and appropriated $250,000 for a "fire-proof building for the use of the National Museum."

Based on plans drawn by the Army Corps of Engineers' General Montgomery C. Meigs, designer of the Pension Building (now the National Building Museum), Adolph Cluss and Paul Schulze designed the National Museum in a style they labeled "modernized Romanesque." The building was constructed in 15 months at a cost of $310,000—$3 per square ft. The structure is the least expensive and most quickly built project the federal government has ever undertaken. At the time, the museum was one of the most modern buildings in the country. The public got its first peek on March 4, 1881, when the building hosted President Garfield's inaugural ball.

The expo bequest increased the size of the Smithsonian's collection fourfold and broadened its focus from natural history to history and technology. Over the years, the National Museum has housed specimens and exhibits now located in other Smithsonian museums. Rockets, once displayed in the yard along the National Museum's west side, were relocated in 1976 to the newly built National Air and Space Museum. Some of the artworks hanging in the National Museum of American Art and the National Portrait Gallery were first displayed in the National Museum. So too were anthropological and scientific specimens now in the National Museum of Natural History.

At some point, the facility was renamed the Arts and Industries Building, and the structure was remodeled to provide office space for the growing number of Smithsonian programs.

## Exterior

The AIB is constructed of red brick and Ohio sandstone. Its design was intended to emulate Victorian structures such as the Dresden Museum. The trussed roof, with more than 26 surfaces, is a maze of turrets and gables. The museum's main entrance is on Jefferson Dr. A second entrance is from the Enid A. Haupt Garden. The Independence Ave entrance is kept locked.

Over the main entrance is a sculpture of three women entitled *Columbia Protecting Science and Industry* (1881; Casper Buberl). Columbia is at the center, her arms stretched over the heads of the seated figures of Industry, to the right, who is holding a surveying tool, and Science, to the left, reading a book. A statue of Spencer Fullerton Baird, the Smithsonian's second secretary, is just outside the west entrance.

## Interior

**Ground level.** The floor plan of the AIB resembles a fan. At the center is the rotunda; from there exhibition halls extend in four directions. Entering from Jefferson Dr brings visitors into the North Gallery and the exhibit **Speak to My Heart: Communities of Faith and Contemporary African American Life,** which explores the ways in which individual beliefs have shaped and changed African American history and culture and celebrates the determination of Black congregations and individuals to meet the challenges of a complex society in the new millennium.

Walk south from the Jefferson Dr entrance through the exhibit to **The Old Landmark Made New,** a section about church restoration, renovation, and rebuilding. Displays feature models and photographs of churches that have been rehabilitated. To the east of this is **Community Affirmations of Faith,** which explores individual and group quests for spiritual understanding and fellowship. Highlights are a video about gospel music and displays of vestments worn during worship that employs music.

Continuing south is **A Safe Place to Be,** featuring the church as a haven and a place for personal growth. A display honors women's role in the African American church. To the west is **Faith in Action,** with displays about church outreach ministries and food programs. To the west is **Planting the Vineyards,** which highlights educational efforts and neighborhood revitalization. Throughout the exhibit, video screens enhance the stories of the displays.

Located at the southern end of the exhibit is the museum shop, where books (including those related to Speak to My Heart), crafts, an excellent selection of jewelry, and items featured in the Smithsonian mail-order catalog are available.

At the center of the building is the rotunda, with its geometric stencils on the floor and hall spandrels. An information desk is in the northwest corner and changing exhibits are in other corners. The horticultural display of plants and flowers around the fountain is changed seasonally.

**Discovery Theater,** which presents inventive and theatrical performances for children and parents by mimes, actors, dancers, and puppeteers is located southwest of the rotunda. Restrooms, public phones, and a water fountain are along this corridor, also.

The East, South, and West Galleries contain changing exhibits related to the other museums of the Smithsonian Institution. For information, ☎ 357-4500.

**Second level.** Smithsonian offices are located on the second floor, which are inaccessible to the general public.

**Diversion:**

Cross Jefferson Dr to the **carousel,** just north of the Arts and Industries Building. It operates daily, weather permitting, 10–6 in the summer, 11–5 in winter. A three-minute ride on one of its horses, sea dragons, or zebras costs $1.25; children must be at least 1 year old. The blue-and-yellow–awninged carousel, which is privately owned and operated, was manufactured by Allen Herschell Co. in the 1940s. The organ, c. 1900s, is a Wurlitzer, Model 153.

Return to the south side of Jefferson Dr and walk west to the Smithsonian Institution Building, more commonly referred to as the Castle, and the Smithsonian's first building.

## Smithsonian Institution Building (the Castle)

1000 Jefferson Dr S.W. ☎ 357-2700 or 357-1729 (TTY). Web: www.si.edu. Open daily 9–5:30. Information desk and museum shop, 9–4. Closed Christmas Day. Admission: free. Restrooms, telephones. Wheelchair accessible.

Originally, the Castle (1855; James Renwick; DL) housed all the Smithsonian offices, as well as its laboratory, library, museum, art gallery, and collections. The Castle also served as the home for the institution's first secretary, Joseph Henry, and for the institution's bachelor scientists.

Today, the Smithsonian extends beyond this building and the Mall. There are museums and field research stations in several states and Panama. However, the Castle is still considered the headquarters of the institution. Offices, including that of the secretary of the Smithsonian, are on the upper floors. But the Castle's primary service is as the Smithsonian Information Center.

**Highlights:** The tomb of James Smithson, the man who provided the funds that created the Smithsonian, is in a room just inside the Jefferson Dr entrance. "The Smithsonian Institution," a 20-minute film shown in two theaters, provides an overview to the museum complex and the history and highlights of each museum.

### History

The cornerstone of the Smithsonian Institution Building was laid on May 1, 1847. It was completed in 1855 at a cost of $250,000. A severe fire gutted the upper story of the Castle's main wing and the north and south towers in Jan 1865. Much of the collection from the Smithsonian's 30-year history, including James Smithson's papers and collections and 300 portraits of Native Americans, was destroyed. Within two years, the building and its interior were restored. The Castle was later remodeled and enlarged during the 1880s. (For a detailed history of the Smithsonian Institution see Walk 5: "National Mall: National Gallery of Art and National Air and Space Museum.")

### Washington Notes

Abraham Lincoln is said to have watched the Army Signal Corps practice signaling with lanterns from the Castle's main tower during the Civil War. The towers also housed instruments used to gather weather data for reports published in the *Washington Herald*. The Smithsonian's systematic collection of weather data prompted the creation of the U.S. Weather Bureau.

## Exterior

In contrast to the typical classical style of government buildings in the area—the Treasury Department, the Patent Office, and the General Post Office—Renwick designed the Castle in a Norman style, combining late-Romanesque and early-Gothic elements. Renwick intended this design to express the Smithsonian's educational agenda and to complement Andrew Jackson Downing's plans to relandscape the Mall.

The exterior is sculpted from red sandstone mined from a quarry in Seneca Creek, Maryland. The statue of Joseph Henry (1883; William Wetmore Story) located outside the Jefferson Dr entrance originally faced the Castle, but S. Dillon Ripley, eighth secretary of the Smithsonian, ordered that the statue be turned to face the Mall. Ripley felt that position would be more welcoming to visitors and would stand as a symbol of the institution's expanding breadth.

## Interior

Just inside the Jefferson Dr entrance is a small chamber to the east that contains **James Smithson's Crypt**, a case displaying books from Smithson's library, a sample of Smithsonite (the mineral named after the scientist), a bronze bust of Smithson (1975; Felix de Weldon), and a copy of Smithson's will.

The room was created in 1905, after the Smithsonian was informed by Italian authorities during the previous year that the San Benigno Cemetery in Genoa, Italy, where Smithson was buried, was to be demolished. The institution immediately dispatched a member of its board of regents, Dr. Alexander Graham Bell, to retrieve the crypt and bring it to Washington. The Smithsonian's 1905 annual report stated that Smithson's body, according to medical experts, was "in a remarkable state of preservation." On March 6, 1905, the entire board of regents watched as Smithson's body was reinterred into the original crypt—a tomb that had been carved in 1829 in a neoclassical style. During the chamber's renovation in 1978, scientists from the Department of Physical Anthropology, led by Dr. J. Lawrence Angel, examined Smithson's remains again. They concluded that Smithson had probably been five ft six inches tall, smoked a pipe, had a muscular upper body, and died of natural causes. Exit the chamber and reenter the foyer. Turn south and proceed through the doors and into the Lower Main Hall, the Smithsonian's **Information Center.**

Placed around the room are several kiosks whose interactive touch-screen programs provide information about Smithsonian museums and other capital attractions in six languages (Chinese, English, French, German, Japanese, and Spanish.) At the east end of the room are the two theaters showing 20-minute orientation films about the Smithsonian. Along the corridor between the two theaters are photographs with text explaining the casting and installation of the Smithsonian Bell. In the southeast corner, near the theater entrances, is a museum shop. The room also contains models of the Mall, one of which is tactile and features Braille labels. In the center of the room is the information desk.

Follow the stairs along the south wall of the room to the **Children's Room.** The third secretary of the Smithsonian, Samuel Pierpont Langley (1834–1906), wanted more children to develop an interest in natural science and the Smithsonian's exhibitions. In 1899, he commissioned the Children's Room with the belief that "wonder pave[s] the way to knowledge." For 40 years the room served as a special entrance to the Castle for children and housed displays of birds, shells, butterflies, and other natural history specimens, as well as tanks of live fish. As space in the Smithsonian Building dwindled, the South Yard entrance was closed and the Children's Room was used for storage. In 1985, the room's mosaic floor and the *trompe l'oeil* murals on the walls and ceiling were restored. Historical photographs hanging on either side of the South Yard doorway show the room as it originally looked. Special exhibitions for children have not yet been added.

Exit the Castle through the doorway in the Children's Room and enter the Enid A. Haupt Garden.

## Enid A. Haupt Garden

Independence Ave. ☎ 357-2700. Open Memorial Day–Sept 30 7 A.M.–8 P.M. Open Oct 1–day before Memorial Day 7–5:45. Tours April–Sept Tues and Thurs at 2 (weather permitting). Wheelchair accessible.

The 4.2 acre Enid A. Haupt Garden (1987; Jean Paul Carlhian; landscape architect, Lester Collins) was opened in 1987 as part of the Quadrangle complex. This complex also includes the National Museum of African Art, the Arthur M. Sackler Gallery, and the S. Dillon Ripley Center.

### History

The Enid A. Haupt Garden, an area formerly known as the South Yard, sits atop the roof of the complex's underground parking garage. Eight ft of topsoil was laid over the structure to create the garden, named for its donor, philanthropist Enid Annenberg Haupt. During the Smithsonian's history, the South Yard served several functions, among them being the original site of both the National Zoo and the National Air and Space Museum.

After the Civil War Smithsonian scientists kept many "living" specimens, such as prairie dogs, badgers, lynx, and deer, in a series of pens in the South Yard. Taxidermists, such as William Temple Hornaday, used the animals as models for the stuffed animal exhibits displayed in the natural history wing of the Arts and Industries Building, then known as the National Museum. Hornaday, the Smithsonian's chief taxidermist, traveled to Montana to collect bison skins for the collection. Concerned about the decimation of the bison's population by frontiersmen and sport hunters, Hornaday returned with live animals. In 1887, the "Department of Living Animals" was established in the South Yard. In 1888, E. G. Blackford, a New Yorker, purchased a male and female bison. The Smithsonian gladly added this donated pair to its small herd. Two years later, Congress approved the construction of the National Zoo in Rock Creek Park. The animals were transferred in the 1890s to the zoo's site on Connecticut Ave.

From 1919 to 1976 various exhibits were placed in the yard, even rockets. Some as tall as 70 ft lined the west side of the Arts and Industries Building. After the completion of the National Air and Space Museum in 1976, the South Yard was used as a parking lot. A Victorian garden was added during the U.S. Bicentennial celebrations.

## Grounds

The garden is divided into three theme gardens, each designed to complement an adjacent building. Upon exiting the Castle, the parterre, with Victorian-style urns and benches, suggests the architectural era of the Castle immediately to the south. Turn left and walk east. On the left are topiary bison reminding visitors of the animals that once grazed in the yard. To the right is the Summer Garden, a diamond-shaped area, which borrows inspiration from the 14C Alhambra palace in Granada, Spain, and the Shalimar palace. Granite blocks provide seating around a pool of cascading water. Through the garden is the entrance to the National Museum of African Art. Proceed through the garden, turn right, and walk west back to the parterre. Proceed to the west to the Spring and Fall Garden, which suggests an Oriental influence with its square reflecting pool surrounding a circular island, as well as a modern version of a Chinese moon gate. An entrance to the Sackler Gallery is immediately to the south of this garden. The S. Dillon Ripley Center, which is predominantly office space for the Smithsonian, is the circular glass building just outside the northwest gate of the garden.

### Diversion:

Exit the Haupt Garden through the south gates and cross Independence Ave to **Earth Day Park,** a swath of green space that runs from Independence Ave to C St between the Departments of Transportation and Energy, near the Interstate 395 tunnel. Although the park is used primarily by government employees on lunch break, this place is a nice place to pause.

In 1994, President Clinton encouraged federal agencies to increase "environmentally and economically beneficial practices on federal landscaped grounds." Although Earth Day Park was the vision of Hazel R. O'Leary, former secretary of energy, the park is the result of a partnership of municipal and federal government agencies. Volunteers and employees from the Department of Energy, the Department of Transportation, the District of Columbia Public Works, the General Services Administration, and the National Renewable Energy Laboratory transformed this once vacant lot into Earth Day Park.

Groundbreaking for Earth Day Park took place on Earth Day 1995. The design aimed to employ plants and techniques that require less maintenance than traditional parks or gardens. Dwarf ornamental grass, which requires less mowing and water, was planted. Also, perennial rather than annual flowers were used. The predominant foliage species are drought-resistant and native to the mid-Atlantic region. Solar panels were installed to demonstrate the use of energy in an urban setting. At either end of the park are two photovoltaic panels. When photons, or energy particles, in sunlight hit the panels, particles of energy, called electrons, are released. This reaction creates enough electricity to provide 63 percent of the annual lighting for the park. Earth Day Park was dedicated on Earth Day, 1996.

Return to the north side of Independence Ave and reenter the Haupt Garden. To the east is the National Museum of African Art.

## National Museum of African Art

950 Independence Ave S.W. ☎ 357-4600 or 357-4814 (TTY). Web: www.si. edu/nmafa. Open daily 10–5:30. Closed Christmas Day. Admission: free. Eliot Elisofon Photographic Archives open, by appointment, Mon–Fri 10–4. ☎ 357-4600, ext 281. Warren M. Robbins Library open, by appointment, Mon–Fri 9–5:15. ☎ 357-4600, ext 286. Tours available, ☎ 357-4600, ext 221. Wheelchair accessible; wheelchairs available at the security desk on the ground level. Telephones, restrooms. Museum shop open daily 10–5:15. No flash photography.

The National Museum of African Art (1987; Shepley, Bulfinch, Richardson & Abbott) exhibits art from all parts of Africa, although its collections have in the past focused on regions south of the Sahara. Contemporary art from the entire continent is exhibited in the Sylvia H. Williams Gallery. The museum's entire collection is comprised of more than 7,000 objects.

The Eliot Elisofon Photographic Archives, named for the late *Life* photographer who bequeathed to the museum his portfolio and collection of photographs, slides, and films, houses a research and reference center for visual materials. This facility, coupled with the Warren M. Robbins Library—named for the museum's founder—continues the educational tradition upon which the museum was founded.

**Highlights:** This is the only museum in the country that focuses entirely on African art; it contains a collection of Royal Benin art, central African ceramics, and wooden sculptures. Check the schedule for the storytelling and art workshops for children.

### History

Warren M. Robbins established the Museum of African Art in 1964 as a private, educational institution originally located on Capitol Hill in a row of Victorian townhouses, 316 to 332 A St N.E. Number 316 had been the home of former slave and abolitionist Frederick Douglass. (Douglass moved to Washington in 1870 to edit a newspaper called the *New Era*. He spent the last 25 years of his life in Washington working as an editor, lecturer, and government official for both the District and the federal government.)

In 1979 Congress incorporated the museum into the Smithsonian Institution and the museum was renamed the National Museum of African Art. The current collection is part of a complex known as the Quadrangle museums. This complex, which also includes the Arthur M. Sackler Gallery for Asian Art, the S. Dillon Ripley Center, and the Enid A. Haupt Garden, was constructed to enhance the Smithsonian's focus on non-Western art. The facility was built underground (95 percent of the gallery space is below ground level) for several reasons. Most important, space on the Mall was limited and an aboveground complex of this nature probably would have overpowered the existing adjoining buildings, which the complex was designed to complement. Seven government agencies, each with regulatory power, oversaw the design and construction of the project. The National Museum of African Art opened in 1987.

### Washington Notes

The current location of the National Museum of African Art was once the site of the National Air Museum, the precursor of the National Air and Space

Museum. This World War I–era building was originally used to conduct aircraft experiments. An ironic coincidence is that the Robey and Williams slave pens, Washington's most infamous, were located one block west of the museum's current site along B St South (now Independence Ave) between 6th and 7th Sts.

## Exterior

Designed to complement the Freer Gallery of Art, the exterior of the National Museum of African Art incorporates circular motifs such as the six copper domes of its roof. The entrance pavilion is faced with pink granite from Texas to be compatible with the Arts and Industries Building. The remaining three floors of the complex reach 57 ft below ground.

## Interior

**Ground level.** Enter the museum through the south door adjacent to the Enid A. Haupt Garden. Turn left and walk north past the security desk. The ground floor contains an information desk, checkroom, and elevators and stairs to the other levels. Also here are three sculptures by Nigerian artist Sokari Douglas Camp. Two of these pieces are kinetic and timed to perform at 15 and 45 minutes past the hour during museum hours. Turn right and walk east. At the end of the corridor is the information desk. From the desk, turn south and proceed down the stairs on the right or use the elevators to the left.

**First level.** The four permanent exhibits, which display objects from the museum's collection, as well as the museum shop, are located on this floor. The stairs and elevators are in the center of the building, while the exhibits run along the perimeter of the floor.

At the foot of the stairs is the **The Point of View Gallery.** Displayed here are temporary exhibits or works of art from the museum's permanent collection.

Immediately to the south of the stairs is the **Sylvia H. Williams Gallery,** a space used to show contemporary African arts. Proceed into the Point of View Gallery and turn south into **The Art of the Personal Object.**

This exhibit examines the beauty of utilitarian objects, most of which are from eastern and southern Africa. While many of the items, such as chairs, bowls, pipes, and baskets, were constructed for everyday use, they were also intended to be admired. One of the first objects visitors encounter is a chair shaped like an inverted Y. It was constructed from wood and iron by the Tiv peoples (Nigeria). Turn right and proceed west to a case containing headrests. African headrests are designed to cradle the neck and support the head. Most of these objects are simply designed but feature intricate decorations. The objects were carved from wood by peoples in a variety of African regions such as the Zulu peoples (South Africa), the Makonde peoples (Tanzania and Mozambique), and the Tsonga peoples (Mozambique). Continue west through the gallery. To the left is a case of snuff containers carved from wood, ivory, horn, and fashioned from gourds. Snuff, introduced to Africa by European traders during the 16C, was offered to friends and visitors. Some of the more interesting containers are the ivory, leather, copper, iron, and glass-beaded ones created by the Kipsigis peoples (Kenya); the scraped hide container used by the Xhosa (South Africa); and the glass bottle decorated with glass beads by the Zulu peoples (South Africa). To the south is a collection of stools that are designed for stability and portability. Most were carved from a single piece of wood and feature a handle.

Continue west. On the south side of the gallery is a collection of pipes. The African artists who adopted European designs for their wooden stemmed pipes and clay bowls, added whimsical twists to their designs. For example, there is a terra-cotta pipe created by the Asante peoples (Ghana) in the shape of a toucan. Another has a train engine and caboose on its stem. On the north side of the gallery are wooden combs and snuff spoons, some of which are made of ivory and some of horn.

At the west end of the gallery are objects commonly found in African homes: wooden bowls, drinking vessels, baskets, and containers. All of the objects are highly decorated to marry beauty with functionality. Note the plant-fiber basket of the Pende peoples (Zaire); the gourd and pigment bowl by the Fulani peoples (Chad); and the double wooden bowl of the Tsonga peoples (South Africa). At the end of the exhibit is a corridor leading to the Arthur M. Sackler Gallery. Retrace your steps to the Point of View Gallery.

Proceed north through the Point of View Gallery into **The Ancient Nubian City of Kerma, 2500–1500 B.C.** This small, square gallery shows a semipermanent exhibition of 40 works on loan from the Museum of Fine Arts in Boston. The objects are from Kerma, the capital of the sophisticated Nubian kingdom known to the Egyptians, with whom the Kermians traded, as Kush. Kerma is the oldest city in Africa, aside from sites in Egypt, to be excavated. The objects in this exhibit were excavated between 1913 and 1916; they include jewelry, ceramics, and ivory figurines. To the left of the entrance is a case displaying pottery from the early and middle periods of Kerma (c. 2500–1750 B.C.) to the classic period (c. 1750–1570 B.C.). The pieces from the early and middle periods were colored with red ocher but are characterized by their black rims. The black area was created by inverting the vessel into combustible material, such as animal dung, when the pot was fired. After firing, the Kermians polished the pots by rubbing stones against them. Classic period vessels are entirely red or black. A photograph in this gallery shows mica ornaments found around the skulls of male bodies buried in Kerma. They were once animal-shaped and are believed to have been attached to cloth or leather skullcaps that were placed on the deceased for burial. Other notable objects are in a case against the north wall. There is a necklace of carnelian beads and a copper-alloy dagger with a wood-and-ivory hilt (both c. 1750–1570 B.C.).

Proceed through the west doorway into **The Ancient West African City of Benin, A.D. 1300–1897.** This gallery displays royal art objects from the kingdom of Benin (in present-day Nigeria) that are representative of the city prior to British colonial rule. The exhibit includes symbolic images of kings and their attendants—cast-metal heads, plaques, and figures. It is organized in three sections: the Oba (objects owned by or depicting the ruler of Benin); the Court (objects used by or depicting members of the royal court); and Foreigners (objects depicting Europeans or their influence). The gallery opens with the Oba, who the Benin people believed was a living god with power over life and death. Against the east wall is the head of Oba (18C), a cast–copper-alloy and iron-inlay symbol of status and kingship. This piece was probably displayed on an altar honoring the Oba. Next to this is a copper-alloy figure of an Oba (19C), with markings on the forehead made of iron inlay. The staff in his left hand was believed to add to the power of his words; the figure once held a sword in his right hand. Another Oba object is the copper-alloy altar bell (18C–19C), whose clapper is iron inlay. Quadrangle bells, placed at ancestral altars, were rung to draw the ancestor's attention to the descendant's prayers and sacrifices. Smaller versions were worn by Benin soldiers as identification or for spiritual protection. Continue west to the **Court** area, which displays objects used to show status and depict the life of court members. Copper palace plaques (16C–17C), such as the ones hanging on the wall, show narrative scenes of battles or hunts. The size of the figures in court or military regalia alludes to a figure's rank. The backgrounds of flowers, known as river leaves, refer to Olokun, god of the seas. Olokun is ritualistically tied to the Oba and wealth. At the south end of the gallery is the third section, Foreigners. Images on the palace plaques depict French, Dutch, and English traders and military. They are shown with longer noses, straight hair, and European-style clothing and equipment such as muskets. Retrace your steps to the Point of View Gallery. Immediately turn east, then north, and enter **Images of Power and Identity**, the museum's largest exhibit.

Images of Power and Identity shows more than 100 important works of art from the permanent collection. Objects, grouped by room according to where they originated and to their cultural origin, are presented from West Africa to East Africa. The first room contains art from **Western Sudan**. Sculpture from this region is often angular and elongated. Anatomical details are minimally suggested, unlike pieces from other African regions, which tend to be more explicit. The objects' surfaces are usually either matte or encrusted. In the case at the center of the room are terra-cotta figures depicting an equestrian and an archer (13C–15C). Their dress suggests ceremonial military costumes, and it is believed they represent the warriors of the court of Sunjata (c. 1210–60). On the east side of the room are headdresses (chi wara kun) of the Bamana peoples of Mali, constructed from wood, iron, and fiber. These pieces were worn in ceremonies praising good farming practices, so the headgear combines the horns of an antelope, the body of an aardvark, and the skin of a pangolin—all animals that dig in the earth.

Proceed north into the next room, which displays objects from the **Guinea Coast**, a region extending from Guinea-Bissau through southwest Nigeria. The carved wooden objects in the room are naturalistic in subject matter and are painted with earth-tone pigments. Many celebrate leadership. In the southwest corner is a wooden shrine figure (a-Tshol) of the Baga peoples (Guinea), representing the spirit of lineage. Family members would appeal to these figures in times of need such as during harvesting or illness. In a case against the north wall is an iron altar (asen) of the Fon peoples (Ouidah). The seated figure represents a deceased person; the male and female figures represent his family. Other imagery refers to the deceased's religious beliefs, occupation, and heritage.

Continue east to the room with objects from the **Yoruba** peoples (Nigeria), one of Africa's most prolific manufacturers of art. Yoruban sculptures are used during rituals and ceremonies to honor ancestors, reinforce values, and promote fertility. The Palace Door (1910–14; Olowe of Ise), created with wood and pigments, is one of a pair that originally hung in the arinjale's palace at Ise. Scenes depict an actual event: the first visit of a British traveling commissioner to the Ekiti-Yoruba kings in 1899. The panel at the top, with the mothers and babies, represents the king's or the kingdom's fertility. The most significant panel is the second from the top because it is the most detailed and, when the door was installed, was at eye level. Shown on horseback, the arinjale's hand is extended to welcome the commissioner, who is depicted on the other door (not displayed). Along the left side of the door are 13 pairs of heads representing prisoners. On the bottom panel is a decapitated woman who had been sacrificed. Wooden vultures once pecked at her body.

In a case next to the door is *Bowl with Figures* (c. 1925; Olowe of Ise). This bowl, probably carved for a person of status or for a shrine, was used to offer kola nuts to guests or deities. Proceed south. In the case facing west is a 20C glass-beaded crown *(ade)* by the Yoruba peoples of the Ijebu region (Nigeria). A Yoruba king wore a beaded crown to signify he could trace his ancestry to Oldudua, the mythical founder of the Yoruba. The faces represented all kings, past and present. The veil protects the king's visitors from the supernatural powers believed to radiate from his face.

Continue south. The crocodile headdress, perhaps created by the Ejagham peoples (Nigeria and Cameroon), is comprised of wood, antelope skin, palm fiber, bamboo, metal, and pigments. It was worn by young girls in coming-of-age ceremonies and was intended to discourage inappropriate behavior. In a case at the center of the south end of the room is a harp of the Zande peoples (Zaire) made from wood, animal hide, and metal. Note the carved knob depicting a human head that caps the neck of the instrument.

(The museum is in the process of updating its labeling to reflect the fact that in 1997 Zaire changed its name to the Democratic Republic of the Congo and is commonly referred to as Congo [Kinshasa], which distinguishes it from the neighboring Republic of the Congo, which the museum refers to as Congo [Brazzaville]).

In the southwest corner of the room is a figure (19C) fashioned with wood, textile, glass beads, shells, and brass by the Bamum peoples (Cameroon). This figure holds his chin in his left hand, a gesture symbolizing respect for others.

Proceed east to the next room, which displays objects from the **Lower Zaire and Kwango River Basins.** Three major categories of objects found in this region are: woman and child figurines, which are metaphors for societal fertility; power figures used as protective devices; and regalia and emblems, such as staffs and jewelry, which validate power and authority. Note the mask *(Hemba* or *Geemba)* of the Suku peoples (Zaire). The bell-shaped helmet masks decorated with animal figures are used for puberty rituals for young boys. Continue east into the next room, **Eastern Zaire River Basin.**

Along the west wall is the mask *(mwaldi)* of the Tetela peoples (Zaire), constructed from wood, pigment, kaolin, and raffia, worn by a diviner in rituals celebrating the new moon, an event believed to ensure health, wealth, and fertility.

At the center of the room is a figure constructed of wood, metal, and shell by the Songye peoples (Zaire). It was used by an elder to protect the community against harm and to ensure general success. Medicines were once stored in the figure's abdominal cavity. Proceed south and then turn east into the room displaying art from **southern and East Africa.** Note, along the west wall, the wooden throne of the Luguru peoples (Tanzania). The female figure on the backrest may symbolize the maternal lineage of the tribe. On the south wall, note the red glass-beaded hat created by the Topotha peoples (Sudan). Hats such as this were worn by men of wealth and status. On the east wall is a brass processional cross from Ethopia (20C). Ethiopians have drawn on Christianity from various traditions since the 4C. Priests place crosses such as this one on staffs as they lead processions from a church to outside gatherings.

Continue east. To the north is a stool of the Kwere peoples (Tanzania) carved from a single piece of wood. The intricate design and structure indicate that it was probably made for a person of high status and wealth. The flags on the east wall are emblems of the Asafo military companies, which, though established to counterbalance the ruling elite, more often performed civic and religious functions. The British Union Jack is commonly found in the upper-left corner of Asafo flags made from the mid-19C until Ghana was granted independence in 1957. The top flag was created by the Fante peoples (c. 1910). At its center is probably Kweku Amamfe, one of the original pre-Fante inhabitants of the region. The seven smaller figures around him represent those who conquered Kweku.

Exit the gallery to the south. On the east side of the corridor is the museum shop. On the west side are stairs to the second level.

**Second level.** Temporary exhibitions are housed on this level as well as a lecture hall, a workshop, the Warren M. Robbins Library, and the Eliot Elisofon Photographic Archives. The library contains more than 20,000 volumes about African art and culture. The photographic archives holds more than 300,000 photographic prints and transparencies, plus film footage, videos, and documentary films about African art.

**Third level.** A small installation here displays **Ceramic Arts of the National Museum of African Art,** with traditional and modern ceramic pieces from different regions of the continent. This level also contains the reflecting pool and access to the S. Dillon Ripley Center.

Walk west through Haupt Garden to the Arthur M. Sackler Gallery. The Sackler can be accessed through the doorway located at the west end of the Art of the Personal Object gallery or by heading west across the Enid A. Haupt Garden. The ground level entrance to the Sackler Gallery is directly opposite the entrance to the National Museum of African Art.

## Arthur M. Sackler Gallery

1050 Independence Ave S.W., ☎ 357-2700 or 357-1729 (TTY). Web: www.si. edu/asia. Open daily 10–5:30. Closed Christmas Day. Admission: free. Daily walk-in tour information available at information desk in Entrance Pavilion. Group tours by appointment. Special groups must reserve in writing four weeks in advance. Write to: Tours, Arthur M. Sackler Gallery, Smithsonian Institution, Washington, D.C. 20560. Wheelchair accessible. Wheelchairs available. Gallery shop open 10–5:30. Library open Mon–Fri 10–5. ☎ 357-4880. Photography allowed unless noted. Use of a tripod must be cleared in advance by the Office of Public Affairs, ☎ 357-4880.

The Arthur M. Sackler Gallery (1987; Shepley Bulfinch Richardson & Abbott) exhibits objects from Asia and the Near East from ancient times to the present and plays an important role in educating visitors about the art and cultural heritage of this region.

**Highlights:** Chinese bronzes, Buddhist and Hindu sculpture, Persian and Indian paintings and manuscripts, the Taj Mahal Emerald (which weighs 141.13 carats), and a changing selection of loan exhibitions.

Throughout the year the Sackler has Saturday programs for children related to specific exhibits or permanent parts of the collection. These may include constructing paper versions of objects featured in exhibits, storytelling, or musical pieces and dance. ImaginAsia, an educational program for children of ages

6–12, is held on Sat and Sun from Sept to June and during the week in July and Aug.

### History

Dr. Arthur M. Sackler was a medical researcher, publisher, and art collector from New York City. In 1982, he donated more than 1,000 masterpieces to the Smithsonian Institution as well as $4 million for a new building in which to expand the Smithsonian's collection of Asian art. Sackler initiated numerous philanthropic projects in the arts, sciences, and humanities. The Arthur M. Sackler Museum, part of a $73.2 million complex, opened to the public on Sept 28, 1987. In addition to Sackler's contribution, funding also came from the Smithsonian Institution and from private sources.

Dr. Thomas Lawton, then director of the Freer Gallery, was chosen to jointly serve as director of the Sackler. He combed through Sackler's collection, selecting objects for the new museum that he felt would complement the collection of the Freer Gallery. In Oct 1988, Lawton retired to resume his research of ancient Chinese art and was replaced by Dr. Milo C. Beach, then the assistant director of the Sackler Gallery.

Since the gallery's opening, additions through purchases and donations have expanded the collection's focus. The Henri Vever Collection, an assemblage of Islamic art from the 11C to 19C, is one such acquisition.

## Exterior

The Sackler Gallery is one of four facilities in the Quadrangle complex. (The National Museum of African Art, the S. Dillon Ripley Center, and the Enid A. Haupt Garden comprise the other three.) The Entrance Pavilion, visible from the street, offers admission to the gallery from Independence Ave. The façade for this part of the building is gray granite from Minnesota, chosen to complement the granite façade of the Freer Gallery. The roof, adorned with pyramid shapes, was designed to complement the diamond motif on the neighboring Arts and Industries Building.

## Interior

**Ground level.** Enter the gallery, turn right, and proceed north into the entrance pavilion where the information desk and storage lockers are located. From the information desk, turn left and proceed down the stairs to the first level.

**First level.** Exhibition galleries and the gallery shop are on this level. Although the museum does have a permanent collection, much of the art on display is changed at six-month intervals. A corridor at the west side of the floor leads into the Freer Gallery.

Turn right and enter the gallery to the south, **Puja: Expressions of Hindu Devotion.**

*Puja* is the Hindu act of paying homage to god through prayer, song, and rituals. This reverence is typically paid with the assistance of objects such as sculpture, vessels, or graphic arts. This exhibit explains the tradition of *puja* and displays objects steeped with a divine link. To the right of the entrance are bells Hindus rang to "awaken senses" before worship. Visitors are invited to ring the bells or touch a bronze sculpture representing Nandi, Shiva's bull, for good luck. Nandi symbolizes single-minded devotion and the strength of faith. At the center of this room, south of the Nandi sculpture, is a re-creation of the central sanctum of a shrine to Shiva. Among the objects in the temple are a bronze incense burner (18C) and a water-drip vessel (16C) that depicts Karttikeya, Shiva's son, riding a peacock. The water in the vessel drips onto the linga during *puja* to anoint it and to honor Shiva.

Walk through the doorway to the southeast and into the small theater on the right. The theater shows a 12-minute video featuring members of the local community and some of its rituals. Exit the theater to the east.

The next room displays sculptural symbols and representations of Shiva, who is sometimes shown in human form. His four arms symbolize his superhuman power; in three hands are attributes: His trident is used to ward off demons, his rosary beads represent transcendence, and the rattle creates life. Naga, a cobra around his neck, signifies fertility and strength. To his side is Parvati, his wife and the Mother of All Creation. She complements Shiva's masculine attributes and represents a balance of opposites. Their elephant-headed son, Ganesha, is known as the Remover of Obstacles and he assures success to new endeavors. Also in the room are linga covers such as the one made of brass (17C; Maharashtra). These are placed over the linga to protect it.

Continue east into the next room. To the left is a hands-on resource area with books, puzzles, and objects relating to Hinduism. The sculptural objects in this room demonstrate the physical characteristics of the god Vishnu, his wife Lakshmi, and their incarnations. Vishnu is the god of home and family values. He is recognizable by the four objects he carries: a discus, conch shell, club, and lotus. Lakshmi, often shown standing on a lotus, or holding lotuses, is the goddess of abundance and prosperity. The reincarnated couple is also depicted as Rama and Sita or as Krishna and Radha. Note the bronze lampstand (18C; Himachal Pradesh) in the form of Garuda, the winged mount that Vishnu rides. At the east end of the room is a two-minute video showing a *puja* being performed in the Rajasthan home.

Proceed east into the next room. On the north wall, behind small wooden doors which visitors can open, is a re-creation of a household shrine. It contains a fossilized shell, a bronze with the footprints of Vishnu (18C; Himachal Pradesh), a vessel for holy water, and a spoon for ladling the holy water. This gallery also displays 19C ceremonial sandals created from bronze, wood, silver, and ivory. These strapless sandals, *padukas*, are worn by priests who have vowed not to wear leather. On the opposite wall are 19C brass spiritual masks resembling animal heads, such as bulls and boars. People in the coastal Indian city of Karantaka used these masks to worship spirits, *bhutas*, who are invoked to ensure welfare, regulate weather, ward off disease, settle family disputes, and provide healthy offspring.

Continue east into the next room which focuses on Devi, a goddess who takes diverse forms and is worshiped by Hindus. Among her many incarnations, she is often shown with a lotus, the symbol of creation, and a trident, which she uses to ward off evil. In the southwest corner of the room is a recreation of an outdoor shrine to the goddess Kali-Ma, the divine being who causes and cures diseases. Shrines such as this one are set up near natural landmarks such as trees, rocks, and rivers, and these shrines are often cluttered with terra-cotta elephants. Kali-Ma rides an elephant in her nightly quest against evil. In the southeast corner of the room is a two-minute video showing a *puja* where the goddess Chandi is invited to enter a tree that is believed to hold the spirit of the community. A doorway at the east side of the room leads into the National Museum of African Art. Continue viewing the Sackler by returning through the Puja exhibit.

Walk south and enter **Sculpture of South and Southeast Asia.** The first part of this multiroom gallery displays **arts of Cambodia.** Buddhism and Hinduism arrived in the Khmer Empire (9C–1431), now part of modern-day Cambodia, via Indian merchants. The Cambodian religious objects are less voluptuous than figures created by Indian artists, but the shapes, including animal-shaped vessels, are similar. Note the sandstone lintels (c. 11C–13C) against the south wall. These were placed over doorways and entrances to temples. In the one displayed, the male figures hold a lotus flower, a god's throne. The sandstone goddess figure (10C) is missing her arms and hands, making her identification impossible since goddesses are recognized by the items they hold. Walk west into the room containing **Indian sculptures of a Hindu temple.**

The stone figures in this room once adorned the walls and niches of temples. In the southwest corner is a statue of Ganesha (13C; Mysore region), the elephant god whose blessing brought good fortune and prosperity. To the left of Ganesha is a bronze representation of Shiva (c. 13C–14C). Bronze sculptures of Shiva were given as offerings by wealthy devotees. Against the north wall note *Vishnu with Avatars* (11C), in which Vishnu holds a discus and mace in his upper hands. At one time the figure in this statue probably held a conch shell and a lotus in his lower hands. The attendants flanking this representation are the goddesses Saravati (holding a lute) and Lakshmi (has a lotus). The incarnations, or avatars, associated with Vishnu are carved in low relief around the panel. Clockwise, beginning at the bottom left, are a fish, tortoise, boar, man-lion, dwarf, Roma, Parasurama (with the ax), Balarama (with the plow), Buddha, and Kalki (the man riding the horse).

Continue west into the corridor. Set into the west wall of the corridor is a fragment of a colorful tile mosaic (1480–81) salvaged from the shrine of Zayn al-Mulk in Iran. The gift shop is also along the west side of the corridor. Across from the gift shop entrance are restrooms, water fountains, and elevators.

From the mosaic, turn south and proceed into a temporary exhibition gallery where works of art from the Islamic world are usually on view.

The **Taj Mahal Emerald** (c. 1630–50; Mughal period) is in a case along the east wall of the first corridor leading to this gallery.

**For Shah-Jahan.** Shah-Jahan, fifth ruler of the Mughal dynasty established in 1526 by his great-grandfather. Shah-Juhan ruled the kingdom from 1628 to 1658 and was known for his ambitious architectural programs such as the Taj Mahal—the tomb he built for his wife, Mumtaz Mahal, and himself. He collected gems and patronized artists known for their perfection. This hexagonal Colombian emerald weighs 141.13 carats and is carved on one side with a stylized lotus, a poppy plant, and a third, unidentifiable flower. Scholars believe the three flowers represent the unity of the Shah-Jahan empire. This jewel was most likely worn as a pendant around the shah's neck.

Continue east into Metalwork and Ceramics from Ancient Iran. Most of the objects which still exist from western Asia prior to 4000 B.C. are metalwork and ceramics. The objects displayed in these two galleries are from a period between 2300 and 100 B.C. and they illustrate the use of pyrotechnology. Many objects were originally made with metal. Later ceramic was more commonly used because it was less expensive than metal and could be manipulated to resemble metal surfaces. The finials (1000–650 B.C.), or ornamental pole tops, in the case along the south side of the room were created with copper alloy and used by the peoples of Luristam in the Zagros Mountains of western Iran. These finials resemble demons and are flanked by panthers or by trees and goats. Vegetation symbolizes fertility and the demons suggest magical powers. The copper animal-shaped pendants (1000–650 B.C.) along the west wall were found in tombs and are believed to be charms buried with the dead to provide protection or luck. At the center of the room is a ceramic gazelle rhyton (500–300 B.C.), an animal-shaped drinking vessel.

Proceed east into the next room. Ancient Iranian ceramics are often rounded shapes with long, pointed spouts. They are adorned with animal decorations or are in the shapes of birds, camels, or turtles, and have smooth surfaces with a metallic sheen. The colors are created by manipulating the kiln conditions during firing. The objects in this exhibit are from an area of northern Iran bordering the Caspian Sea. Many were buried in tombs, but others were used in religious ceremonies. Note the beak-spouted pitcher and the bull-shaped vessel (both c. 1350–800 B.C.) along the north wall.

Return west to the previous room. Turn north and enter the Sculpture of South and Southeast Asia gallery. Turn right and proceed east to the end of the room. Turn left and walk north past the stairway to the gallery at the north end, The Arts of China.

Each room in **The Arts of China** focuses on a period and medium of art. The first room, **Ancient Chinese Art: 4th Millennium to 3rd Century A.D., displays jades from Neolithic cultures (5000–1700 B.C.**), most of which were used in religious, court, or burial rituals and were symbols of social and political status. Note the jade weapons (13C–12C B.C.), such as an ax and Halberd blades, as well as the religious and ornamental pieces like the disks, called *bi,* and bracelets. The early cast-bronze vessels, including wine and food containers, are from the 15C–14C B.C.

Proceed north into the room containing objects from the **Shang dynasty** (c. 1700–1050 B.C.), the first historically documented dynasty in China. Animal shapes, such as birds, tigers, and fish, were common motifs for jade pieces and bronze vessels from 1300 to 1050 B.C. These jades were usually worn as pendants, whereas the bronze vessels were used in religious ceremonies. Note the jade waterbird (11C) and fish (11C).

Continue north, through the room of **Western Zhou** (c. 1050–771 B.C.) works, and turn west into the room of **Eastern Zhou dynasty** (c. 771–221 B.C.). The tomb figure (4 B.C.) is made from wood, pigment, and deer antlers. Figures such as this one signified deities and were placed in tombs to protect the body and the tomb from evil spirits. On the south wall, note the set of six bronze, clapperless bells (6 B.C.) believed to have been important parts of religious rituals. The bells were probably rung by a hit from a wooden mallet.

Walk south into **Buddhist Art in China.** Buddhism arrived in China during 1C A.D. The objects in this gallery, which change periodically, illustrate the merging styles of Chinese and Indian elements in Buddhist art.

Head west into **Later Chinese Art,** which begins with the Song dynasty (960–1279). During this period there was a shift in the political system. Power was given to scholars rather than inherited by families. The scholars, who advised the emperor, were trained in literature, history, and philosophy, and were often patrons of art who practiced painting and calligraphy. These scholars, as well as the imperial family and wealthy merchants, commissioned many paintings, pieces of furniture, jades, and lacquerware. In this room and the adjacent room to the north are objects from the Song, Yuan (1279–1368), Ming (1368–1644), and Qing (1644–1911) dynasties, and also the Republic period (1911–present). In the north room look for the six-post canopy bed (17C) created from rosewood. Canopy beds were treasured household items. Note the geometric design of the railing, which represents begonia flowers; the panels beneath the canopies suggest magnolia blossoms.

Exit this gallery to the west and enter the corridor. A hallway to the west joins the Freer Gallery. Elevators on the east side of the corridor provide access to the ground, second, and third levels of the Sackler.

**Second level.** The second level has one large gallery used for temporary and traveling exhibits. On the south side of the level is the classroom where **Imagin-Asia** and other activities take place. The **research library,** which is the largest Asian art library in the United States, consists of archives and slides; it serves both the Sackler and Freer Galleries. The collection consists of nearly 60,000 volumes, about half of them in Chinese and Japanese.

**Third level.** The Sculpture Court is located at the center of this level. Access to the S. Dillon Ripley Center is on the south side of the floor.

To continue to the Freer Gallery of Art, exit the Sackler Gallery into the Haupt Garden and walk north to Jefferson Dr. Walk west to the north entrance of the Freer Gallery. Visitors may also walk through the first-level exhibition gallery **Luxury Arts of the Silk Route Empires,** which includes works from both the Sackler and the Freer Galleries. On view are 1C–7C objects such as silver and ceramic vessels, carried along the trade routes that linked the Mediterranean regions with eastern Asia. At the west end of the corridor is an elevator.

Take the elevator or marble staircase to the first level of the Freer. Turn left (from the elevator) and walk west to the intersection, then turn right. If climbing the marble staircase, take two rights at the top and climb a short flight of stairs to the corridor. At the end of this corridor is the Freer museum shop. Climb the stairs to the west of the shop. These stairs lead to the ground level of the Freer Gallery, where most of the art is displayed.

## Freer Gallery of Art

Jefferson Dr at 12th St S.W. ☎ 357-2700 or 357-1729 (TTY). Web: www.si. edu/asia. Open daily 10–5:30. Closed Christmas Day. Admission: free. Daily tour schedule listed at information desk. Group tours available by appointment. Request permission four weeks in advance. Write: Tour Scheduler, Freer Gallery of Art, Smithsonian Institution, Washington, DC 20560. Gallery shop located on Mall side, second level. Open daily 10–5:30. Archives and slide library open by appointment, except federal holidays. ☎ 357-4880, ext 343. Wheelchair accessible. Restrooms and checkrooms. Use of tripod photography must be cleared in advance by Office of Public Affairs, ☎ 357-4880.

The Freer Gallery of Art (1913, planned; 1916–23, constructed; Charles Adams Platt; 1993 restoration, Shepley Bulfinch Richardson & Abbott; Cole & Denny / BVH) is considered to house one of the world's finest collections of Asian art. Its collection spans six millennia and represents the cultural and art heritage of China, Korea, Japan, South and Southeast Asia, and the Near East. Additionally, the Freer contains early Egyptian and Christian art, as well as 19C–20C American art, including the world's most comprehensive collection of works by James McNeill Whistler. As the collection is so large, only a small portion (less than 5 percent) is displayed at any given time.

**Highlights:** Whistler's only existing interior decor design, *Harmony in Blue and Gold: The Peacock Room,* is permanently installed in Gallery 12. Other highlights include Japanese folding screens, Persian manuscripts, Korean ceramics, and Chinese jades.

### History

The Freer Gallery of Art was the Smithsonian's first art museum when it opened in 1923—and for 40 years it was the Smithsonian's only art museum. The gallery's unique combination of American art and Asian art reflects the personal tastes of the museum's founder, Charles Lang Freer (1854–1919), a Detroit industrialist who made his fortune in railcar construction. He retired from the American Car and Foundry Company at age 44 and devoted his remaining years to collecting art.

Freer's acquisition of Asian art was aided by Ernest Fenellosa, a scholar of Asian art and faculty member at Harvard University and the Fine Arts Academy of Tokyo, who advised Freer and introduced him to art dealers. In 1887, Freer made his first Asian acquisition—a Japanese fan. Although that piece was purchased in New York, Freer visited Asia five times in his lifetime.

Freer was also friends with James McNeill Whistler (1834–1903). The two met in London in 1887 when Freer knocked on the expatriate artist's door to introduce himself. Freer quickly became Whistler's most important patron, buying 100 paintings and more than 1,000 graphics, as well as the Peacock Room. Today, the Freer Gallery contains the world's most extensive collections of Whistler's art.

In 1904, Freer informally proposed his ideas for a museum to President Theodore Roosevelt. Freer planned to donate his personal collection of 7,500 objects, a building, and an endowment for the study and acquisition of Asian art. The gift became official that same year despite strict restrictions Freer insisted the Smithsonian uphold: None of the objects may be loaned to other museums, nor may any works belonging to other museums be displayed in the gallery. Most important, none of the objects Freer donated could be sold, though he arranged for an annual endowment for acquiring new works. Today, the collection contains more than 28,000 works.

Freer planned to ask Stanford White (1853–1906), a leading 19C architect, to design the gallery. Before Freer could approach White, the architect was fatally shot at a party on the rooftop of New York City's Madison Square Garden. Several years passed before Freer asked New York architect Charles A. Platt (1861–1933) to design a structure to house his collection. Though Freer thought a "Tudor-Gothic" structure would best suit his collection, Platt designed an Italian Rennaissance–style building to complement the neighboring Smithsonian Castle and Department of Agriculture buildings. Ground was broken in Sept 1916, but construction ceased six months later with the onset of World War I. In 1918 building resumed, and the gallery opened to the public in 1923. Sadly, Freer had died in 1919.

In 1923, the gallery's East Asian Painting Conservation studio was founded to keep the collection in optimal condition. In 1951, the need to historically analyze the collection led to the establishment of the Freer Technical Laboratory.

The Freer Gallery of Art closed in the fall of 1988 for a four-year renovation project. The project included cleaning and restoring the exterior, massive renovation of the interior, construction of a marble-and-limestone gallery leading to a new exhibit area connecting the Freer and Sackler Galleries underground, creation of the Freer Auditorium, and the refurbishment of outside pathways. The expansion also increased the storage, conservation, and technical research areas by 70 percent.

## Exterior
Freer worked closely with architect Charles A. Platt to design this simple and symmetrical one-and-a-half–story building. The design is based on a Florentine Renaissance palazzo constructed around an interior courtyard. While the exterior is Stony Creek granite from Massachusetts, the courtyard is faced with white marble from Tennessee. The main entrance faces the Mall and is fashioned with three arches and Doric pilasters. A wheelchair-accessible entrance is located on Independence Ave.

Displayed outside the Jefferson Dr entrance is *Twisted Form (Traveler's Guardian Spiral)* (1981; Shiro Hayami), a granite sculpture set on an Agi stone base.

## Interior
**Main level.** Enter the Freer Gallery through the Jefferson Dr entrance and proceed into the foyer. To the right is the information desk and a touch-screen kiosk providing information about Charles Lang Freer, the collection, and the building. To the left is a checkroom and stairs leading to the lower level. There are 19 galleries on the main level, all of which display objects from the Freer collection. Paintings, lacquerware, and other light-sensitive objects are changed every six months, and occasional thematic exhibitions present the collection's breadth.

Proceed up the stairs to the center of the south wall. Beyond the glass walls is the courtyard, open to the public during special events and warmer months. Plans are under way to allow public access to the courtyard, which has been closed for decades due to the effects of outside atmosphere on the art displayed inside.

Galleries 1 and 2, to the right, display **Chinese ceramics** with green and blue Celadon glaze. The exhibit begins on the east side of the room and chronologically traces the evolution of this glazing process. The stoneware lion-shaped stand (c. 265–317) was manufactured during the Western Jin dynasty in the Zhejing Province of China; it was one of the original pieces donated by Freer. At the center of the room is a stoneware basin from the same period and region, decorated with animal masks.

Proceed north into Gallery 2. On the east wall is a porcelain dish (1723–35) created during the Qing dynasty in the Jiangxi Province. Cast in the imperial kiln, its colors represent a revival of Longquan-type wares; the decoration at the center is of a dragon floating amid clouds. At the west end of the gallery are 12C–13C funerary jars. Return to Gallery 1 and exit into the corridor. Turn right and walk to Galleries 3 and 4.

These galleries display **Arts of the Islamic World,** a 60-piece exhibition that includes a changing selection of Koran pages, metalwork, glass, and ceramics.

Return to the corridor and proceed south. Galleries 5–8, on either side of the hall, display **Japanese Art. Screens** are shown in Gallery 5, to the left. These folding screens, called *byobu*, partioned rooms and served as art. The panels, constructed from paper, were fastened to wood lattice work. The Freer's collection of some 125 folding screens is among the finest and largest in an American museum. The selection of screens displayed changes every six months, as do those items displayed in Galleries 6, 6A, and 7, due to light sensitivity.

From the corridor, proceed into Gallery 8, **Japanese Ceramics from Seto and Mino.** Seto, Mino, and Sanage are Japan's oldest ceramic industry centers. Sanage introduced glaze, Seto developed tea ceremony ceramics, and Mino created new glazes and designs. These revolutionary steps resulted in the rise in popularity of the tea ceremony during the 16C. Among the objects are sake ewers, tea bowls, and decanters.

Proceed through the east doorway into Gallery 9, **Korean Ceramics,** composed of items made between 200 and 1900. Displayed are tableware for the wealthy classes, Buddhist cinerary urns, and vessels used by peasants. A porcelain jar (c. 1900), decorated by leafy branches of a fruit plant called Buddha's Hand, was cast at a kiln near the northwest coastal city of Haeju. There's also a stoneware wine ewer (c. 1250) with a design representing the petals of two lotus buds. The sister of this ewer was uncovered from the tomb of a prince who died in 1257 on Kanghwa Island during a Mongolian raid.

Return to the corridor and walk east, past the Independence Ave entrance on the right, to Galleries 10 and 11, which display **American art** by Abbott Handerson Thayer, Dwight William Tryon, Thomas Wilmer Dewing, and James McNeill Whistler.

Continue to Gallery 12 in the southeast corner of the museum where the **Peacock Room** is installed. It was designed by interior architect Thomas Jeckyll in the 1870s as a dining room for Frederick R. Leyland, an English shipowner. Jeckyll installed a system of decorative shelving to display Leyland's collection of Chinese blue and white porcelain. *The Princess from the Land of Porcelain* (1863–64; James McNeill Whistler) hung above the fireplace and was the centerpiece of the room. Jeckyll hung the walls with 17C Dutch leather. Whistler, whom Leyland had hired to decorate the entrance hall of his home, did not think the color of the leather or its pattern of red and yellow flowers complemented *The Princess.* Leyland agreed to let Whistler make some changes in the color scheme, but Whistler went far beyond their agreement. When Leyland was away, Whistler painted golden peacocks on the room's shutters and doors and retouched the walls and ceiling with metal leaf and a peacock-feather pattern. Leyland initally refused to pay for the additional work, claiming Whistler undertook the project without permission. In retaliation, Whistler painted a pair of fighting peacocks on the wall opposite *The Princess.* Around the feet of one angry bird are silver shillings, a reference to the money Leyland refused to pay. Another allusion to Leyland are the silver feathers on the peacock's throat that resemble the ruffled shirts Leyland typically wore. Whistler called the mural *Art and Money; or, The Story of the Room.* Freer purchased the room in 1904 and had it reinstalled in his Detroit home, where it was used to display his collection of ceramics. The porcelain currently displayed on the shelves is from the Kangxi era (1662–1722) of the Qing dynasty, the same type of wares that Leyland collected.

Exit into the corridor, turn right, and walk north. Galleries 13–16 display **Chi-**

nese art. To the left, in Gallery 13, changing selections of Chinese paintings are shown.

Across the hall, in Galleries 14 and 15, is **Ancient Chinese Pottery and Bronze.** Clay, jade, and bronze were the dominant materials used in Chinese art, partucluarly vessels such as pots and funerary urns, from 4000 B.C. to the early A.D. centuries. The objects displayed are from a transitionary period between the end of the Neolithic pottery tradition and the emergence of metalworking (c. 2000 B.C.). The exhibits stop at the end of the Bronze Age and the rise of glazed stoneware (c. A.D. 200). Among the inlaid bronzes representing the early period are a wine container (c. 400 B.C.), a decorative chariot fitting (c. 300–250 B.C.), and a lavish canteen (c. 300–250 B.C.). Other objects include Han dynasty glazed pottery (206 B.C.–A.D. 220), an incense burner (c. 200–100 B.C.), and white pottery created with white clay. Proceed through the north doorway into Gallery 16, where **Charles Lang Freer and Egypt** presents a small part of Freer's Egyptian collection.

Return to Gallery 15 and walk west into the corridor. Turn right and proceed to Gallery 17, **Buddhist Art.** Just outside the exhibit entrance, and opposite it at the west end of the hall, are two wooden statues (14C) that once guarded the entrance of Ebaradera, a Japanese Buddhist temple near Osaka. Proceed into the gallery. To the right is *Life of Buddha* (late 2C–early 3C), a stone frieze depicting four major events in the life of Buddha. From left to right, they show Buddha's birth from his mother's side; his defeat of demonic forces led by the Evil One, Mara, preceding his enlightenment; Buddha preaching his first sermon; and Buddha reaching nirvana, the release from the cycle of rebirth. Along the east wall is a bodhisttva (late 12C). The figure, representing an enlightened being, is seated in a lotus-shaped throne. The halo behind the figure represents the light surrounding the deity. Statues like this were displayed at altars in Japanese Buddhist temples. The Chinese adopted the Indian practice of carving cliffs and cave walls to serve as sacred chapels. The carvings along the north wall are from the caves in Xiangtangshan, an area between the Hebei and Henan Provinces. Rulers of the Northern Qi dynasty (550–577) sponsored the creation of these relief murals, which were influenced by murals created during the Gupta dynasty (320–647). At the center of the right panel, *Western Paradise* (c. 570), is the Buddha of Infinite Light, referred to as Amitabha in Indian culture, lord of the Pure Land called Western Paradise. He is presiding over a pond and watches newly born souls emerge from lotus blossoms. The mural is the earliest known depiction of Western Paradise in Chinese art. The left panel, *Heavenly Buddhist Gathering* (c. 570), depicts a party attended by Buddhas, bodhisattavas, and blessed souls.

Continue west into **South Asian Art,** Gallery 18. Among the objects displayed is a bronze statue of Nandi (13C–14C), the bull ridden by the Hindu god Shiva. During temple festival processions in south India, devotees pulled statues such as this through towns on wooden chariots so others could receive the blessing of seeing the god. This blessing was known as taking *darshan.*

Walk west into Gallery 19, now reserved for changing thematic exhibitions from Asian cultures.

Exit the gallery and turn right. Proceed down the stairs and enter the Jefferson Dr entrance foyer. To go to the gift shop, turn right and continue down the stairs.

**Second floor.** At the foot of the stairs, turn left. The **museum shop** is on the left. To reach the Meyer Auditorium or the elevators to the other floors, turn right.

Walk south and before reaching the steps to the auditorium, turn left and proceed to the elevator. There is no exhibition space on this level.

**First floor. Meyer Auditorium,** used for the Freer's and Sackler's free public programs of film, dance, music, and lectures, is located in the southeast corner.

**Level S.** A corridor connecting the Freer Gallery of Art to the Arthur M. Sackler Gallery is on this level.

The Smithsonian Metro station (Blue/Orange Line) is located on the Mall, one block west of the Freer Gallery of Art. To continue to the next walk, go north across the Mall to the Museum of Natural History.

# 7 · National Mall: National Museum of Natural History and National Museum of American History

Metro: Blue/Orange Line to Federal Triangle or Smithsonian; Green/Yellow Line to Archives/Navy Memorial.
Bus: 13A, 13B, 13M, 32, 34, 35, 36, 52, 54, 62, 64, P2, P6, S2, or S4.

## National Museum of Natural History

Constitution Ave at 10th St N.W. ☎ 357-2700, 633-9126 (Spanish), or 357-1729 (TTY). Web: www.mnh.si.edu. Admission: free. Open daily 10–5:30. Closed Christmas Day. Free guided tours Mon–Thurs 10:30 and 1:30; Fri 10:30 only.

The Discovery Room, an area enabling visitors to handle objects from the collection, is on the first floor. ☎ 357-2747. Open Tues–Fri 12–2:30; Sat–Sun 10:30–3:30. Summer hours: daily 10:30–3:30. Free passes distributed daily at room entrance. Children must be accompanied by an adult. The new Discovery Center houses the Atrium Café and the Samuel C. Johnson Theater, a state-of-the-art facility showing IMAX 2D and 3D films. The theater box office is open daily from 9:45; first show is at 10:10, last show at 6:40. ☎ 633-7400.

Telephones, restrooms. Cafeteria and museum shops. ATM.

Wheelchair entrance at Constitution Ave. Handheld photography permitted.

With more than 121 million objects in its collection, the National Museum of Natural History (1911; Hornblower & Marshall; 1965 wings, Mills, Petticord and Mills; DL) maintains by far the largest part of the Smithsonian's collection. The museum focuses on understanding the natural world and humanity's part in it.

**Highlights:** African Voices explores the peoples, history, and culture of the vast African continent. The Janet Annenberg Hooker Hall of Geology, Gems, and Minerals displays the famous Hope Diamond, a 45.52-carat blue diamond. More than 5 million visitors annually view the exhibits in the O. Orkin Insect Zoo, a collection of live and model insects. Dozens of dinosaur skeletons are displayed in the Dinosaur Hall. The bull elephant in the museum's rotunda serves as an unofficial museum symbol. Children are especially fond of the hands-on activities in the Discovery Room and of the Dinostore. The Discovery Center, which opened in summer 1999, includes a 487-seat IMAX theater, an enlarged gift shop, and the Atrium Café.

## History

After the United States celebrated its 100th anniversary in 1876 with the Centennial Exposition in Philadelphia, Spencer F. Baird, the assistant secretary of the Smithsonian, convinced dozens of foreign exhibitors to donate their collections to the Smithsonian. Baird, however, recognized that there was not enough storage space in the Smithsonian Institution Building, the facility's first building, which was constructed in 1855 and commonly referred to as the Castle. Baird lobbied for a new building. Congress quickly appropriated funds for a new building to be called the National Museum. (It has since been renamed the Arts and Industries Building.) Ground was broken in 1879 and the building completed in 1881. On March 4, 1881, President James A. Garfield held his inaugural ball in the new museum. Shortly thereafter the exhibits were installed and the building opened to the public.

In 1897 Charles Doolittle Walcott, director of the U.S. Geological Survey and the acting assistant secretary of the Smithsonian, convinced Congress to appropriate $8,000 for the construction of additional galleries to the National Museum's four main exhibit halls. Walcott also reorganized the museum into three departments: Anthropology, Biology, and Geology.

In 1903 Congress appropriated $3.5 million for the construction of the second National Museum building. Ground was broken on June 14, 1904, and the cornerstone laid on Aug 21, 1905. Construction was completed on June 20, 1911, but the daunting task of moving the collections across the Mall began as early as 1909.

Though the new building was filling up quickly with natural history and scientific specimens, works of art were also being installed. In 1903 Harriet Lane Johnston willed her art collection to the Corcoran Gallery of Art with the proviso that it would be transferred to a national gallery of art should one ever be established. The Corcoran refused the bequest and Johnston's lawyers approached the Smithsonian. Since the institution's charter included a provision for art, the National Gallery of Art was hastily created, and Johnston's gift became the core of the collection.

With this addition, the Smithsonian administration conceptually separated the Natural History Building from the National Museum. On March 17, 1910, the National Gallery of Art and the Natural History Building, both divisions of the National Museum, opened to the public. (In 1937, after Andrew Mellon offered the necessary money and art for a suitably important National Gallery of Art, the National Museum renamed its collection the National Collection of Fine Arts. During the mid-1960s the National Collection was relocated to the old Patent Office between 7th and 9th Sts on F and G Sts N.W.) In 1918 the National Museum closed to the public in order to house 3,000 government workers from the Bureau of War Risk. The museum reopened a year later.

In the 1930s Congress authorized the construction of additional wings to the Natural History Building. However, the Depression and World War II set back those plans for 30 years. Finally in 1961 and 1963 new wings were added to the east and west sides of the building.

As the already massive museum collections continued to grow, Congress, on June 28, 1955, approved a plan to build the Museum of History and Technology on the site west of the Natural History Building. Now called the National Museum of American History, the building was dedicated on Jan 22, 1964.

The museum is continuing its renovation plans. In 1997 the redesigned Janet Annenberg Hooker Hall of Geology, Gems, and Minerals opened; in 1999 the stonework and marble columns of the rotunda were cleaned. The elephant's pedestal will be a replica of the Angolan landscape with a cutaway showing biological and geological strata. A new permanent exhibit, African Voices, opened in Dec 1999, and a new Hall of Mammals is scheduled to open in 2003.

## Exterior

This understated, neoclassical building was constructed with interior walls of red brick. The façade of the ground floor is pink granite from Massachusetts. The first and second floors are faced with white granite from Vermont, and the white granite covering the third floor is from North Carolina. Aside from the Corinthian capitals, the most unique architectural feature is the Roman-style dome.

On pedestals on the west and east side of the steps leading to the Mall entrance are geological samples. At the west end is a 2.25-billion-year-old specimen of banded iron ore from Jasper Knob in Ishpeming, Michigan. At the east side are two specimens of 200-million-year-old petrified wood from the Triassic period. The chunks were found near Arizona's Petrified Forest National Park.

A path through the block-long Butterfly Habitat Garden links Madison Dr with Constitution Ave on the east side of the museum. The garden features four habitats frequented by butterflies: wetlands, meadows, woodlands, and backyards. Each illustrates the relationship between plants and butterflies. Plaques throughout the garden identify plant species and explain the relationship between the habitat and the butterflies.

Proceed north through the Butterfly Habitat Garden. At Constitution Ave turn west and enter the museum at the north entrance.

## Interior

**Ground floor.** Inside the Constitution Ave entrance is an information desk staffed by docents. At the east end of the lobby, towering one story into the stairwell, are two Haida **totem poles** carved late in the 19C from western red cedar. An accompanying video explains the ceremonial significance of totem poles and the craft of carving. To celebrate the raising of a totem pole, the Haida would hold a potlatch, a feast of several days duration with dances and plays. Near the totem poles on the east wall are sections of petrified trees. Against the wall are cases of bugs, minerals, and aboriginal pottery.

A second set of cases stands at the west end of the lobby. These cases exhibit arrowheads, bones, and Native American costumes. Restrooms flank the central corridor leading south. The security office is at this end of the lobby.

Just before the entrance to the central corridor is a bust of Spencer F. Baird, who served as assistant secretary of the Smithsonian from 1850 to 1878 before becoming the secretary from 1878 to 1887. Baird is considered the unofficial founder of the National Museum of Natural History.

Follow the corridor south. Along the west wall is an ATM, and on the east wall opposite it is the Visit Planning Kiosk. The kiosk offers information helpful to planning a day's activities in the museum, including news of special programs, recently opened exhibits, and IMAX showtimes. The museum shop, which sells CDs, T-shirts, science kits, books, and other items, is located on the east side of the hallway. On the west side is the entrance to the Atrium Café, where hot, cold, grilled, and rotisserie selections are available in a beautifully open setting at the ground level of a six-story atrium.

The Atrium Café is part of the **Discovery Center** (1999; Hammel Green and Abrahamson of Minneapolis and Keyes Condon Florence Architects, Washington, D.C.), an 80,000-square-ft, free-standing structure that opened in the West Court in the summer of 1999. The new Discovery Center reflects the architecture of the surrounding museum, which was built in 1911, with brick and stone walls, terrazzo flooring, and arched windows and doorways. The Samuel C. Johnson Theater, a state-of-the-art IMAX cinema, with a screen six-stories high, presents films on natural and cultural history. The museum's own IMAX 3D production, *Galapagos,* premiered here in the fall of 1999 for an extended stay. The entrance to the theater box office is on the first floor of the museum, just off the rotunda in the Native Cultures of the Americas Hall. Visitors can also enter the center on the ground floor, by taking the stairs or elevator in the café to the theater level.

In the center of hall is the Smithsonian **rai,** a circular stone, or "coin," resembling a giant doughnut. The stone was quarried in 1904 and sold to the Smithsonian in 1962 by a Balibat community on Yap, an island west of Guam.

The escalator leads to the rotunda on the first floor. On the south side of the escalators, in the area beneath the rotunda, is Baird Auditorium, where the museum presents films and slide lectures most Fridays at noon. Flanking the halls on either side of the auditorium are cases displaying **Birds of the District of Columbia Region.** This exhibit shows hundreds of mounted birds ranging from the Atlantic Ocean to the Allegheny Mountains.

Take the escalator to the first floor.

**First floor.** Rotunda. In the center of the rotunda is an **African bush elephant** standing on a platform that suggests the Angolan savanna. This bull was 50 years old when it was killed in 1955 by Hungarian big-game hunter J. J. Fenykovi in Angola. At the time it weighed eight tons, and 23 attendants were needed to carry the skin. It took Smithsonian taxidermists 16 months to create the model on which the skin is mounted. On display in the rotunda since 1959, the elephant has come to symbolize the Smithsonian's holdings.

With the elephant are plants and animals of the savanna, including a black-backed jackal scurrying into his den, a puff adder with raised head, a pack of dung beetles, and various birds, including the Lilac-Breasted Roller, whose raucous rak-rak sounds can be heard. Around the base of the platform, information stations tell the story of the species represented, with videos showing dung beetles carting away elephant dung to eat and build with (especially fascinating to kids), baboons swinging through the trees, and elephant families on the move.

The information desk is located in the southeast corner of the rotunda. Corridors to the east, west, northeast, and northwest lead into exhibits. To the south is the entrance from the Mall, flanked by two pairs of elevators. For chronological purposes, the best place to start is with the exhibit in the southeast corridor.

**Earliest Traces of Life.** This exhibit sketches the evolution of life on land from single-cell organisms into plants, amphibians, reptiles, and dinosaurs. The mural on the north entrance wall depicts Earth as scientists believe it looked 3.5 billion years ago. To the south of the entrance a time line beginning 4.6 billion years ago with the birth of the solar system chronicles the development of life on Earth. Displayed in the exhibit is one of the world's oldest fossils, a 3.5-billion-year-old mass called a stromatolite, which was built by microorganisms. Walk north into the next gallery.

**A Grand Opening: Fossils Galore.** This gallery focuses on the emergence of hard-shelled life (versus the previous era of only soft-bodied life), which occurred in the Paleozoic era, 570 million years ago. A U-shaped group of group of three cases at the center of the gallery displays fossils from the renowned Burgess Shale, sedimentary rock that preserves even delicate species from this transitional period in remarkable detail. Two fossils cut from a 440-million-year-old section of sea floor hang on the gallery's west wall. Thousands of specimens of animal and plant life are embedded in the sediment. Look closely to see the fossilized shells and wormlike creatures. To the east, a hall leads into a two-story room containing reconstructed dinosaurs. To the west, a hall returns to the rotunda. Continuing chronologically, walk east, then turn south.

**Conquest of Land.** This exhibit traces a series of adaptations made by early life forms. Discussed are lobe-finned and lung fish, creatures that could remain out of water longer than other species. There is a model of a eurypterid, one of the first species to make the transition from water to land and an ancestor of scorpions. Eurypterids are believed to have developed air-breathing abilities similar to those arachnids even though they lived in shallow water.

Follow the ramp south. The mural on the south wall depicts Earth 425 million years ago before life began to live on land. While the Silurian seas teamed with life, the mural illustrates a landscape without land creatures. A brief video shows the behavior of mudskippers, modern-day creatures resembling the eurypterid. Head east.

**Before the Dinosaurs.** This exhibition ties the development of the first forests and flowering plants to the emergence of early amphibians and reptiles. Models show how early plants evolved. Among the fossilized plants displayed are a sphenophyllis, a plant that lived 310 million years ago. The east end of the exhibit focuses on the development of amphibians such as Trimerorhachis and the Acroplous. Turn north.

**Reptiles—Masters of the Land.** This is the dinosaur exhibit. At the center of the room are reconstructed skeletons of several beasts including a Stegosaurus stenops, an Allosaurus, and a Triceratops elatus. Illustrated placards show how these beasts appeared with muscles and flesh, how they interacted with other dinosaurs, and what they might have eaten. Follow the hallway north into **Ancient Seas.** Backtrack to the entrance of the Ancient Seas exhibit, which traces the path of life's evolution in water.

The **Ancient Seas** exhibit begins in the Paleozoic era, 570–230 million years ago, when creatures with shells and hard skeletons, such as trilobites, brachiopods, and crinoids, were prominent. Just inside the entrance from the rotunda is a three-dimensional reconstruction of reef life 250 million years ago during the Mesozoic era. The exhibit details how early fish emerged 230–65 million years ago; a video depicts the emergence of land masses. With the beginning of the Cenozoic era, 65 million years ago, came the birth of whales, sea cows, seals, sea lions, mollusks, and clams.

Visitors in both the Ancient Seas and Reptiles—Masters of Land exhibits can peek into a working fossil lab showing Smithsonian scientists and volunteers cleaning fossils and performing various tests. Through the north doorways in the

Ancient Seas, Reptile—Masters of Land, and Fossil Plants exhibits is Mammals in the Limelight.

**Mammals in the Limelight.** This exhibit displays the skeletons of animals that lived between the time of dinosaurs and the Ice Age. Appearing about 200 million years ago, several of the mammals alive during the Mesozoic, Paleocene, and Eocene periods are reconstructed from skeletons dating 5–37 million years ago. Among the skeletons is a Stegomastoden, a tusked elephant from one million years ago. Small creatures such as canines and ancestral varieties of modern-day hoofed animals are reconstructed. Behind each display a mural illustrates what the animal probably looked like.

**Ice Age.** This gallery opens with a cast of a 24,800-year-old mammoth tusk engraved by a prehistoric man. This item illustrates both the emergence of man and his early dominance over the environment. Also at the entrance to the exhibit are Pleistocene horses. Among the other reconstructed skeletons are giant ground sloths, armadillos, and a saber-toothed cat. These animals appear similar to their modern-day counterparts. Perhaps the most dramatic skeleton is that of a woolly mammoth, a creature looking like a hairy elephant. A brief display details glaciers and land bridges, geological formations that enabled migrations. **Climax of the Ice Age: 20,000 Years Ago** addresses the causes and effects of ice ages.

**What's New in Human Evolution** features a time line tracing the history of man from Australopithecine to modern Homo sapiens. Displayed are early tools made from stones carved into blades, axes, and other sharp objects, as well as art objects such as wall paintings. The exhibit ends with a full-scale re-creation of a 70,000-year-old Neanderthal burial site. In the hallway north of the Ice Age exhibit are restrooms.

In the next hall is a major, new permanent exhibit, **African Voices.** This 6,500-square-ft exhibition examines the historic diversity, dynamism, and global influence of Africa's peoples and cultures within the realm of family, work, community, and the natural environment.

To enter the exhibit through its "official entrance," retrace your steps through the Ice Age, Mammals, and Ancient Seas exhibits, turn right (north), and walk through the Asian and Pacific Cultures gallery.

Throughout the exhibit, visitors find personal accounts from contemporary interviews and literary works, as well as cultural voices from proverbs, prayers, folktales, songs, and oral epics. Recorded voices, over 400 objects, powerful images, and creative interactive displays convey how people in Africa live their daily lives and confront the challenges of the 21st century.

The exhibition is laid out in the form of a rectangle, with a **History Corridor** running down the center and four thematic galleries opening off it: **Wealth in Africa, Living in Africa, Working in Africa,** and **Global Africa.** At the end of the History Corridor is Freedom Theater, and next to that is the Learning Center.

Those with very young children might want to consider entering the exhibit through its official exit, from the Ice Age dinosaur hall. To the right of this exit is the **Learning Center,** where touch-screen TVs explain in simple terms African history and culture and the conundrum of race in our own society. A wonderful introduction piece by Whoopi Goldberg explains to children the seemingly unexplainable—how race used to be considered a barometer of a person's worth. Looking at these may make it more interesting and more understandable for a child under 10 going through the exhibit.

Upon entering the exhibit from the official entrance, pick up a copy of *African Voices Family Guide,* which gets children involved in the exhibit through questions about what they're seeing. To the left of the entrance is a multiscreen television with scenes from African life. "Hear us, our African voices speak across a vast continent." Watching these scenes and listening to the multiple voices is an excellent introduction to the variety of the customs and lifestyles of this continent that encompasses 54 countries, over 800 languages, and 1,000 ethnic groups in a landmass three times the size of the United States.

To the right of the entrance is the **Focus Gallery,** a space dedicated to temporary exhibits. Through Dec 2000, the work of Nigerian sculptor Lamidi Olonade Fakeye is on display.

The History Corridor takes the visitor chronologically through the history of Africa, from the origins of human life to the present day. **Five Million Years Ago** tells the story of the beginnings of human life and includes among its displays a fisherman's knife that is 70,000–90,000 years old. **3100 B.C.E. to 350** highlights the civilizations that flourished along the Nile River—Nubia to the south and Egypt to the north—with murals depicting how these two cultures traded, warred, and intermarried.

On the right is the entrance to Wealth in Africa, where various objects demonstrate how exchanges of valued objects build relationships between people and also how valued objects represent Africans to their neighbors. Among the objects displayed are a Tunisian wedding headdress and tunic (mid-20C) made of cotton and wool, elaborately decorated with sequins and silver and gold threads. A Tunisian bride wears these when the marriage contract is signed and when she moves to her husband's house. Also on display are a Kibango staff (19C) made of wood, copper, and iron, with carved figures telling the story of a king's path to power, and a coffin in the shape of a KLM 747 jumbo jet made by Paa Joe, a master carpenter from Nungua, Ghana, where designer coffins have become common and are often in the shape of vehicles, animals, or farm produce.

Next to the coffin display is an exhibit about the currency of African countries, accompanied by a display giving children a chance to match the photos of elephants and giraffes with the currencies that feature those animals.

Wealth is also measured in items for trade or sale, like mud cloth from Mali, which uses mud dye to form elaborate designs on white cotton. Across from the currency exhibit is a display about mud cloth (now featured in runway fashions in Europe and America), how it is made, and the various designs that are used. For centuries, Bamana people in Mali have used mud cloth (also called *bògòlanfini*) to mark major life transitions. The patterns refer to Bamana culture and history.

Across from this is **Market Crossroads,** which re-creates the bustle of a market in Accra, Nigeria. A television screen continuously runs a film of the real market, while visitors examine the displays here of yams, kola nuts, and housewares that are for sale, as well as hear the voices of present-day merchants explaining how they make their living.

Next to the market display is a station with headsets where visitors can listen to a musical tour of the continent by pushing buttons in various areas on a map.

Return to the History Corridor where **200 B.C.E.–1400** tells the history of the ancient cities in Niger Valley and the valley's three successive empires—Ghana,

Mali, and Songhai—through murals and maps. **1086–1238** depicts the era when the African Muslims ruled Spain. On display are objects such as a wood lute (late 19C), also called an *oudh*, that was played with a quill from an eagle's feather and a 13C Spanish painting showing two Muslims playing chess.

Turn to the left, and Living in Africa, in order to see an *aqal*, a Somali portable house made of arched acacia roots and insulated with woven mats. On an accompanying video screen a Somali woman explains how the women of her tribe are in charge of erecting and dismantling these structures, which are carried from place to place on the backs of camels. Displayed next to this are two monumental wooden doors (c. 1900) from Zanzibar that were attached to a house made of coral stone. Traditionally, across the top of the doors the owner would have a proverb engraved.

Copper wall plaques are across from the doors along with masks representing Benin's warlike history as well as its carving crafts, with tribal chiefs depicted in martial stances. On the other side of this display, in the History Corridor, **1800s–early 1900s** tells how trade with the rest of the world transformed Africa. Exports such as elephant tusks and rubber helped pay for the continent's largest import, guns. The story told here relates how African rulers tried to maintain favorable terms of trade with Europeans while also maintaining control of their countries' destinies.

Next along the corridor is **1500s–1860s,** which chronicles the slave trade, begun by the Portuguese, fueled by wars between tribes on Africa's west coast, and supported by American traders. **1896** tells of Ethiopia's defeat of the invading Italian Army at the Battle of Adwa, a victory by Emperor Menelik II still celebrated in Ethiopia. At the end of the History Corridor is **Late 1800s–1990,** the story of colonialization yielding to independence in Africa as one by one the European powers withdrew, usually peacefully. Photographs on the walls show the first parliament to meet following Namibia's independence.

To the right, Working in Africa displays traditional crafts such as pottery and textiles, and films show scenes from one of Africa's biggest trades—tourism. There are also still photos of the traditional ceremony initiating adolescent Maasai boys into the warrior rank and a Kenyan man's face ruff (similar to a frame made of feathers) used during the ceremony.

To the left of 1896 is a display about slavery in the American South. The voices of African Americans speak the words of their ancestors, describing the horrors of slavery. Nineteenth-century manacles and shackles are displayed, along with pictures drawn by slaves depicting their brutal treatment. Next to this, in stark contrast, are the adornments worn by the celebrants of the Afro-Brazilian nature-based religions, which were developed between the 16C and 19C by the 3½–5 million slaves carried to Brazil from Africa. An elaborate head-to-toe straw-and-velvet body mask, worn to represent the god Omolu, and a broom are displayed, along with beautifully carved brass pieces, such as a sword, a fan, and a crown that was worn by female celebrants.

Next to this is a small photographic exhibit about African Americans in Washington, D.C., from the earliest free settlers to Frederick Douglass to Washington's current African American community.

To the right, at the end of the History Corridor, is **Freedom Theater,** a semicircular theater showing two films: "Atlantic Slave Trade" (18 minutes), about the slaves brought to North, Central, and South America, and "Struggle for Freedom" (20 minutes), about the country of South Africa's hard-earned triumph over oppression. Freedom Theater is part of Global Africa, which addresses the challenges facing Africa today, including the very difficult issue of health care. A film shows how nurses bring health care to the continent's most remote corners, where children and adults die of AIDS, malaria, and diarrhea at alarming rates.

Straight ahead from Global Africa and a little to the right, next to the exit, is the Learning Center and its touch-screen TVs.

Walk back through African Voices to tour the Asian and Pacific Cultures gallery.

**Asian and Pacific Cultures.** This gallery focuses on the daily life of Asian, Indian, and Pacific cultures. The Asian gallery has cultural objects from Japan, China, and Korea. A map on the west wall lists dozens of Asian languages. Among the exhibits are Chinese kitchen utensils, a shrine to Confucius, ivory art pieces, and a re-creation of rooms in a Korean house. Other cases display Chinese writing instruments such as printing blocks, inkstones, and calligraphy brushes, as well as musical instruments such as a brass hooked trumpet, a long zither (lute), and pan pipes. Among the exhibits are a model of a Japanese Shinto shrine and textiles from the Ryukyu Islands. A case on the north side of the gallery re-creates a famous scene from *Second Return to the Palace,* a Chinese opera. The woman, representing the queen mother, is emotionally torn between her loyalty to her father, the male on the left, and her love for her son. In another case, just inside the gallery's entrance, is a suit of Japanese Samurai armor. The suit was presented to President Theodore Roosevelt on Sept 5, 1905, by the emperor of Japan after the Portsmouth Peace Conference, which ended the Russo-Japanese War. The helmet was constructed between 1532 and 1555. The face mask, called a *mempo,* was made between 1800 and 1854. The suit was used between 1850 and 1875.

The latest gift on view in the gallery is a collection of contemporary ceramics made by Korean artists and donated to the museum by the National Museum of Korea.

In the hallway west of Asian Cultures are several displays. The trade map on the east wall catalogs the contributions made by Asian cultures to Western civilization through trade, including the provision of cotton, flax, hemp, and animals such as goldfish, pigs, and sheep.

Colorful textiles from India, Pakistan, and Bangladesh are in a case south of the stairwell. Displayed in the center of this foyer is the ceremonial costume of the Fijians, a black-and-white cloth called *masi,* which is fashioned from bark. Tribal chiefs wore these valuable possessions when hosting guests.

The Asian Cultures gallery continues with Thai craftwork. Many of the items displayed were gifts from Thai kings to U.S. presidents during the 19C, including silver snuffboxes and dishes, lacquered boxes inlaid with mother-of-pearl, and enameled teapots. A Sindhi home in Pakistan is re-created on the west wall. Stringed musical instruments from India such as *chikara,* an *esrar,* and an *ektara* are also displayed.

The Pacific Cultures area to the south focuses on the native people of Indonesia, Melanesia, Polynesia, Micronesia, Australia, New Zealand, and the Philippines. Cases exhibit Malaysian shadow puppets, Australian aborigine tools, and cultural objects such as wigs, a cord used to strangle enemies, and a chief's turban from Fuji. Models of boats, reed hats, and fish traps represent Micronesia's fishing industry. A map just north of the rotunda entrance to the exhibit pinpoints the Pacific Islands groups: Indonesia, Melanesia, Micronesia, and Polynesia. Greeting visitors at the north entrance is a 19C statue from Easter Island weighing several tons. Slightly northeast of the statue, convenient to the rotunda, an enclosed courtyard leads to new restrooms, including a wheelchair-accessible restroom open to both men and women.

Enter the rotunda. The gallery to the west of the escalators and the Pacific Cultures area is for special exhibitions. Continue west to the entrance of the next gallery.

**Native Cultures of the Americas.** The main entrance to the Johnson IMAX Theater can be found just inside this hall to the west. The exhibit itself, which is organized by region, begins with Eskimos. Displayed are Arctic and subarctic Eskimo clothing, weapons, and sleds. Two new exhibit cases flank the theater entrance. One case illustrates the diversity of native peoples with a beaded Athapaskan chief's coat, a Yup'ik haw mask, a Tlingit chief's rattle, and objects from other cultural groups. In the companion case, finely woven baskets, an open-crowned hunting visor, gutskin bags, and an ancient burial mask will help tell the story of the native people of the Aleutian Islands. The Eastern Woodlands culture section follows. A birch bark canoe, baskets, clay pipes, and straw dolls are among the representative items. One case displays early lacrosse sticks. Originally, lacrosse balls were buckskin, and the sticks were fashioned from wood and leather netting. A diorama shows Captain John Smith trading with the Powhatan Indians on the James River in 1607. A small plaque tells the important role these Native Americans played in saving the early settlers from starvation.

Made from 14 buffalo hides and decorated with porcupine quills, the Plains Indian tipi, in a case on the west wall, was part of the Smithsonian's Centennial Expo in 1876. Other Plains Indian items include ceremonial costumes, examples of quillwork and beadwork, and feather bonnets. Clothing, armor, and weapons represent tribes from the Northwest Coast. The gallery leads to a corridor that runs west to east.

To the east of this exit, a shellacked black marlin hangs above the black marlin exhibit. A marlin skull and attached bill are displayed in a case. A three-minute video shows ways scientists learn about marlin and other fish.

Follow the corridor west, continuing with the Native Cultures of the Americas gallery. Two totem poles stand at the entrance to this gallery. The poles flank either side of a case displaying masks from several Northwest (U.S.) tribes. An elevator bank is north of this display.

Pomo Indian baskets, shell money, ceremonial costumes, and a placard discussing food-gathering practices represent tribes from California. The section featuring Southwestern tribes displays Florida Seminole Indian clothing, Navaho blankets, a diorama of a Hopi Indian apartment, and Zuni pots. Other exhibits focus on pueblo construction and the importance of corn. A Mohawk basket maker talks about her craft in a five-minute video.

In the midst of case upon case of earth-tone objects is an exhibit of dramatic, skeleton-like papier-mâché figures from Mexico, outfitted with brightly colored blankets, sombreros, and guitars. Store owners in Mexico City would attract customers to the market on Holy Saturday, the day before Easter Sunday, by using firecrackers to explode these figures representing Judas.

Ornamental fans, religiously significant figures, and a variety of baskets are featured in the section devoted to Middle and South American tribes. On display are colorful blankets and belts woven by Chile's Aracanian women, skilled weavers of sheep and llama wool.

**Discovery Room.** Tucked into the northwest corner of this wing, the Discovery Room offers hands-on activities for adults and children. Here visitors can handle artifacts and objects similar to the ones in the museum's exhibits. Walk south.

**Tigers!**—on view indefinitely—explores the behavior of tigers in their native habitat. The diorama features a tiger lunging after a deer. The pouncing Indian tiger, killed in its homeland after savagely attacking numerous people, was given to the museum in 1967. Fiberglass whiskers replace the original hairs plucked by visitors. One video highlights the conservation efforts at Chitwan National Park in Nepal, and the other video follows a Bengal tiger hunting his prey.

**Great Mammals of North America** closed in Sept 1999 to accommodate the creation of a new Hall of Mammals. This gallery, and two adjoining hallways, featured dioramas of mammals—warm-blooded animals with backbones and hair who nurse their young. The exhibit also addressed classification and adaptation. The hallways included mounted bison, mountain lions, wolves, a grizzly bear, American elk, a black bear family, moose, and bighorn sheep.

Walk north and turn west.

**Sea Life: Exploring Marine Ecosystems.** The ecosystems of a kelp forest along Maine's rocky coast and a Caribbean reef are simulated in this gallery. A number of computer kiosks and hands-on activities illustrate the impact of humans on such fragile environments. Also, a 92 ft long blue whale hangs from the ceiling. Continue west into **At Home in the Sea,** which focuses on squid, walruses, and sea otters. Visitors can explore these animals' habitats and eating habits, and view specimens. Exit this gallery through the north doorway. Turn east.

**Birds of the World.** This gallery features hundreds of mounted birds. The first case, to the north, displays large birds of African marshes collected and donated to the museum by Colonel Theodore Roosevelt, who was later elected president of the United States. Specimens represent each of the continents as well as provide examples of migratory birds and birds with unusual feeding and reproductive habits. Between cases containing birds from Madagascar and New Zealand is a case of extinct birds. Structure and evolution—how birds evolved from reptiles—is discussed in a case west of the one featuring Australian birds. Next are the birds of Asia and Africa, as well as a case about migration. Birds are classified into 27 orders and 171 families. The main group of 26 orders is exhibited on the north wall. On the south wall is the remaining order: songbirds. Birds of Europe and South America are displayed in the cases continuing east. Species characteristic of North America and birds of "Paradise" follow. A magnificent male peacock is on display. In the last case, just before the exit into the rotunda, there are birds of the Antarctic: a family of penguins.

Exit the Birds of the World Gallery into the rotunda. Turn north and climb the stairs immediately to the left to the second floor.

**Second floor.** At the top of the stairs walk west.

**South America: Continent and Culture.** This exhibit illustrates man's relationship with the Earth by focusing on four environmental zones in South America: grasslands, tropical forests, mountain valleys, and coastlands. Each area shows how man used the region's resources during the prehistoric, colonial, and modern eras.

The **grasslands** of southeast South America are discussed first. The exhibit opens with a diorama of a Tehuelche Indian on horseback using boleadoras, triangle-shaped weapons made from rope and stones. In the 19C Indians in Patagonia hunted prey such as rheas and llamas by throwing these weapons. Placards explain man's farming and hunting practices.

Included in the **tropical forest** display are ceremonial dance costumes of Waiwai men: headdresses, nose ornaments, armbands, and dance paddles. Other Waiwai artifacts are spears and bows, which accompany a description of Waiwai hunting practices. A case on the south wall displays Waiwai daily dress: necklaces strung with monkey teeth, and a woman's glass-bead apron. Large vessels and pottery shards of Napo and Marajoara tribes are in a case on the north wall.

A re-creation of an Andean market is part of the **mountain valley** section. Two women seated on burlap sacks barter vegetables; a man, drinking *hicha,* an Andean beer, offers an alpaca for trade; a market stall features handcrafts such as pottery, dolls, sandals, and blankets. A nearby case displays artifacts from Incan sites. On the south wall is a re-creation of a stucco-and-stone colonial church façade. Behind the glass arches are examples of primitive metallurgy—copper pins, silver animals, gold figurines, and bronze axheads—and various textiles.

A wooden sailing vessel from Playas, Ecuador, is beached on a re-created shoreline in the **Pacific coastlines** area. This and other objects demonstrate the indigenous peoples' use of the sea's resources. Shells, artwork inspired by sea creatures, and various tools used to fish are among the items exhibited. Walk west to the end of the corridor.

**Origins of Western Cultures.** This exhibit links the development of civilizations at the end of the Ice Age—11,000 years ago—to those of 500 years ago in western Asia, northern Africa, and Europe. The basis of cultures shifted from hunting to farming and from camps to cities. The exhibit opens with artifacts from the Ice Age, spanning a period from 30,000 to 11,000 years ago.

A new photo exhibit, **Frozen In Time: The Iceman,** describes the discovery and study of a 5,300-year-old mummy frozen in an Alpine glacier. Depicted is how scientists, using a wide range of techniques, are reconstructing one individual's life during Europe's Copper Age. The exhibit features a touchable replica of the copper ax blade found with the iceman's remains.

A diorama shows two cave dwellers creating a cave painting. There are tools made from from animal bones and explanations of humanity's shift from hunting to farming. A diorama of an early farming community, Ali-Kosh in the Zagros Mountains of Iran, shows women weaving reeds into a roof to cover a mud-brick dwelling being built by several men. Nearby is a case of vessels fired in early kilns and chipped stone tools such as saws and projectile points.

**From Village to City** covers the period from 5,000 to 2,500 B.C. Stone woodworking tools, daggers, and axes from western Europe are displayed. This section of the exhibit chronicles the emergence of cities such as Mesopotamia. A small theater continually shows a film featuring Gilgamesh (a legendary king of early Mesopotamia), Bronze Age tombs, and topics related to ancient Egypt.

The next section of the exhibit portrays the development of political structures and organizations. Cases display school and economic tablets and ownership seals as well as highly decorated Egyptian coffins and death masks. In addition to two re-creations of tombs from the early Bronze Age (3,050–2,950 B.C.), there are cases of Aegean sculpture from 3,000 to 2,000 B.C. and objects from Mycenaean Greece, 1,500 to 1,100 B.C. The Greeks were active traders.

The final section of the exhibit, **Trade and Empire,** discusses the emergence of bazaars and nomadic traditions. There were two basic elements to the nomadic tradition: tents and animal herds. Both people and animals adapted to frequent movement. Among the artifacts on display are Byzantine pottery shards, ancient coins and seals, works of Roman glass, and Ptolemaic paper. A theater at the end of the gallery shows films about ancient Egypt.

At press time visitors to the Western Cultures Gallery had to retrace their steps through the exhibit to continue with other exhibits. Head south.

**Bones.** This exhibit opens with a case displaying skeletons of marsupials such as a koala bear and a gray kangaroo. Using models and skeletons, some cases address various evolutionary adaptations made by animals. The exhibit displays hundreds of skeletons from every order (a scientific classification of the animal kingdom), including primates, rabbits, bats, even- and odd-hoofed mammals, running birds, amphibians, and reptiles.

**Reptiles.** The first case presents the origins of herpetology, the study of reptiles. On the west wall is a diorama of the Florida Everglades, a region offering subtropical climate and habitat for these cold-blooded creatures. Among the vertebrates displayed are an alligator, several snakes, and frogs. Among the mounted reptiles are Komodo dragons, a king cobra, and iguanas.

**O. Orkin Insect Zoo.** Visitors will hear the sounds of crickets, katydids, and cicadas before reaching the gallery. One of the most popular areas of the museum, the insect zoo receives five million visitors annually. The zoo focuses on exotic and common insects as well as the role insects play in the world and their relationships with plants, animals, and humans. Live specimens from ponds, deserts, rain forests, and backyards are kept at the zoo. Visitors can peer at black widow and tarantula spiders, centipedes, hermit crabs, praying mantids, and scorpions. Hands-on exhibits include a 14 ft model of an African termite mound that kids can crawl through. There is a live beehive in a wall built to resemble a tree; a tube links the hive to the natural world, and hundreds of bees buzz back and forth. A rain forest is re-created at the end of the exhibit. The sound system plays simulations of the sounds of the upper and lower rain forest canopy. There are three daily **tarantula feedings:** Mon–Fri 10:30, 11:30, and 1:30; weekends and holidays 11:30, 12:30, and 1:30.

Return to the rotunda and walk counterclockwise around the rotunda.

**Janet Annenberg Hooker Hall of Geology, Gems, and Minerals.** This hall is a comprehensive Earth-science complex that explores the solar system and topics such as volcanoes, earthquakes, metals, and mineral formation. The interactive exhibits include hands-on displays and multimedia presentations.

There are three entrances to the hall. Proceed to the middle entrance, the **Harry Winston Gallery.** There are six natural treasures located in the room. In the northwest corner the 1,300-pound quartz crystal formed by silicon and oxygen merging in the hot water under the Earth's crust was extracted from the Otjua mine in Karibib, Nigeria. Walk east toward the 324-pound sheet of nearly pure copper found in the White Pine mine of Michigan. The black areas on the sheet are rock. If the sheet were to be melted down, it could coat more than 2.5

million pennies. At the center of the room is the 45.52-carat **Hope Diamond,** the world's largest faceted blue diamond.

> ### Washington Notes
> The Hope Diamond has long been considered cursed. One of the first persons to wear the diamond—Marie Antoinette, wife of King Louis XVI of France—was executed during the French Revolution. Mrs. Evalyn Walsh McLean was among the last of the private owners. She too experienced coincidental tragedies. Shortly after purchasing the diamond, McLean's mother-in-law unexpectedly died. Her young son was hit by a car and died soon thereafter. Later, her husband became involved in the Teapot Dome scandal and went bankrupt. He was declared insane and eventually died in an asylum. McLean sold the jewel to Harry Winston, a New York jeweler, who donated the piece to the Smithsonian in 1958, where, mineral scientists say, it has brought nothing but good luck.

In the southwest corner of the room is a slab of granite gneiss from Sri Lanka. Its various pink and gray shades reveal that this specimen was created by a combination of layers from the Earth's crust. Also in this corner is a sandstone concretion that looks like an artist's creation. It was discovered in Fountainbleau, France, and is a natural formation of tiny crystals of quartz sand. Walk east to the Tucson meteorite. These two sections once formed the core of an asteroid 4.6 billion years old. They were found in the 1700s in the area now known as Arizona. Blacksmiths used the pieces as anvils.

Walk south into the gallery that displays a dazzling selection of gems from **the National Gem Collection.** The collection includes more than 7,500 gemstones ranging in size from one-half carat to a 23,000-carat topaz. Among the displayed objects are "celebrity jewels," such as the 172-diamond necklace and diamond-and-turquoise tiara given by Napoleon (1769–1821) to his second wife, Empress Marie Louise. There are also raw and cut gems such as sapphires, emeralds, and rubies. Highlights include the **Hooker Emerald Brooch,** a 75.47-carat Colombian emerald surrounded by 138 diamonds weighing a total of about 13 carats; the **Hooker Diamond,** a starburst design of 50 matched diamonds totaling 24.5 carats, designed by Cartier, Inc.; the **Star of Asia,** a 330-carat sapphire noted for its rich color and large size, which once belonged to the Maharajah of Jodhpur; the **Chalk Emerald,** a 37.8-carat Colombian emerald nestled in a 15-carat cluster of 60 pea-shaped diamonds; as well as the **Pink Diamond,** 2.9 carats, and the **Red Diamond,** 5.03 carats, both notable for their rare color. A large crystal ball is also exhibited. Turn east into the Minerals and Gems Gallery.

This gallery displays specimens from the 300,000 items in the **National Gem Collection.** The exhibit, which discusses how fluid, heat, and pressure create and change gems and minerals, organizes objects by shape, diversity, growth, and color. For visitors with limited time, follow the **Fast Track tour** that runs the length of this and the following galleries down the center of each room. This route covers key geologic themes and takes visitors past highlights of geological specimens. Adjoining alcoves provide more in-depth information than the regular exhibit. The case addressing shape informs visitors that gems are shaped by their atoms, which link together in identical, repeating units. Specimens include pyrite, calcite, and wulfenite. Atoms also determine color by absorbing or reflecting light. Impurities in stone give the same minerals different shades. There is also a case of **Amazing Gems,** those which have unique characteristics such as shimmering surfaces. Pegamatites are coarse-grained rocks created by molten rock or magma beneath the Earth's surface. Specimens include beryllium, phosphates, topaz, and tourmaline.

To the south visitors can walk through pockets of re-created mineral veins in the **Mine Gallery** to see how ores are extracted. Visitors see a zinc mine, a semiprecious gem mine, a copper mine, and a lead mine.

Turn north and proceed into the **Plate Tectonics and Meteorites Galleries.** The **Plate Tectonics Gallery** explains how geological phenomena such as earthquakes and volcanoes are the result of shifting plates of crust on the Earth's surface. A theater shows films about the creation of land masses through these processes.

Walk west into the **Moon, Meteorites, and Solar System Gallery.** Through films, interactive exhibits, and touchable specimens, the gallery explores the birth of our solar system. Rocks from Mars, which scientists believe fell to Earth more than 13 million years ago, and rocks from the Moon are displayed. Visitors can also touch meteorites, see effects of meteorite impacts, and learn how the Earth and its moon were formed.

Return to the rotunda through the west doorway.

Exit the National Museum of Natural History from the Mall exit. Walk west on Madison Dr to the National Museum of American History.

## National Museum of American History

14th St and Constitution Ave N.W. ☎ 357-2700 or 357-1729 (TTY). Web: www.americanhistorysi.edu. Open daily 10–5:30. Closed Christmas Day. Extended spring and summer hours determined annually. Admission: free. Times and topics for guided tours available at the information desks daily 10–4. Tours for the visually impaired Mon–Fri 10–2 (must be arranged one week in advance). ☎ 357-1481 or 357-1563 (TTY). Loop-amplification in the auditorium for the hearing impaired. Sign language and oral interpreters. Wheelchairs available.

At the Hands-On Science Center children and adults can perform wet chemistry experiments, measure radioactive hot spots, and perform other experiments. Open Tues–Fri 12:30–5; Sat–Sun 10–5. Closed Mon and holidays. Children under 13 must be accompanied by an adult. Tickets available on a first-come basis at the center's door. At the Hands-On History Room kids can play with 19C toys such as mechanical piggy banks and old-fashioned bicycles. Open Tues–Sun 12–3. Tickets available at the room's entrance on a first-come basis. Children ages 5–12 must be accompanied by an adult. No children under 5.

Restrooms, telephones, ATM. Cafeteria and Palm Court Ice Cream Parlor, which serves sandwiches and light refreshments. Photography and video are permitted in the museum with hand held cameras. Some exceptions exist, so check at the information desk.

The National Museum of American History (1964; Steinman, Cain & White), formerly the Museum of History and Technology, focuses on the history and heritage of American culture and the American experience. The museum offers exhibitions about American arts and crafts, industry, agriculture, armed forces, and political history, as well as cultural history.

**Highlights:** Some of the permanent exhibits include the original Star-Spangled

Banner flag, first ladies' gowns, and a Model T Ford. Items from popular American television programs on display include Archie Bunker's chair, Howdy Doody, and Oscar the Grouch. Favorite items in the Icons of American Culture exhibit are Dorothy's ruby red slippers from *The Wizard of Oz*, Dizzy Gillespie's trumpet, and a baseball autographed by Babe Ruth.

Preserving the Star-Spangled Banner allows visitors to follow the progress of the three-year conservation of the flag through floor-to-ceiling glass walls that look into the conservation laboratory. The conservation process is slated for completion in 2002, at which time a new exhibition will open, featuring the flag that flew over Fort McHenry in 1814. Communities in a Changing Nation explores the concept of the promised land through three distinct groups: Jewish immigrants in Cincinnati, industrial workers and managers in Bridgeport, and free blacks and slaves in Charleston.

For kids, the museum offers two interactive labs: the Hands-On Science Center and the Hands-On History Room. The information desk has four family guides. Two are related to specific exhibits and geared to younger children; the other two present overviews of the museum that are geared to older children.

### History

Around the turn of the century, the National Museum established the Department of Engineering and Industries to document the history of technology, invention, and engineering. Objects in the collection included items from the National Cabinet of Curiosities, a collection that was transferred to the Smithsonian from the U.S. Patent Office in 1858 (and again in 1903 and 1926), and exhibits from the 1876 Centennial Expo in Philadelphia. The staff continued to amass thousands of objects for the Smithsonian.

Leonard Carmichael succeeded Alexander Wetmore on Jan 2, 1953, when Wetmore stepped down to resume his work with the Natural History Museum's Division of Birds. The seventh secretary of the Smithsonian had definite plans for the institution, as well as for the newly established National Museum of History and Technology. He immediately began lobbying Congress for a building to house the new museum. In June 1955 Congress appropriated funds to erect the National Museum of History and Technology Building on the west side of the National Museum of Natural History.

Construction progressed smoothly and the building was dedicated on Jan 22, 1964, nine years after building began. In the early 1970s the museum acquired the archives of the Science Service, a wire service founded in 1921 to popularize science. The collection included thousands of photographs about such subjects as civil and mechanical engineering, medicine, and chemistry.

In Oct 1980, to better reflect its mission, the Museum of History and Technology changed its name to the National Museum of American History. The museum is responsible for preserving, researching, and exhibiting all aspects of American history and culture. In addition to the artifacts, the museum makes a concerted effort to represent American history through music, storytelling, and other public programs.

## Exterior

The building, a monolithic Beaux-Arts structure, is faced with rose-white Tennessee marble. Located on the west side of the building is an original amphitheater and a 19C bandstand from Illinois that features pastel colors and ginger-bread detailing. Outside the Mall entrance, which leads to the second floor, stands *Infinity* (1967; José de Riviera). The sculpture turns very slowly, completing a full revolution every six minutes. The piece was the first item of abstract art commissioned by the federal government. Constitution Ave provides access to the first floor. *Gwenfritz* (Alexander Calder), a 40 ft tall sculpture by Alexander Calder, is located at Constitution Ave and 14th St.

## Interior

**Lower level.** The cafeteria is located at the west end of this level. At the east end are the security office plus the bookstore, which sells books about American history, political science, and culture; games and toys; music; folk art; and jewelry. An ATM is at the foot of the stairs, near the elevators.

**First floor.** The Carmichael Auditorium is located south of the **West Virginia Country Store and Post Office,** an actual working U.S. post office dating from the 1850s. The post office is open Mon–Fri 9:15–5:15; it's closed Sat and Sun. Across the lobby is the Taylor Gallery, which is used for special exhibitions. The information booth is located in the center of the lobby. Walk south.

**A Material World.** At the center of the museum's first floor, this exhibit displays more than 600 objects designed to teach visitors about the materials commonly used in art and manufacturing and how these reflect and are affected by economics, politics, and society. Rather than documenting who used an object or what it was used for, this exhibit focuses on what it is made of. Some of the materials represented are: wood, cast iron, steel, stainless steel, aluminum, polyester, and plastics. This exhibit is intended to be a precursor to the museum's other exhibits: to get visitors to consider what materials have been used during various points in history and why. Exhibits surround an inlaid marble compass in the floor. A Materials Panorama chronologically displays everyday items such as fans, telephones, a movie projector, a jukebox, surfboard, and television, illustrating how materials and design have evolved from the 1700s to the 1980s. There are also bicycles from 1869 to 1953, such as the 1869 Velocipede made from hickory, iron, and bronze, as well as a 1953 Schwinn Panther composed of steel, rubber, and plastic. Also displayed are washing machines. The set opens with the "Union" (1860), a cast-iron basin with a wood-handled press. This exhibition is expected to be dismantled sometime between 2000 and 2001.

To the south are the **Palm Court Ice Cream Parlor** and restrooms. The parlor serves ice cream sundaes as well as soups, salads, and sandwiches.

Turn east and enter the East Wing, where A Material World continues. On the left is the *Swamp Rat XXX,* the first drag racer to exceed 270 mph and the winner of major races in 1986–87, including the National Hot Rod Association's World Championship. Designer Don Garlits employed aerodynamic and space-age materials such as Kevlar, carbon fiber, and aluminum alloys to achieve the car's light weight. An accompanying video addresses the design and materials involved in building dragsters.

At the east end of the hall is **John Bull,** the oldest locomotive in operating condition. Built for the Camden and Amboy Railroad of New Jersey by R. Stephenson and Company in 1841, this self-propelled engine pulled freight and passengers between New York and Philadelphia until 1865. The locomotive is positioned on the

Philadelphia and Reading Railroad Bridge, built in 1845 from an innovative design that coupled iron and wood.

**Hall of Agriculture.** This exhibit displays the machines used to plant, harvest, and plow American farmlands. At the entrance is the International Harvester Model 1486 (1979), a tractor owned by Gerald McCathern of Hereford, Texas. McCathern used it to plow his fields before driving it 1,800 miles to Washington, D.C., to participate in the 1979 American Agriculture Movement demonstration (See "Washington Notes" in "Department of Agriculture" section). This tractor features modern technology such as a 156-horsepower, diesel, turbo-charged engine; 12 gears; and air-conditioning; an AM/FM radio; and a cassette deck. Just inside the exhibit is a Huber Steam Tractor (1924), which burned 100 to 150 pounds of coal per hour but could only travel at 2 mph. Behind this tractor is a case of about 50 patented varieties of barbed wire used by cattle ranchers and farmers to confine animals and protect crops. Next to this case is a brass sphere, the Borden's Vacuum Pan. In 1853 Gail Borden developed condensed milk in this pan. This was an important step for the dairy industry as it allowed milk to be powdered and stored without refrigeration.

The largest piece of equipment in the hall is the monstrous Combined Harvester-Thresher (1886). Designed by Benjamin Holt, who later founded Caterpillar Tractor, this combine had to be pulled by 20 horses. It was used to cut and winnow crops. Other machinery in this area includes: a colonial wooden plow, an 1887 cradle scythe, the 1942 "Old Red" harvester that ushered in the end of labor-intensive cotton production, and a 1924 John Deer. Exit to the south and turn left.

**American Maritime Enterprise.** The history of America's water-borne commerce is the focus of this exhibit. There are more than 100 ship models from oceangoing ships to those used on lakes, rivers, and canals. Among them are the *Mayflower* and modern cargo ships. The power plant from the 1804 *Little Juliana*, and machinery salvaged from the U.S. Coast Guard tender *Oak* are in a reconstructed engine room. Other exhibits focus on wartime shipbuilding, luxury liners, whaling vessels and commerce, China trade, and the life of a seaman. One highlight is a walk-in model of a 1970s Towboat Pilot House. Towboats are used by river pilots to push barges. An accompanying video illustrates how these boats work and contribute to commerce. In a section called **Preventing Disasters,** there is a lighthouse's medium-size Fresnel lens (c. 1872), a lens incorporating several prisms that project an intense light beam from a small light inside the lens. This lens served on Bolivar Point at the entrance of Galveston Bay from the 1870s to 1933. It crowned the 117 ft tower and could be seen from 21 miles away. Also here is a 1930s lighted bell buoy that was once stationed at the mouth of the Elk River, near Turkey Point in the Chesapeake Bay. As the buoy rolled with the waves, the clapper of its bell would sound. Two hatches in the base provide access to the batteries that powered its light. Exit to the south and turn left.

**Road Transportation.** The museum owns more than 40 antique cars, including the 1893 Duryea, the 1894 Haynes, and a **1913 Model T Ford.** The museum also displays vehicles from earlier times, such as a 1770 horse-drawn carriage. Other road vehicles include: velocipedes, high-wheelers, and motorcycles. Some highlights are daredevil Evel Knieval's customized 1972 Harley-Davidson, which was used for several of his stunts, and General Motors' Sunraycer

(1987), an aluminum-and-Kevlar, solar-powered car that won the 1987 World Solar Challenge by two and a half days in Australia. Although the car averaged 41.6 mph during the race, this vehicle later set the world's solar-powered car speed record at 75.276 mph. There are 8,800 solar cells on its body. The forerunner to the modern motorcycle was the Roper Steam Velocipede (c. 1869; Sylvester Roper), a steam-powered vehicle made from iron and wood. Beside it is a Harley-Davidson motorcycle (1942), a model popular for Army service, recreational use, police service, and with couriers. This example was built for the president of Guatemala. To the right of the Harley is a blue, bullet-shaped Yamaha SR185 (1982) motorcycle that was modified by the Rifle Fairing Company. This model achieved 372 miles per gallon in the 1983 Vetter High-Mileage Contest. (The vehicles in this exhibit are periodically rotated in and out of the hall so that the museum can display more of its collection.)

Turn north. On the right the White Motor Bus (1917), a 15-passenger bus used on Charles Street in Baltimore from 1917 to 1922, has solid rubber tires and acetylene headlamps, which were later replaced by electric lamps. Continue north to the Freightliner Tractor (1950). This diesel engine tractor features a cab-over-engine design that permits the driver to haul longer trailers yet remain within legal length limits. Along the north wall are cases of bus fares used from 1920 to 1960 and a 1948 Tucker Sedan. One of the most unique vehicles in this hall is **Dave's Dream.** David Jaramillo bought this car in 1978 and began converting it into a lowrider. *Lowriders,* a term which defines both the driver and car, are vehicles with modified frames and suspensions that drop the car to just inches above the pavement. These cars feature a rebuilt engine that is usually chromed, a hydraulic system, and reupholstered interiors; this model features red velour. Exit Road Transportation through the east doorway and walk south.

**Railroad Hall.** Several railroad cars and engines are displayed in this gallery. The *1401* is a Pacific-type steam locomotive built in 1926 for the Southern Railway. At one time this class was among the most popular for passenger trains. The 1851 *Pioneer,* weighing 12½ tons, was used for 40 years on the Cumberland Valley Railroad in Pennsylvania. Other trains in the hall include an eight-wheel passenger coach from 1836, a Seattle cable car from 1898, and a diorama of New York's Third Avenue in 1880 with models of vehicles used in urban transit. Walk up the stairs to the west.

**Civil Engineering: Bridges and Tunnels.** Visitors see the evolution of bridge and tunnel design and building materials from Roman days to the present. Among the displays are models of arch, truss, cantilever, and suspension bridges. Other models include famous bridges and tunnels such as Pont du Gard in France, built between 27 B.C. and A.D. 14, and New York's Lincoln Tunnel and Brooklyn Bridge. Another highlight of this gallery is a walk-through model of a 19C English timber tunnel. Dioramas illustrate how rock beneath London was hollowed to create subway tunnels. Walk West.

**Power Machinery.** Displayed in this gallery are early examples of the attempt to harness power. Visitors learn about the development of engines and see models and full-size steam, Diesel, and gasoline engines, steam pumps, steam turbines, and internal combustion engines. Proceed north.

**Electricity.** This exhibition has three distinct sections tracing the history of electrical power. The beginning section, **First Views,** focuses on Benjamin Franklin and electrostatics. Next, **Lightning a Revolution** highlights Thomas

Edison and the development of electric power. Finally, the **Demonstration Center** offers periodic demonstrations of electrical devices. Among the displays is a 1908 vacuum cleaner, an electric elevator, Westinghouse watt meters used to gauge electrical consumption, and early generators and transformers. The collection of light bulbs illustrates the evolution of this common item. Continue west to the hallway and turn south.

**Engines of Change: The American Industrial Revolution, 1790–1860.** This exhibit takes visitors through the American Industrial Revolution, a period of dramatic change. Its six sections focus on the lives and products of craftspeople, factory workers, inventors, and entrepreneurs who were affected for better or for worse by the modernization of society. The gallery opens with a re-creation of the Crystal Palace, the site of the 1851 World's Fair in London. American technology won international recognition at this historic event. Cases feature American medal-winning inventions such as the Colt Revolver (patented in 1836) and the Burt Solar Compass (1836). In the center of this anteroom, hidden by a red velvet screen, is the *Greek Slave* (1843; Hiram Powers), a statue of a female nude originally displayed at the Corcoran Gallery. Despite great controversy (see "Washington Notes" in the "Corcoran Gallery" section), critics awarded Powers accolades for its form and style. Engines of Change traces the evolution of America from an agricultural society to a manufacturing society. The focus is on factories and textile mills. More than 250 objects are displayed, in addition to a re-created 1850 machine shop and a clockmaker's shop. Linked to this gallery is **On Time,** a new permanent exhibition that opened in Nov 1999, the 116th anniversary of Standard Railway Time and the beginning of uniform national time in America. On Time explores the ways Americans have measured, used, and thought about time during the past 300 years. Many of the displayed objects will be "virtually" showcased via interactive computer stations.

Return to the main hallway. Proceed west through A Material World. Continue west to the escalators. Displayed in cases at the bottom of the escalators is a rotating exhibit of items from popular television shows. The collection includes Oscar the Grouch *(Sesame Street),* Archie Bunker's chair *(All in the Family),* one of Mr. Rogers's sweaters, and Howdy Doody, the beloved puppet from a 1950s kids' show. Walk north.

**Information Age: People, Information, and Technology.** This exhibit explores the impact of information technology on American society during the past 150 years. The gallery itself uses state-of-the-art technology as a teaching tool. Visitors receive a bar-coded brochure upon entering the exhibit. A computer network links the interactive workstations, video, film, and audio recordings throughout the gallery. After using any of the stations, visitors can scan their bar code through a supermarket-like scanner. At the end of the exhibit they receive a printout outlining the steps they took through the gallery. Among the activities available are fingerprint analysis and talking over the same telephone wire used by Alexander Graham Bell.

The gallery opens with **People, Information, and Technology, 1835–1939.** This section addresses information processing and the emergence of instantaneous communication. Visitors can listen to radio programs such as *The Shadow, Burns and Allen,* and *Superman.* **World War II: The Information War, 1940–1945** opens with a six-minute black-and-white newsreel about the war. A re-created Combat Information Center enables visitors to learn about radar and sonar. Other items include a machine developed to help decipher the German ENIGMA code.

**People, Information, and Technology, 1946–Present** features early televisions airing the Kennedy-Nixon debates, *Captain Kangaroo*, and other early programs. This section also exhibits early consumer electronics, high-fidelity records, color TVs, and personal computers.

The beginning years of the computer business is the focus of **Foundations, 1946–1960.** Among the artifacts on display are early computers such as those used to provide electronic surveillance and weapons control during the Cold War.

The significance of computers in American culture is the focus of **Into the Mainstream, 1961–1975.** The interactive workstation in this section enables visitors to scan and analyze their fingerprints to understand the importance of the FBI's National Crime Identification Center's use of fingerprints. Martin Luther King, Jr.'s killer, James Earl Ray, was tracked and caught using this computerized system. The **Control Center** enables visitors to answer simulated 911 emergency calls. In the theater at the south side of the gallery a 10-minute video illustrates how integral computers have become to modern American life. Exit through the south door.

**Science in American Life.** This exhibit, exploring the way science has changed American life since the 1870s, traces historically significant milestones in science. The **Hands-On Science Center** allows visitors to perform various experiments, such as testing water, detecting radioactivity, and exploring DNA testing.

The exhibit is presented chronologically in six sections: **Laboratory Science Comes to America, 1876–1920; Science for Progress, 1920–1940; Mobilizing Science for War, 1940–1960; Better than Nature, 1950–1970; Science in the Public Eye, 1970–Present;** and **Looking Ahead.** Looking Ahead focuses on the future of science, particularly biotechnology. At the conclusion of this gallery, visitors can participate in an ongoing opinion poll concerning science.

The exhibit starts by detailing the trust Americans developed in science as a problem solver and promoter of a better future. The more than 900 objects in the exhibit include a re-created laboratory, a fallout shelter, and a 1950s kitchen and living room. Another area highlights the scientific achievements of minorities and women.

Next to this exhibit is the **Hands-On Science Center,** open to ages 5 and older accompanied by an adult. Visitors can participate in science experiments and activities, such as measuring distance with a laser or using orange peels to smell the difference between mirror molecules. Passes are required and are handed out at the door on a first-come, first-served basis.

**Second Floor. Ceremonial Court.** This re-creation of the White House Executive Mansion includes original furnishings, presidential memorabilia, and White House china. Among the articles displayed that belonged to presidents are Jimmy Carter's hymnal, Woodrow Wilson's golf bag, John F. Kennedy's life preserver from the presidential yacht *HoneyFitz*, and Bill Clinton's Timex Ironman watch. Among the presidential state gifts are rifles, swords, and a lacquered inlaid mother-of-pearl box. Also displayed are examples of American art glass, jewelry, silver, stoneware, and painted tinware.

Next to this exhibit is **First Ladies: Political Role and Public Image.** This three-part exhibit shows the evolution of the role of the president's wife. The exhibits are **The First Lady: Political Role; The Gown Gallery,** which includes the gowns of Betty Ford, Nancy Reagan, Barbara Bush, and Hillary Rodham Clinton; and **The First Lady: Shaping a Public Image.**

**From Parlor to Politics: Women and Reform in America, 1890–1925.** The parlor, The tenement, and Hull House illustrate how women's changing social and family roles have affected modern society. Between 1890 and 1925, more than 23 million immigrants from Europe came to the U.S. in search of a better life. Many of these immigrants suffered harsh working conditions and were crowded into run-down tenements. A typical six-story tenement had four apartments of three rooms per floor, with two communal toilets, few windows, no electricity, and ten to twenty people per apartment. Infant mortality was high and poverty rampant.

Many middle- and upper-class American women met in their parlors to devise ways of assisting those less fortunate than themselves. Women planned campaigns to lobby for major social, political, and economic reforms, working to improve health care through clinics and nutrition programs, and devising ways to finance kindergartens and playgrounds in poor neighborhoods. Sometimes women worked in groups of as little as three or four; sometimes they formed organizations that grew to national prominence. One such organization, the National Congress of Mothers and the Mothers' Club, with nearly 200,000 members, lobbied for foster homes to replace orphan asylums and for equal parental guardianship. In 1924, this congress became the PTA (Parent-Teachers Association).

Many of these well-meaning women, in their earnest desire to abolish the conditions in the tenements, set up "Americanization" programs to assimilate new arrivals into what these women saw as the superior American way of life. One woman who didn't exactly see things that way was Jane Addams, who, along with Ellen Gates Starr, established the Hull House Settlement in Chicago in 1889. The purpose of Hull House was to bring reformers into the poor and immigrant neighborhoods to live and to work. Addams felt that different classes could learn from one another, and she called Hull House a "neighborhood household." She saw it as a place where the values of the home could extend into public life. Hull House provided basic classes in nutrition, cooking, cleaning, and hygiene, as well as a place for community groups to meet. There was even a theater where performances served as both an educational forum and a place for new immigrants to express their cultural heritage. Addams was awarded the Nobel Peace Prize in 1932.

In order to exit, visitors must retrace their steps. After exiting this gallery, turn to the right to **After the Revolution: Everyday Life in America, 1780–1800.** A multimedia program describes the era and its three major cultural groups: Native Americans, Europeans, and Africans. The exhibit focuses upon the Delaware farm family of Thomas and Elizabeth Springer and their two daughters, African Americans in the Chesapeake area, a Virginia planter family, the Seneca nation of the Iroquois Confederation, the Massachusetts merchant family of Samuel and Lucy Colton, and the major urban center of Philadelphia. The exhibit includes the Springer log cabin, tools, housewares, textiles, and religious objects.

Next to the exhibition is the **Hands-On History Room,** where visitors 5 and older accompanied by an adult can step back in time and try on colonial dresses, work on handcrafted shoes, decorate a Pueblo Indian pot, or learn by playing with a variety of other objects.

Upon leaving this last exhibit, head toward the west wing of the museum and the first right entrance.

**American Encounters.** This historical exhibit was created to commemorate the Columbus quincentenary. American Encounters looks at historical and contemporary issues and explores the positive and negative dynamics and effects of encounters between Native Americans, Hispanics, and Anglo-Americans in New Mexico's Rio Grande Valley. The 3,800 ft area features videotaped interviews from the residents of an Indian pueblo and a Hispanic village. Visitors learn about the communities' cultures. The display contains eight sections: **New Mexico: Past, Present, and Future, Khapo'o: Santa Clara Pueblo, Pueblo Resistance and Self-Determination, Christianization: Faith and Defiance, A Hispanic Community: Chimayo, Hispanic Resistance and Self-Determination,** and **Tourism.**

Head south, then west.

**Field to Factory: Afro-American Migration, 1915–1940.** This gallery, tracing the period when more than a million blacks left the South and moved north, explores the hardships and strengths of southern life, the personal decision to migrate, and northern city life. Among the items are a 1920s Maryland sharecropper's house; a replica of separate black and white entrances to the Ashland, Virginia, train station; objects from a beauty salon run by a black woman; and a re-creation of a Philadelphia row house.

At the entrance to the exhibit is **Sitting for Justice: The Greensboro Sit-in of 1960,** an exhibit of the actual Woolworth's lunch counter from Greensboro, North Carolina, where four African American students staged a sit-in on Feb 1, 1960, after being refused service because of the store's whites-only policy. Hundreds joined the four students, and in July of that year the counter was finally desegregated.

Exit through the north doorway, then turn west to the **Star-Spangled Banner** lab and exhibition, where visitors can follow the progress of the historic $18 million conservation of the Star-Spangled Banner. The museum's staff are vacuuming the surface of the flag, removing dirt and dust, and are also adding a support fabric called crepeline to particularly weak areas of the flag. A gantry (a giant aluminum structure) is extended over the flag so that technicians may reach every area of the surface without damaging it.

This is the flag that flew over Fort McHenry and inspired Francis Scott Key's poem, which was later set to music and became the U.S. national anthem. The flag, passed down through the Armistead family in the 1800s, came to the Smithsonian in 1907. In the summer of 1982, the flag underwent major preservation. The flag, with its fifteen stars and stripes, was made by Mrs. Mary Pickersgill in 1813. The banner is 30 by 34 ft, handsewn from English wool bunting, with cotton stars and backed by Irish linen. It weighs 300 pounds.

In 2002, a new exhibition featuring the flag is set to open. Both same-day and advance passes will be available. For same-day entry passes, go to the Star-Spangled Banner kiosk on the second floor (the same floor as the lab) near the Mall entrance. Distribution times are at 10 A.M. for entrance between 10:30 and 1:00 P.M., and at 1:00 P.M. for entrance between 1:30 and 5:00 P.M. There is a limit of six passes per person. For advance passes, call TicketMaster, ☎ (800) 551-7328.

### Washington Notes

Key, a Georgetown lawyer and a civilian, was on an American ship in the Chesapeake when the British attacked Fort McHenry outside Baltimore on Sept 13, 1814. Because the British seemed unbeatable, Key was surprised when in the morning the American flag was still flying over the fort. The American troops, under Major George Armistead, had withstood the attack. Inspired, Key wrote a poem, "The Defence of Fort McHenry," which the *Baltimore Patriot and Evening Advertiser* published a week after the battle. Later on, the words were set to the tune of the well-known English song "To Anacreon in Heaven." In 1931 Congress declared the "Star-Spangled Banner" to be the U.S. national anthem.

**Third Floor.** Turn west at the top of the escalator.

**Ella Fitzgerald: First Lady of Song** features costumes, awards, photos, recordings, scrapbooks, sheet music, and personal memorabilia from the 60-year career of this extraordinary singer. Particularly enjoyable is an ongoing video of Ms. Fitzgerald singing as only she could.

**Musical Instruments.** This three-room gallery displays western European and American instruments. Some date to the 17C, while many of the Gibson and Fender guitars are from the 1950s and 1960s. The cases of stringed instruments—such as the 17C–18C Antonio Stradivari pieces—are temporary. However, the display of organs, harpsichords, and pianos is permanent. Head north into the second room. The small stage at the east side of this room is used for concerts and recordings. The windows at the west end of the room offer a great view of the Washington Monument. Continue north into a long, narrow room. A computerized player piano offers visitors a choice of several songs.

Continue north.

Next to the dollhouse is **Icons of American Popular Culture,** where one of the museum's most popular items is on display—**Dorothy's ruby red slippers** from the 1939 movie *The Wizard of Oz.* Also here are Michael Jordan's jersey, Indiana Jones's jacket and hat, Dizzy Gillespie's trumpet, Minnie Pearl's hat, a baseball autographed by Babe Ruth, Muhammed Ali's boxing gloves, Arthur Ashe's tennis racket, and a phaser from the original *Star Trek* television series.

Next to the escalator bank is a dollhouse created by Francis Bradford that depicts the ideal home of wealthy Americans during the early 1900s. Bradford donated the house to the Smithsonian in 1951.

Walk south from the escalator.

**Hall of Printing and Graphic Arts.** This hall, which examines the history of prints and printing techniques, is organized in four sections: an 1885 print shop complete with a (Ben) Franklin Press and a Common Press, a 19C foundry that cast type by hand, an 1865 job shop, and a newspaper office from 1885. The exhibit addresses the four methods of printing: relief, intaglio, lithographic, and stencil. There are also linotype machines, a Bruce typecasting machine, and dozens of 19C presses. In the **DigiLab,** which opened in fall 1999, visitors explore modern imaging technology by manipulating images of Superman using scanners, computers, and other digitally based computer equipment. Reenter the lobby and head east.

**Hall of Textiles.** Many aspects of textiles are presented, including the arduous process of making cloth in colonial days. Placards discuss American use of textiles such as wool. A highlight is the **display of quilts** and the discussion of their emergence during the 18C. Follow the corridor north, passing the restrooms.

**Money and Medals.** This gallery shows the evolution of money and monetary exchange. The **Gold Room** dazzles with coins and currencies form dozens of nations. The gallery traces the history of money from the early use of shells and skins; colonial money in England, France, and Spain; as well as money used during the Civil War and Reconstruction. A section about the United States Mint explains its founding and also illustrates U.S. coin designs. Counterfeit coins and paper money are displayed. Follow the corridor south, then turn east.

**We the People: Winning the Vote.** This exhibit examines the Constitution as a living document. Political processes and social developments such as voting rights and freedom of speech are featured. At the entrance is a glass model of the Capitol assembled from 1972 to 1975. The first section of the exhibit, **Promoting the Candidates,** has objects used by political candidates, including items from George Washington's 1789 inauguration as well as golf balls with candidates' faces. **Television and Politics** addresses the emergence of presidential debates and displays chairs and lecterns used during the Ford-Carter and Dole-Mondale debates in 1976. **Convention** discusses the political and sociological importance of political rallies and conventions. Proceed north.

**Armed Forces History.** This exhibit uses uniforms, weapons, flags, and ship models to illustrate the origins of armed forces and the life of a soldier. At the entrance is the first American flag referred to as Old Glory. It was made for merchant ship captain William Driver in 1824. The gallery features George Washington's field headquarters tent, U.S. Army swords from 1832 to 1902, and a Revolutionary War vessel. One case displays Old World weapons, including a breastplate and an English suit of armor. The exhibit includes information on the origins of the U.S. Army, Marines, and Coast Guard; the development of the U.S. Navy during the Civil War; as well as artifacts from World War II and the Vietnam War. The extensive World War II exhibit (**World War II G.I.: The American Soldier**) displays temporary barracks (c. 1943), U.S. military pistols and rifles, and interactive "tools of war" such as land mines called Bouncing Betties. The Vietnam War section (**Personal Legacy: The Healing of a Nation**) is the most moving. Objects left by visitors to Washington's Vietnam Memorial from 1982 to 1991 include dog tags, uniforms, letters, and medals. Opening in April 2000 and continuing for 18 months is **Fast Attacks and Boomers: Submarines in the Cold War.**

**A More Perfect Union: Japanese Americans and the U.S. Constitution** explores the internment of Japanese Americans during World War II. Video interviews with Japanese Americans who were interned and a life-size re-creation of one of the camp's cabins illustrate the spartan realities of camp life.

Also on the third floor is the gunboat *Philadelphia* and the Firearms Gallery, which is to the left of the exit of the last exhibit. The **National Firearms Collection** features miniatures and life-size versions of weapons such as the M9 pistol, the M16 rifle used in Vietnam, as well as Confederate and Colonial rifles. The *Philadelphia* was a Continental gondola built and sunk in 1776; it is the oldest American man-of-war in existence. Adjoining cases display artifacts retrieved from the wreck, including pewter spoons, ax heads, and uniform buttons.

The nearest Metro station is Smithsonian/Mall (Blue/Orange Line). Exit the National Museum of American History and head south, crossing the Mall.

To continue to the next walk, exit the museum via the Constitution Ave lobby and walk west one block to the Ellipse, 1600 Constitution Ave. The Ellipse, which is on the north side of Constitution Ave, is the open grassy area south of the White House.

# 8 · The Ellipse and 17th Street Sites

Metro: Blue/Orange Line to Farragut West or McPherson Square. Bus: 32, 34, 36, 38B, 42, 52, 54, 80, G8, N2, N4, N6, S2, S4, or X2.

## The Ellipse

The Ellipse, 1600 Constitution Ave, is a 17-acre oval that is part of President's Park South, a 54-acre grassy park south of the White House. The Ellipse serves as ceremonial grounds for the White House, and sometimes political demonstrators also make use of the grounds to rally for their causes.

### History

When L'Enfant was mapping out the capital, the site of the Ellipse was marshy lowland, boggy with stagnant water from nearby Tiber Creek and flood waters from the Potomac. L'Enfant included this area as the vast President's Park in his 1791 plan for the city. However, these wetlands posed health risks and in the first years of the 19C, President Jefferson built a low stone wall to separate the land from the White House.

In 1815 the Washington Canal was created. It flowed along the southern border of the park, which is present-day Constitution Ave. For a long time the park remained undeveloped. During the Civil War Union troops camped in the area and their horses, mules, and cattle grazed on the site. The Ellipse area also became known as the White Lot, named for the whitewashed fence to the south that separated the White House ground from the troops and their livestock.

The Washington Canal, created to transport goods, was never a success. Local residents used the canal as a dumping ground and sewer. The accompanying stench was often so strong, especially in the heat of summer months, that President Lincoln took refuge at times on the other side of the city.

In 1866 the city decided to fill in the marshy land of the Ellipse. In 1879–80 dirt excavated during the construction of Pennsylvania Ave and the Old Executive Office Building was used as fill. Native trees were added to create shade. By the end of the 19C, the "White Lot" became a popular public attraction, hosting baseball games, tennis, and croquet matches. In the 1920s the Ellipse was converted into a parking lot as, at the time, the city lacked parking spaces for the increasingly popular automobile. It wasn't until the mid-20C that the Ellipse officially became ceremonial grounds for the White House.

## Statues

There are a number of sculptures and monuments around the Ellipse. Marking the south border of the Ellipse, on the southeast and southwest corners at Constitution Ave, are the **Bulfinch Gatehouses** (1828; Charles Bulfinch). These gatehouses originally served as guardhouses to the Capitol. They were transported to the Ellipse after the Capitol grounds were relandscaped in 1874. Stains on the sandstone structures mark the water level to which the Potomac River once climbed.

Walk north along 15th St. Midway through the block, on the left, is the **Boy Scout Memorial** (1964; Donald DeLue). Marking the site of the First National Boy Scout Jamboree in 1937, the memorial commemorates the 50th anniversary of the Boy Scouts of America. The allegorical bronze sculpture features two 12 ft high neoclassical figures representing "the sum of great ideals of past civilizations, developed through the centuries and now at best as delivered by American Manhood and Womanhood to the present generation." A contemporary Boy Scout, representing all Scouts, walks into the future between them. The figures stand on a pedestal engraved with the Boy Scout oath. An elliptical pool at the foot of the statue reflects the sculpture.

Proceed north through the Ellipse. The **Ellipse Visitor's Pavilion,** open Tues–Sat 8–4, has an information desk, restrooms, telephones, and a refreshment window.

Walk west along Ellipse Dr to the four-ft-high, pink granite stone. Called the **Zero Milestone,** it marks the meeting of the north and south meridians of the city and was used in the capital's planning; it's also the point for the measurement of distance from Washington, D.C., to other destinations on U.S. highways. This marker was donated by the Lee Highway Association and dedicated on July 4, 1923. Just south of the Zero Milestone is the **National Christmas Tree,** a blue spruce transplanted here on Oct 11, 1978. During the holiday season it is strung with lights.

Continue west. In the northwest corner of the Ellipse, between Ellipse Dr and E St, is the **Butt-Millet Memorial Fountain** (1913; Daniel Chester French). This eight-ft-high, neoclassical marble fountain was funded by friends of Major Archibald Willingham Butt and Francis Davis Millet, both of whom died on the *Titanic* in 1912. Millet, a decorative artist, and Butt, a military aide to Presidents Taft and Roosevelt, were prominent citizens of Washington at the time of their death.

Turn south and walk across the Ellipse to Constitution Ave, then turn west to the **Settlers of the District of Columbia Monument** (1936; Carl Mose). This granite shaft is a memorial to the original 18 landowners of the area that became the District of Columbia. Donated by the National Society of the Daughters of the American Revolution, the structure features four relief panels representing the corn and tobacco farmed on the land, as well as the turkey and herring found in the wild. Walk west along Constitution Ave to the southwest corner, where the **Second Division Memorial** (1936; James Earle Fraser) is located. Composed of immense granite portal fronts, guarded by a large hand gripping an 18 ft high flaming sword, the monument symbolizes the American forces blocking the German troops entry into Paris. Two wings have been added since its construction in 1936—one on the west for World War II and another on the east for the Korean War.

### Washington Notes
Two homeless men were nearly entombed in this memorial in 1962 when the Korean War addition was built. Construction workers were laying an eight-inch-thick slab of granite in place when they heard rustling noises inside and discovered the men.

Cross 17th St to the Organization of American States.

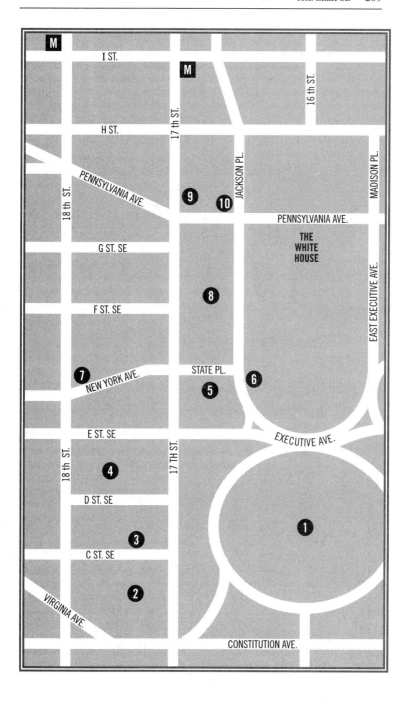

## *Organization of American States/House of the Americas*

17th St. and Constitution Ave N.W. ☎ 458-3000. Web: www.oas.org. Open Mon–Fri 9–5:30. Visitors may stroll the grounds freely but must sign in to visit the interior lobby and the Hall of the Americas, which is on the second floor. Group tours can be arranged by calling the Office of External Relations, ☎ 458-3927. Wheelchair accessible. The Organization of American States (OAS) is the world's oldest regional international organization. Housed in the white marble House of the Americas (1910; Albert Kelsey and Paul P. Cret; DL), it is devoted to peaceful relations and economic cooperation among the 35 member countries who represent Central, South, and North America, and the Caribbean. The grounds include a number of sculptures and gardens, as well as the Art Museum of the Americas and the Van Ness Carriage House.

### History

The First International Conference of American States, held in Washington in 1889–90, founded the International Union of American Republics. Its central office became known as the Pan American Union in 1913. Because of the union's increasing activities, it needed a larger headquarters.

The land for the new building was donated by the U.S. government. Andrew Carnegie contributed $750,000 for the building. Its cornerstone was laid May 11, 1908, and the structure was dedicated July 26, 1910. In 1948, at the Ninth International Conference in Bogota, Columbia, the charter of the OAS was adopted. The OAS succeeded the Pan American Union as the international organization of the Americas.

### *Washington Notes*

The site of the House of the Americas was previously home to two of Washington's most important early buildings: the David Burnes House, built in 1750, and the Van Ness Mansion, completed on the same plot in 1816.

"Crusty Davey" Burnes, a cantankerous Scotchman, was one of the capital city's first and largest landowners. His property included what became the central portion of the city on either side of Pennsylvania Ave. When the new government, under the leadership of George Washington, attempted to purchase Burnes's land for the new capital, Burnes drove a hard bargain, enraging George Washington. When Burnes finally did sell part of his land, he received the best per-acre rate the government paid. Burnes continued to grow tobacco on his remaining holdings, about 600 acres (which included the site now occupied by the OAS), until his death in 1799.

In the early days of the capital, Burnes's house was a gathering place for many members of Congress, especially eligible bachelors who were interested in Burnes's only child, Marcia, whose charms were enhanced by her father's money. From his deathbed, he reputedly told the 17-year-old Marcia, "You have been a good daughter; you'll now be the richest girl in America." At the time of her father's death, Marcia was worth about $1.5 million. Burnes is buried in Rock Creek Cemetery.

Marcia married New York congressman John Peter Van Ness in 1802. They contracted Benjamin Henry Latrobe to build a Greek revival mansion which, upon its completion in 1816, was considered the most expensive private home built in America. The house included hot-and-cold running water in every room, apparently an American first. Van Ness eventually became mayor of Washington in 1830.

Marcia and their daughter were victims of the cholera epidemic of 1832. Van Ness died in 1846. The Van Ness family tomb, designed by George Hadfield, is now in Oak Hill Cemetery.

After Van Ness's death, the property was acquired by Thomas Green, a prominent newspaper editor from Richmond. The Burnes's house was demolished in 1864. Following the Civil War, the property deteriorated and was used in succession as a German beer garden, a botanical nursery, headquarters of the city street cleaners, and the Columbia Athletic Club. In 1907 the Van Ness Mansion was razed, leaving only the carriage house standing.

There is a legend that the original conspiracy against Abraham Lincoln, in which the conspirators apparently intended to kidnap Lincoln rather than kill him, included a plan to hide the president in the Van Ness wine cellar.

## Exterior

The building is a combination of Spanish and French Renaissance styles, incorporating white marble from Georgia and black marble from the Andes, representing the styles of North and South America.

*Queen Isabella I,* (1966; José Luis Sanchez) a life-size bronze statue, dominates the plaza fronting the entrance. She wears the crown of Castille and a mantle emblazoned with the crests of Aragon and León. In her hands, a dove emerges from a promegranate. She was a gift of the Institute of Spanish Culture in Madrid and dedicated by the Spanish foreign minister on April 14, 1966, the old calendar's 475th anniversary of Columbus's first sighting of the New World.

The building's entrance features three arched doorways flanked by female allegorical statues representing North and South America. To the left, *South America* (1910; Isidore Konti) holds a boy representing South America's young state of development. Directly above this sculpture are two panels related to South America. The upper panel is *South American Condor* (1910; Solon Borglum) a high-relief medallion. Beneath it, the panel *The Meeting of Bolívar and San Martín* (1910; Isidore Konti) depicts an important event in South America's struggle to free itself from Spanish rule.

To the right in *North America* (1910; Gutzon Borglum), a draped female stands beside a young boy. The woman holds a torch in her right hand.

Two reliefs representing North America adorn the wall above the sculpture. The uppermost, *North American Eagle* (1910; Solon Borglum), is a medallion. The lower panel, *Washington's Farewell to His Generals* (1910; Gutzon Borglum), depicts Washington taking leave of his men near the conclusion of the American Revolution.

The gardens surrounding the building contain many pieces of sculpture worth noting. On the grounds to the north of the entrance is a concrete replica of *The Prophet Daniel*, a work by Brazil's first important sculptor, Antonio Francisco Lisboa (better known as Aleijinho). The original, sculpted in soapstone in 1805 near the end of Lisboa's career, was part of his group of 12 carvings of prophets. These represent some of the finest pieces of the Brazilian baroque style. The replica was a gift of the Brazilian government in 1962.

The bronze high-relief panel of *Rubén Darío* (1967; Juan José Sicre) in the south garden was erected by the OAS to honor Darío, the brilliant Nicaraguan poet and literary critic, who is arguably the most important author in the Spanish tongue in modern times. It marks the 100th anniversary of his death. The relief portrait is mounted on a rectangular concrete panel held aloft by four concrete posts. Urns flank both sides of the work.

The bronze bust of *José Cecilio del Valle* (1967; Juan José Sicre) is in the rear garden on the north side. Placed by the OAS in 1967, the work commemorates del Valle's inter-American system designed to foster peace and commerce within the Western Hemisphere. Born in Honduras c. 1777, José Cecilio del Valle was a Central American statesman, lawyer, and newspaperman who used his influence to promote Central American unity. He proposed a single legislature for the area. Before his death, in 1834, he served as the president of Guatemala.

The south side of the rear garden features a bronze bust of Cordell Hull, secretary of state under Franklin Delano Roosevelt and a champion of Roosevelt's "good neighbor" policy. Hull won the 1945 Nobel Peace Prize for his role in creating the United Nations. The sculpture, a copy of a 1945 piece by Bryant Baker, was placed in 1956 to commemorate Hull's contribution to Pan-American unity and international peace.

## Interior

The interior of the main building is distinctly Latin American in character. The glass-canopied **Aztec Garden**, just past the lobby, is a lush tropical patio featuring tropical vegetation, such as cacao, rubber, palm, and coffee trees. The most historically significant tree, the huge "Peace Tree," was grafted from a fig and a rubber tree, and was planted by President Taft in 1910 to symbolize the marriage of North and South American cultures.

The courtyard's most conspicuous element, *The Aztec Fountain* (1910; Gertrude Vanderbilt Whitney), stands eight ft tall with two basins decorated by hieroglyphics from pre-European South and Central America. Three figures, one each from Mayan, Aztec, and Zapotecan civilizations, support the basins. Water falls to the fountain's base from eight heads that represent the Mayan and Aztec deity Quetzalcoatl, the feathered serpent. A Mexican star centers the base of speckled pink-and-white marble.

Tiles reproducing mosaics and archeological fragments from pre-European Mexico, Guatemala, and Peru pave the courtyard. These include Mayan wall decorations from the Mayan ruin Palenque in Southern Mexico, tiles from the Mayan ruin Copan in Honduras, and tiles from the pre-Inca ruin Tiahuanaco in Bolivia. The coats of arms of the original member nations decorate the courtyard's ceiling molding.

Part of the second floor, accessible by a staircase on either side of the lobby, is open to the public. The **Hall of the Americas**, a vaulted columned room, contains three Edward Caldwell and Company crystal chandeliers. Adjacent to the hall, the **Old Council Room** (Miranda Room) features low-relief friezes of events in the history of the Americas.

## Art Museum of the Americas

201 18th St N.W. ☎ 458-6016. Open Tues–Sun 10–5. Closed Mon and holidays. Displays works by Latin American and Caribbean artists. This museum is located in a small building behind the main headquarters, on the corner of 18th St and Virginia Ave N.W.

**Highlights:** Works by Tamayo, Siqueiros, Matta, Soto, and Portina.

The Art Museum of the Americas originally served as the residence of the OAS secretary general. The museum, the first in the world dedicated exclusively to works of art from throughout the Americas, displays many traveling exhibits and maintains a collection of close to 2,000 pieces.

The **Carriage House** of the Van Ness Mansion, located on the northwest edge of the property, now contains administrative offices for the museum.

Walk north on 17th St. Cross C St. On the left is the headquarters of the Daughters of the American Revolution.

## Daughters of the American Revolution (DAR) National Society Headquarters

1776 D St N.W. ☎ 879-3254. Web: www.dar.org. Museum gallery open Mon–Fri 9–4; Sun 1–5. Tours of period rooms, Yochim Gallery, and library balcony Mon–Fri 10–3; Sun 1–5. Closed Sat, holidays, and two weeks in April. Admission: free, donations accepted.

Quilt-study workshops on the first Thurs of the month. Reservations required. Wheelchair entrance, 1775 C St N.W. Call in advance for assistance ☎ 879-3241.

Memorial Continental Hall Library. Entrance on D St. Open Mon–Fri 9–4. Closed weekends, holidays, and April. Admission: fee. More than 120,000 volumes in the collection concern genealogical research.

DAR's headquarters has grown into a block-long complex comprising a museum, 33 period rooms, and a genealogical library—all housed in Memorial Continental Hall (1910; Edward Pearce Casey; DL)—and the 4,000-seat meeting hall, Constitution Hall (1929; John Russell Pope; DL). The DAR mission is threefold: historical, educational, and patriotic. The organization's main goal is to perpetuate the memory of the men and women who fought for America's independence by collecting and preserving historical and biographical records, documents, and relics. The DAR's collection contains more than 30,000 objects.

**Highlights:** Geneological and historical documents in the library. In the museum, noteworthy items include the Paul Revere beaker and silver teapot, and several period rooms—including the Oklahoma colonial kitchen, the Georgia tavern, the D.C. room, and the New Hampshire attic, which has a display of 18C and early-19C doll carriages and toys.

### History

In 1890 the Sons of the American Revolution held their first national convention in Louisville. Women were excluded, prompting Mrs. Mary S. Lockwood and three other female descendants of the Revolution to organize the Daughters of the

American Revolution. By 1899 the DAR had collected nearly 50 objects including manuscripts, porcelain, furniture, and silver, which the society stored at the Smithsonian Institution. Envisioning their own national headquarters, the women raised money for the next four years in order to buy land and construct a building. When enough funds were raised, Edward Pearce Casey was hired as the architect. The building site had formerly been the property of Thomas Carbery. A prominent local businessman, Carbery sat on the board of the Washington Monument Society and served as mayor of Washington in the 1820s.

During the first year of construction, the DAR held its annual Continental Congress (during the anniversary of the Battle of Lexington, the week of April 19) in the building, even though its roof was incomplete. (This meeting is now conducted in Constitution Hall.) The structure—Memorial Continental Hall—was completed in 1910. The gavel (a tool used by Masons to fit stone) that laid the cornerstone of this building was the same one used by George Washington to lay the Capitol cornerstone in 1793.

The hall attained National Historic Landmark status when it hosted the 1921 Conference for Limitation of Armament between the U.S., Great Britain, France, Italy, and Japan—the first disarmament agreement between major powers. A plaque commemorating this event hangs in the library.

The DAR decided to build an additional hall when the auditorium in Memorial Continental Hall became too small for the growing number of members. Constitution Hall was added in 1929 by John Russell Pope, as a memorial to the Constitution. It was dedicated on April 19, 1929, on the 154th anniversary of the Battle of Lexington. Carved on the hall's cornerstone, laid on Oct 30, 1928, are the words: "Memorial to that Immortal Document the Constitution of the United States in which are Incorporated those Principles of Freedom, Equality, and Justice for which our Forefathers Strove."

The facility soon became a cultural venue for Washington, hosting artists, lecturers, and classical and rock concerts.

### Washington Notes

One of Constitution Hall's most famous concerts is one that never occurred. In 1939 African American contralto Marian Anderson was contracted to sing for the Easter Sunday celebration. But the DAR balked, insisting their facilities were for whites only. Repulsed by such racism, Mrs. Eleanor Roosevelt resigned from the organization and asked Secretary of the Interior Harold Ickes to arrange for the concert to be held on the steps of the Lincoln Memorial. More than 75,000 people came to hear Anderson sing.

The DAR, later embarrassed by its position, permitted Anderson to perform in 1943 for the United China Relief organization.

## Exterior

**Memorial Continental Hall**'s white marble architecture and decoration reflect the DAR's patriotic mission. The structure is an example of Beaux-Arts architecture. The original entrance, which faces the Ellipse, has a monumental porte cochere, or carriage entry, with large-scale steps. The C St entrance, a semicircular portico with a balustraded terrace, is dominated by 13 Greek columns symbolizing the original 13 colonies.

Adjacent to Memorial Continental Hall, a garden on C St between 17th and

18th Sts features a nine-ft-high marble sculpture dedicated to the *Founders of the DAR* (1929; Gertrude Vanderbilt Whitney). The monument portrays a woman with outstretched arms, cloth draping below, and a horizontal background stele with engraved bronze medallions memorializing the four founders: Mary Desha, Eugenia Washington, Ellen Hardin Walworth, and Mary Smith Lockwood.

**Constitution Hall** is a rectangular building constructed with Alabama limestone. The hall features a main entrance supported by Ionic columns, and bronze doors. A 90 ft wide pediment of the American eagle rests above the columns, with the dates of the signing of the Declaration of Independence (1776) and the Treaty of Paris (1783) to its south and north, respectively. Behind the columns, on the building's façade, immense five-ft-tall relief panels portray allegorical neoclassical figures. Both the carvings of the pediment and the panels were executed on the site by Ulysses A. Ricci after the hall's construction.

Three pairs of symmetrical bronze doors lead into the hall. An inscription above the center door quotes George Washington speaking to the Constitutional Convention in 1787: "Let us raise a standard to which the wise and honest can repair. The event is in the hands of God."

## Interior

Memorial Continental Hall was originally designed as an auditorium for the society's annual Continental Congress. In the late 1940s, the chairs were removed to make room for the library, but the room's original architecture, including the stage and floor, was retained. Impressive high-arched walls covered in custom-decorated plaster enclose the room. Tiered balconies line the walls, receiving diffused sunlight from the glass ceiling partitioned with delicate ironwork.

The front focal wall features a portrait of George Washington by Rembrandt Peale, as well as flags representing the 13 original colonies. Opposite this wall the official Great Seals of the first 13 states are painted on wooden shields.

The **Library** contains one of the largest collections of geneological materials in the United States. Established in 1896 with 125 books in order to provide records by which the society's genealogists could verify prospective members' lineages, the collection now includes more than 120,000 volumes covering state, county, town, and church records. More than 10,000 men and women use the collection each year. Alex Haley researched part of his novel *Roots* at this facility.

The **Museum** is located in Memorial Continental Hall. The collection contains 50,000 items of 18C–19C ceramics, silver, furniture, paintings, and textiles, donated mainly by members and supporters of the society.

In a three-room area on the first floor, the DAR features its permanent collection and temporary exhibitions. Particularly noteworthy in the permanent collection are the Paul Revere silver beaker and teapot located in the rear room, the case on the left. The ceramics collection includes a selection of blue-and-white Staffordshire decorated with portraits of American society, as well as Spode, Chinese export porcelain, Blue Canton, and Nankin china.

Perhaps the most unique feature of the museum is the collection of **33 period rooms.** Created as a fund-raiser for the hall, the period rooms were purchased and designed by each state, and in some cases reflect the state's culture.

A sampling of 10 to 15 of these 18C and 19C rooms, scattered on four levels throughout the complex, are presented on a guided tour. Highlights include: the Oklahoma Kitchen (lower level), a colonial kitchen; Peter Tondee's Tavern (lower level), a Savannah, Georgia, pub; District of Columbia Room (first floor); and the New Hampshire Attic (third floor), an array of 18C and early-19C doll carriages, toys, and porcelain, bisque, and papier-mâché dolls.

The **Oklahoma Kitchen** displays furnishings as well as copper, brass, and cast-iron kitchen and domestic utensils from 18C and 19C colonial America. Displayed also are a butter churn, dough box, spinning wheel, and candle molds. In that era the open-hearth fireplace functioned as both a cooking area and a source of heat and light.

**Peter Tondee's Tavern,** the Georgia Period Room, is based on the actual "long room" in a tavern in Savannah. This historic tavern, open from 1770 to 1785, was a frequent meeting place for the Sons of Liberty, a group formed in response to the Stamp Act. At this tavern, the first reading of the Declaration of Independence in Georgia took place on Aug 10, 1776.

The **District of Columbia Period Room** is a parlor featuring furniture of an affluent household in the early 1800s. Note the English painted maple chair, believed to be part of the Tayloe family's set of 16 in the Octagon at New York Ave and 18th Sts.

Visitors can find their own state's contribution in the remaining period rooms: the Alabama Period Room, an antebellum parlor (1820–50); the California Period Room, an upper-middle-class parlor from the 1860s, mixing Mexican, Far East, and Chinese objects; the Colorado Period Room, decorated with 19C furnishings (currently used as a conference room); the Delaware Period Room, a recently updated late-18C study; the Illinois Period Room, a multipurpose early-19C parlor; the Indiana Period Room, an east coast private library during the early Federal period; the Iowa Period Room, a parlor (1770–1810) with some of the oldest objects in the museum; the Kansas Chapel, a smaller version of the Sargent Chapel in the Central Congregational Church in Topeka; the Kentucky Period Room, a parlor (1830) that features a scroll-back neoclassical sofa made around 1810; the Louisiana Period Room, arranged like a gallery, displaying Native American, French, and Acadian objects; the Maine Period Room, an early-19C parlor; the Maryland Period Room, a parlor from around 1830 that includes Baltimore painted furniture; the Massachusetts Period Room, a bed chamber from 1775 based on the Hancock-Clarke home in Concord; the Michigan Period Room, a library (1790–1830) with a collection of tin-glazed earthenware from the mid-1700s; the Missouri Period Room, a mid-19C parlor in rococo revival style; the New Jersey Period Room, suggesting an English council chamber from the late 1600s; the New York Period Room, an 1820 parlor; the North Carolina Period Room, a formal dining room (1780–1850s); the Ohio Period Room, a mid-19C parlor with a collection of American glass; the Pennsylvania Period Room, with late-18C and early-19C furnishings; the **Pennsylvania Foyer,** the entrance to the DAR library, which is elaborately decorated to harmonize with the building's Beaux-Arts design; the Rhode Island Period Room, which displays American- and European-made musical instruments from the 18C and 19C; the South Carolina Period Room, a brightly painted half–bed chamber (1810–20); the Tennessee Period Room, featuring a portrait of Andrew Jackson (1830–32) by Ralph E. W. Earl; the Texas Period Room, a German-influenced bedroom (1850–80); the Vermont Period Room, an early-19C parlor with Bennington and Rockingham pottery; the Virginia Period Room, a dining room (1790–1810), which features a cast-iron fireback that belonged to George Washington's parents; the West Virginia Period Room, a parlor from 1790 that has an American-made pianoforte and chamber organ; and the Wisconsin Period Room, a one-room home (1680–1720).

A **walk-in gallery** is located on the lower level hallway, between the North Carolina and Louisiana Period Rooms. Recently conserved items are displayed alongside unrestored objects. A section of the gallery chronicles furniture design. Often displayed (items are rotated) are a mahogany high chest built around 1776 in Newport, Rhode Island, and an elegant reverse-curve sofa, c. 1770s from Philadelphia.

For children, the **Touch of Independence** area is located outside the New Hampshire Attic and contains reproduction objects to play with. Childrens' programs "The Colonial Adventure" and "The Colonial Child" cater to ages 5–7 and 7–11, respectively.

Recently renovated Constitution Hall's auditorium has a 33 by 52 ft stage and a capacity of 4,000. Its patriotic symbols include a replica of the Great Seal of the United States centered over the stage. Lining the seal are 12 Revolutionary War battle flags. Twin Ionic columns are located on both sides of the stage, each crowned with a gold-leafed American bald eagle. The 25 ft long blue curtains are decorated with gold stars and medallions. Fifty-two boxes, adorned with state seals, line the hall in a U-shape. Both the president of the United States and the president general of the DAR have boxes named in their honor.

Other rooms in the building include the President General's Reception Room and a page's lounge used for meetings and recitals.

Continue north on 17th St to the American Red Cross.

## American Red Cross

430 17th St N.W. ☎ 639-3300. Web:www.redcross.org. Visitors Center, 1730 E St N.W. Open Mon–Fri 9–4. The main building is open to visitors by appointment only.

The American Red Cross (1915–17; Trowbridge & Livingston, architects; Boyle-Robertson Company, builder; 1929, Goodhue Livingston; DL), a three-building white marble complex. The main building, a stately white structure fronted by an impressive colonnade, has the familiar red cross on its pediment. This symbol has been associated with emergency services to victims of war and natural disasters since 1881.

**Highlights:** Photographic stories of those helped by the Red Cross.

### History

The American Red Cross traces its origins to 19C Europe and the founding, in 1863, of the International Committee of the Red Cross by Henry Dunant. Dunant, a Swiss businessman, had witnessed the 1859 Battle of Solferino in northern Italy, an engagement in which 40,000 men were killed or wounded and left without help. At the committee's first conference, it adopted as an emblem the red cross on a white field, the reverse of the Swiss flag.

Dunant's ideas became the origins of the Geneva Conventions, the international treaties designed to protect the victims of war. The treaties have been continually expanded and revised since Dunant's time, and today bear the signatures of 188 governments.

The American Red Cross owes its existence to the efforts of Clara Barton, the former Massachusetts schoolteacher and federal government worker who became known for her work tending the wounded on the battlefields of the American Civil War. After the war, she left for Europe and, after learning of the Red Cross movement there, stayed and joined the relief efforts for the civilian victims of the Franco-Prussian War. When she returned home, Barton led the movement that persuaded the U.S. government to sign the Geneva Conventions. On May 21, 1881, the American Association of the Red Cross was established. Due to the organization's conspicuous service and success, the U.S. government granted the American Red Cross a charter in 1900, making the volunteer entity responsible for providing aid to the U.S. armed forces and relief to victims of disaster. Barton served as its head until 1904.

In 1917, the Red Cross moved into their national headquarters building, a practical monument to honor the women of the North and South who served the wounded during the Civil War.

## Exterior

The **Gardens** behind the Red Cross building on 17th St feature two sculptures and one memorial. *The Red Cross Men and Women Killed in Service* (1959; Felix de Weldon), is a seven-ft-tall bronze sculpture group dedicated to the volunteers who gave their lives in the service of the Red Cross. General Mark Clark presented the piece to Roland Harriman, chairman of the National Red Cross, on June 25, 1959. The sculptor sought to capture the spirit and strength of people striving to preserve human life and lessen suffering during wartime. At the center a Red Cross woman is comforting a wounded man who is being carried by two male figures. The wounded figure's helplessness is underscored by the muscular strain evident in the arms that lift him.

Across from this sculpture stands a monument titled *Jane A. Delano and the 296 Nurses Who Died in Service in World War I* (1933; Robert Tait MacKenzie). Delano was the founder of the Red Cross Nursing and Health Services, and a casualty of World War I. The monument was dedicated in 1933. The figure, veiled and draped, stands seven ft tall and reaches with outstretched hands to symbolize compassion. The phrase inscribed on the monument's marble base is from Psalm 91. Nearby, a memorial honors the Harvard Field Hospital Unit (Sept 1939–July 1942). This group staffed a prefab hospital in England from Sept 1939 to July 1942. A plaque honors Red Cross workers who died in Vietnam.

On the lawn, to the north of the 17th St building, is a sculpture by Armenian artist Friedrich Sogoyan depicting a woman embracing a child. The work honors the victims of the Dec 7, 1988, earthquake in Armenia and commemorates the humanitarian relief efforts of the Red Cross. The sculpture was dedicated on March 15, 1991.

The interior of the main building is no longer open to the public. However, just off the second floor lobby is the Board of Governors Hall, which features three ten-ft-tall Tiffany windows representing the theme of ministry to the sick and wounded. These may be viewed by appointment, but only by large groups. For information, ☎ 639-3300. From the front of the main building, walk west one-half block on E St to 1730 E St N.W. This stately marble building was constructed in 1928 and was originally the headquarters of the District of Columbia chapter of the Red

Cross. Currently there are plans to turn the building into a visitors center and museum by the summer of 2002. Just north of the American Red Cross, across E St, is the Corcoran Gallery.

## Corcoran Gallery of Art

500 17th St N.W., at 17th St and New York Ave N.W. ☎ 639-1700. Web: www.corcoran.org/cga/index.htm. Open Mon and Wed–Sun 10–5; Thurs 10–9. Closed Tues, New Year's Day, and Christmas Day. Admission: adults, $3; seniors and students, $1; children under 12, free; family groups, $5. Guided tours (45 minutes) of the permanent collection: daily except Tues at noon; Thurs also at 7:30. Group tours upon request Tues–Fri. Lectures, films, and exhibition-related workshops are held regularly. "Jazz at the Corcoran" Wed 12:30–1:30 in Armand Hammer Auditorium. "Gospel Brunch" Sun 10:30–2. ☎ 639-1786.

Café des Artistes open daily (except Tues) 11–3; Thurs 11–8:30. Serves breakfast, lunch, and tea; dinner on Thurs, Sun brunch 10:30–2. Beaux-Arts Bar open Thurs 5–8:30. Museum shop open during gallery hours.

Restrooms, telephones. Wheelchair accessible.

The Corcoran Gallery (1897; Ernest Flagg; 1928, Charles Platt; DL) is nationally respected for its collection of American art. Besides displaying its own collection, the Corcoran hosts temporary shows of students and professors of the Corcoran School of Art, as well as traveling exhibits. The Corcoran, which holds a wide variety of art and photography courses for adults and children, also usually hosts family art programs every other Sun. Reservations are required.

A major addition to the Corcoran Gallery and the Corcoran College of Art and Design is in the process of being designed by Frank O. Gehry, the award-winning architect who designed the Guggenheim Museum Bilbao, Spain, which opened in 1997. The new Corcoran facilities are expected to be completed in late 2003 or early 2004.

**Highlights.** *The Greek Slave* by Hiram Powers, *Niagara Falls* by Frederic Edwin Church, the Clark collection, and the Salon Doré.

### History

William Wilson Corcoran (1798–1888) was a Washington banker who, with his partner George Riggs, founded the Corcoran and Riggs Bank. In the 1840s the pair made a fortune selling war bonds. Riggs and Corcoran had negotiated a contract with the American government to be the exclusive agents of war bonds in Europe. These bonds, which were being sold to fund the Mexican War, were as unpopular with the American population as the war itself. Europeans, on the other hand, invested heavily in the certificates. Corcoran and Riggs reportedly made more than $1 million from their sales. During trips abroad Corcoran was introduced to European art and architecture.

As his collection grew, Corcoran hired James Renwick to design and build a gallery. This building is now the Renwick Gallery of the Smithsonian Institution (see "Renwick Gallery," later this walk). Construction of the building was interrupted by the Civil War. Because of Corcoran's Southern sympathies (not uncommon among the citizens of Washington), the federal government appropriated the building shortly after its completion for use as offices for Union officers and as a supply depot.

Although founded in 1869, the museum's interior was not finished until 1874, when it opened to the public. It is one of the three oldest museums in the United States. The collection was comprised of Corcoran's personal art collection, valued at the time at $100,000. The gallery's mission was "to be dedicated to art, and used solely for the purpose of encouraging the American genius in the production and preservation of works." Corcoran also bequeathed a $900,000 endowment.

The collection, and the Corcoran School of Art, quickly outgrew their home. Ernest Flagg, a recent graduate of the Ecole des Beaux-Arts, was commissioned to design a new building. The new Corcoran Gallery was dedicated on Feb 22, 1897. By this time the collection had nearly doubled to 700 works.

Ten years later the gallery held the first of its biennial series with the Exhibition of Contemporary American Oil Painting. This series, which continues today, promotes the works of American painters, realizing William Corcoran's wish that American art be justly recognized on a level with the best art in the world.

A wing was added on the west side of the building in 1928 to accommodate a collection donated by William Andrews Clark, a senator from Montana. Clark, who grew up on a farm in Pennsylvania and taught school in Missouri, had earned his fortune by discovering copper in Montana. His extensive art collection included works by many European masters, including Daumier, Degas, Rembrandt, and Turner. Clark's collection also featured Persian carpets, stained glass, tapestries, lace, ceramics, and other antiquities. The Clark Wing houses the Corcoran's European painting collection.

In 1930, the board of trustees decided to refocus the gallery's purpose and concentrate on establishing the best possible American art collection, only acquiring foreign works if an unusual opportunity presented itself. In 1974 the American collection was reorganized chronologically to display its development. This collection now includes nearly 5,000 works, and the entire permanent collection has more than 11,000 works.

More than 300,000 people visit the museum annually. Currently, under the direction of David Levy, the Corcoran is particularly strong in contemporary and avant-garde art exhibitions.

### Washington Notes

The Corcoran Gallery was the site of a homoerotic photography exhibition by Robert Mapplethorpe in 1989. The show was canceled due to controversy. The cancellation created even more controversy and led to debates about art, morals, and freedom of expression.

## Exterior

The Beaux-Arts building features Georgia white marble on a base of Milford pink granite. The roof is copper. Inscribed above the main entrance is an abbreviated version of the gallery's mission: "Dedicated to Art." Under the building's cornice are the names of 11 artists: Phidias, Giotto, Dürer, Michelangelo, Raphael, Velásquez, Rembrandt, Rubens, Reynolds, Allston, and Ingres.

## Interior

The two-story building has a grand staircase. In the south atrium the frieze running under the balcony is a cast of the Elgin marbles, the frieze taken by Lord Elgin from Athens's Parthenon and put in the British Museum.

The permanent collection is shown on the first floor on a rotating basis. Generally, the collection begins with a representative group of 18C portraits, including John Singleton Copley's *Thomas Avery II.* Among important late-18C and early-19C holdings are Samuel F. B. Morse's *The Old House of Representatives,* depicting a congressional session in 1822; Frederick Edwin Church's *Niagara Falls* (1857); and Rembrandt Peale's gigantic *Washington Before Yorktown.*

*The Greek Slave,* by American artist Hiram Powers, stands out among the museum's sculptures. This marble nude, part of Corcoran's original collection, caused much controversy when it was first displayed at the old Corcoran Gallery, now the Renwick Gallery.

The American collection is perhaps most well known for its 19C works, which include almost all the masters. Note John Singer Sargent's *The Oyster Gatherers of Cancale,* Mary Cassatt's *Susan on the Balcony with Her Dog,* and Winslow Homer's *A Light on the Sea.*

Holdings from the 20C represent major modern figures, among them Stuart Davis, Edward Hopper, Mark Rothko, Andy Warhol, and Helen Frankenthaler.

A rotunda just off the main staircase leads to the **Clark Wing,** housing Clark's private collection of European works, including Dutch, Flemish, and French Romantic paintings. The Clark Wing also contains the Walker Collection donated by Edward C. and Mary Walker, a group of French impressionist paintings that includes works by Renoir, Monet, and Pisarro.

Included in the Clark Wing is the gilded 18C Salon Doré. In 1768 Pierre-Gaspard-Marie Grimod, comte d'Orsay, commissioned artists to create this gilded room in the ground floor bedroom of the house. Clark purchased the room in 1904 for installment in his Fifth Ave home in New York. Élie Janel carved the trophy panels, which represent military arms, music, arts and sciences, and peace and love. Hugues Taraval painted the ceiling mural, the *Apotheosis of Psyche.*

Note the Hemicycle Gallery situated at the northern end of the second floor's main gallery. Hidden away for more than 50 years as part of the adjacent school, it is now used to display student and local artists' works.

Recent and upcoming exhibits include Annie Leibovitz (Oct 1999–Feb 2000), which featured more than 100 photographs by the renowned photographer; Arnold Newman: Sixty Years (March–June 2000), more than 160 photographs taken between 1938 and 1998; Norman Rockwell: Pictures for the American People (June–Sept 2000), the first major exhibit dedicated to "the people's artist" in 30 years.

**Diversion:**
Cross 17th St to the **First Infantry Division Monument,** 17th St and State Place, N.W. This monument honors soldiers in this division of the U.S. Army who died in combat. The west wing, dedicated in 1957, honors soldiers killed in World War II. The east wing, erected in 1977, honors those killed in Vietnam. A column at the center of the monument honors the U.S. Expeditionary Forces who died in battle from 1917 to 1919 during World War I. Their names are inscribed on plaques around the base. A winged figure, facing south, stands atop the column.

Return to the west side of 17th St. Walk west along New York Ave to the Octagon.

## Octagon

1799 New York Ave N.W. ☎ 638-3105. Open Tues–Sun 10–4. Closed Mon and federal holidays. The basement, first floor, and second floor are open to the public. Museum staff offices are located on third floor. Wheelchair accessible only on first floor.

The Treaty of Ghent was signed in this historic house (1801; William Thornton; DL). The property is owned and operated as a museum by the American Institute of Architects. Exhibitions focus on architecture, decorative arts, and Washington history.

Currently in the planning stages is a future renovation of the Ice House, which is located behind the Octagon. The Ice House would be turned into a greeting station and a gift shop for visitors.

### History

George Washington encouraged Colonel John Tayloe III (1771–1828) to purchase land and build a home in the new Federal City. Tayloe obliged him by buying Lot 8 in Square 170 for $1,000 from Gustavus W. Scott in April 1797. Tayloe chose the lot because of its proximity to the President's House (as the White House was then called), which was under construction at the time. Tayloe's home, designed by Dr. William Thornton, architect of the Capitol, was completed in 1801. One of the first architect-designed town houses in the United States, Tayloe's home's original cost was estimated at $13,000, but after completion three years later, the bill totaled $35,000—an amazing amount in that era.

At the time of its construction, the Octagon was a country house, three miles from the bustling port city of Georgetown. Tayloe had inherited thousands of acres of land in Virginia and hundreds of slaves. After completion of the house, he and his wife, Ann Ogle, would split their time, living in Mt. Airy, Virginia, during the summer months and Washington in the winter.

#### Washington Notes

The house immediately became a center of society in the new capital. Visitors included James Madison, Thomas Jefferson, James Monroe, General Lafayette, and many others. John Tayloe and his wife, Ann, were well-known pillars of the District's social scene. When John Tayloe entered his famous trotters in the annual Jockey Club meets, politics came to a halt as the Congress and all public officials gathered at the race track.

The Octagon is probably most famous as the temporary residence of President Madison, who signed the Treaty of Ghent here on Feb 17, 1815, ending the War of 1812.

With the War of 1812 and the British invasion of Washington, the Tayloes left the city, renting the Octagon to French Minister Louis Serurier, who occupied the house at the time of the British attack. Serurier sent a messenger to General Ross, the British officer orchestrating the burning of the President's House, asking for armed protection of the Octagon. Ross assured the French minister that the diplomatic quarters were going to be respected as if the French monarch himself resided there. Hence, the Octagon wasn't burned while the White House and other buildings were torched. While the White House was being rebuilt, the president and Dolley Madison resided at the Octagon.

From 1855, when Anne Ogle Tayloe passed away, to the end of the century, the Octagon fell into disrepair. It was used as the U.S. Hydrographic Office, then served as a girls' school, and later was rented out to families. In 1897 the American Institute of Architects (AIA) leased the house, then purchased it in 1902.

Under the ownership of the AIA, the Octagon underwent several renovations. Initially the AIA used the Octagon as its headquarters, but eventually it constructed another, larger building on the east side of the property. In 1968 the AIA transferred ownership of the Octagon to the American Architectural Foundation (AAF), a nonprofit educational organization. Two years later the Octagon opened to the public as a museum of architecture and design. The AAF completed the most recent renovations in 1955.

## Exterior

The mansion is actually not an octagon—it has six sides. The building is called the Octagon because it has eight angles. It was designed to fit the acute angle at the intersection of New York Ave and 18th St. The front and center of the mansion is a circle with two balanced rectangles angled off its sides. Two unmatched triangles fill the remaining space.

The light and elegant American Federal design marked a sharp break in Thornton's work at the time. Among his past designs were the European-styled Library Hall and the Georgian and neoclassical Capitol Building.

The Ionic column capitals in the mansion's portico are made of imported English Coade stone, an imported earthenware substance. The Octagon has the largest known collection of original surviving Coade stone architectural ornament in the U.S. A pitched roof, replacing the original flat one in 1816, was reshingled by the AAF during the 1995 restoration.

## Interior

The Octagon's interior layout was based on the mansion's functions at the time. All public rooms, except for the Treaty Room, were located on the first floor. The main bedrooms and an upstairs parlor were located on the second floor. Additional bedrooms and tutor's quarters were built on the third floor. The basement housed the kitchen and servants' quarters. (The slaves' quarters were above the laundry, an outbuilding on the property.)

The large, **circular entryway** in which public officials and guests were greeted still contains its original gray-and-white marble floor and has two cast-iron coal stoves imported from Scotland. Just past the entryway is an impressive oval staircase with mahogany-and-iron balusters that winds its way up to the third floor.

The **drawing room,** to the right of the staircase, was the most important room in the house and features a view of the White House, the Capitol, and the Potomac. This room, as well as the dining room on the opposite side of the house, both contain original, intricately carved Coade stone mantels.

The **dining room** is furnished with simple, classically designed Federal furniture. Decorating the walls are Gilbert Stuart's portraits of John and Ann Tayloe.

The **Treaty Room,** where the War of 1812 was ended on Feb 17, 1815, with President Madison's signing of the Treaty of Ghent, is located on the second floor in the circular room directly above the entryway. Scholars believe that the treaty was signed on the circular table.

The Tayloes's master bedroom, adjacent to the study on the east side, is larger than the other bedrooms on the second floor, which are currently used as galleries. The third floor rooms, which now serve as museum offices, were smaller bedrooms for family members and tutors.

One of the more interesting design aspects of the Octagon's layout is the intricate detailing in the **basement,** which housed the kitchen and servants' hall. The floor is bricked in a herringbone pattern. The ceiling is double-layered. One layer of wood comprises the floor above, while a second made of wood and plaster beneath it insulates the chambers. This technique, called nogging, was used to prevent noise from the busy kitchen below rising to the public rooms.

The basement also contains a cistern once used to pump water for use throughout the house and a large wine cellar. The servants were kept as inconspicuous as possible. A separate staircase to the dining room was constructed for them, away from the main stairs. Two jib doors in the dining room, and a smaller pantry next to the dining room, allowed servants to serve the guests conveniently without using formal entryways.

### Washington Notes

For an example of how legends can outlive facts, especially in a rumor mill such as Washington, consider the story of the Tayloe daughters. Supposedly in the early 1800s one of Tayloe's daughters fell from the top of the spiral staircase to her death. The accident reportedly occurred after a heated argument with her father over her British boyfriend. Legend has it that on stormy nights her ghost can be heard re-creating the fall with a shriek and a thud. Also another of Tayloe's daughters supposedly died on these stairs after the War of 1812. Sources at the time claim that she had come to ask her father's forgiveness after marrying against his wishes. Colonel Tayloe pushed her aside and she tumbled down the stairs, breaking her neck. Supposedly, her spirit also haunts the house. The fact that both daughters died elsewhere has not hampered the enthusiastic retelling of the ghoulish legend of the stairs in many books and ghost tours of Washington, D.C.

Proceed east along New York Ave. Cross 17th St and walk north.

## Old Executive Office Building

17th St and Pennsylvania Ave N.W. ☎ 395-5895. Admission: free. Ninety-minute tours available Sat at 9, 10, 10:30, and 11. Reservations required; book three to four weeks in advance. Sign language tours available with sufficient notice. Call or write to: Preservation Office, Room 576, Old Executive Office Building, Washington, DC 20503, with name, date of birth, country of citizenship, and social security number. Wheelchair accessible. No public facilities. No photography or video cameras.

Originally built for the staff of the State, War, and Navy Departments, the Old Executive Office Building (OEOB) (1875–88; Alfred B. Mullett; DL) now houses various agencies of the executive branch, including the White House Office, the Office of the Vice President, the Office of Management and Budget, and the National Security Council. Once slated for demolition, the building is considered by many to be the best surviving example of French Second Empire architecture in the U.S.

### History

From 1799 until the 1820s a complex of four two-story brick buildings surrounded the White House. These buildings housed the Treasury, State, War, and Navy Departments. When the Treasury Department Building burned down for the second time in 1833, plans to fireproof government buildings were discussed.

The War Department Building, which also housed the Navy and State Departments, had been torched once by the British in their Aug 1814 attack on Washington. Since fireproof (or at least fire-resistant) construction materials were available—as was evidenced by the Robert Mills–designed Treasury Building and the Washington Monument—Congress decided it was vital to house sensitive government material in fireproof buildings. Although several options were presented for a new State, War, and Navy Department building, plans were interrupted by the Mexican War in 1846, and then by the Civil War.

After the State Department Building was razed in 1866 to provide space for the north wing addition of the Treasury Building, the State Department temporarily relocated to the D.C. Orphans Asylum. But it wasn't until 1869, when the continued growth of the State, War, and Navy Departments had put the Executive Office's buildings in a state of cluttered confusion, forcing some departments to rent additional office space elsewhere, that a plan to create a single structure to house all three departments was developed.

In Dec 1869, under the direction of Secretary of State Hamilton Fish, a commission was assembled to oversee the project. Supervising architect of the Treasury Alfred B. Mullett designed a building plan, and in March 1871 Congress approved construction at a cost of $500,000. The new fireproof building was to be built on a plot west of the White House where the previous War and Navy Departments were located.

Construction went slowly. The architectural design was elaborate and much of the progress depended on how fast granite could be quarried and cut. Progress was further complicated by cost overruns. Eighteen separate appropriations were required to keep up with additional costs. In 1888, 17 years after construction had begun, the building was completed at a final cost of $10 million.

Mullett supervised construction until Dec 1874 when he resigned after the new secretary of the treasury, William Bristow, revoked Mullett's authority to certify disbursements. Of the three wings in Mullett's design, only the south wing had neared completion at the time. Following two interim supervisors, Colonel Thomas Casey, construction supervisor for the Washington Monument, took over in 1877 and remained until the project's completion in 1888. He successfully reduced costs and streamlined Mullett's intricate details while remaining faithful to Mullett's design.

### Washington Notes

In 1889 Mullett sued the U.S. government for $160,000 for professional services rendered in the construction of the OEOB. He claimed that his work on the project was above and beyond his duty as supervising architect of the Treasury. Mullett lost the case. The court decision, paired with his wife's mental illness, the decline of his architectural practice, and a lawsuit against him, drove Mullett to suicide in Oct 1890.

The State Department occupied the building in 1875. When reports of the opulence of State Department offices reached the Navy and War Departments, they ordered Casey to provide their offices with lavish furnishings as well. The navy began occupying the east wing in 1879.

Within the first decades of the 20C, the departments had outgrown their new building. In July 1918 occupancy reached an all-time high of 4,500 employees, and the departments began renting additional space. The navy moved out in 1918, followed by the War Department in 1938. The State Department relocated to Foggy Bottom in 1947. The building's name was changed once again to the Executive Office Building.

### Washington Notes

Several presidents, writers, and Washingtonians were outspoken about what they considered to be Mullett's eyesore. Herbert Hoover criticized the OEOB as an "architectural orgy foisted on Washington," and President Harry S. Truman labeled it "the greatest monstrosity in America." Henry Adams condemned the structure as an "architectural infant asylum." Never at a loss for cynicism, Mark Twain added his two cents, calling it "the ugliest building in America." In 1957 President Eisenhower's administration recommended that the building be razed; however, the cost of demolition was too high and the plan was abandoned. In 1971 destruction of the building became impossible when it was declared a National Historic Landmark.

Few physical alterations have been made to the building during its lifetime. In the 1960s the subsurface areas of the south courtyard were reconstructed, and in the 1970s an auditorium was installed on the fourth floor of the north wing's central pavilion. In the 1980s a historic restoration was undertaken. The State and War Departments' libraries have been restored as well as the secretary of the navy's office, the Indian Treaty Room, and several corridors and stairways. In 1986, the National Security Council moved in.

### Washington Notes

More than 1,000 treaties have been signed in the building. Some of the important historical events include the signing of the Bretton Woods Treaty (1944), the Treaty of Versailles (1919), and the United Nations Declaration (1942), the televising of the first presidential press conference (Jan 19, 1955), and the revoking of the diplomatic papers of the Japanese on Dec 7, 1941, after the bombing of Pearl Harbor.

Seven men who became president had offices here—Theodore and Franklin Roosevelt, William Taft (whose pet cow Pauline grazed on the south lawn), Dwight Eisenhower, Lyndon Johnson, Gerald Ford, and George Bush.

## Exterior

When the building was completed, it was the largest office building in the U.S. The six-story structure boasts four-ft-thick Virginia granite walls. Two stories are simply styled but support three highly decorated stories and the two-story mansard roof. An equally high central pavilion rises from the main entrance, distinguished on each level by a portico and Doric or Ionic colonnades. There are 900 exterior columns, more than 550 rooms, and nearly two miles of marble corridors connecting them. Hundreds of windows have varying segmental, triangular, and straight hood molds. Large white chimneys break the roofline.

Though dozens of cannons and guns once decorated the exterior, many were melted as scrap metal to support various war efforts. The two that remain on the north side of the building were seized in the Spanish-American war. In the north pediment of the wing that housed the War Department, there is a suit of armor flanked by a cannon, cannon balls, and assorted medieval weapons.

The planters were added by building superintendent Douglas McArthur in 1913.

## Interior

An outstanding architectural feat at the time, the OEOB successfully integrated such technological advances as fireproofing, heating, ventilation, and plumbing with French Second Empire design.

Visitors are generally surprised at the elaborate and elegant detailing planned by Mullett, the original architect and designer, and his successors, Thomas Casey and Richard von Ezdorf, who put the kind of pizzazz most often associated with Austro-Venetian palaces into this democratic work station. Marble floors, ornate bronze balusters, and granite, spiral staircases that lead to skylit domes, some with stained glass and others with gold leaf, are just some of the accoutrements. The libraries feature lacy, tiered wrought-iron balconies, and Minton tile floors.

> ### Washington Notes
> President Franklin Roosevelt requested that all the building's swinging doors be removed after visiting British Prime Minister Winston Churchill was accidentally hit by a door as an aide exited an office. The handrails leading from the second to the fourth floors were installed at the request of the portly William Taft, who at 300 pounds had difficulty climbing the stairs.

The south wing, the most time-consuming and costly of the building's three wings, was the only wing whose construction Mullett oversaw. Consequently, Mullett's design is most visible here. Elaborately furnished and decorated originally at a cost of $75,000, the south wing includes the Secretary of State's Office, the Diplomatic Reception Room, and the State Department Library—now the **White House Library and Research Center.** Originally constructed entirely of cast iron, the White House Library features a vaulted ceiling, an intricate iron balcony, and an English Minton tile floor.

In the original plan for the south wing, there were no passageways between this and the two other wings in an effort to maintain "the quiet and privacy which are essential to the proper conduct of business in the Department of State," which included the office of the president. However, a congressional ruling in 1882 required that the barriers be removed.

The east wing was constructed over a seven-year period. The **Indian Treaty Room** is used for conferences, press interviews, and entertaining. When the Navy Department occupied this wing, the room was used as the Navy's Library Reception Room. The room has marble walls, Minton-patterned tile floors, and ornate bronze lighting fixtures. Framing the room is a balcony with a wrought-iron railing woven with nautical decorations and sea horses. Overlooking the room are mermaidlike sculptures symbolizing liberty, war, peace, industry, arts, and sciences. These 800-pound bronze figures were created by von Ezdorf, who employed children as his models.

The **Vice President's Office** was originally used by the secretary of the navy. The ceiling is covered with gold leaf and the china cabinet belonged to Ulysses S. Grant. The parquet floor is crafted from mahogany, cherry, and maple. Its fireplace mantels are constructed from black Belgian marble. The hand-stenciling on the ceiling and desk dates to Franklin Roosevelt's administration. Beginning with Truman, each vice president has left his signature in the desk's top drawer.

The north wing was completed in two years and seven months. Similar in design to the south wing, the stairways in the north wing are circular (unlike the south wing's elliptical ones), which simplified and expedited construction.

The west and central wings, built on the site of the old Navy Department Building, were the final wings to be completed (in Jan 1888). The west wing features the **Secretary of War's Office Suite,** the only rooms in the building not designed by Mullett or von Ezdorf. Stephen Decatur Hatch of New York City decorated these rooms in heavy ornamentation, using dark hardwood paneling.

The **War Department Library** is decorated with fireproof cast iron in classical, Gothic, Moorish, and other styles. The iron, electroplated to resemble bronze, brass, and black iron, gives the effect of a mixture of metals.

Walk north on 17th St and cross Pennsylvania Ave.

## Renwick Gallery

Pennsylvania Ave at 17th St N.W. ☎ 357-2700 or 357-4522 (TTY). Web: www.nmaa-ryder.si.edu/collections/index.html. Open daily 10–5:30. Closed Christmas Day. Admission: free. Guided tours at 10, 11, and 1. Sign language tours and oral interpreters available with reservation. ☎ 357-2531 or 357-4522 (TTY). Wheelchair accessible—ramp located at Pennsylvania Ave entrance, lower level. Wheelchairs available.

Telephones, restrooms, museum shop. On two Thurs per month, at lunchtime, the Renwick sponsors a film called *The Creative Screen.* To receive a calendar of monthly events, send your name and address to: Office of Public Affairs, Room 182, National Museum of American Art, Smithsonian Institution, Washington DC 20560. The Renwick also has crafts demonstrations on Sat afternoons. Call for information.

The Renwick Gallery of the National Museum of American Art (1859; James Renwick; DL), an adjunct of the Smithsonian Institution's National Museum of American Art, displays American crafts dating from 1900 to the present.

**Highlights:** The gallery houses the nation's premier collection of American crafts with about 450 objects of glass, ceramic, wood, fiber, and metal. Pieces from the permanent collection, featuring works by Albert Paley, Harvey Littleton, and Peter Voulkos, are shown on a rotating basis. The Grand Salon, decorated in the lavish style of the 1860s–1870s, has been given a major renovation and reopened to the public in spring 2000. When the National Museum of American Art (see Walk 13: "Judiciary Square/Chinatown Area") closed in Jan 2000 for a three-year renovation, a selection of its 19C works were hung in the Grand Salon.

### History

The Renwick was built in 1858–59 by William Wilson Corcoran, the founder of Riggs Bank and a philanthropist, to house Corcoran's $100,000 art collection. The French Second Empire–style building was designed by 27-year-old James Renwick, Jr., who was well known for designing the Smithsonian Castle.

Corcoran wasn't the first to use his new building, however. Only a few months before construction was completed, the Civil War erupted and the federal government appropriated the building. It was used as a depot and headquarters for the quartermaster general of the Union Army, Montgomery C. Meigs. To prevent the government from seizing his house on the corner of H St and Connecticut Ave, Corcoran leased it to the French minister, Marquis de Montholon. Corcoran, a Confederate sympathizer, waited out the war in Europe.

Corcoran returned in 1869 and incorporated the Corcoran Gallery of Art in 1870, the same year New York's Museum of Modern Art and Boston's Museum of Fine Arts were opened. It was Washington's first art museum.

> #### Washington Notes
> Although Corcoran founded his gallery in 1869, the museum's interior was not fully completed until 1874. Corcoran opened the gallery on Feb 20, 1874, with a gala ball to benefit the Washington Monument. The event coincided with a three-day celebration of Washington's "new era." President and Mrs. Grant, as well as many of Washington's most distinguished citizens, attended the event. Outside the picture-lined halls of the Grand Salon, a Mardi Gras parade marched through the streets as all of Washington celebrated the completion of the wood paving of Pennsylvania Ave and the passage of Washington's Territorial Act, which declared self-rule for the District.

Having outgrown its building, the Corcoran Gallery moved to its present location, 17th St and New York Ave, in 1897. Two years later the U.S. Court of Claims moved into the old gallery, and Corcoran eventually sold the building to the government in March 1901 for $300,000. The court occupied the building until 1964. In 1965 the building was transferred to the Smithsonian Institution and renamed the Renwick Gallery in honor of its architect. Designated as an arts, crafts, and design museum, it opened to the public in Jan 1972.

> #### Washington Notes
> The building that now houses the Renwick Gallery was one of the Lafayette Square buildings named by the McMillan Commission to be razed in the name of progress. (This group of architects and landscape designers obviously didn't care for James Renwick's designs; his Smithsonian Castle was also listed for destruction.) As the General Services Administration and Congress were preparing to demolish the building, the Kennedy administration saved the building by adding it to their Lafayette Square restoration project.

## Exterior

Renwick modeled his design after a style developed for the Tuileries addition to the Louvre Museum that was completed for the Paris Exposition of 1855. Both Corcoran and Renwick had visited the Louvre and admired its mixture of architectural motifs. The style came to be known as Second Empire and can be seen in the Old Executive Office Building across the street.

The Renwick's façade of brick and stone appears as it did in the mid-19C. In 1976, when stones falling from the building became a hazard, all potentially dangerous stones were removed and replaced, duplicating the color and texture of the originals. In the 1880s and 1890s the original second-story niches held 11 statues of famous artists created by Moses Jacob Ezekiel. The artists, chosen by Corcoran, were Phidias, Raphael, Michelangelo, Dürer, Titian, da Vinci, Rubens, Rembrandt, Utrillo, Canova, and Thomas Crawford. Crawford, the sole American, was esteemed by Corcoran as the greatest contemporary sculptor. These statues can now be found in the Norfolk (Va.) Botanical Gardens. During the tenure of the U.S. Court of Claims, these niches were knocked through to create windows, six of which have been retained.

The four highest points of the building are topped with pavilions designed with intricate ironwork. This decoration is repeated in the elaborate stone carvings surrounding the second-story mantel. A stone inscription "Dedicated to Art," as well as a four-ft-wide portrait medallion of Corcoran and his monogram enshrouded in laurel leaves, are centered above the entrance.

To distinguish the museum as distinctly American, Renwick used red brick rather than European sandstone. Shucked corn and tobacco leaves decorate the capitals of the columns instead of the typical acanthus leaves.

## Interior

The two-storied museum contains a series of 20- and 30-ft-ceilinged gallery rooms, as well as two period rooms, the Grand Salon and the Octagon Room, decorated in the style of the 1860s and 1870s.

Temporary exhibitions are displayed on the first floor as well as in two gallery rooms on the second floor. A rotating selection of the permanent collection is normally displayed in the gallery rooms running between the Grand Salon and the Octagon Room on the second floor.

The permanent collection of roughly 300 objects features Albert Paley's *Portal Gates* (1974), a hand-forged, steel-and-brass doorframe with a remarkably fluid and original design; Mary Lee Hu's *Choker* (1978), a woven silver, gold, and copper decorative neckpiece; Peter Voulkos's *Rocking Pot* (1956), a free-form expressionistic stoneware piece; Michael Hurwitz's *Rocking Chaise* (1989), a flawlessly crafted rocking chair, made out of mahogany, steel pipe, and milk paint; and Richard Mawdsley's *Feast Bracelet* (1974), a miniature artistic table setting forged from sterling silver, with jade and pearls.

The James Renwick Alliance, a national nonprofit organization founded in 1982, has played an important role in acquiring works, donating more than $220,000. Other important artists represented in the collection are Dale Chihuly, Mark Lindquist, Anni Albers, Wendell Castle, and William Harper.

Temporary exhibitions run throughout the year. Past exhibitions have included Louis Comfort Tiffany's masterworks, the pottery of George Ohr, beads in contemporary American art, new American furniture, and fiber art by Lenore Tawney.

The **Grand Salon** is located at the top of the staircase. This gallery, originally known as the Main Picture Gallery, displayed W. W. Corcoran's collection of paintings. They were hung above the wainscoting, out of the line of sight, in a popular method called "skying." The watercolor illustration by James Renwick hanging in the room serves as a guide to the room's intended design. In the 1870s elaborate plasterwork was added to the ceiling, cornice, and frieze. Now paintings on loan from the National Museum of American Art, from its 19C American collection, hang where Corcoran's paintings were once displayed. Three paintings here are on loan from the Corcoran Gallery: *William Wilson Corcoran* (1870) by William Oliver Stone, *The Helping Hand* by Emile Renouf, and *The Trial of Queen Katherine* by Edwin Austin Abbey.

The room remains decorated in a French salon style authentic to the mid- to late-19C. All of the furniture except the room's large chest was previously owned by Richard Rush, a former member of the Smithsonian's board of regents. Pieces on display include gilt chairs and sofas, marble-topped cabinets with gilt bronze fittings and inlaid patterns of brass and tortoise shell, popular in France in the 17C.

Velvet-covered benches surround the pedestals of the bronze torches. These 1860 figures holding now-electrified gaslights are signed by the French sculptor Paul Dubois and caster Ferdinand Barbedienne. Reproduced bentwood chairs are like those designed by Michael Thonet.

Along the south wall, four tall display cases, once belonging to the Smithsonian Castle, date to the 19C. The cases exhibit works of porcelain, enamel, and glass from the John Gellatly Collection of the National Museum of American Art and from the National Museum of American History's collection.

Opposite the Grand Salon is the **Octagon Room,** designed specifically to exhibit W. W. Corcoran's most important and provocative work, *The Greek Slave* (now at the Corcoran Gallery), by American sculptor Hiram Powers.

> ### *Washington Notes*
> Since this nude statue embarrassed the genteel Washington community, Corcoran established separate viewing hours for men and women and charged a $.25 admission. Visitors were required to be at least 16 years old.

According to James Renwick's plan, the Octagon Room, the building's focal point, has six sides—not eight as the name suggests. The room's crystal-and-gilt chandeliers date from the mid-19C, and the room is decorated in the Renaissance revival style. In the center of the room stands the "Berlin Vase," painted after the frescoes *Aurora* and *Self-Portrait* by 17C painter Guido Reni. The furniture includes a rosewood cabinet. The custom-woven upholstery and drapery fabrics were reproduced from documented ones in the Smithsonian collection. The carpet, also custom-made for the room, complements the plaster ceiling decoration above it.

Upcoming exhibits include Spirited Objects: Traditional Craft for the 21st Century (Oct 2000–Jan 2001), presenting the finest contemporary examples of traditional American crafts such as Pueblo earthenware pottery and Appalachian split-oak basketry; and George Catlin's Indian Gallery (Nov 2000–April 2001), an unparalleled collection of 445 paintings created by the lawyer-turned-painter during the years 1830–36.

## Blair House

Proceed east along Pennsylvania Ave. A few houses on the left is the Blair House, 1651 Pennsylvania Ave N.W. (1824; architect unknown). Known as the Presidential Guest House, Blair House incorporates four separate houses: the original Blair House and the adjacent Lee House (both on Pennsylvania Ave), and two houses on Jackson Place. It is not open to the public.

### History

Blair House, built in 1824 by Dr. Joseph Lovell, the first surgeon general, was a mirror image of the nearby Ringgold-Carroll House, 1801 F St N.W. When Lovell died in 1836, the house was sold to Francis Preston Blair, Sr., for $6,500. Blair had earned a fortune in Washington real estate as well as from his newspaper, the *Congressional Globe,* a paper that enthusiastically supported Jacksonian Democracy. Blair and his son Montgomery Blair served as advisors to several presidents.

In 1843 Blair built a house next door to his own for his daughter Elizabeth Blair Lee and her new husband, Samuel Phillips Lee, cousin of Robert E. Lee. Elizabeth Blair Lee grew friendly with President Jackson. The president expressed his feelings by presenting Lee with his late wife's wedding ring.

Two years later Blair permanently moved to his 200-acre summer estate, Silver Spring, just north of Washington, near what is now Georgia Ave. Montgomery Blair, an attorney who represented Dred Scott and later served as postmaster general, then moved into the Blair House.

### Washington Notes

Abraham Lincoln often stopped by the house during neighborhood walks, and several historic political decisions were made in the house. At the request of President Lincoln, the young Blair met with Robert E. Lee, then commandant of West Point, at the Blair House to offer Lee the command of the Union troops. Citing his southern roots, Lee refused. After agonizing about the decision at his Arlington home, Lee packed his gear and headed for Richmond to command the Confederate Army. Another Civil War commission was accepted at the house, however. In 1861 David Glasgow Farragut was appointed commander of the Union attack on New Orleans.

In the years before the federal government purchased the Blair House, it was leased to several cabinet members and other political and military figures. George Bancroft, known as the "father of American history" for his extensive writings, lived in the house for a year. During that time he founded the United States Naval Academy in Annapolis, Maryland. Succeeding him as a tenant was Thomas Ewing, the first secretary of the interior. Ewing's daughter Ellen later married Lieutenant William Tecumseh Sherman in the house.

The house remained in the Blair family until 1942 when the government purchased it and its 18C–19C antique furnishings for $142,000. Blair House was acquired to serve as the president's guest house and was connected by interior doorways with the adjacent Lee House in 1943, which the government had also purchased the year before.

### Washington Notes

From 1948 to 1951, President Harry Truman and his family resided in Blair House while the White House was being renovated. On Nov 1, 1950, a pair of Puerto Rican nationalists stormed the Blair House with guns. Oscar Collazo and Grielio Torresola were hoping to draw attention to the problems their island was experiencing. The two never made it past the entrance. Torresola was killed by White House Secret Service Agent Leslie Coffelt, who died from bullet wounds. Collazo was also shot, but survived to stand trial. Although convicted and sentenced to death, the nationalist's sentence was lessened to life in prison by Truman. A plaque on the door commemorates Coffelt's service.

In 1960 the U.S. government purchased the two adjacent Victorian houses on Jackson Place to be used as additional guest houses. In 1982, after a series of structural problems, Blair House was declared unsafe. The building was closed and the White House ordered an extensive renovation as well as the construction of a two-story wing and the connection of all four guest houses. Reopened in 1988, Blair House continues to operate as the President's guest house.

### Washington Notes

Eleanor Roosevelt is often credited as the motivator to purchase a separate residence for dignitaries visiting Washington. According to legend, Mrs. Roosevelt bumped into White House overnight guest Winston Churchill in his nightshirt. When the first lady asked the British prime minister why he was wandering the halls in the middle of the night with a burning cigar and a snifter of brandy, he replied, "To see Franklin." Apparently, the two had been carousing late into the night and Churchill wanted to continue, whereas the president sneaked off to bed. Mrs. Roosevelt shooed Churchill back to bed, replying, "Oh no, you're not. You've kept him up half the night as it is. Now please just go back to your room and let him rest."

## Exterior

Blair House was built in the Federal style with a scored stuccoed façade. Two Victorian-style houses, at 700 and 704 Jackson Place, are now annexed to either side of the original two-story family home.

## Interior

Blair House was closed in 1982 after the discovery of a natural gas leak. In May 1982 major renovations began. With a $9.7 million congressional grant, as well as $5 million in private donations, the buildings were given a face-lift. Structural problems were corrected, a new wing was added to the complex, and under the direction of interior designers Mario Buatta and Mark Hampton, the interiors were fully renovated.

Blair House now provides 70,000 square ft of living space, including 35 bathrooms and 7 guest bedrooms. In the 112 rooms of the four-house complex 2,150 yards of carpet were laid, 96 curtains hung, and 1,860 yards of decorative trim added to upholstery. The goal was to present an authentic and traditional American decor for foreign visitors, using as many of the original Federal furnishings as possible.

In the Blair family's original dining room English Chippendale chairs are covered with needlepoint seats. The rear drawing room features the Blair's original chandelier and fireplace. Above the mantel hangs a portrait of Daniel Webster, secretary of state from 1841 to 1843.

Rooms of note include the high-ceiling study dedicated to President Truman, who used it as an office. A portrait of Francis Blair painted by Thomas Sully in 1845 hangs here as well. A three-room suite, refurbished more lavishly than the rest of the house, was created for the primary guest.

The nearest Metro Station is Farragut West (Blue/Orange Line). Walk west to 17th St. Turn right and walk north two blocks. The Metro Station is located on I St. To continue to the next walk, cross Pennsylvania Ave. Walk east, pass the White House, and enter East Executive Park on the right. The Visitor's Entrance to the White House is halfway through the park on the right.

# 9 · The White House and Lafayette Square

Metro: Blue/Orange Line to Farragut West or McPherson Square.
Bus: 32, 34, 35, 36, 38B, 42, 52, 54, 80, G8, N2, N4, N6, S2, S4, or X2.

## The White House

1600 Pennsylvania Ave N.W. ☎ 456-7041 (24-hour recording); (800) 717-1450; 456-2121 (TTY). Web: www.whitehouse.gov. Open Tues–Sat 10–12. Closed Sun–Mon, holidays, and for official functions. Admission: free.

Timed, day-of, first-come, first-served tickets required year-round. Tickets for self-guided tour available beginning at 7:30 A.M. at the White House Visitor Center, 15th and E Sts N.W. ☎ 208-1631. Open daily 7:30–4. Metro: Blue/Orange Line to Federal Triangle or Red Line to Metro Center. Four-ticket limit per person. Everyone, including children, needs a ticket. Tickets for guided tour, known as VIP tickets, should be requested four to six months in advance from your congressperson.

Wheelchair accessible through public entrance on Executive Ave. No tickets necessary. Four visitors may enter with each handicapped person. No public restrooms. No photography or videotaping.

Self-guided tour: Enter White House through East Wing; view Vermeil Room and Library; visit East Room, Green Room, Blue Room, Red Room, and State Dining Room, and Cross Hall; exit through North Portico. Tour time: about 15–20 minutes. U.S. Secret Service Tour Officers are located in each room to answer questions.

VIP Tours guided 8:15–8:45 by U.S. Secret Service Tour Officers, although questions are not answered until the end. Enter White House through East Wing; visit Vermeil Room, China Room, Diplomatic Reception Room, Library, East Room, Green Room, Blue Room, Red Room, State Dining Room, and Cross Hall; exit through North Portico. Group size: 60–80 people.

Special events include: Easter Egg Roll on the South Lawn on Easter Mon; children aged 3–6 permitted to participate in activities; no adults admitted without a child. Garden tours of approximately 40–45 minutes held on designated weekends in Oct and April; no tickets necessary. Candlelight tours 5–7 on designated evenings in late Dec.

Note: Watch the 35-minute film "Within These Walls" at the White House Visitor Center. It provides an excellent introduction to the White House, depicts each room on the tour, and details the building's history, architecture, renovations, decor, and historical significance. The Visitor Center has exhibits on the first ladies,

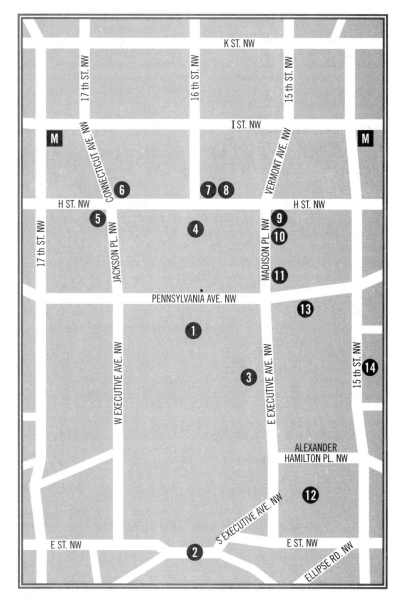

the construction and renovation of the White House, and also presents a video of Mrs. John F. Kennedy's televised tour of the White House. Wheelchair accessible. Restrooms, museum shop.

The White House (1792; James Hoban; DL) has served as the official residence

| | |
|---|---|
| 1 White House | 8 St. John's Parish House |
| 2 Zero Milestone Marker | 9 Cutts-Madison House |
| 3 East Executive Park | 10 Tayloe House |
| 4 Lafayette Square Park | 11 Treasury Annex Building |
| 5 Decatur House | 12 Sherman Park |
| 6 U.S. Chamber of Commerce Building | 13 Treasury Building |
| 7 St. John's Church | 14 Old Ebbitt Grill |

for every president but George Washington. It is the oldest public building in the city.

**Highlights:** The China Room, Diplomatic Reception Room, the East Room, the Blue Room, and the State Dining Room.

#### History

On July 16, 1790, the U.S. Congress passed an act determining the region near the banks of the Potomac River as the nation's capital. This act also empowered George Washington to select the exact location for the Federal City and oversee the future city's design. French engineer, Pierre L'Enfant, created a city plan based upon two focal points: the Capitol Building and the President's House.

In June 1791 Washington reviewed L'Enfant's proposed site for the White House and suggested that the president's house be moved to higher ground closer to Rock Creek and to the trading post of Georgetown. Washington preferred the newer site for its downhill view of the Potomac River. The 255 acres in the area where the White House would be built was purchased from Ninian Beall.

Because L'Enfant never produced a design for the White House (he was fired), at the suggestion of Thomas Jefferson in 1792, Washington and the commissioners for the District of Columbia announced a design contest. The winner was promised either $500 or a medal of the same value. One entry, based on Palladio's Villa Rotunda near Vicenza in Italy, was designed by Thomas Jefferson, who entered it anonymously under the initials "A.Z." On July 17, 1792, James Hoban, a self-taught Irish architect practicing in Charleston, South Carolina, won the contest. He chose a gold medal worth less than $500 and requested the remaining amount in cash.

Hoban's design was based on Leinster House in Dublin and other Anglo-Irish Georgian country houses in the British Isles. With great ceremony the cornerstone was laid on Oct 13, 1792, on the 300th anniversary of Columbus's landing in America. According to the Charleston (South Carolina) *City Gazette and Daily Advertiser,* the only detailed report of the occasion, a grand procession led by the Freemasons began in Georgetown and continued to President's Square (now Lafayette Square Park). After a speech by Peter Casanave, master of the lodge, a brass plaque was placed under the cornerstone with the inscription "This first stone of the President's House was laid the 13th Day of October, 1792, and in the 17th Year of Independence of the United States of America." The names of George Washington, James Hoban, Peter Casanave, and construction commissioners were also inscribed. Efforts made on several occasions to locate this original plaque have been unsuccessful.

Hoban also laid the cornerstone to the U.S. Capitol along with President Washington in Sept 1793. He also served as superintendent for much of the Capitol's construction.

During construction, the White House grounds were cluttered with building materials and shacks for workers. The three kilns that produced all the bricks for the White House and other federal buildings stood where the north grounds of the White House are today. Hoban recruited stonemasons from Edinburgh, Scotland, many of whom lived in shanties in President's Square. The stone for the foundations and façades was delivered by boat, up the Potomac, from Aquina Creek Quarry in Stafford County, Virginia. In 1798 the building's exterior was whitewashed to seal the Aquina sandstone, giving it the white appearance from which its name was later derived. Much of the timber came from North Carolina and Virginia. Mount Vernon and Stratford Hall plantations also contributed lumber to the project.

When Washington left office in 1797, the walls were standing and the roof was framed. During the next three years workers installed windows and plastered the interior. John Adams, the second president, moved into the White House on Nov 1, 1800, before the building was completed, for the last four months of his term. Mrs. Adams came to the presidential mansion two weeks after her husband, exhausted by her journey from Boston. Her coach often lost its way, and at times the road was so overgrown with brush that a man was forced to sit on the coach and chop away branches.

### Washington Notes

The succeeding president, Thomas Jefferson, originally dismissed the White House as "big enough for two emperors, one Pope, and the grand Lama." Jefferson opened the house in the mornings to visitors, a tradition that continues.

President Jefferson and Benjamin Latrobe added the East and West Terraces. Although Jefferson also added landscaping, his work is hardly evident today since Andrew Jackson Downing was commissioned in 1849 to relandscape the grounds.

James and Dolley Madison moved into the house in 1809. On Aug 24, 1814, British forces under Rear Admiral George Cockburn torched the White House. The exterior sandstone and interior brickwork were the only remnants, saved by a violent thunderstorm that extinguished the flames. While the Madisons moved into the Octagon House, Hoban reconstructed the White House in addition to two adjacent executive offices from 1815 to 1817. Hoban reconstructed the damaged walls, coating them with whitewash.

In Sept 1817 President James Monroe, like President Adams before him, moved into an unfinished house. With a $20,000 grant from Congress, Monroe furnished the house with china, silver, and gilded furniture from French and Georgetown cabinetmakers. A few years later, in 1824, Monroe enlisted Hoban to add the semicircular South Portico. The North Portico was added by Hoban in 1829.

### Washington Notes

Agreeing with Jefferson's democratic stance that the president's house should be accessible to the people, President Jackson held an open reception at the White House after his inauguration in 1829. Unfortunately, the people trampled the president's lawn and flowerbeds in order to meet Jackson and eat the free refreshments. "The rabble," as the crowd was later referred to, mobbed Jackson, pinning him against the wall in the oval drawing room. Escaping through a window leading onto the South Portico, Jackson rushed back to his temporary residence at the Gadsby Hotel.

There were dangers of other sorts. Well into the 19C the White House was an unhealthy place to live. Until 1859 sewage from the White House drained into the marshy Ellipse behind the White House and the dirty and foul-smelling Washington Canal joined the Potomac not far away. The city dump, at the bottom of 17th St, was also close by.

Indoor bathrooms and running water came to the White House in 1833, and gas lighting in 1848. The first truly efficient heating and central plumbing systems were installed in 1853 for President Franklin Pierce. Benjamin Harrison introduced electric lighting to the house in 1891.

As the nation's power and wealth expanded, so did Washington's importance. In 1860 President Buchanan sponsored two important social events: the arrival of Japanese dignitaries and a visit from the Prince of Wales, the future King Edward VII. In the following years, the Civil War brought strife to the nation.

### Washington Notes

President Lincoln signed the Emancipation Proclamation from his second-story office in the White House. Troops were housed in the East Room when the war first began, the same room where thousands of mourners filed by Lincoln's body after his assassination. Sixteen years later, the White House entered another period of mourning when James A. Garfield fell to an assassin's bullet.

When Grover Cleveland moved into the White House in 1885, he became the second bachelor president. In 1886, however, he married Frances Folsom in the Blue Room. Cleveland is the only president to have been married in the White House. Rutherford B. Hayes is the only president to be sworn into office at the White House.

Prior to President Theodore Roosevelt's election, the house was officially called the Executive Mansion, but was popularly known as the White House. In 1901 Roosevelt made the the White House name official. During his term, Congress appropriated funds for extending and remodeling the residence. In 1902 workers refurbished the house and built new offices for the president and for staff. By 1909 more space was needed. The West Wing offices were enlarged and the now famous Oval Office was added. The current Oval Office dates from an enlargement of the West Wing that took place in 1934.

### Washington Notes

The President's desk, presented to President Rutherford B. Hayes by Queen Victoria, was fashioned from timbers of the British ship HMS *Resolute*. President Kennedy retrieved the desk from storage. The desk was also used by Presidents Carter and Reagan.

In 1927 a third floor was added to the White House for more residential space. In 1934, Franklin Roosevelt expanded the West Wing once again. During World War ll the president built the East Wing, a movie theater, and air-raid shelters. In 1948 Harry S. Truman built a second-story balcony on the South Portico. From 1949 to 1952 the Trumans lived in Blair House, across Pennsylvania Avenue, while the White House was being renovated. The art and furnishings were removed. The interior was gutted; all interior walls and ceilings ripped out; a new basement poured; a new foundation laid; and steel frames set in place to take the burden of weight off the walls. The Trumans moved back into the White House in 1952.

Succeeding administrations have given a more formal, elegant image to the White House. In 1961 Jacqueline Kennedy advertised globally for any of the house's original furniture in an effort to authentically redecorate the neglected interior. Americans nationwide were able to view her accomplishment in the first-ever televised tour of the White House. In 1984 a visitor's entrance was constructed south of the East Wing. Recent renovations include the 1995 refurbishing of the Blue Room.

### *Washington Notes*

The White House has a rich history of ghost tales ranging from knocks on doors to actual appearances by dead presidents. Only two presidents have died in the building—William Henry Harrison in 1841 from pneumonia contracted during his long inaugural address, and Zachary Taylor nine years later from a gastrointestinal disruption brought on by a combination of ice milk and cherries overzealously consumed at an Independence Day celebration. Caroline Harrison (wife of Benjamin Harrison) passed away in the White House in 1892, as did Ellen Axson Wilson (first wife of Woodrow Wilson) in 1914. Two presidential children also died here. Willie Lincoln succumbed to a feverish cold at age 12. Calvin Coolidge, Jr., died at the age of 16 from a streptococcal infection.

President Lincoln's ghost inhabiting the White House is a famous Washington story. Visitors, presidents, their families, and some White House staff tell tales of their encounters with Abraham Lincoln. Many years ago Queen Wilhelmina, from the Netherlands, reportedly heard a knock on the door of her room, the Rose Room, in the middle of the night. She opened the door and found herself face to face with the towering apparition of the former president.

Winston Churchill refused to sleep in the Lincoln Bedroom or even provide an explanation, except to say the room made him uncomfortable. In the bedroom, used by Lincoln as a study, Lincoln signed the Emancipation Proclamation. According to legend, several days before his assassination, Lincoln dreamt that he walked into the East Room and found mourners surrounding a casket. A mourner informed him that the president had died.

Presidents Theodore Roosevelt, Dwight Eisenhower, and Harry Truman have all either encountered the ghost or felt his presence. Grace Coolidge is said to have seen the apparition "in black, with a stole draped across his shoulders to ward off the drafts and chills." Several staff members have met the ghost in the halls of the White House, including one of Eleanor Roosevelt's secretaries, who saw Lincoln's ghost pulling on a pair of boots in the Lincoln Bedroom. FDR's valet—claiming to have seen Lincoln—ran screaming from the house, into the arms of a security guard.

Other apparitions and stories include tales of Andrew Jackson and his laughter emanating from the bed in the Rose Room. People have reported seeing Abigail Adams carrying her laundry through the East Room. Some have claimed that the ghost of a British soldier walks the grounds with a torch in hand. He supposedly died there during the War of 1812. Reputedly, Mrs. Lincoln sometimes heard the spirit of John Tyler wooing his 20-year-old wife.

## Exterior

The White House is five times smaller than the veritable palace James Hoban planned. Hoban's design didn't fit with popular, 18C democratic opinion. The White House is a rectangular sandstone building with a circular portico to the south and a rectangular portico to the north. The roof is surrounded by a balustrade, and porticos include Ionic pilasters. The rounded South Portico features a rooftop balcony. On the opposite side of the building the North Portico supports a simple undecorated pediment.

Windows on the first level are adorned by alternating round and triangular pediments. Flanking the main structure to the east and west are one-storied wings connected by pavilions. Intricate carvings frame the double entrance doors. Surrounding the White House is the President's Park, 18 acres of grass, flower gardens, trees, and fountains.

The building is most remarkable for its stonework, the finest example of the craft in the country during the 18C. Portions of these handcarved stone walls remain today. If the stonemasons were being paid by the job, they often carved into the stone "banker marks," or small carved designs identifying their work so they could be paid.

Between 1976 and 1996 the exterior sandstone of the White House was restored. Workers began by removing more than 28 coats of paint from the intricately carved stones, some layers dating back to the paint that concealed the stones charred from the fire of 1814.

### Washington Notes

The grounds are maintained to standards set in 1935 by the Olmsted Brothers, a landscape architecture firm. Each president plants a tree on the grounds. Among the most famous is the magnolia planted by Andrew Jackson. Official functions, such as bill signings, occur in the Jacqueline Kennedy Garden on the east side of the White House, as well as in the **Rose Garden** on the west side.

Roses were first planted in this area in 1913 by Ellen Axson Wilson. The Rose Garden has been used as a reception area by several presidents. Visitors welcomed here include foreign dignitaries, Medal of Honor recipients, and astronauts. Other notable events in the Rose Garden have included the appointment of the first woman to the Supreme Court, state dinners, and the wedding of President Nixon's daughter Tricia.

## Interior

There are 132 rooms on four floors: the ground floor, state floor, second floor, and third floor. Visitors on self-guided and VIP tours are permitted to view and enter rooms on the ground and state floors. The second and third floors are used by the president and family as their residence and for entertaining official guests.

*White House (South Lawn view). Courtesy of the Washington, D.C., Convention &*
*Visitors Association.*

Famous rooms located on these upper floors are the Lincoln Bedroom, the Treaty Room (which was used as a Cabinet Room from 1865 to 1902), and the Queen's Bedroom. Executive offices are located in the West Wing as well as in the Old Executive Office Building. The first lady's staff's offices are located in the East Wing.

The tour begins in the East Wing Lobby, which has exhibits on White House history and seasonal celebrations. The lobby, built in 1942, is decorated with alternating portraits of presidents. The East Colonnade also features a small theater. The Press Room is located in the West Colonnade. From the lobby, visitors proceed through the glass-enclosed colonnade to the ground floor.

**Ground floor corridor.** Traditionally, portraits of first ladies hang in this corridor, as well as other areas of the house.

The **Library.** This room contains books on history, biography, fiction, and science written by American authors. The paneling in this room, as well as in the Vermeil and China Rooms, was salvaged from 1817 timbers and placed here during the Truman renovation (1948–52). Over the mantel hangs *The Cincinnati Inquirer* (1883; William Harnett).

The two portraits of Native Americans, *Eagle of Delight* and *Wicked Chief,* are by Charles Bird King. The paintings are from a set of eight portraits commissioned in 1821 by the American Indian Archives in Georgetown. The originals, kept in the Smithsonian Castle, perished in the fire of 1865.

Duncan Phyfe, a New York cabinetmaker, produced much of the Library's furniture. The red painted wooden chandelier came from the family of James Fenimore Cooper, author of *The Last of the Mohicans.*

The looking glass (mirror) on the north wall between the two windows is an unusual piece from the Federal period. An American eagle adorns the top of the glass. Painted in the rare eglomise style, the eagle was painted in reverse on the glass. Six matching Phyfe "cross-banister" chairs are in front of the windows and a Phyfe drum table is in the center of the room. The English silver-plate Argand lamps on the mantel were a gift from the Marquis de Lafayette to General Henry Knox, Washington's secretary of war. A lighthouse clock made by Simon Willard rests on a bookshelf. A bell is enclosed within a fragile glass dome, and the medallion at the bottom depicts the Marquis de Lafayette.

The **Vermeil Room** is also the Gold Room. Refurbished in 1991, this room serves as a showcase for the collection of vermeil (gilded silver) given to the White House in 1956 by Mrs. Margaret Thompson Biddle. The collection, complemented by the yellow paneled walls, includes pieces by Paul Storr, an English Regency silversmith (1771–1844); and Jean-Baptiste-Claude Odiot, a French Empire silversmith (1763–1850). Other pieces are reproductions of President Monroe's gilt flatware.

Douglas Chandor's portrait *Eleanor Roosevelt* (1949) is here. The painting features multiple portraits of Mrs. Roosevelt and the first lady's inscription: "A trial made pleasant by the painter. Eleanor Roosevelt." Joining Mrs. Roosevelt are a collection of other first ladies: *Lou Henry Hoover* (1950; Richard Brown; a copy after the original, 1932; Philip de Laszlo), *Jacqueline Kennedy* (1970; Aaron Shlikler), *Claudia (Lady Bird) Taylor Johnson* (1968; Elizabeth Shoumatoff), *Patricia Ryan Nixon* (1978; Henriette Wyeth), and *Nancy Davis Reagan* (1987; Aaron Shlikler).

The **China Room.** In 1917 Mrs. Woodrow Wilson chose this room to house and display the growing collection of White House china. When the room was redecorated in 1970, the red color scheme was retained. The red theme is carried throughout the room in the 20C Indo-Ispahan rug and the velvet-lined cabinets. The fact that red is this room's traditional color can be verified by the painting of Mrs. Calvin Coolidge by Howard Chandler Christy. The pair of Chippendale side chairs (c. 1760–85) were used by George Washington and John Adams when the presidential residence was in Philadelphia. The painting above the mantel, *View on the Mississippi Fifty-seven Miles below St. Anthony Falls, Minneapolis,* by Ferdinand Richardt, was completed in 1858 in honor of Minnesota's statehood.

Almost every president is represented by state or family china or glassware. The collection begins chronologically, to the right of the fireplace. Until Mrs. Benjamin Harrison took an interest in the china in 1889, no one valued the historical importance of the pieces. Mrs. William McKinley and Mrs. Theodore Roosevelt continued the project. Prior to the Wilson administration, presidential china was manufactured abroad, usually France or England. The designs featured patriotic symbols; the American eagle appears on many sets. The most flamboyant china belonged to the Hayeses. Their china features flora and fauna, including a strutting wild turkey.

The **Diplomatic Reception Room.** This former boiler-and-furnace room, one of the three oval rooms in the White House, now serves as a drawing room and south entrance to the White House for family and new ambassadors arriving with their credentials. President Franklin D. Roosevelt delivered his Fireside Chats from this room in the 1940s.

In 1960, the room was furnished in the Federal style and redone in a gold-and-white motif. The Aubusson-style rug, woven especially for this room, has borders with the emblems of the 50 states. The wallpaper, called "Views of North America," by Jean Zuber et Cie, was first printed in Rixheim, Alsace, in 1834. The 32 scenes derived from engravings made in the 1820s, including the Natural Bridge of Virginia, Niagara Falls, New York Bay, West Point, and Boston Harbor. Gilbert Stuart's portrait of George Washington hangs over the mantel. Stuart painted three different portraits of Washington: the Vaughan painting, the Lansdowne, and the Athenaeum. This version (a copy of the Athenaeum portrait) was donated to the White House in 1949.

Proceed up the stairs in the corridor to the state floor. The tour continues in the East Room.

The **East Room.** Hoban originally designed this room as the "Public Audience Room," and it is the largest room in the White House. The room usually does not contain much furniture, and is traditionally used for large events such as dances, dinner parties, concerts, weddings, press conferences, and bill signings. Slain presidents traditionally lie in state in this room.

A 1902 renovation added the Fontainebleau parquet oak floor, electric lights, upholstered benches, and three Bohemian cut-glass chandeliers. The wood-paneled walls contain eight relief insets illustrating classical scenes. The four fireplaces' marble mantels were installed during the Truman renovation (1948–52).

Eric Gugler designed the Steinway piano, the 300,000th made, as well as the gilt American eagles decorating the piano. Dunbar Beck added folk dancing scenes to its decoration. The Steinway company donated the piano to the White House in 1938.

### Washington Notes

The full-length portrait of George Washington is the only known object to have remained in the White House since 1800. (This is not the Lansdowne portrait.) Dolley Madison rescued it and the cabinet's papers when the British invaded Washington in 1814. She removed the canvas, which was intact on its stretcher, and escaped from the invading troops, fleeing to upper George-town in her carriage.

A portrait of Martha Washington (1878; Eliphalet F. Andrews) hangs beside the Washington portrait. John Singer Sargent painted the portrait of Theodore Roosevelt in 1903.

The **Green Room.** Thomas Jefferson used this room as a dining room. Today, it is used as a parlor. In 1971, the Green Room was completely refurbished in the Federal style (1800–15) and the delicate green shade that Mrs. Kennedy chose in 1962. The green, beige, and coral draperies are careful reproductions of a design shown in an early-19C periodical. The French cut-glass-and-ormolu chandelier was added in 1975. Most of the mahogany furnishings are pieces attributed to the New York workshop of Duncan Phyfe. Some of his works, constructed in 1810, include a Sheraton secretary bookcase, worktables with hidden compartments, and a pair of rare benches with reeded edges that sit in the window niches.

In 1818 the Italian white marble fireplace mantel was purchased for the State Dining Room and moved here in 1902. Gilbert Stuart's portrait of Louisa Catherine Adams, wife of then secretary of state John Quincy Adams, hangs above George H. Durrie's *Farmyard in Winter* (1858). Mrs. Adams posed for the portrait four years before her husband became president. His portrait was also painted by Stuart. Below President Adams's portrait is John Singer Sargent's *The Mosquito*

*Net* (1912). A 1767 portrait by David Martin of Benjamin Franklin reading beside a bust of Isaac Newton hangs over the mantel. A portrait of James K. Polk by George P. A. Healy and a portrait of Benjamin Harrison by Eastman Johnson hang above the left and right doors, respectively. Other noteworthy pieces include *Independence Hall in Philadelphia* (1858–63; Ferdinand Richardt), *Lighter Relieving a Steamboat Aground* (1847; George Caleb Bingham), and *Bear Lake, New Mexico* (1930; Georgia O'Keeffe).

Another highlight is the 1785 silver Sheffield coffee urn. It was owned by John Adams and is monogrammed with "JAA" for John and Abigail Adams. The French candlesticks on either side of the urn were used by James Madison.

The **Blue Room.** The room, designed by Hoban as an "elliptical saloon," was used to receive guests. It was christened the Blue Room in 1837 after President Van Buren had it painted and upholstered in this color. In 1995 its French Empire decor was refurbished. President James Monroe had ordered mahogany furniture for the White House but these gilded pieces arrived instead. The decorative themes complementing the Bellangé chairs and sofas include acanthus foliage, imperial eagles, wreaths, urns, stars, and classical figures.

The portraits in the room include *Thomas Jefferson as Vice President* (1800; Rembrandt Peale), *John Adams* (1793; John Trumbull), *James Monroe* (1816; Samuel F. B. Morse), and *John Tyler* (1859; George P. A. Healy). A double-paneled looking glass surmounted by American eagles hangs above the Carrara marble mantel. The Hannibal clock on the mantel was created by Denière and Matelin and purchased by President Monroe in 1817. The woven oval rug reflects English designs of 1815.

### *Washington Notes*

President Grover Cleveland married Frances Folsom on June 2, 1886, in the Blue Room. Cleveland is the only president to have married while in office. Traditionally, during the winter holiday season, the White House Christmas tree is set up in the center of this room.

The **Red Room.** The Red Room, one of the four state reception rooms in the White House, has typically been used as a parlor. John Adams ate his breakfasts here, Dolley Madison hosted Wed evening receptions here when this was her "Yellow Drawing Room," and Rutherford B. Hayes took his oath of office on March 3, 1877, in the Red Room.

When Gilbert Stuart's portrait of George Washington hung here during President Polk's and President Tyler's terms, this room was referred to as the Washington Parlor. It is decorated in the American Empire style of 1810–30. The room displays many noteworthy furnishings by the French cabinetmaker Charles-Honoré Lannuier. Highlights include the mahogany sofa table to the left of the fireplace and the mahogany secretary bookcase between the windows. The most important piece of American Empire furniture in the White House collection is Lannuier's labeled marble-top gueridon, or small round table, opposite the fireplace. The mahogany table has a trompe l'oeil top of marble inlaid in geometric patterns. Bronze-doré female heads support the carved and reeded legs. The marble mantel is the sister of the one in the Green Room. President Vincent Auriol of France presented the Louis XVI musical clock to the White House in 1952.

Paintings in the room include *Dolley Madison* (1804; Gilbert Stuart), *Rocky*

*Mountain Landscape* (1870; Albert Bierstadt), *Indian Vespers* (1847; Alvan Fisher), and a portrait of John James Audubon (1826; John Syme).

The **State Dining Room.** The State Dining Room can seat 140 guests. During Theodore Roosevelt's administration a moose head and other big game trophies were mounted on the walls. In 1981, the Queen Anne–style chairs were re-upholstered in gold horsehair material and silk-damask draperies were installed. A contemplative portrait of Abraham Lincoln, (1869; George P. A. Healy) hangs above the bison-head marble mantel. A quote from John Adams is inscribed on the mantel: "I Pray Heaven to Bestow the Best of Blessings on THIS HOUSE and on All that hereafter Inhabit it. May none but Honest and Wise Men ever rule under this Roof."

In 1998, a major renovation of the room was completed. The walls were re-painted, the drapes replaced, and the gilt was removed from the side tables (1902; designed by Stanford White) to reveal the original mahogany.

Set into the Tennessee marble floors of the Cross and Entrance Halls are the major construction and renovation dates of the White House. Walk north through Cross Hall into Entrance Hall. Exit the building through the doorway to the north.

Two rooms not on the tour are the Oval Office and the Lincoln Bedroom.

The **Oval Office.** Built in 1909 and moved in 1934 from the center of the West Wing to the southeast corner, the Oval Office is used by the president for formal meetings with visiting chiefs of state and heads of government. The decor of the room changes with the administration. President Clinton chose to use a desk given to President Rutherford B. Hayes by Queen Victoria in 1880. The desk was constructed from oak timbers from the HMS *Resolute,* a ship American whalers re-covered from the Arctic. The panel adorned with the presidential coat of arms in the desk's kneehole was carved for President Franklin D. Roosevelt. The presidential seal is also woven into the oval carpet. Above the marble mantel, which has been a fixture of the office since 1909, is a portrait of George Washington by Rembrandt Peale. Other artwork includes *The Three Tetons* (c. 1895; Thomas Moran), *City of Washington from behind the Navy Yard* (1833; George Cooke), *The Bronco Buster* (Frederic Remington), *The Avenue in the Rain* (Childe Hassam), and a bronze bust of Benjamin Franklin (Jean-Antoine Houdon). Boston cabinet-makers built the mahogany case for the clock that stands along the east wall in the early 19C.

The **Lincoln Bedroom.** The furnishings reflect the American Victorian era (1850–70). Although the room is now primarily used as a guest bedroom for friends and family of the president, Lincoln used this room as an office and Cabinet room. President Truman had the room redecorated to reflect the Lincoln era. The rosewood bed is eight ft long and six ft wide. Although Lincoln probably never slept in the bed, the piece is thought to have belonged to the set that Mrs. Lincoln bought for the house in 1861. The ornate carving on the bed and on the rosewood marble-top table of birds, grapevines, and flowers is typical for the period. One of five holograph copies of the Gettysburg Address is displayed on the desk. The speech was dedicated at the national cemetery in Gettysburg on Nov 19, 1863. This is the only copy signed and dated by President Lincoln.

Located on the North Ellipse is the **Zero Milestone,** a four-ft-high shaft of pink granite that stands on the north and south meridian of the District of Columbia.

This is the official starting point for measurement of highway distances from Washington, D.C. On July 7, 1919, the first transcontinental motor convoy started from this point on its way to San Francisco. The National Highway Marketing Association marked the spot with a temporary plaster monument. Congress authorized the erection of a permanent marker on June 5, 1920, but one wasn't placed until three years later. The Lee Highway Association donated the current monument as a gift to the city of Washington. The monument features a bronze compass on top.

Exit the White House grounds through East Executive Park, between Pennsylvania Ave and Hamilton Place N.W. The park is open daily 6 A.M.–11 P.M. and was developed in 1989 by the National Park Service. There are interactive informational kiosks, as well as public restrooms and benches. Also, a copy of the Liberty Bell is displayed. Walk north to Pennsylvania Ave. Turn left and proceed to Lafayette Square Park, between 15th and 17th Sts N.W. and H St and Pennsylvania Ave N.W., which features several statues of historically significant figures such as Andrew Jackson and heroes of the War of 1812.

## Lafayette Square Park

### History

Before the creation of the District of Columbia, this seven-acre plot was farmland and an apple orchard belonging to the Pierce family of Charles County, Maryland. In the 1790s, as part of L'Enfant's plan, the land was purchased for $469 and became a section of the 80-acre presidential park that was to surround the White House. Initially neglected, the land later served as the site of White House construction workers' temporary camp in the 1790s, a racetrack in 1797, an open-air marketplace, and finally, during the War of 1812, an encampment for British soldiers. At one point the park had a small zoo containing deer and prairie dogs. Eventually nearby residents complained about the emanating stench, and the animals were removed.

In the early 1800s President Jefferson decided that the presidential park ought to be accessible to the public. He ordered Pennsylvania Ave extended into this part of town and the parcel north of the White House transformed into a public park named President's Square. In 1824 the Marquis de Lafayette, a Frenchman who was commissioned at the age of 19 to the American Navy during the Revolution, visited Washington for the second time. During his stay President's Park was renamed to honor him.

After the White House, the first important building constructed on the square was St. John's Church, designed by Benjamin Latrobe and built in 1816. Two years later, Commodore Stephen Decatur also bought property on the square. Commodore Decatur commissioned Benjamin Latrobe, architect of the Capitol and St. John's Church, to build his home. Latrobe's work is featured on three sides of the square—the South Portico of the White House, St. John's Church, and the Decatur House.

Richard Cutts, Dolley Madison's brother-in-law, constructed his residence on the northeast side of what is now Madison Place. Cutts was the first of a number of wealthy and prominent citizens who built residences on Lafayette Square. In the following years prominent Washingtonians continued to build in the neighborhood. Among them was Benjamin Ogle Tayloe, son of John Tayloe, owner of the Octagon at New York Ave and 18th St. Benjamin Tayloe's house, which is now government-owned, was located next to the Cutts residence on Madison Place.

Another property owner was William Wilson Corcoran, Washington's "first philanthropist" and founder of the Corcoran Gallery of Art, one of the first modern art museums in the country, and Riggs Bank. He purchased the home of Daniel Webster and hired James Renwick, architect of the Smithsonian Castle, to remodel the structure. With its completion in 1849, the property became the city's first Victorian mansion.

### Washington Notes

During the late 19C Washington was jolted with the news of an affair, a jealous husband, his murderous rage, and the resulting criminal trial. Teresa Sickles, wife of New York congressman Daniel Sickles, and Attorney General Philip Barton Key, son of Francis Scott Key, composer of the *Star-Spangled Banner,* frequently met for secret rendezvous in the Sickleses' home, as well as more obscure locations such as Congressional Cemetery.

To signal Key that her husband was away, Mrs. Sickles would hang a handkerchief from her bedroom window on Madison Place, adjacent to Lafayette Square. Thus informed, the lover would walk across Lafayette Square for their tryst.

According to legend, when Congressman Sickles learned of the affair, he forced a detailed written confession from his wife. He also had her wave her hanky to summon Key, but as Key crossed Lafayette Square, Sickles intercepted him. With several witnesses present, Sickles shot the defenseless Key three times. Key died on the steps of the nearby exclusive Washington Club.

In court, Sickles's lawyer argued that his client's mind was "affected" and passion overtook reason. With the absence of any legal recourse against Key, an all-male jury concluded that Sickles was justified in defending his honor. The trial drew national attention not only for its first successful use of the "insanity plea" but because the details of Mrs. Sickles's scandalous affair were widely publicized. In fact, the acquittal further convinced many Americans living outside of the capital of the depravity of Washington society. Legend has it that Key's ghost can be spotted in Lafayette Square walking hastily to meet his lover.

In 1902 the McMillan Commission presented plans to the Congress calling for the destruction of the square and surrounding buildings, including St. John's Church, in order to make way for blocks of big buildings. Due to lack of interest and funds, the plan was abandoned.

The square continued to be the choice neighborhood for many of the nation's most distinguished families until the 1920s when other areas of town became fashionable. After the 1920s many of the residences on the square were razed in the name of progress. Large government buildings, such as the U.S. Chamber of Commerce and U.S. Court of Claims, were erected in their places.

It wasn't until the early 1960s, following interest in the park by the Commission of Arts, that improvements to the area were made. In 1962 Congress approved several bills for the full restoration of the existing buildings and further beautification of the square. Changes included the creation of brick paths and double fountains at the north and south ends of the park. The $435,550 project was funded privately by Paul Mellon's organization, the Old Dominion Foundation.

### Washington Notes

One of the often overlooked legacies of Jacqueline Kennedy was her effort to preserve historic Washington architecture. She urged husband President John F. Kennedy to initiate the Pennsylvania Ave redevelopment plan. Her first design project in the District was the preservation of the buildings surrounding Lafayette Square, including the Old Executive Office Building (see Walk 8: "The Ellipse and 17th Street Sites") and the building that is today the Smithsonian's Renwick Gallery.

## Statues

In 1853 in conjunction with a large public works program, President Fillmore commissioned Andrew Jackson Downing to redesign Lafayette Square. His plan, modeled after the work of the famous British landscape gardener and author Humphrey Repton, combined both formal and informal park architecture. Winding gravel paths were created along with a wide straight aisle on line with the entrance to the White House. Trees and flowers were planted, and park sculptures planned.

To honor the first Democrat elected president, the Jackson Democratic Society raised funds to erect a statue of Andrew Jackson. An 1848 Congressional resolution required that some of the statue's configuration include metal from cannons captured during the War of 1812. The statue, *Andrew Jackson* (1853; Clark Mills), was unveiled as the park's centerpiece in 1853. The work depicts Jackson astride his horse, doffing his hat. The statue faces south; some say Jackson's frozen image is saluting the president in the White House.

### Washington Notes

For previous bronze sculptures, the American government commissioned French, Italian, and German artists. Clark Mills, however, a self-taught sculptor, was American. He built a furnace and studio near the square (where the Treasury Building stands today) and cast the work in ten pieces, using 15 tons of bronze melted down from cannons Jackson captured from the British during the War of 1812 in the Battle of Pensacola (Florida) and the Battle of New Orleans. Mills also trained a horse to remain standing on its hind legs, which allowed Mills to study its balance of weight and muscle configuration.

His piece was the first equestrian statue designed, cast, and erected by an American sculptor. Mills's success proved that bronze works could be accomplished in America by an artist without traditional European training. Congress admired the work and offered Mills a $20,000 bonus for the statue as well as a commission to design a statue of George Washington; Mills's rendering of Washington is located in Washington Circle in Foggy Bottom.

During the 20C four additional statues were placed in the park. The figures represent generals from France, Germany, and Poland who provided military advice to the U.S. during the American Revolution: Lafayette, Rochambeau, von Steuben, and Kosciusko. In 1891 a statue was erected in the southeast corner of the park for its namesake, Marquis de Lafayette. Originally placed facing the White House on the south side of the Jackson statue, the statue was moved when officials realized that it blocked the White House's view of the Jackson statue.

Two French artists collaborated to create the Lafayette statue. Standing atop a white marble base, Lafayette wears civilian clothing. He has a cloak draped over his left arm, and his right arm is outstretched. He is shown petitioning the French National Assembly for aid for the Americans. At the foot of the pedestal, a bare-chested female figure symbolizing America offers a sword to Lafayette. Tongue-waggers joke that if America could speak she'd say, "Give me back my clothes and I'll give you your sword."

In the early 1900s, to create symmetry, other statues were erected in the remaining three corners of the park. The first, *Comte de Rochambeau* (1902; J. J. Fernand Hamar) is a memorial to a commander of the Royal French Expeditionary Force. Located in the southwest corner, the statue, a replica of one in Rochambeau's birthplace in Vendome, France, is surrounded by figures symbolic of the friendship between America and France.

A memorial to Major General Friedrich Wilhelm von Steuben (1910; Alber Jaegers) was erected in the northwest corner. The eight-ft-high sculpture commemorates this German officer and aide-de-camp of Frederick the Great whose knowledge of military techniques greatly benefited the American cause. Persuaded to help the American cause by Benjamin Franklin during his tenure as minister to Paris, von Steuben, a master of drills, fashioned the volunteers into a military force during the winter at Valley Forge.

Also in 1910 the memorial to General Thaddeus Kosciuszko (1910; Antoni Popiel) was presented to the U.S. by the Polish National Alliance of America and placed in the northeast corner of the square. This work commemorates the Polish patriot who fought for America's freedom, as well as for Poland's own independence from Russia in 1784.

### Washington Notes

Kosciuszko, also interested in the freedom of blacks in America, donated the proceeds of the sale of 500 acres of land in Ohio awarded him by the U.S. Congress toward the establishment of the Colored School in Newark, New Jersey. This was the first school for blacks in the country.

Northwest of the Jackson statue is a bench known as the Bernard Baruch Bench of Inspiration. Baruch, who ran the War Industries Board during World War I, was an advisor to several presidents from Woodrow Wilson to John F. Kennedy. He often sat at this bench during the day to reflect. The bench was dedicated in 1960 on the financier-statesman's 90th birthday.

At the south side entrance to the park the two ornamental bronze urns were cast for the park in 1872 by the Navy Yard in Washington. Reminiscent of the classical urns at Versailles, these pieces were included in Downing's plan for the park.

Head to the northwest corner of the park to the Decatur House.

## Decatur House

748 Jackson Place, N.W. ☎ 842-4210. Web: www.decaturhouse.org. Open Tues–Fri 10–3; Sat–Sun 12–4. Closed Mon, Thanksgiving, Christmas, and New Year's Day. Admission fee. A 45-minute guided tour of the eight interior period rooms is available by reservation. Purchase tickets in the museum shop at 1600 H St N.W., open Mon–Fri 10–5; Sat–Sun 12–4.

The brick Decatur House, (1818; Benjamin Latrobe; DL) is a reminder of one of the earliest, and certainly the most prominent, neighborhoods of the emerging capital. Decatur House was the third building and first private residence to be erected on Lafayette Square. It has served as the home of many important historical figures including statesmen, congressmen, and a vice president. The structure houses a museum featuring period decor and furniture.

The Decatur Carriage House, 1610 H St N.W., ☎ 842-4210, was the site of a number of service buildings for the Decatur House. Currently it is used to host museum programs, public and private receptions, and business meetings.

**Highlights:** The family quarters on the first floor and the formal ballroom on the second floor. Gift shop has interesting items.

### History

Navy Commodore Stephen Decatur, Jr., and his wife, Susan Wheeler, moved to Washington in 1816. Decatur was a naval hero who had won battles with the Barbary pirates, as well as against the British in the War of 1812. Because of his rising position in Washington society, Decatur chose to build a home in Lafayette Square, which, with its proximity to the White House, would soon become a posh enclave for the capital's elite. Decatur also asked the well-regarded Benjamin Latrobe, architect of the Capitol, to create the design. Decatur wanted a home reminiscent of the neoclassical homes he knew in Philadelphia. The house, which was built in 1818–19 at a cost of between $10,000 and $20,000, was funded with prize money awarded to Decatur for his naval conquests in the War of 1812.

### Washington Notes

In 1819, Decatur and his wife moved in with high expectations for the new capital and their own social and political position. But troubles lay ahead. Decatur also invested in 60 other Washington properties, plus a farm in Anacostia. Like many other speculators in the city's early days, Decatur put himself deeply in debt. The Decaturs occupied the house for a mere 15 months before Decatur died of wounds inflicted in a gentleman's duel on March 22, 1820. His nemesis was Captain John Barron, who had been court-martialed for his absence from a battle during the War of 1812. Barron had officially tried to clear his name but the navy refused to reinstate his commission.

Barron sought satisfaction from Decatur, who had been on the Board of Navy Commissioners and voted against Barron. The two met on a dueling field known as the Valley of Chance in Bladensburg, Maryland. Though both men were wounded, only Barron survived. (Within a year after the house was completed, its architect, Latrobe, also met his demise, after a bout with yellow fever.)

Decatur was, and remains, the youngest man to be commissioned as a captain in the U.S. Navy, and his naval career, however brief, was distinguished. Still, there may have been some reluctance on the part of the navy to pay up when Decatur submitted a $200,000 bill for the battle in which he captured a prize British ship, the *Macedonia*. There are no records of Decatur ever receiving his share of the money, and this may explain his wife's overwhelming indebtedness following his death.

Grief-stricken and in debt, Decatur's young widow, Susan Wheeler Decatur, auctioned many of the furnishings and moved to a small house in Georgetown. To earn her own living expenses she rented the Decatur House to a series of U.S. and foreign dignitaries, including Henry Clay, Martin Van Buren, and Edward Livingston.

In 1836 the home was sold to millionaire hotelier John Gadsby, who wished to improve his social position by buying into this tony enclave. Gadsby brought his slaves with him. Their quarters were attached to the house, which probably did not endear him to his neighbors. Following Gadsby's death, the house was again rented, this time to Louisiana senator Judah P. Benjamin. Benjamin, a Jew, was shunned by Washington's anti-Semitic society. When the Civil War broke out, Benjamin became secretary of war for the Confederacy. The Federal government confiscated the Decatur House and used the mansion as a headquarters for the 79 soldiers and officers of the Union Army's Subsistence Department.

In 1872, the home was sold to Edward Fitzgerald Beale, a Western frontiersman, diplomat, and entrepreneur, who had made a fortune in the California gold rush by supplying prospectors. With the election of Ulysses Grant, Beale served as Grant's ambassador to Austria and Hungary.

### Washington Notes

Beale initiated the U.S. Army's Camel Corps in the deserts in New Mexico and Arizona. Beale reasoned that in the arid southwest these desert beasts would prove superior to horses. Beale, however, hadn't anticipated the animals' often uncooperative nature nor the fact that their hooves were too soft for the hard American desert. When the experiment proved unsuccessful, President Lincoln disbanded the American Camel Corps.

Beale and his wife, Mary Edwards Beale, refurbished the exterior and interior of the house, adding Romanesque revival stone trim to the façade, installing gas lights, and commissioning the impressive parquet floor in the second-floor north drawing room. The Beales frequently hosted social gatherings of Washington's elite, a tradition carried on by their son Truxton Beale. Truxton Beale served as an ambassador to Persia and later Romania. His second wife, Marie Oge Beale, was an intimate friend of Alice Roosevelt Longworth and a major Washington hostess, throwing soirees for the diplomatic corps and Washington society until the outbreak of World War II.

In 1956, after the home had been in the Beale family for 84 years, Marie Beale bequeathed Decatur House to the National Trust for Historic Preservation. The historic home was opened to the public as a museum in the early 1960s.

## Exterior

The main façade is a symmetrical square interspersed with nine windows of varying heights. In 1872, shortly after purchasing the house, Edward Beale added exterior brownstone decoration, in keeping with the Victorian era. It was removed by Marie Beale in 1944.

The formal garden in the rear of the house features a red brick herringbone walkway leading to a fountain. Azaleas and dogwoods flourish in early spring, and mature elms form a natural canopy throughout the summer. Originally this decorative garden served as a vegetable garden and livestock area.

## Interior

The house has four levels, two of which are open to the public. The first floor of this brick row house depicts the home as it appeared when occupied by its first owners, Stephen and Susan Decatur, while the second floor evokes the occupancy of the Beale family. The juxtaposition provides a good sense of how style in the capital changed from the republic's early years to the late 19C.

**Note:** The interior of Decatur House is currently under revision, as evidenced by uncovered brick surfaces in many of the rooms. As discoveries are made about the previous functions of rooms, contents may change.

The **entrance hall** is an impressive example of Benjamin Latrobe's neoclassical style, featuring wide arches and a circular ceiling that creates a simple grandeur. The painting of Decatur House (1822; E. Vaile) presents a view of the front of the house and its surrounding acreage at the time of its early occupancy.

**Stephen Decatur's office** features an Empire-style clock (c. 1800), a collection of items from Decatur's sea travels, medals, a sword and sheath presented to him by Congress, dueling pistols, and the tabletop desk his father, also a war hero, used in the Revolutionary War. Next to the desk is an original copy of a Washington newspaper, the *National Intelligencer,* dated Dec 14, 1820.

Across the hall are the **family quarters.** These would have been closed to all but the most intimate of friends. (All other Decatur guests were ushered upstairs to be received formally.) The parlor and dining room are simply decorated. The portraits of Susan and Stephen Decatur are attributed to Gilbert Stuart. Two interesting charcoal portraits by noted artist Charles B.J.F. St. Memin are also here. Dating to approximately 1795, these depict Decatur's sister, Ann Pine, and her husband, Captain James McKnight. He was killed in a duel in 1802, and she died in 1818. St. Memin is also credited for an engraved miniature portrait of Stephen Decatur, Sr., displayed in the china cabinet. Note, also, Decatur's tabletop desk, given to him by the crew of his ship. The Chinese sewing table (c. 1800) was an engagement gift from Decatur to his first ladylove (pre-Susan). The chairs and table (c. 1800–1820) belonged to the Decaturs. The dining room features portraits of Stephen's parents, a punch bowl honoring his father's 25 years in the navy, and silver trays commemorative of Stephen's naval accomplishments.

At the foot of the **grand staircase** is a photographic display of those who have lived in the house. Here, also, is a series of paintings of the house in Marie Beale's time, including one of her and Alice Roosevelt Longworth having lunch in the garden. On the first staircase landing are two Ming vases. At the top of the stairs is a model of the sloop-of-war USS *Constellation,* a tricornered chair from which Marie Beale used to greet her guests, a Waterford crystal chandelier, and a mirror with an elaborate frame carved from one piece of wood by a crewman from one of Edward Beale's ships. (Beale also served in the navy for a time.)

The grand staircase leads to the **second floor.** The second floor collection focuses on the Beale family, especially Marie Beale and her prominent entertaining in Washington society. The **morning room** represents the Beale family library, as well as Marie's office. On the desk next to her typewriter are the two books Marie Beale wrote, *Flight Into America's Past* and *The Modern Magic Carpet*. The loving cups came from Marie's riding competitions; the horse portraits were gifts from Ulysses S. Grant to his friend, Edward Fitzgerald Beale. The monogrammed silver set (c. 1880) has small bears on top of the teapots and sugar bowls, a reminder of the bear as a symbol of California, where the Beale family made its fortune. Featured, also, are several pieces of Belter furniture.

The **formal ballroom** is graced with a painted ceiling, a crystal, etched-glass chandelier (c. 1876) from the Philadelphia Exposition, an antique Steinway grand piano (1872), a handcarved Japanese table (c. 1875), Florentine oil paintings, and a portrait of Marie Beale by San Francisco artist Theodore Wores. The most notable feature of the adjoining **dining room** is its beautiful parquet floor inlaid with 16 native woods and a central mosaic of the California state seal. The impressive candlesticks (1880) standing on either side of the entryway are reproductions of Venetian originals admired by Truxton Beale.

Although the other floors of the mansion are closed to the public, a service stairwell extending from the first to the fourth floors allows a peak at the upper floors. This tightly spiraled stairway was used by the servants and family to access the bedrooms on the third floor and the garret.

Cross H St and walk east to the **U.S. Chamber of Commerce Building** (1922; Cass Gilbert), 1615 H St N.W. Gilbert constructed the building with the same cornice lime used in the Treasury Annex, across Lafayette Square Park. Designed to complement the White House and other buildings in the neighborhood, the U.S. Chamber of Commerce Building does not have much to interest visitors except for the Daniel Webster Dining Room, the library, and the Hall of Flags. The Daniel Webster Dining Room, located near the main lobby, is used by senior staff to entertain guests. The decor and furnishings are representative of styles from the 18C and 19C.

A mural shows a historic Lafayette Square c. 1840, as viewed from the North Portico of the White House.

There are two notable features in the library. One is the ceiling design, created by artist Ezra Winter, who also painted the murals in the reading rooms in the Library of Congress–John Adams Building. The second item is Daniel Webster's rosewood-and-mahogany desk.

Several presidents have held press conferences and hosted dignitaries in the Hall of Flags, which features flags of 12 world explorers: Columbus, Cabot, Vespucci, Hudson, Cartier, La Salle, Ponce de León, de Soto, Magellan, Drake, Balboa, and Cortés. The ceiling is inscribed with the achievements of these gentlemen, who are credited with the initial development of and trading with the New World.

### History

The U.S. Chamber of Commerce was established in April 1912 at the request of President William Howard Taft, who felt there ought to be a single voice for the U.S. business community.

The building was constructed as a result of the 1902 McMillan Plan's edict to unify the architecture around Lafayette Square by creating governmental buildings. Cass Gilbert, architect of the Supreme Court Building, designed the Chamber building as a four-story structure (two additional floors were added in 1957). The cornerstone was laid in 1922.

### Washington Notes

This area was once the site of the homes of Daniel Webster and John Slidell. Webster's home, which was awarded to him by admirers, was where Webster and Henry Clay negotiated the 1850 Compromise. The house was later William Wilson Corcoran's home. Slidell was a senator from Louisiana and the Confederate minister to France. He is remembered for the Mason-Slidell controversy, which almost brought the British Empire into the Civil War on the South's side.

Henry Adams and his wife, Marian "Clover" Adams, moved into the Slidell House in 1877. On a Dec day in 1883, Adams's wife died in her bedroom—presumably a suicide. Adams, who had been away on business, was so grief-stricken by her death that he commissioned Augustus Saint-Gaudens to sculpt *Grief*, a statuary marker for her grave in Rock Creek Cemetery. For years the Slidell House was reputedly haunted by Mrs. Adams's spirit.

The houses were bulldozed in 1922 to clear the site for the U.S. Chamber of Commerce Building.

For a discussion of the Hay-Adams Hotel, see Walk 14: "16th Street N.W."

Proceed east on H St. Cross 16th St.

## St. John's Church

1525 H St N.W. ☎ 347-8766. Open Mon–Sat 9–3. Guided tours Sun after the 11 A.M. service. Sunday services at 8, 9, and 11; weekday services at 12:10. The balcony is only open to the public during services and tours.

St. John's Church (1815–16; Benjamin Latrobe; DL) is known as the Church of Presidents because every president has attended a service here since it opened in 1816. Presidents Madison, Monroe, Jackson, Van Buren, Harrison, Taylor, Tyler, Fillmore, and Buchanan were parishioners. St. John's Church, one of the first churches built in the capital, is the second oldest building on Lafayette Square (the White House is oldest).

### History

The population of the neighborhood around Lafayette Square, then called President's Park, grew rapidly after the War of 1812. In 1814 a group of wealthy residents gathered funds to purchase a plot of land on which to build a second Episcopalian parish. (The first was Christ Church on Capitol Hill.) They hired Benjamin Latrobe, the architect who restored the Capitol and the White House after the War of 1812. Latrobe sketched the building as a Greek cross and ads were placed in the *National Intelligencer* soliciting a builder. The cornerstone was laid on Sept 14, 1815, and construction was completed the following June.

### Washington Notes

In 1816 Latrobe described his accomplishment to his son Henry, "I have just completed a church that made many Washingtonians religious who have not been religious before." Latrobe was so proud of the church that he refused to accept payment. He also served as the parish's first organist and choirmaster.

James Madison was the first president to become a member of the church. Since that time, pew 54 has been designated the President's Pew, as it is marked with a brass plaque. Legend has it that when St. John's mourns the death of an important American, ghosts of "six great Washingtonians" now unknown appear at midnight, briefly paying their respects in the "President's Pew."

James Renwick was hired in 1883 to enlarge the interior and renovate the exterior. Only a few of Renwick's plans were carried out; the rest were vetoed. One of Renwick's changes was to add a Palladian window above the altar.

## Exterior

St. John's is classically styled. Latrobe built the original church in the form of a Greek cross, but this was later hidden by the addition of the tower and Latrobe's Doric-columned Greek porch. Although the church has undergone several enlargements and alterations, its appearance remains much as it was in 1822, when a triple-tiered steeple by an unknown designer was erected above the west transept.

### Washington Notes
St. John's 1,000-pound bell was cast by Paul Revere's son using British cannon confiscated during the War of 1812.

## Interior

Most remarkable are the stained glass windows, many designed and constructed in France in the 1880s by Madame Veuve Lorin, curator of stained glass windows at the Chartres Cathedral in France. Most of the windows, planned by James Renwick, depict the New Testament stories of Jesus and St. John. President Chester Arthur donated a window on the south side of the church in memory of his deceased wife. He asked that it be placed in that location so he might see sunlight shining through it from his White House study across the square. Chester felt it would remind him of his wife, Ellen Lewis Preston, a choir singer, whom he met at the church.

Other windows to note: In the organ bay to the right of the altar are the *Good Samaritan* window donated in memory of Charles Henry Crane, surgeon general during the Civil War, and *Peter and Jesus Walking on Water,* donated in memory of Admiral Joseph Smith. Located in the south transept is *Madonna of the Chair,* created by Charles Winston, after Raphael's painting. The current sanctuary arrangement employing a freestanding altar was completed in 1969.

## St. John's Parish House

Immediately to the east is the St. John's Parish House (1836; Mathew St. Clair Clark; DL). It functions as an office building and meeting place for the parish clergy and staff of St. John's Church and is open Mon–Thur 9–4; Fri 9–3. Closed weekends. Free parking is available on Sun at 1625 I St.

### History

The house was built in 1836 by Mathew St. Clair Clark. Once a clerk in the House of Representatives (1822–35), Clark was fired by the incoming Jackson administration. Nonetheless, Clark had ambitious plans for the construction of the mansion, hiring the finest craftsmen and using the best quality materials. When Clark's investments collapsed and he went bankrupt, he sold his recently completed house to Joseph Gales, editor of the *National Intelligencer*, who later leased the property to the British government and moved to the nearby Decatur House.

> ### Washington Notes
> During the 1840s Lord Alexander Baring Ashburton, a British minister, used the house as the British Embassy while settling the Maine–New Brunswick border dispute with American secretary of state Daniel Webster. The ensuing months on the square were reportedly festive. Webster and Ashburton treated each other to exceptional meals—Ashburton's French chef serving Continental cuisine, while Webster offered a wide variety of the local specialties, such as Maryland crabs, Chesapeake ducks, and Virginia terrapin.

Afterward, the house switched hands several times before being purchased in 1853 by Miss Sarah H. Coleman for $30,000. It remained in her sister's family, the Freemans, until 1940 when the estate was bought for $1 million by the American Federation of Labor (AFL). This organization swapped the house with St. John's Church in 1954 for St. John's Rectory and Sunday School Hall, 819 and 821 16th St, respectively. In 1974 the Parish House was designated a National Historic Landmark.

## Cutts-Madison House

Cross H St. At the southeast corner of H and Madison Place N.W. is the Cutts-Madison House (1820; Richard Cutts; DL). Although this building has been incorporated into the U.S. Court of Claims complex and is closed to the public, the house has an interesting history.

### History

The home was built in 1820 by Richard Cutts, a congressman from Massachusetts, but it was brought to life by his sister-in-law, Dolley Madison. In 1836, after her husband, President James Madison, died, the house was given to Dolley Madison as repayment for a debt owed to her husband. Dolley Madison was considered one of the city's most popular hostesses. Although she was born to sober Quaker parents, Madison was regarded for her lavish parties and outfits, in spite of the fact that when she moved into the house on Lafayette Square in the fall of 1837, Dolley Madison was 70 years old.

> ### Washington Notes
> Mrs. William Seaton, a guest to the White House in 1812, described Dolley's New Year's Day dress as "a robe of pink satin, trimmed elaborately with ermine, gold chains and clasps about her waist and wrists, and upon her head a white satin and velvet turban with a crescent in front and crowned with nodding ostrich plumes."

Madison was plagued by the spendthrift habits of her son by her first marriage, Payne Todd, and was forced to rent the house intermittently between 1839 and 1843. In 1844, she sold Montpelier, the Virginia estate where she and her husband had lived, and moved into the Lafayette Square house permanently. Friends, knowing of her financial difficulties, helped. Daniel Webster regularly sent baskets of provisions. In May 1848, the house caught fire and Madison refused to leave until the trunk containing her husband's papers was safely outside. She died in July 1849.

In 1851, Captain Charles Wilkes, who had commanded a South Seas expedition famous at that time, bought the house. When he left it to serve in the Civil War, he turned the house over to the federal government, and it became headquarters for General George B. McClellan of the Union Army. After the war ended, Rear Admiral Wilkes (he was promoted), took possession of the house, living in it until his death in 1877.

In 1878, Wilkes's heirs sold the house to the Cosmos Club—a group of scientists, scholars, and artists—for $40,000. The club also purchased the adjoining Tayloe House. The Cosmos Club later relocated to 2121 Massachusetts Ave N.W. (see Walk 16: "Dupont Circle West Area").

Although the building's Federal-style symmetry and basic design are still evident, the house has been drastically altered. Originally the entrance faced the square where a bay window now juts out, and there was an attic floor topped with a gabled roof.

## Tayloe House

Proceed south along Madison Place to the Tayloe House (1828; Benjamin Tayloe; DL), 21 Madison Place N.W. The house is part of the U.S. Court of Claims complex and is not open to the public, but the building's history is worth noting.

### History

Benjamin Ogle Tayloe, second son of Colonel John Tayloe, proprietor of the nearby Octagon, built this home in 1828. Tayloe lived here with his family until his death in 1868. At this home he hosted Washington's elite, as well as international diplomats and dignitaries. The three-story, Federal-style mansion was decorated with fine furniture, paintings, and other artwork that Tayloe had collected in his world travels.

#### Washington Notes

Among prominent visitors to the home was President William Henry Harrison, who ventured out of the White House for the last time before his death to visit the Tayloes. Harrison reportedly stopped by to request the address of the Tayloe's family physician and to inform Tayloe of the appointment of his brother Edward as secretary of the Treasury.

In 1862 Anthony Trollope, the British author, was a guest of the Tayloe family and wrote, "I spent more hours in your house than in any other in Washington, and certainly felt myself more at home there."

After Tayloe's death, the house was occupied by a series of politicians, and served as an annex to the Cosmos Club, which was headquartered in the Cutts-Madison House next door. At the end of the 19C, during the McKinley administration, the Tayloe House was dubbed the Little White House. Senator Mark Hanna, who resided there at the time, hosted hearty breakfasts of corned beef hash for the capital's most powerful residents. Nicknamed Uncle Mark, Hanna is best known for his role in McKinley's 1896 campaign, when he outspent the opposing candidate, William Jennings Bryan, by $25 to $1.

Behind the Tayloe and Cutts-Madison Houses is an Eduard L. A. Pausch copy of *Grief*, the sculpture Henry Adams commissioned Augustus Saint-Gaudens to create in honor of Adams's deceased wife.

### Washington Notes

A plaque on the courtyard's south wall indicates the site where Commodore John Rodgers built his home in 1831. Lewis Payne, a coconspirator of John Wilkes Booth, attempted to assassinate W. H. Seward, secretary of state, in the house on April 14, 1865, the same night President Lincoln was slain. Seward's son arrived to help his father, but only after Seward had already been stabbed three times.

The house was later razed by U. H. Painter to build the Lafayette Square Opera House, a brick, terra-cotta, and mackite building, which opened Sept 30, 1895. The facility was renamed the Belasco Theatre in 1905. Members of the armed forces frequented the establishment's 1942 incarnation as the Steel Door Canteen. The building was torn down in 1964 for the 1967 construction of the U.S. Court of Claims.

Continue south along Madison Place to the **Treasury Annex Building,** Madison Place at Pennsylvania Ave N.W. This six-story building, faced with Bedford limestone from Indiana quarries, is an extension of the Treasury Building, located across Pennsylvania Ave N.W. from the annex. It is not open to the public and is a product of the 1902 McMillan Plan to line Lafayette Square with columned neoclassical structures. Although the plan wasn't completely carried out, three buildings were constructed: the Treasury Annex, the U.S. Chamber of Commerce, and the Veterans Administration Building.

### Washington Notes

The Freedman's Savings and Trust Company, founded to serve freed slaves and blacks, occupied the site from 1865 to 1874. Frederick Douglass served as the bank's last president. Despite Douglass's efforts, the financial panic of 1873 swallowed all of the savings the black depositors had made and the bank folded.

The federal government purchased the building in 1882, and it was used as office space until 1899 when it was torn down to make room for the annex. The Treasury Annex was completed in 1919 to provide office space for the overflowing Treasury Building and the growing Treasury Department.

Cross Pennsylvania and reenter Executive Park. Proceed south to **Sherman Park,** between Hamilton Place and E. St N.W. In the center of the park is a 14 ft tall bronze statue of General William Tecumseh Sherman (1903; Carl Rohl-

Smith). The statue of the Civil War hero was placed on a rise where Sherman is believed to have watched a parade in March 1865 of 200,000 soldiers of his Army of the West returning from the Civil War.

The elaborate monument includes a mosaic listing the general's battles and a chronology of his military assignments. At the foot of the statue on the terrace, four standing soldiers represent the branches of the army: infantry, artillery, cavalry, and engineers. On the west side of the statue is War, a bound woman standing above the corpse of a soldier.

Turn north to the Treasury Building.

## Treasury Building

1500 Pennsylvania Ave N.W. Guided 90-minute tours focusing on architecture and history are conducted every other Sat at 10, 10:20, 10:40, and 11. Reservations must be made one week in advance by telephone. For 24-hour information and reservations, ☎ 622-0896 or 622-0692 (TTY). For security reasons, name, date of birth, and social security number of each visitor must be provided when you call. Photo identification must be presented on day of the tour. Photographs may be taken in public areas only. Video cameras are not allowed.

**Highlights:** The ornate Salmon P. Chase Suite, the Andrew Johnson Suite, and the Cash Room.

### History

The Treasury Building (1833; Robert Mills, Thomas Ustick Walter) houses the oldest executive department, created even prior to the nation's independence. The responsibilities of the United States Treasury began on July 23, 1775, just a few days after the Battle of Bunker Hill, when the Continental Congress in Philadelphia decided to raise money by printing $2 million in bills redeemable on faith in a successful outcome of the American Revolution. The department employed 3 printers and 28 people to sign and number the new currency.

As the country developed, the functions and the organization of the Treasury changed. On Sept 2, 1789, the First Congress of the United States established a permanent institution for the management of government finances. Nine days later it appointed Alexander Hamilton to the post of secretary of the Treasury.

When the capital city moved from Philadelphia to the banks of the Potomac, the department of the Treasury relocated with it. Its first home, a Georgian-style building designed by George Hadfield, was torched by the British in 1814; its second structure, designed by James Hoban, was destroyed by arsonists in 1833. Some historians believe that former President and then–Massachusetts congressman John Quincy Adams participated in the futile, all-night water bucket brigade to save the building.

### Washington Notes

Congress and President Andrew Jackson's administration debated the placement of the new Treasury building for six months. Finally Congress recommended the site of the previous Treasury Department, but offered the final decision to Jackson. Two days later a frustrated Jackson marched out of the White House and thrust his walking stick to the ground to indicate the location on which he wanted the building constructed. This placement blocked the view between the Capitol and the White House; some speculate that this was what Jackson wanted after his arguments with Congress.

Robert Mills, architect of the Washington Monument and the Patent Office Building, was commissioned in 1833 to design the new Treasury building. He was hired for his expertise in fireproof buildings. Mills planned a three-story building stretching along 15th St. Construction began shortly after his appointment, but the project was halted by Congress, who protested that the lost view interrupted L'Enfant's plan. Congress insisted that the project be redesigned or relocated. Mills refused, continuing construction on east and center wings. Mills, however, was fired in 1851.

Thomas Ustick Walter handled the several structural additions and architectural details added through 1869. When the Treasury Building was finally completed, it was one of the world's largest office buildings. Aside from its various financial functions, the Treasury Building has served as an Army barracks during the Civil War and a temporary White House for Andrew Johnson after Lincoln was assassinated. The Cash Room was the scene of Ulysses Grant's inaugural ball.

## Exterior

The large, Greek revival building covering two city blocks is constructed from granite. Its sparing ornamentation gives it an austere and somber look. The structure was built over a period of 33 years. Mills's original plan was a T-shaped structure with an Ionic colonnade running along 15th St. However, when the Treasury Department had grown too large for the building, Thomas U. Walter designed an addition in 1855. Three wings on the south, west, and north sides enclose the original building, resulting in a rectangular structure with two interior courtyards.

The building's most impressive exterior feature is the colonnade running the entire length of the east front. Each 36 ft tall column was carved out of a single block of granite. The capitals feature federal symbols such as an eagle and a hand clenching a Treasury key.

## Statues

The bronze sculpture *Alexander Hamilton* (1923; James Earle Fraser) stands at the south entrance between E. Executive Ave and 15th St. This monument honors the first secretary of the Treasury. Considered one of Fraser's best portraits, the ten-ft statue illustrates Hamilton in 18C dress, his long dress coat in one hand and a cornered hat in the other. The inscription reads, "He smote the rock of the national resources and abundant streams of revenue gushed forth. He touched the dead corpse of the public credit and it sprang upon its feet."

The donor of the statue has never been revealed. News accounts, however, reported that the donor was an unnamed, mysteriously veiled woman who was present at the dedication ceremony.

### Washington Notes

In 1947 a bronze statue of Albert Gallatin (1761–1849) was erected on the north side of the building to balance that of Alexander Hamilton. Also sculpted by James Earle Fraser, this eight-ft structure was proposed by Democrats who disputed the idea that the Republican Hamilton should be the only secretary of the Treasury to be memorialized. The Democrats argued that Gallatin, secretary of the Treasury in 1801, was worthy of the honor since he inherited a $14 million national debt from former Secretary Hamilton. Within six years Gallatin had paid the debt and created the first Treasury Department surplus. The Republican-dominated Congress at the time approved the statue's construction on the condition that it be funded by private funds.

## Interior

Restoration of the Treasury's interior began in 1985.

**Salmon P. Chase Suite.** Located in the southeast corner of the third floor, this is the office where Secretary of the Treasury Salmon Chase (1808–1873) worked. Originally from Keene, New Hampshire, Salmon Chase spent much of his life in Ohio. An attorney, Chase served in the U.S. Senate from 1849 to 1855, was governor of Ohio from 1856 to 1860, and worked in Lincoln's administration as secretary of the Treasury.

> ### *Washington Notes*
> Great changes were made during Chase's tenure, most of which concerned the Civil War. To help finance the war, Chase mandated the Legal Tender Act of 1862, creating a "greenback" currency without a gold or silver standard. In Feb 1863, Chase established a national banking system, putting an end to the previous system in which some states and banks printed their own money. Other accomplishments during Chase's term were the creation of the Bureau of Engraving and Printing to produce federal notes and the Bureau of Internal Revenue—now the IRS—to collect income tax to finance the Civil War. Chase resigned in June 1864 because of difficulties with President Lincoln. Chase went on to become Chief Justice of the U.S. Supreme Court during the Reconstruction era.

The suite, designed in the 1850s by Goldsborough Bruff, a Treasury draftsman, includes an elaborately decorated office and reception room. Restored to its original rococo revival style, the suite contains typical 19C furniture. The freehand allegorical murals representing treasury and justice have been restored. The carpet is a reproduction cut-pile Wilton. Hanging above the mantelpiece in the reception room is a portrait of financier Jay Cooke, a key aide to Chase. Bruff's decorative touches and symbols are noteworthy. Bruff traveled to California in 1849, bringing back images of Native Americans, buffaloes, and nuts and berries that he used to decorate the mirrors, cornices, and lighting fixtures.

**Secretary's conference and reception rooms.** Located adjacent to the secretary of the Treasury's office are the secretary's conference and reception rooms, separated by a modern kitchen and foyer. Renovated as typical 19C public rooms, the interior design is American Renaissance revival, a style popular from the 1860s–1880s.

The walls and ceilings accurately duplicate the color and painting schemes of the original wing. Plaster cornices have been painted to resemble walnut and are distinguished by the Treasury Department seal surrounded by flags and stars. Five Renaissance revival gas chandeliers and antique white metal and brass wall sconces light the rooms. Wool Wilton and Brussels carpets in 19C patterns, woven in strips on looms, then sewn together as they originally were, cover the floors. Elaborate lace window draperies flow from carved wood and gilt cornices.

The rooms' furnishings come from the Treasury's collection and from acquisitions. Treasury collection pieces include the reception room's large mahogany bookcase with a U.S. shield, mahogany side chairs marked with the U.S. insignia in the configuration of a dollar sign, and a 24 ft long conference table. Purchases include two Renaissance revival parlor suites upholstered in beige-, red-, and green-striped fabric—one decorated with the American eagle and shields, the other with gilded shields and metal plaques.

Paintings in the conference room include portraits of George Washington (Gilbert Stuart) and Salmon Chase (Thomas Sully). In the reception room a marble female bust, *America,* bears a charm necklace inscribed with the names of American presidents. Possibly made to commorate the 1876 Centennial, this bust was created in Florence, Italy, in the 1870s. A series of vignettes running through both rooms are products of the Bureau of Engraving and Printing. In the niche of the foyer note the plaster bust of Alexander Hamilton, modeled after a marble bust by Giuseppe Cerrachi (1751–1801). Excluding the marble bust of *America,* all works of art are from the Treasury collection.

The **Andrew Johnson Suite** has an important place in history.

### Washington Notes

Within five hours after President Lincoln's assassination, the succeeding president, Andrew Johnson, held his first cabinet meeting in this room in April 1865. For six weeks President Johnson worked in Secretary of the Treasury Hugh McCullough's reception room so that Mrs. Lincoln wouldn't feel rushed out of the White House. It was here that Johnson held his first official function of his presidency, a reception for foreign ambassadors. He also issued a $100,000 warrant for the arrest of Confederate president Jefferson Davis, who was suspected of conspiring in Lincoln's assassination. Note Jefferson Davis's teapot, which is in the shape of a train. The teapot was looted from the Confederate White House and presented to Andrew Johnson.

The suite was restored in Renaissance revival style to match the original design by French émigrés Pottier and Stymus. Solid furniture and austere pale colors create a soft and classical atmosphere. Note the two-planed mirror in the reception room, which reflects two different views of the room. It was devised to avoid a structural column directly in front of the mirror, positioned there because the room was once part of a larger lobby.

**Hugh McCullough Suite.** This office is ornamented with gilded and ebonized details. The star carpet, a cut-pile Wilton, is an accurate reproduction of the original. The renovation-designer Scalamandre created the sofa and blue draperies from historical documents. Curtain cornices are all handcarved from black walnut. An original Treasury desk serves as the room's centerpiece. The couch, also an original, features a shield carved in the middle of its back. Above the couch, a framed engraving displays past secretaries of the Treasury surrounding Abraham Lincoln in the center.

**Burglar-proof vault.** Discovered during the 1985 renovation, this vault was sandwiched between later vault extensions and had been hidden for more than 80 years. Originally designed in 1862 by Isaiah Rogers, the supervising architect of the Treasury, the vault's unique construction improved upon existing vault systems. The lining is comprised of two interposing layers of cast-iron balls, contained between the traditional alternating plates of wrought iron and hardened steel. These loosely held balls rotate upon contact with a drill or other tool and prevent a burglar from penetrating the vault.

The four vaults in the northwest corner of the north wing were designed to be used by the treasurer of the United States and the comptroller of the currency, whose offices were directly above and below them. Money is no longer stored in the Treasury Building, nor are the vaults in use.

**Cash Room.** Alfred Mullett, designer of the north wing, decorated this room in 1869. Created as a roofed version of an Italian palazzo, a traditional bank design in Europe at the time, this Italianate revival style features rich materials and elaborate ornamentation. Mullett's intention was that it should "in the purity of its design, and by the avoidance of all shams and imitations of materials, be emblematic of the dignity of the nation and the stability of its credit." Declared the most expensive room in the world at its opening, Mullett used seven varieties of imported and domestic marbles.

The room was created to house the Treasury's banking room, which functioned principally as a "banker's bank," supplying area banks with currency while also providing some public services. By the 1970s, however, its cost of operation had grown too great, and the room was converted into a meeting room. By that time its appearance had greatly deteriorated.

In the 1985 restoration wall-to-wall carpeting was removed and a new marble floor composed of the original Carrara and a Vermont red Lisbon marble pattern was laid down. The authentic gilded ceiling was duplicated using bronze paint, and egg and dart details were replicated in the ceiling coffers. Three bronze gaslight chandeliers, replicated from the originals, are suspended from the ceiling, the largest weighing 1,500 pounds. Framing the room is an ornate bronze railing. Its wheat, corn, cotton, and grape motifs symbolize the abundance of the agricultural economy, the shell and starfish designs stand for commerce, and the staff and snakes (the "caduceus") represent the Marine Hospital Service, once a bureau of the Treasury. The room's clock is thought to be one of the first electric clocks in Washington.

### Washington Notes

While still under construction the Cash Room was used for President Ulysses S. Grant's disastrous inaugural ball on March 4, 1869. It was to be a dazzling affair—2,000 tickets were sold (each admitting one man and two women) at $10 apiece. Dining rooms were set up downstairs, reception rooms on the lower level, and the marble floor was covered with polished wood for dancing to the tunes of the U.S. Marine Corps Band. Huge portraits of the Goddess of Liberty and Abraham Lincoln faced each other on opposite sides of the room, and gas jets outside spelled "PEACE" in nine-ft-high letters.

As evening wore on, however, the room became crowded and stuffy. Women fainted. The *New York Tribune* later reported that "There were no seats at all and tired ladies subsided in ungraceful groups on the floor." When the meal was served less than half of the guests were able get through the door, and reportedly some hungry men stampeded the kitchen for food.

When guests attempted to leave, they found their checked coats and hats in unorganized heaps. The *Tribune* reported that some stayed until four in the morning searching for their belongings, while others went outside in the raging snowstorm with no coat at all. Without a system for calling cabs and carriages many guests ended up leaving the chaotic ball on foot in the snow and slush.

Cross 15th St to the Old Ebbitt Grill.

## Old Ebbitt Grill

675 15th St N.W. ☎ 347-4801. Open daily for breakfast, lunch, and dinner. The menu, which changes daily, includes homemade pastas, seafood, hamburgers, and sandwiches. There is a seasonal oyster bar.

### History

William E. Ebbitt opened the Ebbitt House as a boarding house near what is now Chinatown in 1856. The inn's bar was popular with statesmen and military heroes. Presidents Grant, Andrew Johnson, Cleveland, and Theodore Roosevelt are also said to have frequented the establishment.

During the early part of the 20C the Ebbitt, as it's known, relocated to a converted haberdashery at 1427 F St N.W. At this location it competed with the Rhodes Tavern, which stood on the corner of F and 15th Sts N.W. According to legend, British generals toasted one another at the Rhodes while watching the White House burn in the distance. President McKinley is rumored to have lived in the Ebbitt House during his tenure in Congress. Caleb Willard purchased the boarding house from Ebbitt but kept Ebbitt's name for the business. When guests outnumbered rooms at Caleb's family's hotel, the Willard, a block away, patrons were sent to the Ebbitt House.

In 1970 the Ebbitt was closed by the Internal Revenue Service and possessions parceled as lots were auctioned to settle a $7,412 tax claim. Stuart Davidson and John Laytham, owner of Clyde's of Georgetown, offered to buy the Ebbitt's collection of antique beer steins. When the auction proceeds fell short of the lien, the entire property was put on the block.

The Ebbitt moved again in 1983 into the former home of the B. F. Keith Theater, a Beaux-Arts vaudeville theater where George Burns and Gracie Allen as well as other greats once performed. The Ebbitt's F St location was razed for the construction of the National Press Club.

## Interior

The bar and restaurant's interior is decorated in a Victorian style and has the feel of a turn-of-the-century gentleman's club. Animal heads mounted above the bar are reputedly the trophies of Teddy Roosevelt. The wooden bears are said to have adorned Alexander Hamilton's private bar. The antique clock above the revolving door was salvaged from the Ebbitt's previous location. The marble staircase and iron-spindled rail were removed from the neighboring National Metropolitan Bank.

The bar is mahogany and modeled after the bar from the F St location. Charles B. Shefts carved the mirrors and windows, including the three that separate the bar and restaurant. Those three depict the White House, Capitol, and Treasury

Building. The main dining room has antique gas chandeliers and fixtures, replicated Victorian bentwood chairs of a New York Central Railroad dining car, English lace curtains, and a handlaid, oak plank floor. Paintings by Kamil Kubik on the north wall depict patriotic scenes near the White House, Supreme Court, and the Library of Congress.

Grant's Bar on the south side of the atrium features a ceiling mural and an artistic rendering of the famous Mathew Brady photograph of General Grant. Behind the bar the oil painting of a nude reclining near a lily pond was painted about 1900 by Jean-Paul Gervais. Two paintings of the Ebbitt at its F St location hang near the entrance to Grant's Bar.

The Cabinet Room, a downstairs dining area, features six paintings by renowned bird-painter Robin Hill.

The nearest Metro station is Federal Triangle (Blue/Orange Line). Walk south on 15th St. to Pennsylvania Ave. Turn left and walk east on Pennsylvania Ave to 12th St. Cross Pennsylvania Ave and continue south on 12th St. The Metro station is on the right.

# 10 · Monuments and Memorials

Metro: Blue/Orange Line to Smithsonian.
Bus: 13A, 13B, 13M, 52, or V6.

## *Washington Monument*

15th St and Constitution Ave, N.W. ☎ 426-6841. Web: www.nps.gov/wamo. Open daily 9–5; last elevator at 4:45. Extended hours April–Aug 8 A.M.–12 A.M.; last elevator at 11:45 P.M. Closed Christmas Day. Admission: free. Timed passes required all day. Ticket kiosk on 15th St opens at 8:30 A.M. (7:30 April–Sept) for same-day, first-come, first-served tickets. Advance tickets available for nominal charge from TicketMaster. ☎ 432-SEAT or (800) 505-5040.

Visitors to the monument are ushered to and from the top by elevator. While the stairs have been closed to the general public since 1976, hour-long walking tours down the monument's 897 stairs are offered on Sat at 10 and 2, staff permitting. These first-come, first-served tours enable visitors to see some of the 192 carved memorial stones that states and countries donated to help build the monument. These donors include all 50 U.S. states, various municipalities, private organizations, individuals, the Cherokee nation, and some foreign governments. Note that the walk down is strenuous and recommended only for people in good health.

**Note:** A $5 million restoration of the monument began in Jan 1998 and is scheduled to be completed in July 2000. At times the monument was closed to visitors. Throughout the project the monument was cloaked in scaffolding and a blue fabric decorated with a grid design resembling the mortar and stone pattern of the monument.

Only a handful of landmarks in the United States are as familiar as the Washington Monument (1848–54; 1878–84; Robert Mills; DL). At a height of 555⅛ ft, this obelisk is one of the largest masonry structures in the world. It was erected to honor George Washington, the nation's first president.

**Highlights:** The views from the 500 ft high landing near the top.

*Washington Monument. Courtesy of the Washington, D.C., Convention & Visitors Association.*

### History

In 1783 the Continental Congress voted to honor George Washington with a statue of the first president mounted on horseback. Although Washington objected to spending federal money for such a project, he approved a site chosen by Pierre L'Enfant—the crossing of the western axis of the Capitol with the southern axis of the White House.

When Washington died in 1799, popularity grew for the planned monument. In 1804, Thomas Jefferson, then president, placed a marker at the proposed site,

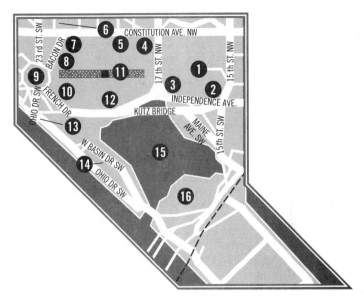

1 Washington Monument
2 Sylvan Theater
3 Commodore John Paul Jones Memorial
4 Lock Keeper's House
5 Constitution Gardens
6 Albert Einstein Memorial
7 Vietnam Veterans Memorial
8 Vietnam Women's Memorial
9 Lincoln Memorial

10 Korean War Veterans Memorial
11 Reflecting Pool
12 D.C. War Memorial
13 John Ericsson Monument
14 Franklin Delano Roosevelt Memorial
15 Tidal Basin
16 Thomas Jefferson Memorial

which was on the banks of the Potomac River. As the land was quite marshy, Jefferson's stone sank. (A marble stump, placed on Dec 2, 1889, in the field northwest of the Washington Monument, denotes the spot where Jefferson's marker disappeared.) Proposals for a memorial were repeatedly made in 1816, 1819, 1824, 1825, and in 1832, the centennial of Washington's birth. Instead of an equestrian statue Congress explored the possibility of a mausoleum "to be of American granite and marble in pyramidal form." Virginia officials and Washington's descendants, however, refused to relocate Washington's body from its crypt at Mount Vernon.

In 1833 a group of affluent citizens, as well as Washington's fellow Freemasons—led by George Watterson, Librarian of Congress—formed the Washington National Monument Society. This group assumed responsibility for funding and overseeing the creation of the monument. Americans were asked to contribute $1 each, the equivalent of about $15 today. In 1836 a national design competition was held. The trustees chose a design by Robert Mills.

Mills, a respected architect with experience designing monuments, had in 1815 designed the nation's oldest monument honoring Washington, the memorial in

Baltimore. Mills's new design called for a 500 ft tall obelisk protruding from a 110 ft tall, circular Greek temple that would house statues of national figure-heads and notable persons in U.S. history. The statues would be placed in 30 niches behind the temple's columns. The highlight of the monument would be a classical statue of Washington wearing a toga and driving a chariot.

In the 12 years between conception and the beginning of construction, Mills's plans were altered dramatically due to fund-raising troubles. George P. Marsh, U.S. minister to Italy, is credited with suggesting the construction of a simple marble obelisk. Finally, on July 4, 1848, ground was broken on a higher, solid site, 350 ft east of L'Enfant's intended placement.

### Washington Notes

In honor of Washington's involvement with the Freemasons, the Masonic trowel used during the monument's 1848 ceremonies was the same Washington used during the Capitol's cornerstone ceremonies. A time capsule was tucked in the cornerstone containing information about the United States and the Washington family, American currency, a Bible, newspapers, and the initial "Programme of the Organization of the Smithsonian Institution." Among the thousands in attendance was a little-known congressman named Abraham Lincoln.

To lessen the cost the Monument Society invited states, countries, and dignitaries to donate blocks of marble to be set in the shaft's interior wall. One of the largest controversies surrounding the monument was a marble slab from Rome's Temple of Concord provided by Pope Pious IX. The American Party (also called the Know Nothing Party), who were anti-Catholic and antiforeign, burglarized the monument in 1854, confiscating the stone and tossing it into the Potomac River. In 1892, divers discovered the "Pope Stone" under Long Bridge. Shortly thereafter it was stolen again and has never been recovered. In 1982 the Vatican donated a replacement stone that is a replica of the original.

### Washington Notes

Work on the monument came to a halt in 1854 because of a lack of funds and many disagreements among Monument Society leaders. The outbreak of the Civil War further delayed construction. The monument stood unfinished, at 156 ft tall, for the next 22 years. Never at a loss for words, writer Mark Twain referred to the incomplete monument as "a factory chimney with the top broken off" and described the area surrounding it as "cow sheds around its base . . . and tired pigs dozing in the holy calm of its protecting shadow." During the Civil War, the monument was also dubbed the Beef Depot Monument. Thousands of cattle grazed in the area before being slaughtered to feed Union troops.

During the 1870s several new design proposals for the monument were considered, but a decision was finally made to continue with Mills's modified plan. After the 1876 Centennial, Congress passed legislation, which President Grant signed, approving funds to complete the project.

Lieutenant Colonel Thomas L. Casey of the U.S. Army Corps of Engineers was named to head the final stages of construction. One of his first moves was to add a concrete skirt around the base to stabilize the foundation. In 1880 marble from the Maryland quarry that had supplied the first 150 feet was unavailable. Matching marble was acquired from a Massachusetts quarry. By Aug 9, 1884, the monument reached the 500 ft mark. The remaining 48 ft of the monument was fashioned solely from marble that was again available from the Maryland quarry. The newer stone had weathered to a different shade, so the two periods of construction are noticeable on the building's exterior.

On Dec 6, 1884, the aluminum metal apex, 5.6 inches on each base side, 8.9 inches high, and shaped like a small pyramid, was set on top of the monument. Engraved on the apex are the names of the engineers and notables who had completed the monument, and one side has "LAUS DEO" ("praise God") engraved on it.

On Feb 21, 1885, President Chester A. Arthur, the vice president who was inaugurated after President James A. Garfield's assassination, officially dedicated the Washington Monument. It had cost $1,870,710. The interior of the monument opened to the public on Oct 9, 1888. Today more than 1 million people visit the monument annually.

## Exterior

The façade of the Washington Monument is white marble from Maryland and Massachusetts. In 1959, 50 flagpoles flying the Stars and Stripes were placed around the perimeter of the monument's concrete skirt. A plaque acknowledging Alaska and Hawaii is located in the monument's lobby.

**Dimensions.** Height: 555 ft 5.9 inches (according to satellite measurement taken in summer 1999). Width at base of shaft: 55 ft 1.5 inches; width at 500 ft: 34 ft 5.5 inches. Thickness of walls at base: 15 ft; thickness of walls at 500 ft: 18 inches. Depth of foundation: 36 ft 10 inches. Weight of monument: 81,120 tons.

## Interior

Granite blocks and eight wrought-iron columns serve as structural supports. A wrought-iron staircase winds to the top but is only accessible to visitors on special tours. The original elevator was steam-powered. The first electric elevator operated from 1901 to 1959. The current elevator shoots visitors to the top of the monument in 75 seconds; the descent takes only 65 seconds.

The Statue of George Washington in the waiting room of the monument is a bronze replica of a marble statue sculpted in 1787 by Jean-Antoine Houdon, the original of which stands in the state capitol in Richmond, Virginia. The monument's statue, dedicated in 1994, is 6.8 ft tall, weighs 800 pounds, stands on a marble pedestal, and faces east toward the Capitol.

The area at the top of the monument is cramped, dimly lit, and often cold and damp. Tucked into one corner is a tiny museum shop, which sells Washington, D.C.–related trinkets, books about George Washington, and models of the monument.

Four windows provide panoramic views of the city. Placards below each window identify many of the major buildings visible from each vantage point. Views (counterclockwise east to south) include the Mall, the Capitol Building and other Capitol Hill sites; downtown Washington and the White House; Georgetown and Washington Cathedral; and the Potomac River, northern Virginia, and National Airport.

Note: Even with timed tickets, there can be a wait to ride the elevator to the top.

The viewing area at the top can get crowded, the windows are sometimes dirty, and clouds or fog can obscure the scenic view. The second-best view in Washington, D.C., is often less of a hassle: Ride to the 270 ft high observation gallery of the Old Post Office tower (see Walk 12: "Federal Triangle and Old Downtown").

To reach the **Sylvan Theater,** walk southeast from the monument toward the 15th St ticket kiosk. The wooden open-air stage, located at the bottom of the hill, is used for musical performances and theatrical productions. The United States Marine Corps Band performs several free, evening performances during the summer season. For information, ☎ 619-7222.

Follow the sidewalk away from Sylvan Theater, due west (toward the Lincoln Memorial). Upon reaching 17th St., head south. The **Commodore John Paul Jones Memorial** (1912; Charles Henry Niehaus, sculptor; Thomas Hastings, architect) is at the southernmost point of the street. The centerpiece of the monument is a bronze statue of Jones in period naval attire. His left hand rests on the hilt of his sword and his right is clenched. On either side of the pedestal, water spurting from the mouths of two dolphins flows into pools on the west and east sides of the monument. A relief on the south side of the monument depicts Jones hoisting the American flag on a U.S. battleship. Above the relief are his words: "Surrender? I have not yet begun to fight!" Jones uttered this pledge in the 1779 battle during which his ship, the *Bonhomme Richard,* was almost destroyed before eventually defeating its English attacker. Also carved into the marble monument: "In Life He Honored the Flag / In Death the Flag Shall Honor Him."

### Washington Notes

Although Jones (1747–1792) was an American naval commander during the Revolutionary War, he died in poverty in Paris, France, in 1792, after having served as an admiral in the Russian Navy. In 1905 Jones's remains were discovered in a cask of rum buried in a small Parisian cemetery. His remains were shipped to the United States and reinterred at the United States Naval Academy in Annapolis. In 1906, Congress appropriated $50,000 to construct this memorial to honor Jones. It was completed in 1912.

Head north on 17th St, passing the Reflecting Pool. The **Lock Keeper's House** (also called Bullfinch Gatehouse because of the decorative sculpture on its façade done by Charles Bullfinch) is at the southwest corner of the intersection of 17th St and Constitution Ave N.W. The gate's twin stands on the corner of 15th St and Constitution Ave N.W. Constructed around 1835, this fieldstone cottage was built to shelter the keeper of Lock B. The façade is marked "Weighing Station for the Washington Canal." Constitution Ave was once the Washington branch of the Chesapeake Canal. This eastern section emptied into Tiber Creek and the Potomac River. (See "National Mall: History" in Walk 5.) The lock keeper recorded the passage of canal boats and collected tolls. The house, used as a toolshed, is not open to the public.

Find the path behind the Lock Keeper's House and follow it west into Constitution Gardens.

## Constitution Gardens

Constitution Ave and 17th St N.W. Admission: free. Concession stand open 9:30–6. Restrooms. Wheelchair accessible. For information on Ranger tours, which are subject to staff availability, call ☎ 426-6841.

Constitution Gardens (1974–76; Skidmore, Owings and Merrill) is a 52-acre man-made park north of the Reflecting Pool and parallel to Constitution Ave. A. J. Downing and Calvert Vaux, landscape architects, envisioned the Mall to have features like this park: meandering paths, a small lake, groves of trees, and lots of green space. Constitution Gardens commemorates the 56 idealists who signed the Declaration of Independence. A memorial honoring them is located on the island near the north bank of the lake.

**Highlights:** The memorial commemorating signers of the Declaration of Independence. The Vietnam Veterans Memorial is at the west end of the gardens.

### History

About 400 years ago, the Potomac River flowed over present-day Constitution Ave before heading east along what is now 17th St. Mud flats covered the area where Constitution Gardens is today, and a series of canals ran along Constitution Ave and 17th St. In 1815 Tiber Creek was transformed into the Washington Canal. Never a successful route for transporting goods, the Washington Canal was abandoned as rail routes became more popular. The canal became an open sewer and a health hazard. In 1871 the Washington Canal was filled in and renamed B St, which later became Constitution Ave. In 1874 Congress appropriated funds to dredge the Potomac River to make it more navigable and to enable boats to moor along Maine Ave. Mud from the river's bottom was used to fill the marshland that is now Constitution Ave.

For years the U.S. Fish Commission used the area for propagating ponds for European carp. On June 6, 1900, an act was passed to develop this area into a scenic and recreational park. By 1901 work had begun on West Potomac Park, but it was curtailed because of World War I and World War II. During the war years the site had temporary buildings, known as tempos, as well as parking lots for employees of the army and navy. The last of these structures was removed in 1971.

In 1972 President Richard Nixon authorized construction of a park as a Bicentennial project. Work began in 1974 and Constitution Gardens were dedicated on May 27, 1976. The gardens commemorate the events relating to the Revolution and the founding of the nation. In 1978 legislation was passed to construct the 56 Signers of the Declaration of Independence Memorial. Also, on July 1, 1980, Congress designated two acres of the park for the Vietnam Veterans Memorial. (See "Vietnam Veterans Memorial," later this walk.)

By 1982 the Declaration of Independence Memorial was completed. Set on an island accessible by a wooden bridge, the memorial is a semicircular grouping of 56 red marble stones arranged in 13 groups—symbolic of the 13 colonies. Etched in each stone is a signer's name, occupation, hometown, and signature. The 6½-acre lake is stocked with koi and smallmouth bass. Among the birdlife that can be spotted in the park are Canada geese, mallards, gulls, and night herons.

### Washington Notes

In the late 1980s ducklings began disappearing from the lake in Constitution Gardens. Police believed someone was sneaking into the park at night and snatching the fowl. After the National Park Service drained the lake, it was discovered that catfish were swallowing the small birds whole.

Two other memorials are slated for placement in the gardens. One is the **Black Revolutionary War Patriots Memorial,** which will honor the estimated 5,000 African American soldiers and sailors who served in the American Revolution, as well as the tens of thousands of slaves who ran away to freedom and filed petitions for liberty. It will be placed on the south side of the small lake. The memorial design, by Edward Dwight, Jr., calls for two curving and rising walls. On the north wall men, women, and children will be depicted in bas-relief in acts of wartime courage. The granite wall to the south will have quotations from African American patriots. The estimated $6 million for the memorial is being raised through private donations.

A site at the east end of Constitution Gardens has been designated for the **Martin Luther King, Jr., Memorial.** A leader of the 1960s civil rights movement, Dr. King is especially known for his inspirational "I Have A Dream" speech, which was delivered in Washington, D.C., at the Lincoln Memorial.

Cross Constitution Avenue and walk west. The **Albert Einstein Memorial** (1979; Robert Berks) is outside the National Academy of Sciences at 2101 Constitution Ave N.W. The 21 ft tall, bronze statue portrays Einstein holding a notebook containing his mathematical equations and studying more than 2,700 celestial bodies (steel pins peppering a black granite sky). Berks signed his name on one of Einstein's legs. (See Walk 18: "Foggy Bottom.")

The **National Academy of Sciences** often holds free art exhibits. Open weekdays 8:30–5. ☎ 334-2000.

Cross Constitution Ave to the south side of the street and walk west to Henry Bacon Dr. Follow this street south to the entrance to Constitution Gardens on the east side of the street.

## The Vietnam Veterans Memorial

Constitution Ave and Henry Bacon Dr N.W. ☎ 634-1568. Web: www.nps.gov/vive. Open 24 hours a day, year-round. Rangers are posted at the memorial 8 A.M.–12 A.M.

The Vietnam Veterans Memorial (1982; Maya Ying Lin), commonly known as the Wall, is along this path, northeast of the Lincoln Memorial. The names of American soldiers who were killed during the war, were prisoners of war, or remain missing in action are chronologically listed on the black granite V-shaped memorial.

### History

In 1979 Jan Scruggs, an infantry corporal during the Vietnam War, headed an effort to establish a memorial to Vietnam veterans. On July 1, 1980, Congress set aside two acres of Constitution Gardens for the memorial. Scruggs and Washington–based veterans organized the Vietnam Veterans Memorial Fund to estab-

*Vietnam Veterans Memorial. Courtesy of the Washington, D.C., Convention &*
*Visitors Association.*

lish a monument to honor veterans and to heal the nation. The group solicited donations from corporations, foundations, unions, veterans, civic organizations,
and more than 275,000 Americans. No federal funds were used to construct the
$7 million memorial.

A national design contest was held. Applicants from around the nation submitted 1,421 proposals. The guidelines were strict: The memorial must be reflective and contemplative in character, must harmonize with the natural
surroundings and neighboring national memorials, must include the names of all
who were killed or remain missing, and must not make any form of political statement about the war.

A 21-year-old Yale University architecture student, Maya Ying Lin, the daughter of Chinese immigrants, won the competition with her design of a simple, V-
shaped, polished black granite wall inscribed with the names of the initial 57,939
servicemen who were killed, missing in action, or were prisoners of war. The wall
now contains 58,209 names. Lin's philosophy was that "the names would become the memorial." One wing of the wall points toward the Lincoln memorial,
while the other stretches east toward the Washington Monument. Each wing
grows in height until the two wings converge at the vertex. To blend the wall with
its natural surroundings, the wall is slightly burrowed into the ground. Lin saw
this as emblematic of a healing process. "Take a knife and cut open the earth," she
said, "and with time grass would heal it."

Maya Lin hardly expected the controversy that ensued. Supporters found the
memorial moving, while others saw the dark, brooding, granite block as fore-
boding and morose. Some critics called the monument "a tombstone" and "a
black gash of shame and sorrow." To appease those dissatisfied with the wall,
artist Frederick E. Hart was commissioned to create a sculpture that would add a

human element. His *Three Servicemen* (1984; Frederick E. Hart) depicts three young and proud servicemen—one African American, one white, and one Hispanic. Their gazes, cast to the wall, evoke weariness and valor. The sculpture was placed near a flagpole that flies the American flag 60 ft above the servicemen's heads. The base of the pole displays the emblems of the nation's five armed forces.

On March 11, 1982, Lin's design was approved, and work began on March 26. The wall was dedicated Nov 13, 1982. Hart's piece was dedicated during the fall of 1984. Thousands of visiting veterans and tourists discovered the memorial's true gift: involvement. Many visitors touch the name of a relative or friend. Others leave flowers, flags, pictures, letters, and personal items. These are collected nightly by National Park Rangers. An exhibit displaying some of the collected objects was at the Smithsonian's Museum of American History in the fall of 1992, the tenth anniversary of the Vietnam Veterans Memorial.

**Rubbings.** The National Park Service encourages rubbings of names from the Vietnam Veterans Memorial. Rangers supply special graphite pencils and commemorative rubbing paper at the information booth located near the *Three Servicemen* sculpture. The Park Service appreciates the use of graphite pencils to preserve the memorial. Rangers can provide ladders to reach names; they are also willing to make the rubbings for visitors who are unable to do it themselves.

**Chronology.** The names on the memorial wall are listed chronologically, beginning in 1959 and ending in 1975. For each day of the war, the names are listed alphabetically. The chronology starts at the vertex and continues to the end of the east wing. The list begins again at the top of the west wall and advances chronologically to the end of the wall. Books listing the names and how to find them are located at either end of the memorial. A computer in the information booth has the names on a databank.

**Symbols.** Next to each name is a symbol: A diamond denotes a soldier killed in action (KIA); a cross denotes the soldier as missing in action (MIA) or as a prisoner of war (POW). Approximately 1,300 names have a cross beside them. If a soldier were to return home alive, a circle would be inscribed around the cross. If a soldier were to return dead, a diamond would be superimposed over the cross.

**Dimensions.** The walls of the memorial measure 246.75 ft long, meeting at the vertex at an approximately 125-degree angle. At the vertex, the walls are 10.1 ft high. Extending 35 ft into the bedrock below the wall are 140 black granite pilings. The granite for the wall was quarried from Bangalore, India; the rock was cut and finished in Barre, Vermont. The inscriptions were grit-blasted in Memphis, Tennessee; the height of individual letters is .53 inch, with a depth of .038 inch.

## Vietnam Women's Memorial

At the east end of the Wall is the Vietnam Women's Memorial (1993; Glenna Goodacre), 21st St and Constitution Ave N.W. ☎ 634-6841. Web: www.nps.gov/vive/wommem.htm. The memorial is open 24 hours a day, year-round. Rangers are posted at the memorial 8 A.M.–12 A.M.

### History

When the Vietnam Veterans Memorial was dedicated in 1982, the women who had played a part in the war were almost completely excluded. In 1984, Diane

Carlson Evans cofounded the Vietnam Women's Memorial Fund to establish a women's memorial. The Vietnam Women's Memorial was dedicated on Nov 11, 1993, Veteran's Day.

Designed by Glenna Goodacre, the bronze sculpture depicts three field-hospital nurses in fatigues aiding fallen soldiers. One woman cradles a wounded soldier in her arms while seated on a pile of sandbags. An African American woman is looking skyward, as if searching for an approaching helicopter. A third woman kneels behind the other two, staring into the helmet of the fallen serviceman. Eight yellowwood trees are planted around the memorial as a tribute to the eight servicewomen who were killed in action during the Vietnam War. The statue is 6.8 ft tall and weighs one ton.

Follow the paved path west to the Lincoln Memorial.

## Lincoln Memorial

23rd St and Constitution Ave N.W. ☎ 426-6895. Web: www.nps.gov/linc. Open 24 hours daily, year-round. National Park Service Rangers available 8 A.M.–12 A.M., except Christmas Day. Wheelchair accessible. Restrooms. Museum shop.

One of Washington's best-known landmarks, the Lincoln Memorial (1922; Henry Bacon, architect, Daniel Chester French, statue sculptor, Ernest C. Bairstow, stonework; DL) is a modern interpretation of a Greek temple. A colonnade of 38 fluted columns surrounds the memorial. Inside sits the famous statue of Abraham Lincoln.

**Highlights:** The statue of Abraham Lincoln, famous quotes from his speeches, and Guerin's murals.

### History

Suggestions for a memorial honoring Lincoln began shortly after his assassination. Two years later, in March, 1867, Congress established the Lincoln Monument Association. When the McMillan Commission announced in 1901 that the memorial would be placed in West Potomac Park, controversy ensued. The park, which had been under the Potomac River until the late 19C, remained marshy. The Speaker of the House, Illinois Congressman "Uncle Joe" Cannon, was one of the most outspoken opponents of the West Potomac Park site, vowing: "So long as I live, I'll never let a memorial to Abraham Lincoln be erected in that goddamned swamp." Other proposed sites included the spot where Union Station was later constructed and Meridian Hill on 16th St.

Many design proposals were submitted. One of John Russell Pope's four proposals was a pyramid with Doric porticoes, and the automobile manufacturers lobbied for a 72-mile road stretching from the Capitol to Gettysburg, Pennsylvania, lined with statues of prominent Americans.

Congress passed legislation to construct the Lincoln Memorial in Feb 1911. Architects Henry Bacon and John Russell Pope were invited by the congressional committee to submit plans for the monument. Bacon's neoclassical design was chosen, and on Jan 29, 1913, he submitted his final plan for Congress's approval. The memorial is Bacon's coupling of a Greek Doric temple capped with a Roman-style attic.

Despite the initial opposition to West Potomac Park, ground was broken there

*Lincoln Memorial (interior and sculpture). Courtesy of the Washington, D.C., Convention & Visitors Association.*

on Feb 12, 1914. This site put the memorial in line with the Capitol, Washington Monument, and the home of Robert E. Lee (Arlington House) across the Potomac River in Arlington National Cemetery. The slight hill the memorial sits atop is mud dredged from the Potomac reinforced with the sandstone columns used in the 1836 construction of the colonnade on the Department of the Treasury Building. (The sandstone columns were replaced with granite in 1907.)

Within a year the cornerstone was set. In Dec 1914, the commission asked Daniel Chester French, chairman of the Commission of Fine Arts, to sculpt the statue of Lincoln for the monument's chambers. The commission also chose Jules Guerin to design and create two murals for the chamber's endwalls.

French studied photographs of Lincoln, as well as a plaster "life mask" cast by sculptor Leonard Volk in 1860, to learn Lincoln's physical characteristics. Finally deciding to portray Lincoln seated, French made a series of models of the statue. "What I wanted to convey was the mental and physical strength of the great war president and his confidence in his ability to carry the thing through to a successful finish." French had planned to create a ten-by-ten-ft statue, but when the model was placed in the memorial, French realized that it was dwarfed by the massive memorial. French and the other planners decided to double the size of the statue. The Piccirilli brothers, who helped French carve the Georgia marble for the statue, estimated the cost to be $46,000 for the statue and $15,000 for the pedestal. Early in 1920, workmen began assembling the 28-piece statue at the memorial. It was completed the following May.

### Washington Notes

The Lincoln Memorial was dedicated by Supreme Court Chief Justice William Howard Taft, head of the commission, on Memorial Day, May 30, 1922. A sad irony is that on the day of dedication African Americans who came to honor the Great Emancipator were forced to sit in a segregated section. Dr. Robert Moten, president of Tuskegee Institute, was scheduled to speak during the ceremony. Moten, however, found himself ushered away from the stage by foulmouthed Marines, who dragged him to an all-black section of the crowd that was separated from the rest of the audience by a road.

The Lincoln Memorial has since become a symbol for equality and civil rights. In 1939 when Marian Anderson was denied the chance to sing at the Daughters of the American Revolution Constitution Hall because she was an African American, First Lady Eleanor Roosevelt resigned as a member of the DAR and asked Secretary of the Interior Harold Ickes to arrange for Anderson to use the Lincoln Memorial steps as her stage. The famous contralto sang to a crowd of more than 75,000 people on Easter Sunday, 1939.

Years later, in 1963, 250,000 Freedom Marchers gathered at the Lincoln Memorial. The Reverend Dr. Martin Luther King, Jr., delivered his famous "I Have a Dream" speech from the memorial's steps on Aug 28, 1963.

### Washington Notes

The Lincoln Memorial was the victim of friendly fire during World War II. Government officials, fearing an attack on Washington, installed guns on the roofs of several government buildings. A soldier manning one of these guns atop the Department of Interior Building accidentally fired a round of ammunition at the Lincoln Memorial. The shot damaged the roofline where the state seals of Maryland, Texas, and Connecticut are displayed. The damage was repaired and is barely visible today.

## Exterior

Constructed with Colorado-Yule marble (exterior) and Indiana limestone (interior walls and columns), the Lincoln Memorial resembles the Parthenon, the temple to the goddess Athena on the Acropolis in Athens, Greece. The 36 states listed above the 38 columns surrounding the walls of the memorial represent the states in the Union at the time of Lincoln's death in 1865. The attic walls above the frieze list the 48 states of the Union and their dates of admission, c. 1922. Alaska and Hawaii are dedicated with inscriptions on the terrace leading to the memorial. The carving on the frieze and attic wall decorations are Ernest Bairstow's work.

## Interior

The statue and murals are located on the chamber level, as is the bookstore. On the lower level are restrooms and an exhibit. Due to asbestos contamination, the caves under the memorial are no longer accessible.

Below the murals are paragraphs from Lincoln's Second Inaugural Address (north wall) and the Gettysburg Address (south wall). Evelyn Beatrice Longman worked on the addresses under the direction of Daniel Chester French.

**The Statue.** Daniel Chester French's design for the Lincoln statue portrays Lincoln as a strong but brooding president. If the statue were to come to life and Lincoln were to unfold his gangly limbs, he would stand 28 ft tall.

> **Washington Notes**
> French had a son who was deaf, so the sculptor was familiar with sign language. The statue's left hand is shaped to make an *A* while his right forms an *L*.

The statue was constructed from 28 blocks of Georgia marble. On the wall behind Lincoln is the inscription: "In this Temple, as in the hearts of the people, for whom he saved the union, the memory of Abraham Lincoln is enshrined forever."

**The Murals.** The mural *Emancipation* is on the south wall and *Unification* is on the north wall. The 600-pound canvases were painted by Jules Guerin using oil paint that had been mixed with wax and kerosene. *Emancipation,* placed above the Gettysburg Address, symbolizes the freeing of a race. Guerin painted the Angel of Truth, with wings spread, offering freedom and liberty to a slave. To the left of the angel is a group representing justice and law, while on the right the collection of characters symbolize immortality. Guerin depicted the unity of North and South in *Unification,* which is placed above the president's Second Inaugural Address. The figures to the left of the Angel of Truth, who is joining the hands of the laurel-crowned North and the South, represent fraternity, unity, and charity.

The murals are currently undergoing a ten-year restoration process. The fine arts restoration firm of Cunningham-Adams is stabilizing the murals' cracked and flaked paint and painstakingly removing dirt, in the process, revealing the rich vibrancy of Guerin's original work.

**Lower lobby.** This area is accessible from the entrance to the south of the foot of the steps leading to the memorial chamber. The restrooms, water fountains, and elevator are here. A small exhibit, **The Lincoln Legacy,** traces the history of civil rights in the United States as well as the history of the Lincoln Memorial and the man it honors. The impetus for the exhibit, and $62,000 of its cost, came from high school students nationwide in the early 1990s who felt that the civil rights movement should be mentioned in the Lincoln Memorial.

Washington honored the memorial's architect and the statue's designer by naming streets after them. Henry Bacon Dr runs one block from Constitution Ave between 21st and 23rd Sts. A similar one-block street, Daniel Chester French Dr, runs parallel to the other and leads to Independence Ave.

A site at the eastern end of the Lincoln Memorial Reflecting Pool has been chosen for the **World War II Memorial** designed to honor those who served in uniform and those who served on the home front during World War II. In June 1999, the National Capital Planning Committee approved a preliminary design featuring two tall arches and a series of stone pillars. Fund-raising for the estimated $100 million memorial continues. Groundbreaking is planned for Veterans Day 2000 and completion for Veterans Day 2002.

## Korean War Veterans Memorial
Independence Ave at the Lincoln Memorial, in West Potomac Park. Open 24 hours daily, year-round, except Christmas Day. Rangers are posted at the memorial 8 A.M.–12 A.M. ☎ 619-7222. Web: www.nps.gov/kwvm. Information booth with touch-screen computer databases of Korean War casualties. Wheelchair accessible.

Follow the paved path south of the Lincoln Memorial's steps to the Korean War Veterans Memorial (1995; Cooper & Lecky, architects; Frank Gaylord and Louis Nelson, sculptors). This memorial features a highly polished wall, but this one is decorated with faces of soldiers. The most prominent part of the Korean War Veterans Memorial is the bronze sculpture group of platoon soldiers making their way through a field.

**Highlights:** The larger than life-size sculpture group of platoon soldiers.

### History
The veterans of the Korean War felt forgotten after the dedication of the Vietnam Veterans Memorial in 1982 and the announcement of a future World War II memorial. In 1985 the Korean War Veterans Association was organized. On Oct 28, 1986, Congress authorized the American Battle Monuments Commission to establish a memorial to honor the American veterans of the Korean War. President Ronald Reagan approved the resolution, which permitted placement of the memorial on the Mall. A site just north of Independence Ave, in a grove of trees, was selected.

Setbacks such as fund-raising and design conflicts delayed construction. The four professors who had submitted the winning design in 1989 proceeded to sue the federal government because alterations were made by another design firm. That firm, Cooper & Lecky, is credited with the final design of the memorial. President Bill Clinton and Kim Young Sam, president of the Republic of Korea, dedicated the memorial on July 27, 1995, the 42nd anniversary of the armistice that ended the war.

Frank Gaylord was asked to sculpt 19 statues, a unit of soldiers on patrol. These seven-ft-tall, stainless steel figures were placed in a gently sloping, triangular area, the Field of Service. The haunting, slightly larger than life-size figures are dressed in battle fatigues covered by ponchos and are carrying rifles. The soldiers have tired, weary looks. Their stance, attire, and faces suggest the harsh conditions of war. At the tip of the triangle, engraved in granite flush with the ground, is the tribute, "Our Nation honors her sons and daughters who answered the call to defend a country they never knew and a people they never met." An American flag hangs half-mast overhead. A granite strip along the walkway lists the 22 countries who were involved in the United Nations effort in Korea.

Louis Nelson created the mural etched on the 164 ft polished black granite memorial wall. Sandblasted into the block are images of the people who served: nurses, soldiers, chaplains, airmen, and sailors. The faces were sculpted from photographs of real, unidentified people who were involved in the conflict. On the east end of the wall is an inscription inlaid with silver, "Freedom Is Not Free." This protrudes into a half-crescent reflecting pool, the Pool of Remembrance. Adjacent is a curb inscribed with the casualty figures—the number of U.S. and UN troops dead, missing, captured, and wounded. A grove of trees that encircles the pool provides a peaceful setting.

### Washington Notes

When the 19 statues depicting the soldiers who fought in the Korean War reflect in the wall, their numbers double to 38. This number is a metaphor for the 38th parallel, the longitude established as the border between North and South Korea in 1945.

Walk along the stone path south of the Reflecting Pool. The **Reflecting Pool** (1919; Henry Bacon) runs from the foot of the Lincoln Memorial to the edge of 17th St. The original plan for the pool, developed in 1902 by the McMillan Commission, was for a cross-shaped pool. During World War I, however, construction was halted, so the pool remained a rectangle. During the war years the Mall was used for temporary army and navy buildings, called tempos. Bridges connecting the tempos stretched across the width of the Reflecting Pool. Although the remaining tempos weren't removed until 1971, the bridges were taken down shortly after the end of the war.

Continue east along the Reflecting Pool to the **D.C. War Memorial** (1930; Frederick H. Brooke), located just north of Independence Ave., to the right of the path. This classical-style pantheon pays tribute to citizens from the District of Columbia who served in the armed forces during World War I. Inscribed in the cornerstone are the names of the 26,000 Washingtonians who lost their lives during the war. The memorial was dedicated on Armistice Day, 1931, by President Herbert Hoover.

Walk south to Independence Ave and turn right. At the intersection of Independence Ave and Ohio Dr, near the Potomac River, is the **John Ericsson Monument** (1926; James Earle Fraser, sculptor; Albert Ross, architect). Ericsson (1803–1889), a Swedish American inventor, is remembered for building the *Monitor*, which battled the Confederate ship *Merrimac* during the Civil War. This was the first known battle between two ironclad vessels. Ericsson also revolutionized navigation by inventing the screw propeller. The statue of Ericsson is seated. On a pedestal above him are three statues, the incarnations of vision (a woman), adventure (a Viking), and labor (an iron molder). The figures lean against the Norse Tree of Life.

Follow Ohio Dr. south until it intersects with W. Basin Dr. Head northeast on W. Basin Dr to the Franklin Delano Roosevelt Memorial.

## *Franklin Delano Roosevelt Memorial*

1850 W. Basin Dr S.W. ☎ 619-7222. Web: www.nps.gov/fdrm. Open 24 hours daily. Staffed by National Park Service Rangers 8 A.M.–12 A.M. daily, except Christmas Day. Admission: free. Wheelchair accessible. Restrooms. Information center and bookshop open 9–9 daily, except Christmas Day.

The FDR Memorial (1997; Lawrence Halprin, architect; George Segal, Robert Graham, Neil Estern, Thomas Hardy, and Leonard Baskin, sculptors; John Benson, stone carver) is located on the southwest bank of the Tidal Basin, south of Independence Ave and north of the 14th St Bridge. The FDR Memorial consists of four outdoor sculpture courts called rooms. The memorial honors the 32nd president of the United States, a man who was elected to an unprecedented four terms in office. FDR helped the country struggle through the Great Depression and World War II. The 7½-acre memorial is the first major national memorial to honor a 20C president, as well as the first to honor a president's wife.

**Highlights:** FDR's quotes and sculpture by George Segal, Leonard Baskin, Neil Estern, and others, which depict ordinary people living in extraordinary times.

### History

The completion of a memorial to FDR took nearly 50 years and $48 million. A few years before his death, FDR confided to Supreme Court Justice Felix Frankfurter that he wanted a modest memorial—a stone set in the lawn in front of the National Archives. FDR died in 1945. In 1946 Congress voted to create a Roosevelt memorial, but the Franklin Delano Roosevelt Memorial Commission was not established till nine years later. In 1959 the site in West Potomac Park, between the Tidal Basin and the Potomac River, was approved. This spot was the last site determined by the McMillan Plan for monument placement.

The first of several design competitions was held in 1960. A design by William Pedersen and Bradford Tilney was chosen over 547 other submissions. The design called for a circular formation of concrete tablets inscribed with FDR quotations. Critics dubbed it "Instant Stonehenge," and Roosevelt's descendants also disliked the design. After numerous revisions the design was rejected by the Commission of Fine Arts in 1965.

Another architect, Marcel Breuer, was invited to submit an idea in 1966. Breuer's idea was to group triangular granite slabs around a stone cube engraved with a likeness of Roosevelt. A year later, this too was rejected. The commission asked prominent architects and landscape architects to compile a list of possible designers. From a list of seven, San Francisco–based landscape architect Lawrence Halprin was selected in 1974. The FDR Memorial Commission selected sculptors for the art works in 1977. In 1978 the FDR Memorial Commission and the Commission on Fine Arts approved Halprin's design. Nine years after President

Ronald Reagan approved construction of the memorial, ground was broken in 1991. Construction began three years later.

Halprin describes the memorial as a "walking environmental experience." It is laid out in four chronological rooms, north to south, each dedicated to one of FDR's terms. Halprin used stonework, landscaping, water, sculpture, and quotations to reflect the social, economic, and cultural changes during FDR's presidency. To resemble the stonework of the Roosevelt Estate in Hyde Park, New York, Halprin chose carnelian granite quarried from Milbank, South Dakota. It took 2½ years and 210 trips for the trucks to cart the 6,000 tons of reddish-pink granite from the quarry to Washington.

The memorial, incorporating the artistic work of six artists, was intentionally designed to be accessible to people with disabilities. A statue of Eleanor Roosevelt shows her wearing a typical ensemble of simple clothes. However, so as not to offend animal-rights groups, the statue lacks the fur collar typically worn by Eleanor Roosevelt. Several pillars with Braille lettering and tactile images were incorporated for the visually impaired.

Even though FDR was wheelchair-bound during part of his political career, he originally was not depicted in a wheelchair, a fact that angered many people with and without disabilities. In response to this, in 1998 it was announced that the main entrance of the memorial would be reconfigured to create an additional outdoor room of granite that would have a bronze, human-scale statue of Roosevelt sitting in the small wheelchair he invented. Architect Lawrence Halprin, sculptor Robert Graham, and stone carver John Benson will create the addition. The statue is to be placed facing the memorial's entrance in order to underscore the fact that Roosevelt used a wheelchair before he became president.

## Exterior

The memorial is about 800 ft long. Four outdoor rooms are separated by 12 ft high walls. The texture of the walls and the use of water suggest different events and moods in the country during FDR's presidency. The memorial incorporates 9 artworks and 6 waterfalls plus 21 Roosevelt quotations that were carved into the granite walls by master stone carver John Benson. Benson also carved the inscriptions on the John F. Kennedy Memorial at Arlington National Cemetery.

**Room 1: The Early Years (1932–36).** Just before the entrance is a small building that houses the bookshop, restrooms, information center, and an exhibit about FDR (See "Interior"). Eagle Alcove, named for the bas-relief interpretation of the presidential seal when FDR took office, marks the entrance to Room 1. This room focuses on FDR's early presidency and the launching of New Deal programs. On the south wall is the 30 ft bas-relief *The First Inaugural* (Robert Graham), which depicts FDR waving from an open car to crowds watching his first inaugural parade. The piece is meant to convey a sense of optimism. Carved into the wall is a quote from a speech given before the 1932 Democratic National Convention: "I pledge you, I pledge myself, to a new deal for the American people." The water in the fountain to the west of the bas-relief cascades quietly to symbolize the healing effect water had throughout FDR's life, particularly during his tenure in the navy and while in Warm Springs. Visitors walk through the first of two meditative gardens to Room 2.

**Room 2: Social Policy (1936–40).** This room addresses the Great Depression and the hope engendered by FDR's social programs. Visitors first encounter three

THEY (WHO) SEEK TO ESTABLISH
SYSTEMS OF GOVERNMENT BASED ON
THE REGIMENTATION OF ALL HUMAN
BEINGS BY A HANDFUL OF INDIVIDUAL
RULERS... CALL THIS A NEW ORDER.
IT IS NOT NEW AND IT IS NOT ORDER.

*FDR Memorial (Room 3: The War Years). Photo credit: Terry J. Adams, National Park Service.*

artworks by George Segal representing hope, hunger, and despair. The first, *Fireside Chat*, is a life-size statue of a seated man listening to a fireside chat. Nearby is a fireside chat phrase, "I never forget that I live in a house owned by all the American people and that I have been given their trust." Against an adjoining wall is *The Breadline*, a line of five statues waiting for food. *The Rural Couple* represents not only farmers, but the nation's weary, hardworking population.

Robert Graham's five bas-relief panels of faces, hands, and people pay tribute to FDR's New Deal social programs. Five pillars are lettered with Braille and are touchable. The fountain's water, flowing smoothly over several steps, symbolizes dams built by the Tennessee Valley Authority. In the second meditative garden, which leads to Room 3, visitors encounter piles of broken blocks of rough granite engraved with the words "I," "Hate," and "War."

**Room 3: The War Years (1940–44).** All of the imagery in this room suggests war's turbulence. The waterfall roars and the granite is rough. A nine-ft statue of a seated and caped FDR is placed against the south wall. His Scottish terrier, Fala, guards FDR's feet. The scattered granite blocks evoke the rubble remaining after bombings. The quotations express FDR's anger about the war. Inscribed is a quote from FDR's March 15, 1941, address to White House correspondents: "They (who) seek to establish systems of government based on the regimentation of all human beings by a handful of individual rulers . . . call this a new order. It is not new and it is not order." A recessed meditative area divides Rooms 3 and 4.

**Room 4: Seeds of Peace (1944–45).** In addition to reflecting peace and optimism, the fourth room honors FDR's life and legacy. One wall has part of an address FDR had prepared for an April 13, 1945, speech that he didn't have the chance to make: "The only limit to our realization of tomorrow will be our doubts of today. Let us move forward with strong and active faith." The 30 ft bas-relief *Funeral Cortege* (Leonard Baskin) is above a pool called Grand Finale. Baskin's work shows mourners following behind the horse-drawn carriage conveying Roosevelt's coffin. Around the corner, on a west wall, is a Neil Estern statue of Eleanor Roosevelt placed in front of a UN emblem. She is honored for her humanitarianism. Carved into the risers of a short staircase are significant dates in FDR's personal and presidential life.

## Interior

In the foyer of the building that houses the bookshop is a small exhibit about FDR. On the wall a time line chronicles the major events of his presidential terms, and there is also a replica of his wheelchair. A placard explains that FDR personally designed the chair using parts of a commercial wheelchair and a kitchen chair. The bookshop sells materials—including books, videos, and posters—about FDR, Eleanor Roosevelt, and the memorial.

## Tidal Basin

Follow the sidewalk south along the Tidal Basin. Paddleboats can be rented by everyone in the Tidal Basin during warm weather 10–6. ☎ 484-0206.

**Highlights:** The springtime display of hundreds of blossoming cherry trees.

### History

The Tidal Basin was created in 1897 as part of the Army Corps of Engineers Potomac River dredging project. (See "Constitution Gardens" and "Hains Point.") This roundish body of water was designed to "flush" the adjoining Washington Channel, inhibiting the accumulation of silt. During high tide and when the Potomac River floods, water from the river enters the Tidal Basin. As the water recedes, it enters the Washington Channel and protects moored and traveling boats from getting beached or running aground.

From 1917 to 1925, there was a popular whites-only beach near where the Jefferson Memorial was later built. It featured a bathhouse and diving platform moored in the basin.

## Cherry Trees

Part of the Tidal Basin and Jefferson Memorial's fame lies in the springtime blossoming of the world-renowned cherry trees. Several individuals deserve the credit for these trees. In 1885 Mrs. Eliza Ruhamah Scidmore began a 24-year project to plant cherry trees along the reclaimed banks of the Potomac. In 1902, while in Japan, Department of Agriculture official David Fairchild admired the many waterways and avenues lined with the fragile, blossoming trees referred to by the Japanese as the Royal Flower. In 1906 Fairchild imported 100 trees to plant in the yard of his Chevy Chase home, and he encouraged his community to plant more. The Chevy Chase Land Company ordered 300 trees to be planted around the city. Fairchild, in an alliance with Susan B. Snipe, supervisor of School Gardens in Washington, developed a plan to have a schoolchild from each school in the district plant one tree on their school's grounds on Arbor Day, March 27, 1908. The children planted 150 cherry trees.

The Arbor Day ceremony attracted the attention of First Lady Helen Herron Taft, who, like Fairchild and Scidmore, wanted to beautify West Potomac Park. Together with Colonel Spencer Cosby (superintendent of Public Buildings and Grounds), Mrs. Taft asked Fairchild to design plans for the park. Fairchild proposed planting cherry trees, and Mrs. Taft ordered 90 American-grown, double-flowering Japanese cherry trees to be planted for a total cost of $106.

Dr. Jokichi Takamine, a Japanese chemist (known for his discovery of adrenaline) learned of Washington's Arbor Day cherry tree project while visiting the capital in 1909. Takamine proposed to Mr. Midzuno, the Japanese counsel in New York, a gift of cherry trees as a gesture of friendship from Tokyo. In 1909 the city's mayor responded with a generous shipment of 2,000 trees, but the trees, infected with insects, failed their agricultural inspection. The trees were destroyed and the Japanese government sent a second shipment of 3,000 cherry trees within weeks. This time, every tree passed inspection. On March 27, 1912, First Lady Taft and Viscountess Chida, wife of the Japanese ambassador, planted the first two cherry trees on the northern bank of the Tidal Basin as a "living symbol of friendship between the peoples of Japan and the United States."

In 1965 the Japanese government presented another 3,000 trees to the United States. Lady Bird Johnson and Mrs. Ryuji Takeuchi, wife of the Japanese ambassador, reenacted the 1912 planting. The Japanese government presented 100 more trees in 1997. These were planted around the Washington Monument.

Washingtonians have been enamored with the trees since their arrival. In 1935 civic groups organized the Cherry Blossom Festival, an annual two-week springtime event that brings thousands of spectators to the area. The festival begins every year with the lighting of a 300-year-old Japanese stone lantern, a 1954 gift from Japan commemorating the 100th anniversary of the Treaty of Peace, Amity, and Commerce between the U.S. and Japan.

Walk across to Ohio Dr and remain on the sidewalk which continues to the Jefferson Memorial.

## *Thomas Jefferson Memorial*

South end of 15th St S.W. ☎ 426-6841. Web: www.nps.gov/thje. Open 24 hours daily. National Park Service Rangers staff the memorial 8 A.M.–12 A.M. daily, except Christmas Day. Bookstore in lower lobby. For information on Ranger programs, call ☎ 426-6821.

The Thomas Jefferson Memorial (1943; John Russell Pope, Otto R. Eggers, and Daniel P. Higgins, architects; DL) honors the third president of the U.S., a man who drafted the Declaration of Independence, negotiated the Louisiana Purchase (which doubled the size of the country), and dedicated himself to educating the masses by establishing the University of Virginia. The domed circular building was designed to resemble the rotunda Jefferson designed for the University of Virginia. A bronze statue of Jefferson (1943; Ruldoph Evans) stands in the center of the memorial. A.A. Weimann designed the pediment.

### History

In 1934 Congress created the Thomas Jefferson Memorial Commission, whose mission was to locate a site for the memorial, solicit a design, and oversee the memorial's construction. Initial locations on the Mall, in Lincoln Park, and along the banks of the Anacostia River were rejected, so the Commission reverted to the 1901 McMillan Commission recommendation. That plan had outlined a kite-shaped design for future monuments so that each monument would be visible from every other monument. The Lincoln Memorial was constructed at the top of the kite at the west end, and the Jefferson Memorial was built at the tip of the south wing.

Although it didn't take as long to complete (nine years from proposal to completion) as the Washington and Lincoln projects, the Jefferson Memorial experienced its share of controversies. One criticism concerned John Russell Pope's design based on the Roman Pantheon, which was classical rather than American in style. Pope incorporated the rotunda because it had been a favorite design element of Jefferson's. Jefferson had used rotundas in his plans for the Virginia Capitol Building, his Monticello home, and the University of Virginia. Jefferson's democratic ideals made him an admirer of ancient Rome's politics and architecture. Other critics noted that the memorial's placement would block the White House's view of the Potomac River. However, the most widely publicized controversy surrounded the cherry trees planted in 1912, some of which had to be destroyed. Despite these concerns Pope's proposal was accepted.

On Nov 15, 1939, President Franklin Delano Roosevelt laid the cornerstone using the same silver gavel Washington had used to place the cornerstone of the Capitol. That same gavel had also been used to lay the cornerstone of the Washington Monument. A wooden gavel from an elm tree Jefferson had planted at Monticello was also used. Placed into the 11-ton Vermont marble cornerstone were copies of the Declaration of Independence and the U.S. Constitution, Jefferson's writings, and the Nov 15 editions of local newspapers.

Pope passed away before construction began; colleagues Otto Eggers and Daniel Higgins saw the project to completion. The memorial was dedicated on April 13, 1943, the 200th anniversary of Jefferson's birth.

In 1938 more than 100 sculptors submitted designs for the statue of Jefferson. Rudolph Evans's design for a 19 ft high portrait statue was selected. The U.S. was involved in World War II during the memorial's construction and there was a wartime restriction on metals, including bronze, so the statue of Jefferson initially placed in the memorial was plaster. A bronze statue replaced it in 1947.

*Jefferson Memorial with Tidal Basin. Courtesy of the Washington, D.C., Convention & Visitors Association.*

### Washington Notes

In 1972, thirty years after the memorial's dedication, another complication arose. Frank W. Fetter, a professor at Northwestern University, noticed that Jefferson's writings about liberty displayed around the memorial were inaccurate. Apparently, space on the memorial's walls was limited, so with the encouragement of the building's architects, the quotes were shortened and their punctuation changed. The National Park Service, who maintains the memorial, decided to leave the quotations as they were.

## The Building

There are four entrances, one from each direction, behind the memorial's colonnaded shell. These entrances not only provide interesting views of the 19 ft tall statue of Jefferson, but also afford views of the Mall. The main, or north, entrance of the memorial faces the Tidal Basin. Entering from here, visitors notice the sculpted marble pediment, *The Drafting of the Declaration of Independence* (1943; Adolph A. Weinman), above the entryway. The scene depicts Jefferson standing before the four men appointed by the Continental Congress to help him draft the Declaration of Independence; if viewed from the steps, Benjamin Franklin and John Adams sit to Jefferson's left, Roger Sherman and Robert R. Livingston are to Jefferson's right.

## Interior

The memorial's interior is dominated by Jefferson's statue, which stands on a six-ft black Minnesota granite pedestal.

**The Panels.** The interior walls of the memorial feature four panels inscribed with quotations outlining Jefferson's philosophies. The southwest wall houses the first in the sequence, an excerpt from the Declaration of Independence. The second set of inscriptions was drawn from the Act for Religious Freedom, which was written by Jefferson and passed by the Virginia Assembly in 1779. The northeast wall is inscribed with six quotations taken from Jefferson's *Summary Views, Notes on Virginia*, two letters written in 1786, and a paragraph he penned shortly before his death. The quotes reveal his thoughts on slavery and education. Jefferson believed that the general education of the people was necessary for an efficient government. Jefferson, one of the country's first abolitionists, spoke openly of slavery's incongruity in a democratic government.

The fourth wall is dedicated to Jefferson's views on change within a democracy. "I am not an advocate for frequent changes in laws and constitutions, but laws and institutions must go hand in hand with the progress of the human mind"—this quotation was taken from a 3,000-word letter Jefferson sent to Samuel Kercheval in 1816. A fifth quote, at the base of the dome, is from a letter Jefferson wrote to Benjamin Rush in 1800: "I have sworn upon the altar of God eternal hostility against every form of tyranny over the mind of man."

Renovations in 1998 added new exhibits, including a time line and informational videos.

Walk south from the Jefferson Memorial into East Potomac Park. **Hains Point** lies at the southern tip of East Potomac Park. This artificial peninsula is named for Army Corps of Engineers Major General Peter C. Hains. Between 1882 and 1890, Hains supervised a project that dredged the channel in the Potomac River and laid the resulting mud over 300 acres of parkland. Congress passed the legislation calling for the dredging and elevation of the flats after a flood in Feb 1881 caused the waters to reach almost to the foot of Capitol Hill.

During the 1920s when vacationing by car became popular, the government used 60 acres of the peninsula as campgrounds for tourists. The site had tennis courts, a golf course, and the Potomac Speedway. Today, the campgrounds and speedway are gone. But there still are tennis courts, plus a driving range and public golf course.

> ### Washington Notes
>
> One of Washington's more unique attractions is *The Awakening* (1980; J. Seward Johnson, Jr.), an aluminum sculpture portraying a giant reclining man struggling to lift his buried body from the ground. Only his right knee, right arm, left hand, and bearded face have emerged. Johnson's piece was placed at Hains Point in 1980 after the International Sculpture Conference. The placement was considered temporary, and Congress has approved the construction of a Peace Memorial Garden on the site.

The nearest Metro station is Smithsonian/Mall (Blue/Orange Line). Return to the Jefferson Memorial and proceed northeast on Basin Dr. This road turns into Raoul Wallenberg Place after Basin Dr crosses over the Tidal Basin outlet. Continue north on Raoul Wallenberg Place (also marked as 15th St). To use the Metro, turn east onto Independence Ave and proceed for three blocks. To continue to Walk 11, walk east to 14th Street. Proceed north on 14th St to the Bureau of Engraving and Printing.

# 11 · Bureau of Engraving and Printing and U.S. Holocaust Memorial Museum Area

Metro: Blue/Orange Line to Smithsonian.
Bus: 13A, 13B, 13M, 52, V6, 32, 34, 36, or 38.

## Bureau of Engraving and Printing

14th and C Sts S.W. ☎ 874-3019 or 874-3188. Web: www.moneyfactory.com. Closed Christmas Day, New Year's Day, and federal holidays. Admission: free, though ticket required. Request same-day and next-day tickets at ticket booth on Raoul Wallenberg Place. Opens at 7:45 A.M. Opens for evening tour tickets at 3:30. Tours: April 14–Sept 26 every ten minutes 9–2; Oct 1–March 31 every ten minutes 9–2 (no tickets required). Evening tours: June 2–Aug 29 every ten minutes 4–7:30. Tours in French, German, Japanese, Spanish, and Hebrew upon advance request. Accommodations for hearing-, sight-, and physically impaired upon advance request. Wheelchair accessible.

The Bureau of Engraving and Printing (BEP) (1914; James Knox Taylor) designs, engraves, and prints U.S. securities—including paper currency, Treasury bonds, and U.S. postage stamps—and other assorted items for the federal government, such as White House invitations, identification cards, and diplomas.

**Highlights:** Watching currency being printed. Purchasing bags of shredded bank notes at the gift shop.

### History

The Bureau of Engraving and Printing was started on Aug 29, 1862, as the six-person First Division of the National Currency Bureau. The operation was located in the basement of the main Treasury building. Four women and two men separated, sealed, and numbered the $1 and $2 state-chartered notes produced by private banknote printers.

The Treasury Department began printing U.S. paper currency in the fall of 1863. It was recommended a year later that the Bureau of Engraving and Printing of the Treasury Department be created. Congress agreed by passing the Appropriation Act of March 3, 1869. By 1877 all U.S. currency was printed by the bureau.

From 1879 until 1914 the bureau's administration and presses were housed in the building now known as the Auditor's Building. (See "Auditor's Building.") As the bureau grew to keep up with the United States's booming economy, the bureau quickly outgrew the auditor's facility. The current location was constructed between 1911 and 1914. This facility has been the home for the Bureau of Engraving and Printing since March 19, 1914. The bureau's annex, directly across 14th St, opened in 1938. It is not accessible to the public.

#### Washington Notes

When the bureau was located in the building now known as the Auditor's Building during the late 19C, the bureau had 250 presses. These presses rolled out approximately $5 million every 28 days. Today, the bureau's presses run 24 hours per day, seven days per week. As of 1985, more than 23 million notes valued at more than $66 million were printed annually. Less than a decade later, during 1992, 8.5 billion notes were printed with a face value of more than $103 billion.

## Exterior

The bureau's building—with its barred windows, surveillance cameras, and tight security—resembles a federal penitentiary. As this facility was constructed with limited financial resources during World War I to house what is essentially a factory, the exterior is not as ornately designed as other federal buildings.

## Interior

Since the tour generally runs only 20–25 minutes, on busy summer days most visitors spend more time waiting in line on the covered walkway leading from 14th St to the entrance of the Bureau of Engraving and Printing Building than in the facility. The bureau has recognized this frustrating dilemma and addressed it with an opportunity to educate visitors about the history of currency through a series of videos and tubelike exhibit cases.

Displays include **silver certificates** (the first U.S. security to bear the slogan "In God We Trust"), engraver's tools, and printing plates, as well as examples of the bureau's work, including postage stamps and White House invitations. A kiosk traces the **history of paper currency**, beginning with the "Flying Money" of the 618–907 Tang dynasty of China through colonial money to modern security measures designed to deter counterfeiting. The videos share the steps involved to produce "greenbacks" and the history of the bureau, as well as currency trivia.

Two printing presses, a transfer press, and a more modern intaglio press, are exhibited beside a re-creation of President Lincoln signing the bill that authorized the production of U.S. currency. Another video, on a large-screen television just before the beginning of the tour, relates the history of U.S. currency from Lincoln's signature through the engraving process to modern-day production.

Follow the red line and placards of over-size $100 bills through the corridors to watch the presses and examiners from behind glass windows. The first viewing area reveals a stockpile of ink drums. U.S. currency is printed in two ink colors, green on the back side one day, black on the face side the next day.

At the next stop visitors see four **high-speed, sheet-fed intaglio presses printing $1 bills;** 8,000 sheets of 32 notes each are printed per hour. The engraved plates are pressed against the sheets with 20 tons of pressure to ensure the intricate designs are transferred completely. Posted below the window is a sheet displaying which bills each machine is producing.

At the viewing area for $10 bills, visitors learn that U.S. paper currency is comprised of 75 percent cotton and 25 percent linen and that the BEP prints an estimated $444 million per day. About 95 percent of these notes are used to replace currency already in circulation. Forty-eight percent of the notes BEP prints are $1 bills, typically used for 22 months before being removed from circulation and shredded by Federal Reserve banks. An audio voice-over discusses each process of a note's production in depth and is illustrated with stories from BEP employees.

The next step involves **trimming and scanning** for imperfect notes (known as

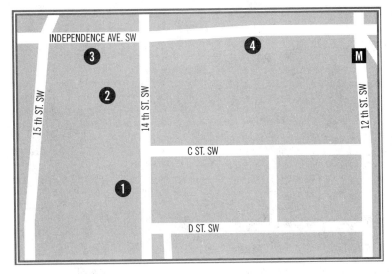

1 Bureau of Engraving and Printing

2 U.S. Holocaust Memorial Museum

3 Auditor's Building

4 Department of Agriculture

mutts)—those with ink spots, smears, discolorations, or irregular cuts. This is followed by **overprinting.** The presses with green ink add serial numbers and Treasury seals, while the presses with black ink add Federal Reserve seals and district numbers. **Cutting** by guillotines follows. The notes are then sorted into units of 100 notes, banded, and packaged into stacks ("bricks") of 4,000 bills. After the bricks are shrink-wrapped they are finally ready for distribution to the 12 Federal Reserve banks.

The tour ends at the bottom of an escalator leading into the **Visitor's Center** and **gift shop.** Reproductions of historical bills, sets of stamps and U.S. minted coins, presidential portraits, as well as the ever-popular baggies of **shredded money** are on sale. Additional videos at kiosks around the room address restoring damaged currency, designing and printing stamps, and security measures.

Exit the Bureau of Engraving and Printing and continue north on 14th St.

## U.S. Holocaust Memorial Museum

100 Raoul Wallenberg Place S.W., between 14th and 15th Sts near Independence Ave. ☎ 488-0400 or 488-0406 (TTY). Web: www.ushmm.org. Open daily 10–5:30. Closed Yom Kippur and Christmas Day. Admission: free. Passes for permanent exhibition are timed at 15-minute intervals 10–4:15 and available daily at 10 A.M. Lines start at the 14th St entrance about 8:30 A.M. Passes distributed on first-come, first-served basis. Each person in line may obtain up to four tickets. Pro-Tix sells passes in advance for a nominal charge; limit ten passes per group. ☎ (800) 400-9373. Museum Café, in museum annex, serves light lunch items and prepackaged kosher entrées 8:30 to 4:30. Coatcheck, restrooms, telephones,

*U.S. National Holocaust Memorial Museum (14th St entrance). Photo credit: Beth Redlich. Courtesy of USHMM Photo Archives.*

museum shop. No video or audio recording. Photography not permitted in galleries; flash photography not permitted in Hall of Remembrance. Wheelchairs and baby carriers available. Allow two to three hours to view the exhibit.

The 14th St entrance brings visitors directly onto the first floor. If passes have been reserved, they can be picked up at a counter to the right of the main doors. Also to the right are the stairs that lead to the concourse level, where restrooms are located. The museum shop is to the left of the main entrance. All visitors must pass through a metal detector, and bags and parcels are subject to X ray.

The U.S. Holocaust Memorial Museum (1993; James Ingo Freed of Pei Cobb Freed & Partners, Notter Finegold + Alexander Inc.) serves as a national memorial to the millions of people persecuted and murdered during Nazi tyranny from 1933 to 1945. The museum's primary purpose is to teach visitors about this tragedy, to encourage them to consider the moral issues raised by the Holocaust, and to remember the victims.

**Highlights:** Aside from the memorable, emotionally charged Permanent Exhibit, attractions include the Wexner Learning Center, an interactive computer-based research center; Remember the Children: Daniel's Story, an exhibit about a child's view of the Holocaust; the Hall of Remembrance; and the Wall of Remembrance.

### History

In 1980 Congress unanimously passed an act creating the United States Holocaust Memorial Council. The council was charged with establishing a living memorial to honor the millions of Jews and other victims of persecution by the Nazis prior to and during World War II. Though the museum was built on federally donated land, the museum was constructed with private funds.

The architect, James Ingo Freed, was mandated by the council to design a building that would be "visually and emotionally moving in accordance with the solemn nature of the Holocaust." Freed's goal was to create a relationship between the building design and the exhibitions inside. According to Freed, "There are no literal references to particular places or occurrences from the historic event. Instead, the architectural form is open-ended so the museum becomes a resonator of memory." To develop his ideas for the design and to determine which materials would be appropriate to use, Freed visited several Holocaust-period ghettos and camps.

The museum was constructed on a site that once was used by temporary buildings of the Bureau of Engraving and Printing. The site was dedicated on April 22, 1993. Since its opening the museum has had more than 10 million visitors, 80 percent of whom are non-Jewish. Nearly half a million children visit the museum each year.

### Washington Notes

The section of 15th St that runs west of the museum was renamed Raoul Wallenberg Place to honor the Swedish diplomat who smuggled several hundred Hungarian Jews to safety.

## Exterior

Freed has explained that he wanted the musuem's design to disturb visitors. The building has an industrial, penitential feel. The north side's brick towers hint at sentry towers. The other three sides of the building are limestone. The main entrance on 14th St is a limestone-and-brick rectangular wedge. Paneless windows in the screen have a ghostly feel. The brick and limestone were used to complement the neighboring Bureau of Engraving and Printing Building as well as other nearby buildings.

Near the Raoul Wallenburg Place entrance is the six-sided Hall of Remembrance. In the Eisenhower Plaza is one of the museum's four site-specific, commissioned artworks: a sculpure by Joel Shapiro, *Loss and Regeneration* (1993). It was created in memory of the children who perished in the Holocaust. Etched into the exterior walls of the museum is a quote from General Eisenhower during his April 1945 visit to the Ohrdruf camp. It serves as a testimony to the atrocities the liberators uncovered. A second quote was spoken by President Ronald Reagan on Oct 5, 1988, at a cornerstone dedication.

At the north side of the Plaza is the museum annex.

## Interior

To suggest a cold, harsh world in which things have gone wrong, Freed used industrial materials such as bricks, rivets, bolted metals, and steel plates. Reenforcing this feeling are the odd angles in the stairway and other areas of the main atrium. The prisonlike, factory feeling is also underlined by the catwalks and exposed beams.

**First floor.** Visitors enter the building from the 14th St side to the first floor, moving through a canopied entrance and crossing over a raw steel platform to the **Hall of Witness.** In this lobby and waiting area a large glass skylight supported by interior steel beams presses against the interior brick walls, creating a sense of oppressiveness. Metal railings, a massive black granite wall, and industrial metal-colored doors conjure the feel of prisons and factories. In the center of the hall is the information desk. No pass is required for this area.

To the north of the information desk is **Remember The Children: Daniel's Story,** a special hands-on exhibit that explores the devastating effects of the Holocaust as told from the perspective of a young boy in Nazi Germany. Designed for children ages 8 and older, the exhibit is based on experiences of the children who survived the Holocaust and wrote about what happened to them between 1933 and 1945. Daniel, an 11 year old when the Nazis first come to power, is a composite of many children of the Holocaust. While walking through the exhibit, visitors first see Daniel's comfortable middle-class home and learn about his mother, sister Erica, and father. Then, the increasing restraints of Nazi policies are told from Daniel's viewpoint. He is not allowed to go to school, he loses his friends, he has to move to a ghetto, and he is separated from his mother and sister at the concentration camp. Visitors are invited to look through Daniel's diary (a handwritten book in each of the rooms) as he records his feelings and fears. Photographs (none too graphic for children) and spoken narrative tell the story. At the end of the exhibit, visitors—especially children—are invited to express their feelings about the exhibit by writing a card and tacking it onto a bulletin board provided. A memorial to the 1.5 million children who died in the Holocaust, this is an unforgettable experience for all audiences, and a precursor to the main exhibit. A prototype of Remember the Children: Daniel's Story originated at the Capital Children's Museum some years ago.

From the Hall of Witness, walk down the stairs to the **concourse level** and the **Wall of Remembrance (Children's Tile Wall),** which is composed of more than 3,000 tiles painted by American schoolchildren to commemorate the children who died in the Holocaust. Above the tiles is a quote by Yitzhak Katzenelson, "The first to perish were the children . . . From these a new dawn might have risen." Many of the tiles depict children crying or in the camps, while others are hopeful, such as the one showing the Star of David and the Christian cross framing the words "Working Together."

Across from the Wall of Remembrance is a photographic display about Oskar Schindler, the German manufacturer whose famous list saved over 1,000 Jews from the camps.

Other rooms on this level include classrooms (part of the Gonda Education Center), the 178-seat Helena Rubenstein Auditorium, the 414-seat Joseph and Rebecca Meyerhoff Theater, and the Sidney Kimmel and Rena Rowan Special Exhibition Gallery. This level also has temporary exhibits.

**The Permanent Exhibit: The Holocaust** is a three-floor comprehensive history of the "Final Solution" created with the use of artifacts, photographs, films, and eyewitness testimonies. The exhibit is divided into three sections that chronologically depict life before the Holocaust in the early 1930s, continue through the Nazi rise to power and the subsequent tyranny and genocide, and conclude with the liberation of the camps and the trials of Nazi officials. The Permanent Exhibit is not recommended for children under the age of 11. The exhibit begins on the fourth floor and ends on the second.

Before entering the elevator on the first floor, pick up a passportlike identification card from the boxes along the wall just before the elevator bank. To personalize the visit, each card shows a photo and name of a real person who experienced the Holocaust. Prior to exiting each of the three sections of the exhibit, check the card to learn what happened to this person during those years.

During the elevator ride to the fourth floor and the beginning of the exhibit, a brief newsreel film is shown. Images of emaciated concentration camp prisoners and a voice-over by a horrified American soldier who helped liberate a camp in 1945 are an effective introduction. The soldier wonders how such horrors could have happened.

**Fourth floor.** Exit the elevator. Visitors see ceiling-high black-and-white photographs of inmates of Ohrdruf, one of many concentration camps established in Germany and the countries it occupied. An equally eerie presence is the haunting black metal wall to the right. Letters spelling *THE HOLOCAUST* have been cut out of it. Behind black bars are the blue-and-gray-striped uniforms worn by camp prisoners. These seem to float in space. A 13-minute film, "The Nazi Rise to Power," relates the story of a young Adolf Hitler and his rise from a lowly soldier to the powerful leader of Germany.

**Nazi Assault, 1933–1939.** Through photographs, narrative, and film, the Nazis spread their racism, anti-Semitism, and extreme nationalism. In 1933, when Hitler was appointed chancellor, there were 29 million Jews in continental Europe. Eleven of the 37 German Nobel Prize winners prior to 1933 were Jews. Most Jews in Germany considered themselves members of their society, committed to their country. The exhibit shows how through one disturbing incident after another, the rights and the identity of German Jews as Germans were whittled away. Between 1933 and 1939 the Nazis enacted more than 400 laws that defined and segregated German Jews.

**The Science of Race** addresses the forced sterilization programs that were carried out in an attempt to "purify" the German population. "Anti-Semitism" is a film about the history of this racist movement and the resulting genocide. A Jewish lawyer speaks with assurance that, as citizens, they will be able to address these wrongs through the court system, but this hope is smashed by the Nuremberg Laws in 1935, when it was declared only those of "German or kindred blood" could be citizens. This excluded Jews, some of whose families had lived in Germany for generations. Films of the May 1933 book burning are shown (books by Helen Keller and Ernest Hemingway were among those destroyed), where in one day, 25,000 books were burned in Berlin. Photographs and circulars distributed at the time attest to the penalties heaped on those who socialized or "mated" with Jews. Look at the faces of the jeering crowd in a photograph of a woman being marched through the street wearing a sign that says, "I am a German girl and I allowed myself to be defiled by The Jew."

Continue on to **"Night of Broken Glass,"** *Kristallnacht* **1938.** Photographs depict a synagogue before and after the destruction of Jewish property. Excerpted histories from those who lived through the destruction are shown. The Jewish population was penalized $400 million to pay for the damage done to their own property. From here enter the room depicting **Operation T4,** the systematic killing of the handicapped, organized and carried out by German physicians who said that the money spent on care of the handicapped could be better spent on newlyweds.

Exhibits detail the beginning of the war, Jewish refugees' search for lands to emigrate to, and the lack of response by President Franklin Delano Roosevelt.

Cross the glass **Bridge of Villages.** On the glass are etched the names of towns and cities whose Jewish communities were wholly or partially lost in the Holocaust.

The **American Responses** has newsreels and newspapers examining America's response to Nazi persecution of its Jewish citizens. Individual booths with headphones and television screens tell the story of failed diplomacy and timidity that continued during the years prior to and during the Final Solution. From here enter a small room where black-and-white photographs taken by Roman Vishniac in Poland, Russia, and the Ukraine between 1935 and 1939 are displayed. Vishniac, one of the foremost photographers of prewar Jewish life in eastern Europe, brings to life the harshness of existence in the faces of young children and old men.

Other black-and-white images illustrate the somber and terrified faces of hundreds waiting in lines to be shuttled to ghettos and death camps. These images contrast with the "before" photos of Ejszyszki, a Polish village. **Tower of Faces: The Ejszyszki Shtetl Collection** is housed in a red brick tower that has the ominous shape and feel of a smokestack. Jews had lived in the small town of Ejszyszki (or Eishyshok in what is now Lithuania), near Vilna, for more than 900 years. In 1939, the Jewish population of 3,500 was a majority in the town, which was famous for its Talmudic academy and wide range of cultural and political organizations. It is chilling to realize that in two days in Sept 1941 almost the entire population was massacred by Nazi soldiers. Only 29 of the town's 3,500 Jews survived.

### Washington Notes

One of the children saved from the massacre and in hiding until the Allied liberation in 1944 was the creator of the collection of photographs, Dr. Yaffa Eliach. Eliach and her family hid for years in a cave under a pigsty. This collection of photos (which continues down to the third floor) was a labor of love and determination by Dr. Eliach, whose grandfather and grandmother, both photographers, took most of the photographs of the more than 100 families included in the collection. Over a 17-year period, Dr. Eliach (who is a writer, historian, and professor at Brooklyn College in New York, and creator of Brooklyn's Center for Holocaust Studies) pored over diaries, letters, and birth and marriage certificates, putting together a history of the town where she was born and which she saw destroyed as a child. In her researches she also garnered hundreds of photographs (sometimes donated, sometimes paid for with her own money) displayed here. Eliach has described the people of Ejszyszki as "complicated, contradictory, multifaceted, and fascinating, true representatives of the family of man in all its complexity." That complexity is displayed here, in the faces of giggling teenage girls, husbands and wives in their twilight years together, dignified town officials, and children, such as the two boys with their skis, the older one with his arm protectively around the shoulder of the younger. What is chilling to realize is that all of these people were murdered. Dr. Eliach's collection personalizes the Holocaust by literally putting faces on the tragedy.

**Third floor.** The exhibit continues on the third floor with **"FINAL SOLUTION," 1940–1945.** Visitors learn how the Nazis systematically deported Jews and others to ghettos, then to the concentration camps, where the implementation of the "Final Solution" was handled at the killing centers. Given that few countries were willing to provide haven for the Jews (as proven by the Evian Conference), the Nazis began to plan what was called the Final Solution to the Jewish question, or *Judenfrage.* The methodical gassing of Jews began on Dec 8, 1941, at a death camp in Chetmno, Poland.

Before Jews were deported to the camps, they were put into ghettos. **Ghettos, 1939–1944** describes through photographs, artifacts, and film the lives of the Jews living in these sealed towns. More than 2 million Jews were eventually removed from the ghettos to be deported to the death camps, beginning with the elderly, children, and the sick.

Evocative descriptions of life in several ghettos are featured. By the summer of 1942, there were more than 400 ghettos in eastern Europe, imprisoning over 2 million Jews and 8,000 gypsies.

A casting of the largest remaining segment of the **Warsaw ghetto wall** (the original was 11 ft high, with barbed wire on top) introduces visitors to perhaps the most famous of the ghettos. Before the war, the city of Warsaw contained the largest concentration of Jews in Europe. In 1940, the ghetto was established in the city and sealed. For two years, the Jews of Warsaw lived eight to a room, with no fresh food or clean water. Disease and starvation killed those who weren't deported to the death camps. In May 1942, a tragically brave uprising by the remaining Jews was defeated when the ghetto was set afire, building by building, and then razed.

A milk canister from the Oneg Shabbat Archive is shown here. In May 1940, Emanuel Ringelblum, a Jewish historian, began collecting and recording information about the Warsaw ghetto, collecting items such as underground newspapers, notices from the Jewish Council (every ghetto had a council that helped organize ghetto life), and reports on resistance organizations. For safety, the archives were placed in metal containers, which were then hidden in places around the ghetto. Two milk canisters (one of them displayed here) were found after the war.

Continue to the display of the Czech town of **Theresienstadt.** From 1941 to 1945, 140,000 Jews were interned here; 16,872 survived the war. Theresienstadt had a rich cultural life, with a lending library of 60,000 volumes. Its 15,000 children attended school, painted pictures, and wrote poetry, before being deported to the camps, where almost all of them died. Prior to a Red Cross visit, the Nazis planted gardens, painted houses, and stocked the cafés with food and drink—all of which disappeared once the Red Cross inspectors left.

Displays about Lodz, Cracow, and Tarnow are also here, with photographs, artifacts (an iron hospital door from Lodz, a synagogue window from Cracow, a cemetery gate from Tarnow), and films.

Exit the ghetto display. Next, visitors come to a wooden boxcar resting on train tracks. Visitors must walk through this car to get to the rest of the exhibit. **Boxcar No. 31599 G** is a 15-ton *Karlsruke* freight car, one of several types used to deport Jews to the death camps. Leather suitcases belonging to those once herded inside are piled on either side. Passengers were packed in 100 to a car. Sometimes the train would halt for several hours or days and sit at stations, while those packed inside froze in winter cold or suffocated in summer heat, with no food, water, or means of sanitation. A survivor tells of the bonds that grew between people: "Everybody said farewell to life through his neighbor."

Walking through the boxcar, come to **Who Shall Live and Who Shall Die,** where the process known as *Selektion* separated those who were gassed immediately upon arrival at the camp (the sick, elderly, pregnant women, and young children) from those who would be worked to death. At the height of operation, the camps numbered in the thousands and contained more than 700,000 prisoners. Besides Jews, there were also gypsies, Russian POWs, political prisoners, Jehovah's Witnesses, and homosexuals interned in the camps. A wall of photographs of camp prisoners with shaved heads and bleak, staring eyes leads the way to a casting made from the entrance gate to the most famous of the camps, Auschwitz-Birkenau. Walk under the inscription over the gate: *"Arbeit macht frei,"* or "Work Will Make You Free," a sign at the actual camp entrance.

**Voices from Auschwitz** is a glass-enclosed room in which visitors can listen to oral histories of survivors. One woman, for example, talks about "the stink, the fear, the selections . . . mostly, mostly death in the gas chambers."

Across from Voices From Auschwitz is a re-creation of prisoners' quarters at the camp, with actual bunk beds from the camp. Auschwitz operated for five years. More than 400,000 prisoners were registered; thousands of others were killed upon arrival. Those not killed had their heads shaved, were issued a ragged uniform (one survivor speaks of the women getting only a loose dress and slippers, but no underwear), and had identification numbers tattooed on their left forearm. Against one wall is a scale model of Crematorium II, one of the camp's four killing centers. The scale model, sculpted by Mieczystaw Stobierski in stark white, shows dozens of people arriving, then undressing, then struggling for life in the death chamber as the Zyklon B pellets dropped from the ceiling, killing them within a few minutes; finally, the bodies are removed to the crematorium chamber, where gold teeth and fillings are removed. The crematoriums burned about 1,000 bodies a day.

Across from the sculpture is a casting of a gas chamber door from one of the death chambers at Majdanek, complete with a small glass peephole for SS guards to look through. Some of the most graphic displays, such as photos of the disfigured victims of Joseph Mengele's "medical experiments" appear behind "privacy walls," enabling visitors to view only those they want to see. Other artifacts displayed here include a casting of a Majdanek table used in the extraction of gold fillings from the dead bodies, and four ceiling-high concrete posts used to hold electrified barbed wire at the camps.

From the Auschwitz portion, walk across another glass-covered passageway where the names of Jewish victims of the camps are etched into the glass. From here enter a room in which are piles of shoes taken from Jewish prisoners. On the wall is etched a poem by Moses Schulstein, a Yiddish poet: "We are the shoes, We are the last witnesses, / We are shoes of grandchildren and grandfathers from Prague, Paris, and Amsterdam / And because we are only made of fabric and leather / And not of blood and flesh, each one of us avoided the hellfire."

Next, behind a privacy wall, is a disturbing, panoramic photograph of the hair shorn from 40,000 deportees. The Nazis sold such hair to private firms to make felt slippers, bumpers for boats, and stuffing for mattresses.

Walk through the bottom half of the Ejszyszki Shtetl Collection to the stairs leading down to the second floor and the final portion of the exhibit. In the lobby is *Consequence* (1993; Sol LeWitt), five large squares of varying hues bordered in black.

Exit under the brick archway connected to steel scaffolding and take the stairs down to the second floor. In the lobby here before the entrance to the continuation of the exhibit is the wood-and-fiberglass piece *Memorial* (1993; Ellsworth Kennedy).

**Second floor.** On the second floor is **Last Chapter,** exhibits about those who tried to help their Jewish neighbors, the liberation of the camps, the war crimes trials following the war, and survivors' efforts to rebuild their lives.

The exhibits tell the stories of the French village of Le Chambon, which hid several thousand Jews from the Nazis; the U.S. War Refugee Board that finally, beginning in 1944, helped rescue as many as 200,000 European Jews; Raoul Wallenberg, the Swedish diplomat based in Budapest who saved thousands of Jews by forging their passports; the government of Bulgaria, which enacted harsh anti-Semitic laws but refused to deport its Jewish population to the camps, saving its entire native Jewish population from extermination; and Zegota, a Polish Catholic organization that hid 2,500 Jewish children in Polish homes.

A small wooden boat is on display, one of dozens used by the government of Denmark to transport its Jewish citizens to Sweden (Denmark was occupied by the Germans; Sweden was unoccupied), saving 90 percent of its Jewish population. Across from it is a wall with names and photographs, honoring those individuals who risked their lives trying to save eastern European Jews.

From here enter a room devoted to the liberation of the camps and the horrors found there by American soldiers. This room contains graphic film and photographs of camp survivors. Visitors exit the room into a long hallway. On one side are television screens with films about the war crimes trials (headsets provide the narrative). On the other side is a display focusing on the 1.5 million children who died in the camps. Artwork by the children of the Theresienstadt ghetto is displayed.

Exiting the hallway, visitors pass by the poem attributed to Martin Niemoller, an anti-Nazi German pastor: "First they came for the socialists and I did not speak out because I was not a socialist, / Then they came for the trade unionists and I did not speak out because I was not a trade unionist, / Then they came for the Jews and I did not speak out because I was not a Jew, / Then they came for me—and there was no one left to speak for me."

The final room of the exhibit contains a display about the travails of survivors trying to find a new life in a new world, as well as a small photographic display about the creation of Israel. Also here is a theater showing the film *Testimony,* in which camp survivors relate their experiences.

Exiting the exhibit, visitors pass by the seal of the United States and the words "For the dead and the living we must bear witness." Cross a hallway containing the flags of Jewish resistance groups to the hexagonal **Hall of Remembrance.** On its black walls in raised letters are the names of the camps. An eternal flame burns above a stone tomb containing dirt from the death camps and above it on the wall are these words from Deuteronomy: "Only guard yourself and guard your soul carefully, lest you forget the things your eyes saw, and lest these things depart your heart all the days of your life. And you shall make them known to your children, and to your children's children." Visitors are able to light candles in areas along the walls and sit here and reflect.

Across from the hall is the **Wexner Learning Center,** containing a survivor's registry and touch-screen computer stations that aid in research of the Holocaust through text, photographs, maps, films, oral testimonies, and music.

Take the stairs back down to the first floor to exit the museum.

Exit the U.S. Holocaust Museum onto 14th St and walk north.

## Auditor's Building

201 14th St S.W. at Independence Ave. ☎ 205-1680. Open Mon–Fri 8–4. Closed Christmas Day, New Year's Day, and federal holidays. Admission: free. Very limited public access.

The Auditor's Building (1880; James Hill; 1989 renovation, Notter Finegold + Alexander Inc.) is a red brick building that runs the length of one block of Independence Ave between 14th St and Raoul Wallenberg Place. The building was constructed between 1878 and 1880 to house the Bureau of Engraving and Printing. The bureau outgrew the building, however, and in 1914 it moved to a site further south on 14th St. The Auditor's Building is so named because the next governmental tenants were auditors with the Navy, Treasury, and State Departments, as well as the Internal Revenue Service. Today, the U.S. Forest Service, a division of the Department of Agriculture, is the building's sole tenant.

### History

The federal government originally hired private contractors to print American currency. Toward the end of the 18C, however, the government decided this was no longer viable. Beginning in 1862, limited operations for the Bureau of Engraving and Printing were housed in the basement of the old Treasury Building. This six-person operation primarily handled the final steps, such as separating, sealing, and numbering the privately printed bills before public distribution. A year later, the bureau began printing currency. By 1877, all American currency was printed by the bureau.

In 1869 Congress appropriated $300,000 to build a "plain, substantial fireproof building" in which to relocate the agency. Although the bureau chief, Edward McPherson, had recommended building the structure north of Independence Ave in line with the Department of Agriculture and Smithsonian buildings on the Mall, the eventual site—on the south side of Independence Ave, then called B St—was purchased for $27,537 from William W. Corcoran, a philanthropist.

James Sherman, secretary of the Treasury, appointed James G. Hill as the designer of the new facility. Plans continued to be drawn as construction began. The architect remained only one step ahead of the builders. With finishing work still to be completed, the Bureau of Engraving and Printing moved into the building between June 1 and July 6, 1880. Until 1914 all American currency, most postage stamps, White House invitations, and bonds were printed in this facility.

Although additions—including new wings—were gradually made, in 1907 the government recognized the bureau had outgrown the building. Construction began on another building in 1911, and the bureau relocated to its current location in 1914.

### Washington Notes

If the 1901 McMillan Commission Plan for the redesign of the Mall had been followed faithfully, the Auditor's Building would have been razed. In fact, the building was threatened again in 1966 when the Master Plan for the District scheduled its demolition. Miraculously, the building survived to see its designation as a Category III landmark of the District of Columbia.

## Exterior

Plans for the building specified "repressed machine brick," most of which are dark red and laid in Flemish bond, a mixture of black mortar and black sand.

For security reasons only one main entrance was included in the design; it is at the corner of 14th St and Independence Ave.

The architectural plans also called for a clock to be installed in the four round openings in the tower. None were ever installed, and glass plates have been placed there instead.

## Interior

Ironically, during the years that the Bureau of Engraving and Printing occupied this building, visitors were granted greater access than that extended today. From behind wire screens on the second floor, visitors could watch currency being printed. The bureau chief complained in 1880 that, for security reasons, a separate stairway should be added to keep visitors and employees apart.

Currently, the only area open to the public is the tiny, first-level **Visitor's Center.** There are two exhibits on display. One addresses the four seasons in Washington, D.C. The latter discusses the role and responsibilities of the U.S. Forest Service. Families may want to add this building to their tour for the free educational materials, activity booklets, and goody bags that include maps of U.S. forests, a poster of Smokey Bear, and pens or pencils emblazoned with the Forest Service logo.

Exit onto 14th St. Walk north to the corner of 14th St and Independence Ave.

## *Department of Agriculture*

14th St and Independence Ave S.W., Room 103-A. ☎ 690-4750. Open Mon–Fri 9–5. Closed Christmas Day, New Year's Day, and federal holidays. Admission: free. Restrooms. Wheelchair and handicapped accessible.

The building on the northeast corner is the Department of Agriculture (1905; Rankin, Kellogg & Crane). Cross 14th St, then turn north and cross Independence Ave. Walk one block north on 14th St. Turn right at the sand-and-pebble path leading east along the Mall. Enter the Department of Agriculture through the glass doors on the north side of the building. The Visitor's Center at the Department of Agriculture, to the left of the entrance, offers hands-on activities that teach visitors about the department and how it helps the American people, as well as foreigners who buy exported goods.

### History

President Lincoln founded the Department of Agriculture (USDA) in 1862 as the "people's department." At that time about 90 percent of the American population was involved in agriculture in some way, if not actual farmers. (Less than 2 percent of today's population are farmers. However, American citizens are affected in one way or another by the practices of the "people's department" whether it is through food, clothes, or housing.)

The Department of Agriculture Complex was the first project of the McMillan Commission to be built on the south side of the Mall. A heated debate ensued as to the best location for this building. Ultimately, President Theodore Roosevelt stepped in to prevent its construction in the middle of the Mall. A cornerstone was finally laid in 1905 on a site that had previously been used for Smithsonian greenhouses and propagating gardens. As with many federal building projects, the construction was underbudgeted. Finally, the Department of Agriculture Complex was completed in 1930.

The current white marble, Beaux-Arts building replaced the Agriculture Department Building, which stood from 1868 to 1930 in the area between the new Department of Agriculture Building and Jefferson Dr. That building's gardens, greenhouses, and outbuildings stretched across the Mall to Constitution Ave. The outbuildings contained exhibitions designed to educate visitors about the Department of Agriculture's publicly unrecognized influence in modern life, much the way the Visitor's Center does today.

> ### Washington Notes
> Also in the vicinity of the Department of Agriculture was a popular tourist attraction: the General Noble Tree House. This was a dubious tribute to John Noble, who served as secretary of the interior from 1889 to 1893 and is perhaps best remembered for his enthusiastic support of legislation to preserve American forests. The Tree House was fashioned from a 2,000-year-old, 300 ft high, 26 ft wide giant sequoia cut from General Grant National Park in California. Its trunk was hollowed out and the tree itself was cut into pieces that could be easily transported and reassembled in Washington. It was disassembled in 1932 and destroyed in 1940 after years in storage.

Early in Feb 1979, an estimated 2,000 farmers from around the country motored into Washington on tractors and other farm equipment. Part of the American Agriculture Movement, the farmers were demonstrating for higher farm prices. Washington's police corralled the vehicles in an area outside the Department of Agriculture using Metro buses and garbage trucks. The protest lasted for weeks, and when temperatures dropped at night, the USDA invited camping farmers to sleep in its offices. An unanticipated debacle occurred. Many farmers made long-distance phone calls at the expense of Uncle Sam. Shortly thereafter, the USDA kept its doors locked at night. A blizzard blanketed the city on Feb 19, and some farmers were permitted to use their tractors to help plow roads leading to hospitals and other emergency facilities. In the meantime, local residents had been visiting the Mall to see the farm equipment; often children were offered tractor rides.

### Exterior
A whimsical detail to look for: Above the columns on the two lower wings, facing the Mall, are images of children holding banners that read "Cereals," "Forests," "Flowers," and "Fruits."

### Interior
The **Visitor's Center,** Room 103-A, is the only publicly accessible area in the Department of Agriculture Complex. The center was designed to educate visitors about the department and its function. A series of **Discovery Drawers** contain natural elements such as pine cones and minerals, as well as man-made or culti-

vated products such as cotton. Nutritional guidelines and information cards explain the significance and the Department of Agriculture's role in developing these products. Exhibits concern each division of the department such as the Forest Service. Videos and kiosks address natural resources, discoveries, consumer protection, and farming. Many of the kiosks are equipped with Soundstix, an audio system providing spoken information on particular topics. There is a toy model of a dairy house and farm.

To continue to the next walk, proceed two blocks north on 14th St, crossing the Mall, to the intersection of 14th St and Constitution Ave N.W. Walk one block west on Constitution Ave to 15th St, then two blocks north on 15th St to Hotel Washington.

# 12 · Federal Triangle and Old Downtown

Metro: Blue/Orange Line to McPherson Square.
Bus: 32, 34, 36, or 38.

In 1926 when the U.S. celebrated its 150th anniversary, the ostensible goal of the Federal Triangle Project was to erect massive buildings capable of housing the offices of the federal government. But the unstated goal was far more impressive: to express in limestone, granite, aluminum, and bronze the spirit and purpose of American democracy. Between 1929 and 1938, as the country struggled with an economic depression, Americans nevertheless undertook a phenomenal project to construct monumental office buildings along the convergence of Pennsylvania Ave (beginning at 15th St N.W.) and Constitution Ave (at 6th St N.W.), an area known as the Federal Triangle.

## Pennsylvania Avenue

### History
In 1806 a visitor to the newly established U.S. capital wrote: "Except some houses uniformly built, with some public-houses, and here and there a little grog shop, this boasted [Pennsylvania] Avenue is as much wilderness as Kentucky. Some half-starved cattle browsing among the bushes present a melancholy spectacle to the stranger, whose expectation has been warmed up by the illusive descriptions of speculative writers. So very thinly is the city peopled that quails and other birds are constantly shot within a hundred yards of the capitol."

What was later to be dubbed America's Main Street had been named for the state in which the federal government was located prior to 1800. When John and Abigail Adams arrived in 1789 to survey what would be their new home, the capital still qualified as a small town, with 3,000 residents. The federal government consisted of five departments—State, Treasury, War, Navy, and Post Office—with a total of 137 clerks.

Among those 3,000 residents, however, were businessmen with a canny sense of what the capital could become. Pennsylvania Ave had been envisioned by L'Enfant as a broad vista serving both as a thriving commercial district and as a processional route between the Capitol and the White House, then called the

President's House. Early travelers, however, found a rutted, dusty road that in places gave way to grazing cows, vegetation, and even in some spots, crops cultivated by skeptical farmers. It wasn't until Thomas Jefferson arrived as president in 1801 that the avenue was graded for the first time.

### Washington Notes

Jefferson, envisioning a grand boulevard, appropriated $11,702 to plant Lombardy poplar trees along Pennsylvania Ave, fashioning it after Rome's Appian Way. Unfortunately, the trees disappeared one by one for firewood, the president calling them "daily falling sacrifices . . . to the necessity of the poor." It was Jefferson who unintentionally started the tradition of inaugural parades when a crowd gathered to follow him home after his swearing in at the Capitol.

By 1835, Pennsylvania Ave was lined with hundreds of Federal row houses, two to four stories high. The avenue also had hotels, shops, theaters, and the Central Market, located between 7th and 9th Sts, which offered fresh produce to hundreds of shoppers every day between dawn and noon. (When this market burned down in 1870, architect Adolph Cluss designed a turreted, brick market for the site. The new Central Market opened in 1872 and was state-of-the-art, with stalls for 1,000 vendors, 8 electric elevators, and Washington's first cold-storage vault.)

Pennsylvania Ave, however, was far from a grand boulevard. In 1845, a lady guest at the National Hotel (corner of 6th and Pennsylvania) stepped into a puddle on the avenue and sank in three feet of mire. The outcry that followed prompted Congress to appropriate money to make Pennsylvania Ave navigable. In 1847, cobblestones were laid, but as late as 1860 pigs had the run of the avenue.

During the Civil War, the avenue had two distinct looks. On the north side (the right side of the street looking toward the White House) were hotels and businesses such as Mathew Brady's photograph studio, but on the avenue's south side were dingy shacks, saloons, and houses of prostitution. Poor drainage had ruined the avenue's cobbled pavement, so that once again the street became a dirt road, dusty in dry weather and muddy in the rain.

### Washington Notes

Prostitutes lined the avenue between 10th and 15th Sts. Reputedly, they were nicknamed hookers after their customers, the divisions of General Joseph Hooker's troops quartered nearby.

Because of the many crimes committed in this area, it became known as Murder Bay. When another rough neighborhood near the Capitol, Swampoodle, was cleaned up, the inhabitants moved to Murder Bay, making it even more dangerous. A guide to Washington warned, "If you are so lost to all self-respect as to go there to witness drunkenness, ribald song, vulgarity, immodesty and all the other vices, do not, as you value truth and honor, take any innocent youths with you. It has been the ruin of thousands of the bright and talented young men of this city. Watches, honor and happiness have been left there innumerable times."

By 1873, Pennsylvania Ave was an eclectic mix of sheds and coal yards interspersed with busy markets, shops, banks, restaurants, theaters, liquor stores, and still-thriving houses of prostitution. Frequent floods and motley crowds drove

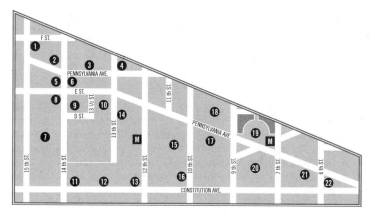

1  Hotel Washington
2  Willard Hotel
3  National Theatre
4  Warner Theatre
5  Pershing Park
6  Freedom Plaza
7  Dept of Commerce (Herbert Clark Hoover) Building
8  National Aquarium
9  District Building
10  Ronald Reagan Building
11  U.S. Customs Service/Dept of Labor
12  Departmental Auditorium
13  ICC Building
14  Ariel Rios Building
15  Old Post Office
16  IRS
17  Dept of Justice
18  J. Edgar Hoover FBI Building
19  Market Square/Navy Memorial
20  National Archives
21  FTC
22  Mellon Fountain

the tonier merchants to higher ground near F St. Still, as the city and the federal government grew, workers leaving their jobs in the afternoon strolled along the avenue, shopping, meeting friends, and riding the trolley cars that had begun running in the late 1850s. The financially successful trolley lines debuted as cars drawn by horses over rails. The trolleys changed briefly to a cable system until they were electrified in 1898.

In 1899, in an attempt to revive the area, the Romanesque revival (Old) Post Office Building was built on the former site of some of the most dilapidated structures. In 1904 the Beaux-Arts District Building (later renamed the John A. Wilson Building) was constructed in the area.

### Washington Notes

In 1909 the body of the avenue's designer, Pierre-Charles L'Enfant, was brought from Maryland, where he had died in poverty in 1825, to lie in state in the Rotunda of the Capitol. From there the body was brought down Pennsylvania Ave to Arlington National Cemetery for reinterment.

It wasn't until the Public Buildings Act of 1926, when Congress approved the Federal Triangle Project, that L'Enfant's vision of a grand vista began to become a reality. Between 1917 and 1926, the federal government had doubled in size. It was imperative that major federal government departments have more organized space. Using the rule of eminent domain, the federal government took over 70 acres, bounded by Pennsylvania Ave, Constitution Ave, and 15th St. As a result of the $50 million project, seven neoclassical buildings, extending from 15th St on the west to 6th St on the east, were built between 1929 and 1938.

> ### Washington Notes
> It's easy to forget that the creation of these massive federal buildings meant the destruction of an entire neighborhood. In the early 1900s Washington's Chinatown was a prosperous commercial and residential section of Pennsylvania Ave, stretching from 3rd to 6th Sts N.W. The Federal Triangle Project, backed by the law of eminent domain, required the entire community to relocate itself. The Chinatown community moved to the area around 6th and H Sts N.W.

Secretary of the Treasury Andrew W. Mellon picked architect Edward H. Bennett of the Chicago firm of Bennett, Parsons & Frost as his architectural adviser. Most of the architects chosen for the project had been educated at the Ecole des Beaux-Arts in Paris. Although most of the buildings are six stories high, the architects were instructed to obscure the uniform height and classic stone façades with porticoes, and colonnades were used to mask the buildings' modern steel-frame construction. The original Federal Triangle plan called for the demolition of the (Old) Post Office Building and the District (Wilson) Building, but the cost of demolition was too high and the funds ran out.

Following World War II and into the 1960s, the avenue again went through a period of deterioration and upheaval. The city itself was changing—first with the flight of white, middle-class residents, and then their black counterparts in the 1970s and 1980s, to the more inviting suburbs springing up in Virginia and Maryland. The avenue was still the hub of federal government activity during the day, but at night it was dark and quiet, except for some restaurant and theater patrons.

In 1964 the avenue looked so shabby it was suggested that Lyndon Johnson's inaugural parade be moved to Constitution Ave. In 1968, following the assassination of Martin Luther King, Jr., riots broke out ten blocks away, and federal troops were called in to restore order. Although no physical damage was done to America's Main Street, the psychic damage to the city as a whole was devastating. Businesses followed residents to "better" sections of town or to the suburbs. An inventory of the avenue found that the remaining businesses included six bars, one bedding outlet, a burlesque house, six coffee shops, three fireworks stands, six discount stores, twelve wig shops, six liquor stores, three palm readers, seven porno shops, and one religious organization.

At the request of President John F. Kennedy, the President's Council on Pennsylvania Avenue came together informally to discuss ways of improving conditions on the avenue. After the president's assassination, the group officially became the Temporary Committee on Pennsylvania Avenue. Although hundreds of ideas were submitted for action, none were approved and the committee disbanded. In 1974, with the nation's Bicentennial approaching, the committee regrouped as the public/private Pennsylvania Avenue Development Corporation.

The result is a dramatically revitalized Pennsylvania Ave, including Freedom

Plaza (between 13th and 14th Sts), Market Square (between 7th and 9th Sts), the Ronald Reagan Building and International Trade Center, which opened in 1998, and the Federal Building Complex, where renovation was completed in 1999.

## Hotel Washington

15th St and Pennsylvania Ave N.W. ☎ 638-5900. Web: www.hotelwashington. com.

From the McPherson Square Metro station, walk south on 15th St three blocks to Hotel Washington (1917; John Carrére and Thomas Hastings; renovation 1985, Pennsylvania Avenue Development Corporation; Mariani and Associates, preservation consultants; Ivan Valtchev, materials conservator), the city's oldest continuously operating hotel.

**Highlights:** The view of the city from the Sky Terrace restaurant atop the hotel.

### History

This choice location was the site of the Kennedy House, built around 1850, when the area was a fashionable residential neighborhood known for its good rabbit hunting. In 1875, banker and financier William Wilson Corcoran replaced the house with the Greek revival Corcoran Office Building. Just before President Woodrow Wilson's inauguration on March 5, 1917, the building was razed to make way for the Hotel Washington, but not before bleachers were erected on the vacant lot for citizens to watch the inaugural parade.

> ### Washington Notes
>
> Because of the hotel's proximity to both the White House and the Capitol, the Hotel Washington has often served as the residence for the city's prominent government officials and guests. This includes the National Turkey, who resides at the hotel each year on the night before he joins the president at the White House, when the president officially declares the beginning of Thanksgiving Day weekend.
>
> At one time, the hotel was the residence of 50 congressmen and five senators. It was in the hotel's bar that John Nance Garner received the telephone call offering him the office of vice president under Franklin Delano Roosevelt. Its location near theaters such as the National, Warner, and the now-defunct Poli has also made it popular with performers, including comedians Will Rogers, George Burns and Gracie Allen, bandleaders Jimmy Dorsey and Duke Ellington, and actor John Wayne.

The Hotel Washington's crest is an adaptation of George Washington's family crest. The hotel's shield has two red bars (symbolizing courage) and three red stars ("influence which shines from afar") but replaces the Washington family's traditional eagle, raven, or dove with a swan representing beauty, grace, and nobility. It was on Hotel Washington's corner (15th and Pennsylvania) that the city's first electric street light was placed, in Oct 1881.

## Exterior

The ten-story-plus-terrace hotel was designed in a European style inspired by Italian Renaissance forms. The building has a steel frame and is faced with rusticated ashlar stone on the first three stories and brown brick above. The most unusual feature of the façade is the frieze encircling the building. Representations of George Washington, Abraham Lincoln, Thomas Jefferson, and other prominent Americans were executed by Italian artisans using the ancient technique of sgraffito, in which designs are scratched through layers of plaster impregnated with colors.

## Interior

The hotel has 350 guest rooms. The Sky Terrace restaurant on the roof of the hotel offers an impressive view of the city and its monuments. The restaurant's open-air dining experience is popular with Washingtonians.

> **Washington Notes**
> Facing the hotel's F St side is the Metropolitan Square office complex. Affixed to the corner of the building is a bronze plaque commemorating the fact that this is the site where Rhodes Tavern once stood. The three-story brick tavern, built in 1799, served as Washington's city hall at one time and stood along the inaugural route of every president from Thomas Jefferson to Ronald Reagan. After an unsuccessful battle by preservationists, which included a court suit that attempted to save the tavern as a historic landmark, it was razed in 1984.

From the entrance on 15th St, walk south to Pennsylvania Ave.

## *Willard Hotel*

14th St and Pennsylvania Ave N.W. ☎ 628-9100.
  Around the corner from the Hotel Washington is another famous Washington hostelry, the Willard Hotel (1901; Henry Hardenbergh; renovation 1979–86, conceptual design by Vlastimil Koubek with Hardy Holzman Pfeiffer Associates; restoration, Stuart Golding; Oliver Carr Company, managing partner).
  **Highlights:** The ornate lobby and Peacock Alley.

### History

Originally this was the site of the City Hotel, whose owner hired a Hudson River steamer steward as manager in 1847. Three years later the steward, Henry Willard, bought the hotel, gave it his name, and brought his brothers into the business. The old Willard Hotel was small and elegant and known for its distinguished guests, among them writer Nathaniel Hawthorne, who stayed at the Willard while covering the Civil War for *Atlantic Monthly* magazine. Regarding the hotel's place in Washington social life, Hawthorne commented, "This hotel, in fact, may be much more justly called the center of Washington and the Union than either the Capitol, the White House, or the State Department. . . . You are mixed up with office seekers, wire pullers, inventors, artists, poets, . . . until identity is lost among them."

> **Washington Notes**
> President Ulysses S. Grant chose the Willard lobby to escape the pressures of office with a brandy and a cigar, but soon found himself approached by power brokers hawking their causes. As a result, the term *lobbyist* was

coined. Traditionally, the hotel has provided a presidential suite for the president-elect on the eve of his inauguration. Abraham Lincoln had to be smuggled into the hotel in 1861 because of threats of assassination. He and his family of five stayed ten days at the hotel, and he paid his bill (a total of $773.75, including meals) when he received his first paycheck as president.

## Exterior

The current building, opened in 1901, was designed by Henry Hardenbergh (also the architect of New York's Plaza Hotel and the original Waldorf-Astoria) in the Second Empire Beaux-Arts style. Its steel frame (one of the first in Washington) is covered with a rusticated limestone base and a shaft of light-colored brick and terra-cotta, channeled to resemble the stone masonry below. On the Pennsylvania Ave entrance four Doric columns rise three floors to an entablature and balustraded parapet topped with stone urns. Pediments, iron balconies, and ten large dormers decorate the exterior, all of these topped by an ornate mansard-roofed penthouse.

## Interior

Closed in 1968, the Willard was considered for demolition when it was declared a National Historic Landmark. Saved through the intervention of the Pennsylvania Avenue Development Corporation, the current building was opened in 1986 as the Willard Inter-Continental Hotel. Noted areas include the **main lobby,** with its 35 different types of marble, and **Peacock Alley,** a promenade through the lobby of the hotel from Pennsylvania Ave to F St. The restoration added four pavilion-like areas on the west side for restaurants and shops.

The Willard Hotel has 340 guest rooms, each unique in design and decor.

> ### Washington Notes
>
> Several well-known literary and political works have been written at the Willard Hotel. In 1861, Julia Ward Howe was awakened in her room by Union soldiers singing the popular "John Brown's Body." Howe immediately wrote the words to "The Battle Hymn of the Republic." A little over 100 years later, in Aug 1963, Martin Luther King, Jr., wrote the inspiring "I Have a Dream" speech in a room at the Willard. Mark Twain, who liked to sit in Peacock Alley, wrote portions of several works while in residence.

**Diversion:**

One block east on the south side of Pennsylvania Ave is the **National Theatre** (1321 Pennsylvania Ave N.W.; ☎ 628-6161; Web: www.nationaltheatre.org). A National Theatre has occupied the same site since 1835, but the present structure is the sixth. The original 1835 Greek revival theater was the scene of President Polk's inaugural ball in 1845. Soon afterward, the theater was destroyed by a fire, as were three subsequent theaters on the site. (Theaters in those days were particularly susceptible because of all the flammable materials used in the sets and the curtains.) The fifth National Theatre, a five-story, Italianate structure, advertised an asbestos stage curtain and seated 1,900. This theater lasted until 1922, when a new theater was built using steel beams to comply with the new building code. The National was converted to a movie theater in 1948 when prominent actors and playwrights boycotted it because of the city's segregation policies. The

National reopened as a "legitimate," and integrated, theater in 1952 and has continued in operation ever since.

The theater is adjacent to **The Shops at National Place** (1982; Frank Schlesinger), a complex of shops, businesses, and the Marriott Hotel, bounded on the east and west by 13th and 14th Sts and on the north and south by Pennsylvania Ave and F St.

One block further east is the **Warner Theatre** (1924; C. Howard Crane and Kenneth Franzheim; 1989 restoration, Shalom Baranes and Pei Cobb Freed and Partners) (1299 Pennsylvania Ave N.W.; ☎ 626-8271; Web: www.warnertheatre.com). This theater is a remnant of the heyday of Hollywood studios when theaters were built to showcase films. The restoration restored the gilt ceilings, impressive chandeliers, and grand lobby.

From in front of the Willard Hotel, walk south to where Pennsylvania Ave is split by **Pershing Park** (1981; M. Paul Friedberg; Jerome Lindsay, associated architects), which is between 14th and 15th Sts. On the 15th St side of the park are shaded areas with benches and a large pond, complete with ducks. On the 14th St side is Robert White's statue of General John Joseph "Black Jack" Pershing (1865–1948), commander of the American Expeditionary Forces in Europe during World War I. To the right of the statue is a granite wall with a map of Europe and a description of several of America's war campaigns.

Walk through the park to Pennsylvania Ave at 14th St and look east to **Freedom Plaza** (1980; Venturi, Rauch & Scott Brown; George E. Patton, landscape architect). At one end of the plaza is an inlaid rendition of L'Enfant's capital city plan in black-and-white stone. Framing the giant map are paving stones incised with quotes about the District. At the other end of the plaza is a bronze statue of Count Casimir Pulaski (1910; Kasimiriez Chodzinski). Pulaski, a Polish brigadier general, gave up his rank and, ultimately, his life to fight for America's freedom in the Revolutionary War.

From Pershing Park, walk south across E St.

## Department of Commerce Building (Herbert Clark Hoover Building)

409 15th St N.W., between 15th and 14th Sts on the east and west and between Constitution Ave and E St on the north and south. ☎ 482-2000. Web: www.doc.gov.

The White House Visitor Center has timed tickets for tours of the White House. Open 7:30 A.M.–4 P.M. Mon–Fri; in peak season, tickets may be gone by 8:30 A.M. ☎ 456-7041.

The National Aquarium (Room B-077) is on the 14th St side. ☎ 482-2825. Open daily 9–5. Closed Christmas Day. Admission fee. Wheelchair accessible.

When completed in 1932, the Herbert Clark Hoover Building (1927–32; York and Sawyer; Louis Ayes, supervising architect; James Earle Fraser, sculptor), more commonly known as the Department of Commerce Building, was the largest government building in the U.S., with 37 acres of floor space and 8 miles of corridors. It cost $17 million.

**Highlights:** The Great Hall, now the White House Visitor Center, which distributes tickets to the White House, and the National Aquarium, which has shark feedings on Mon, Wed, and Sat at 2 P.M.

**History**

The Department of Commerce and Labor, established in 1903, split into two separate departments in 1913 at the urging of labor leaders who felt the department's interests were too strongly in tune with those of big business.

> ### *Washington Notes*
> On the west section of this site was the home of the Capital Bicycle Club, razed in 1928. During the 1880s and '90s, the most popular sports for Washington's well-to-do were rowing and bicycling. The Capital Bicycle Club, a three-story Romanesque revival building, was known as the finest bicycle clubhouse in America. Cyclists would start on 15th St, opposite the Ellipse, for a Sun morning run that could stretch as far as the Shenandoah Valley in Virginia.

## Exterior

The Department of Commerce Building is constructed of Indiana limestone and has a red tile roof. The center section along 14th St has a colonnade of 24 Doric columns and 8 relief panels, as does the corresponding center section on E St. The relief panels represent the agencies of the Commerce Department at the time the building was completed. A flaming torch is carved on the side of each panel. On the 15th St side, four projecting Doric colonnades support large triangular pediments, each cradling a heroic sculptural group. Both the E St and Constitution Ave elevations have a central colonnade. On every side of the building, Roman and Egyptian busts are distributed between the windows, and limestone urns decorated with lions and eagles sit at several of the entrances. The main entrances have massive bronze doors decorated with sheaves of wheat. Other entrances have inscriptions by famous Americans apropos of the department's agencies. Abraham Lincoln's statement "The Patent System Added The Fuel Of Interest To The Fire Of Genius" is above the 15th St entrance nearest the intersection of 15th and E Sts.

## Interior

The building is designed as a rectangle, within which are six interior courts. On E St is the entrance to the **Malcolm Baldridge Great Hall.** Baldridge was secretary of commerce from 1981 to 1987. The Great Hall, with its elaborate ceiling and stenciled archways, is a massive Beaux-Arts space, which for years served as the Patent Search Room as well as the site of grand Washington balls. The hall now has the **White House Visitor Center.**

## The National Aquarium

In the basement of the Commerce Building on the 14th St side is the National Aquarium (Room B-077), now celebrating its 125th anniversary. The aquarium, with both freshwater and saltwater tanks, houses more than 270 different species of fish, invertebrates, amphibians, and reptiles.

### History

The U.S. Commission of Fish and Fisheries was established in 1871 and located in Wood's Hole, Massachusetts, where it was equipped with steamships and specially constructed railroad cars for research purposes. The aquarium was founded here in 1873. In 1877, Congress granted the commission 20 acres of land on the Washington Monument grounds for a hatchery. The commission, renamed the Bureau of Fisheries, was placed under the Department of Commerce in 1909. The aquarium was included when the building was erected.

## John A. Wilson Building

Across 14th St on Pennsylvania Ave is the **District Building** (1904; Cope and Stewardson architects; Adolph De Nesti, sculptor; 1999 renovation, Kendall/ Heaton Associates) at 1350 Pennsylvania Ave N.W., now renamed the John A. Wilson Building in honor of the former City Council chairperson and civic leader. This "upstart monstrosity," as many called it soon after its completion, has been scheduled for demolition many times. When the renovation is complete in 1999, the District's City Council is slated to return to its offices in the building.

> ### Washington Notes
> In March 1977, Hanafi Muslims attacked the District Building, as well as the B'nai B'rith headquarters (1640 Rhode Island Ave N.W., ☎ 857-6600) and the Islamic Center (2551 Massachusetts Ave N.W., ☎ 332-8343). A radio reporter was killed and two people were seriously injured, one of them city councilperson Marion Barry. The siege ended the following morning, when diplomats from the embassies of Iran, Pakistan, and Egypt negotiated the surrender of the Muslims to authorities. Barry was elected mayor in 1978 and served from 1978 to 1990. He was arrested for cocaine possession and served time in prison. Afterward he was elected to the City Council, serving from 1992 to 1994, and then he was reelected mayor, serving from 1994 to 1998.

### Exterior

The building is an elaborate English Renaissance revival structure, constructed of white marble over a gray granite base. Above the main entrance on Pennsylvania Ave is the sculpture *Law and Justice* (1908; Adolph de Nesti). One the left, a reclining woman carries the scales of justice, while another woman to her right holds the scroll of law. Between them is an elaborate cartouche containing the seal of the District of Columbia, surmounted by a marble eagle. At the building's attic level are 28 statues of heroic, sculpted male and female figures representing the arts, commerce, science, and statesmanship.

### Interior

To maximize the amount of natural daylight, the building employs a U-shaped plan above the first floor.

## Ronald Reagan Building and International Trade Center

1300 Pennsylvania Ave N.W., from 13th to 15th Sts on Pennsylvania Ave. ☎ 312-1399. Food court, Lower Level C, 14th St entrance, open Mon–Fri 7–4.

The newest and final addition to the Federal Triangle is the Ronald Reagan Building and International Trade Center (1998; Pei, Cobb, Freed & Partners in association with Ellerbe Becket, architects and engineers). The building is surrounded on two sides by the Federal Building Complex, a group of four connected structures originally built as the Department of Labor, the Departmental Auditorium, the Interstate Commerce Commission, and the Post Office Building.

Situated where a Grand Plaza was designated in the original Federal Triangle plans, the Ronald Reagan Building and International Trade Center is the second largest U.S. government building. (The Pentagon is the largest.) The building has 13 floors, 5 of which are below ground. The structure houses the Environmental Protection Agency, the U.S. Customs Service, the Agency for International Development, and the Smithsonian Institution's Woodrow Wilson International Center for Scholars, as well as commercial office space.

### *Washington Notes*

Some felt it to be ironic that this huge and expensive building was named for a president who abhorred big government and governmental waste. The building was completed four years behind schedule, with a total cost of $818 million, $446 million more than original estimates. Republican Representative John Duncan from Tennessee called the project "the biggest boondoggle to come down the pike in a long time." Nancy Reagan spoke at the building's dedication on May 5, 1998. President Reagan, suffering from Alzheimer's disease, was not present.

### History

In the 1860s on the southwest corner of 13th St and Pennsylvania Ave was the Southern Railway Building, headquarters for one of the leading newspapers of the day, the *National Republican.* Prior to work on the site, an archaeological dig uncovered part of a petrified tree believed to be 65 million years old, plus more than 250,000 remnants of city life from the 1860s, including perfume, beer, and liquor bottles.

## Exterior

The base of the building is granite, with the upper portions made of limestone from the same Indiana quarry as the Federal Triangle buildings constructed 60 years earlier. Also matching the other structures are the terra-cotta tiles on the building's five-acre roof. The lead architect, James Ingo Freed, has described the building's exterior design as "a contemporary reading of the neoclassical style." There is no fluting on the columns and pilasters; the building's massive size is softened by its smooth curves and open spaces. Standing in the plaza in front of the building's 14th St entrance, a visitor can look east through the building site to 12th St, a distance of three football fields.

This 14th St plaza is graced by the **Oscar S. Straus Memorial Fountain** (1947; John Russell Pope; Eggers and Higgins; Adolph Alexander Weinman, sculptor), which has been restored and returned to its original location on 14th St. Authorized by Congress in 1921, this bronze-and-marble monument to one of America's leading diplomats was not constructed until 1947 because of indecision over the site and delays caused by World War II. Oscar S. Straus (1850–1926), a German immigrant, grew up in Georgia and was a lawyer and businessman in New York City. He served as ambassador to Turkey in the late 1880s and early 1900s, and between 1902 and 1926 he represented the U.S. before the International Court of Arbitration at The Hague in the Netherlands. He also served as the first secretary of commerce and labor, under Teddy Roosevelt.

The sculpture consists of three parts, a fountain and two groups of statues representing justice and reason. The three-tier central fountain is inscribed "Statesman, Author, Diplomat." The group of bronze figures on the left represents religious freedom. A child holds the open book of religion, with the inscription "Our Liberty Of Worship Is Not A Concession Nor A Privilege But An Inherent Right." To the right is a seated man representing reason, accompanied by a child, the Genius of Capital and Labor. Reason holds symbols of capital and labor: a purse, key, and hammer. Below is the inscription "The Voice Of Reason Is More To Be Regarded Than The Light Of Any Present Inclination."

In the **Woodrow Wilson Plaza,** a four-acre courtyard separating the Ronald Reagan and Ariel Rios Buildings, are two mammoth sculptures. *Federal Triangle Flowers* (commissioned 1993; Stephen Robin) is composed of two ten-ft-high cast-aluminum and granite flowers, a rose and a lily, lying on stone pedestals. Across from them is *Bearing Witness* (commissioned 1993; Martin Puryear), a bronze piece standing 40 ft high.

### Interior
Inside the 14th St entrance is a cone-shaped, horizontal glass skylight rising 125 ft above a 170 ft diameter atrium. The skylight contains 1,240 pieces of glass and covers an entire acre. A section of the Berlin Wall is at the top of the staircase on the 14th St side. At the south end of the atrium is *Route Zenith* (commissioned 1993; Keith Sonnier), a neon artwork that has a metal armature supporting vertical tubes of brilliant yellow, red, and blue lights.

A food court, located on Lower Level C, leads to the Woodrow Wilson Plaza and the Federal Triangle Metro station.

## Federal Building Complex
Cupping the Ronald Reagan Building, between 12th and 14th Sts on Constitution Ave, is the Federal Building Complex (1935; Arthur Brown, Jr.), which is made up of the U.S. Customs Service Building (originally slated for the Department of Labor), the Departmental Auditorium (also called the Andrew Mellon Auditorium), and the Interstate Commerce Commission (ICC) Building on Constitution Ave (the three built at a cost of $11,012,538). The Ariel Rios Building (formerly the Post Office Building), on 12th St between Constitution and Pennsylvania Aves, faces the Reagan Building. The Rios Building cost $10,800,000.

### History
Arthur Brown, Jr., was chosen to design the rear of the massive Federal Building Complex. He designed the complex with the Departmental Auditorium as the center anchor, its Doric temple façade complemented by Doric colonnades on each end of the Department of Labor building and the ICC.

### U.S. Customs Service Building
The U.S. Customs Service (1301 Constitution Ave N.W.; ☎ 566-8195; Web: www.customs.ustreas.gov) was established in 1927 as the Bureau of Customs and redesignated the Customs Service in 1973. Customs enforces customs treaties, seizes contraband, and assesses and collects customs duties.

The building was originally intended to house the Department of Labor (now at 200 Constitution Ave N.W., ☎ 219-6666, Web: www.dol.gov), which was established in 1913. Farm labor leaders lobbied for a separate entity devoted solely to the protection and advancement of labor. The bill establishing the department was signed into law by President William Howard Taft just two hours before he left office.

## Exterior

On the southwest corner, 14th St and Constitution Ave, of the U.S. Customs Service Building is the pediment *Abundance and Industry* (1935; Sherry Fry). A reclining female nude representing abundance and industry is flanked by rams representing productivity and security. The woman holds a vase from which pours the fruits of industry.

Walk a half-block east on Constitution to a second pediment, *Labor and Industry* (1935; Albert Stewart). A nude male reclines against a large bull. A sheaf of wheat is at one corner and a millstone at another. Under the pediment is an elaborate frieze extending the entire length of the building. The sculptured relief panels consist of neoclassical heads and skulls of animals, vases, shields, helmets, anchors, and cornucopias. The keystone figures over the first-floor windows are of alternating allegorical neoclassical heads.

### Washington Notes

Pause a moment and look east towards the Capitol, imagining that it is 1855. The swampy and foul Washington Canal (later B St, and then Constitution Ave) cuts through the area. On the Mall to the right is the partially built Washington Monument, which will not be completed for another 30 years. Across the flat, open space east of the monument is the Smithsonian Castle, alone except for a few cows grazing the surrounding grassy area.

## Andrew W. Mellon/Departmental Auditorium

Continue east on Constitution Ave a half-block to the Andrew W. Mellon/Departmental Auditorium, currently closed for proposed renovation. Originally named the Interdepartmental Auditorium, it became the Andrew W. Mellon Auditorium, and now is referred to as the Connecting Wing (CW) Building.

### Washington Notes

Governmental events held here include the first Selective Service lottery, presided over by President Franklin D. Roosevelt in Oct 1940, and the signing of the North Atlantic (NATO) Treaty by President Harry S. Truman and foreign ministers of 11 European nations in 1949.

## Exterior

A two-story rusticated base supports six monumental Doric columns. The central figure on the pediment is *Columbia* (1935; Edgar Walter). On her right is an eagle, symbol of the United States, and next to that a nude soldier on horseback and a reclining woman surrounded by books. On Columbia's left there is a nude youth, and next to him a nude female rides a bull and carries a sheaf of wheat, while a male holding a large hammer reclines in the corner.

## Interior

The auditorium's relief panel consists of *Washington Planning the Battle of Trenton* (1935; Edmond Romulus Amateis) and *Washington in Public Service and Agriculture* (1935; Edmond Romulus Amateis). The six-by-ten-ft panel presents Lieutenant General George Washington with his horse during the Revolutionary War. Washington is charting his course for the Battle of Trenton. On the left is Major General Nathaniel Greene; seated in the foreground is Major General John Sullivan. General Greene's face is that of the building's architect, Arthur Brown, while General Sullivan has the face of sculptor Edgar Walter. This panel is one of the few featured in the Federal Triangle that actually represents an historical event from American history, rather than an allegorical event. In the spandrels, agriculture is represented on the left by a female figure holding a sheaf of wheat, and public service is represented on the right by a female figure holding a fasces, a Roman symbol of authority.

## Interior

The interior of the Departmental Auditorium is currently closed to the public. The inside has been described as "incurably ceremonial, not appropriate for budget hearings."

Continue east on Constitution Ave to the corner of 12th St. The **Interstate Commerce Commission Building** (☎ 565-1696) is the third building in the complex. The ICC was created by the Act to Regulate Commerce in 1887. The agency became known by its current title in 1920. The ICC enforces federal laws dealing with trade among the states. The building is currently under renovation. When completed in the summer of 2000, the building will house offices of the Environmental Protection Agency.

## *Ariel Rios Building*

Turn north onto 12th St and walk to the **Ariel Rios Building** (formerly the Post Office Building; 1934; Delano and Aldrich), which is shaped like a scripted *X* and faces the Ronald Reagan Building. The building has a post office (1100 Pennsylvania Ave N.W.; ☎ 523-2571; open Mon–Fri 6 A.M.–6 P.M.; Sat 6 A.M.–3 P.M.). The south side of Ariel Rios houses sections of the Environmental Protection Agency; the north side has been under renovation and began a phased occupancy in June 1999. The building was renamed in Dec 1985 to honor Ariel Rios, an Alcohol, Tobacco, and Firearms agent who died in the line of duty in 1982.

## Exterior

The 12th St façade is decorated with three projecting Ionic colonnaded pavilions. The pediment above the center pavilion, *The Spirit of Civilization and Progress* (1934; Adolph Alexander Weinman) depicts a gracefully gowned woman, representing the spirit of progress and civilization, who holds a torch and a winged sphere. On her right is a young man with a scroll and a book; on her left is winged Mercury, messenger of the gods, who symbolizes the post as quickener of commerce. To the left of this group are two rearing horses held in check by a powerful male figure, symbolizing mail delivery by land; to the right, seahorses, driven by a Triton and accompanied by dolphins, symbolize mail delivery by sea. In the right-hand corner are a male figure and winged genie controlling the wires of electrical communication; in the left corner a reclining winged figure with eagles symbolizes mail delivery by air.

## Old Post Office Building and Pavilion

1100 Pennsylvania Ave N.W., at 12th St and Pennsylvania Ave N.W. ☎ 289-4224. Web: www.oldpostofficedc.com. Open Mon–Sat 10–9; Sun 12–8. Tower open summer 8 A.M.–10:45 P.M.; winter 10 A.M.–5:45 P.M.; closes in inclement weather. ☎ 606-8691.

For the best view of the entire Federal Building Complex, the Ariel Rios Building, and the new Ronald Reagan Building, cross 12th St and take the glass elevator to the clock tower of the **Old Post Office Building and Pavilion** (1899; Willoughby J. Edbrooke, supervising architect; 1982 restoration, Arthur Cotton Moore/Associates). The building has a bank, restrooms, a while-you-wait shoe repair, a Ticket Place (Tues–Sat 11–6, ☎ 842-5387), shops, and a food court where concerts are often given in the evening.

**Highlights:** The clock tower's 270 ft high observation deck provides the second-best view of the city. Although the Washington Monument may provide the best view, the lines are considerably shorter at the clock tower. There are occasional evening concerts.

### History

Like the District Building, the Old Post Office Building has been scheduled for demolition several times. Almost before it was completed the building was viewed as a dinosaur because of its Romanesque revival style. Some critics felt the design conflicted with the Federal Triangle's proposed designs. Because of lack of funds during the Depression, the building was never razed. In the 1970s, historic preservationists led by Nancy Hanks, head of the National Endowment of the Arts from 1969 to 1977, prevented this building from being destroyed. The NEA's offices as well as other offices and retail shops are located in the building.

### Washington Notes

George Washington thought an efficient mail service was so important he personally helped in surveying postal routes. In 1782, the U.S. Continental Congress decreed that private letters could not be opened by postal authorities, a novelty among nations at that time. In 1789, when Samuel Osgood was appointed the first postmaster general, there were 75 post offices in America and fewer than 2,000 miles of post roads. In 1829, the postmaster general was made a member of the president's cabinet. For a history of the U.S. Postal Service, visit the Postal Museum (see Walk 1: "Capitol Hill North and East").

### Exterior

The building is constructed of gray granite. Above the seventh floor the cornice has steep roofs, gabled dormers and spires over the corner turrets, and rounded, arched molds over rectangular windows. From the recessed portion of the Pennsylvania Ave façade, the clock tower rises to 315 ft.

Within the tower are the Congress Bells, given to Congress by the Ditchley Foundation of Great Britain in 1976 to celebrate the Bicentennial. In 1983 the bells were permanently housed in the clock tower. The ten bells range from 581 to 2,953 pounds and are replicas of the bells in London's Westminster Abbey. The

*Old Post Office. Courtesy of the Washington, D.C., Convention & Visitors Association.*

bells can be heard on some Thurs evenings when the Washington Ringing Society practices. Otherwise, the bells are rung only at the opening and closing of Congress or on other auspicious occasions, such as when the Redskins won the Super Bowl in 1983, 1988, and 1992.

In front of the Old Post Office Building is a statue of Benjamin Franklin (1889; Jacques Jouvenal, sculptor; J. F. Manning, architect), which was donated to the city by Stilson Hutchins (1839–1912) in the name of America's newspaper publishers. Hutchins, after graduating from Harvard University, became a journalist and founded four newspapers, among them the *Washington Post*. (The old *Post* building was located across the street, at the present site of the J. Edgar Hoover FBI Building, 935 Pennsylvania Ave N.W., 10th St and Pennsylvania Ave.) In Jan 1889, the eight-ft-high marble statue honoring one of America's first and most illustrious journalists was unveiled by Mrs. H. W. Emory, Franklin's great-granddaughter.

## Interior

Inside the main entrance is an antique mailbox, for show only. The impressive atrium is 99 by 190 ft and 160 ft high. The atrium's decorative sculpture, balconies, and murals can best be viewed when taking the glass elevator to the top of the atrium. A second elevator takes you up to the tower's 270 ft high **observation deck.** A narrow staircase leads down to the bell chamber.

The ground floor food court with its many eateries is a good place to grab an inexpensive snack.

## *Internal Revenue Service Building*

1111 Constitution Ave N.W., between 10th and 12th Sts. ☎ 622-5000. Web: www.irs.ustreas.gov. Continue east on the south side of Pennsylvania Ave to the Internal Revenue Service (IRS) Building (1930–35; Louis A. Simon, supervising architect). The main façade faces Constitution Ave. The building is currently under partial renovation.

## Exterior

Because the IRS is a bureau and not a department, its building is less decorative than those of its Federal Triangle neighbors. The only ornamentations are a simple Doric colonnade on the Constitution Ave side and rows of fluted Doric pilasters on the 10th and 12th St and Pennsylvania Ave façades. Carved above the main entrance on Constitution Ave is Oliver Wendell Holmes's maxim, "Taxes Are What We Pay For a Civilized Society."

### History

Prior to the Civil War, government revenue was obtained as much from customs duties as from internal revenue. Now almost all federal income is from income taxes. The first income tax was levied in 1861 for a brief period. Another income tax was levied in 1894, but the Supreme Court declared it unconstitutional. In 1913, an amendment to the Constitution authorized Congress to levy income taxes, and the Internal Revenue Service was created.

### *Washington Notes*

On this site in the early 1800s was Carusi's Assembly Rooms, popularly known as Carusi's Saloons. Inaugural balls for John Quincy Adams (president 1825–29) through James Buchanan (president 1857–61) were held here. Gaetano Carusi and 17 other musicians were originally recruited at the request of Thomas Jefferson to upgrade the Marine Band. But upon their arrival in the capital, they were told the marine commandant had rejected Jefferson's suggestion. Carusi (and later his sons) set up shop as a music-and-dancing master on Pennsylvania Ave. This was also the site of the Cholera Hospital, where many of the 1,000 Irish immigrants working on the roadbed of Pennsylvania Ave died of the disease in the 1832 cholera epidemic.

## Interior
The four inner courtyards are not open to the public. There used to be a visitor's gallery that had a copper still, which may have belonged to George Washington.

## Department of Justice Building
Continue east on Pennsylvania Ave to 10th St N.W. and the Department of Justice Building (1934; Borie, Medary, and Zantzinger; Carl Paul Jennewein, sculptor) at 950 Pennsylvania Ave N.W. ☎ 514-2000.

### History
The Office of the Attorney General was created by Congress in 1789. In 1870, Congress created the Department of Justice under the attorney general to handle the legal problems that arose following the Civil War. The department enforces federal laws and provides legal advice for the president and the heads of the executive departments of the government. The attorney general has the power to appoint a special prosecutor when deemed necessary. In clearing the block to build the Justice Building, it was necessary to demolish a theater called the Old Bijou, which had been on that site since Civil War days.

### Exterior
The building is made of limestone with a granite base and constructed around a center area called the Great Court. The building has Ionic colonnades on the 9th St and Pennsylvania Ave façades and spare blocklike fluted pilasters along the 10th St and Constitution Ave façades. Above the Constitution Ave entrance the relief panel *Law and Order* (1935; Carl Paul Jennewein) consists of five-ft-high neoclassical figures standing below a quote from the Roman writer Pliny (A.D. 23–79), which translates as "By law and order all is accomplished." Only the central figure, a youth, faces front. He represents opportunity and stands between two Doric columns that represent uprightness and faith in the future. Behind the columns a laurel and an oak tree symbolize civil and military valor. To the left and right of the youth stand two female figures, representing peace and prosperity. Opportunity, peace, and prosperity result from the balance of law and order, which are represented by the two nude males standing on the far left and right of the central grouping. The law figure holds a parchment and a sword, while the order figure clasps a staff with a snake coiling around the bottom, a symbol of wisdom.

The influence of Art Deco on this building is reflected in the extensive use of aluminum decorative torcheres and monumental doors. Each torchere has sculptured designs of a buffalo, a dolphin, and a bird. A pair of lion medallions adorn the 10th St façade. Carved relief panels alternate over the fifth-floor windows, depicting Viking ships and scales of justice.

On the Constitution Ave side is a statue of Nathan Hale (c. 1915; Bela Lyon Pratt). The statue is behind a railing so it is difficult to see many of the details and impossible to read the inscription on the pedestal, which states: "Nathan Hale / Captain Army Of The United States / Born At Coventry Connecticut June 6, 1755 / In The Performance Of His Duty He Resigned His Life A Sacrifice To His Country's Liberty At New York September 22, 1776."

> ### Washington Notes
> Captain Nathan Hale (1755–1776) is one of America's most famous Revolutionary War spies. Caught by the British, he uttered the memorable words "I only regret that I have but one life to lose for my country" before he was hanged.

## Interior
The department has a gross floor area of 1,237,000 square ft. The building is not open to the public.

## *J. Edgar Hoover FBI Building*
935 Pennsylvania Ave N.W., between 9th and 10th Sts. Tours Mon–Fri 8:45–4:15. ☎ 324-3447. Directly across the street on the north side of Pennsylvania Ave is the J. Edgar Hoover FBI Building (1967–72; C. F. Murphy). Walk one block north to E St to the tour entrance. FBI agents, sometimes nicknamed the Feds (or G-Men after the 1935 James Cagney movie), battle racketeers, crime syndicates, terorrists, and other bad guys. Because the tours are a popular tourist attraction, especially in spring and summer, it's best to schedule a tour three months in advance. For same-day admission, line up at 7 A.M., but there may not be any spaces left. Note: In 1999 because of threats to security, the FBI suspended tours. Check to see if the tours are once again available.

**Highlights:** Recognize anyone on the "Ten Most Wanted List"? Watch technicians at the DNA and blood labs at work, look at hordes of confiscated weapons, and witness a firing range demonstration.

### History
The Federal Bureau of Investigation (FBI) was created as a part of the Department of Justice in 1908. Since its inception, 46 agents have lost their lives in the line of duty. The FBI currently has 11,000 agents; 1,700 of them are female. Mandatory retirement age for agents is 57.

## Exterior
The building has an unadorned, severe façade. The upper floors of the 11-story building sit on stiltlike columns. The original intention was to form an open arcade with shops and restaurants, but FBI Director J. Edgar Hoover vetoed this because of security concerns. The buff-colored precast window frames are set into cast-in-place corner piers.

## Interior
Note: The following is a description of highlights of the FBI tour from before tours were suspended. If and when tours are reinstated, these features may change because of security concerns.

The tour guides provide a brief history of the FBI. Near the beginning of the tour is a death mask of gangster John Dillinger. Note the bullet hole in the center of the forehead from Dillinger's 1934 shootout with FBI agents. Visitors walk past more than 5,000 weapons and other items confiscated from drug dealers, including a stuffed Alaskan Kodiak bear worth $20,000. The collection of FBI movie posters includes one for the 1935 Cagney classic *G Men*. Glass windows provide a look at technicians working in the DNA laboratory. The tour ends with a bang (and often a bull's-eye) as agents demonstrate firearms skills by aiming revolvers and automatic weapons at torso-shaped targets.

Continue east on Pennsylvania Ave to the offices and restaurants of **Market Square** (1990; Hartman-Cox Architects; Morris Architects, associated architects), between 7th and 9th Sts.

## U.S. Navy Memorial and Naval Heritage Center
701 Pennsylvania Ave N.W. ☎ 628-3557. Open Nov 1–Feb 28 Tues–Sat 9:30–5; March 1–Oct 31 Mon–Sat 9:30–5. Admission: free. Web: www.lonesailor.org.
   The center of Market Square is dominated by the U.S. Navy Memorial and Naval Heritage Center (1990; Conklin Rossant; Stanley Bleifeld, sculptor).

### Exterior
Dominating the memorial's outside amphitheater is a 100 ft diameter, 108-ton granite map, the largest map in the world. It was created with liquid-jet cutting methods considered a breakthrough in stone cutting. Framing the map are two sculpture walls with 22 bronze reliefs commemorating events in naval history or honoring aspects of naval service. Standing at the entrance to the memorial is *Lone Sailor* (1987; Stanley Bleifeld), a seven-ft-tall bronze statue.

### Interior
In the **Navy Memorial Log Room,** visitors can look up the service records of more than 200,000 naval personnel, living and deceased. The 250-seat **Arleigh and Roberta Burke Theater** shows the 36-minute film *At Sea,* produced by the same company that did the popular Air and Space Museum's *To Fly.* The film is a visually impressive look at life aboard a modern aircraft carrier. On the **Gallery Deck** (downstairs) there are interactive video kiosks displaying photos and text on naval ships and aircraft, model ships, and naval artifacts and presentations of naval history from the Revolution to the present.

#### Diversion:
Before crossing Pennsylvania Ave to the National Archives, consider the **Temperance Fountain,** (c. 1880; Henry Cogswell, designer; sculptor unknown), 7th St and Pennsylvania Ave N.W., at the intersection with Indiana Ave. Henry Cogswell, a San Francisco dentist, made his fortune in real estate and mining stocks. Cogswell donated fountains, at a cost of about $4,000 each, to cities that would accept them. Each of the fountains have sculpted marine and animal life—this one has a bronze water crane—and a statue of Cogswell himself, with full beard and frock coat. He holds a temperance pledge in one hand and an empty water glass in the other. Other cities gifted with Cogswell statues include Buffalo, New York; Fall River, Massachusetts, home of Lizzy Borden; Pawtucket, Rhode Island; and San Francisco. The drinking fountain here no longer works, as the District stopped providing ice for the Victorian-period cooling device built into the base.

Next to the Cogswell fountain is the **Stephenson Grand Army of the Republic Memorial** (1909; Rankin, Kellogg & Crane, architects; John Massey Rhind, sculptor). The Grand Army of the Republic was a Civil War–era organization dedicated to the assistance of permanently wounded soldiers and the widows of fallen Union servicemen. The memorial, erected by the organization to honor its founder, Dr. Benjamin F. Stephenson (1823–1871), is a 25 ft high granite shaft with bronze figures on each of its three sides. The soldier and sailor, in Civil War Union uniforms, symbolize fraternity; below them is a bronze medallion portrait of Dr. Stephenson and two badges of the Grand Army. The woman holding the shield and sword represents loyalty; the woman protecting the child represents charity.

Turn north and face the red brick Victorian building (c. 1880s; Alfred B. Mullet) at the corner of 7th St and Indiana Ave with "Fireman's Insurance Co." carved on its 7th St façade. The structure currently houses a Starbucks coffee shop.

### Washington Notes

In 1889, the same storm that killed 2,000 residents of Johnstown, Pennsylvania, caused the Potomac to overflow its boundaries. More than two ft of water stood at the intersection of 7th St and Pennsylvania Ave, and some businesses conducted their transactions from second-story windows, dealing with customers in boats.

# National Archives

700 Pennsylvania Ave N.W., at 8th St and Constitution Ave N.W. ☎ 501-5400. Web: www.nara.gov. Exhibition Hall open daily; winter 10–5:30; April 1–Labor Day 10 A.M.–9 P.M. Closed Christmas Day. Central research and microfiche research rooms open Mon and Wed 8:45–5; Tues, Thurs, and Fri 8:45 A.M.–9 P.M.; Sat 8:45–4:45. Research rooms closed on Sun and federal holidays. Admission: free. The Archives's holdings are available for research purposes to anyone over 16 with a valid photo ID. ☎ 501-5400.

Walk to the corner of 8th St and Pennsylvania Ave. A strategic location in L'Enfant's original city plan, the site is midway between the Capitol and the White House. This is one of the reasons it was chosen as the site of the National Archives (1935; John Russell Pope; Adolph A. Weinman, James Earle Fraser, and Robert Aitken, sculptors).

**Highlights:** The Declaration of Independence, the Constitution, the Bill of Rights.

### History

The National Archives is responsible for protecting, sorting, and cataloging the important papers of the United States. The Archives's major records date back to 1774 and reflect the nation's civil, military, and diplomatic activities. In addition to the Declaration of Independence (1776), the Constitution (1789), and the Bill of Rights (1791), the Archives is also home to 5 million photographs, 82,000 reels of film, and 70,000 sound recordings, as well as the Louisiana Purchase Treaty signed by Napoleon Bonaparte, the documents signed by Japan to surrender after World War II, and the Emancipation Proclamation (1862). Also available in the genealogical records are U.S. Census Records up to 1920, ships' passenger lists, and veterans' lists dating back to the Revolutionary War.

Thomas Jefferson expressed a concern about the preservation of documents when he warned, "Time and accident are committing havoc on the originals deposited in our public offices." Plans for a national archive were first considered in 1810 and again before World War I in response to a number of fires in government buildings. The project was delayed when the war began, and discussion did not resume until the Federal Triangle Project was conceived.

The Archives was built on the site of the Center Market, designed by Adolph Cluss and opened in 1872. The market was the center of the city's commercial life through the 1920s. Adjacent to the market, where Constitution Ave now runs, was the Washington Canal, whose barges delivered fresh fish daily to the market.

The Archives was designed by John Russell Pope, who also designed the National Gallery of Art (see Walk 5: "National Mall: National Gallery of Art and National Air and Space Museum"), the Jefferson Memorial (see Walk 10: "Monuments and Memorials"), and Constitution Hall (see Walk 8: "The Ellipse and 17th Street Sites"). Pope was a fellow of the American Academy in Rome in 1895 and attended the Ecole des Beaux-Arts in Paris in 1900.

Considering the fact that the interior of the Archives had to be designed to store an unknown quantity of existing records with room for an unknowable number of future records, the planners managed to allocate space with foresight and practicality. However, the building was designed and construction begun before an archivist had been appointed. When the first archivist of the U.S., R. D. W. Connor, came on board, he and his staff immediately perceived difficulties with the design, and construction delays ensued. The building's cornerstone was laid by President Hoover in Feb 1933. Among the items contained in the cornerstone are a Bible, copies of the Constitution and the Declaration of Independence, an American flag, and a copy of each of Washington's daily newspapers. To ensure the durability and permanence of the building, the structure has 21 levels of steel and concrete stack areas, with no windows and a temperature control system.

The Archives also operates the national Presidential Library system and publishes the *Federal Register,* a daily record of government orders, regulations, and proclamations. In addition, the National Archives oversees 12 regional archives and 14 records centers across the country.

### Washington Notes
In Dec 1952 the Declaration of Independence, the Constitution, and the Bill of Rights were brought from the Library of Congress to be permanently placed in the Archives. These documents were transported in an armored Marine Corps personnel carrier accompanied by a color guard, ceremonial troops, the Army Band, the Air Force Drum and Bugle Corps, two light tanks, four servicemen with submachine guns, and a motorcycle escort.

## Exterior

There are 72 Corinthian pillars, each 52 ft high, grouped in colonnades around the building's four façades. All of the sculpting was done on-site by sculptor James Earle Fraser and his assistants, among them his wife, Laura Gardin Fraser. The figures in the pediment above the Constitution Ave entrance are noteworthy for their fluidity. *The Recorder of the Archives* (1935) features an elderly man seated on an architectural throne that rests on two reclining rams, symbols of parchment. Above the rams is a decorative frieze based on the flower of the papyrus plant, the symbol of paper. Paper and parchment together make possible the housing of the documents in the Archives. On either side of the Recorder are figures receiving documents. Each stands in front of a winged horse, or Pegasus, the symbol of aspiration. Behind these figures are groups of people acquiring and contributing records and documents. Groups of dogs (some modeled on Fraser's household pets) at each end symbolize guardianship.

Standing sentinel at the bottom of the steps leading to the Constitution Ave entrance are two eight-ft-tall limestone figures, *Heritage* (female) and *Guardianship* (male), both executed in 1935. The male figure holds the helmet of protection in one hand, and the fasces, the symbol of unified government, in the other. The inscription, attributed to Thomas Jefferson, reads "Eternal Vigilance Is The Price Of Liberty." The female figure holds a child and a sheaf of wheat in her right arm, while her left hand rests on an urn, the symbol of the home. The inscription reads "The Heritage Of The Past Is The Seed That Brings Forth The Harvest Of The Future." On the base of *Guardianship* are low-relief carvings of weapons and helmets.

Around the attic frieze of the building's four façades are 13 medallions, each eight ft high, representing the 12 departments of the federal government that contributed their records to the Archives. One medallion is for the Great Seal of the United States. These were sculpted by James Earl Fraser and Robert Aitken. Aitken, who also sculpted the two 12 ft neoclassical figures *Past* and *Future* (1935), which are on the Pennsylvania Ave side by the main entrance, made some mistakes sculpting the Great Seal. Among these are the incorrect position of the eagle's head and the arrangement of emblems, the laurels and arrows, in its talons.

## Interior

From the Constitution Ave side enter the **Exhibition Hall.** Just inside the doorway on the marble floor is a bronze circular inlay in low relief of four winged figures representing legislation, justice, history, and war and defense.

The rotunda has a 75 ft half-domed ceiling. The centerpiece of the National Archives, the case displaying the **Declaration of Independence,** the **Constitution,** and the **Bill of Rights,** is in the **Circular Gallery.** To the left and right of the case are the two sides of the Great Seal of the United States.

> ### *Washington Notes*
> The three documents are enclosed in a bulletproof, helium-filled case that is covered with a green ultraviolet filter to protect the documents from aging due to light and air exposure. Each night (and on Dec 25, the only day the Archives is closed) the documents are lowered into a 50-ton, bombproof vault, about 22 ft below the floor of the Exhibition Hall.

To the left and right of the case are 34 ft murals, *The Declaration of Independence* and *The Constitution* (both by Barry Faulkner). Also displayed is a 1297 version of the Magna Carta, on loan indefinitely from billionaire Ross Perot. The gallery to the left of the entrance has changing exhibits from the permanent Archives collection.

## Diversion:

On the grassy plot in front of the National Archives Building on the Pennsylvania Ave side is an easily overlooked memorial. In Sept 1941, speaking to his friend

Supreme Court Justice Felix Frankfurter, Franklin Roosevelt said that "If any memorial is erected to me, I know exactly what I should like it to be. It should be a block about the size of this [his desk] and placed in the center of that green plot in front of the Archives Building." In April 1965, FDR got his wish. Since then, the need was felt to erect a more elaborate memorial. The Franklin Delano Roosevelt Memorial (see Walk 10: "Monuments and Memorials") opened in 1997.

## Federal Trade Commission Building

Cross 7th St east on Pennsylvania Ave to the Federal Trade Commission (FTC) Building (1938; Edward H. Bennett) between 6th and 7th Sts on Pennsylvania Ave, ☎ 326-2222. Also called the Apex Building because of its location at the apex of the Federal Triangle, the FTC Building was almost abandoned because of the financial demands of the Depression. As a result of the economic crisis, the building was stripped of much of its planned classical detail.

### History

The Federal Trade Commission, established by an act of Congress in 1914, protects U.S. trade and commerce against unlawful restraint and monopolies. The FTC protects the public from deceptive methods of advertising and packaging of consumer goods and from the improper use of consumer credit account data.

### Washington Notes

On the site of the FTC Building in the 1880s stood the Fortune Gambling Hall. It was so popular with congressmen that often the Speaker of the House sent a page there to round up enough congressmen for a quorum. This was also the site of the Baltimore and Pacific Railroad Station where President James A. Garfield was shot on July 2, 1881. Garfield had only been in office four months when he was shot by an angry office seeker as the president was about to catch a train.

### Exterior

The building is made of limestone resting on a granite base. The rounded corner facing the Capitol is accentuated with an Ionic colonnade stretching from the third floor to the cornice line. On each side of the curved corners stands a mammoth statue—12 ft high, 15 ft in length—of a workhorse being held in check by a muscular man. Michael Lantz, a WPA instructor from New York who won a $45,000 competition for the sculptures, dubbed them *Man Controlling Trade* (1942), symbolic of the FTC controlling monopolies. The four aluminum doors (1938; William M. McVey, sculptor), two on the Pennsylvania Ave side and two on the Constitution Ave side, have panels showing sailing ships, freighters, and an airplane—symbols of both the old and the new means of conducting trade.

### Diversion:

Cross north to the corner of 6th St and Pennsylvania Ave, across from the FTC Building. Here stood the National Hotel, one of Washington's major hotels from 1816 until well into the 1850s. Andrew Jackson stayed here, walking from the hotel to the Capitol for his inauguration. On that same block, at 625 Pennsylvania Ave, Civil War photographer Mathew Brady had his studio. It occupied the three floors above Gilman's Drugstore, a shop known for its ornate vaulted ceiling.

## Andrew W. Mellon Memorial Fountain

To end the tour, walk east on Pennsylvania Ave to the Andrew W. Mellon Memorial Fountain (1952; Otto R. Eggers, architect; Sidney Waugh, sculptor), situated on the triangle bounded by Pennsylvania and Constitution Aves and 6th St. Donated by his friends at a cost of $300,000, this was, at the time, the largest fountain basin ever cast in bronze. It consists of three tiers of bronze basins, with cascades of water flowing into a low granite-curbed pool. On the floor of the basin, zodiac signs are carved in high relief. The symbols are arranged so that the ram, the sign of Aries, is touched by the sun's rays on the vernal equinox, March 21. The sign faces the rising sun from then until April 20.

The fountain provides a stone bench, a spot of shade, and the coolness of water on a hot Washington summer day.

### History

Andrew W. Mellon (1855–1937) was a financier, industrialist, and statesman. He served as secretary of the Treasury from 1921 to 1932 and was ambassador to Great Britain from 1932 to 1933. His collection formed the basis for the National Gallery of Art. Mellon coordinated the design and placement of the buildings in the Federal Triangle Project, insisting on a unified treatment and the use of buff-colored limestone rather than granite or marble.

### Washington Notes

*Washington, D.C.: City and Capital*, the Federal Writers' Project guide to Washington written in the 1930s and published in 1942, provides a contemporary view of the Federal Triangle Project. The guide states: "Though still pointed to with official pride, the Triangle has had in recent years a very poor press. The location is usually described as atrocious city planning and the common attitude toward the monumental office buildings is simply satirical. . . . The cost of these structures, not counting land and furnishings, is approximately $78,000,000—enough to buy each employee a modest cottage costing almost $3,000. Each weekday morning 30,000 workers leave their homes, converge on this area, and disappear into the monumental buildings. Each weekday afternoon, at almost the same hour, they reappear on the streets, and fight their way across the business section toward home. Underground parking facilities in some buildings are not nearly sufficient, and the flood of humanity clogs the transportation systems, all of which operate above ground."

To continue to the next walk, proceed one block east on Pennsylvania Ave to 5th St, then turn north and walk three blocks on 5th St to Judiciary Square.

# 13 · Judiciary Square/Chinatown Area

Metro: Red Line to Judiciary Square.
Bus: D1, D3, or D6 on E St N.W.

The corridor running from Judiciary Square through East Downtown to New York Ave continues to change and rejuvenate. The center of federal and local courts, Judiciary Square is generally considered to be the 19 acres bounded by 4th and 5th Sts between D and G Sts N.W. This section also has a rich ethnic heritage as the place where many of the city's 19th century immigrants made their homes and opened businesses. An early commercial district, once a center for businesses owned by German, eastern European, and Jewish merchants, the area west of Judiciary Square continues today as Washington's Chinatown. The relatively recent opening of the MCI Center added a renewed vitality to the 7th St commercial artery that extends from Market Square on Pennsylvania Ave to Mount Vernon Square. Along with the area's theaters and art galleries, the basketball games, new restaurants, shops, and clubs create more reasons for people to be downtown in the evening. (Downtown Washington is generally defined as the area north of the Mall between the White House and the Capitol.) Anthony Williams, the District's mayor, and the D.C. Financial Control Board have unveiled plans to turn an area extending from the new convention center site at Mount Vernon Square to N. Capitol St into a high-tech corridor of media and technology companies. Planners are calling this area NoMa, for "North of Massachusetts Ave." The plan includes retail shops, a theater, and housing units, as well as a new City Museum to be located across from the new Convention Center.

### History

In 1800, one of Washington's new residents sarcastically spoke of it as "the best city in the world. We want nothing here but houses, cellars, kitchens, well-informed men, amiable women, and other little trifles of this kind, to make our city perfect." Most of these "little trifles" would arrive in abundance in the next several decades, but in 1800 the population of Washington and the surrounding territory, including Alexandria and Georgetown (separate at that time), was 14,093. By 1820, the population rose to 33,039. By 1870 the population nearly tripled following the Civil War. In the first half of the 19C, the city had as much farmland as it did residential clusters, hotels, and boardinghouses; the business community was just getting started.

It is thought that the three-acre plot called Judiciary Square, with its proximity to the Capitol, was intended by L'Enfant as the site of the Supreme Court. Instead, in 1820 Washington's City Hall was built on that site. During the 19C, prominent residences as well as hotels and businesses surrounded the city's grandly Greek revival–styled seat of government. The city's first jail, located at 4th and G Sts N.W., cost $38,000 in 1840. The City Hospital, located behind City Hall, was built in the 1840s. At the beginning of the 20C, City Hall, the hospital, the jail, and the Pension Office Building (now the National Building Museum) were the area's only public buildings.

To the west of Judiciary Square, businesses developed along 7th St N.W., which was ideally located as a major business thoroughfare. Farmers from Maryland and Washington County to the north brought their produce to town via the road that ran into 7th St. This route continued on 7th St to the Center Market on Pennsylvania Ave and on to the Potomac River waterfront in Southwest Washington. The importance of this street was obvious to the city's developers. In 1845, 7th St was paved with cobblestones, making it more attractive both to businesses and their patrons. In 1862, one of the city's first horsecar lines ran along 7th St. In 1890, cable cars took over this route. F St, stretching across the city east to west,

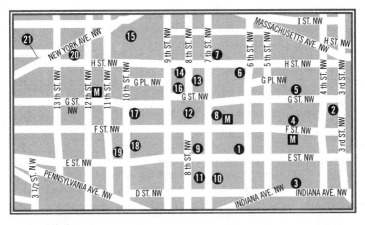

1 National Law Enforcement Offices Memorial
2 Adas Israel Synagogue
3 Old City Hall
4 National Building Museum
5 General Accounting Office
6 Mary Surratt House
7 Friendship Arch
8 MCI Center and Discovery Channel Store
9 General Post Office Building
10 Gallery Row
11 Lansburgh Building
12 Old Patent Office (National Portrait Gallery and National Museum of American Art)
13 Calvary Baptist Church
14 Greater New Hope Baptist Church
15 Washington Convention Center
16 Martin Luther King Library
17 St. Patrick's Catholic Church
18 Ford's Theatre
19 Petersen House
20 National Museum of Women in the Arts
21 New York Avenue Presbyterian Church

was also an important route, partly because its ridgetop location made it safe from Tiber Creek's periodic flooding.

In the early 1800s the residences around 7th and F Sts housed the craftsmen and laborers who built the government buildings. As the city developed, more merchants appeared, often living in rooms above their shops, and the downtown area expanded. Blodgett's Hotel was constructed in 1795 at 8th and E Sts N.W. When the building was destroyed by fire in 1836, a General Post Office Building replaced it, opening in 1842. A new Patent Office, built between 7th and 9th Sts and F and G Sts N.W. opened in 1867. Office buildings, such as the Le Droit Building at 802–810 F St N.W., went up, as did boardinghouses along E, F, and G Sts. Churches and schools were built to accommodate the rapidly growing population.

### *Washington Notes*

The area has connections to Abraham Lincoln and to the Civil War. Lincoln prayed at the New York Presbyterian Church, 13th St and Pennsylvania Ave N.W., and was assassinated in Ford's Theatre, 10th and G Sts N.W. It was at Mary Surratt's boardinghouse, 604 H St N.W., that Lincoln's assassination was planned. Most of the section's public buildings served as hospitals during the Civil War. Red Cross founder Clara Barton and poet Walt Whitman were among those who administered to the neighborhood's patients.

After the Civil War many immigrants, mostly Germans and Jews, opened businesses in the area, including major department stores such as Kann and Sons on 8th St and Lansburgh's on 7th St. In the 1930s, Chinese immigrants established a community along H St N.W. Washington's first Chinese community had begun on 4½ St in the 1880s. By 1908, Chinatown, with a population of 400, included Pennsylvania Ave from 3rd to 6th Sts. By 1928, the population had grown to 600, and Chinatown was a thriving district of drugstores, grocery markets, tailor shops, and restaurants. In 1931, however, Chinatown was slated for demolition to make way for the Federal Triangle Project. Two of the community's tongs (family associations) secretly negotiated through real estate agents for large blocks of buildings along H St, and the new Chinatown was born. Today it continues as a viable part of the Washington community.

Downtown remained a strong commercial center between the wars. However, the attractions and development of the suburbs following World War II and the completion of the Capital Beltway in 1964, which made commuting to downtown jobs easier than before, enticed many of the area's residents to relocate outside of the city's boundaries. This caused the failure of many local businesses. As a result, entire blocks of the neighborhood deteriorated into boarded-up stores and low-rent hotels, especially after the 1968 riots that erupted following the assassination of Dr. Martin Luther King, Jr., in 1968. The 1976 opening of the Metrorail system, the 1979 development of Gallery Row (401–413 7th St N.W.), and the 1983 completion of the Washington Convention Center in 1983 began a gradual revitalization. The rejuvenation of Pennsylvania Ave in the last 20 years has also helped, including the 1992 reopening of the restored Lansburgh Building as a mixed commercial and residential space. The 1997 debut of the MCI Center gave the area additional panache.

If arriving from the Federal Triangle walk, continue east one block on Pennsylvania Ave to 5th St, turn north and walk three blocks to Judiciary Square. Otherwise, begin this walk at the Judiciary Square Metro station, which comes up to street level on Judiciary Square facing E St.

## National Law Enforcement Officers Memorial

F St between 4th and 5th Sts N.W. Visitors Center two blocks west at 605 E St N.W. ☎ 737-3400. Web: www.1nleomf.com. Admission: free. Open Mon–Fri 9–5; Sat 10–5; Sun 12–5. Guided tours April–Oct on Sat 11–2. Gift shop. Wheelchair accessible. The National Law Enforcement Officers Memorial (1991; David Buckley, architect; Ann Hawkins, Raymond Kaskey, and George Car, sculptors) is located directly on the square. Judiciary Square's three acres, valued at more than $20 million, were donated by the federal government to serve as a memorial. The square was chosen because of the area's historical association with the criminal justice system. Two three-ft-high walls, consisting of 128 marble panels, display the names of more than 15,000 police officers killed in the line of duty since 1794. Flanking this are four groups of bronze lions and cubs, which represent the protective role the police play in society and symbolize the officers' strength, courage, and valor. An inscription reads: "It Is Not How These Officers Died That Made Them Heroes, It Is How They Lived."

**Diversion:**
Walk east one block to 3rd St, then north two blocks to G St and the **Adas Israel Synagogue (Lillian and Albert Small Jewish Museum and the Jewish Historical Society)** (1876; architect unknown; 1975 restoration; Leon Brown, architectural supervisor; DL), 701 3rd St N.W. ☎ 789-0900. Open Sun–Thurs 12–4. This two-story, Colonial-style structure is the oldest building constructed as a synagogue in the city.

### History

The Adas Israel Congregation was formed in 1869 when 35 members of the Washington Hebrew Congregation left that membership over religious differences. After years of meeting in members' homes and rented quarters, a new synagogue was dedicated at 8th and D Sts N.W. in 1876 in the presence of President Ulysses S. Grant and other dignitaries. A semicircular stone below the roof line has the equivalent date–5636–in the Jewish calendar. In 1908, the congregation moved to a bigger synagogue at 6th and I Sts N.W., and the building was used by various other religious groups until 1946, when it became a grocery store and carryout. Although the first floor was considerably altered, the synagogue proper on the second floor remained intact and still contained the original *aron kodesh*, the Torah Ark. In 1968, when the entire block was scheduled for demolition to make way for the headquarters of the area's transit authority, a group of Washingtonians worked to raise funds to buy a new site. In 1969, the 270-ton brick building was lifted onto huge dollies and moved three blocks away. After a five-year restoration, the building opened as the Lillian and Albert Small Jewish Museum and the Jewish Historical Society, which was founded in 1960. The Adas Israel Congregation now occupies a site at Connecticut Ave and Porter St N.W.

Walk south on 4th St N.W. to the park on the northeast corner of 4th St and Indiana Ave and the sculpture *Guns Into Plowshares* (1997; Esther and Michael Augsburger, sculptors), a metal wave covered with handguns in various stages of conversion to smooth metal. The plaque identifies the piece "as a symbol of hope from the friends and supporters of InterChurch, Inc" to the city of Washington.

Continue west on Indiana Ave.

## Superior Court of the District of Columbia Building

451 Indiana Ave N.W. ☎ 628-1200. Lobby open to the public Mon–Fri 8:30–5:30.
Directly next to the park is the Superior Court of the District of Columbia Building, formerly the **Old City Hall** (1820; George Hadfield; DL). This building is considered by many to be one of the finest examples of Greek revival style in Washington.

### History

This was the first building erected in Washington to house the District government. Architect George Hadfield, a protégé of Benjamin West, came to America in 1795 to serve as the superintendent of the Capitol, which was still under construction. Unfortunately, after differences with the Capitol's designer, William Thornton, Hadfield resigned. His most famous designs are the Old City Hall and Arlington House, the home of Robert E. Lee, now part of Arlington Cemetery.

The City Hall had a difficult start. Funds for the project were quickly depleted and a lottery scheme to raise additional monies failed. Congress reluctantly allocated $10,000, with the stipulation that one wing of the structure be for federal offices. The cornerstone was laid in 1820, and the building was proclaimed as "an edifice devoted to municipal purposes, to be the seat of legislation and of the administration of justice for this metropolis."

### Washington Notes

Several famous trials were held here, including those of Charles Guiteau and former mayor Marion Barry. In 1881, during Guiteau's 72-day trial for the assassination of President James Garfield, Guiteau published in a local paper his choices for the new president's cabinet. In 1990, Barry's trial on cocaine possession lasted two months. He was convicted on one charge while the jury deadlocked on 12 additional charges. Barry served six months in prison, was released, and then was elected to the District's City Council, where he served from 1992 to 1994. In 1994, Barry was reelected mayor.

## Exterior

The central section is distinguished by a Greek Ionic portico with recessed, round-headed windows at first-floor level and flanked on two sides by wings with Ionic columns and arched doorways. From the building's terraced entry, there is an unbroken view of Constitution Ave and the East Building of the National Gallery of Art.

## Interior

The main lobby is graced with marble floors and two marble columns, on either side of which are stairways with brass-railed iron balusters. The marble stairs rise to landings, then branch and rise again to meet in a central balcony on the top floor.

Two pieces of sculpture grace the Old City Hall site. *Abraham Lincoln* (1868; Lot Flannery) was erected by the citizens of Washington to honor its fallen president. Fund-raising was begun within days of the 1865 assassination, and the statue was dedicated on the third anniversary of Lincoln's death in 1868. Flannery, a local sculptor who had known Lincoln, chose to depict the president simply— Lincoln stands with his right arm extended and his left arm resting on a fasces (the Roman emblem of leadership). When the courthouse was enlarged in 1919, the statue was temporarily placed in storage. Officials decided the statue was no longer needed since the Lincoln Memorial was under construction. However, a public outcry on the statue's behalf returned it to its original site with a new inscription: "This Statue Erected by the Citizens of the District of Columbia April 15, 1868, Re-erected April 15, 1923 under Act of Congress of June 21, 1922."

Public outcry of a different sort greeted the **Joseph Darlington Fountain**

(1923; Carl Paul Jennewein). Walk west to the northeast corner of 5th and D Sts. The inscription at the base of this nonworking fountain reads "This Monument Has Been Erected by the Friends of Joseph Darlington, 1849–1920, Counselor, Teacher, Lover of Mankind." The life-size gilded bronze figure of a nymph and a fawn rest on an octagonal pedestal. Darlington was being honored for his personal and professional integrity, as well as for his deep religious convictions. It was the convictions of his fellow Baptists, offended by the statue's nudity, that caused the furor when the statue was unveiled. Jennewein responded that the nymph was the perfect divine work, "direct from the hand of God instead of from the hands of the dressmaker." Legend has it that one morning the statue was discovered clothed in gingham.

From the Darlington Fountain, walk north on 5th St to the National Building Museum.

## National Building Museum

401 F St N.W., between F and G and 4th and 5th Sts N.W. ☎ 272-2448. Web: www.nbm.org. Open Mon–Sat 10–4; Sun noon–4. Closed Thanksgiving, Christmas Day, New Year's Day. Tours weekdays at 12:30; weekends at 12:30 and 1:30. Suggested donation. Gift shop and snack bar. Wheelchair accessible.

Originally constructed to house the Pension Bureau responsible for dispersing military pensions, the National Building Museum (1887; Montgomery C. Meigs, architect; Casper Buberl, sculptor; 1989, restoration architecture by Keyes Condon Florance, with Giorgio Cavaglieri as associate architect; DL) houses a museum devoted to the building craft. Restored to its original grandeur in 1989, the building is considered to be one of the most beautiful in Washington.

**Highlights:** The Great Hall, with its central fountain and its 75 ft high columns. "Arches and Trestles: The Tension Builds," a lecture given for children every Sat from 2:30 to 2:50 P.M., demonstrates how a building remains standing. *Patterns That Thump, Bump and Jump,* available for a nominal fee in the gift shop, is a children's booklet explaining basic architecture and construction.

### History

Upon entering the Great Hall it's very hard to imagine that this museum has been a government office building for virtually all of its history. Built to contain a Pension Bureau overwhelmed by the needs of more than 500,000 veterans and their dependents from the Revolutionary War, the War of 1812, the Mexican War, and the Civil War, the Pension Building was commissioned by Congress in 1881 and completed in 1887.

Architect Montgomery C. Meigs was quartermaster general of the United States Army when he was assigned the task in 1881 of constructing "a fireproof building of brick and metal" on a budget of between $250,000 and $300,000. Meigs, who studied engineering and architectural design at West Point, already had several successful designs to his credit, including the city's aqueduct system, the Cabin John Bridge (at 220 ft in length, the longest masonry arch in the world before 1900), and the extension of the U.S. Capitol, including designing the crane that made construction of the great cast-iron dome possible.

Meigs's efficient use of budget and space was demonstrated during the Civil War when he constructed barracks and supply depots for almost a million troops, inexpensively, efficiently, and quickly. After the Civil War, Meigs traveled in Europe to recover from the grief of losing his son in the conflict. On these trips Meigs studied Italian Renaissance architecture. These journeys helped prepare him for his next two projects: the Arts and Industries Building (then called the National Museum Building) of the Smithsonian Institution and the Pension Building (which would become the National Building Museum).

> ### Washington Notes
> For many years, the Pension Building was jokingly referred to as Meigs's Old Red Barn. Not everyone liked the building. During a tour of it, General Phil Sheridan, Meigs's Civil War comrade in arms, was asked for his opinion. Sheridan replied, "I have one fault to find with it. It's fireproof."

One other fault the building is reputed to have—it's haunted. In 1917, a guard on the all-night shift reported that he saw the veins in the simulated onyx of one of the Great Hall's mammoth columns arrange themselves into the shape of a buffalo head. The next morning, the guard learned that Buffalo Bill Cody, a guest at the first inaugural ball held in the Great Hall, had died the previous evening. Late on a summer's night in 1972, a guard looked up from his newspaper to see a man in a light-colored suit moving toward one of the stairways. The man, who had a peculiar kind of walk, didn't respond to the guard's telling him he wasn't supposed to be in the building after hours. When the guard approached him, the man turned and the guard, as he explained later to officials at St. Elizabeth's Hospital (for the mentally ill), saw in the man's eyes the fires of hell and smelled the stench of the dead. Historians of the Pension Building speculated at the time that the intruder might have been the ghost of James Tanner, one of the first pension commissioners and a veteran of the Second Battle of Bull Run (Manassas), where he lost both his feet; this would explain the peculiar walk. No one, however, speculated on the nature of Mr. Tanner's transgressions, which would have associated him with the fires of hell.

Meigs created an elegant and innovative building with thoughtful touches. The offices placed around the perimeter had plenty of light and fresh air. The steps have wider than usual treads and shallow risers, thus making them more easily climbed by men using crutches, a fact of life for many war veterans.

The Pension Bureau outgrew the building in a little over 25 years. After the Pension Bureau merged with other agencies to form the predecessor of the Department of Veterans Affairs in 1926, the General Accounting Office (GAO) took over the building. The GAO placed desk cubicles in the Great Hall, strung light fixtures across its open spaces, and placed filing cabinets in the fountain. In 1950 the GAO moved into new headquarters across the street. Various agencies, including the Civil Service Commission and the Superior Court of the District of Columbia, occupied the building until 1980, when the National Building Museum was created and restoration work began. The museum opened to the public in Oct 1985.

## Exterior

Meigs's inspiration for the Pension Building was the 16C Palazzo Farnese in Rome, the largest and most famous of all Renaissance palaces, whose dimensions Meigs eventually doubled for the Pension Building, creating a structure 400 by 200 ft. Avoiding expensive building materials, Meigs worked imaginatively with factory-made terra-cotta and painted plaster on brick surfaces. The foundation is stuccoed rubble stone walls about four ft thick, supported by concrete footings about six ft wide and three ft deep. The exterior brick walls are 75 ft high and over two ft thick, with 27 window bays on both the north and south façades, 13 on the west and east, and an entrance in the center on all four sides.

The exterior's most extraordinary feature is Casper Buberl's buff-colored terracotta frieze, modeled after the frieze on the Parthenon in Greece. The Pension Building's frieze glorifies military service. Three ft high and 1,200 ft long, Buberl's frieze, extending all around the building between the first and second levels, depicts military units from each of the armed forces. Buberl first created each design in clay, then made a plaster cast from which a repeat plaster cast was made, into which the terra cotta was pressed to make the clay casts for the 28 panels, each two to four ft in length.

Each of the four entrances (called gates by Meigs, perhaps an allusion to a fort) also has work by Buberl representing aspects of military service. On the north is the **Gate of the Invalids,** presided over by Justice; on the west is the **Gate of the Quartermaster,** presided over by Minerva, goddess of wisdom; on the south is the **Gate of the Infantry,** presided over by Truth; and on the east is the **Naval Gate,** presided over by Mars, god of war. Allegorical figures, such as Athena, fill the spandrels created by the entrance arches.

## Interior

One of the most beautiful spaces in Washington, the museum's interior consists of the **Great Hall** (116 by 316 ft) and its balconies of office space. By placing offices around the perimeter, Meigs created a healthful environment at a time when civil servants worked in dark, stuffy rooms with no fresh air. The 75 ft high Corinthian columns are among the tallest indoor columns in the world. Each column is constructed of 70,000 bricks and is painted to look like Siena marble.

> ### Washington Notes
> The Great Hall, with its 28 ft central fountain, has been the site of 14 presidential inaugural balls. The first was in 1885 for Grover Cleveland, before construction was completed. A temporary roof was built over the open courtyard, a wooden floor laid over the dirt, and decorations concealed the unfinished interior.

In the 234 niches above the center court are busts (1984; Gretta Bader) created from eight prototypes representing Americans "who created the built environment of the United States." These include an 18C bricklayer, a 19C architect, and a 20C construction worker. These are the second set of figures. The first set was made from molds of Native Americans lent by the Smithsonian Institution and molds of others, including casts of Meigs, his father, and his wife. After the installation Meigs was angered to learn that some of the figures were of heads of federal prisoners. These remained until the early 20C. Photographs taken in 1923 show the niches empty, but when the busts disappeared and where they went is not known.

Several interesting plaques adorn the walls. The plaque on the south entrance wall notes that the 1883 revenues of the U.S. were $398,287,582 and expenditures for pensions was $99,460,000, or almost a quarter of the nation's revenues. (This plaque also contains the error of listing George F. Edmunds as vice

*National Building Museum (Great Hall). Photo credit: Jack E. Boucher, HABS.*

president when he was actually president pro tempore of the Senate.) A plaque at the west entrance commemorates the building's completion in 1887, and beneath it is a glazed tintype of Abraham Lincoln. A similar tintype of Ulysses S. Grant is at the east entrance.

The museum has a series of changing architectural exhibits as well as a small permanent display, **Washington: Symbol and City,** a study of the growth of the capital.

**Diversion:**
Directly across G St from the National Building Museum is the **General Accounting Office** (1951; Gilbert Stanley Underwood, architect; Joseph Kiselewski, sculptor), 441 G St N.W., ☎ 512-4800, Web: www.gao.gov. This was the first block-shaped federal government building in the city, a direct result of advances in office lighting that allowed workers sufficient illumination without depending on natural light. Underwood, who served as supervising architect in the Federal Works Agency until federal architectural functions were taken over by the General Services Administration, also designed the State Department Building. On either side of the front entrance are 9 by 15 ft, Art Deco–style bas-reliefs depicting people at work. On the west side are professionals; on the east side are laborers.

## Chinatown

To enter the Chinatown area, exit the National Building Museum on G St, walk a half-block west on G St to 5th St, one block north on 5th to H St, then turn west on H St. There are no street signs on any corner at this intersection.

One block west is **604 H St,** currently Go-lo's Restaurant, but this site was the **Mary Surratt House,** 541 H St, during the Civil War. Mrs. Surratt, a widow with a grown son, ran a boardinghouse. Among the visitors to the Surratt house was John Wilkes Booth. At this house Booth and several of Surratt's boarders (including, allegedly, Surratt's son, John) plotted Abraham Lincoln's assassination. Booth and his conspirators originally intended to abduct Lincoln and exchange him for Confederate prisoners, but Lee's surrender brought despair and a change of plans.

> ### Washington Notes
> The plaque placed on the site by the Chi-Am Lions Club refers only to the abduction plot and not to the assassination. Following the assassination, John Surratt fled to Canada. He was brought back for trial two years later but walked free when the jury couldn't agree on a verdict. Surratt spent the latter part of his life on the lecture circuit, talking about his experiences. His mother was arrested immediately following the assassination, tried with several of the other conspirators, and hanged. She protested her innocence to the end.

Continue west on H St. Notice the money and dog figures carved in the red brick sidewalk. At the intersection of 7th and H St is the **Friendship Arch** (1968; Alfred H. Liu), a gesture of goodwill between the "sister" cities of Beijing, People's Republic of China, and Washington, D.C. Using *duo gong* carved wood systems that don't allow use of nails or other metal connectors, Liu balanced seven roofs weighing 63 tons with a steel-and-reinforced-concrete base and created the largest single-span Chinese archway in the world. The arch is 47 ft high and 61 ft wide. Included in the brightly multicolored arch are 58 animal models, 12 dragons in the round, and 272 painted dragons, plus motifs of clouds, medallions, and lotus.

> **Washington Notes**
> The archway, a public relations coup for Mayor Marion Barry and the District government, was not met with enthusiasm by all in the Chinese community. As a symbol of harmony with the Chinese Communist government, the Friendship Arch conflicts with the sentiments of many Chinatown residents and business leaders who have strong ties with the Nationalist Chinese party in Taiwan.

**Diversion:**
Continue west across 7th St to the **Adams National Bank.** The sign in the window explains how the bank was renovated using the principles of *feng shui* (pronounced "phong shway"), an ancient Chinese philosophy used to determine the most propitious placement of a dwelling's entrances.

## MCI Center

601 F St N.W., between F and G Sts N.W. and 6th and 7th Sts N.W. ☎ 628-3200. Web: www.mcicenter.com. Open daily 9 A.M.–11 P.M. Tours of the facility daily on the hour 10–4. Admission packages vary.

Turn south on 7th St and walk two blocks to the MCI Center (1997; Ellerbe Becket, architect; Architects and Engineers of Kansas City). The professional sports arena also has shops and restaurants, which are open to non–ticket holders. Walk past the G St entrance to the center and note the neon sign with "MCI Center" in Chinese letters.

### History

When Abe Pollin, chairman of the Board of the Washington Sports and Entertainment Limited partnership and a prominent Washington businessman and booster, opened the MCI Center for business on Dec 2, 1997, it was a giant step in an ambitious plan to revitalize the downtown area. The Downtown Business Improvement District (BID) was formed in July 1997 to create "a safe, clean, more attractive user-friendly downtown . . . a vibrant center of the city and region . . . a downtown that is a world class destination." Property owners within the BID 120-block area have agreed to tax themselves to raise the funds to improve transportation and parking, as well as improve signage and security and provide assistance for the homeless.

### Interior

This five-acre futuristic sports arena and food and retail center is home to Washington's male basketball NBA team (the Wizards), male hockey NHL team (the Capitals), and female basketball WNBA team (the Mystics). The center has overhead and touch-screen monitors, printers, and sound and e-mail connections (arenaNet information kiosks).

**Level G, the Event Floor.** On this level is the space used for all sports events.

**Level 1, the Main Concourse.** The main entrance is on F St; side entrances are on 7th and 6th Sts. On this level you'll find the entrance to the Discovery Channel Store Destination DC, restaurants, and food facilities. It features **video walls**—27-inch monitors stacked like a tic-tac-toe board present upcoming events and short films of historical moments in Washington sports, entertainment, and politics. There are ticket windows and event seating.

**Level 2, Club Concourse.** On this level there are event seating, a continuation of the Discovery Channel Store Destination DC, and more restaurants and food facilities.

**Level 3, Suite Concourse.** This level features event seating in suites costing $160,000 or more per year, continuation of the Discovery Channel Store Destination DC, and the **MCI National Sports Gallery** (admission varies). The Sports Gallery is a 25,000-square-ft attraction that offers sports memorabilia such as a 1909 T206 Honus Wagner baseball card (valued at $675,000) and virtual reality sports theme games.

**Level 4, Upper Concourse.** Continuations of the Discovery Channel Store Destination DC and the Sports Gallery occupy this level, along with more food facilities.

**Levels 5 and 6, Upper Press.** This level contains press rooms and announcers' booths.

ArenaNets placed throughout the main and upper concourses offer instant trivia games and generate digital postcards that put visitors' faces into scenes with star athletes. These stations also include information on the Washington, D.C., area, including local restaurants, hotels, and transportation.

## Discovery Channel Store

The Discovery Channel Store Destination DC (601 F St N.W., ☎ 639-0908, Web: www.flagship.discovery.com, open Mon–Sat 10–9 and Sun 12–6, closed Christmas Day) is a 30,000-square-ft, four-level store that offers educational material, toys, games, and books interestingly exhibited using multimedia and interactive displays. The themed store "time travels" the shopper from the first floor, which deals with prehistoric items and things from deep beneath the earth's surface, to the top level, which features items about the far reaches of the universe.

**Level 1, Paleo World.** Fossils, gems, and jewelry are sold here. Highlights include **Discovery Rex,** a cast of the world's largest Tyrannosaurus rex skeleton ever assembled, and the interactive **Dinosaur Dig,** which culminates in finding a T-rex.

**Mezzanine, Ocean Planet.** Along with sea-life exhibits, ceramics, clothing, toys, and models of famous shipwrecks are for sale on this level.

**Level 2, Wild Discovery World Cultures.** A **giant ant colony** is a highlight. Gardening books and travel items are among the merchandise for sale.

**Level 3, Sky&Space Science Frontiers.** On display here is an authentic World War II B-25 bomber cockpit. Model planes, science kits, and telescopes are available for sale.

**Level 4, Discovery Channel Theater.** "Destination D.C.," a 15-minute film about Washington, D.C., is shown here on the hour and half hour. An admission is charged.

## *General Post Office Building*

Walk south on 7th St to the General Post Office Building (1839–42; Robert Mills; 1855–60, Thomas U. Walter; Montgomery C. Meigs, superintendent of construction; Guido Butti, sculptor; DL) at 7th and 8th Sts between E and F Sts N.W. Most recently this building housed the International Trade Commission. The building has been vacant for many years but is now being considered for purchase by a national hotel chain. A bronze plaque near the E St entrance states: "In

1800 building erected on this site by Samuel Blodget [*sic*] was the scene of the first theatrical performance given in Washington. From 1812 to 1836 it sheltered the City Post Office and for part of that period the Post Office Department and the Patent Office and here after the burning of the Capitol the Congress of the United States was convened Sept 19th 1814."

### History

Samuel Blodgett, Jr., was one of Washington's most adventurous land speculators and at one time owned 494 acres in the city. He built Blodgett's Hotel, at 8th and E Sts N.W., in 1795. On Aug 22, 1800, he opened the United States Theatre, a small playhouse located in the property, which was Washington's first theater. Because it proved to be financially unsuccessful, Blodgett closed the theater on Sept 19, 1800. Blodgett's property was the largest privately owned building in the Federal City for its first 20 years. After Blodgett went bankrupt in a lottery scheme, the federal government purchased the building in 1810 to house the Post Office Department and the Patent Office. (Blodgett died penniless in Baltimore in 1814.)

### Washington Notes

During the War of 1812, when the British burned many government buildings in 1814, this structure housed the Patent Office. Its hundreds of models of inventions were saved through the intervention of Dr. William Thornton. (In addition to being the architect of the Capitol, Thornton was also at one time or another commissioner of the Federal City, superintendent of the Patent Office, and vice president of the District Medical Society.) Thornton literally threw himself in front of a cannon as the British commander prepared to blow up the building and its treasures. Afterward, Thornton recalled for the local newspapers that he persuaded the British officer that "to burn what would be useful to all mankind, would be as barbarous as formerly to burn the Alexandrian Library, for which the Turks have since been condemned by all enlightened nations." Moved, the British officer did not burn the building, and the patents and inventions were saved.

After the War of 1812, the Capitol and White House were in ruins, and Congress met briefly in this building. In 1836, what war couldn't accomplish, carelessness did. A servant accidentally placed hot fireplace ashes in a wooden box, and the building was destroyed by fire, taking with it more than 10,000 Patent Office specifications, 9,000 drawings, and 7,000 models of inventions. The current building was begun in 1839 by architect Robert Mills, who also designed the Patent Office (now the National Portrait Gallery and the National Museum of American Art), the Treasury Building, and the Washington Monument. Mills is considered by many to be the first great American-born professional architect. (Unfortunately, he wasn't as talented with his bookkeeping and was repeatedly investigated by Congress.) In 1836 Mills was appointed by President Andrew Jackson as federal architect of public buildings, a post he held for the next 15 years. Until 1897, the building housed the Post Office Department and the City Post Office.

### Washington Notes
The General Post Office was the site of the first public telegraph office in the U.S. The first telegraph message—"What hath God wrought!"—was sent from this building by Samuel F. B. Morse on April 1, 1845.

The General Post Office did its duty during the Civil War, serving as a barracks, hospital, and supply depot. The army used the cellar to store provisions. Heavy barrels of coffee, rice, and other staples were rolled up the marble stairs and carted away in commissary wagons. When the news came of Lee's surrender, 3,500 candles lit the windows of the Post Office, and hung across its façade was a large transparency showing a mail carrier and the words, "Behold, I bring you good tidings of great joy."

## Exterior
Robert Mills worked on the structure's south portion from 1839 to 1842. Mills's original design was of a U-shaped building facing E St between 7th and 8th Sts. A major addition by Thomas U. Walter in 1855 changed the building into a rectangle that extended to F St. The building, based on a traditional Renaissance palazzo, was the first use of the Italianate style for an important public building in America.

The addition Walter made to the building tripled the length of the eastern and western façades and created a new northern façade, interjecting subtle changes to the exterior. Mills's main (south) front has a three-columned portico of fluted Corinthian columns framed by single pilasters. Mills included an arched opening into the courtyard on the west for the transport of mail in and out of the building. Sculptor Guido Butti created the figures for the arch's keystone and spandrels. The keystone represents fidelity. On the left spandrel, a female figure with feathered wings represents electricity; she holds a lightning bolt in her right hand and a scroll in her left hand. The right spandrel features a male figure, whose wings are webbed, holding a locomotive; he represents steam.

The site will once again be that of a hotel, as the GSA (General Services Administration) is leasing the building to a four-star hotel for the next 50 years.

Continue south two blocks to the 400 block of 7th St, at one time the heart of the former commercial/residential mix in this area.

### Diversion:
General Post Office architect Thomas Walter lived around the corner at 614 F St, the abolitionist newspaper *National Era* was published at 427 F St, Clara Barton rented rooms at 488½ 7th St, and Samuel Morse labored over his new telegraph machine in a building that stood on 7th St between E and F Sts.

In 1979, as part of the downtown revitalization project, a series of art galleries, **Gallery Row** (Hartman-Cox, architects; Oehrlein & Associates, preservation architects), 401–413 7th St N.W., opened. Five run-down 19C buildings were shored up and connected by a link building (409 7th St) that houses a four-story rotunda and lobby.

Next to Gallery Row is the **DC UNITE Sculpture Park** (Web: www.

essentialism.com), founded by local metal sculptor Robert T. Cole in Oct 1997 to give other sculptors a public arena for their work. The D.C. Commission on the Arts and Humanities provided some financial assistance to pay for the rehabilitation of the space, including the chain-link fencing and green vinyl grass, and the GSA (General Services Administration) assisted with lighting and electricity.

## Lansburgh Building

Another step in the downtown revitalization was the opening across the street of the Lansburgh Building (1992; Graham Gund) at 420–480 7th St N.W. The Pennsylvania Avenue Development Corporation (a 1974–96 joint venture of private and public industry) renovated this former department store, creating residential and commercial space. The Lansburgh Building has 385 rental apartments, ground-floor retail space, and the Shakespeare Theatre (450 7th St N.W., ☎ 547-3230, Web: www.shakespearedc.org), one of the country's major Shakespearean theaters.

### History

The three Lansburgh brothers—Gustav, Max, and James—began their retail business in Washington in 1859, operating several small establishments throughout the city. Following the Civil War, the brothers consolidated their holdings at a new location, 515 7th St N.W., and renamed their business the Metropolitan Dry Goods Store. In 1882 they moved their business to 420–424 7th St N.W. and changed the name to Lansburgh & Brothers Department Store. Their 24,000 square ft of retail space featured the only elevator in a commercial building in town. By 1925, the store grew to 268,000 square ft and employed 500 people. Lansburgh's was innovative, selling related items in the same department, such as men's shoes with men's suits, and it also created a Service Department to aid the customer. Lansburgh's later expanded into suburban malls, but those stores couldn't survive the influx of national chains such as Bloomingdale's, and its downtown store could not overcome the decay of the 7th St corridor. The Lansburgh chain closed in 1973.

### Exterior

The six-story building was built in three stages: The 1916 and 1924 structures were designed by the architectural firm of Milburne & Heister & Co.; Clifton B. White designed the 1941 addition. The 8th St façade is divided into twelve segments by five-story arcades. These arcades are detailed with bas-relief ornaments. Each segment contains three windows, except for the wider eastern bay of the north façade, which has four. The E St façade is similar to that of the 8th St one except it consists of only two arched segments of unequal widths. On both the 8th and E St façades the entire first floor is a series of show windows for retail and commercial businesses.

Continue south to the corner of 7th and D Sts. Walk west on D St to 8th St, then north on 8th St. Notice the whimsical 8th St façade of the PEPCO (Potomac Electric Power Company) Building, with its trompe l'oeil windows and colonnades.

**Diversion:**
On the southwest corner of F St and halfway up the block on F St is the **Le Droit Building** (1875; James H. McGill) at 802–810 F St N.W. In its heyday this was one of the area's finer commercial structures. In the 1980s the building was used for artists' studios. In summer 1999 the Le Droit Building and the Atlas Building next door (corner of 9th and F Sts N.W.) were sold to a developer, whose plan is to renovate the buildings for office, retail, and residential use.

When the Le Droit Building was in use, the large display windows on its second floor provided steady light for its first office workers and for the artists that followed a century later. Even in its dilapidated condition, the building's Italianate details, including the Corinthian entrances and bracketed frieze, give it a faded dignity.

One block west, on the southeast corner of F St is the **Riggs National Bank Building** (1891; James G. Hill; 1926, addition to west end; Arthur Heaton, architect). Vacant for almost a decade, this Romanesque revival building, with its façade of gray rock-faced granite ashlar and layers of round-arch windows, is now a Courtyard by Marriott hotel (Courtyard Washington Convention Center), whose most interesting feature is its breakfast café in the old bank vault. Also undergoing renovation, across the street on the northeast corner of F St, is the former **Masonic Hall** (1868; Adolph Cluss and Joseph Wildrich von Kammerrheuber). In 1876 the Prince of Wales feasted here with prominent Washingtonians, and for decades debutantes "came out" at dances held in the hall. In 1908, the Masons moved to 13th St and New York Ave (now the home of the National Museum of Women in the Arts), and in 1921 this structure became Lansburgh's Furniture Store, which it remained until 1973, when the Lansburgh chain closed. Now renamed 901 F Street at Gallery Place, the building, transformed into retail and office space by Martinez & Johnson Architects, opened in the fall of 1999.

# Old Patent Office (National Portrait Gallery and National Museum of American Art)

Continue north on 8th St to the Old Patent Office (1836; Ithiel Town and William P. Elliot, Jr.; 1836–40, 1849–52, Robert Mills; 1852–57, Edward Clark and Thomas U. Walter; 1880s, Adolph Cluss and Paul Schulze; 1969, Faulkner, Stenhouse, Fryer; Faulkner and Underwood; Victor Proetz; Bayard Underwood, restoration; Caspar Buberl, sculpture for the Great Hall; DL), between 7th and 9th Sts and between F and G Sts N.W., now the **National Portrait Gallery** and the **National Museum of American Art.** Both facilities are Smithsonian Institution museums. In Jan 2000, this building closed for three years of major renovations.

> ### *Washington Notes*
> Walt Whitman helped nurse wounded soldiers in the Patent Office when it served as a hospital during the Civil War. His poem "The Wound-Dresser" is based on his nursing experiences. In later years, Whitman spoke of the haunting images of the anguished faces of the wounded men as they lay on the rows and rows of cots reflected in the glass of the cabinets holding the patent models. Clara Barton, founder of the American Red Cross, worked in the Patent Office from 1854 to 1857 as a clerk but was fired for her aboli-

tionist sentiments. She returned during the war to nurse the wounded. Walt Whitman also worked in the building in the Bureau of Indian Affairs (the Department of the Interior had offices here) and he was fired in 1867 after the publication that year of a revised edition of *Leaves of Grass,* a book many considered scandalous.

The gallery leading from the Great Hall on the third floor was called the Lincoln Gallery because it was the site of Lincoln's second inaugural ball in 1865. The event was a benefit for the families of Union soldiers, and several thousand joined the evening's festivities. Walt Whitman, who attended this event, wrote: "I have been up to look at the dance and supper-rooms, for the inauguration ball at the Patent Office; and I could not help thinking what a different scene they presented to my view a while since, fill'd with a crowded mass of the worst wounded of the war, brought in from second Bull Run, Antietam, and Fredericksburg. To-night, beautiful women, perfumes, the violin's sweetness, the polka and the waltz; then the amputation, the blue face, the groan, the glassy eye of the dying, the clotted rag, the odor of wounds and blood, and many a mother's son amid strangers, passing away untended there . . ."

### History

Following the devastating fire in 1836 that destroyed most of America's patent documents and models, President Andrew Jackson selected an architectural design by Ithiel Town of New York and William P. Elliot, Jr., of Washington for a Patent Office building that would house patent materials and also art and historical artifacts, including paintings by Gilbert Stuart and John Singleton Copley and the Declaration of Independence.

The collection increased so much that before the Civil War more than 1,000 boxes were transferred for storage to the new Smithsonian building on the Mall. Jackson also endowed Robert Mills with the authority "to aid in forming the plans, making proper changes therein from time to time, and seeing to the erection of said buildings in substantial conformity to the plans hereby adopted." In other words, he could butt in as often as he liked, which he proceeded to do, causing a very public architects' war that went on for some years, almost until Mills's death in 1855.

The initial plan for the Patent Office Building was for a rectangular structure with a courtyard, which could be built wing by wing, as space was needed and resources became available. The south façade (F St) was constructed in 1836, followed by the east (7th St) in 1852, the west (9th St) in 1856, and the north (G St) in 1867. The only wing not made of marble is the south façade, which was subsequently painted white both to mask and protect its Virginia sandstone.

When the building was completed in 1867, it was the largest office building in Washington. It is considered one of the finest examples of Greek revival architecture in the U.S. For the next ten years, the Patent Office Building was one of the city's major tourist attractions. But in 1877 a fire destroyed 100,000 patent models and portions of the south and west wings, which were remodeled during the 1880s. Through the years, more than 500,000 patents were issued to inventors such as Alexander Graham Bell and Thomas Edison. In 1932, the Civil Service Commission moved into the building. In 1953, a bill was introduced in Congress to demolish the building and put up a parking lot. President Eisenhower intervened, and the building was transferred to the Smithsonian Institution, under whose authority it remains.

## Exterior

Each of the walls on the four façades are accented with wide Doric pilasters. In the center are giant Doric colonnaded porticoes crowned with simple pediments. On the north and south the porticoes have eight columns, and on the east and west they have six.

Thomas Walter took over as architect in 1852. (Robert Mills was removed from the project while he underwent his fourth congressional investigation over alleged misuse of funds. Mills was eventually exonerated, but this investigation ended his career as a public architect.) Walter introduced the shallow pediments above the pavilions on the north and west wings.

## Interior

The interiors of the four wings differ in their architectural styles and their use of space. When Mills took over in 1849, he included a double, semicircular, three-story flying marble staircase projecting from the north wall. This graceful staircase provides an elegant center to the gallery leading up to the Great Hall on the third floor.

The interiors were designed to display patent models, as well as provide office space. One visitor found that "side by side with the greatest inventions of the age, are some of the craziest products of the human brain.... One is surprised at the wisdom and foolishness of man's intellect.... From the fool's point of view it would seem that when an idea of a patent creeps into an inventor's head, common sense flies out the window."

After the fire of 1877, a Victorian style was adopted for the Great Hall on the south wing's third floor (National Portrait Gallery). The Cluss and Schulze design used cast-iron columns on top of square piers to support the iron balconies in the side areas. The relief panels and portraits were designed by Casper Buberl and cast in white cement. The four portraits are of early American inventors: Benjamin Franklin, Thomas Jefferson, Robert Fulton, and Eli Whitney. The panels are allegorical depictions of fire, electricity and magnetism, and water (north wall), and of agriculture, industry and invention, and mining (south wall). The Minton tile floor is original. The stained glass windows and paint-and-stencil designs were included in the 1976 renovation.

## National Portrait Gallery

Entrance on F St. ☎ 357-2700. Web: www.npg.si.edu. Open daily 10–5:30. Closed on Christmas Day. Wheelchair accessible. Gift shop. Shares cafeteria.

**Note:** In Jan 2000, this museum closed for a three-year renovation.

**Highlights:** (old collection before current renovation) Gilbert Stuart's "Lansdowne" *George Washington* and the Hall of Presidents.

### History

The concept of a national portrait gallery goes back to the Revolutionary War, when Charles Willson Peale, noted American painter and portraitist, took up the mission of creating a gallery to portray the great men of his era. In 1857, Congress commissioned George Peter Alexander Healy to paint a series of presidential portraits for the White House. More than a century later, in 1962, an act of Congress created the National Portrait Gallery, describing it as "a free public museum for the exhibition and study of portraiture and statuary depicting men and women who have made significant contributions to the history, development, and culture of the people of the United States, and the artists who created such portraiture and statuary." Today the gallery's collection consists of more than 4,000 images in a wide range of media.

## National Museum of American Art

Entrance on G St. ☎ 357-2700. Web: www.nmaa.si.edu. Open daily 10–5:30. Closed Christmas Day. Wheelchair accessible. Gift shop. Cafeteria.

The National Museum of American Art (NMAA) houses the largest collection of American art in the world—35,000 works reflecting American's ethnic, geographic, cultural, and religious diversity.

**Note:** In Jan 2000, this museum closed for a three-year renovation.

**Highlights:** (old collection before current renovation) The Gilded Age collection, including Abbott Henderson Thayer's *Angel* and stained glass windows by John La Farge; James Hampton's room-size *The Throne of the Third Heaven of the Nations Milennium General Assembly.*

### History

The origins of the collection date back to 1829, when Washington resident John Varden decided to create a permanent museum with his collection of European art. Varden kept his collection in his home, but exhibited the collection in 1841 in the newly constructed Patent Office Building. In 1858, many items from the Patent Office, including some works from Varden's collection, were moved to the newly opened Smithsonian Institution, and from 1865 until the end of the century most of the artwork was placed in the Library of Congress or on loan to the Corcoran Gallery of Art.

In 1906, the gift of a benefactor (Harriet Lane Johnston, niece of President James Buchanan and an art collector) focused attention on the need for a National Gallery of Art to house these gifts and others. From 1910 to 1968, the collection was in a specially designed gallery in the Smithsonian's Natural History Museum. As Andrew W. Mellon claimed the name National Gallery of Art for his gift to the nation, the collection's name changed to the National Collection of Fine Art in 1957 when the Old Patent Office Building was turned over to the Smithsonian. In 1980 the name was changed to the National Museum of American Art.

The museum has taken as its mission "a commitment to the diversity of American art and to the understanding, enjoyment, and preservation of America's great visual achievements."

Around the corner from the museum and gallery is the landmark **Victor Building,** 9th and H Sts N.W. One of the oldest buildings in the downtown area, the Victor Building was constructed by Washington patent attorney Victor J. Evans. Evans gave a major collection of Native American artifacts to the Smithsonian's Museum of Natural History. For many years the Victor Building was occupied by Central Liquors, a large liquor store.

The Smithsonian purchased the structure in summer 1999. The Renaissance revival façade has been preserved, while the interior of the building has been gutted. The Smithsonian plans on using a portion of the building to house employ-ees of both the Museum of American Art and the Portrait Gallery, and to open a portion of the renovated building to the public as a new Center for American Art. At this facility the public will be able to search a database of 500,000 items and use image collections for research. Relocating the museum and gallery employees to the renovated Victor Building will give the museum and gallery an additional 60,000 square ft of space for exhibitions and public events.

**Diversion:**
Walk one block north to the **Calvary Baptist Church** (1866; Adolph Cluss; 1894, James G. Hill; 1925–29, Arthur Heaton) at 755 8th St N.W., ☎ 347-8355. This church has a long tradition of activism. The red brick Victorian structure was built by a small number of pro-Union and antislavery Baptists. Their social pro-gressiveness continued after the Civil War. In 1885 a member of the church, Dr. E. M. Gallaudet, after whom Gallaudet College is named, founded the city's first mission for the hearing-impaired at the church. In 1864, Woodward Hall, de-signed by James G. Hall, was added as a Sunday school building. The building was named for a philanthropic member of the congregation, S. W. Woodward of the department store chain Woodward & Lothrop. Another addition is the Green Memorial Building (1925; Arthur Heaton). The 5,000-pipe Mohler organ in the sanctuary was the largest in Washington when it was installed in 1927.

Continue north one block to the **Greater New Hope Baptist Church** (1897; Stutz and Pease) at 816 8th St N.W., ☎ 842-1036. Originally built for the Wash-ington Hebrew Congregation, this strongly Byzantine-like church has minaret towers, octagonal open belfries, and a large Star of David window. The synagogue was sold to the Greater New Hope Baptist Church in 1955.

Walk west one block to 9th St and the **Washington Convention Center** (1983; Welton Becket); 900 9th St N.W., ☎ 789-1600, Web: www.dcconven-tion.com. A modern design of glass and preformed concrete, the Convention Cen-ter is Washington's major facility for national and international meetings and expositions. The facility spans nearly 10 acres, has 380,000 square ft of exhibit space, and hosts an average of 30 conventions a year.

Coming in 2003 is a new convention center, which will be twice as large as the existing one. The new facility is being built at Mount Vernon Square, 9th and L Sts N.W. When that center opens, the old facility will close. Currently the City Coun-cil is trying to decide how the old convention center building will be used.

The old **Carnegie Library** (1903) at Mount Vernon Square, which is bounded by 7th St N.W. on the east, 9th St N.W. on the west, and Mount Vernon Place N.W. on both the north and south sides, is slated to reopen in 2003 as a city mu-seum operated by the Washington Historical Society. The museum will house Dis-trict archives and artifacts and also have a multimedia theater and a Visitors Center.

## Martin Luther King Library
901 G St N.W. ☎ 727-1126. Web: www.dclibrary.org/mlk. Opens at 10 A.M. Mon–Sat; noon on Sun. Closing hours change periodically.

From the National Portrait Gallery, turn west on G St and walk one block to the Martin Luther King Memorial Library (1972; Ludwig Mies van der Rohe). Wash-ington's central public library is home to two outstanding collections: the **Wash-**

**ingtoniana Collection** of materials pertaining to the city's history and the **Black Studies Collection** of materials pertaining to both local and national African American history. This glass-box building was one of the last projects designed by Ludwig Mies van der Rohe before his death in 1969. The *American Institute of Architects Journal* described the library as "unadorned, its beauty being revealed in its quiet and harmonious proportions." Facing a large plaza (where a good number of the city's homeless spend their days) the G St and the 9th St façades are raised on stilts, with the ground level enclosed by a cream-colored brick exterior wall placed behind a row of steel columns.

The city's public library system was begun in the early 1890s when a citizens' group presented a collection of 12,000 books to the city to start a public library. (The first nonpublic library was established at 13th St and Pennsylvania Ave N.W. in 1812; it was open two days a week for two hours only to shareholders.)

Directly across the plaza from the library is the **Mather Building** (1917–18; Clarence G. Harding) at 916–918 G St N.W. Now owned by the University of the District of Columbia and boarded up, this office building, with its Gothic facing of white glazed terra-cotta, very likely housed law offices and real estate–related businesses in its day.

Continue west on G St to 10th St and turn south.

**Diversion:**
At the corner of 10th and G Sts is **St. Patrick's Roman Catholic Church** (1884; architect unknown), 619 10th St N.W., ☎ 347-2713. This church was founded at the urging of James Hoban, architect of the White House, for the Irish stonemasons who worked on the federal buildings. The property was purchased in 1794 for £80 sterling. By 1810 the church had a brick building for services. St. Patrick's was the first church in Washington to possess an organ.

> ### *Washington Notes*
> For part of the Civil War, St. Patrick's served as a hospital. Mary Surratt, one of its parishioners, was hanged in 1865 for the assassination of Abraham Lincoln. Pastor Jacob Walter defied public opprobrium to stand next to her on the gallows.

In 1872, the cornerstone for the present Victorian Gothic revival–style building was laid. The church was completed in 1884. The exterior of the church is made of blue-gray gneiss and trimmed with buff-color sandstone and polished rose-and-gray granite. The interior of the church, accented with Carrara, Vermont, and Mexican marble statues, was renovated for the parish's 1994 bicentennial.

## Ford's Theatre
511 10th St N.W. ☎ 426-6924. Web: www.nps.gov/foth. Open daily 9–5 except Christmas Day and except when there are matinees and rehearsals in the theater. Self-directed tour all day. Fifteen-minute narratives at quarter past the hour for the first three and the last three hours of operation. Wheelchair accessible. Bookstore and museum.

Walk two blocks south on 10th St to Ford's Theatre (1863, James J. Gifford, architect; 1968, Macomber & Peter; William Haussman, restoration; DL). Petersen House (DL; 516 10th St N.W.; same phone number as Ford's Theatre) is directly across the street. Because Ford's Theatre and Petersen House are among the most popular attractions in the city, there are plans that, beginning in spring 2000, admission will be by timed tickets. A National Park Service attendant hands out same-day, timed tickets, starting at 9 A.M. daily.

America has lost four presidents to the assassin's bullet (Lincoln, Garfield, McKinley, Kennedy), but Petersen House—where Lincoln died—is the only site preserved as it was at the time of the assassination. Lincoln was shot on April 14, 1865, and died the next morning.

**Highlights:** The museum in the theater's basement. The presidential box, in the main part of the theater, which is furnished much as it was the night Lincoln was assassinated.

### History

John T. Ford, a theatrical entrepreneur successful both in Philadelphia (then America's leading theater town) and Baltimore, saw opportunities for big profits in Washington City, which had thousands of Union troops and fashionable residents. Ford bought the First Baptist Church from its congregation and built Ford's Theatre on the site. He also bought the building next to the theater (where the ticket office is now). Ford's son, Harry, who helped manage the theater, lived on the upper floors, while downstairs on the ground floor was the Star Saloon, where John Wilkes Booth, Lincoln's assassin, had a drink just before entering the theater the night of the assassination. One of the leading matinee idols of his day, the 26-year-old Booth, a staunch Southern sympathizer, was one of the highest-paid actors in the country, earning $20,000 in 1863. Booth knew Ford and Laura Keene, the lead actress in *Our American Cousin,* the play being performed when he shot Lincoln.

On the evening of April 14, 1865, Lincoln entered the president's box to thunderous applause from the audience. About an hour after the president's arrival, Booth entered the box from the back, shot Lincoln with a small pistol through the back of the head, stabbed the president's guest, and leapt from the box to the stage, crying "Sic semper tyrannus!" ("Thus always to tyrants!") The spur on Booth's boot caught in the American flag draped over the front of the president's box, causing Booth to fall on the stage and break his leg. Booth stumbled off the stage in front of a horrified audience and past old friends and fellow players backstage who had no idea what had just happened.

Dr. Charles Leale, a 23-year-old assistant surgeon with the United States Volunteers, rushed to the president's box, saw the seriousness of the wound, and advised against trying to transport the president down the bumpy cobblestones of Pennsylvania Ave to the White House. A Swedish tailor named William Petersen had a boardinghouse across the street, which was popular with Union soldiers. Leale had Lincoln carried there.

As the president lay in a coma, First Lady Mary Todd Lincoln sat in the front parlor, weeping uncontrollably. The bedroom next to the parlor was taken over by Secretary of War Edwin M. Stanton, who immediately began taking statements from those present. Throughout the night, members of the president's cabinet and his friends made their way to the little house on 10th St to say their good-byes, while a large crowd waited outside in the rain. When Lincoln died in the early morning hours of April 15, General Stanton said, "Now he belongs to the ages."

Meanwhile, Booth made his getaway out of the city and into rural Virginia, where he was shot ten days later while trying to escape from a burning barn. The bullet pierced Booth's spine, paralyzing him from the neck down. As he lay dying, he asked one of the soldiers to raise his hands so he could see them. Staring at his hands, he said, "Useless, useless," and died.

Ford's Theatre was closed immediately following the assassination. When Ford tried to reopen the theater in July 1865, the ensuing threats of violence caused the federal government to cancel the performance. One year later, in 1866, Ford sold the building to the government. (Ford was a major contributor to the statue of Abraham Lincoln that now stands in front of the Superior Courthouse of the District of Columbia.) The War Department used the theater building to house the Record and Pension Bureau and the Army Medical Museum. The museum moved out in 1887, and the War Department left in 1893 after the collapse of the interior. In 1933, the National Park Service (NPS) took over the building. In 1964, the NPS received approval to restore the building to its original condition using Mathew Brady photographs of the interior. In 1968, Ford's Theatre reopened, and in 1990, the basement museum opened.

The death of the president in a theatrical establishment was a scandal in many parts of the nation. In Detroit, a preacher told his congregation, "Would that Mr. Lincoln had fallen elsewhere than at the very gates of hell—in the theater. How awful and severe the rebuke which God has administered to the nation for pampering such demoralizing places. The blood of Abraham Lincoln can never be effaced from the stage!"

### Washington Notes

There are several odd coincidences connecting Abraham Lincoln and John Wilkes Booth. Booth was known to Lincoln, who, as a great lover of theater, went to plays whenever he had the chance. After seeing Booth perform in 1864, Lincoln invited him to a White House reception. Booth never responded to the invitation. Several weeks before the assassination, Booth rented a room in Petersen's boardinghouse—the same room in which the president died. On the day Booth's brother Edwin, another leading actor of the time, was being buried in New York in 1893, all three of the upper floors of Ford's Theatre, then a government office building, collapsed into the basement, killing 22 workers and seriously injuring 68 more.

## Interior

The self-guided tour of Ford's Theater consists of a simple U-shaped walk from the back of the theater to the front, a view of the **president's box** (which has the original sofa and portrait of George Washington), and a tour of the **basement museum.** Most of the museum's artifacts are from the collection of O. H. Oldroyd, a great admirer of Lincoln. The items were displayed in Lincoln's childhood home in Springfield, Illinois, for ten years before being placed in the Petersen House. When the basement museum opened, the collection moved to Ford's Theatre.

Included in the collection are the playbill from the performance on the night of the assassination, the pistol and dagger used by Booth, and a sleeve of the president's coat, torn from his body as he was carried from the theater. Large glass cases exhibit photographs of the conspirators, personal items from Lincoln and his wife and children, and political memorabilia of the time.

## Petersen House

The Petersen House, also known as The House Where Lincoln Died, has been restored to its original appearance and contains antique furniture from the period. The rugs and wallpaper are reproductions of the originals. On the self-guided tour visitors view the front parlor where Mary Todd Lincoln waited, the bedroom/parlor where General Stanton worked through the night, and the back bedroom where the president lay. The walnut, four-poster bed is a copy of the original. Two prints of paintings by Rosa Bonheur hang above the bed, as they did the night Lincoln died.

# National Museum of Women in the Arts

1250 New York Ave, N.W. ☎ 783-5000. Web: www.nmwa.org. Open Mon–Sat 10–5; Sun noon–5. Closed Thanksgiving, Christmas Day, and New Year's Day. Admission: donation. Guided tours by appointment. Wheelchair accessible. Museum shop and café. Library available by appointment.

Walk south one block to E St, then walk three blocks west to 13th St, and then two blocks north to New York Ave and the National Museum of Women in the Arts (NMWA) (1907–8; Wood, Donn & Deming; Waddy B. Wood, architect in charge; 1987 renovations, Keyes Condon Florance Architects; DL). NMWA's mission is to showcase and support women's artistic endeavors in all media. NMWA has more than 2,500 works in its permanent collection by over 600 women artists from some 25 different countries. The Library and Research Center holds the world's most comprehensive source of information on women in the arts.

**Highlights:** Hollis Sigler's *To Kiss the Spirits: Now, This Is What It Is Really Like* (second-floor landing), the Eulabee Dix collection of miniature portraits (fourth floor), and the Library and Research Center.

### History

The structure was built as a Masonic lodge. President Theodore Roosevelt presided over the laying of the cornerstone in 1907, using the trowel George Washington, a Mason, used to lay the cornerstone of the Capitol in 1793. From 1910 to 1921, the upper two floors were used by George Washington University's Law School, and in 1916 the first-floor auditorium was remodeled to show silent films. From 1942 to 1983, the building housed the Pix Movie Theatre and then the Town Theatre. In 1968, the Town renovated its interior to accommodate a wider screen and stereophonic sound, but by then the neighborhood had become run-down. Lack of business finally closed the Town Theatre in 1983.

The following year the building was bought for the purpose of housing the National Museum of Women in the Arts, and an extensive interior renovation was undertaken. A Washington architectural firm designed the interior in consultation with museum specialist David Scott. James Madison Cutts designed the two-level trapezoidal marble stairway leading from the Great Hall to the mezzanine. The original ceiling was retained and restored. In 1993, the property next to the museum was purchased and renovated; it opened in 1997 as the Elisabeth A. Kasser Wing.

In the early 1960s, the museum's founder and principal benefactor, Wilhelmina "Billie" Cole Holladay, and her husband, Wallace, perceived a general lack of interest in women artists. When the Holladays returned from a European trip, they discovered they could find nothing in any of the major art history texts about the women artists whose works they'd just seen in European museums. (H. W. Janson's standard text *History of Art* didn't include any women artists—not even the much cited Mary Cassatt—until the third edition was published in 1986.) In the 18C and 19C women were frequently barred from art schools and art societies, and, as the Holladays learned, even into the mid-20C, women's work did not always garner the respect it deserved. The Holladays began collecting art by women from all eras, determined to found a museum dedicated to honoring and supporting women in the arts. Their collection formed the nucleus of NMWA's permanent collection.

## Exterior

This Renaissance revival–styled, steel-framed building with its Indiana limestone, terra-cotta, and light gray brick façade is built on a trapezoidal site formed by the intersections of 13th St, New York Ave, and H St. Large doors rounded at the top and windows accent the building's massive base. A colonnade flanked with piers lines the superstructure. Above the attic level, a decorative terra-cotta frieze encircles the building.

## Interior

Enter the main lobby. The gift shop is on the east side and the information desk and **Education Resource Center** are straight ahead. The center has explanatory materials for adults and books and hands-on activities for children. From the Resource Center, turn west to the **Lockheed Martin Great Hall.** (Martin Marietta Corporation was one of the museum's original sponsors.) Walk to the center of the hall and turn east. On the east wall of the mezzanine is the wide screen used by the Town Theatre to show movies. Look up at the gilded ceiling with its three ornate crystal chandeliers. Note the stone escutcheon with an enormous *M* in its center, a reminder of the building's original Masons. Climb the stairs to the mezzanine, where temporary exhibits are shown next to the museum's restaurant.

Proceed up the stairs to the second floor (elevators are located at both ends of the building) to the temporary exhibits. These focus on individual artists or on the work of women from a particular country or region.

Continue up the marble staircase to the landing between floors to *To Kiss the Spirits: Now, This Is What It Is Really Like* (1993; Hollis Sigler), a lovely yet unsettling painting of angels ascending a golden staircase that stretches from a mundane suburban housing development to a dark blue sky. The painting is a finale to Sigler's series *Breast Cancer Journal: Walking with the Ghosts of My Grandmothers,* which examined the high incidence of breast cancer in America in terms of Sigler's own experience with the disease.

Continue up to the third floor to selections from the museum's **permanent collection.** In the gallery to the left of the stairs is *Sheep by the Sea* (1869; Rosa Bonheur). Bonheur, who was trained by her father, is recognized as the great animal painter of the 19C. (A print of one of her paintings hung over the bed in which Abraham Lincoln died.) In pursuit of her art, she visited horse fairs and slaughterhouses, places women were not generally allowed. In order not to cause comment, Bonheur dressed as a man (for which she needed legal authorization), which caused comment anyway.

*Lady with a Bowl of Violets* (1910; Lilla Cabot Perry), an American impressionist work, is one of the museum's most popular paintings. This painting incorporates influences from American, French, and Japanese art. Perry, an American, spent ten years living next door to Monet at Giverny. What she learned about impressionism she brought back to the turn-of-the-century Boston School of painters. In 1898, Perry and her family moved to Japan. Perry brought impressionism to Tokyo, while also absorbing Japanese influences.

Continue into the adjoining gallery to *Love's Young Dream* (1887; Jennie Augusta Brownscombe). The Norman Rockwell of her time, Brownscombe specialized in the sentimental genre painting that was popular in America at the same time as the impressionist movement was taking hold in Europe. *Love's Young Dream* was one of the most popular of Brownscombe's magazine illustrations and typical of the artist's nostalgic portrayal of 19C American life.

In the gallery to the right of the stairs is *Bacchus #3* (1978; Elaine Fried de Kooning). De Kooning was a major player in the abstract expressionist movement in New York in the 1950s and the wife of abstract expressionist painter Willem de Kooning. The figures of the drunken god and his handmaidens are transformed into energized spirals of line and color. Nearby is *Indian, Indio, Indigenous* (1992; Jaune Quick-To-See Smith), a Native American artist whose paintings address the myths of her ancestors in the context of current issues. Included in this "narrative landscape" are the masthead of a reservation newspaper, photocopies of George Catlin's drawings of Native Americans (displayed in the National Museum of American Art), a portion of a U.S. map, pictographs of bear, deer, and a coyote, and a painted bust.

In an adjoining gallery is *Portrait of a Noblewoman* (1580; Lavinia Fontana), a "dowry" portrait whose purpose was to record the valuables the woman brings to the match. This includes a heavily embroidered overdress and the gold and ruby jewelry she wears. Her right hand caresses a small lapdog, a representation of marital fidelity. Maria Sibylla Merian, whose illustrations for the book *Dissertation in Insect Generations and Metamorphosis in Surinam* (1719) are on display here, is considered one of the foremost painters of flowers, fruits, insects, and reptiles. Her paintings and copperplate engravings contributed not only to the artistic world but also had enormous impact on the study of natural sciences.

Also on the third floor is the **Rose Bente Lee Sculpture Gallery,** where a changing selection of sculpture from the museum's permanent collection is exhibited.

On the museum's fourth floor is NMWA's **Library and Research Center,** and the **Eulabee Dix Gallery** (directly ahead upon exiting the elevator), where Dix's miniature portraits painted on ivory are displayed, along with special exhibits. The fifth floor houses the museum auditorium and staff offices.

Take the elevator down to the mezzanine level and stop by the **Radice Room,** tucked into the southwest corner. Here is the whimsical ceramic *Oeuf l'arche de Noe* (c. 1951) by Lourdes Rodriguez.

If you wish to go to the nearest Metro station, exit the museum through the main door onto H St. Walk a half-block west to the corner. Two blocks south from here is the Metro Center station (Blue/Orange/Red Lines).

**Diversion:**

Walk west on New York Ave one block to the **New York Avenue Presbyterian Church** (1950; Delos H. Smith); 1313 New York Ave N.W. ☎ 393-3700. Web: www.nyapc.org. This church is often called the Church of Presidents because so many presidents have worshiped here. There are tours on Sun following the 9 and 11 A.M. services. The sanctuary is open Mon and Tues until 9; Wed, Thurs, and Fri until 5; a tour guide is available.

> ### Washington Notes
>
> Abraham Lincoln was a regular attendee during the Civil War, although he never became an official member of the congregation. He would often slip in the side door to his pew for a brief prayer. Lincoln held the strong conviction that a man should stand during his prayers and he did so, even though the custom was for the congregation to remain seated while praying. In the sanctuary is a window portraying Abraham Lincoln standing during prayer.

The New York Avenue Presbyterian Church was formed in 1859 from the union of the F St Associate Reformed Presbyterian Church and the Second Presbyterian Church. The F St Associate Church was begun in 1793 by the Scottish stonemasons and carpenters working on the construction of the White House. They worshiped in a carpenter shop temporarily erected on the White House grounds and later in a corner of the Treasury Building. In 1859, they united with the Second Presbyterian Church, which had been founded in 1819. In 1820, the Second Presbyterian Church purchased the present site from Richard Cutts, brother-in-law of Dolley Madison. A church resembling the current one was built.

When a hurricane-like windstorm blew off the wooden steeple in 1896, the steeple and a set of chimes were given to the church by the Robert Todd Lincoln family. In 1950, it was determined the congregation needed more space, and a new, bigger but similar-looking church was erected.

To continue to the next walk, from 13th St and New York Ave proceed a half-block north on 13th St to H St, then three blocks west on H St to Lafayette Square.

# 14 · 16th Street N.W.

Metro: Red Line to Farragut North or Blue/Orange Line to Farragut West.
Bus: D2, D4, X2, 38B, or 80S.

Sixteenth St, which runs north from the White House for about seven miles to the District's border with Maryland, is a major city thoroughfare. An eclectic mix of gracious turn-of-the-century homes, now converted to offices, embassies, and residences, line the street along with apartment buildings, churches, and row houses. The street's history is as mixed as its architecture. The southern portion of the street—from Lafayette Park to Meridian Hill—went from outlying farmland prior to the Civil War to an upscale enclave by the turn of the century. With the Depression and other economic shifts, some of the mansions were carved up into boardinghouses for a working-class population, others became offices, and some were returned to their former glory. The 16th St area is home to many newly ar-

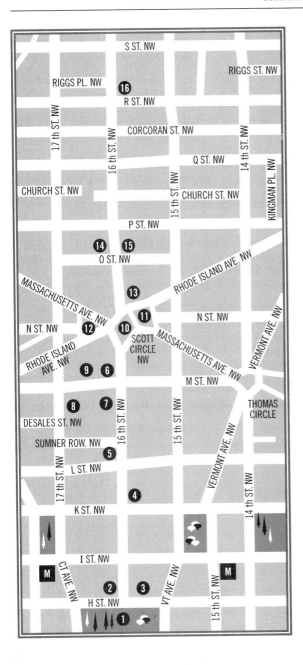

1 Lafayette Square
2 Hay-Adams Hotel
3 St. John's Parish House
4 St. Regis Hotel
5 The Presidential
6 The Jefferson
7 National Geographic Society
8 Explorers Hall
9 Metropolitan African Methodist
   Episcopal Church

10 Scott Circle
11 Memorial to Dr. Samuel Hahnemann
12 Statue of Daniel Webster
13 General Scott Building
14 National Wildlife Federation Building
15 Susan Shields Residence
16 The Chastleton

rived immigrants in Adams Morgan (see Walk 15: "Adams Morgan") as well as working- and middle-class families along other stretches. Along 16th St, perhaps more than in other areas of the city, people of differing backgrounds and economic situations come together in lively neighborhoods.

### History

Much of the upper 16th St area in the early 19C was part of Mount Pleasant, a farm owned by Georgetown merchant Robert Peter. In 1816 Commodore David Porter built a large home at the top of Meridian Hill, which takes its name from the fact that the hill is situated on the official meridian of the U.S., established Dec 20, 1793, on the north-south axis from the White House. Porter's house burned down in 1863. Up until the 1870s the land between Lafayette Square and Meridian Hill was sparsely developed with only a few homes and shanties. Here, as in many of the other undeveloped areas of the city, the lanes were muddy, animals roamed freely, and garbage proliferated. The state of 16th St was indicative of the problems of the city at large; Vermont senator George F. Edmunds complained of "the infinite, abominable nuisance of cows, and horses and sheep and goats, running through all the streets of this city, and whenever we appropriate money to set up a shade tree, there comes along a cow or a horse or a goat, and tears it down the next day."

To address these problems, a public improvement board was established in 1871, with Alexander "Boss" Shepherd as chairman. Shepherd spent nearly $20 million, many millions more than had been appropriated. Despite the fact that his overspending bankrupted the city, Shepherd did much to improve it—paving roads, laying gas pipes, and creating sewer systems (see Walk 16: "Dupont Circle West Area"). Shepherd's improvements helped spur building booms throughout the city.

In 1887 more than 2,450 building permits were issued. The trend was to purchase large chunks of land for development. Pacific (Dupont) Circle, Kalorama Heights, Chevy Chase, Cleveland Park, and stretches along Massachusetts Ave underwent major development. In 1887 former Missouri senator John B. Henderson and his wife, Mary Foote Henderson, bought numerous lots along 16th St with the intention of transforming it into a grand "Avenue of the Presidents" lined with embassies. On a six-acre plot the Hendersons built a huge Romanesque revival mansion designed by E. C. Gardner, which became known as Boundary Castle. While only a small portion of the Henderson home remains—a section of retaining wall on 16th St between Florida Ave and Belmont St—16th St owes much of its character to Mrs. Mary Foote Henderson's vision. Development at first was slow, especially since 16th St was not graded or paved until after 1900.

In 1898 the Hendersons retained architect Paul Pelz to design (but not build) a grand, new presidential mansion for the summit of Meridian Hill. In the early 1900s Mrs. Henderson had architect George Oakley Totten design and build nine mansions that she hoped to lease to embassies. Socialites and government officials occupied these houses and others, and some embassies eventually moved to the area also. To further beautify the neighborhood, Mrs. Henderson proposed a park for Meridian Hill in 1906, which the Commission of Fine Arts approved in 1914. Meridian Hill Park (1913; George Burnap; 1919–30; Ferruccio Vitale; completed by Horace W. Peaslee) features a cascading water staircase based on those in 17C Italian and English gardens.

The city was undergoing development in other areas as well. The 1893 Chicago World's Fair inspired many to make Washington, D.C., a beautiful capital. In 1901 Michigan senator James McMillan sponsored a resolution to establish the McMillan Commission to plan improvements for the city's park system. Private developers, encouraged by the McMillan Commission, constructed many new buildings.

Through 1929 16th St between Lafayette Park and Scott Circle remained zoned as a residential area, the only such zoning in the immediate vicinity of the White House. In the 1930s house assessments increased, owners sold their properties, and hotels and apartment buildings were constructed on lots that once housed mansions. Though altered over the years, 16th St still features some of the city's finest early-20C architecture, including many buildings with rich and colorful histories.

## Hay-Adams Hotel

Begin at Lafayette Square (see Walk 9: "The White House and Lafayette Square"). Continue east along H St to the Hay-Adams Hotel (1928; Mirhan Mesrobian; DL) at 800 16th St N.W., ☎ 638-6600. The hotel was built in the Italian Renaissance style. Inside, ceiling treatments include Tudor, Elizabethan, and Italian motifs. The Hay-Adams's two restaurants are favorite spots among the Washington elite for power breakfasts, lunches, and dinners. The Lafayette Restaurant (open for breakfast Mon–Fri 6:30–11:30; Sat–Sun 7–10:30; for lunch Mon–Fri 12–2; for dinner daily 6–10; for brunch Sat–Sun 11:30–2; reservations suggested) is light and airy with seven windows facing the White House. Off the Record (open Mon–Fri 4:30 P.M.–12 A.M.; Fri–Sat 4:30 P.M.–1 A.M.), which has the air of a gentleman's club with wood paneling, fireplaces, and couches, offers a light lunch-and-dinner menu as well as evening piano tunes. The hotel's 143 guest rooms and suites provide views of the White House and St. John's Church.

### History

The Hay-Adams Hotel was built on the site of the former homes of John Hay and Henry Adams. Hay, Lincoln's private secretary and secretary of state under Presidents William McKinley and Theodore Roosevelt, and Adams, great-grandson of John Adams, purchased adjacent lots on the corner of H and 16th Sts N.W. in 1884. The Hay and Adams families were close friends. To convince John Hay to build the double houses, Adams wrote to Hay saying "I need not say how eager I am to spend your money to have you next door. I would sacrifice your last dollar."

Adams commissioned architect Henry Hobson Richardson, a classmate at Harvard, to design homes for the two men. The homes soon became centers of Washington social life and hosted notable artists, writers, and politicians. In 1905, upon Hay's death, the house was given to Senator James Wolcott Wadsworth, who had married Alice Hay, John Hay's daughter. When Adams died in 1918, his home became the Brazilian Embassy.

Developer Harry Wardman purchased the properties in 1927 and demolished the two houses. In their place, with the help of architect Mihran Mesrobian, he built the Hay-Adams House, which opened in 1928 "to provide for the socially elite as well as men and women who loom large in the country's life." The hotel had cost $90,000 and featured walnut wainscotting, decorative ceilings, and intricate architectural details. Among the guests were Charles Lindbergh, Amelia Earhart, Sinclair Lewis, and Ethel Barrymore. Two years after opening, the Hay-Adams boasted the first air-conditioned dining room in Washington.

The Depression ended the era of elegance and opulence in the District, but the hotel was able to maintain its reputation. The hotel was bought and sold by several developers until David Murdock finally purchased it in 1983. That same year he began renovations. In 1989, a group of private investors formed the Hay-Adams Limited Partnership, which continues to operate the hotel today.

> ### Washington Notes
> During the early 1980s, Colonel Oliver North housed and entertained potential donors to the Iran-Contra cause at the Hay-Adams Hotel. Presumably, North chose this hotel because of its proximity to his office at the Old Executive Office Building, as well as for the hotel's historic reputation and lavish style.
>
> Coincidentally, during the 1860s this area was the location of other clandestine activity. The site of the hotel was once the home of sociable widow Rose O'Neal Greenhow. Greenhow was a Confederate spy who "entertained" Union soldiers and officers in her home. Legend has it that secrets leaked to her and passed to Confederate General Beauregard in code enabled Beauregard to prepare his troops for the skirmish known as the Second Battle of Bull Run.

### Exterior

The hotel represents a blend of English and Italian Renaissance architecture from several periods. The nine-story building is divided into three vertical segments. The middle structure, or pavilion, features five horizontal bands—a base, a top segment, and three two-story sections in the classical style.

### Interior

The hotel lobby, dining room, and lounge have intricate ornamental ceiling work and paneling.

For St. John's Parish House, see Walk 9: "The White House and Lafayette Square."

## St. Regis Hotel

Continue east on H St to 16th St. Turn left, or north, on 16th St and walk to the St. Regis Hotel (1925; Mihran Mesrobian; 1987 renovation, Brennan Beer Gorman) at 923 16th St N.W., ☎ 638-2626.

## History

The St. Regis Hotel, formerly the Sheraton-Carlton, and originally the Carlton, was built on the site of Nicholas Anderson's former residence. The Anderson family had sold the property in 1918; the house had several owners before Anna C. Walker bought it on May 1, 1924, and sold it the same day to Henry Wardman. Wardman leveled the house in Feb 1925 to make way for the hotel.

A relatively small facility designed for an elite clientele, the Carlton had 257 rooms. Each room was as large as two to six typical hotel suites and featured walnut furnishings, a grand piano, oversize bathtubs, and telephones in the bathrooms. The hotel was advertised as "uncompromisingly exclusive."

### Washington Notes

Having made his fortune by working—he was a tradesman—Wardman was denied entry into Washington's elite social circles. It was rumored that Wardman built the hotel in reaction to this exclusion.

Wardman lost the Carlton Hotel and most of his other properties in 1932, as a result of the Depression. The hotel survived because of labor leaders John L. Lewis (United Mine Workers) and Philip Murray (Congress of Industrial Organizations), who, along with the United Steel Workers, set up headquarters in the building and maintained official suites.

During Franklin Delano Roosevelt's presidency, the Carlton served as entertainment headquarters for State Department functions. Located only two blocks from the White House, the Carlton was a favorite dining spot for diplomats and government officials.

### Washington Notes

One famous noontime frequenter of the Carlton was World War I hero General John Pershing. President Truman utilized the Carlton for social functions while the White House was being restored in the 1950s. Representative Edward A. Kennedy of New Jersey died after falling six stories into the hotel's south courtyard. Kennedy supposedly had walked through a wall of glass after turning the wrong direction in a darkened hallway.

The Washington Sheraton Corporation bought the Carlton in 1954, renamed it the Sheraton-Carlton, and in 1958 remodeled it. In 1987 the hotel underwent a $16 million renovation. In April 1999, the hotel became the St. Regis.

## Exterior

The hotel, designed in the genre of small, exclusive European hotels, such as Claridge's of London, incorporates Italian Renaissance details but places them in a simpler, classical context. Mesrobian created three horizontal layers, according to classical tradition. The structure rises from granite to limestone to brick, becoming more intricate and decorative with each layer.

## Interior

Not much remains of the building's original interior. The Art Moderne Lounge featured neon, red-and-white upholstered chairs, and a "revolving servidor" bar which, in compliance with D.C. law, separated the bartender from the clients via a revolving door. The original sea nymph statue and fountain in the garden were replaced by a bronze cherub. Both of these architectural changes occurred during the Carlton's 1958 remodeling.

## The Presidential

Continue north on 16th St and proceed one block to the Presidential (1922; Appleton P. Clark, Jr.) at 1026 16th St N.W., a private, cooperative residence.

### History

The wealthy widow Mrs. Clara R. Dennis built this structure as an investment shortly after the District Zoning Board decided to allow apartment houses south of Scott Circle. Because Dennis hoped that the $350,000 apartment building would house President Harding's cabinet members and their families, she named the building the Presidential. When the building opened in 1923, it contained 46 rental units, ranging from kitchen-less bachelor apartments to large, luxurious units. Like the Jefferson up the street, the Presidential was one of the city's most prestigious apartment houses in the 1920s. It offered the services of doormen, maids, and round-the-clock elevator attendants. The building has since been converted to a cooperative apartment house with offices on the first floor.

### Interior

The elegant lobby remains intact. It features a black-and-white marble parquet floor and an ornamental plaster ceiling with gold-leaf highlights styled in the genre of late-18C English country houses. The Presidential remains one of the oldest and most elegant buildings in this section of the city.

Cross the street and continue one block north to the Pullman Mansion (1910; architect unknown) at 1119 16th St N.W. The mansion was built by Mrs. George M. Pullman, widow of the sleeping-car magnate. Mrs. Pullman never occupied the house. The grand, stone mansion and other buildings on the property have been used as offices by the Soviets and later the former-Soviet governments for decades.

## The Jefferson

Continue north on 16th St to the Jefferson (1923; Jules Henri de Sibour), 1200 16th St at 16th and M Sts N.W., ☎ 347-2200. Now a hotel, the building was constructed as a luxury apartment building.

### History

Located four blocks from the White House, the Jefferson housed members of Washington society during the 1920s. Construction of the 100-room Jefferson Apartments cost an estimated $450,000. In 1931, General A. R. Glancy purchased the building. During World War II military troops lived in the Jefferson. In 1955, the building was transformed into a hotel called the Jefferson. Actors and dignitaries stayed at the hotel in the late 1950s and 1960s. Attorney Edward Bennett Williams, former owner of the Baltimore Orioles, bought the hotel in the 1970s and invested $7 million in renovations and the purchase of antiques for the guest rooms and public spaces.

### Washington Notes

During the Reagan Administration, the Jefferson was known by some as the White House North because many top government officials stayed there. Oliver North secretly resided at the Jefferson during the Iran-Contra trials. George Bush's family booked most of the hotel for Bush's presidential inauguration.

In the 1990s President Clinton's political consultant Dick Morris was caught having an extramarital affair at the hotel. To impress his mistress, Morris allegedly let her listen in on confidential phone calls with the president. As a result of the incident, Morris resigned from the presidential team.

## Exterior

The Beaux-Arts building features an entry embellished with stonework and an arched glass overhang.

## Interior

The formal lobby features pilasters, fine plasterwork, and an ornamented barrel-vaulted ceiling modeled after the dome of Thomas Jefferson's Monticello.

# National Geographic Society

Also at this intersection is the National Geographic Society's headquarters at Hubbard Memorial Hall (1902; Hornblower & Marshall, exterior; 1904; Allen and Collens, interior), 16th and M Sts N.W. This building is not open to the public. Explorers Hall, the society's public museum, 1145 17th St N.W. at 17th and M Sts N.W., is open Mon–Sat 9–5; Sun 10–5. The museum is closed on Christmas Day. Admission is free. ☎ 857-7588. Web: www.nationalgeographic.com. The building also houses the *National Geographic* magazine offices.

### History

The National Geographic Society was founded in 1888 by a group of scientists meeting at the Cosmos Club. Hubbard Memorial Hall was dedicated to the memory of their first president, Gardiner Greene Hubbard, who had come to Washington to work with his son-in-law, Alexander Graham Bell, on Bell's scientific experiments. Hubbard was president of the society until his death in 1897.

Conceived as a scholarly organization, the society had a small membership in its early years. The *National Geographic* magazine, which was initially published sporadically, helped increase membership. When Alexander Graham Bell took over as president in 1897, he wanted to increase membership so that members' dues could fund the society's scientific explorations. To do this, Bell wanted to change the format of the magazine so that it would appeal to more than just scientists and explorers. He saw the magazine as a vehicle for bringing the wonders of the world and of exploration to the average person. In 1899, Bell hired 23-year-old Gilbert Grosvenor to assist with the magazine; Bell named Grosvenor editor of *National Geographic* magazine in 1903. Grosvenor transformed the magazine from a technical journal into an extraordinarily popular magazine.

Hubbard Hall was built as a meeting site for the scientific community.

> **Washington Notes**
> Mrs. Gertrude Hubbard's and Mrs. Mabel Hubbard Bell's vision of the build-
> ing conflicted with that of the first architects. The women, who preferred a
> simpler design for the windows and balcony, replaced Hornblower & Mar-
> shall, who were allowed to finish the exterior, with the firm of Allen & Collins,
> who completed the interior.

As *National Geographic* magazine's popularity soared, membership in the National Geographic Society skyrocketed from 2,700 in 1904 to 150,000 in 1912.
To serve the membership, the society increased its staff, outgrowing its facilities
at Hubbard Hall. A new building, designed by the architectural firm of Arthur B.
Heaton and built on land adjacent to Hubbard Hall, was completed in 1913. In
1931 an administrative building was added to the complex. A building for editors
was completed in 1948, and in 1961 construction began on the ten-story building on 17th St N.W. (Edward Durell Stone) that now houses Explorers Hall. The
editors' wing and the northwest section of the 1913 building were razed in 1981
to make room for a building completed in 1984 that contains offices and a 400-
seat auditorium.

In the late 1990s, National Geographic Society membership reached 9.5 million.

## Hubbard Hall

### Exterior
The Italian Renaissance–style Hubbard Hall is a white brick building trimmed in
white limestone. Note the arched second-floor windows and the balcony facing
16th St N.W.; these were the sources of controversy during the design phase.

### Interior
Hubbard Hall's entry and stair hall includes a gracious double staircase and an
impressive skylight. The library/boardroom contains the original board table
around which the scholars sat at the Cosmos Club when planning to establish the
National Geographic Society. Hubbard Hall displays five N. C. Wyeth paintings in
the stairwell and library entrance: *The Discoverer, Caravels of Columbus, Through
Pathless Skies to the North Pole,* and the two *Maps of Discovery*. The building is not
open to the public.

## Explorers Hall
The National Geographic Society museum occupies the ground floor of the ten-
story building at 17th and M Sts N.W. **Geographica** is an interactive learning
center drawing from anthropology, undersea archaeology and exploration,
botany, and astronomy. The **exhibition hall** features rotating exhibits relating to
cultural and scientific themes. The society store sells an extensive array of gifts
and National Geographic Society publications.

The National Geographic Society hosts lectures and other programs for adults
and children, including lively programs on Sat mornings for children 8 and up. An
admission fee is charged; society members receive a discount.

## Metropolitan African Methodist Episcopal Church
Not far from the National Geographic Society, on the south side of M St between
16th and 17th Sts N.W., is the historic Metropolitan African Methodist Episcopal

(AME) Church (1886; Samuel Morsell), 1518 M St N.W. The church is still active and open to the public. Guided tours are available by appointment. ☎ 331-1426.

### History
The Metropolitan AME Church was founded in 1838 by African Americans dissatisfied with racial segregation at Ebenezer Methodist Episcopal Church in Washington. The group first met behind a small building off of L St, near 15th St N.W., a block from the present church. The church had two forerunners, the Israel Bethel AME Church, founded in 1821, and the Union Bethel AME Church, which was founded in 1838. The Baltimore Conference of the African Methodist Episcopal Church officially sanctioned Union Bethel on July 6, 1838, and, in 1872, authorized the name change to Metropolitan AME and the construction of a new church in Washington.

> ### Washington Notes
> Frederick Douglass attended the consecration ceremony. He worshiped at the Metropolitan AME and often lectured there as well. Douglass donated the two silver candelabra in the chancel. Douglass's funeral was held at the church in 1895. Funeral services for Blanche Kelso Bruce, the first African American to serve a full term in the U.S. Senate, were held at the church in 1898.

In the 1860s, the basement of the building housed one of the nation's first free schools for blacks. The church organized the Union Relief Association during the Civil War, collecting food, clothing, and other goods for the influx of freed slaves. The prestigious Dunbar High School for African Americans, named after the nationally renowned black poet Paul Lawrence Dunbar, held graduation ceremonies at the Metropolitan AME for a number of years. Many prominent Americans, including several presidents, have spoken or worshiped at the Metropolitan AME, including Presidents McKinley, Theodore Roosevelt, Taft, Carter, and Clinton, first lady Eleanor Roosevelt, the Reverend Jessie Jackson, Mary McLeod Bethune, Joel Elias Spingarn, Hubert H. Humphrey, and John Mercer Langston.

## Exterior
The red brick church with granite trim is Victorian Gothic, a style typical of the late 19C.

## Interior
The church sanctuary features distinctive stained glass windows. A circular window on the M St side memorializes the first 15 AME bishops. Windows on the 15th and 16th St sides are dedicated to AME annual conferences. The fellowship hall below the sanctuary is named in honor of Frederick Douglass.

## Scott Circle
From the M St exit of the church, walk to 16th St. Continue north on 16th St to Scott Circle, at the intersection of Massachusetts and Rhode Island Aves and 16th St N.W.

### History
Pierre L'Enfant had envisioned a circle and a park at the site of what became Scott Circle. Despite the fact that the surrounding area had little development

and no paved roads, a monument to General Scott was erected in 1874. Over the years most of the site's proposed parkland was usurped by developers. As a result, Scott Circle has virtually no surrounding parkland. The 16th St tunnel beneath Scott Circle was built in 1942.

## Description

The Scott Circle area has three memorials. Located in the center of the circle is a bronze equestrian statue of **Lieutenant General Winfield Scott** (1786–1866), hero of three wars—the War of 1812, the Mexican War, and the Civil War. Henry Kirk Brown cast the statue of General Scott from cannons captured by Scott during the Mexican War. Brown's initial model featured Scott astride his favorite steed, a small mare, instead of the more typical pose of a general riding a fierce stallion. When Scott's descendants objected, Brown compromised, creating a stallion with the body of a mare.

In the triangle east of Scott Circle, created by the intersection of Corregidor St and Rhode Island and Massachusetts Aves N.W., the American Institute of Homeopathy dedicated the memorial to **Dr. Samuel Hahnemann** (1900; Charles Henry Niehaus, sculptor; Julius F. Harden, architect), the German physician who founded the homeopathic school of medicine. Hahnemann (1775–1843) developed his homeopathic theory in the 1790s, while practicing medicine in Leipzig; the theory is based on his "law of similars," which states that diseases are cured by introducing the afflicted individuals to drugs that create symptoms similar to those of the disease. Hahnemann also discovered that physicians of his day were administering a much higher dosage of drugs than was needed. Leipzig druggists forced Hahnemann out of town after physicians reduced their prescription dosages and the druggists lost business. The memorial, in the shape of a Greek exedra, or curved bench, features a life-size sculpture of Hahnemann posed in deep concentration. Four bronze panels represent different stages of his life, as student, chemist, teacher, and practicing physician.

A statue of **Daniel Webster** (1900; Gaetano Trentanove) is located in the triangular park west of Scott Circle, which is created by the intersection of Rhode Island Ave and 16th and Bataan Sts N.W. Stilson Hutchins, founder of the *Washington Post,* gave the statue of legendary orator and statesman Daniel Webster (1782–1852) to the city. Hutchins lived at 1603 Massachusetts Ave, across from the park, for many years. A bronze relief panel depicts Webster's famous reply to Robert Young Hayne of South Carolina in 1830, in which Webster declared that the secession of a state from the Union is illegal. In addition to Webster, John C. Calhoun, and Hayne, almost 100 figures are represented in the relief. Carved above the panel are Webster's words "Liberty and Union, Now and Forever, One and Inseparable."

Facing Scott Circle is the **General Scott Building** (1940–41; E. C. Ernst, architect; Robert O. Scholz, builder), 1 Scott Circle N.W., at the corner of 16th St and Rhode Island Ave N.W. It is a private condominium residence. The General Scott was one of many Art Deco apartment buildings constructed during the pre–World War II era in Washington, D.C. It is named for the general whose statue occupies Scott Circle. Coincidentally, the building opened in 1941 during the centennial anniversary of Scott's first year as a general of the U.S. Army. Known for its sun-filled apartments, the General Scott remains a first-class building after its conversion to a condominium in 1982.

### Washington Notes

Tenants of the General Scott managed to prevent their building from being sold in the early 1980s by forming a committee to buy out the prospective investors. The buyout process lasted two and a half years and cost $300,000 (about $4,000 per tenant). As owners, the tenants converted the building into condominiums.

## Exterior

Typical of the Art Deco style, the building is faced in cream-colored brick, has strong vertical and horizontal patterns, and features Art Deco motifs at the top of the black marble entry pilasters. The General Scott has five projecting pavilions, a rounded bay overlooking the corner of 16th St and Scott Circle, and an aluminum marquee.

## Interior

The Art Deco lobby features a step-down area with recessed dome, bowed reception desk, and pink marble floor. Most of the apartments were designed as efficiencies that contain a solarium partitioned by glass walls, a Murphy bed, wood block floors, and tiled bathrooms.

Just north of Scott Circle is the **National Wildlife Federation Building** (1988), 1400 16th St N.W., at the corner of 16th and O Sts N.W., ☎ 797-6800. Displayed across the building's façade are 13 bas-relief panels transferred from a 1961 building that previously occupied the site. The panels depict wildlife species native to different regions of the United States. Illinois mosaic and mural artist Lumen Martin Winter carved the 176 wildlife creatures in white Carrara marble. The panels were dedicated by John F. Kennedy during the original building's dedication. The National Wildlife Federation was the first organization dedicated to the conservation of wildlife and natural resources in America. Its headquarters now are located in suburban Virginia. Resources for the Future co-owns the 16th St building.

## Susan Shields Residence

Directly across 16th St is the Susan Shields Residence (1888; Samuel Edmonston, architect; Charles Edmonston, builder) at 1401 16th St N.W., offices of the Embassy of Kazakhstan.

### History

Mrs. Susan Shields, widow of former Norfolk newspaper publisher William B. Shields, built the house to help further business for her son-in-law, William B. Gurley, who worked in real estate, insurance, and local securities. Mrs. Shields hired architect Samuel B. Edmonston, a follower of Henry Hobson Richardson, to design the structure. It is believed that she was the first woman to seek a building permit in Washington, D.C. Mrs. Shields's daughter, Elizabeth, inherited the house when her mother died in 1900. In 1901 Elizabeth deeded the estate to relatives, who sold it to William Scully in 1902.

An Irish resident alien, Scully became a millionaire after buying land in the American western frontier in the 1850s. Since Scully's family dreaded the prospect of frontier life, they moved to Washington, where Scully bought his first home in the United States, the Shields residence. After making improvements to the house, Scully leased it to Michigan senator Russell A. Alger in 1903. Scully moved to England, planning to return to Washington after Alger's lease was up, but he died in England in 1906. Mrs. Scully and her children moved back into the Shields house after Senator Alger's death in 1907.

In the following years Mrs. Scully occupied the house sporadically, frequently leasing it to others. In 1910, Vice President James S. Sherman and his wife became tenants. Sherman died in 1912—the only U.S. vice president to die in office—but Mrs. Sherman remained in the house until 1914. Over the years, the house had a wide variety of occupants: the Netherlands legation was based there from 1918 until 1920, and Senator Thomas F. Bayard, Jr., of Delaware lived in the house from 1924 to 1929. Margaret Calvert ran the building as a boardinghouse, the Calvert House, from 1936 to 1938. With the death of Mrs. Scully and her heir, Frederick Scully, in 1942, the house was sold in 1944 to Hallie and Alvin Black, who continued the boardinghouse. The house had been vacant for five years when, in 1976, the Catholic Archdiocese sold it to lawyers William B. Ingersoll and Stuart M. Bloch. Architects Henry Grant Ingersoll and Glenn Chen Fong oversaw restoration of the building to its original condition. Ingersoll and Bloch sold the building to the Embassy of Kazakhstan in 1998.

## Exterior
The understated brick Romanesque revival building has a tower, projecting bays, gables, and dormers. The windows are relatively small and without stained glass.

## Interior
The entry is wrapped in rich wood paneling and ornate floral plasterwork. A stained glass skylight softly lights the space. A large central staircase features a landing where, it is said, Vice President Sherman stood to greet guests.

## National Association for the Education of Young Children
Continue north on 16th St to 1509 16th St N.W. (1909; Averill, Hall, and Adams; 1979 renovation, Mariani and Associates), the second building from the corner of 16th and P Sts N.W. and headquarters for the National Association for the Education of Young Children (NAEYC).

### History
Built as a seven-story luxury apartment building by painter and etcher John Taylor Arms, the building initially featured two three-bedroom apartments and five four-bedroom apartments. Each apartment included a drawing room, a library, two baths, a balcony, a kitchen, two pantries, servants' rooms, and servants' baths. The drawing rooms featured ornamental plaster cornices and classical fireplaces with gas logs. Each library also had a gas log fireplace, as well as glazed cabinets, a wall safe, an elaborate beamed ceiling, and a wrought-iron chandelier.

During the Depression Washington's real estate market bottomed out, and in 1932 the building was converted into a boardinghouse. Seven years later it was transformed again, becoming the Alturos Hotel. After decades of deterioration, the once-elegant building became the Christian Inn, a youth hostel, in 1971. Jeffrey Cohen bought the structure in 1979 and began renovations, including the addition of an external, brick-faced elevator bay and restoration of the fireplace mantels, cornices, and other details in the drawing rooms and libraries. The remainder of each floor was turned into office space. The building was reopened in 1981 for use as office space. In the early 1990s the NAEYC took over the building for use as its headquarters. The NAEYC (Web: www.naeyc.org) is dedicated to the healthy development and constructive education of all young children.

## Exterior

The red brick and limestone building is Georgian revival in style. The top floor has a limestone face and cornice with classical detailing. The tripartite windows have limestone and terra-cotta surrounds.

## Interior

The entrance hall is fashioned of stone imported from Caen, France. The space features a frescoed, vaulted ceiling. Although the interior has been converted to office space, the renovation preserved some of the building's original detail.

For the Carnegie Institution of Washington, 1530 P St N.W., and the Cairo, 1615 Q St N.W., a condominium residence, see Walk 17: "Dupont Circle East."

Continue north on 16th St to the **Chastleton** (1920; Philip M. Jullien; 1986 restoration), 1701 16th St N.W., at the corner of 16th and R Sts N.W. This ornate, Gothic revival apartment building cost $1.7 million. The structure features balconies and gargoyles on the façade and intricate plaster ceilings in the lobby, lounge, dining room, and first-floor hallways.

The building has changed hands many times through the years, losing some of its luster along the way. In the 1970s developer Virginia Page bought it, with the intention of restoring its luxury status. The restoration was completed in 1986.

> ### Washington Notes
> Among the building's famous owners were Mr. and Mrs. Alfred Dupont, who owned it for a few months in 1922, and Harry Wardman, who owned it from 1926 to 1932. Wardman also owned the Wardman Park, the Carlton, the Somerset House, the Hay-Adams, and the Roosevelt, all of which he lost during the Depression.

To continue with the next walk, proceed north on 16th St to the National Scottish Rite Center at 1733 at 16th St N.W.

# 15 · Adams Morgan

Metro: Red Line to Dupont Circle.
Bus: 42, L2, L4, S2, or S4.

The name Adams Morgan wasn't attached to a neighborhood until 1958. Bounded by New Hampshire Ave and R St to the south, 16th St to the east, Harvard Ave to the north, and Rock Creek Park and Connecticut Ave to the west, Adams Morgan has long been one of Washington's culturally significant areas. Initially an enclave of the city's elite, Adams Morgan has since become Washington's most vibrant ethnic melting pot, a residential area with a strong Hispanic, black, and white population, as well as a bustling commercial area that features dozens of restaurants, clubs, vintage clothing stores, health food shops, and boutiques. The heart of Adams Morgan is at 18th St and Columbia Rd N.W.

Parking is always a problem in this bustling neighborhood. At night, as in other city areas, be careful on side streets; sometimes there are purse snatchings and muggings. The best way to enjoy the area's restaurants and clubs at night is to arrive and depart by cab.

Three important factors in the development of Adams Morgan were the introduction of streetcar lines, the building of the Taft Bridge over Rock Creek, and the influx of Latino immigrants.

### History

Adams Morgan was initially part of a land patent known as Widow's Mite that was owned in the mid-1600s by John Longworth. Longworth came to America in 1637 as an indentured servant. In 1666 it is recorded that "Mrs. Longworth's children" were killed by Indians, and upon her death the land went to her nephew. By the early 1700s the patent had been divided into a few large estates. The area, high on a hill, offered pleasant summer breezes that provided an escape from the city's muggy lowlands as well as a view of the growing Federal City. Dr. William Thornton, the architect of the Capitol, was one of the region's farmers; he owned a 56-acre parcel of land. In the early 1800s, while the Federal City was being created, this area was mostly ignored, as it was far from the developing city.

Commodore David Porter became the first notable to actually live in the area. In 1816 for the sum of $13,000 (prize money from his naval battles during the War of 1812) he purchased 157 acres on what is now Meridian Hill and built a large, wooden mansion, reportedly designed by George Hadfield, on the current site of Meridian Hill Park. In 1822, Columbia College was established by the Baptist Church along the area's eastern boundary. In 1825, John Quincy Adams purchased a small grist mill in Rock Creek (Adam's Mill Rd is named for this mill), and in 1829 Adams leased the Porter estate. During the Civil War, both the college campus and the Porter mansion were used to house Union officers. In 1873, Columbia College relocated to Foggy Bottom in northwest Washington and eventually evolved into George Washington University (see Walk 18: "Foggy Bottom").

Adams Morgan remained largely rural until the latter half of the 19C when four separate neighborhoods took shape: Meridian Hill to the south, Lanier Heights to the north, Washington Heights west of 18th St, and Kalorama Heights west of Columbia Rd.

Meridian Hill was named for the stone placed on it during early surveys of the Federal City to mark a true meridian line. One of its most famous residents in the 1880s was Cincinnatus Heine Miller (1841–1913), the "Poet of the Sierras," who wrote under the pseudonym of Joaquin Miller. Miller was best known for his poetic account of his life among the Indians, *Songs of the Sierras* (1876). Miller, who built a cabin on 16th St, was quoted as saying, "The President's House is at one end of Sixteenth Street and mine is at the other, but while I own a cabin, the President has only his cabin-et." Miller's cabin had fewer amenities than the president's house; its walls were layered with newspapers and rejection slips (for his poetry) to keep out the cold. Miller was a society favorite and he thought that fit-

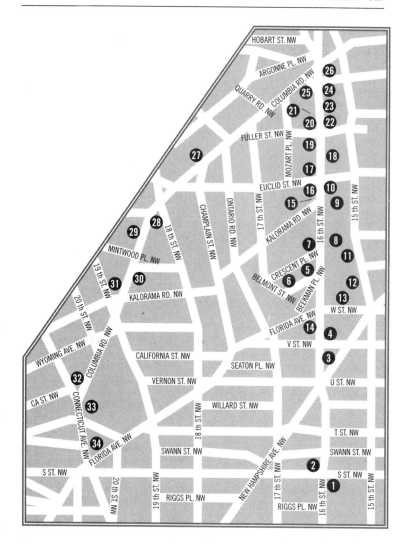

ted him for the office of ambassador to Japan. When he lobbied for the post and was rejected, Miller left Washington for good.

In 1873, Thomas Morgan built an estate, called Oak Lawn, in the area's southwest corner, then known as Washington Heights. In 1880, George Brown Goode, a scientist influential in the development of the Smithsonian Institution, built his home in the northern part of the area, Lanier Heights. Goode had the first streets put in the area and bought and sold lots to many of his associates.

The most important arrival to the area came in 1888, when former senator John Henderson and his wife, Mary, bought six acres at what is now the corner of

1 National Scottish Rite Center, Library, and Museum
2 Universalist National Memorial Church
3 The Balfour
4 Roosevelt Hotel
5 White-Meyer House
6 Meridian House
7 Meridian Mansions (the Envoy)
8 Meridian Hill Park
9 *Joan of Arc* sculpture
10 *Serenity* statue
11 *Dante* statue
12 *James Buchanan Memorial*
13 *Armillary Sphere*
14 Meridian Hill Park exit
15 Park Tower
16 Embassy of Ghana
17 Pink Palace (Inter-American Defense Board)
18 Warder-Totten House
19 Embassy of Poland
20 Embassy of Italy
21 Scottish Rite Temple
22 Embassy of Spain
23 Embassy of Mexico
24 All Souls Church Unitarian
25 Unification Church, Washington Chapel, Church of Jesus Christ of Latter-Day Saints
26 National Baptist Memorial Church
27 Avignon Freres
28 Knickerbocker Theatre
29 Woodley Apartments
30 Norwood Apartments
31 Wyoming Apartments
32 Statue of Major General George B. McClellan
33 Washington Hilton and Towers
34 Boundary St

Florida Ave and 16th Sts N.W. and proceeded to build what came to be called Boundary Castle (see Walk 14: "16th Street N.W."). Henderson was the Missouri senator who drafted the Thirteenth Amendment, which abolished slavery.

A visionary of sorts, Mrs. Henderson spent the next 30 years trying to bring the center of the city to her doorstep. With architect George Oakley Totten, Jr., she built a series of mansions that she proposed to sell or lease to embassies. Totten had been a student of H. H. Richardson, and his buildings have the same romantic, villa-inspired qualities characterized by Richardsonian architecture. Together with his patroness, he transformed 16th St and Meridian Hill into one of the most elegant areas of the city. Their first project was the Venetian-inspired Pink Palace, at 2600 16th St N.W. What eventually became the Embassy of Spain, at 2801 16th St N.W., was first offered to the government by Mrs. Henderson as a residence for the vice president. In 1912, she lobbied successfully to have the name 16th St changed to the Avenue of the Presidents. It only remained that for one year, however, in the face of critics who called the change "pompous, ostentatious, affected."

In 1890 Congress acquired 2,000 acres to the west of 16th St to establish Rock Creek Park and the National Zoo, and it changed the name of Boundary St to Florida Ave. That same year, the Rock Creek Railway extended its service down Florida Ave from Connecticut Ave over to 18th St and north on 18th St to Columbia Rd. In 1897, the Metropolitan Railroad extended its line from the intersections of Florida and Connecticut Aves north along Columbia Rd to 18th St. The increased rail service made the area more accessible to city dwellers and workers.

In 1906, Mrs. Henderson proposed an urban park opposite her "castle" on 16th St, and Meridian Hill Park was approved by the Commission of Fine Arts in 1914. By the mid-1920s, the area was a graceful enclave of beautiful mansions and elegant parks, with commercial and retail establishments nearby to cater to the wealthy tastes of the residents. Furriers, clothiers, and caterers such as Avignon Freres set up shop for their exclusive clientele. Nightclubs flourished, and theaters offered live entertainment and movies.

Segregation and high rents limited the access of African Americans to the area. The major black presence consisted of the servants who commuted here each day to serve their affluent employers. In the 1920s, some wealthy citizens purchased property and set aside low-rent districts to keep domestic help closer at hand.

World War II brought considerable change to the area, as it did to most of the city. A citywide housing shortage coupled with lack of zoning restrictions meant extensive subdivisions of the larger homes. The influx of lower-income residents, as well as the development of national highways and a car-dominated society, resulted in the exodus of Adams Morgan's affluent to the developing Washington suburbs. By the 1950s, the area had become the home of low- and middle-income, ethnically diverse groups.

The 1950s also saw the beginning of a Hispanic immigration to Adams Morgan that would transform it into the center of Washington's Latino community. Many shops and restaurants opened or were converted to serve the needs of this burgeoning population, as well as those of new Vietnamese and Ethiopian residents. In the late 1950s, the designation Adams Morgan first came into use, through the community activism of area leaders. Federal plans for urban renewal and school integration prompted residents to band together to have a voice in the future of the neighborhood. In 1958, the principals of the area's two most prominent schools, the African American Morgan School (named after the early settler Thomas Morgan) and the predominantly white Adams School (named after John Quincy Adams) were instrumental in organizing the Adams Morgan Better Neighborhood Conference. That same year the Adams Morgan Community Council was formed, and the neighborhood's present boundaries were defined.

The 1960s saw another major influx of Hispanic residents, most of them newly arrived from Central and South America. Some were employed in the Latin American embassies on 16th St, but the majority were political and economic refugees. Washington's existing Spanish-speaking population had until that time consisted mainly of those affiliated with embassies, students attending local universities, and white-collar Mexican Americans who had come to the area in large numbers to fill the federal jobs created during the New Deal and World War II. But this middle- and upper-middle-class population in the late 1950s was joining other city dwellers in the exodus to the suburbs. Now Adams Morgan was a magnet for a different Hispanic population, considerably less-educated immigrants—some legal, some illegal—from countries suffering economic and political turmoil.

Today the Hispanic population is more than 250,000. Cubans came here in the 1960s, followed by large numbers of South Americans in the 1970s. A large population of Latin and Central Americans migrated to the District in the 1980s. Puerto Ricans, a minority group in Adams Morgan, produced many of the leaders of Washington's Spanish-speaking community. The best known was Carlos Rosario, often referred to as the Godfather of the community. Rosario, who served in the Army in World War II and came to the U.S. in 1950, was instrumental in the establishment of the D.C. Office of Latino Affairs, originally called the Office of Spanish-Speaking Affairs when it was established in 1969.

In the 1980s the neighborhood experienced a new wave of settlers—the affluent, mostly white upper-middle class who wanted to live in a diverse and lively residential area. While the neighborhood welcomed these people, there was some concern that gentrification would diminish the very diversity these newcomers

·were seeking. It seems unlikely this will happen. The restaurants and stores as well as the activities sponsored by neighborhood churches are strongly Latino-oriented, even as greater numbers of Asian immigrants join the community.

In May 1991, rioting broke out in the Mt. Pleasant neighborhood north of Adams Morgan, with some of the looting spilling into the shops and restaurants along the 18th St and Columbia Rd corridors. The disturbances grew out of complaints from the Latino community about their treatment by the D.C. police. For a brief time, Adams Morgan's retail community felt the impact of reluctance by outsiders to come into the area at night, but the community soon recovered. Adams Morgan continues to offer a rich blend of cosmopolitan clubs and ethnic restaurants.

> ### Washington Notes
> Trendy Adams Morgan has appeared as background in several films. Examples include scenes with Tom Cruise in *A Few Good Men*, Clint Eastwood in *In the Line of Duty*, and a memorable scene in *Dave* when Kevin Kline and Sigourney Weaver demolish the song "Tomorrow" in front of the Argentine Grill on 18th St.

## National Scottish Rite Center

Walk north on 16th St to the National Scottish Rite Center, Library, and Museum (1911–15; John Russell Pope; Adolph Alexander Weinman, sculptor), 1733 16th St at the corner of 16th and S Sts N.W. ☎ 232-3579. Web: www.srmason-sj.org. Open to the public Mon–Fri 8–2. Admission is free; guided tours are available.

### History

The building is headquarters for the Scottish Rite, one of the two branches of the Blue Lodge or Symbolic Freemasonry. The Masons are a fraternity whose goals incorporate fellowship, education, and community service. Scottish Rite Freemasonry took hold in the New World in 1783 with the creation of a Lodge of Perfection in Charleston, South Carolina. In 1801, the Supreme Council of the 33rd and Last Degree for the United States was established in Charleston. The 16th St building serves as executive offices for the first Supreme Council of the world, an organization whose influence extends to all Supreme Councils that trace their origins to Charleston.

The first Freemasons were 17C stonemasons who worked on houses, churches, and cathedrals. They formed craft guilds. The guild ceremonies still are part of the Fraternity of Freemasonry. In 1884, after the Civil War, Scottish Rite leaders transferred their central operations from Charleston to new headquarters at 433 3rd St in Washington. The council remained there until moving to the 16th St location in 1915.

Sovereign Grand Commander James D. Richardson was actively involved with construction of the 16th St headquarters building. A Tennessee congressman for 20 years, Minority Leader, and Democratic Caucus nominee for Speaker of the House, Richardson retired from politics in 1905, devoting the rest of his life to Scottish Rite Freemasonry. In 1910, Richardson selected John Russell Pope as architect for the new building. The next May, Norcross Brothers of Worcester, Massachusetts, builder for famed architect H. H. Richardson, was signed. Construction cost an estimated $1,100,000.

### Washington Notes

In accordance with Masonic tradition, the Bible used at the presidential inauguration of George Washington (a Freemason) and the gavel that Washington used to lay the cornerstone of the U.S. Capitol were used at the Oct 18, 1911, ceremony to lay the new building's cornerstone.

**Highlights:** The ornate exterior and the Freemasonry library, as well as the largest collection in the U.S. of books by and about poet and Mason Robert Burns.

## Exterior

The building resembles the Hellenistic temple-tomb of King Mausolos at Halicarnassos, which was built around 350 B.C. in what today is Bodrum, Turkey. The **sphinxes** (1915; Adolph A. Weinman) flanking the entry to the terrace symbolize power (left) and wisdom (right). On each base are inscriptions in Phoenician characters (the names of the columns that stood in front of Solomon's Temple) and Egyptian hieroglyphics (the quotation "He hath established it in strength"). Thirty-three ft tall fluted pilasters support a pyramidal roof. Pope, with the advice of local architect and Mason Elliott Woods, incorporated some basic symbolism, but the majority of the decorative details were planned by the grand commander of the lodge, George Fleming Moore, after the architectural design was completed.

## Interior

The interior includes the main ceremonial room, executive chamber, offices, a library, banquet hall, museum rooms, and galleries displaying memorabilia of sovereign grand commanders. The most ornate room in the building occupies the entire top floor. This chamber hosts Supreme Council meetings, which are held every two years.

Some of the galleries are devoted to specific collections, such as the **Goethe Collection,** which contains most of the English editions of *Faust.* In addition, the collections contain information on famous Masons. The **Albert H. Hanauer Collection of Mark Pennies,** an emblem given to a candidate who has attained the degree of Royal Arch Mason, features items from 1899 to 1925. The **Robert Burns Library** houses America's largest collection of books by and about the poet and Mason. The **Albert Pike Room** exhibits manuscripts, photographs, and personal belongings of the Civil War general, author, and one-time sovereign grand commander. The **J. Edgar Hoover Law Enforcement Museum** displays memorabilia from the career of the FBI director, and the **Burl Ives Collection** honors the folksinger and actor. (Both Hoover and Ives were Masons.) The **Library** has more than 175,000 books about Freemasonry, along with ornamental objects relating to Freemasonry.

## Universalist National Memorial Church

Cross 16th St and continue north to the Universalist National Memorial Church (1926–30; Allen and Collens) at 1810 16th St N.W. ☎ 387-3411.

### History

Washington's original Universalist community had no church of its own until the mid-1870s. Universalist ministers preached in the city throughout the 1860s.

Following the Civil War, Universalists worshiped at the Unitarian Church at 6th and D Sts N.W. The first permanent Universalist organization, the Murray Universalist Society, was founded in 1869 and had 59 members.

> **Washington Notes**
> Walt Whitman occasionally participated in the Murray Universalist Society. Well-known Universalists include Benjamin Rush, signer of the Declaration of Independence; Clara Barton, founder of the American Red Cross (whose portrait hangs in the 16th St Church); Owen D. Young; Horace Greeley; and Stanley K. Hornbeck, ambassador to China.

The society worshiped at members' homes and at other churches and temples until 1874, when the first Universalist church in Washington, the Church of Our Father (1874; Adolf Cluss) was built at 13th and L Sts N.W. This church was used until 1925.

Ideas for the construction of a Universalist National Memorial Church in Washington were discussed in 1867 during the Universalist General Convention in Baltimore. The original funds collected for the national church were, however, redirected to rebuild a Chicago church ruined by fire. After World War I, the plan to establish a national church was revitalized. In 1921, money set aside for the project was deployed for disaster relief work after an earthquake in Japan where Universalist missionaries were stationed. Meanwhile, a site was purchased on New Hampshire Ave for construction of the national church. In 1925, the Universalists sold the New Hampshire Ave site to raise funds. Over the next two years the Universalists purchased the 16th St property, on which several row houses were located.

Dr. Frederick Perkins, chairman of the Universalist Church's Committee on Church Architecture, was chosen as minister of the Universalist National Memorial Church and chief overseer of its construction. It was not until 1928 that the Universalists had gathered enough money to begin construction. On April 28, 1928, the cornerstone was laid. On Palm Sunday, 1930, Dr. Perkins held the first service in the church.

## Exterior

The brick, Romanesque-style building's most outstanding feature is by an unknown artist—the tympanum of the Peace Tower portal—which depicts Christ in glory surrounded by the symbols of the evangelists. The Peace Tower, a memorial to Owen D. Young, was dedicated on Oct 27, 1929. Young served as chairman of the board of General Electric from 1920 to 1930 and he was instrumental in the founding and development of RCA and NBC. Young, a devoted Universalist, organized relief efforts to Europe following World War I. Known as the Young Plan, it was a predecessor to the Marshall Plan that followed World War II. A street-level inscription reads, "This tower dedicated to the ideal of international justice and world peace is a loving and grateful tribute to Owen D. Young who inspired by faith in the constructive power of human brotherhood contributed his rare talents of mind and heart to the healing of the nations devastated by the World War. Peace on earth among men of good will."

## Interior

A Celtic cross, stained glass windows, and impressive stone carvings are the primary decorative elements of the church interior. All of the stained glass windows are symbolic and nonfigural. The three chancel windows represent the Universalists' central doctrine, "Now abideth faith, hope, love, and the greatest of these is love." The large clerestory windows on each side of the sanctuary represent the life of Jesus. The lower windows in the side aisles portray the history of Christianity. Those in the baptistry relate to children and the rite of baptism. All of the windows were made by Calvert, Herrick & Reddinger of New York City. Calvert made many visits to France's Chartres Cathedral and was asked to employ Chartres's reds and blues when creating the Universalist windows. The stone carving in the church is handsome as well. Note the capitals, chancel rail, pulpit, lectern, the arch behind the communion table, and the Celtic cross, which hangs in the center against a background of Tiffany mosaics.

## *The Balfour*

Continue north on 16th St to the Balfour (1900; George S. Cooper), 2000 16th St N.W., at the corner of 16th and U Sts N.W., a private condominium residence.

### History

Originally known as the Westover, the building's original, large, five-bedroom apartments have been reconfigured over the years into smaller units. Opened as an upscale rental building in 1901, the Westover changed its name to the Balfour in 1909 because there was another Westover on Pennsylvania Ave.

The name Balfour was indicative of the times. An English-sounding name was thought to add prestige to a building. The Balfour was named for Arthur James Balfour, the first earl of Balfour and acting British prime minister from 1902 to 1905.

### Exterior

The Balfour is designed in the Beaux-Arts style popular in the early 1900s. The first floor, fashioned in limestone, features a porch that shelters the wide entrance. Two oriel windows rise from the second to the fourth story of the building.

### Interior

Now a condominium building, the Balfour has about 55 units. The lobby's floor of off-white stone tiles features a border of red and gold stone in the Greek key pattern popular in the early 1900s. In the lobby a marble staircase stretches from the lobby to the first landing.

Cross 16th St and walk to the northeast corner of 16th and V Sts N.W. to the **Roosevelt Hotel** (1919; Appleton P. Clark, Jr.) at 2101 16th St N.W. Originally called the Hadleigh, the building opened in 1920 as a luxury apartment hotel. In 1924 the name was changed to the Roosevelt, in honor of President Theodore Roosevelt. Clark's design has five wings. A rooftop garden had been planned for the building, but the idea was dropped after Mrs. John B. Henderson complained that the garden would block the view from the future Meridian Hill Park.

### Washington Notes

The Roosevelt was a popular residence for members of Congress around 1926, when the old Congress Hall apartment-hotel was demolished to make way for the Longworth Building. Until as recently as the mid-1950s, the building was the setting for fashionable concerts and dances, featuring top entertainers such as Ray Charles, Nat King Cole, and Benny Goodman. After its heyday, the building became a residence for senior citizens. Now vacant, it is owned by the city's housing department. Much of the original detailing and plasterwork is gone, having been removed in the 1960s.

## Meridian International Center

1630 Crescent Place N.W. ☎ 667-6800. Web: www.meridian.org. Grounds open Mon–Sun 8–5. For tours of the building, ☎ 667-6800. Galleries of both houses with rotating exhibitions open Wed–Sun 2–5. Admission: free. For concert schedule, ☎ 667-6800. For information about tours of the galleries of both houses, ☎ 939-5595, as the houses close to the public for special occasions.

Continue north on 16th St N.W. to Crescent Place, where there are several significant buildings. The White-Meyer House (1911; John Russell Pope; 1934 renovation, Charles A. Platt; DL) at 1624 Crescent Place N.W. and the Meridian House (Irwin B. Laughlin House) (1920–29; John Russell Pope; DL) at 1630 Crescent Place N.W. together form the Meridian International Center, a nonprofit, cultural, and educational organization devoted to promoting international understanding through the exchange of ideas and art. The center provides services to foreign visitors and diplomats, and presents conferences, art exhibitions, lectures, world affairs programs, and seminars.

### Washington Notes

The White-Meyer House was built on the historic farmlands of Meridian Hill. Cincinnatus ("Joaquin") Miller—horse thief, journalist, lawyer, judge, world traveler, and poet—lived there in a log cabin during the early 1800s. Having spent much of his time in America's West, though, the "Poet of the Sierras" soon found Washington to be too crowded and returned to the West. In 1912, Miller's log cabin was moved to Rock Creek Park.

## White-Meyer House

### History

Henry White, formerly the U.S. ambassador to France, purchased the property at 1624 Crescent Place N.W. in 1910. White married Emily Vanderbilt Sloane in 1920. The couple hosted many diplomatic and political functions at the 1624 Crescent Place residence. Among their distinguished guests were France's leader during World War I, Henri "the Lion" Clemenceau, British statesman Lord Robert Cecil, Senator Henry Cabot Lodge, and President Warren G. Harding.

After White's death in 1927, his son took over the property and two years later leased it to Eugene Meyer, then head of the Federal Farm Loan Board. Myer went on to become the owner of the *Washington Post* and bought the property in 1934. Charles A. Platt, architect of the Freer Gallery, remodeled the house. Following Myer's death in 1959 the Antioch School Law Library rented the property until it was purchased by Meridian International Center in 1987.

## Exterior

This was the first of two mansions designed by Pope on Meridian Hill. Built in the style of an English Georgian country house, with a Tuscan garden, the building has five bays with attached single-bay wings. Many of the windows have iron grilles and louvered shutters. The north entrance, which faces Crescent Place, features a large double entrance oak door; Ionic columns support a semielliptical bow over the southern entrance's French doors. The bow forms a shallow second-floor balcony overhanging this entrance. Tennis courts and an accompanying shelter were added in 1939. A brick retaining wall was built along the street frontages in 1961.

## Interior

The north entrance leads to an open **Reception Hall,** one of the two largest spaces in the residence. The hall's floor has a pattern of limestone and slate black squares and a crystal chandelier. From the hall there are entrances to the library and the dining room. The **library,** which opens onto a terrace overlooking the city, has walnut paneling and bookcases. There is a green-veined fireplace mantel. The library, loggia, and drawing room to the left of the gallery are also open to the public. The **dining room** has a brass-finished globe chandelier hanging from a plaster sunburst. The dining room was the site of many strategic meetings of the French Mission during World War I.

## *Meridian House (Irwin B. Laughlin House)*

The 1630 Crescent Place mansion was built by Irwin Boyle Laughlin, who served as secretary of the Embassy of London (1912–17), minister to Greece (1924–26), and ambassador to Spain (1929–33). Laughlin's primary objective in creating the building was to house his substantial collection of 18C and 19C French and Italian artwork and Oriental porcelains. Money apparently was no object; the 18C French-style house cost an estimated $350,000. The quality of design, materials, and workmanship was exceptional. When Laughlin died in 1941, the house was left to his wife. In 1960, the American Council on Education purchased the property and established the Washington International Center. In 1961, the Meridian House Foundation took over the property, and in 1992 it became the Meridian International Center.

## Exterior

Two terra-cotta sphinxes once flanked the entry terrace. They and the original loggia chandelier are now at Dumbarton Oaks in Georgetown. Some paintings and porcelains from Laughlin's collection remain in the house (most notably the large Oriental vases in the gallery). Each side of the house is five bays wide, with simple molded entablature dividing the two main stories. Fine limestone was used for the walls and sculptural details. The north entrance, which faces Crescent Place, has a large double oak door divided into three paneled sections.

## Interior

The north entrance leads to an open **Reception Hall,** which has a floor decorated in a pattern of white and gray slate, mirror-paneled closet doors, and a Waterford crystal teardrop chandelier. The curved stairways have elaborately carved newel posts. The loggia, dining room, drawing room, and library may be entered from the hall. The **loggia** functions like a sunroom; it has raised wall panels and two wood candelabra carved to resemble fanciful trees. A 16C English Mortlake tapestry portraying Alexander the Great meeting Diogenes graces the **dining room.** To create the effect of an unbroken line of bookshelves in the **library,** the door leading to the gallery is treated to resemble additional bookshelves.

## Meridian Mansions (The Envoy)

Walk along Crescent Place to its intersection with 16th St N.W. and the Meridian Mansions (1918; Alexander H. Sonnemann), now the Envoy, at 2400 16th St N.W.

### History

Meridian Mansions was constructed by real estate developers William and Edgar Kennedy. The Italian Renaissance building cost $950,000, making it the most expensive apartment building in Washington at that time. Along with luxury apartments and a large lobby, the building had two ballrooms, a grand dining room, and rooftop pavilions. In addition, it had its own power plant, a three-story parking garage with chauffeurs' and servants' quarters above, and tennis courts on the garage roof. The building included 190 units: 78 large apartments for permanent residents and 112 furnished bedrooms and efficiencies for transients.

Located in one of the most exclusive areas of town, Meridian Mansions flourished until the Depression; the building was completely booked for its first 12 years and had a long waiting list. Diplomats and members of Congress often gathered at Meridian Mansions during this time. The Bolivian Legation rented quarters in the building in 1921; as recently as 1956, 32 foreign countries rented units in the building.

The Kennedy family fortune was lost during the Depression, and Meridian Mansions was taken over by Metropolitan Life Insurance Company. The building was sold in 1936, renamed the Hotel 2400, and redecorated; an Art Deco–style nightclub was added. In 1956 Hotel 2400 was sold; two years later, under government ownership, the hotel was converted into one of D.C.'s first integrated apartment-hotels. New York Congressman Adam Clayton Powell tried unsuccessfully to buy the building in 1962 for use as a retirement home for the poor. New York investors bought it for $2.2 million in 1964. The group changed the building's name to the Envoy Towers and spent $2 million to revamp the property as a 334-unit apartment building. After the mortgage was foreclosed in 1967, the government bought the building at public auction. The building was used temporarily to house Washingtonians displaced during the riots of 1968. Developer David Clark bought the building in 1979, changed its name to the Envoy, restored the lobby, and reconfigured the building. The changes eliminated the ballrooms and public dining room. In 1981 the Envoy reopened as a 303-unit condominium. When the condo venture failed, investors bought the Envoy, which is now operated as a luxury rental apartment building.

## Meridian Hill Park

Proceed along 16th St to Meridian Hill Park (1913; George Burnap; 1919; Ferruccio Vitale; completed over the next 20 years by architect Horace W. Peaslee and the U.S. Commission of Fine Arts; DL) at 16th and W Sts N.W. The park, bounded on the west by 16th St, on the east by 15th St, on the south by W St, and on the north by Euclid St, is one of the city's bonafide treasures. Sadly, it is also a park with a history of drug activity, making it unwise to visit the park alone or in the evening. At the top of the hill one can see impressive views of downtown.

**Highlights:** The park's most beautiful feature, a cascading water staircase, was based on a similar staircase at the 17C Italian Villa Aldobrandini at Frascati.

### History

The Mt. Pleasant Farm of Peter Hill originally occupied the Meridian Hill site. Robert Peter of Georgetown owned the estate and surrounding land. His son sold it to Washington Bowie in 1811, and Bowie in turn sold it to Commodore David Porter, a U.S. naval officer who gained notoriety for putting his men in high-risk situations. In 1820, the financially destitute Commodore Porter sold the land to John Quincy Adams through a second party. During the Civil War, the Massachusetts Brigade and the New York 77th Regiment occupied the property. A fire destroyed the estate in 1863. Four years later, the land was subdivided; plots were sold for 10 cents a square ft.

### *Washington Notes*

The name Meridian Hill comes from a proposal, supported by Thomas Jefferson, to establish a meridian, or longitudinal base, through the White House. The park is on the meridian line. A plaque at the park's upper entrance notes an 1816 marker for the meridian.

Until 1887, the Meridian Hill area continued to resemble a farm. When former Missouri senator John B. Henderson and his wife came to the Meridian Hill area in 1888, 16th St's transformation to a grand entry to Washington, D.C., began. The Hendersons built an elegant mansion on Meridian Hill that came to be known as Boundary Castle. After Senator Henderson's death, Mary Foote Henderson continued her efforts to develop 16th St and establish Meridian Hill Park.

### *Washington Notes*

Mary Foote Henderson was known not only for her active role in the development of 16th St but also for being an outspoken woman who often disagreed and clashed with D.C.'s local government. She proposed numerous ideas for 16th St that never materialized. These include placing a double row of presidential and vice presidential busts along 16th St, building the Lincoln Memorial on Meridian Hill, erecting a commemorative arch to Thomas Jefferson, and building a Presidential Palace on Meridian Hill to replace the White House. She succeeded in changing the name of 16th St N.W. to Avenue of the Presidents on March 4, 1913, but the name was changed back on July 21, 1914.

Mrs. Henderson's plan for a park met universal approval. She sold the 12-acre property to the federal government in 1910 for $490,000. Meridian Hill Park stands as a testament to Mary Foote Henderson's determination to bring grandeur and style to the 16th St area during the early 1900s. After her death in 1931, the 16th St area declined until the late 1980s, when restoration efforts began.

## The Park

The Italian Renaissance–style park features an upper terrace, a stepped cascade of water, and a pool below. Its design also includes Art Deco and Islamic elements. Meridian Hill Park was first designed by George Burnap in 1913, but the design was revised over the next 25 years by architect Horace W. Peaslee, landscape architect Ferruccio Vitale, and the Commission of Fine Arts. After a rocky period of funding shortfalls, court injunctions, vandalism, and neglect, the park was officially completed in 1936. The use of exposed aggregate concrete for the park represented the first use of this material in North America and remains one of the finest examples of this application.

Enter the 12-acre park at the corner of Euclid and 16th St. This initial flat section of a broad grassy promenade extends to the crest of the hill. The bronze sculpture *Joan of Arc* (1922; Paul Dubois) is a replica of the statue in front of Rheims Cathedral in France and a gift from the women of France to the women of America. The nine-ft equestrian statue depicts Joan (1412–1431) leading the French troops into battle against the Burgundians.

The statue *Serenity*, located in the northwest corner of the park, honors the memory of Lieutenant Colonel William Henry Scheutze, who was the navigator of the USS *Iowa* during the Spanish-American War, fought in the Battle of Santiago, and was a member of the expedition to retrieve the bodies of the lost Arctic explorers of Jeanette. The statue was presented by millionaire and friend Charles Deering in 1928.

Walk down the two sets of massive concrete steps to the first broad terrace and Ettore Ximenes's *Dante* (1920), located in the Italianate gardens. The medieval Italian poet, best known for his *Divine Comedy*, is represented wearing a scholar's gown and a victor's laurel and holding his most famous work. The 11½ ft bronze figure was a gift to the park on behalf of Italian Americans by Carlo Barsotti, editor of an Italian American newspaper in New York City. The dedication was held in 1921, the 600th anniversary of the poet's death. That same year a replica statue was unveiled in New York.

Continue down the steps to the bottom of the hill and the *James Buchanan Memorial* (1930; Hans Schuler). A bequest for a memorial honoring the 15th president of the United States was left by his niece and White House hostess Harriet Lane, but Congress acted so slowly to fulfill her request that construction on the memorial was started only a few weeks before the 15-year time limit ran out. In the bronze eight-ft statue Buchanan is seated on a white marble pylon, flanked on either side by two granite allegorical figures, Law (male) and Diplomacy (female). The *Buchanan Memorial* faces a reflecting pool with water lilies. To its right is the sculpted basin at the bottom of the central cascade.

Walk back toward 16th St. Along this path is the southern garden and the *Armillary Sphere*, which was fashioned by Carl Paul Jennewein after Manship's sculpture of the ancient astrological instrument design. The sphere found frequent use in 17C Europe as a model for understanding the Ptolemaic system, in which the Earth is the fixed center of the universe. Work on the statue was interrupted in 1929 due to funding problems but was finished in 1931 after Miss Bertha Noyes donated $15,000 for its completion, dedicating it to her sister, Edith Noyes. The Meridian Hill Park niche and fountain by Carl Mose was dedicated to the memory of Mary F. Henderson in 1935.

## Park Tower

From the bottom terrace, exit the park at the intersection of 16th St and Florida Ave, the former site of the Boundary Castle. Incongruously attached to a retaining wall that ends on Euclid St are two Romanesque towers that served as the gateway to the estate, the only remaining portion of Mrs. Henderson's massive rusticated Seneca brownstone mansion. Continue up the hill on 16th St N.W. to the Park Tower (1928–29; William Harris) at 2440 16th St N.W. The building, the second from the corner of 16th and Kalorama Sts N.W., on the west side of 16th St across from the park, is a private condominium residence.

### History

The Park Tower is an early example of Washington's Art Deco–style buildings. When the building opened in 1929, its units were rentals. Restoration of the building earned a 1987 award from the Art Deco Society of Washington. The Park Tower now is a 114-unit condominium.

## Exterior

One aspect of the building's exterior sets it apart from other Art Deco structures: Colored brick dominates the building, unlike most Art Deco structures, which are faced in tan-colored brick.

## Interior

The lobby features large chandeliers, a fountain, and vintage Art Deco furnishings.

Continue north on 16th St to the **Embassy of Ghana** (1907–8; George Oakley Totten, Jr.) at 2460 16th St N.W., on the corner of 16th and Kalorama Sts N.W. across from the park, ☎ 686-4520, built originally as the Embassy of France in the Louis XIV style. The use of the corner tower was common in Paris due to the triangular sites created by the street patterns. Totten uses the tower as a hinge between the sides of the building, which have triple-bay façades and open balconies. The exterior of the building is limestone cut in ashlar blocks; the balustrades, capitals, decorative panels, and the entablature are molded terra-cotta.

## The Pink Palace

On the west side of the street is what has always been called the Pink Palace (1905–6; George Oakley Totten, Jr.), 2600 16th St N.W., at the corner of 16th and Euclid Sts N.W., ☎ 939-6600. Now, though, it is more of a cream palace. Currently it is the headquarters of the Inter-American Defense Board (IADB), an international organization that serves as an advisory board to the Organization of American States (OAS).

### History

This building is noteworthy because it was the first collaborative effort of Mrs. Henderson and her architect, Totten. Mrs. Henderson hoped to attract distinguished public figures to her 16th St properties and she succeeded at the Pink Palace. The building's first occupants were Oscar S. Straus and his family. Straus was secretary of commerce and labor under President Theodore Roosevelt and, while in residence at the Pink Palace, entertained the president many times. Other occupants included Franklin McVeaugh, secretary of the Treasury under President William H. Taft, who lived here from 1909 to 1911, and Mrs. Delia Field, widow of Chicago department store magnate Marshall Field, who lived here from 1914 to 1937. Field hosted Edward, Prince of Wales, during his first visit to the U.S. in 1919.

The IADB leased the building in 1949; three years later, the Organization of American States purchased it. The IADB renovated the building during the 1980s.

## Exterior

Totten designed the mansion in the style of a 15C Venetian palazzo. The building has had many tenants who made many changes in its exterior. In 1984 all but one of the original balconies were removed, and an addition was built on the west wall. (It was at that time the building was painted cream.) Still remaining are its most admired features—the Venetian Gothic trefoil (imitating a leaf with three sections) arches on the second- and third-story windows. The ground level is made of polished Beaver Dam marble, and the upper stories are brick covered with marbelized plaster.

## *Warder-Totten House*

A significant property across from the Pink Palace is vacant and in disrepair. The Warder-Totten House (1885–88; H. H. Richardson; 1915; 1923; George Oakley Totten; DL), at 2633 16th St N.W. in the middle of the block, includes the former residence of George Totten and a reconstruction of H. H. Richardson's Warder House, which was moved from 1515 K St N.W. Antioch School of Law was the last tenant; the property is vacant, badly damaged by fire, its windows and doors left open to the elements. On the D.C. Preservation League's list of "most endangered places," the house is privately owned and has been vacant for more than ten years.

### History

The home of George Oakley Totten, Jr., occupied this site. Totten (1866–1939), architect of grand residences—many intended to be used for embassies and legations—and the "official" architect for Mrs. John B. Henderson, designed the house. From 1897 to 1939, Totten served as the American delegate to the International Congress of Architects, assigned to Brussels, Paris, Madrid, London, Vienna, Rome, and Budapest throughout his career. During World War I Totten served as a major in the Army Corps of Engineers. In 1908, he went to Turkey to design the American chancery and a residence for Prime Minister Issez Pasha. Sultan Abdul Hamid appointed Totten as the "private architect to the Sultan of Turkey" but was overthrown in 1909 in favor of a constitutional government.

Totten's 16th St home included the main house, which he designed and expanded for eight years, and a garden along the street frontage. In 1921 Totten bought a Japanese tearoom from Chicago businessman Charles T. Yerkes, for which he created a two-story "tea and attic room" addition.

Three years later, Totten took on the purchase and reconstruction of H. H. Richardson's Warder House. In Jan 1923, news spread about the imminent destruction of the north side of the 1500 block of K St N.W., including the Warder House. Interested citizens devised ways to preserve the block's more historic buildings. Totten bought Warder House materials from the wrecking company, numbered and stored the pieces, and reconstructed the massive mansion on the site of his garden, effectively casting his own home in shadow.

Reconstructing the Warder House as the Richardson Apartments cost Totten an estimated $175,000. He hoped the building—which contained offices and luxury apartments—would be rented for use as a foreign legation.

The Ecuador legation rented space in the building from 1933 to 1934, and the Dominican legation was located there from 1936 to 1939. Senator Hiram Bingham, the explorer who had discovered the fortress city of Machu Picchu in Peru, was Totten's most famous resident; Bingham lived in an apartment in the building from 1927 to 1934.

Totten subdivided the building to create additional apartments during the 1930s, when luxury apartments were difficult to rent. In 1936, he donated his Japanese tearoom to Choate School in Connecticut. Two years later, in financial ruin due to the Depression, Totten lost his architectural practice, and Fidelity Philadelphia Trust took over his property.

In 1942 the property was sold to Henry G. Slaughter, who increased the number of apartments to 15. From 1942 to 1943, the military and air attaché of the Polish Embassy lived at the Richardson. After Henry J. Kaiser, acting trustee for the Permanente Foundation, bought the building in 1946, it was converted for use as the Kabat-Kaiser Institute Clinic. In 1953, the National Lutheran Council bought the building for office use. The Urban Law Institute of Antioch College purchased the building in 1972 to house the Antioch School of Law.

## Exterior
The style of the Totten house is 18C and early-19C Georgian mixed with Spanish colonial.

## Interior
When Totten lived in the house, from 1915 to 1938, it included a living room, dining room, sunroom, the two-story addition for the Japanese tearoom, plus a ceramics studio.

Continue north on the west side of 16th St to the **Embassy of Poland** (1909–10; George Oakley Totten, Jr.) at 2640 16th St N.W., on the corner of 16th and Fuller Sts N.W., ☎ 234-3800. Totten had a gift for expressing French historical styles in innovative ways. His third Meridian Hill building was this Louis XVI–styled, three-bay house with an understated elegance. Although built in 1910, the building was apparently unoccupied, except for a brief residence by the ambassador from imperial Russia, until 1919, when Mrs. Henderson sold it to the Polish government.

Directly across Fuller St, also on the west side of 16th St, is the **Embassy of Italy** (1923–24; Warren and Wetmore) at 2700 16th St N.W., ☎ 328-5500. A trained architect, Gelasio Caetani, Italy's ambassador to the United States in 1924, was reportedly involved in the design of this Italian Renaissance structure, working closely with New York architects Warren and Wetmore. A wide belt course separates the ground level from those above, and the smooth limestone walls are accented by the projected triangular pediments of the main-story windows.

Continue north on 16th St to the **Scottish Rite Temple** (1938–39; Porter, Lockie and Chatelain) at 2800 16th St N.W., ☎ 232-8155. This is the local Masonic temple, not to be confused with the national temple farther south on 16th St. Perhaps the most striking feature of the Scottish Rite Temple is John Joseph Earley's concrete-and-stone mosaic above the handleless bronze door. Pulsating rays of autumnal color surround a bronze eagle and are framed by a filigreed bronze screen of animals symbolic in Masonic rites. The monolithic building, raised on a terrace five ft above the sidewalk and set back, is composed of two intersecting sections—a 70 ft cube that rises above and extends slightly in front of a rectangle that extends back 129 ft. The 81-room temple cost $350,000 to build.

Across 16th St is the **Embassy of Spain** (1921–23; George Oakley Totten, Jr.; 1926 remodeled; 1926 chancery; Jules Henri de Sibour) at 2801 16th St N.W., ☎ 452-0100. It was built by Mrs. Henderson and extensively remodeled by the government of Spain when they bought it in 1926. Both the chancery at the back of the property and the main building have been renovated several times. The embassy building is constructed of stuccoed brick and has a mansard roof.

Continue north on 16th St to the **Embassy of Mexico** (1910–11; Nathan C. Wyeth), 2829 16th St N.W., ☎ 728-1628, which was originally built as the residence of Secretary of the Treasury Franklin MacVeagh. Wyeth's design in buff-colored brick set this structure apart from its lavishly embellished neighbors. When the home was bought by the government of Mexico in 1921 to serve as its embassy, the Tuscan porte cochere was added to the stark front façade. The building serves as the Mexican Cultural Institute, a nonprofit organization dedicated to promoting Mexico's art and culture.

## All Souls Church Unitarian

Continue north. Across Columbia Rd at 16th and Harvard Sts is All Souls Church Unitarian (1924; Shepley; Coolidge and Shattuck), ☎ 332-5266. Office hours are Tues–Fri 10–6. Tours can be arranged. Shepley's variation is a large service wing with a courtyard that is perpendicular to the church's main façade.

### History

The building is the place of worship for the First Unitarian Church of Washington, which changed its name to All Souls Church in 1877 in order to incorporate. In 1911 the already expanding membership increased dramatically with the presidential inauguration of the church's most famous member, William H. Taft. As a result, the church building at 14th and L Sts N.W. was no longer big enough for the congregation. Plans were drawn up for a new church in 1913, only to be put aside when World War I was declared.

After the war, interest in the new church building resurfaced. In a shrewd maneuver, the Unitarians razed the 14th St building, replaced it with a business structure, and sold the 14th St building and lot for a healthy profit. This money, along with donations and loans was enough to fund a new church building. In 1920 the 16th St N.W. land was purchased from Mrs. Henderson.

The 1920 competition held for the design of All Souls Church stipulated that the structure "typify Unitarian ideas and ideals, harmonize with the architecture of Washington and fit into the surroundings of the chosen site." The winner of the competition was Henry Shepley, grandson of architect H. H. Richardson and member of the Boston firm of Coolidge and Shattuck. His model was the baroque

London church St. Martin-in-the-Fields, designed by James Gibbs in the early 1700s. The new All Souls Church was dedicated on Sun, Oct 24, 1924. President and Mrs. Coolidge, and William H. Taft, then chief justice of the Supreme Court, attended the ceremony. The structure included a sanctuary, office space, parlor space, and Pierce Hall.

### Washington Notes

Pierce Hall functioned as a large auditorium, complete with motion picture projection booth. The Sun evening movie hour, with accompanying music from the Tulloch organ, soon became a popular weekly event.

The 16th St church incorporates a bell cast in 1822 by Joseph Revere, son of American Revolutionary hero Paul Revere. The bell is still used today.

## Exterior

Shepley designed the stone-and-brick church to resemble St. Martin-in-the-Fields in London's Trafalgar Square. This type of parish church design was popular throughout the 18C and early 19C in much of the eastern United States.

## Interior

A youth club uses the subsanctuary gymnasium. A sanctuary, balcony, stage area, classrooms, and Pierce Hall occupy the rest of the church.

### Washington Notes

All Souls Church has attracted many prominent Washingtonians, including Frederic A. Delano of Washington's Planning Commission; department store owner Julius Garfinkel; Dr. Percival Hall, president of Gallaudet College; William Howard Taft, whose funeral ceremonies were held here in 1930 before interment at Arlington National Cemetery; Democratic presidential candidate Adlai Stevenson; and former D.C. mayor Marion Barry. Today the integrated church is a popular place of worship for many of Washington's prominent African Americans.

Also on 16th St near the intersection with Columbia Rd is the **Unification Church, Washington Chapel, Church of Jesus Christ of Latter-Day Saints** (1932–33; Young and Hansen) at 2810 16th St N.W., ☎ 462-5770. Two of Brigham Young's grandsons worked together on this structure, which is reminiscent of the Mormon temple in Salt Lake City; Don Young was the architect, and Mahonri Sharp Young created the mosaic of Christ over the main entrance. The bird's-eye marble used for the exterior veneer was quarried in Utah. The architectural style is a mix of classical elements, such as the pilasters, and medieval touches, such as the buttresses.

Catercorner across 16th St is the **National Baptist Memorial Church** (1922–26; Egerton Swartwout), 1501 Columbia Rd N.W., at 16th St and Columbia Rd N.W., ☎ 265-1410. The congregation was incorporated in 1906, and a neo-Gothic mission church designed by George W. Stone, Sr., and called Immanuel Baptist was built here in 1909. In designing a replacement church, Swartwout took as his inspiration John Nash's Church of All Souls in London. President Warren G. Harding did the groundbreaking for this largely neoclassical structure in 1921, and the cornerstone was laid in 1922, but the church wasn't dedicated until 1933.

National Baptist Memorial Church is an excellent example of an urban church adapting to its community. Four other congregations worship here: First Haitian Baptist Church, Ignesia Bautista (a Latin American Baptist church), Tigrigna Evangelical Church (an Eretrian Baptist church), and Covenant Community Church. In addition, several community organizations make their headquarters here, including a refugee-assistance group funded by Catholic charities and the Academy of Hope, an organization that offers computer training and helps new arrivals qualify for the General Education Diploma (high school equivalency diploma).

Continue east on Columbia Rd to its intersection with Euclid St and the **Avignon Freres** shop, 1775 Columbia Rd, in the middle of the block between Champlain and Euclid Sts N.W. Established in 1918, this was one of the area's most elegant caterers. The shop has adapted to the changing times and today specializes in fine pastries and baked goods.

The southwest corner of 18th St and Columbia Rd, now occupied by Crestar Bank, 1800 Columbia Rd N.W., was once the site of the **Knickerbocker Theatre** (1917; Geare), one of the town's fanciest and most elite movie houses until a snowy evening in 1922, when it became the site of one of Washington's worst disasters.

### Washington Notes

Opened in 1917, the Knickerbocker was a neoclassical showpiece with a capacity for 1,700 patrons. On Jan 27, 1922, a storm began that covered the city with 28 inches of snow. Two days later, a Sat, the Knickerbocker opened as usual for business. At 9:10 P.M., near the end of the silent film feature, the ceiling cracked and fell, dropping tons of steel, masonry, and snow on the helpless audience below. Ninety-eight people died, and 136 more were seriously injured when they were trapped beneath the debris. Subsequent investigations determined that the contractor had secured the roof's beams a mere two inches into the wall instead of the required eight. Although architect Reginald Geare was cleared of any culpability for the horrible collapse, he never recovered from the shock and committed suicide in 1927.

Continue south on Columbia Rd to its intersection with Mintwood Place N.W. and the **Woodley Apartments** (1903), 1851 Columbia Rd N.W., the first apartment building on Columbia Rd and now used by the Russian government as a trade mission. Mintwood Place before and after World War II was known as Admiral's Row because of all the navy personnel who lived in its pastel town houses. Senator Thomas Gore, grandfather of author Gore Vidal and the first blind senator to serve in Congress, lived at 1863 Mintwood Place from 1907 to 1921. Most of these buildings are now apartments and condominiums. What was known as General's Row is only a block away on Biltmore St. Many of the town houses formerly lived in by Pentagon personnel have been torn down to make way for modern apartment buildings.

Continue south on Columbia Rd to its intersection with Belmont St N.W. and the **Norwood Apartments** (1917), 1868 Columbia Rd N.W., ☎ 265-5600, noted for its decorative plasterwork.

### Washington Notes

Representative William Bankhead, who at one time was Speaker of the House, lived here, but his fame was eclipsed by that of his actress daughter Tallulah, known for her foghorn voice and her role in Alfred Hitchcock's *Lifeboat*.

Continue south on Columbia Rd to the **Wyoming Apartments** (1905; Simmons; DL) at 2022 Columbia Rd N.W., ☎ 332-1900, one of several fine apartment houses in the area built before World War II. Stanley Simmons, a prominent local architect at the turn of the century, designed several residences and apartment buildings in the area. Most of his designs favor the eclectic Beaux-Arts style and are made of stone or light brick.

### Washington Notes

The Wyoming is known as the former home of Dwight and Mamie Eisenhower, who lived here in the late 1920s to early 1930s when Ike worked in the War Department. The tale told is that during those days the Eisenhowers were so poor Ike walked to work to save money, and Mamie, who grocery-shopped at what is now Fort McNair, would take a cab only as far as Florida Ave and walk the rest of the way to save the cost of crossing a taxi zone.

Continue south on Columbia Rd to the island formed by the intersections of Columbia Rd, Connecticut Ave, and California St. There is a bronze statue of Major General George B. McClellan (1907; Frederick MacMonnies, sculptor; James Crocoft, architect). McClellan (1826–1885), known for his inaction as the head of the Union Army in the early years of the Civil War, stands permanently entrenched by urban traffic. The statue appears isolated, and it takes some fancy footwork to get to it. MacMonnies won a 1902 competition (judged by, among others, the architect Charles F. McKim and sculptors Daniel Chester French and Augustus Saint-Gaudens) to create the nine-ft statue, which was exhibited at the Paris Salon of 1906 before being shipped to the U.S. in 1907. The richly decorated Beaux-Arts pedestal has cannons, flags, and arms, with eight escutcheons naming McClellan's battles. An inscription reads: "Erected by the Society of the Army of the Republic and the Congress of the United States 1907."

Continue south on Connecticut Ave to the **Washington Hilton and Towers** (1965) at 1919 Connecticut Ave N.W., ☎ 483-3000. According to city lore, this was the site of an oak tree designated as an Indian "treaty tree" by the chief of the Anacostia Indians. It was better known to locals as the site of the National Masonic Lodge from 1922 to 1945. Frank Lloyd Wright designed a building he called the Crystal Palace to be built here after the lodge was torn down; but the city fathers feared it would dominate the city skyline, so the project was scrapped.

### Washington Notes

It was outside the Washington Hilton that John Hinckley shot President Ronald Reagan, Press Secretary James Brady, a Secret Service agent, and a Washington police officer on March 30, 1981.

Continue south on Connecticut Ave. Pause near its intersection with Florida Ave and look down Connecticut Ave toward the center of the city. Until the 1920s, most Washingtonians lived below what was then called Boundary St (named Florida Ave in 1890). This was the northernmost point on L'Enfant's map of the Federal City, and basically remained so until the advent of the automobile and a comprehensive public transportation system.

To continue with the next walk, proceed south on Connecticut Ave for several blocks to Dupont Circle.

# 16 · Dupont Circle West Area

Metro: Red Line to Dupont Circle.
Bus: G2, D1, D2, D3, D6, L2, or 42.

## Dupont Circle

Dupont Circle, loosely bounded by U St on the north, 17th St on the east, Rock Creek Park on the west, and K St on the south, has developed from a nonresidential outpost of the Federal City in the mid-1800s to a bustling commercial center with shops, restaurants, and museums. Coexisting with the area's commercial and residential elements is a community of foreign diplomats whose embassies and chanceries are located along Embassy Row in the grand mansions that once housed the city's wealthiest residents during the winter social season. Dupont Circle also has a reputation as a gathering place for the area's homosexual community.

### History

Dupont Circle was one of Pierre L'Enfant's original seven circles in his plan of Washington City, but for the first 70 years of the city's history, this neighborhood remained relatively undeveloped. Old Slash Run, also called Shad Run, ran within a block of the circle. When it rained, this stream became a torrent, causing problems for those wanting to cross it. Slash Run also had a foul odor as the creek carried offal from the city's slaughterhouses. Until 1870 there really wasn't much reason to come to this area, especially since the center of the residential city and its government buildings was miles to the south and east. Dupont Circle was considered the edge of the city; Boundary St (Florida Ave) served to mark the line between developed and undeveloped land. But beginning in 1871, the reason for the interest in the area was land speculation.

In 1871, Alexander "Boss" Shepherd was appointed executive director of the city's Board of Public Works. In this capacity, and as territorial governor (1872–74), Shepherd's goal was to improve the city as rapidly as possible. Coincidentally, at that time Shepherd was also a member of a real estate consortium that began buying land near the circle for 10–25 cents a ft. Soon after these purchases Shepherd ordered major improvements in the area, among them the elimination of Slash Run (it was buried in conduits and sewer pipes), the construction of a metal-truss bridge on P St connecting Dupont Circle to Georgetown's bustling commercial area, as well as the landscaping of the intersection of Massachusetts, New Hampshire, and Connecticut Aves and 19th and P Sts, thus creating the circle, which was designated a federal park. It was called Pacific Circle because of its western location.

When Shepherd built his own mansion at the corner of Connecticut Ave and K

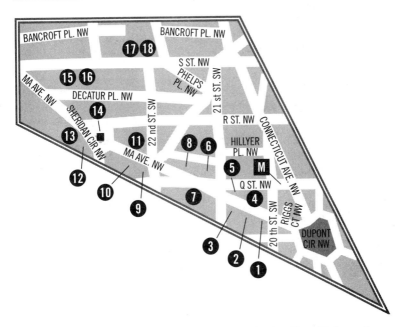

1 Blaine Mansion
2 Beale House
3 Walsh-McLean House
4 Hdqtrs of the Church of the Savior Ecumenical Church
5 Westin Fairfax Hotel
6 Phillips Collection
7 Anderson House (Society of the Cincinnati)
8 Townsend House (Cosmos Club)
9 Alexander Stewart House
10 Chancery of Ireland
11 Hennen Jennings House (Embassy of Greece)
12 Edward Everett House (Embassy of Turkey)
13 Alice Pike Barney House
14 Sheridan Circle
15 Woodrow Wilson House
16 Textile Museum
17 Thomas Gales House (Union at Myanmar Embassy)
18 Residence of Irish Ambassador

St, not far from Pacific (later Dupont) Circle, accusations were made that the area was chosen for street paving and lighting, sewers, and other civic improvements before other, more established neighborhoods because Shepherd lived there. Nevertheless, others soon followed Shepherd, taking up residency in the area.

### Washington Notes

Alexander Robey "Boss" Shepherd, a controversial figure, was hailed by some as "a latter day L'Enfant, with more brains and more power," and denounced by others for bankrupting the city. Along with the Dupont area improvements, Shepherd authorized the paving of roads, the planting of 50,000 trees, and the installation of gaslights. These improvements and others cost the city almost $20 million in three years. As a result of the city's debts, Congress established a Board of Governors to oversee the city. Boss

Shepherd, who had used much of his own money to improve the city and to speculate in land development, was broke. He sold his property to settle his debts and moved to Chihuahua, Mexico, where he discovered a silver and gold mine, thus once again becoming a rich man.

Shepherd's improvements led to substantial investment in the area. In 1873, Senator William Morris Stewart of Nevada built a palatial residence called Stewart's Castle by some, but Stewart's Folly by others because of its isolation. Stewart spent $225,000 on the Second Empire–style structure and another $100,000 to furnish it. The house stood at the site of Riggs National Bank, on the corner of 20th St and Massachusetts Ave. Stewart eventually found his "castle" too expensive to maintain. In the 1890s he rented it to the Chinese for their mission, and later he sold the building.

In 1874, the Metropolitan Railroad Company's streetcars began service in the area, making the circle easily accessible to the rest of the city. In 1875, when the British legation moved into its new Second Empire–style structure west of Connecticut Ave on N St, it enhanced the area's reputation as a growing and chic region. The wealthy built mansions along the avenues, and the middle and working classes (tradesmen and servants, over half of whom were African American, or immigrants from Great Britain, Ireland, and Germany) lived along the adjoining streets.

Joseph Moore in his *Picturesque Washington* (1884) described the area: "It is on this spacious plain, but a few years ago an almost valueless area of swamps, that those palatial mansions, the pride and boast of the capital, are erected. Here are the residences of the wealthiest citizens and those of the millionaires from different sections of the United States who make Washington their winter home. . . . On every side is a dazzling spectacle of luxury and grandeur, and one can obtain by a stroll through the avenues and streets, a realization of the enormous wealth that is centering in Washington at this present time." Many of the wealthy residents lived in the area only during the winter season, using their mansions to entertain the city's influential residents. By the turn of the century, several foreign missions, such as those of Austro-Hungary, Spain, and Switzerland, had relocated near the circle, adding a cosmopolitan allure.

Although the racial mix shifted so that white residents outnumbered their African American counterparts, a substantial black presence remained. Just before World War I, black professionals moved into the eastern part of the neighborhood, and the 1700 block of U St became known as Strivers Row. Segregation was the rule, however, and the black and white communities developed as separate entities. The Dupont Circle Citizens Association served white citizens, and the Midway Civic Association served African Americans.

By the 1920s, many of the circle's affluent citizens had left the area or their property had been sold by their heirs. Income and property taxes were a blow to the area's upper class. Once the wealthier families left, property values began to fall. Some of the mansions were demolished. In the 1930s and '40s the middle-class presence in Dupont Circle increased. More mansions were demolished to make room for office buildings or were converted to foreign embassies. In the 1950s and 1960s, the city in general, and not just the Dupont Circle area, lost residents to the suburbs. As property values continued to fall around Dupont Circle, the residential profile changed in large part from middle-class to proponents of the "counter-culture." Artists, who could find affordable rents in the area, gave a boost to the visual and theatrical arts, which had been part of Dupont Circle since the 1940s. Art galleries, artists' studios, and small theaters proliferated. In the late 1960s Dupont Circle also became the site of many civil protests. Anti–Vietnam War demonstrations became common, hippies hung out at the fountain and lived in the row houses that had been converted to apartments. Also in the 1960s, further changes occurred when large office buildings appeared north and south along Connecticut Ave in place of the mansions and row houses.

In the mid-1970s, property values began to increase, as the circle's historical neighborhoods once again attracted middle-class families. In 1978, the Dupont Circle area was designated as a historic district, with its outer boundaries at Florida and Rhode Island Aves, 17th, 21st, and 22nd Sts. The Strivers section was excluded from the designation, but finally gained historic status in 1985 (outer boundaries at Florida and Rhode Island Aves, 16th, 22nd, T, and N Sts). Dupont Circle today hosts a lively mix of nationalities and an impressive array of businesses, residences, galleries, stores, and restaurants.

> ### Washington Notes
> The gay community has for a number of years maintained a strong presence in Dupont Circle. Gays celebrated the District's first Gay Pride Day just north of the circle on S St in 1975. The celebration is now held annually in this area, usually around 24th and N Sts N.W.

## Dupont Circle Memorial Park and Fountain
Start at the Dupont Circle Memorial Park and Fountain (1921; Daniel Chester French), located in the traffic circle at the intersection of Massachusetts, New Hampshire, and Connecticut Aves and 19th and P Sts.

### History
In 1882, Congress chose the circle as the site for a memorial statue of Rear Admiral Samuel Francis Du Pont, a Civil War hero who entered the navy as a boy of 12 in 1818 and died in 1865. The statue, erected in 1885, proved unpopular. The admiral's niece, wife of a Delaware senator, suggested that the Du Pont family buy the statue from the government and put in its place a more pleasing work of art in the admiral's honor. Congress agreed and commissioned Daniel Chester French (who also designed the Lincoln Memorial and the Lincoln sculpture) to design a fountain.

There are two tunnels beneath the circle. Originally built in 1949 to relieve trolley line congestion, the tunnels were boarded up in 1962 when trolley service ended. In Feb 1995, Dupont Down Under, a collection of fast-food stands and retail shops opened. The food stands were housed in fake "streetcars," and photographs of the tunnel's history lined the walls. Unfortunately, the venture failed to attract sufficient customers, and Dupont Down Under closed.

## The Fountain
The Dupont Memorial Fountain cost the Du Pont family $77,521. The 17 ft high white marble fountain has two basins. The lower basin, which forms the work's base, measures 35 ft 10 inches in diameter; the upper basin, supported by a cylindrical shaft, measures 14 ft across. The shaft's three carved figures, one male and

two female, represent the sea, the stars, and the wind, reflecting Admiral Du Pont's Naval service. The inscription around the lower basin reads: "Samuel Francis Dupont, Rear Admiral United States Navy, 1803–1865. This memorial fountain replaces a statue erected by the Congress of the United States in recognition of his distinguished service."

## Embassy Row

The Dupont Circle neighborhood is known for its heavy concentration of embassies, particularly along Massachusetts Ave.

### Washington Notes

The United States didn't send, or receive, ambassadors until 1893—more than a century after the country's birth and 93 years after Congress moved into the Federal City. America's legation ministers who worked abroad also served in a diplomatic capacity. Congress had to be talked into posting ambassadors and would only send them to leading European countries and three Latin American nations. The first ambassador to be received in the U.S. was Sir Julian Pauncefote of Great Britain, who was received by President Grover Cleveland in 1893, just one day before the French ambassador presented his credentials.

By the 1940s many countries established their embassies in the mansions along Massachusetts Ave, causing the area to be nicknamed Embassy Row. The area was replete with diplomats, their entourages, and their limos. By the 1960s, many Washingtonians complained about the "chancery sprawl." Since the 1980s, construction of new embassies has been limited to downtown sites and those west of Connecticut Ave.

### Washington Notes

Diplomats stationed in Washington have a reputation for driving too fast and getting away with it, since diplomatic license plates on a car very often result in diplomatic immunity from speeding tickets. Things weren't much different at the turn of the century. In 1890 the Washington Star reported, "Some diplomats are addicted to much faster driving than the law permits. One attaché drives a beautiful stallion [along] the avenues at break-neck speed: another secretary of legation has a playful way of riding his horse up to the doors of shops across the sidewalks."

Some diplomats in those days were equally unhappy to be here. Because of the oppressive humidity in the summer, the British stationed here received hazardous duty pay. "What have I done to deserve such a place of exile!" was Minister Barcourt of France's reaction to being stationed in the District at the turn of the century. The reaction of another French minister, named Prevost, was a bit more strong—he committed suicide. In his diary he wrote that he "suffered from the heat of mid-summer and couldn't stand the iced drinks."

## Blaine Mansion

From the fountain at Dupont Circle, walk west to the southwest corner of Massachusetts Ave and 20th St to the oldest surviving mansion in the neighborhood, the Blaine Mansion (1881; John Fraser) at 2000 Massachusetts Ave N.W.

## History

At the age of 21, James Blaine married Harriet Stanwood in 1851 and received financial help from her family to pursue a career in journalism, which exposed him to politics. By 1856, Blaine had helped found the Republican Party and was a party delegate from Maine. In 1858, he was elected to the House of Representatives, and in 1869, he served as Speaker of the House. Blaine and his peers were responsible for the metamorphosis of the Whig Party into the Republican Party, maintaining many tenets of the Whig philosophy, including a strong opposition to slavery. Blaine served as secretary of state under Presidents James Garfield (1881) and Benjamin Harrison (1889–93), both of whom beat him in the race for their party's presidential nomination. In 1884, Blaine ran unsuccessfully for president against Grover Cleveland. Blaine, who died in 1893 at the age of 62, contributed significantly to the shaping of America's foreign policy. He broadened and strengthened ties with South America, presided over the first Pan-American Congress, and backed the theory of reciprocal trade treaties.

The Blaines purchased the land from a family friend, William Walter Phelps, in 1881, and a building permit was issued in June 1881. The Blaines moved into their house in Dec 1882, but their new house proved too expensive to maintain. Consequently, the Blaines moved to a residence in Lafayette Square in 1883. Levi Leiter of Chicago, a partner with Marshall Field in retail, leased the property for a year while his own mansion was being constructed.

### Washington Notes

George Westinghouse leased the Blaine house in 1898, before eventually buying it in 1901. An inventor since his youth, Westinghouse built a rotary engine by the age of 15. He went on to patent the air brake for trains, receiving praise for using interchangeable parts and for using a standardized design. The pioneering inventor founded the Westinghouse Electric Company, which built the generators that powered the hydroelectric plants at Niagra Falls, the New York City and Paris subways, as well as the Metropolitan Railway of London. When Westinghouse died in 1914, ownership of Blaine House passed to his son, who didn't live there. In 1920, Henry B. Spencer bought the house, converting it into three family apartments in 1921. In 1948, the building was renovated and converted into office space.

## Exterior

The building is two and a half stories tall, with its main entrance facing Massachusetts Ave. The primarily brick and terra-cotta structure features molded brick patterns, seven chimneys, a mansard roof, and a tower. A large wood porte cochere (carriage entrance) extends toward the avenue from the building's eastern façade.

Walk west on Massachusetts Ave about a half-block to the **Beale House** (1898; Glenn Brown; DL) at 2012 Massachusetts Ave N.W., national headquarters of the National Federation of Business and Professional Women's Clubs/USA Business and Professional Women's Foundation since 1956. This imposing five-story brick-and-sandstone structure, designed in the Georgian and Renaissance revival styles that were much in vogue at the turn of the century, was originally built for the Joseph Beale family. In 1904, the house was purchased by Samuel Spencer, a former partner of J.P. Morgan and Company, who later became the first president of the Southern Railroad. The house has oak flooring, Italian marble fireplaces, plaster friezes and moldings, Ionic columns, and a mahogany-and-walnut grand staircase. Intricately detailed wrought-iron gates enclose the front entrance. The walkway leading to this entrance is lined with bricks noting the names of those who contributed to the building's second renovation.

## Walsh-McLean House

Continue west a half-block to the **Walsh-McLean House** (1903; Henry Anderson; DL) at 2020 Massachusetts Ave N.W., now the Indonesian Embassy. This ornate structure, with its Renaissance baroque, Louis XVI, and Art Nouveau influences (called "a fabulous eclectic pile" by *Washington Post* architecture critic Benjamin Forgey), was the scene of privilege and parties created by enormous wealth. It was also the site of events of enormous bad luck for Irish immigrant Thomas Walsh and his family.

### History

The house, according to daughter Evalyn Walsh in her memoirs, "expresses dreams my Father and Mother had when they were poor in Colorado." Born in 1851 in Tipperary, Thomas Walsh came to this country in 1870 and 26 years later struck it rich in the gold fields of Colorado. Considered one of the richest men in the world, Walsh chose Danish architect Henry Anderson to design the Washington showplace with a ballroom, three-story center hall, and a carved Art Nouveau mahogany balustrade. Upon completion in 1903, the unfurnished house cost $835,000. The furnishings were also elaborate, with a dining service of gold made from nuggets taken from Walsh's Camp Bird Mine in Ouray, Colorado. Legend has it that a slab of gold was built into the mansion's foundations. Walsh's parties were elaborate, expensive, and attended by many notables of the age, among them Admiral George Dewey and King Leopold of Belgium.

In 1905, Evalyn and her brother Vinson were in an automobile accident. Evalyn was badly injured and Vinson was killed. The death of his son and his daughter's injuries changed Walsh from an outgoing host to a gradual recluse. He died in seclusion in 1910, two years after Evalyn had eloped with *Washington Post* heir Edward Beale McLean, who bought Evalyn the supposedly unlucky Hope Diamond (on display at the Smithsonian Institution's Museum of Natural History since 1958).

### *Washington Notes*

The McLeans, though extraordinarily wealthy, did not seem to escape the curse of the Hope Diamond. While in possession of the diamond, one of their tragedies was the death of their son Vinson, who was named for Evalyn's brother. To prevent him from being kidnapped, the McLeans kept Vinson guarded at all times. In 1919 while trying to get free of supervision, Vinson ran from his guards into the street and was killed by a car. Edward was implicated in the Teapot Dome Scandal in 1923 during Warren G. Harding's administration. (The secretaries of the interior and the navy resigned over the scandal involving the leasing of federal oil reserves—one in Teapot Dome, Wyoming—to private oil producers.) By 1933, Edward's nerves were shattered. He was declared insane and committed to an asylum in Baltimore.

In the 1930s and '40s, the home was used for Red Cross activities and the Washington Civic Theater. In 1951 Evalyn Walsh sold the property to Indonesia.

## Exterior

This tan brick mansion is three and a half stories tall. Its walls are trimmed with three bands of limestone contrasting with brick. Other distinctive features: the second-story open gallery, a carriage porch on the west façade, and the east façade's projecting conservatory, which features stained glass windows.

## Interior

Highlights include the three-story entrance hall crowned by a stained glass skylight and the Louis XVI drawing room, with its ornate woodwork and plaster, gilt pilasters, and ceiling mural, *Eternity of Angels*. The music room features solid mahogany woodwork.

Across the street, at 2025 Massachusetts Ave N.W., is the **Headquarters of the Church of the Savior Ecumenical Church** (1885; W. Bruce Gray), a Romanesque–Queen Anne mansion built by Samuel M. Bryan in 1885 and one of the few surviving buildings by architect W. Bruce Gray. The eclectic, asymmetrical design includes a conical tower on the structure's west side. The building also features stained glass and a recessed main entrance.

Cross 21st St to 2100 Massachusetts Ave N.W., ITT Sheraton's **Westin Fairfax Hotel.** Opened in 1927, this landmark hotel has been a favorite of Washington society and popular political figures.

> ### Washington Notes
> Vice President Al Gore lived here as a child. The hotel's fine restaurant, the Jockey Club, opened on the eve of John F. Kennedy's inauguration and was the favorite lunch spot for two first ladies, Jacqueline Kennedy and Nancy Reagan.

## *Phillips Collection*

1600 21 St N.W. ☎ 387-2151. Web: www.phillipscollection.org. Open Tues–Sat 10–5; Sun 12–7. Summer hours may differ. Admission: contribution requested. Thurs 5–8:30 is Artful Evenings, with musical entertainment and cash bar. Closed New Year's Day, July 4, Thanksgiving, and Christmas Day. Tours Wed and Sat at 2. Gallery Talks on first and third Thurs of the month at 12:30. Free concerts Sept–May Sun at 5. Restrooms, museum gift shop, café (luncheon and light fare Tues–Sat 10:45–4:30; Sun 12–6). Wheelchair accessible. Children's guidebook available.

Cross Massachusetts Ave and continue north a half-block to America's first museum of modern American art, the Phillips Collection (original house, 1897; Hornblower & Marshall; fourth story added, 1915; McKim, Mead and White; annex and glass-enclosed connecting bridge, 1960; Wyeth and King; 1989; Arthur Cotton Moore). The Phillips has a fine collection of 19C and 20C European and American art displayed in an intimate residential environment. Until the 1950s, the Phillips was the only museum in town where 20C American modern art was regularly exhibited.

**Highlights:** Pierre Auguste Renoir's *The Luncheon of the Boating Party,* Vincent Van Gogh's *The Road Menders* and *House at Auvers,* as well as Paul Cézanne's *Self Portrait.*

## History

To anyone familiar with Washington's climate it may be difficult to believe, but it was the local weather that brought the Phillips family to Washington. A doctor advised Duncan and his wife, Eliza, that a warmer climate than their native Pittsburgh would be good for them, and friends recommended a season in Washington. They moved to the city the winter of 1896, which turned out to be extremely mild, so they decided to settle here and had this house built.

The Phillips Collection began as a memorial to the beloved father and brother of the museum's founder, Duncan Phillips. Phillips, scion of a family whose fortune was made in steel, began collecting art after his graduation from Yale University in 1908. With his brother James, he convinced his parents to set aside $10,000 annually to buy paintings. When his father, Major Duncan Clinch Phillips, died in 1917, and his brother James died 15 months later in 1918, Duncan Phillips, with his mother, Eliza Irwin Laughlin, decided to create the Phillips Memorial Art Gallery in their honor. In 1920, a skylighted gallery and storeroom above the library were added to the house to provide more space, and the initial collection of 250 paintings was opened to the public. A year later, Duncan married Marjorie Acker, a young painter. They offered art classes and purchased paintings by emerging artists for their "encouragement collection."

Originally, the collection contained only American artists, including 20 paintings the family brought from Pittsburgh when they moved to Washington. Phillips later broadened the collection by adding European artists. The collection's organization, which juxtaposed contemporary and classic works, strongly reflected Phillip's taste and artistic curiosity. In the 1920s, the collection grew rapidly. On a trip to Europe in 1923, Duncan Phillips saw Renoir's *The Luncheon of the Boating Party* and soon afterward bought it for $125,000. This became the cornerstone of the collection and helped establish the museum as a serious collection. The Phillips, great enthusiasts of American modernists, bought several works of John Marin, Georgia O'Keeffe, Marsden Hartley, and Arthur Dove. Duncan Phillips also published respected criticisms that helped promote an understanding of modern art.

By the 1930s, the number of works had reached 600, and the two display rooms were insufficient to handle the collection. The Phillips decided to move out of their home and convert the entire house into a museum. The collection again outgrew its surroundings in the 1960s. When a new wing was annexed at 1612 21st St N.W. to house part of the permanent collection and to create space for temporary exhibitions, the museum was renamed the Phillips Collection. In 1966, Duncan Phillips died at the age of 80, leaving the direction of the museum to Marjorie. She served as director until 1978, and was succeeded by her son Laughlin.

Laughlin began to transform the museum from a personal home collection to a public state-of-the-art museum, a process that would eventually cost $12 million. In 1983–84, the museum was renovated to include a new electrical system, climate-control, and a modern security system. In 1987, Phillips began renovation on the old annex. The renovated Goh Annex, named for Mr. and Mrs. Yasuhiro Goh, major donors to the museum, opened in 1989. In 1992, Laughlin retired after serving 20 years as director and was succeeded by Charles Moffett, former senior curator of the paintings at the National Gallery of Art, who became the first nonfamily member to serve as director. Since 1972, more than 100 works have been purchased, including a Jackson Pollock, three Diebenkorns, a Picasso, and a Matisse. In June 1998, Jay Gates assumed the Directorship of the Phillips Collection. Previously the director of the Dallas Museum of Art and the Seattle Museum of Art, Gates plans to "lead the museum into the next century with a strong exhibition program."

## Exterior

Hornblower & Marshall, the architects of the original 1897 Phillips home where the museum opened in 1921, drew elements from both the Georgian revival style and the succeeding Federal style. The main façade is asymmetrical and balanced by a wide Palladian window occupying the first-story bay. There is also a touch of the Richardsonian Romanesque style in having the building set on a high basement of rock-faced sandstone. The Italian Renaissance–style library wing has bracketed window frames and heraldic devices carved in stone below a large, square bay window. In 1920, a skylighted second story was added, and in 1923 a mansard roof was added to the original house. In 1960, Wyeth and King designed the Goh Annex, which was renovated by Arthur Cotton Moore in 1989. The annex is divided into four levels. Over the front door is a bas-relief of a bird (Pierre Bourdelle) in flight, taken from one of Duncan Phillip's favorite paintings by Georges Braque.

## Interior

Please note that at the time of this writing the Phillips is undergoing renovations in the galleries in both the original Phillips mansion and in the Goh Annex. It is very likely that during and after the renovations the order of galleries and the paintings displayed will have changed from the information listed here. During these renovations the doors of the mansion at 1600 21st St N.W. have been reopened as the main entrance. Also, there will be a new exhibit, *Renoir to Rothko: The Eye of Duncan Phillips*, that highlights the development of the museum.

Duncan Phillips envisioned an environment different from the normal museum experience for the display of his collection. "Instead of the academic grandeur of marble halls and stairways and miles of chairless spaces, . . . we plan to try the effect of domestic architecture, or rooms small or at least livable, and of such intimate, attractive atmosphere as we associate with a beautiful home."

Just outside the main entrance (located in the Goh Annex) is Alexander Calder's layered pyramid *Pagoda* (1963). Duncan Phillips enjoyed moving paintings from gallery to gallery, curious to see how they would appear in different settings. This practice continues today. Generally, the first floor of the **Goh Annex** displays mid-20C works, with a separate room displaying four major works by Mark Rothko. The second floor of the annex usually displays the permanent collection's 19C European works, particularly impressionist and postimpressionist paintings. This floor also includes the permanent **Renoir Room** in the rear center, featuring *The Luncheon of the Boating Party* (1881; Pierre Auguste Renoir). Also in this area are two important works of Vincent Van Gogh's—*The Road Menders* (1889) and *House at Auvers* (1890). At the rear of the floor is a gallery given over to rotating displays of photographs, works by contemporary artists, and works from the permanent collection. The annex's third floor is for major temporary and traveling exhibits.

From the third floor of the annex, walk south through the skywalk to the upper second floor of the original building. In the first gallery is Pablo Picasso's bathing scene *The Blue Room* (1901). Continue south, taking the steps down to the lower second floor, to works by European and American modernists and early- to mid-20C American artists. At the bottom of the stairs to the right is a small gallery containing *The Dream* (1939; Marc Chagall). Across the hall is the **Klee Room** with such Paul Klee works as *The Way to the Citadel* (1937) and *Arab Song* (1932), which was prompted by Klee's travels in Tunisia.

Take the main staircase down to the first floor to displays of 19C and 20C European and American works, including those of French and American impressionists. Hanging above the stair landing is Alexander Calder's tin-and-wire *Only One Bird* (1952). At the bottom of the stairs, turn south into the **Gerald J. Miller Gallery.** Highlights include Hilaire-Germain-Edgar Degas's *Women Combing Their Hair* (1875) and *Dancers at the Bar* (c. 1900) and Eugene-Louis Boudin's *Beach at Trouville* (1863). In the adjoining **Charles Englehard Foundation Gallery** is Edouard Manet's *Spanish Ballet* (1862) and Jean-Baptiste Chardin's still life *A Bowl of Plums* (c. 1728).

Duncan Phillips was very interested in color, as exemplified by the extensive collection of Pierre Bonnard paintings, one of the largest collections of the artist in North America, including Bonnard's *Circus Rider* (1894) and *Woman With A Dog* (1922). Also displayed in this gallery is *Self Portrait* (1898; Paul Cézanne).

Walk north, past the main lobby stairs to the **Robert and Arlene Kogod Gallery,** which includes in its American collection Maurice Prendergast's *Ponte della Paglia* (1899), Winslow Homer's *Girl with a Pitchfork* (1867), William Merritt Chase's *Hide and Seek* (1888), and Thomas Eakins's *Miss Amelia Van Buren* (c. 1891). Continue north into the **Music Room,** where Sunday concerts have been held since 1941. Turn and face the entry. On one side hangs El Greco's *The Repentant St. Peter* (1600–1605 or later). On the other side hangs Francisco José De Goya's older and more peasantlike Peter in *The Repentant St. Peter* (c. 1820–24). Walk to the far end of the gallery and its beautifully ornate wood-carved fireplace. Next to it is hung Georges Braque's abstract *The Round Table* (1929).

The stairs from the rear of the Music Room lead up to the second floor of the Goh Annex. Returning south through the Music Room to the main lobby leads to the stairs down to the ground floor. Here are the gift shop, café, and another exit.

## Anderson House (Society of the Cincinnati)

2118 Massachusetts Ave N.W. ☎ 785-2040. Open Tues–Sat 1–4. Admission: free. Self-guided tours (maps available). Guided tours Tues–Sat 9:30 and 3, by appointment for groups of 15–45.

Exiting the museum, walk south a half-block on 21st St to Massachusetts Ave. Cross the avenue to the headquarters of the Society of the Cincinnati, also known as Anderson House (1902–5; Arthur Little and Herbert Brown). The expansive mansion built by Larz Anderson III, minister to Belgium and ambassador to Japan, houses the Society of the Cincinnati, an organization founded by commissioned officers of the American Continental Army and their French allies after America's victory in the Revolutionary War. Membership in the society is passed down to the eldest male son of an officer who served in the Continental Army. The society's name comes from Quinctius Cincinnatus, a 5C B.C. Roman general who defeated invaders but shunned personal glory and reward. George Washington served as the society's first president.

**Highlights:** A house museum of intricate architectural detail and grand proportions, this home features 17 kinds of marble, coffered ceilings, and elaborate plasterwork. The art includes sculpture by Thomas Crawford, creator of *Freedom* atop the Capitol dome, murals by American painter Henry Siddons Mowbray, and a collection of Asian objets d'art culled from Anderson's tenure as ambassador to Japan from 1912 to 1913.

### History

Larz Anderson III was a descendant of Lieutenant Colonel Richard Clough Anderson, a founder of the Society of the Cincinnati. When Larz Anderson and his wife, the writer Isabel Weld Perkins, built this house, they intended it to one day house the society, of which Anderson was a member.

Anderson served in the U.S. diplomatic corps and as a soldier during the Spanish-American War. He married Isabel, the daughter of Commodore George Hamilton Perkins and heiress to a $17 million fortune, in 1897. In 1911, Anderson served as minister to Belgium and, in 1912, as ambassador to Japan. Between 1905 and 1937, the Andersons lavishly entertained Washington society and foreign dignitaries. Larz died in 1937, and in 1939 Isabel donated the building and most of its contents to the Society of the Cincinnati. The society also maintains an extensive library on the American Revolution.

> ### *Washington Notes*
> The Andersons donated St. Mary's Chapel at Washington National Cathedral, where their bodies are entombed.

## Exterior

Brick and stone make up the principal elements of this Renaissance revival house (138 ft wide by 106 ft deep by 66.6 ft tall). The U-shaped structure is flanked by two massive wings extending from the house's central body. The central section's two-story portico, with its Corinthian columns and pilasters, dominates the front courtyard. A carved tympanum with the society's eagle crest decorates a portico pediment.

## Interior

Sometimes grand and sometimes gaudy, Anderson House reflects a pre–World War I opulence. The rooms feature English baroque and French 18C embellishments. Built as a private residence by the Andersons at an approximate cost of $800,000, the house was used only during the Washington social season's winter months. Rooms are open to the public on the first and second floors.

Anderson House unfolds in a series of antechambers and passageways. Rooms seem to dissolve into one another, and moods change. Begin in the **Entrance Hall.** On the south wall, immediately opposite the front door, is a white marble bust of George Washington (by Thomas Crawford), the first president-general of the Society of the Cincinnati. Beneath the bust is a replica of the Diamond Eagle, called the Hoyt Eagle, which was presented to General Washington by the French naval officers who participated in the Revolutionary War. The Society Eagle is a decorative motif throughout Anderson House. To the right of the Washington bust is the Flag of the Society, designed in 1786 by a committee of society members. The alternating blue and white stripes represent the alliance between America (blue) and France (white). A circle of 13 stars representing the 13 colonies surround the Society Eagle in the blue canton. Over the main entrance door, note the painted greeting: "Through this door come and welcome be, our friends and guests most cordially."

Turn west and enter the **Choir Stall Room,** so called because of its late-Renaissance wooden choir stalls (dated 1580–1600) from an unidentified Italian church. The 15 stalls are carved walnut with fluted Ionic column pilasters. The wall and ceiling murals were completed in 1909 by Henry Siddons Mowbray (1858–1928). The mural depicts awards and decorations bestowed upon Ambassador and Mrs. Anderson as well as organizations to which they belonged.

Continue west to the **Great Stair Hall,** which has marble door frames, an antique fireplace, faux-marble window frames, and trompe l'oeil murals (1909; Oreste Paltrinieri). The "wood" shutters and "sculpted" eagles are trompe l'oeil works. The mural above the fireplace depicts the military societies connected with the Andersons, including the Society of the Cincinnati, the Star of the Loyal Legion, and the Cross of the Spanish-American War. The flags represent the ranks of general (reached by several of Anderson's ancestors) and commodore (Isabel's father). The sword represents the army, and the anchor the navy. The ambassador's silver box and papers represent diplomacy. The Andersons' initials, used as a decorative element throughout the house, appear in the ceiling niches near the staircase. The large glass display case on the west wall contains guns and swords from the John du Mont Revolutionary War Period Armament Collection.

At the south end of the hall is the entry to the **Billiard Room,** reserved for special exhibitions. From the Great Hall proceed to the foot of the **Great Staircase.** On the first landing is the massive *The Triumph of the Dogaressa Marianna Foscari—1424* (1882; José Villegas y Cordero) measuring 12 by 20 ft. On a table beneath the painting is a Baccarat crystal eagle. (The president of the glassworks Cristallerie de Baccarat, Count Rene de Chambrun, was a member of the society.) This large, lead crystal eagle with its three-ft wingspan was given to the society in 1966 as "a token of gratitude of the French people toward the United States" for U.S. aid during the two world wars.

At the top of the Great Stairs three Russian icons (17C and 18C) are displayed between two ornately carved marble doorways. Through these doorways, enter the **Key Room,** a reception hall named for its marble floor pattern in the Greek key motif. On the walls are murals (1909; H. Siddons Mowbray) of American military events connected with the Andersons. The north wall mural (between the doors) symbolizes the end of the American Revolutionary War; George Washington gives the Marquis de Lafayette a certificate of Society of the Cincinnati membership. Figures representing fame and peace hover above the group. The west wall mural represents the 1787 settling of the territory north and west of the Ohio River, which was designated by Congress as the Northwest Territory.

### *Washington Notes*

General Arthur St. Clair, a society member, was the Northwest Territory's first governor-general. He had the name of the territory's headquarters changed from Fort Washington to Cincinnati. The Anderson family lived in Cincinnati, Ohio, for generations before moving to Washington, D.C., in the early 1880s.

On the south wall is a mural related to the Civil War, some of it allegorical (the Angel of Freedom removing the chains of slavery) and some of it depicting actual events—such as the firing on of Fort Sumter, whose commander was Major Robert Anderson, Larz Anderson's great uncle. On the east wall is an allegorical rendition of the Spanish-American War in which Anderson served as captain and assistant adjutant general of the Second Division of the Second Army Corps. In the display cases are examples of Chinese and Japanese lacquerwork dating from the 17C to the 19C. Above each of the room's four doorways is a marble pediment, in the center of which is an intricately carved marble basket of flowers.

Walk north into the **French Drawing Room,** decorated in the French regency and Louis XV styles. The raised plaster work is covered with 23-karat gold leaf. The display cases have late-19C Chinese Ch'ing dynasty jade trees. Many of the leaves, petals, and flowers are made from precious and semiprecious minerals. The fireplace mantel is flanked by two cases containing pieces of branching red coral. In the west wall case is a Tibetan gilded bronze helmet (c. 1610), which the Andersons bought from a priest while on a visit to Nepal, probably in the late 1800s or early 1900s. (They were among the first Americans to visit that country.) The 17C Brussels tapestries once hung in Venice's Gambara Palace.

Continue north to the **English Drawing Room,** named for its paintings by English painters Sir Joshua Reynolds (1723–1792) and Sir Thomas Lawrence (1769–1830). After dinner, Isabel and the ladies would retire to this room, while Larz and the gentlemen might go downstairs to the room directly below for a game of billiards. Antique fans such as those in the display cases were sometimes given by Isabel to her guests as party favors. Return south through the French Drawing Room and turn west into the **Olmsted Gallery,** paneled in American brown oak and decorated with 17C Brussels tapestries. The life-size wood carvings depicting the *Last Supper* and *The Kiss in the Garden* are from a 16C Spanish church. At the east end of the gallery is a Vargueno, a Spanish cabinet-on-chest of drawers designed to hold valuable documents and objects and to be transported easily by its handles on each side.

Turn south to the entrance to the **Dining Room,** which is paneled in French walnut and has a green Carrara marble floor. The five tapestries (completed in 1625; woven in Brussels) were commissioned by King Louis XIII of France. They relate the story of the goddess Diana, then shift to focus on King Henry II, king of France from 1519 to 1559, and his mistress Diane de Poitiers. On the west walls hang portraits of Larz (c. 1906; José Villegas y Cordero) and Isabel Anderson (c. 1900–1901; Cecilia Beaux).

From the Dining Room, take the red-carpeted East Staircase to the ground floor. At the bottom of the East Staircase, turn east into the **Ballroom,** 60 ft long by 30 ft wide by 30 ft high. On the south wall four Verona red antique marble columns support the Musicians' Gallery. Along the upper walls of the Ballroom are several series of Japanese screens, depicting the 18C city of Kyoto and scenes from Japanese mythology. On the east end of the Ballroom, beneath the Musicians' Gallery, is the (roped off) original **Library,** paneled in English brown oak.

Exit the Ballroom south to the **Winter Garden Room,** with its Mowbray murals and bronze fountain. The figure in the Italian bronze water fountain holding a harpoon represents *Young Neptune Fighting the Monsters of the Deep* (1899; A. Apolloni) and was the subject of a children's book Isabel wrote called *The Great Sea Horse,* published by Little, Brown and Company in 1909. At the west end of the room are murals by H. Siddons Mowbray that depict locales in the city which interested the Andersons, including the Chevy Chase Country Club, the zoo, and the Old Soldiers' Home.

## Townsend House (Cosmos Club)

Leaving Anderson House, walk a half-block west to the intersection of 22nd St and Massachusetts Ave and cross to the Cosmos Club, or Townsend House (1899–1901, 1904; Carrère and Hastings; 1958 alterations, Horace W. Peaslee; DL) at 2121 Massachusetts Ave N.W., a Louis XV mansion with Beaux-Arts touches, housing a club of distinguished writers, scholars, scientists, and artists.

### History

After retiring as president of the Erie and Pennsylvania Railroad, Robert H. Townsend commissioned the architectural firm of Carrère and Hastings to turn the Second Empire–styled Curtis Justin Hillyer mansion, built in 1873, into a manor home. Mrs. Mary Townsend insisted on incorporating the former home into the new one because of a childhood superstition that she would "encounter evil" if she ever lived in a completely new house. Her precautions apparently didn't work because a year after the house was completed Robert Townsend died from head injuries suffered in a riding accident. Mary Townsend remained here after his death, spending most of her time hosting extravagant parties. A vast kitchen downstairs and various pantries provided for frequent dinners, receptions, and supper parties; the house had enough china for 1,000 guests. In one year, Townsend spent nearly $240,000 on entertainment alone.

Townsend's daughter, Mathilde, rumored to be among the richest women in Washington, married Peter Goelet Gerry of New York in 1910. Despite the *Washington Star's* blessing as "the most brilliant marriage [in] years," Townsend divorced Gerry in 1925 to marry Sumner B. Welles, who later became undersecretary of state for President Franklin D. Roosevelt. Welles took an active part in Roosevelt's foreign policy, accompanying him in 1941 to meetings with Winston Churchill concerning the historic Atlantic Charter, and drafting proposals later used as guidelines for the formation of the United Nations. Mathilde and Sumner Welles resided at this address until 1949, when Mathilde died while on vacation in Switzerland. In 1950, the Cosmos Club (created in 1876) bought the mansion from Welles for $364,635.

> ### Washington Notes
> Carrère, one of the building's architects, was a Cosmos Club member from 1905 to 1911. Other members of note have included Presidents William Howard Taft, Herbert Hoover, and Woodrow Wilson, and authors Herman Wouk and Sinclair Lewis, as well as more than 80 Nobel and Pulitzer Prize winners. In the late 1980s, the club's men-only policy was changed to allow women members.

### Exterior

The building's five sections—the central block incorporates much of the original Hillyer mansion, wings, and garden walls—are of equal width but unequal height. Five massive Corinthian pilasters and elaborate window frames flank the center portion, which has large windows dominating each of three bays.

# Interior

The interior of the house uses elements of 18C French, English, and Germanic styles. A 1901 magazine article described the house as having "a series of charming vistas in which the color schemes blend warmly and naturally from the heavy, rich green of the Library to the elegant red and gold of the second salon, then the lighter, more delicate silver of the first salon to the festive white and gold of the ballroom."

# Alexander Stewart House

Continue west on Massachusetts Ave a half-block to its intersection with 22nd St and the Alexander Stewart House, currently the residence of the ambassador from Luxembourg (1908; Jules Henri de Sibour and Bruce Price), at 2200 Massachusetts Ave N.W.

### History

In 1908, Alexander Stewart, a Wisconsin congressman who made his fortune in timber, had the present structure built at a cost of $92,000, then one of the costliest mansions in the area. After his death from a fall during a visit to a paper mill in 1912, his family sold the property in 1921 to H.R.H. Charlotte, the grand duchess of Luxembourg, for only $40,000. The coat of arms of her principality is cut in stone above the door. In 1955, Luxembourg purchased the property at 2210 Massachusetts Ave N.W. to serve as its embassy and bought this house (for $160,000) from the grand duchess for the ambassador.

## Exterior

To make the most of the triangular site, the architect joined all three façades on the ground level. The two upper floors are connected by spandrel sculpture and ornamental panels. The Louis XVI style is evident in the sunken windows framed by vertical panels.

Continue west a half-block to the **Embassy and Chancery of Ireland** (1908–9; William P. Cresson) at 2234 Massachusetts Ave N.W. The Sheridan Circle façade has three bays. The single bay facing 23rd St is as wide as the entrance bay and has a projecting balcony supported by garlanded brackets on the second level.

Across the street on the north side of Massachusetts Ave is the **Hennen Jennings House,** now the Embassy of Greece (1906; George Oakley Totten, Jr.), at 2221 Massachusetts Ave N.W. Hennen Jennings made his fortune as an engineering consultant to British gold mining interests in South Africa. The family sold this Italian Renaissance revival structure to the Greek government in 1935. The top two floors serve as living space for the ambassador and his family.

### Washington Notes

Jennings is one of several businessmen whose mining-related fortunes enabled them to build the mansions that later became embassies. Thomas Walsh's (McLean) mansion houses the Embassy of Indonesia (2020 Massachusetts Ave N.W.), the home of John Jay Hammond is now the Embassy of France (2221 Kalorama Rd N.W.), and W. W. Lawrence's home is the Embassy of Portugal (2125 Kalorama Rd N.W.).

From the corner of Massachusetts Ave and 23rd St, walk west a half-block to 1606 23rd St N.W., the **Edward Everett House,** now the Embassy of Turkey (1910–15; George Oakley Totten, Jr.). This French Renaissance and Georgian–style house is Sheridan Circle's largest mansion. "Cost is no object! And style and design are up to you" were the instructions given by Edward Hemline Everett to architect Totten in 1910. Everett made his money in Texas oil, Missouri beer, and from the patent of a crimped bottle cap that sealed beer and soft drinks. Totten's nickname was the Bottle-Top King.

Everett lived in the house until his death in 1929; the family sold the house to the Turkish government around 1933. The east façade is distinguished by an imposing central block. The semicircular façade has a Corinthian colonnade. The limitless budget bought the house granite walls, an orante ballroom with coffered ceiling, a handcarved staircase, a basement swimming pool, and a roof garden.

## Alice Pike Barney House

Around the corner, at 2306 Massachusetts Ave N.W., is the Alice Pike Barney House (1902; Waddy B. Wood), once the home and studio of American artist and playwright Alice Pike Barney. This house and its furnishings were acquired by the Smithsonian Institution's National Museum of American Art in 1971. The property is currently closed and for sale. Between 1899 and 1924, Barney was a major artistic force in Washington and one of the city's most extraordinary women.

### History

Alice Pike Barney was a turn-of-the-century artist, dramatist, producer, social activist, and philanthropist. Born in Ohio in 1857, she was the daughter of a millionaire businessman who built Cincinnati's first opera house and the Grand Opera House in New York. While in London in 1874, she met the adventurer Henry Morton Stanley ("Dr. Livingston, I presume") when Stanley was preparing to leave on an expedition to Africa. In spite of the fact that she and Stanley signed a marriage contract, Alice married Albert Clifford Barney, an Ohio millionaire, in 1876. For the next 12 years, the Barneys divided their time between Cincinnati, New York, and Europe, where Alice enrolled in a painting class in Paris. One of her paintings was accepted by the Salon des Beaux-Arts in 1887, and later she studied with James McNeill Whistler. The Barneys' D.C. home, Studio House, became the site of plays, concerts, lectures, poetry readings, and dance performances. Barney wrote plays and enlisted the wealthy and/or talented to perform in them, including a one-time appearance by Sarah Bernhardt. She designed the sets and costumes for a ballet in which Anna Pavlova toured the U.S. in 1915. In 1924, Barney moved to Los Angeles, where she continued to paint and write until her death there in 1931. Buried in Dayton, Ohio, her gravestone reads, "Alice Pike Barney, The Talented One."

### Exterior

Wood gave this house a Spanish flavor, with its curvilinear gable and yellow stuccoed-brick façade. The center bay's prominence is reinforced by a recessed fourth-story loggia. The building's handcrafted appearance, for instance, with its mosaic set in the wall above the secondary entrance, is in stark contrast to the prevailing style of Dupont Circle's Beaux-Arts buildings.

Barney's house faces **Sheridan Circle,** which has the bronze sculpture of Civil War general Philip Sheridan (1908; Gutzon Borglum). Sheridan, hat in hand, reins in his galloping horse, a stance reminiscent of the one he took in a battle in Winchester, Virginia. Sheridan called back his retreating men, who then won the fight.

### *Washington Notes*

Borglum, who also carved Mt. Rushmore, used the general's son Philip Sheridan, Jr., a second lieutenant in the army, as the model. It's hard to say who was more popular in his day—General Sheridan or his horse. The horse, originally called Rienzi, was renamed Winchester in honor of the war victory. The steed was known all over the North for his courage during battle. Winchester was later mounted and displayed at the Smithsonian Institution's Museum of American History. General Sheridan, however, is buried in Arlington Cemetery.

**Diversion:**
This diversion takes visitors past the Islamic Center, the Kahil Gibran Memorial Garden, the British Embassy, and the U.S. Naval Observatory.

Four blocks northwest of Sheridan Circle on Massachusetts Ave is the **Islamic Center** (1949–57; Mario Rossi; Egyptian Ministry of Works; Irwin S. Porter and Sons; 1953; mosaics by Joseph Farley Studio).

2551 Massachusetts Ave N.W. ☎ 332-3451. Open Mon–Sat 10–5, excluding times of prayer. Wheelchair accessible. For exhibitions, donations accepted. Bookstore. Prayer services are held five times a day: dawn, noon, afternoon, sunset, and night. Visitors are asked to dress properly; women should not have bare legs or arms.

The Islamic Center was one of the first mosques and Islamic centers in the United States. After World War II, ambassadors who lived in the Washington area and represented the leading Islamic nations wanted a place to worship. The government of Egypt purchased the site, and other Islamic nations contributed to the building costs. The Egyptian Ministry of Works commissioned Italian architect Mario Rossi to design the facility. The complex includes a director's office, a library, and a bookstore, with the mosque in the center. The semicircular niche used by the imam (prayer leader) points in the direction of Mecca. The building features modern renditions of the traditional forms of Islamic architecture. The minaret is 160 ft high. The interior courtyard is decorated with blue and gold mosaics. The Persian rug is a gift from the former Shah of Iran and the two-ton copper chandelier is a gift from Egypt. Arabic calligraphy decorates the ceilings.

Cross Glover Bridge (1940), a 420 ft long single-span bridge above Rock Creek Park, and walk two blocks to the **Kahlil Gibran Memorial Garden** on the 3100 block of Massachusetts Ave N.W., a park that is open 24 hours. Dedicated to the Lebanese poet in 1991, the park includes a fountain and a bust of the poet. Limestone benches engraved with Gibran's poetry are situated in a wooden grove. This is a nice setting for some quiet contemplation, except during rush hour when Massachusetts Ave is noisy with streams of cars.

From the park continue north on Massachusetts Ave one and a half blocks to the **British Embassy** (1927–31; Sir Edwin Lutyens; 1957, chancery annex, Eric Bedford; 1966, William McVey, sculptor), at 3100 Massachusetts Ave N.W., ☎

462-1340. This was the first embassy built north of Sheridan Circle. The chancery faces Massachusetts Ave, and the ambassador's residence is set at a right angle to the chancery, creating a U-shaped complex in the style of an 18C country estate. Above the roof of the chancery portico are two Art Moderne crouching lions, and Art Deco lanterns light the chancery courtyard. Queen Elizabeth II laid the cornerstone for the chancery in 1957. To the east of the Main Gate is a statue of Winston Churchill, his right hand raised in a V for Victory salute. In his left hand is a walking stick and cigar. Buried in the ground beneath the statue are soil from Churchill's mother's Brooklyn home, from Churchill's birthplace at Blenheim Palace, and from the rose garden at Churchill's Chartwell home. A time capsule in the statue's base is scheduled to be opened in 2063, the 100th anniversary of President John F. Kennedy conferring honorary U.S. citizenship on Churchill.

### Washington Notes

In 1997 the embassy was the site of an outpouring of grief over the death of Princess Diana. Thousands of Washingtonians stood in line for hours to sign the embassy's book of condolences, and the embassy's steps were covered with flowers.

Continue north on Massachusetts Ave one very long block to the **U.S. Naval Observatory** (1887–93; Richard Morris Hunt).

3450 Massachusetts Ave N.W., at Observatory Circle and Massachusetts Ave at 34th St N.W. ☎ 762-1438. Web: www.usno.navy.mil. Free 90-minute tours every Mon night at 8:30, except federal holidays. Not open to the public at other times. Note: The tour includes much walking on hilly areas in the dark, and during the winter it can get very cold in the telescope dome areas.

The Naval Observatory is one of the oldest scientific agencies in the country; the observatory's commander reports directly to the oceanographer of the navy. The observatory is the source for all standard time in the U.S. and is the sole authority in the country for astronomic data required for navigation, civil affairs, and legal purposes. The Naval Observatory is one of the few institutions in the world that continually determines the coordinate positions of the Sun, Moon, planets, and stars.

In 1893 the Naval Observatory moved to this site from its first location in Foggy Bottom on 23rd St (see Walk 18: "Foggy Bottom"). At that time this area of Massachusetts Ave was rural, well beyond the city pollution that had interfered with the work at the old observatory. Richard Morris Hunt designed most of the observatory's buildings. One of the most controversial for its era was the four-part **James Melville Gilliss Building** (1892), which has a central portion and three wings, one of which has a revolving dome housing a 12-inch refractor telescope. The observatory also has the 26-inch refractor telescope Dr. Asaph Hall used in 1877 on the old observatory grounds to discover the two moons of Mars.

The **Vice President's House** (1891–92; Leon B. Dessez) is located on the grounds of the observatory. From 1893 to 1928 the superintendent of the observatory lived in this late-Victorian–style house. Then the house became the official home of the chief of Naval Operations and the building was called Quarters A. In 1974 Congress designated the property as the official residence of the vice president and his family. Despite the navy's attempt to discourage this change by testifying that the roof leaked and the dining room only seated 18, Vice President Walter Mondale and his family moved in. Mrs. Joan Mondale inaugurated a program of borrowing art from museums around the country in order to display the work of U.S. artists.

To continue with this walk from the diversion, walk south on Massachusetts Ave to its intersection with 24th St N.W.

# Kalorama

Walk west on Massachusetts Ave two blocks to 24th St, then turn north and walk one block to S St. This is the Kalorama section of Washington, originally settled by Joel Barlow in 1807.

### History

Barlow, a Yale graduate and a poet fluent in many languages, made his fortune in shipping in Europe. His support of the French Revolution earned him the title of Citizen of France—an honor given to only four other Americans (George Washington, Alexander Hamilton, James Madison, and Thomas Paine). Before settling in Washington City, Barlow served as America's minister to France. Barlow wanted to name his estate Belair but "I find that name has been already given to many places in Maryland and Virginia, so by the advice of friends we have changed it to one that is quite new—Calorama—from the Greek signifying fine view, and this place presents one of the finest views in America."

## *Woodrow Wilson House*

2340 S St N.W. ☎ 387-4062. Web: www.nationaltrust.org. Open Tues–Sun 10–4. Closed Mon and national holidays. Admission fee. Restrooms. Wheelchair accessible. Gift shop.

From the intersection of 24th and S Sts, turn east on S St and walk a half-block to the Woodrow Wilson House (1915; Waddy B. Wood; DL) at 2340 S St N.W. This was the home of our 28th president, Thomas Woodrow Wilson, from 1921, when he left office, to his death in 1924, and the home of his widow, Edith Bolling Wilson, until her death in 1961. Following her death, the house and its furnishings were turned over to the Trust for Historic Preservation, which operates the museum.

**Highlights:** The house offers an intimate look at a president in retirement as well as American life in the 1920s.

### History

Born in Virginia, Woodrow Wilson considered himself a southerner. He was the first southerner elected president following the Civil War. After college Wilson went to law school, but instead of practicing law he earned his Ph.D. in philosophy. As a professor he taught at Bryn Mawr, Wesleyan, and Princeton. Wilson is the only U.S. president with an earned Ph.D. Wilson became president of Princeton, followed by governor of New Jersey, and then president of the United States from 1913 to 1921. Wilson's first wife died during his first year as president. Wilson then married Edith Bolling Galt, whose first husband owned the jewelry store Galt & Brothers (still in operation at 607 15th St N.W.). Edith Galt was 16 years Wilson's junior.

Following the end of World War I, Wilson traveled to Europe, the first seated president to do so. He wanted to bring about "open covenants of peace openly arrived at." He returned with a treaty that included the creation of the League of Nations. Led by Henry Cabot Lodge, Congress objected to what they saw as a means for drawing the U.S. into European entanglements. In 1919 Wilson took his case to the people on a whistle-stop train tour. The rigors of meeting with officials, greeting crowds, and writing speeches at night took its toll. On Oct 2, Wilson suffered a stoke that paralyzed his left side. Returning to the White House, Wilson served the remainder of his term from his bedroom, which he never left for the 17-month remainder of his term.

Warren G. Harding was elected president in 1920 and took office in 1921. Wilson went directly from the White House to this building, his new home, the only president to retire in Washington. The house was built by Henry Fairbanks, a New York businessman, at a cost of $75,000. Fairbanks, who lived in the house from 1915 to 1921, sold it to the Wilsons for $150,000. It's thought that the Wilsons used the $50,000 he had received with the Nobel Peace Prize and $100,000 collected by wealthy friends to buy the property. Edith Wilson was a wealthy woman from her first marriage, but the president refused to use any of his wife's money.

A luggage-lift built for Fairbanks was converted into an Otis elevator, thus allowing Wilson to maneuver himself through the five-story house. Their social life during his retirement years was restricted to family members and close friends. Wilson died in 1924, and a private wake was held in the house. The only public viewing of the casket was when the funeral cortege wound its way up Massachusetts Ave to the Washington National Cathedral, where Wilson is buried. Wilson is the only president buried in the city of Washington. Edith Wilson remained in the house until 1961, an active member of Washington society. Her last official occasion was having Jacqueline Kennedy to lunch following the inauguration of John F. Kennedy as president. Mrs. Wilson died the day they began to lay the piling of Wilson Bridge, the only Washington monument to her husband.

### Washington Notes

Warren Harding died while in office and was succeeded by his vice president, Calvin Coolidge. When Wilson died in 1924, Coolidge appointed Henry Cabot Lodge as the official representative of the government at the funeral. Mrs. Wilson was so offended by the idea that the man who had so vitriolically attacked her husband over the League of Nations might attend his funeral that she wrote to Lodge requesting that he not come. Lodge stayed away. Some speculate that Lodge's appointment was a faux pas on the part of the Republican president; others think it was a petty slap at a Democratic rival.

### Exterior

Edith Wilson described the property as "a home suited to the needs of a gentleman." The front façade has three Palladian windows outlined by fluted stone arches. A columned portico and circular entrance driveway complete the Georgian revival design. A drive on the west side of the building leading to the garage was installed by the Wilsons, who needed the space for the president's Rolls Royce.

### Interior

The tour begins in the front entrance **foyer.** It was here the president did his daily therapy, consisting for the most part of walking back and forth. On the west side of the foyer is the gift shop, which during Fairbanks's day was the ladies parlor and was used as a storeroom by the Wilsons. On the east side is the **library** (originally the gentlemen's parlor), used as an office by Edith's brother Randolph Bolling, who served as Wilson's personal secretary during the president's retirement. A baseball from an Army–Navy game played in London in 1918 and signed by King George V sits on the mantel. A portrait of Wilson's first wife, Ellen Axson Wilson, hangs over the fireplace. A 20-minute video is shown prior to touring the rest of the house.

Exiting the library, take the foyer to the stairs leading to the second floor. At the bottom of the stairs stands a hand-cranked Victrola the Wilsons used frequently to listen to the operatic arias of Enrico Caruso. Wilson loved vaudeville and theater and, in his healthier days, would attend performances whenever possible. Along the stairs are portraits of Edith's family. (She was a direct descendant of the Indian princess Pocohantas.) The grandfather clock on the landing between floors was a housewarming gift to the president from Mrs. Wilson.

### Washington Notes

On a table in the second floor hallway is the Hammond typewriter the president used to draft the Versailles Peace Treaty in 1919.

The first room entered on the second floor is the **drawing room,** which displays gifts from foreign leaders—including framed photographs of Britain's King George V; his wife, Queen Mary; and Edward, Prince of Wales. The tiled portrait of St. Peter was a gift from Pope Benedict when the Wilsons visited Rome in 1919.

Next to the drawing room is the president's **study,** or library, where he spent most of his time. Most days Edith would join him for lunch here, and in the evenings they would read. The movie projector was a gift from actor Douglas Fairbanks, Sr., and a Georgetown theater owner kept the Wilsons well supplied with movies to watch. (The screen was pulled down from the ceiling in front of the bookshelves.) The high-backed chair in front of the fireplace was used by the president at cabinet meetings in the White House. The map on the wall shows the boundaries of Europe the president proposed at Versailles following the war. (These borders were not adopted by the European allies.) The walls are covered with canvas, which has been painted to look like leather.

From the library walk into the **solarium.** The large windows on its south side face the garden. An interior Palladian window on the north side faces the staircase and the downstairs foyer. Walk from the solarium into the **dining room.** A portrait of Edith Wilson (1920; Seymour M. Stone) hangs over the fireplace. A Brazilian rosewood dining table and silver Tiffany candle holders trimmed with burgundy fringe set the formal tone; Wilson insisted on wearing a dinner jacket whenever he dined here.

Returning to the second-floor hallway, take the stairs up to the third floor. At the top of the stairs is Robert Vonnoh's portrait of the first Mrs. Wilson and their daughters having tea. In **President Wilson's bedroom,** the bed is a replica of the Lincoln bed in which the president slept at the White House. The shell casing from a bullet on the mantelpiece is a memento of the first shot fired by American doughboys in World War I. In Wilson's closet hang overcoats plus a wombat fur coat from Australia. Next to this is the **nurse's room,** where a full-time nurse lived.

**Mrs. Wilson's bedroom** across the hall has her comfortable armchair and the sewing machine she used to make items for servicemen during World War I. A 1930s Atwater Kent radio is on the table near her bed, as is her appointment book for the year of Wilson's death, 1924. Portraits of Pocohantas hang on the wall.

Take the metal back stairs down to the **pantry** and **kitchen.** In the kitchen are a cast-iron coal and gas stove, an icebox (ice blocks went on one side, perishables on the other), and a wall cabinet with several sets of dishes used at various times during Mrs. Wilson's residence. The pantry has a collection of Campbell's soups, Dole pineapples, and Kellogg's Corn Flakes, all in their original 1920s containers.

> ### Washington Notes
>
> When Wilson first entered national politics in 1912, there were many requests for his photograph, and much copy was written about his good looks. As president, Wilson received hundreds of portraits of himself, many of them folk-crafted pieces with his image sewn, enameled, carved, cut, and fired onto ceramic tiles. He quickly tired of having to graciously acknowledge these gifts and once remarked to his secretary, "No, I will not lie to these people. They ought to do something honest like digging ditches."

Exiting the Wilson House, walk east on 24th St less than a half-block to the Textile Museum.

## Textile Museum

2320 S St N.W. ☎ 667-0441. Web: www.textilemuseum.org. Open Mon–Sat 10–5; Sun 1–5. Closed on national holidays and Christmas Day. Admission fee. Restrooms, gift shop, library, and bookstore.

George Hewitt Myers, a financier and heir to the Bristol-Myers pharmaceutical fortune, opened the Textile Museum (1908, west building; Waddy B. Wood; 1912, east building; John Russell Pope) in 1925 to house and display his growing collection of fine rugs and fabrics. At that time, the collection consisted of 275 rugs and 60 textiles acquired during Myers's travels. By the time of his death in 1957, the collection had increased to nearly 500 rugs and more than 3,500 textiles. The museum now has 15,000 textiles and 1,800 Oriental carpets. Handmade textiles from the Near East, Asia, Africa, and the indigenous cultures of the Americas are highlighted. The collection can be categorized as classical and court textiles, classical carpets, pre-Columbian textiles, Eastern hemisphere ethnographic rugs, Western Hemisphere ethnographic textiles, and Southeast Asian textiles. In addition to the permanent collection, the museum presents exhibitions of textile traditions not represented in its own collections, such as American quilts and the works of contemporary fiber artists from around the world.

**Highlights:** The museum's collection, only a small portion of which is on display, contains more than 15,500 handmade textiles and Oriental carpets dating from 3000 B.C. to the present.

### History

George Myers purchased his first Oriental rug for his dormitory room at Yale in 1898. He became intrigued by rugs and textiles. Myers and his wife, Louise Chase Myers, moved to Washington, had the house at 2310 S St built by John Russell

Pope as a residence, and bought the house next door at 2320 to use as a museum. Myers developed textile conservation and education programs and traveled the world lecturing and collecting, bringing together a network of scholars, authorities, and collectors.

## Exterior
The 1908 structure has elements of the colonial revival style coupled with Beaux-Arts touches such as a swan's neck frame for the window. On the second level of the front façade is a Palladian window.

## Interior
On the west wall of the vestibule is a bronze bas-relief of George and Louise Myers. On the southeast side of the entranceway is the **George Hewitt Myers Room,** now a meeting room but formerly the family parlor. Fluted pilaster and acanthus leaf motifs in the ceiling cornice decorate the walls. Italian walnut paneling and oak floors complement this room and the **Margaret Dodge Garrett Room** on the southwest side of the entrance. The Garrett Room has a French-influenced fireplace. The garden, entered from this room, originally offered a clear view of the monuments of Washington, but much has since been blocked by tall buildings and maturing trees.

From the entrance, walk through the office space—which displays maps, pamphlets, and photographs of the house during Myers's time—and up the stairs to the room opening on the northwest front. The **Joseph V. McMullan Galleries,** reserved for temporary exhibits, have 10 ft ceilings in the front section and 20 ft ceilings in the back section. Walk east through the McMullan Galleries to the **Long Gallery.** This connects to the **Pugh Galleries,** which are also used for temporary exhibits. The stairs to the second floor lead to the **Activity Gallery,** a hands-on space that allows the visitor to see and feel different weaves, dyeing processes, fiber, felt-making, and embroidery. Next to this is the **Collections Gallery,** where selections from the permanent collection rotate.

## The Collections
The **classical and court textiles** collected by Myers include textile fragments from archaeological sites. The museum's Greco-Roman, Coptic, and Islamic textiles from Egypt form a unique collection. Under Myers's direction, the museum became and continues to be the leading center for the cleaning, study, analysis, and preparation of archaeological textiles. The museum's collection of **classical carpets** contains two of only ten known 15C Spanish armorial rugs, a collection of "Dragon" rugs from the Caucasus. The museum's **pre-Columbian textiles** collection dates from 600 B.C. to A.D. 1532. The **Southeast Asian textiles** collection contains the somber, dark cotton ikats that Myers preferred to the silks and metallic textiles from Indonesia. Many of the museum pieces from Malaysia, Thailand, Taiwan, and Laos are considered irreplaceable.

Exit the museum on S St and walk east three blocks to the **Union at Myanmar Embassy,** or the Thomas M. Gales House (1902; Appleton P. Clark, Jr.), at 2300 S St N.W., the earliest of Georgian revival mansions on S St. A broad, curved Ionic porch shelters a Federal-style doorway. The pedimented dormer windows reflect the Georgian style. Continue east to the **Residence of the Irish Ambassador**

(1924; Waddy B. Wood) at 2244 S St N.W. This building has a recessed attic story and an elegant, semicircular limestone porch with six unfluted Corinthian columns.

Continue on S St to Mitchell Park, the 2200 block, probably the only public park to have a dog's grave in the sandbox.

> ### Washington Notes
> Around the turn of the century, Morton and Elizabeth Mitchell purchased this plot, intending to build a home. When their 14-year-old poodle, Bock, died, the Mitchells buried him on the land in the area they envisioned as the backyard. When Morton Mitchell died, his widow lost interest in the house. In 1918 she gave the land to the city as a park with the stipulation that Bock's grave should be preserved. As a result, a fence encircles his grave, keeping him safe from playful children.

Continue east on S St to the corner of 21st St. Turn south and walk one block to 21st and R Sts. Then walk a half-block west on R St to the Fondo del Sol Visual Arts Center at 2112 R St N.W., ☎ 483-2777. Open Tues–Sat 12:30–5:30; closed Sun, Mon, and national holidays. Contribution requested. Established in 1973 as a nonprofit arts organization directed by artist and community members, Fondo del Sol is dedicated to presenting and preserving the cultural heritage and arts of the Americas. Changing exhibits focus on contemporary artists, and the facility has a small permanent collection of Columbian art, as well as contemporary and folk art. The center also sponsors concerts, lectures, and an annual Caribbean Festival, which features outdoor music, dance, and lots of food.

To continue with the Dupont Circle East tour, walk to Connecticut Ave and the Dupont Circle Building at 1350 Connecticut Ave N.W.

# 17 · Dupont Circle East

Metro: Red Line to Dupont Circle.
Bus: G2, D1, D2, D3, D6, L2, 42, N2, or N4.

### History
See "History" in Walk 16: "Dupont Circle West Area."

## Dupont Circle Building
Walk south toward Connecticut Ave to the Dupont Circle Building (1931; Mihran Mesrobian) at 1350 Connecticut Ave N.W. This office building, situated on the tip of an island formed by the intersection of 19th St and Connecticut Ave, is wedge shaped with its narrow end facing the circle. The 12-story building's decorative pattern of limestone and pink brick deflects attention from the structure's size. Mesopotamian friezes and bas-relief also adorn the building.

### History
Mesrobian, an Armenian from Turkey, designed this structure as an elite, 700-unit apartment building. During World War II it housed government agencies, in-

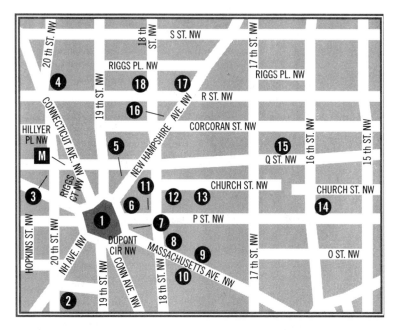

1 Dupont Circle Fountain and Circle
2 Heurich Mansion (Historical Society of Washington, D.C.)
3 Thomas Gaff House
4 Fraser (Thropp) House
5 Woman's National Democratic Club
6 Washington Club (Patterson House)
7 Sulgrave Club (Wadsworth House)
8 National Trust for Historic Preservation
9 Brookings Institution
10 Clarence Moore House
11 William Boardman House
12 St. Thomas Episcopal Church
13 Church Street Theater
14 Carnegie Institution of Washington
15 Cairo Apartment Building
16 Perry Belmont House (International Eastern Star Temple hdqtrs)
17 Thomas Nelson Page House
18 National Museum of American Jewish Military History

cluding the Office of Civil Defense, which was headed by Eleanor Roosevelt. Following the war, the building was converted into office space. For the next 40 years, the Dupont Circle Building was the haven for activist public interest and nonprofit organizations and small entrepreneurs. The 1948 presidential campaign office of Thomas E. Dewey was located here. In 1986, the building was sold and renovated; it reopened as an upscale office building.

Directly across 19th St is the **Euram Building** (1970; Hartman-Cox) at 21 Dupont Circle N.W. Designed by the local architectural firm Hartman-Cox, this building innovatively mixes glass, brick, and concrete.

Continue clockwise around the circle to New Hampshire Ave, turn south and walk one block to the Heurich Mansion, headquarters of the Historical Society of Washington, D.C.

## Heurich Mansion

1307 New Hampshire Ave, N.W. ☎ 785-2068. Web: www.hswdc.org. Open Mon–Sat 10–4. Self-guided tours (maps provided). Admission fee. Library with extensive collection of historical books, records, and documents pertaining to city history open Wed–Sat 10–4.

This grand Victorian mansion (1892; John Granville Meyers; DL) in the Romanesque revival style served for 53 years as the home of Christian Heurich, German immigrant, master brewer, and Washington philanthropist. Virtually unchanged on the ground floor, the house now welcomes the public as the headquarters of the Historical Society of Washington. However, that will be changing. In 1998 Congress gave the Historical Society the building previously known as the Carnegie Library at Mount Vernon Square (8th and L Sts N.W.), as well as the funds to open the City Museum there in 2003. The entire collection of the Historical Society, including the office, archives, special collections, and library, will be moved to this building, which will feature exhibits on the history of the city of Washington. The Heurich Mansion will remain under the direction of the Historical Society. It will be renovated and serve solely as a historic house open to the public for tours.

**Highlights:** The first floor has lavishly ornamental wood carving, particularly in the music room. The third-floor library has an extensive collection of books, articles, and materials pertaining to Washington, D.C.'s history. Throughout the year the society sponsors programs for children 7–12 that revolve around Samantha Parkington, the Victorian doll of the American Girls Collection of books and dolls. Participants receive a special tour of the mansion as if they were accompanying Samantha, a guest who is visiting friends in the house, along with her aunt Cornelia. Children learn about life in 1904, the year of Samantha's visit, make a Victorian keepsake to take home, and are served refreshments.

### History

Perhaps the most accomplished brewer in Washington history, Christian Heurich, born in Haina near Roemild, Germany, in 1842, emigrated to the United States in 1866. He came with a little over $200 in gold he had saved during the previous seven years. Twenty-four years later, his brewing company was valued at over $800,000. When he first arrived in the U.S., Heurich, who learned the art of brewing in Germany, took a job in a Baltimore brewery and went to English classes at night. In 1870, he visited Washington and saw how quickly the city was growing. Heurich knew a burgeoning market when he saw one. In 1872, with a partner from Baltimore, he leased the run-down Schnell Brewery at 20th St N.W. between M and N Sts, a largely rural area of the city near Pacific (Dupont) Circle. Heurich later wrote "that section of the city at the time was but sparsely inhabited and the little cluster of buildings in the neighborhood of the dilapidated looking sheds which composed the brewery stood sort of by themselves. All around were fields, many of them cultivated; the land from Massachusetts Avenue to Q Street and from 20th to 22nd Street was farmed at the time by my father-in-law-to-be. . . . Cornstalks of the last harvest lay on the edge of [what is now] Dupont Circle!"

In 1873, when brewery owner George Schnell died, Heurich married Schnell's widow, Amelia. With her money he bought out his partner and renamed the brewery Christian Heurich's Lager Beer Brewery. By 1882 the brewery produced about 30,000 barrels annually. In 1893 Heurich moved his brewery to Foggy Bottom to the site now occupied by the Kennedy Center.

In 1879 Amelia Heurich purchased the present building's site for a home for her and her husband. Before detailed plans were created, Amelia died of pneumonia. In 1887 Heurich married his second wife, Mathilde Daetz, the sister of the brewery's secretary/treasurer. In 1892, the Heurichs commissioned John Granville Meyers to design a grand mansion on the New Hampshire Ave site. The firm of August Grass was hired to carve the oak and Philippine mahogany woodwork; Hayward & Hutchinson handled the marble, tile, and mosaic flooring; and the New York interior design firm of Charles H. Huber Brothers was given $10,000 with which to furnish the rooms. In 1894 the Heuriches moved into the lavish home. Mathilde's health, weakened from an earlier miscarriage, was further jeopardized by a carriage accident; she died in Jan 1895.

In 1899, at the age of 57, he married the 33-year-old Amelia Keyser, niece of his first wife. By 1908, they had three children. Heurich served on the Board of Trade, the Board of Commerce, the Columbia Historical Society (later the Historical Society of Washington), the Board of Directors for the German Orphans Home, and a host of other philanthropies. Heurich twice refused knighthoods offered him by Duke George II for charitable works he had funded in his native Haina and Roemild. Heurich felt that a knighthood was inappropriate for an American citizen.

When Prohibition came to Washington in 1917, two years before the rest of the country, and the brewery business took a downturn, Heurich retired to Bellevue, his Maryland farm, to raise dairy cattle. The brewery resumed production in 1933 and would operate until 1956. Heurich died in 1947 at the age of 102. Amelia lived in the house until her death at the age of 89 in 1956, at which time the Historical Society of Washington was given the property and the contents of the house.

## Exterior

Some architectural critics, such as Pamela Scott and Antoinette Lee, consider the mansion to be "the finest of Meyers's 115 known Washington buildings, the culmination of a thirty-year career." Other critics, such as Richard Howland, label the house as "beer barrel baronial." The New Hampshire Ave façade, made of dark, rough-faced, squared ashlar stonework, is the most elaborate, with a porte cochere defined by Romanesque round arches and double columns. A corner tower rises from ground level to above the primarily mansard-style roof. The remaining façades, made of smooth, red brick, have projecting, gabled bays. All around the exterior are deeply cut, interlaced leaf designs, stone gargoyles, and whimsical animals.

## Interior

Seven rooms are open to the public, each with ornately carved fireplace mantelpieces. (The house has 17 fireplaces, never used because the Heuriches had a central steam heating system installed. Radiators are hidden in most of the rooms.)

The triangular **main hall** has a Japanese temple vase and an Italian suit of armor. Leading to the upstairs offices is a curving brass, onyx, and marble staircase. The floor features a marble mosaic pattern, and the walls are stucco with plaster medallions painted antique silver. Off the main hall to the right is the museum shop, formerly the **library.** This room has an oak desk, complete with antlers, created in 1872 by a German cabinetmaker in Bozeman, Montana, as a gift for President Ulysses S. Grant. The ceiling canvas depicts art, industry, commerce, geography, and literature, and the wall frieze portrays famous historical figures, including George Washington.

The **parlor** to the left of the main hall is used only for formal occasions. The blue damask and gilt French rococo revival furnishings and painted canvas ceiling are in the style of a Louis XV grand salon. The light fixtures are original, combining both gas and electric lighting. Continuing east off the main hall is the **drawing room.** The walls are stenciled and shaded to imitate folded damask drapery. Note the miniature balconies of ornately carved wood above the doorways.

At the end of the main hall is the **dining room,** which leads to the conservatory on the east and the music room on the west. The dining room was used by the Heurich family for dinner, but breakfast and lunch were taken downstairs in the basement *Bierstube* (beer room). The elaborate oak table and Jacobean chairs were carved by cabinetmaker August Grass; the pastel-tiled fireplace was created by the firm of Hayward & Hutchinson. The 15-light gas-and-electric chandelier is from Vienna.

From the dining room can be seen the roped-off **music room,** with its carved mahogany musicians' balcony. The Steinway parlor grand piano is decorated with gold leaf and painted flowers; the walls and ceiling are enlivened with musical motifs. At the far eastern end of the house is the **conservatory.** The fountain is a memorial to the Heuriches' first daughter, who died in infancy. The plaster walls were molded to imitate bark, and the floors were covered with tile for roller skating and riding toy cars.

The Heuriches, along with their wealthy neighbors, spent summers away from the city. In June and July, the Heuriches resided at their country home in Prince Georges County, Maryland (now a fully developed suburb of Washington), and every Aug they traveled in Europe.

The tour continues in the basement, where a family breakfast room and kitchen have been re-created.

Walk north on 20th St three blocks to the southwestern corner of the intersection of 20th and Q Sts and the **Thomas T. Gaff House** (1904; Bruce Price and Jules Henri de Sibour) at 1520 20th St N.W., currently the Embassy of Colombia. This elegant residence echoes the styles of a 16C and 17C French château. A brick pattern trimmed in limestone and terra-cotta blocks decorates the façade. Entrance to the house is through an extended vestibule featuring a glass canopy.

Continue north on 20th St to its juncture with Connecticut Ave, the main commercial artery of the Dupont Circle area. Shops and ethnic restaurants line this stretch of the avenue. The area on Connecticut north of the circle retains many of the classical revival homes built during the neighborhood's heyday. Though adapted now for commercial purposes, these buildings still convey a sense of Dupont Circle's opulent past.

Cross Connecticut Ave at R St to the **George S. Fraser,** or **Scott Thropp House** (1890; Hornblower & Marshall), at 1701 20th St N.W. Designed to serve as a residence for George S. Fraser, the 16,500-square-ft house represents a unique merger of Richardsonian Romanesque, Italian Renaissance, and colonial American styles. The three-story, square mansion has red brick façades, an English basement constructed of pink granite, a tiled and hipped roof, and a balustraded entrance portico featuring 12 Romanesque columns. A Palladian window outlined in pink granite stands above the entrance portico and is fronted by a square balustrade. Bands of pink granite surround the building and serve as lintels and sills. Fraser, a New York merchant, sold the home to Miriam Douglass Thropp, wife of iron magnate and Pennsylvania congressional representative Joseph E. Thropp in 1901. After Miriam's death in 1930, the home was converted into the Parrot Tearoom and Boardinghouse. In 1995, it became Washington headquarters for the Church of Scientology.

## Woman's National Democratic Club

Cross 20th St to Connecticut Ave and walk one block south to Q St. Turn east on Q St and walk one block to its intersection with New Hampshire Ave. On the southwest corner of the intersection is the Woman's National Democratic Club (WNDC), formerly the Whittemore House (1892–94; Harvey Page), at 1526 New Hampshire Ave N.W. The club is closed to the public, but the gift shop is open to the public at selected times. The WNDC—a political, social, and cultural club whose members are prominent Washington women—lobbies for projects supported by the Democratic Party. The house was built by Sarah Adams Whittemore, cousin of the historian and novelist Henry Adams and descendant of President John Adams. Perhaps the home's best-known resident was John C. Weeks, a banker, congressman, senator, and secretary of war under Presidents Harding and Coolidge. The building was purchased by the WNDC in 1927.

### Exterior

The building's exterior employs a distinctive multihued Roman brick, which came from a small, rare deposit of clay in New Jersey that was never produced again. A copper, semicircular bay overhangs the main entrance; a shingled roof extends to shelter the bay. The octagonal tower is echoed by octagonal bronze bays on each façade. The windows have leaded glass in diamond patterns. This was one of the first buildings in the city to be wired for electricity.

### Interior

A self-guided tour booklet is available from the front desk. The booklet describes in detail the many rare and interesting objects found in each of the rooms. Note that not one room in the original building is shaped as a rectangle or square. The rooms are named for well-known Democrats. **Marjorie Meriweather Post** donated much of the furnishings for the drawing room named after her, including a rose damask settee and a grand piano with an oil painting of Mrs. Post hanging on a nearby wall. Also in this room are a Hepplewhite-style, inlaid mahogany wall mirror given by Mrs. Harry Truman and an autographed portrait of James Monroe. Among the items in the **First Ladies' Room** are two autographed photos of Rosalind Carter and a Chippendale, inlaid mahogany wall mirror given by Eleanor Roosevelt. The **Adlai Stevenson Room**, a 1967–68 addition, is used for speakers, luncheons, and large meetings. Upstairs the **library** contains a carved chest from the cedar tree from the Heritage, Andrew Jackson's Nashville estate, and a desk that belonged to Frances Perkins, secretary of labor under Franklin D. Roosevelt and the first woman cabinet member. The **Daisy Harriman Room,** named for the club's first president, contains Oriental lamps donated by Jacqueline Kennedy. The **Hamlin Room** (formerly the second drawing room) has an elaborate plaster ceiling decorated with a musical motif in each corner. Designed by Nathan Wyeth, the ceiling was most likely a tribute to Sarah Adam Whittemore's career as an opera singer.

## Washington Club (Patterson House)

Walk south on New Hampshire Ave to Dupont Circle and continue one block around the circle to the intersection of P St and Dupont Circle and the Washington Club, or Patterson House (1903; McKim, Mead, and White; Stanford White, chief architect; DL), at 15 Dupont Circle N.W., ☎ 483-9200. Tours Sept–May on Mon, Wed, and Fri 9:30–11:30.

Built as a social palace for Chicagoan Mrs. Robert "Cissy" Patterson, daughter of Joseph Medill, editor and publisher of the *Chicago Tribune*, this neoclassical masterpiece was designed by famed New York architect Stanford White. The Washington Club, one of the oldest women's clubs in America, was founded in 1891 as a women's literary and educational club.

### History

Joseph Medill, editor and publisher of the *Chicago Tribune*, built this house for his daughter in 1903. The daughter, whose married name was Patterson, had two children, Joseph Medill and Elinor (sometimes spelled Eleanor), who was often referred to as Cissy. According to Cissy, the house was built to please her mother because Washington provided an atmosphere "where any woman with money and talent" could build a grand house and "become an important hostess." In 1904, Cissy married Count Josef Gizycka of the Austro-Hungarian court in this house. The marriage ended badly. In 1907, Cissy fled with their daughter Felicia to England and, in 1908, Count Gizycka kidnapped the 3-year-old Felicia and took her to Russia with him. After Cissy's mother wrote a letter to President Taft requesting that he intercede, the president wrote to Czar Nicholas, who ordered that Gizycka return Felicia to her mother. Cissy divorced Gizycka in 1910 and for the next 15 years alternated between her homes in Chicago and Washington.

In 1925, Cissy married Elmer Schlesinger, a New York corporate lawyer, who died four years later. Following the advice of her friend, publisher William Randolph Hearst, Cissy decided to pursue a career in journalism and was appointed the editor of the *Washington Herald,* where her column (entitled "Interesting But Not True") bolstered the paper's popularity. Eventually Cissy, who resumed her former name (Elinor Medill Patterson) accumulated stock in various newspapers through inheritance and purchases. By 1942, she had bought both the *Chicago Tribune* and the *Washington Herald,* from which she created the popular *Times-Herald.*

When Cissy died in 1948, she left an estate valued at $17 million to her family and donated this residence and its contents to the National Red Cross. The Red Cross eventually auctioned off the residence to the Washington Club.

### Washington Notes

From March to Sept 1927, this house served as a temporary White House for the Coolidges while the White House was undergoing renovation. While in residence, the presidential couple entertained the decade's most famed hero, aviator Charles Lindbergh.

## Exterior

The marble and glazed terra-cotta façade of this neoclassical mansion was intended by White to give the house a "light and rather joyous character." The main façade's rich ornamentation features a Greek key string course and third-story windows crowned by a female mask flanked by scrolls and crowned by a torch. A black enamel double door serves as the main entrance. The loggia above the entrance has Ionic columns. The two-story addition on the P St side was constructed in 1955.

## Interior

The ground-floor foyer contains a 15C Italian-style mantel and a white marble staircase. The second floor's main rooms—a dining room, drawing room, and a ballroom with a musicians' gallery—radiate out from a central hall.

## Sulgrave Club (Wadsworth House)

Continue clockwise around Dupont Circle to its intersection with Massachusetts Ave, turn south on Massachusetts Ave and walk a half-block to the Sulgrave Club, or Wadsworth House (1900; Frederick H. Brooke; DL), at 1801 Massachusetts Ave N.W. The Sulgrave Club is a private women's club.

### History

Countess Marguerite Cassini, a frequent visitor to this house, which occupies a full block, felt the building "had somehow the shape of a boat," with its prow headed directly towards Dupont Circle. The house was built for Henry Wadsworth, who owned and managed large agricultural properties in Genessee Valley, New York, and his wife, Martha, a St. Louis socialite. According to the Countess Cassini, it was Martha Wadsworth who actually designed the mansion. The architect, Frederick Brooke, also designed the District of Columbia War Memorial in West Potomac Park and was the American architect of the U.S. Embassy in Great Britain. The Wadsworths lived here until 1918, when they donated the house to the Red Cross. In 1932, Mabel Boardmen purchased the house for $125,000 so it could be used as a private women's social club.

### Washington Notes

The club's name comes from the ancestral home of George Washington, Sulgrave Manor. The club uses Washington's coat of arms as a seal.

## Exterior

The three-and-a-half–story building's eclectic style combines 18C French and English elements. The house is built of limestone and rusticated yellow brick and has a mansard roof. The ground floor central façade bay on Massachusetts Ave was originally a carriage entrance. In 1932, this entrance was filled in and a porch added. The present entrance, created during a 1952 renovation, consists of a limestone stoop and eight glazed French door panels. The windows on the second level have French doors after the Louis XVI period, and the Palladian window over the entrance is symmetrically fluted by Ionic columns.

## Interior

Though modified over the years, many features of the building's original interior remain, including an 18C English-inspired pentagonal stairhall, an oval salon, and a gilded ballroom. The fourth-floor servants' quarters are now guest rooms. Two circular rooms—the drawing room overlooking Dupont Circle and the morning room facing the intersection of 18th St and Massachusetts Ave—occupy two points of the building's triangular layout.

## National Trust for Historic Preservation

Continue east on Massachusetts Ave a half-block to the intersection of 18th St and Massachusetts Ave and the National Trust for Historic Preservation, formerly the McCormick Apartments (1916–17; Jules Henri de Sibour; DL), at 1785 Massachusetts Ave N.W. ☎ 588-6000. Web: www.nthp.org. Lobby open Mon–Fri 9–5. Guided tours must be arranged in advance.

### History

This elegant five-story Beaux-Arts structure was built by Stanley McCormick, whose father, Cyrus McCormick, invented the mechanized reaper and founded the International Harvester Company. The entire building originally contained only six apartments, which were designed to serve as luxury living spaces—two on the first floor and one on each of the remaining floors. The larger apartments contained six bedrooms and measured 11,000 square ft. The ceilings were more than 14 ft high. Some of Washington's most influential citizens lived here at one time or another—among them the founder of Dumbarton Oaks, Robert Woods Bliss; art dealer Lord Joseph Duveen; U.S. ambassador to Luxembourg and hostess Perle Mesta; and Andrew Mellon.

> #### Washington Notes
> Art dealer Lord Duveen, who knew of Mellon's passion for collecting fine works of art, deliberately rented the rooms beneath Mellon's apartment. Duveen hung some of his finest pieces in these rooms, gave Mellon a set of keys, and invited him to browse whenever he was in the mood. This ingenious plan paid dividends when Mellon agreed to purchase 24 paintings and 18 sculptures for $21 million. These works eventually became part of Mellon's gift to the nation, the National Gallery of Art.

In 1941, the government essentially commandeered the building and forced all the residents out so the space could be used for offices as part of the war effort. Following the war, the government converted the building into commercial office space. In 1950, the American Council on Education bought the building. In 1970, they sold it to the Brookings Institution, which occupied Mellon's apartments and rented the rest of the building to other organizations. In 1977, the National Trust for Historic Preservation purchased the building.

## Exterior

The building has a raised basement, a concrete foundation, and a mansard roof. Limestone highlights the three façades on Massachusetts Ave, P St, and 18th St. The building's decor also features entablatures, relief panels, and ornately carved structural features such as the balconies' stone supports.

## Interior

In 1977 the National Trust made an effort to restore many of the rooms. Consequently, the former Mellon apartment on the top floor retains much of its original appearance, despite the fact that it has been used as office space. From the apartment's oval reception room, doors lead to a salon and a 45 by 24 ft living room that occupies much of the Massachusetts Ave side of the apartment. This is now a boardroom with a 20 by 24 ft adjoining salon. The north corridor still contains built-in cedar closets.

Continue east a half-block on Massachusetts Ave to the **Brookings Institution,** the influential national research center and think tank, at 1775 Massachusetts Ave N.W. Founded by Robert S. Brookings in 1916, it was one of the nation's first public policy research organizations. With nearly 70 scholars on its staff, the institution conducts a variety of analytical research projects on topics such as economics, foreign policy, congressional reform, education, and health care. Its publications are read worldwide.

Cross Massachusetts Ave at 18th St and walk east to the **Clarence Moore House** (1906; Jules Henri de Sibour) at 1746 Massachusetts Ave N.W., the Embassy of the Republic of Uzbekistan. This Beaux-Arts structure was built by Clarence Moore, a West Virginia tycoon who made the unfortunate decision to return from Europe on the maiden voyage of the *Titanic.* Luckily (for them), the pack of English hounds, 12 Welsh pony mares, the stallion, and 8 Irish hunting hounds he had bought for the Chevy Chase Hunt had been sent on another ship. The walls of the mansion combine buff brick with carved limestone highlights. The structure's second and third stories feature French windows that open onto balconies; the second-story balconies are limestone, and the third-story ones are wrought iron.

Return west to 18th St for one block, cross Massachusetts Ave, and walk north on 18th St one block to P St and the **William J. Boardman House** (1893; Hornblower & Marshall), the Embassy of the Democratic and Popular Republic of Algeria and headquarters for the Iraqi Interests Section. (Iraq no longer has an embassy in Washington because it no longer has diplomatic relations with the U.S.) This building combines Italian Renaissance and Richardsonian Romanesque features. Warm yellowish-brown Roman bricks create a subdued tone and blend with sandstone and terra-cotta details. A ground floor, single-story bay window crowned by an Ionic balustrade, apparently copied directly from Florence's Piti Palace, projects toward P St. An archway with handsome carved details, built to handle carriages, serves as the mansion's entrance. The third story has a balustraded balcony that overhangs the first floor's projecting bay.

Walk north one block on 18th St to Church St, then turn and walk east a half-block on Church St to the ruins of **St. Thomas Episcopal Church** (1894–99; Theophilus P. Chandler) at 1772 Church St N.W. This neo-Gothic structure was virtually destroyed by arson in 1970. The parishioners opted to maintain the ruins as a park, and the result is a striking space with a garden and benches. The church's altar and eastern wall remain intact. St. Thomas Hall remains in use for church activities.

### Washington Notes

For years President Franklin D. Roosevelt worshiped at St. Thomas Episcopal Church.

Walk east on Church St a half-block to the **Church Street Theater** at 1742 Church St N.W. Throughout the 1970s this was the home of the New Play-wrights' Theater, one of the city's first small theaters. This is the edge of one of Washington's theater districts, an area that runs along 14th St between P and S Sts. Stages here include Woolly Mammoth Theatre (1401 Church St N.W.), Studio Theatre (1333 P St N.W.), and Source Theatre (1835 14th St N.W.).

Continue east a half-block to the intersection of Church St and 17th St, turn south onto 17th St, walk a half-block to P St, and turn east on P St. Walk one block on P St to the northeast corner of P and 16th Sts to the **Carnegie Institution of Washington** (1908–10; Carrère and Hastings) at 1530 P St N.W. In 1902, industrialist millionaire Andrew Carnegie donated funds to create a facility dedicated to the accumulation and propagation of knowledge in the field of science. The Carnegie Institution has since become an international center for research in physical and biological sciences.

## Cairo Apartment Building

Turn north on 16th St, walk one block to its intersection with Q St, then west on Q St a half-block to the Cairo Apartment Building (1894; Thomas Franklin Schneider; 1972; Arthur Cotton Moore) at 1615 Q St N.W.

### History

In 1894, Thomas Franklin Schneider was given a permit to construct a $425,000, 100-unit, 350-room luxury apartment building that was 14 stories and 165 ft tall. It was the largest nonpublic structure in the city and the first to use a steel frame. Because of the Cairo's size, the building was nicknamed Schneider's Folly. In addition to 100 apartment units, the building also offered a public dining room, a ballroom, a lobby with ornate public parlors and waiting rooms, a drugstore, a bowling alley, and billiard rooms. The Cairo was lit solely by electricity, unusual at the time.

> ### Washington Notes
> The Cairo's height proved highly controversial. Residents complained that the building blocked light and views and was out of scale with the rest of the neighborhood and the city. Architects were outraged by its "ugly appearance." The city fire department was concerned because the building exceeded the reach of firefighting equipment. In response to the outcry, in 1894, the District commissioners limited the height of buildings according to their use and the width of the street on which they were built. (This regulation didn't affect the Cairo, whose permit had already been issued.) In 1898 and 1910, Congress supported local building codes and set limits of 90 ft for residential buildings and 110 ft for commercial buildings, except along wider avenues, such as Pennsylvania Ave, where buildings up to 130 ft were allowed. The 1989 Height of Buildings Act further ensured the Washington skyline wouldn't be dominated by skyscrapers.

The Cairo remained in the Schneider family until 1955, when Schneider's daughters and heirs sold it following the neighborhood's decline after World War II. In 1972, the deteriorated building was sold to the Inland Steel Development Corporation, which hired local architect Arthur Cotton Moore to modernize it.

The interior was gutted and many of the original features, such as the ornate lobby and the intricate elevator cages, were eliminated. New units were created and much of the rear courtyard was converted to garden and duplex apartments. In 1979, the Cairo was converted to condominiums.

## Exterior
Schneider was heavily influenced by the design of Louis Sullivan's Transportation Building, which Schneider saw at the 1893 World's Columbian Exposition in Chicago. The Cairo, built on a concrete-and-limestone foundation, is U-shaped, with a façade decorated by limestone and Moorish-influenced reliefs on a buff brick surface. Birdlike gargoyles support the stone balconies. The flat roof once featured a garden filled with tropical plants.

## Interior
Moore's 1970s renovation resulted in a mix of 66 efficiency, 44 one-bedroom, and 66 two-bedroom units.

Continue west on Q St one block to the intersection of Q and 17th Sts. The homes on the 1700 block of Q St N.W. were also designed by Thomas Franklin Schneider in the late 1890s and early 1900s. These display a wide variety of Victorian influences. Some also have a protruding window called an Oriole window, the forerunner of the bay window that is so popular in Washington.

## Perry Belmont House
Turn north onto 17th St, walk one block, and then turn west onto Corcoran St. Continue west one block on Corcoran to its intersection with New Hampshire Ave and the Perry Belmont House (1909; Etienne Sanson and Horace Trumbauer) at 1618 New Hampshire Ave N.W., the national headquarters of the **International Eastern Star Temple** since 1935. The Order of the Eastern Star is the women's organization associated with the Masons. The house itself was modeled on 18C French designs.

### History
Perry Belmont, the son of New York financier August Belmont and the grandson of Commodore Matthew Perry, served as the congressional representative from New York between 1881 and 1887 and as minister to Spain from 1888 to 1889. In 1906 Belmont purchased the entire block between New Hampshire Ave, 18th St, and R St, and commissioned Sanson to design a showplace. (Belmont had become familiar with Sanson's work in cities such as Paris and Madrid, while he was in Europe.) The house, which was estimated to have cost between $500,000 and $1.5 million, became one of the premier social centers in the city. By 1929, however, the Belmonts had moved out. Perry Belmont tried to convert the house into luxury apartments in 1935 but was unsuccessful. Later that year the Order of the Eastern Star purchased the house for $100,000.

### Washington Notes
The Belmont House has served several diplomatic functions. In 1917 the Special Japanese Mission resided here for six weeks. The Italian War Mission, the British Mission, and the president of Brazil utilized the house as

well. In Nov 1919, Edward, Prince of Wales resided here during his official state visit.

## Exterior

The Belmont house is a two-and-a-half–story, gray stone structure featuring an ornamented porte cochere. Corner pavilions, embellished with entablature at the second level, stand on each of the structure's sides. The mansard roof, partially obscured by a balustraded parapet that features decorative urns, gives way only above the port corchere, where it becomes flat.

## Interior

The original interior was lavish, with marble floors and stairs, and rooms for entertaining decorated with mirrors, gilt, and brocade. The most impressive room was the 78 by 33 ft ballroom, which featured red brocade walls and an expansive skylight.

## Thomas Nelson Page House

Walk north on New Hampshire Ave to the intersection with R St and the Thomas Nelson Page House (1896; McKim, Mead and White) at 1759 R St N.W. Designed by Stanford White, this Georgian revival mansion served as the home of writer Thomas Nelson Page, considered in his time a spokesman for the Old South.

### History

Thomas Nelson Page came from an affluent Virginia family that included Carters, Lees, and Randolphs. A graduate of the University of Virginia's law program, Page began practicing in Richmond in 1874 and also at that time started writing and publishing stories about the antebellum South. These were highly successful, and Page became known as a spokesman for the aristocratic, pre–Civil War South. In 1893, he married Florence Lathrop Field and relocated to Washington, where the couple established themselves as part of Washington society. In 1913, President Woodrow Wilson, a fellow Virginian, appointed Page ambassador to Italy. Page returned to the United States in 1919 and died three years later.

## Exterior

This four-and-a-half–story house has five sides of irregular length. The brick façades feature Flemish bond above a granite base and limestone details in the form of banding; lintels and chimney caps decorate the structure. A Doric cornice complements the mansard roof, and molded cornices highlight the dormers' gables.

## Interior

This house was designed for large-scale entertaining and is centered around an open-well staircase that leads to a spacious hall on each floor. The electric elevator was part of the original construction.

## National Museum of American Jewish Military History

1811 R St N.W. ☎ 265-6280. Web: www.penfed.org/jwv/home.htm. Open Mon–Fri 9–5; Sun 1–5. Closed Sat and Jewish and federal holidays. Admission: free. Group tours available with reservation. Archives and library available.

From the Page House, turn west on R St. A half-block past the intersection of R and 18th Sts is the National Museum of American Jewish Military History, headquarters of the **Jewish War Veterans (JWV) of the United States of America.** The JWV, one of the oldest active veterans groups in the U.S., was formed by 60 Civil War veterans in 1896. The museum, opened in 1984 by the JWV, presents historical exhibits documenting the role of Jewish American men and women in the armed forces. Two levels of galleries display changing exhibits of the museum's collection from the Civil War to the present. **Rescue and Renewal: GIs and the Displaced Person** focuses on the role of Jewish military in aiding those displaced by war. The museum's archive welcomes contributions relating to the Jewish role in American history.

To continue with the next walk, proceed two blocks west on 18th St to 20th St, then four blocks south on 20th St to the Dupont Circle Metro station. Take the Red Line to Metro Center, then the Blue or Orange Line to Farragut West Metro station.

# 18 · Foggy Bottom

Metro: Blue/Orange Line to Farragut West or Foggy Bottom.
Bus: 30s line (32, 34, 36, or 38) on Pennsylvania Ave N.W.

For most of its first 200 years, this now-fashionable area of northwest Washington unofficially called Foggy Bottom was a business and industrial neighborhood peopled mainly by immigrant laborers and the city's lower-income residents. Its fluid boundaries are generally considered to be 18th St (by the Old Executive Office Building), Constitution Ave (across from the Mall), 26th St (bordering Georgetown), and Pennsylvania Ave (at Washington Circle).

The area supposedly got its nickname from the mix of fog that settled over the adjacent swampy land near the Potomac River and the smog that arose from the area's factories and breweries. Today the area is an eclectic collection of Victorian town houses, post-1950s high-rises, and office buildings peopled by university students and government workers. The Kennedy Center attracts theatergoers and music lovers. Foggy Bottom has metamorphosed from swamp to swank and is still suffering growing pains as preservationists spar with developers.

### History
Until major redevelopment began in the 1950s, Foggy Bottom was a rarity in Washington—an ethnic neighborhood (Adams Morgan developed its ethnic identity a bit later). Foggy Bottom's German and Irish enclaves gave the area a prosperity distinctively different from that enjoyed by its neighbor, Georgetown. The houses built here were, for the most part, small and plain, but they were affordable to the people who worked in the nearby factories.

In 1765, German immigrant Jacob Funk purchased 130 acres and subdivided them into 234 lots. He called the area Hamburg although others insisted on calling it Funkstown. He sold the lots to Maryland speculators, who intended to resell rather than settle in the area. Funk did settle here, building a large brick house near the Potomac River between what are now 22nd and 23rd Sts.

In 1791, all private property within the surveyed boundaries of the new capi-

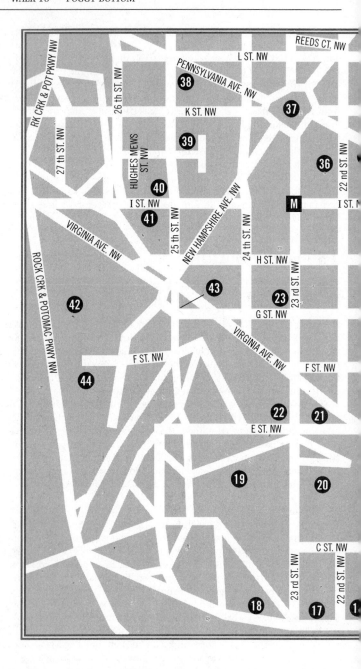

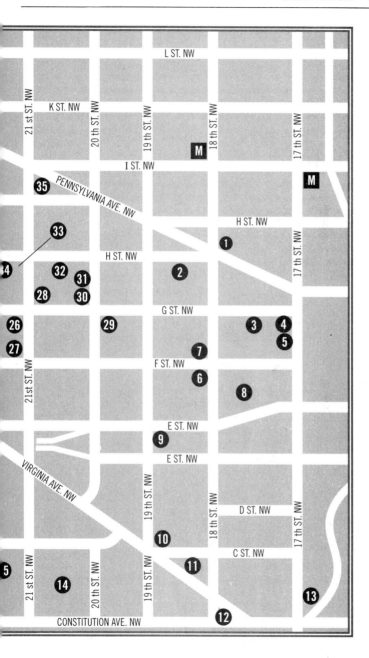

| | |
|---|---|
| 1 National Permanent Building | 23 St. Mary's Church |
| 2 World Bank | 24 GWU's Veterans' Memorial Park |
| 3 Liberty Plaza | 25 School Without Walls |
| 4 Federal Home Loan Bank Building | 26 GWU's Strong Hall |
| 5 Winder Building | 27 GWU's Lenthall Houses |
| 6 General Services Administration | 28 GWU's Woodhull House |
| 7 Marshall/Ringgold House | 29 United Church |
| 8 American Institute of Architects | 30 GWU's President's House |
| 9 Rawlins Park | 31 GWU's Law Center |
| 10 Department of Interior Building | 32 GWU's University Yard |
| 11 Statue of Simón Bolivar | 33 GWU's Lisner Auditorium |
| 12 Statue of José Artigas | 34 GWU's Hippo Sculpture |
| 13 Van Ness Mansion | 35 Arts Club of Washington |
| 14 Federal Reserve Building | 36 GWU Hospital |
| 15 National Academy of Sciences | 37 Washington Circle |
| 16 Albert Einstein Memorial | 38 St. Stephen Martyr Church |
| 17 American Pharmaceutical Assn | 39 Snow's Court |
| 18 Braddock's Rock | 40 822–828 25th St N.W. |
| 19 Old Naval Observatory | 41 2503–2507 I St N.W. |
| 20 State Department Building | 42 Watergate |
| 21 Pan American Health Organization | 43 Statue of Benito Juárez |
| 22 Columbia Plaza | 44 Kennedy Center |

tal was bought by the government and then sold at public auction, the proceeds going toward construction of public buildings such as the Capitol and the President's House.

In 1791, when George Washington was supervising the purchase of lots for the new Federal City, he had some particular concerns about Hamburg, since it had been an established town for almost 30 years. In a letter dated Feb 17, 1791, Washington wrote, "The Maryland Assembly has authorized a certain number of acres to be taken without the consent of the owners or making compensation as therein provided. . . . I will, therefore, beg the favour of you to take measure immediately for buying up all the lots you can in Hamburg, on the lowest terms you can, not exceeding the rate of 25 pounds the acre." Washington himself bought one lot in Hamburg, which he willed to his wife's grandson, George Washington Parke Custis.

L'Enfant's plan of the city noted two sites in the Foggy Bottom area: what is now Washington Circle, which he envisioned as the center of a fashionable residential neighborhood, and a small hill fronting the river, labeled Reservation Number Four, which L'Enfant designated as a military fort ideally situated to defend the city from invasion by river. Today this site is occupied by the Naval Medical Command, previously called the Naval Observatory. Thomas Jefferson, admiring the view from the top of the hill, wanted this site for the Capitol, but L'Enfant and George Washington favored Jenkins (now Capitol) Hill. Foggy Bottom's hill for some years was left unused, except as a trysting place for lovers.

Robert Peter, one of Georgetown's leading citizens and its first mayor, built a plantation called Mexico near the Rock Creek. In 1797 Peter built three blocks of three-story houses along present-day K St between 24th and 25th Sts. Each block had two houses. Peter moved his six sons (one of whom was married to Martha Washington's granddaughter) and their families into these houses.

At the time Foggy Bottom was a sparsely populated residential area whose inhabitants, besides the Peters, included a carpenter, an architect, a pump borer, a stonecutter, an African American family, and a German family. Foggy Bottom soon had warehouses; shipping provided employment, as did Coningham's Brewery, located on what is now Constitution Ave between 21st and 23rd Sts.

Soon after the turn of the century, Western Market was built on the triangle formed by the intersection of Pennsylvania Ave with 20th and I Sts. The market brought people from nearby areas into Foggy Bottom. In 1807, a glass factory called the Glass House went up along the river at the foot of 22nd St, employing between 100 and 200 men, many of them glassblowers from Bohemia.

A tributary nicknamed Slash Run—because it carried off the drainage from the town's slaughterhouses—flowed through Foggy Bottom along L St to its outlet at Rock Creek, near the head of 23rd St. The Glass House closed during the financial panic of 1837 and reopened as a roofing factory in 1860. When a fire gutted this building, the site reopened as a fertilizer plant. Foggy Bottom was known primarily as a foul-smelling industrial area. Foggy Bottom was still sparsely populated in the years prior to the Civil War, with only 40 households in 1822.

Far removed from the social life of downtown and separated from the prosperity of Georgetown, Foggy Bottom still provided habitable dwellings and steady employment. However, crime and rats were concerns for residents. A gang of boys calling themselves the Round Tops, the name locals gave to the area now encompassing Washington Circle and environs, terrorized the neighborhood. After a heavy rain, swarms of rats infested the muddy streets and Slash Run.

The creation of the Chesapeake and Ohio Canal proved a catalyst for development in Foggy Bottom. By 1850, the C&O ran from Georgetown to Cumberland, Maryland, with a connecting canal running along the Potomac River at Foggy Bottom to the mouth of the Washington Canal (now Constitution Ave) just south of the White House. By 1860 the number of Foggy Bottom households increased to 175. Almost half of these residents were unskilled laborers who were able to find work in the new industries cropping up along the riverfront: three lime kilns, an icehouse, a wood yard, and a shipyard.

In 1856 the Washington Gas Light Company built gas storage tanks at the intersection of Virginia and New Hampshire Aves. For the next 100 years, this building and its malodorous vapors dominated Foggy Bottom and kept it a working-class neighborhood.

During the Civil War, Camp Fry and Camp Fuller were located in Foggy Bottom. The two camps took up most available land to the river, with their barracks, barns, and corrals. Camp Fry was a housing facility for the Veteran Volunteer Corps, invalid soldiers who served as guards at government buildings. Camp Fuller served as the largest supply center for the Army of the Potomac, housing thousands of horses, mules, and supplies.

### *Washington Notes*
In Dec 1861, a fire in Camp Fuller's stables killed almost 200 horses. Over 1,000 other horses were spared by being cut free, and these galloped off all over the city, some even making it as far as Capitol Hill before being recaptured.

Following the Civil War, Foggy Bottom continued to be a factory workers' community. The introduction of the streetcar and the trolley system enabled the more well-to-do to move to outlying areas of the city, where there was less congestion and pollution. This left the older areas of the city to newly arrived skilled and unskilled laborers, who in Foggy Bottom were mainly German and Irish immigrants.

Most of the Irish, who worshiped at St. Stephen's, worked at the gasworks. Most of the Germans, who worshiped at the United Church, worked at Foggy Bottom's two breweries: the Abner Drury Brewery and the Heurich Brewery. The Heurich Brewery on 25th St, owned by a German immigrant named Christian Heurich, remained on the site until 1961, when it was demolished to make way for the Kennedy Center. The brewery had the capacity to produce 5,000 gallons of ale, porter, and lager beer a day. The site also had an ice-making plant and, in 1897, a beer-bottling plant was added.

### Washington Notes

Many of the poor lived in alleys in dwellings less than 30 ft wide that had no sewers, water, or light. Crime was a problem. Some alleys, such as Snows Court, were considered too dangerous to enter by outsiders. Foggy Bottom policemen in those days wore helmets and carried nightsticks. Some patrolled on horseback. One of these mounted officers, Pat Creigh, known as the Mayor of Foggy Bottom, trained his horse to break up crowds by grabbing offenders' coat collars. Social reformers worked to improve the unhealthful living conditions. In 1892 Congress banned further construction of houses in alleys. At the time about 1,500 people already lived in alleys in Foggy Bottom. They were not helped by the new legislation.

Until Prohibition in 1918, the breweries continued to provide employment. During Prohibition, money could only be made from producing cider or soft drinks, and later, 3.2 percent beer. The Abner Drury Brewery hobbled along until 1922 making soft drinks. Although Heurich's Brewery couldn't afford to convert to nonalcoholic production, their ice plant carried the business until 1933, when the brewery reopened.

In 1881, Congress appropriated funds to dredge the swampy land near the river. By the turn of the century East and West Potomac Parks had been created. In 1911, West Potomac Park had been chosen as the site of the Lincoln Memorial, and its dedication in 1922 brought a new élan to the area. George Washington (GW) University relocated from downtown to 20th and G Sts in 1912. Between 1927 and 1959, GW University constructed nine large campus buildings.

The expansion of Rock Creek Pkwy and the Mall in the 1930s added greenery to Foggy Bottom's south and west. In 1947, the gasworks were dismantled, freeing the land bordering the river for development. That same year, the State Department relocated from the Old Executive Office Building to 22nd and C Sts, bringing with it a monumental style of governmental architecture and a middle-class legitimacy to what had become a run-down area. How run-down was made evident in a 1944 survey by the Washington Housing Association, which found that out of the 186 dwelling units in the blocks bordered by Virginia and New Hampshire Aves and 23rd St a quarter had no water and a fifth no electricity.

The last gas tanks were removed in 1954, spurring development and remodeling. Upper-middle-class residents began renovating the tiny row houses once home to factory workers, and large-scale developers began tearing down other row houses to replace them with buildings in the international style of concrete-and-glass, rectangular structures.

The social price of this urban refinement was the dislocation of lower-income residents, mostly African Americans. Potomac Plaza, built near the site of the former gasworks in 1955, had apartment condominiums ranging in price from $9,000 to $34,000. Houses that had sold for as little as $800 in 1950 were going for $12,500 to $42,000 by 1960, following renovation. Rising real estate values and property taxes made the change swift and thorough. In 1950, Foggy Bottom was predominantly lower-income African American; in 1960, it was upper-income and predominantly white.

There were also major public works undertaken, such as the Theodore Roosevelt Bridge, the Virginia Ave Tunnel under 23rd St (with 23rd St expanded in the process), and the Whitehurst Freeway (named after Herbert C. Whitehurst, former director of the District Highway Department), which meant the demolition of many of the town houses and residences.

In 1965, the Watergate apartment complex opened. Efficiencies started at $20,000 and penthouses cost ten times as much. By the time of its completion in 1970, the Watergate complex consisted of two apartment buildings, two office buildings, a luxury hotel, two shopping areas, and several restaurants. The John F. Kennedy Center for the Performing Arts (derogatorily called by some "the box the Watergate came in") was begun a few years later, on the site of the old Heurich Brewery.

Local residents, especially those who had taken a chance on the area in the 1950s and early '60s, investing in property and making renovations, were alarmed at the rapid appearance of the big office and apartment buildings. Concern over growth continues to this day, with George Washington University the developer most often at odds with the community. There are still some streets where row houses built for factory laborers charm passersby—in particular, along the 2400 and 2500 blocks of I St. But these are surrounded by the eclectic post–World War II buildings that have taken over the area originally settled by Mr. Funk and Mr. Peter.

Exit the Farragut West Metro station on 17th St and walk two blocks south to Pennsylvania Ave, then one block west to the intersection of 18th and H Sts with Pennsylvania Ave and the **National Permanent Building** (1977; Hartman-Cox Architects) at 1775 Pennsylvania Ave N.W. The American Institute of Architecture in *Guide to the Architecture of Washington, D.C.* calls this building "one of the city's few truly epochal structures," a major influence "on virtually all subsequent (intelligent) design in the District." That is because this columned office building with its mansard roof was one of the first designed to also fit in with the neighboring buildings.

Diagonally across the street is the **World Bank** (1987; Hellmuth, Obata & Kassabaum) at 1818 H St N.W., ☎ 477-1234. The World Bank comprises five organizations: the International Bank for Reconstruction and Development (IBRD), the International Development Association (IDA), the International Finance Corporation (IFC), the Multilateral Investment Guarantee Agency (MIGA), and the International Center for Settlement of Investment Disputes (ICSID). The bank's purpose is to stabilize the economic growth of developing countries by lending money both to governments and to the private sector.

Walk south on 18th St one block to G St, then east on G St a half-block to the entrance to **Liberty Plaza,** an open courtyard designed by Sasaki Associates as an informal meeting place between the commercial office building on the north and the Winder Building on the south.

The **Federal Home Loan Bank Board** (1977; Max O. Urbahn Associates), the L-shaped office building at 17th & G Sts N.W., with shops at street level and offices above, was built so as not to overpower its ancestral neighbors, the Winder Building and the Old Executive Office Building across the street.

The **Winder Building** (1848; R. A. Gilpin; DL), 600 17th St N.W. at 17th and G Sts N.W., houses the offices of the U.S. Trade Representative. The five-story building has little ornamentation. Four years after its completion in 1848, the building was purchased by the War Department, which used it as U.S. Army headquarters during the Civil War.

### Washington Notes
Both Winfield Scott and Ulysses S. Grant had their offices here. Supposedly, President Lincoln often came here late at night to speak with prisoners of war held in basement cells.

Architecturally, the building is of importance because it was the first structure in the city to use a fireproofing technique that employed cast-iron beams with segmental brick vaults between them. James Renwick partially used this technique when constructing one of the Smithsonian buildings.

From the Winder Building's front entrance on 17th St, walk south a half-block to F St, then west one block to 18th St and the **General Services Administration** (GSA) (1915–17; Charles Butler; Ernest C. Bairstow, sculptor) at F St between 18th and 19th Sts N.W. ☎ 708-5082. Web: www.gsa.gov. Built to house the Department of Interior, which was here until 1936, the structure housed the Federal Works Agency and then the GSA when it was formed in 1949. The GSA supports government operations by providing products and services amounting to $40 billion annually. When the bid for the building came in under the appropriated funding, the developers substituted limestone for the intended gray brick exterior. An interesting feature is its E-shaped floor plan, which allows abundant natural light for the interior offices. The eagle over the central cornice was carved by sculptor Ernest C. Bairstow, who also carved the limestone panels in the sixth-story frieze and the ornamental work of the F St entrance.

Facing the GSA on F St's north side is the **Marshall/Ringgold House** (1825; Tench Ringgold, original owner and builder; 1860, architect unknown; 1911, Jules Henri de Sibour; 1985, various architects) at 1801 F St N.W. Even though it's currently used as the offices of an international foundation, this multiperiod house is a refreshing bit of residential charm amidst the area's massive office buildings.

### Washington Notes
A prominent figure in the early 1800s, Ringgold was a member of the team designated to oversee restoration of the buildings burned by the British in 1814. His daughter, because of a dwindling fortune, was compelled to take in boarders, but only those befitting her station. These included future president Martin van Buren, Civil War general George McClellan, and Chief Jus-

tice of the Supreme Court John Marshall, who lived here from 1801 until his death in 1835, the years he served on the Court.

As originally built, the structure was two stories tall and flat-fronted. The columned bay entrance was designed by Jules Henri de Sibour in 1911 for the Countess of Yarmouth, a noted Washington hostess.

Walk south on 18th St one block to the intersection of 18th and E Sts with New York Ave. Turn east on New York Ave and walk a half-block to the **American Institute of Architects** (AIA) (1972–74; The Architects Collaborative; 1989, interior renovation by Malesardi & Steiner; 1993, library expansion by The Architects Collaborative, Malesardi & Steiner) at 1735 New York Ave N.W. ☎ 626-7492. Web: www.aiaonline.com. This is an early example of a "background" or "wraparound" building connected to a historic building, in this case the Octagon (see Walk 8: "The Ellipse and 17th Street Sites"). The spatial geometry–based design of the Octagon (a circle, two rectangles, and a triangle) is complemented by the graceful curvature of the AIA headquarters. A garden walkway connects the two structures built 173 years apart, yet presenting a unified sense of composition.

From the AIA, turn west on New York Ave and walk a half-block to 18th and E Sts, then a half-block south on 18th St to **Rawlins Park** (1938; John Kirkpatrick, landscape architect; 1973, Joseph A. Bailey, sculptor) at D and E Sts between 18th and 19th Sts N.W., an oasis with shade trees and a fountain. Major General John Aaron Rawlins (1831–1869) grew up in Galena, Illinois, and was a neighbor and friend to Ulysses S. Grant. By the time the Civil War broke out, Rawlins had already spent three years in California panning for gold and several years in Illinois studying law. An avid supporter of the Union cause, Rawlins was appointed by Grant to be his aide-de-camp and remained one of the general's closest advisors throughout the war. In 1869, Rawlins was named secretary of war by President Grant, but he died five months later of tuberculosis. Bailey portrays Rawlins with his field glasses in one hand and his sword in the other.

## Department of Interior Building

1849 C St N.W. ☎ 208-3100. Web: www.doi.gov. Museum open Mon–Fri 8:30–4:30. Closed weekends and holidays. Admission: free. Other building artwork can be viewed only on an accompanied tour scheduled two weeks in advance. ☎ 208-4743. Library open 7:45–5. Indian arts and crafts shop open 8:30–4:30. National Park Service Information Office open 9–3. Cafeteria. Restrooms. Wheelchair accessible. Must have picture ID for entrance to the building.

Directly across from Rawlins Park is the E St entrance to the Department of Interior Building (1935–36; Waddy B. Wood; paintings and sculptures, various; DL). The main entrance is reached by continuing south on 18th St one block, past Constitution Hall (see Walk 8: "The Ellipse and 17th Street Sites"), to the C St entrance of the building. One of the lesser-known Washington treasures, this government office building has the functionality of a civil service agency and the heart of an art museum. The museum has displays, videos, crafts, and metal silhouettes (cutouts depicting various departmental functions), plus a collection of Depression-era murals unparalleled in the city.

**Highlights:** The murals depicting Native American life, located in the South Penthouse on the eighth floor.

### History

In 1849, Congress created the Department of the Interior to address the difficulties presented by the Republic's rapid western expansion. Interior was given the mandate to explore the western territories, manage national parks, and oversee territorial governments, thus earning it the nickname The Department of Everything Else. At one time or another it was in charge of the Patent Office, the Pension Office, the Education Department, the Agriculture Department, Homesteading and Railroads, and Washington, D.C.'s police department and water system. By the 1930s, the department had outgrown its headquarters (the current GSA Building at 18th and F Sts N.W.) and had offices scattered around the city. President Franklin Roosevelt's progressive secretary of the interior, Harold Ickes, began lobbying Congress for a new building. When Congress refused, Ickes was successful in having the building constructed as part of the Public Works Administration.

Secretary Ickes helped oversee the construction, insisting on spacious central corridors, open courtyards, and central air-conditioning (a major innovation at the time). Ickes strongly felt that comfortable employees were more productive. He also requested space for the promotion and sale of Indian arts and crafts. Mrs. Ickes was a strong spokesperson for Native American human rights.

The Interior Building contains more Section of Fine Arts (a Depression art project operating at the same time as the Works Project Administration, or WPA) artwork than any other government building. The Interior Building is second only to the Post Office Building (Franklin Square Station) in the number of artists from this program whose work is on display. Muralists, sculptors, and painters decorated the building's interior with illustrations of the department's mission. Ickes personally approved each artistic rendering. More than 2,200 square ft of walls in the cafeteria, the arts and crafts shop, and the employees' lounge were devoted exclusively to Indian artists, specifically six artists from the Navajo, Apache, Potawatomi, Pueblo, and Kiowa tribes.

The building's escalators, rooftop promenade, employee gymnasium, and penthouse radio studio broke new ground in office design. The current Interior Department consists of a number of bureaus and offices, including the Bureau of Indian Affairs, the Bureau of Land Management, the Bureau of Reclamation, the U.S. Fish and Wildlife Service, the U.S. Geological Survey, the Minerals Management Service, the National Park Service, the Office of Surface Mining, and the Office of Insular (island) Affairs.

### Washington Notes

The only bullet fired in the city of Washington in World War II was accidentally fired by a soldier stationed on the rooftop of the Interior Building. The bullet hit the Lincoln Memorial, chipping the word "Wisconsin."

## Exterior

The building features Indiana limestone above a pink granite base. Its design reflects the Moderne style popular in the 1930s. A central hall runs north to south, and six wings cross it running east to west. These wings, seven stories above the pavement and rigidly and identically Spartan in design, provide the building's most notable façade. The building is seven stories high, with an eighth-story setback over the connecting wings. The north and south façades have recessed porches, each featuring massive three-story posts, with a heavy cornice above and a two-story attic with a monumental frieze. The C St frieze features the seals of the 13 original states.

## Interior

There is much artwork throughout the building as well as such decorative details as bronze grilles, ornamental plaster moldings, and marble floors. Inside the main entrance on C St, leading to the lobby, are grand bronze doors, their transoms embellished with Roman grate designs. The marble lobby is dominated by a bronze bas-relief, 54 inches in diameter, of the departmental seal, which depicts a grazing buffalo with the sun rising behind mountains in the background. On the west side of the lobby is the department's library containing several hundred thousand volumes; on the east side is the auditorium. In the main corridor, the departmental symbol of the American buffalo is repeated in the marble relief sculptures of Boris Gilbertson. On the east side is *American Bison* (1939) and on the west side is *American Moose* (1939).

Enter the **museum** from the main corridor. Many of the exhibits are originals from the museum's 1938 opening, accompanied by current explanations of the perceptions and prejudices of that era, particularly as they relate to race and conservation. The museum offers an overview of the department's history and activities, with exhibits on Native Americans, western expansion, national parks, and the measuring and employment of America's natural resources. The galleries to the left and right of the central hallway have dioramas and videos.

On the left of the museum's entrance is a pictorial display explaining the department's main focus of development, conservation, and recreation and also the department's relationship with Native American tribes.

The first gallery on the left of the hallway is the **Bureau of Indian Affairs (BIA) Gallery.** The bureau's past is represented by a mounted American bison head, a birch bark canoe, and a diorama of Window Rock, Arizona, the Navajo tribal capital, in 1938. Intricately cut silhouettes from the 1930s, made from sheet metal dipped in plastic and backlighted to appear two-dimensional, depict five Native American tribes in traditional 19C scenes, while the video shows Native Americans today acting as partners with the BIA to revive economies and preserve their languages. Art by Indian women includes woven Cherokee baskets by Lucy George and wood animal carvings by Amanda Crowe.

Across the hallway is the **National Park Service Gallery.** The gallery has silhouettes depicting parkland activities, a video about balancing preservation and recreation in the national parks, and a display of original art posters of national park scenes by Charley Harper. Harper's posters continue in the hallway that leads to the next gallery.

The **Bureau of Land Management Gallery** describes homesteading, surveying methods, land management, the administration of federal laws relating to the public domain, and the origins of land grant colleges. A bronze sculpture, *The Old Bearing Tree* (1984; Jim McNealey and Ken Omsberg), and equipment such as a zenith telescope and a "Diamond A" branding iron used in the West are also featured.

In the hallway leading to the next galleries are four paintings by William Henry Jackson (1843–1942) depicting scenes from four major surveys: the Hayden Survey, 1871 (an official exploration of what would become Yellowstone National Park; the photographer in the background is Jackson); the Powell Survey,

1869–72 (exploration of the Canyon of the Colorado River); the King Survey, 1867–69 (a geological exploration extending along the 40th parallel to the eastern base of the Rocky Mountains); and the Wheeler Survey, 1873–75 (of the 100th meridian, near Corn Mountain, a sacred mesa of the Zuni people).

> ### Washington Notes
> William Henry Jackson's long life was an adventurous one. He served in the Union Army during the Civil War, was a pioneer on the Oregon Trail, and went on an around-the-world expedition in the 1890s. For the Hayden exploratory survey he photographed the Teton and Wind River Ranges and Colorado's Central Rockies. When he was commissioned in 1935 to do these paintings for the new Interior Building, an age requirement had to be waived because Jackson was 92 years old at the time. He died at the age of 99 and is buried at Arlington National Cemetery.

The next galleries are the **U.S. Geological Survey Galleries.** On the left are displays relating to topography and oil fields. To the right are displays of crystals, ores, and minerals, as well as information about the eruption of Mount St. Helens in 1980 and a dinosaur painting (1920s) by Charles Knight.

In the hallway leading to the Bureau of Mines gallery are paintings of pioneer life in the 1800s American West by Wilfred Swancourt Bronson. The **Bureau of Mines Gallery** has a diorama of the devastation of an early mine explosion and exhibits describing the development of safety procedures and strategies for conservation in mining.

The **Bureau of Reclamation Gallery** on the right has a diorama of Hoover Dam. From there walk to the **U.S. Fish and Wildlife Service Gallery.** The exhibits here focus on conservation. Displayed is a collection of paintings and illustrations of departmental artist Bob Hines, a protégé of conservation pioneer Rachel Carson.

The **Office of Insular Affairs Gallery,** the final gallery, features storyboards of morality tales, or fables, carved on wood pieces and executed by artists in the 1950s and '60s such as Kerradel Eterochel, Baules Sechelong, Rechucher Charlie Gibbons, and Ngiraibuuch Skedong.

Most of the building's **Depression-era murals and sculptures** can only be viewed on a guided tour. Two murals are in the cafeteria, which is open to the public.

**Basement.** In the courtyard of the basement cafeteria are two unusual and compelling pieces of life-size bronze sculpture. *Negro Mother and Child* (1940; Maurice Glickman) was at the time of its creation one of the few monuments to African Americans in Washington. When first exhibited, it received acclamation from both the public and the New York art critics. The original plaster cast of the sculpture is located in the library of Howard University, given to Howard after the work was rejected by the National Museum of Art. Also in the basement courtyard is *Abe Lincoln* (1940; Louis Slobodkin), a lanky depiction of the future president as farm hand. Winner of a contest for sculptural work to be displayed at the U.S. Building at the World's Fair in 1939, Slobodkin's work was erected in a pool of water with flowing fountains. But when the artist and his wife went to see it on opening day, it had disappeared. Edward Flynn, U.S. Commissioner General to the fair, had had the statue removed because it "was too big, far too high and hid all the lighting." Incredibly, the sculpture was never found and was presumed to have been destroyed. The present statue was made from one or two original plaster casts, created without the aid of models, photographs, or any biographical information on Lincoln.

The mural *Incident in Contemporary American Life* (1942; Mitchell Jamieson), to the right of the south entrance, vividly recalls an important incident—the crowd reacting to the emotional impact of Marian Anderson's concert at the Lincoln Memorial in 1939.

### Washington Notes

When Marion Anderson was denied use of Constitution Hall by the Daughters of the American Revolution solely because of she was African American, Secretary Harold Ickes, working with Eleanor Roosevelt, provided the Lincoln Memorial for the concert. Jamieson chose to concentrate on the mixed crowd of 75,000 who attended, rather than the performer. The young woman seated at the top of the steps in the foreground is the artist's sister, the elderly woman standing beside her is his mother, and the seated woman with braids holding a baby is Mary McLeod Bethune, a prominent civil rights leader.

**First floor.** Four panels comprising one of the building's most evocative murals—*The Negro's Contribution in the Social and Cultural Development of America: Education, the Arts, Religion, and Science* (1943; Millard Owen Sheets)—are located on walls near the foot of the Grand Staircase. All portray African American subjects. *Education* is on the southeast wall, *Arts* on the southwest wall, *Religion* the northeast wall, and *Science* the northwest wall.

**Second floor.** *The Construction of a Dam* (1939; William Gropper), across the south end of the main corridor, has been reproduced more than any other mural of its time. Three eight-ft-tall panels separated by fluted pilasters illustrate the incredible engineering undertaking that is the construction of a great dam. Inspired by the construction of the Grand Coulee Dam on the Columbia River and the Davis Dam on the Colorado River, Gropper depicts the power of common labor, as men grapple with machinery to defeat the natural forces of rock and water.

**Third floor.** Mary Ogden Abbott's teakwood sculpture *Indian Doors* (1961), at the south end of the main corridor at the entrance to the office of the director of the National Park Service, was donated by the artist to the department for the 1976 Bicentennial. One of the few pieces by women artists in the building, the panels reflect the artist's impression of Plains Indians. Henry Varnum Poor's mural *Conservation of American Wildlife* (1939), at the north end of the main corridor, shows John J. Audubon and Henry Thoreau, among others, studying and making notes on natural surroundings. Incongruously, Daniel Boone also makes an appearance, complete with rifle. Others in the 9 by 42 ft fresco are working in a duck preserve, releasing banded birds, and scattering corn to attract waterfowl.

**Eighth floor.** The Native American murals in the South Penthouse, painted in 1939–40, attest to Ickes's devotion to his employees, as this area was the Employees' Lounge. Woodrow Wilson Crumbo's *Potawatomie Life* includes *Buffalo Hunt, Deer, Courting, Flute Player* (music was an important element in Potawatomie ceremonies), *Peyote Bird* (a tribal symbol), and *Wild Horses*. The grouping of subjects called *Navajo Scenes* by Gerald Lloyde Nailor uses the symbols of a Navajo sandpainting in *The Hunting Ground*, depicts Navajo women in traditional dress in *Preparing Yarn for Weaving*, and portrays dances initiating children into the home of the gods in *Initiation Ceremony*. In Allan C. Houser's murals *Apache Scenes: Singing Love Songs* a young boy follows the girl he admires when she leaves camp and sings to her. Houser's *Apache Round Dance* and *Sacred Fire Dance* both revolve around what is now called the Devil Dance.

Velino Shije Herrera, along with Nailor and Houser, was a student of the Indian school of painting in Sante Fe, New Mexico. His *Pueblo Life* includes *Buffalo Dance, Buffalo Chase, Pueblo Woman and Child, Pueblo Corn Dance, Women Making Pottery* (Herrera's mother was a potter), *Pueblo Girls Carrying Water,* and *Pueblo Symbols: The Eagle Dance Design* and *The Shield Design*. A major renovation and conservation project for these murals, which had worn away considerably in spots, was undertaken in Jan 1996 with $250,000 provided by GSA. The renovation was completed in May 1998.

Exit the Interior Building on C St and cross to the park and the **Statue of General Simón Bolívar** (1959; Felix W. de Weldon; Faulkner, Kingsbury, and Stenhouse, architects), a gift to the United States from Venezuela. At 27 ft high the work is one of the largest equestrian statues in the U.S. Bolívar (1783–1830) was known as the Liberator for ending Spanish colonial rule in Venezuela, Colombia, Ecuador, Peru, Bolivia, and Panama. De Weldon, who also did the U.S. Marine Corps War Memorial at Arlington National Cemetery (popularly known as the Iwo Jima Memorial), has Bolívar wearing the gold medal given him by Lafayette, sent by George Washington Parke Custis, adopted grandson of the first president. The statue, bronze on a base of black Swedish marble, is flanked by a marble walk and six fountains representing the countries Bolívar freed.

Continuing in the path of South American freedom fighters, walk south a half-block on 18th St, crossing Virginia Ave to Constitution Ave and the **Statue of General José Artigas** (1950; Juan M. Blanes), Father of the Independence of Uruguay. This nine-ft-high bronze statue was paid for by the contributions of Uruguayan school children (with the help of the Uruguayan Chamber of Deputies). Perhaps as a reminder that the U.S. hasn't sole claim to the name America, the inscription on the statue base reads: "From the people of Uruguay to the people of the United States. Liberty of America is my dream and its attainment my only hope."

### Washington Notes

Artigas, a passionate Federalist, was reputed to carry a copy of the U.S. Constitution with him at all times. He spent his life fighting for freedom for the people of Uruguay. He died at the age of 86 in 1850.

**Diversion:**

Walk one block east on Constitution Ave to 17th St. Here from the early to the late 1800s stood the Van Ness Mansion. General John Peter Van Ness was a congressman from New York who married Washington heiress Marcia Burns. The house, designed by Benjamin Latrobe, was described at the time by a city resident as "probably not excelled by any private building in this country."

From the Artigas statue at 18th St and Constitution Ave, walk two blocks west on Constitution Ave, past the House of the Americas (see Walk 8: "The Ellipse and

17th Street Sites"), to the **Federal Reserve Building** (1937; Paul Philippe Cret; John Gregory, sculptor) at 20th St and Constitution Ave N.W., ☎ 452-3000, a white marble rendering of fiscal solidity if there ever was one. This is the last building to be constructed along Constitution Ave west of 17th St. Cret, who also designed the Folger Library and the House of the Americas, won the competition held for the building, partly because of his design's "purity of line." Two bronze fountains in small garden settings border a terraced marble plaza leading to steps to the central portico, where four square pilasters support a flat cornice. Ornamentation is minimal. The marble stairs have 18 stars in sets, bronze window grilles cover the two-story-high windows, and lion head knockers hang on massive bronze doors. A six-ft-high American eagle by Sidney Waugh is perched over the Constitution Ave doorway. On each side of the C St entrance are two high-relief panels by John Gregory. Each features a seated woman in classical dress. The woman on the right (east) represents America, her hand supporting the United States seal. The woman on the left (west) supports the Federal Reserve Board seal with her right hand, and her left holds the caduceus of Mercury, Roman god of commerce. The caduceus was a gift from Apollo, a magic wand that allowed Mercury to turn anything into gold.

Continue west on Constitution Ave one block to the **National Academy of Sciences (NAS) Building** (1924; Bertram Grosvenor Goodhue; Lee Lawrie, sculptor; 1962–70, Wallace K. Harrison) at 2101 Constitution Ave N.W. ☎ 334-2000. Web: www.nas.edu. This organization was created by Congress in 1863, with a charter signed by President Lincoln, "to investigate, examine, experiment, and report upon any subject of science or art." The National Academy of Engineering, the Institute of Medicine, and the National Research Council also share this building. The academies and the institute are honorary societies that elect new members each year. More than 120 Nobel Prize winners are members of the NAS. Each year more than 200 NAS studies are conducted on a wide range of topics in the fields of science, technology, and health.

Designed in the classical style, but without columns or pediments, the building's white New York Dover marble has mellowed to a pale gold. The window grilles and sliding doors are bronze, and the roof is copper. Lee Lawrie's eight-ft-high low-relief bronze panels are located between the windows on the Constitution Ave façade. These panels depict those involved in the progress of science from ancient to modern times. Represented are Euclid, Hippocrates, Aristotle, Benjamin Franklin, Leonardo da Vinci, Galileo Galilei, and René Descartes. The building's eaves are decorated with alternating copper figures of an owl and a lynx, signifying wisdom and observation. A coiled serpent at each corner also represents wisdom. Below the cornice is a quote from Aristotle (in Greek): "The search for truth is in one way hard and in another easy. For it is evident that no one can master it fully nor miss it wholly. But each adds a little to our knowledge of nature, and from all the facts assembled there arises a certain grandeur." The embossed entrance doors depict episodes in the history of science.

From the front of the NAS Building, walk west on the pathway a few yards to the **Albert Einstein Memorial** (1979; Robert Berks), situated on the southwest corner of the NAS grounds in a grove of elm and holly trees. Einstein, who revolutionized scientific thought with his concepts of space, time, mass, motion, and gravitation, is depicted sitting on a semicircular three-step bench of North Carolina white granite. At his feet is the visible universe, portrayed in a circular sky map made of Norwegian emerald pearl granite and embedded with more than 2,700 small metal studs representing the celestial bodies positioned as they were at noon on April 22, 1979, when the memorial was dedicated. The bronze sculpture (labeled "lumpy mashed potatoes" by some) is 21 ft high, weighs 7,000 lbs, and is supported by a subbase consisting of three concrete caissons sunk to bedrock at a depth of 25 ft.

From the Einstein Memorial, continue west on Constitution Ave one block to the **American Pharmaceutical Association Building** (1933; John Russell Pope; Ulysses A. Ricci, sculptor) at 2215 Constitution Ave N.W. ☎ 628-4410. Web: www.aphanet.org. The inscription above the front entrance reads: "This building is dedicated to those who have contributed their knowledge and endeavor to the preservation of public health and to the further advancement of science in pharmacy." Designed in the neoclassical style, the Vermont marble building has an unadorned, windowless central projecting pavilion with four pilasters at the center. Flanking the bronze entrance door are massive bronze lamps and above these are six-ft-high by four-ft-wide bas-relief panels. One panel depicts a youth in classical dress holding a bowl with an old man looking over his shoulder. The youth symbolizes progressive spirit and the old man is the pioneer who observes the advances resulting from his earlier research. Beneath the two figures is the Greek word for *pharmaceutical*. The other panel features a young woman dressed as a classical figure with an invalid male looking over her shoulder. The woman symbolizes hope, leading the invalid toward a lamp that symbolizes the light of curative knowledge. The woman holds the Staff of Aesculapius, the Roman god of healing. The inscription reads "Light and Hope." Money for the building came from subscriptions from 14,000 druggists nationwide in the early 1930s.

Continue on Constitution Ave a half-block to 23rd St and cross at the traffic light to the grassy island bordering the ramp to the Theodore Roosevelt Bridge. Walk up the island (west) about a half-block to **Braddock's Rock,** in colonial times part of a large rock mass that jutted like a natural wharf or quay into the deep water of the Potomac River. The Potomac shoreline in that era was at the bottom of 23rd St.

### Washington Notes

The plaque here chronicles the belief that it was in this area that British General Sir Edward Braddock landed in April 1755 with troops and colonials, including Lieutenant George Washington, who was commander in chief of the Virginia militia. From here they began their march into the interior to rid it of the French, who were settled at Fort Duquesne (now Pittsburgh). On July 9, the force was ambushed by the French and their Indian allies, and Braddock and more than 700 of his men were killed. It was Lieutenant Washington who led the survivors back to safety—the beginning of his acclaimed military career.

## Old Naval Observatory

23rd and C Sts, N.W. ☎ 762-3248. Tours available if scheduled in advance.

Walking east back down the grassy ramp island, cross 23rd St and walk north up 23rd St a half-block to the Old Naval Observatory (1843–1930s; several architects; Roland Hinton Perry, sculptor; DL), now site of the Naval Medical Command, the administrative offices of the Naval Medical Center in Bethesda, Maryland.

**Highlights:** The observatory room on the second floor.

### History

The highest hill in Washington has had many names, including Peter's Hill, Reservation Number 4, Windmill Hill, Camp Hill, University Square, and Observatory Hill. In the late 1700s, it belonged to Robert Peter and was part of his Mexico plantation. After its sale in 1791 to the U.S. government, Pierre L'Enfant chose the hill as the site of a major military installation, but George Washington wanted the site for a national university. Then called University Square on some maps, the hill awaited funding for Washington's dream, but this never came to fruition.

### *Washington Notes*

Marines who had come from Philadelphia with the new government lived here for two years, giving the site the name Camp Hill. The marines proved to be terrible neighbors, plundering local houses for food and taking target practice in the middle of the night. The first Marine Band concert was held here to assuage the neighbors.

Following the War of 1812 the marines moved out, and the area became an overgrown meadow where lovers met. In 1844, the Naval Observatory was constructed here, the first scientific structure built by the federal government, but the observatory almost didn't get built. President John Quincy Adams, an amateur astronomer, remarked on America's scientific inferiority to Europe, saying, "It is with no feeling of pride as an American that the remark may be made that on the comparatively small territorial surface of Europe there are existing more than one hundred and thirty of these lighthouses in the skies; while throughout the whole American hemisphere there is not one." Yet Congress repeatedly voted down funding for an observatory. Appropriations came when Naval Lieutenant Louis Goldsborough convinced Congress and the Board of Navy Commissioners that naval instruments, such as charts and instruments, should be housed in one depot to be repaired and properly calibrated. To do this required frequent celestial observations, as precise time could only be determined by observing the transit of a star across the local meridian. An Italianate-style structure constructed of yellow brick with a 23 ft diameter revolving dome made of wood and sheathed with copper was built to house the 9.6-inch, German-made equatorial refracting telescope. The dome revolved on six 32-pound cannonballs set in a grooved cast-iron rail.

### *Washington Notes*

The city quickly became used to having the observatory on the hill. Passersby would set their watches at noontime when, to mark the hour, a large black ball dropped from a pole on top of the dome.

Matthew Fontaine Maury, the first superintendent of the observatory, became known as the Father of Oceanography for his pioneering work in hydrography, astronomy, and meteorology in his 17 years as superintendent. But the Civil War brought an end to his work. A native Virginian, Maury reluctantly resigned his commission the day following Virginia's vote to secede from the Union. In 1873 the observatory acquired the largest refracting telescope in the world. It was used to discover the moons of Mars in 1877. By 1893, however, the Foggy Bottom smog and city lights made it increasingly difficult for the observatory to function at full capacity, so it was moved to higher ground on Massachusetts Ave, where it remains today.

From 1894 to 1902, the Naval Museum of Hygiene was located in the observatory building. This facility was a pioneer in environmental and occupational medicine. Studies were conducted on the purity of water systems aboard naval vessels and at shore installations and on the healthfulness of work spaces in government buildings. In 1902, the museum became officially known as the U.S. Naval Museum of Hygiene and Medical School, and it was called the Medical School and Naval Hospital until 1917. As the facility expanded, the ten-acre tract proved insufficient. After a 1930 study recommended razing all the buildings, including the observatory, the facilities were moved to a 247-acre tract of land in nearby Bethesda, Maryland. The Naval Medical Center and the Bureau of Medicine and Surgery moved its offices into the hill buildings, which later came to be known as the Naval Medical Command.

### Washington Notes

In 1987, when the Soviet Union launched a rocket to one of the moons of Mars, attached to the rocket's exterior was a metal plate copy of the page from the observatory's log book noting the discovery of that moon 110 years earlier.

Directly in front of the observatory building, now called **Building 2**, is Louis R. Metcalf's statue of Dr. Benjamin Rush (1904). Rush (1745–1813), a Princeton graduate, was a member of the Second Continental Congress, a signer of the Declaration of Independence, and served for a time as surgeon general. He was known for his humanitarian concerns, which included the education of women, the cofounding of the first American antislavery society, and the opening of America's first public health clinic in 1786. A close friend of Thomas Jefferson's, Rush was treasurer of the U.S. Mint for 16 years before his death in 1813. This statue was erected by the American Medical Society in 1904. At that time, the hill was the site of the Museum of Hygiene, and Rush was renowned for being ahead of his time in urging clean operating rooms and sterilized instruments. The Latin inscription on the Indiana limestone pedestal literally translates to "Study without a pen is dreaming," meaning that if a scholar doesn't record his findings, they're meaningless.

## State Department Building

2201 C St N.W. ☎ 647-4000. Web: www.state.gov. Diplomatic Reception Rooms tours Mon–Fri 9:30, 10:30, and 2:45 P.M. By appointment only, at least two months in advance during the April–Oct season. ☎ 647-3241. No same-day tours at any time. Photo ID must be presented at desk. Restrooms. Wheelchair accessible.

Descend the hill to the main gate of the Old Naval Observatory and cross 23rd St to the tour entrance of the State Department Building (1941; Gilbert Stanley Underwood and William Dewey Foster; 1958, Graham, Anderson, Probst and

White with A. R. Clas, associate architect). The State Department Building is a high-security facility not open to tours, except for the reception rooms on the eighth floor, which feature one of the finest collections of 18C American furniture and 18C and 19C American art works.

**Highlights:** The 18C and 19C period pieces and the Thomas Jefferson State Reception Room.

### History
The Department of State is the oldest department in the executive branch. The first State-like department was the Committee on Secret Correspondence (established in 1775), which developed into the Committee for Foreign Affairs. In 1781, the Continental Congress created a Department of Foreign Affairs and appointed Robert Livingston as the first minister of foreign affairs; he was succeeded by John Jay in 1784. With the adoption of the U.S. Constitution in 1789, Congress included the Department of Foreign Affairs as part of the executive branch. The name of the department was changed from that of Foreign Affairs to State because certain domestic duties were assigned to it, such as preservation of the laws of the United States. There have been 64 secretaries of state. The first was Thomas Jefferson, and the most current is Madeleine K. Albright, who is also the first woman to serve in this position.

## Exterior
The State Department Building was built in two sections, 18 years apart. During World War II, department employees increased from fewer than 1,000 to more than 7,000, and even the 47 separate offices scattered in buildings throughout the city didn't have enough room for all the personnel. With the emergence of the U.S. as a world leader, it was decided the Department of State deserved a central location where all its personnel and functions could be consolidated. The initial plans were for the department to share the new War Department Building being built in Foggy Bottom from designs made by Underwood and Foster in 1941 on the eve of the war. But an impatient War Department decided to build the Pentagon across the Potomac River in Arlington, and the State Department inherited its current location, the former site of the Old Glass Works. The first of the two sections (the block facing 21st St) has a rough limestone finish and polished granite in the spandrels between the metal casement windows. A dramatic portico of four stark piers four stories high draws the eye to the center of the 21st St façade. In 1958, extensions on the west and the south were built, creating entrances on C, 23rd, and E Sts. Built in the modern style of the 1950s, the smooth limestone-sheathed structure is punctuated with two-pane casement windows.

## Diplomatic Reception Rooms
These rooms are truly an American treasure, created through the magnanimity of generous citizens and foundations using absolutely *no* tax dollars. The collection of 18C and 19C American furnishings and art is valued at more than $90 million. The inspiration for the transformation of the reception rooms from their "early airport decor" of the 1950s to their present glory came from the collaboration of Clement E. Conger, chairman of the department's Fine Arts Committee and collection curator, and architect Edward Vason Jones. They designed and remodeled these rooms over a 15-year period between 1965 and 1980. The purpose

was to showcase American culture and American craftsmanship; with only a few exceptions everything in these rooms was made in America. The rooms are used by the president, vice president, members of the cabinet, and the secretary of state to entertain more than 80,000 guests each year; more than 60,000 visitors tour them annually.

The tour begins in the **Edward Vason Jones Memorial Hall,** named in honor of the rooms' architect and modeled after the drawing room of Marmion, an 18C house in King George County, Virginia. The chandeliers are 18C English cut glass. The mahogany side table is unique for its time period (1755–75) and place of origin (New York) because of its cabriole legs and its serpentine front rail.

Continue into the **Entrance Hall.** The paneled interior is based on Carter's Grove (1751–53) and Westover (1674–1744), two distinguished plantation houses on the James River in Virginia. A highlight is the bombé secretary (desk) and bookcase signed in three places on the inside by Benjamin Frothingham in 1753, making this the earliest dated bombé piece in the U.S. The six Chippendale chairs are from the home of Francis Scott Key (see Walk 20: "Georgetown West"). The Philadelphia origins of the Chippendale highboy are evidenced by the peanut carved on the apron, a signature of 18C Philadelphia craftsmen. The breakfront containing American silver is the only American Chippendale breakfront in the collection; the other three are British. The three-piece tea set was a gift to Daniel Webster in 1828, possibly to celebrate the publication of his monumental dictionary. The French-made clock by Bourghelle is known as one of the most intricate clocks to have been produced in this country in the 18C. Around the main dial are subsidiary dials for, among other things, relating information about the tides and the position of the planets.

The passageway leads into the **Gallery,** the first of the rooms to be renovated. Palladian windows were installed at each end of the long, narrow room. This room serves as an exhibition gallery for portraits, landscape paintings, and American Queen Anne and Chippendale furniture, including pieces by John Townsend and John Goddard of Newport, Rhode Island. One of the most valuable pieces in the collection is the small bombé chest with a serpentine front, rococo pulls, and handles. It is crafted of fine mahogany by a Newport craftsman. One of Gilbert Stuart's *George Washington* (1795) portraits is here, as are two portraits by John Singleton Copley. At one end of the gallery is *Alice Hooper* (1763), painted before Copley had any formal training. Compare it to *Mrs. John Montresor* (c. 1778) at the other end of the gallery, painted after Copley had two years of formal training in London. Also on display is a 65-piece dinner service of green-and-white pattern china.

Continue into the **John Quincy Adams State Drawing Room,** where guests are received at official luncheons and dinners. The portrait of Adams (1816; Charles Robert Leslie) is remarkable because, it was said at the time, this was the closest Adams ever came to laughing. Charles Willson Peale's portraits of George and Martha Washington (c. 1795–98) are here, as is a curiosity by Benjamin West called *The American Commissioners* (painted after 1820). The intention was to paint a portrait of the British and American diplomats present at the signing of the Treaty of Paris in 1782 that ended the Revolutionary War. The Americans (John Jay, John Adams, Benjamin Franklin, Henry Laurens, and Temple Franklin) showed up, but the British didn't. The painting was left with an unfinished look and the title *The American Commissioners.* Gilbert Stuart's portrait of John Jay (1783), considered one of his finest, was acquired at auction in 1986 for

$999,000. Two other pieces are of particular note: the English desk (c. 1780) on which the Treaty of Paris was signed and Thomas Jefferson's architect table, used in his Philadelphia apartment while attending the Continental Congress. It is likely portions of the Declaration of Independence were drafted on this table. Jefferson preferred to stand as he worked, which the adjustable drawing board allowed. On this same table, in 1971, President Richard M. Nixon signed into law the Twenty-sixth Amendment, lowering the voting age to 18.

The fireplace screen is handcarved. These screens were more than decorations. The ladies of the day put melted wax and even flour on their faces to hide their blemishes. At social functions, the ladies would gather near the fireplace because the rooms were inevitably cold. The screens enabled the women to be warmed at the fire without having their makeup melt. One of the most valuable pieces of china in the collection is in the corner breakfront: a saucer that was part of a "State" series given to Martha Washington. The service had the names of all the states inscribed around the border and an "M.W." monogram in the center. In this same breakfront is George Washington's Order of the Cincinnati Chinese export porcelain dinner service, commemorating the surrender of British General John Burgoyne and the end of the Revolutionary War. Note the Chinese features of the soldiers. This is because the Chinese artists who painted the porcelain only knew how to draw Oriental features.

The **Thomas Jefferson State Reception Room** is considered a masterpiece of neoclassic design. This is not surprising, since Edward Vason Jones used the same design books as Jefferson. The room has Doric entablature, pedimented glass doors, triple-sash windows, and an 18C Carrara marble mantel. The mahogany-and-maple floor is copied from Jefferson's home at Monticello. The bust of Benjamin Franklin (c. 1778; Jean-Antoine Houdon) was completed in the artist's Paris studio. Two items of particular note are the knife box and William Thornton's portrait of Jefferson. The sterling silver knife box, holding 72 knives, was made in England in 1797–98 and is one of only two known examples in the world. The portrait of Thomas Jefferson (c. 1815–16; Dr. William Thornton, the architect of the Capitol) is a copy of one executed by Gilbert Stuart in 1805. The portrait is notable because of its simplicity. Jefferson is presented sans wig. Compare this portrait to the replica of Peale's portrait (1791) in this room.

The final room on the tour, and the largest, is the **Benjamin Franklin State Dining Room,** named for the "Father of the American Foreign Service." The portrait of Benjamin Franklin by David Martin over the mantel is a contemporary replica of the original painted from life in 1767 in London. The clock on the mantel beneath Franklin's portrait is a gilt bronze clock, made in Paris (c. 1805), with a statue of George Washington standing beside it. The Savonnerie-style carpet was made on a single loom and weighs more than 8,000 lbs. Designed for the 96 by 46 ft room, the carpet incorporates the Great Seal of the United States (also depicted in plaster and gilt on the ceiling), symbols of the four important crops of the early Republic, the four seasons, and 50 stars representing the states of the Union. Eight Adam-style cut-glass chandeliers were also made especially for the room. Approximately 5 to 15 functions are held in this room each week.

Continue north on 23rd St one block to the headquarters of the **Pan American Health Organization (PAHO)** (1964; Roman Fresnedo-Siri, design architect;

Justement, Elam, Callmer & Kidd, architects) at 523 23rd St N.W. ☎ 974-3000. Web: www.paho.org. Here also is the regional office for the **Americas of the World Health Organization** (Web: www.who.org). The mission of the PAHO, which was founded at the Second International Conference of American States in Mexico in 1902, is to "promote and coordinate the efforts of the countries of the Regional of the Americas to combat disease, lengthen life, and promote the physical and mental health of their people." PAHO's 35 member governments sponsor programs to deal with basic problems such as nutrition, disease, and environmental pollution. Uruguayan architect Fresnedo-Siri won a $10,000 international competition to design a building to fit the triangular plot bounded by 23rd and E Sts and Virginia Ave.

Continue north on 23rd St a half-block to **Columbia Plaza** (1963; Keyes, Lethbridge & Condon) at 2400 Virginia Ave N.W., ☎ 293-2000, the only realized portion of a "packaged living" project conceived in the 1940s, which was to have included four groups of high-rise apartments and a hotel surrounding a commercial plaza.

# George Washington University

Continue north one block to 23rd and F Sts and the beginnings of the area encompassing George Washington (GW) University/Hospital/Law Center (1850s–present; George S. Cooper; Victor Mindeleff; Albert L. Harris; Arthur B. Heaton; Alexander B. Trowbridge; Waldron Faulkner; Mills, Petticord and Mills; Keyes Condon Florance; Skidmore, Owings and Merrill), bounded by Pennsylvania and Virginia Aves and 19th and 24th Sts N.W. ☎ 994-0175. Web: www.gwu.edu.

**Highlights:** St. Mary's Episcopal Church (located amidst the campus buildings) and George and Martha Washington's River Horse statue at the corner of 21st and H Sts N.W.

### History

Even though George Washington's first attempts to have a university situated on Observatory Hill failed, he did not give up. Washington left 50 shares of stock in the Potomac Company for the endowment of a university. A precursor of the C&O Canal, the Potomac Company, established in 1785, dissolved in 1828, causing Washington's stocks to become worthless. But before this happened, a university had been established. In 1819, the Reverend Luther Rice, agent for the Baptist General Convention, purchased 47 acres of land north of what was then called Boundary St (now Florida Ave N.W.) between 14th and 15th Sts for construction of what became Columbian College. In 1821, President James Monroe signed the act of Congress that created the college.

Columbian College was composed of a preparatory school and theological and classical departments. Total fees were less than $200 a year, and $10 was required for pocket money.

The college's first graduating class, in 1824, consisted of three seniors, and the ceremony was witnessed by President James Monroe, his cabinet, and the Marquis de Lafayette as guest of honor. The assembly was entertained by the Marine Band, and dinner was at the college president's home on campus. In 1825, the medical school was founded, and in 1826, the Law Department. When the Civil War broke out, most students left to join the Confederacy, as did many members of the faculty. During the war, much of the campus was taken over for use as hospitals and barracks.

By the late 1800s, the college had become a university with graduate-level courses and was centralized in a downtown location at 15th and H Sts. In 1881, women were admitted to the university on a trial basis, but the law school declined to admit them with the reasoning that it "was not required by any public want." In 1898, the University Hospital opened on H St between 13th and 14th Sts. In 1904, Columbian University became George Washington University. In 1912, the first of its departments was established in Foggy Bottom, and most of its facilities were located there by the 1930s. In 1954, the university abolished all restrictions on minority-student admissions. During the years of the Vietnam War, many students were active in the antiwar movement. Two thousand attended an on-campus rally in 1968 to hear Jerry Rubin and Abbie Hoffman speak; Maury Hall was seized and temporarily shut down in 1969; and in 1970, students went on strike to protest the invasion of Cambodia.

During the 1980s and into the '90s, protests of another sort have been occurring in the university buildings, where officials have met with community activists trying to work out an agreeable middle ground regarding campus expansion. Currently, the university is the largest institution of higher education in Washington, with about 7,000 undergraduate students studying in 79 majors and 9,000 graduate students. GW's 90 buildings situated on 43 acres make it the second largest landowner (after the U.S. government) in Foggy Bottom.

Walking around the GW campus involves walking around much of what is left of the Foggy Bottom residential area. From 23rd and F Sts, continue north on 23rd one and a half blocks to **St. Mary's Episcopal Church** (1886; James Renwick; DL) at 730 23rd St N.W., ☎ 333-3985, the first African American Episcopal Church in Washington, D.C. The church is open to visitors.

In the 19C, a separate congregation was the only solution to the restrictions placed upon African Americans in houses of worship. African Americans were relegated to pews located in remote corners of the church, received communion after whites, and sent their children to segregated church studies. The first church on this site, known as St. Mary's Chapel for Colored People, was formerly the chapel attached to Kalorama Hospital, which was about to be razed. A parishioner of St. John's Episcopal Church donated the lot, and Secretary of War Edwin M. Stanton, another St. John's parishioner, had the chapel taken apart, loaded on wagons, and rebuilt on this site. By 1882, the structure was already too small for its worshipers. St. John's Church engaged James Renwick to design a new, larger church. Renwick's Gothic design has simple lines accented by a picturesque tower. The stained glass windows were designed and executed by Lorin of Chartres, France. Ethnic subjects chosen for the windows include St. Cyprian, the African bishop and martyr. The handcarved oak pews, patterned tile and red marble floors, and polychromatic stenciling of the walls were all gifts from members of the parish. A bronze plaque on the west wall honors those who died in the two world wars.

From St. Mary's entrance, walk south a half-block on 23rd St to G St, then one and a half blocks east on G St to the university's **Veterans' Memorial Park,** established in 1996 to honor those students who died in the service of their country, with its abstract iron sculpture *Remember, Stick Together* (1983; Chris Gardner). Across the street on the south side of G St is the District's **School Without Walls High School,** which allows advanced-level students to set their own curriculum under faculty guidance.

Continue east on G St to the southwest corner of the intersection of 21st and G Sts and **Strong Hall** (1935). A gift to the university from Mrs. Henry Alvah Strong, this was the first residence hall built specially for women. Note the stone insert in the wall facing the intersection: "Erected by a woman's altruism and understanding. Dedicated to the growth of the human spirit that God and the state may be served by noble women." This red brick colonial structure, topped by a solarium, was intentionally built in the style of what was then a residential neighborhood.

Turn south on 21st St and walk one block to 606–610 21st St N.W., the **Lenthall Houses** (c. 1800; John Lenthall; DL). Originally built by Lenthall, superintendent of construction of the U.S. Capitol, these red brick, Federal-style homes were on 19th St near G St, but were moved in 1978 to make way for a World Bank annex. These are university-owned and used as residences for visiting faculty. Some of the oldest buildings in the city, the houses reflect the best of their time, with their restrained and well-proportioned features. Lenthall family members lived in no. 606 for over 100 years.

Walk north on 21st St a half-block to the intersection with G St. On the northeast corner at 2033 G St N.W. is the **Woodhull House** (1855), a red brick, Italianate-style building, detailed in stone, terra-cotta, and wood. The building serves as headquarters of the university police force. This was the home of General Maxwell Van Zandt Woodhull, a brevet brigadier general in the Union Army at the age of 21. The house was given to the university by Woodhull's son in 1921. The junior Woodhull was a trustee of the university who urged its relocation to Foggy Bottom.

Walk east on G St one block to the intersection of 20th and G Sts. On the southeast corner stands the **United Church** ("Die Vereinigte Kirche") (1892) at 1920 G St N.W., ☎ 331-1495, which was founded by the Germans who lived and worked in Foggy Bottom. The lot was sold to a group of German Lutherans by Jacob Funk in 1768, and the Concordia Lutheran Evangelical German Congregation was founded. John Philip Sousa was baptized here in 1854. The present church was erected on the site in 1892, and English services were added in 1909. The reality of a dwindling residential neighborhood, as office buildings replaced houses, brought about a merger with the United Methodist Congregation in 1975 to form the United Church. Two German services are held each month.

On the northwest corner of the intersection of 20th and G Sts are two adjoining houses, **2003 G St N.W.** (1892; Victor Mindeleff and Theodore A. Harding) and **700 20th St N.W.** (1892; George S. Cooper and Theodore A. Harding). Both contain university offices, although for part of this century, 700 20th St served as the university president's house. These typical row houses of the late 1800s are made of brick with sandstone trim and feature Second Empire–style mansard roofs.

Continue north on 20th St a half-block to the university's **National Law Center,** which includes the neo-Georgian **Stockton Hall** (1925; Arthur B. Heaton), named for Rear Admiral Charles Herbert Stockton, university president from 1910 to 1918, and the **Jacob Burns Law Library** (1967; Mills, Petticord and

Mills; 1984 expansion, Keyes Condon Florance Architects). The brick and sandstone creates a monochromatic effect. The building has faux attic dormers.

Continue north on 20th St a half-block to H St. Turn west on H St and walk a half-block to **University Yard,** a sort of central campus in this urban setting. The statue of George Washington is a cast bronze copied from the original marble statue by Jean-Antoine Houdon (1741–1828) for the state capitol in Richmond, Virginia. The statue was purchased by the university in 1932 on the occasion of George Washington's bicentennial. The university is the D.C. representative for the All-America Rose Selections (AARS), and the roses featured in the yard are AARS award winners.

Continue west on H St a half-block to the boldly geometric **Lisner Auditorium** (1946; Waldron Faulkner; DL) at 730 21st St N.W., ☎ 994-1500, named for its donor and university trustee, Abram Lisner. One of the oldest and largest stages in the city, the Lisner hosts more than 200 performances annually of everything from opera to ballet to pop to jazz.

### Washington Notes

In front of the Lisner, on the corner of 21st and H Sts, is a curiosity: a small bronze hippopotamus. A gift from university president Stephen Joel Trachtenberg to the class of 2000 in 1996, the hippo has become an unofficial university mascot. The plaque relates the fanciful tale of "George Washington's River Horse," saying that the Potomac River once had so many hippos that George and Martha watched them cavorting from the porch at Mount Vernon. Martha's grandchildren tried to lure the beasts to shore to pet their noses for luck, and the presence of the hippopotamuses was credited with enhancing the fertility of the plantation. A short poem sums it up: "Art for wisdom, Science for joy, Politics for beauty, And a Hippo for Hope." Of course, there never were any hippopotamuses in the Potomac River, but that doesn't stop students from rubbing the hippo's nose for luck before exams and ball games.

In 1999 the university purchased the former Howard Johnson Hotel (more recently called the Premier Hotel), at 2601 Virginia Ave N.W., with plans to turn it into housing for freshman students. Located across the street from the Watergate hotel and apartment complex, the Howard Johnson property played a small part in that historic episode. Lookouts armed with binoculars occupied Room 723 on the night of June 17, 1972, ready to warn the Watergate burglars if the police appeared. GW plans to set aside the seventh floor for 40 students enrolled in the yearlong course America after Watergate: How Watergate Changed Us Politically, Socially, and Culturally. Room 723 will be decorated with Watergate memorabilia.

Walk two blocks north on 21st St to Pennsylvania Ave.

### Diversion:

On Pennsylvania Ave, walk east one block to the intersection of Pennsylvania Ave with 20th and I Sts and the **Arts Club of Washington** (1802–6; Timothy Caldwell, owner and builder; 1988 façade restoration, Davis Buckley; DL) at 2017 I St N.W., ☎ 331-7282. The club offers live performances of jazz and classical music, art exhibits, and literary readings, all of which are open to the public. Designated as the Caldwell-Abbe House on the National Register of Historic Places, this building, one of the city's earliest residences, was intended by its builder to be "the handsomest house in the capital city." To that end Caldwell included expensive exterior ornamentation and finely carved interior woodwork. The project proved so expensive that Caldwell was forced to sell the masterpiece when it was completed.

### Washington Notes
When James Monroe was secretary of state, he and his wife lived here, filling the house with the furnishings acquired during Monroe's stay in Paris. In 1817 the house served for a time as Monroe's "White House," while the damage done to the original President's House when the British burned it in 1814 was being repaired. Meteorologist Cleveland Abbe, head of the U.S. Weather Bureau in the 1890s, lived here from 1877 to 1916. Abbe is known mainly for pioneering the concept of daily weather forecasts (which makes him the Father of TV Weathermen).

In 1916, two groups of Washington artists bought the house to establish the Arts Club of Washington. Known for its focus on painting, sculpture, music, and drama, the club was the first in the city to admit women as full-fledged members. In the 1920s, the MacFeely House was linked to the Monroe House to provide space for the club's expanding programs.

From 21st and Pennsylvania Ave, turn northwest and walk two blocks to the emergency entrance of George Washington University Hospital (1948; Federal Works Agency), main entrance at 901 23rd St N.W., ☎ 994-1000.

### Washington Notes
President Ronald Reagan was brought here on March 30, 1981, after being shot by John Hinckley.

The Medical Department of GW University was established in 1826. The Columbian College Infirmary began in 1844 as the capital's first general hospital and one of the nation's earliest teaching hospitals. The University Hospital's Surgery Unit, established in 1966, was one of the first in the U.S. to offer one-day care for minor surgical procedures. More than 17,000 patients are admitted to the hospital each year. Another 48,000 patients are treated in the Ronald Reagan Institute of Emergency Medical Services, and the Ambulatory Care Center handles more than 350,000 outpatient visits annually. In 1997, George Washington University and Universal Health Service, Inc., entered into a management agreement (20 percent university, 80 percent Universal Health Services) to operate George Washington University Hospital. In 1998, the partnership announced that a $96 million replacement hospital would be built on 23rd St across from the current hospital building.

Directly north of the hospital is **Washington Circle.** The statue *George Washington* (1860; Clark Mills) depicts Washington at the Battle of Princeton in the winter of 1776 trying to advance his horse, which is rearing at incoming cannon fire. The city's first horse racing course was located in this vicinity.

From Washington Circle walk west on Pennsylvania Ave to the corner of 25th St and **St. Stephen Martyr Church** (1867; Adolf Cluss and J. W. Kammerheuber; new building 1961, Donald S. Johnson and Harold L. Boutin; Felix G. W. de Welden, sculptor) at 2436 Pennsylvania Ave N.W., ☎ 785-0982. Established to accommodate the Irish Catholic workers living and working in Foggy Bottom, the original neo-Gothic structure cost $60,000. Anxious Pastor John McNally would stand outside the Gas Company on payday to collect contributions. In 1961 a contemporary-style church was dedicated. A heroic ceramic statue of St. Stephen by Felix G. W. de Welden dominates the main façade of the church. An elliptical concrete arch frames a 35 ft jeweled glass window. The 70 ft white, pre-cast concrete bell tower is topped with a 20 ft gold cross.

From the corner of 25th St and Pennsylvania Ave, walk south a half-block to **Snow's Court** (c. 1860), an alley off 25th St N.W. These simple brick houses were some of the first alley dwellings in Foggy Bottom. Built about 12 ft wide by 26 ft deep, these dwellings, now gentrified, originally housed some of the city's poorest residents.

Continue south on 25th St a half-block to the rows of houses at **822–828 25th St N.W.** (DL). These examples of what is called the urban vernacular style, or modest working-class style, were built between 1874 and 1884. Number 822 is the most stylistically ambitious of the group, with its windows and door capped with brick lintels in the Second Empire style.

Continue south on 25th St a half-block, turn west on I St to the 2500 block of I St where closely abutting, modest row houses are flanked by larger houses at either end. Numbers **2503–2507 I St N.W.** (c. 1911; DL), designed by Thomas Francis, Jr., differ from their neighbors by having large projecting square bays. Across the street, no. **2506** is distinguished by a decorated cornice and three brackets supporting corbeled eaves. Number **2508** was designed and built by Peter McCartney, Foggy Bottom's best-known builder, whose skill with brick and wood is evident in the corbeled brick cornice and delicate jigsaw work above the windows, as well as by the delicate columns flanking the entry. McCartney also designed and built **2530–2532**, two attached houses connected by a ground level, arched opening that accesses the rear yards. Both houses have intricate brick cornice work.

## Watergate

Take the curved driveway next to 2532 I St that runs behind the houses and walk southeast one block to the intersection of 25th St and Virginia Ave and the Watergate (1963–67; Luigi Moretti; Milton Fischer, associate architect) at 2500–2700 Virginia Ave and 600–700 New Hampshire Ave N.W., ☎ 338-3008. This well-known building stands on the site of the old Washington Gas Light Company's storage tanks. Just as the gas company defined the working-class character of Foggy Bottom, Watergate defines the neighborhood's new identity—large-scale buildings and wealth. The Societa Generale Immobiliare of Rome, an Italian investment corporation, underwrote the project, and Italian architect Luigi Moretti undertook the design of what he saw as a departure from the angular Washington architectural style. His five curvilinear buildings are placed amid landscaped gardens and a below–street level shopping center. Horizontal ribbon windows and balconies reinforce the graceful curves.

**Washington Notes**

The Watergate complex is best known as the site of the break-in of the Democratic National Committee in the early morning hours of June 17, 1972. The resulting hearings and criminal investigation led to the resignation of Richard M. Nixon on Aug 9, 1974. Nixon was the first (and only) U.S. president to resign.

From the Watergate, cross 25th St and proceed northeast on New Hampshire Ave to the **statue of Benito Juárez** (a copy of an original made in 1895; Enrique Alciati; Louis Ortiz Macedo, architect). Juárez (1806–1872) was the Zapotec Indian who became the leader of Mexico's democratic movement. He was declared president twice in the turbulent history of Mexico's democracy, and he is remembered for his passionate advocacy of independence under constitutional law and equal rights for the poor. This 12 ft bronze statue was part of an exchange of gifts between the people of the United States (who gave a statue of Abraham Lincoln, now standing in Mexico City) and the people of Mexico in 1969. At the back of the base an urn is buried containing soil from Oaxaca (Juárez's birthplace), where the original statue is located.

# John F. Kennedy Center for the Performing Arts

2700 F St N.W. ☎ 467-4600. Web: www.kennedy-center.org. Tours daily 10–1, except Christmas Day. ☎ 416-8341. The several theaters showcase plays, musicals, ballet, modern dance, opera, and musical and symphonic performances. The center has three main stages–the Concert Hall, the Opera House, and the Eisenhower Theater—and two smaller stages—the Terrace Theater and the Theater Lab. Millennium Stage offers free performances of music, dance, and storytelling in the Grand Foyer daily except Christmas Day. The American Film Institute, a research center for American film, has a 224-seat theater with over 700 screenings a year. ☎ 828-4000. Performing Arts Library open Mon–Fri 12–5. Three restaurants. Restrooms. Wheelchair accessible.

Walk southwest on New Hampshire Ave one block to the John F. Kennedy Center for the Performing Arts (1971; Edward Durell Stone).

**Highlights:** The Israeli Lounge adjacent to the Concert Hall, the African Lounge adjacent to the Opera House, and the view from the Roof Terrace. Note: The Kennedy Center lounges are open to the public only during tours, not during performances.

### History

In 1962, President John F. Kennedy stated, "I am certain that after the dust of centuries has passed over our cities, we, too, will be remembered not for our victories or defeats in battle or in politics, but for our contribution to the human spirit." At that time the National Cultural Center legislation signed into law by President Eisenhower was already four years old, but little progress had been made toward the construction of a performing arts center. The Kennedy Center wasn't dedicated until 1971, 13 years after the act was passed. Richard Coe, drama critic emeritus of the *Washington Post*, remarked, "The Perils of Pauline pale beside the birth pangs of the Kennedy Center."

Various sites were chosen, then changed, including the current site of the Smithsonian's Air and Space Museum. Finally, the site of the old Heurich Brewery was deemed the best choice. Edward Durell Stone's final plans projected the building to cost $31 million. When President Kennedy was assassinated in 1963, Congress passed an act naming the center in the slain president's honor. In 1965 President Johnson turned the first shovelful of earth. Three years later, construction began after a series of labor disputes were resolved and funds were raised for the original $31 million plus an additional $50 million for landscaping and an underground garage.

One of the first countries to generously contribute to the center was Italy, which donated 3,700 tons of Carrara marble, valued at more than $1.5 million, for the exterior and interior of the building. On Sept 8, 1971, the Kennedy Center debuted with the premiere performance of Leonard Bernstein's *Mass* in the Opera House. The next night the Concert Hall was dedicated with a performance by the National Symphony, which makes its home at the Kennedy Center. In Oct, the Eisenhower Theater was christened with a performance of Ibsen's *A Doll's House.*

## Exterior

This was one of Stone's last major works, an enlarged version of the low-slung box-shaped form he used for the U.S. Embassy Building in New Delhi. The Kennedy Center structure has a surrounding single row of thin columns supporting an overhanging roof. The general critical judgment of the building is that it is a modern rendition of a classic Washington monument. Those who don't like the rectangular lines derisively refer to it as "the box the Watergate Complex came in."

## Kennedy Center Entrance Plaza

The bronze sculptures *America* and *War and Peace* (1969; Jurgen Weber) are Germany's gift to the Kennedy Center. These allegorical sculptures consist of two mammoth panels attached to the front of concrete piers. In *America,* a crowd of nude, starving Europeans eagerly await the unloading of grain from an American freighter. Huge flames and smoke envelop the *Statue of Liberty,* and the piece ends with warships and a rocket to the moon. *War and Peace* also alludes to violence in the modern world. A person is trapped in an underground bunker while the city burns above him; a murder is happening in a bombed-out building. Then comes peace—a nursing baby and its family, people singing, and finally, a party of can-can dancers, a jazz band with Louis Armstrong on trumpet, and the Greek god Pan playing the saxophone. One art critic dubbed it "Comic strips in bronze."

## Interior

Tours of the center don't follow any set path. What is seen in which order depends on where other groups are at any given time. However, all tours start at the Information Desk in the Hall of States and end on the Roof Terrace and progress from the main floor to the Terrace level.

From the east side Entrance Plaza enter the **Hall of States** through the door that is farthest north (closest to the Watergate complex). Beginning on the right, facing the plaza, are the flags of all 50 states, placed in the order of their admission into the Union. Included as well are the flags of the District of Columbia and the five territories of Puerto Rico, the Virgin Islands, Guam, American Samoa, and the Commonwealth of North Mariana Islands.

The **American Film Institute** is located just inside the plaza door, and the **Information Desk** is in the center of the hall. In the **Hall of Nations,** located at the opposite end of the building, the flags are of those nations where the U.S. has diplomatic missions (as of 1994). The flags are hung in alphabetical order beginning on the right, facing the plaza. Both halls feature part of the center's 19,000 square yds of rich, red carpeting, with walls and floors of Carrara marble. From the Hall of Nations walk west toward the **Grand Foyer**, the building's most glamorous space. This 618 ft long hall extends the entire length of the building on the west side. The hall is 40 ft wide and 63 ft high. (The Washington Monument could be laid on its side in here and have 75 ft to spare.) The 60 ft high windows are hung with gold metallic-weave draperies. Running the length of the foyer are Sweden's gift to the center: 18 Orrefors crystal chandeliers that are 15 ft long, 7 ft wide, and weigh 1 ton each. Their total of 8,000 lights shining through 16,000 double prisms are reflected in the foyer's 58 by 9 ft mirrors—a gift from Belgium—that flank the entrance to the Opera House.

The focal point of the foyer is the bust of John F. Kennedy (Robert Berks), the design and the construction of which took more than six years. Working with lighting genius Abe Feder, Berks designed special ceiling spotlights to throw two beams of light onto the bust and give the impression the face is changing expression with the time and light of day. The foyer is the site of the **Millennium Stage**, a venue offering free concerts every day at 6 P.M. Performers cover a wide range of disciplines; among them have been jazz pianists, folklorists, and college choirs. No tickets are required.

At the southern end of the Grand Foyer is the **Concert Hall.** Seating 2,442, the Concert Hall is the largest of the performing spaces. Its 1997 renovation included installing a state-of-the-art acoustical system. The chandeliers were a gift from Norway, and the 4,000-pipe organ was a gift from the Filene Foundation. Adjacent to the Concert Hall is the **Israeli Lounge,** a gift from Israel. Three Israeli artists carved and painted the walls and the ceiling with scenes of Biblical stories. Nechemia Asaz used walnut wood highlighted with brass and copper to carve ancient musical instruments mentioned in the 150th Psalm. Yehezkil Kimchi sketched the history of Israel in sepia ink on nylon and silk panels. Shraga Weil highlighted the ceiling with brilliantly colored paints and 22-karat gold leaf to illustrate scenes from the Old Testament. On the doorpost of the lounge is the traditional mezuzah, a tubular case holding a rolled-up bit of parchment with verses from the book of Deuteronomy asking for blessings for the room. Near the lounge entrance is Luxembourg's gift to the center: Lucien Wercollier's pink marble sculpture *Ascension.* In the same area is a gift from Great Britain, Dame Barbara Hepworth's bronze sculpture *Figure.* Opposite these is *Apollo X 1970,* a gift from Switzerland created by artist Willy Weber, who exploded dynamite on both sides of a 500-pound sheet of steel to create the irregularly shaped curves, craters, and bumps.

Walk north through the foyer to the **Opera House,** the second largest performing space in the center (2,350 seats). The Opera House's walls, floors, curtain, and ceiling are reflected in the 50 ft sunburst crystal chandelier, a gift from Austria. The Opera House is the home of the Washington Opera Company and the site of the Kennedy Center Honors Gala, which is televised each year. Two tapestries by Henri Matisse, *Birds of the Air* and *Fish of the Sea,* hang at opposite ends of the box-tier level. The **African Lounge,** entered from the box-tier level, was a gift from many African nations to express their grief over the death of President Kennedy. Hung with tribal cloth hangings and tapestries, the room has a subdued feel. The statue *Mother Earth* by Dr. Oku Ampofo of Ghana stands in the center of the room. The 12 ft high lounge doors were carved from the wood of a 700-year-old tree by Nigerian artist Lamidi Fakeye.

Continue walking north to the **Eisenhower Theater.** The smallest of the main level performing spaces, with 1,100 seats, the theater has a wood-paneled interior and a steel fire curtain weighing 6,000 lbs. Cyprus's gift to the center is an amphora (a two-handled jar with a narrow neck) that dates back to about 800 B.C. Egypt's gift, presented in Oct 1975 by Mrs. Anwar Sadat, is an alabaster vase once owned by King Djeser of the Third Dynasty, c. 2680 B.C. In the stairwells are Mexico's gift: two tapestries from artist Leonardo Nierman, *Poem to Fire One* and *Poem to Fire Two.*

Take the elevator in the Hall of States to the Roof Terrace level and the **Terrace Theater.** A gift from the people of Japan in honor of the American Bicentennial, this silver, lavender, and purple-accented room seats 513. The evening of its dedication, the theater was purified in an ancient Shinto ritual performed by a 36-man Grand Kabuki Troupe that included two "Living National Treasures" of Japan, actor/dancer Nakamura Kanzanburo and musician Hinatayu Takemoto.

In the center of the Roof Terrace level is the the **Theater Lab,** used for experimental productions and the Young Playwrights Festival. For a year and a half in the 1980s, this was the home of the ill-fated American National Theater project under the direction of Peter Sellars (the director, not Peter Sellers the actor). At the opposite end of the lobby, the **Performing Arts Library** has 5,000 books and periodicals and more than 6,000 recordings and videotapes. The center's three restaurants are located on the south side on this level. These include the Roof Terrace Restaurant (dinners; lunches only on matinee days), the Encore Café (casual fare), and the Hors D'Oeuverie (cocktails and light fare).

Step out onto the **Roof Terrace.** From the east, look out at the Foggy Bottom neighborhood, a mix of massive federal and association buildings, small row houses, and the large buildings of George Washington University. From the west, there is a nice view of the Georgetown harbor.

The next walk begins in Georgetown at the Dumbarton Bridge, also called the Buffalo Bridge, at 23rd and Q Sts N.W. Walk northwest on New Hampshire Ave four blocks to Washington Circle, then north on 23rd St five blocks to Q St.

# 19 · Georgetown East

Metro/Bus: There is no Metrorail service to Georgetown. The nearest stops are Blue/Orange Line to Foggy Bottom (from there take the 30s bus on Wisconsin Ave) or Red Line to Dupont Circle (from there take the G2, which continues through Georgetown on P St, or the D1/2/5/6, which continues through Georgetown on Q St).

## Georgetown
Established before the Federal City, Georgetown dates back to 1751. This area, bordered by the Potomac River on the south, Rock Creek on the east, Georgetown University on the west, and Burleith, a residential area, on the north, has always possessed its own style, which is part of its charm. Commercially, Georgetown has

changed from an 18C shipping port and trade center to a shopping and entertainment mecca. As a community it has changed from a sleepy, ethnically and socially mixed village to a cosmopolitan enclave for middle-class families, students crammed into row houses, as well as for many of Washington's wealthy elite.

**Highlights:** Georgetown features buildings from many periods, revealing an architectural continuity that is difficult to find elsewhere in the city. Georgetown has elegant and historic mansions such as Tudor Place, as well as 18C and 19C town houses, Oak Hill Cemetery, Georgetown University, several locks of the C&O Canal, and the Old Stone House, the oldest house in the District. There are also barge rides on the C&O Canal and summer concerts at Washington Harbour, plus music clubs, trendy bars and restaurants, and shopping, shopping, shopping.

### History

The Potomac River played a major role in Georgetown's creation. Georgetown was first the site of the Tohoga village of the Anacostan Indians, who recognized the advantages of the location: From here they could navigate the Potomac River and trade with other tribes. ("Potomac" is from an Algonquin word meaning "trading place.") After the Anacostans moved on in the 1600s, the land remained relatively deserted until around 1700, when grants with titles like The Widow's Mite, Poor Tom's Last Shift, Knave's Disappointment, and Plain Dealing were awarded to individuals, and the settlement of Georgetown by Europeans began.

Ninian Beall, a Scottish merchant, eventually became an important landowner, but he started his career as an indentured servant in Maryland. Beall had fought on the side of King Charles I against Cromwell at the Battle of Dunbar (1650), and following the defeat had been sold into servitude to a planter in Barbados and then to Maryland. Following five years of indenture, Beall was given 50 acres of land. He became an Indian fighter and then a negotiator, as well as a major landowner, and was appointed commander of Maryland's provincial forces under the restored monarchy of Charles II. Beall named his land the Rock of Dunbarton. (It wasn't until about 1800 that the spelling "Dumbarton" came into use.)

Beall and others, including Scottish merchant George Gordon, owned the land where the Potomac reached its uppermost navigable point. By the mid-1700s this area became a major port for Maryland's tobacco. In 1745, when a Maryland law required that a tobacco inspection house be created, Gordon's warehouse, located southwest of the intersection of Wisconsin Ave and M St, was used. In 1751 after some merchants petitioned the Maryland legislature to lay out a town, the legislature purchased 60 acres of land, some from George Gordon's Rock Creek Plantation and some from George (son of Ninian) Beall. Most likely Georgetown was named after King George II, but some historians suggest it may have been named for landowners George Gordon or George Beall. The original borders of the "town of George" were N St (north), Jefferson St (east), and 34th St (west).

The town was laid out in 80 lots of equal size. Streets were named according to the English custom of referring to pertinent activities. Wisconsin Ave was High St to the north and Water St to the south; M St was Bridge St to the east and The Falls to the west.

### Washington Notes

Prior to the Revolution the black population, including slaves as well as free blacks, accounted for about a third of Georgetown's residents. In 1795 the

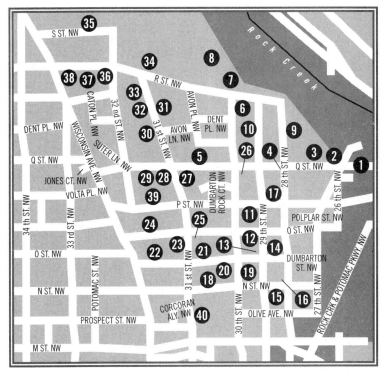

1 Buffalo Bridge
2 Mt. Zion Cemetery, 27th & Q
3 Dumbarton House, 2715 Q
4 Robert Dodge House, 1534 28th
5 Cooke's Row, 3007–3027 Q
6 K Graham's house 2920 R
7 Oak Hill Cemetery, 3001 R
8 Montrose Park, 30th & R
9 Evermay, 1628 28th
10 Mackall Mansion, 1623 29th
11 Alger Hiss house, 2905 P
12 Mt. Zion Community House, 2906 O
13 Mt. Zion Church, 1334 29th
14 Scheele's Market, 1331 29th
15 2806/2808/2812 N St
16 Kesher Israel (28th & N)
17 Gunbarrel Fences, 2811 P
18 N St houses,
    3014/3017/3033/3038/3041–45
19 Colonial Apts, 1311 30th
20 Kissinger et al. and fire station seal
    house, 3018 Dumbarton
21 Brown and Kelley, 3035/3037
    Dumbarton
22 Dulles et al., 3107 Dumbarton
23 Christ Church, Georgetown, 31st & O
24 Greely house, 3131 O
25 Laughlin Phillips house, 3044 O
26 Francis Dodge House, 1537 30th
27 Dodge House, 1531 31st
28 K. A. Porter, 3112 Q
29 Sevier Place, 3124 Q
30 Tudor Place, 1644 31st
31 Biddle house, 1669 31st
32 Taft house, 1688 31st
33 Carpenter Gothic house, 1696 31st
34 Dumbarton Oaks, 31st & R
35 E Taylor house, 3240 S
36 Fortas house, 3210 R
37 Halleck house, 3238 R
38 Georgetown Library, R & Wisconsin
39 Georgetown Presbyterian Church,
    3115 P
40 Georgetown Post Office, 1221 31st

community passed an ordinance prohibiting the assembly of more than seven free black men at a time. There were even cases of free blacks being taken from their families and forced into indenturement. Slave dealer John Beattie established his business in Georgetown in 1760 at the site of what is now the 3200 block of O St.

Georgetown's port during the Revolutionary War served as a base of supplies and munitions. John Yoast's gunsmithery produced many of the muskets carried by the Colonial Army. In 1789, Georgetown was officially incorporated, with Scotsman Robert Peter as its first mayor. His son, Thomas Peter, would later marry George Washington's granddaughter, Martha Parke Custis, and build one of Georgetown's most beautiful homes, Tudor Place.

In the early years of the Republic, Georgetown thrived. By 1791, Georgetown was the largest tobacco market in the state of Maryland and perhaps in the U.S. Georgetown had trade, socially prominent families, acceptable housing, and the capital's only cultural center, Georgetown College, which was established in 1789. In contrast, the Federal City at this time comprised more muddy fields and hopes than substantial government buildings and houses. Secretary of the Treasury Oliver Wolcott wrote these laments to his wife: "There are few houses in any one place, and most of them small, miserable huts. . . . The only resource for those who wish to live comfortably [not in boardinghouses] will be found in Georgetown, three miles distant, over as bad a road in winter as the claygrounds near Hartford."

George Washington wanted land in Georgetown, then part of Maryland, to be part of the new capital. Some landowners balked at parting with their property for what they considered below-market prices. Uriah Forrest, Revolutionary War hero, member of the Continental Congress, and successful merchant, held a dinner at his home (at what was later 3350 M St) attended by George Washington and those whose land Washington wanted for the capital. A compromise was reached. The agreement was finalized the following evening at Suter's Tavern, located somewhere in the vicinity of Grace Episcopal Church.

In 1791 two Marylanders—Andrew Ellicott, veteran of the Revolutionary War and surveyor of portions of the Mason-Dixon Line, and Benjamin Banneker, a free black man educated by the Ellicott family—were appointed to survey the boundaries of the future District of Columbia. As declared in 1791, the new capital included Washington City, as well as the port towns of Georgetown, with a population of approximately 3,000, and Alexandria, with a population of about 5,000. (In 1846 Alexandria retroceded to Virginia.) Regardless of its inclusion in the new District, Georgetown continued to operate politically, socially, and economically as an independent entity and it continued to thrive.

### Washington Notes

Not everyone was enamored of Georgetown. Abigail Adams, newly arrived wife of President John Adams (served 1797–1801), in a letter to her sister dated Nov 1800, wrote, "The ladies from Georgetown and in the 'city' have many of them visited me . . . but such a place as Georgetown! It is the very dirtyest Hole I ever saw for a place of any trade or respectability of inhabitants. It is only one mile from me, but a quagmire after every rain. . . . The Capitol is near two miles from us. As to roads, we shall make them by the fre-

| quent passing before winter! But I am determined to be satisfied and content, to say nothing of inconvenience, etc."

By the late 1820s, Georgetown's economic position suffered due to the decline of the tobacco trade, the rise of business in other parts of the District, and the construction of the Long Bridge, which is at the site of today's 14th St Bridge. The bridge connected Alexandria directly with the capital, thereby diminishing Virginia's trade with Georgetown.

Georgetown placed its faith for economic revival in the creation of the Chesapeake and Ohio Canal. The C&O Canal's goal was to create a trade route linking Maryland with the Ohio settlements. Construction began in 1828 and was aborted in 1850 with the canal reaching only to Cumberland, Maryland. Despite the shortened route, the canal did for a while boost Georgetown's trade. In the 1870s—the canal's golden age—ships brought coal, wheat, limestone, lumber, and produce to the area. Schooners from Maine sailed down with ice and then filled their hulls for the return trip with coal from Cumberland. The increased prosperity led to the building of hundreds of fashionable Victorian houses in the last decades of the 19C. Unfortunately, the C&O coincided with the coming of steamships, which made deeper ports more desirable, and the advent of the railroad. On the same day ground was broken for the canal, Charles Carroll of Carrollton, Maryland, broke ground for America's first railroad, the Baltimore and Ohio. Railroads could transport goods faster and cheaper.

The Civil War (1860–65) brought many changes to Georgetown, a largely Southern town. Many local churches served as hospitals and even Tudor House, the grand mansion of the Peter-Custis family, quartered Union soldiers. Confederate troops disrupted shipping routes and vandalized warehouses, further interfering with Georgetown's trade economy.

### Washington Notes

By the late 19C, Georgetown's African American population lived in what was known as Herring Hill, a 15-block area south of P St between Rock Creek Park and 29th St, named after the main food staple the families fished from the creek. More than 1,000 black families lived in Georgetown; the majority were cooks, domestics, and gardeners, but some were tradesmen and landowners.

In 1867, almost two years before the Fourteenth Amendment granted African Americans full citizenship, Congress enfranchised black citizens of what would soon be the District of Columbia. Thousands of blacks voted in the 1867 elections, and in 1868 blacks were elected to local office for the first time. A year later there were seven African American members of the City Council. In 1870, the council prohibited discrimination in hotels, bars, restaurants, and places of amusement.

When the Georgetown-Tenallytown Railroad, a pioneer electric trolley, was completed in the 1890s, it brought people from the District-Maryland line in the north to amusements on M St and businesses on K St along Georgetown's waterfront. But by 1915, Washington's commercial center had moved downtown, suburban developments became the fashionable places to live, and a new harbor in southwest Washington became the city's shipping center.

By 1920 Georgetown changed to an industrial area that had power plants, meat-rendering factories, and other "less desirable" businesses. The panache was gone. In the 1930s Georgetown's low prices and once charming architecture appealed to preservationists, but large-scale restoration efforts were halted by World War II. After the war, rezoning was created to promote residential instead of industrial use of buildings. In 1950 Congress passed the Old Georgetown Act, which made Georgetown a historic district. During the 1950s many of Georgetown's African American homeowners moved out of the area. Some were tempted by high prices for their town houses as well as by bigger homes and better schools in the surrounding suburbs, and some were forced out by tax increases. In the 1970s and 1980s trendy shops, restaurants, and bars sprang up to cater to the increasing number of college students and singles working in the city. Georgetown's commercial vitality makes it a magnet for both city dwellers and suburbanites, a popularity modern Georgetowners sometimes have trouble coping with, but one that would have certainly appealed to the town's original merchant settlers.

> ### Washington Notes
> Georgetown is home to some of Washington's most celebrated citizens, including Katherine Graham, *Washington Post* publisher and Pulitzer Prize winner; former *Post* editor Ben Bradlee and author Sally Quinn; celebrity biographer Kitty Kelly; and *Winds of War* author Herman Wouk.

Take the G2 bus that runs along P St N.W. in Georgetown to 26th and P Sts. Walk one block north on 26th St to Q St. Turn east on Q St and walk one and a half blocks to the **Dumbarton Bridge** (1914; Glenn and Bedford Brown, father and son architects; D. E. McComb, engineer), also called **Buffalo Bridge,** which spans Rock Creek Park and Pkwy. It was built to link downtown Washington, through the Dupont Circle area, to Georgetown. The bridge measures 261 ft long by 50 ft wide by 65 ft high. Its design, constructed in sandstone and reinforced concrete, strongly reflects Romanesque influences, particularly in the scale of the arches supporting the roadway. The design is said to echo that of the Ponte Maggiore Bridge, which spans the Tronto River in Italy.

The structure's decoration, however, is distinctly American. Eight-ft-tall bronze American bison (1914; Alexander Phimister Proctor) flank the eastern and western approaches to the bridge, and a representation of a life mask of Kicking Bear, a Native American chief, adorns each of the bridge's 56 corbels. Note Proctor's name etched into the base of the bison on the northwest corner of the bridge. He was known for the statues of animals, cowboys, and Native Americans he created for the Chicago Columbian Exposition of 1893.

## Mt. Zion Cemetery

Continue west on Q St one block to Mt. Zion Cemetery (DL), behind 2515–2531 Q St N.W., ☎ 723-8478. This is one of two adjacent cemeteries established in the 1800s for the burial of free blacks. For those who are interested in old cemeteries, Mt. Zion is worth the visit.

### History

In 1842, the Female Union Band Society, an association of women church members, bought property adjacent to what was then the Old Methodist Burying

Ground for the purpose of providing burial space for black families living in Georgetown. In 1849 Oak Hill Cemetery opened and became the preferred burial spot over the Old Methodist Burying Ground, which was subsequently leased to the Mt. Zion Church for the sum of $1 for 99 years. Together the Female Union Band Cemetery and Mt. Zion Cemetery from the oldest predominantly black burying ground in the city. Burials ceased in 1950. The cemetery was placed on the National Register of Historic Places in the 1970s.

At the intersection of 27th and Q Sts, turn north on 27th and walk through the apartment building parking lot to Mill Rd, which runs behind the apartments. Turn east on Mill Rd and walk the length of the building, about one block, to a dead end, then up a small embankment to what at first glance looks like a park area. In this L-shaped cemetery, clusters of graves are scattered across a wide area. Walk west, then south, and come out at the entrance to the parking lot, back onto 27th St.

## Dumbarton House

2715 Q St N.W. ☎ 337-2288. Walk-in tours Tues–Sat 10:15, 11:15, and 12:15. Closed in Aug, Thanksgiving Day and weekend, and Dec 25–Jan 1. Donation requested. Wheelchair accessible.

Walk south through the parking lot to Q St. Continue west on Q St a half-block to Dumbarton House (1799–1805; architect unknown; 1928, Fiske Kimball and Horace W. Peaslee, restoration architects). The house is a museum serving as the headquarters for the National Society of the Colonial Dames of America (NSCDA), an association of women who trace their descent from a relative in the American colonies prior to the Revolutionary War. The museum's collection of furniture, paintings, textiles, silver, and ceramics—many of them contributed or on loan by members of the society—were all made and used during the Federal period.

**Highlights:** Of particular note are the garden and the Charles Willson Peale painting of Benjamin Stoddert's children featured in the dining room. Two annual programs target families and children. The May puppet show aims at prekindergartners to fourth graders, and the December open house features Federal-era holiday traditions, quill writing, and storytelling.

### History

Dumbarton House is built on land that was originally part of the Rock of Dunbarton patent awarded to Ninian Beall in 1703. Beall's grandson, Thomas, sold four and a half acres of the tract to the mayor of Georgetown, Peter Casenave, for $600 in 1796. Casenave sold it almost immediately to Uriah Forrest and Isaac Pollock. Samuel Jackson bought the property in 1798 and began to construct what he called Cedar Hill. One year later he sold the land to Philip Fitzhugh. The property changed hands several times over the next four years, and in 1805 was sold for taxes to Comptroller of the Currency Gabriel Duvall, who in turn sold it to Joseph Nourse, the first registrar of the Treasury.

### Washington Notes

Nourse had the mammoth task of moving the nation's early financial records from Philadelphia to Washington. He held the office of registrar for 40 years, hiring so many of his relations while in the post that when President Andrew Jackson "requested" his resignation, Jackson referred to it as "clearing out the Noursery."

Nourse completed the house and lived there with his family until losing a large part of his wealth. Nourse sold the property to Charles Carroll, relative of a signer of the Declaration of Independence and owner of a paper mill on Rock Creek. Carroll renamed the house Belle Vue, a name retained until 1890. Carroll played host to Dolley Madison, wife of President James Madison (served 1809–17), on her flight from Washington City when the British burned the White House in 1814. Belle Vue remained in the Carroll family until 1841, when it was sold to Mrs. Lydia Newbold Whital of Philadelphia, who left it to her daughter, the wife of Charles Rittenhouse, whose daughter, "Miss Loulie," spearheaded the drive in the early 1900s to create Montrose Park. In 1915, the house was moved 100 yds to the west so that Q St could be cut through to Dumbarton Bridge. In 1928, the property was purchased by the NSCDA, who restored it to its early-19C character, named it Dumbarton House, and opened it to the public in 1932.

### Washington Notes

In 1817 Joseph Nourse purchased an 82-acre parcel of land, in what is now upper-northwest Washington, that he called Mt. Alban after the Mt. St. Alban in Hertfordshire where he was born. Today this is the site of Washington National Cathedral (Cathedral and Massachusetts Aves N.W.) and St. Alban's Church and school. Nourse's great-granddaughter, Phoebe Nourse, a schoolteacher, stated that upon her death the 40 gold dollars she left should be the beginning of a fund "For a Free Church on Alban Hill." Other donations followed and St. Alban's, the first free Episcopal church in the Diocese of Washington, opened in 1852.

### Exterior

Originally, Dumbarton House was built as a rectangular block with two bayed windows, two wings, and connecting hyphens. When the house was reconstructed following its move in 1915, the two wings were rebuilt, the central portion of the structure was lowered, and second stories were added to portions of the wings, substantially changing the original architectural composition. The garden behind the house contains plants and flowers from the Federal period.

### Interior

Visitors view the house on a guided tour. A central hall extends through the house, with two large rooms on either side opening into each other and onto the hall. The front (south) rooms are square shaped, and the rear rooms with the bowed bays look out over the garden. All the floors are original to the house, as are the delicate plaster cornices. The carved mantelpieces are of the period but from other sources.

The formal drawing room to the right of the entrance is called the **Blue Parlor,** taking its name from the blue damask fabric used to cover the cushions of the mahogany chairs. The mantelpiece design of urns, garlands, and pineapples is a frequently used period symbol of hospitality. Adjoining the Blue Parlor, on the north front of the house, is the **Music Room.** Note the late-18C, cobalt blue glass, Russian chandelier. The painting over the mantel, *The Troublesome Generation* (c. 1830; George Cooke, a Georgetown grocer), of a young girl and a young boy with his spelling medal proudly displayed has been cited as a portrait of George Washington's great-niece, Harriet Washington, and her brother Lawrence, but there is no basis for this.

Across from the Blue Parlor is the **Library.** The Chippendale mahogany English breakfront contains a 1792 edition of the *Encyclopedia Britannica* and an 1808 first edition of Chief Justice John Marshall's *Life of George Washington.* Adjoining the Library on the north end of the house is the **Dining Room.** Most notable is the painting of the children of Benjamin Stoddert (1789; Charles Willson Peale) above the sideboard. Stoddert was secretary of the navy under President John Adams; Q St was originally named Stoddert St in his honor. In the background of the painting is the earliest-known painted view of Georgetown's harbor and the island now known as Roosevelt Island, then called Mason Island for its owner James Mason. The weeping willow behind the children is a symbol of mourning, included because the children's grandmother had recently died. On the dining table is laid out the fine Chinese export porcelain dinner service of Martha Washington's granddaughter, Eliza Custis Law.

### Washington Notes
In 1804 Mrs. Law became the first woman in the new Federal City to be divorced. Due to the far-sightedness of her step-grandfather, George Washington, a prenuptial agreement protected her Custis inheritance.

Since, in colonial America, closets were taxed as rooms, cupboards and linen presses were used instead. On the **Second Floor Landing** a Chippendale mahogany linen press holds a quilt made by Martha Washington. On the bed in the bedroom above the Blue Parlor is a white muslin dress owned by Martha Washington and remade for her granddaughter Eliza Custis Law. On the windows of the bedroom above the Dining Room hang Venetian blinds (which were invented before the Revolutionary War), and displayed on a mannequin is Martha Washington's traveling cloak of olive green padded and quilted silk. The other room on the second floor is used for exhibits featured throughout the year.

Continue west half a block to the southwest corner of Q and 28th Sts and the **Robert Dodge House** (1854; Andrew Jackson Downing and Calvert Vaux) at 1534 28th St N.W. In the early 1800s, Francis Dodge, Robert's father, was one of Georgetown's most prosperous merchants and, until his death in 1851, one of the town's most prominent citizens. He said he wanted all his children (he had 11) to marry in his lifetime, and five of them obliged him in 1847 by marrying in a joint ceremony held at four o'clock in the morning so they could catch the early stage to Baltimore. Robert Dodge served as engineer for the C&O Canal.

The house was originally designed in the Italiante style, but graceful towers and balconies, arched verandas, and ironwork gave way in later years to changing tastes and urbanization. After 1900, the house stood vacant until World War II, when it opened as a nightclub called the Carcassonne. Sometime in the 1960s, its west end was subdivided into two modern town houses.

Continue west on Q St one and a half blocks to **Cooke's Row** (1868–69; Starkweather and Plowman) at 3007–3027 Q St N.W., another example of the Italiante style. Henry Cooke was a financier and one of the city's first commuters, traveling downtown to his office as president of the First National Bank of Washington on 15th St. Cooke commissioned four sets of twin dwellings, Italian villa–style in the center, Second Empire on either end, making eight units. The structures boasted many luxuries, including walls 10 inches thick inside and out, finished basements, 12 ft high ceilings, second-floor bathrooms, front porches (now gone), and dumbwaiters. The villas didn't sell and, when his bank failed in the financial panic of 1873, Cooke turned seven of the eight residences over to receivers, and he and his wife moved into 3007 Q St. Cooke died in 1881 at the age of 56. His wife continued to live at 3007 for 20 more years, making her living as a dressmaker. The differing styles of architecture lend a quirky yet picturesque look to the block.

> ### Washington Notes
> Bob Woodward, who with Carl Bernstein broke the Watergate story in the *Washington Post*, lives at 3027 Q with his wife, writer Elsa Walsh. Muckraking author Sinclair Lewis lived for a time at 3028 Q St.

Walk east a half-block to the corner of 30th and Q Sts and then north on 30th two blocks to **2920 R St N.W.** (c. 1780), home of Katherine Graham, publisher emeritus of the *Washington Post* and Pulitzer Prize winner. This is one of the oldest residential sites in Georgetown and was originally part of the Rock of Dunbarton grant. Thomas Beall built the house soon after he inherited the land in 1780. In 1815, the property went to Thomas's daughter Eleanor, wife of George Corbin Washington, great-nephew of George Washington. During the Civil War, Senator Jesse Bright of Indiana lived here. Ousted from the Senate for his Southern leanings, he departed for home and left the property untended. Colonel William "Wild Bill" Donovan, creator of the Office of Strategic Services (precursor of the Central Intelligence Agency) during World War II, purchased the property in 1929. In 1946, it was bought by Philip and Katherine Graham.

## Oak Hill Cemetery
Directly across from Graham's house on the north side of R St are the entrance gates to Oak Hill Cemetery (1849) at 3001 R St N.W. Open Mon–Fri 10–4. Closed weekends and holidays. Visitors are requested to check in at the Oak Hill Cemetery Gatehouse for a map of the cemetery grounds.

### History
During the Civil War, R St (then called Road St) was a favorite afternoon jaunt, especially after the new Georgetown Reservoir opened in 1860. A *Washington Star* newspaper article reported that "hundreds of visitors to Washington, D.C., ride over weekly to view it [the reservoir] and the picturesque cemetery as well, and the fine view of the Union Army's fortifications in Virginia so clearly discernible from the Heights." The picturesque Oak Hill Cemetery is on 15 acres of land that was previously owned by Richard Parrott and was part of his Parrott's Woods. The cemetery was founded by Washington banker (Riggs National Bank; see Walk 20: "Georgetown West") and philanthropist (Corcoran Gallery of Art; see Walk 8: "The Ellipse and 17th Street Sites") William Wilson Corcoran, who bought the land in 1848 from George Corbin Washington, grandnephew of George Washington, and endowed the nonprofit cemetery with a trust fund. It was chartered by Congress and named for the grove of huge oak trees that still stand among its

17,000 graves. Until it was a cemetery, this land was a fairgrounds and picnic area, with annual Fourth of July celebrations held among its trees. Currently, there are no spaces available in the cemetery, but a new renovation project is expected to create new interment spaces in the near future.

## Grounds

The cemetery extends along the western bank of Rock Creek, across four plateaus separated by terraced ravines. Standing at any point in the cemetery, the visitor is surrounded by clusters of monuments, columns, pedestals, angels, and obelisks engraved with the names of Georgetown's famous families. Because of the irregularity of the paths, visitors should use the map available at the Gatehouse to find various graves.

One of the most interesting burial sites is that of **Bishop William Pinkney** (1810–1883), whose life-size marble statue was erected in 1883 (sculptor unknown) as a tribute from his life-long friend, W. W. Corcoran. Pinkney was the fifth Protestant Episcopal bishop of Maryland and was known for his charitable works. The inscription at the base of the statue is typical of Victorian hyperbolic cemetery prose.

Also noteworthy is the monument (1882; Moffitt and Doyle) for **John Howard Payne** (1791–1852), a highly successful actor, playwright, and theater manager who eventually drifted into debt but was rescued through the efforts of his friend Daniel Webster, who secured for him a position in the U.S. Foreign Service. Payne died while serving as U.S. consul in Tunis in April 1852 and was buried in that city's Protestant cemetery. Payne would have stayed in relative obscurity in Tunis except that one of his plays contained a little ditty called "Home, Sweet Home!"—a particular favorite of Corcoran's. Corcoran had Payne's body exhumed and brought to Oak Hill, where it was reinterred in a formal ceremony attended by President Chester A. Arthur, General William T. Sherman, as well as cabinet members and justices of the Supreme Court. The inscription on the base of the 12 ft high marble monument reads: "Sure when thy spirit fled, / To realms beyond the azure dome, / With arms outstretched God's angels said, / Welcome to Heaven's Home, Sweet Home."

The **Van Ness Family Mausoleum** (c. 1825; George Hadfield, architect; sculptor unknown; DL), a sandstone-and-brick monument, was originally built for $30,000 and located in a small cemetery on H St in downtown Washington. The mausoleum was moved to its present location in 1872. John Peter Van Ness, a congressman from New York, married Marcia Burns in 1802 and became one of the wealthiest landowners in Washington. This structure, which contains the remains of John Peter and four other family members, was modeled after the ancient Temple of Vesta in Rome. William Corcoran is also buried at Oak Hill, as are Dean Acheson, secretary of state under President Harry Truman; the Reverend Stephen Balch, pastor of Georgetown Presbyterian Church; Alexander de Bodisco, ambassador from Russia; Uriah Forrest; Philip Graham, *Washington Post* publisher; Edward Linthicum, one-time owner of Dumbarton Oaks; Mrs. E.D.E.N. Southworth, romantic novelist; and Joseph C. Willard, owner of the Willard Hotel.

## Gatehouse

The three-story, red brick **Oak Hill Cemetery Gatehouse** (1850–53; George F. de la Roche) resembles a miniature Italian villa, with a pedimented tower, window hood molds, buttress caps, and decorative horizontal molding around the tower. The gatehouse bell, no longer in use, called the workmen to a grave when the funeral procession was approaching.

## Chapel

James Renwick's **Oak Hill Cemetery Chapel** (1850; DL), northeast of the main gate, is the only known example of Renwick's Gothic revival church design in Washington. This one-story, rectangular structure, measuring 23 by 41 ft and constructed of Potomac gneiss, is graced with four Gothic windows on the sides, separated by buttresses.

Exit the cemetery through its elaborate ironwork main gates onto R St, turn north and walk a half-block to **Montrose Park,** which is open until dark (restrooms and telephone available). This land was originally known as Parrott's Woods. Richard Parrott built his home here about 1806 and called the house Elderslie. Parrott also had his rope-making business on this site. In 1814, Parrott lost all his money and moved away. Elderslie sat deserted until William Boyce purchased the house in 1837 and renamed it Montrose. When Boyce was killed in a railroad accident in 1858, his widow moved to England and the house again sat deserted. In 1900, the road at the farthest west end of the property was officially designated Lover's Lane. In 1905, Sarah Louisa Rittenhouse (Miss Loulie to her friends), daughter of Charles Rittenhouse and former resident of Dumbarton House, decided at the age of 58 to find a play area for the neighborhood's children. She wanted the grounds of the old Montrose mansion. For five years she repeatedly petitioned Congress to appropriate funds for the park. Finally, in 1910, a bill was enacted. The property was purchased for $110,000, and the mansion was torn down. Miss Loulie was honored by the Georgetown Garden Club when it dedicated the astrolabe memorial (west of the entrance) to her for her perseverance in creating a park in Georgetown. Montrose Park is currently maintained by the U.S. Park Service.

Exit the park on R St and walk east one block to 29th St.

### Diversion:

Continue east on R St one block to 28th St, turn north on 28th St and walk a half-block to **Evermay** (1801; Nicholas King; DL) at 1628 28th St N.W. Evermay is not open to the public and the house is just barely visible from the street, but Evermay's history makes it an interesting diversion. Note the bronze plaque on the wall next to the entrance: "Samuel Davidson, a Scot of original character, purchased the site and built Evermay 1792–1794. . . ."

#### History

In 1801 Samuel Davidson hired Nicholas Hedges, a Georgetown carpenter, to build the house. Hedge received $897.40. The interior was not completed until 1818. Davidson, a bachelor, left his estate to his nephew with the condition that Grant assume the surname of Davidson, which he did. (This required a special act of Congress, approved and signed by President Madison.) Grant died in 1832, and upon the death of his widow in 1851, the property passed to her daughter, Eliza Davidson Dodge. In 1876 Evermay was the home of retired Union general Henry Hayes Lockwood, who fought at Gettysburg and whose son accompanied the Greely expedition in search of the North Pole. The McPherson family, who owned the property in the 1870s, made many changes, adding Victorian verandas and balconies. In 1923 Ambassador F. Lammot Belin and his wife bought the property and began restoring it to much of its original design, removing many of the Victorian additions. Evermay remains in the Belin family.

## Exterior

This is one of the largest surviving plots of open land in the area (3.72 acres). Evermay is a five-bay, two-and-a-half–story, Flemish-bond brick house with three dormer windows and a gabled slate roof with four interior end chimneys. The main house is connected by hyphens to wings on either side, which were later additions.

From the intersection of 29th and R Sts, turn south on 29th and walk a half-block to 1623 29th St N.W. and what was formerly the **Mackall Mansion** (c. 1717). The north wing is the only part remaining from the original house, which is thought to be among the oldest structures in Georgetown. It was probably built by the Beall family. The current house was built c. 1820 by Benjamin Mackall.

**Diversion:**
At the intersection of 29th and P Sts, turn west. Two doors from the corner is **2905 P St N.W.**, the former home of alleged Russian spy Alger Hiss.

Continue south on 29th to O St, then west a half-block to the **Mt. Zion Community House** (1810–11) at 2906 O St N.W., ☎ 337-6711, which is open by appointment. Thought to be the only remaining medieval English–style brick cottage in Washington, this property's first African American owner was a freed woman, Abigail Sides, who purchased it in 1849. Purchased by Mt. Zion United Methodist Church in 1920, the cottage housed the first black library in the District. Prior to the 1985 restoration, the house was in poor condition. In addition to being a meeting space, the cottage houses old photographs, manuscripts, church records, and artifacts from the early days of the African American community in Georgetown.

## *Mt. Zion United Methodist Church*

Walk a half-block east on O St to 29th St, then one block south on 29th to Mt. Zion United Methodist Church (founded 1816; current church building built 1884; V. E. Koerber; DL) at 1334 29th St N.W., ☎ 333-9435. Tours are available by reservation. Mt. Zion United Methodist Church has been an integral part of the Georgetown community for the past 180 years.

### History

The first black church in Washington, Mt. Zion had its genesis in a meeting in 1814 of about 125 dissatisfied black members of the Montgomery St Church (today known as the Dumbarton Ave United Methodist Church). Angered at the attitude of Montgomery St members toward their "coloured brethren," the dissidents purchased a lot on Mill St (now 27th St) near West St (now P St). The African American parishioners built a church they called the Meeting House and the Little Ark. Because of laws at the time, white ministers from the parent church served as pastors for many years. In 1864, Mt. Zion welcomed its first black pastor, the Reverend John H. Brice. In 1880, the Little Ark burned to the ground, after which the congregation met for a time in the Good Samaritan Hall, located at what is now the 1500 block of 26th St N.W. In 1875, the congregation purchased the present site from Alfred Pope, a former slave who became a successful black businessman. Construction of the church began, with much of the workmanship being done by black artisans, among them one of the pastors, the Reverend Alexander Dennis, and his associate, the Reverend Edgar Murphy. The present church was dedicated on July 8, 1884.

Since its inception the Mt. Zion congregation has served the religious, social, and educational needs of the black community in Georgetown and later the city of Washington. Mt. Zion's Sabbath School, established in 1823 when there were no educational facilities for black people in Washington, had a large enrollment of adults as well as children.

### Washington Notes

Mt. Zion, which served as a way station in the Underground Railroad, used a vault in its cemetery to hide runaway slaves. The archives and an in-depth history of the church are available at the Mt. Zion Community House at 2906 O St N.W.

Across the street from Mt. Zion Church, at 1331 29th St. N.W., is **Scheele's Market,** a tiny store (three aisles wide) that has served the neighborhood since 1895.

Continue south on 29th St one and a half blocks to N St, then east a half-block to **2806–2812 N St N.W.** These three houses (there is no 2810) are among the best examples of Federal architecture in Georgetown. The buildings, constructed between 1813 and 1817, feature Flemish-bond brickwork; semicircular, keystoned glassed transoms; and gabled roofs. Numbers 2806 and 2808 are essentially identical, except that they are mirror images. Number 2812 is larger and is referred to as the **Decatur House** because it is thought that Susan Wheeler Decatur, widow of American naval hero Stephen Decatur, lived here. Decatur was killed in a duel in 1820.

Continue on N St a half-block to the northwest corner of 28th and N and **Kesher Israel Congregation–Georgetown Synagogue** (congregation founded 1911, synagogue built 1931; architect unknown) at 2801 N St N.W., ☎ (recorded information about services) 333-4808. To make an appointment to see the inside of the synagogue, ☎ 333-2337. Kesher Israel has served the needs of the Orthodox Jewish population of Georgetown for more than 80 years. The first members of the congregation were merchants who had moved from Southwest Washington, bought stores along M St, and lived above their stores. The interior was designed according to Orthodox tradition; the men sat downstairs and the women sat in the upper balcony of the sanctuary.

### Diversion:

Continue north on 28th to P St, then west a half-block to 2803–2811 P St N.W. and the **Gunbarrel Fences** of Reuben Daw. Daw, born in Cornwall, England, in 1808, came to the U.S. with his family in 1817. By 1834, Daw had a prosperous gun and locksmith business on M (Bridge) St. For some years, he and his family lived in the Old Stone House (see Walk 20: "Georgetown West"), where his second daughter was born in 1835. He built the house at 2811 in 1843; 2803 and 2805 followed a few years later. When the Mexican-American War ended in 1848, Daw bought a large lot of gun barrels that had been put up for sale as surplus and used them to fashion the fences that span the three properties.

### Washington Notes

The house at 2805 P St was once occupied by former secretary of state Dean Acheson.

From Kesher Israel Synagogue at 28th and N Sts, walk west on N St two blocks to 30th St. N St is one of the most historic thoroughfares in Georgetown, and this block has many of its most historic homes. The **Laird-Dunlop House** (1799; attributed to William Lovering) at 3014 N St N.W. is currently home of *Washington Post* vice president at large Benjamin Bradlee and his wife, writer Sally Quinn. The central, original portion of the house was built by wealthy tobacco merchant John Laird, and inherited by his son-in-law, Judge James Dunlop, a chief justice of the Circuit Court and a first cousin of the Peter family of Tudor Place. James Dunlop married Laird's daughter Barbara. President Abraham Lincoln's eldest son, Robert Todd Lincoln (onetime secretary of war, former ambassador to England, and the only one of Lincoln's four sons to live to manhood) bought the house in 1915 and added the wing and the porch. Robert Lincoln lived here until his death in 1926.

The **Thomas Beall House** (1794; architect unknown) at 3017 N St. N.W. is typical of New England seacoast mansions of the Federal era. It was later bought by Major George Peter, who fought in the War of 1812.

### Washington Notes

Jacqueline Kennedy bought this house when she moved from the Averell Harrimans' house after her husband was assassinated. She moved to New York City in less than a year because of the large numbers of gawkers.

The **Beall Mansion** (possibly 1760s; architect unknown) at 3033 N St N.W. is one of the oldest brick houses in Georgetown. The central portion may have been built by George Beall in the 1760s or it may have been built by one of Beall's sons. Records show that Thomas Beall inherited the property in 1780 and in 1786 gave it to his brother George Beall, Jr.

The **Romulus Riggs House** at 3038 N St N.W. was built by Riggs, a Washington businessman, in 1816. He was the brother of Elisha Riggs and half-brother of George W. Riggs, founder (with W. W. Corcoran) of the Riggs National Bank.

### Washington Notes

U.S. statesman Averell Harriman and his wife, Pamela, the ambassador to France, owned the house when Jacqueline Kennedy lived here with her children soon after President Kennedy's assassination in 1963.

The **Wheatley Town Houses** (1854–59; Francis Wheatley) at 3041–3045 N St N.W. were built by Francis Wheatley, a wealthy lumber merchant from Charles

County, Maryland, who lived in 3045. These town houses are noted for their early use of sculptural stone and cast iron.

Walk east on N St a half-block to 30th St and then walk north a half-block to the **Colonial Apartments** (1820; restored 1953, architect unknown) at 1311 30th St. From 1826 to 1861, this was Miss Lydia English's Georgetown Female Seminary, where the daughters of some of Georgetown's finest were educated. Following the defeat of Union forces at the First Battle of Bull Run (called the Battle of Manassas by Confederate forces), the building was commandeered for use as an Army hospital. Miss English opened another school for a few years at 2812 N St (the Decatur House). After the war, that building was converted into apartments.

Continue north on 30th St one block to Dumbarton Ave, then west a half-block to **3018 Dumbarton Ave N.W.**

> ### Washington Notes
> At different times Felix Frankfurter (former justice of the Supreme Court), Henry Kissinger (secretary of state under Presidents Nixon and Ford), and Cyrus Vance (secretary of state under President Carter) lived here.

Note the fire station seal on the wall over the garage. In the early 1800s, each citizen was required to have one leather bucket for each story of his house and to subscribe to a particular fire station, which would be responsible for making sure his house didn't burn down. As proof of subscription, homeowners put their fire station's seal on their houses.

Continue west on Dumbarton a half-block to the semiattached town houses at **3035–3037 Dumbarton Ave N.W.**

> ### Washington Notes
> J. Carter Brown, director emeritus of the National Gallery of Art, resides at 3035 and the popular biographer Kitty Kelley lives at 3037.

Walk one block to **3107 Dumbarton Ave N.W.,** which has been home to John Foster Dulles (secretary of state under President Eisenhower), Bert Lance (advisor to President Carter), and Harold Ickes (advisor to President Clinton), but even more remarkably for Georgetown, this house has a double garage.

Walk a half-block east back to 31st St, then north a half-block on 31st to **Christ Church, Georgetown** (1885; Cassell and Laws) at 31st and O Sts N.W., ☎ 333-6677. Organized in 1817, the church's members were primarily from southern Maryland. As a result, many had problems living in Georgetown during the Civil War. But when President Lincoln was assassinated, the congregants passed a resolution stating that "[their] horror is all that the heart can feel and more than the tongue can utter," and they tolled the church bell for two hours on the day of Lincoln's funeral. The first church, built in 1818, was Georgian. Alterations made in 1867 changed the façade to match the Victorian style fashionable among churches then. The present church with its Gothic design dates from 1885.

### Diversion:
Continue west on O St a half-block to **3131 O St N.W.** and the former home of Arctic explorer Adolphus Greely, who also served as a major general in the U.S. Army and helped found the American Geographical Society.

On the southeast corner directly opposite Christ Church, Georgetown is **3044 O St N.W.**, the home of Laughlin Phillips, chairman of Phillips Gallery. Continue east on O St one block to 30th St, then north on 30th two blocks to the southeast corner of 30th and Q Sts and the **Francis Dodge House** (1850–53; Downing, Vaux) at 1537 30th St N.W. Francis Dodge, Jr., was forced to sell the house in 1863 because of financial difficulties. Henry Cooke bought the mansion in 1864. Cooke frequently hosted President Ulysses S. Grant here. The structure has now been divided into condominiums.

Walk west on Q St a half-block to the southeast corner of 31st and Q Sts to yet another **Dodge House** (original house on this site bought in 1810; architect unknown; current house, 1897, George Cooper) at 1531 31st St N.W. This was the site of the original Dodge farm and the home of Francis Dodge, Sr., patriarch of the family that controlled so many of Georgetown's commercial interests. When Francis died in 1851, he was one of the wealthiest men in Washington, worth more than $300,000. Six years later, after the financial panic of 1857, the Dodge brothers, except for Robert, lost their wharf properties and sold their vessels to Yankee shippers from New England. With the Dodge trade gone, the port of Georgetown fell into decline.

### Washington Notes
John F. Kennedy lived across the street at 1528 31st St when he first came to Washington as a congressman from Massachusetts's 11th District.

Continue west a half-block on Q St to **3112 Q St N.W.**, the former home of *Ship of Fools* author Katherine Anne Porter. Two houses west on Q St is the **Bowie Sevier Place** (1800–1805; Washington Bowie; 1890, architect unknown; 1957, Horace Peaslee) at 3124 Q St N.W., whose center original portion is often cited as one of the best examples of Georgian architecture in Georgetown. At one time the property stretched the entire block. The garden landscaping is reputed to have been laid out by Pierre L'Enfant. The house was built by Washington Bowie, a wealthy Georgetown shipowner and godson of George Washington, as well as a member of the same family as Colonel James Bowie, hero of the Alamo, and Colonel Rezin Bowie, probable inventor of the bowie knife. In the 1980s the property became the Episcopal Church Home for Women. Currently, there are plans to remove the two wings and renovate the original portion as a private residence.

## Tudor Place
1644 31st St N.W. ☎ 965-0400. Tours Tues–Fri at 10, 11:30, 1, and 2:30; Sat hourly from 10 to 4. Reservations suggested.

Walk east on Q St to 31st St, then north a half-block to the entrance of Tudor Place (east and west wings built c. 1795; architect unknown; center portion and hyphens completed 1816, William Thornton; DL). Among the grand houses of Georgetown, Tudor Place stands out for its graceful neoclassical design, dramatic south façade, and for its association with many of the most illustrious names from America's early history, including Washington, Lee, and Lafayette. But perhaps even more distinctive is the fact that this beautiful home remained intact and in the possession of the same family for 180 years, an extraordinary circumstance in a city where real estate speculation was rife. When touring with kids, request the booklet written for children about Tudor Place and its residents.

**Highlights:** The architecture, furnishings, and gardens.

### History

In 1797, Thomas Beall sold the parcel of land where Tudor Place now stands to Francis Lowndes, a tobacco exporter, who began construction of two wings of what was to be an imposing house. By 1802 Lowndes was gone, the two wings were completed, and Thomas and Martha Peter were living in the west wing, using the east wing as a stable. Martha "Patsy" Parke Custis was the granddaughter of Martha Parke Custis Washington and step-granddaughter of George Washington. Thomas was the son of Georgetown's first mayor, Robert Peter. After George Washington's death in 1799, Patsy was left a generous legacy; she and Peter purchased Tudor Place in 1805 and selected William Thornton as their architect. Thornton was also the architect of the U.S. Capitol and head of the Patent Office. When Tudor Place was completed in 1815, it became the social and political center of the new Federal City.

> ### Washington Notes
> When Lafayette visited in 1824, he gave Patsy the engraving of himself that hangs in the drawing room.

Patsy's brother, George Washington Parke Custis, had married Mary Fitzhugh and used his legacy from George Washington (1,200 acres on the Virginia heights across the Potomac River from Georgetown) to build a mansion he called Arlington. His daughter Mary Anna Custis married Robert E. Lee in 1831. When General Lee assumed command of the Confederate forces at the beginning the Civil War, Mary Anna was forced to flee Arlington. She asked her cousin Britannia Peter Kennon to save what treasures she could from the house before the Union Army took possession, and Britannia (middle name Wellington) was able to bring back two wagonloads to Tudor Place. Britannia was one of three daughters of Patsy and Thomas Peter, the other two being Columbia Washington and America Pinckney. When Britannia's husband, Commodore Beverley Kennon, was killed in an explosion during a pleasure cruise on the Potomac in 1844, she and her daughter returned to Tudor Place, where Britannia would reign as mistress until her death at the age of 96 in 1911.

It was Britannia's indomitable spirit that saved Tudor Place during the Civil War. The Peter family was known to be sympathetic to the Southern cause (they had slaves until 1862). Tudor Place was slated to be turned into a Union soldier's hospital. To prevent this, Britannia offered Tudor Place as a home for Union officers for the duration of the war, a situation that must have been difficult to endure, especially since two of the Peter cousins were hung as Confederate spies in 1863 in Tennessee. (A framed photograph of the hanging bodies is in one of the bedrooms, along with the men's spurs on the mantel.)

In 1867, Britannia's daughter, Martha "Markie" Kennon, married her cousin Armistead Peter, and after Britannia's death in 1911, Armistead Peter, Jr., purchased Tudor Place from his siblings. In 1960, Armistead Peter III inherited Tudor Place, and in 1966 he created the Tudor Place Foundation to ensure the preservation of the house and grounds. When he died in 1983, the foundation assumed control of the estate, and in 1988 Tudor Place opened to the public.

## Exterior

The north façade is rather plain. The entrance doorway has a semicircular glassed transom. By contrast, the south façade is dominated by a two-story circular, domed temple porch supported by four Doric columns. The connecting hyphens on the south façade are three bays wide.

## Interior

Visitors see the house on a guided tour. All of the floors are original to the house, and all of the doors, many of which slide into the door frames, are of curly (or tiger) maple. Tudor Place appears as the home of a patrician family.

The **entrance hall** extends through the house to the south façade with its floor-to-ceiling bay windows, which can be lifted to serve also as doors. In the hall are Federal period gilt-framed mirrors, a piano that belonged to Thomas Peter, and an elaborate bronze gasolier (a chandelier using gas instead of candles). To the east of the entrance hall is the **drawing room,** where General Lafayette was entertained.

To the west of the hall in the **parlor** is a reproduction of George Washington's love letter to Martha from Philadelphia, the Washingtons' fireplace andirons and China from Mount Vernon, as well as a mahogany desk that belonged to Francis Scott Key. West of the parlor is the **dining room.** The mahogany chairs around the table belonged to George Washington. In the **upstairs hall,** on a chest owned by George Washington, is a waxwork (wax figures enclosed in glass depicting classical themes) given to George Washington by a New York tavern owner. **Britannia's bedroom** on the southeast is as it was when she died in 1911 and includes a rosewood wardrobe (c. 1800).

> ### Washington Notes
> On the windowsill of the southwest bedroom is a white petticoat that Britannia and her sisters used to wave to signal their cousin Mary Anna Custis at Arlington House across the Potomac.

Exit Tudor House on 31st St. Walk north to **1669 31st St N.W.,** a red brick structure, the former home of Francis Biddle, attorney general under Franklin Roosevelt. A half-block north is **1688 31st St N.W.,** the home of Senator Robert Taft in the 1940s and '50s. Continue north a half-block to R St. Just before the intersection of 31st and R Sts, note the pink Carpenter Gothic house at **1696 31st St N.W.** and its plaque acknowledging that the house has been "recorded by the Historic American Buildings Survey of the U.S. Department of the Interior for its archives at the Library of Congress," a designation enjoyed by many of Georgetown's architecturally distinctive houses.

## Dumbarton Oaks Museum and Gardens

Garden entrance at 31st and R Sts N.W. ☎ 339-6410. Web: www.doaks.org. Garden open daily April–Oct 2–6; Nov–March 2–5. Admission: April–Oct $4, children and seniors $3; Nov–March free. For questions about accessibility, ☎ 339-6410.

Museum entrance at 1703 32nd St N.W. Museum open Tues–Sun 2–5. Admission: free, but donations accepted. Closed on national holidays.

Directly north of the intersection across R St are the gates leading to the entrance to Dumbarton Oaks Museum and Gardens (1800; architect unknown; 1920s garden landscaping, Beatrix Farrand; 1963 pre-Columbian collection wing, Philip Johnson; 1963 garden library wing, Frederick Rhinelander King; DL).

**Highlights:** In addition to functioning as Harvard University's center for Byzantine studies, Dumbarton Oaks provides important resources on the subjects of pre-Columbian studies and the history of landscape architecture. The museum has a noted pre-Columbian and Byzantine collection.

### History

The land Dumbarton Oaks sits on was part of Ninian Beall's original 1703 patent. In 1800 Beall's grandson sold 20 acres to William Hammond Dorsey, who built the house. Dorsey's debts forced him to sell the house in 1805 to Robert Beverley. In 1822 Beverley gave the estate to his son, who was married to a daughter of Georgetown's Peter family. The following year the son sold the estate to the Calhoun family, and it became the home of Vice President John C. Calhoun. In 1828 the house was sold to Brooke Mackall and in 1846 to Edward Linthicum, a prosperous Georgetown merchant. Throughout this buying and selling, the house had a succession of architectural adjustments, including the additions of a round tower, an octagonal cupola, and a French Second Empire–style mansard roof.

In 1920 the estate was bought by career diplomat Robert Woods Bliss and his wife, Mildred Barnes Bliss, heiress to the Fletcher's Castoria fortune. The Blisses were stepbrother and stepsister. They restored the mansion to its original style, renamed it Dumbarton Oaks, added a music room, and in 1940 added a separate wing to house their Byzantine collection. In 1940 the Blisses gave to Harvard University—Robert Bliss's alma mater—Dumbarton Oaks and their Byzantine collection, followed by their pre-Columbian collection and books on garden history and landscaping design. In 1963 a wing was added to house the pre-Columbian collection and another wing to house the garden library.

### *Washington Notes*

In 1944 the United Nations Conference, held in the Music Room, laid the foundations for the international organization's creation following World War II.

## Exterior

The main house is Federal style, with a neo-Georgian wing on the west built to house the landscape and garden library. The wing built to house the pre-Columbian collection is a modern interpretation of a Byzantine church plan and has eight circles arranged in a square configuration around a central circle. Each of the sections around the perimeter is topped by a low dome.

## Grounds and Gardens

The gardens were laid out by Beatrix Farrand with input from Mildred Bliss. The 16-acre property includes ten acres of formal gardens and more than a dozen different garden areas, including a series of terraces on the eastern slope of the hill. Highlights of the garden include the **Orangery,** attached to the main house, the walls of which are covered by a spreading fig; the **Rose Garden,** which contains nearly 1,000 varieties of roses; the **Urn Terrace,** with its pebble mosaics and English ivy; the **Fountain Terrace,** which features a huge English beech, two lead fountains, and a number of seasonal flowers; a miniature Roman-style **amphitheater** overlooking a small pool; the tree-shaded **Ellipse,** with its central Provençal fountain; and the Pebble Garden.

> ### Washington Notes
> Dumbarton Oaks's long musical tradition has included performances in the Music Room by noted artists. Polish pianist and statesman Jan Paderewski often played in the room, and his autograph appears on the grand piano. Igor Stravinsky, a friend of the Blisses, premiered some works here and composed his noted Dumbarton Oaks Concerto for the Blisses' 30th anniversary.

## The Collections

The **Garden Library** contains thousands of books on flowers and local birds, many rare works of the 15C and 16C, architectural books of the 18C, and early botanical works on the medicinal uses of plants. The Garden Library is open only by appointment to qualified researchers.

The noted **Byzantine Collection,** begun by the Blisses, has more than doubled in size since 1940. The collection contains mainly small, luxurious objects made of silver, gold, bronze, cloisonné enamel, and ivory, as well as several illuminated manuscripts. Large pieces, such as pavement mosaics from Antioch and sculptures from the late-Roman and early- and middle-Byzantine periods, are also included. Although the primary focus is on the Byzantine period (4C–15C), the museum has some Western medieval and Ptolemaic Egyptian art.

In the **Courtyard** are works created either chronologically earlier than or located on the edge of the Byzantine Empire. The central open area within the square colonnade features mosaics from Antioch, Roman sculpture, Ptolemaic Egyptian sculpture, a lead sarcophagus from Syria, and a bronze South Arabian Horse (late 2C–3C). The aisle areas display Roman glass, bronzework, sculpture, and portraiture, as well as examples of ancient Near Eastern and Greek art.

The **Textile Gallery** displays rotating selections of Byzantine and Islamic fabrics, such as fragments of curtains and wall hangings in wool, linen, and silk. Small exhibitions from the extensive collection of Byzantine coins (about 12,000 total) are occasionally on view.

The **Byzantine Gallery** displays artifacts from the Byzantine, or Eastern Roman, Empire (330–1453) period—jewelry, ivorywork, mosaics, ecclesiastical bronzes, icons, manuscripts, a sarcophagus, and pottery. The highlight of the gallery is the **Sion Silver Treasure,** the essential liturgical vessels used to celebrate the Eucharist, known in the Orthodox Church as the Divine Liturgy. The holy vessels include three ornately beautiful patens, each decorated with a gilded chrismon, the monogram of Christ (the first two letters of his name in Greek: chi and rho). Patens such as these were used to hold a whole loaf of leavened Communion bread and are still a tradition in many Orthodox Christian communities.

The **Music Room** features a 16C stone chimney piece from the Château de Theoban in southwest France, an 18C oak parquet floor, and a ceiling copied from a painted wooden ceiling in the Château de Cheverny, a 16C castle in the

Loire Valley, France. El Greco's *The Visitation* (1610) is on display here, along with the 16C statue *Virgin and Child* by Tilmann Riemenschneider.

**The pre-Columbian Collection.** The Blisses' interest in pre-Columbian art began in Paris in 1912 when they saw their first pieces. Two years later they acquired a **jadeite figure** of a standing man from the Olmec culture of Mexico that is still one of the finest pieces in the collection (Room II). During the succeeding years, the Blisses collected objects made in Mexico, Guatemala, Costa Rica, Panama, Colombia, and Peru before the Spanish conquest. **Room VIII** displays artifacts from the Aztec culture, the last dominant indigenous Mexican power before Cortez's Spanish forces invaded their land in 1519. Small carvings of Aztec gods, such as Tlaxolteotl, the goddess of filth who absorbed the sins of humanity, as well as gold necklaces, earrings, and lip plugs done by the lost-wax process are displayed.

**Room I** holds treasures from Teotihuacan, Mexico's first great city, whose golden age lasted from A.D. 300–600. Depictions of the Rain God and Feathered Serpent dominate this collection. Frescoes and stone masks are also on display. **Room II** displays the works of the Olmec, Mexico's first known civilization (1200–300 B.C.). Finely carved jade figures, ceremonial axes, and plaques offer testimony to the Olmec's level of sophistication. The symbol of the werejaguar (combining the features of a jaguar and a human infant) dominates Olmec art and is used in many of the pieces. Mayan works fill **Rooms III** and **IV.** Mayan civilization (A.D. 300–900) spread from eastern Mexico to northern Central America. The Dumbarton collection includes bas-reliefs, polychrome pottery, and carved works of jade and shell. The bas-reliefs recorded the actions of different rulers of city-states, displaying the Mayans' literate and historic sensibilities.

**Room V** displays products of central Veracruz's lowlands during their golden age (A.D. 300–900), specifically yokes, *palmas,* and *hachas.* The stone yokes are thought to be interpretations of the protective belts worn by players during ceremonial ball games. *Haches,* thin stone ax heads, and *palmas,* or palms, adorn the yoke in front of the player's waist. The games were extremely serious: losing players were usually put to death.

The gold of Costa Rica, Panama, and Columbia dominate **Room VI.** Gold ornaments and jewelry reflected status and often served as rewards in the early cultures of these countries. Also on display are repoussé gold ornaments, as well as cups representing gods and mythical creatures created by the Chavin, Peru's earliest great culture (900–200 B.C.). **Room VII** displays the funerary pottery of Peru's Moche (A.D. 1–660) and Nazca (400 B.C.–A.D. 500) civilizations. The Huari, who came to dominate Peru (A.D. 540–1000), are represented here by ceramics, shell mosaics, featherwork, and pile cloth hats. Small pieces of bronze, silver, and gold, as well as tapestry shirts represent the Inca, powerful militaristic rulers of western South America.

The wrought-iron gates at the estate's entrance on R St are topped with gilded finials representing a sheaf of wheat, and carved on the wall plaque at the 32nd St entrance is "Quod severis metes" ("As ye sow, so shall ye reap"). Each visitor to Dumbarton Oaks, and each scholar who researches in its libraries, reaps the benefits of the Blisses' collection.

Exit the museum on 32nd St.

**Diversion:**

Walk north on 32nd St a half-block to S St, then west a half-block to **3240 S St N.W.** This was the residence of Elizabeth Taylor and Senator John Warner when they were married.

From the Dumbarton Oaks Museum exit, walk south on 32nd St to the intersection of 32nd and R Sts. The yellow home on the southwest corner, **3210 R St N.W.,** was formerly the home of Supreme Court justice Abe Fortas.

Continue west a half-block on R St to the **Halleck House** (1854; architect unknown) at 3238 R St N.W. Built in 1854 by an Alabama family, the house was rented for the duration of the Civil War (the family having returned to Alabama) by the Union's chief of staff, Lieutenant General Henry Halleck. The neighbors disapproved when a detail of enlisted men were quartered in the rear barracks. Reveille and taps were played every morning and evening, and the troops marched up and down Road (R) St. After the war, the house served as a summer home for Ulysses S. Grant.

Continue west on R St a half-block to the **Georgetown Regional Public Library** (1935) at R St and Wisconsin Ave N.W., 3260 R St N.W., ☎ 282-0220, located on the site of the dismantled Georgetown Reservoir on what was originally known as Lee's Hill. In 1860 the Washington Aqueduct pumped 10,000 gallons of water per hour into the Georgetown Reservoir. Montgomery Meigs designed the aqueduct and supervised its construction. The million-gallon capacity reservoir (100 ft in elevation) was only used from 1859 to 1897, when it was replaced by a larger reservoir at Fort Reno.

Walk around the back of the library to the parking lot. On the east side of the parking lot is an open gate leading to a pathway and steps down to Reservoir Rd and Wisconsin Ave. From the top of the steps, look across to Rosalyn, Virginia, to the north and the spire of Georgetown University's Healy Building to the west.

Take the steps down to the intersection of Reservoir Rd and Wisconsin Ave. Turn east on Reservoir Rd and walk one block to 32nd St. Turn south on 32nd St and walk two blocks to 32nd and P Sts. At one time 32nd St was a main route and went all the way through to M (Bridge) St. Along these two blocks of 32nd are some of Georgetown's most charming Federal structures.

At P St, turn east and walk a half-block to **Georgetown Presbyterian Church** (1821; William Archer; 1873, architect unknown; 1956 restoration, Lorenzo Winslow) at 3115 P St N.W., ☎ 338-1644. The church was founded in 1780 to meet the needs of Georgetown's large Scottish population. Founder and church pastor for 52 years, Dr. Stephen Bloomer Balch also served as a Revolutionary War officer and an educator. The first church, which was designed by William Archer, stood on the corner of Bridge and Washington Sts (M and 30th Sts) and was informally called the Bridge St Church. In 1873, the church was moved to West St (now P St), rebuilt in a Victorian style, and named the West St Church. In 1895, when West St became P St, the church became the Georgetown Presbyterian Church. In 1956 the building was restored to the original colonial style.

Continue east on P St a half-block to 31st St. (This is the next intersection; there is no street sign.) Turn south on 31st St and walk three and a half blocks to the **Georgetown Custom House,** now the **Georgetown Post Office** (1856–57;

Ammi B. Young; DL) at 1221 31st St N.W., ☎ 523-2405, which is open Mon–Fri 8–5:30 and Sat 8:30–2. One of several standardized types of customhouses developed by Young, supervising architect of the Treasury from 1852 to 1862, this Renaissance revival–Italian palace structure was the second customhouse located in Georgetown. Georgetown was established as a port of entry to the U.S. by an act of Congress in 1779.

### Washington Notes

By 1856, when the question of where to build a permanent customhouse for Washington was referred to the Senate Committee on Commerce, the committee reported, "There is nothing that can be called commerce in Washington, and there is something of it in Georgetown."

Congress appropriated $65,000, and the customhouse was completed in 1858. The first floor was used as a post office. (Georgetown had had a post office since 1776 but no permanent building to house it.) On the second floor were the customhouse officials as well as the Corporation of Georgetown, the mayor's office, and the council members and aldermen. In 1913, President Taft ordered a reorganization of custom districts, and the port of Washington became part of a district that included Maryland, Washington, and Alexandria, Virginia. In 1967, the customhouse moved out of its second-floor space.

If you wish to continue with the Georgetown West walk, proceed a half-block south to 31st and M Sts, then one block east to 30th and M Sts.

# 20 · Georgetown West

Metro/Bus: See Walk 19: "Georgetown East."

Whereas a walk through east Georgetown is in large measure a walk through the personal lives of the town's earliest and often wealthiest citizens, a walk through west Georgetown takes the visitor through more of the commercial history of the town and the forces that shaped its early character.

Begin at the intersection of 30th and M Sts, on the northwest corner. This is where Alexander Beall, town clerk, began his survey of the 60 acres of the town of George in 1751. In the 1790s, this corner was the site of the home of Thomas Sim Lee, friend of George Washington, twice governor of Maryland, and delegate to the Continental Congress in 1783–84. The southeast corner of 30th and M Sts is the former site of the **Union Tavern** (and hotel), which was built by John Suter in 1796. The tavern was destroyed by a fire but rebuilt in 1836 and was later remodeled into stores. In 1936 all except the west wing was demolished.

### Washington Notes

On Feb 8, 1798, George Washington recorded in his diary, "Dined at the Union Tavern," and in 1799 an elaborate birthday ball was held for Washington in the tavern's upstairs ballroom. This is believed to have been the last public function attended by Washington, who died that same year.

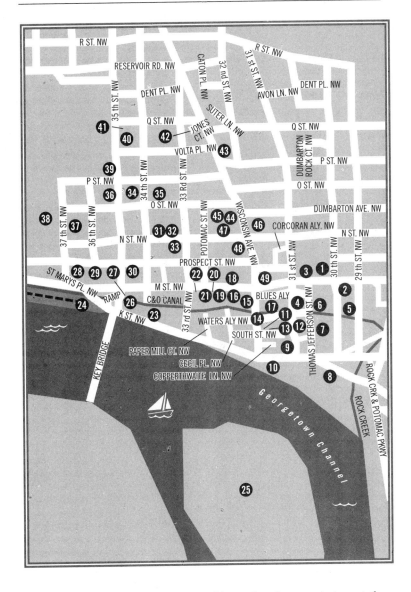

In 1800 President John Adams lodged here when he came to inspect the progress of the new Federal City being built to the east of Georgetown. Other guests included Napoleon's minister Talleyrand, inventor Robert Fulton, author Washington Irving, and others who, in those early days of the capital, preferred the comforts of Georgetown to roughing it in Washington City's boardinghouses. Reports of the tavern in contemporary accounts indicate it was the size of a large

1 30th & M, NW corner
2 30th & M, SE corner
3 Old Stone House
4 Masonic Lodge
5 C&O Canal/Visitor's Center
6 Jefferson St Bridge
7 Duvall Foundry Building
8 Washington Harbour
9 Suter's Tavern site
10 site of Bayou Club
11 Georgetown Incinerator
12 site of Hollerith Tabulating Machine Co.
13 Grace Episcopal Church
14 Wisconsin Ave Bridge
15 site of Vigilant Firehouse
16 Georgetown park
17 Blue's Alley
18 site of Dr. Thornton's house
19 Clyde's
20 Georgetown Policing Center
21 Georgetown Market House
22 Forrest-Marbury House
23 Francis Scott Key Park
24 Key Bridge-Canoe House
25 Theodore Roosevelt Island

26 Old Transit Building
27 75 Steps
28 site of Southworth house
29 Prospect House
30 Halcyon House
31 Cox's Row
32 JFK house
33 Dr. Balch's house
34 3400 O St
35 Bodisco House
36 Holy Trinity Church
37 GU's Village B
38 Georgetown University
39 Visitation Preparatory School
40 Volta Bureau
41 Longden House
42 Georgetown Lutheran Church
43 Neam's Market
44 site of Doc's Pharmacy
45 St. John's Episcopal Church
46 Au Pied de Cochon
47 Smith's Row
48 site of Stohlman's Bakery
49 Riggs Bank

hotel, extending a half-block on M (Bridge) St and one entire block south toward the river.

> ### *Washington Notes*
> Napoleon's younger brother, Jerome Bonaparte, was a guest at Union Tavern in 1803, when he married a famous Baltimore beauty, Elizabeth Patterson. Miss Patterson was famous not only for her beauty but also for her habit of wearing as few clothes as possible. From a description of the time: "She has made a great noise here, and mobs of boys have crowded around her splendid equipage to see what I hope will not often be seen in this country, an almost naked woman. . . . Her dress was the thinnest sarcenet . . . there was scarcely any waist to it and no sleeves; her back, part of her waist and her arms were uncovered and the rest of her form visible."
> Near the present-day site of Grace Church Episcopal (1041 Wisconsin Ave N.W.) was Suter's Tavern, also called Fountain Inn. Built in the late 1700s by Robert Peter, Georgetown's first mayor, the inn was frequented by the more wealthy of the town. About a block to the south of Suter's Tavern was Sailor's Tavern, suitable for the waterfront crowd. About a block to the north of Suter's was City Tavern, which catered to commercial travelers, and north of City Tavern was Montgomery Tavern, which hosted farmers who came to sell their produce on market day.

## *Old Stone House*

Continue west a half-block on M St to the Old Stone House (1766; Christopher Layman; DL) at 3051 M St N.W. ☎ 426-6851. Open Wed–Sun 10–4. Closed holidays. Admission: free. The only surviving pre–Revolutionary War building in Washington, this simple stone structure stands on Lot no. 3 of the 80 lots surveyed in 1751.

**Highlights:** 18C architecture and gardens.

### History

Christopher Layman, a cabinetmaker, began construction of the house in 1764. Layman was from Pennsylvania, which probably explains why the structure is similar to those constructed by German settlers in eastern Pennsylvania. In 1766 his widow, Rachel, completed the front portion of the structure. In 1767 Cassandra Chew, the new owner, added the rear wing. The paneling and mantel in the dining room were brought from the Chew family's former home on what is now 29th St N.W. Chew and her two daughters lived in the house until 1808, when it became the home of the eldest daughter, Mary, and her husband, Richard Smith. Reuben Daw, a Georgetown landowner, gunsmith, and locksmith, lived here for a time, as did a variety of other artisans during the 1800s, when the building served as a combination home and shop. A used-car dealership was on the site when the National Park Service acquired the property in 1950.

## Interior

Five rooms are open to the public. A National Park Service attendant is available to answer questions. The floors, the fieldstone walls, and the paneling are original. The ground-floor entry leads directly into the kitchen, which has a large working fireplace and reproductions of utensils used during the Federal period. Proceed south to the front of the house facing Wisconsin Ave and the shop area. An iron stove and reproductions of carpenter's tools are displayed. Walk back to the kitchen and up the narrow stairs to the second-floor dining room on the east side of the house. The stoneware and earthenware were found by archaeologists excavating the ground floor and date from the period. The 18C mantel is by Robert Adam. The two bedrooms on the west side of the house are furnished simply with quilt-covered beds. Behind the house is a garden frequented by Georgetown picnickers and tourists alike. The trees and flowers are faithful to the late 1700s.

Walk west to the traffic light at the intersection of 31st and M Sts, cross the street and walk east one block to Thomas Jefferson St (the Old Stone House faces Thomas Jefferson St, but jaywalking in M St traffic is very dangerous), then south one block to 1058 Thomas Jefferson St, at the intersection of Thomas Jefferson St and the C&O Canal towpath. From 1810 to 1840, this was the **Masonic Lodge** of Georgetown. In 1830, the first floor was used to sell "Belfast Liquors and Beer," even though the building was used by the Masons for their lodge until 1840. This is thought to be the oldest former Masonic lodge still standing in Washington. Currently, the building serves as the offices of a publishing firm.

## C&O Canal

C&O Canal Visitor's Center at 1057 Thomas Jefferson St N.W. ☎ 653-5190. Web: www.nps.gov. Open Wed–Sun 9–4:30. Admission: free. Restrooms. Gift shop. Rides on mule-drawn barges through the locks of the canal Wed–Fri 11 and 2:30; Sat–Sun 11, 1, 2:30, and 4. Fee charged for barge rides.

Walk east one block along the towpath to the **C&O Canal Visitor's Center.**

Staffed by the National Park Service, the center has exhibits about the C&O Canal (DL) and an interesting selection of reproduction period toys, including marbles and wooden harmonicas, as well as children's books, such as *America's Earliest Canals*, about the canal era. The Chesapeake and Ohio Canal project was initiated to provide a commercial waterway for the exchange of goods between the city of Washington and western Pennsylvania, via the Potomac and Ohio Rivers (see "Georgetown: History" in Walk 19: "Georgetown East"). When construction stopped in 1850, the canal only reached as far as Cumberland, Maryland. The towpath is a favorite hiking and biking trail. Mile-markers lead the way out of Georgetown, past the impressive Great Falls of the Potomac, through the scenic valleys of the Appalachians, and into the mountainous areas of western Maryland.

**Highlights:** The mule-drawn barge rides April through Oct and the pleasant walks and picnic spots.

### History

Until it closed in 1924, the C&O Canal was not only a commercial link for Georgetown but also a supply lifeline for the communities along its route. The canal opened as sections were completed: Georgetown to Seneca, Maryland, in 1831; to Harpers Ferry, West Virginia, in 1833; near Hancock, Maryland, in 1839; and ending at Cumberland, Maryland, in 1850. Although laborers began digging the canal with picks and shovels in 1828 the same day as tracks for the Baltimore and Ohio Railroad were begun, the railroad reached Cumberland first. Eventually, rail travel, which wasn't as handicapped by dry spells, floods, and winter freezes as the canal, made the canal transport of goods impractical. After flood damage, the canal closed in 1924.

In 1850, the existing canal averaged 40–60 ft wide by 6 ft deep and included stone aqueducts and a remarkable 3,118 ft long brick-lined tunnel. Water levels were adjusted by 74 lift locks for a 605 ft difference in elevation between the western terminus in the mountains and Georgetown in the east.

Although the citizens of Georgetown appreciated the importance of the canal to the city's economy, some citizens complained of the rowdy behavior of some of the bargemen. Not all barge operators were rowdy, however. Families were a large part of the canal operation. Sons and daughters worked on the barges along with their fathers. Wives sometimes helped steer the boats and children drove the mules, walking or riding for long hours in all kinds of weather. Boats traveled for an average of 18 hours a day, 7 days a week. One captain attested to the value of family workers, saying, "The women and the children are as good as the men. If it weren't for the children, the canal wouldn't run a day."

During the Civil War, Union soldiers camped in the area and bathed in the canal, further annoying Georgetown's genteel citizens. A *Washington Star* writer complained, "What aggravates the matter is that the bathers range themselves along the towpath in the costume of the Greek slave, minus the chain and in attitudes anything but peaceful and becoming."

### Washington Notes

The survival of the canal is largely due to the efforts of the late Supreme Court justice William O. Douglas. In the early 1950s, many wanted to turn the canal into a parkway. In March 1954, Douglas, a conservationist, led a hike of government officials along the towpath to Great Falls, Virginia, convincing them to refurbish the canal, which had fallen into disrepair.

**Diversion:**
For those interested in exploring the canal or the Potomac River, **Thompson's Boat Center,** 2900 Virginia Ave N.W., ☎ 333-4861, at the intersection of Rock Creek Prkwy and Virginia Ave, rents boats. **Fletcher's Boat House** at 4940 Canal Rd N.W., ☎ 244-0461, rents bicycles and canoes from March to mid-Nov, weather permitting. Fletcher's also sells bait, tackle, and fishing licenses; bass, bluegill, perch, and catfish can be caught. There are grills and tables nearby. To get to Fletcher's Boat House, walk two miles west of Key Bridge on the canal path to the old stone building that is the boathouse.

Return west along the canal towpath to Thomas Jefferson St. (Many of the houses built along the towpath were built on speculation in the 1870s for Georgetown's artisans and laborers and are now used as offices.) Turning south, cross the canal on the **Jefferson St Bridge.** The bridge's original stone construction was completed in 1830, then replaced with a raised iron span in 1867. Portions of the original supports remain.

Continue south on Thomas Jefferson St to the **Duvall Foundry Building** (1973–76; ELS Design Group, Arthur Cotton Moore/Associates; landscape architecture, Sasaki Associates; Vlastimil Koubek, architect) at 1055 Thomas Jefferson St N.W. The Foundry was a sand-and-gravel plant that at one time had also served as a veterinary hospital for canal mules. The Foundry has a mall of shops, movie theaters, and restaurants on the first two levels and several floors of offices.

Continue south on Thomas Jefferson St one block to K St and the waterfront. Directly south on K St is **Washington Harbour** (1987; Arthur Cotton Moore/Associates; J. Seward Johnson, Jr., sculptor) at 3000 K St N.W., ☎ 944-4242. Hourly riverboat tours of the Potomac leave from Washington Harbour throughout the year, ☎ (301) 460-7447. In the early 1900s, this was the site of cement and dredging operations. In the 1950s, the Georgetown waterfront was still an active, unattractive industrial center. The commuter bypass, the Whitehurst Freeway, cut off a large part of the waterfront's view of Theodore Roosevelt Island. In the 1970s a congressional task force was set up to explore the possibilities of a waterfront park that would also include office and residential space.

Washington Harbour's tan brick-and-limestone structure contrasts with the Federal style so predominant in Georgetown. Four structures, two on either side of Thomas Jefferson St, are accented by towers, domes, and curved shapes. The crescent plaza has a fountain. Placed throughout the complex are the realistically human bronze figures by sculptor J. Seward Johnson, Jr. A wooden boardwalk runs along the river's edge, providing a walkway for pedestrians, a path for bikers, and a pier for boats whose owners come to Washington Harbour to dine at the waterfront restaurants.

### *Washington Notes*
President and Mrs. Clinton occasionally have had Sunday brunch at the Sequoia restaurant at 3000 K St N.W.

From Washington Harbour, walk west one block along the river to 31st and K Sts, the supposed site of **Suter's Tavern,** built by Georgetown mayor Robert Peter and run by John Suter for the well-to-do of the town. There are also various other locations along the waterfront that are thought to have been the site of this historic tavern.

> ### Washington Notes
> It was in Suter's Tavern on March 30, 1791, that local landowners met with George Washington for the second time (the first meeting was a dinner hosted by Uriah Forrest the evening before). The landowners agreed to sell their land for $66.67 per acre and to retain half the building lots marked off from their former lands.

Stand at the corner of 31st and K Sts. The buildings to the west toward Key Bridge are renovated warehouses. The last three at the end of the row once belonged to the Dodge family. A Washington landmark, the Bayou Club, known for its live blues, rock, and other types of music, was located at 3135 K St N.W. The Bayou opened in 1953 and closed on Dec 31, 1998. The entire 3100 block of K St has been sold to Milennium Partners and Eastbanc, Inc., who are in the process of building a 93-room Ritz-Carlton hotel, a 3,000-seat Loews Theaters multiplex, 10,000 square ft of retail space, and 30 luxury residences.

From 31st and K Sts, walk north on 31st St one block to South St, then one block west to the Georgetown Incinerator, another one of the supposed sites of Suter's Tavern. This four-story industrial structure was built in 1932 and operated until 1971. It sits on an acre of land that is part of the development project mentioned above. Plans call for the 150 ft tall chimney to become a wine-and-cigar bar.

### Diversion:

From 31st and K Sts, walk north on 31st one block to 1054 31st St N.W. From 1892 to 1911, this was the site of **Herman Hollerith's Tabulating Machine Company.**

> ### Washington Notes
> Hollerith was an engineer working for the Census Bureau in 1884 when, on a train trip to the West, he noticed the system conductors used to identify passengers—they punched physical characteristics, such as dark hair or light eyes, onto passengers' tickets (to thwart robbers and stowaways). Hollerith decided the tabulation of the national census could be sped up immeasurably by using tabulated cards punched with identifying information about each person. Hollerith developed a prototype battery-operated tabulating machine to do the job. Further adjustments and the invention of a keyboard punch machine enabled him to win the competition for counting the 1890 census, in which the 62.5 million nationwide count was completed in only six weeks, many months faster than a lower number had been tabulated by hand in 1880. More contracts followed. In 1911 Hollerith sold his company, which became the International Business Machines Corporation (IBM) in 1924.

Directly southwest of the Georgetown Incinerator on South St is **Grace Episcopal Church** (1866–67; rectory, 1895; parish hall, 1898; architects unknown; DL) at 1041 Wisconsin Ave N.W., ☎ 337-7100. Take the stone steps and enter the grounds from the back of the churchyard. This community-oriented, activist church, presently also home to the Georgetown Ministry Center, a facility to aid the homeless, and yet another proposed site of the elusive Suter's Tavern, began as a mission chapel in 1855 for the workers of the C&O Canal. The present church was built with the help of a $25,000 loan from Henry Cooke, Washington financier and builder of Cooke's Row. The rectangular, gable-roofed church is interesting architecturally not only because of its Gothic revival style but because of its resemblance to James Renwick's 1850 Oak Hill Cemetery Chapel. In the southwest corner of the churchyard is a 12 ft high granite cross inscribed "In memory of our boys who made the supreme sacrifice in the Great War / Jesu mercy." The church is also the site of classical concerts and performances by area professional theaters.

From the front entrance of the Grace Episcopal Church grounds, take the stone steps down to Wisconsin Ave. Walk north on Wisconsin Ave across the **Wisconsin Ave Bridge** (1831), the only intact bridge of its period. Immediately across the bridge is an iron-fenced square of grass on which sits an eight-ft-high granite obelisk celebrating the commencement of the C&O Canal on July 4, 1828. The marker was found in an old mill on the waterfront in 1889 and erected here in 1900 by H. P. Gilbert at his own expense to honor the canal.

Directly north of the obelisk is Papa Razzi restaurant at 1066 Wisconsin Ave N.W., the former site of the Vigilant Firehouse (DL). Subscription to a firehouse in the 1800s was a form of fire insurance. The iron plaques on the fronts of houses indicated which fire company was responsible for putting out a fire. When the Vigilant Fire Company organized in 1817 (note the carving near the roof: "Vigilant instituted 1817"), it was the first in Georgetown. In 1868 Vigilant (named after its fire engine), became the first firehouse in Georgetown to have a steam engine. The building ceased to function as a firehouse in 1883. Carved in stone beneath the restaurant's framed menu and all but obliterated is "Bush, The Old Fire Dog Died of Poison July 5th 1869 R.I.P." Besides the Vigilant Firehouse, Georgetowners had a choice of four other companies—the Columbian, the Mechanical, the Western Star, and the Eagle.

## Georgetown Park

3222 M St N.W., ☎ 298-5577. Open Mon–Sat 10–9; Sun 12–6. Restrooms. Food court. Restaurants.

Next door is the east entrance to Georgetown Park (1982; Alan J. Lockman/Lockman Associates; Chloethiel Woodard Smith & Associates, architectural consultants; Clark Tribble Harris & Li, interior design). The mall is built on the site of Georgetown's first tobacco warehouse, which later became the Capitol Transit Company. The M St façade and the old retaining wall overlooking the canal were retained while the interior was renovated to create a multilevel, neo-Victorian, skylighted shopping center with dozens of stores, plus restaurants and cafés. A small museum on the second floor of the mall displays unearthed artifacts and a pictorial history of Georgetown. On the ground floor near the steps by the food court is another of J. Seward Johnson, Jr.'s realistic bronze figures, *Out to Lunch* (1979).

Exit Georgetown Park onto Wisconsin Ave, using the exit near the entrance to the parking garage. Directly across Wisconsin Ave to the east is the alley where you can find the entrance to Washington's most celebrated mainstream jazz club, **Blues Alley**, 1073 Wisconsin Ave N.W., ☎ 337-4141, which has been attracting jazz afficionados since 1965. Charlie Byrd, Sarah Vaughan, and Wynton Marsalis have all played here.

Continue north a half-block on Wisconsin Ave to M St. This is the commercial heart of Georgetown. Walk west on M St a half-block. On the north side of M St is the former site of **Dr. William Thornton's house** at 3219 M St N.W. Thornton lived here with his wife in 1793, but eventually moved to the Federal City to be nearer his architectural projects, which included the Capitol. The house has long since been torn down and the buildings now on the site house a men's clothing shop and an Italian restaurant.

A half-block further west on the south side of M St is **Clyde's Restaurant** at 3236 M St N.W., ☎ 333-9180, created in 1963 by Washingtonian Stuart Davidson, who felt Washington needed a good saloon. In the 1960s Georgetown was a picturesque area of secondhand clothing shops, boutiques, bookshops, and antique stores. Parking was only a problem on weekends. Clyde's started the evolution that ended all that. Patterning itself after P.J. Clarke's in New York City, Clyde's became a stylish hangout to meet, greet, and eat.

> **Washington Notes**
> The gold record hanging over the bar is the Starland Vocal Band's "Afternoon Delight," inspired by the title of Clyde's special happy hour menu.

Next door to Clyde's is the **Georgetown Community Policing Center** at 3242 M St N.W., ☎ 333-1600, whose irregular hours of operation are necessitated by the fact that it's manned by volunteers. When open it has brochures of area attractions.

## Georgetown Market House

Continue west on M St to 3276 M St N.W. and the Georgetown Market House (1865; architect unknown; 1992 restoration, Clark Tribble Harris & Li; Jack Ceglic, designer; Core Group, PC, associate architects; DL), now an upscale **Dean & Deluca Food Emporium** store open Sun–Thurs 10–8, Fri–Sat 10–9 (espresso bar open Sun–Thurs 8–8; Fri–Sat, 8 A.M.–9 P.M.).

### History

The first market on this site, and the first public market of record in Washington, opened in 1795. A year later the market was torn down, and a new market was built. By the end of the Civil War, the 1796 building was so run-down that it was razed, and a new market (the current building) was erected in 1865. The market contained 22 stalls, including those of butchers, fishmongers, and dairy farmers. Sometime in the early 1900s, the market closed and was intermittently vacant and occupied by small businesses, including an auto parts shop.

In 1992, Dean & Deluca renovated the interior, left the exterior intact, and reopened the market. The red brick building is distinguished by the brick pilasters that separate round-arch window openings.

## Forrest-Marbury House

Continue west on M St two blocks to 3350 M St, the Forrest-Marbury House (1788–92; architect unknown; 1988 restoration, Geier Brown Renfrow Architects; DL), now the Embassy of Ukraine.

### History

Uriah Forrest was a shipping merchant, landowner, mayor of Georgetown, a statesman, and a Revolutionary War hero who lost his leg at Brandywine.

> ### Washington Notes
> Perhaps Forrest's greatest contribution was made on the evening of March 29, 1791, when he brought together over a sumptuous 16-course dinner a group of landowners and his friend and former commander, George Washington. Forrest was known for his charm and for his lavish entertaining. It was at this dinner that an agreement was reached regarding the sale of the land that would become the city of Washington. The agreement was sealed at Suter's Tavern the next night.

From 1800 to 1835 the estate was the residence of William Marbury, first president of the Farmers and Mechanics Bank (now Riggs Bank), who is famous for his suit to retain a judgeship awarded him by President John Adams. *Marbury v. Madison* was the first case involving a constitutional question of any importance to come before the Supreme Court. In 1803 the decision established the doctrine of judicial review. (Marbury was awarded the judgeship.)

During the Civil War, Marbury's son John and his family, who were strongly pro-South, lived here. The emotional explosiveness of the time is attested to by the fact that John Marbury's daughter was arrested for putting flowers on the grave of one of Jefferson Davis's children buried in Oak Hill Cemetery. Mrs. Marbury, alerted to the fact that Union soldiers were coming to the house to search for other evidence of treason, sewed letters she had received from nephews in the Confederate Army into an armchair cushion. The house was sold by the Marbury family in 1895 and was occupied by a succession of stores and clubs until 1991, when it sold for $4.1 million at a foreclosure auction.

## Francis Scott Key Park

Continue west on M St a half-block to the Francis Scott Key Park at the east entrance to Key Bridge (dedicated 1993), established in honor of the Georgetown philanthropist and amateur poet, best known as the author of "The Star-Spangled Banner."

> ### Washington Notes
> While negotiating for the release of an American prisoner in Baltimore during the War of 1812, Key was temporarily held by the British when they launched their attack on Fort McHenry in 1814. The fact that the fort's flag was still flying at dawn following a night of strong bombardment by the British inspired Key to write the poem "The Defence of Ft. McHenry." The poem was later set to the tune of "To Anacreon [a lyric poet of ancient Greece] in Heaven" by John Stafford South, a song of an English social club called the Anacreontic Society.

Key was three times the U.S. attorney for the District of Columbia, a negotiator with Indian tribes in the area, founder of Christ Church in Georgetown, and active in antislavery causes. He died of pneumonia while on a trip to Baltimore in 1843 at the age of 64. He and his family (he had 11 children) lived in a house about 100 yds west of the park in a house torn down in 1949 to make way for the Whitehurst Freeway.

### Washington Notes

Key's son, Philip Barton Key, was killed by Congressman Daniel Sickles in 1859 over an affair with Sickles's wife. Sickles was acquited on the grounds of "temporary aberration of mind"—the first time this defense was used. Sickles went on to lose a leg in the Civil War battle at Gettysburg. Sickles donated his leg to the Army's National Medical Museum, where it was preserved. Sickles was named minister to Spain by President Ulysses S. Grant. Key's grandson, John Ross Key, was a Washington scenic painter.

## Key Bridge

From the park, walk to Francis Scott Key Bridge (1917–23; Nathan C. Wyeth, architect; U.S. Army Corps of Engineers, District Engineer Major Max C. Tyler), named for "Star-Spangled Banner" composer Francis Scott Key.

### History

Little Falls Bridge, the first bridge across the Potomac, was built by the Georgetown Bridge Company in 1791 at Little Falls, about five miles above Georgetown and the site of the current Chain Bridge. (The C&O Canal towpath goes under Chain Bridge.) The second bridge across the Potomac was the Aqueduct Bridge, designed by Major William Turnbull and constructed between 1833 and 1843. This bridge, also called the Water-trough Bridge, was built to allow barges from the C&O Canal to bypass the port of Georgetown. The barges went from the canal waters to the Virginia side and the deepwater port of Alexandria, bypassing Georgetown. During the Civil War the bridge was drained and covered with planks for permanent use as a roadway for Union troops. After the war the planks remained, and exorbitant fees were charged by the company that owned the bridge, hindering Georgetown's trade with northern Virginia farmers. In 1888 the government opened the bridge to toll-free traffic, and Georgetown commerce once again prospered.

As the city grew, the Aqueduct Bridge become inadequate, and the Key Bridge was begun in 1917 about 100 ft east of the Aqueduct. Several lives were lost during its construction. The 1,650 ft long bridge, with its five arches and open-ribbed spandrels (the triangular space between the curve of an arch and the rectangular framework surrounding it), was opened for traffic on Jan 17, 1923.

From the center of Key Bridge, looking east you see the Kennedy Center, Theodore Roosevelt Island, and Washington Harbour. To the west, on the Georgetown side of the river, is the Washington Canoe Clubhouse.

### Washington Notes

In the center of the river between the clubhouse and the Virginia shore is **Three Sisters Island** (or **Rocks**), three large granite rocks jutting out of the river. During the Civil War, this was the halfway point for Union Army deserters and Confederate Army escapees from a Union prison in Georgetown. The swimmers would tie their boots and trousers around their waists, swim to the island, rest, then resume their swim to the Virginia shore and possible freedom. Meanwhile, atop a flagpole tower on Mt. Alto, sat a scout with a telescope. When he sighted a swimmer, he would signal another scout, and the word would be passed to soldiers at the Aqueduct Bridge, who would greet the swimmer as he straggled up out of the water onto the shore.

The success of these soldiers in at least getting to the other side of the river belied the curse of Three Sisters Island, which goes back to before the settlement of Georgetown. Captain John Smith, exploring the area in the early 1600s, wrote in his diary about the sobbing sounds heard near the rocks and referred to the legend of the three Indian sisters who died trying to avenge the deaths of their lovers by another tribe. Overcome by the river's swift current, the sisters clasped their arms together and, just before they drowned, shouted the curse that no one would ever cross the river at that point. The morning after their deaths, according to legend, three granite boulders appeared on that spot in the river.

While on the bridge, turn south and take a moment to look at the Old Transit Building and its clock tower, better appreciated from this distance.

**Diversion:**
East of Key Bridge on the Potomac River is **Theodore Roosevelt Island** (DL). ☎ (703) 285-2603. Web: www.nps.gov. Open dawn to dusk. Restrooms. Check the schedule for Ranger-led tours.

**Highlights:** Theodore Roosevelt statue and nature trails.

### History

Originally granted by Lord Baltimore to Captain Randolph Brandt (or Burnett) in 1681 for his bravery in fighting Indians, the 91-acre wooded island was sold by the captain's descendants to George Mason, son of the Virginia statesman George Mason (1725–1792), whose writings and political leadership made him one of the most influential figures of the pre-Revolution era. The younger George Mason's son, General John Mason, built a family plantation on the island and and named it Analostan, from the same Indian source as *Anacostia.* Mason imported Merion sheep from Spain and operated a ferry to Georgetown.

A visitor to the island in 1816 described it as a very pleasant place: "We walked to the mansion under a delicious shade. The blossoms of the cherry, apple, and peach trees, of the hawthorn and aromatic shrubs, filled the air with their fragrance [sic]. . . . The view from the spot is delightful. It embraces the picturesque banks of the Potomac, a portion of the city, and an expanse of water. . . . Numerous vessels ply backwards and forwards to animate the scene."

On this island, Mason entertained many of Georgetown's elite residents, and in 1789 Louis-Philippe (the future "citizen-king" of France) came to dinner. In 1832, the Mason family left the island, leasing it to Richard Southern, who farmed the land. The Southern family lived on the island ten years, until it passed from the Mason family's possession.

General Mason's son, James Murray Mason, was a member of the U.S. Senate from 1847 until 1860, when he left to become part of the Confederate government. He was appointed commissioner of the Confederate States to Great Britain and, along with John Slidell, commissioner to France, was taken off the British ship *Trent* by a Union ship of war and held captive for a time. After the war he lived in Alexandria, but legend has it that he never forgave the Union and would turn his back to the Capitol whenever he sat on his front porch.

During the Civil War, it is said that the island housed a Union Army unit of African Americans. The Strathmore family bought the island in the late 1800s and transformed it once again into a showplace, with a 14-room house in the center of the island, a barn, and a fine boathouse. The house was burnt to the ground, and the family forced to flee for their lives across the river to Georgetown and later back to England. The fire apparently resulted from the elopement of the eldest Strathmore daughter with an English gentleman named Savoy to whom her father objected. When Savoy sent Indian messengers (Analostans, still residing in the area) to the island to inform Eileen he was coming for her, Strathmore had them killed. So the night of Eileen's elopement, the Analostan chief torched the house to revenge the deaths of his men.

The home and grounds eventually decayed, and the island became a popular recreation area for Georgetowners. The Washington Gas Light Company bought the island in 1913 with the intention of erecting a gas plant, but the plan failed to materialize. In 1931 the Theodore Roosevelt Association purchased the island and gave it to the National Park Service.

### *Washington Notes*

Originally, the plans for Roosevelt's memorial called for a 67 ft sphere, a vehicular approach, and a 200-car parking lot on the tiny island. Roosevelt's notoriously plainspoken daughter, Alice Roosevelt Longworth ("If you can't say anything nice about someone, come sit by me"), wasn't at all pleased with the prospect. In an interview with the *Washington Post* in 1960, Ms. Longworth admitted she had been consulted about plans, "but I was too horrified even to think about them. I only wondered why they hadn't thought to add Muzak. . . . There are too few areas in this country now where one can walk and enjoy wildlife in its primeval state. . . . That lovely, wild island should be left just as it is." To a large extent, it has been.

When the McMillan Plan was adopted for the city of Washington at the turn of the century, Roosevelt Island was designated to remain a natural setting and an area of recreation, accessible by ferry and walkway from Georgetown. The island is crisscrossed by a number of pathways. In the center of the island is the **Theodore Roosevelt Memorial** (1967; Eric Gugler, design; Paul Manship, sculptor). A 17 ft bronze statue of Theodore Roosevelt in a characteristic speaking pose—teeth bared, fist raised in emphasis—faces an oval plaza with a 40 ft wide reflecting pool. Two granite monoliths, 20 ft high by 10 ft wide, rise on either side of the statue, bearing inscriptions of Roosevelt's visionary words on preserving the environment.

Roosevelt Island can only be reached by boat or by a bridge from the Virginia bike path. Walk across Key Bridge, then turn east on the path just before the first traffic light on the other side of the bridge. Follow the path about 100 yds to the footbridge connecting the island to the Virginia shore.

Hiking/touring the island's 2.5 miles of trails takes the visitor through three different terrains—swamp, marsh, and upland forest. The upper trail coils around the island's woods, through elms, tulip trees, oaks, and red maples. The lower trail, which has a tendency to wash out after rains, runs along the shoreline. Red and gray fox are sometimes sighted in this area. Although the island has no formal picnicking areas, picnics are permitted. Fishing is permitted with a valid D.C. license, but there are no rental facilities for poles and equipment on the island.

Cross M St at 34th St and continue west on M St to the **Old Transit Building** (1895–97; Waddy B. Wood) at 3600 M St N.W., now officially called the **Car Barn** and an office building. This was originally built as a transfer, terminal, and storage center for streetcars from Virginia and trolley lines from suburban Maryland and downtown Washington. (If the garage door is open, trolley tracks leading into the building can be seen.) When the two systems were phased out in the 1960s, the city's bus lines operated from here. The most impressive feature of the brick-and-stone building, whose north section reaches back to Prospect St four stories above M St, is its 140 ft high brick clock tower, which once contained passenger elevators. The M St façade is distinguished by red brick turrets projecting through and above the red tile roof.

Continue west a half-block on M St to 36th St, where cars come off the Whitehurst Freeway onto Canal Road (M St). Turn north.

### Washington Notes

To the rear of the gas station and adjacent to the Car Barn are the 75 steps made famous in the film *The Exorcist*. Local coaches often use the steps as a training challenge for their teams.

Proceed up the steps to the corner of 36th and Prospect Sts. (If the steps appear too daunting, go east on M St a half-block to 35th St, then north one block to Prospect, then west one block to the intersection of 36th and Prospect, and look down the steps.) For *The Exorcist,* a temporary addition was made to the exterior wall of the house next to the steps. **Prospect Cottage,** a Carpenter Gothic cottage, once stood on this site. It was owned by the prolific novelist, Mrs. E.D.E.N. (Emma Dorothy Eliza Nevitte) Southworth (1819–1899), who wrote 60 novels, most of them romances of Southern life. The house was torn down in 1941 and replaced by the two brick houses currently on the site.

### Washington Notes

This area was once called Holy Hill because of the strong Catholic presence of Georgetown University, Visitation School, Holy Trinity Church, and the many Catholic residents attracted by the nearness of these institutions.

## Prospect House

Walk east on Prospect St one block to 3508 Prospect St N.W. and Prospect House (1788–93; architect unknown; DL), an excellent example of the houses Georgetown's first merchants built for themselves.

### History

There is some question as to who had the house built, but its second owner was Commodore Charles Morris. His daughter eloped with W. W. Corcoran, who became one of the richest men in Washington, but at the time of his marriage was a dry goods clerk. During the Civil War, Prospect House was owned by William Whiton, a railroad engineer who participated in General Tecumseh Sherman's destructive March to the Sea. In 1868 the house was sold to Minnesota sawmill owner and flour merchant Franklin Steele. Prospect Place was restored in the 1930s, and in the 1940s was the residence of President Harry Truman's secretary of defense James Forrestal. While the White House was being renovated in 1949 and the Trumans moved to Blair House, Prospect House was used as the government's guest house. The Shah of Iran and Field Marshall Viscount Montgomery, famed tank commander of World War II, were hosted here.

## Exterior

The entrance of this Flemish-bond brick house is trimmed with reeded pilasters, and the house has a semicircular leaded-glass fanlight.

## Halcyon House

Continue east one block to Halcyon House (1787; architect unknown; DL) on the corner at 3400 Prospect St N.W. It was the home of Benjamin Stoddert, a shipping merchant in partnership with Uriah Forrest and the first secretary of the navy, under President John Adams.

### History

The halcyon is a fabled bird with the power to calm the wind and the waves during the winter solstice and consequently, a favorite of those, like Stoddert, in the maritime industry. A prominent citizen, Stoddert was one of the men who incorporated the Bank of Columbia to finance land transactions for the growing Washington City, and he also was one of George Washington's pallbearers. Although prosperous for a good part of his life, by 1801 Stoddert's finances were shaky due to land speculation. He was forced to mortgage his home to the same Bank of Columbia he had helped found. His daughter and son-in-law lived in the house following Stoddert's death in 1813. Between 1900 and 1938 the house was at the mercy of its eccentric owner Albert Adsit Clemons, a compulsive renovator. Living in the basement with a carpenter, Clemons spent 38 years in nonstop alterations. Clemons is said to have believed that he wouldn't die as long as he kept building onto the house. Clemons and the carpenter enclosed the entire building, subdivided the rooms, added new stairwells, a chapel, and a ballroom, creating rooms within rooms and endless corridors. Clemons also was a compulsive shopper, collecting such a mass of antiques and bric-a-brac that he had to purchase two nearby houses to store them all. When he died, an inventory of his possessions included eleven sandstone griffins, Samurai armor, and a row of seats from Ford's Theatre. Four years after Clemons's death, Halcyon House was purchased by Dorothy Sterling, wife of the former U.S. ambassador to Sweden. Sterling modernized and restored part of the mansion. It has since been sold several times, including to Georgetown University, who used the property as dormitory space for female students. The house is currently privately owned.

### Washington Notes

The hauntings of Benjamin Stoddert were one of Georgetown's favorite ghost stories before Albert Clemons began his renovations, and following his death, Clemons supposedly joined Stoddert in his ghostly visits. Stoddert was most often reported walking the halls or sitting in a captain's chair by the window looking out toward the river, as he often had done in life. Clemons wasn't seen so much as his presence felt, usually when the electric lights would go off for no apparent reason, since Clemons had rejected electricity during his life. Also reported in Halcyon House were the spirit of an old woman who rearranged bedcovers, the face of an old man outside an upstairs window, a young girl in period dress, and moaning and sobbing sounds heard in the basement, which may have been used as a stopover in the Underground Railroad by slaves escaping via the river from Virginia.

## Exterior

In spite of Clemons, the house retains a good deal of its original Georgian style, particularly on the south façade facing Prospect St, although the iron balconies are Southern colonial style.

From the corner of 34th and Prospect Sts, turn north on 34th St and walk one block to N St. On the southeast corner of N St is **Cox's Row** (1815–18; John Cox, owner-builder; DL) at 3331–3339 N St N.W., built by Georgetown mayor Colonel John Cox. Cox entertained Lafayette during the French hero's visit to Washington at 3337 N St. Cox also lived for a time at the Cedars, which stood on the current site of the Duke Ellington School for the Arts at 35th and R Sts N.W. Mayor of Georgetown from 1823 to 1845, Cox was known as something of a dandy, described by a contemporary as someone who would "saunter down town in silk stockings and pumps, not getting a spot upon himself, while other men would be up to their ankles in mud." The early Federal period is reflected in the doors and windows set flush with the outer walls, the delicately carved garlands of leaves and flowers, and the semicircular fanlights above the doors.

Walk east on N St a half-block to **3307 N St N.W.** (1812; William Marbury, owner-builder). This was the home of John F. Kennedy and his family when he was elected president of the United States. The formal, red brick house was built by William Marbury (of the Forrest-Marbury House) and was said to be a favorite of Jacqueline Kennedy's. The senator supposedly bought the house for her as a present when she was in the hospital after the birth of their daughter, Caroline. During the Civil War, St. John's Episcopal Church rented the house for use as a rectory.

Across the street at **3302 N St N.W.** is the former home of Dr. Stephen Bloomer Balch (1747–1833), founder of the Georgetown Presbyterian Church, and once the home of Helen Montgomery. Note the plaque.

### Washington Notes

After the election, reporters camped outside Kennedy's home, awaiting word of the president-elect's cabinet appointments. The Montgomery family served the reporters hot coffee and allowed them to use the house's phones, eventually installing two extra phone lines. The grateful reporters dedicated the plaque which reads: "In the cold winter of 1960–61 this house had an important role in history, from it was flashed to the world news of pre-inaugural announcements by President John F. Kennedy. Presented by the grateful newsmen who were given warm haven here by Miss Helen Montgomery and her father, Charles Montgomery."

Walk west on N St one block to the intersection with 34th St, then north one block on 34th St to O St and **3400 O St** on the northwest corner, built during the War of 1812 and onetime residence of former senator and vice presidential candidate Lloyd Bentson.

## Bodisco House

Walk east on O St a half-block to the Bodisco House (1815; Clement Smith, owner-builder) at 3322 O St N.W., once the home of the Russian legation but more famous as the site of the fairytale romance of Baron Alexander de Bodisco, the imperial Russian minister to the United States, and Georgetown native Harriet Brooke Williams. Williams married the baron in 1849 when he was 62 and she was 16.

### History

Two stories are told of their first meeting. The more common story has them meeting in this house at a Christmas party de Bodisco gave for his nephews, then students at Georgetown College. A more intriguing tale is that related by one of Harriet Williams's schoolmates at the Georgetown Seminary: "One day as the minister [de Bodisco] was driving by the seminary at noon, as he often did, the young ladies were being dismissed. . . . He rode in an open barouche, drawn by four white horses, two postilions in livery behind, two drivers in front, Bodisco sitting on the backseat. They were an imposing sight, moving slowly along to catch a good view of the girls. Miss Williams, full of fun, said, so I have heard, 'Girls, shall I stop the Russians?' and immediately stepped into the street, in front of the horses, and stooped down to tie her shoe. All were astonished at the action, but as she looked up, so full of mischief, the minister was captivated. Not many months after they were married."

The second story illustrates the much needed spunk Harriet Williams had to marry a much older man against the wishes her family. She may have been persuaded by the baron's argument to her family that "she might find someone younger and better looking, but no one who would love her better." The ceremony took place in June 1840 at St. John's Episcopal Church, with an elaborate reception held here. Further festivities celebrating the union lasted a full month, including dinner at the White House. The marriage was brief (de Bodisco died in 1854) but by all accounts happy. They had six children. Harriet Williams de Bodisco later married a young English Army officer, Captain Douglas Gordon Scott, and returned with him to England, where she remained until her death.

### Exterior

The house, with its pedimented portico and graceful twin stairs, is representative of late-Federal architecture.

Continue east on O St two blocks to **Holy Trinity Church and School** (original church building, 1794; Alexander Doyle, probable architect; current church building, 1846–49; architect unknown; rectory, 1869; Francis Staunton) at 36th and O Sts N.W., ☎ 337-2840. This was the first Catholic church in Washington, and for more than 100 years after its establishment in 1794, it was the only place that African American Catholics could worship in Georgetown. However, the black parishoners had to stand in the center of the nave with those who couldn't afford to rent pews. Later the African American congregants sat in an extension of the choir loft, which they entered by a separate stairway. The original church building (1794), at 3525 N St N.W., serves as the parish center. The current church building (1846–49), at 3513 N St N.W., was used as a hospital for wounded Union soldiers coming back from the First Battle of Bull Run (called the Battle of Manassas by the Confederacy). A "deadhouse" was constructed behind the church to handle the large numbers of wounded who died in the hospital. Abraham Lincoln attended a funeral at Holy Trinity, and John F. Kennedy often worshiped here with his family.

> ### Washington Notes
> A spiritual dilemma arose for Holy Trinity in 1978, when it announced plans for a major renovation of the church's interior at a cost of $400,000. The Community for Creative Non-Violence (CCNV), an advocate organization for Washington's homeless that ran a shelter near Capitol Hill, led by activist Mitch Snyder, approached the church and said that $80,000 of the money raised for church renovations should be given to CCNV to renovate its homeless shelter. Holy Trinity declined and Snyder protested, saying the church was out to "maim and torture" the needy. Members of the parish raised $5,000 for CCNV but this didn't stop CCNV members from picketing the church and voicing protests during Mass. Finally Snyder went on a hunger strike that lasted more than 40 days but did not cause Holy Trinity to change its stand. The church did agree to work in partnership with CCNV on various programs for the homeless, and Snyder gave up his fast. At the time, the situation raised many questions about the moral issues faced by urban churches, trying to balance the community's spiritual needs with the churches' often more immediate physical needs.

From Holy Trinity Church at 36th and O Sts, walk west on O St to Georgetown University's student-housing complex **Village B** (1983; Hugh Newell Jacobsen) on 37th between N and O Sts N.W., an example of modern Georgetown structures designed to both complement and enhance their Federal-style surroundings. The half-block complex emulates the Italianate style popular in Georgetown before the Civil War. The buildings also have Federal features adapted by Jacobsen so that they fit in with the character of Georgetown.

## Georgetown University
37th and O Sts N.W. ☎ 687-0100. Public information booth in the west gatehouse of the main gate. Hours vary. Web: www.georgetown.edu.

Directly across the street from the complex, at the intersection of 37th and O Sts, are the front gates of the Main Campus of **Georgetown University** (1789). Georgetown University (GU) is the oldest Catholic university in the country and a Jesuit-run center of learning open to all faiths since its inception. The 104-acre campus includes 61 buildings, a 407-bed teaching hospital, and student residences that house over 4,200 of the university's 12,000-plus students. The

Georgetown mascot, the hoya, is derived from the Greek and Latin phrase *hoya saxa* (loosely translated as "what rocks!"), which possibly originated from a cheer referring to the stones of the school's outer walls. Georgetown's list of well-known graduates is long and impressive—it includes President Bill Clinton; Attorney General Janet Reno; George Mitchell, former senator and mediator of the 1998 peace accord in Ireland; Don McHenry, former ambassador to the United Nations; James Webb, former secretary of the navy; Senator Patrick Leahy of Vermont, Representative John Dingell of Michigan, Representative Frank Wolf of Virginia, Supreme Court justice Antonin Scalia, William Peter Blatty, author of *The Exorcist;* Maria Shriver, NBC-TV news commentator; and basketball players Patrick Ewing, Alonzo Mourning, and David Wingate.

**Highlights:** Gaston Hall, Old North (the oldest building on campus), and Dahlgren Chapel of the Sacred Heart.

### History

Georgetown University was founded by the Reverend John Carroll in 1789. Carroll (1735–1815), a native Marylander (his brother Daniel Carroll owned the plantation that included the future Capitol Hill), had intended to remain in Europe as a teacher in Jesuit colleges, but the suppression of the Jesuit order in 1773 brought him back to the American colonies. Carroll actively supported the colonies' fight for independence, in part because the new nation would guarantee freedom of worship and the right to vote for Catholics. When Carroll was appointed as the first head of the American Church in 1784, he immediately set in motion the founding of a liberal arts college for men. (Women were not admitted until 1969.) In 1789, Carroll obtained the deed to 60 acres of ground on a hill overlooking Georgetown for the price of £75. Proximity to Holy Trinity Church, then under construction, and the "Salubrity of Air, Convenience of Communication and Cheapness of Living" made this, in Carroll's view, an excellent choice for the college. In 1792, construction was begun on the Old North Building, and George Washington addressed the student body from its porch in 1797. Until the Jesuits officially established themselves in the U.S. in 1805, the college fell under the governorship of the Corporation of the Clergy of Maryland. In 1815, Congress raised the status of the institution from a college to a university. Determined that the school be open "to Students of every religious Profession," Carroll sought diversity in the student population. In the first ten years nearly one-fifth of the students were Protestants, and by the 1830s Jews were attending Georgetown University also.

### Washington Notes

During the Civil War, Georgetown students were overwhelmingly pro-South, with four out of five of those who fought in the war fighting on the Confederate side. In May 1861, the 79th New York Division took up residence on campus. The Union soldiers spilled grease on the floors, stole guitars and violins, ripped out doorframes, and used the dining tables as butcher blocks, according to a bill sent to Quartermaster General Montgomery Meigs requesting that the government move the troops and pay for the damages. Meigs replied that the college was on property used on a tax-free basis and he refused to pay, but he did move the 79th New York elsewhere.

In the fall of 1862, several university buildings were turned into hospitals to handle the wounded from the Second Battle of Bull Run/Manassas. At one point, enrollment was down to 17 students, but Georgetown survived the war, and its postwar population became increasingly more Northern. In 1866 the school adopted its official colors of blue and gray to symbolize the reunion of the North and the South. In 1873, the Reverend Patrick Healy (1834–1908) became Georgetown's president, the first African American president of a major university. Healy transformed Georgetown from a small body of higher education to a major educational and spiritual center by expanding the curricula as well as the medical and law schools, which had been founded in 1849 and 1870, respectively.

The university continued to expand until the Depression, when enrollment dropped, only to explode following World War II with the G.I. Bill. The present hospital complex was opened in 1947.

## Campus

The Main Campus is bounded by Reservoir Rd (GU Hospital is at 3700 Reservoir Rd N.W.) on the north, M St on the south, Glover Archbold Park on the west, and 37th St on the east.

Enter the campus through the main gates at 37th and O Sts N.W. and stop at the Visitors Center (west gatehouse) for information and a campus map ($1). In the center of **Healy Circle** is the life-size bronze statue of Georgetown's founder, John Carroll (1912; Jerome Connor). The campus's oldest buildings (Healy Hall, Dahlgren Chapel, Ryan Hall, and Old North) form a quadrangle, with **Healy Hall** (1879–1909; J. S. Smithmeyer and Paul J. Pelz; DL) its eastern boundary.

At its highest point, Healy Hall, a Flemish Romanesque building rises more than 300 ft over the Potomac River. Made of dark gray Potomac gneiss ashlar, Healy Hall has numerous dormers, cupolas, and towers, as well as a number of imaginative copper gargoyles. The 200 ft clock spire is composed of a rectangular base of three stories: The first level has two slit windows and is separated from the second level by a continuous layer of sandstone. The third level has the clock face on the east and west sides. A spire is located at the southwest corner of the building. Healy's most famous space is **Gaston Hall** (named for its first student, William Gaston of North Carolina, who was elected to Congress in 1813), which has ornate classical murals created by Bavarian-born Jesuit Francis Schroen. The hall has been the setting for speeches by U.S. presidents and other world figures, as well as musical performances ranging from Rostropovich to Muddy Waters. The hall is open to the public only for scheduled events.

> ### *Washington Notes*
> The two canons in front of Healy are relics from the two ships, the *Ark* and the *Dove*, that brought the first Maryland colonists and Jesuits to America in 1634.

From the front of Healy Hall, take the stone steps to the front entrance, walk through the entrance hall, and take the hallway to the left. Halfway down the hallway take the first door to the right out into the square, which has a fountain and tree-shaded benches. This square is formed by the four-building quadrangle of Healy, Old North, Ryan Hall, and Dahlgren Chapel. **Old North,** to the east of Healy in the square, is the oldest building on campus. Built in 1795, designed in the Federal style, and made of red brick, Old North has a central five-bay projecting pavilion and a one-story wooden porch (from which George Washington addressed the students and faculty when his nephews Augustine and Bushrod were students here). At the entrance is a bronze plaque commemorating the 1,138 Georgetown students who died in the Civil War. To Healy Hall's north is **Dahlgren Chapel of the Sacred Heart,** a gift to the university from Mrs. John Vinton Dahlgren in memory of her infant son. The cross above the altar is from the earliest days of the Maryland colony. The chapel is one of the most visited buildings on campus because of its beautiful stained glass windows and pipe organ, and because many moviegoers remember it from *The Exorcist.* To the west of Healy is **Ryan Hall** (1904; architect unknown), once used for classrooms and now the residence of the campus's Jesuit faculty and administration.

Exit Healy Hall onto the central campus. To the south is the **Joseph Mark Lauinger Memorial Library** (1970; John Carl Warnecke), named in honor of the first Georgetown University graduate to die in Vietnam. Creation of this building was the subject of a passionate debate that included the city's Fine Arts Commission, the Citizens Association of Georgetown, the National Planning Commission, the university, and others. The structure's modern design is in strong contrast to its neighbors. On the fifth floor of Lauinger Library is Georgetown University's **Special Collections Room.** Changing exhibits highlight Georgetown's collection of papers and documents from the world of letters and the arts. One item in the university's collection considered too valuable to display here is the original manuscript of Mark Twain's *Tom Sawyer,* a gift to the university from Mrs. Nicholas Brady of New York.

**Diversion:**
On the northwest side of the campus is the **Georgetown University Astronomical Observatory** (1841–44; James Curley, S.J.; DL), the third-oldest observatory in the U.S. Built before the U.S. Naval Observatory and the Harvard Observatory, this Greek revival–style building was the site of important astronomical advancements. Its designer, Father James Curley, was a self-taught mathematical genius who was the first to calculate the latitude and longitude of the District of Columbia. In 1888, research conducted at the observatory by Father John Hagen established the fact that the position of the earth on its axis of rotation is not a constant. Father Hagen's assistant, Father George A. Fargis, invented the first practicable instrument for photographing star transits, a predecessor of the Baker-Nunn camera. The building no longer functions as an observatory because of interference from the glare of city lights. The astronomy club and the physics department use the building, which is not open to the public.

On the same side of the campus, across from the Georgetown University Medical Center on Reservoir Rd between 39th and 44th Sts, is an entrance to **Glover-Archbold Park,** a 183-acre enclave extending from the southern end of the C&O Canal to Massachusetts Ave near Ward Circle, ☎ 426-6834. Financier and philanthropist Charles C. Glover and philanthropist Anne Archbold donated the land so that it would remain "in its natural state for a bird sanctuary and for the enjoyment of people." The National Capital Region of the National Park Service maintains the park. The main park path follows Foundry Branch, a small stream. Other paths wind through groves of trees.

Another diversion from Georgetown University's northwest campus is the

**Duke Ellington School of the Arts.** From Reservoir Rd at the entrance to the medical center, turn east and walk three blocks to the corner of 35th and R Sts N.W. (Reservoir Rd becomes R St at this corner). The neoclassical building on the hill (formerly Western High School) is the Duke Ellington School, a testament to the dedication and determination of its founder, Peggy Cooper Cafritz. An arts magnet school founded in 1974 that draws many of its students from some of Washington's most troubled neighborhoods, Ellington offers its students a full load of college preparatory courses and specialized classes in dance, music, literary arts, museum studies, theater, visual arts, and vocal music. More than 90 percent of the Ellington School's students are accepted to colleges, and other students go on to work with professional companies such as the American Ballet Theater and the New York Metropolitan Opera. Actress/choreographer Debbie Allen was one of the Ellington's well known teachers. The current enrollment is about 500 students.

## Georgetown Visitation Preparatory School

1524 35th St N.W. ☎ 337-3350. Web: www.ee.cua.edu/~georgvis.

Exit Georgetown University from the main entrance onto 37th St and walk north one block to P St, then two blocks east on P St (there are no street signs; 37th St curves around the university and a stone wall runs on the north side of the street, becoming a red brick wall on the second block) to 35th St and Georgetown Visitation Preparatory School (Chapel of the Sacred Heart, 1825; Father Joseph Picot de Cloriviere; Monastery, 1857; architect unknown; Academy Building, 1874; Norris G. Starkweather; DL) home of the second-oldest convent in the U.S. and one of the oldest schools for women in the country.

### History

The Georgetown Academy for Young Ladies was established in 1799 by three American "Pious Ladies"—Alice Lalor, Maria Sharpe, and Maria McDermott—under the sponsorship of Georgetown College president Leonard Neale and their spiritual director, Father Joseph Picot de Cloriviere. The three women were formally professed as Sisters of the Visitation (a French order not previously established in the U.S.). The purpose of the academy was to educate young Christian women.

### Washington Notes

In July 1993, on a day when the thermometer reached 100 degrees in Washington, a fire that began in the attic of the Academy Building during renovations completely gutted the inside of that building. Half of the city's 54 fire trucks responded to the blaze, which took more than three hours to bring under control. School archivist Sister Mada Anne ran up three flights of stairs toward the fire to retrieve the school's vow book (containing records of vows taken by every nun in the convent since 1816) and two student needlepoint samplers from 1799, which depict scenes from the school. Because of the rapid spread of the fire, the rest of the school's archives were destroyed.

## Campus

Walk south on 35th St, past the Federal-style Monastery, then the classically Gothic Chapel of the Sacred Heart and the ornately Victorian Academy Building.

The verse carved above the chapel entrance, "Vovete et reddite Domino Deo vestro," translates as "Make vows to the Lord, your God, and fulfill them." Two new buildings on the campus are the Catharine E. Nolan Performing Arts Center (1998), a 16,000 square ft, two-level facility seating 500, and a 25,000 square ft Fisher Athletic Center. The latter includes a 500-seat playing court, lockers, classrooms, and conference facilities. KressCox Associates, P.C., designed both buildings.

## Volta Bureau

Directly across from the main gates of Visitation, on the east side of 35th St, is the Volta Bureau (1894–96; Peabody and Sterns; DL) at 1537 35th St N.W., ☎ 337-5220.

> ### Washington Notes
> Alexander Graham Bell (1847–1922) established the Volta Bureau with the $10,000 Volta Prize he was awarded by the French government in 1880. The Volta Prize was created by Napoleon I to honor the Italian physicist who invented the electric battery.

The property serves as headquarters for the **Alexander Graham Bell Association for the Deaf,** a clearinghouse for information about scientific advancements and medical aids for the hearing-impaired. Bell's parents, Professor and Mrs. Alexander Melville Bell, moved to 1525 35th St N.W. in 1879, and Melville's brother, David Bell, soon afterward moved to 1521 35th St N.W. Melville Bell was a professor of physiology in Edinburgh, Scotland, and perfected a system of visible speech for the hearing-impaired. While teaching his father's methods in Boston, Alexander Graham Bell met and married one of his pupils, Mabel Hubbard, daughter of Gardiner Greene Hubbard, founder of the National Geographic Society.

The small museum inside the building is open to the public Mon–Fri 9–3:30. Photos of the Bell family and hearing-aid devices are displayed. Upon request visitors can view a brief video about the Bell Association.

> ### Washington Notes
> Author and Nobel Prize winner Sinclair Lewis worked as an assistant clerk and office boy at the Volta Bureau for $15 a week in 1910. Lewis left the apparently boring job and the city after six months, but returned to Washington ten years later to write *Main Street* while living at 1814 16th St N.W.

Continue on 35th St a half-block north to the **Longden House** (1853; George Longden, owner-builder) at 1555 35th St N.W., home to Thomas Jefferson's granddaughter Mrs. Septimia Randolph Meikleham from 1877 to 1882.

> ### Washington Notes
> When Mrs. Meikleham's husband, Dr. David Meikleham, died in 1849, Mrs. Meikleham was left with three children to support and little means to do so. In 1880, as Jefferson's only surviving grandchild and in need of funds, Mrs. Meikleham sought a stipend from Congress. At that time, her daughter Esther was a clerk in the Patent Office and had to support her mother and an

invalid sister and brother on $1,000 a year. Congress eventually denied Mrs. Meikleham her stipend, and she died in 1887 while residing at 1429 Q St N.W.

Walk north to the corner of 35th and Q Sts, turn east on Q St, then walk three blocks to Wisconsin Ave, then walk south on Wisconsin Ave one block to **Georgetown Lutheran Church** (established 1769; fourth and present church, 1914) at 1556 Wisconsin Ave, N.W., ☎ 337-9070. A church made of hewn logs, thought to be the first church in Georgetown, was originally constructed on this site in 1770. The lot had been donated by the land's owners, Charles Beatty and George Fraser Hawkins, who in 1769 specified, "Four of said lots we give to public uses, to wit: one for building on a church for the use of the Church of England, one of a Calvinist church, one for a Lutheran church, and the other for a market house."

Continue south on Wisconsin Ave into the commercial district of Georgetown. At the corner of Wisconsin Ave and P St stands **Neam's of Georgetown** (3217 P St N.W., ☎ 338-4694), a neighborhood market since 1909, offering quality produce, baked goods, and meat.

Continue south on Wisconsin to the southwest corner of Wisconsin Ave and O St and 1344 Wisconsin Ave N.W., the former site of what was called Doc's Place for almost 50 years but was officially the **Georgetown Pharmacy.** Pharmacist "Doc" Dalinsky sold ice cream and cigarettes to Franklin Delano Roosevelt when FDR came to visit his son James at 3331 O St. In the 1960s and '70s, Doc served Sunday brunch to regulars such as David Brinkley, Art Buchwald, and Herman Wouk. When too many came to gawk at the celebrities, Doc stopped serving brunch in 1979 and finally sold the place in 1984.

## St. John's Episcopal Church
Turn west on O St and walk one block to St. John's Episcopal Church (1796–1806; Dr. William Thornton; 1870, Starkweather and Plowman) at 3240 O St N.W., ☎ 338-1796, one of the oldest Episcopal churches in the city and one that has seen its share of good times and bad.

### History
According to a book published by the church in 1998, the building was not constructed from a plan suggested by Dr. William Thornton, architect of the Capitol, as has often been stated. Dr. Thornton did submit a plan, but none of his suggestions were used. Sometime in 1796 funds ran out and building ceased, to be resumed in 1803, when the exterior of the church was completed. The current foundation, walls, roof, and bells are of this original church. Regular services began in the summer of 1804. Early members included the families of Thomas Corcoran, Francis Scott Key, and William Marbury. Bank failures in the 1820s left St. John's in precarious financial shape. In the early 1830s the building was partially abandoned. Birds flying in and out of its rafters earned it the nickname Swallow Barn, and in 1834 it became the studio of a German artist named Ferdinand Pettrich. In 1836 W. W. Corcoran paid the church's delinquent taxes, and by the fall of 1838 the church had been restored to a usable condition.

In the 1850s, St. John's, concerned about the number of impoverished African Americans in Georgetown, opened a free school "for the purpose of imparting religious instruction to the coloured portion of the congregation." In 1864 a school for former slave children was opened in the basement. The church was renovated in 1870 and the rectory completed in 1874, both designed by architect Norris G. Starkweather; the mosaic tile floors were added in 1909. The present tower and belfry, designed by Walter Peter, were put in place in 1924.

### Washington Notes

In 1996, the Reverend Margaret Graham became the first woman to serve as rector of St. John's. In 1997, the church accepted Dr. Albert Scariato as its first openly gay ordained clergyman.

From St. John's, walk east to Wisconsin Ave, then south on Wisconsin Ave to 1335 and the **Au Pied de Cochon** restaurant, the site of the spy thriller with the comic ending.

### Washington Notes

On the evening of Nov 2, 1985, Vitaly Yurchenko, the highest-ranking KGB official ever to defect from the USSR to the U.S., was at dinner with his CIA escort. Yurchenko excused himself from the table, slipped out of the restaurant into a crowd, grabbed a taxi, and went to the Soviet Embassy, where he renounced his defection. The Au Pied de Cochon subsequently introduced a drink called the Yurchenko Shooter, consisting of equal parts Stolichnaya vodka and Grand Marnier.

Continue south on Wisconsin Ave to the southwest corner of N St and Wisconsin Ave and **Martin's Tavern** at 1264 Wisconsin Ave N.W., a restaurant/pub established in 1933 and a favorite of the university crowd.

**Diversion:**
Walk west on N St one block to 3249 N St N.W., a red brick apartment house, which during the Civil War was the residence of Samuel Hein, who ran a soup kitchen for Northern troops in his yard. On the south side of N St in this block is **Smith's Row** (3255–3263 N St N.W.), a group of Federal-style homes built in the early 1800s.

### Washington Notes

Herman Wouk, best-selling author of *The Caine Mutiny* and *The Winds of War*, lives at 3255, on the end of the row. John F. Kennedy lived at 3260 in 1951. He planted a magnolia tree and had the living room converted into a bedroom so he wouldn't strain his back using the stairs.

At the intersection of N St and Wisconsin Ave, cross to the southeast corner. Pause a moment to look down the hill along Wisconsin Ave to the Potomac River and Roosevelt Island. This is the route Maryland farmers took to bring their produce to port in the earliest days of Georgetown, and their wheels turned it into a road. It is the road up which General Braddock and his troops marched in 1755 on their way to defeat by the French in Pennsylvania. This is the street, then called High St, that the wounded Union soldiers were carried along in wagons in the aftermath of the First Battle of Bull Run (Manassas), as businesses and houses on both sides of the avenue became makeshift hospitals. And this is the avenue that is closed to traffic (along with M St) every Halloween as thousands pour into Georgetown to celebrate All Hallows Eve.

Walk south a half-block down the hill and look across the street at the ornate façade of **1254 Wisconsin Ave N.W.** (DL), now a clothing store but until 1957 a popular confectionary. A previous building on the site housed Arnold's Bakery in the 1820s, which was subsequently bought by the May family. Mrs. May was aunt to Frederick Stohlman, who inherited the business and the building from her in 1845. He had the current red brick Victorian building erected in the 1880s (architect unknown) and opened Stohlman's Bakery, which eventually became Stohlman's Confectionary. When the store closed in 1957 the interior, with its Victorian ice cream parlor fittings, was given to the Smithsonian Institution for display.

Continue south on Wisconsin Ave as it curves down the hill to the intersection of M St and Wisconsin Ave. At the northeast corner is the **Farmers and Mechanics Branch, Riggs Bank** (1922; William J. Marsh and Walter Peter) at 1201 Wisconsin Ave N.W., ☎ (301) 887-6000. In 1840, W. W. Corcoran and George W. Riggs became partners, acquired the assets of the defunct Bank of the United States, opened the bank of Corcoran and Riggs, and proceeded to make a fortune by bankrolling the Mexican War for the U.S. government. In 1854, Corcoran retired. In the ensuing years, the establishment known as Riggs Bank became one of the strongest banks in the country. Distinguished by its stately gold-leaf dome, the building has long been one of Georgetown's most recognizable sites. A lantern lights the dome, and, at the cornice, a clock with a design of garlands and swags underneath faces the intersection. Two great Corinthian pillars support the cornice and frame the building's entrance.

To continue to the next walk, take any of the 30s buses on Wisconsin Ave to Washington National Cathedral.

# 21 · Washington National Cathedral

Metro: Red Line to Tenleytown-AU. Walk south on Wisconsin Ave. It's about a 25-minute walk to the National Cathedral.
Bus: From Georgetown take any of the 30s buses heading north on Wisconsin Ave.

Massachusetts and Wisconsin Aves N.W. ☎ 537-6200. Web: www.cathedral. org/cathedral. Visiting hours Mon–Sat 10–4:30; extended summer hours vary. Good Shepherd Chapel open 6 A.M.–10 P.M. for private prayer. Gardens open daily until dusk. Medieval Workshop for families Sat 10–2. Guided tours Mon–Sat 10–11:30 A.M. and 12:45–3:15 P.M. Admission: donation requested.

Worship services—Sun: regular services at 8, 9, 10 (except in July and Aug), 11 A.M.; Evensong at 4 P.M.; Holy Eucharist on the first, third, and fifth Sun of the month at 6:30 P.M.; Taizé service on second and fourth Sun of the month at 6:30 P.M. Mon–Sat: Holy Eucharist at 7:30 A.M., noon; cathedral intercessions at 2:30; evening prayer at 4; compline at 8:45 P.M. (Mon–Fri).

Cathedral Boy's Choristers sing Evensong Mon–Wed 4 P.M.; Girl Choristers

Thurs 4 (Sept–May). Organ demonstrations Wed 12:45 P.M. The carillon is played Sat 12:30 P.M. Numerous special musical events include visiting choirs and musicians. Cathedral shops: Museum Store, Gatehouse Shop (in season), Herb Cottage, and Greenhouse open 9:30–5 daily, except Christmas Day and New Year's Day. ☎ 537-6267.

Restrooms, telephones. Wheelchair accessible. Wheelchairs available. Sandwiches and other refreshments available in Museum Store.

The Washington National Cathedral (1906–90; 1906–17, George Frederick Bodley and Henry Vaughan; 1921–42, Philip Hubert Frohman, E. Donald Robb, and Harry B. Little; Philip Hubert Frohman, chief architect; 1942–71, Philip Hubert Frohman; 1971–73, James E. Goodwin, superintending architect; 1973–81, Howard B. Trevillian, Jr., superintending architect; 1981–90, Anthony J. Segreti, superintending architect; DL) is the sixth largest cathedral in the world and the second largest in the U.S. The official name of the facility is the Cathedral Church of St. Peter and St. Paul. It is the seat of the bishop of the Episcopal Diocese of Washington. Daily worship services follow The Episcopal Book of Common Prayer. The cathedral, which took 83 years to build and is in the shape of a cross, extends more than 500 ft from its eastern apse to west façade; its principal architectural style is Gothic. The top of the central tower, the Gloria in Excelsis, is the highest point in Washington at 676 ft above sea level.

**Highlights:** Philip Hubert Frohman's design and Frederick Hart's sculptures at the building's west façade; 16C Flemish tapestries; the tomb of the only president to be buried in the District, Thomas Woodrow Wilson; the great organ, an Aeolian Skinner with more than 10,000 pipes; and the stained glass Space Window, which has a piece of moon rock.

### History

The cathedral's history begins with the founding of the nation's capital. It is said that when George Washington and Major Pierre L'Enfant planned the city, they rode north from the thriving port of Georgetown to visit their friend Joseph Nourse, secretary of the Treasury. Nourse's home was on the highest spot in the area. Nourse told the president and L'Enfant of his dream that one day a church would rise on what was then his land.

It wasn't until 1891, however, when a group of influential Washingtonians met in the home of Charles C. Glover, a prominent banker, that the dream of a cathedral on this spot began to become a reality. On Jan 6, 1893, the Protestant Episcopal Cathedral Foundation was created by an act of Congress and the charter signed by President Benjamin Harrison.

By 1898, the first bishop of Washington, Henry Yates Satterlee, had secured all of the 57 acres on Mt. St. Alban needed for the site for the sum of $245,000. Satterlee was determined that the cathedral be a "House of Prayer For All People." Those words are emblazoned on the cathedral banner.

In 1907, the first architects of the cathedral, Englishman George Bodley and Henry Vaughan, an Englishman by birth who came to the U.S. as a young man, submitted their plans. On Sept 29, 1907, the foundation stone, part of which came from a field near Bethlehem, was laid before a crowd of more than 10,000. President Theodore Roosevelt delivered the address. In 1912, Bethlehem Chapel was opened for services. Following the death of architect Henry Vaughan in 1917

*Washington National Cathedral. Courtesy of the Washington, D.C., Convention &
Visitors Association.*

(George Bodley had died in Oct 1907) and completion of the second phase of construction in 1919, building was halted. In 1921, the Boston architectural firm of
(Philip Hubert) Frohman, (E. Donald) Robb, and (Harry B.) Little was selected by
the cathedral governing body to oversee the completion of the construction, and
work was resumed in 1922 with the building of the Great Choir foundation.
Frohman altered the Bodley-Vaughan design extensively by increasing the height
of the tower, extending the buttresses, altering the nave, and changing the design
of the west façade.

The cathedral's third bishop, James Freeman, raised enough money to keep
work going through the Depression, and the north porch was completed by the
time of America's entry into World War II in 1941. In 1942, E. Donald Robb died

and Philip Hubert Frohman became the cathedral's chief architect, a position he would hold until 1971, the year before his death. (Harry B. Little died in 1944.)

> ### Washington Notes
> Frohman, a Roman Catholic, spent most of his career designing an Episcopal cathedral. He died as a result of injuries sustained after he was hit by a car while crossing a street near the cathedral. Frohman is buried in the cathedral crypt.

Francis Bowes Sayre, Jr., began a 27-year career as dean of the cathedral in 1951. Dean Sayre was the grandson of Woodrow Wilson, who was buried in Bethlehem Chapel in 1924, and now rests in the Wilson Bay on the cathedral's nave level. Sayre supervised much of the carvings, stained glass, and other decorative items. The nave was completed in time for America's Bicentennial. The cathedral's first African American bishop, John Walker, who also served as dean, raised a good deal of money, enough to complete the Pilgrim Observation Gallery by 1982. In that same year, the cathedral opened its doors to people of all faiths in a memorial service for Anwar Sadat and services for the hostages in Iran. On Sept 29, 1990, the last stone finial, weighing 1,008 pounds, was placed atop the south tower's southwestern pinnacle. President George Bush addressed the crowd.

The National Cathedral has been the site for services for many national leaders. The funerals of President Dwight Eisenhower, Secretary of Commerce Ron Brown, Supreme Court Justice Thurgood Marshall, and Ambassador Pamela Harriman were held at the National Cathedral. There have been many weddings of prominent people, including the wedding of Albert Gore, Jr., and his wife Tipper, Robert and Elizabeth Dole, and the wedding of the Gores' daughter, Karenna.

## Exterior and Grounds

From Wisconsin Ave the visitor sees the front of the cathedral. The best way to take in the size and splendor of this Gothic wonder is to walk around the cathedral, beginning at the northwest corner. It's best to begin by looking at the lowest stained glass windows and at some of the 106 gargoyles and grotesques. Walk to the top of the north side ramp, face the door, and look up. The first gargoyle is a dapper gentleman with lots of teeth and hair whose half-glasses help him read the book he's holding. To the left of this is a cat in a tree gazing intently at a nearby mouse. Continue east to the gargoyle depicting the cathedral's master stone carver Roger Morigi. This affectionate depiction celebrates his devilish nature with a cleft foot, horns, and a curly tail. Continue east to the north transept.

**North transept.** This was the first completed entrance into the main level of the cathedral. The outside arched niches honor women with statues of (left to right) St. Elizabeth, the mother of John the Baptist; Mary Magdalene; St. Agnes; St. Cecilia; St. Monica, mother of St. Augustine of Hippo; St. Hilda, the Abbess of Whitby; and St. Catherine of Sienna. The tympanum over the door represents St. Mary and the Christ child, surrounded by shepherds and the Magi. Directly beneath on the post between the two doors is a statue of St. Anne, the mother of St. Mary.

A cloister connects the north transept to the cathedral's Administration Building; another cloister connects the apse with the Administration Building. An angle formed by the cloisters and the cathedral itself is a cloister garth. The large abstract fountain in the center of the garth (1969) is the work of sculptor George Tsutakawa and its bronze sheen and flowing water make this a serene stop for visitors.

From the north cloister one may enter the cathedral at crypt level or go up a flight of stairs to the north transept entrance on the nave level. However, continue east around the exterior of the building and pass by (on the left) the College of Preachers, a graduate education center for clergy of all denominations. Next is the Cathedral Library, which houses offices, including those of the Cathedral Choral Society. At the east end of the apse, between the arches of the flying buttresses, are statues of St. Peter, St. John, and St. Paul. On the frieze below the apse parapet are the words of the angels from the Book of Revelation: "Alleluia, the Lord God omnipotent reigneth, alleluia."

Continue around the apse to the South Rd. On the left is Sayre House, the former residence of the dean, now the offices of the National Cathedral Association and the Cathedral's Development Department. On the right is the entrance to Bethlehem and the other crypt chapels. Walk west along the South Rd to Pilgrim Steps. The bronze equestrian statue of George Washington (1959) is by Herbert Haseltine. From the South Rd look up to see the Gloria in Excelsis Tower, which has both a 53-bell carillon and a 10-peal bell. The tower is decorated with 396 carved angel figures symbolizing the seraphim and cherubim surrounding the throne of God. From South Rd, above a flight of steps is the south transept porch.

**South transept.** This graceful portal has intricately carved decorations. The Last Supper is depicted above the entrance. Christ dominates the scene, surrounded by his 12 apostles. Three scenes from the story of the Emmaus road (1959) by sculptor Heinz Warnecke are carved beneath the major scene. The piece is considered to be one of Warneke's most outstanding works.

Surrounding the oak doors are statues of eight biblical figures. From the right the statues are: the widow who gave her mite, the sick spirit, Lazarus, and blind Bartimaeus. On the left are: the boy with loaves and fishes, Nicodemus, the woman by the well, and Judas Iscariot. Forty-four angel figures are carved into the arches directly over the entrance.

Head west on the South Rd. On the left is the **Bishop's Garden,** which has flowers, shrubs, and plants laid out according to medieval garden design. The **Shadow House** gazebo has benches. Visitors are welcome to eat lunch in the garden (beware of bees).

Continue west to the **Herb Cottage,** a gift shop specializing in herbs, potpourri, and decorative home and kitchen items. The building was originally intended as the cathedral's baptistry. Next to the Herb Cottage is Church House, formerly the bishop's home and now the offices of the Episcopal Diocese of Washington.

Turn north to the front of the building and face the **west façade.** Created by the last architect of the cathedral, Philip Hubert Frohman, the west façade is considered to be a masterpiece of Gothic design. The theme is the Creation. The west rose window depicts the creation of light; the carved tympanum shows the creation of man and woman—struggling half-formed figures reaching out from the void toward the warmth of the sun. Below this huge carving stands a statue of Adam. Both the tympanum and the trumeau statues (1982) are the work of sculptor Frederick E. Hart, who also carved the bronze sculpture of three soldiers at the Vietnam Memorial. Carvings above the north and south doors depict the creation of night and day. Statues in the trumeau niches are of St. Peter in the northwest entrance and of St. Paul in the south.

The massive bronze gates (1975) are the work of German sculptor Ulrich Henn and were cast in England. The north pair tells the story of Abraham and Isaac, and the two south gates depict three vignettes from the life of Moses. Surrounding these Old Testament figures are flowers and foliage from North and South America. Henn's gates are unusual because they are pierced, with figures and flowers visible from both sides, unlike most gates, which are solid and feature the sculpture only on one side. Enter through the plate glass doors into the narthex.

## Interior

**Narthex.** This porch, donated in memory of Jesse Ball duPont, features a mosaic floor of state seals, the seal of the District of Columbia, and the cathedral seal. In the center is the Great Seal of the United States. The flags down the center aisle represent the 50 states, territories, and the District of Columbia, and are placed in the order in which each entered the Union.

The stained glass windows—there are more than 200 in the cathedral—on the clerestory level represent teachings of the Old Testament up to the crossing, after which the windows depict New Testament stories. Windows in the middle level from the south side toward the west doors celebrate religious painters, including Rembrandt; musicians and painters such as Bach, Merbecke, and Vaughn Williams; artisans and craftsmen; scientists and technicians; and poets and writers such as Dante and John Milton. On the north side, the windows at the crossing from east to west feature Joan of Arc, labor and social reform, agriculture and maritime labor, a tribute to Air Force general Henry White, servants of God, Socrates and Christ in the Philosopher's Window, and the YWCA Window.

On the south end of the narthex is the **Rare Book Library.** Opened in 1965, the library's exhibit room is wood paneled with oak pilasters and beams. The focal point of the room is a limestone exhibit case carved with delicate finials and small faces. The **main exhibit room** contains the library's treasure: a first edition of the King James Bible printed in London in 1611. In addition to rare books, changing exhibits and collections are displayed here. Next to the main exhibit room is a Gothic cloister featuring carvings of medieval monks: a scholar reading, a manuscript reader, and a glassblower.

Begin the tour of the cathedral interior by going south from the center aisle to the Washington Bay.

**George Washington Bay.** The gray-toned, abstract stained glass window (1976) by Robert Pinart, depicts "Birth of a New Nation." To the right on the west wall is a white Vermont marble statue of George Washington (1947) designed by Lee Lawrie. The 7½ ft tall figure rests on a pedestal 2 ft high. The paneled alcove's carvings depict the life of the patriot. Over the entrance to the office door is a carving symbolizing Washington's life as a soldier and a farmer. There are depictions of the family's coat of arms and the façades of Washington's home, Mount Vernon, and Independence Hall in Philadelphia.

From the Washington Bay, walk east down the south aisle to the **Maryland Bay,** which has symbols of the state in its stone carvings and in the stained glass windows. Walk past the **Folger Bay,** whose windows portray the Lewis and Clark expedition; the **Glover Bay,** whose windows feature the National Cathedral founders, led by Charles C. Glover; and the **Warren Bay,** in memory of Charles Warren, an attorney and historian. Next is the Wilson Bay.

**Woodrow Wilson Bay.** Containing the tomb of the 28th president, Woodrow Wilson, this bay commemorates the life and times of this crusader for peace. When Wilson died in 1924 his body was buried in Bethlehem Chapel and moved here when the bay was completed in 1956. On the tomb itself rests a crusader's sword, in memory of his valiant fight for peace. Thistles at the cross-shaped hilt represent his Scottish heritage. On the face of the sarcophagus, toward the center aisle, are three seals: Princeton University, the state of New Jersey, and the United States. Wilson was president of Princeton and the U.S. and was a one-term governor of New Jersey. The walls bear inscriptions from Wilson's First Inaugural Address, his war message to Congress, his speech submitting the Versailles Peace Treaty to the Senate, and his last published words. The stained glass windows, by Ervin Bossanyi, symbolize war and peace as perceived within the Christian faith. Edith Bolling Galt Wilson died in 1961 and is buried in the crypt below the president's tomb.

Above the tomb is the window unofficially referred to as the **Space Window.** (The official name is the Scientists and Technicians Window.) Photographs taken during space travel inspired Rodney Winfield to create the dark spheres punctuated by tiny white stars and the thin white line of a spaceship trajectory. In the center of the large red sphere is a sliver of moon rock brought by the crew of *Apollo XI* at the time of the window's dedication in 1973.

Continue east on the south aisle past the **Lee-Jackson Bay,** memorializing two great Southern Civil War generals, Robert E. Lee and Thomas "Stonewall" Jackson. Continue past the wrought-iron gate at the the **Mellon Bay,** named for industrialist and philanthropist Andrew Mellon. To the right is the baptistry, whose massive font is carved from pink Tennessee marble. The needlepoint, windows, and stone carvings all depict symbols of baptism. Turn left and walk to the center aisle of the cathedral. Look to the west and the Creation Rose Window situated high on the west wall.

**The Creation Window.** (1976) Based on the verse in the Book of Genesis that contains "Let there be light," Rowan LeCompte's masterpiece is a ten-petal rose window with 10,500 pieces of colored glass. The window has been called the jewel of the cathedral.

Turn around and walk east back to the center directly at the bottom of the high altar stairs. The inlaid **Jerusalem Cross** is the cathedral's special symbol. The cross features the symbols of St. Peter (the keys of the kingdom) and St. Paul (book and sword). The official name of the cathedral is Cathedral Church of St. Peter and St. Paul.

**The crossing.** This is, in a sense, the center of the cathedral where the interior of the building is at its tallest. The four huge piers rise 98 ft—approximately ten stories—from this level. From their bases deep beneath the cathedral to their tops, each pier is 324 ft tall. Face west toward the Creation Window, turn right and look high on the north wall to the second rose window, **the Last Judgment Window** (1933). In the center of Lawrence B. Saint's window a life-size Christ holds the scales of justice and is seated on the throne of judgment. The fires of hell burn beneath him; the gates of heaven are above him.

Turn toward the south wall to the third rose window, **The Church Triumphant** (1962), by Joseph Reynolds and Wilbur Burnham. The imagery from the Book of Revelations embodies St. John's vision of the throne of God in heaven. In the center is God the Father surrounded by the 24 elders of the church.

Turn east toward the sanctuary. Placed at the top of the stairs is the rood screen. In the Middle Ages, cathedrals were places of commerce and culture as well as worship. To separate the more public or commercial part of the cathedral (nave) from the high altar, a screen was put up. The word *rood* is from the Old English word for wood. In Christian lore, the rood is the cross.

To the right of the chancel steps is the **Canterbury Pulpit,** from which the sermon is preached during services. The stone for the pulpit came from the bell tower of Canterbury Cathedral in England.

### Washington Notes

It was from this pulpit that Archbishop Desmond Tutu of South Africa addressed congregants, the Reverend Billy Graham preached, and in 1968, the Reverend Dr. Martin Luther King, Jr., delivered his final Sunday sermon before being assassinated three days later.

Carved in England, the figures depict the history of the English Bible. The pulpit stands ten ft high on its stone pillars. Three panels depict, from left to right, Venerable Bede, an 8C churchman, dictating from his deathbed a translation of the Gospel into Anglo-Saxon; the archbishop of Canterbury handing the Magna Carta to King John for his signature; and the martyrdom of William Tyndale, the first man to translate, print, and distribute the entire Bible in English. The lectern has carvings of Moses, King David, Elijah, St. Luke, St. Peter, St. Paul, and St. John the Divine.

Walk south to the first of five chapels on the nave level.

**War Memorial Chapel.** As the name suggests, this chapel is dedicated to the men and women who lost their lives in service to the U.S. during wartime. Many of the objects inside the chapel, such as the needlepoint kneelers, were given by the people of Great Britain to the people of the United States in gratitude for American aid during and after World War II. One of the kneelers originally here was made by Queen Mother Elizabeth and is now on display in the Rare Book Library. On the communion rail is a small carved statue of St. George, the patron saint of England. To the left of the altar a needlepoint hanging, the Tree of Life, features the seals of the 50 states surrounded by those of the five armed services. The seals from each side of the $1 bill are featured in the upper corners. Over the high altar is a sculpture of the suffering Christ (1968), designed by British artist Steven Sykes. The chapel windows (1949) portray themes of freedom and sacrifice, including the supreme sacrifice of Christ upon the cross, as well as sacrifice made in war. The windows were created by Reynolds, Francis, and Rohnstock of Boston. To the left in the War Memorial Chapel is a statue of the Christ child (1934) by Mary Aldrich Fraser. Christ is holding out his hands in welcome to the Children's Chapel.

**Children's Chapel.** With arms open wide, Christ seems to be inviting children into their own special church. The windows (1936), by Henry Willett, tell stories of the child Samuel and the boy David. There is a depiction of Jesus saying, "Suffer the little children unto me." The small figures above the panels are of St. Peter and St. Paul. In the center of the altar screen is Christ with St. Mary and St. John. The needlepoint kneelers feature baby animals and the wrought-iron gates (1935; Samuel Yellin) show off fantastic birds, bugs, and other creatures.

Exit the Children's Chapel into **St. John's Chapel,** donated by the parents of Norman Prince to honor his memory. Prince was an American pilot who founded the Escadrille Americaine (the Lafayette Escadrille) in World War I. Walk east toward the altar. Notice the red needlepoint history kneelers on the chairs; each features symbols from the life of a famous American. High on the south wall are windows that illustrate the miracle of Christ in 28 medallions, created by Lawrence Saint. The statue and tomb of Norman Prince (1936) are by Paul Landowski. At the base of the reredos, which was carved in place and took two years to complete, is Jesus seated next to St. John during the Last Supper. Above this scene is Christ on the cross flanked by St. John and St. Mary. From St. John's Chapel, walk up the stairs to the high altar.

**The chancel and sanctuary.** The rail separating the chancel from the sanctuary is called the communion rail. Carved into it are 11 male figures representing the apostles—one wooden block at the north end of the railing has been left blank to symbolize the unfinished character of Judas Iscariot.

The main altar is called the **Jerusalem Altar** because it is made up of stones from quarries outside Jerusalem. Ten small stones from the Chapel of Moses on Mt. Sinai represent the Ten Commandments and are set into the flooring in front of the altar. These stones are covered by a needlepoint rug made by Episcopal and Presbyterian women from Pennsylvania. The altar cross, nearly six ft high, is made of wood, brass, and crystal.

Over the altar is the Ter Sanctus ("thrice holy") reredos, featuring Christ in Majesty surrounded by 110 people who lived exemplary lives. These are the prophets of the Old Testament and Christian saints from every age. On each side of the center panel, three carvings represent quotations from the 25th chapter of St. Matthew: "For I was hungry and ye gave me meat; I was thirsty and ye gave me drink; I was a stranger and ye took me in; naked, and ye clothed me; I was sick and ye visited me; I was in prison and ye came unto me."

To the left is the **Glastonbury Cathedra,** a massive stone chair made from stone from Glastonbury Abbey in England. *Cathedra* means "Bishop's chair" and is the word from which *cathedral,* "the place of the bishop," is derived. The inscription on the cathedra represents the guiding principles for Christian unity, according to the Episcopal Church: "Holy Scripture and Apostolic Creed + Holy Sacrament + Apostolic Order."

Looking west toward the rood screen one can see the choir area with its oak choir stalls. The seats of the stalls feature needlepoint kneelers embroidered with the seals of all the dioceses and missionary districts of the Episcopal Church. On the left side of the choir is the **Great Organ,** which has 10,651 pipes. The smallest pipe is 3 inches long and the longest is about 32 ft long.

**St. Mary's Chapel.** Exit the chancel to the left and take three steps down to the chapel memorializing the life of the mother of Jesus. The events of Mary's life are carved on the linden wood reredos, which is painted gold with highlights of blue and rose, St. Mary's colors. In the two center scenes Mary holds out the young savior, presenting him to the world, and she also stands in grief at the foot of the cross. The stained glass windows are known as the **Parable Windows** since each portrays a parable of Jesus. Larz Anderson III, a former ambassador to Japan, and his wife are interred in the tomb at the north wall. Ambassador Anderson donated the 16C Flemish tapestries depicting the biblical story of David and Goliath. The Andersons are also known for their residence at Dupont Circle, the Anderson House.

**Holy Spirit Chapel.** Exit St. Mary's Chapel. To the right is Holy Spirit Chapel. Named for the Holy Ghost, much of the chapel's ornamentation features the dove, a symbol for the Holy Spirit. Noted painter N. C. Wyeth worked on the oak-paneled reredos (1936) displaying Jesus, angels praising the Lord in song, and seven small doves symbolizing the sections of the confirmation prayer. This chapel is closed to tour groups but remains open to those wishing private reflection.

Walk west down the north outer aisle to the **Kellogg Bay,** which honors the diplomat and statesman Frank Kellogg. The windows (1949; Reynolds, Francis and Rohnstock) reflect Kellogg's desire for peace. On the east wall is a statue of Dr. Martin Luther King, Jr., preaching his last Sunday sermon, given at the cathedral in 1968. Next is the **Humanitarian Bay,** honoring servants of mankind such as George Washington Carver and Albert Schweitzer. Continue west. The **Henry White Bay** memorializes the former member of the 1918 Peace Commission. The windows (1954; Henry Lee Willett) have symbols of the League of Nations and the United Nations.

The **Bettelheim Bay** is named for Edwin Sumner Bettelheim, noted author and soldier. The windows (by Rowan and Irene LeCompte) celebrate "America the Beautiful." West of this is the **National Cathedral Association (NCA) Bay,** honoring NCA members from all parts of the U.S. The windows (1963; Ervin Bossanyi) feature Christian women as lifegivers, healers, and teachers. The **Dulin Bay** windows (1970; Albert Birkle) portray the words of the 23rd Psalm. The **Frohman Bay** honors the primary architect of the cathedral, Philip Hubert Frohman. Near the west end of the north aisle is a memorial to the 16th president, Abraham Lincoln.

**Abraham Lincoln Bay.** This bay was donated by Lincoln's granddaughter and his great-grandson. The poignant bronze sculpture, by Walker Hancock, shows the young Lincoln as he was leaving Illinois on his way to Washington and the presidency. In the floor in front of Lincoln is a seal made of Lincoln-head copper pennies. To the right, clasped hands symbolizing peace between the North and the South after the Civil War are carved into the tympanum over the north door. Below this carving are words from Lincoln's Second Inaugural Address: "With malice toward none."

Exit the north aisle by the west doors and turn left. Continue walking south through the narthex to the **Churchill Porch,** which honors the English politician and statesman. From here take an elevator to the **Pilgrim Observation Gallery** to enjoy the spectacular views of Washington and the cathedral's flying buttresses. When exiting the elevator, take a left and then a right down the steps leading into the **Museum Store,** which sells guidebooks, postcards, religious books, art, and sculpture, as well as snacks. Walk east through the shop and descend a flight of stairs to the **Visitors' Lounge** on the right. Volunteers can answer questions and visitors can sign the visitors' book and review the posted schedule of events. Turn around and walk east. The three chapels on this (crypt) level of the cathedral tell the story of the three chapters of Jesus' life: his birth, death, and resurrection. On the left is a chapel dedicated to the story of Jesus' death and burial.

**The Chapel of St. Joseph of Arimathea.** One descends into this space as if going into a tomb. Located directly below the crossing and formed by the four piers supporting the central tower, this chapel is in the shape of a Greek cross. The chapel is named for the man who gave up his tomb for the crucified Christ. Legend has it that he was the first missionary to England and that he founded Glastonbury Chapel in England, the site from which the stone for the cathedral's cathedra came. The mural (1939; Jan Henrik de Rosen) describes the crucifixion. Beginning in the upper left corner are the empty crosses of Calvary. Below them are St. John and St. Mary—her grief symbolized by the sword in her heart. At her feet is the sorrowful Mary Magdalene. Christ dominates the center of the mural, and behind him stands an angel with feet of fire. Leading the way into the tomb is Nicodemus, followed by St. Joseph of Arimathea holding the golden chalice, or Holy Grail. The right foreground portrays a Roman soldier. At the back of the chapel, behind the wrought-iron gates, is the cathedral's columbarium. On a pillar to the left of the gates, designated by a plaque both in English and in Braille, are the ashes of Helen Keller. Approximately 180 people are buried in the National Cathedral, most of them in the columbarium.

Exit the chapel by going up the south stairs and turn right to the **Resurrection Chapel.** This Norman chapel is in memory of the second bishop of Washington, Alfred Harding. Bishop Harding, his wife, and his son are buried in the tomb at the southwest corner of the chapel. Designed by W. Douglas Caroe, the tomb is an example of early Celtic design. A mosaic (1951; Hildreth Meiere) depicting the Resurrection is located above the altar. The risen Christ bears in his hand the cross and banner of victory. At the right are two sleeping soldiers; at the left, an angel kneels in front of an empty open tomb. A brilliant sun rises against a vibrant blue sky. On the walls a series of mosaics (1964; Rowan and Irene LeCompte) portray the appearances of Christ after his resurrection. The baptismal font was designed by cathedral architect Philip Hubert Frohman and was carved by Edward Ratti, who was later baptized using it.

Leave the chapel, turn right, and walk east to the **Bethlehem Chapel.** Dedicated to the birth of Jesus, this small chapel was for many years the only completed portion of Washington National Cathedral. The foundation stone was laid under the high altar in Sept 1907. In the niches on the south wall are carved figures of King David with his harp and Ruth with a sheaf of wheat. The Indiana limestone reredos depicts the birth of Christ. Surrounding the stable tableau are the four authors of the Gospels: Matthew, Mark, Luke, and John. The chapel is dedicated to the first bishop of Washington, Henry Yates Satterlee. He and his wife are buried in a vault behind the altar. Over the vault is an alabaster tomb bearing a likeness of the bishop. The windows in the chapel (by John Lisle) grace the ambulatory behind the altar, telling the story of the birth of Jesus with great care and detail. They were made in England in 1912.

Continue west to the **Chapel of the Good Shepherd,** a tiny bay reserved for private prayer. The statue of Christ the good shepherd (1976) was carved from pink granite by Walker Hancock. Good Shepherd Chapel is directly beside the exit to the north porch of the cathedral.

To continue to the next walk, take any of the 30s buses on Wisconsin Ave to Wisconsin Ave and Albemarle St and the Tenleytown–AU Metro station. From here take the Red Line to the Woodley Park–Zoo Metro station.

# 22 · Woodley Park, National Zoo, and Cleveland Park

Metro: Red Line to Woodley Park–Zoo.
Bus: L2, 92, or 96.

Woodley Park and Cleveland Park are residential neighborhoods that stretch along Connecticut Ave for nearly one and a half miles, from Rock Creek Park on the south and east to as far west as Wisconsin Ave at Cleveland Park's northwestern boundary. The National Zoological Park, located off Connecticut Ave in adjacent Rock Creek Park, is just south of the boundary between the two neighborhoods. Woodley Park is to the south of the zoo and Cleveland Park is to the north. As their names suggest, these areas were first known for their sylvan setting, their woods and elevation offering cooler and healthier air than the heart of the Federal City.

At the beginning of the 19C the neighborhoods and the zoo were Washington County farmland, but by the century's end these areas had become part of the District of Columbia. Woodley Park takes its name from Woodley Oaks, a former country estate; Cleveland Park is named in honor of President Grover Cleveland, who had a summer home here. In the 20C the neighborhood burgeoned. Electric streetcars on Connecticut Ave brought people to the area and made commuting to downtown easy. Developers built houses and large apartment buildings to serve the growing federal work force, and merchants established businesses. Today Woodley Park and Cleveland Park retain much of their early character and original architecture.

**Highlights:** The National Zoological Park; Hillwood Museum and Gardens, which has Russian icons, china, and objects designed by Carl Fabergé; many Art Deco–inspired buildings.

### History

In 1830 English author Frances Trollope described the area now encompassing Woodley Park and Cleveland Park as "a beautiful line of hills behind Washington, which form a sort of undulating terrace on to Georgetown; this terrace is almost entirely occupied by a succession of Gentlemen's Seats." The area's first documented resident was General Uriah Forrest, a Revolutionary War veteran, shipping merchant, Georgetown mayor, Continental Congress delegate, and friend of George Washington and Pierre L'Enfant. In 1792, Forrest and two partners purchased the area, which was then part of rural Maryland, and named it Pretty Prospects. By 1794, Forrest and his family had built Rosedale, their farmhouse. For the Forrests, Rosedale and its woods were a respite from their house in the busy port of Georgetown.

During the first part of the 19C Pretty Prospects was subdivided, and other men of distinction built houses. Uriah Forrest's brother-in-law, Philip Barton Key, an attorney, congressman, United States Circuit Court chief justice, and son of Francis Scott Key, purchased land and built Woodley, a Georgian country mansion. Key and his family lived here from 1806 until his death in 1817, when Key's wife moved to Georgetown.

1 Omni Shoreham Hotel
2 Taft Bridge
3 Duke Ellington Memorial Bridge
4 Woodley Park Business District
5 2606 Connecticut Ave N.W.
6 2602 Connecticut Ave N.W.
7 Wardman Tower (Marriot Wardman
   Park Hotel)
8 2800 Woodley Rd N.W.
9 Swiss Embassy
10 Woodley (Maret School)
11 Cathedral Mansions
12 2929 Connecticut Ave N.W.
13 National Zoological Park
14 The Kennedy-Warren
15 Klingle Valley Bridge

16 Newark St
17 Rosedale
18 Cleveland Park Business District
19 Uptown Theater
20 Park and Shop
21 Cleveland Park Fire House
22 Yenching Palace
23 Adas Israel Congregation
24 Broadmoor
25 Sedgwick Gardens
26 Tilden Gardens
27 Hillwood Museum and Gardens
28 Howard University School of Law
29 Edmund Burke School
30 Intelsat Building
31 University of the District of Columbia

### Washington Notes

Several presidents, including Martin Van Buren, James Buchanan, and Grover Cleveland, used Woodley as a summer house while they were in office. The former site of Woodley is now the Maret School.

Forrest Hill, built in 1869 by George Forrest Green, the grandson of Uriah Forrest, began as a simple oblong farmhouse built of stone. In 1885, after President Grover Cleveland married the stylish Frances Folsom, he purchased the house during his first term in office to use as a summer residence. Cleveland renamed the house Oak View and had it remodeled by architect William M. Poindexter to reflect Victorian taste. Poindexter added wooden double-tiered porches, fanciful trim, turrets, and a red-painted roof that led to the house's popular name, Red Top. When Cleveland lost his bid for reelection, he sold Oak View. Located between today's Newark St and Woodley Rd, the house fell into disrepair and was razed in 1927, but the Cleveland Park neighborhood retains the name of the president who lived there.

Twin Oaks is the only remaining original summer home in the area. Built in 1888 by Gardiner Green Hubbard, a lawyer and founder of the National Geographic Society, the house served as a hilltop retreat from his Dupont Circle town house. The colonial Georgian revival–style edifice was a gathering place for Hubbard's entire family, including his son-in-law Alexander Graham Bell. Bell had been a teacher of Hubbard's daughter, who was deaf, and had married prior to his inventing the telephone and establishing the first telephone company, which was financed by Hubbard. Secluded from street view, Twin Oaks at 3225 Woodley Lane, is now owned by the Taipei Economic and Cultural Representative Office in the United States.

In the late 19C the region of estates underwent many changes. The post–Civil War building boom encouraged development outside of the original bounds of L'Enfant's city. In 1890 Congress established Rock Creek Park and the National Zoological Park, and by 1892 bridges had been built over Rock Creek at Calvert St and over the Klingle Valley and the electric streetcar lines running on Connecticut Ave. The Highways Acts of 1893 and 1898 extended the city to include Woodley and Cleveland Parks. Developers pitched upper Connecticut Ave as a suburb within easy reach of downtown by streetcar but, as one real estate agent stated, "free from the annoyances of the city as if it were in the heart of the Adirondacks." Easy access to downtown jobs brought quick development to the area.

In 1895 the Cleveland Park Company began building houses on Newark St. Each house was individually designed by a leading architect until 1909, when Ella Bennett Sherman, a New York–trained artist and wife of Cleveland Park Company president John Sherman, took over. The developers also built a heated stone lodge as a community center and place to wait for the streetcar, a fire station that doubled as a police station, and a stable for common use. These have all been razed. Cleveland Park was a success. The houses, expensive for their era, attracted professionals, business leaders, and many scientists from the National Bureau of Standards and the U.S. Geological Survey, which were located at the time just north of Cleveland Park.

Woodley Park began around 1905 with the construction of row houses as well as some single-family homes. Built by several architects and developers, the houses, modeled after English town house neighborhoods, were more affordable than those in Cleveland Park. Developers promoted the neighborhood as being within easy reach of Rock Creek Park and the Million Dollar Bridge (the Taft Bridge), which opened in 1907.

Both neighborhoods grew rapidly in the first decades of the 20C. With the influx of government workers, particularly during World War I, there was a demand for housing, and several glamorous apartment buildings were constructed. Owners of single-family homes, however, raised concerns about rising noise and traffic. In the 1920s zoning regulations were passed restricting construction of apartment houses to Connecticut Ave and allowing commercial establishments only in several stretches along Connecticut Ave. Connecticut Ave became one of the most fashionable apartment house corridors in the District of Columbia. Many of the buildings had doormen, dining rooms, ballrooms, elevators, and beauty parlors.

Except for a short hiatus during the worst years of the Depression, apartment houses and businesses proliferated along Connecticut Ave during the 1930s and 1940s. The demand for apartments continued to grow as an influx of workers arrived in Washington to staff new federal agencies. Several of these buildings, constructed in the Art Deco style, survive today, albeit in a somewhat less grand fashion.

The growing popularity of the automobile also affected this area. In 1930, one of the first planned shopping complexes in the nation, the Park and Shop, opened at the corner of Connecticut Ave and Ordway, featuring off-street parking for several stores.

Following World War II, many politically savvy newcomers to the neighborhoods joined with longtime residents to discourage the destruction of old houses and their replacement with new developments, a trend that continued into the 1980s. In the late 1980s, sections of the neighborhoods were declared historic districts and placed on the National Register of Historic Places. As a result, Woodley Park and Cleveland Park retain much of their original charm.

## Omni Shoreham Hotel

From the Woodley Park–Zoo Metro station, walk a half-block south on Connecticut Ave to Calvert St, then a half-block west on Calvert St to 24th St and the Omni Shoreham Hotel (1930; Joseph Abel; 1935 addition, Dillon and Abel), 2500 Calvert St N.W., ☎ 234-0700.

Built to rival the Wardman Park Hotel one block to the north, the Omni Shoreham is an Art Deco–style building with a jaunty combination of buff-colored brick, round bays, horizontal lines and a general lack of fussiness.

### History

When it first opened, the Shoreham consisted of apartments and hotel rooms and featured such modern amenities as public dining rooms, a glassed-in swimming pool, a ballroom replicating the design of the Oval Office, a terrace overlooking Rock Creek Park, a basement garage, push-button elevators, a nightclub, and an outdoor course for the newly popular sport of miniature golf.

The hotel was immediately successful, drawing many famous guests such as Gary Cooper, Marlene Dietrich, Henry Ford, and Marilyn Monroe, as well as several U.S. presidents. The Blue Room, the Shoreham's nightclub, was rated among the city's best. Bing Crosby and Frank Sinatra performed at the Blue Room. John

F. Kennedy took Jacqueline Bouvier here during their courtship. By the mid-1950s the apartments had been converted to hotel rooms and many of the original residents had moved to the Shoreham's rival, the Wardman Park. Currently, the hotel is owned and operated by the Omni chain. In 1998–99 the Omni Shoreham underwent an elaborate restoration.

> ### Washington Notes
> The Shoreham debuted with a gala on Halloween night, 1930. Headliner Rudy Vallee was paid $9,000 to cancel a New York appearance to perform at the opening. Vallee and his band, the Connecticut Yankees, headed for Washington on a chartered airplane, but bad weather caused delays. The waiting crowd drank bootleg liquor and received updates from aviator Amelia Earhart, a Shoreham guest. By the time Vallee arrived it was nearly 4:15 A.M. He was only able to perform for about 15 minutes before having to head back to New York by train. Nonetheless, the crowd was pleased and the Shoreham received the publicity it sought.

## Taft Bridge

Walk one block east on Calvert St. To the south on Connecticut Ave is the Taft Bridge (1907; Edward P. Casey). Stretching across the Rock Creek Valley to connect Woodley Park to the neighborhoods of Sheridan-Kalorama and Kalorama Triangle, this bridge was the first to provide access to lower Connecticut Ave for the first time, spurring development along upper Connecticut Ave. When erected, the Taft Bridge was one of the first and largest precast concrete bridges in the world. On each end of the bridge are pairs of **lions** (1906; Roland Hinton Perry), each 12 ft long. (Perry is also known for the Court of Neptune Fountain outside the Jefferson Building of the Library Congress.) Made of precast concrete, a material that has proved not particularly suitable for such use, the lions have required much repair over the years.

The ten-ft-tall iron **eagle lampposts** lining both sides of the bridge were designed in 1906 by Ernest C. Bairstow, a sculptor who specialized in architectural decorations. Originally known as the Million Dollar Bridge, this bridge's name was changed in 1931 to honor William Howard Taft, former U.S. president and chief justice of the Supreme Court.

Walk one block east on Calvert St to the **Duke Ellington Memorial Bridge** (1935; Paul C. Cret). Originally known as the Calvert St Bridge and renamed for the jazz musician and Washington native in the 1980s, this bridge replaced an outdated truss bridge that had stood at this location since 1891. The Ellington Bridge, designed not to overpower the Taft Bridge, features fewer decorative elements. The limestone panels' four low-relief works are *Modes of Travel* (1935; Leon Hermant). Each one depicts a neoclassical figure with either a locomotive, plane, ship, or automobile.

From the intersection of Connecticut Ave and Calvert St, turn north. The 2600 block of Connecticut Ave is part of the **Woodley Park Business District.** The majority of these commercial buildings were built in the 1920s and 1930s as modest structures with limestone façades, parapet roofs, and classical details such as floral medallions. The building at **2606 Connecticut Ave N.W.** (1921; architect unknown), a narrow one-story brick structure with finials topping its parapet roof, was the first commercial structure built in the Woodley Park Business District. Currently, the restaurant Jandara occupies the structure, which has been sightly altered and, unfortunately, painted purple. Other buildings, such as 2602 Connecticut Ave N.W., now Salon Roi, were residences before being converted for retail use.

### Washington Notes

The mural of Marilyn Monroe (1981; John Bailey) painted on the side of 2602 Connecticut Ave N.W. (and visible from the intersection of Connecticut and Calvert) was a 40th birthday gift from Charles Stinson to Roi Bernard, a Marilyn Monroe memorabilia collector and the proprietor of Salon Roi.

## Wardman Tower

Continue two blocks north on Connecticut Ave to Woodley Rd. On the southwest corner is the Wardman Tower (1928; Mihran Mesrobian), 2660 Woodley Rd N.W., once a residential apartment wing adjacent to the largest and grandest apartment-hotel in the District of Columbia, the now-demolished Wardman Park Hotel (1918; Frank R. White). It was the success of Wardman Park that prompted the building of the Shoreham Hotel. Both buildings were modeled after a country resort. The Georgian revival–style Wardman Tower combines red brick, limestone trim, projecting bays, Palladian windows, and chimneys, all set off by white woodwork. Previously known as the Annex, Eastern Wing, and the Congressional Wing, the Wardman Tower was renamed in 1878 in honor of its developer, Harry Wardman. The Wardman Tower was famous as the home of many high-ranking government officials; it was said to have housed more presidents, vice presidents, and cabinet members than any other apartment house in the District. Notable residents have included presidents Dwight Eisenhower, Herbert Hoover, and Lyndon Johnson, as well as Clare Boothe Luce, Adlai Stevenson, and Supreme Court chief justice Earl Warren. Beginning in 1973 the apartments were converted into hotel rooms. Currently, the Wardman is part of the large Marriott Wardman Park Hotel complex that includes a modern structure (1980; Hellmuth, Obata, Kassabaum) built on the site of the original Wardman Park Hotel. The long corridor lined with Palladian windows once connected the Wardman Tower to the Wardman Park Hotel.

### History

When built by developer Harry Wardman in 1918, the Wardman Park Hotel was the largest apartment-hotel in the city. Called Wardman's Folly because of its remoteness from the center of Washington, the hotel, offering apartments as well as hotel rooms, was surrounded by parklike grounds. With such luxuries as a dining room, tea room, billiard parlor, roof garden, Turkish bath, and a grocery store, the hotel flourished and led to construction of the Wardman Tower. The success boosted Wardman's career, and he became one of Washington's most prolific developers. Wardman, who immigrated to the United States from England at age 17 and got his start working as a carpenter, built approximately 400 apartment buildings, 2 embassies, 4,000 houses, 12 office buildings, 8 hotels, 2 clubs, and 2 hospital buildings in the first decades of the 20C before his death in 1938.

### Washington Notes

Prominent Washington hostess Perle Shirvin Mesta lived at the Wardman Tower. Born into an Oklahoma family in the real estate, oil, and hotel businesses, Perle Shirvin married Pittsburgh industrialist George Mesta and moved to Washington in the 1920s. Mesta's specialty was giving lively parties, but she also ran her husband's business after his death, became an important Democratic fund-raiser, and befriended many members of Congress before being appointed the first U.S. minister to Luxembourg in 1949. She was also the basis for Sally Adams, the main character in Irving Berlin's Broadway musical *Call Me Madam*. Adams, played by Ethel Merman in the play's 1950 opening, was a party-loving Washington hostess who held ambassadorial duties in a small European duchy.

Turn left on Woodley Rd and walk three blocks west. At the southwest corner of Woodley Rd and 29th St is the apartment house at **2800 Woodley Rd N.W.** (1941; George T. Santmyers). The building is a prime example of streamlined Art Deco style. The façade employs horizontal rows of metal-framed windows, zigzag spandrels, and buff-colored brick. The building retains many features of its original lobby, including the curvilinear wood-veneered pillars, mirrored surfaces, and recessed lighting.

Walk one block north on 29th St. At the southwest corner of 29th St and Cathedral Ave is the **Swiss Embassy** (1959; William Lescaze), 2900 Cathedral Ave N.W. The Swiss Lescaze was one of the first architects to bring European modernism to the United States. This austere-looking building has exposed skeletal elements and sweeping glass walls. The sculpture in front of the embassy is *Eurythmie* (1955; André Ramseyer).

Walk one block west on Cathedral Ave. At 3000 Cathedral Ave N.W. is **Woodley** (1806; Philip Barton Key, owner-builder; 1952 adaptation, architect unknown), the Georgian manor house built by Philip Barton Key, an attorney, congressman, United States Circuit Court chief justice, and son of Francis Scott Key. The house, which is not open to the public, has a large central structure, classic porticoes at the front and rear, arched windows, and fanlight doorways. The sections of Woodley that still exist have become part of the administration building of the Maret School. Constructed on land purchased from Key's brother-in-law Uriah Forrest, Woodley was one of the earliest houses in the area. Several presidents used Woodley as a summer home while they were in office, including Martin Van Buren, James Buchanan, and Grover Cleveland. The neighborhood of Woodley Park takes its name from this estate.

Return three blocks east on Cathedral Ave. At the northwest corner of Cathedral and Connecticut Aves is **Cathedral Mansions** (1924; Wardman and Wagaman), 2900 Connecticut Ave N.W., a series of buildings that continues along Connecticut Ave to Devonshire Place. Built on a tract of land once considered for the National Cathedral, the complex includes three separate and similarly designed Georgian revival–style brick buildings, with pedimented dormers, quoin-block corners, and limestone trim. When completed in 1924, at a cost of $4 million, Cathedral Mansions was considered the largest apartment house complex south of New York. The middle building, where the Zoo Market and Zoo Bar are now located, originally contained services such as a drugstore, delicatessen, and pastry shop. The northernmost building, painted beige, is now a condominium.

Walk north on Connecticut Ave. The apartment house at **2929 Connecticut Ave N.W.** (1936; Joseph Abel) with its angular lines is an example of Art Deco influenced by the international style. The intact original lobby has a nautical theme and rounded pillars, indirect lighting, and shiny metal rails and trim.

Continue one and a half blocks north on Connecticut Ave to the entrance to the National Zoological Park.

## National Zoological Park

3001 Connecticut Ave N.W. ☎ 673-4800; 673-4717. Web: www.si.edu/natzoo. Open daily; May 1–Sept 15 grounds open 6 A.M.–8 P.M., animal buildings open 10–6; Sept 16–April 30 grounds open 6–6, animal buildings open 10–4:30. Closed Dec 25. Admission: free. Weekend guided tours available by advance reservation. ☎ 673-4955. Wheelchairs available. Restrooms, telephones, ATM, restaurants, bookstore, gift shop. Stroller rental available. Limited parking available, at hourly rate.

Encompassing 163 acres abutting Rock Creek Park, the National Zoological Park, part of the Smithsonian Institution, is today one of the most highly regarded zoos in the world. Consistently a popular destination since its opening in 1891, the zoo has evolved from a menagerie nestled amid picturesque woodlands to a leading research center conducting pioneering programs in the areas of wildlife preservation, breeding, genetics, animal behavior, veterinary medicine, nutrition, and ecology. The modern National Zoological Park stresses that it is a biological park whose goal is to present the complex relationship among all living things. The National Zoo also maintains a 3,200-acre conservation research center, closed to the public, in nearby Front Royal, Virginia.

Two paths slope downhill from Connecticut Ave to Lion/Tiger Hill. Olmsted Walk, the zoo's main path, winds past all the indoor exhibits except the Bird House and Amazonia. The Valley Trail is steeper than Olmsted Walk and includes the major aquatic exhibits plus Birds and Amazonia. Wheelchair users should be cautious on the Valley Trail.

**Highlights:** For many years the zoo's most popular attraction was Hsing-Hsing, the last of the two giant pandas given to the United States by the People's Republic of China in 1972. The 28-year-old Hsing-Hsing was euthanized on Nov 28, 1999; he had been suffering from progressive kidney failure and arthritis associated with old age. The Komodo dragons, the world's largest lizards, are also popular, as are Amazonia, a simulated rain forest, and the Think Tank, which examines animal intelligence. Those interested in Public Works Administration art should visit the Elephant House and the Reptile House. The zoo is also a great place for children to learn about other species. Check with the Visitor Center for the times of daily feedings and demonstrations. The Amazonia Science Gallery has interactive displays geared for ages 4–12.

### History

Although there were no plans for a zoo when the Smithsonian Institution was established in 1846, the National Zoological Park became an important part of the Smithsonian. In the late 19C, interest in establishing the zoo was initiated by William Hornaday, the chief taxidermist at the U.S. National Museum, now the Museum of Natural History. Hornaday was responsible for creating lifelike mounted (stuffed) pieces for the museum's animal exhibit. He kept a small number of live specimens for study. In 1887, after a trip to the quickly disappearing western frontier, Hornaday organized his live specimens into a trial zoo he called the Department of Living Animals. He exhibited several bison, an eagle, a bear, and a badger on the Mall behind the Smithsonian Castle. Hornaday, who wanted to create a national preserve for all disappearing North American animals, led the Smithsonian efforts to establish a zoo as "a home and a city refuge for the vanishing races of the continent." This concept of a zoo with a scientific purpose was novel. Most zoos of that era presented animals for public exhibition; circuses presented animals as performers. The trial zoo proved popular. On March 2, 1889, President Cleveland signed a bill into law establishing the National Zoological Park to be built on lands purchased by federal funds. The Smithsonian Institution was to run the zoo, but it was to be financed by both the federal and District of Columbia governments.

Wooded Rock Creek Valley was chosen as the site, and noted landscape architect Frederick Law Olmsted was consulted on the zoo's layout. When the directors of the project abandoned their original concept of a scientific refuge for the popular concept of exhibiting animals, Hornaday resigned. William Blackburne, who had been a cat handler for the Barnum & Bailey Circus, was hired as head keeper. From the time he accepted his job, Blackburne never took a day off until his retirement; he is widely credited with holding the zoo together in its early years.

In 1890 the animals housed on the Mall had been transported to the zoo in borrowed circus wagons. On April 30, 1891, the National Zoological Park opened. Three structures were built to house animals, including a stone Carnivora House (1891; William R. Emerson), a log cabin–like Buffalo House (1891; William R. Emerson), and an octagonal Elephant Barn (1891; Glenn Brown), all now razed. Initially there were no funds for animal acquisitions. As a result of donations the zoo obtained two of their finest early animals, Dunk and Golddust, Indian elephants given by James E. Cooper, proprietor of the Adam Forepaugh Circus. Alexander Graham Bell donated mandarin ducks and President Grover Cleveland donated a golden eagle that had been bestowed on the nation, as well as many dogs. In 1893, the zoo also set up a short-lived arrangement with the Forepaugh Circus. The zoo would house the circus animals over the winters and in return would keep any live births. By 1895, the National Zoo was permanent home to 520 species and continuing to expand. In 1902, a 150 ft long Great Flight Cage, designed by Glenn Brown, was built, followed two years later by the Small Mammal House, designed by Hornblower & Marshall. The Great Flight Cage was later razed, but the Small Mammal House still exists; it currently contains the zoo's Think Tank exhibit.

In 1915 Soko, the largest chimpanzee in captivity, was obtained, and in 1928, N'Gi, the first gorilla, began a reign as the most popular animal in zoo history, surpassed only by the giant pandas that arrived in the 1970s. In 1925 the zoo's superintendent, William Mann, persuaded several business leaders to finance collecting expeditions. Walter Chrysler subsidized a six-month collecting expedition to present-day Tanzania that yielded more than 1,000 animals, the National Geographic Society underwrote a 1937 trip to the Dutch East Indies, and Harvey Firestone, Jr., funded a 1940 expedition to Liberia.

As a result of the New Deal's Public Works Administration funding, several structures were built, including the Bird House (which is still in use), the Reptile House (also still in use), and the Pachyderm House (now the Elephant House), as well as several smaller buildings. Funds from the Public Works of Art Project and Treasury Relief Art Project financed artists who created elaborate carvings on the Reptile and Pachyderm Houses as well as zoo sculptures.

The short-lived prosperity of the zoo ended with World War II. During the war years international expeditions were halted. Venomous snakes were moved to midwestern zoos less vulnerable to bomb attack. Local grocery stores donated food unfit for human consumption to help alleviate animal food shortages. After the war, despite the worsening of the zoo's physical plant, the zoo's programs moved toward conservation, research, and education. In 1958 two zoologists invented the Cap-Chur gun, used to immobilize animals with tranquilizing darts, paving the way for more convenient interzoo animal breeding loans. Also in 1958, zoo neighbors, members of the Cleveland Park Citizens Association, founded Friends of the National Zoo (FONZ) to support zoo programs. Today FONZ operates the zoo's concessions, using profits for research and education programs.

In the 1960s the zoo became more of a scientific park. By the end of the decade, all zoo expenses had became part of the Smithsonian Institution budget, increased funding had been obtained, and new exhibits were designed with fewer visual barriers and more attention to the animal's natural habitats. Zoo programs expanded into animal breeding, reproductive biology, animal behavior, exotic animal medicine, nutrition, and ecology. In 1974 the zoo opened a 3,200-acre Conservation Research Center in nearby Front Royal, Virginia, where animals roaming freely in more natural conditions were more likely to breed, realizing for the first time Hornaday's dream of the zoo as an animal preserve. The National Zoo is active in animal preservation programs, including reintroducing captivity-bred animals into their native habitat, and loaning animals for breeding purposes as part of the Species Survival Plans.

In the 1980s and 1990s the zoo became more of a biological park, presenting ecosystems and the complex relationships between all living things. According to Zoo Director Michael Robinson, the zoo is "determined to put life back together" and "pay tribute to the long interaction between our own species, humankind, and the rest of the living world that is reflected in the arts and much of our culture."

### Washington Notes

In his quest for zoo funds Superintendent William Mann often had to be creative. At a 1926 Smithsonian conference attended by the U.S. director of the budget, Mann set up a small exhibit of zoo animals that included a mynah bird. When the budget director walked by, the bird asked, "How about the appropriation?" When the director said "That's impertinent!" the bird replied, "So's your old man." Even though Mann claimed not to know how the bird learned such language, the zoo received $40,000 more than what was expected that year.

## Grounds

Enter the zoo grounds from Connecticut Ave. The Visitor Center, where wheelchairs can be obtained, is the first building on the left. From there, follow the path of **Olmsted Walk** through the zoo. The first exhibit along this route is the Cheetah Conservation Station, a simulation of African plains and home to the fastest land mammals. Zebras are housed in an adjacent area. Next along the path is the former Panda Pavilion. It is currently closed. The **American Prairie** exhibit, in an adjoining area, features bison, prairie dogs, and prairie ecosystems.

Continue along Olmsted Walk to the **Elephant House** (1938; Edwin Clark), home to the largest land mammals. Originally known as the Pachyderm House, this building was constructed with Works Progress Administration monies provided under the New Deal. The demilune limestone bas-relief panels above the outside doors depict groups of prehistoric ancestors of modern elephants. Charles Knight, a noted author and lecturer, designed the panels and Erwin Frederich Springweiler sculpted them. Knight also designed the floor's colorful mosaic medallions depicting modern mammals. Along with elephants, the structure houses giraffes, the tallest mammals, as well as hippos and rhinos.

Exit the Elephant House and continue ahead to the Bactrian Camels and beyond that to the **American Indian Heritage Garden,** an exhibit describing how Native Americans have used plants as both food and medicine. The adjacent building, the **Small Mammal House** (1936; Edwin Clark), was built with Public Works Administration funds. The structure houses a range of creatures, including sloths and monkeys. The life-size bronze *Giant Anteater* (1928; Erwin Frederich Springweiler) in front of the building was funded by New Deal Public Works of Art and Treasury Relief Art Projects monies.

Continue along Olmsted Walk to the **Great Ape House** (1981; Wilkes and Faulker), home to gorillas, the largest primates, and to orangutans. These animals sometimes climb poles and cross a cableway to the Think Tank exhibit, which examines animal intelligence.

Next on the route is Gibbon Ridge, a large cage housing white-cheeked gibbons, the fastest canopy-living primates. Continue to the Reptile House, now called the **Reptile Discovery Center** (1930; Albert Harris), a fanciful structure built with Public Works Administration monies. The ornately carved stone entry portal (1930; John Joseph Earley) features turtles at the base of the columns, frogs at the top of columns, and lizards at the corners just below the pediment, as well as bronze snake-shaped door handles and ceramic door panels depicting reptiles. The structure features Komodo dragons. The National Zoo was the first to breed these largest and heaviest of lizards outside their Indonesian homeland. The backyard leads to the **Invertebrate Exhibit,** the most diverse exhibit at the zoo, showcasing creatures without backbones. Visitors can observe leaf-cutter ants, live corals, sea stars, and many other creatures from one-celled organisms to octopuses. The Pollinarium, at the end of the exhibit, explores plants and the animals that pollinate them, such as butterflies and hummingbirds. In the warmer months visitors can observe a hive of live bees.

Exit the Reptile House. Continue along Olmsted Walk to the old Small Mammal House (1904; Hornblower & Marshall), home to the monkey collection for 60 years. The building's distinctive finials depict lynx, foxes, and bears designed by Laura Swing Kemeys. The structure now houses the **Think Tank,** an innovative exhibit that examines animal thinking and how animals communicate with one another. There are videos, interactive exhibits, and the opportunity to watch scientists communicate with the orangutans in a computer-generated symbolic language.

Exit the Think Tank. Continue along Olmsted Walk to the Servals (African wildcats with black-spotted, tawny coats). Follow the path by the servals and enter **Great Cats** at the white tiger area near Predators. Renovated and reopened in

1998, Great Cats presents three outdoor habitats totaling 30,000 square ft. Lions and tigers are here from about 7 A.M. to 6 P.M. The habitats have oak trees for shade and bamboo thickets for shelter. Follow the curving 900 ft Great Cats Trail along the perimeter of the exhibit. Three stops along the walkway allow for closer views of the animals. A *machan,* a viewing platform, looks out over the tiger moat. At the Tiger Kids Stop, there is shade, water, and a clear overlook of the exhibit. Enter the Predator Alcove. A large bronze cast of a skull of a Tyrannosaurus rex, a fierce carnivore predator, found in Montana is displayed. The great cats are the largest land-living pure carnivores alive today. A Great Cats Conservation Theater is currently in the planning stages. Follow the curving 250 ft Tiger Tracks walk along Lion/Tiger Hill. Walk in the footprints of a tigress to the tiger exhibits and the Tiger Conservation area. Along the way are various engaging elements for kids. Children can match their hands to a tiger paw and press a button to hear a tiger roar.

Next along the route is the **African American Heritage Garden,** featuring plants important in African American culture. Continue to the Bears, and then to the Bat Cave. Continue along Olmsted Walk to the Mane Restaurant. Across from it is the sculpture *Wrestling Bears* (1935; Heinz Warneke), another result of the New Deal Public Works of Art and Treasury Relief Art Projects. Last along Olmsted Walk is an information booth. Turn right past the booth and walk along the **Valley Trail** back through the zoo.

The first exhibit along this path is **Amazonia,** a re-creation of a tropical river and rain forest with 350 plant species. Animals include Goeldi's and titi monkeys, a sloth, tropical tanagers, and dart-poison frogs. The Amazonia Science Gallery, attached to Amazonia, aims at children ages 4 to 12. The Science Gallery has interactive computer programs, videos, microscopes with specimens such as insect parts, and presentations by zookeepers and scientists.

Exit Amazonia and continue to the **Bear Line,** which exhibits spectacled bears and a Kodiak bear, the largest terrestrial carnivore. Next along the Valley Trail are Seals and Sea Lions, followed by Red Wolves, then Beavers, Otters, and Bobcats. Continue to the **Free-Ranging Tamarins** (summer only). These animals, whose numbers are dwindling in the wild, are part of a zoo breeding program. The animals are given training on how to survive in the wild and then reintroduced to the Brazilian rain forest.

Follow the Valley Trail to the exhibit of Birds, home to the Andean condor, the largest living raptor. Continue to the Australia Pavilion, where the red kangaroo, the largest kangaroo and the largest marsupial is exhibited. Follow the path through the **Wetlands** exhibit, a natural habitat for more than 39 waterfowl species, including the trumpeter swan, the largest waterfowl. Continue to the **Bird House** (1927; Albert L. Harris), home to the goliath heron, the largest heron, and the kori bustard, one of the heaviest flying birds. Adjacent is the Flight Exhibit (1963; Richard Dimon of Daniel, Mann, Johnson and Mendenhall), where birds are in an expansive aviary. Retrace the path through the Wetlands exhibit to the Valley Trail. Follow its path to the Bongos and Tapirs. Then exit the zoo at Connecticut Ave.

### Washington Notes

The famous Smokey Bear lived at the National Zoological Park. He came to the zoo in 1950 as a 4-month-old cub with a singed paw, having been rescued from a forest fire in New Mexico's Lincoln National Park. Smokey became such a popular symbol of the U.S. Park Service's campaign to prevent forest fires that a separate zip code was created for him to handle the extensive amount of mail he received. The original Smokey Bear died in 1976.

## The Kennedy-Warren

Walk north on Connecticut Ave to the Kennedy-Warren (1930; Joseph Younger; 1935 addition, Alexander H. Sonnemann, supervising architect) at 3133 Connecticut Ave N.W. This apartment building is a fine example of Aztec Art Deco, a style characterized by geometric forms, iron grillwork, metal panels, sunrise patterns, and zigzag decorative bands. The Kennedy-Warren apartment house was considered one of the best addresses on Connecticut Ave when it opened in 1930. Today it is perceived as the finest Art Deco apartment building ever constructed in Washington. Many of the original architectural details are intact. The façade has an innovative use of aluminum, in the elaborate spandrels and streamlined marquee. The stylized medallion and decorative colored glasswork above the curved entrance are notable as is the building's distinctive color created by the use of three shades of buff-colored brick. Also notable are the tower's high-relief limestone carvings of two imposing griffins, as well as the pairs of geometric eagles and stylized medallions near the entrance. The lobby has sleek geometric metal railings, decorative copper elevator doors, and marble-faced columns, but the lobby has lost the splendor of its original walnut-veneer walls and sophisticated painted zigzag decoration on the beamed ceiling.

### Washington Notes

The Kennedy-Warren was also noteworthy for its pioneering features. The building had the nation's earliest forced-air cooling system. Large fans at the rear of the building pulled cool air from adjacent Rock Creek Park up into the hallways and then into apartments through above-door louvers.

The Kennedy-Warren also featured a uniformed doorman, dining rooms, lounges, a two-story ballroom, and a basement parking garage. The building as it appears today is only half of the original design. In late 1931, after the builders for whom the building is named, Edgar S. Kennedy and Monroe Warren, Sr., went bankrupt, construction of planned rear and south wings halted. The mortgage company assumed management of the building. Although apartments were difficult to rent during the first years of the Depression, by 1935 conditions improved and the rear wing was built. During World War II the Kennedy-Warren was home to many wives of admirals and generals stationed overseas. By 1943 the waiting list numbered more than 5,000 people. The building is run by the mortgage company that assumed management in 1931. The forced-air cooling system is still being used effectively, events continue to be celebrated in the ballroom, and plans are under way to restore some of the building's original features and begin construction of the south wing.

### Washington Notes

When designing the elaborate interior details for the Kennedy-Warren, architect Joseph Younger called for metalworkers to make a mold from the best-quality aluminum orange juice squeezer obtainable. From the mold aluminum ornaments were made to cap the staircase newel posts.

Continue north on Connecticut Ave across the **Klingle Valley Bridge** (1931; Paul Cret), between Klingle Rd and Macomb St, a single steel arch span that replaced an earlier 1891 bridge. The bridge's geometric railings and monumental limestone urns topped by fluted glass lanterns complement the Kennedy-Warren. This bridge is considered to be the north-south boundary between Woodley Park and Cleveland Park.

Continue north another block on Connecticut Ave. Turn west onto Newark St. Walk three blocks. The first commercially developed thoroughfare in Cleveland Park, **Newark St** was begun by the Cleveland Park Company in 1895. The eclectic mix of house styles ranges from Queen Anne to mission revival. Different architects designed the homes until 1909 when Ella Bennett Sherman, an artist and wife of Cleveland Park Company president John Sherman, took over. Her simplified and refined versions of the Queen Anne style are unique to Cleveland Park. Referred to as cottages by the Shermans, the houses employ asymmetry, a variety of window shapes, broad overhanging eaves, wood porches, and a combination of wood shingles, clapboard, and stucco. Especially distinctive is the applied rope-dipped-in-plaster decoration. Today many of the Sherman designs survive and can be seen at **2930, 2934, 2940, 3038, 3042,** and **3121 Newark St N.W.**

### Washington Notes

One of the most famous residents of Cleveland Park was Arctic explorer Edward Peary, who lived at 2940 Newark St N.W. Peary asked the zoo to temporarily house his sled dogs, and they became part of the dog exhibit that lasted from 1896 into the 1920s. When the neighbors complained about the barking, the exhibit was moved to the center of the zoo.

Continue west two blocks. At 3501 Newark St N.W. is **Rosedale** (1794; Uriah Forrest, owner-builder), a farmhouse built by General Uriah Forrest, veteran of the Revolution, shipping merchant, mayor of Georgetown, Continental Congress delegate, and friend of George Washington and Pierre L'Enfant. Forrest and his family are the first documented inhabitants of the area that became Woodley and Cleveland Parks. In 1792, Forrest and two partners purchased land, which was then part of rural Maryland, and named it Pretty Prospects. Rosedale was built in the typical 18C style as a series of connected clapboard, L-shaped structures with brick chimneys and a covered front veranda. Forrest descendants resided at Rosedale until 1917. Today the house, still surrounded by trees, is occupied by the International Exchange—Youth for Understanding. The grounds are open to the public, but the buildings are not.

Walk five blocks east on Newark St to Connecticut Ave, then turn north on Connecticut and walk five blocks. The 3300–3500 blocks of Connecticut Ave comprise the **Cleveland Park Business District.** Most of the buildings date from the 1920s through the 1940s and are a mix of architectural styles. At the northwest corner of Connecticut Ave and Newark St, shops on the ground level of the Art Deco–style apartment building the **Macklin** (1939; Mihran Mesrobian) begin the strip of limestone-façaded retail establishments that stretch to the **Cleveland Park Post Office** (1940; C. Meigs). The post office is a classic

Moderne–style structure with a smooth façade, rounded pilasters, bands of windows, and streamlined lettering. Across the street, **3415–3417 Connecticut Ave N.W.** (1936; A. S. J. Atkinson), where the Aroma Company and Ritz Camera now are, feature Art Deco–stylized aluminum panels above their windows.

At 3426 Connecticut Ave N.W., the **Uptown Theater** (1936; John Jacob Zink) is the only large, one-screen Art Deco–era movie theater remaining in the city. Designed by an architect whose specialty was movie houses, the Uptown's powerful stepped façade makes use of horizontal and vertical striations on limestone and brick, zigzag and sunburst banding, narrow windows with stylized floral-etched glass, a sleek aluminum marquee, and a neon sign.

> ### Washington Notes
>
> Crowds came to the Uptown's opening in 1936. The featured film, *Cain and Mabel,* starred Marion Davies and Clark Gable. Nostalgia enthusiasts flocked to the reopening held after restoration in 1991, at which the uncut version of the controversial film *Spartacus,* starring Kirk Douglas and Jean Simmons, was screened. In May 1999 dozens of *Star Wars* enthusiasts camped out for days to attend the premiere of George Lucas's *The Phantom Menace.*

Continue north a half-block to 3507–3523 Connecticut Ave N.W., the **Park and Shop** (1930; Arthur B. Heaton). This red brick colonial Georgian revival edifice has gabled dormer windows and a swan's neck pediment above the entrance closest to Connecticut Ave. The Park and Shop was one of the first shopping malls in the country built to accommodate cars.

The **Cleveland Park Fire House** (1916; Snowden Ashford) at 3522 Connecticut Ave N.W. is a colonial Georgian revival structure. The firehouse has a limestone string course, quoin-block corners, and brick chimneys. The firehouse was the first edifice in what is now the Cleveland Park Business District. Next door at 3524 Connecticut Ave N.W. is the **Yenching Palace** (1945; R. C. Archer, Jr.), a Chinese restaurant that is an example of an Art Deco–style storefront typical of the late 1930s and 1940s. The façade has an aluminum cornice, glass block, diamond-shaped windows, stylized gold-tone decorative banding, black Vitrolite glass, and a large neon sign.

> ### Washington Notes
>
> An often-repeated local story, for which there is no published corroboration, is that during the Cuban Missile Crisis in 1962 Yenching Palace was the site of secret negotiations between representatives of President John F. Kennedy and Soviet Premier Nikita Khrushchev. Supposedly, it was here that the agreement to the conflict's end was reached and a war averted.

Continue north on Connecticut Ave to its intersection with Porter St.

## Adas Israel Congregation

On the southeast side of Connecticut Ave and set back from the street is a triangular plot of land, bordered by Quebec St N.W. and Porter St N.W. This is the site of Adas Israel Congregation (1951; Frank Grad & Sons, Newark, N.J.; 1958, religious school built, architect unknown; 1988, renovation and expansion), 2850 Quebec St N.W., ☎ 362-4433. The synagogue, designed in a 1950s rectangular style, is faced with granite and has five pairs of heavy bronze doors that lead to a red marble lobby. A building-size menorah faces Connecticut Ave.

### History

Adas Israel was established Dec 31, 1869, as an orthodox congregation when several members left the Washington Hebrew Congregation, which was becoming too liberal for them. The members met in their homes and in rented quarters until 1876, when a new synagogue was dedicated at 8th and D Sts N.W. In 1908 the synagogue relocated to 6th and I Sts N.W. In the 1920s the congregation began its gradual shift toward a Jewish conservative theology. Adas Israel, the largest conservative congregation in the D.C. area, has a membership of more than 1,800 families. It relocated to its present location in 1951. (See "Lillian and Albert Small Jewish Museum and the Jewish Historical Society" in Walk 13: "Judiciary Square/Chinatown Area.")

Across the street from Adas Israel on the northeast corner of Porter St and Connecticut Ave is the **Broadmoor** (1928–29; Joseph Abel), 3601 Connecticut Ave N.W. When the Broadmoor opened in 1925 it was one of the very first apartment houses on upper Connecticut Ave. The building is an imposing example of Gothic revival style, with its castlelike porte cochere, limestone panels with carved heraldic decoration, battlements, and rough tapestry-finish brick. The Broadmoor was originally a full-service building, offering maid and valet service, hotel rooms, a restaurant, parking garage, barber shop, and newsstand. During the World War II housing shortage, some of the public corridors and space on the ground floor were converted to sleeping quarters for women officers of the navy and army. The Broadmoor was named after the noted Broadmoor Resort in Colorado Springs.

### Washington Notes

Like other luxury apartments, the Broadmoor has housed some famous residents. During World War II Archduke Otto of Hapsburg, claimant to the Austro-Hungarian throne, lived here, and his younger brother, Felix, was an occupant until he was drafted into the United States Army. Senator Huey Long of Louisiana, always accompanied by three bodyguards, maintained an apartment at the Broadmoor at the time of his 1934 assassination in Baton Rouge. Locals say that the building's bar, the Silver Grill, was the hangout of Washington's baseball team, the Senators, during the 1930s, when many of the players and their manager lived at the Broadmoor.

Walk two blocks north on Connecticut Ave to Sedgwick St. On the southwest corner is **Sedgwick Gardens** (1932; Mihran Mesrobian) at 3726 Connecticut Ave N.W., one of Washington's Aztec Art Deco–style treasures. White brick, stepped marble panels, triangular cornice projections abutting wrought-iron railings, and carved limestone panels depicting stylized figures are incorporated in its unique façade. The limestone porte cochere has streamlined octagonal columns, geometric lamps, zigzag and panther decorative bands, and two sculptures of robed women holding medieval staffs. Inside Sedgwick Gardens its original lobby, which has been described as "a potpourri of Romanesque and Byzantine," is intact except for a fountain. The lobby has grillwork railings, limestone, marble columns with elaborately carved capitals, round archways, and a six-sided skylight. When Sedgwick Gardens opened, its services included 24-hour porters, a doorman, valet parking, a sprinkler system on the roof for cooling top-floor apartments in the summer, and a formal garden.

Continue one block north on Connecticut Ave to Tilden St. At the southwest corner is **Tilden Gardens** (1929; Parks and Baxter; Harry L. Edwards, associate architect), 3000 Tilden St N.W. One of the first apartment houses constructed on upper Connecticut Ave, this is a complex of six Tudor revival–style buildings. The buildings have rough tapestry-finish brick, multiple chimneys, stucco, and gabled roofs. They were described as "stark and expressive of a new age" when Tilden Gardens opened.

Walk east three blocks on Tilden St. At Linnean Ave turn north and walk two blocks.

## Hillwood Museum and Gardens

4155 Linnean Ave N.W. ☎ 686-8500. Web: www.hillwoodmuseum.org. Has been closed for restoration until summer 2000, with public programs continuing. Upon reopening, open Tues–Sat by appointment only. Closed during Feb. Admission: A donation from adults and from students is requested; visitors may request a refund of the donation at the end of the tour. Tour includes access to gardens, a 50-minute film, and a 90-minute guided tour of the house. Children under 12 not admitted to house. No photography permitted in house. House mostly wheelchair accessible. Restrooms. Telephones. Museum shop. Public programs.

Hillwood Museum and Gardens (1926; Jack Diebert; 1957, Alexander McIlvaine; 1965, Perry Wheeler, landscape architect; 1985 Native American building, O'Neil & Manion Architects, Pa.; 1986 café, O'Neil & Manion Architects, Pa.; 1998 restoration, Oehrlein & Associates Architects and Bowie Gridley Architects, PLLC), are a testament to the collecting passion of its former owner, Marjorie Merriweather Post, heiress to the Post cereal fortune. The house and nearly 25 acres surrounding it were purchased by Mrs. Post in 1955 and transformed into a lavish spring/fall residence for entertaining, as well as a showplace for her extensive collection of 18C and 19C French and Russian decorative arts. The Georgian revival style–structure's gardens include many azaleas, a French garden, Japanese garden, and rose gardens. The collection consists of groups of European porcelains including a large selection by the noted French factory of Sevres, as well as several sets of imperial Russian dinner services; about 90 objects by Carl Fabergé, jeweler to the imperial Russian court; Russian icons; and gold and silver ecclesiastical objects. In addition the mansion has Beauvais tapestries, portraits of Russian czars and czarinas, Chinese jades, a collection of lace, and the elegant garments worn by Mrs. Post. About 20 percent of the Russian pieces were bought by Mrs. Post when she was married to her third husband, Joseph E. Davies, the first ambassador to the Soviet Union. Mrs. Post's will provided for Hillwood and its gardens to become a museum after her death, stipulating that the collection be kept perpetually intact.

After a two-year renovation Hillwood is expected to reopen in summer 2000. The new Visitor Orientation Center houses a theater, the reservations office, and the museum shop. More signs in the gardens will enable visitors to better identify plants and flowers. The French-style parterre garden is being restored to its appearance during Marjorie Merriweather Post's lifetime and the greenhouses are being improved to provide better conditions for the orchids and other tropical plants. There will be two new gatehouses for visitors and improved parking facilities.

**Highlights:** Hillwood has a noteworthy collection of Russian icons and art, reputedly the largest assemblage outside of Russia, and lovely gardens. Standout pieces are a gold and diamond chalice commissioned by Catherine the Great in 1791; four porcelain dinner services commissioned by Catherine the Great; a diamond crown worn by Alexandra at her 1894 wedding to Nicholas II, the last Russian monarch; two imperial Russian Easter eggs made by Carl Fabergé; and *The Boar Wedding* by Konstantin Makovsky, a painting depicting 17C Russian court life.

## History

Born in 1887, Marjorie Merriweather Post was the daughter and only child of Charles William Post, the founder of the Postum Cereal Company and inventor of Grape Nuts and Postum, an instant coffee substitute. Post prepared his daughter to assume leadership of the family business. Upon his death in 1914, Marjorie became the sole owner and operator of the Postum Cereal Company.

After two daughters and a 14-year marriage to Edward Bennett Close, Post divorced Close in 1919 and married Edward F. Hutton the following year. By 1923, Hutton was chairman of the board of Postum and, with Marjorie's influence, led the company to acquire Frosted Foods, which produced Birds Eye products and eventually became General Foods. With Hutton, Marjorie had one daughter, Nedenia, who later took the stage name Dina Merrill and has gone on to a successful career as a film and TV actress. Post and Hutton owned the Sea Cloud, the largest private yacht in the world, and several properties, including Topridge, a camp in the Adirondacks; Hillwood, a house on Long Island; and Mar-a-Lago, a winter residence in Palm Beach, Florida. In 1935 Marjorie and Hutton divorced. Shortly thereafter she married lawyer Joseph E. Davies, who was appointed the first ambassador to the Soviet Union by President Franklin Delano Roosevelt in 1936. It was during her time in the Soviet Union with Davies between 1936 and 1938 that Marjorie acquired about 20 percent of her collection of Russian objects.

As a result of the Russian Revolution, the Soviet government confiscated religious items from Russian nobility, selling the items to raise money and to destroy traces of both religion and imperial Russia. Upon returning to the United States, Marjorie and Davies lived in Cleveland Park where Marjorie continued to purchase objects for her collection. In 1955, at the time of her divorce from Davies, Marjorie purchased the property that is today Hillwood Museum and Gardens, transforming the house, originally called Abremont (which means wooded arbor), into a residence that doubled as a showplace for her extensive collections. She had the house enlarged to include paneling and other elements taken from European castles and châteaus, and she created elaborate gardens with the assistance of the landscape architect, Perry Wheeler, who was best known for the White House Rose Garden. She renamed the estate Hillwood. With 36 rooms and 6 baths, Hillwood was listed in a 1961 tax assessment as the costliest home in Washington. In addition to 30 gardeners, Post employed a staff of 35 for the house and her lavish entertaining. In 1964 after her divorce from her fourth husband, Pittsburgh industrialist Herbert A. May (whom she had married in 1958), Marjorie took her maiden name.

Marjorie Merriweather Post resided at Hillwood until her death in 1973. Her will bequeathed Hillwood with its collection and grounds to the Smithsonian Institution, which administered the collection for several years before returning it to the Marjorie Merriweather Post Foundation of the District of Columbia. Hillwood Museum and Gardens opened to the public in 1977. An extensive restoration began in 1998 and is expected to last until summer 2000.

### Washington Notes

For many years Post volunteered at the Red Cross and supported the Boy Scouts of America. In a socially unpopular move, Post invited returning Vietnam veterans to Hillwood for a celebration in their honor.

Continue two blocks north on Linnean Ave. Turn west on Upton St and walk two blocks. Visible through the trees to the north of Upton St is the rear of the **Howard University School of Law** (c. 1930s–1940s; architect unknown) at 2900 Van Ness St N.W. The school, housed in a large Tudor revival–style building situated on 22 acres, is part of Howard University, a traditionally black, private, coeducational institution chartered by Congress in 1867. Howard University's main campus is located in the Shaw area of northwest Washington. The Howard University School of Law opened in 1869 and later moved to this location.

### Washington Notes

Howard University School of Law has had many notable students and faculty. These include Supreme Court Justice Thurgood Marshall; Charles Hamilton Houston, the strategist in the *Brown v. Board of Education* case; Gabrielle Kirk McDonald, a judge on the International Criminal Tribunal for the Former Yugoslavia; and Vernon Jordan, Jr., chairperson of the Clinton/Gore transition team and a close personal friend of President Clinton.

Continue walking west on Upton St to the **Edmund Burke School** (date and original building architect unknown; 1985 addition, Keyes, Condon and Florence) at 2955 Upton St N.W., ☎ 362-8882. Established in 1968 as an independent high school for grades 9–12 by Jean Mooskin and Dick Roth, the Edmund Burke School currently educates children in grades 6 through 12.

Continue on Upton St to Connecticut Ave, turn north, and walk one block. At 3400 Connecticut Ave N.W. is the **Intelsat Building** (1987; John Andrews International, Ltd.; Notter Finegold + Alexander, associate architects). Intelsat is a 110-nation cooperative that owns and operates communications satellites. The building's space-age appearance reflects its high-tech mission. The structure has a series of mirrored glass block towers and octagonal sections lined with reflective solar sunscreen-equipped windows designed to maximize solar energy and natural cooling. The interior of the building houses atrium gardens, and its roof features a sodded garden. All the Intelsat offices have windows with views. WJLA-TV, the local ABC affiliate (Channel 7), leases space in the Intelsat Building.

Walk six blocks north on Connecticut Ave to Van Ness St. At the northwest corner is the **University of the District of Columbia (UDC)** (1972; Bryant and Bryant, Ellerbe Becket, Inc.), 4200 Connecticut Ave N.W. The university's 21-acre campus stretches behind Connecticut Ave. Its twelve concrete buildings combine blank façades and dark glass windows. The University of the District of

Columbia was established in 1976 as a land-grant institution bringing together Federal City College, Washington Technical Institute, and District of Columbia Teachers College. UDC is the only public institution of higher education in the District of Columbia. The university is the nation's first exclusively urban land-grant university.

### History

In 1963, President John Kennedy appointed a commission to study the District's inadequacies in the area of public education. The commission found that the needs of District residents, often poor and unable to afford the private universities and colleges in Washington, called for improvements in public higher education. The Public Education Act of 1966 created two schools—Federal City College and Washington Technical Institute—both of which opened in 1968. (So many students applied to the Federal City College its first year that admission had to be determined by lottery.) In 1969, the District of Columbia Teachers College, the city's oldest teacher-training institution, came under the jurisdiction of the District's Board of Higher Education. Washington Technical Institute received accreditation in 1971; Federal City College in 1974. The year after limited home rule was granted to the District of Columbia in 1975, a mandate for consolidation of the three schools was authorized by the D.C. City Council. A Board of Trustees took office in May 1976. In Aug 1977 the schools were consolidated into the UDC.

That same year, Lisle Carleton, Jr., was appointed UDC's first president, a post he held until 1982. Carter and subsequent presidents have struggled to establish UDC's identity as a university while at the same time dealing with a series of administration-faculty differences about the way the university should be run. Today, under President Julius F. Nimmons, Jr., Ph.D., who was appointed in 1998, UDC continues to "strive for excellence in meeting the higher education needs and aspirations of the people of the nation's capital at the lowest possible cost to the students." UDC frequently struggles with budgetary problems. In 1999 Mayor Anthony Williams suggested relocating the UDC campus to the less-costly Anacostia area. After student and faculty protest, the idea was abandoned.

On the east side of Connecticut Ave, across from the UDC campus at Upton St, is the Van Ness–UDC Metro station. To continue to the next walk, take the Red Line to Metro Center, and from there the Green Line to the Shaw–Howard University Metro station at 7th and R Sts. From there, walk south on 7th St one and a half blocks to Rhode Island Ave, and then west on Rhode Island Ave six blocks to Logan Circle.

# 23 · Shaw and LeDroit Park

Metro: Green Line to U St/African American Civil War Memorial/Cardoza or Shaw–Howard University.
Bus: Any of the 50s lines.

A tour of the Shaw and LeDroit Park sections of Washington brings visitors an awareness of an era of African American pride and accomplishment and also shows visitors the results of decades of despair that have plagued these areas.

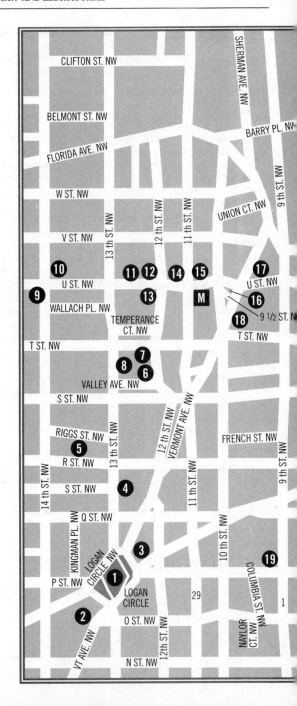

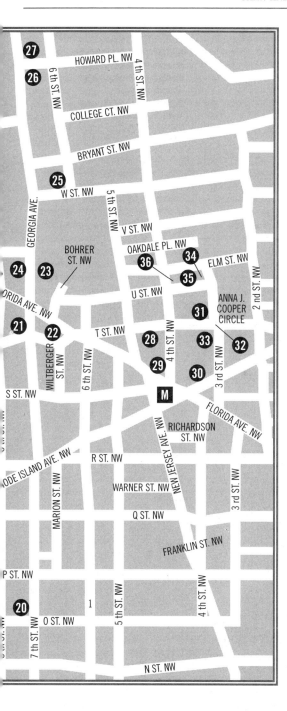

1 Logan Circle
2 Mary McLeod Bethune Museum and Archives
3 Smith-Mason Gallery
4 site of Camp Barker
5 site of MuSoLit Club
6 Thurgood Marshall Center
7 Duke Ellington home
8 Whitelaw Hotel
9 14th & U Sts
10 Reeves Center
11 Lincoln Theatre
12 Ben's Chili Bowl
13 True Reformers Hall
14 Industrial Bank
15 Bohemian Caverns
16 African Am. War Memorial
17 Scurlock Photo Studio
18 site of Grimke Elementary School
19 Shiloh Baptist Church
20 O Street Market
21 site of Waxie Maxie's
22 Howard Theatre
23 Howard University Hospital (Griffith Stadium)
24 Church of God
25 home of Will Marion Cook
26 Miner Teacher's College
27 Howard University (Howard Hall, Founders Library, Rankin Chapel)
28 home of Walter Washington
29 site of Harrison's Cafe
30 site of McClelland home
31 Cooper home
32 Cooper Circle
33 Terrell home
34 Brooke home
35 Fleetwood home
36 Dunbar home

Today, both Shaw and LeDroit Park are the focus of a determined movement by city leaders and local organizations to restore the boarded-up buildings and vacant lots in what was the business, retail, and entertainment center of the city's African American community for more than 40 years. In Nov 1998 mayor-elect Anthony Williams and the D.C. Financial Control Board unveiled plans to turn Georgia Ave on either side of Howard University into a center for African American civic and cultural organizations. Dilapidated buildings will be cleared to make room for these organizations.

# Shaw

### History

The name Shaw comes from Colonel Robert Gould Shaw, the white commander of the black regiment known as the 54th Massachusetts during the Civil War. The name was first given to a junior high school in the area. Prior to 1966, those living in the area usually identified themselves by the neighborhood they lived in or the closest major thoroughfare, such as Logan Circle or 14th and U Sts. When the city government and the National Planning Commission in 1966 applied for an urban renewal grant for the area, they needed a name. The commission decided the attendance boundaries of Shaw Junior High School would be used to geographically define the area (between N. Capitol and 15th Sts on the east and west and Florida Ave and M St on the north and south), and the name Shaw was chosen.

However, the area known as Shaw has strong historical ties with its border neighborhoods of LeDroit Park, Bloomingdale, Howard University, Mount Vernon Square, and Columbia Heights, and parts of these neighborhoods are often also labeled Shaw. To many, the area is best known by its commercial and entertainment center for so many years, U St.

When the city of Washington was established in 1791, this area was farmland owned by five men, two of whom were the real estate developer Samuel Blodgett (see Walk 13: "Judiciary Square/Chinatown Area") and Georgetown merchant Robert Peter (see Walk 19: "Georgetown East"). Boundary St (Florida Ave) was then just a dirt road leading to Bladensburg, Maryland.

The Civil War brought major changes to Shaw, as it did to every other section of the city. Federal troops were housed here for a time and former slaves who had escaped from Confederate states found shelter in the "wilds" of this relatively undeveloped area. In 1862, streetcars began to operate along 7th and 14th Sts, and Shaw landowners, seeing the possibilities, began to sell their lots. Shaw grew from south to north, with the northern section described in 1870 as still "in the woods." But under the regime of Alexander "Boss" Shepherd (see Walk 16: "Dupont Circle West Area") in the early 1870s, the city government made significant improvements in the quality of Shaw life, surfacing roads, sweeping streets, planting trees, and installing gas lamps, water mains, fireplugs, and sewers. All manner of city residents—black and white of all classes—made their way to Shaw to rent, buy, or build homes. Many of the brick row houses lining the streets of Shaw today were constructed between 1875 and 1900.

In the community's early years, Shaw attracted black and white residents of all classes. Even as late as the World War I years (1914–18), Shaw remained racially mixed, though increasingly less so, with neighborhoods of white government workers and professionals adjacent to their black counterparts. However, it was between the years of 1880 and 1920 that Shaw gradually became the city's largest and most affluent African American community, having the most significant concentration of black businesses in Washington.

Immediately following the Civil War, African American male city residents were given the right to vote, and they responded by registering in large numbers. For a period of time segregation abated between 1866 and 1874 as African American constituents were elected and appointed to local offices. The new officeholders helped pass laws prohibiting segregation in housing. Unfortunately, when Congress changed the District's government from a territorial one to a commission in 1874, the white commissioners represented the interests of the white community better than they represented the needs of the black residents. After 1874 segregated housing became widespread again. The strong influence on city government policies African American Washingtonians had exerted would not be felt again until the 1970s.

But African Americans continued to be attracted to the city for its good schools and housing, despite segregation. In 1908, although the population of the city was about one-third African American, only 9 of the 450 employees at the District government center offices were black. Beginning in the 1890s, jobs that had traditionally gone to African Americans, such as recorder of deeds (a post held by Frederick Douglass) and assistant district attorney, were given to white residents. In 1908, of the 881 employees of the city post office, only 134 were black; of the fire and police departments' 1,229 employees, only 48 were black.

Increasingly denied access to the use of and the development of businesses and entertainment spots in other parts of the city, African Americans turned to Shaw, particularly U St between 7th and 14th Sts, as a place of opportunity and acceptance. Although African American Washingtonians in those years never gave up their commitment to full integration and equal rights, at the same time they realistically created an area of the city where they could prosper and live in peace as a community.

Although it was difficult at first for African Americans to find the money for business development, institutions such as the 12th St YMCA (formerly the Anthony Bowen YMCA, now the Thurgood Marshall Center for Service and Heritage), the True Reformers Hall, the Whitelaw Hotel, the Union League, and perhaps most important, the Industrial Savings Bank were eventually financed and built by African Americans. A list of Shaw area businesses between 1910 and 1920 gives testament to the strength of the African American community: 47 hairdressers, 19 barbers, 44 eateries, 31 groceries, 11 undertakers, 10 pharmacies, 10 printers, 10 shoemakers, 10 upholsterers, 8 bakers, 7 cigar and tobacco shops, 6 pool halls, 5 photographers, 5 tailors, 5 florists, 4 jewelers and watchmakers, 4 employment agencies, 3 insurance agencies, 3 real estate agencies, 3 oyster, clam, and fish dealers, 2 dry cleaners, and 2 architects.

As one longtime resident recalled many years later, "If you were on U Street, you didn't need to go elsewhere. It was all right there for you. Blacks had a society put together on this street. You didn't realize you were in a segregated situation. We knew where to go and what to do."

As much as the community was proud of its strong commercial center, it perhaps was even prouder of the influence U St and its night spots had on the black entertainment industry. Homegrown talent such as Duke Ellington, Pearl Bailey, and Billy Eckstine all got their start here. U St had three first-run movie theaters, and all of them let out at the same time, their patrons pouring into the street and into the clubs along Washington's "Black Broadway." The Howard Theatre, at 7th and T Sts, opened in 1910, making it the oldest legitimate theater specifically for African Americans in the U.S. (The Apollo in New York City opened in 1930.) Entertainment was a huge economic force in Shaw in the years prior to World War II.

Just as all economic classes mingled in the residential areas, so too did they at the night spots. A former resident recalled, "If you went to the Lincoln Theatre, you wouldn't know if you were sitting next to the bootblack or the president of Howard University. So you would conduct yourself accordingly. You would think, this is a human being, so I'm going to treat him as if he was the president of the university, because he might be."

In 1919 race riots against African Americans erupted in D.C. on July 19 and continued until July 23. This was part of what was called the Red Summer because of the amount of bloodshed that occurred in riots against African Americans across the nation that summer following World War I. In Washington, a mob composed mainly of white military personnel attacked black men in several parts of the city as retaliation for an alleged offense of one black man against a white woman. When the rumor spread that U St would be the next mob target, an estimated 2,000 armed Shaw residents, some veterans of the war, lined U St ready to defend their families and property. The white rioters didn't show.

This was a time of overt racism across the U.S. The lynching of African Americans occurred with alarming impunity, and the Ku Klux Klan, experiencing a spurt of public approval, was given permission to march in full regalia down Pennsylvania Ave. The sitting president, Woodrow Wilson, introduced a series of legislative acts that would have further limited the civil rights of black Washingtonians, including laws that would have segregated the civil service and the streetcars. (These were already segregated in practice.) The African American community responded by establishing organizations such as the Washington chapter of the National Association for the Advancement of Colored People (NAACP), which by 1916 had become the largest chapter in the country. Shaw's residents drew strength from the cohesive fabric of their community, a community justly proud of the care provided for its children. (Shaw's schools were considered among the best for African Americans in the country.)

Change came following World War II. Forced into a relatively small area by segregationist policies, residents of Shaw and surrounding black enclaves felt overcrowded even before the war. When the Supreme Court overturned racially restrictive covenants in 1948, many of Shaw's residents took advantage of the opportunity to move. Affluent African Americans left for those areas of the city and suburbs providing larger, more luxurious homes. Businesses followed their best customers, and the Shaw area began a gradual decline. Single-family homes were converted to multiple-unit dwellings, and the density of the neighborhood increased as services decreased.

By the 1960s, Shaw, mired in poverty and unemployment, was ripe for redevelopment. Local organizations such as the Model Inner City Community Organization (MICCO) were determined that, whenever possible, Shaw properties would be renovated rather than torn down, which resulted in the flavor of the historical community remaining intact.

The location of a major District government office building in the heart of Shaw (the Franklin Reeves Center at 14th and U Sts) and the opening of the U St Metro station have contributed to a regeneration of Shaw. Other factors spurring the resurgence of Shaw are the desirability of in-city housing to escape clogged rush hour routes and the construction of the new Washington Convention Center at Mount Vernon Square, on the outer edge of Shaw. The center is projected to pump $1.1 billion in revenue into the area its first year; businesses are moving back in anticipation of the Shaw renaissance.

**Highlights:** Mary McLeod Bethune Museum and Archives and Howard University.

## Logan Circle

From the Shaw–Howard University Metro station at 7th and R Sts, walk south on 7th St one and a half blocks to Rhode Island Ave, and then west on Rhode Island Ave six blocks to Logan Circle (DL) at the junction of Rhode Island and Vermont Aves N.W. and 13th and R Sts N.W. Identified by Pierre L'Enfant as one of the "special places" in his plans for the city, the eight-block Logan Circle area features well-preserved Victorian architecture, with 60 percent of its residences built between 1874 and 1887. During the Civil War, the area (then called Iowa Circle) was farmland on the edge of the city, where newly freed slaves lived in shanties. Civic improvements brought by the regime of Alexander "Boss" Shepherd made this a prime residential area and many of the city's white upper-middle-class citizens moved in. But by the turn of the century, streetcar lines and encroaching communities to the north brought an influx of residents from elsewhere, and the circle's residential make-up changed as middle-class African American families moved into the neighborhood.

In 1901, a bronze equestrian statue of **John A. Logan** (1901; Franklin Simmons; Richard Morris Hunt) was dedicated in the circle (although the name wasn't changed to Logan Circle until 1930). Logan, a Civil War general, was the senator from Illinois credited with introducing the legislation that established

Memorial Day. For the statue of Logan, New England sculptor Simmons worked with the Parisian-trained architect Hunt, who previously had designed the base of the *Statue of Liberty.* Their creation is unique among statues in Washington in that it is made entirely of bronze. High-relief panels on two sides depict Logan's war experiences, with allegorical figures on either end and eagles at the corners of the entablature.

After World War II, Logan Circle, which had been one of the centers of African American social, cultural, and intellectual life in Washington, began to decline, as the wealthier African American families moved to the suburbs and lower-income black families moved in. Many of the large houses on the circle became boardinghouses and apartments, some with absentee landlords who didn't always maintain the properties. In the late 1960s, restoration began on many of the residences. In 1972, Logan Circle (with 132 of its adjacent residences) was declared a historic district.

## Mary McLeod Bethune Museum and Archives
1318 Vermont Ave N.W. ☎ 673-2402. Open Mon–Sat 10–4:30; summer Mon–Sat 10–4. Admission: free. Guided tours available for minimal fee.

From Logan Circle, walk south on Vermont Ave one and a half blocks to the **Mary McLeod Bethune Council House National Historic Site** (1870s; William Roose, probable architect; DL), the home from 1936 to 1949 of the internationally known educator and presidential advisor, who died in 1955 at the age of 80. The 25-minute video about the educator's life is aimed at children, and the gift shop features a selection of books about Bethune and African American history.

### History
The 15th of 17 children born to former slaves, Bethune recognized at an early age the necessity of education. In 1904, on a budget of $1.50, she founded the Daytona Normal and Industrial Institute for Negro Girls, a one-room school that had orange crates for furniture and five students. In 1924, Bethune was elected president of the National Association of Colored Women and ten years later, along with Lucy Diggs Slowe (the first dean of women at Howard University), founded the National Council of Negro Women. That same year, Bethune became Special Advisor for Minority Affairs to President Franklin Roosevelt and in 1936 was appointed director of Negro affairs in the National Youth Administration. Bethune was also a wife (Albertus Bethune in 1898) and mother (Albert McLeod Bethune), as well as a businesswoman—at one time, Bethune served as director of the Afro-American Life Insurance Co., Inc.

Bethune's dedication to young people is carved on the base of the statue erected in her honor in Lincoln Park (see Walk 1: "Capitol Hill North and East"): "I leave you love. I leave you hope. I leave you the challenge of developing confidence in one another. I leave you a thirst for education. I leave you a respect for the use of power. I leave you faith. I leave you racial dignity. I leave you a desire to live harmoniously with your fellow man. I leave you, finally, a responsibility to our young people." Bethune died in Daytona Beach, Florida, where she is buried on the campus of Bethune-Cookman College. From 1943 to 1966 the Vermont Ave house was the headquarters of the National Council of Negro Women.

The Vermont Ave property now houses the **National Archives for Black Women's History,** the largest collection of documents relating to African American women in the country. The museum, administered by the National Park Service since 1966, features temporary exhibits and sponsors cultural and educational series.

From the museum, return to Logan Circle and walk a half-block east on Rhode Island Ave to the former site of the now-defunct **Smith-Mason Gallery** (1207 Rhode Island Ave N.W.). Here Helen Mason, an art teacher in the District public schools, and her real estate executive husband, James, opened a contemporary art gallery in 1967 to exhibit the work of African American artists and conducted art classes on weekends. The Smith-Mason Gallery, along with the Barnett-Aden Gallery, located in the Bloomingdale section near N. Capitol St N.W., were two of the very limited number of galleries open to African American artists.

From the gallery site return to Logan Circle (a half-block west on Rhode Island Ave) and walk north on 13th St one block to Q St. Between Q and R Sts and 12th and 13th Sts was the site of **Camp Barker,** a Civil War military barracks created to house runaway slaves who had come to Washington in the first months of the war.

> ### Washington Notes
> Duff's Green Row (now the site of the Library of Congress) on Capitol Hill had been their original refuge, but following an outbreak of smallpox the former slaves were moved here. In 1862 the citizens of Washington organized the Freedmen's Relief Bureau to give refugees from the South, as organizers stated, "clothing, temporary homes, and employment and, as far as possible, to teach them to read and write, and bring them under moral influences." Camp Barker became one of the central locations for this effort. Between April and Oct 1862, residents of the camp grew from 400 to over 4,200. Protection from bounty hunters (any slave, even on free soil, could legally be taken into custody to be returned to his or her master) and free medical care at the Freedmen's Hospital (established in 1862) proved a powerful draw to this area.

At 13th and R Sts, walk west a half-block to the former site of the **MuSoLit Club** (1327 R St N.W.), currently a Howard University fraternity house for Omega Beta Sigma.

> ### Washington Notes
> In the early 1900s the MuSoLit Club was one of the area's premier *mus*ical, *so*cial and *lit*erary clubs. Founded at the turn of the century by Francis L. Cardozo, Sr., one of Washington's education pioneers (and father of four daughters, one of whom married the actor/singer Paul Robeson), the MuSoLit Club was for men only and avidly Republican, sponsoring an annual Lincoln-Douglass birthday celebration every Feb that was one of the social highlights of the year. There were many such African American social clubs in the area, among them the middle-class Bachelor-Benedicts, which presented young debutante women to society, and the Jack and Jill Club for children of the well-to-do.

## Thurgood Marshall Center for Service and Heritage
Return east to 13th and R Sts, then walk north on 13th St two blocks to 13th and S Sts. Turn east on S St and walk one block east to 12th St, then a half-block

north on 12th St to the original site of the Anthony Bowen YMCA (1912; William Signey Pittman; DL) at 1816 12th St N.W., the first YMCA in the U.S. established for "colored men and boys," and has recently been renovated as the Thurgood Marshall Center for Service and Heritage.

### History

Originally known as the 12th St YMCA and then the Anthony Bowen YMCA, the center was founded and designed by African Americans (Anthony Bowen founded it; Pittman designed it) and built with community funds matched by philanthropists John D. Rockefeller and Julius Rosenwald (of Sears, Roebuck and Company). Founded by Bowen, a former slave and prominent educator and religious leader, in 1853, the YMCA was housed first on 11th St N.W. and later at the True Reformers Hall on U St N.W. Following a community fund-raising effort, President Theodore Roosevelt laid the cornerstone of the 12th St building on Thanksgiving Day, 1908. Construction was completed four years later. (Bowen died in 1871.) The Y became the first full-service building for African American men, offering lodging, sports (basketball, indoor golf, swimming), and social and civic events that drew people from around the city.

The poet Langston Hughes lived here briefly in the 1920s. For 70 years the Y provided services to the Shaw community. The Y sent young men to Union Station to meet trains, directing African American travelers coming into a segregated city to appropriate hotels and restaurants. In 1972, the Y was renamed the Anthony Bowen YMCA. Ten years later the Metropolitan Washington YMCA declared the building unsafe and closed it. In 1994, the building was declared a National Historic Landmark. Groundbreaking for the multimillion-dollar Thurgood Marshall Center was in Sept 1998. The new facility, which opened in Feb 2000, houses social and civic organizations. The center also hopes to include an interactive museum focusing on the history of the Shaw community.

## Duke Ellington Home

Continue north on 12th St a half-block to the intersection of 12th and T Sts and 1212 T St N.W., the childhood home of Edward Kennedy "Duke" Ellington (1899–1974), jazz composer and performer.

### History

Ellington, whose nickname came from his impeccable dress and sophisticated manner as a young man, took piano lessons at the urging of his mother, who wanted to keep him off the streets and out of trouble. But his passion for baseball was strong, too, and he spent his summers selling ice cream at Griffith Stadium. Although Ellington won a scholarship to Pratt Institute in New York City to study art, he chose instead to drop out of high school and study piano. Soon he had formed one of the leading society bands in Washington and from there he catapulted to fame at Harlem's Cotton Club. In 1943, Ellington became the first nonclassical musician to perform at Carnegie Hall. A prolific arranger and composer of more than 6,000 works, Ellington composed (often with collaborators, such as Billy Strayhorn) classics such as "Satin Doll," "Mood Indigo," and "Don't Get Around Much Anymore." Jonathan Yardley of the *Washington Post* wrote, "There are more sounds of America in his music than in anyone else's. [No one else] left so incredibly rich and varied a legacy. He was our one true giant, and it's about time we said so."

Walk west one block on T St to the northeast corner of 13th and T Sts and the Whitelaw Apartments, formerly the **Whitelaw Hotel** (1920; Isaiah T. Hatton; DL), at 1839 13th St N.W. At one time the Whitelaw was the only major hotel serving African American visitors to Washington.

> ### Washington Notes
> Local legend has it that the hotel name is a pun on the so-called white laws that prevented African Americans from staying at segregated Washington hotels. Actually, the hotel was named after its builder, John Whitelaw Lewis, founder of the Industrial Savings Bank. Band leader Cab Calloway, boxer Joe Louis, and scientist George Washington Carver stayed at the Whitelaw, which was also the scene of dances and debutante balls.

During the Depression, the hotel became an apartment hotel for low-income families, and by the late 1960s the property had fallen into disrepair. The city closed the property in 1977. The property has been restored and is a middle-income apartment house.

## 14th and U Sts

Continue north on 13th St two blocks to U St, then west on U St to the corner of 14th and U Sts, the commercial heart of Shaw.

### History

At one time 14th St north of U St was a 20-block-long retail strip with some of the area's finest stores catering to both elite and middle-class clientele. By the 1950s, the area had a more Southern, rural, blue-collar atmosphere, but was still a strong commercial area. During the Civil Rights movement of the early 1960s, Martin Luther King, Jr.'s headquarters for the Poor People's Campaign was at the corner of 14th and T Sts. The riots following his death in April 1968 almost completely wiped out the 14th St commercial corridor. Three days of rioting and burning along 14th St, 7th St, H St N.E., and from 3rd St to Bladensburg Rd left 12 people dead, 1,200 injured, and property losses in the tens of millions.

U St was also a bustling center of activity with social clubs and nightclubs. It was on U St in 1938 that African Americans gathered to celebrate Joe Louis's victory as the heavyweight champion of the world.

Prior to 1968, 14th St businesses were grossing $75–100 million. By 1970, nearly 90 businesses had closed, and receipts totaled less than $4 million.

## *Franklin D. Reeves Municipal Center*

The opening of the Franklin D. Reeves Municipal Center (1986; VVKR, Devereaux & Purnell, Robert Traynham Coles; 1997, Walter Kravitz, sculptor) on the southwest corner of 14th and U Sts brought some commercial rejuvenation. Named for the first African American member of the Democratic National Committee, the Reeves Center was established here to bring city services to the neighborhood.

### Exterior

A prominent feature of the building is its gabled glass-and-polished-steel corner pavilion.

## Interior

Dangling from the ceiling in the atrium are the dancing figures of *U Street Sound* (1997; Walter Kravitz)—several brightly colored, translucent figures between 8 and 20 ft high. The red, blue, green, purple, and pink figures are made of polycarbonate, the shatterproof plastic used in bulletproof windows. The figures suggest a chorus line and jazz musicians, creating a tribute to the area's rich history as a musical center.

## Lincoln Theatre

Walk east on U St one and a half blocks to the Lincoln Theatre (1922; Reginald Geare; 1994, Mary Oehrlein; DL) at 1215 U St N.W., ☎ 328-6000, the only remaining major movie palace from U St's heyday.

### History

The Lincoln Theatre was designed as a cinema-vaudeville house, providing both live and film entertainment. Following its opening in March 1922, the *Washington Bee* newspaper described it as "perhaps the largest and finest theatre for colored people exclusively anywhere in the United States." Here, African American audiences could see first-run movies on a 40 ft movie screen, rather than waiting for the segregated downtown movie houses to conclude their runs before getting the films. (Movie houses in other parts of the city were closed to African Americans.) The Lincoln had a 27 by 38 ft stage flanked by fluted Corinthian columns, high ceilings from which hung elaborate chandeliers, and a terrazzo floor. When a $7 million renovation was begun in 1994, it was found that much of the interior of the theater had remained intact. The stage, columns, elaborate chandeliers, floor, and ornate plasterwork seen today are all original to the theater.

> ### Washington Notes
> Ralph Bunche (1904–1971), the first African American awarded the Nobel Peace Prize (in 1950, for his mediation of the 1948 Arab-Israeli War settlement), was refused admission to a theater downtown. He walked to another theater nearby, asked for the ticket in French, and was allowed in because the cashier thought he was part of a foreign legation.
>
> In 1939 Bunche and other Howard University faculty boycotted Gone With the Wind when it opened at the Lincoln Theatre because of the film's depiction of blacks. As Bunche remembered, "All the maids got off Thursday and came to the movie and said we were crazy—that's how slavery was. We just told them to go back and wash some windows and we kept on picketing."

A popular ballroom located behind the theater and connected to it by a tunnel was the Lincoln Colonnade, where entertainers such as Duke Ellington, Lena Horne, Pearl Bailey, Bessie Smith, and Billy Eckstine played. The Colonnade was torn down in the 1960s, and the Lincoln Theatre closed in 1979. Now operated by the U St Theatre Foundation, the Lincoln Theatre reopened in 1994, bringing back live entertainment to Shaw.

Next door to the Lincoln Theatre is another Washington institution, **Ben's Chili Bowl** at 1213 U St N.W., which is still serving customers after more than 40 years. The District's first silent movie theater, the Minnehaha, was located on this site; its façade is still visible behind the restaurant's sign. Ben and Virginia Ali operate this gastronomical landmark, the home of the halfsmoke and "the Finest Hot Dogs and Chili Served with a Touch of Class." Bill Cosby courted his wife, Camille, here and still stops by when in Washington.

Across the street from Ben's Chili Bowl, on the northeast corner of 12th and U Sts, is the former site of the **True Reformers Hall** (1903; John A. Lankford) at 1200 U St N.W., now in disrepair, but at the beginning of the century the property was "the best office, store, hall, and lodge room building that the Negro owns in the United States," according to the *Washington Bee* newspaper. Built by the United Order of True Reformers, a benevolent society, the hall was the meeting place of local fraternal groups. An armory in the basement was used by the First Separate Battalion, the city's African American National Guard unit. The Knights of Pythias bought the building in 1917 to be used as their temple, and in the years after World War I the second-floor auditorium became a dance hall. In later years the hall was a recruiting station for the armed forces in World War II and was home to the Metropolitan Police Boys Club No. 2, the only boys club between the wars that would admit African American children. Through the years the building has been occupied by a number of community organizations and commercial concerns. The property is in the process of being restored.

Walk east on U St to the corner of 11th and U Sts and the **Industrial Bank of Washington** at 2000 11th St N.W., another example of an enterprise built and owned by African Americans. The Industrial Savings Bank, founded by John Whitelaw Lewis in 1913, stood at this site. The bank closed during the bank crisis of 1932. Two years later Jesse Mitchell opened the Industrial Bank of Washington.

### Washington Notes

The Industrial Bank was a life force for the Shaw area. Although blacks could make deposits in white banks, it was difficult for them to get loans. The Industrial Bank of Washington, with its strong depositors' base, lent money to African American entrepreneurs and helped the Shaw business community thrive.

Across the street from the bank, at 2001 11th St N.W., is **Bohemian Caverns,** one of the most famous of the dozens of cabarets, jazz clubs, supper clubs, dance halls, and cafés that dotted the area in the glory days of Washington's Black Broadway. After undergoing a $2 million renovation, Bohemian Caverns reopened in the summer of 1999.

### Washington Notes

Entertainer Pearl Bailey, who performed at the Caverns in the 1930s, recalled in a magazine article that "Monday night [the Caverns] was so exciting. Whoever was playing at the Howard, Duke Ellington or whoever it was, would come over to the Caverns after they finished playing on Monday night. Everybody wanted to be there. See, it was a chance to see everybody get loose after their stage performance, just play and have a good time."

Other area clubs from that bygone era remain only a memory: The Club Bengasi at 1425 U St featured Nat King Cole; the Lincoln Colonnade, Cab Calloway; the Dance Hall at 9th and V Sts, Louis Armstrong; the Jungle Inn at 12th and U Sts, Jelly Roll Morton; and Murray's Palace Casino, Duke Ellington and Charlie Barnett.

Continue east on U St to its intersection with Vermont Ave. Facing the entrance to the U St/African American Civil War Memorial/Cardoza Metro station is the **African American Civil War Memorial** (1998; Ed Hamilton, sculptor; Edward D. Dunson, designer; Devereaux & Purnell), slated for completion in 2000. Other than the monument to Robert Gould Shaw and the troops of the 54th Massachusetts Regiment, there have been no notable monuments to the service of African Americans in the Civil War. This has been the case even though black soldiers served against greater odds than their white counterparts—if captured, they were more likely to be killed; if wounded, they were less likely to receive medical attention. For much of the war they were paid less. Few of them became officers. Future plans for the memorial include semicircular walls engraved with the names of the 208,000 African American soldiers and sailors and their mostly white officers who served with the Union Army, along with a visitor's center where individuals may research their relatives who fought in the war. The 11 ft high bronze statue features life-size relief figures of three soldiers and a sailor on one side and a family on the other.

The dedication of the Civil War Memorial is further indication of a new vibrancy and determination in the Shaw and LeDroit Park areas of the city of Washington.

Continue east on U St one and a half blocks to the northeast corner of 9th and U Sts and the former site of **Scurlock Photo Studio** at 900 U St N.W., now a boarded-up building. For 59 years, Addison N. Scurlock chronicled the institutions and faces of black Washington. Scurlock opened this studio in 1911 after winning the gold medal for photography at the 1907 Jamestown Exposition.

## Grimke Elementary School

Walk south on 9th St one block to T St, then west on T St one block to Vermont Ave, then north on Vermont a half-block to the former site of **Grimke Elementary School** at 1923 Vermont Ave N.W., which now houses offices of the D.C. Department of Corrections and the D.C. Fire Department.

### History

The Grimke family was influential in Washington's African American community as educators and civic and religious leaders. The Grimke brothers, Archibald and Francis, were the acknowledged slave sons of a wealthy South Carolina planter. Upon his death, they were freed and sent to Lincoln University in Pennsylvania in 1866. Their aunts, Angeline Weld and Sarah Moore, famous abolitionists, supported their education. After graduating from Princeton Theological Seminary, Francis took over the pastorate of the 15th St Presbyterian Church at 15th and R Sts N.W. in 1878 and for almost 60 years led the church in its fight for equal rights in the nation's capital. Archibald, the second African American to graduate from Harvard Law School, moved to Washington in 1905, where his daughter Angeline became a poet and respected teacher at Dunbar High School. Grimke served as head of the Washington branch of the NAACP, as well as president of the American Negro Academy.

**Diversion:**
Walk south on Vermont Ave a half-block to T St, then east on T St one block to 9th St, then south on 9th St five blocks to the intersection of 9th and P Sts and **Shiloh Baptist Church** at 1500 9th St N.W., ☎ 232-4200. Throughout Shaw and LeDroit's history, churches have been at the center of the life of these communities. The first schools for African Americans were established in church basements prior to Congressional authorization for public education for black children in 1862. Church leaders became political and community leaders.

A 1957 survey counted 108 religious institutions in the Shaw area. Since 1924, Shiloh Baptist Church has been at the center of community spirituality and activism. The church was founded by 300 members of the Shiloh Baptist Church who left Fredericksburg, Virginia, in 1862 at the invitation of the Union troops preparing to attack the city. Shiloh's congregation organized one of the first Sunday schools for African Americans in the city. The present church building was acquired in 1924. When a member of the previous church on the site set fire to the sanctuary, services were held at the Howard Theatre during the repair work. Today, Shiloh's 800-seat auditorium is filled to overflowing on Sun with those who come to hear the congregation's ten choirs.

From Shiloh Baptist Church, walk south on 9th St one block to O St, then east on O St two blocks to the corner of 7th and O Sts and the **O St Market,** one of the city's three remaining 19C market buildings. (The other two are Eastern Market on Capitol Hill and Georgetown Market, now the site of a Dean & Deluca food emporium.) Built in 1888, the market thrived for years as a place where residents could buy fresh produce. It was closed in 1968 following the riots, but an African American developer, James Adkins, reopened it in 1980. Though it was subsequently sold to another owner, the market continues to operate every day but Mon.

From the former site of Grimke Elementary School, walk south a half-block on Vermont Ave to T St, then east on T St three blocks to 7th St, then a half-block south on 7th St to the vacant lot, the former site of **Waxie Maxie's** at 1836 7th St N.W., a record store that became a 7th St landmark. When it opened in 1938, the store (then called the Quality Music Shop) needed police to control the crowd that turned out for the longest "jam session" in D.C. history, running continuously from 3 P.M. Fri afternoon to 3 A.M. Sat morning. Live storefront radio broadcasts featuring performers such as vocalists Sarah Vaughn and Margaret Whiting were also crowd pleasers. At one time, Waxie Maxie's, owned by jukebox entrepreneur Max Silverman, had 25 stores in the Washington area. The 7th St store was burned to the ground during the 1968 riots and all stores at other locations have also gone out of business.

## Howard Theatre
Walk a half-block north on 7th St to T St, then a half-block east on T St to the Howard Theatre (1910; architect unknown; DL) at 624 T St N.W., now closed to the public but for 60 years the queen of Washington's Black Broadway.

### History
The oldest major African American theater in the U.S. (predating New York's Apollo by 20 years), the Howard Theatre opened in 1910. The Italian Renais-

sance–Beaux-Arts auditorium seated 1,200, with a balcony and eight boxes, and backstage there were dressing rooms for 100 performers. For its first 20 years the theater booked vaudeville acts and circus road shows, but then it closed in 1929 after the stock market crash. The Stiefel brothers bought the theater in 1931, and Duke Ellington headlined the gala reopening. The Howard had four shows a day and sometimes, for extremely popular acts, eight shows. The theater was never torched during the 1968 riots, but the deteriorating neighborhood and the rise in crime kept audiences away. The Howard finally closed in 1970.

### Washington Notes

Although Washington remained a segregated city until after World War II, the performers and the audiences were integrated. White bandleaders like Woody Herman, Stan Kenton, and Artie Shaw brought their bands to the Howard. The Howard weathered the changing musical tastes of its community and its times, going from Sarah Vaughan and Ella Fitzgerald to Smokey Robinson and the Miracles, James Brown, and the Supremes, who gave their first theater performance at the Howard in Oct 1962.

Walk a half-block west on T St to 7th St, then one block north on 7th St to U St. It was at this intersection that Shaw residents made their stand during the 1919 riots. Here 7th St becomes Georgia Ave.

## Howard University Hospital

Continue north on Georgia Ave to Howard University Hospital at 2401 Georgia Ave N.W., ☎ 865-6100, a 400-bed acute-care facility. The hospital is the U.S.'s largest privately owned African American health care institution and a major graduate training center for African American physicians and dental specialists. Successor to the Freedmen's Hospital, whose mission was providing health care to newly freed slaves, Howard University Hospital spearheads a number of community efforts to educate city residents about prevention and wellness, focusing primarily on cancer, AIDS, hypertension, and health care for young people.

### History

The Freedmen's Hospital was founded in 1862, and for more than 100 years served the African American community. Funded by the Freedmen's Bureau, the hospital treated nearly 23,000 patients its first year. Dr. Alexander T. Augusta, the highest-ranking black officer in the armed forces in 1863, was the first African American superintendent of Freedmen's. In response to the need for trained black medical professionals, Freedmen's and the Howard University College of Medicine were joined in 1869 (Freedmen's becoming the university's teaching hospital) and Dr. Augusta was offered a faculty position—the first African American to hold such a position at any medical school in the U.S.

### Washington Notes

From the beginning the hospital was integrated. Until Washington's hospitals were integrated in the 1950s, Freedmen's was the only place in the city where African American doctors and nurses could be trained or African American patients could receive treatment.

Freedmen's was associated with some of the most important medical professionals of the day, including Dr. Charles Drew, one of the pioneers in the development of blood plasma. Dr. Daniel Hale Williams, founder of Chicago's Provident Hospital, performed the first successful heart surgery in America at Freedmen's in 1893.

By the 1960s, however, community needs had put a tremendous strain on Freedmen's resources, and the Department of Health, Education, and Welfare took over the administration of the hospital. President John F. Kennedy signed legislation officially transferring Freedmen's Hospital to Howard University. In 1975, Howard University Hospital was officially opened on the site of the old Griffith Stadium. The hospital treats over 100,000 patients a year.

Note also that officially Howard University uses the spelling "Freedmen's" for Freedmen's Hospital, and Arlington National Cemetery officially uses "Freedman's" for Freedman's Village. However, in the 19C spelling was somewhat casual, and documents sometimes have different spellings for these sites.

**Griffith Stadium** was named after Clark Griffith—player, manager, president, general manager, and owner of the city's only major league baseball team, the Washington Senators. The stadium was also home to the Washington Redskins, the professional football team that came to Washington from Boston in 1937. Griffith Stadium housed Washington's baseball and football teams until 1961. It was demolished in 1965.

### Washington Notes

The stadium, unlike most of the city, was integrated well before the 1950s. Despite this, many black Washingtonians opted to sit together in an area called the Pavilion along the first base line. Although no African Americans played in major league baseball until 1947, Griffith Stadium did host local African American baseball teams and the National Negro League. Popular local African American teams such as the LeDroit Tigers, the Washington Pilots, and the Washington Elite Giants often drew bigger crowds than the Senators.

On opening day in 1912, President Howard Taft threw the first ball from a special box in the stands, initiating the tradition of having a president throw the first pitch of the baseball season.

## Church of God

Directly across from the hospital, at 2030 Georgia Ave N.W., is the Church of God, known previously as the Temple of Freedom Under God, Church of God, home of the world-famous evangelist Elder Lightfoot Solomon Michaux (1885–1968).

### History

In his 1968 obituary Michaux was described as a "religious leader, gospel song popularizer, showman, real estate developer, and friend of presidents." Michaux founded his temple in a Georgia Ave storefront in 1928 and shortly after began his "Happy Am I" radio program on station WJSV in Alexandria, Virginia. (The call letters stood for Willingly Jesus Suffered Victory over the grave.) When CBS picked up the program, opening with the lines "God furnishes the spirit, Elder Michaux and his church the enthusiasm, and the Columbia Broadcasting System the service. . . . Well, Glory!" Michaux and his choir, the Cross, became world famous.

A committed showman, Elder Michaux held baptism ceremonies for hundreds of people at Griffith Stadium in 1938. Healing ceremonies were also held at Griffith, with those healed often dashing the bases on a "home run for Jesus." In 1933, during the Depression, his church took over operation of a lunchroom, renamed it the Happy News Café, and offered lunches for a penny apiece. In 1940 Michaux nominated Eleanor Roosevelt for the vice presidency at the 1940 Democratic Convention. The present church was built in 1958.

Walk one block north on Georgia Ave to W St, turn east on W St, walk one block to 6th St, then a half-block north on 6th St to 2232 6th St N.W., the site of the home of **Will Marion Cook** (1869–1944), a violinist, composer, and musical director whose musicals won acclaim in London and New York. The son of John H. Cook, dean of Howard University Law School, and husband of Abbie Mitchell, who sang "Summertime" in the original Broadway production of *Porgy and Bess*, Cook organized one of the first jazz bands in the country in 1905.

### Washington Notes

In 1912 Cook conducted what was called "the formal coming-out party" for African American music when he led the 125-piece Clef Club Orchestra at Carnegie Hall. Cook's musicals *In Dahomey* and *In Abyssinia* played in London and New York, and his *Bandana Land* created the cakewalk (dance) rage in New York society.

Walk a half-block south on 6th St to W St, then a half-block east on W to 520 W St, former site of the original Freedmen's Hospital. The building is now Howard University's College of Medicine Administration Building.

Return one and a half blocks west on W St to Georgia Ave, then walk two blocks north on Georgia Ave to the **Miner Teachers College Building** (DL) at 2565 Georgia Ave N.W. From the early 1870s through World War II, the Miner Teachers College (originally called the Miner Normal School) produced most of the African American elementary school teachers employed by the District public school system. The school's founder was a white teacher from upstate New York, Myrtilla Miner. She first went to Mississippi to teach young slaves. Finding that an impossibility because of the laws, Miner moved to Washington in 1851 and established the Colored Girls School, partly with a $1,000 contribution from the proceeds of Harriet Beecher Stowe's recently published *Uncle Tom's Cabin*. The school, located between 19th and 20th Sts and N and O Sts N.W., encountered strong opposition. White residents feared that if the school were successful, it would bring even more African Americans to a city with a rapidly growing black population. Some also felt that it was dangerous educating African Americans beyond their current social and political possibilities. Violence was threatened and rocks thrown. Miner told a friend she went to bed each night "in expectation that the house would be fired before morning." Miner's fragile health deteriorated to the point that she had to close the school in 1860, and soon afterward Miner died at the age of 49. Congress voted to reopen it in 1863, and in the 1930s reorganized it into a four-year college. Eventually, Miner Teachers College merged with other institutions to become the University of the District of Columbia. In 1998, this historic landmark building was acquired by Howard University, and discussions are now under way to convert the property into a museum.

## Howard University

2400 6th St N.W. ☎ 806-6100. Web: www.howard.edu. Offices open Mon–Fri 9–5. Closed holidays. Free guided campus tours available for prospective students through the Office of Student Recruitment. ☎ 806-2752. Restrooms, buildings, and facilities are wheelchair accessible.

Continue one block north on Georgia Ave to the entrance to the 89-acre campus of Howard University (1867–68; architect unknown; 1934–39, Albert I. Cassell; DL) at Howard Place and Georgia Ave.

**Highlights:** Howard Hall and Founders Library.

### History

Established in 1867, Howard University is one of the country's oldest and most respected universities dedicated to the education of African Americans and other historically disenfranchised groups. During its 133-year history, the university has grown from a single-frame building to 95 buildings on five campuses, with 12 schools and colleges serving 11,000 students. Howard University has produced more African American Ph.D.'s than any other institution in the world, and its faculty is the largest assembly of African American scholars and Ph.D. degree holders at any college or university in the country.

Howard University has the nation's only African American academic medical center, Howard University Hospital, and the only African American–owned public broadcasting television station, the award-winning WHUT. The university's current president is H. Patrick Swygert, a graduate of the university and its law school.

### Washington Notes

Famous graduates include diva Jessye Norman; Supreme Court justice Thurgood Marshall; producer/dancer Debbie Allen; Pulitzer Prize–winning writer Toni Morrison; the U.S.'s first African American ambassador to the United Nations, Andrew Young; and Ossie Davis, famed actor, author, and teacher.

On Nov 20, 1866, a 30-member board of the First Congregational Society met with the idea of creating a theological seminary to train African American men as preachers to minister to the newly freed slaves and those African Americans born free. The institution was to be called Howard Theological Seminary, after General Oliver Otis Howard (1830–1909), a member of the Congregational board, Civil War hero, commissioner of the Freedmen's Bureau, and longtime advocate for the improvement of the lives of African Americans.

When the board next met, on Dec 4, 1866, their goals had expanded to include educating African American teachers at a proposed Howard Normal and Theological Institute for the Education of Teachers and Preachers. Doubts still existed in some circles of society about the ability of African Americans to handle a liberal arts education, but with the opening of universities such as Shaw in Raleigh, North Carolina, and Morgan in Baltimore, the Congregational Society decided to make the now-named Howard University a full-fledged liberal arts institution. The society's stated goal was to create an institution of the "higher grade for training colored preachers and teachers to help uplift some of the four million recently emancipated slaves and a quarter of a million Negroes who had been born

HOWARD UNIVERSITY, WASHINGTON, D. C.

*Howard University, 1884. Courtesy of the Washingtoniana Division, D.C. Public Library.*

free." On March 2, 1867, Howard University was founded by an act of Congress and subsequently approved by President Andrew Johnson. The act stated that the university's mission was to educate "Negroes" and "youth," with no restrictions as to race nor gender.

In May 1867, four students, white daughters of faculty members and trustees, enrolled for Howard's first term. By the end of the first term, 94 students had enrolled. The university acquired 150 acres for the campus. This was a much larger plot than was needed, but John A. Smith, owner of the property, would only sell if the university bought the entire lot because he feared construction of a black university would ruin the property's value. The university later sold portions of the plot to finance the school's growth.

On March 19, 1867, the Reverend Charles Boynton became the university's first president but resigned after only 150 days because of discord with General Howard. Boynton believed in fundamental differences between the races and advocated separate worship. He also feared an "amalgamation" of the races. Howard strongly disagreed. Byron Sunderland, one of the city's ardent abolitionists, assumed the post in Aug 1867. General Howard succeeded Sunderland in 1869 and served until 1873, all the while modestly objecting to having the school named after him.

In 1879 Congress authorized a special appropriation for the university. In 1928 the charter was amended to authorize an annual federal appropriation for construction, development, improvement, and maintenance of the university.

In 1926, Howard's first African American president, Dr. Mordecai Wyatt Johnson, took office. At that time, none of the eight schools and colleges that made up Howard University's curriculum had received national accreditation. At the end of Dr. Johnson's term 34 years later, ten schools and colleges within Howard University had attained this goal. By 1940, the faculty, which had at one time been predominantly white, was 91 percent black.

Dr. James M. Nabrit succeeded Dr. Johnson as president in 1960. In 1961, the university acquired the Freedmen's Hospital, which had served as the teaching hospital for the Howard University Medical School since 1869. Under the leadership of James Cheek, president from 1969 to 1989, Howard University made many great advances, but also attracted controversy. During these years, the student body increased by a third to 13,000, the number of faculty doubled, and seven new schools opened within the university, as did a hotel, TV station, radio station, and book publishing operation.

Some questioned Cheek's practices, accusing him of being highly political, secretive, and excessive in spending university funds. Finally in 1989, after Cheek backed the appointment of Republican Party chairman Lee Atwater (remembered by many as masterminding a racially charged campaign ad during the 1988 presidential election) to the board of directors, students stormed the administration building and demanded Cheek's removal. Cheek stepped down and was replaced by Franklyn Jenifer. Jenifer closed down what he viewed as weak departments, raised admissions standards, improved the physical conditions of buildings and housing facilities, and instituted more frequent faculty evaluations. In 1995, current president H. Patrick Swygert assumed the presidency.

## The Campus

The university campus has three buildings of particular note: Howard Hall, Founders Library, and the Andrew Rankin Memorial Chapel. To get to **Howard Hall** (607 Howard Place) from the main entrance to the campus on Georgia Ave, walk east on Howard Place to 6th St, then north a half-block. Howard Hall is on the left, next to the Mordecai Wyatt Johnson Administration Building. Howard Hall was built in 1869 (architect unknown; DL) and is the only remaining original university structure. This well-proportioned, three-story, Second Empire building was originally the home of General Oliver Howard, and when first built dominated the hilltop overlooking the city. Its walls are constructed of hollow white bricks later painted red. Pressed-metal dormer window frames adorn the attic story and the tower. The tower also features lacy ironwork atop a slated mansard roof. When General Howard, the last surviving Civil War general, died in 1909, the university bought the building and for many years used it to house the Conservatory of Music, as well as the African Language Center. The hall was designated a historic landmark in 1974.

From Howard Hall, walk a half-block southeast, cross 6th St, go through the large gate, then proceed east for a half-block. **Founders Library** (1929–37; Louis E. Fry, Sr.), the colonial revival–styled building on the right, at 500 Howard Place between Rankin Chapel and the Undergraduate Library, was named to honor the university's founders. Although African American architect Albert I. Cassell was superintendent of buildings and grounds at Howard University and developed its 20-year building plan, a member of Cassell's Washington firm, Louis E. Fry, Sr., designed the Founders Library. Fry's design was based on that of Independence Hall in Philadelphia. Fry's variations include a third story and limestone trim used extensively for carved frames and swags in the pediments of the gabled wings. The library's tower is 165 ft high, with an open, copper-roofed cupola above the clock. The library occupies the site of the original Main Building.

> ### Washington Notes
> Founders Library contains the Moorland-Springarn Research Center, one of the largest collections of historical materials documenting the history and culture of black people from Africa, South America, the Caribbean, and the U.S.

The **Andrew Rankin Memorial Chapel,** a half-block south of Founders Library, was completed in 1895 with funds donated by the widow of Howard University president Jeremiah E. Rankin's brother. Eleanor Roosevelt, President John F. Kennedy, and Dr. Martin Luther King, Jr., are among those who have spoken from the chapel's pulpit. Entrance to this neo-Gothic brick building is through a rock-faced granite-pointed archway upon which simple floral motifs are carved. A shingled broach spire tops the square tower.

In 1998 the university broke ground for two new library facilities: the Louis Stokes Health Sciences Library, on W St N.W. between 4th and 5th Sts on the main campus, and the Law Library, at 2929 Van Ness St N.W., on the west campus. These new digital information centers will significantly enhance the university.

# LeDroit Park

### History

Less than one square mile in size, this tiny community began as a white enclave in what was then still farmland. Originally part of Washington County north of the Federal City's Boundary St (Florida Ave), LeDroit Park was the site of Campbell Military Hospital (which became the Freedmen's Hospital in 1865) and was later owned by Howard University. LeDroit Park was designed to be "a beautiful little village" on the edge of a burgeoning city.

Founded in 1873, the 55-acre tract, bought from Howard University, was in the shape of a triangle. Its developers were Amzi L. Barber, a white ministry graduate of Oberlin College who became a faculty member of Howard University, and Andrew Langdon, Barber's white brother-in-law and son of New York real estate developer LeDroit Langdon, after whom the development was named. The streets were deliberately laid out at an angle, to distinguish the area from the rest of the city and to discourage through traffic. There were five streets running north and south—LeDroit Ave (now 2nd St), Harewood Ave (now 3rd St), Linden St (now 4th St), Larch St (now 5th St), and Juniper Ave (now 6th St)—and three streets running east and west—Maple Ave (now T St), Spruce St (now U St), and Elm St (still called Elm).

Architect James H. McGill designed the houses using elements of Eastlake, Second Empire, Italianate, Queen Anne, and Gothic revival architectural styles. All the homes featured what has been called "an exuberance of detail," apparent in the window moldings, brackets, cornices, cupolas, towers, ornate porches, decorative metal work, and patterned slate on the roofs. The development included an ornamental park complete with fountain and landscaping at 3rd and T Sts.

Lawyers, doctors, government administrators, and teachers, some of them affiliated with Howard University, all of them white, purchased the 64 LeDroit Park homes that had been built by 1887.

When McGill ceased building, other developers filled in the lots of LeDroit Park and adjacent neighborhoods with row houses. The earlier row houses were detailed two- and three-story Queen Anne buildings with projecting bays, ornamental iron steps, handrails, and fences, often featuring a mixture of slate, stone, and terra-cotta. By the turn of the century, the row houses built had plain wall surfaces and metal cornices.

Part of LeDroit Park's charm was the fact that despite its proximity to downtown Washington, it retained a rural, village flavor through landscaping and gardens. No fences were permitted, and residents prided themselves on their flower gardens. A former resident recalled, "The gardens were wonderful. You could smell the flowers the minute you crossed 6th Street." The development was separated from its neighbors (especially Howardtown, an African American residential area founded in 1870 to the north) by a wood-and-cast-iron fence that went from 7th St to 3rd St and from Florida Ave to Elm St, with gates and watchmen stationed at entrances on Florida Ave and Elm St.

The fence meant residents of Howardtown, going south to downtown Washington, had to walk around LeDroit Park. When Howardtown residents began jumping the fence at night, LeDroit residents hired a night watchman. Matters escalated until the summer of 1888 when an angry mob of African Americans tore down the fence. Residents wrote to Barber, "The rights of residents and property holders of LeDroit Park have been again outraged by the tearing down of the fences across Linden and Elm Streets which protect our property against trespass," and four days later a barbed wire fence was erected. It, too, came down. After a series of lawsuits, the fence was legally demolished in 1901, and foot traffic through LeDroit Park became common.

In 1893 Octavius A. Williams, a barber who worked in the Capitol, became the first African American resident of LeDroit Park. Neighbors reacted with hostility. Williams's daughter recalled in later years, "just after we moved in and were having dinner one night, someone fired a bullet through the window." Her father left the bullet in the wall for years "so his grandchildren could see it." One year later, a second African American family moved into the neighborhood. Robert Terrell, a Harvard University graduate and principal of the M St High School, and his wife, Mary Church Terrell, a foreign language teacher who would one day be a leader in the civil rights and suffragette movements, were at first denied residence. They were only able to purchase a home through a white real estate agent ally who bought the house and then transferred the title to them.

By 1900, a small group of African American upper- and middle-class homeowners had established themselves in LeDroit Park. By World War I LeDroit Park had become one of the most prestigious and desirable African American neighborhoods in the city. Adjacent to the U St area and to Howard University, LeDroit Park became the preferred home of black Washington's intellectual and cultural elite. Poet Paul Laurence Dunbar wrote of this area, "Here comes together the flower of colored citizenship from all parts of the country." Lilian Thomas Burwell, herself an artist and niece of the artist Hilda Wilkinson Brown, speaks of Dunbar's home as "a cultural meeting place" and relates that the "proximity of LeDroit Park to the Howard Theatre at 7th and T Sts fostered a constant, if temporary, influx of musicians into the neighborhood." Among them were Lionel Hampton, Lucky Millander, Count Basie, Duke Ellington, vocalist Ruth Brown, and Earl "Fatha" Hines.

The area began to change in 1919 with the construction of Griffith Stadium, a 34,000-seat ballpark, home to the Washington Senators baseball team. From 1919 until the stadium was torn down in 1965 (to make room for Howard University Hospital), LeDroit Park residents, especially those living on U St whose backyards were abutted by the stadium's center field fence, had to make seasonal adjustments to the noise and crowds. Change continued during the Depression, when the National Capital Housing Authority built public housing units just to the north of LeDroit Park, hurting property values. During World War II, the government built two large apartment units to house government workers in the same area. In 1948, when the Supreme Court abolished segregated housing, upper- and middle-class families grabbed the opportunity and moved to more affluent areas of the city. The McGill houses were subdivided into apartments, and lower-income families began to move into the area. Howard University bought the government workers' buildings, turning them into dormitories. By the 1960s Howard University owned more than 40 percent of LeDroit Park's houses, some of which were allowed to fall into disrepair. The university also changed the character of the neighborhood with construction of large-scale buildings for both the university and its medical school. The area became troubled, with frequent vandalism and crime.

In the early 1970s Bennetta Bullock Washington, whose family had lived in LeDroit Park since 1918, and her husband, Walter Washington, the city's first African American mayor, mobilized other concerned residents to form the LeDroit Park Civic Association. The association lobbied for increased police protection and improved government services, and in 1972 the association initiated the LeDroit Park Historic District Project, which led to the designation of LeDroit Park as a historic district on the National Register in 1974. Today, LeDroit Park seems on the verge of a renaissance as growing numbers of young professionals buy and renovate the area's historic town houses.

From the entrance to Howard University at Howard Place and Georgia Ave, walk south on Georgia Ave six blocks to T St, then east on T St two and a half blocks to the home of **Walter E. Washington** at 408–410 T St N.W. In 1975, Washington became the city's first elected mayor in more than 100 years. He had already served as appointed-mayor under Presidents Johnson and Nixon before being elected under the newly granted Home Rule. The house at 408 T St was originally owned by the Reverend George O. Bullock, pastor of the Third Baptist Church. Bullock's daughter Benetta received her doctorate from Howard University before serving as principal of Cardozo High School and director of the federal government's Women's Job Corps. When Benetta Bullock married Walter Washington, they became one of the city's most influential couples, working for the empowerment of the African American community.

Continue east to the corner of 4th and T Sts, turn south on 4th St, and walk one block to the corner of 4th St and Florida Ave, the former site of **Harrison's Cafe,** 455 Florida Ave N.W., one of the community's most popular restaurants for nearly half a century. Founded in 1920 by Robert Hilliard Harrison, who learned about the art of fine cooking from his wealthy employers while traveling in Europe, the café's menu ranged from lobster to (reputedly) the best 20-cent hamburger in town. When Harrison died in 1957, he left the café to two longtime employees, who kept it open until 1962.

Walk southeast on Florida Ave one block to Rhode Island Ave, then one block north on Rhode Island Ave to its intersection with 3rd St and the former site of the **David McClelland residence,** now a Safeway. McClelland, one of the original partners in the development of LeDroit Park, built a sumptuous Italianate mansion here. The home was surrounded by grounds that included orchards extending four blocks to what is now Elm St. The African American Elks Columbian Lodge No. 85 bought the home in 1925, and it became known as the Old Elks Home, a central meeting place in the community. In 1968, the mansion was torn down and the present Safeway store built. Safeway plans to close this facility.

Walk one block east on Rhode Island Ave to 2nd St, then one block north on 3rd St to T St and 201 T St N.W., the former home of educator and author **Anna Cooper** (1858–1964). Cooper was born a slave and in 1879 was widowed at the age of 21. In 1884, she became one of the first African American female graduates of Oberlin College. For nearly 40 years, Cooper taught Latin at M St High School; she also served as its principal from 1901 to 1906.

### Washington Notes

Cooper secured assurances from Harvard, Yale, and other Ivy League universities that her students would be considered for scholarships and admission if they passed an entrance exam. Under her guidance, two of her students were the first to be admitted to Harvard without having studied at an academy or preparatory school.

In 1925, at the age of 67, Cooper completed her doctoral degree at the Sorbonne, having defended (in French) her dissertation, "The Attitude of France in Regard to Slavery [American] During the Revolution." Cooper served as president of the Frelinghuysen University, which was located at this site and held adult education classes for African Americans. Cooper continued to devote her life to racial pride and accomplishment and died in 1964 at the age of 105.

A half-block north of the house is **Anna Cooper Circle,** named in her honor. This circle, part of the original LeDroit Park design, at one time had a fountain and gardens. In 1982 the circle, which had a road for cars, was filled in, and the present brick pathways and gardens were installed.

Catercorner to the circle is the former residence of **Robert and Mary Church Terrell** (DL) at 326 T St N.W., now a boarded-up building on the D.C. Preservation League's list of "most endangered historical places." In 1895 Mary Church Terrell (1863–1954) was the first African American appointed to a school board. As a member of the Washington school board she was instrumental in the establishment of the National Association of Colored Women in 1897; she also worked with Susan B. Anthony for three decades in the women's suffrage movement. In 1909 Church Terrell was a member of the committee that laid the foundation for the organization of the National Association for the Advancement of Colored People (NAACP), and during World War I she worked on behalf of those African American servicemen who were refused service in Washington's public places.

At the age of 76, Church Terrell wrote her autobiography, *A Colored Woman in a White World,* for which her friend H. G. Wells wrote the preface. Then in 1950, when Church Terrell was in her 80s, she took on one of her most significant struggles—integration of the restaurants in the nation's capital. In 1907 she had written, "As a colored woman I may walk from the Capitol to the White House, ravenously hungry and abundantly supplied with money with which to purchase a meal, without finding a single restaurant in which I would be permitted to take a morsel of food, if it was patronized by white people, unless I were willing to sit behind a screen." A report issued by President Harry Truman's Committee on Civil Rights in 1947 spoke of the "shamefulness and absurdity of Washington's treatment of Negro Americans."

### Washington Notes

Not much was done about integrating restaurants until 1950, when Church Terrell and three others respectfully requested service at Thompson's Restaurant on 14th St and were denied. They immediately filed suit against Thompson's for violating the "Lost Laws" of 1872–73, statutes mandating equal treatment in public places. In the landmark 1953 Supreme Court case, *District of Columbia v. Thompson Co.*, the court declared the Lost Laws had never been repealed and were therefore enforceable. The resulting integration of city restaurants did not bring about the massive closings that had been anticipated.

Robert Terrell (1857–1925) served as the first African American judge on the Municipal Court of the District of Columbia.

Walk east to Cooper Circle at T St, then north on 3rd St to 1938 3rd St N.W., former residence of **Edward Brooke,** the first African American elected by popular vote to the U.S. Senate. Brooke grew up in this house, selling ice cream and hot dogs at nearby Griffith Stadium during the summer and attending Shaw Junior High School and Dunbar High School. He was awarded the Bronze Star during World War II and in 1962 was elected attorney general of Massachusetts. In 1966 Brooke was elected as a moderate Republican to the U.S. Senate, where he served for two terms. He was the first senator to call for President Richard Nixon's resignation during the Watergate scandal.

Return south a half-block on 3rd St to U St, then walk a half-block west on U St to 319 U St N.W., now part of an urban renewal housing project but formerly the site of the residence of **Christian Fleetwood.** Fleetwood (1840–1914) was among the first African Americans to be awarded the Medal of Honor for his service in the Civil War. Even with this highest honor and with the support of every officer in his unit, Fleetwood's application for a commission in the U.S. Army was turned down. As a boy, Fleetwood had been educated by a local doctor (behind locked doors), which prepared him to enter what is now called Lincoln University in Pennsylvania. Fleetwood worked for the War Department for 30 years and was instrumental in organizing African American militia and National Guard units in Washington. His wife, Sara, entered the first nursing school class at Freedmen's Hospital at the age of 55 and became its first African American superintendent of nurses in 1901.

Next door is 321 U St N.W., formerly the site of the residence of **Paul Dunbar,** the first African American to achieve international renown as a poet. Born in 1872, Dunbar attended school in Dayton, Ohio, where he was a friend of the

Wright brothers. Following the successful publication of two books of poetry, Dunbar moved to Washington. Suffering from the tuberculosis that would eventually kill him at the age of 34, Dunbar worked as a clerk at the Library of Congress while absorbing the influences of black Washington.

To continue with the next walk, proceed east for one block on U St N.W. to the intersection with Florida Ave N.W. Turn right (southeast) onto Florida Ave and continue for two blocks to the intersection with 7th St N.W. Turn right (south) onto 7th St and continue one and a half blocks to S St N.W. and the Shaw–Howard University Metro station. Take the Green Line to Fort Totten Metro station. At Fort Totten, take the Red Line to the Brookland–CUA stop.

# 24 · Brookland

Metro: Red Line to Brookland-CUA.
Bus: H2, H4, G8, or 80.

As recently as the turn of the century, Brookland was farmland. Slowly, the region attracted those who wanted an airy retreat in the country and an escape from Washington's sweltering summers. As the city grew, a subdivision of the original property was created, linking Brookland with the downtown area. Brookland is a vital, racially mixed, middle-class neighborhood and an enclave of religious and educational significance.

Although beautiful and removed from Washington's downtown, Brookland's streets vary substantially in their degree of safety. When walking here, exercise caution.

**Highlights:** Brookland harbors Catholic and Trinity Universities, the Franciscan Monastery of the Holy Land, and the Basilica of the National Shrine of the Immaculate Conception.

### History

Prior to the 1840s, farms predominated in this rural area outside the boundaries of L'Enfant's Federal City. The largest farm belonged to Nicholas Queen, a successful innkeeper. When his daughter, Anne Margaret, married Colonel Jehiel Brooks, Queen gave them 185 acres of his 1,500-acre estate. He later divided the remainder of his property into farms for his other children and grandchildren.

Colonel Brooks, the namesake of the present-day neighborhood, was a colorful and industrious character. Shortly after his marriage to Anne, President Andrew Jackson appointed Brooks Indian agent to the Caddo Indians, requiring them to move to Red River, Louisiana. In 1834 Brooks turned down an appointment as governor of Louisiana so that he and his wife could return to their family in the Washington area. Soon after their return, they began building a manor home on their land. Their Greek revival mansion was completed in 1840. Inspired by the clean, crisp air in the area, the Brookses dubbed their home Bellair. The Brookses reared five children in Bellair. Colonel Brooks maintained friendships and corresponded with many influential people, including Presidents Tyler and Polk. His letters are held in the archives of nearby Catholic University.

By the 1850s, the city began to encroach upon the estate. The Columbia Ceme-

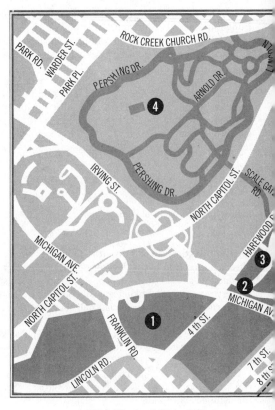

1 Trinity College
2 Catholic University of America
3 Basilica of the National Shrine of the
  Immaculate Conception

4 U.S. Soldiers' and Airmen's Home
5 Bellair (Brooks Mansion)
6 Franciscan Monastery Memorial
  Church of the Holy Land

tery, an integrated burial ground, moved from the city to just south of Bellair, around present-day Rhode Island Ave. In 1873, in order to serve the farmers, the Baltimore and Ohio Railroad created Brooks Station near the manor. In 1885, Catholic University of America was established to the west of the farm.

After Colonel Brooks died in 1886, his heirs sold the property, and a subdivision marketed under the name Brookland began. The arrival of the streetcar in 1889, which connected Brookland to the city proper, spurred settlement. By 1891, Brookland, attracting middle-class Washingtonians, had a population of about 700. A Baptist church and school was established.

The presence of Catholic University, and later Trinity College (1899) and the Basilica of the National Shrine of the Immaculate Conception (1919), brought many Catholics into the neighborhood, earning the area the unofficial title of Little Rome. During the early 1900s, Brookland remained primarily white and pri-

marily segregated, but blacks were always a vital part of the community. In the 1930s Pearl Bailey lived for a time at 1428 Irving St. After World War II, more blacks moved into the area, but some white residents resisted the change. Sterling Brown, a Howard University professor and poet, noted that after he moved into the area many white families moved out.

In the '60s, blacks countered by forming the Brookland Neighborhood Civic Association. Symbolic of the neighborhood's—as well as the country's—change during the 1960s, the first black cabinet member, Robert Weaver, John F. Kennedy's secretary of housing and urban development, resided in Brookland while in office.

Today, the racially diverse neighborhood strives to maintain its historic sites and charm. Urban blight has threatened Brookland's charm, but its residents have remained steadfast.

## Trinity College

125 Michigan Ave N.E. ☎ 884-9700. Web: www.trinitydc.edu.

Begin the tour from the Brookland-CUA Metro stop. From the CUA exit, walk onto Michigan Avenue and proceed west to Trinity College (1899–1909; Edwin

F. Durang and Son of Philadelphia; 1920–24, Maginnis and Walsh; mosaics designed by Bancel La Farge; stained glass by Connick of Boston; 1929, landscaping, Olmsted Brothers) One of the first Catholic women's colleges in the United States, Trinity College is a liberal arts Catholic college offering weekday and weekend undergraduate programs to women and coeducational graduate programs. The more than 1,500 students currently enrolled at Trinity come from over 30 states and 12 foreign countries.

### History

In 1897, Sister Mary Euphrasia, superior of the N. Capitol St Convent, wanted to establish a summer girls' academy. She consulted with Sister Julia McGroaty, provincial superior of the Sisters of Notre Dame de Namur, who expanded the plans to the creation of a full-fledged women's college since, at this time, Catholic University did not accept women. Sister Julia consulted with Monsignor Thomas J. Conaty, the rector of Catholic University.

Despite considerable opposition from the Catholic Church, Sister Julia's idea was eventually adopted, and in 1900 Trinity College opened. The first class graduated in 1904. In 1997, Trinity College began celebrating its Centennial Era (1997–2000), marking the centennial of the college's founding in 1897 to the arrival of its first students in 1900.

Visible from Michigan Ave, the **Notre Dame Chapel** is Trinity's most significant building, offering a fine example of Byzantine architecture. Constructed of Kentucky limestone, the chapel features a red tile roof and a low saucer dome 67 ft high above a cylindrical base. The decor highlights the Virgin Mary. A relief of Mary and the Christ child sitting on a throne decorates the west portico, and scenes from her life dominate the stained glass. There are mosaics by Bancel and Thomas La Farge, and stations of the cross executed in Algerian onyx by Albert Atkins.

## Catholic University of America

620 Michigan Ave N.E., at Michigan Ave and 4th St N.E. ☎ 319-5000. Web: www.cua.edu. University offices open Mon–Fri 9–5. Closed holidays. Restrooms, telephones, cafeteria, bookstore. The Rat, the cafeteria located in the University Center, is open Sept–mid-May Mon–Fri 11–11; Sat 12–11; Sun 1–10; closed in summer. The Cardinal's Nest, a food court located in the University Center, is open Mon–Fri 9:30–2:30 throughout the summer; longer hours during the school year. Free guided campus tours are available but must be prearranged through the Admissions Office. The university's restrooms, buildings, and facilities are wheelchair accessible.

Return to Michigan Ave and retrace your steps to Harewood Ave. Turn left, or north, on Harewood onto the main campus of the Catholic University of America (CUA). This 144-acre university, which holds a papal charter, remains the only university in the United States established by U.S. Catholic bishops and is the national university of the Catholic Church.

**Highlights:** Caldwell Hall, McMahon Hall, and Mullen Library.

### History

In 1866, the Catholic bishops of the United States decided to establish a university to promote higher education for the clergy. At the Third Plenary Council in

1884, Bishop John Lancaster Spalding, of Peoria, Illinois, convinced the other bishops that founding a university rather than an expanded seminary would do more to promote Catholicism. A monetary gift from Mary Gwendoline Caldwell, of Newport, Rhode Island, made establishing the university possible. On April 10, 1887, the Catholic Church founded the Catholic University of America, registering an incorporation in the District of Columbia on April 21, 1887. Pope Leo XIII approved the university's first constitution on March 7, 1889, and on Nov 13, 1889, 37 students entered CUA, attending classes in what is now Caldwell Hall and the School of Religious Studies.

Expansion included the creation of the School of Law in 1898, and in 1930, the establishment of the Graduate School of Arts and Science and the School of Engineering and Architecture. Today the university has ten schools including music, nursing, library and information science, and social service.

The clash between Catholicism's conservative stance on such social issues as birth control, abortion, and gay rights and more liberal approaches has led to friction between some students, faculty, and the church. CUA welcomes students of all religious faiths.

### Washington Notes

In 1937, shortly after American University's graduate school voted to admit blacks, CUA allowed blacks into its School of Social Work. In 1948 CUA became the only university in the District other than Howard University to open all its schools to blacks.

Even though the campus address is 620 Michigan Ave N.E., the main entrance is on Harewood Rd. From Michigan Ave, turn north onto Harewood Rd and from that turn east onto Catholic University campus. The roads on the campus aren't named, so directions are given using adjacent buildings. Coming off Harewood Rd onto the campus, pass Ward Hall. The second building to the left of Ward Hall is **Caldwell Hall** (1889; Baldwin and Pennington), CUA's first building. Named after benefactor Mary Gwendoline Caldwell, this Richardson Romanesque building stands across from the Basilica of the National Shrine of the Immaculate Conception.

Exit Caldwell Hall and walk back to Ward Hall. From the front of Ward Hall turn left toward McMahon Hall. At McMahon Hall, bear right toward Mullen Library. **Shahan Hall** (1949; Frederick Vernon Murphy) and **Keane Hall** (1958; Thomas H. Locraft) are directly behind Mullen Library. Both buildings echo the Italian Romanesque features of the shrine. The designers of both buildings taught at CUA. Murphy founded CUA's architecture department in 1911 and served as its chairman until 1950, and Locraft succeeded Murphy in that position.

## Basilica of the National Shrine of the Immaculate Conception

400 Michigan Ave N.E., at Michigan Ave and 4th St N.E. ☎ 526-8300. Web: www.nationalshrine.com. Open daily April 1–Oct 31 7–7; daily Nov 1–March 31 7–6. Admission: free. Restrooms, telephones. Cafeteria open Sun 7:30–3; weekdays 7:30–2. Gift shop and bookstore hours vary. During the school year: open Mon–Tues 8:30–6:30; Wed–Thurs 8:30–5:30; Fri 8:30–5:00; Sat 10–2. Summer: open Mon–Tues 9–6; Wed–Thurs 9–5; Fri 9–4; closed Sat–Sun. Free

guided tours are available Mon–Sat 9–11 and 1–3; Sun 1:30–4 approximately every half hour. Advance reservations are available.

The Basilica of the National Shrine of the Immaculate Conception is fully wheelchair accessible. Handicapped restrooms are located at the east entrance on the Crypt level. Ramps to the Crypt Church and an elevator are located on either side of Memorial Hall.

Return to Harewood Rd. Immediately in view and adjacent to CUA's campus is the prominent domed building, the Basilica of the National Shrine of the Immaculate Conception (1920; Maginnis, Jr., and Murphy; 1959; Kennedy), the largest Roman Catholic church in the Americas. The church honors Mary, in her role as patroness of the United States. The National Shrine, elevated to Minor Basilica status in 1990 by Pope John Paul II, is a major Washington landmark.

**Highlights:** This impressive church features a varied collection of 20C mosaics, stained glass windows, and 60 chapels and 6 oratories reflecting the Catholic Church's devotion to Mary.

### History

Catholic immigrants arriving in the New World brought with them many of the external trappings and devotions unique to their faith. Among these was the belief in the Virgin Mary's central role in the life of the church. In 1792, John Carroll, the first Catholic bishop of the United States, declared Mary the protector of the new nation. Years later, in May 1846, 19 Catholic bishops petitioned Rome to officially recognize this position. In 1847, Pope Pius IX granted the petition, proclaiming Mary, in her title of the Immaculate Conception, patroness of the United States.

Following the Pope's proclamation, the Church hierarchy in the United States advanced the idea of creating a national shrine, dedicated to Mary, in the nation's capital. In 1913, Bishop Thomas J. Shahan, the fourth rector of the Catholic University of America, presented a plan for construction of the current basilica to Pope Pius X. Pius X enthusiastically endorsed the proposal and made the first donation of $400 toward the costs of construction. Following this meeting, Shahan began a national fund-raising drive. On Sept 23, 1920, James Cardinal Gibbons, archbishop of Baltimore, laid the cornerstone of the shrine.

The construction of the National Shrine was completed in stages. In 1922, work commenced on the Crypt Church, located on the lower level. As construction continued, American Catholics were eager to utilize this new national center. The first mass was celebrated in the Crypt Church on Easter Sun, 1924, fully two years before the church was completed. By 1931, construction had moved beyond the confines of the Crypt Church to encompass most of today's Crypt level, including Memorial Hall, the Chapel of Our Lady of Lourdes, and, following Bishop Shahan's death in 1932, the Founder's Chapel, which contains Shahan's remains.

During the years of the Depression and World War II, construction on the National Shrine came to a virtual halt. Work resumed in 1954 when Archbishop John Noll of Fort Wayne, Indiana, and Archbishop Patrick O'Boyle of Washington, D.C., revived the nation's interest in the project. The construction of the shrine's Great Upper Church was entrusted to the John McShain Company of Philadelphia. The company had earlier constructed the Pentagon and the Jefferson Memorial. Eugene F. Kennedy, Jr., served as supervising architect. In an amazing feat of engineering, the exterior façade of the Great Upper Church was erected in five years. On Nov 20, 1959, Francis Cardinal Spellman, archbishop of New York, dedicated the completed National Shrine of the Immaculate Conception.

While construction of the exterior façade and most of the Great Upper Church was complete, much work remained on the shrine's interior. The multiethnic and diverse American Catholic community sought to represent the immigrant nature of their nation within the walls of the basilica. Their efforts resulted in the construction of 60 chapels and 6 oratories reflecting devotion to Mary found in all corners of the world. The latest chapel, dedicated Aug 1997, honors Mary as mother of Africa and attracts thousands of African American Catholics each year. In Nov 1999, a massive sculpture entitled *The Universal Call to Holiness* was dedicated. Today several projects remain to be completed at the shrine.

## Exterior

The Basilica of the National Shrine of the Immaculate Conception is the largest Catholic church in the Americas and the eighth largest church in the world. Its exterior design reflects the Byzantine-Romanesque architectural style of the earliest Christian churches and buildings found throughout the Mediterranean. The National Shrine has a 329 ft bell tower and a sparkling blue and gold dome visible from miles around.

On the south façade of the **Great Upper Church,** a Latin cross stands directly above the main entrance to the shrine. Below it, two eagles stand on each side of a traditional symbol of Mary. The tympanum over the center doors depicts the Annunciation, when angels told Mary that she would bear the child Jesus. Below, written in stone, is the traditional Catholic invocation: "Hail Mary, Full of Grace, The Lord is with Thee." The four panels to the left of the doorway depict significant Old Testament women, while the panels to the right depict women important in Jesus' life. Carvings on both sides of the giant arches represent the apostles and various prominent figures in Biblical history.

The east façade draws on the theme of faith. Carvings and reliefs on this side of the National Shrine illustrate the history of the Catholic faith in America. Depicted on the exterior wall are the founding of Maryland and Columbus's discovery of the New World. The east portico contains several mosaics further depicting scenes from American Catholic history.

The north exterior wall is dominated by the central figure of Mary, queen of the universe. Above this figure, stands a 16 ft stone cross that bears the Greek inscription for "Jesus Christ Conquers."

The less-visited west façade illustrates the theme of charity. Important carvings include Christ healing a paralytic and Pope Leo XIII holding his important document on social justice. The mosaics in the east portico were donated by American Catholics serving in the military. Scenes depict the Daughters of Charity caring for the wounded in the Civil War and an army chaplain on the battlefield.

The **Great Dome** of the shrine features colorful polychrome tiles whose letters *A* and *M* (for Ave Maria) intertwine. The dome is further adorned with traditional symbols of Mary, including the fleur-de-lis, the cedar of Lebanon, the tower of ivory, and the star of the sea. Atop the great dome is a 14 ft gold-leaf cross.

The **Knight's Tower,** a gift of the Knights of Columbus, was completed in 1959 and dedicated on Sept 8, 1963. The 329 ft tower ranks second only to the Washington Monument as the city's highest structure. The tower houses 56

French bronze bells. The bells range in size from the largest, weighing 7,200 pounds, to the smallest, weighing 21 pounds. The carillon is operated by a wooden keyboard located within the playing cabinet at the 200 ft level of the tower.

## Interior

Corresponding to the shape of the Latin cross, the shrine contains 2 central worship spaces (the Crypt Church and the Great Upper Church), 60 chapels, and 6 oratories.

The **Crypt Church,** on the lower level, is modeled after the Roman Catacombs and provides an intimate location for quiet reflection. Able to seat more than 400 people, the Crypt Church contains an impressive display of stonework. The intricate pattern of the floor is comprised of more than 40,000 individual pieces of marble. Fifty-eight columns support the tile ceiling with its ceramic depiction of the members of the Holy Trinity. At the center of the church is the Mary Memorial Altar, carved from a single piece of Algerian onyx.

> ### Washington Notes
> An Indiana schoolgirl, Mary Downs, conceived of the idea of all American women named Mary contributing to a shrine memorial. This altar is the gift of 30,000 women named Mary who responded to this appeal.

The **Great Upper Church,** which seats more than 2,000 people, is designed to impress the visitor with its huge columns, arches, and stained glass windows. Towering above the north apse of the Great Upper Church is the mosaic of *Christ in Majesty.* The largest mosaic of Christ in the world, it was completed in 1959, the gift of an anonymous donor. On the southern interior wall, work has recently finished on *The Universal Call to Holiness* sculpture (1999; George Carr), which depicts an important theme of the Second Vatican Council.

The National Shrine's 60 chapels and 6 oratories are located on both the upper and lower levels. They are representative of the immigrant cultures that united in their faith to form the American Catholic community. Examples include the Chapel of Our Lady of Hope, dedicated to a Marian devotion in Pontmain, France, and donated by Mr. and Mrs. Bob Hope, and the Oratory of Our Lady of Good Health, Vailankanni, donated by American Catholics of Asian Indian descent.

## U.S. Soldiers' and Airmen's Home

From the shrine, go west on Michigan Ave (or on Irving St, depending on where you exit the shrine) to N. Capitol St, then north on N. Capitol St to the U.S. Soldiers' and Airmen's Home (1851–57; Barton S. Alexander), 3700 N. Capitol St, at Rock Creek Church Rd and N. Capitol St N.W. Inaccessible to the general public, this facility, one of three military asylums established by Congress in 1851, is the only one in operation today.

### History

Secretary of War James Barbour recommended in 1827 that Congress establish an asylum for aged and disabled soldiers. No progress was made until 1848 when General Winfield Scott, after taking Mexico City during the Mexican War, levied a $150,000 tribute from the conquered city. Scott deposited this in the Bank of America, New York City, "to the credit of the Army Asylum, subject to order of

Congress." On March 3, 1851, under the leadership of Senator Jefferson Davis, Congress passed a bill authorizing asylums to be built in the District of Columbia, in New Orleans, and in East Pascagoula, Mississippi. Only the D.C. asylum lasted past 1860.

The asylum opened on Dec 24, 1851, in temporary quarters on 17th St N.W. In June 1852, the asylum was relocated to its present site, a 256-acre estate purchased from George Riggs.

Residents lived first in Anderson Cottage (formerly called the Corn-Riggs House). In 1857 residents moved into the completed Main Building, later renamed Sherman South. Providing uninterrupted service since 1851, the asylum has grown from housing 127 people in 1859 to nearly 3,000 residents today.

### Washington Notes

President Buchanan spent the summers from 1857 to 1860 at Anderson Cottage to escape Washington's unpleasant, humid downtown. From 1862 to 1864, President Lincoln lived at the cottage from midsummer to Nov. While there in 1862, after learning of General Lee's defeat at Antietam, Lincoln penned the second and final draft of the Emancipation Proclamation. Presidents Hayes and Arthur also summered at the cottage.

There are four buildings of historical significance at the asylum. The **Anderson Cottage** (1843; architect unknown), originally George Riggs's summer home, is a two-story Gothic house with wrought-iron porches, white lattice windows, and gingerbread trim. The original red brick walls were stuccoed in 1897. **Sherman South** (1857; Barton S. Alexander), or Main Building, is a three-story Norman Gothic building. Architect of the Capitol Edward Clark added the third story and a belfry in 1872. The Gothic revival cottages **Quarters 1** and **Quarters 2** (1857; Barton S. Alexander), which housed the asylum governor and secretary-treasurer, retain their original exterior.

## Bellair

Return to Michigan Ave and walk several long blocks east on Michigan, back past Catholic University, to Monroe St. Walk three blocks east on Monroe to 9th St. The area enclosed by 9th and 10th Sts on the east and west, Monroe St to the south, and Newton to the north marks the heart of the Brookses' original farm and the site of Bellair, which stands in the center of this property.

Bellair, also known as the Brooks Mansion (1840; architect unknown), served as home to the Brookses until 1886, when the Marist Society bought the home to use as a college; the Marist Society created an addition in 1894 (architect unknown). The three-story, brick manor's walls were originally stuccoed, and the main entrance has Doric columns. A cupola crowns the original wing. The southern extension built of brick by the Marists is roughly the same size as the original manor.

In 1905 the Marists sold the property to the Benedictine Sisters, who founded St. Benedict Academy. Brookses' grandchildren studied here. The academy operated until 1928 when the building was turned into a convent, which occupied the manor until 1970. The building, owned by the University of the District of Columbia, is currently vacant and for sale.

## Franciscan Monastery Memorial Church of the Holy Land

1400 Quincy St N.E. ☎ 526-6800. Web: www.pressroom.com/~franciscan. Open daily 9–5. Closed Easter, Thanksgiving, Christmas Day, and New Year's Day. Admission: free. Mon–Sat tours given hourly 9–4, except noon; Sun 1–4. Restrooms, telephones, gift shop. Shop open 9–5, except Good Friday. Daily mass services open to the public.

Walk southeast on Monroe St to 14th St. Turn left and proceed north to Quincy St and the Franciscan Monastery Memorial Church of the Holy Land, American headquarters for the Order of St. Francis and dedicated to the support of schools, missions, and programs in the Holy Land. The monastery houses relics of Catholic saints, as well as replicas of Holy Land shrines.

**Highlights:** Replicas of Rome's Catacombs and of sites sacred to the Catholic Church, including the Garden of Gethsemane, the Grotto of Lourdes, and the Holy Sepulchre.

### History

This site was originally part of a tract of land given to George Calvert, first Lord Baltimore, by King Charles I of England in 1632. Through the years it passed into other hands and finally was the property of the McCeeney family. In 1897, Father Godfrey Schilling, a Franciscan, acquired the McCeeney estate in order to build a Franciscan monastery. The Catholic Church guaranteed trusteeship to the Franciscans for 700 years.

Schilling renamed the hill where the monastery stands Mt. St. Sepulchre. Construction began in 1898, and in 1899 the monastery was dedicated. Its purposes are to preserve the Holy Land's shrines, to make these shrines accessible to those in America who could not go abroad to visit the original ones, to provide charitable services, and to provide financial support for the Franciscans.

### Exterior

The gate, at Quincy and 14th Sts, features a statue of St. Bernadine of Sienna. The Rosary Portico, which surrounds the monastery, is adorned with colonnades with red roof tiles. This area includes replicas of the Garden of Gethsemane, the Tomb of the Blessed Virgin, the Grotto of Lourdes, and the Chapel of St. Anne. A statue of St. Christopher bearing Christ upon his shoulders is inside the portico near the entrance of the church. The flowers and shrubbery contribute to the monastery's peaceful setting.

The Byzantine-style church (1899; Aristides Leonori) echoes Italian Renaissance structure, consisting of a five-fold cross plan crowned by a dome and cupola.

### Interior

The monastery is impressive with many chapels, shrines, and features such as stained glass windows that depict the three orders of St. Francis.

Enter by the main gate and walk straight ahead toward the monastery. Approaching the monastery, bear to the left and enter the gift shop. Walk through the gift shop to the hallway, and down the hallway to a lobby where the guided tours of the monastery begin. The first room on the tour, the **Chapel of St. Joseph**, celebrates the foster father of Jesus. A statue in the chapel depicts Joseph holding the infant Jesus. Bas-reliefs show the marriage of Mary and Joseph and the flight from Jerusalem.

Leave the chapel through the door on the right. The **Altar of Thabor,** honoring Christ's transfiguration, is immediately outside this exit. Beneath the altar, a reproduction of the **Holy Sepulchre** in Jerusalem, the site believed to be where Christ was interred, celebrates his death and resurrection. In front of the altar is a Palestinian marble reproduction of the **Stone of Anointing.** The original in Jerusalem is said to mark the spot where Christ's body was prepared for burial.

At the center of this room, which conforms to the shape of a cross, is an impressive **altar** with a canopy supported by four bronze pillars. Each pillar is adorned with figures of three of the twelve apostles. This altar, which honors the Trinity, is modeled after the Papal Altar in St. Peter's in Rome.

To the right is a chapel that contains the **Altar of St. Francis of Assisi,** dedicated to the saint who founded the Franciscan Order. This altar's bas-relief panels depict important moments in St. Francis's life. Exit through the left passage so as to reenter the main area. Built into the wall, the **Altar of the Holy Ghost**'s bas-reliefs depict Christ sending the apostles out to preach and St. Francis giving his first followers their missions.

The chapel to the left of this altar houses the **Altar of Calvary,** a replica of the altar in the Holy Land that marks the site of Jesus' crucifixion. A break in the marble to the right of the room's opening symbolizes the crack caused by the earthquake following Christ's death. A detailed bas-relief shows Christ's last moments on the cross.

Leave through the door facing the altar and descend the steps outside to the **Shrine of the Scourging** and the **Coronation Shrine.** Statues here represent Jesus after his whipping at the hands of the Romans and then after the crown of thorns had been placed on his head.

Return to the main room and enter the chapel to the right of the top of the stairs, the **Chapel of St. Anthony,** where a statue shows Anthony embracing the young Jesus. Panels depict Anthony healing the sick and giving food to the poor.

Exit on the far side to the **Sacred Heart Altar,** which celebrates Christ's love for humankind. Descend the stairs in front of the altar to the grotto area. The first area, the **Grotto of Nazareth** copies the Shrine of Annunciation in Nazareth and commemorates Mary's learning that she would give birth to the Savior. To the right of the stairway, the **Catacombs** reproduces a small section of the Roman site where early Christians worshiped and interred their dead. A passage here leads to the **Martyr's Crypt,** a facsimile of a Catacombs chapel. Encased in the altar's wax figure are relics of St. Benignus brought from Rome. The crypt leads to the **Purgatory Chapel,** behind which the Catacombs continue. Two additional chapels are dedicated to St. Cecilia and St. Sebastian. The final stop, the **Grotto of Bethlehem,** reproduces the Grotto of the Nativity in Bethlehem.

To continue to the next walk, National Arboretum, it is advisable to take a cab.

# 25 · National Arboretum

**A note on transportation:** Public transportation may be used to get to the arboretum; however, this very worthwhile attraction is located in an area of town less safe than the more common tourist areas downtown. It is best to visit here by driving or by taking a cab and arranging ahead of time for the cab to wait or to return at a specified time, as cabs can be difficult to find in this neighborhood.

Metrorail and bus: Blue/Orange Line to Stadium-Armory. Transfer to Metrobus B2, get off at Bladensburg Rd and R St, and walk 300 yds west on R St to the R St Entrance Gate.

If driving, the arboretum is located on New York Ave (Rte 50) east from downtown, just past Bladensburg Rd in northeast Washington. Use the New York Ave entrance located on a service road paralleling New York Ave.

3501 New York Ave N.E. ☎ 245-2726. Web: www.ars-grin.gov/na/. Grounds open daily 8–5. Closed Christmas Day. National Bonsai and Penjing Museum open daily 10–3:30, except Christmas Day. Administration Building open weekdays 8–4:30; weekends March–mid-Nov 9–5. Arbor House Gift Shop open March 1–Dec 24 10–3. Tram tour weekends only spring through autumn 10:30, 11:30, 1, 2, 3, and 4; fee charged. For tours, classes, and lectures, ☎ 245-4521. Restrooms. Picnic areas. Wheelchair accessible.

The National Arboretum (DL), a research-and-education facility of the Department of Agriculture's Agricultural Research Service, is a living museum covering 444 acres. The property has experimental seedlings and an array of flowers in season. A leading horticultural facility, the arboretum has a dozen specialty gardens.

The stated mission of the arboretum is "serving the public and improving our environment by developing and promoting improved landscape plants and new technologies through scientific research, educational programs, display gardens, and germplasm conservation." In contrast to the research done at the Department of Agriculture's research center in Beltsville, Maryland, research at the arboretum is restricted to the field of ornamental plants.

**Average blooming dates (sampling):** Jan/Feb (conifer foliage and cones, holly in fruit, winter jasmine, Japanese apricot); March (sweetbox, cornelian cherry, pussy willows, daffodils, woodland wildflowers); April (crocus, magnolias, crabapples, flowering cherries, azaleas); May (rhododendrons, mountain laurel, iris, tulip trees, peonies, lilacs); June (magnolia, lilies, herbs, dogwood); July (hibiscus, crape myrtle, boxwood, annuals, prairie wildflowers); Aug (waterlilies, sweet pepper bush, cardinal flower, plumleaf azalea); Sept (hibiscus, firethorn in fruit, autumn crocus, osmanthus); Oct (fall foliage, dogwood in fruit, native witchhazel, conifer foliage and cones); Nov (ornamental grasses, conifer foliage and cones, viburnum and dogwood in fruit); Dec (holly and heavenly bamboo in fruit, Japanese apricot, wintersweet).

**Highlights:** National Bonsai and Penjing Museum and the National Capitol Columns.

### History

Established by an act of Congress in 1927, the National Arboretum was initially allocated $300,000 and assigned the goal "to conduct research, provide education, and to conserve and display trees, shrubs, flowers and other plants to enhance the environment." The site chosen was Mt. Hamilton, formerly part of the city's fortifications during the Civil War and the second highest point in Washington (after Mt. Alban and the Washington National Cathedral). At the time of purchase, the land was used for farming.

The idea for a national arboretum had been discussed since 1917, but action was delayed because of World War I. After the war, money was a problem. However, the idea of an arboretum continued to be strongly supported for two basic reasons: national pride and research.

Two years after the 1927 act of Congress establishing the arboretum, plans were still being discussed. An *Evening Star* newspaper article in 1929 quoted the president of the Carnegie Institution (see Walk 17: "Dupont Circle East") as strongly supporting the project because the populace needs to understand that "a large part of our heritage is already gone. . . . We lack one thing that is fundamental, and that is a laboratory in which [scientists] can work—a place of trees, an arboretum into which they can bring all kinds of trees from all parts of this country and from other countries to study them."

Between 1935 and 1940, the Civilian Conservation Corps was brought in to dig ponds and build roads. Meanwhile, a committee was meeting to decide on the scope of the arboretum's research. The committee appointed F. V. Coville as acting director from 1929 to 1937; he was succeeded in 1937 by B. Y. Morrison. Plantings (some brought from other areas of the country) began in the early 1940s, and the azaleas were planted between 1947 and 1949. It was in 1949, with the blooming of the azaleas, that the arboretum was opened for the first time to the public. Visitors could come on weekends. In 1951, Morrison officially became director of the arboretum. In 1952, the dogwood plantings began.

From the beginning, funding was an issue. In 1959 the Department of Agriculture wanted to cut the facility's appropriation by $185,000, explaining that the money was needed elsewhere in the department. The arboretum's budget was not cut. That same year the arboretum, finally with enough funds to do so, opened to the public on a full-time basis.

The arboretum also had to fend off requests for its land. In 1970, Martha Mitchell, wife of Attorney General John Mitchell, proposed that some of the arboretum acreage be used to build a guarded compound for cabinet officers and their families. Later that same decade, Washington Mayor Marion Barry proposed the use of arboretum land to build an amusement park. Intense lobbying on the part of First Lady Betty Ford, among others, helped defeat the idea.

The growing environmental movement of the 1960s and the gift of the core bonsai collection by the people of Japan in 1976, has increased the arboretum's stature, as has its many community-related projects. The arboretum's Youth Garden program gives urban youngsters a garden plot in which to grow vegetables. About one million people visit the arboretum each year.

The facility's scientists study the development of trees, shrubs, and floral plants. Through a program of testing and genetic improvement, plants have been developed at the arboretum that have superior survival characteristics. Research has also developed new methods of plant disease detection and control.

To see the complete 444 acres, it's necessary to have a car or be an accomplished hiker. About 30 percent of the arboretum grounds are naturally wooded areas. However, without a car, it's still possible to see a lot of the arboretum by taking the tram tour and by enjoying the sites within walking distance of the Administration Building. Because the neighborhood that the arboretum is situated in is less safe than other tourist areas, it is wise to see the arboretum by taking a guided tram tour instead of venturing on one's own.

The New York Ave entrance leads directly to a parking lot and the **Administration Building** (1964; David Norton Yerkes of Deigert and Yerkes and Associates), a $1.3 million facility housing administration staff offices, space for changing exhibits, the arboretum library, and a 150-seat auditorium. Surrounding this contemporary-style building is a pool featuring water lilies and exotic Japanese koi fish.

From the Administration Building, walk east to the **National Bonsai and Penjing Museum,** the largest North American collection of trees artistically trained in the bonsai and penjing styles. The collection is housed in four complementary pavilions: the **Mary E. Mrose International Pavilion** and the **Chinese Pavilion** (1996; JT Associates in collaboration with Lee/Liu Associates, Inc.), the **Japanese Pavilion** (1976; Masao Kinoshita of Sasaki & Associates), and the **John Y. Naka North American Pavilion** (1990; Masao Kinoshita with Urban Design Collaborative International). Each pavilion has its own meditative garden.

The National Bonsai Collection began in 1976 when 53 bonsai and 5 viewing stones were presented as a gift of the people of Japan, through the Nippon Bonsai Association, in commemoration of America's Bicentennial. In the spring of 1998, 7 additional bonsai (after a year in quarantine) were given to the collection by the same association, and 2 others soon after by the American bonsai master John Naka, whose self-portrait hangs in the museum. Trees of more than 30 species are in the collection, ranging in age from 15 to more than 350 years, and measuring on average one to two ft in height.

*Suiseki* (viewing stones) are naturally formed stones admired for their beauty and power to suggest a scene from nature. Created by nature and unaltered by people, *suiseki* depict the art of nature. Viewing stones come in all sizes from as small as four inches to as large as four ft.

Enter the museum through the **Ellen Gordon Allen Entrance Garden,** which is landscaped with Japanese plants such as Japanese cedars and wildflowers. The garden leads into a courtyard. From here, enter any of the four pavilions. The **Penjing Collection,** which has a pagoda-like entrance, includes trees ranging in age from 15 to 100 years, among them a Chinese elm and a golden larch. Penjing is the Chinese art of growing a plant or group of plants and stones together to re-create a scene in nature. Penjing has been appreciated for more than 1,200 years.

In the Bonsai Collection is the oldest tree in the museum—a Japanese white pine more than 350 years old. This pine was a gift from the imperial household, as was a 180-year-old red pine, the first bonsai of the Imperial Collection ever to leave Japan. The North American Pavilion is named in honor of John Y. Naka and reflects the diversity of the North American landscape and climate. The collection includes an upright cypress, a California juniper, and a redwood. The Mary E. Mrose International Pavilion features special exhibits related to the museum.

From the museum, cross Meadow Rd to the **National Herb Garden,** two and a half acres featuring 800 kinds of herbs in theme gardens that highlight herbal uses such as for fragrances, medicines, dyes, and spices. The **Rose Garden** next to the Herb Garden is filled with more than 100 varieties of heritage roses. Helpful signs are posted throughout, such as "Bee Aware! Construction Zone! Carpenter bees won't sting you! The male bees want to know who is in their territory but they do not have stingers. The female bees are only interested in constructing nests. Look up to see their perfectly round holes in the unpainted wood."

From the Herb Garden, continue south across the meadow facing the garden to the **National Capitol Columns,** 22 sandstone Corinthian columns that until 1958 formed part of the East Front of the U.S. Capitol. The columns provided a backdrop for the inaugurations of presidents from Andrew Jackson (1829) to Dwight Eisenhower (1957). Each of the columns, part of the reconstruction following the burning of the Capitol in 1814, was constructed of a single piece of sandstone quarried from the Aquia Creek quarry located 40 miles from Washington in Stafford County, Virginia. The Washington Canal (now Constitution Ave N.W.) was used to transport the sandstone to the foot of the Capitol. In 1958 the columns were replaced by marble columns.

After the columns were replaced, arboretum board member Ethel Garrett lobbied to have the columns removed from storage and placed in the arboretum. In 1990, after $2 million in private donations, the National Capitol Columns were officially dedicated as part of the National Arboretum. Russell Page was selected to design the landscaping for the columns' setting, but he died soon after beginning the project. Russ Hanna and Pat Faux were chosen to complete the project and made alterations to Page's design.

Notice that on many of the sandstone slabs (formerly steps of the Capitol building) used on the ground there is a number. This is the identification mark of the artisan who carved the slab. Memorial stones with the names of national and local contributors form the periphery of the column landscape.

From the National Capitol Columns, walk west across the meadow to Eagle Nest Rd and the **sandstone sculpture** formed by a capital and a base of one of the Capitol columns. All the columns were handcarved. An Englishman, George Bladen, was in charge of the stonecutters. An Italian, Giovanni Andrei, oversaw the carvers. On average, it took a carver six months to complete one Corinthian capital.

Walk north along Eagle Nest Rd to Meadow Rd and the circle in front of the Administration Building. From here, turn west and walk a few yds on Meadow Rd to the booth where tickets are sold for the **tram tour.** Continue a few yds farther to the **Arbor House,** and the tram pickup site. This area has a gift shop, soda machines, public phone, and restrooms.

The tram tour highlights the major areas of the arboretum. Adjacent to Arbor House is **Friendship Garden,** a collection of perennials that was a gift from the National Council of State Garden Clubs, Inc. The **National Boxwood Collection** (Azalea Rd), one of the most complete collections of boxwoods in the world, covers five acres and contains more than 100 species and varieties.

Plantings of crabapples and magnolias lead to the **Azalea Collections** (Azalea

Rd). In late April each year, more than 12,000 azaleas (with some dogwoods and cherries among them) provide one of Washington's most dazzling spring displays. The plants bloom along the sides of the road and in the **Morrison Azalea Garden,** which has a lace bark pine as well as some small redwoods.

The **National Grove of State Trees** (just off Azalea Rd), a 30-acre representation of America's forests, has trees from every state and the District of Columbia. (In this area are facilities for picnicking.) Past the grove and across the meadow are the National Capitol Columns.

The **Native Plant Collections** (Crabtree Rd) has wildflowers, shrubs, and trees representing a number of east coast ecosystems. The collection includes the **Fern Valley Trail,** a half-mile of woodlands and wildflowers. **Beech Spring Pond** (Valley Rd) provides a haven for migrating Canadian geese, and beyond it is the **Grecian Love Temple.** Flowering crabapples and weeping beech trees lead to the ten-acre **Holly and Magnolia Collections** (Holly Spring Rd). The magnolias bloom in spring.

The **Asian Collections** (Hickey Hill Rd) feature plants from Japan, China, and Korea in a dramatic setting overlooking the Anacostia River. The collection has a Chinese pagoda.

Along Hickey Hill are the remnants of the arboretum's camellias, those that survived the brutal winter of 1977. Scientists are studying these to find out what made them so hardy. Farther along Hickey Hill Rd is the **Dogwood Collection** and another overlook above the Anacostia River.

Beyond this is a grove of redwoods and then the **Conifer Collections.** The cone-bearing evergreens include the **Gotelli Dwarf and Slow-Growing Conifer Collection.** Gotelli, a building contractor who collected the conifers over a 15-year period as a hobby, donated his collection of 1,500 specimens in 1964. Represented here are 30 genera (a biological category ranking below a family and above a species), including fir, cedar, false cypress, juniper, spruce, pine, yew, and hemlock.

Facing New York Ave is the **Historic Brickyard** (DL), started in 1909–10 and operated until 1972. One of the more than 100 brickmaking operations in and around the city, the brickyard operated until 1972. The United Clay Products Co. operated the facility under that name, as well as under the names Hudson Brick and Supply Co., District Tile and Brick Co., and the United Brick Corporation. The clay deposits from the Anacostia River made this an ideal site for brickmaking, and at one time the company was turning out about 140,000 bricks a day. The operation closed down in 1972, and the federal government bought the 35-acre property in 1976 for $5.5 million. Arboretum management eventually hopes to turn the facility into an educational center.

Beyond the brickyard are the crepe myrtle breeding ground and an oak along Meadow Rd considered to be more than 200 years old. Among the tree's roots have been found buttons from the uniforms of Civil War soldiers, probably the same soldiers who manned the fortifications of this hill overlooking the city of Washington.

If you wish to continue with the next walk, the Anacostia River precludes being able to walk to Kenilworth Aquatic Gardens from the National Arboretum.

In order to get from the National Arboretum to Kenilworth Aquatic Gardens by public transportation, leave the arboretum from the front gates on New York Ave, cross New York Ave, walk north to 33rd St, then proceed one block on 33rd St to South Dakota Ave. From there catch the H2 bus marked "Westfront Circle." Take the H2 to the corner of South Dakota Ave and Bladensburg Rd and catch the B2 bus marked "Anacostia." Take the B2 to the corner of Pennsylvania and Potomac Aves. From there catch the V7 marked "Deanwood" to the Deanwood Metro station (Orange Line). From the Deanwood Metro station at Minnesota Ave and Polk St, walk one block north on Polk St to Kenilworth Ave. Cross Kenilworth and Polk becomes Douglas St. Walk two blocks north on Douglas St to Anacostia Ave and the entrance to the gardens.

# 26 · Kenilworth Aquatic Gardens

**A note on transportation:** Getting to Kenilworth Aquatic Gardens by public transportation requires caution, as these areas of town are less safe than those most frequented by tourists. A cab ride from downtown Washington takes about 20 minutes. By car from downtown Washington, take New York Ave east (it becomes Rte 50). After crossing the Anacostia River, turn right on Kenilworth Ave (Anacostia Pkwy). Turn right on Douglas St to Anacostia Ave. Turn right again into Kenilworth's parking area on the left. There is a proposed plan to develop the Anacostia Riverfront. This would probably make the aquatic gardens more accessible.

Metro: Orange Line to Deanwood.

Anacostia Ave and Douglas St N.E. ☎ 426-6905. Web: www.nps.gov. Open daily 7–4. Closed Christmas Day. Visitor's Center open daily 8:30–4. Admission: free. National Park Service tours summer weekends at 9 and 11; June–Aug and early morning hours best time to visit. Annual Water Lily Festival the last Sat in July. Restrooms. Wheelchair accessible.

The only national park devoted entirely to water plants, Kenilworth Aquatic Gardens encompasses 12 acres of ponds surrounded by 71 acres of tidal marshes on the east bank of the Anacostia River. What began as the hobby of a Civil War veteran and later developed into a thriving business has become a sanctuary for wildlife and water lilies in the middle of a busy residential and commercial sector of the city.

**Highlights:** The South American *Victoria amazonica* tropical lily.

### History

Walter B. Shaw, a Civil War veteran, started the lily ponds after he lost his right arm in battle. He learned to write with his left hand and worked as a letter writer for the U.S. Treasury Department in Washington, D.C. In 1880 he met and married a local woman, Lucy Marie Miller, and bought from her father a 30-acre farm along the east bank of the Anacostia River. Shaw had a fondness for water lilies, an inquisitive mind, and a gift for recognizing a good business opportunity.

Shaw imported 12 white lilies from his native Maine and planted them in an unused ice pond on the farm. During the years that followed, he learned more about water lilies and became interested in hybridizing. His collection of water lilies grew, and eventually his hobby became his business. Shaw dredged pools on his farm, planted and developed more exotic varieties, and sold his plants out of a truck. His daughter Helen Fowler assisted him.

In 1912 Helen Fowler succeeded her father as manager of the business known as W. B. Shaw Lily Ponds. She continued his search for more exotic plants, importing lotuses from the Orient, blue lilies from the Nile, and varieties native to South America. Shaw died in 1921.

> **Washington Notes**
> In the 1920s it became the fashion in D.C. to stroll around the lily ponds on Sun morning. Thousands of visitors, including President Coolidge and his wife, would walk the paths between the ponds and watch the flowers open to the sun.

In the 1930s, however, the ponds were threatened with destruction when the Army Corps of Engineers decided to dredge the Anacostia River and reclaim the marshes surrounding the gardens. Helen Fowler rallied support for the ponds and, with the aid of the Kenilworth Citizens Association, lobbied Congress so successfully that in 1938 the federal government agreed to buy the gardens for $15,000. The National Park Service was given responsibility for the gardens, which were renamed Kenilworth Aquatic Gardens in honor of the community that had grown up around the Shaw farm. Today, the gardens have more than 100,000 water plants.

From the Deanwood Metro station at Minnesota Ave and Polk St, walk one block north on Polk St to Kenilworth Ave. Cross Kenilworth and Polk becomes Douglas St. Walk two blocks north on Douglas St to Anacostia Ave and the entrance to the gardens.

## The Gardens

The ponds feature both hardy and tropical water lilies, lotuses, and aquatic plants such as bamboo, wild rice, water primrose, and rose mallow. Native trees include river birch, red maple, willow, elm, ash, sycamore, and sweetbay magnolia. Animals in the park include bullfrogs, toads, snapping turtles (including the park mascot, Buster), sunfish, water snakes, green heron, red-winged blackbirds, muskrats, squirrels, raccoons, and opossums.

It's the flowers, though, that amaze when they're in bloom. In mid-June, day-blooming lilies, some 70 varieties in all, are at their peak. In late July and early Aug, in the early morning hours, it's possible to see more than 40 varieties of day-blooming tropical water lilies open. The lotus blossoms, some as large as basketballs, rise from stalks almost six ft tall.

The entrance to the gardens is down a gravel path from the parking area that leads to the **Visitor's Center.** The center's displays explain the history of the gardens. A map and a brochure are available, and a National Park Service attendant is on duty to answer questions.

Exit the Visitor's Center and walk east toward the ponds and pathways that run between and around them.

The majority of the ponds contain **water lilies** (genus *Nymphaea*, after the female sprites of ancient myth who inhabited lakes and streams). The plants are grouped into hardy and tropical varieties. Both types grow in shallow, slow-moving bodies of water, usually from tubers rooted in the mud. The leaves form underwater and grow toward the surface and the sun. The flowers bloom for 3 to 14 days, opening and closing in response to light.

Hardy lilies have round leaf pads with smooth edges; their flowers peak in June and July. Among the varieties featured in the garden are pink opal, which has coral red flowers; sumptuosa, which has strawberry pink flowers with orange stamens; and sunrise, which has canary yellow curved petals.

**Tropical lilies** are stored in greenhouses in the winter, then moved outdoors in May. The leaf pads of tropical lilies have rippled edges; their flowers peak in July and Aug. One of the most dramatic is *Victoria amazonica* from South America (featured in the ponds adjacent to the river at the far end of the gardens), whose platterlike leaves with upturned edges may reach six ft across. Other varieties, planted in the ponds nearest the river bank at the far end of the gardens, are Texas shell pink, which has light pink flowers; General Pershing, which has deep pink flowers with dark green leaves tinged with purple and spotted underneath; and blue beauty, which is ten inches across and has yellow stamens and violet tips.

The **lotus plants,** located at the rear of the two ponds nearest the Visitor's Center, are particularly interesting. The pink-tinged East Indian lotus (genus *Nelumbo*) on view descends from ancient plants whose seeds were recovered in 1951 from a dry Manchurian lake bed. A National Park Service botanist induced germination of the 350–375-year-old seeds, believed to be the oldest viable seeds ever found. Lotus plants have waxy leaves and beautiful flowers. Eastern religions use the lotus as a sacred symbol. Hindus believe Brahma was born from the heart of a lotus, and the Buddha is often shown seated on a lotus. The Chinese saw the flower as a symbol of purity. The Egyptian queen Cleopatra was said to have favored the lotus above all other flowers, and its form is often featured in Egyptian temple columns.

The ponds also have cattails and yellow flag iris along the pool edges. There are more than 40 species of birds in the gardens at different times of the year.

# 27 · Anacostia

Metro: Green Line to Anacostia.
Bus: A2, A4, A6, A8, B2, P2, P6, P18, W2, W6, W14, or 94.

Anacostia was recognized by Pierre L'Enfant and Thomas Jefferson as an area excellently situated to serve as both a naval base and a commercial port. But neither of these functions ever materialized and Anacostia, Washington's first "suburb," was left to its own devices for much of the city's history—part of the District of Columbia in matters of law and taxes, but set apart by a river and often by economic and social prejudice. Anacostia, which has both middle-class and poor neighborhoods, is generally considered to include all the communities of far southeast Washington that lie east of the Anacostia River and south of Pennsylvania Ave.

**Highlights:** The Frederick Douglass Home (Cedar Hill) and the Smithsonian's Anacostia Museum and Center for African American History and Culture.

### History
Anacostia is thought to have been the landing site of the English explorer Captain John Smith, who sailed up the Potomac and "discovered" the centuries-old Native

American village Nacotchtank on its banks. In his *Historie*, Smith wrote, "The river above this place maketh his passage down a low pleasant valley overshadowed in manie places with high rocky mountains; from whence distill innumerable sweet and pleasant springs."

In 1632, English trader Henry Fleet revisited the Nacostines, as he called them, and began trading with the friendly natives. It is from permutations of *Anaquashtank*, meaning "town of traders," that the name *Anacostia* developed. Sixty years later, the native people had been wiped out by war and diseases brought by the Europeans, but the name remained. Anacostia Park is located on the old Nacotchtank grounds, along E. Capital St from Pennsylvania Ave to the Naval Annex. The park has eight miles of woods, fields, and walking trails.

The English soon discovered Anacostia's fertile land was ideal for growing tobacco, and by the mid-17C tobacco plantations farmed by slaves dotted the area. In the late 18C, when tobacco growing was no longer productive, farmers, such as James Barry, who owned a large farm in the area, turned to wheat, corn, and maize.

In 1799, the Navy Yard was built on the northwestern bank of the Anacostia River. Instantly the city's largest employer, the yard was the site of the design and construction of large vessels, and plans were made to create a strategic port, hidden from enemy warships approaching from the Potomac. Unfortunately, steady silting of the river from the overfarmed land around it made the Anacostia River too shallow to hold 19C warships. The bustling commercial and military port never materialized. Instead of an asset, the Anacostia River became a physical barrier separating Anacostia from the rest of the city.

In the 1820s, Anacostia's Good Hope was the first community around the main road from southern Maryland to Washington. Initially owned by major slaveholding families, the land was gradually divided into smaller plots that were rented or sold. In a memoir written in 1900 about Old Anacostia, one former resident described his town: "The Good Hope Tavern was at the juncture of the Good Hope and Marlboro Roads at the top of Good Hope Hill. . . . It was the rendesvous [sic] of the Gentlemen of Washington and the country around in their meets for fox hunting and it was a beautiful sight of a frosty October morning to see superbly mounted men in crimson and top boots surrounding the old Hostelrie making the echoes ring with their fox horns and encouraging the half hundred hounds in their grumblings and bayings. All independent gentleman of that date joined in such amusements, and it was not thought to be an ungentlemanly diversion to attend a cock, dog or bear fight."

In 1850, the Allen African Methodist Episcopal Church was built in Good Hope by freed blacks. More than a third of America's freed blacks lived in Maryland and Virginia at that time, and many of them made their homes in Anacostia. Anacostia's economy was growing, providing employment opportunities, as small businesses such as blacksmith shops and taverns made Anacostia a convenient way station en route to the city of Washington. The Navy Yard also continued as a major employer, having been rebuilt following the War of 1812.

Expecting the nation's capital to develop southeastwardly, real estate investors purchased much of Anacostia's farmland in the 1800s. One of these speculators was Georgetown resident William Marbury of *Marbury v. Madison* fame.

### Washington Notes

In 1801, in a series of "midnight" appointments, outgoing President John Adams named Marbury a local justice of the peace. When President Thomas Jefferson took office, he instructed Secretary of State James Madison to refuse to give Marbury his commission. Marbury sued Madison, and in 1803 the Supreme Court denied Marbury his appointment and declared the suit unconstitutional, thereby expanding the Court's powers of judicial review.

Another land speculator, Philadelphian John Van Hook, entered into a partnership with Anacostia residents John Fox and John Dobler to establish the Union Land Association. In 1854, the association bought 100 acres of Anacostia for $1,900, then divided the tract into 700 lots, calling the new subdivision Union Town. (Today, its boundaries would be Good Hope Rd on the north, W St on the south, Martin Luther King Ave on the west, and 16th St on the east.) Calling Union Town "the most beautiful and healthiest neighborhood in Washington," the association advertised its suburban development, Washington's first, as "Homes for All." This was belied by the boldly stated restrictions prohibiting sale, rental, or lease of property to Jews, African Americans, and those of Irish descent.

Due to the economic skittishness of the pre–Civil War years, Union Town was slow to develop. Confiscation of much of Anacostia for defense of the capital during the war contributed to Union Town's problems. The Union Land Association declared bankruptcy in 1877.

### Washington Notes

In 1877 African American orator and statesman Frederick Douglass purchased Van Hook's Hill, the site of a home Van Hook had built for himself, renamed it Cedar Hill (after all the beautiful cedar trees on the property), and broke Union Town's color barrier. After the war, Congress officially changed Union Town's name to Anacostia to avoid confusion with several other Uniontowns. Today, what was Union Town is known as Old Anacostia.

After the Civil War thousands of recently freed African Americans needed housing. In 1865 the Bureau of Refugees, Freedmen and Abandoned Lands, commonly known as the Freedmen's Bureau, purchased the 375-acre James Barry Farm. The land was then divided into one-acre lots that were sold to African Americans for $125–300, along with enough lumber to construct a small house. Payments could be made in 24 installments. By 1868, 300 of the lots were sold, and the Barry's Farm community of 500 African American families was created. Later the area would be divided and the other half was named Hillsdale. Barry's Farm had a Baptist church and a school for 150 students.

White and black communities developed separately in Anacostia. Many residents were blue-collar laborers employed at the Navy Yard or the U.S. Government Insane Asylum (now called St. Elizabeth's Hospital), which opened in Anacostia in 1855. In the 1870s, Anacostia benefited from the city improvements undertaken by Alexander "Boss" Shepherd, head of the Board of Public Works. Streets were paved, public transportation was introduced, and a new 11th St Bridge was built, better linking Anacostia with downtown.

### Washington Notes

The previous 11th St Bridge was part of the escape route used by John Wilkes Booth on the night of April 14, 1865. After assassinating President Abraham Lincoln, Booth rode out of town over the 11th St Bridge and out Good Hope Rd.

Despite these developments in the 1870s, by the 1890s Anacostia lagged behind other city neighborhoods in street improvements, main waterlines, and clean wells. Residents formed separate, racially segregated community associations to lobby for aid. The Barry's Farm/Hillsdale Civic Association served blacks, and the Anacostia Citizens' Association served whites. Anacostia remained sparsely populated until the 1920s and 1930s, when the government built several housing developments in the area. Construction of the Suitland Pkwy, however, in the 1940s physically divided the Barry's Farm and Hillsdale communities, weakening the neighborhood's stability.

Housing developments continued to be built in Anacostia during the 1940s, '50s, and '60s. The Federal Housing Administration constructed several garden apartments as well as more than 900 units of public housing, creating a shift from single-family homes to multiple-family units. Some of these public housing units built in the late 1960s were created to house the large numbers of area African Americans dislocated as a result of the development of Southwest Washington. Rapidly, a neighborhood that had included both black and white families became predominantly black. In 1940, 20 percent of Anacostia's population was African American; by 1970, blacks constituted 96 percent of Anacostia residents, many of these in the lower-income sector. Businesses failed, crime rose, and in the past 20 years parts of Anacostia have become strongholds of poverty and despair.

Residents rightly point out that city government policies have not dealt with the lack of employment in the area. In 1999, however, when Mayor Anthony Williams proposed creating jobs by relocating government offices and the campus of the University of the District of Columbia to Anacostia, residents elsewhere in the city protested, and Williams was forced to reconsider.

But the area is also graced with strong community organizations, which are demanding social assistance programs that will provide Anacostia residents with better schools and good jobs.

### Washington Notes

In 1932, World War I veterans camped out on the Anacostia Flats, now a part of Anacostia Park, demanding the bonus payments they'd been promised by Congress for their service in the war. In a move that shocked the nation, the veterans were forcibly dispersed by troops led by General Douglas MacArthur, an action, along with the woes of the Depression, that contributed to President Hoover's defeat.

John Hinckley, Jr., the man who shot President Ronald Reagan in 1981, remains a patient at St. Elizabeth's Hospital. Another famous patient was the poet Ezra Pound. Pound was committed to St. Elizabeth's following his trial for treason against the U.S. government. During World War II, Pound made pro-Fascist radio broadcasts from Italy critical of U.S. policy. Pound remained at St. Elizabeth's from 1943 to 1958.

# Frederick Douglass National Historic Site (Cedar Hill)

1411 W St S.E. ☎ 426-5961. Web: www.nps.gov/frdo. Open daily spring–summer 9–5; fall–winter 9–4. Closed Thanksgiving, Christmas Day, and New Year's Day. Admission: free. Tours given on the hour beginning at 10, except from noon to 1; last tour at 4 (April–Oct), at 3 (Nov–March); tour fee charged. Gift shop. Visitor Center and first floor of the house wheelchair accessible. Restrooms.

To get to Cedar Hill by car from the Mall travel south on 9th St to I-395 north, exit onto I-295 south across the bridge, exit onto Martin Luther King, Jr., Ave, turn left on W St, and proceed three blocks to Cedar Hill parking lot.

By Metrorail and bus, take the Green Line to the Anacostia station, then take the Mt. Rainier B2 bus to Cedar Hill. Local tour companies also have tours to Cedar Hill.

**Note:** Be aware that Anacostia is not as safe a section of the city as the usual tourist areas.

### History

Frederick Douglass was born Frederick Augustus Washington Bailey in 1818 on a Maryland plantation, the slave of the overseer. It's thought he was born on Valentine's Day (Feb 14), since he was referred to by the other slaves as the "Valentine gift." Separated from his mother, Harriet—a slave—at birth, he hardly knew her nor his white father. In his first autobiography, Douglass wrote, "I never saw my mother . . . more than four or five times in my life . . . and each of these times was at night. She was hired by a Mr. Stewart, who lived about 12 miles from my home. She made her journey to see me at night, traveling the whole distance on foot, after the performance of her day's work in the field. . . . She would lie down with me, and get me to sleep, but long before I waked she was gone."

Douglass spent his early years with his grandparents, Isaac and Betsy Bailey, but was separated from them at the age of 8 when he was chosen to be the companion of a white boy at the home of a Mr. Hugh Auld in Baltimore. About first meeting Auld's wife, Sophia, Douglass wrote, "And here I saw what I had never seen before; it was a white face beaming with the most kindly emotions."

Finding Douglass quick to learn, Mrs. Auld began to teach him to read and write. Her husband severely reprimanded her, protesting that if Douglass learned these skills "there will be no keeping him." There wasn't. In 1833 Douglass was moved to a nearby plantation and there deemed unmanageable, after which he was hired out to what was called a slave-breaker. This was a man who made his reputation by being able to starve and whip the most stubborn slave into submission. He starved and whipped Douglass, but to no avail. Douglass was returned to Baltimore, where his owner, despairing of ever making any money from Douglass's labors, rented him to a ship's caulker, who taught Douglass the caulking trade.

Around this time Douglass met his future wife, Anna Murray, a free daughter of former slaves. Douglass had taught himself to read and write (and would eventually speak five languages), and he and Anna made plans for a life together.

In 1838, Douglass, disguised as a sailor, escaped from Baltimore to New York City, where Anna joined him and they were married. Anna paid for more than half of Douglass's train fare by selling her feather bed and giving him her savings from nine years work as a domestic servant. From New York, they traveled to New Bed-

*Frederick Douglass National Historical Site (Cedar Hill). Photo credit: Terry J. Adams, National Park Service.*

ford, Massachusetts, where Douglass worked on the ships. It was here, to avoid capture as a runaway slave, that Douglass adopted his new last name, taken from Sir Walter Scott's poem *Lady of the Lake*.

It was also here that Douglass became active in the abolitionist movement. The leader of the movement, William Lloyd Garrison, heard Douglass speak at a rally and hired him as a speaker for the Massachusetts Anti-Slavery Society. Between 1841 and 1847, Douglass's reputation as an orator began to grow. Frustrated by the fact that people refused to believe he could have been born a slave, Douglass published his first autobiography, *Narrative of the Life of Frederick Douglass*, which became a best-seller and made Douglass popular in the elite social circles of the North. But even as the darling of society, Douglass could still be captured by the slave hunters—who now knew where to find him—and returned to his owner.

To protect Douglass, the Massachusetts Anti-Slavery Society sent him to England and Ireland to speak on behalf of the abolitionist movement. Douglass, in favor of equal rights for everyone, was one of the earliest and most vocal of male supporters of women's suffrage, and while in England Douglass also spoke in favor of Irish home rule. In 1847 Douglass returned to America, settling in Rochester, New York, after his English friends bought his freedom and provided him with the money to launch a newspaper, the *North Star*, named for the star slaves used as a point of direction in their flight to freedom.

At the outbreak of the Civil War, Douglass asked Lincoln to recruit freed African

American men for the Union Army. Lincoln hesitated for two years, but after the Emancipation Proclamation the call went out: "Men of Color, to Arms!" Two of Douglass's sons fought in the war; both survived. Following the war, Douglass's popularity as a speaker led to a tireless schedule of speaking engagements, which were followed by a series of public and diplomatic appointments, including U.S. marshall and record keeper of the District of Columbia.

When their home in Rochester burned to the ground in a mysterious fire, the Douglass family moved to Washington, D.C., to 316 A St N.E. In 1877, they bought Cedar Hill in Anacostia for $6,700, a home in a previously "whites only" neighborhood. Douglass had made a fortune through his three autobiographies and his speaking.

Anna died in 1882, and in 1884 Douglass married one of his assistants, Helen Pitts, who was white. Although this caused considerable controversy at the time, Douglass shrugged it off, saying that his first wife had been the color of his mother and his second wife was the color of his father.

Although Douglass himself was respected and prosperous, he saw that this was not so for all the African American people and he spoke out about the "abandonment" of African Americans by their government. In 1889, at the age of 71, Douglass was appointed minister to Haiti, but he resigned the post within two years and returned to Cedar Hill. On Feb 20, 1898, after attending a women's rights rally, Douglass died of a heart attack at his home. Private services for the "Sage of Anacostia" were held at Cedar Hill, and then a horse-drawn hearse carried his body through the city to the Metropolitan A.M.E. Church (1518 M St N.W.), where his funeral was attended by government dignitaries, colleagues in the fight for civil rights, and members of the African American community. Douglass was 77 years old. He is buried with his first wife, Anna, at Mt. Hope Cemetery in Rochester.

Following Douglass's death, Helen Pitts Douglass worked tirelessly to preserve Cedar Hill, which she hoped to make "the Mount Vernon" of the African American people. In 1900 she established the Frederick Douglass Memorial and Historical Association, which, due to financial difficulties, joined with the National Association of Colored Women's Clubs in 1916. Maintaining the house and grounds proved to be an overwhelmingly expensive project, and in 1962 President John F. Kennedy signed a bill giving responsibility of the site to the National Park Service. It took ten years to restore the house to its original appearance before it opened to the public in 1972.

## Exterior

This Gothic revival brick structure (1855–59; architect unknown; DL) was built by investor John Van Hook between 1855 and 1859. Van Hook moved into what was then a 14-room house in 1863. In 1877, the Union Land Association declared bankruptcy, and the deed to the house was taken over by the Freedman's Savings and Trust, of which Frederick Douglass was president. Douglass bought the 9¾-acre property for $6,700 and a year later added another 5¾ acres to the estate. Douglass would spend the last 18 years of his life here. Between 1879 and 1881, he built a rear wing containing a kitchen, pantry, and laundry on the first floor and bedrooms on the second. The grounds were enhanced with more trees, a fruit orchard, vegetable garden, and a grape arbor. A carriage house was added to the back of the house.

## Interior

There is a Visitor Center off the parking lot, where those taking the tour initially gather. Here one may see a short film on the life of Frederick Douglass, as well as photographs of his children and exhibited items dealing with his accomplishments and the period of history in which he lived.

About 90 percent of the furniture and decorations presently in the house were there when the Douglass family lived in the house. The rugs, wallpaper, and drapery are not original to the house, but are representative of the period.

The guided tour of the house begins in the **east parlor,** the room reserved for entertaining. The checker set was handcarved by Douglass. The portraits are of Douglass, his first wife, Anna, and Senator Blanche K. Bruce of Mississippi, who was best man at Douglass's second wedding and a pallbearer at his funeral.

**Library.** Douglass came to the library after breakfast and he worked up to five hours a day. It was here he wrote his third autobiography, *The Life and Times of Frederick Douglass.* On the wall around his desk are portraits of those with whom he labored for civil rights: Susan B. Anthony, William Lloyd Garrison, and John Brown. The more than 1,100 books cover the fields of politics, history, government, law, philosophy, and theology. The rolltop desk contains Douglass's pens, ledger books, and a diary written in Santo Domingo in 1871.

**West parlor.** This was the family parlor, where the children played the piano and Douglass played Scottish dance tunes on his violin. The cane resting against the chair belonged to Abraham Lincoln and was given to Douglass by Mrs. Lincoln after her husband's death.

> ### Washington Notes
> Douglass's grandson Charles, a violinist, was the first African American musician to tour Europe.

From the upstairs hallway, family and guests would disperse, according to Victorian custom, to the men's rooms on the east side of the house or the women's rooms on the west side. In the **men's guest bedroom** is a small desk given to Douglass by his friend Harriet Beecher Stowe, author of *Uncle Tom's Cabin.* In the **women's guest bedroom** is a cane-bottomed chair original to the house, as is the portrait of Elizabeth Cady Stanton, a friend of Douglass. The porcelain hair receiver on the dresser was used by women to store the hair taken from their brushes and combs, to be used for making switches or for hair art, which was popular at the time. There was no electricity or running water in these rooms. There were also no closets—closets were taxed as separate rooms, so armoires were used to store clothing.

**Anna Douglass's bedroom.** Anna lived here only four years before she died. Suffering from arthritis and rheumatism, she used the "invalid's chair" to move closer to the window when she wanted the warmth of the sun. When she died in 1882, Douglass closed the room and refused to have it opened. He called her "the anchor of my life."

**Frederick Douglass's bedroom.** The lithograph on the wall between the doorway and Douglass's bed shows him at about age 22. The clothes displayed all belonged to Douglass, as did the dumbbells, which he used for exercise. The bed is shorter than Douglass's six-ft-plus height because it was believed back then that it was healthier to sleep sitting up, propped up by stacks of pillows.

**Nursery.** As Douglass's 4 children and his 21 grandchildren lived nearby, there were always small children staying at Cedar Hill. One photograph in the room is of Douglass' casket surrounded by flower arrangements in the west parlor, where his body lay in state for three days; the other is of his funeral procession in front of the Metropolitan A.M.E. Church.

Next door is the **bedroom of Haley George,** a grandson who spent so much time at Cedar Hill he had his own room (also used by other guests). Haley taught school in the District of Columbia for 46 years and was elected mayor of Highland Beach, Maryland.

**Helen Pitts Douglass's bedroom.** Helen was 20 years younger than Douglass and she could trace her family back to the *Mayflower.* She first met Douglass when she was 15 years old and he spoke at her father's home in Rochester. She was a graduate of Mt. Holyoke Female Seminary and worked for Douglass when he was the recorder of deeds for the District of Columbia. Regarding the controversy of her marriage to Douglass, she said, "Love came to me, and I was not afraid to marry the man I loved because of his color." The sewing machine and typewriter belonged to Helen.

Return downstairs. The **pantry** contained preserved foods and an icebox similar to the one displayed. Made of oak with a galvanized tin interior, the icebox kept things cold with a 25-pound block of ice on top. The ice-cream maker is also typical of the period. The Douglass family was well-to-do; this is reflected in the fact that they had three servants and that their **kitchen** was modern for its time, with a cooking range, a pie safe, and a dry sink. It was called a dry sink because there was no running water in the house. Water was brought from outside the house and dumped into the sink.

Next to the kitchen is the **laundry room,** which contains the only indoor source of water for the house, the cistern. Rainwater, which collected in a reservoir, was used for chores such as washing windows and scrubbing floors. Several irons are displayed.

Return to the original section of the house and walk to the **dining room,** the largest room in the house. Douglass and Anna liked to entertain guests. Instead of strong liquor, cocoa, coffee, and tea were served. The china on the table is original to the house. The lamp hanging in the hallway was put there by Helen to honor Douglass's memory.

Behind the house is a reconstruction of Douglass's growlery. The original was destroyed by Hurricane Hazel in 1956. The growlery was Douglass's retreat from family and friends. Probably built by Van Hook as a storage shed, Douglass converted it into a study with a desk, a stool, and a black mohair couch. He added a skylight and a fireplace, but no windows, since views might have distracted him from his work.

From the Douglass Home, walk south on W St one block to 16th St, then east on 16th St three blocks to Good Hope Rd. At 16th St and Good Hope Rd, take the W6 bus marked "Anacostia Shuttle" to the Anacostia Metro station (Green Line). From there, catch the W2 bus marked "Washington Overlook," which stops across the street from the Anacostia Museum.

**Note:** Walking between the Frederick Douglass Home and the Anacostia Museum is not advised.

## Anacostia Museum and Center for African American History and Culture

1901 Fort Place S.E. ☎ 287-2061. Web: www.si.edu/anacostia. Open daily 10–5. Closed Christmas Day. Gift shop. Wheelchair accessible. Smithsonian shuttle service from the Museum of Natural History (10th St and Constitution Ave N.W.) available, ☎ 357-2700. As of press time, the museum was closed for a $5.9 million renovation. It is scheduled to reopen in spring 2001.

When the Anacostia Museum (1987; Keyes Condon Florance) was founded in 1967, it was the first federally funded community-based institution in the country. Today, coupled with the Center for African American History and Culture located in the Arts and Industries Building on the National Mall, the museum is "a national resource devoted to the identification, documentation, protection and interpretation of the African-American experience, focusing on Washington, D.C., and the Upper South." The geographic area covered includes Maryland, Virginia, North and South Carolina, and Georgia. The museum also deals with contemporary urban issues—such as housing, economic development, and health care—and the impact these issues have on the African American community. This is a relatively small museum, with only one floor with one main gallery (directly facing the main door) and a small community gallery (where community-related exhibits are often displayed) to the side. But its exhibits are timely and richly representative of its surrounding community, as well as of the African American community as a whole.

**Highlights:** The museum's changing exhibits.

### History

The Anacostia Neighborhood Museum opened in 1967 in the renovated site of the George Washington Carver Theater. It was the idea of Smithsonian Secretary S. Dillon Ripley, a tangible effort on the part of the Smithsonian Institution to broaden its service to both a local neighborhood and a group that had not traditionally been part of the Smithsonian's constituency. The museum had work areas for arts and crafts activities, a small zoo, a science corner, touch boxes and books for children, a country store, astronauts' space suits, and a space capsule. Within a year of its opening, the staff, responding to feedback from the community, shifted the focus to topics rarely explored in traditional museums: prison reform, relationships between black men and women, the achievements of African American women, the role of African Americans in westward expansion. Public response was overwhelming, and the museum began to broaden its mission, while it shortened its name to the Anacostia Museum. In 1987, the museum moved about one mile east to its present site in Fort Stanton on land donated by the National Park Service.

The museum is involved in a number of ongoing research projects. **Black Mosaic: Community, Race, and Ethnicity Among Black Immigrants in Washington, D.C.** examines the family and community life of Afro-Latino and Caribbean people, with research jointly conducted by the museum staff and community scholars trained in oral history and video documentation. So far, the project has resulted in a groundbreaking exhibition of diverse community life, with more than 200 oral interviews, photos from more than 40 families, and 5,000 slides.

The museum's current major research project and accompanying exhibit, on display at the Arts and Industries Building on the Mall, is **Speak to My Heart: Communities of Faith and Contemporary African American Life,** which examines the challenges and changes of the past 25 years in the black community and the role of the church in addressing issues such as AIDS, homelessness, and youth violence.

In Dec 1999, the Anacostia Museum and Center for African American History and Culture closed for renovations, which are planned to take 14 months. Reopening is scheduled for spring 2001. During this time, some of the museum's exhibits are on display at the Smithsonian's Arts and Industries Building.

## Fort Stanton Park

Three blocks south of the Anacostia Museum on Morris Rd are the remnants of Fort Stanton (DL), located behind Our Lady of Perpetual Help Church at 1600 Morris Rd S.E. One of 68 forts built during the Civil War to protect the city from Confederate attack, Fort Stanton's purpose was to protect the Navy Yard and the two bridges across the Potomac and Anacostia Rivers. Battery Ricketts, which was used for the storing of ammunition, is the only remaining part of the fort. Now a park, the Fort Stanton site is under the jurisdiction of the National Park Service.

### History

Named for Edwin M. Stanton, U.S. attorney general from 1860 to 1862 and secretary of war from 1862 to 1868, Fort Stanton had a perimeter of 322 yds. It was designed for 18 guns and a garrison of 270 artillerymen and 215 infantrymen. From the fort, troops had a panoramic view of the city, as well as of Alexandria, Virginia, to the south and Bladensburg, Maryland, to the northeast.

Fort Stanton was closed in March 1866, and its materials sold at auction or returned to the government for other uses. In 1901 the McMillan Park Commission proposed establishing park areas at former fort sites, creating a scenic parkway encircling the city. In the 1920s the National Capital Park and Planning Commission studied this proposal. In 1933 20 fort sites were transferred to the jurisdiction of the National Park Service. Although urban development prevented the proposed scenic parkway, some of the fort sites, such as Fort Stanton, became parks.

Northeast of Fort Stanton Park, Kingman and Heritage Islands in the Anacostia River have been designated as the proposed site of the **National Children's Island,** a commercial recreational and educational park for children. This plan has been under consideration for more than 15 years. The proposed 45-acre facility will feature rides and exhibits on space exploration, sports, medicine, communications, music, and magic, using simulators, 3-D movies, and virtual reality entertainment. Although the project's backers claim that the National Children's Island would provide more than 1,000 jobs and generate $9 million in tax revenue, the City Council has voted against the proposal because of financial and environmental concerns. The Control Board has withheld approval because of concerns about financing. As of this writing, the project is on hold.

**Diversion:**
From Fort Stanton Park at 16th and Morris Rd, take the W2 bus to Milwaukee Place and Martin Luther King, Jr., Ave and St Elizabeth's Hospital, 2700 Martin Luther King, Jr., Ave S.E., ☎ 562-4000. **Note:** This area can at times be unsafe, so it's probably better to take a cab from Fort Stanton Park to St. Elizabeth's Hospital. However, cabs are not always cruising this area, so consider hiring a cab to go to both places.

## St. Elizabeth's Hospital

St. Elizabeth's Hospital (DL) provides in- and out-patient psychiatric care. The hospital was the first mental health facility created with public funds and a pioneer for the humane treatment of patients. It consists of more than 125 buildings on 364 acres. The grounds are of interest to Civil War enthusiasts as more than 300 Union and Confederate Civil War soldiers are buried on site. Although in the past the hospital has conducted tours of its Civil War Cemetery and small museum of 19C medical memorabilia, including items belonging to founder Dorothea Dix, because of budget cuts tours are currently infrequent. Those interested should not just drop by, as the hospital discourages unscheduled visits. Call ahead to see if a tour is available.

**Highlights:** Civil War Cemetery and the room American poet Ezra Pound stayed in when he was a patient.

### History

In the 1840s and 1850s New England social activist Dorothea Lynde Dix crusaded for the humane treatment of the mentally ill. Typically, in asylums and almshouses the insane were "confined . . . in cages, closets, cellars, and pens," a situation that horrified Dix. She lobbied President Millard Fillmore to create a national institution to provide "the most humane care and enlightened curative treatment of the insane." In 1852, with the president's support Dix convinced Congress to purchase 364 acres of wooded land known as "St. Elizabeth's tract" for the proposed Government Hospital for the Insane, the first mental health facility sponsored by public funds.

In 1855, slaves loaned by Maryland farmers and hospital patients completed a first structure, the 250-bed Center Building.

### Washington Notes

West Lodge, the second building finished in 1856, housed a separate ward for black patients. This gave St. Elizabeth's the distinction of being, according to the superintendent at the time, "the first and only provision for the care of colored insane in any part of the world."

Other firsts claimed by St. Elizabeth's include the use of psychoanalysis, dance therapy, psychodrama, and hydrotherapy. The hospital quickly expanded to include a small railway connecting a bakery, a brick kiln, a toy factory, and a 400-acre farm three and a half miles away—all used for patient vocational training. The Government Hospital for the Insane had been designed to treat any mental patient who had served in the military as well as D.C. residents, but during the Civil War St. Elizabeth's set up additional wards to fit artificial limbs on soldiers and sailors who had lost an arm or a leg.

When recuperating soldiers found out that Jesuit priests accompanying the original Catholic settlers of Maryland had named the promontory overlooking the Potomac and Anacostia Rivers after the Hungarian Princess Elizabeth who cared for lepers, paupers, and the insane, the soldiers began referring to the hospital as St. Elizabeth's in their letters home. In 1916 Congress officially changed the hospital's name to St. Elizabeth's, a more neutral title than Government Hospital for the Insane.

### Washington Notes

More than 300 Union and Confederate soldiers who did not survive medical treatment are buried on the hospital's grounds, including three members of the first black regiment, the 54th Massachusetts Volunteer Infantry. The movie *Glory* dramatized the story of the 54th regiment.

In 1987, Congress transferred the management of the hospital from the federal to the District government.

The hospital also cares for inmates who have been found to be criminally insane. The most well known of these is currently John Hinckley, Jr., who shot and wounded President Ronald Reagan, Press Secretary James Brady, a D.C. police officer, and a Secret Service agent on March 30, 1981.

### Washington Notes

Hinckley was not the first would-be presidential assassin housed at St. Elizabeth's. The seventh patient sent to St. Elizabeth's in 1855 was Richard Lawrence, who attempted to murder Andrew Jackson at the Capitol, but his two flintlock pistols misfired.

On Sept 10, 1991, St. Elizabeth's Hospital became a National Historic Landmark.

## Exterior

There are more than 125 buildings on the hospital grounds, many of them reflecting Victorian architectural styles. The red brick **Center Building** (1856–60) was designed in the collegiate Gothic style.

## Interior

Center Building now houses administrative offices and, in what once served as the superintendent's suite, the **hospital museum.** The museum displays antique hospital documents, memorabilia, photographs, and a room-size model of the hospital that was seen at the 1876 Centennial Exhibition in Philadelphia. There is also period furniture, much of which was made from trees on the hospital grounds.

### Diversion:

**Bolling Air Force Base,** which is parallel to S. Capitol St and Malcolm X Blvd, is located on the east end of Anacostia. It is bordered on the north where the Potomac and Anacostia Rivers meet, on the west by the Anacostia Freeway, on the south by Laboratory Rd, and on the east by the Potomac River. Bolling Air Force Base is not open to the public. If you wish to proceed to Bolling Air Force Base, it is advised that you do so by cab.

Bolling Air Force Base is home to the 11th Wing, a Direct Reporting Unit (DRU). The 11th Wing is called the Chief's Own because it provides direct support to the U.S. Chief of Staff. Bolling was activated in 1918 and became the center of early military aviation. General Billy Mitchell and Colonel Charles Lindbergh flew at Bolling.

### Washington Notes

Many flights that were aviation firsts took off from this base, including the first night flights and the first around-the-world flights. The base is named after Colonel Raynal C. Bolling, the first senior Army Air Corps officer killed in action in World War I.

To continue to the next walk, it is advised that you take a cab either into Southwest Washington to Jefferson Dr and 12th St N.W., or to the Anacostia Metro station on Howard Rd. From the Anacostia station, take the Green Line to L'Enfant Plaza.

# 28 · Southwest Washington

Metro: Blue/Orange Line to Smithsonian, Yellow/Blue Line to L'Enfant Plaza, Green Line to Federal Center SW or Waterfront.
Bus: V6, V7, V8, A42, A46, A48, P1, P2, or 70.

Southwest Washington is bounded by Independence Ave on the north, S. Capitol St on the east, Greenleaf Point (the confluence of the Potomac and Anacostia Rivers) on the south, and 14th St on the west. Southwest Washington's waterfront is one of the liveliest places in the city on weekends, when neighborhood restaurants feature live jazz and great seafood. The city's fish market sells fresh fish seven days a week, but on weekend mornings be prepared for traffic jams along Water St as locals angle for the best catch.

Probably more than any other section of the city except for the Federal Triangle, Southwest's development has been interfered with by the federal government. Southwest, one of the earliest sections of the city to be settled, might have become a popular residential area early in the city's history, but the government built and then all but abandoned a canal through the area, cutting the Southwest off from the rest of the city. The Southwest was largely ignored by the city until the 1950s, when the area's dilapidated condition became an embarrassment. In the 1950s thousands of families and hundreds of shops were displaced. The subsequent federal government plan (see "History") and the resulting upheaval made Southwest what it is today: an unusual combination of picturesque waterfront, public housing, and affluent high-rise apartments, bordered by federal government complexes.

### History

An English visitor in 1795 wrote this description of Southwest Washington: "The private houses are all plain buildings; most of them have been built on speculation, and still remain empty. The greatest numbers, at any one place, is at Green Leaf's Point, on the main [Potomac] river, just above the entrance of the eastern branch. This spot has been looked upon by many as the most convenient one for trade." The new Americans weren't the first to recognize the area's location as a prime one for trade. Native American tribes had traded along the rivers for hundreds of years before the arrival of Captain John Smith in 1608. By the time Pierre L'Enfant drew his city plan, Southwest's strategic military position was apparent. L'Enfant designated what was then called Turkey Buzzard's Point, later to be called Greenleaf Point, as a military site, which it has been since 1791. Initially a fort occupied the site, then a military arsenal and a federal prison, and today Fort McNair is located there.

The city's early speculators also saw the Southwest as prime territory for the development of homes. With its river view and its trading establishments, the area was envisioned to rival Georgetown. Land speculators began buying lots. In Sept 1793 James Greenleaf made a deal with the new government. In exchange for being allowed to purchase 6,000 lots with partners Robert Morris and John Nicholson of Philadelphia at a reduced rate, Greenleaf agreed to construct ten houses a year for seven years. Just four years after purchasing the 6,000 lots, Greenleaf and his associates were bankrupt. Greenleaf, especially hard hit, spent a year in debtors' prison. Still, a biography written about him in 1901 seems to indicate his reputation, at least in some quarters, remained admirable. "Wealth he had and better, learning; learning he had and better, culture; culture he had and better, character. Judge Wylie . . . told me: 'Greenleaf was a great lawyer and a noble character.' "

### Washington Notes

Before his financial demise, Greenleaf and his associates built a series of elegant houses in Southwest that still stand as a testament to his civic optimism. Wheat Row, a group of houses at 1315–1321 4th St S.W., was built in 1794. This is the oldest extant row house group in the city. Around the corner from Wheat Row is the Duncanson–Barney House at 468–470 N St S.W., also built in 1794. Both are now part of the Harbour Square apartment complex.

In addition, Greenleaf built what was known as the Honeymoon House for his friend Thomas Law and Law's new bride, Eliza Parke Custis, granddaughter of Martha Washington. Although the couple resided in Honeymoon House only a few months, their lavish entertaining set a tone for Southwest that most assumed would continue. It didn't. The Law house, however, remains; it's part of the Tiber Island apartment complex. Even though several other prominent citizens had built their homes in Southwest (among them Robert Brent, the first mayor of the city), by the early 1800s Southwest was still a neighborhood consisting mainly of simple cottages and frame row houses.

As people of affluence moved to other areas of the city, Southwest's property values fell, putting the houses within the reach of laborers and other low-income residents. This group lacked the political clout to stop the federal government from building the Washington Canal (now filled in as Constitution Ave) through their neighborhood in the early 1800s. The original intent of the canal was to attract trade. The canal, part of the grand plan of rebuilding the capital after the British invasion of 1814, was designed by Benjamin Latrobe. "We are going this Summer to cut a Canal from the Potowmac thro' the heart of our city to the Har-

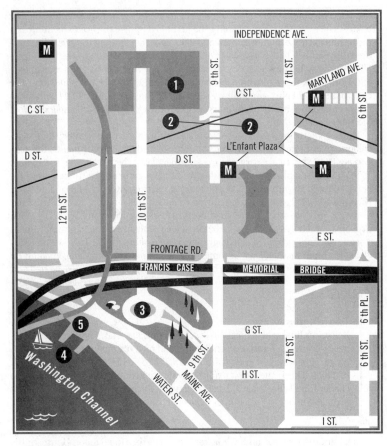

1 Forrestal Building (Dept of Energy)
2 L'Enfant Plaza
3 Benjamin Banneker Park
4 Capital Yacht Club
5 Municipal Fish Market
6 Women's *Titanic* Memorial
7 Fort McNair
8 Wheat Row
9 Edward Simon Lewis House
10 Duncanson-Barney House
11 Tiber Island
12 Waterside Mall
13 Thomas Law House
14 St. Augustine's Episcopal Church
15 Arena Stage/Kreeger Theater
16 Town Center Plaza
17 Southeastern University
18 St. Dominic Church
19 HUD Building

bor or Eastern Branch," Latrobe wrote in 1810. The canal ran in a straight line between the Ellipse and the Capitol and then split in two, one passage cutting through the area that is now Fort McNair, the other entering the Anacostia River near the Navy Yard. Thomas Law, former Southwest resident and the canal's chief promoter, planned to run packet boats between the Ellipse and the Navy Yard, "a

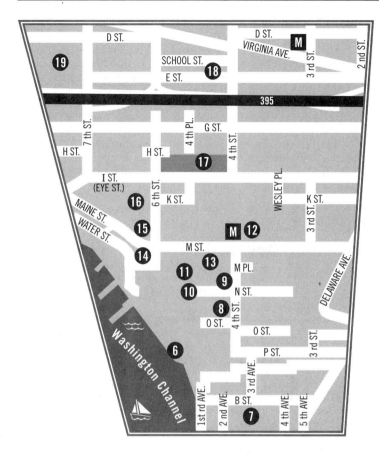

conveyance which may be rendered more economical and comfortable than the hackney coach." But things didn't work out as planned.

Poorly designed, the canal proved navigable only by small, narrow boats with limited cargo space. This made transporting goods not as economical as envisioned. The government refused to widen or deepen the canal, citing insufficient funds for the effort and for the frequent dredging the canal required. Traffic on the canal declined. The canal became a decaying, foul-smelling health hazard and was eventually condemned and covered over. The major effect of the canal was to isolate Southwest, often referred to as "the island."

Before the Civil War, when slavery was legal in the capital, slaves were held in the northern end of Southwest Washington before being sold or transported to other states.

### Washington Notes

Where the Federal Aviation Administration Building now stands, near L'Enfant Plaza between 7th and 9th Sts on Independence Ave, is the site of

Robey's Slave Pen, described by an English visitor in 1835 as "a wretched hovel . . . surrounded by a wooden paling 14 or 15 feet in height with posts outside to prevent escape, and separated from the building by a space too narrow to permit of free circulation of air." In 1848, 77 African American slaves escaped on board a ship called the *Pearl*. When the ship was about 140 miles from Washington, it was forced to take shelter in a cove from high winds. As a result, the ship was captured and the African Americans returned to the slave pen, despite publicity and protest of local and national abolitionists.

Fifteen years later, in the 1850s, Anthony Bowen (see Walk 23: "Shaw and LeDroit Park") was running a section of the Underground Railroad from his home in the same area of what is now L'Enfant Plaza, on E St between 9th and 10th Sts.

Before the Civil War, Southwest had a large number of African American residents. During the Civil War the African American population grew to almost 40 percent of the Southwest population. From the Southwest's docks hundreds of ships bearing arms, supplies, and troops began their journey south during the Civil War. Greenleaf Point was the site of the Washington Arsenal, a gun and powder factory. An explosion killed 21 women workers during the war.

### Washington Notes

Also on Southwest's docks the wounded were unloaded to await transport to city hospitals. Walt Whitman described this scene in May 1862: "Two boatlands came about half-past seven last night. A little after eight, it rained a long and violent shower. The pale, helpless soldiers had been debarked, and lay around the wharf. . . . All around—on the wharf, on the ground, out on side places—the men are lying on blankets, old quilts, etc., with bloody rags bound 'round heads, arms, and legs. The attendants are few, and at night few outsiders also; only a few hardworked transportation men and drivers. (The wounded are getting to be common, and people grow callous.)"

In the thirty years following the Civil War, the population of Southwest nearly doubled. The new arrivals were mainly African American laborers. Hundreds of tiny alley dwellings sprang up to accommodate them. In the early 1870s, the Washington Canal was finally covered over and new streetcar lines connected Southwest with the rest of the city. But in 1873 tracks for the Baltimore and Potomac Railroad were laid along Maryland and Virginia Aves, again isolating Southwest from the city's more middle- and upper-class neighborhoods.

Beginning in the 1880s, Jewish immigrants from Germany and eastern Europe began settling in Southwest along 4½ St (now 4th St) and 7th St. They established tailor shops, dry goods stores, and "mom and pop" grocery stores, often living above their shops. Clarke's Market on Maine Ave had a person who would kill chickens, certifying that they were kosher.

### Washington Notes

Rabbi Moses Yoelson led the Talmud Torah Congregation (informally known as the E St Shul) and lived at 713 4½ St. Yoelson's son was entertainer Al (Asa) Jolson, famous for starring in the first talking motion picture, *The Jazz*

*Singer,* and for his blackfaced vaudeville renditions of songs such as "Mammy." When *The Jazz Singer* made him a fortune in 1927, Jolson moved his parents out of Southwest because of its deteriorating conditions and rising crime rate.

By the early 1900s the residential areas of Southwest suffered from the encroachment of large federal office buildings and from the noise, congestion, and dirt created by blocks of warehouses and freight. By 1930, the population, which had been around 35,000 in 1905, had fallen to 24,000. Most of Southwest's white population lived on the west side of 4½ St, while most of Southwest's black population lived on its east side. But whites and blacks did stand together to demand civic improvements. In 1934 the white Citizens' Association and the black Civic Association came together successfully to convince the city government to have 4½ St paved, widened, and lit, and its name changed to 4th St.

### Washington Notes

This victory was followed by a parade, recalled by one resident as "the first time that Negroes and whites paraded together in the history of Washington."

In the 1930s the national media ran stories on the rundown Southwest alley dwellings. New Deal housing authorities, proud of other New Deal successes, planned improved housing for Southwest's low-income residents. Even so, the federal government contributed to the further decline of Southwest's neighborhood by tearing down more than 40 Victorian row houses to widen Independence Ave for traffic. It was also in the 1930s that a new federal building program was enacted involving what was called the Southwest Rectangle, an area bounded by Independence Ave, 14th St, the Southwest Freeway, and 2nd St. The Department of Health and Human Services, the Department of Agriculture South building, and the Bureau of Engraving and Printing Building were constructed during this time. In the 1950s, as part of an experiment in urban renewal, Southwest Washington was changed. Unfortunately, those solutions eventually created urban blight. The government's plans did not take into consideration the feelings the residents had for their homes. Even in economically depressed sections, neighbors looked out for one another and knew each other. This was a community where people grew up together, married, and stayed. However, despite Southwest Washington's social cohesiveness, the area lacked political power.

In 1946, Congress chartered the Redevelopment Land Agency (RLA) and gave it the power to condemn, redesign, and rebuild neighborhoods. In 1949, the National Housing Act provided money to RLA for slum clearance, redevelopment, and low-rent public housing. An early plan for Southwest Washington called for the rehabilitation of existing structures where possible, coupled with building new ones where necessary. This was rejected as too costly. In 1953, President Dwight Eisenhower requested the New York development firm of Webb & Knapp to prepare a plan. Heading Webb & Knapp's planning staff was I. M. Pei, who, together with Chicago architect Harry Weese, unveiled a plan in early 1954 that called for a mix of high-rise apartment towers interspersed among groups of town houses (an innovative mix of building types for its time), the complete redevelopment of the waterfront, the creation of "super blocks" by closing many of the streets, and the construction of a shopping mall to serve as the town center. The tailors, the dry goods, the mom and pop stores were out.

There was much rejoicing over the demolition of Southwest—by nonresidents. A 1964 article in the *Washington Post,* with its subhead "From Our City's Decay and Squalor Came a Blueprint For the Nation," gleefully declared, "The first rotten tenement crashed to the ground in 1954, signaling the death of the old Southwest." Another such signal was the construction of the Southwest Freeway, which necessitated displacing hundreds of families from their homes. Despite lawsuits, clearance began in 1953 and many of the homes and stores were gone by the end of that year. An article in the *Washington Star* quoted an aged, black store owner: "Well, it seems like they're handin' out a passel o' joy and a passel o' sorrow." Southwest businesspeople lost their case in the Supreme Court, where an opinion prepared by Justice William O. Douglas (who saved the C&O Canal) denied that the condemnation of their property was unfair or arbitrary.

By 1960, most of old Southwest was gone, and in some quarters there was much jubilation and self-congratulation. That same 1964 *Washington Post* article continued, "The success of the new Southwest is mirrored in the comments of its residents: 'It's Georgetown with new buildings and closet space. . . . It's a prestige area, because of the high rents.' The area has appealed primarily to young people, both married and unmarried, who enjoy the bustle of city life. . . . The racial composition of the Southwest, once 76 percent Negro, has been completely reversed. It is now 90 percent white. But integration has worked, has worked well. Nowhere is this more evident than at the various project pools, where white and colored tenants swim and sun-bathe [*sic*] together unselfconsciously. . . . But the problems of the area are heavily outweighed by the contribution it makes to the city's life. At a net cost of $72 million to American taxpayers, the new Southwest has added to the beauty of the city and hugely broadened its tax base. It has also become a very pleasant place to live."

But an estimated 15,000 poor African Americans lost their homes, as well as a number of white, middle-class residents who had chosen Southwest for its convenience. A 1966 study of displaced Southwest families found that "they resent more than ever before the forced disintegration of the social milieu which was theirs in the old Southwest."

In the years since its rise from the old Southwest, the new Southwest has continued to be gentrified in places. Waterfront restaurants attract residents and tourists every weekend, as does the fish market at the base of Water St. Arena Stage has become a Washington landmark. Even if on the whole, Southwest's architecture leans towards the bland, 1960s suburban style, Southwest's residents are well-situated for enjoying the waterfront and for commuting to work in downtown Washington. Its neighborhood associations are active, and its numerous Metro stations make the Southwest easily accessible.

### Washington Notes

Until 1989 only the state of Washington did not have an avenue named after it in the nation's capital. Whether this was to avoid confusion with the name of the city is not known, but C. S. Wetherell, a 67-year-old retired Coast Guard captain and lifelong state of Washington resident, took it upon himself to lobby for a reversal of this slight. On Nov 16, 1989, Canal St S.W., a four-block path between Independence Ave and S. Capitol St, was renamed Washington Ave.

**Highlights:** The Municipal Fish Market off Maine Ave on Water St, Women's *Titanic* Memorial at the end of Water St, an evening of theater at Arena Stage.

# Forrestal Building (Department of Energy)

From the Smithsonian Metro station at Jefferson Dr and 12th St N.W. (on the Mall), walk south one block past the Department of Agriculture's Administration Building (1905; Rankin, Kellogg & Crane; sculpted pediments by A. A. Weinman) and South Building (1930–37; designed in the offices of the Supervising Architect of the Treasury). Walk to 12th St and Independence Ave S.W., then one block east on Independence to the Department of Energy in the Forrestal Building (1970; Curtis and Davis, Fordyce and Hamby Associates, Frank Grad and Sons) at 1000 Independence Ave S.W.; ☎ 586-5000; Web: www.doe.gov.

## Department of Energy

The Department of Energy (DOE) has its origins in the Manhattan Project, the government-sponsored program that developed the atomic bomb during World War II. In 1946, the Atomic Energy Commission was established to maintain civilian government control over the field of atomic research and development. In response to changing circumstances, the Energy Reorganization Act of 1974 created two agencies: the Nuclear Regulatory Agency to regulate the nuclear power industry and the Energy Research and Development Administration to manage nuclear weapons, naval reactors, and energy development programs. Three years later, Congress responded to the energy crisis by creating a unified energy organization called the Department of Energy. Today, the department's mission is defiend as "contributing to the future of the nation by ensuring our energy security, maintaining the safety and reliability of our nuclear stockpile, cleaning up the environment from the legacy of the Cold War, and developing innovations in science and technology."

### History

In 1848, two Greek revival row houses were built on this site by Gilbert Cameron, a master stonemason from New York brought to Washington in 1847 by James Renwick, Jr., to oversee the cutting of the stone for the Smithsonian Castle. (Cameron also built the original Scott Hall of the Soldiers' Home.) Cameron used one of the houses as a residence, the other as a rental property. The houses, known as Cameron Row, lasted until 1941, when they, along with about 40 other Victorian houses and several churches, were razed to widen Independence Ave. During World War II, a temporary government building called Escanaba Hall stood on this site, serving as a dormitory for the Coast Guard personnel training in the Washington Channel.

## Exterior

These are actually three buildings: The 660 ft long main building faces Independence Ave, a taller annex is behind the main building, and there is a separate cafeteria building. When the design for the Forrestal Building was unveiled in 1965, it was described as "a split structure, half on one side of 10th St, and half on the other. A bridge will connect the two sections, running over 10th St at the height of a four-story building—36 ft. The revamped 10th St is to be a broad Mall-type thorofare [*sic*] and the main entrance to the redeveloped Southwest area." To preserve the Independence Ave view of the Capitol, the architects put two floors underground and raised the structure on stilts.

### Washington Notes
When unveiling the plans for the Forrestal Building at a White House meeting with representatives of the American Institute of Architects, President Lyndon Johnson proclaimed, "This structure will be one of our very finest buildings in the federal complex, and I want it to have one of the finest names I know." The building is named for James Forrestal (1892–1949), first secretary of defense (July 1947–Aug 1949) when that department was created after World War II. Forrestal had been secretary of the navy from 1944 to 1947, and the stresses of the war followed by those of the developing Cold War in the late 1940s led him to suffer a nervous breakdown. Forrestal committed suicide by jumping from a window at Bethesda Naval Hospital in 1949.

## Interior
In the main building's lobby an exhibit details the DOE's mission and gives a brief history of the Forrestal Building. Also on display is a bronze portrait bust of James Forrestal (1972; Nicolaus Koni), created by the Hungarian artist known for his portrait bust of Marian Anderson at Lincoln Center in New York. Outside the DOE main entrance doors facing L'Enfant Promenade is *Chthonodynamis* (Robert I. Russin), a granite representation of the ancient Greek concept of the energy of the earth and humanity's attempt to contain its awesome forces.

Walk two blocks south along L'Enfant Promenade to a wide granite court that marks the entrance to **L'Enfant Plaza** (1965; I. M. Pei & Partners; Araldo A. Cossutta, Partner In Charge; 1970–73, Hotel and West Office Building, Vlastimil Koubek), an office, hotel, and retail complex that was originally intended to serve all Southwest but today functions mainly as a business and shopping center for the surrounding federal office buildings.

### Washington Notes
Before the Civil War, this area was residential. The east end of the plaza is the site of the home of Anthony Bowen and the Underground Railroad "station" he operated.

The L'Enfant Promenade in the original design was a 1,200 ft long mall, and L'Enfant Plaza was envisioned as a cultural and convention center, with a hotel, theater, and outdoor cafés. By the time construction began, the plans had changed. L'Enfant Plaza is now primarily a hotel-and-office complex, with a 100,000 square ft underground shopping mall. The steps immediately at the entrance of the plaza lead down into the shopping area, an underground warren of retail shops and restaurants.

Continue south one block to the termination of the promenade and **Benjamin Banneker Park,** a circular plaza and fountain overlooking the waterfront and

Maine Ave. The park is named in honor of the African American who, along with Andrew Ellicott, in 1791 surveyed the ten square miles that would become the city of Washington. Banneker (1731–1806) was a free resident of Maryland who, in spite of a lack of formal education, became an accomplished mathematician, astronomer, and almanac writer. Annually between 1792 and 1797, Banneker published an almanac for which he calculated and predicted the positions of the Sun, Moon, and planets. Walk through the park, which is operated by the National Park Service, to the south end, which has a wonderful view of the Washington Channel, the waterfront docks and restaurants and, to the west, the Thomas Jefferson Memorial.

# The Waterfront
Walk down the hill from the park to 9th St S.W. and its intersection with Maine Ave.

### History
The street was called Water St until it was renamed Maine Ave in 1938. The original Maine Ave, which ran parallel with the Maryland Ave on the east end of the Mall, was eliminated to enlarge the Mall and allow further development of the Smithsonian Institution. During the redevelopment of Southwest in the 1960s, another street was created running along the dock area, and thus Water St again came into existence. Maine Ave and its waterfront was one of the most intense areas of debate during the redevelopment process in the 1950s and '60s. This was once a thriving dock area—a center for Washington's fish, oyster, and crab business—where fishermen sold their daily catch off their boats. During World War II, the area was used for Coast Guard training. In 1945, the U.S. District Engineers' Office developed a five-year improvement program designed to "give Washington one of the finest water fronts [sic] anywhere," according to a 1945 article in the Sunday Star. The plan included, among other things, a pier "designed to accommodate two separate excursion lines . . . [with] Colonial-Style offices, storehouse and comfort stations . . . which will be used to take care of small, ocean-going freighters and inland craft carrying produce and freight." Also planned was a yacht basin whose completion "will afford Washington yachtsmen a total of 356 berths . . . and has every prospect of being one of the finest—if not the best—facility of its kind in the country."

Because the costs involved were prohibitive, these plans did not materialize. In the 1950s and '60s, the 13-acre waterfront strip once again became a focus of redevelopment. Most of the buildings were leveled. These included the mammoth Terminal Refrigerating & Warehousing Corporation building that filled the block then bounded by 11th, 12th, E, and F Sts. (All those streets in this area were replaced or rerouted by the Southwest Freeway.) The corporation building had a hexagonal clock tower with a bell, resembling a ship's bell in tone, that would strike every hour on the hour. New restaurants went up, and some work was done to improve the marina and docks. One major change was the emphasis on low-scale buildings with open areas so that the view of the channel could be enjoyed by more Southwest residents.

In the 1990s, the city came up with a plan to move the Municipal Fish Market inside under two glass-enclosed pavilions, as well as create a fishing pier and an amphitheater surrounded by shops and restaurants. Opposition from the fish

*Sixth Street Wharf (Southwest waterfront), 1863. Courtesy of the Washingtoniana Division, D.C. Public Library.*

market vendors, who saw their rents going up, and nearby residents, who saw loads of tourist buses coming into their neighborhood, put a hold on that plan, at least for the time being. But it's likely a new plan will appear, as the waterfront is viewed by the city as a "potential gold mine of tax revenue."

Walk west along the marina, past Phillips Flagship Restaurant, to the **Capital Yacht Club,** founded in 1892 by nine local yachtsmen aboard one of the first gasoline-powered yachts to sail on the Potomac. In the Yacht Club's early years, when members had large sailing boats, the club sponsored the 140-mile Annapolis Race, a nautical test of nerve and skill that was discontinued during World War I. These days the club hosts many transient boats during boating season, from 15 to 250 ft, and has a full dock staff on duty every day of the year. The club is active locally, hosting annual events such as Flag Raising, Blessing of the Fleet, Fourth of July BBQ, the Commodore's Ball, and the Police and Firemen's Picnic.

Continue walking west through the Yacht Club's parking lot to the **Municipal Fish Market,** a roughly two-block area of fish and seafood vendors in roofed stalls lining Water St. The original market, a colonial revival–style building, was constructed in 1916 at a cost of $185,000 and became legally the "sole wharf for the landing of fish and oysters for sale in the District of Columbia." Here also was the Office of the District Market Master of the Department of Weights, Measures and Markets, and surrounding that was the city's largest wholesale food market, handling almost 75 percent of the food consumed in Washington. During the 1930s, an average of 715 boats annually sailed up the Washington Channel to the market delivering or selling directly off their boats 10 million pounds of fish, oysters, clams, and crabs from the Eastern Shore, Chesapeake Bay, and the Rappahannock River. The original market building was razed in 1960. Today, most of the produce sold here is brought in by refrigerated trucks from Chesapeake Bay.

From the front of the market, turn east and walk along Maine Ave, with its fine collection of mainly seafood restaurants, although new nonseafood restaurants are appearing, such as H.I. Ribster's and Creole Orleans. The Channel Inn Hotel, the only waterfront hotel, has 100 guest rooms and includes the Pier 7 Restaurant. Small parks also dot the waterfront between Maine Ave and Water St. The park at 6th and Water Sts displays the sculpture *The Maine Lobsterman* (1959; Victor Kahll) facing the channel, a gift from the state of Maine.

On either side of this park are docked the *Spirit of Washington* and the *Odyssey*, both of which leave from this point on Potomac River cruises. Next to these are the headquarters of the District of Columbia Harbor Police and Fire Patrols. At the end of Water St is Washington Channel Park, which then becomes Waterside Park (1967–68; Sasaki, Dawson and Demay) in front of the Waterside Towers complex. Across the channel from Waterside Park is East Potomac Park, whose tip is Hains Point.

The walkway along Water St ends at the RMS *Titanic* Monument (1931; Gertrude Vanderbilt Whitney), known as the **Women's *Titanic* Memorial.** This pink granite sculpture is dedicated "To the brave men who perished in the wreck of the Titanic April 15, 1912. They gave their lives that women and children might be saved" erected "by the women of America." The monument, now under the auspices of the National Park Service, was approved by an act of Congress in 1917, and the Women's *Titanic* Memorial Association raised $59,000 to pay for the memorial's completion. The stone bench surrounding the male figure with outstretched arms was designed by Henry Bacon, designer of the Lincoln Memorial. Until 1968, the monument was located at Rock Creek and Potomac Pkwy.

## Fort McNair

Turn east at the monument and walk one block on P St along the red brick wall that encloses **Fort Lesley J. McNair** (1908; McKim, Mead and White; DL) at 4th and P Sts S.W. ☎ 545-6700. The fort stretches from here to the end of Greenleaf Point. A military reservation was located here in 1791, making this site one of the oldest posts in the U.S.

### History

During the British invasion of the city in 1814, the arsenal and all its original structures were destroyed when powder hidden in a well was accidentally ignited. In 1826, the first federal penitentiary was built here, and in 1898 the forerunner of today's Walter Reed Army Medical Center was located on the post. Major Walter Reed conducted much of his research here.

In 1948, the post was renamed in honor of the commander of the Army Ground Forces during World War II, Lieutenant General Lesley J. McNair. McNair was killed by friendly fire at Normandy in 1944, the highest-ranking officer in the armed forces to die in that manner.

The Beaux-Arts **Roosevelt Hall** (1908; McKim, Mead and White), currently undergoing renovation, houses the National War College, established as the Army War College in 1901. The college is now part of the National Defense University (Web: www.ndu.edu), which was established in 1976 and brought together the Industrial College of the Armed Forces, the National War College, the Information Resources Management College, and the Institute for National Strategic Studies at Fort McNair, as well as the Armed Forces Staff College in Norfolk, Virginia. The army's vice chief of staff resides at Fort McNair (the chief of staff resides at Fort Myer, adjacent to Arlington Cemetery in Virginia), as do the soldiers of Company A, 3rd U.S. Infantry, known as the Commander-in-Chief's Guard. The grounds of Fort McNair are open to the public on weekdays from 9 to 5, but the buildings are not.

> ### Washington Notes
> The 1865 trial and execution of four of the conspirators in the assassination of President Abraham Lincoln took place at the U.S. Penitentiary, located on the northern end of the fort's grounds. The conspirators, except for Mary Surratt, had 32-pound iron balls attached to their left legs and were handcuffed. More than 300 witnesses were called to testify at the long and sensational trial, attended by such luminaries as General George Armstrong Custer and his new bride. The trial ended on June 30, when George Azteroth, Davis Herold, Lewis Powell, and Mary Surratt were sentenced to death. One week later, on July 7, the four were hanged and immediately buried in the prison yard near the scaffold. (A tennis court now occupies the site.) Four years later, the bodies were returned to the families, and Mary Surratt was buried in Mt. Olivet Catholic Cemetery in northeast Washington. John Wilkes Booth's body had been brought to the penitentiary immediately following his death and buried on the grounds. His body was also later released to his family. He is now buried on what was the family home in Maryland.

Turn north onto 4th St. Until 1934, this was called 4½ St. Until the redevelopment of the 1950s and '60s this street was the main economic district of Southwest. Walk a half-block on 4th St to **Wheat Row** (1794; James Greenleaf; 1966; Chloethiel Woodard Smith & Associated Architects; DL) at 1315–1321 4th St S.W., four 18C buildings that escaped the wrecker's ball during redevelopment. One of the first of Greenleaf's speculative housing projects, Wheat Row is named after the first inhabitant of no. 1315, John Wheat. These Georgian-style houses are distinguished by their 12-bay row of windows, lintels with keystones, and arched lintels over the fanlights. Along with the Lewis House at 456 N St S.W. and the Duncanson-Barney House at 468–470 N St S.W., Wheat Row was incorporated into the Harbour Square apartment complex in 1966.

From 4th St, walk a quarter-block to N St, then turn west on N St and walk a half-block to the **Edward Simon Lewis House** (1817; architect unknown; 1966; Chloethiel Woodard Smith & Associated Architects; DL) at 456 N St S.W., a fine example of the early-19C brick houses of Washington. The house was converted into apartments in the 1920s, and in the 1930s one of its tenants was journalist Ernie Pyle, who would gain fame as a World War II correspondent. The house was converted to a single-family dwelling in the Harbour Square complex in 1966.

Continue west on N St to 468–470 N St and the **Duncanson-Barney House** (1794; James Greenleaf; 1966; Chloethiel Woodard Smith & Associated Architects; DL). Originally occupied by Captain William Mayne Duncanson, an early Washington speculator who like so many others did not do very well, the house was later used for the Washington Sanitarium, a home for the indigent elderly, and as the Barney Settlement House. In 1966, it was incorporated into the Harbour Square complex.

Catercorner to the Duncanson-Barney House is the N St side of **Tiber Island** (1965; Keyes, Lethbridge and Condon), an apartment complex bounded by M, N, and 4th Sts and the waterfront. Tiber Island was the winner of the first RLA design competition during Southwest's redevelopment. Of particular interest are its juxtaposition of high-rise apartment towers and low-rise town houses, its central plaza covering a parking garage, and its limited range of colors and materials that contribute toward a cohesive look.

Return east on N St to 4th St and then north on 4th St one block to M St and the **Waterside Mall** (1972; Chloethiel Woodard Smith & Associated Architects) at 400 M St S.W., a suburban-style shopping center stretching for ten acres between 4th and M and 6th and I Sts. This mall has never really caught on with local residents nor attracted major retailers other than Safeway. Although conveniently located on top of a Metro station (Waterfront-SEU), Waterside Mall's low shopper turnout has been a problem from the beginning, as were the early confrontations between residents and developers, unable to agree on what kinds of stores the neighborhood needed. Today, the mall serves mainly workers from adjacent office buildings.

On M St, turn west and walk one block to 6th St, then turn south on 6th St and walk through the Tiber Island complex to the **Thomas Law House** (1796; attributed to William Lovering; DL) at 1252 6th St S.W., one of the first houses built in Southwest and now a community center for Tiber Island residents. When Thomas Law married Eliza Parke Custis, Martha Washington's granddaughter, Elizabeth was 19 and Thomas was 39. They spent their honeymoon here, from the spring of 1796 to that fall, and so the house was nicknamed the Honeymoon House. Law and his wife soon moved to a new house in the city. In 1816, Richard Lee, uncle of Robert E. Lee (who would also marry into the Custis family), a member of the first Congress and influential in bringing the capital here, bought the house and lived in it until his death in 1827. From 1827 until 1897, a junk dealer named Edmund Wheeler lived here; his shop was located nearby. From 1919 to 1956, the mansion was a clinic for Hadley Memorial Hospital. In 1965, the building was turned into the Tiber Island's community center.

Return to M St, which becomes Maine Ave at the intersection with 6th St. On the southwest corner is **St. Augustine's Episcopal Church** (1966; Alexander Cochran) at 600 M St S.W. For the first six years of the parish's existence, it held services at the old Hogate's Seafood Restaurant, located across the street from the current restaurant on Maine Ave, leading to the church's nickname of St. Hogate's. Church plans were approved by the RLA in 1963, and the building was dedicated in 1966. Inside is an 11C baptistry of either Norman or northern European origin.

## Arena Stage

Directly across from St. Augustine's is Arena Stage (1961; Harry Weese & Associates) at 6th St and Maine Ave (1101 6th St S.W.; ☎ 488-3300; Web: www.arenastage.com) and its adjoining **Kreeger Theater** (1970; Harry Weese & Associates). Cofounded in 1950 by Zelda Fichandler (with whom the theater is strongly identified), her husband Thomas C. Fichandler, and Edward Mangum, Arena Stage began the regional theater movement in this country and was the first theater outside New York City to win a Tony Award. From 1950 to 1955,

Arena was housed in the Hippodrome Theatre, a former movie house at 9th St and New York Ave N.W., with ticket prices in the $2.50 range.

**Washington Notes**
Arena was the first theater in Washington to open to integrated audiences.

The 1956 through 1961 seasons were spent in the converted Hospitality Hall of the old Heurich Brewery on the site of what is now the Kennedy Center. The 500-seat theater-in-the-round was nicknamed the Old Vat in reference to the brewery's huge kettles and as a pun on Britain's Old Vic theater. In 1961, Chicago architect Harry Weese created the company's first permanent home, Arena Stage. Needing an inexpensive structure, Weese chose to achieve an elegant effect through the use of simple materials, such as exposed concrete and sheet metal roofing painted dark gray, and he used this idea again when designing the Kreeger Theater addition in 1970. In 1976, Arena opened a third stage, the Old Vat Room, an intimate space for small-scale productions. The Fichandler Stage is in-the-round and the Kreeger has a modified thrust stage. Now in its fifth decade, Arena has had only three artistic directors: Zelda Fichandler for 43 years, Douglas C. Wager for the next seven, and, beginning with the 1997–98 season, Molly Smith. Arena attracts more than 250,000 patrons annually to its eight-play seasons.

**Washington Notes**
The name Arena Stage was chosen instead of Arena Theater because when the building opened in 1961, the District's building code required a theater to have a proscenium arch and a fire curtain, difficult to manage with a theater-in-the-round. Hence the choice of name.

Walk north on 6th St a half-block to **Town Center Plaza** (1961–62; I. M. Pei & Partners) at 1000 6th St S.W., winner of a Federal Housing Authority Honor Award. These are the only apartments in the redevelopment area that don't have balconies and don't incorporate town houses into the complex.

Continue north on 6th St a half-block to the corner of 6th and I Sts and **Southeastern University** at 501 I St S.W. (☎ 488-8162; Web: www.seu.edu), a private university founded in 1879, with an emphasis on liberal arts and business education. The university is job-oriented, preparing its students for positions in business and public service. Its president, Dr. Charlene Drew Jarvis, is also a member of the District of Columbia's City Council. The university currently has an enrollment of more than 700 students from more than 40 nations and the greater metropolitan area.

## St. Dominic Church

Turn west on I St and walk one block to the intersection with 7th St, then north on 7th St two blocks to E St, then east on E St one block to St. Dominic Church (1875; P. C. Keeley) at 630 E St S.W., ☎ 554-7863, established in 1852 by the Dominican Fathers. Ground for the original Gothic-design church was bought from Georgetown College (later University) for a little over $5,000. Built in 1853, the church was outgrown by the its parishioners in 12 years. Because of lack of funds, completion of the present Victorian Gothic church in 1875 required active participation by members of the parish who were skilled construction workers. A fire in 1885 destroyed the entire interior of the church, with only the walls left standing under a shattered roof. Another fire in 1929 damaged the roof, and water damage in the interior destroyed the organ, thought to be one of the finest in the city at the time. The church itself escaped the wrecker's ball during redevelopment, but its priory, school, and convent for the nuns who taught at the school were all demolished to make way for the Southwest Freeway.

St. Dominic Church, made of granite from the quarries of Port Deposit, Maryland, is 200 ft long by 90 ft wide and can seat 1,400. Its most distinctive feature is the beauty of its 57 stained glass windows. The grand altar windows, the rose window, the St. Peter and St. Paul window, and the Dominican shields all date from the 19C. The 24 windows along the side of the church, those in the chapels, and the rear balcony window were designed by Edward W. Heimer and Company Stained Glass Sudio in Clifton, New Jersey, in 1965.

## HUD Building

From the front of the church, walk north on 6th St to D St where it crosses with Virginia Ave, turn west on D St and walk one block to 7th St, then north on 7th St one block to the Department of Housing and Urban Development (HUD) Building (1968; Marcel Breuer & Associates; Nolen, Swinburne & Associates; 1998 front plaza design, Martha Schwartz) at 451 7th St S.W.; ☎ 708-1422; Web: www.hud.gov.

Breuer's concrete honeycomb building, with its deeply modeled window panels, is easily one of Southwest's most architecturally interesting buildings. It was commissioned in 1963 and was one of the first structures to go up after President John Kennedy issued his directive on "Guiding Principles for Federal Architecture," intending to raise the aesthetic standards of federal buildings. Breuer had designed a similar curvilinear structure for the UNESCO headquarters in Paris in 1958. The style of the building provides the maximum amount of natural light in restricted office space; at the same time it complements the curves of the adjacent Southwest Freeway. One of the guiding principles of Kennedy's directive was that a percentage of construction costs be devoted to artistic embellishments.

Thirty-five years later, in 1998, HUD followed the guidelines when it unveiled landscape architect Martha Schwartz's "mechanical trees" on the building's front plaza facing 7th St. These aluminum structures are 38 ft in diameter, tautly covered in sheets of white vinyl, and supported 18 ft above ground by shiny stainless steel poles. Lit from within, the spheres emit a phosphorescent glow in the dark, adding an eerie note of drama at night to the empty spaces created by the surrounding mammoth government buildings. Originally, the spheres were supposed to be in brilliant hues of orange, red, yellow, and cobalt blue. But HUD Secretary Andrew Cuomo felt the hues made too strong an artistic statement, and so the color was changed to pearlescent white. Part of this plaza renovation was to have included a gigantic backlighted mural designed by Schwartz of blown-up images of HUD's accomplishments, but this was canceled for budget reasons.

The Department of Housing and Urban Development was established in 1965. Its mission is to prevent housing discrimination, oversee public housing projects throughout the country, and expand the availability of mortgage funds for moderate-income families by using government guaranteed mortgage-back securities.

To continue to the next walk, proceed to the L'Enfant Plaza Metro station and take the Blue Line to Arlington Cemetery.

# 29 · Arlington: Arlington National Cemetery and Related Sites

Metro: Blue Line to Arlington Cemetery.
By Tourmobile: Tourmobile (☎ 554-5100) runs tour buses to Arlington National Cemetery.

## Arlington Memorial Bridge

If traveling by Metro, take the Blue Line to the Arlington National Cemetery stop and walk east toward the Arlington Memorial Bridge (1926–32; McKim, Mead and White; Carl Paul Jennewein and Alexander Phimister Proctor, sculptors; 1951, James Fraser and J. H. Friedlander, equestrian statues; DL). If you are coming from the Mall area near the Lincoln Memorial, walk around the circle to the entrance to the bridge.

Arlington Memorial Bridge (Web: www.nps.gov) was built as a symbol of the reunification of the North and South following the Civil War. The bridge was originally proposed in 1901 as part of the McMillan Commission's plan for city beautification. An old wooden bridge stood on the site, held in place mainly by the rocks that were dumped around its piers each year. This rock-piling had created an unintentional dam that caused problems downriver. The bridge, often in disrepair, caused huge traffic jams because of its dilapidated condition.

### Washington Notes

In 1921, when President Warren G. Harding and other dignitaries were held up in a three-hour traffic delay on their way to the dedication of the Tomb of the Unknown Soldier (as it was then called), the decision was made to go ahead with the McMillan Commission's recommendation for a new bridge.

Memorial Bridge has nine segmented arches, increasing in length from 166 ft at the ends to 184 ft in the center. The arches vary in height from 28 ft at the ends to 35 ft in the center. The bridge itself is 2,163 ft long. The reinforced concrete framework has a veneer of North Carolina granite. The bridge, built at a cost of $14.75 million as a drawbridge, was dedicated by President Herbert Hoover on Jan 16, 1932.

On the bridge's pylons are eight-ft disks with massive eagles sculpted by Carl Paul Jennewein. On either side of the disks are equally large sculpted fasces, symbols of power and authority in ancient Rome. Six-ft bison keystones are found at the apex of the pylons. These were carved by Alexander Proctor, who also did the bronze bison on the Dumbarton Bridge in Georgetown (see Walk 19: "Georgetown East"). Original plans for the bridge included a row of neoclassical statues along each side of the bridge, but this idea was abandoned as construction costs rose. Flanking the east end of the bridge and the Rock Creek and Potomac Pkwy terminus are four equestrian statues of gilded bronze. The two statues *Music and Harvest* and *Aspiration and Literature* are collectively titled *The Art of Peace* (1951;

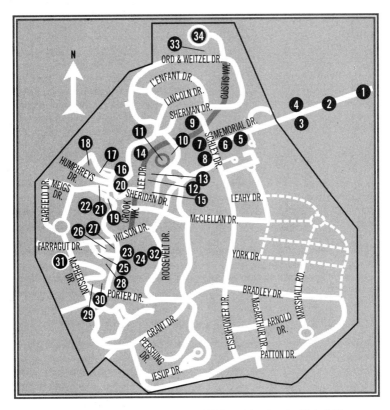

1 Arlington Memorial Bridge

2 Memorial Dr

3 *The Hiker* (United Spanish War Veterans Memorial)

4 Seabees Memorial

5 Admiral Richard E. Byrd Memorial

6 101st Army Airborne Division Memorial

7 Schley Gate

8 Women in Military Service for America Memorial

9 William Howard Taft grave

10 Oliver Wendell Holmes grave

11 John F. Kennedy grave site

12 Robert F. Kennedy grave site

13 Mary Randolph grave site

14 Robert E. Lee Memorial (Arlington House)

15 Pierre L'Enfant grave site

16 Tomb of the Unknown Civil War Dead

17 Memorial to Pan Am Flight 103

18 Anita Newcomb McGee grave site

19 Philip Kearny grave site

20 Montgomery Meigs grave site

21 Abner Doubleday grave site

22 George Washington Parke Custis grave site

23 Memorial amphitheater

24 Tomb of the Unknowns

25 USS *Maine* Memorial

26 *Challenger* Memorial

27 Iran Rescue Memorial

28 Audie Murphy grave

29 Nurses Memorial

30 John Foster Dulles grave

31 Confederate Monument

32 Joe Louis grave

33 Netherlands Carillon

34 U.S. Marine Corps Memorial

James Fraser), and *The Art of War* (1951; J. H. Friedlander) consists of the two statues *Valor* and *Sacrifice*. These statues were gifts from the people of Italy to the people of the U.S. The sculptors were commissioned in 1925, but the statues were not erected and dedicated until 1951, after being cast and gilded in Italy. (The gilding was restored in 1971.) *Music and Harvest* shows the winged horse Pegasus (from Greek mythology) between a male figure with a bundle of wheat and a sickle and a woman with a harp. In *Aspiration and Literature* Pegasus is flanked by figures holding a book and a bow. *Valor* has a male equestrian striding forward with a shield, accompanied by a female. *Sacrifice* portrays the earth as a standing female looking up to the rider, who is Mars, the Roman god of War. Each of the four granite pedestals bears 36 gilded bronze stars representing the states of the Union at the end of the Civil War.

**Diversion:**
Four miles south by car on George Washington Memorial Pkwy is **Ronald Reagan Washington National Airport** (1940; Howard Cheney, architect for the Terminal Building; 1997; Cesar Pelli & Associates, architects for the New Terminal). There is also a Metro station (Blue/Yellow Line) for the airport.

### History
Unofficially known as Gravelly Point when it first opened (and unofficially as National Airport today), the airport is built on a site historically linked with the surrounding area. In 1746, John Alexander, of the family after which Alexandria, Virginia, is named, built a mansion here he called Abingdon. In 1778, the mansion was purchased by John Parke Custis, son of Martha Washington, for his bride Eleanor Calvert, daughter of the fifth Lord Baltimore. In 1829, the house served as a retreat for President Andrew Jackson. During the Civil War it was owned by Confederate Major Bushrod Hunter and his son; because of this it was confiscated by the Union government. In 1930, the house, owned by the Richmond, Fredericksburg & Potomac Railroad, burned in a brush fire. The foundations and a chimney were preserved by the Society for the Preservation of Virginia Antiquities. The remains are on high ground west of the present terminal building, preserved as part of the Airports Authority's Capital Development Program.

Hoover Field, which opened in 1926, was Washington's first major airport facility; it was followed in 1927 by the nearby Washington Airport. Located near the site of the present-day Pentagon, the two merged in 1930 to become Washington-Hoover Airport. This combined facility was hampered by the high-tension electrical wires on the highway that paralleled the airport and by the tall smokestack nearby. The airport's only runway was intersected by the heavily traveled Military Rd, and guards were posted to flag down traffic during takeoffs and landings.

In 1938, President Franklin Roosevelt chose the current site for a facility that would be safer and more convenient for air traffic. Washington National Airport, dedicated in 1940, cost $12.5 million to build and was constructed mainly with WPA (Works Progress Administration) labor. American Airlines made the first official landing with a plane piloted by Bennett H. Griffin, who became airport manager in 1947. As Americans took to the skies following World War II, the airport expanded repeatedly, with new buildings and runways added throughout the 1950 and early '60s.

In 1987, the federal government relinquished direct control over National Airport (and Dulles International Airport in Virginia) to the Metropolitan Washington Airports Authority. In the early 1990s, plans for the New Terminal were formulated. Cesar Pelli & Associates describe their terminal design as being based on a 45 by 45 ft repetitive structural steel bay that establishes scale, flexibility, and architectural proportions. Each bay is a dome with a central glass oculus. The 1 million-square-ft terminal opened in July 1997 with 35 new gates and a 1,600 ft concourse designed to accommodate approximately 16 million passengers annually. The terminal features works by 30 artists in the form of medallions, murals, friezes, and balustrades.

Cross Memorial Bridge and look to the right. In the distance is Washington National Cathedral and nearer is the curved façade of the Watergate, the boxy exterior of the Kennedy Center, and the dome of the Old Naval Observatory (see Walk 18: "Foggy Bottom"). Note that the Washington, D.C., side of the bridge rests on **Columbia Island,** an attenuated strip of land about a mile long that separates Washington from Virginia by the Boundary Channel. Boundary Channel Bridge carries Memorial Ave across the narrow channel between Columbia Island and the Virginia shore. The bridge's central arch spans the channel, and its design complements that of Memorial Bridge, with identical balustrades, benches and lampposts.

Traffic leading on and off Memorial Bridge is always heavy, and caution should be exercised when crossing the road. From Columbia Island, walk onto Memorial Dr, which leads to the cemetery gates. This drive is known informally as the **Avenue of Heroes** because of a series of monuments lining its path. The first, and perhaps most famous, is **The Hiker** (1965; Theodora Alice Ruggles Kitson). This eight-ft bronze sculpture was erected by the United Spanish War Veterans and affiliated organizations to honor the more than 450,000 veterans of the Spanish-American War and the Philippine Insurrection (1898–1902), about 15,000 of whom were still living at the time of the dedication in July 1965.

Also along the drive is the Seabees Memorial (the U.S. Naval Construction Battalion, or C.B.), which has the inscription "With willing hearts and skillful hands, the difficult we do at once, the impossible takes a bit longer."

Continue west on Memorial Dr to the **Admiral Richard Evelyn Byrd, Jr., Memorial** (1961; Felix de Weldon). In May 1926 Admiral Byrd (1888–1957) and his copilot, Floyd Bennett, flew from Norway to the North Pole. Byrd also made several expeditions to the Antarctic; the first was in 1928. During World War II Byrd served on the Chief of Naval Operations staff. In 1961 the National Geographic Society erected the life-size statue of Byrd. The inscription reads, "Upon this bright globe he carved his signature of courage." Continue west to the **101st Army Airborne Division Memorial.** Sculptor Bernhard Zukerman created the large bronze eagle with uplifted wings to symbolize the 101st, known as the "Screaming Eagles." The still-active division fought in World War II and the Vietnam War. The base is inscribed with Major General William Lee's Aug 1942 prediction that the 101st "has no history but has a rendezvous with destiny."

In the middle of the Avenue of Heroes is the entrance/exit to the Arlington Cemetery Metrorail stop (Blue Line) and across from it the entrance to the **Visitor Center.** Stop in here for a map of the cemetery, which is absolutely essential, as many of the streets are unidentified. (This is also one of only two restroom stops in the cemetery. The other is at Arlington House.) The Visitor Center has a bookstore and an exhibit, on view through at least 2002, that tells the story of **taps**, the bugle piece (or call) played at every U.S. military funeral (an average of 30 times a day at Arlington Cemetery) and one of the most recognizable pieces of music in America. Along with the story of the origin of taps during the Civil War, on display are bugles and trumpets from all U.S. wars, including a bugle made of plastic during World War II (when brass was in short supply), as well as the bugle played at the funeral of President John F. Kennedy in 1963.

From the Visitor Center, take the marked Pedestrian Walkway to the west end of Memorial Dr, where there are the two gated entrances to the cemetery. On the north is **Schley Gate**, named for Admiral Winfield Scott Schley of the Spanish-American War, and on the south is **Roosevelt Gate**, named for President Theodore Roosevelt. In the center of each gate is a gold wreath with a diameter of 30 ft. Set within the Schley Gate wreath are the seals for the U.S. Navy and the U.S. Coast Guard; within the Roosevelt Gate are the seals for the U.S. Marine Corps and the U.S. Army. (The U.S. Air Force hadn't yet been established when the gates were installed in 1932.)

Between the gates is a **hemicycle** (a semicircular retaining wall) that rises 30 ft high and is 226 ft in diameter. Dedicated in 1932 at the time of the cemetery dedication, the hemicycle (DL) was intended to be the ceremonial entrance to Arlington National Cemetery. However, in 1938, it was decided that the hemicycle interfered with the view from Arlington House to the Memorial Bridge, so the hemicycle was covered with ivy in an attempt to lessen the impact. The hemicycle was never completed. In its center is the Great Niche with a bas-relief of the Great Seal of the United States; to its north, the seal of the Department of the Navy; to its south, the seal of the Department of War (now called the Department of Defense).

## Women in Military Service for America Memorial

☎ (800) 222-2294 or (703) 533-1155. Web: www.womensmemorial.org. Open daily Oct–March 8–5; April–Sept 8–7. Closed Christmas Day. Gift shop. Restrooms. Wheelchair accessible.

At the foot of the hemicycle is the Women in Military Service for America Memorial (1997; Marion G. Weiss and Michael A. Manfredi). This is the nation's first major national memorial honoring the more than 1.8 million women who have served in America's defense.

At the memorial's dedication, Colonel Kelly Hamilton of the U.S. Air Force said, "Duty, Honor, Country—what an overwhelming rush of energy. Standing shoulder to shoulder in a sea of women veterans, I am overwhelmed by the legacy that surrounds me. Immersed in history, past, present, future, I am one among many committed to serving America."

**Highlights:** The view from the Upper Terrace, looking back toward the Robert E. Lee Memorial (Arlington House) and the Kennedy grave, looking down at the Women in Military Service Memorial, and looking across to the city of Washington. The Hall of Honor and the Computer Register. The information desk, which has special materials for children, including a crossword puzzle with answers to questions about women in the military that can be found in the exhibits.

### History

The creation of the memorial was the result of more than ten years of work by military veterans, male and female, and by the Women in Military Service for American Memorial Foundation, which was headed by retired Air Force Brigadier General Wilma L. Vaught, one of the most decorated women in U.S. military history. Following the 1982 approval by the American Veterans Committee (AVC) of the memorial to women, the AVC lobbied Congress for approval. In 1986, Congress unanimously approved a bill, later signed by President Ronald Reagan, for the establishment of the Women's Memorial. In 1987 the foundation began fundraising.

In 1989, there was a national competition to design the memorial, open to all U.S. citizens 18 and older. There were two basic criteria: The view lines from the Lincoln Memorial to the Kennedy grave site and Arlington House had to be maintained, and the design had to "blend harmoniously" with the other memorials. In Nov 1989, the team of architects led by Marion G. Weiss and Michael A. Manfredi won. Their original design called for tall glass spires that would rise from the hemicycle's upper terrace and glow softly at night, but this idea was eventually dropped because of concerns that the illuminated spires would overshadow the historic memorial corridor that runs from the Capitol to the Lincoln Memorial to the JFK grave site and Arlington House.

The dedication in Oct 1997 was a four-day celebration, with a candlelight march from the Lincoln Memorial to the Women's Memorial. Vice President Al Gore officiated at the ribbon-cutting ceremony on Oct 18, 1997, which was attended by more than 36,000, including thousands of veterans.

> #### Washington Notes
>
> When walking around the semicircular Exhibit Gallery, approaching the Register Room, notice the line of polished black granite leading to the room. This is a physical rendering of the historic line that extends between the Lincoln Memorial and Arlington House, symbolically linking the North and the South following the Civil War. From here, the line symbolically extends upward through the Kennedy grave site to Arlington House.

## Exterior

The **fountain** and **reflecting pool,** directly in front of the memorial, represent the coming together of water and light. The fountain has more than 200 jets of water, created to suggest the "individual voices of women blending in a collective harmony of purpose . . . brought together and come to rest in the 80 ft in diameter reflecting pool." A plaza named the **Court of Valor** forms a semicircle fronting the memorial.

## Interior

The 33,000-square-ft facility houses a 196-seat theater, the Hall of Honor, a conference room, gift shop, and exhibit gallery. The gift shop and restroom facilities are located in the lobby. Across from the information desk is the donor wall listing those who contributed $10,000 or more to the construction of the monument and states that have honored their women veterans. Walking clockwise around the interior semicircle, you'll come first to the **theater,** where a film chronicling women's place in the nation's wars runs every 12 minutes. Outside the theater on the wall is a rendition of the U.S. Postal Service stamp honoring America's servicewomen.

Continue clockwise to the **Computer Register.** Continuously scrolled on its three screens are the names and records of every woman registered with the memorial. Type in a name on one of 12 keyboards to bring up a servicewoman's record, if she has registered. Along the opposite wall and around the semicircle is the **Exhibit Gallery,** which consists of 16 alcoves of temporary exhibits that tell the story of women in the military, from the Revolutionary War to the present.

> ### Washington Notes
> The Exhibit Gallery features such women as Sybil Ludington, who rode 40 miles on horseback—farther than Paul Revere—in 1777 to warn people around Ludington, Connecticut, that the British were attacking; Sarah Osborne, a cook for the Continental Army during the American Revolution who carried food between the campfire and the trenches in buckets and lived to be 103; Dr. Mary Walker, awarded the Medal of Honor for tending to wounded soldiers during the Civil War; Irish immigrant Jennie Hodgers, who enlisted in the army as "Albert Cashier" and fought in World War I; four field nurses in World War I who, after their ship was torpedoed, spent 12 days in an open life raft before rescue; Phoebe Jeter, who commanded a platoon of 15 men assigned to identify incoming Scud missiles and destroy them during the Gulf War and the first woman in her battalion to earn an Army Commendation medal while in Saudia Arabia; as well as representative women who served in Korea, Vietnam, Panama, and the Gulf War.

Walk along the gallery and look up toward the skylights, which have quotations etched on them about the honor of serving one's country. When the sun hits the skylights, the reflections form the words that can be read on the marble gallery wall.

At the end of the semicircle is the **Hall of Honor.** Servicewomen who were killed in action, died in the line of duty, were prisoners of war, or recipients of the nation's highest award for service and bravery are honored here. Flags of the 50 states, the District of Columbia, and the U.S. territories were donated by the National Society of the Daughters of the American Revolution and the poles they hang on by the United Daughters of the Confederacy. The large block of Colorado Yule marble against the wall is the "Sister Block" of marble to that used in the Tomb of the Unknowns.

Exit the underground spaces and walk up the outside stairs (or take the elevator inside the facility) to the **Upper Terrace.** The stairway entries represent women "breaking through barriers in the military." From the stairway, look down through the skylights into the Exhibit Gallery to see the quotations again. The Upper Terrace affords the same unimpeded view of Washington as can be seen from higher up on the ridge at the Kennedy grave site and Arlington House.

In 2000, the memorial will mount a major exhibition on the anniversary of the beginning of the Korean War, honoring those women who served in Korea and at home. The exhibition will become a permanent part of the memorial.

## Arlington National Cemetery

Located off Memorial Dr in Arlington, Virginia, made accessible via the Memorial Bridge west of the Lincoln Memorial. ☎ (703) 697-2131. Web: www.

arlingtoncemetery.com or www.mdw.army.mil/cemetery.htm. Open daily Apr–Sept 8–7; Oct–Mar 8–5. Tour buses (for a fee) shuttle between four stops inside cemetery gates: Visitor Center, John F. Kennedy grave site, Tomb of the Unknowns, Robert E. Lee Memorial (Arlington House).

From the Women's Memorial, turn right and enter Arlington National Cemetery (established 1862; Arlington House renovations by George Hadfield, 1820; *Kearney*, 1914, Edward Clark Potter; *Meigs*, 1865, Theophilus Fisk Mills; Memorial Amphitheater, 1921, Frederick D. Owens; Tomb of the Unknowns, 1931, Lorimer Rich; Thomas Hudson Jones, sculptor) through the Schley Gate.

**Highlights.** Tomb of the Unknowns, Arlington House, graves of President John F. Kennedy, Jacqueline Kennedy, and Senator Robert Kennedy.

### History

In 1669, Robert Howsen, a ship's captain, was granted a 6,000-acre tract for bringing colonists to Virginia. That tract included what are now Alexandria and Arlington, Virginia. The Alexandria family later bought and named part of the tract Alexandria, while farther north John Parke Custis, the son of Martha Washington and Daniel Parke Custis, bought 1,110 acres of the tract in 1776 and named it Arlington, after an older family property on Maryland's Eastern Shore. When John Parke Custis died of camp fever while serving as an aide to George Washington at Yorktown, two of his children, George Washington Parke Custis (6 months old) and Nellie (2 years old) went to live with their grandmother and her second husband, George Washington, at Mount Vernon.

George Washington Parke Custis inherited the Arlington land upon the death of his grandmother in 1802. He began to develop what would be a living monument to George Washington. He gathered a collection of treasured memorabilia that had belonged to the general and his wife, including a china punch bowl given to Washington by French naval officers, pieces of a china set presented to the Washingtons by the Society of the Cincinnati, and the bed on which Washington died (now at Mount Vernon). Custis himself is thought to have drawn the original plans for Arlington House. (In 1820 the house was remodeled by architect George Hadfield.) A bachelor when construction began, Custis was married and father to four children 14 years later when construction was completed. Custis's wife, Mary Lee Fitzhugh, shared bloodlines with several of the first families of Virginia, including one of its most illustrious, the Lee family.

#### *Washington Notes*

George Washington Parke Custis entertained visitors and distinguished guests. He even had his photograph taken by Mathew Brady. Often Custis, an amateur playwright and artist, pulled out the tents used by George Washington at Yorktown, erected them on the lawn, and spun stories about his famous "father" while playing his violin. Custis, known for giving away his collected Washington memorabilia to his guests, gave the Marquis de Lafayette, who had served with Washington during the war, a Masonic sash and an umbrella during Lafayette's two visits.

The only one of Custis's children to survive into adulthood, Mary Anna Randolph Custis fell in love with Robert E. Lee, a distant cousin and childhood friend, and son of Henry "Light Horse Harry" Lee, a Revolutionary War hero and friend of George Washington. On June 30, 1831, Robert E. Lee, a handsome young army lieutenant, and Mary Anna married at Arlington House. As a military man (Lee had graduated second in his class at West Point), Lee knew the strategic value of Arlington House, with its immense view of Washington and the Potomac River. In 1853, Mary Lee Custis died. When George Washington Parke Custis died four years later, on Oct 10, 1857, Robert E. Lee took over the estate, its grounds, and its slaves.

The attention Lee received from capturing John Brown in 1859 brought him a military transfer to Texas. South Carolina seceded in Dec 1860. On Feb 1, 1861, Texas followed.

### Washington Notes

By March 1, Lee was back at Arlington, dealing with the care of his arthritis-stricken wife and the possible secession of his home state, Virginia. Lee had been granted command of the First U.S. Calvary by the newly inaugurated President Abraham Lincoln and was offered the field command of the U.S. Army, which was certain to invade Virginia as soon as Virginia's secession was officially voted upon. On April 20, 1861, after two days spent considering the matter, Lee wrote a brief, formal letter to the secretary of war, resigning his commission as colonel of the First Regiment. "Though opposed to secession and deprecating war, I could take no part in an invasion of Southern States." On April 19, 1861, with the Civil War just days old, Virginia seceded.

Robert E. Lee left Arlington House on April 22, 1861. His wife wouldn't see him again for 14 months. On April 27, Lee wrote to his wife, "War is inevitable and there is no telling when it will burst around you. . . . You have to move and make arrangements to go to some point of safety. . . . The Mount Vernon plate and pictures ought to be secured. Keep quiet while you remain, and in your preparations. . . . May God keep and preserve you and have mercy on all our people."

The Lee family moved from Arlington on May 15, 1861, taking with them only a few of George Washington's paintings and the family silverware. On May 24, Federal troops claimed Arlington House and its grounds for Union military headquarters.

Concerned for her home and her family's Washington memorabilia, Mrs. Lee expressed the hope to those in command that the Washington family artifacts be preserved. Efforts were made, but the task soon became impossible. (It was said that cups from the Washingtons' china set were being sold on the streets of Washington by peddlers.) The remaining possessions of the Lee, Custis, and Washington families were collected and stored in the U.S. Patent Office; but countless heirlooms had disappeared. In the fall of 1861, Lee again wrote to his wife: "It is better to make up our minds to a general loss. They cannot take away the remembrance of the spot, and the memories of those that to us rendered it sacred. That will remain to us as long as life will last, and that we can preserve."

### Washington Notes

On June 7, 1862, the U.S. government passed "An Act for the Collection of Direct Taxes in the Insurrectionary Districts of The United States." This law taxed "insurrectionary property" and land according to its valued worth.

The tax had to be paid in person by the legal titleholder or the land and properties were subject to seizure. Arlington House was valued at $26,810 and a tax of $92.07 was levied. Mrs. Lee, the legal titleholder, too frail to risk passing enemy lines in order to make payment, authorized her cousin, Philip R. Fendall, to travel to Alexandria, with the necessary funds. However, the payment was refused, probably on the technicality that Fendall was not the legal titleholder. The taxes were declared delinquent. As a result, on Jan 11, 1864, the Arlington estate was offered for sale at a public auction where the tax commissioners, representing the U.S. government, were the only bidders. The estate, with its 1,100 acres, mansion, and all outbuildings, was bought by the government for its assessed value "for Government use, for war, military, charitable and educational purposes." Although not aimed directly at the Lee family, the insurrectionary taxation law resulted in Arlington House officially becoming the property of the U.S. government.

The Union also passed a National Cemetery Act in 1862 allowing the president unlimited power to claim any land fit for use as a burial ground. During the early years of the Civil War fighting had centered around the city of Washington, and there was an urgent need for cemeteries. By the spring of 1864, more than 8,000 soldiers had been buried in the Soldiers' Home Cemetery. In 1864, Quartermaster of the U.S. Army General Montgomery Meigs (later architect and builder of what is now the National Building Museum) suggested that 200 acres surrounding Arlington House be used for a cemetery. There has long been historical debate whether Meigs's proposal was a matter of the practical use of unused land or a vengeful blow toward a despised enemy. Meigs did lose his son, John Rodgers Meigs, in the war (both father and son are buried in the cemetery), but this loss was not until five months after the burials had begun. It is known that Meigs, a native of Augusta, Georgia, never forgave his fellow Southerners who committed their loyalties to the Confederacy.

### Washington Notes
The first documented burial at Arlington occurred a month before official approval was given. On May 13, 1864, Private William Christman, a Pennsylvania farmer and member of Company G of the 67th Pennsylvania Infantry, was interred at Arlington National Cemetery. (Christman's grave remains in Section 27, along with other fallen Civil War soldiers.) It is also said that the first soldier buried at Arlington was a Confederate prisoner, L. Reinhardt of the 23rd North Carolina Regiment. From May to June of 1864, 2,619 soldiers were buried on the grounds; 231 of these were African American soldiers. By the end of the Civil War, 16,000 graves were situated around Arlington House.

In April 1866 a burial vault, 20 ft across and 10 ft deep, was erected in what used to be Mrs. Lee's rose garden (Section 26, Grid QR-32/33). The Tomb of the Unknown Civil War Dead is inscribed: "Beneath this stone repose the bones of two thousand one hundred and eleven unknown soldiers gathered after the war from the fields of Bull Run, and the route to Rappahannock. Their remains could not be identified, but their names and deaths are recorded in the archives of their country: And its grateful citizens honor them as of their noble army of martyrs. May they rest in peace; September A.D. 1866."

### Washington Notes

During the Civil War years, Arlington not only became a national cemetery and a strategic military encampment but also a refuge for freed slaves. Following the Act of Emancipation in April 1862, thousands of former slaves made their way to Washington, joining those slaves who had been freed by Union troops. Federal troops freed slaves with the rationalization that they were "contraband"—a phrase coined by Union General Benjamin Franklin Butler. This equated slaves with guns, ammunition, horses, and carriages. Because the city rapidly ran out of space to house the new arrivals, a camp in the area now encompassing Sections 8, 47, and 25 along Eisenhower Dr was established. The temporary camp, also the home of the former slaves of Robert E. Lee, grew to become a permanent encampment called Freedman's Village.

The village, dedicated on Dec 4, 1863, was under the jurisdiction of the U.S. Army until March 1865 when the Bureau of Refugees, Freedmen, and Abandoned Lands (known as the Freedmen's Bureau) assumed jurisdiction. For almost 30 years the 1,100 residents of Freedman's Village were served by a school with 900 pupils (both adults and children); a training center for blacksmiths, wheelwrights, carpenters, shoemakers, and tailors; a home for the aged and disabled; a hospital with 50 beds and a staff of 14; farms producing corn, wheat, and potatoes; and several churches. (Note: The village at Arlington was called Freedman's Village, although it was sometimes referred to as Freedmen's Village. The freed slave village near Howard University was called Freedmen's Village.) In the years following the war, however, the spirit of support for former slaves decreased and with it public funding. On Dec 7, 1887, the remaining residents were notified they had 90 days to vacate the premises, as the federal government took possession of the land for the national cemetery. Today, 3,800 slave graves rest in Section 27, the "contraband" section.

Robert E. Lee never tried to regain his home and he resisted any reclamation attempts, in order to heal the wounds of the Civil War. Lee and his wife lived the rest of their lives on the campus of Washington College (now known as Washington and Lee University) in Lexington, Virginia. Lee, who served as president of the college for the final five years of his life, died there (his last words were "Strike the tent") in 1870. Mary Anna Randolph Custis Lee died three years later.

A few months before she died, Mrs. Lee returned to Arlington House to see the remnants of her home. Selina Gray, Mrs. Lee's most trusted slave, was still living on the property and recognized Mrs. Lee as she sat in her carriage. Because she was by now totally paralyzed and unable to walk, Mrs. Lee couldn't enter the house, but she could see from the carriage that the mansion was in complete disrepair. She wrote that she would not have recognized it except for a few oak trees that "had been spared and the trees planted on the lawn by the General and myself. . . . My dear home was so changed it seemed but a dream of the past."

### Washington Notes

The Arlington estate was left to the Lees' son, George Washington Custis Lee. After a long legal battle that ended in the Supreme Court in Oct 1882,

Custis Lee was granted the right to evict any trespassers on his land. He chose not to disturb the interred at Arlington. Instead he settled for a compensation fee of $150,000, turning the land over to the government on May 14, 1883. In 1925, Congress designated Arlington House as a permanent monument to Robert E. Lee and provided for restoration of the house to its pre–Civil War condition. The memorial opened to the public in 1929. Jurisdiction of the property was handed over to the National Park Service by the U.S. Army in 1933.

At the end of the Civil War, Arlington National Cemetery harbored the remains of 16,000 soldiers. Today more than 245,000 veterans and their families rest among the cemetery's 612 acres. There are dead buried at Arlington from every war in which American troops have fought. With an average of 20 burials every weekday, cemetery officials estimate its lots will reach full capacity around the year 2020.

Not all veterans are eligible for burial at Arlington Cemetery. Those who aren't can have their cremated remains placed in the columbarium at the cemetery. Those eligible for ground burial are: retired military who are receiving a pension (active duty time is required, other than for training); recipients of the Purple Heart, Silver Star, Distinguished Service Medal, Distinguished Service Cross (Air Force Cross, Navy Cross), and the Medal of Honor; POWs who died after 1993; veterans who were discharged with a 30 percent or more disability prior to Oct 1, 1949; those who died while on active duty; the dependent child or legal spouse (allowed since 1888) of an active duty service member, but not if the spouse has remarried; and the legal spouse of someone already buried at the cemetery.

Veterans and service members being buried at Arlington National Cemetery receive standard military honors, which consist of body bearers, a firing party that fires a three-rifle volley, and a bugler who plays taps. A chaplain is provided for the service, and presents the flag to the next of kin.

From Schley Gate, walk along Schley Dr to just beyond its intersection with Custis Walk. On the left is a stepped pathway up the hill to the grave site of **William Howard Taft** (Section 30, Grave S-14, Grid YZ-39/40), 27th president of the United States and Chief Justice of the Supreme Court. Taft was also civilian governor of the Philippines and secretary of war under President Theodore Roosevelt. Taft is also remembered for being so heavy (over 300 pounds) that he couldn't fit in the White House bathtubs.

Continue along Schley Dr to its intersection with Sherman Dr, then turn left on Sherman Dr and continue to the intersection with Sheridan Dr. Follow the signs toward the Kennedy grave site, but before reaching it turn left on Sheridan Dr to Section 5. In this section, in the corner nearest the pathway leading up to the Kennedy grave site, are the graves of four Supreme Court justices and one admiral (Grid VW-36/37). **Oliver Wendell Holmes, Jr.** (1841–1935), was a Civil War veteran of the 20th Massachusetts Volunteers and was wounded three times. Known as the Great Dissenter during his 29-year tenure on the Supreme Court, he became the oldest person to serve on the court at the age of 91. On one side of **William O. Douglas**'s (1898–1980) tombstone is "Private, U.S. Army" and on the other is "Associate Justice, U.S. Supreme Court, 1939–1975." **Thurgood Marshall** (1908–1993) was the first African American appointed to the Supreme

Court and served as an associate justice from 1967 to 1991. **Warren Earl Burger** (1907–1995) was chief justice of the Supreme Court. Admiral **Hyman G. Rickover** (1900–1986), was "Father of the Nuclear Navy." His tombstone makes note of the fact that he had "63 Years of Active Duty." Rickover was a native of czarist Russia, from which he emigrated with his family at the age of 6.

Continue up the path to the **John F. Kennedy** grave site (Section 45, Grave S-45, Grid UV-35/36), the most visited grave in Arlington Cemetery.

> #### Washington Notes
> John F. Kennedy (1917–1963), 35th president of the United States, enjoyed coming to Arlington House to look across the Potomac at the city of Washington. For this reason, Jacqueline Kennedy chose this site at the base of the hill below the house.

The first set of stairs leads to a stone terrace where, on a low wall, are etched seven of the president's most famous quotes. Another short flight of steps leads to the marble plateau where the eternal flame burns above the graves of the president, two of his children (who died in infancy), and Jacqueline Kennedy Onassis. Facing JFK's grave site, the pathway to the left leads to the grave site of **Robert F. Kennedy** (1925–1968), the president's younger brother and a candidate for the Democratic Party's nomination for the presidency when he was assassinated in Los Angeles in 1968. A simple white cross marks his grave. Opposite the cross is a low wall inscribed with Robert Kennedy's words the night of Martin Luther King, Jr.'s assassination (just a few months before his own): "Let us dedicate ourselves to what the Greeks wrote so many years ago: to tame the savageness of man and make gentle the life of this world. Let us dedicate ourselves to that, and say a prayer for our country and our people."

Facing President Kennedy's grave site, a stepped pathway on the right leads up the hill to Arlington House. Just before the final set of steps to the house, on the left, is the grave of **Mary Randolph** (1762–1828).

> #### Washington Notes
> Mary Randolph was the first person known to have been buried on the Arlington estate. A cousin of Thomas Jefferson and Robert E. Lee and a direct descendant of Pocahontas, Randolph, according to her tombstone, died "a victim to maternal love and duty." This epitaph was written by her disabled son, Burwell Starke Randolph, who as a U.S. Navy midshipman fell from a mast and suffered severely disabling injuries. His mother cared for him until her death. During her life, Mary Randolph was the best-selling author of a how-to book called *The Virginia Housewife,* a domestic guide that included recipes, instruction on candlemaking, herbal cures, and the correct preparation of a turtle for cooking.

## Robert E. Lee Memorial (Arlington House)

☎ (703) 557-0613. Open daily April–Sept 9:30–6; Oct–March 9:30–4:30. Closed Christmas Day and New Year's Day. Admission: free. Restrooms. Bookstore. Memorabilia museum.

A few more steps up the path is the Robert E. Lee Memorial (Arlington House) (1802–18; George Washington Parke Custis, owner-builder; renovations in 1820,

George Hadfield). Officially designated as the Robert E. Lee Memorial in 1972, Arlington House, for more than 40 years the home of the Custis and Lee families, is a fine example of Greek revival architecture. Eight Doric columns support a massive buff pediment. The stuccoed brick structure has balancing wings on either side of the central portion, with a portico 60 ft wide and 25 ft deep. Inside, high ceilings, wide arches, and broad cornice moldings reflect the grand scale of the exterior.

Arlington House was built in part as a tribute to George Washington by his step-grandson, George Washington Parke Custis. The property became instead the place to honor the memory of a man, Robert E. Lee, who put his conscience before his country, knowing it could mean the forfeit of an entire way of life for himself and his family. As with Washington and Custis, admiration for Lee is tempered by the fact that his way of life included owning slaves and that the cause he fought for was, in part, the cause of perpetuating the buying and selling of other human beings. Paradoxically, Custis called slavery "the mightiest serpent that ever infested the world" and was a member of the American Colonization Society, organized to send freed slaves back to West Africa. In his will Custis stipulated that his 55 slaves should be freed upon his death, unless the estate was in debt, in which case the slaves should be freed five years after his death. There was a debt, and so Lee kept the slaves the extra five years, until 1862. Lee sent letters of manumission from the battlefield for each of the estate's 55 slaves.

### Washington Notes
At the crest of the hill in front of Arlington House is the grave site of **Pierre L'Enfant** (1754–1825), a granite slab raised on six legs. Overlooking the city he designed, L'Enfant was originally buried where he died, impoverished and embittered, at Chilham Castle in Prince George's County. His remains were reinterred at Arlington Cemetery by the Daughters of the American Revolution on April 28, 1909. Note the error on the inscription, which attributes to him the rank of major in the U.S. Engineers. L'Enfant was a captain in the U.S. Engineers, not a major. (He held the temporary rank of brevet major in the U.S. Army during the Revolutionary War.) The error hasn't been corrected because of fear of disfiguring the stone.

## Interior
Most of the furnishings are copies of the originals. By the time Congress approved restoration in 1925, most of the furnishings had either gone to Mount Vernon, to museums, or to the Lee heirs. In 1934, restoration passed from the War Department to the National Park Service, which found a crumbling, decaying building and restored it.

Typical of its period, Arlington House has a long central hall from the front of the house to the back. A family dining room and parlor are on the north side, a long drawing room is on the south side, and a stairway at the west end leads up to the second floor. In the south wing, beyond the drawing room, is the formal dining room, an adjoining study, and a conservatory. The Custis family bedroom and sitting room are in the north wing, which also has a small sewing and schoolroom. A service hall in the north wing accesses a stairway to the basement and the winter kitchen.

In the entrance hall is a copy of Charles Willson Peale's portrait of George Washington, made by Ernest Fischer for the Lees. The painting to the left of it is a copy of the equestrian portrait, *Washington at Yorktown,* that George Washington Parke Custis considered one of his finest.

The **family parlor** and the **dining room** were the center of family life for the Lees and Custises. On the north wall of the parlor above the fireplace is the original portrait of Mary Anna Randolph Custis (1831; August Hervieu) painted just before her marriage to Lee. The Lees were married in this room in June 1831. The traveling desk belonged to Lee, who was an avid correspondent with his family. The green silk-upholstered furniture was acquired by the Custises around 1825. The Custises imported the Carrara marble mantels in both rooms from Italy. The dining room table would have had a cloth beneath it, called a crumb cloth, covering the floor. The knife box is from Mount Vernon. The white Canton china is a reproduction of the set used by the Lees. Several of the silver pieces, also reproductions, have the Lee crest, a squirrel.

In the **study** is the desk used by Lee when stationed in Baltimore for four years to supervise the construction of Fort Carroll. Custis used the adjoining **morning room** as his painting studio. Custis's *Battle of Monmouth* displayed here was intended for the U.S. Capitol but was returned when John Trumball's paintings were used instead. After Custis's death, Mary Lee used this room to edit her father's memoirs and to paint. The Lees decorated the more formal parlor, called the **white parlor,** with crimson upholstered furniture they had brought with them from West Point. The marble mantels were designed in New York City.

The **bed chambers** upstairs open onto the upper hall. In the **Lees' bedroom** in the southwest corner, Lee wrote his letter of resignation from the U.S. Army. The room beside it on the south side is the **bedroom of Lee's sons**—Custis, Rooney, and Robert, Jr. Next to the boys' room is a guest room, a small chamber created by Mary Lee by combining two dressing rooms and having a doorway cut into the upper hall. Across the hall is the **bedroom of Lee's daughters**—Agnes, Annie, and Mildred. The small sculpture on the mantel, the *Three Graces,* was a gift from George Washington Parke Custis to his granddaughters. The sketch of the bedroom made by one of the Union soldiers who occupied the house is sarcastically titled *Roughing it at Arlington.*

Downstairs in the north wing of the house is the **kitchen** and the mansion's first **bathroom,** which Lee had installed with modern fixtures. This was the first section of the house to be built, and George Washington Parke Custis and his wife lived here during the early years of the mansion's construction. Fourteen fireplaces and one stove heated this wing. The kitchen was used both for cooking and for laundry.

Behind the house is a small **museum** highlighting the Lee family (two of his cousins signed the Declaration of Independence) and containing Lee memorabilia such as his mess kit. Across the yard from the museum are the **south slave quarters** and the home of Seline Gray and her family. Gray was the servant to whom Mary Lee entrusted her keys to the parts of the Washington Treasure (George Washington artifacts) that couldn't be transported with Mary and the children when they left in May 1861. Adjacent to the slave quarters is Mary Lee's garden.

Walk through the garden to an alcove encircled by trees. In the center is the **Tomb of the Unknown Civil War Dead.** Next to the tomb site is the **Old Amphithe-**

**ater and Rostrum.** The recently renovated Old Amphitheater is used for memorial services and other special events smaller in scope than those held in the new amphitheater. General James Garfield (who would later be the 20th president of the U.S.) spoke at the Old Amphitheater on the occasion of its dedication, May 30, 1868, Decoration Day (now called Memorial Day). The structure, which seats 1,500, was designed for burial ceremonies but also provided a popular meeting place. Its latticed roof, supported by a colonnade, grew thickly covered with vines and sheltered the rostrum from which many of the great orators of their day spoke, including William Jennings Bryan, before the new amphitheater was built in 1921.

From here, cross Sherman Dr and walk down the path to the Old Administration Building (a large white structure). In front of this building stands the **Memorial to Pan Am Flight 103** (Grid O-34/35). Two hundred seventy Scottish stones compose a memorial cairn (the Scottish word for a memorial mound made of stones) honoring the 270 people killed in the terrorist bombing of the Pan American Airlines flight over Lockerbie, Scotland, on Dec 21, 1988.

Continue west on Humphreys Dr to the grave of **Anita Newcomb McGee** (1864–1940), the first female army surgeon. From here walk back down Humphreys Dr to its intersection with Wilson Dr and turn right onto Wilson. Just before the intersection of Lee, Meigs, and Wilson Drs is the bronze statue of Major General **Philip Kearny** (1914; Edward Clark Potter). Unknown by most Americans today, this Union general was famous in his time as a fearless fighter, beloved by his men. Kearny, a millionaire who chose to become an army officer, was always the first to lead the charge. He lost his left arm in the Mexican War. During the Second Battle of Bull Run (Manassas), Kearny charged too far ahead of his troops and was killed. Lee returned Kearny's body, his sword, and his horse under a flag of truce.

> ### Washington Notes
>
> Two military legacies evolved from Kearny's military service: His division, the Third Division of the Army of the Potomac, wore red patches on their caps to create an esprit de corps. The shoulder patch used in today's army evolved from this custom. Each of the men in his division was awarded a cross of honor, or medal, distinguishing him as being a member of the fallen general's division. Known as Kearney's Cross, the medal was later presented to all soldiers who showed exceptional valor in battle. This cross evolved into the Medal of Honor, the highest decoration an American soldier can receive.

From the Kearny statue, walk west on Meigs Dr to Section 1. Near the middle of the section (N-32/33, Grave 1) are the gravestones of Quartermaster General **Montgomery Meigs** (1816–1892) and his son John (1842–1864). A huge granite monument marks the grave of Montgomery Meigs, "Soldier, engineer, architect, scientist, patriot," and the man who made the decision to bury the war dead at Arlington. The Major **John Rodgers Meigs** monument (1865; Theophilus Fisk Mills) depicts the young soldier as he was found lying on the field near Harrisonburg, Virginia, where he was shot by Confederate guerrillas, his gun lying beside him.

***Washington Notes***
Nearby is the gravestone of **Abner Doubleday** (1819–1893) (Grid N-32/33, Grave 61), a West Point graduate who fought in many of the major battles of the Civil War, including Fort Sumter, Antietam, and Gettysburg. One of baseball's biggest myths is that it was created by Abner Doubleday, a conclusion reached by a special commission in 1908, whose purpose was to determine baseball's origin. Despite its common acceptance, there are no historical facts that substantiate this claim. Doubleday left behind many journals and letters, in which he never once mentioned baseball.

Cross Meigs Ave to Section 13. At the far end on the crest of a hill are two graves shaded by trees with an iron gate around them. Here lie **George Washington Parke Custis** (1781–1857) and his wife, Mary (1788–1853).

## Memorial Amphitheater

Walk back to the Kearny statue and from there turn right onto Sheridan Dr. Walk down the hill on Sheridan to Crook Walk and follow the sign to the Tomb of the Unknowns, reached by going down and then up a series of stepped pathways. Approach the tomb through Memorial Amphitheater (1921; Frederick D. Owens) (Grid S-23/25). Due to the increasing number of visitors attending Arlington around the turn of the century, a new, larger amphitheater was authorized by Congress on May 30, 1908. President Woodrow Wilson laid the cornerstone on Oct 15, 1915. Items sealed inside the cornerstone include a Bible, a 1914 map of Washington, an autographed photograph of President Wilson, and copies of the Declaration of Independence, the Constitution, and L'Enfant's design for Washington.

Construction went slowly, and the new amphitheater was not dedicated until Memorial Day, 1921. Above the stage are Abraham Lincoln's words at Gettysburg: "We here highly resolve that these dead shall not have died in vain." A Latin quote from Horace's *Odes* (III, 2, 13) is etched above the west entrance of the amphitheater: "Dulce et decorum est pro Patria more"; this means "It is sweet and fitting to die for one's country." Around the exterior wall above the colonnade are the names of 44 battles in which Americans have fought, from the Revolutionary War through the Spanish-American War. On the second floor of the memorial lies the **Medal of Honor Room,** a space displaying the names of the medal's recipients.

## Tomb of the Unknowns

Walk through the amphitheater to the Tomb of the Unknowns (1931; Lorimer Rich; Thomas Hudson Jones, sculptor)—also known as the Tomb of the Unknown Soldier—dedicated to those servicemen whose remains never returned to American soil. The original idea of the tomb arose after the end of World War I. The United States felt that a memorial for slain soldiers should be erected like those in Europe. The tomb honors the patriotic spirit of soldiers from every war Americans have died in except the Revolutionary War. The first unknown soldier (from the Battle of the Marne, France, in World War I) was laid to rest Nov 1921 in a ceremony led by President Warren G. Harding at the new Memorial Amphitheater. Congress did not authorize completion of the monument until 1926. President Woodrow Wilson signed the legislation to create the memorial on his last day in office. Since then, every president has visited the Tomb of the Unknowns at least once a year.

The white marble sarcophagus has a flat-faced form and has neoclassical pilasters along the sides. Sculpted into the east panel, the one facing Washington, D.C., are three Greek figures representing peace, victory, and valor. Inscribed on the tomb are the words "Here rests in honored glory an American soldier unknown but to God." The sarcophagus was placed above the grave of the unknown soldier of World War I. West of this unknown soldier are the crypts of the unknowns from World War II, Korea, and Vietnam. These three graves are marked with white marble slabs. The Vietnam unknown was laid to rest at the tomb on Memorial Day, 1984. President Reagan presided over the funeral.

### Washington Notes

The Vietnam unknown soldier was eventually identified. On June 30, 1998, based on DNA testing, scientists identified the soldier as Air Force First Lieutenant Michael Joseph Blassie, who was shot down near An Loc, Vietnam, in 1972. His remains were returned to his family. In Sept 1999, during a ceremony attended by veterans, families of MIAs, and Defense Secretary William S. Cohen, a new inscription "Honoring and Keeping Faith With America's Missing Servicemen" was dedicated. As a result of modern forensic tools and techniques, it is unlikely that other unidentified remains will be added to the tomb.

The Tomb of the Unknowns is guarded 24 hours a day by the Third U.S. Infantry. During daytime the changing of the guard takes place every half hour from April 1 through Sept 30 and every hour on the hour from Oct 1 through March 31. The guards change at two-hour intervals during night hours year-round.

### Washington Notes

The guard paces from his post and across the crossway in 21 steps, turning to pause while facing the memorial for 21 seconds. Turning once more, the guard pauses for another 21 seconds before repeating the process. This is symbolic of the military's highest honor, the 21-gun salute.

The marble relief on the face of the 9 ft high by 11 ft wide by 16 ft deep tomb depicts the male figure of Victory, symbolic of valor, offering a palm branch with the female figure of Peace to the third figure, an American soldier. The sculptor, Thomas Hudson Jones, was chosen from among 75 others who competed for the honor of decorating this solemn tomb.

Across Memorial Dr in Section 24 is the **USS *Maine* Memorial** (Grid MN-23/24). The sinking of the USS *Maine* was a major factor in drawing the U.S. into the Spanish-American War. Sunken by a Spanish submarine mine on Feb 15, 1898, the *Maine* lost 266 crewmen, 229 of whom are buried at Arlington. Of these, the identities of 62 are known; the rest are unknown. The *Maine's* original mast, which stood in Havana Harbor for 12 years before it was removed to Arlington, projects upward from a battleship turret at the monument's base. The names of the known servicemen are inscribed around the turret. The monument was built by Norcross Brothers of Worcester, Massachusetts. The base is granite and the walls are marble. Welded into the inner door of the memorial is half of the ship's bell, which has the inscription "USS Maine, Navy Yard, New York, 1894."

> ### Washington Notes
>
> During World War II, the monument's turret served as a temporary tomb for the remains of world leaders who had died while seeking sanctuary in the U.S. Among these were Manuel Quezon y Molina, president of the Philippines, who fled to the U.S. after the Japanese seized his homeland. Molina died in exile in 1944. Also here at one time was exiled Polish President Ignace Paderewski. Paderewski requested that he be buried at Arlington until "Poland is free." His body was removed in June 1992 for reinterment in his native Poland.

Walk down the hill from the *Maine* Memorial. On the right in Section 46 are two other emotional memorials. One is the ***Challenger* Memorial** (Grid NO-23/24), in honor of those who died when the space shuttle exploded: "In grateful and loving tribute to the brave crew of the U.S. space shuttle Challenger 28 June 1986." The crew members who died aboard the *Challenger* were commander Francis R. "Dick" Scobee, pilot Michael J. Smith, mission specialists Ellison S. Onizuka, Judith A. Resnik, and Ronald E. McNair, payload specialist Gregory B. Jarvis, and schoolteacher Christa McAuliffe. The unidentified remains were placed in a common grave. The identified remains of two crew members are in separate graves at Arlington: Scobee (Section 46, Grave 1129-3) and Smith (Section 7A, Grave 208-1).

Next to the *Challenger* Memorial is the **Iran Rescue Memorial** (Grid OP-23/24). The white stone marker fronts a bronze plaque with the names of three marines and five airmen who lost their lives on April 25, 1980, in the rescue attempt of the 53 American hostages being held in Iran. The mission failed when two aircraft collided while trying to rendezvous at a covert desert location.

Return to Memorial Dr and turn right to a small pathway of steps in Section 46. Only two small American flags distinguish this grave from others. **Audie Murphy** (1924–1971) (Grave 366-11, Grid OP-23/24), World War II's most decorated soldier, is buried here. After his service Murphy became a movie actor. By the time Murphy turned 21, he had been wounded three times in battle and had received three medals from France and one from Belgium, boosting his medal count to 28 and making him the most decorated soldier in the U.S. Army. One of ten children deserted by a sharecropper father in rural Texas, Murphy tried to join the marines at the age of 16 in 1942 but was too short; he ended up in the army. He won his Congressional Medal of Honor for action in France in 1945 when, from the inside of an abandoned burning tank destroyer and with a single machine gun, he stalled the advance of six German Panzer tanks and 250 infantrymen for more than an hour. After the war, Jimmy Cagney encouraged Murphy to try acting. Murphy went on to appear in more than 40 films, including *To Hell and Back,* the screen adaptation of his war memoirs, and John Ford's *The Unforgiven,* in which Murphy played third lead to Burt Lancaster and Audrey Hepburn. Murphy died at the age of 46 in a plane crash near Roanoke, Virginia.

From Murphy's grave continue west on Porter Dr to just before the intersection with McPherson Dr and the **Nurses Memorial** (1938; Francis Rich) (Grid M-

19/20). Rich's sculpture of a nurse stands on a rise above the graves of nurses who served in the armed forces. In 1970 the memorial was rededicated to include nurses in the air force and all nurses who have served since 1938.

Turn right (east) at the intersection with Lawton Dr and walk to the grave of **John Foster Dulles** (1888–1959) (Lot 31, Grid MN-20/21). An army major during World War II, Dulles assisted with negotiations that led to the peace treaty with Japan. Dulles, as President Dwight Eisenhower's secretary of state, was an important force in creating America's foreign policy in the early Cold War years. Backtrack on Lawton Dr to McPherson Dr and turn right (north). Continue to Jackson Circle and the **Confederate Monument** (1914; Moses Ezekiel) (Grid I-23). In June 1900 Congress authorized a section of Arlington Cemetery to be devoted to the Confederate dead. A total of 482 soldiers from other grave sites within the cemetery and from other burial grounds in Virginia and Washington, D.C., were reinterred by the end of 1901. Their pointed gravestones (legend has it that the points were to prevent "Yankees" from sitting on the markers) form concentric circles around the Confederate Monument—a woman representing the South, who extends a laurel wreath toward the fallen soldiers. Ezekiel, who was also a Confederate soldier, is buried at the base of the monument.

Continue north on McPherson Dr. Turn right onto Farragut Dr. Cross Memorial Dr and follow the path around the amphitheater to Section 7A. On the corner of this section, near a group of benches, is the grave site of **Joe Louis (Barrow)** (Grid U-24, Grave 177), former heavyweight boxing champion of the world. Scoring 22 knockouts in 25 championship title defenses, the "Brown Bomber" held the world title longer (1937–49) than any other fighter in history. While fighting in World War II as an enlisted man, Louis boxed 96 exhibition bouts, raising $100,000 in relief funds for the army and navy.

Straight ahead is the intersection with Roosevelt Ave. Follow the avenue back to the Visitor Center and to the exit.

### Diversion:

Some Revolutionary War soldiers are buried at Arlington Cemetery. These veterans were reinterred at Arlington Cemetery; nine of them are buried in Section 1 between Arlington House and the Fort Meyer Gate. These include William Ward Burrows, the oldest member of the U.S. Marine Corps buried at Arlington (Section 1, Lot 301-B); Joseph Carleton, a paymaster (Section 1, Lot 299); John Follin, a sailor who was captured by the British and held as a prisoner of war for three years (Section 1, Lot 295); and John Green, colonel of the Tenth Virginia Volunteers and one of the earliest to be buried at Arlington (Section 1, Lot 503).

Additional graves of notables include Lieutenant Commander Roger Bruce Chaffee, U.S. Navy, Apollo astronaut who died while performing test operations for the *Apollo* 1 space mission (Section 3; Grave 2502-F); Lieutenant Colonel Virgil I. "Gus" Grissom, U.S. Air Force, Apollo astronaut, the second American in space on the Mercury mission, 1961, and first person to make two space trips on the two-man Gemini flight, 1965 (Section 3, Grave 2503-E); Robert Todd Lincoln, son of President Abraham Lincoln (Section 31, Lot 13); General John J. "Black Jack" Pershing, commander of the American Expeditionary Forces in France, World War I, and general of the Armies of the United States (Section 34, Grave S-19); Walter Reed, a pioneering 19C bacteriologist who discovered that malaria was caused by mosquitoes instead of by contaminated water (Section 3, Lot 1864);

General Philip Henry Sheridan, U.S. Army, a Civil War general (Section 2, Lot 1); Daniel "Chappie" James, Jr. (Section 2, Lot 4968-B, Grid V-33), the first African American four-star general; and British Field Marshal Sir John Dill (Section 32, Lot S-29, Grid X-33), who served on the World War II Allied Combined Chiefs of Staff.

To reach the U.S. Marine Corps War Memorial (Iwo Jima Memorial) and Netherlands Carillon from Arlington National Cemetery, exit the grounds through the Ord and Weitzel Gate.

# U.S. Marine Corps War Memorial and Netherlands Carillon

Administrated by the National Park Service, Superintendent, George Washington Memorial Pkwy, Turkey Run Park, McLean, VA. ☎ (703) 285-2598. Web: www.nps.gov. Open daily. Admission: free. Carillon concerts held May–Sept on Sat and national holidays; 2–4 P.M. in May and Sept; 6–8 P.M. in June, July, and Aug. Marine Corps sunset review May–Aug on Tues at 7 P.M. No reservations required.

## *Netherlands Carillon*

The Netherlands Carillon (1954; present tower 1960, Joost W. C. Boks) is a large instrument, played by professional carillonneurs. The carillon consists of 49 bells, tuned to a chromatic scale, housed in a 127 ft tall bell tower. The largest bell is 6 ft 9 inches in diameter and weighs 12,654 pounds; the smallest is 9 inches in diameter and weighs 37.5 pounds. The 49 bells give the carillon the ability to play one note more than four octaves. During concerts, visitors are invited to enter the tower to observe the carillonneur and enjoy the view of Washington, D.C.

### History

The carillon is dedicated "from the people of the Netherlands to the people of the United States." It was a gift from Netherlands to express thanks for help received during and after World War II. The idea originated with G. L. Verheul, a government official, and was endorsed by Queen Juliana. When visiting the United States in 1952, Queen Juliana presented President Truman with a small silver bell as a token of the carillon that was being built, and these words: "To achieve real harmony, justice should be done also to the small and tiny voices, which are not supported by the might of their weight. Mankind could learn from this. So many voices in our troubled world are still unheard. Let that be an incentive for all of us when we hear the bells ringing."

In 1954, the carillon bells were installed in a temporary tower in West Potomac Park and in 1960 were moved to the present tower built near the U.S. Marine Corps War Memorial. The dedication was held May 5, 1960, the 15th anniversary of the liberation of the Netherlands from the Nazis.

### Exterior

The bell tower, designed by Joost W. C. Boks, a leading Netherlands architect, is 127 ft high, 25 ft deep, and 36 ft wide. The tower is an open steel structure, reinforced with steel plates coated with a bronze, baked-enamel finish. There is a glass-

*U.S. Marine Corps War Memorial (Iwo Jima Memorial). Photo credit: Terry J. Adams, National Park Service.*

enclosed playing booth 83 ft above the ground. The tower is situated in a plaza that is enclosed by a low wall of lava stone. Paul Konig, a Dutch sculptor, designed the two bronze lions guarding the steps to the plaza. In the spring, the grounds bloom with 18,000 tulips.

## U.S. Marine Corps War Memorial
Across a stretch of grass is the U.S. Marine Corps War Memorial (1954; Horace W. Peaslee; Felix W. de Weldon, sculptor). Although the memorial depicts the well-known raising of the U.S. flag on Iwo Jima during World War II, the memorial is dedicated to all Marines who have died in combat since 1775.

### History
Iwo Jima, a small island in the Pacific, was a strategic part of the U.S. battle plans to end the war in the Pacific during World War II. On Feb 19, 1945, the Fourth and Fifth Marine Divisions were sent to capture Mt. Suribachi, the highest peak on the island. After four days of fighting, the extinct volcano was in the possession of the Marines, who raised the flag on the volcano's peak.

Joe Rosenthal, a news photographer, photographed the flag raising, a picture that earned him a Pulitzer Prize. The inspiring photo caught the imagination of sculptor Felix W. de Weldon, who constructed a model. The three survivors of the battle—Pfc. Rene A. Gagnon, Pfc. Ira Hayes, and PhM. 2/c John H. Bradley, USN—posed for the sculptor, who used their facial features. Since the other three men—Sergeant Michael Strank, Corporal Harland H. Block, and Pfc. Franklin R. Sousley—were killed in later phases of the battle, de Weldon sculpted their faces from photographs. The casting process took three years. The memorial, designed by Horace W. Peaslee, was begun in Sept 1954 and dedicated by President Eisenhower on Nov 10, 1954, the 179th anniversary of the Marine Corps. The $850,000 cost of the memorial was donated by U.S. Marines, their families, and their friends.

## Exterior

The individual figures are 32 ft tall and modeled after the five soldiers and one navy corpsman who raised the flag at Iwo Jima. Hayes is the figure farthest from the flagpole; Sousley to the right front of Hayes; Strank on Sousley's left; Bradley in front of Sousley; Gagnon in front of Strank; and Block closest to the bottom of the flagpole. The canteen held by the figures would hold 32 quarts of water, and the M-1 rifle is 16 ft long.

The six figures stand on a rock slope rising six ft from the Swedish granite base. Inscriptions around the base list every major Marine Corps engagement since its founding in 1775, as well as this dedication: "In honor and in memory of the men of the United States Marine Corps who have given their lives to their country since November 10, 1775." There is also a tribute from Rear Admiral Chester W. Nimitz to the men who fought on Iwo Jima: "Uncommon valor was a common virtue."

A cloth flag flies from the 60 ft bronze flagpole 24 hours a day as the result of a presidential proclamation on June 12, 1961.

To continue with the next walk, return to the Arlington National Cemetery Metro Station and take the Blue Line to Rosslyn.

# 30 · Arlington: Newseum

Metro: Blue/Orange Line to Rosslyn.

Freedom Forum World Center, 1101 Wilson Blvd, Arlington, VA. ☎ (703) 284-3544 or 888-NEWSEUM. Web: www.newseum.org. Open Wed–Sun 10–5. Closed Thanksgiving, Christmas Day, and New Year's Day. Admission: free. Restrooms. Gift shop. Café. Wheelchair accessible.

The only interactive museum of news, this inventive and unique museum offers visitors a behind-the-scenes look at how and why news is made. The Newseum is a rewarding experience for anyone curious about news gathering. Visitors can see themselves on tape as reporters and newscasters; experience the major news stories of history through multimedia exhibits, artifacts, and memorabilia; and see today's news as it's happening on a block-long Video News Wall. The Newseum, located on the first three floors of the Freedom Forum World Center, is funded by the Freedom Forum (formerly known as the Gannett Foundation), a nonpartisan foundation dedicated to free press and free speech.

## History

The genesis of this $50 million, 72,000-square-ft museum was in a meeting called in 1991 by Allen H. Neuharth, founder of *USA Today* and former chairman of Gannett Company. Neuharth challenged the board members of his new foundation, the Freedom Forum, to "think big," and after four days of meetings the idea of a museum that would "wed history to future technology" was born. The Newseum took six years to complete, including two years of development. A team of Freedom Forum members, journalists, museum professionals, writers, educators, historians, and technical experts labored on what they called "a high-tech hybrid—history museum, live-news aquarium, special news auditorium and educational experience." The Newseum team created a master plan that architect Appelbaum translated into a physical design. Freedom Park, an outdoor exhibit displaying artifacts that demonstrate the ongoing struggle for freedom, opened in 1996. Almost a year later, on April 18, 1997, the Newseum opened.

The Newseum (1997; Ralph Appelbaum Associates) is two blocks east from the Rosslyn Metro station on Wilson Blvd. The museum is heavily staffed. After entering on **Level I,** be prepared to be approached by a succession of Visitor Services representatives who will point out the News Byte Café, hand out maps of the Newseum, describe what's available on the other levels and how to reach them, and point out the **Internet terminals** behind the café. The terminals access a number of news-related sites. Representatives are available on each of the three floors throughout the exhibits.

Take the escalator to **Level II** to the **Domed High-Definition Video Theater.** Every 20 minutes a film narrated by Charles Kurault answers the question "What is news?" by showing clips from major news events of the past century. (The theater exits on Level III.) Across from the theater is the **Newseum Store,** which offers an interesting selection of news-related items, including reproductions of vintage newspapers and magazines. In the center of the floor between these is the **Birthday Banner Station,** where newspapers of a particular day and year can be brought up on the screen and copies purchased.

To the right of the Birthday Banner Station is the **Interactive Newsroom,** an array of hands-on news experiences and multimedia exhibits that enable visitors to be reporters, editors, photographers, radio sportscasters, and TV newscasters and make the hard decisions about how to cover a news story, what to include, what to photograph, and how to meet deadlines and space limitations by using personal judgment rather than personal opinions. As a radio sportscaster, a visitor can enter a glass-enclosed soundbooth, watch a sports event, and record his or her version of the action as it happens. As a TV newscaster, a visitor can read news using a TelePrompTer. Tapes of both radio and TV performances can be purchased, as well as magazine covers featuring a visitor. At the **Ethics Center,** a touch-screen computer enables visitors to decide journalistic questions related to topical news. Tours of the fully operational **Broadcast Studio** are given hourly. Also, special broadcasts are taped here. See the schedule posted near the studio entrance.

**Level III** has the **News History Gallery** and the **Video News Wall,** a 126 ft long multiscreen video display of the world's news. Beneath the screen, on Level II, is a display of the day's front pages from 70 U.S. and international newspapers.

The **History Gallery** is a collection of objects and displays, historic broadcasts, newspapers and magazines, and editorial cartoons from ancient times to the present. In the **Early News Gallery** are examples of early news reports, such as Sumerian cuneiform tablets (2176–562 B.C.), Asian and African drums, and the spread of news by conch shell and bronze bells. Reported here is the fact that Cicero, the Roman philosopher, complained that the daily handwritten "acta" copies received by citizens were too full of what he called "tittle-tattle" on divorces and gladiator fights.

The **News History Wall,** which is divided into 12 segments, documents the history of news, the people who created it, and the context in which they worked. The segments cover a 500-year period, beginning with the first newspapers in 1500, through the so-called jazz journalism of the 1920s to the rise of television in the 1950s and '60s, and into the next millennium with digital news. Among the artifacts on display are Paul Revere's glasses, Charles Dickens's pen, one of only nine known 18C wooden printing presses in existence, a newspaper printed in Stalag Luft III in Germany by American POWs during World War II (giving whatever news they had heard about the outside world and detailing the daily life of the prisoners), the microphone used by Edward R. Murrow to report the bombing of London (radio clips of this and other famous broadcasts can be heard), columnist Ernie Pyle's typewriter, and the first color studio cameras used by CBS for Walter Cronkite's news broadcast (clips of famous TV broadcasts can be viewed). Minitheaters at either end of the History Wall hallway present special reports and interviews with reporters on how major stories such as Watergate were covered.

Take the steps near the **News Globe,** which is lined with the names of daily newspapers throughout the U.S., back down to Level II.

Near the theater exit is the door leading outside to **Freedom Park,** which is located on the overpass between 1100 and 1101 Wilson Blvd. Freedom Park is a moving tribute to those who have fought for or sought freedom. It is open daily from dawn to dusk. Admission is free.

The **Journalists Memorial** (1996; Ralph Appelbaum Associates; KCE Structural Engineers), at the highest point in the park, honors those who have died while reporting the news. One hundred forty-nine glass panels currently feature the names of 1,150 journalists who were killed between 1812 and 1998. The supporting stainless steel structure is engineered to withstand hurricane-force winds, the total weighing approximately 10,000 pounds. Each year new names are submitted by individuals or organizations and chosen by the Committee to Protect Journalists for inclusion in the memorial.

On adjacent plazas there is a collection of international icons representing the struggle and victory of freedom over oppression. Items displayed include: segments of the Berlin Wall, which came down in 1989; a toppled statue of Lenin from the town of Tevriz, which is 1,300 miles from Moscow (the toppled statue represents the people's push for freedom); Warsaw ghetto cobblestones used in desperation by Jewish defenders against Nazi tanks; a bronze cast of a South African ballot box; a kayak paddled by a Cuban refugee from Cuba to the U.S. in 1966; a bronze cast of Martin Luther King, Jr.'s jail-cell door from King's 1963 incarceration in Birmingham, Alabama; replicas of suffrage banners used by women rallying for the right to vote; and a Native American "talking circle" of stones symbolizing the tradition of free speech.

To continue to the next walk, proceed two blocks west on Wilson Blvd to the Rosslyn Metro station and take the Blue Line to the Pentagon station.

# 31 · Arlington: The Pentagon

Metro: Blue/Yellow Line to Pentagon.
Bus: Many buses go to the Pentagon. Among them are the 13A, 13B, 13M, 16B, 16C, 24, and 25.
Car: From Washington, D.C., take I-395 south, exit 8, South Pentagon Parking. Turn right at first stop sign and right on Army-Navy Dr. Paid parking is available on the right near Macy's. A pedestrian tunnel under I-395 leads to the Pentagon.

Located in Arlington, Virginia, immediately west of the Potomac River. ☎ (703) 695-1776. Web: www.defenselink.mil/pubs/pentagon. For tour information, write to Director, Pentagon Tours, Room 1E776, 1400 Defense Pentagon, Washington, DC 20301-1400. Guided tours take 90 minutes and are available Mon–Fri 9:30–3:30. Closed all federal holidays. Admission free, but bring photo ID for all persons over 16 years of age. Restaurants, gift shop, restrooms, water fountains. Note: No weapons or videotaping is allowed inside the Pentagon. Photographs are allowed, but no photographs of personnel in uniform are permitted.

The Pentagon (1941–43; Lieutenant Colonel Hugh Casey and George Bergstrom) houses the Department of Defense, which coordinates all branches of the United States military. The Pentagon is both a building and a symbol. The building, an engineering marvel, is the largest office building in the world, measuring 6½ million square ft and housing 23,000 employees. The floor space of the Pentagon is three times that of the 102-floor Empire State Building. The distance around the outer ring of the building is almost one mile. The Pentagon has more than 100,000 miles of telephone cable, enough to wrap around the world four times. There are 7,754 windows in the building, a total glass area of 7.1 acres. The massive building has come to be associated with the military might of the U.S.

**Highlights:** The building itself, displays of some of the 7,500 paintings of the Air Force Art Collection, the Coors Collection, 86 paintings from the 1,034 Time-Life paintings of World War II.

### History

General Brehon B. Somervell first proposed a monumental building to house the entire War Department in 1939 in a report to the secretary of war. Somervell's concern was that the delays resulting from the wide dispersal of personnel over 20 buildings in Washington, D.C., were "embarrassing in peacetime and may be inadvisable in the event of an even relatively minor emergency." In 1941, a site was chosen at Arlington Farms.

On Fri, July 17, 1941, Somervell directed his staff, headed by Lieutenant Colonel Hugh J. "Pat" Casey and George Bergstrom, a consulting architect, to have plans for a building to house the War Department on his desk the following Mon morning. Born over the course of a weekend, the Pentagon's unique shape was a result of trying to accommodate the original building site, which was bordered on five sides by roads. Although the building site was eventually changed, the shape of the building remained the same.

Construction began on Sept 11, 1941, with a 24-hour-a-day building schedule employing 3,000 men. When the Japanese bombed Pearl Harbor (Dec 1941) the need for the building intensified, and at one point there were 15,000 employees working around the clock to finish the structure. Staff began occupying the building on April 29, 1942, although the building was not completed until Jan 15, 1943, just 16 months after the start of the project. A building of this size would normally take four years to complete. The total cost of the project was $83 million. In 1947, the armed forces were unified under the Department of Defense and the Pentagon became the headquarters for the entire military of the United States.

Due to wartime economies, no elevators were installed in the original building. Employees used the original 31 stairways.

### Washington Notes

Although an executive order dated June 25, 1941, outlawed discrimination in the federal government, the placement of the Pentagon in Virginia, which required equivalent, but separate, facilities for white and black persons, posed problems. Separate eating facilities were planned in the basement for blacks, and four restrooms were planned for each of the five axes of the building. Reportedly, President Roosevelt put an end to this practice before it started when he toured the nearly completed building and questioned the need for these facilities. Separate signage was never posted, and segregation was abandoned before it ever began at the Pentagon.

Although most of the Pentagon is austere, two dozen corridors were decorated at the request of Secretary of Defense Donald H. Rumsfeld in 1976, when the Pentagon opened for tours to celebrate the nation's Bicentennial. A dozen of these corridors are included in current Pentagon tours.

The Pentagon began a 12-year renovation in 1997, which may alter the path of the tour occasionally to accommodate construction activities. Tours may also be modified to avoid stairs to allow for wheelchair access.

## Exterior

The Pentagon was originally conceived as a three-story structure, but five stories were built. The style has been labeled "stripped classicism," popular in federal buildings of the 1930s–1950s. Classic design elements, such as symmetry, were employed but simplified. The five-sided building actually consists of five concentric rings connected by diagonal corridors and separated by light wells.

Because of the shortage of building materials due to World War II, reinforced concrete and Indiana limestone were chosen to minimize the amount of steel used in the structure. Six hundred eighty thousand tons of sand and gravel were dredged from the nearby Potomac River and processed into the 435,000 cubic yards of concrete that make up the Pentagon's walls.

## Interior

Although the floor space of the Pentagon totals 17.5 miles, any office can be reached within ten minutes because of the configuration of the connecting corridors.

Visitors enter from the Metro entrance to the **Concourse Area,** which is the only area civilians may enter without an escort. Here visitors must register for tours.

The **Main Corridor** (E ring), entered from the security area, consists of shops and food establishments for employee use. Facilities provided for Pentagon employees include shops, dental and medical offices, a library, and a day-care center.

Walk down the corridor to the right and then left into the Pentagon tours area. On the right wall of the ramp are paintings from the **Coors Collection** by George L. Skypeck. These depict the missions and campaign medals of American military personnel in each conflict since World War II. Collages depicting aspects of daily life in each branch of the armed forces are featured around the corner.

At the top of the ramp, the seals of the four branches of the military and the Coast Guard are prominently displayed along with portraits of the current highest-ranking officials in each branch. Guides explain the civilian and military chain of command beginning with the president of the U.S. The service flags of the military are displayed, with the flag of the United States always displayed to the left. The flags are arranged in order of seniority of service beginning with the army and ending with the Coast Guard. The Coast Guard is listed last because it is operated under the Department of Transportation. In times of war, the Coast Guard flag would be moved up and positioned between the army and Marine Corps.

To the right is a small theater showing a 12½-minute movie about the Pentagon, its construction, history, and ongoing mission. Exit the theater from the back, turn right, and walk to the top of the ramp, where various military awards are displayed. On the left in the cases are models that depict the evolution of aircraft from the 1903 Wright brothers' plane to modern space exploration vehicles.

Walk left to the **Air Force Art Collection Corridor.** The collection of 7,500 paintings portrays the missions and the evolution of the air force. Only a portion of the collection is displayed. On the left are the 12 Outstanding Airmen of the Year, selected from the air force, National Guard, and reserve forces, based on job performance, leadership ability, personal improvement, and community service.

The 992 African American combat pilots known as the Tuskegee Airmen because of their training at the Tuskegee Army Air Field in Alabama are featured in a portrait and four paintings on the right.

### Washington Notes

The Tuskegee Airmen flew more than 500 missions in World War II, and their service was a key factor in President Harry S. Truman's decision to integrate the military in 1947.

Farther along the corridor on the left wall are portraits of three of the five Vietnam flying aces. An aviator must have shot down five enemy aircraft to be declared an ace. The red stars in the background denote the number of "kills" attributed to each aviator. The two other aces of the Vietnam War were naval aviators.

### Washington Notes

On the right is a portrait of General Daniel "Chappie" James, Jr., the first African American to reach the rank of four-star general. He was also a Tuskegee Airman.

Walk left to the **Air Force Executive Corridor,** also known as the Arnold Corridor. Portraits of former air force chiefs of staff line the right wall, and paintings depicting the evolution of air power line the left. The air force chief of staff's office is along this corridor.

On the left is a portrait of General Henry "Hap" Arnold, the air force's first and, so far, only five-star general. He graduated from West Point, was taught to fly by the Wright brothers, and was the first man to deliver mail by air. General Arnold is the only five-star general to have served in two branches of the military, the Army Air Corps and the air force. General Arnold's nickname—Hap—was earned because he always had a smile on his face. Display cases on either side of the portrait display a career time line for General Arnold.

On the right is the office of the current secretary of the air force.

### Washington Notes

The first woman to serve as secretary of any branch of the military was Dr. Sheila Widnall, who served as secretary of the air force.

Next is the **POW Alcove,** which is dedicated to prisoners of war in Vietnam. Visitors are asked to remove their hats and observe silence. On the right is a portrait of Maxine McCaffrey, who painted and donated more than 60 portraits to the Air Force Art Collection. Directly across the hall on the left is a portrait by McCaffrey of Colonel Robinson Risner, who was a POW in a camp nicknamed the Hanoi Hilton. On the wall in the portrait are Risner's name and the names of other POWs who were held with him.

Just beyond the corridor entrance, on the right, is a portrait of Colonel Ed Hubbard, also a POW in Vietnam. The chute number portrayed in the portrait is 73, which was not his actual chute number (21), but the year he was released from the POW camp. Over Hubbard's shoulder in the clouds are two faces. The one on the right is Colonel Hubbard's face after he stepped off the bus when returning home. The face on the left is a depiction of "Mumbles," Hubbard's prison guard during his captivity. The guard was named Mumbles because neither the prisoners nor other guards could understand a word he said.

Exit the POW Alcove to the left. On the right are photographs and paintings depicting the Air Force Honor Guard. The Honor Guard serves at funerals of heads of state and the air force and at the Tomb of the Unknowns; they also conduct tours at the Pentagon.

Turn right into the **Commandants of the Marine Corps Corridor.** On the walls are portraits of former commandants of the Marine Corps. A plaque beside each features significant events that occurred during their terms. On the right is a portrait of Commandant Alexander Van de Griff, who served during World War II. The first active duty Marine Corps officer to reach the rank of four-star general, Van de Griff was also the recipient of the Congressional Medal of Honor. Also on the right is a portrait of General Archibald Henderson, the fifth commandant of the Marine Corps.

### Washington Notes

A commandant's normal term of office is 3–4 years, but Henderson served 38 years, which earned him the nickname the Grand Old Man of the Marine Corps. In 1829, President Andrew Jackson wanted to abolish the Marine Corps, saying that there was no need for two land-based infantry units. General Henderson fought against the proposal and is credited with saving the

Marine Corps, which was moved under the jurisdiction of the navy in 1834. Henderson was responsible for the Marine Corps uniforms that had large leather collars designed to protect the neck from bayonet attacks and to remind Marines to "hold their heads high." These leather collars were the reason for the Marines' nickname, the leathernecks.

Turn left in the **Navy Executive Corridor.** Lining the corridor on the right are portraits of former secretaries and undersecretaries of the navy. On the left are models of ships from the navy's fleet, including a model of the USS *Constitution,* the oldest ship in the navy. The ship, which was commissioned on Oct 21, 1797, is moored in Boston Harbor. There is also a model of the USS *Harry S. Truman,* the largest ship in the naval fleet and one of eight Nimitz-class aircraft carriers in the fleet.

On the right is the office of the commandant of the Marine Corps, who was housed in the Naval Annex until 1996. Farther up the corridor on the right is the office of the secretary of the navy. Beyond the secretary's office is a model of the USS *Tennessee,* a submarine designed to launch missiles underwater. The *Tennessee* has a crew of 150 and is 170 meters long, taller than the Washington Monument.

Next to the model is a portrait of James Vincent Forrestal, former secretary of the navy. When the National Security Act of 1947 was enacted to create the Department of Defense, Forrestal was appointed the first secretary of that department.

At the end of the corridor, go down the stairway on the right and exit on the third floor. Go left into the **Army Executive Corridor,** which is dedicated to General George C. Marshall. On the right is the **Marshall Alcove,** which commemorates General Marshall's 50 years of service to the U.S. In addition to attaining the rank of five-star general, Marshall served as army chief of staff, secretary of state, secretary of defense, and president of the Red Cross. In the alcove is the Nobel Peace Prize presented to General Marshall in 1953 for the Marshall Plan, which spearheaded the recovery of Europe after World War II.

Go down the spiral staircase on the right and enter the **Time-Life Corridor.** Paintings along the wall depict various scenes in Europe during World War II. At the start of the war the army planned to have paintings done to commemorate various soldiers and battles, but the army had to abandon the plan because of cost. Time-Life volunteered to continue the series at its own cost if the army would supply lodging to the painters. About 1,034 paintings are in the collection, 86 of which are on display.

Continue straight ahead into the **MacArthur Corridor.**

### Washington Notes

At the beginning of the hallway is an army flag with 173 battle streamers, one for each army battle. The colors of the battle streamers have meaning. The red in the streamer for the Battle of Lexington (1775), for example, represents the first blood spilled on U.S. soil; the tan in the latest streamer added represents the desert sand of the Persian Gulf War.

Display cases present chapters of General MacArthur's autobiography and of his 52 years of military service. In the case on the left are service medals awarded for his actions during World War I. These include two Distinguished Service

Crosses, one Distinguished Service Medal, seven Silver Stars, and two Purple Hearts.

Across the hall is a copy of the instrument of surrender signed by the Japanese on Sept 2, 1945, aboard the USS *Missouri* in Tokyo Bay. The fountain pen is one of the pens used to sign the original document. The uniform displayed is the one worn by Gregory Peck when he played the general in the movie *MacArthur*. A display case on the left holds MacArthur's corncob pipe and his uniform. Just beyond is a display noting the achievements of General MacArthur and his father, Lieutenant General Arthur MacArthur; the two of them are the only father and son in U.S. military history to receive the Medal of Honor. Lieutenant General MacArthur received his medal for acts of bravery during the Civil War, and General Douglas MacArthur received his during the defense of the Philippines in World War II.

Directly across the corridor is the **Hall of Heroes**, dedicated to the 3,049 recipients of the Congressional Medal of Honor, the nation's highest military award. Visitors are asked to remove any headgear as they enter. Central to the display are the three versions of the Medal of Honor and the three ways it may be worn. Ninety percent of all Medal of Honor winners receive their medals after their death either because they died while performing the act or because their actions were classified at the time and could not be publicized. The black stars beside some of the names indicate that the recipients received two Medals of Honor for two different acts of bravery. A black asterisk denotes two medals awarded for only one act but from different branches of the service. The blue stars indicate that the Medal of Honor was received from the the president. The back wall has a photograph of the most recent recipients.

Exit the hall and turn right to the **Military Women's Memorial**. Posters on the left wall detail women's involvement in the military. On the right are several display cases highlighting women's achievements. The first, and the newest addition, is a replica of the Vietnam Women's Memorial, erected in honor of the 11,000 women who served during the Vietnam War. The second case tells the story of Dr. Mary Edwards Walker, the only woman to receive the Congressional Medal of Honor.

> ### *Washington Notes*
> A surgeon during the Civil War, Walker would dress as a male Union soldier and sneak out to the front lines to help wounded soldiers. Walker was captured and spent four months in a Southern prison. She was awarded the Medal of Honor on Nov 11, 1865, an action that was revoked in 1917 because she was a civilian and not on active duty. In 1977 the medal was restored to her family.

Prior to World War I, women could work with the military on contracts as specialists but were not allowed to enlist in any branch of the service. During World War I restrictions were lifted, and women could enlist in the navy, Coast Guard, and Marine Corps. In World War II women were also allowed to enlist in the army. Another exhibit case highlights women's achievements in more recent conflicts, including those of Rear Admiral Grace Hopper.

> ### *Washington Notes*
> Known as the Grand Old Lady of Software, Rear Admiral Hopper developed COBOL, a computer-programming language. When Hopper retired from ac-

tive duty, she was recalled four times because of her extraordinary abilities with computers.

Exit the hall. Directly across the concourse is a display about the **Navajo Code Talkers.** The Japanese were expert at breaking combat codes during World War II, so they frequently knew about American soldiers' orders as soon as the orders were transmitted. Phillip Johnson, who had grown up on a Navajo reservation as a child, proposed incorporating the Navajo language to encrypt messages. Because the Navajo have no written language, it was not possible to decode messages. As a result, 480 Navajo Indians were recruited into the Marine Corps, taught military code, and assigned to incorporate the Navajo language into coded messages. After implementing Navajo Code Talk, the Japanese were unable to decode another message for the duration of World War II.

Turn right into the **Flag Corridor.** Lining the walls are the flags and emblems from each of the 50 states and from the U.S. territories. On the right, windows overlook the Pentagon's five-acre central courtyard, which is the largest "no-hat, no-salute" zone in the U.S. military. No headgear is required and lower-ranking officers do not have to salute higher-ranking officers while in the courtyard.

### *Washington Notes*
A favorite story on the Pentagon tour, and a good example of Pentagon humor, is the one about the building in the center of the courtyard, known as the Ground Zero Café. As the tale goes, during the Cold War, when the Russians took aerial pictures of the Pentagon, they saw a small five-sided building surrounded by an immense fortification of five walls. Assuming that this building must house secrets of immense importance, it was made a target of nuclear weapons in case of war. The building is a hot dog stand.

Turn right into the **NATO Corridor,** which honors the various members of the North Atlantic Treaty Organization (NATO), established in 1949 during the administration of President Harry S. Truman. On the left wall are more than 200 images, pictures, maps, and newspaper headlines detailing NATO actions since 1949. On the right are the flags and emblems of the 19 NATO member countries. Three relatively recent NATO members are the Czech Republic, Poland, and Hungary.

Turn left and walk past the cafeteria to the security checkpoint to reenter the tour-waiting area.

### Diversion:
Walk around the Pentagon to the pavilion at the North Parking area. Directly across the parking lot is the **Lyndon Baines Johnson Memorial Grove** (1974; Mills, Petticorde and Mills; Meade Palmer, landscape architect). Because of traffic, travel by car is recommended. By car, turn left from the Pentagon parking area onto Army-Navy Dr. Turn left on Fern St. Turn left at the second stop sign and drive by the front of the Pentagon. Bear right at the fork onto Washington Blvd. Exit at the second exit (20) to the Pentagon North Parking. At the stop sign turn left. The access road dead-ends at Boundary Channel Dr. Parking for the LBJ Memorial Grove is directly across the street.

### History

Lyndon B. Johnson was born on Texas in Aug 27, 1908. After serving as a teacher, he began working as secretary to Texas congressman Richard M. Kleberg in 1931. Johnson was elected as the Texas director of the National Youth Administration in 1935, then won a seat in Congress in 1937. Johnson volunteered for military service after the Japanese bombing of Pearl Harbor and earned a Silver Star. He returned a hero and was elected to the Senate in 1948. After two years he became the Minority Whip, the youngest in Senate history at the age of 42. He became the Majority Leader when the Democrats gained control of the Senate in 1951.

Johnson was selected to be John F. Kennedy's running mate in the 1960 election. After Kennedy was assassinated in 1963, Johnson succeeded him as president. Although environmental awareness was not a major issue at the time, President Johnson established certain environmental guidelines. Claudia "Lady Bird" Johnson, the first lady, created a Highway Beautification Project. This initiative included cleaning up urban and rural roads, reducing billboard advertisements, and planting wildflowers to beautify the country.

> ### Washington Notes
> During his administration, Johnson added 3.6 million acres of land to the National Park System, including the Redwood National Park, Fire Island National Seashore, and Assateague Island National Seashore, which is famous for its wild ponies. He signed the Wilderness Act of 1964, which set forth the idea that some of the nation's land should be preserved in its natural state and remain wild. Johnson also signed into law the Land and Water Conservation Fund, created in 1965, to allow states the means to purchase land to set aside for outdoor activities. Under the Johnson administration, the first water- and air-pollution acts were also passed.

After Johnson's death in 1973, friends and colleagues sought to erect a suitable memorial to this president who championed conservation. The Grove Committee, as it came to be called, wanted to build a living tribute to honor Johnson, and 17 acres were set aside within Lady Bird Johnson Park along the Potomac River to build the memorial. The Memorial Grove was built with private funds.

From the parking area, visitors walk down the stairway to the site of a short orientation video. Access to the grove is via a footbridge over the Boundary Channel. The grove is a living monument designed by Meade Palmer, a Virginia landscape architect. Serpentine paths lead visitors through the grove, which is planted with hundreds of white pines and dogwood trees, as well as azalea and rhododendron bushes. Yellow daffodils bloom in the spring. A slate pathway leads to a paved circle dominated by a red granite monolith chosen to symbolize Johnson's "energy and personality." The monolith, which weighs 43 tons and stands 19 ft tall, was quarried 35 miles from LBJ's ranch home in Texas. Equally spaced around the stone are four granite markers bearing quotations from speeches given by Johnson during his presidency. These express his philosophy on education, environment, civil rights, and the presidency.

# Drug Enforcement Administration (DEA) Museum and Visitors Center

700 Army-Navy Dr, Arlington, VA 22202. ☎ (703) 307-3463. Web: www.usdoj.gov/dea. Open Tues–Fri 10–3. Tours on the hour by appointment only; call between 9–5 weekdays to schedule a tour.

It is easiest to get to the Drug Enforcement Administration (DEA) Museum and Visitors Center (1999; designed by Chris White Designs, Inc.; constructed by Rogay, Inc. and Design and Production, Inc.) from the Pentagon. If walking, leave the Pentagon via the pedestrian tunnel under I-395 and proceed to Army-Navy Dr. If driving, exit the Pentagon via the Pentagon Access Rd and continue south to Army-Navy Dr. Turn left (east) on Army-Navy Dr and continue one block to the intersection with S. Hayes St. If traveling by Metro, take the Blue/Yellow Line to Pentagon City shopping mall; the museum is across the street from Macy's.

The DEA Museum chronicles 150 years of America's complex relationship with illegal drugs. Although the facility is relatively small at 2,200 square ft, the museum's historical photographs and displays are well laid out, interesting, and informative.

**Highlights:** On display are a hollowed-out surfboard and a Harley-Davidson motorcycle used by drug smugglers, along with an assortment of submachine guns used by DEA agents in the 1930s.

## Interior

The museum's entrance is dominated by an **international poster kiosk,** displaying historical posters from around the world aimed at fighting drug trafficking. A 1910 Chinese poster declares that "Working together to fight drugs is a citizen's responsibility."

Straight ahead is a depiction of a 1940s American **drugstore,** with startling revelations about such cultural icons as Coca-Cola and Bayer aspirin. According to the museum, Coca-Cola contained cocaine until 1903 and was advertised as a medicine that would "ease the tired brain, soothe the rattled nerves and restore wasted energy to both Mind and Body." Bayer aspirin was preceded by Bayer heroin, which was advertised as being "highly effective against coughs."

Next to this display is a depiction of a **head shop** from the 1970s, complete with hookahs, bags of marijuana, and rolling papers fashioned after $100 bills with the White House phone number printed in green ink on the front.

Turn north to a scene from a Philadelphia **crack house** in the 1990s—with two small children picking through crack vials—and the chilling statistic that the crack epidemic of the 1980s created about 4 million hard-core addicts. Also included here are a brief definition of addiction and a photo showing 3-D views of a brain's dead cells, the result of cocaine use.

Next is a display explaining the **1840 Opium War,** in which Britain, for economic reasons, went to war with China to prevent that country from closing down its opium trade. When Chinese laborers came to California in the 1850s to work on the railroads, they brought their opium with them. Displayed is a block of opium with the label "Government Opium, Hong Kong."

The remainder of the exhibits spread along the east wall and are arranged in chronological order.

**America's First Drug Epidemic, 1850–1914** details how the Civil War, with its primitive medical treatment, produced thousands of veteran morphine addicts, so many that morphine became known as the Soldier's Disease. But drug use wasn't limited to those at the front, as evidenced by an excerpt from Mary Chestnut's Civil War diary (made famous in the PBS production *The Civil War*): "All day I was in bed—the night before sat up too late hearing Mrs. Davis . . . [who] told me unutterable stories of the War—but I forget after so much opium."

### Washington Notes

By 1900, 1 in 200 Americans was a drug addict; the typical profile was a white, middle-class woman whose addiction began with medical treatment.

Nor were children spared. The turn of the 19C was the heyday of patent medicines, many of which contained addictive drugs. Ads and sample bottles are displayed touting such elixirs as Mrs. Winslow's Soothing Syrup, an opiate-based concoction given to children "for teething pains and to sooth their fussiness." Next to this is a coroner's report from a Minnesota town in 1906 describing a baby's death from the syrup; deaths of this type were not uncommon.

Cocaine was introduced in 1885 as "the first effective local anesthetic," and, even though it was recognized by 1900 as being highly addictive, it continued to be an ingredient in patent medicines such as toothache drops. Displayed are various tins in which cocaine was sold. These were "particularly popular with young boys," especially when advances in manufacturing brought the prices down to a figure children could afford. A display of treatments for addiction to these drugs points out that many treatments simply substituted one drug for another.

The exhibits in **Enforcing New Drug Laws, 1919–1950** demonstrate how the government reacted to the nation's growing drug problem. In 1906 the federal government began regulating drug content and use. The first federal narcotics law was passed in 1914, but that didn't deter the gangsters of the 1920s from creating a flourishing drug trade.

In 1930, the Bureau of Narcotics, forerunner of the DEA, was created. Displayed here are samples of each agent's equipment—a badge, a Thompson submachine gun, and a pair of hand grenades. So successful was the bureau that by the end of World War II the addict population numbered only about 50,000 nationwide.

**Hipsters and the Drug Scene** examines the 1950s version of what would later be called the counterculture. The tragedy of addicted jazz musicians, such as Billie Holliday and Charlie Parker, as well as literary figures, is detailed through photographs and personal quotes. One particularly harrowing remembrance by writer William Burroughs describing his days as an addict begins, "I had not taken a bath in a year or changed my clothes or removed them except to stick a needle every hour in the fibrous grey wooden flesh of terminal addiction."

**Rise of the Modern Drug Culture, 1960s & 1970s** may elicit more chuckles and head shaking than shudders, with its psychedelic posters proclaiming drug guru Timothy Leary's mantra ("Turn on, tune in, drop out") and a not-to-be-missed pair of green snakeskin shoes with two-inch-high platform soles worn by an undercover DEA agent, along with the requisite bell-bottoms. Not so amusing are displays lamenting the loss to drugs of music icons Janis Joplin and Jimi Hendrix, nor the fact that by the late 1960s, drug use was making its way into high schools.

According to the exhibit, drug use in the U.S. peaked in 1979. **The Return of Cocaine and the Rise of the Cartels, 1970s–1990s** depicts how cocaine went from being the "champagne of drugs" among yuppies to the scourge of the urban centers. On display are a Harley-Davidson confiscated in a drug raid and a diamond-studded Colt .45 taken from a dealer.

At the south end of the museum are interactive video kiosks and a small gift shop.

To continue to the next walk, return to the Pentagon City shopping mall and the Pentagon City Metro station. Take the Blue Line to the King St Metro station.

# 32 · Alexandria

Metro: Blue/Yellow Line to King St.
Car: From Washington, D.C., take the George Washington Memorial Pkwy south.

## Old Town

Alexandria is six miles south of Washington, D.C., along the banks of the Potomac River. It was the river and the promise of riches that lured the first settlers to Alexandria's shores in the early 17C. The area grew with the aspirations of its residents. George Washington, a young surveyor's assistant, helped pace off these parcels. The historic Old Town, the original settlement, retains many 18C and 19C buildings. Scores of these have been converted into restaurants and shops. The combination of historic old brick façades and trendy 20C eateries makes Old Town a popular evening destination for Washingtonians. Old Town also has several historic houses and sites.

### History

The land that makes up Old Town Alexandria was originally part of a grant of 6,000 acres made by Governor Sir William Berkley to Robert Howson (or Howsing) in Oct 1669 "for bringing into the Colony of Virginia one hundred twenty persons to inhabit." Within a month, the grant was purchased by Captain John Alexander for 6,000 pounds of tobacco. Some years later, when it was discovered that an earlier grant to this land existed from King Charles to a Mistress Brent in Maryland, Alexander's heirs paid another 10,500 pounds of tobacco for the tract.

By 1732, Hugh West had established a tobacco warehouse at what was called West's Point. Other Scottish merchants established a small settlement around the warehouse called Great Hunting Creek. In 1749, the Virginia Assembly received petitions from several counties to establish a town in the area of Great Hunting Creek. The owners, Hugh West and Phillip and John Alexander, protested the petition because they did not want the new town on their property. Despite their objections, an act of the Virginia Assembly in 1749 established the town of Alexandria on 60 acres at Great Hunting Creek.

> ### Washington Notes
> John West, Jr., the deputy surveyor of Fairfax County, drew up the plan for the town. According to tradition, his assistant for this job was young George Washington, age 17.

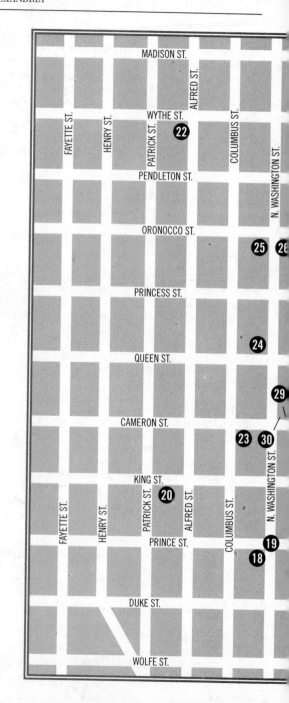

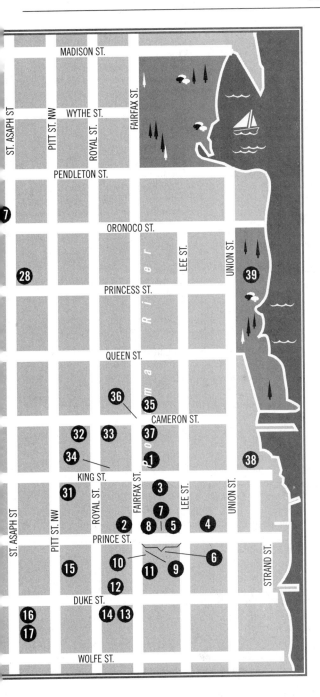

1 Ramsay House Visitors Center
2 Stabler-Leadbeater Apothecary Shop
3 Col. George Gilpin House
4 Captain's Row
5 The Anthenaeum
6 Gentry Row
7 Fairfax Town House
8 Dr. Elisha Cullen Dick House
9 Col. Michael Swope House
10 Green Steam Furniture Works
11 Dr. William Brown's House
12 Dr. James Craik's House
13 Old Presbyterian Meeting House
14 St. Mary's Church
15 St. Paul's Church
16 Lafayette House
17 a "flounder" house
18 The Lyceum
19 Alexandria Confederate Memorial
20 Friendship Firehouse
21 George Washington Masonic National Memorial
22 Alexandria Black History Resource Center

23 Christ Church
24 Lloyd House
25 Edmund Jennings Lee House
26 Lee-Fendall House Museum
27 Boyhood Home of Robert E. Lee
28 Alexandria Jail
29 Lord Fairfax House
30 Gen. Henry Lee House
31 Marshall House
32 Gadsby's Tavern—the S.W. corner of Cameron and Royal Sts
33 City Hall—the S.E. corner of Cameron and Royal Sts
34 Market Square—behind City Hall between Royal and Fairfax Sts on King
35 Anne Lee Memorial Home—N.E. corner of Fairfax and Cameron Sts
36 Bank of Alexandria—S.E. corner of Fairfax and Cameron Sts
37 Carlyle House—next to the Bank of Alexandria
38 Torpedo Factory Art Center
39 Founders Park and Oronoco Park

The town was laid out with ten streets and 84 half-acre lots. Each buyer was restricted to the purchase of two lots. Loyal to England, the colonists named their streets east to the river in honor of royalty—King, Queen, Prince, Princess, and Duke Sts. Cameron and Fairfax Sts were named in honor of Lord Thomas, the sixth lord of Fairfax, baron of Cameron—the proprietor of the Northern Neck, an area on the northern neck of Chesapeake Bay. The road along the river was called Water St and later renamed Lee St in honor of Alexandria's most famous citizen, Robert E. Lee.

Lots were auctioned off July 13–14, 1749, and the proceeds were used to compensate the reluctant founders. It is believed that the town was named in their honor. Since the terms of the sale stated that purchasers had to "build to secure" (construct houses), the area developed relatively rapidly. By 1762, all land from the original sale had been built upon, so more land was acquired from the reluctant Alexanders to expand the town. Alexandria was becoming known because of its port and because the town was situated on the King's Hwy between Williamsburg and New England.

In 1752, when Governor Dinwiddie moved the Fairfax County Court to Alexandria, a courthouse was built at the marketplace. In 1755, Edward Braddock, an English general, made his headquarters in the city while planning his campaign against the French. In 1779, Alexandria was incorporated and made an official port of entry for foreign vessels. The first mayor, Robert Townsend Hooe, was appointed to that position in 1780.

In 1789, Alexandria and a portion of Fairfax County were slated to become part of the Federal City across the Potomac River. Congress officially accepted the land in 1801, and Alexandria became part of the ten-square-mile District of Columbia. In 1804, a yellow fever epidemic ravaged the city, and in 1806, a trade embargo affected profits. In Aug 1814 the British, triumphant after their burning of the White House and surrounding areas, captured Alexandria. The British plundered warehouses, shipping the goods back to England aboard commandeered ships. The British demanded—and received—a large ransom in exchange for not inflicting more damage. In 1827, a fire (called the Great Fire) destroyed 53 houses. In 1834, the completion of the Baltimore and Ohio Railroad to Harper's Ferry diverted much trade from Alexandria to Baltimore's harbor.

In economically depressed Alexandria, the movement to rejoin the commonwealth of Virginia, which had some followers in the 1820s, gained momentum in the 1840s. Burdened by taxes and bereft of state representatives and funds, Alexandria's citizens also worried that continued alliance with the District would lead to giving up their slaves. Abolitionists had succeeded in having Congress prohibit slave owning in the District, a situation that worried many slave-holding Alexandrians. Congress acceded to Alexandria's wishes, passing the Act of Retrocession in July 1846, and Alexandrians voted their approval in Sept. In 1847, the city again became part of Virginia, which started to revive Alexandria by assuming part of the debt for the Alexandria Canal and by providing funds for improvements and railroads.

In 1843 the Alexandria Canal, which had been costly for the city to build, was linked to the Chesapeake and Ohio (C&O) Canal. This connection became even more valuable when the C&O Canal reached the Cumberland Gap in 1850. That enabled barges loaded with coal from the Appalachian highlands to float into Alexandria, creating a thriving coal trade that continued up to the Civil War. By 1853, for example, Alexandria was shipping 16,000 tons of coal monthly. Railroads brought added prosperity to the city. The Orange and Alexandria Line linked the city with the wheat-growing regions of Manassas Gap in Dec 1851, Gordonsville in March 1854, and Lynchburg in 1860. As a result, Alexandria became an important flour-trading port.

When Virginia voted to join the Confederacy on May 23, 1861, Union troops occupied Alexandria the next day in order to protect the Federal government's use of the Potomac River and the city as a supply center.

### Washington Notes

The first casualty of the Civil War occurred in Alexandria. Colonel Elmer Ellsworth, a protégé of President Abraham Lincoln's, was shot when he pulled down an Alexandria inn's Confederate flag. His outraged troops threatened to burn down the city but were prevented from doing this by being moved to a freighter in the river. President Lincoln, a friend of Ellsworth's, rode in the colonel's funeral cortege.

After the war, Alexandria entered a slow decline as more trade was routed through Baltimore. This lack of major industrialization saved the historic area from destruction. In 1960, Alexandria began major historic preservation and renewal efforts, which were intensified for the Civil War Centennial and the nation's Bicentennial in 1976. When Alexandria celebrated its 250th birthday in 1999, the city was justifiably proud of the renewal of Old Town, a successful recreation of colonial and Civil War America that also has nourished a thriving modern-day shopping area.

## Ramsay House Visitors Center

221 King St, Alexandria, VA. ☎ (703) 838-4200. Open daily 9–5. Closed Thanksgiving and Christmas Day. Brochures and information about local attractions, block tickets to local sites, and tours available. Restrooms across the street in the parking garage. Wheelchair accessible.

From the King St Metro station, walk nine blocks east on King St toward the river. If traveling by car from Washington, D.C., turn left at King St and proceed to Fairfax St. The Ramsay House Visitors Center is on the northeast corner. Off-street parking is available nearby, marked by the green *P* signs, but visitors from outside Alexandria can obtain a free permit at the visitors center.

The Ramsay House Visitors Center (1724; William Ramsay) is said to be the oldest house in Alexandria. Tradition has it that after purchasing the lot on King St, Ramsay floated his house upriver from Dumfries, Virginia, to the current site. It is believed that the house incorporated part of an earlier structure, built in 1724. The house changed hands many times during the 19C and 20C, being used as a tavern, a grocery store, rooming house, and cigar factory over the years. The city of Alexandria purchased the property in 1944 and restored it in 1955–56. The house serves as the visitors center for Alexandria.

From mid–March through mid-Nov on weekend nights (Fri–Sat 7:30 and 9 P.M.; Sun 7:30 P.M.; fee charged), the Ramsay House is the starting point for the **Original Ghost and Graveyard Tour** through the "haunted" streets of historic Old Town. Guides in colonial attire lead the one-hour exposé of Alexandria's most famous ghosts. The tour always ends at a graveyard.

### History

William Ramsay, a tobacco trader, was one of the town's original trustees. He came to America from Galloway, Scotland, and settled in Dumfries, Virginia, where he represented a Scottish firm. Ramsay and John Carlyle both moved to Alexandria after the town lots were sold because of Alexandria's harbor.

Ramsay successfully bid for two lots opposite those purchased by Lawrence Washington. The lots were along the town's original waterfront, and it was believed that he built his house facing the river so he could observe trading vessels coming upriver. Ramsay served as a census taker, a member of the Safety Committee, and was Alexandria's first postmaster (from 1770 to 1785). Ramsay married Anne McCarty, a cousin of George Washington on Washington's mother's side. She was praised by Thomas Jefferson for raising more than $75,000 to support the Revolution. Ramsay's son, Colonel Dennis Ramsay, was an officer in the Revolutionary War and became mayor of Alexandria in 1788. Colonel Ramsay was an honorary pallbearer at George Washington's funeral.

### Exterior

The two-story house with a gambrel roof was typical of the building style of the mid-18C. Much of the original house was destroyed in a fire in 1942 but was reconstructed from earlier photographs of the building. The rock foundation of this house would normally be below ground but was exposed when the streets of the city were graded, beginning in the late 1780s. Excess dirt from the regrading efforts was used to fill in the shallow crescent of the riverfront, creating more land.

## Stabler-Leadbeater Apothecary Shop

105–107 S. Fairfax St, Alexandria, VA. ☎ (703) 836-3713. Open Mon–Sat 10–4; Sun 1–5. Closed Wed Nov–March. Admission: shop free; fee for museum.

Exit the Ramsay House, turn right, and walk to the corner. Cross King St, then cross Fairfax St. Turn left and walk to the Stabler-Leadbeater Apothecary Shop, 105–107 S. Fairfax St, which holds the record for the longest family-operated pharmacy in the country. The large glass globes filled with colored water in the window identified it for the illiterate as a pharmacy. By custom, the globes were filled with red water during times of illness in the city, such as the yellow fever epidemic that forced the quarantine of Alexandria in 1804.

**Highlights:** The shop has an extensive collection of 18C and 19C pharmaceutical equipment and supplies.

### History

No. 107 was built by Phillip Dawes, a coppersmith, sometime in the late 1770s or early 1780s. The shop was leased to Edward Stabler, a Quaker pharmacist, in 1792 and was patronized by the Washingtons and Lees, as well as many other gentry. Stabler married Mary Pleasants, and they had five children before Mary died in 1804. Stabler bought no. 107 in 1805.

In 1829, Stabler bought the adjacent lot, no. 105. He married Mary Hartshorne, and they had ten additional children. Mary, a daughter from his second marriage, married John Leadbeater in 1835 and lived for a time in Baltimore. When they returned to Alexandria, Leadbeater joined Stabler in business; that accounts for the name the shop has today.

#### Washington Notes

The shop was a popular gathering place for the community. It is said that J. E. B. Stuart found Robert E. Lee in the shop on Oct 19, 1859, and gave Lee his orders to suppress the uprising in Harper's Ferry.

The apothecary was operated continuously for 141 years, but in 1933 the Depression forced its closing. The Landmarks Society purchased the shop in 1934, and it reopened as a museum. The collection of pharmaceutical equipment and supplies, purchased by L. Manuel Hendler of Baltimore, was loaned to the museum initially and donated in its entirety in 1948.

### Exterior

The three-story Georgian-style building was built with local brick. The exterior was remodeled in the 19C, but it was returned to its original appearance when the shop became a museum.

### Interior

The doors at no. 107 remain closed; the museum must be entered through no. 105. A ten-minute tape (also available in French, Spanish, and Russian) at the entrance to the museum gives a brief history. More than 8,000 objects, such as pill rollers, drug mills, medicinal glassware, and furnishings, are still in place. The shelves and counters were modified in the 1850s and retain their unusual Gothic-style decorations. Many original herbs, potions, and paper labels are still in the drawers, and the shop has a valuable collection of more than 900 handblown medicinal bottles.

Exhibits describe the work and traditions of an apothecary and note the various patrons of the shop. A silver plaque marks the spot Lee was standing when he received his orders to quell the Harper's Ferry uprising.

Two large mortars and pestles remain from the first order placed by Edward Stabler for supplies in 1792. In the center of the shop, two tiles are placed in the center of the counter for the mixing of medicines. One was said to be used for horse medicine and the other for people.

> ### Washington Notes
> Patrons of the shop included George and Martha Washington, Daniel Webster, and the Lee family. One note, dated 1802, includes a request in Martha Washington's own hand for castor oil, and Dr. Elisha Dick ordered Glauber Salts from the shop for use by George Washington shortly before his death.

Exit the shop, turn left, and walk back to the corner of King and S. Fairfax Sts. Cross S. Fairfax St and walk down King St past the house of **Colonel George Gilpin** at 206–208 King St. The double house was originally constructed in 1798 on a lot originally owned by Lawrence Washington. The building is now an art gallery.

### History

Colonel George Gilpin, an aide to General Washington in the Revolutionary War, was one of Alexandria's earliest surveyors and drew the only surviving 18C map of the city. He took an active part in city life, serving as judge of the orphan's court, vestryman of Christ Church, and engineer in charge of paving and grading the streets. As a representative for the Alexandria-Washington Lodge of Masons, Gilpin was elected to serve as an honorary pallbearer at George Washington's funeral. Gilpin also served as Alexandria's postmaster from 1809 until his death in 1813.

Continue to the corner, cross Lee St, walk south one block to Prince St, and turn left. The Federal-style houses that line the 100 block of the cobblestone street are known as **Captain's Row.**

### History

Captain John Harper purchased his home in 1773 and also the land on the north side of Prince St east of Water (now Lee) St. This land, originally underwater, was created when the waterfront was filled in. Harper built a number of small dwellings along the street. The original wood-frame houses were badly damaged in the Great Fire of 1827 but were quickly rebuilt. At this time, no one is sure which dwellings are original and which are post-1827.

Walk to the second residence, no. 127. At the second-floor window is a *busybody*, an arrangement of mirrors that enabled the occupant of the room to discreetly view passersby traveling up and down the street.

## The Athenaeum

201 Prince St, Alexandria, VA. ☎ (703) 548-0035. Open for programs and special exhibitions Wed–Sat 11–3; Sun 1–4. Call in advance about programs.

Return to the corner and cross Prince St. The building with the salmon-colored pillars on the southeast corner is the Athenaeum (c. 1852), currently occupied by the Northern Virginia Fine Arts Association.

### History

A large frame warehouse originally stood on this site. It was replaced by the Athenaeum and occupied by the Bank of the Old Dominion between 1850 and 1852. Some believe that the architect was William Fowle, the bank's president. When Union troops occupied the city in 1861, a bank cashier took the bank's valuable papers and records and buried them. Most Alexandrians sided with the Confederates. The bank served as headquarters for the Commissary Department during the war.

Afterward, the papers were recovered, and the bank paid off its obligations. The building was operated as a bank from 1907 to 1925. It was purchased by the Free Methodist Church of North America and used as a place of worship until the mid-1960s, when it was purchased by the Northern Virginia Fine Arts Association.

## Exterior

The Athenaeum, meaning "Temple of Athena," is an example of the Greek revival architecture that flourished in Alexandria in the late 1840s. Many private homes were built in this style, but only two public buildings—the Athenaeum and the Lyceum. The large exterior porticoes and columns give the building a solid appearance. The salmon color is believed to be the original, as determined by research by the National Park Service.

## *Gentry Row*

The north side of the 200 block of Prince St beyond the Athenaeum was known as **Gentry Row,** where many friends of George Washington resided. Directly across the street was the home of Colonel Robert T. Hooe (200 Prince St).

### History

Colonel Robert T. Hooe moved to Alexandria from Charles County, Maryland, where he had served in the militia and as a member of the local Safety Committee. Hooe was a partner in the firm of Hooe and Harrison, one of several firms employed by George Washington to handle his plantation business. As a result, Hooe was a frequent visitor at Mount Vernon, George Washington's home. Hooe was a board member of the original Bank of Alexandria and was appointed Alexandria's first mayor in 1780. He lived at 200 Prince St from 1780 until his death in 1809. The house was purchased by a bank after his death and remained a bank until 1910. The original house has since been divided into two private residences.

Walk up Prince St to no. 207, the **Fairfax Town House** (c. 1752), built by Colonel William Fairfax on land purchased in the original land auction of 1749.

### History

Colonel Fairfax, cousin to Lord Thomas, had come to Virginia to oversee his cousin's affairs in the New World. When Fairfax died in 1757, he deeded the property to his son, George William Fairfax. George Fairfax and his wife, Sally, lived at

Belvoir plantation, but used the town house when visiting Alexandria. Loyal to the crown, Fairfax and his wife left for England just before the beginning of the Revolution.

### Washington Notes

After his father's death, George Washington (age 11) went to live at Mount Vernon with his brother, Lawrence. Mount Vernon was adjacent to Belvoir, and young George Washington was a frequent visitor to the Fairfax home. Washington and George William Fairfax became good friends and in 1746 they worked together surveying the boundaries of Lord Thomas's proprietary—the Northern Neck, which encompassed approximately a quarter of the land in Virginia. This was the first step in Washington's career as a surveyor.

After the Fairfaxes left for England, George Washington continued to keep in contact with the family but he never saw them again. In 1783, the Belvoir home was destroyed in a fire. In his diary, Washington wrote: "happiest moments of my life had been spent there."

The Fairfax House was sold to Captain John Harper in 1773. Although Harper was a Quaker, he actively supported the cause of the Revolution. He organized two companies of militia in 1775, was a member of the local Committee of Safety, and sailed to Philadelphia to obtain gunpowder for Virginia's troops. Harper turned into a local real estate magnate, buying up available land. He had an unusually large family and was rumored to have left a house to each of his children. His will listed nine daughters and ten sons—and a large amount of real estate that was distributed among them in 1804.

The house was sold again in 1790 to a political refugee from England, William Hodgson. The house remained in Hodgson's possession for 25 years. A reversal of business fortunes finally forced the sale. The house remained a private residence over the years.

Proceed to 209 Prince St, the **Dr. Elisha Cullen Dick House.** The three town houses at nos. 209–213 were built by Captain John Harper and leased to various tenants. Although a brass plaque at no. 209 notes that this was the house of Dr. Dick, much evidence suggests that Dr. James Craik actually rented no. 209 from 1789 until 1793, when he purchased a house at 210 Duke St. Dr. Dick occupied the town house at no. 211 from 1802 until 1820.

### History

Dr. Elisha Cullen Dick and his wife were on their way to South Carolina to establish a new practice when they passed through Alexandria. Armed with a letter of introduction from his family to George Washington, Dr. Dick chose to remain in Alexandria. Dr. Dick was a founder of the Masonic Lodge of Alexandria, as was George Washington. After succeeding Washington as grand master, Dr. Dick participated in the ceremony that established Jones Point as one of the boundaries of the District of Columbia in 1791, as well as the ceremonial laying of the cornerstone for the Capitol Building in 1793. Dr. Dick also performed the Masonic Service at George Washington's funeral.

Dr. Dick's house was so well known that it was frequently used as a marker to direct citizens to other locations on Prince St.

### Washington Notes

Dr. Dick attended George Washington during his last illness as an attending physician to Dr. Craik. According to an old custom, he stopped Washington's bedroom clock at the time of his death—10:20 P.M. The clock was presented to the Masonic Lodge by Mrs. Washington and may be seen on display there.

Directly across the street at 210 Prince St was the home of **Colonel Michael Swope.**

### History

Colonel Swope built no. 210 when he moved from Pennsylvania in 1784, where he had been hailed as a local hero. Swope, a leader of the Pennsylvania Dutch community, was elected to the Pennsylvania State Assembly several times. He served on the Pennsylvania Committee of Safety with Benjamin Franklin and at the age of 50 was the first man to enlist in the Pennsylvania militia at the start of the Revolutionary War.

Colonel Swope was selected with the soldiers of York, Pennsylvania, by George Washington to defend Fort Washington. When the fort surrendered, Swope and some 2,000 soldiers were taken prisoner. He remained a prisoner for five years. After the Revolution, Swope relocated to Alexandria. He and his sons formed a trading concern, which he worked at until his death in 1792. The exterior of the house has remained much the same since that time. The house is privately owned.

Walk to the corner and cross Prince St. The building on the corner of Prince and Fairfax Sts housed the **Green Steam Furniture Works** (c. 1836), Alexandria's largest furniture maker and one of the largest in the South. A bronze of an original advertisement for the company is posted on the building's front.

### History

The Green Family Cabinet Makers was started by William Green in 1817 and continued by his son James. James Green purchased the site for his furniture company in 1836. During the Civil War, the building was used as a Federal prison for Union deserters. The Green family resumed operations afterward, but facing increased competition, closed the company in 1887. Several pieces of furniture manufactured at the Green Steam Furniture Works are on display at the Lyceum.

Walk south on S. Fairfax St to no. 212, **Dr. William Brown's House** (c. 1775).

### History

Dr. William Brown built this frame house over brick. He moved his practice here in 1786 and lived here until his death in 1792.

Dr. Brown served as the physician general and director of hospitals for the Continental Army for two years. He was the author of the first American-written pharmacopoeia and was a vestryman of Christ Church. Dr. Brown also served as president of the board of trustees of the Alexandria Academy.

Continue a half-block on S. Fairfax St to Duke St, then turn east on Duke St to **Dr. James Craik's House** (c. 1783; John Short) at 210 Duke St.

### History

The property was purchased from John B. Murray by Dr. Craik. He moved to the new property in 1795 from a house rented from Captain John Harper on Prince St and resided here until 1809.

Dr. Craik emigrated from Dumfries, Scotland, in 1751. He served in the French and Indian War and during the Revolutionary War was surgeon general of the Continental Army. Reportedly, he ministered to General Edward Braddock as Braddock was dying near Fort Duquesne in the French and Indian War, tended General Lafayette's wounds at Brandywine in the Revolutionary War, and attended both George and Martha Washington at their deathbeds.

### *Washington Notes*

Dr. Craik served as George Washington's personal physician and was with George Washington during every major battle of the war. George Washington referred to him as "my compatriot in arms and old and intimate friend" in his will. He left the doctor a bureau and circular chair, which may be seen at Mount Vernon.

Dr. Craik died in 1814 and was buried in the graveyard at the Old Presbyterian Meeting House.

## Old Presbyterian Meeting House

321 S. Fairfax St, Alexandria, VA. ☎ (703) 549-5570. Web: opmh.org. Open Mon–Fri 9–3. Admission: free.

Walk a half-block west on Duke St to the corner and cross S. Fairfax St. Cross Duke St and walk south several yds on S. Fairfax St to the Old Presbyterian Meeting House (c. 1775; John Carlyle; restored 1835, 1949).

### History

Richard Arell and his wife gave the land to the Reverend William Thoms, the congregation's first pastor, to build a church in 1773. The church was completed sometime after 1775, and the bell tower added in 1790. Upon the death of George Washington, the bell tolled continuously until Washington's funeral at Mount Vernon.

The steeple was struck by lightning on July 16, 1835, and the church burned, leaving only the exterior walls and a small portion of the interior. The church was rebuilt along the original plans, which caused the destruction of a number of graves. The bell was recast and hung in the new belfry in 1843. The church closed its doors in 1889 and was practically abandoned for 60 years. It reopened in 1949.

## Grounds

To the right of the meeting house are the wrought-iron gates that serve as the entrance to the church graveyard. Follow the path back into the graveyard.

The church grounds served as a burial place from 1772 until 1809, when city ordinance prohibited further burials within the town limits. Among those buried in the churchyard are John Carlyle, Colonel Dennis Ramsay, Dr. James Muir, and Dr. James Craik. At the far right is an enclosed grave site, erected April 12, 1949, which marks the Tomb of the Unknown Soldier of the Revolutionary War. The Sons and Daughters of the American Revolution gather here each year to pay tribute during their yearly convocation. A tape at the grave site gives a brief history of the tomb and those buried within the churchyard itself.

### Washington Notes

When the foundation of St. Mary's Catholic Church was dug in 1826, an ammunition chest was unearthed containing human remains with military furnishings. Some believed that the remains were those of a British soldier, possibly one of General Braddock's men. The elders of the Old Presbyterian Church, however, noted that the builders had strayed a bit more than a ft over the property line of the church graveyard, and that the remains were probably a soldier of the Revolution. The remains are now entombed in the churchyard as the Unknown Soldier.

Continue along the path and through the gates at the back of the yard. Turn right and walk up Royal St to **St. Mary's Catholic Church** (c. 1826; 1888) at 302 S. Royal St. A plaque inside a wrought-iron railing gives a brief history.

### History

The first Catholic congregation in Virginia was established in Alexandria in 1793. Tradition has it that George Washington met with Colonel John Fitzgerald on St. Patrick's Day, 1788, and that building a church was discussed. Although not Catholic, George Washington reportedly contributed to the building fund. The original church was built on the southeast corner of Washington and Church Sts, but only the church graveyard remains there today. The earliest portion of the church on this site was built in 1826, and the current granite structure was completed in 1888.

### Diversion:

Walk to the corner of Royal and Duke Sts, then two blocks west on Duke St to S. Pitt St. Cross Duke and walk north on Pitt St to **St. Paul's Church** (c. 1818; Benjamin Latrobe) at 222 S. Pitt St.

### History

The church was constructed after a split in the Episcopal church in Alexandria. The interior was patterned after St. James Church in Piccadilly, London, which was designed by Sir Christopher Wren. When the town was occupied by Union troops at the beginning of the Civil War, the Reverend Kinzey Johns Stewart was dragged out of the church during morning services when he refused to pray for Lincoln. Thereafter the church was seized; it was used as a hospital during the Civil War, with the rectory serving as a commissary.

### Washington Notes

St. Paul's Church is known as the burial place of the "female stranger." As the story goes, a young woman of gentle birth and her husband arrived at Gadsby's Tavern in 1816. The woman was ill with typhoid fever, and her doctor and nurse were sworn to silence regarding her identity. When she died a few weeks later, her husband had a marble tomb erected over her burial site. The husband vanished shortly afterward, leaving a number of debts behind.

From St. Mary's Catholic Church, walk to the corner of Duke and Royal Sts. Cross Royal St, walk two blocks west on Duke St, and cross S. St. Asaph St. The Federal-style brick house on the corner at 301 S. St. Asaph St is the **Lafayette House** (c. 1815–16). It was so called because the owner, Mrs. Thomas Lawrison, lent the house to General Lafayette and his staff during their visit to Alexandria in 1824.

### Diversion:

Walk south on S. St. Asaph St. to nos. **317** and **321.** The houses on these lots are "flounder" houses. Somewhat modified since they were built, the houses, constructed with pitched roofs, were usually set back from the street. The side along the steeper pitch of the roof had no windows, in contrast to the other side, which did—reminding many of the flounder with its eyes on one side. Some explain the architectural style as a way of saving taxes, which were levied on glass window panes. Others explain the modest houses as the easiest type to build to satisfy the legal requirements of "build to secure."

## The Lyceum

201 S. Washington St, Alexandria, VA. ☎ (703) 838-4994. Open Mon–Sat 10–5; Sun 1–5. Closed Thanksgiving, Christmas Day, and New Year's Day. Admission: free. Restrooms and museum shop. Special programs are ongoing, call for details. The Lyceum auditorium is available for rental for events.

Continue west on Duke St one block and cross S. Washington St. Turn right and walk up S. Washington St one block to the Lyceum (c. 1839; attributed to Benjamin Hallowell; restored 1974; Carroll Curtice), Alexandria's history museum.

**Highlights:** The permanent collection spans three centuries of Alexandria history. Highlights include a reproduction of the Hooe drawing room, portraits of the Ramsay family, furniture manufactured by the Green Steam Furniture Works, and the May and Howard Joynt Collection of Alexandria-made silver. These are included in changing exhibits throughout the year. A children's station in the South Gallery provides materials for children to color pictures of colonial life or draw maps of Alexandria. The gift shop sells children's books about colonial life and historical figures.

### History

In 1834, Benjamin Hallowell, a Quaker schoolmaster, and six other culturally concerned Alexandrians formed the Lyceum Company in order to provide lectures and debates on numerous subjects. In 1839, the Lyceum Company joined with the Alexandria Library Company (founded in 1794) to construct a cultural center that would house a lecture hall and the library's collection. The library used the south room on the first floor and by 1857 had grown to 4,600 books. Lectures were given on the second floor by speakers of national fame, including

John Quincy Adams. Debates were held on various questions, but religion and politics were barred as subject matter.

During the Civil War, the Lyceum served as a hospital. After the war, the Lyceum Company was disbanded, and the building was sold to John B. Daingerfield, who converted it into a private dwelling for his daughter and her family. The building was remodeled for office use in 1940. In 1970, the building was purchased by the city of Alexandria; it was restored in 1974.

## Exterior
The Lyceum is one of two public buildings in Alexandria constructed in the Greek revival style. (The Athenaeum is the other.) The pediment front is supported by four fluted Doric columns.

## Interior
Two entrance doors lead into the central hall, which has an information desk. Directly beyond the table, in a smaller hallway, is a rack of brochures for local attractions. The first floor has a museum shop and restrooms. The exhibit hall on the right features temporary exhibitions, such as the history of Alexandria's Jewish residents. The **North Gallery** is devoted to the early history of the region.

The Lyceum has a city map and a display of silver made by Alexandria's silversmiths. One exhibit informs visitors that Alexandria was one of the largest importers of slaves in the country in the early part of the 19C. A reproduction of the drawing room from the Robert T. Hooe mansion dominates the rest of the gallery, with portraits of the Ramsay family also featured. Directly across from the exhibit is a collection of Native American artifacts.

Exit the North Gallery and cross the central hallway to the **South Gallery.** Prominently displayed in the center of the room are three pieces of furniture produced at the Green Steam Furniture Works. The furnishings include an inexpensive wardrobe in the Gothic revival style, dated 1869–79; an Eastlake sideboard, dated 1880–84; and a desk, made to furnish City Hall, dated 1871. The desk was rescued when the building burned down that year; it was discovered in storage at the Ramsay House Visitors Center some years later.

Immediately on the right are exhibits about activities during World War II, including a clipping concerning the Torpedo Factory and an example of the shells produced. Along the wall around the room are displays of a soldier's uniform and equipment from World War II, information about local transportation history, and various items relating to industrial growth in Alexandria.

Exit the Lyceum and walk several yds to the corner of Prince and S. Washington Sts. In the middle of the intersection is the **Alexandria Confederate Memorial** (c. 1889; designed by John A. Elder, executed by M. Casper Buberl). A plaque on the corner in front of the Lyceum provides information about the memorial.

### History
The soldier faces south, his head bowed in sorrow—a scene from the painting *Appomattox* (also by John A. Elder). The memorial commemorates the 100 Confederate dead from Alexandria and was erected on the spot where they assembled to march to war on May 24, 1861. The statue was erected and dedicated on May

24, 1889. Originally, the memorial was surrounded by a 40 by 60 ft grassed area with a fence and gas lamps, but these were removed in order to accommodate modern traffic requirements. Although the statue has been knocked down by careless motorists and has been labeled a traffic hazard by some, an 1890 ordinance by the Virginia Assembly requires that it remain in this spot forever.

## Friendship Firehouse

107 S. Alfred St, Alexandria, VA. ☎ (703) 838-3891. Open Fri–Sat 10–4; Sun 1–4. Closed on Thanksgiving, Christmas Day, and New Year's Day. Admission: free. Walk west on Prince St for two blocks, cross S. Alfred St, then cross Prince St. Walk north on S. Alfred St to the Friendship Firehouse (c. 1855; architect unknown; remodeled 1871; restored 1992).

### History

The Friendship Fire Company was established in 1774; it was the first volunteer fire company in Alexandria. George Washington was a member, and tradition has it that he purchased and presented the company with its first fire engine in 1775, after having seen one demonstrated in Philadelphia. That original engine was sold a number of times before it was returned to Friendship Veterans Fire Engine Company on permanent loan in 1954. Note that the company's fire mark is duplicated in the weather vane atop the cupola.

### Interior

The **first floor** displays manually drawn fire engines, buckets, axes, hoses, and other historic firefighting equipment. At the base of the stairs, the company's fire mark is displayed. Customers subscribed to a fire company, displaying its emblem in case of fire.

Ascend the staircase to the **second floor,** where a book of letters to and from honorary members of the Friendship Fire Company members is displayed. Notables offered honorary membership in the fire company include Winston Churchill, Presidents Herbert Hoover, Harry Truman, Dwight Eisenhower, and George Bush, General Douglas MacArthur, and Washington Redskin players John Riggins and Joe Theisman. Lining the walls are ceremonial objects used by the company, including parade uniforms, capes, and banners.

> ### Washington Notes
>
> A display on the wall notes that George Washington attended a meeting on April 16, 1777, in City Hall, and the Friendship Fire Company was located nearby at Market Square. While the meeting was going on, a fire broke out across the street at McKnight's Tavern at the corner of Royal and King Sts. Friendship Fire Company provided firefighting support, with Washington reportedly manning the pumps.

### Diversion:

Turn left and walk to the corner of King St. Nearby, the George Washington Masonic National Memorial (1932; Helmle and Corbett) can be seen at the top of Shooter's Hill. To visit the memorial, walk six blocks west on King St (three blocks past the King St Metro station) to Callahan Dr.

# George Washington Masonic National Memorial

101 Callahan Dr, Alexandria, VA. ☎ (703) 683-2007. Web: www.gwmemorial. org. Open daily 9–5. Guided tours on the half hour in the morning, on the hour in the afternoon. Restrooms. Wheelchair accessible. Museum gift shop.

**Highlights:** A collection of items used by George Washington, including the chair he sat in as worshiful master and the clock that was stopped at the hour of his death by Dr. Elisha Cullen Dick. Famous paintings include Sir Joshua Reynolds's portrait of Lord Thomas Fairfax and Charles Peal Polk's portrait of the Marquis de Lafayette. A replica of the Ark of the Covenant and a re-creation of King Solomon's Temple are noteworthy, as is the view from the observation level.

### History

When Gerald Alexander and friends made a trip up the shoreline of the Potomac and landed at what would become Alexandria, they noted a ramshackle building occupied by William Shuter, a river man who made his living selling water beer to passersby. Although Alexander owned the land, Shuter held squatter's rights. Alexander offered him the large hill on the other side of the swamp, which bore the name Shuter's Hill thereafter.

> #### Washington Notes
> Following the Revolutionary War, Alexander Hamilton and Thomas Jefferson selected Shuter's Hill for the site of the Capitol Building because of its height and location. Washington objected, fearing that he would be criticized for favoritism because he owned large amounts of land in nearby Virginia and would benefit from the selection.

At the beginning of the Civil War, Union soldiers seized Shuter's Hill and built a fort and observation tower. Named Fort Ellsworth in honor of Colonel Elmer Ellsworth, considered one of the first Union soldiers killed in the Civil War, the fort served as the headquarters for those stationed in Alexandria, and the hill was used to train troops. The guns on the hill were fired daily. Eventually, the constant firing of the guns caused the name to be changed to Shooter's Hill.

In 1909, the Wright brothers made a historic flight from Fort Meyer to Shooter's Hill and back again. The purpose of the flight was to test the Wrights' Military Flyer, the first military aircraft in the world. The plane is on display in the National Air and Space Museum.

Charles Callahan chose the site to be the location of the new lodge hall and museum for the Alexandria-Washington Masonic Lodge. Groundbreaking took place on June 5, 1922, and the cornerstone was laid by President Coolidge in 1923. The building itself took more than ten years to construct; donations were collected from more than 3 million Masons throughout the United States to pay for the memorial.

## Exterior

The Masonic Memorial stands on Shooter's Hill and is modeled after the lighthouse that stood in the harbor at Alexandria, Egypt. The design was modified in 1920 to accommodate the addition of elevators, a tower, and the observation level.

Shooter's Hill is made of clay, part of a prehistoric river. The clay, which remained stable when dry, was kept moist by underground water sources. In order to support the weight of the monument building, a concrete cap was poured over the top of the hill—some nine ft deep in the center—to keep the clay moist at all times.

## Interior

The two lower floors of the memorial are open to the public. The upper tower rooms are included in special guided tours. Visitors enter through **Memorial Hall.** At the far end of the hall, which is lined with Doric columns, is a 17 ft 3 inches tall statue of George Washington, the first worshipful master of the Alexandria lodge.

Along each wall of the hall are two large murals painted by artist Allyn Cox in the 1950s. The mural on the right wall is *George Washington and Brethren in Saint John's Day Observance, Christ Church, Philadelphia, December 28, 1778.* The mural on the left wall depicts *George Washington Laying the Cornerstone of the National Capitol, September 18, 1793.* There are six stained glass windows, three on each side of the hall. Brother Robert M. Metcalf, a stained glass artist, installed the windows, which were designed by Allyn Cox.

Exit Memorial Hall to the left to enter the gift shop. Beyond, on the right, is the entrance to the **auditorium.** Along the back wall are plaques depicting 14 past presidents who were Masons. On the left is the **Lodge Room** and **Hall of Past Masters.**

Descend the staircase to the **lower level.** Turn left and go through the double glass doors. The hallway directly ahead is lined with photographs taken during the construction and dedication of the memorial, and there is an assembly hall that displays dioramas of Washington's life. Prominently displayed in the center is a large Persian rug, produced for Persian royalty in the 1600s. The rug took 12 people 27 years to create.

No visitors are allowed above the lower levels without a tour guide. The tour of the tower levels takes approximately 45 minutes. Most of the memorial's treasures are stored in these upper levels.

### Diversion:

From the Friendship Fire Company, walk north on Alfred St six blocks to the **Alexandria Black History Resource Center** at 638 N. Alfred St, ☎ (703) 833-4356. The building was constructed in 1940 as the Robinson Library, the African American community's first public library in the city. Converted to a community center in the 1960s, the building reopened as the Alexandria Black History Resource Center in 1983. The staff presents lectures, tours of the center, and other activities relating to the history and accomplishments of African Americans in Alexandria. Paintings, photographs, books, and other memorabilia document the African American experience in Alexandria and in Virginia from 1749 to the present.

The center also maintains the **Alexandria African American Heritage Park** (Duke St on Holland Lane), an eight-acre memorial park, one acre of which is a preserved 19C African American cemetery. Six of the known 21 burial sites have intact headstones and are in their original location. There is also a wetland area that has mallards, painted turtles, beavers, and crayfish in a natural habitat.

# Christ Church

118 N. Washington St, Alexandria, VA. ☎ (703) 549-1450. Open Mon–Sat 9–4;
Sun 2–4:30. Admission: free, but donations are accepted. Lectures are presented
by docents. Gift shop in the Parish Hall.

From the corner of King and S. Alfred Sts, walk east one block, cross King St,
and then cross N. Columbus St. Walk north one block to the corner of Cameron
and Washington Sts and the entrance of Christ Church (c. 1767–73; James
Wren). The church is one of two pre-Revolutionary churches remaining in
Alexandria; the other is the Old Presbyterian Meeting House.

### History

John Alexander donated one acre of land to build a permanent church. James Parsons agreed to build the church for £600 but failed to finish the building. John
Carlyle completed the work in 1773. George Washington served as one of the 12
vestrymen of Christ Church, known simply as the Church until 1811. Robert E.
Lee first attended services as a boy and met with Confederate representatives at the
church to discuss taking command of Virginia's forces at the beginning of the
Civil War.

The churchyard served as the town's burial ground until the opening of the
town's Presbyterian church. During the Civil War, many of the gravestones were
looted and the remaining ones stacked against the south wall. When they were replaced, two grave markers of black slate were placed by themselves—that of Isaac
Pierce of Boston (1771) and Captain James Munford of New London, Connecticut (1773). Although not the original burial site of either, legend has it that feelings were running high and the stones, belonging to Northerners, were separated
from those of the local Southern men who had died.

Among those buried in the churchyard are Thomas West; Ann Warren, an actress; Charles Simms, a friend of George Washington's; and Eleanor Wren, wife of
James Wren. A memorial shaped vaguely like the Washington Monument stands
at the far right of the current churchyard—an exception to the town ordinance
forbidding burials within town limits after 1809. Charles Bennett, a benefactor of
the city, was buried here by public decree in 1839.

### Washington Notes

Washington was an original pew holder, having purchased a box pew for £36
15S. He attended Sunday services here before leaving for Philadelphia to take
command of the Continental Army in 1775; he also attended services here on
Christmas Day, 1783, immediately after he had resigned as general of the
army. Washington attended services regularly at Christ Church after 1785. It
is a tradition that U.S. presidents attend a service here on a Sun close to Washington's birthday. On Jan 1, 1942, President Franklin Delano Roosevelt, First
Lady Eleanor Roosevelt, and British Prime Minister Winston Churchill sat in
Washington's pew for the service of a World Day of Prayer for Peace during
World War II. Silver medallions along the back of the pew note the occasion.

## Exterior

The early-Georgian-style church was designed by James Wren, and the initial
building was completed in 1773. The structure was built with local brick laid in

a Flemish bond, its high-arched windows are made of handblown glass, and it has a steep hipped roof. The cupola was believed to have been added in 1799, and the bell tower in 1820.

## Interior

When the church was constructed, the pews were originally boxed pews, intended for ease of listening and protection from the cold. In 1817, the pews were modified to slip pews so the congregation would be facing forward. The galleries were added in 1787 to allow more seating.

The original organ (there have been five) was installed in 1810, and chimneys were added. A glass chandelier, ordered from England, was installed on pulleys in 1817 but has been replaced with a larger, electric model. The original chandelier is hung between two pillars.

Walk up the right aisle and across the front of the church. The two panels flanking the pulpit were installed by John Carlyle, and the lettering completed by James Wren. The panels contain the Apostle's Creed, the Ten Commandments, and the Lord's Prayer. The tablets have never been retouched.

Walk down the left aisle. George Washington's family pew is the box-shaped pew on the right, a combination of nos. 59 and 60, and is marked by a small silver marker. It is the only pew in the church that was not modified from its original box construction. The Lee family pew is on the left side of the aisle, no. 46. Robert E. Lee was confirmed here in 1853. Although the original flooring was brick over flagstone, it has since been replaced with granite. While there were a number of changes to the interior of the church, it was restored in 1890 to its original colonial appearance, much as it may be seen today.

Exit the churchyard at N. Washington St. and walk north to no. 212. At the street is a brass marker denoting the site of the first **Synagogue of the Beth El Hebrew Congregation.** The congregation gathered here in 1859. A synagogue was built in 1871 and was in use until 1954, when the building was razed to make way for new construction.

## Lloyd House

220 N. Washington St, Alexandria, VA. ☎ (703) 838-4577. Open Mon–Sat 9–5. Closed Sun and all major holidays.

At the end of the block on N. Washington St is the Federal-style Lloyd House (c. 1798; John Wise), the main historical branch of the Alexandria Library.

### History

The house, built by John Wise, the owner of Gadsby's Tavern, was rented to James Marshall, assistant judge of the Circuit Court of D.C. in 1802. The house was sold to Jacob Hoffman, former mayor of Alexandria, in 1810. It was later rented to Benjamin Hallowell, who ran the Hallowell School at this location from 1826 to 1832. John Lloyd bought the house at auction in 1832. His wife was the daughter of Edmund Jennings Lee, and Robert E. Lee was a frequent visitor. The Lloyds owned the house until 1918, and it still bears their name.

In 1918, the house was purchased by Albert Smoot, a lumber dealer and mayor of Alexandria. The Smoot family owned it until 1942, when the property became a rooming house, providing housing for many who worked at the Torpedo Factory during the war. Twice the house was saved from demolition by the Historical Society of Alexandria, and in 1969 the property was purchased for use as a historical repository for Alexandria and Virginia history.

The Lloyd House has excellent research materials for genealogists, archeologists, scholars, and historians. The facility also has a fine collection of Civil War materials. In the first-floor library is a small collection of 18C and 19C books from the Alexandria Library Company, a subscription library formed in 1794.

Walk north on N. Washington St two blocks, crossing Queen Stand then Princess St. This section of **Princess St** is designated as a historic street and retains its original cobblestone roadway. Some believe that the cobblestones used on the street were ballast rock from ships around the world. Tradition has it that Hessian soldiers provided the labor to cobble Princess St.

Continue on N. Washington St to the **Edmund Jennings Lee House** at 428 N. Washington St. The house was under construction when Charles Lee purchased it in 1800. Three months later, he transferred ownership to his brother, Edmund Jennings Lee. Lee served as a warden of Christ Church and as Alexandria's mayor from 1815 to 1818.

> ### Washington Notes
> In 1811, Christ Church's right to own land was questioned. Edmund Jennings Lee and Charles Simms, both lawyers, fought as advocates for the church. Eventually, they obtained a special act of Congress to protect the church's right to own property.

## Lee-Fendall House Museum

614 Oronoco St, Alexandria, VA. ☎ (703) 548-1789. Open Tues–Sat 10–4; Sun 1–4. Closed Mon. Admission fee.

Cross N. Washington St. On the southeast corner of N. Washington and Oronco Sts is the Lee-Fendall House Museum (1785; architect unknown; remodeled 1850, Louis A. Cazenove), one of the oldest houses associated with the Lee family in the area.

### History

The house was built in 1785 by Phillip Richard Fendall, cousin of General Henry "Light-Horse Harry" Lee. Fendall was a lawyer, director of the Potomac Canal Company, and a founder of the Bank of Alexandria. Fendall had three wives, all members of the Lee family, including Letitia Lee, Elizabeth Steptoe Lee, and Lee's sister, Mary Lee. In 1792, the house was deeded to Richard Bland Lee. Thirty-seven members of the Lee family lived in the house between 1785 and 1903. General Lee and his wife were frequent visitors. Fendall was also an associate of George Washington's. Washington and his wife dined here nine times.

In 1850 the house was purchased by Louis Cazenove, who renovated the structure using elements of the Greek revival style. This is the period style that the museum retains today.

During the Civil War, the house was seized and used as a hospital from 1863 to 1865. In 1937, John L. Lewis, president of the United Mine Workers, bought the house. Upon his death, the Virginia Trust for Historic Preservation purchased the site.

## Exterior

The Greek revival–style house was built of frame over brick, a typical construction method for that period.

## Interior

Visitors enter at the **main hallway.** The ceiling trim, interior archway, fanlight, and bull's-eye molding were all added during the 1850 renovation.

To the right is the **north parlor,** the formal entertaining area of the house. The furnishings are period pieces, but not original to the house. Many were manufactured at the Green Steam Furniture Works in Alexandria. The portraits of Harriet, granddaughter of Richard Henry Lee, and her husband, Louis Cazenove, are on the far wall.

On the wall, to the left of the fireplace, is a large white button with a handle mounted on a silver plaque. The device was attached to a set of five bells in the kitchen. When the handle was turned, a bell rang. Each bell had a different tone so that servants would know to which room they were being summoned.

The **south parlor,** directly behind the north parlor, served as the informal family room. Portraits of Richard Henry Lee, signer of the Declaration of Independence, and his brother Arthur are on the far wall. The desk was used in the house in the 1830s but was taken to the Lee family estate, Bedford. When Union soldiers burned Bedford, the desk was saved. The upper portion was lost at some point, but scorch marks from the fire can still be seen inside the bottom drawer. The long windows to the sun porch and the part of the sun porch adjacent to this parlor were added in 1850.

The family **dining room** is across the main hallway. The china and silver were owned by the Lee family. On the table is a sardine dish and a multitined fork used to serve them; a china container for condensed milk with its silver serving spoon; and an unusual ceramic dish made to hold cheese. On the wall at the far end of the room is a reproduction of a portrait of Henry "Light-Horse Harry" Lee, from the original painted by Charles Willson Peale.

It was at the Fendall house that Henry Lee composed the Farewell Address Colonel Dennis Ramsay delivered to Washington on the way to his inauguration as president. Henry Lee also composed the eulogy for George Washington while visiting the Fendall house. On the wall beside the entrance is a copy of the *Spectator,* a New York newspaper dated Jan 15, 1800. It reports that Henry "Light-Horse Harry" Lee delivered the eulogy, which contained the famous words, "First in war—first in peace—first in the hearts of his countrymen."

On the wall going upstairs are a series of portraits of various members of the Lee family dating back to the mid-1600s, beginning with Richard "the Immigrant." A certificate at the landing is from the Society of Cincinnati, given to those soldiers who served in the Continental Army and some of their French counterparts. The certificate was presented to General Henry Lee and signed by George Washington. Along the upper stairs are portraits of military generals of the Civil War, including Robert E. Lee.

An elevator was added to the house as well as "modern heating" during the time of John Lewis. The elevator is still in use today. A portrait of John L. Lewis is on the right wall of the landing, in front of the room now used as museum offices. To the left, the **south bedroom** is furnished as the parents' bedroom. The quilt is dated 1873, and the fire screen is typical of the period. The bedroom furnishings are part of a suite, all being of the same machined design. The bedspread was knitted and hand crocheted. The settee was brought to Alexandria by a sea captain who had purchased it in India, although it had been made in England. On the wall next to the doorway leading to the north bedroom is a small oval glass containing a lock of Henry Clay's hair, dated 1846. A closet between the bedrooms has been glassed-in and contains period personal items such as women's hat pins, a "mangler" used to crush cloth, and a glass and silver jar used to collect women's hair.

The **north bedroom** is furnished as a girl's bedroom. A sewing machine with a patent date of 1871 is prominent. Period clothing and sheet music are displayed, as are period underwear and several curling irons. A collection of Lee family dolls and doll houses are on the third floor, which would have been the children's bedroom.

Exit the Lee-Fendall House and cross Oronoco St. At 609 Oronoco St is the **Hallowell School** (c. 1795; William Wilson), which Robert E. Lee attended. Lee returned here from Feb to June 1825 for tutoring to prepare for his entrance exams to the U.S. Military Academy.

### History

Benjamin Hallowell was a Quaker schoolmaster. After moving to Alexandria, he opened his first school in this building in 1820. Robert E. Lee was the 13th student to enroll. Hallowell's school became well known and moved to larger quarters at the Lloyd House, and from there to a converted sugar barn. Hallowell recalls in his journals that the Marquis de Lafayette passed by Hallowell's home on his way to pay his respects to General Henry Lee's widow. Lafayette "made us a graceful bow, not knowing it was to a lady who had been married the day before." Thereafter, Hallowell teased his wife gently, calling her his "Lafayette wife." Hallowell was active in the literary life of the community, instrumental in founding the Lyceum, and established the Alexandria Water Company.

## Boyhood Home of Robert E. Lee

607 Oronoco St, Alexandria, VA. ☎ (703) 548-8454. Open Mon–Sat 10–4; Sun 1–4. Admission charged. Thirty-minute guided tours; last one at 3:30.

The house immediately adjacent to the Hallowell school, no. 607, is the Boyhood Home of Robert E. Lee (c. 1795; John Potts, Jr.). It used to serve as a museum of the Lee family, but the property was recently sold as a private home. As of press time, there are attempts by members of the community to purchase the property and keep it open as a museum.

### History

The house was built in 1795 by John Potts, Jr., on a half-block lot. The property was purchased in 1799 by William Fitzhugh. George Washington was known to have dined here with Potts and with Fitzhugh. On July 7, 1804, Fitzhugh's daughter, Mary Lee Fitzhugh, married George Washington Parke Custis, Martha Washington's grandson. Fitzhugh died in 1809.

Henry "Light-Horse Harry" Lee moved his family from their ancestral Stratford Hall to Alexandria in 1810, leasing a house on Cameron St before moving to this house in 1812. His son Robert E. Lee was 5 years old at the time. After Henry died, his widow, formerly Ann Hill Carter, and her children, including young Robert, lived here until 1825, when Robert left for the U.S. Military Academy at West Point.

## Exterior

The house is a twin of its neighbor, the Hallowell School (no. 607), built in a box-like Federal style with widely spaced windows. The addition of a rear wing created an L-shaped building. The ground-floor kitchen and second-floor nursery occupy the addition. The exterior of the house has been restored to its original condition. The garden has been partially restored.

## Interior

**First floor.** (Note: The following section describes the house when it was open to the public as museum.) To the left of the entrance is the **drawing room,** where Mrs. Henry Lee entertained General Lafayette during his 1824 visit to the U.S. Of particular interest is the fabric "Welcome Lafayette" souvenir preserved in this room.

Across the entrance hall is the **large dining room,** containing the portraits of William Fitzhugh, Fitzhugh's wife, and General Henry Lee. This was also called the formal dining room and was used for guests. Behind the large dining room is the morning room, a gathering place and informal dining room. The family's everyday china (a fine collection of Nanking and Canton) and a book of Homer in both Latin and Greek are displayed here, a reminder that Robert E. Lee could read both languages. On the walls of the hallway leading back to the kitchen are the Lee family genealogies. The kitchen has the original fireplace, with an imported cast-iron oven in one side.

**Second floor.** Take the main staircase to the second floor. The **children's bedroom** features a child-size canopy bed, a rocking cradle, and handmade toys. The **master bedroom** has a portrait of Ann Hill Carter Lee, Robert E. Lee's mother. The **guest room** displays a large canopy bed with portable steps containing a drawer for a chamber pot, and a combination fire screen and gentleman's traveling wash stand called a Beau Brummel.

Walk east on Oronoco St. Cross St. Asaph St, turn right, and walk to 403 Oronoco St, the **Alexandria Jail** (c. 1831; Charles Bulfinch). The original 1831 jail has been enlarged over the years.

> ### Washington Notes
> Jailors were much more lenient in colonial days. Sefer Blouse, a German restaurateur on King St, was arrested for some minor offense. When it was found that the confinement of jail was damaging to his health, he was released each day to take a walk; every night he returned to the jail in time for dinner.

Continue on Oronoco St, crossing Princess and Queen Sts. At Cameron St, cross St. Asaph St and walk west on Cameron to no. 607, the **Lord Fairfax House** (c. 1816; Thomas Yeaton).

### History

Thomas Yeaton built this Federal-style town house in 1816. Although he arrived in Alexandria to work in the shipping business, Yeaton became a builder and an architect. Yeaton designed and built the new burial vault at Mount Vernon. Thomas, the ninth Lord of Fairfax, purchased the house in 1830 and used it as his winter residence. His son, Dr. Orlando Fairfax, lived in the house after his father's death in 1846 until after the Civil War.

Walk up Oronoco St to no. 611, the **General Henry Lee House** (c. 1795; John Brogue). John Brogue, a cabinetmaker, built both nos. 609 and 611 Cameron St. In 1810, General Lee moved his family from Stratford Hall, leasing this house for one year.

### History

Henry Lee was born in Dumfries, Virginia, in 1756. When the Revolution began, he joined the Continental Army as captain of calvary. He was involved in most of the major battles in New York, New Jersey, and Pennsylvania, where he earned the nickname Light-Horse Harry for his daring raids.

"Lee's Legion" was known for its effective use of guerilla tactics. In 1781, Lee resigned his commission due to ill health. From 1785 to 1788, he was a member of the Continental Congress. From 1791 to 1794, Lee served as governor of Virginia. His first wife died in 1789, and he married Ann Hill Carter in 1795. From 1799 to 1801, Lee served in the House of Representatives.

When the War of 1812 approached, Lee accepted a commission as major general. On the way to his command, he stopped to visit a friend, Alexander Contee Hanson, at the latter's house in Baltimore. Hanson was editor of the *Federal Republican*. As a result of articles in the paper, a mob stormed Hanson's house and Lee was wounded. Although Lee went to the West Indies for several years, he never truly recovered from the wound and died in March 1818.

Walk back east on Cameron to St. Asaph St and cross the street. Walk south on St. Asaph St to King St and cross King. Turn east and walk one block, crossing Pitt St. At the southeast corner of King and Pitt Sts was the site of the **Marshall House** (c. 1785), now a Holiday Inn.

### History

Although the building burned down in 1872, the Marshall House earned a place in history during the Civil War. The original three-story brick house, built by John Dundas in 1785, was used at various times as a tavern and a boardinghouse. When Virginia voted to secede on April 17, 1861, the proprietor, James W. Jackson, ran the Confederate flag up the flagpole on the roof. It was said that the flag was so big that it could be seen from the White House across the river. Jackson swore to defend the flag with his life.

On May 13, Federal troops under the command of Colonel Elmer Ellsworth arrived to take possession of the city. One of Ellsworth's first acts was to march his troops to the Marshall House to remove the flag. Jackson was awakened and appeared on the landing with his shotgun. One blast killed Colonel Ellsworth, and Jackson was subsequently killed by Corporal Francis Brownell, who accompanied Ellsworth.

Colonel Ellsworth was considered to be one of the first casualties of the Civil War, and the Union fort built on Shuter's Hill (later known as Shooter's Hill) was named in his honor.

## Gadsby's Tavern

134 N. Royal St, Alexandria, VA. ☎ (703) 838-4242. Open April–Sept Tues–Sat 10–5, Sun 1–5; Oct–March Tues–Sat 11–4, Sun 1–4. Closed Mon. Restrooms and gift shop. Guided tours available; admission fee charged. Restaurant open to the public.

Walk east on King St to Royal St and cross King St. Walk one block north on Royal St to Gadsby's Tavern (c. 1770; probably built by John Carlyle; 1792, John Wise; 1972–76 restoration, J. W. Fauber), one of the most well known of Alexandria's taverns.

### History

The establishment known as Gadsby's Tavern consists of two buildings, the 1770 tavern and the 1792 City Hotel. The buildings are named for John Gadsby, who operated them from 1796 to 1808. Gadsby's establishment was the center for Alexandria's political, business, and social life. The tavern hosted many social events, dancing assemblies, theatrical and musical performances, and meetings. The tavern also served as a gathering place for local residents, a place for travelers to eat and sleep, and a place for merchants to sell their wares.

George Washington frequently enjoyed the hospitality provided by tavern-keepers Mary Hawkins (the original owner), John Wise (who built the City Hotel in 1792), and John Gadsby (who leased the property in 1796). Under Gadsby's management, the establishment gained a reputation for excellence and was recommended by George Washington. General and Mrs. Washington attended the annual Birthnight Ball held in his honor here in 1798 and 1799. The tradition continues today as the Birthnight Ball is re-created on Washington's birthday each year. Other prominent people who were entertained at Gadsby's include John Adams, Thomas Jefferson, James Monroe, and the Marquis de Lafayette.

After serving until the late 19C as a tavern and hotel, the buildings went through a variety of commercial uses and fell into disrepair. In 1929, American Legion Post 24 purchased the buildings, saving them from demolition. In 1972 the buildings were given to the city of Alexandria; they were restored by J. W. Fauber and reopened for the 1976 Bicentennial celebration. The museum receives donations from the community.

### Exterior

The 1770 building is Georgian style. It was known as the City Tavern, A Bunch of Grapes, and the Fountain Tavern. The building was believed to have been renovated or rebuilt by Wise after he purchased it. The 1792 building, in the Federal style, was built by John Wise and opened as the City Hotel.

### Interior

The museum is located at the entrance to the 1770 building, and the gift shop is on the right immediately inside the entrance. On the left of the main hallway is the **Public Tap Room.** The room is set up as it may have been in the 18C, with mismatched furnishings and china. Note that the overturned chair and cracked china may have resulted from a dispute arising over politics, or simply from imbibing a bit too much of the potent punch in the large bowl on the central table.

To the right of the hallway is the **Private Dining Room.** George Washington is known to have enjoyed an excellent meal of canvasback duck, hominy grits, and Madeira wine in this room. The stairway leads to an **Assembly Room** where groups gathered to watch local entertainment. The large room has chairs lining the walls.

Further up the stairway are three dormer **bedchambers.** Travelers to the tavern did not typically rent a room, but rather a place to sleep. A posted advertisement for the period stated that the beds were furnished with clean sheets. For one to a bed, the fee was six pence, but up to three people could share a bed.

The bedchamber is furnished with one bedstead (wooden frame with rope) but two "beds"—mattresses filled with straw. A trunk on the floor was used by travelers to store belongings. On the left is a large bedchamber, with two bedsteads and three beds. A wig stand and curlers, which appear to be pieces of chalk, are displayed.

Walk through a modern passageway to the 1792 building. Walk down the hallway to the left. The doorway on the right leads into the **Ballroom.** Mounted on the wall to the right is a Musician's Balcony, furnished with a chair and music stand. Musicians climbed the ladder in the hall to get to the balcony.

Exit the building and walk to the left. Visitors may choose to enjoy a meal in the public area of Gadsby's Tavern, or continue around the corner up Cameron St. On the left is a set of stairs leading down to a small patio. A view through large windows offers a glimpse into the **ice house,** a relic of prerefrigeration days. A plaque explains that such wells were used in the 18C and 19C to store ice packed in straw during warm months. The well consisted of a shallow brick dome, a circular shaft 15 ft deep and 17 ft in diameter, and a sand-covered floor. A brick tunnel extended from the well to the basement of the tavern.

Ice was used to prepare desserts for the tavern and was also sold to the public, although many complained of the prices charged by Gadsby. His ice was eight cents per pound, while others in the area charged six cents.

Cross Royal St and walk east on Cameron St. **City Hall** (c. 1873; 1961), occupies this block. The building sits on the site of the original Fairfax County Court House Building. In earlier days of the town, the market house, fire engine company, stocks, jail, and a school were located on this site at one time or another. The brick market house built on the site in 1817 burned down in 1871. In 1873, the south side of the current building was erected, and the south addition was added in 1961. The building houses the Alexandria City Government offices.

### Diversion:
Continue to the corner and turn right on N. Fairfax St and walk to **Market Square.** Today, as in colonial times, the square serves as a meeting place and for public programs. The stocks, however, are gone. In their place are a public fountain, surrounded by a brick courtyard and plantings along the borders. Convenient, shaded seating areas invite visitors to linger. Events are scheduled on many weekends throughout the year. Information can be obtained from the Ramsay House Visitors Center.

### Washington Notes
George Washington became a trustee of the market in 1766. He was instrumental in having a law passed that required merchants to have their

measures tested by a single standard yearly. A set of weights purchased from England in 1744 and engraved with "County of Fairfax" were used to test all other measures. Under the same law, hay scales were placed on St. Asaph Street. The set of measures are currently on display at the Masonic Memorial and are known to be the only complete set of English standards in the country.

Continue east on Cameron St and cross N. Fairfax St. Turn left and cross Cameron St. The building on the northeast corner at 201 N. Fairfax St is the **Ann Lee Memorial Home** (c. 1777; John Dalton, Thomas Herbert), now a folk art shop. Ann Lee was Henry Lee's wife and Robert E. Lee's mother.

### History
John Dalton, who purchased the property, began construction but died before the house was completed. His son-in-law, Thomas Herbert, completed the construction and rented the building. It had an unusual L-shaped configuration with frontage on both Fairfax and Cameron Sts. A stable and carriage house were located behind the building.

Captain Herbert Lyle established a tavern in the buildings and ran it for nine years. When he died, George Leigh succeeded him as tavernkeeper from 1787 to 1788 and gave it the name it carried in succeeding years, A Bunch of Grapes. In 1787, the northern mail stage stopped at and departed from the tavern. John Wise operated the tavern from 1788 to 1792, before he purchased what is now known as Gadsby's Tavern. When he changed locations, he took the name with him. Other tavernkeepers followed until 1800.

Many of the local gentry dined here, including Washington, members of the Alexandria Jockey Club, and the directors of the Potomac Company. On April 16, 1789, Colonel Dennis Ramsay, then mayor of Alexandria, delivered his farewell address to Washington on the way to his inauguration from the steps of the building. A bronze plaque on the building identifies it as Wise's Tavern (1788–92), where on April 16, 1789, "George Washington was for the first time publicly addressed as President of the United States."

Miss Fannie Burke purchased the building in 1900 and established a home for the elderly that eventually became a widow's home. In 1916, the building was dedicated as a living memorial to Ann Hill Carter Lee, widow of General Henry "-Light-Horse Harry" Lee, and it has since been known as the Ann Lee Memorial Home.

Cross Cameron St. The building on the southeast corner, 133 Cameron St, was the **Bank of Alexandria** (c. 1807; Thomas Herbert).

### History
The Bank of Alexandria was established by an act of the Virginia Assembly in 1792. The amount required to open the bank was determined to be $150,000, and shares were sold for $200 each. Construction on the building at this site began in 1803 but was not completed until 1807. The banking room occupied the main floor, and living quarters for the cashier and his family were above. The bank failed in 1834, mainly because of heavy investments in the Potowmack Canal Company, in which George Washington was also involved.

### Washington Notes

George Washington was one of the original shareholders of the Bank of Alexandria. One of the first items in his will was the gift of $1,000 or 50 shares of stock in the Bank of Alexandria to the Alexandria Free School for the Education of Poor Boys—specifying that only the dividends could be used. However, he noted that if the bank were in danger of failure, the funds could be reinvested in another public institution. The trustees placed their trust in the bank and lost the total amount of the endowment when the bank failed.

In 1848 the building was purchased by James Green, owner of Green Steam Furniture Works, and converted to a hotel. Additions, since removed, were made in 1855. The property was known as Green's Mansion House Hotel. During the Civil War, it served as a hospital. The building was purchased by the Park Authority in 1970.

## Carlyle House

121 N. Fairfax St, Alexandria, VA. ☎ (703) 549-2997. Open Tues–Sat 10–4:30; Sun 12–4:30. Closed Mon. Guided tours, admission charged. Gift shop.

The property to the right of the bank is the Carlyle House (c. 1752; architect unknown; restored 1970s), former home of John Carlyle, a Scottish merchant.

### History

John Carlyle was born in Carlisle, England. He came to America as a merchant's representative in 1741 and settled in Dumfries, Virginia. He married Sarah Fairfax, the daughter of William Fairfax of Belvoir.

When the first property auction was held in 1749, Carlyle purchased two of the most expensive lots on the waterfront immediately adjacent to Market Square. Carlyle, one of the town's first trustees, was the commissary for the Virginia militia during the French and Indian War and the justice of the peace for Fairfax County. Well-liked among the gentry, Carlyle was an astute business man and a friend of George Washington's.

Carlyle had the grandest house in town, fashioned after a Scottish manor house. When General Edward Braddock visited Alexandria and requested a conference with five of the colonial governors, the meeting took place at Carlyle House on Aug 16, 1755. On that date, it was proposed that the colonies be taxed for the monies needed to support the continuing French and Indian war. This was an early example of taxation of the colonies without representation.

After Carlyle's death, the house was occupied by his daughter, Sarah, and her husband, William Herbert, the president of the Bank of Alexandria. He built the Bank of Alexandria on the corner of the property in 1807. When the house changed hands, James Green made extensive modifications to the house.

During the Civil War, the house was used as a hospital, then passed to a succession of owners. The Northern Virginia Regional Parks Authority purchased the neglected and deteriorated house in 1970. It took six years to restore the building and grounds, which were opened in time for the country's Bicentennial.

## Exterior

Considered the finest early-Georgian-style mansion in Alexandria, the building is the earliest documented house in the city, built between 1751 and 1753. The design is reminiscent of a Scottish manor house. The house is one of the few set far back from the street in violation of a town ordinance. As a trustee, Carlyle had already begun planning his home and exempted himself from the restrictions.

The early-Georgian style is seen in such details as the steep hipped roof, central chimney, and central floor plan. Note the initialed keystone above the front entrance bearing the initials *JSC* for "John and Sarah Carlyle" and the date 1752. The exterior was built out of sandstone from the Aquia (about 30 miles south of Alexandria) quarry, which Sarah's father owned. At the time, it was the only building in Alexandria not built from brick.

## Interior

Enter the building from the left side, through the museum shop, which is housed in the basement. A ten-minute film orients visitors to the time period. The **slave's quarters** are in the room directly ahead.

The narrow slaves' stairs lead to the main floor. **Carlyle's bedroom** is on the right side of the passageway. A locked closet, unusual in colonial days, is built into the wall on the left. Carlyle's bed, the only original piece of furniture in the house, takes up most of the room. A portrait of his mother, Rachel, hangs above the fireplace.

Across the hall is the **dining hall.** The room is featured "at rest" with the table folded and stored against the wall. Two closets are built into the wall on either side of the fireplace, and a sharkskin cutlery holder is displayed on a table near the entrance.

The **lower passage** features a large, painted, oil cloth floor covering, which was typical of the period. Visitors would use the front entrance if they arrived by carriage, or the back entrance if they arrived by boat. The large open passage could be used as a ballroom or family sitting room on hot days.

The doorway on the left leads to the **small parlor,** probably where Carlyle worked on his personal papers. A portrait of his father hangs over the fireplace. Maps are prominently featured on the wall above the desk. The trim color in this half of the house is Prussian blue glaze imported from England.

The connecting doorway leads to the **large parlor,** where the historic meeting of General Braddock with the five colonial governors took place. A gaming table is placed to the left, and a portrait of John Carlyle hangs over the fireplace. John Carlyle had not seen his brother since leaving England in 1741, so he invited him to exchange portraits. He commissioned an Annapolis painter to produce a portrait of himself to send to his brother. When he viewed the picture, he sent it back to the painter stating that he looked too young. The "five o'clock shadow" was added to the portrait, which is a reproduction of the original. The portrait sent by George, his older brother, hangs on the far wall.

Up the stairs is a landing that looks out over what are now buildings, but in Carlyle's day the view would have been of the waterfront and wharf that he built. Many of the panes still feature handblown glass.

The **upper passage** has a painted oil cloth floor covering, chairs, and a small table. On the left is a bookcase with curios, including a silver-and-horn snuffbox featuring the Carlyle family crest.

A small passageway on the right of the upper passage lead to the children's bedrooms. The room on the right is set up as the **girl's bedroom,** with period furnishings, a canopy bed, clothes, and a large clothespress. On the opposite side of the passageway is the **boy's bedroom.** On the right is a collapsible canopy field bed, popular during that era. Two mattresses rest atop a canvas support, lashed to the bed with rope. One mattress is stuffed with horsehair and the other with feathers. A second bed is set up at the foot of the first, for a visiting friend.

The **architectural room** is perhaps the most interesting one in the house. When renovations were under way, this room was not restored. A "summer" beam in the floor, to which joists were attached, is exposed. The walls have been stripped bare, and the original sandstone block and mortar construction of the outer walls as well as the lath-and-plaster ceiling are visible. Brickwork shows how the fireplaces in the house were altered over time—made smaller to accommodate coal as a fuel rather than wood.

The Carlyle House also has an attractive terraced garden.

## Torpedo Factory Art Center

105 N. Union St, Alexandria, VA. ☎ (703) 838-4565. Web: torpedofactory.org. Open daily 10–5. Restrooms. Exit the garden and walk through the adjacent parking lot to exit on Cameron. Walk east on Cameron to N. Union and cross the street. Walk south a half-block to the entrance to the Torpedo Factory (1918), an artists' center with workshops and galleries. Visitors can watch artists create pottery, silk screens, etchings, and other art, as well as purchase items.

### History

On Nov 12, 1918, construction began on a $2.75 million two-building factory complex to build torpedoes. Building No. 1 housed the commissary and actual production facilities. Building No. 2 was a storage building. Nine hundred torpedoes manufactured and stored in the building were sent to England under the terms of the Lend-Lease Act of 1941. When the United States entered World War II in Dec 1941, the facility was in full production. Almost 10,000 Mark XIV torpedoes were made here, as well as other types of weapons for short periods of time. An actual Mark XIV torpedo is located in the building on the first floor, right passageway. Other memorabilia from the period, such as copies of *The Torp*, the torpedo factory newsletter, are displayed.

After World War II, the government used the building as a storage facility for Nazi war records, archives from the Library of Congress, and dinosaur bones from the Smithsonian. In 1969, the city of Alexandria purchased the building for $1.5 million. In 1974, Martin Van Landingham proposed the creation of an art center and became its first director. The Torpedo Factory Art Center opened its doors on Sept 15, 1974.

The artists at the Torpedo Factory must pass a jury review before being allowed to apply for space. More than 160 artists work here, and the work of an additional 1,500 artists is exhibited in the galleries. The facilities include 84 working studios, 8 group studios, and 6 galleries.

## Alexandria Archaeology Museum

On the third floor, in suite 327, is the Alexandria Archaeology Museum, which is open Tues–Fri 10–3, Sat 10–5, and Sun 1–5. It is closed on Mon. In the museum's laboratory, visitors can watch volunteers and archaeologists working on items found in the most recent digs. Museum exhibits highlight recent excavations and research, telling the story of Alexandria's past.

### Diversion:

Exit the Torpedo Factory to the rear onto the wharf area, turn left, and walk down to **Founders Park** and **Oronoco Park.** The waterfront during the 1960s was heavily industrialized and overbuilt. In order to revitalize and rehabilitate the area, both public and private concerns joined together to create the Waterfront Plan in the late 1970s. Under the plan, a network of small parks, both public and private, were created along the water's edge as the opportunity became available. The one binding principle of the plan is that the waterfront must be accessible to the public, regardless of who owns the property. Visitors are invited to stroll along the banks of the Potomac, which played such a prominent part in the settling of the city.

A food pavilion has eateries offering coffee, ice cream, sandwiches, and other snacks.

The next walk, Mount Vernon, is ten miles south of Alexandria. You can get to Mount Vernon from Alexandria by returning to the King St Metro station and taking the Yellow Line to Huntington, then the 101 bus. From Washington, D.C., you can travel to Mount Vernon by boat on the *Potomac Spirit*, which departs daily (mid-March to Oct) from Pier 4, 6th and Water Sts S.W. The hearty traveler can bike there via the Mount Vernon Trail, an 18.5-mile trail connecting Washington, D.C., with Mount Vernon. The trail passes through Alexandria.

# 33 · Mount Vernon

Bus: Metrorail Yellow Line to Huntington, then Fairfax Connector bus 101, which runs once an hour, ☎ (703) 339-7200.
Car: From Washington, D.C., take George Washington Memorial Pkwy south.
Boat: Spirit of Washington Harbor Cruises, ☎ 554-8000; Potomac Riverboat Company, ☎ (703) 548-9000.
Tour bus: Gray Line Bus, ☎ 289-1995; All About Time, ☎ 393-3696; Tourmobile, ☎ 554-7950.

Southern tip of George Washington Memorial Pkwy, 16 miles south of Washington, D.C. ☎ (703) 780-2000. Web: www.mountvernon.org. Open daily April–Aug 8–5; March, Sept, Oct, 9–5; Nov–Feb 9–4. Admission fee charged except for the third Mon in Feb when, in observance of Washington's birthday, admission is free. Restrooms. Wheelchair accessible. Restaurant and cafeteria. Two gift shops. Visitors see the property on a self-guided tour. Guides are available in the rooms to answer questions. An audiotape tour is available for rental.

Outside the entrance gate are located a post office, the Quick Bite snack bar, restrooms, phones, a gift shop, and the Mount Vernon Inn restaurant. No eating, drinking, or smoking are allowed on the grounds. A ticket buys a one-day pass; visitors may get their hands stamped for same day reentry.

Library Collection: A noncirculating collection of manuscripts, books, prints, photographs, newspapers, and Library of Congress microfilm of George Washington's papers are available to visiting scholars by appointment, Mon–Fri 9–5.

Curatorial Collection: Information is available on household and personal possessions of George and Martha Washington, including silver, furniture, china, glassware, miniatures, clothing, jewelry, and military objects.

Transportation around Mount Vernon grounds: A shuttle bus transports visitors from the Crossroads (about a block from the entrance gate) to the Wharf and the Pioneer Farm site every half hour, 9:15–4:45; from the Wharf and Pioneer Farms to the Crossroads every half hour, 9:30–5. Priority given to seniors and others needing assistance.

Archaeological dig: Begun in 1987, a professional staff aided by volunteers has explored the sites of a blacksmith's shop, a slave quarter, a kitchen trash pit, and a composting building. The foundations of two garden-related buildings constructed by Bushrod Washington prior to 1815 have been uncovered in the upper garden area. Volunteers are accepted on weekdays throughout the year, and also on Sat April–Sept 8–4; must be over 16; no experience necessary. Thirty-minute tours offered in Oct only (to celebrate Virginia Archaeology Month) at 11:30 and 2:30 daily.

At Mount Vernon (c. 1730s; architect unknown; additions made between 1750s and 1780s under the supervision of George Washington), George Washington's beloved estate on the Potomac River, visitors are able to glimpse the personal life of the Father of Our Country. George Washington was an 18C gentleman farmer. He fought for the freedom of a new nation while depending on slave labor to advance his own fortune and position. He was a fierce soldier and able strategist who also took great pride in developing crop-rotation schedules that would not deplete his farmland. Washington loved his family and the home he created for them; yet he spent more time elsewhere than in residence.

**Highlights:** The view of the Potomac River, the large dining room on the first floor, the kitchen garden, the 16-sided treading barn. In season at the riverfront pioneer farm, costumed guides smoke hogs and dry tobacco, and kids can try cracking corn, making fish nets, and hoeing the fields. Special programs and walking tours are offered year-round.

### History

John Washington, George Washington's great-grandfather, emigrated from England in 1659, and in 1674, along with John Spencer, was granted 5,000 acres along the upper Potomac River, between Dogue and Little Hunting Creeks. In 1690, the tract was divided between John's son, Lawrence, and the Spencer heirs, and from Lawrence the half of the tract known as Little Hunting Creek Plantation passed to his daughter, Mildred. In 1726, George Washington's father and Mildred's brother, Augustine Washington, bought the plantation from her. Six years later, in 1732, George was born, and in 1735 his family moved to Hunting Creek Plantation, where they lived for five years before moving to a farm in Fredericksburg.

In 1740, George's father, Augustine Washington, deeded Huntington Creek Plantation to George's half-brother, Lawrence, who renamed it Mount Vernon in honor of Admiral Edward Vernon, under whom he had served in the Caribbean. When George was 11 years old his father died and he became very close to Lawrence, living for periods of time at Mount Vernon. At 16, George accompanied Lawrence's friend, George William Fairfax, on a surveying expedition, and at 17, George began his own surveying business. In 1752, Lawrence died, and two years later George began leasing Mount Vernon from Lawrence's widow. Following her death in 1761, George inherited the estate.

Washington's military service under General Edward Braddock during the French and Indian War permitted only brief visits to Mount Vernon between 1752 and 1759. During this time the plantation was managed by Washington's younger brother, John Augustine. After the war, George Washington, now Colonel Washington, returned to Mount Vernon. In 1759 he married a young widow, Martha Dandridge Custis, whom he described as "an agreeable Consort for Life." By all accounts, theirs was a love match. In one of his few existing letters to Martha (she destroyed most of their correspondence shortly before her death), written from Philadelphia in 1775, he wrote, "As I am within a few Minutes of leaving this City, I could not think of departing from it without dropping you a line. . . . I retain an unalterable affection for you, which neither time or distance can change." Martha had two small children at the time of the marriage: Jacky, 3 years old, and Patsy, 1 year old.

When he married, Washington expected to retire from the military and to focus on his farm. But in 1775, Washington was named commander in chief of the Continental Army and wrote to his brother, John Augustine, "I am now to bid adieu to you, and to every kind of domestic ease for a while. I am embarked on a wide ocean, boundless in its prospect, and in which, perhaps, no safe harbor is to be found. I have been called upon by the unanimous voice of the Colonies to take the command of the Continental army."

A distant cousin, Lund Washington, took over running the estate and supervising the north and south wing additions that Washington had begun in 1773. Between 1775 and 1783, the years of the Revolutionary War, Washington was home only twice.

### Washington Notes

Throughout the war, Lund and George corresponded about the estate (apparently even in the 18C construction and renovation took longer than anticipated). In 1775, Lund wrote to General Washington, "The Stucco man is at work upon the dining room. God knows when he will get done."

In 1776, in the midst of the New York campaign, General Washington wrote to Lund regarding the large dining room, "The chimney of the new room should be exactly in the middle of it—the doors and every thing to be exactly answerable and uniform—in short I would have the whole executed in a masterly manner."

In 1783, Washington, having won the Revolutionary War, resigned his commission and once again retired to Mount Vernon to farm. In 1787, however, Washington was called upon to preside over the Constitutional Convention. During these years, Martha was with him a good deal, having left her niece, Fanny Bassett Washington, in charge of the housekeeping.

On Feb 4, 1789, the electoral college voted in the first presidential election, and George Washington was unanimously elected president of the United States, an honor he reluctantly accepted. His journey from Mount Vernon to New York (then the seat of government) turned into a parade, with political leaders, war veterans, and citizens in every town turning out for speeches and ceremonial dinners. Washington was inaugurated in New York City on April 30, 1789. During his eight years as president, he would visit Mount Vernon only 15 times.

In 1797, Washington declined to run for a third term and happily returned to his beloved Mount Vernon. He immediately began making plans for his farm and for repairs on the mansion. He wrote to friends: "I am already surrounded by joiners, masons and painters, and such is my anxiety to be out of their hands that I have scarcely a room to put a friend into, or to sit in myself, without the music of hammers and the odiferous scent of paint."

Unfortunately, Washington had only two and a half years to enjoy his retirement. In Dec 1799, after riding through a rough winter storm, Washington caught a cold and died of a resulting throat infection. He was 67 years old. Martha Washington died three years later in 1802. After her death, the estate was inherited by Washington's nephew, Bushrod Washington, an associate justice of the Supreme Court. Bushrod died in 1829, bequeathing the estate to his nephew, John Augustine Washington, who died in 1832. In 1850, his widow gave the estate to their son, John Augustine Washington, Jr., the last of the Washington family to own it. John Washington, Jr., tried to interest both the federal government and the state of Virginia in maintaining the property as a historic building. Meanwhile, the condition of the building and grounds deteriorated. When Mrs. Louisa Bird Cunningham of South Carolina passed by the mansion in a steamboat and reported its rundown condition to her daughter Ann Pamela Cunningham, the latter founded the Mount Vernon Ladies' Association of the Union in 1853 for the purpose of restoring the Mansion. After raising $200,000 the association was able to purchase the estate in 1858. Immediately afterward, the estate was open to the public.

## Exterior of the Mansion House

Mount Vernon is an outstanding example of colonial architecture. Washington was influenced by English books on design. The house also bears a resemblance to the Governor's Palace in Williamsburg, particularly in the proportions of the wing buildings and in the bowling green—the large, grassy expanse facing the building that seems to correspond to the palace green. According to the Mount Vernon Ladies' Association, the piazza—the porch, or colonnade, facing the river, one of the mansion's most beautiful features—was a major innovation for its time.

When Washington inherited Mount Vernon in 1761, the house was one and a half stories high and had a central hall and four rooms on the first floor. In anticipation of his marriage, Washington began remodeling, enlarging the house to two and a half stories. The south wing was added in 1774, the north in 1776, and the covered walks leading to the dependencies were added between 1778 and 1780. Eighty percent of the buildings now standing are original structures.

## The Grounds and Gardens

In a 1783 letter to a friend, George Washington affectionately boasted about Mount Vernon: "No estate in United America is more pleasantly situated than this. It lies in a high, dry and healthy Country 300 miles by water from the Sea . . . on one of the finest Rivers in the world. . . . It is situated in a latitude between the extremes of heat and cold, and is the same distance by land and water, with good roads and the best navigation [to and] from the Federal City, Alexandria and Georgetown."

Washington landscaped the grounds and gardens during the period between the end of the Revolution in 1783 and his election to the presidency in 1789.

Washington's expertise as a surveyor proved valuable as he reshaped the gardens, created new lawns, and realigned several of the roads and lanes. On the north side, he placed the upper (flower) garden and greenhouse; on the south, the lower (kitchen) garden and the fruit garden nursery. Trees were planted in the deep park on the slope leading from the mansion to the river. Although the bowling green was conceived and begun before the Revolutionary War, it was not completed until 1785. Several of the larger trees were planted by Washington in 1785. Washington kept unimpaired the estate's sweeping vistas of the Potomac and of the Maryland shore opposite Mount Vernon.

A plantation had to be self-sustaining, with every need met by the skills of the family and their servants. Cotton and wool grown on the estate were spun and woven into material for the clothes that were sewn. New shoes were made and old ones resoled. Wine was pressed and whisky distilled. Bricks were molded and fired in kilns. The outbuildings, most of which are original, are situated where they were in Washington's day. In Washington's day four other farms were part of Mount Vernon Plantation, including a woodland. Ten wooded acres were needed annually for each Mount Vernon fireplace; wood was also needed to run the forge, heat water for the laundry, and cure the smokehouse meats.

## North Grounds

A few yards inside the main entrance gate is a tent in which a 30-minute videotape on the life and times of George Washington is presented continuously between April and Oct. Next to the tent are pens with rams and sheep. Nearby, at the **Hands-On Area,** at scheduled times, children can learn how to play hoop and stick, carry water, and find out about 18C classrooms. The shuttle bus drop-off point is next to the Hands-On Area.

From the Crossroads, turn north to the North Lane leading to the mansion. First on the right is the gate leading to the **upper (flower) garden** and **greenhouse.** The original greenhouse was destroyed by fire in 1835, and the present structure has been reconstructed based on period documents. The flowers in the courtyard fronting the greenhouse are labeled.

Continue along the North Lane a few yards to a group of outbuildings, beginning with the **slave quarters.** Washington's attitude toward slavery apparently changed during his lifetime, because in his will he made arrangements for all the slaves he owned to be freed upon the death of his wife. In addition to freedom for his slave valet, William Lee, Washington provided food and clothing and $30 a year for life.

> ### Washington Notes
> In 1799, the year Washington died, there were 316 slaves at Mount Vernon: 70 women and 50 men were field slaves, 50 were trained in crafts or worked in the mansion, and the rest were children and retired slaves. One in every four was a skilled worker, such as a carpenter. When Washington married in 1759, he owned 50 slaves. As his estate grew, he needed more slaves. It took more than 100 slaves to farm the 3,000 acres at Mount Vernon. Each slave worked an average of 25 acres per year.

Slaves were housed in communal quarters such as this one or lived over their place of work, such as the kitchen. Slaves who lived and worked on the outlying farms were not as well treated as those at the Mansion House farm. A Polish visitor of the time described their cabins as "more miserable than the cottages of our peasants."

Next along the lane is the **shoemaker's shop.** The shoemaker, and also the tailor, were full-time workers, sometimes slaves, who maintained the shoes of both the family and the workers. One pair of shoes was given to each slave annually. In one year, according to the records, one shoemaker made 217 pairs of shoes and mended 199 pairs.

Next is the **stove room.** The corner fireplace heated the greenhouse on the opposite side. On the end of the row of outhouses along this lane, is the **Archaeology and Restoration Museum,** which displays artifacts found during the ongoing digs, including blacksmith's tools and buttons. Beyond this on the left of the North Lane is the **ice house,** where chunks of frozen ice cut from the Potomac River in winter were packed in straw to be used throughout the year.

Nearing the mansion along the lane are another group of outbuildings. The **overseer's quarters** were usually used by a husband-and-wife team. He managed both free and slave labor and submitted weekly reports on farm operations, while she handled such duties as milking the cows and churning butter. In the **spinning room** are a selection of antique spinning wheels. Ten or more slaves, often women recovering from childbirth, were constantly employed spinning and knitting. In 1768, 815 yards of linen was produced, 365 yards of woolen cloth, and 40 yards of cotton.

Continue to the **salthouse,** which played a major role in the estate's fishing business. In the spring more than 1 million herring and thousands of shad were caught in the Potomac River, then salted and packed in barrels for sale in the U.S. and abroad. The salt was purchased from Portugal and Liverpool, England.

Continue along the North Lane to the **museum,** which opened in 1999. Included among the exhibits are Jean-Antoine Houdon's bust of Washington (1785), representative pieces of the five sets of china owned by the Washingtons, and a chair cushion worked in cross-stitch by Martha Washington over a period of 36 years.

At the end of the North Lane is the **Mansion.**

## Interior of the Mansion House

The decor reflects the changing styles between 1757, when Washington first decorated the mansion, and 1787, when his last addition was completed. The bright colors seen here were the fashion shortly before Washington's death. Great care has been taken to authenticate the decoration of the mansion, using inventories completed in 1799 and in 1802. Round brushes, like those used in Washington's time, were imported from France for the restoration, and pigments were handground and mixed on the estate. Wallpaper was applied in the 18C manner of using rectangles of approximately 21 by 28 inches with slightly overlapping seams.

Enter the two-story **large dining room,** the last addition to the house. The largest and most ornate room, the dining room was used for large receptions and formal dinners. The bright green color of the walls was chosen because it was believed to aid digestion. Note the absence of a table, and the placement of chairs along the walls. The Washingtons were constant hosts. Washington once noted in a letter that in 20 years, he and his wife had rarely eaten alone. However, they often didn't know how many guests to expect. Rather than set a formal table, trestle tables were used to accommodate however many guests arrived. After dinner these tables were dismantled and the room was used for dancing, which Washington loved.

Wheat was Mount Vernon's chief crop and corn its second. Both are featured in the ceiling motif and mantelpiece design. The elaborately carved mantel and mantelpieces were gifts from an English admirer, Samuel Vaughan. The Hepplewhite sideboards (1797) are by John Aitken of Philadelphia.

### Washington Notes

It was in the dining room in 1789 that Washington was informed he had been elected president, and it was in this room ten years later that his body lay in state for three days following his death.

From the dining room, exit onto the piazza as the Washington family and their guests often did after dinner. There is a spectacular view of the river. From the piazza enter the causeway, or passage or central hall, as it is variously called. The oldest portion of the house, the causeway runs the mansion's full length, from the piazza to the front door, and was often used as a parlor. The original yellow pine wood was painted in 1797 by Washington to resemble mahogany. On the wall near the downstairs bedroom is a key to the Bastille, a gift from General Lafayette in 1790 that was brought to Washington by Thomas Paine, whose writings helped fire the American Revolution. Two impressive plaster lions, listed on an invoice from 1757, are above the double doors leading to the piazza. From here, visitors can view the four adjoining, roped-off rooms.

Prior to 1797 the **little parlor** served as a bedroom, but following the general's retirement the room was employed to entertain guests. Music played an important role in colonial homes such as Mount Vernon, both for entertaining guests and for the refinement of young ladies. The harpsichord (1793; English) belonged to Washington's granddaughter Nelly Custis. The trio of mezzotints, or small oval portraits, of Washington, Franklin, and Lafayette are copies of those that hung in the parlor in Washington's time. The carpet is a reproduction of one used at the mansion.

The more formal Prussian blue **west parlor** features paneled walls and a decorated ceiling. Above the mantel is a carved representation of the Washington family coat of arms. The Chinese export porcelain tea service belonged to Martha Washington, and the urn-shaped silver lamps and silver tray were used in the presidential household.

The family used the **small dining room,** whose green color was enriched by glazing, for small groups. The ornate mantel and decorated ceiling were completed in 1775. The mahogany table is believed to be an original Mount Vernon piece, and five of the nine original Chippendale side chairs are identical and belong to a numbered set.

A common feature in colonial Virginia homes, the **downstairs bedroom** was used as the master bedroom until the south end of the house was completed in 1775. Following the war, the family numbered eight persons, but the Washingtons had more than 400 guests a year. The upholstered chair, an original piece, was Martha's sewing chair.

Take the wide stairs at the west end of the causeway up to the second floor and the bedchambers. Although furnished in the style of the period, only a few pieces are from the original house. In 1784 Lafayette stayed in the northeast chamber. The very small room to the right of this is the only one without a fireplace and was originally part of a storage room. The blue bedroom was so named for the color of its woodwork.

### Washington Notes

The yellow southeast bedroom has etched on one of its windows "Eliza P Custis [age] 10 August 2 1792." Eliza (1782–1832) was another of Martha's grandchildren to live at Mount Vernon for a time.

To the southwest is the room used by Martha's granddaughter Nellie Custis (1779–1852) when she was growing up, and later by Nellie and her family (she married Washington's nephew Lawrence Lewis) before they moved to their house, Woodlawn, which was built on a portion of the Mount Vernon estate. The crib was a gift from Martha Washington on the occasion of the birth of Nellie's first child. In this room, also, is the trunk Martha Washington used in her travels to and from the army's winter quarters during the Revolutionary War. Attached to the lid is Nellie's letter describing watching her grandmother pack and feeling "sadly distressed at her going away." About Mrs. Washington's return, Nellie writes, "Oh how joyfully did I look on to see her cloaths [sic] taken out, & the many gifts she always brought for her grandchildren!"

Follow a hallway from the stairs landing on the second floor to the back of the mansion and the **master bedroom,** which was added in 1774. Washington's study was directly below and could be reached by a set of back stairs. Martha's office was in this room. She managed the complete household whenever she was in residence, often without the aid of a secretary. Martha's French desk in the corner is thought to be the one listed in an inventory of furniture as having been purchased in 1791 from the Comte de Moustier, the first French minister to the United States. On top of the desk is Mrs. Washington's leather key basket, with keys to all the important storage areas. The portraits of her four grandchildren (1795) are by Robert Edge Pine. Those of Nelly and Martha are originals; the other two, copies. The kneehole dressing table is one of the few Virginia-made pieces in the house. The bed is the one on which George Washington died in Dec 1799. Following the general's death, Mrs. Washington moved out of their bedroom, a tribute to a dead husband not uncommon in the 18C. Martha moved to a bedroom on the third floor. In May 1802, Martha Washington died in this bedroom. The third floor is open to the public only during the fall and winter months.

Take the stairs from the master bedroom landing down to **Washington's study.** In 1786 the library book press was installed and the pine woodwork was painted to simulate a finer wood. In this room Washington wrote letters to further the establishment of a democratic government. The bust of Washington is a copy of that carved by Houdon, now in the Mount Vernon museum. In 1797, Washington purchased the Tambour secretary (made by John Aitken of Philadelphia) and desk chair (made in New York about 1790) specially for Mount Vernon. The terrestrial globe (from England in 1790) is also original to the house. Washington's library, inventoried at his death, had 884 bound volumes. The books reflected his interests as a soldier, statesman, farmer, and businessman. This was possibly Washington's favorite room, one that afforded him the privacy his very public life lacked. A relative described it as "a place that none entered" without a direct invitation. Washington began each day here by shaving and dressing at four or five o'clock in the morning.

From the study, walk through the south colonnade to the **kitchen.** The kitchen is detached from the house because of the danger of fires. The kitchen staff consisted of two cooks and two waiters, under the direction of a steward or housekeeper (and Mrs. Washington). Breakfast was at seven (tea, coffee, cold or boiled meat, and mush cakes swimming in butter and honey), dinner was at three (a small roasted pig or a boiled leg of lamb, vegetables, pastries), tea was served at six, and supper at nine o'clock. Next to the kitchen is the **larder** where perishables were kept.

> ### Washington Notes
> Food was always made available to those in need. As Washington wrote to Lund in 1775, "Let the Hospitality of the House, with respect to the poor, be kept up; let no one go hungry away . . . provided it does not encourage them in idleness."

## South Grounds

Exit the mansion on the South Lane to another series of outbuildings. The **clerk's office and quarters** was nearest the house for the sake of convenience. In the **smokehouse** hams and porks were salted, dried, smoked, and preserved. To foil raiders, the smokehouse was built without windows. Two slave women worked in the **washhouse** six days a week. Linens and clothing were immersed in cauldrons of boiling water, then scrubbed with lye or animal fat soap, dried in the laundry yard, and pressed with heated irons. The **coachhouse** was rebuilt on this original site in 1893. Displayed is a riding chair, a small chair mounted on a wagon's base used by George Washington when he was a child. In the **stable** is a rare 18C Powell coach given to Martha Washington during her husband's presidency.

Continue down the South Lane to the **fruit garden and nursery,** a four-acre orchard that produced apples, cherries, peaches, and other fruit used in the kitchen. Directly opposite the entrance to the garden is the lane leading to the **Old Family Vault** or **Tomb,** where George and Martha Washington were originally buried, along with other members of the family. Continue past the Old Tomb to the **wharf** (renovated in 1891 and again in 1991) and its beautiful view of the Maryland shore.

From here walk west to the field area called **George Washington: Pioneer Farmer,** a working exhibit of the methods and crops raised by Washington. When Washington took over the farm at Mount Vernon, he had hoped to make his riches raising tobacco, but he quickly found that tobacco depleted the soil of its nutrients and required about three times the number of slaves than other types of farming. Washington studied agricultural texts, corresponded with other farmers here and abroad, and conducted experiments to discover ways to rotate crops to prevent nutrient depletion. He was especially influenced by the New Husbandry agricultural movement then gaining credence in England. There are also exhibits on cracking corn and making wooden farm implements, plus a ten-minute video on how to make a barn.

Return east to the wharf and then walk north halfway back up the red brick path to the gravel path to the **Slave Memorial and Burial Ground,** in which 50 to 100 slaves are buried. A memorial slab erected in 1929 states: "In memorial of the many faithful colored servants of the Washington family buried at Mount Vernon from 1760 to 1860 their unidentified graves surround this spot." In 1983, a memorial consisting of a small obelisk in the center of a red brick circle was erected by architectural students at Howard University: "In memory of the Afro Americans who served as slaves at Mount Vernon this monument marking their burial ground dedicated September 21, 1983."

From the Slave Memorial, continue west on the path to the **Tomb of George and Martha Washington,** a red brick structure with two marble sarcophagi behind an iron gate. One sarcophagus is inscribed "Washington," and the other "Martha, Consort of Washington." Washington requested this site in his will, but pressure was brought to bear on the family to have his remains removed to Washington, D.C. Mrs. Washington consented and a crypt was provided under the dome of the Capitol, but the project was never completed. In 1830, a drunken employee of the estate broke into the Old Tomb and attempted to steal Washington's skull. As a result, John Augustine Washington III built a more secure tomb and reinterred the bodies there in 1831. The last person buried in the inner vault was Jane Washington, John Augustine's mother, in 1855. Legend has it that the doors were then locked and the key thrown into the Potomac River to prevent anyone from getting into the vault.

From the tomb, continue east on the red brick path to the gravel-pathed South Lane, and from there back up the hill to the mansion. At the bowling green, turn west to the "necessary" (outdoor toilet), built above the garden so that the waste could be collected in wooden tubs and used as fertilizer below. Next to the necessary is the entrance gate to the **lower (kitchen) garden.** This is the starting point for the daily tours of the Landscape and Gardens (at 11, 1, and 3) and Slave Life (10, 12, 2, and 4). This garden produced a range of vegetables including carrots, onions, turnips, beets, cabbage, and cauliflower, depending on the season.

Exit the mansion grounds.

**Diversion:**
The 18.5-mile **Mount Vernon Trail**—administered by the U.S. Park Service, ☎ (703) 289-2502—runs parallel to the **George Washington Memorial Pkwy.** The trail, a popular place for biking and hiking, begins in the Mount Vernon parking lot. The trail descends along a forest route to Little Hunting Creek and Riverside Park and continues to **Fort Hunt Park,** which has 156 acres for picnicking and hiking as well as restrooms and a drinking fountain. Past the park is a view of **Fort Washington,** a 19C fort built to defend against the British, who decided to attack the city via another route in 1814. From the fort the trail continues across Alexandria Ave and on to **Dyke Marsh,** a 240-acre wetland with hundreds of species of birds at different seasons, and then to **Belle Haven,** a popular picnic area adjacent to Dyke Marsh and 7.2 miles from the beginning of the trail.

Cross Hunting Creek and pass Jones Point Lighthouse, once the southernmost corner of the District of Columbia. Next along the trail is the city of Alexandria, and two miles past that is **Daingerfield Island,** which has facilities for picnicking, sailing, fishing, and also a restaurant. Cross Four Mile Run and continue past Ronald Reagan Washington National Airport. About 14.5 miles from the beginning of the trail is **Gravelly Point,** which has a beautiful panorama of the city of

Washington. Continue to the Lyndon Baines Johnson Memorial Grove, part of **Lady Bird Johnson Park.** The park has phones, food, restrooms, and a drinking fountain. Continue to the end of the trail at **Theodore Roosevelt Island** (across the Potomac River from the Kennedy Center) near Memorial Bridge.

This multiuse trail is crowded on nice days with walkers, joggers, and bicycle riders. The easiest place to park your car is at the Theodore Roosevelt Island parking lot near the northern end of the trail. Instead of going over the footbridge to the island, follow the path (and the joggers) near the footbridge. No sign indicates that this is the Mount Vernon trail.

The steepest part of the trail is in the south near Mount Vernon and Fort Hunt Park, about 2.5 miles from Mount Vernon. Allow time to explore Theodore Roosevelt Island, a nature reserve with 2.5 miles of trails.

Be careful along the Mount Vernon bike path as both the trail and the adjacent George Washington Memorial Pkwy are heavily trafficked areas. Mostly the bike trail is separate from the busy road, but at places the path and the road merge, forcing bikers to stop and cross heavily trafficked areas. Many accidents have occurred at these stop signs because bikers and drivers don't look out for each other or don't yield.

**Diversion:**
Woodlawn Plantation and the Pope-Leighey House are three miles from Mount Vernon. At the traffic circle at Mount Vernon, bear to the right and stay in the center lane until the first stop sign. Follow the posted sign pointing to Woodlawn straight ahead on Rte. 235 south. Stay on 235 for three miles, until it intersects with Rte. 1. The entrance to Woodlawn is straight ahead.

# Woodlawn Plantation and the Pope-Leighey House
Rte. 1 and Rte. 235 south. ☎ (703) 780-4000. Web: www.nationaltrust.org. Open daily 10–4. Tours every hour. Admission fee charged. Closed Jan–Feb, Thanksgiving, and Christmas Day. Restrooms at Woodlawn. Gift shop. No eating facilities. Woodlawn is wheelchair accessible on the first floor only; Pope-Leighey not wheelchair accessible.

## Woodlawn Plantation
Woodlawn Plantation (1800–1806; William Thornton) was created by the architect of the U.S. Capitol for the step-granddaughter of the first president. The Pope-Leighey House was created by one of America's signature architects for a man who wrote him a letter asking for a house. Woodlawn Plantation's land was once part of Mount Vernon and was given by George Washington to his step-granddaughter Eleanor Parke Custis (called Nelly) upon the occasion of her marriage to Washington's nephew Lawrence Lewis. (The couple met when Lewis came to Mount Vernon to help run the estate.) Lewis and his bride commissioned Dr. William Thornton, first architect of the Capitol, to design their home. The north wing of the Georgian-style house was completed in 1802, and the Lewis family moved into their hilltop mansion. The remainder of the house was completed over the next four years.

The Lewises were very active in the business and social life of the new capital. After Lawrence's death in 1839, Nelly moved in with her son and daughter-in-law, and Woodlawn was left vacant for seven years. In 1846, the estate was sold at public sale to four Quaker businessmen, who divided it into small farms and created a Quaker community. The first free school in Virginia was established on this site.

A series of owners over the next 100 years helped keep the estate in relatively good repair. In 1951 the National Trust for Historic Preservation took over management of the property, and title to the property was acquired by the trust in 1957. Some of the furnishings of the house, such as the sofa in the hallway and Nelly's harp and needlepoint, are original to the house.

Visitors are free to roam the grounds. The gardens were designed and executed by the Garden Club of Virginia, beginning in 1953. When completed, the garden contained one of the finest collections of heritage (old-fashioned) roses in the eastern United States. Almost all the varieties of roses at Woodlawn today were known before 1850; thus it is possible that Nelly Custis Lewis grew these varieties in her garden. Rose types include gallica, moss, cabbage, tea, China, Bourbon, and damask. Among the heritage roses at Woodlawn are Rosa Mundi, Fanny bias, Stanwell Perpetual, Celestial, Rose of Castile, Harrison's Yellow, and Maiden's Blush.

## Pope-Leighey House

The Pope-Leighey House (1940; Frank Lloyd Wright) is located across the parking lot from Woodlawn. In 1939, Loren Pope, a $50-a-week copy editor at the *Washington Evening Star* newspaper, wrote a letter to Frank Lloyd Wright. The letter began, "Dear Mr. Wright, There are certain things a man wants during life, and, of life. Material things and things of the spirit. The writer has one fervent wish that includes both. It is a house created by you." Two weeks later Pope received a letter from Frank Lloyd Wright. It began, "Dear Loren Pope: Of course I am ready to give you a house."

Pope had tapped into one of Wright's pet beliefs. In 1938 Wright had written, "The house of moderate cost is not only America's major architectural problem, but the problem most difficult for her major architects." The Pope-Leighey House is a physical representation of Wright's concept, called Usonian architecture, that people of modest means were entitled to well designed houses. The house, originally on a lot in East Falls Church, Virginia, cost Pope $7,000, and that included the interior furniture Wright designed. The Pope family moved into the house in March 1941. Three months later the Pope's 3-year-old son drowned in a pond near their home. The Popes remained in the house five years and had two more children, at which point they decided they needed more room. They placed a three-line ad in the newspaper and had almost 100 prospective buyers.

The Popes sold the house to Robert and Marjorie Leighey, who lived in the house for almost 20 years. Soon after Robert Leighey died in 1963, the Virginia Highway Department announced plans to seize the property under eminent domain because of construction of I-66. In 1964, Marjorie Leighey signed an agreement with the National Trust deeding the house to the trust in exchange for a guarantee that the house would be saved. The house was dismantled and moved to the Woodlawn estate at a cost of $48,000. In the early 1990s, when it was discovered that clay in the ground where the house was placed was causing cracks in the foundation, the house was turned and moved about 30 ft, then restored. The cost this time was $750,000, or more than 100 times its original cost.

In 1996, the house was reopened to the public, and Loren Pope attended the ceremonies. The Pope-Leighey House design features many of Wright's innovations, including a flat roof, recessed lighting, a carport, heated concrete slab floors, and windows designed as an integral part of the wall.

# 34 · Additional Sites of Interest in D.C. and Surrounding Areas of Maryland and Virginia

## Additional Sites of Interest in Washington, D.C.

### Foxhall and Wesley Heights
Bus: D5 and D6.

The northwest Washington, D.C., neighborhoods of Foxhall, Foxhall Village, and Wesley Heights are loosely bounded by 44th St on the south, Battery Kemble Park and Nebraska Ave on the north, Canal Rd on the west, and Glover-Archbold Park and Massachusetts Ave on the east. In the late 18C and for much of the 19C they were the sites of country estates. This area is still mostly the refuge of the city's wealthier residents. The neighborhoods have two universities—American University and the George Washington University at Mount Vernon College—and also the Kreeger Museum.

Henry Foxall, who was invited by Thomas Jefferson in 1800 to move his iron foundry to the Federal City, built an estate in the area. Foxall's farmland became Foxhall Village. An early mistake on a road sign changed the spelling from "Foxall" to "Foxhall."

> **Washington Notes**
> Foxall built the Foundry Methodist Church at 14th and G Sts N.W. as an offering of gratitude when the British didn't burn his foundry in 1814. Foundry Methodist Church has been President Clinton's main house of worship during his terms in office.

Farther north was the estate of Benjamin King, called Valley View; it is part of Foxhall now. The area continued to develop slowly until the turn of the century, when farms began to be sold and divided into smaller lots. Foxall's property was sold in 1908, and the house was torn down in 1920.

In 1925, the first residences were built along Reservoir Rd. In 1927, Harry K. Boss began construction of Foxhall Village. Also in the 1920s and into the 1930s, houses were built on 44th St and adjacent areas in this fashionable part of town. Palisades Dairy Farm stood on the site of the present-day Mount Vernon College.

### American University
4400 Massachusetts Ave N.W. ☎ 885-1000. Web: www.american.edu. Radio station: WAMU-FM. Current president: Dr. Benjamin Ladner.

American University (AU) (1891–1902; Henry Van Brunt and Frank Howe; Henry Ives Cobb; Frederick Law Olmsted, landscaping) is one of Washington's major universities. More than 10,000 students are enrolled in undergraduate, graduate, and law school programs. American University offers programs in arts and sciences, business, international service, and public affairs.

AU was founded by Methodist bishop John Fletcher Hurst, who bought 90 acres of farmland in 1890 to establish "a nonsectarian, national university." In 1902, President Theodore Roosevelt laid the cornerstone of McKinley Hall and later served as a member of AU's board of trustees. President Woodrow Wilson spoke at the university's official opening in May 1914, when 28 students, including 4 women, were admitted as the university's first graduating class.

In 1920, graduate schools opened downtown on F St N.W. During World War II, Red Cross volunteers were trained in Hurst Hall, and following the war, President Herbert Hoover served on AU's board of trustees. In 1949, the Washington College of Law, which had been founded by women in 1896, merged with AU to become AU's school of law.

### Washington Notes

In June 1963, President John Kennedy chose AU's commencement to call for an end to atmospheric testing of nuclear weapons as a first step toward halting the escalating nuclear arms race with the Soviet Union. Thirty years later, in 1993, President Bill Clinton chose AU's Centennial Opening Convocation to give the first major economic speech of his presidency.

As with Georgetown and George Washington Universities, American has had its problems dealing with the changing needs of a growing study body within the context of a city neighborhood. For several years, bordering neighborhoods have fought the university's plan to expand its law school facilities, and efforts are being made to find a compromise.

Landscaper Frederick Law Olmsted, along with architects Henry Van Brunt and Frank Howe, developed a campus plan between 1891 and 1896 that envisioned Romanesque revival–style buildings. But this conflicted with the wishes of AU's founder, John Fletcher Hurst, who wanted classically inspired buildings, and for the most part Hurst won. Van Brunt's Hall of History (1898), now called **Hurst Hall,** for example, is neoclassical in style with simple Doric pilasters and Ionic columns. Henry Ives Cobb, who succeeded Van Brunt in 1898, designed the **McKinley Ohio Hall of Government** (1902) as a hinge for two long, rectangular lawns called the Court of Ceremony, the central point for a planned 23 marble and granite buildings, all two stories in height. McKinley Hall was the only one of the 23 ever constructed.

## George Washington University at Mount Vernon College
2100 Foxhall Rd N.W. ☎ 625-0400. Web: www.mvc.gwu.edu.

In 1875 Elizabeth J. Somers founded Mount Vernon Seminary, a school for the daughters of distinguished Washington families. Somers, an 1855 graduate of Wesleyan College, moved the seminary to a site on Nebraska Ave N.W. in 1917. Her students, besides being offered the usual second curriculum, were also offered college-level courses, a situation considered progressive at the time. In 1927 a college-level course of study was formally added to the curriculum.

After World War II, Mount Vernon College (MVC) moved to its present 26-acre location. In 1969, Mount Vernon became an exclusively four-year baccalaureate liberal arts college; in 1993, it added graduate programs. In 1996, Mount Vernon became affiliated with George Washington (GW) University in order to "continue Mount Vernon's historical legacy of educating and developing women as leaders." Through this affiliation, George Washington University female students are able to take GW undergraduate courses on the Mount Vernon campus so that they can experience the distinctive residential life of a small women's college campus.

The campus has several neoclassical style brick dormitories; its newest addition is the **Eckles Memorial Library,** which has over 63,000 titles. Also on campus is the **Florence Hollis Hand Chapel** (1970; Hartman-Cox), which won an award for architectural design in 1971, and **Post Hall** (1957; Arthur T. Davis), an addition to the Academic Building donated by MVC alumna Marjorie Merriweather Post, which is used for wedding receptions and other social events.

## Kreeger Museum

2401 Foxhall Rd N.W. ☎ 338-3552. Web: www.kreegermuseum.com. Museum available by guided tour only. Tours conducted Tues–Sat 10:30 and 1:30. Donation requested. Main level galleries and restroom wheelchair accessible.

The Kreeger Museum (1967; Philip Johnson, with Richard Foster) is the result of the generosity of the late Washington philanthropist David Kreeger and his wife, Carmen. The museum's collection consists of more than 180 works of art from the 1850s to the 1970s.

The Kreeger, which opened to the public in June 1994, is a small jewel of a museum worth venturing off the beaten path to visit. The collection is noteworthy, the setting is unique, and the lack of crowds make viewing the art an enjoyable, intimate experience.

The Kreegers' residence was built with the intention of displaying the art they began collecting in the 1950s. Works by Bonnard, Braque, Cezanne, Corot, Degas, Gauguin, Klee, Man Ray, Miró, Monet, Munch, Picasso, Renoir, and van Gogh are in the collection, as are sculptures by Jean Arp, Alexander Calder, Henry Moore, and Auguste Rodin. The African Collection consists of 29 masks and figural sculptures from west and central Africa representing the traditions of the years 1966–74.

### Exterior

The Kreeger Museum is one of Johnson's early examples of postmodernism. It is organized around the module system, with every room a variation of the dimensions 22 by 22 by 22 ft. The building is faced with travertine, a form of limestone often mistaken for marble (it was the substance used to face the Coliseum in Rome). To soften the lines of the building, Johnson used domes, creating echoes of Byzantine style.

### Interior

David Kreeger was a violinist, so Johnson designed the Great Hall, with its domed 25 ft ceiling, specifically with acoustics in mind. Johnson played his Stradivarius here with musicians Isaac Stern, Pinchas Zukerman, and Pablo Casals, among others. The walls are covered in a natural cotton carpeting that softens harsh sounds, the function also of the museum's screens, which were made from cork balls.

# In Other District Neighborhoods

## *Gallaudet University*

800 Florida Ave N.E. ☎ 651-5000. Web: www.gallaudet.edu. Guided tours available by appointment. Restrooms, telephones, and cafeteria.

Gallaudet University is the only university in the world devoted solely to the education of deaf and hard-of-hearing people. The institution includes a preschool, elementary school, and secondary school for deaf children, an undergraduate school, a graduate school, a College of Continuing Education, and the National Information Center on Deafness.

**Highlights:** The Kendall Demonstration Elementary School, the Model Secondary School for the Deaf, and the National Information Center on Deafness. Campus buildings, including Chapel Hall, College Hall, and the President's House.

### History

Gallaudet traces its origins to the Columbia Institution of the Deaf, Dumb, and Blind—an elementary and secondary school started largely through the efforts of Washingtonian Amos Kendall in 1857. Kendall served as postmaster general for President Andrew Jackson and as the financial consultant of Samuel F. B. Morse, the inventor of the telegraph. In 1856 Kendall began the school on his own estate, Kendall Green, in order to educate five orphaned deaf children. The Columbia school received its charter the following year.

In 1864 the institution received a charter from Congress and became the National Deaf Mute College. Former superintendent of the Columbia Institution, Edward Miner Gallaudet, served as the first president, occupying this post until 1910. Initially, enrollment was 13 students. Gallaudet guided the institution through its early period, expanding its size and mission as the school established a reputation for excellence.

In 1894, the institution adopted the name Gallaudet College, honoring Edward Gallaudet's father, Thomas Hopkins Gallaudet, the founder of the first school for the deaf in the United States in 1817.

In 1988, when the board of trustees appointed a new hearing person as university president, the student body revolted. The university, then its 125th year, had never had a deaf president. The students closed access to the school, picketed the administration, and took their demand for a deaf president to the media. The appointee eventually stepped down, and Dr. I. King Jordan became the first deaf president of Gallaudet.

Gallaudet's undergraduate enrollment is about 1,400, and the graduate enrollment is about 575. Of approximately 230 faculty members, about 35 percent are deaf or hearing-impaired.

### *Washington Notes*

In 1894, the Gallaudet football team conceived a method for preventing its plays, which had to be signed, from being read by opposing teams. The method, which involved circling, or huddling, around their quarterback to screen the opposition's view, is now an integral part of the game.

Much of the original campus—designed by Frederick Law Olmsted, designer of the Capitol Grounds, and Calvert Vaux's company in 1866—still stands.

From Florida Ave N.E., walk north onto the campus and proceed to Lincoln Circle. The center building on the circle facing Florida Ave is **Chapel Hall** (1871; Withers). Designed as the centerpiece of the college, the hall is one of the most significant examples of high Victorian Gothic revival architecture in Washington. The exterior retains its original appearance. The walls include brownstone, Ohio sandstone, and pink granite detailing. Red and gray slate create an interesting contrast on its roof. The building has a clock tower.

Immediately to the left or west of Chapel Hall is **College Hall** (1877; Withers, Friedrich, and Myers), also an example of high Victorian Gothic revival style. The east wing, designed by E. S. Friedrich, dates to 1866. The central block, conceived by F. C. Withers, was completed in 1877 by overseeing architect J. C. Myers. Like Chapel Hall, College Hall incorporates various materials of differing color to create a contrast.

West of College Hall, on the university's southwest corner just 60 ft north of Florida Ave, stands the **President's House** (1868; Withers). This red brick Gothic revival structure includes numerous brownstone accents and various decorative and functional features such as dormer gables and chimneys.

Other points of interest on campus include the houses located north of the President's House on Faculty Row. These were built from 1867 to 1875. Immediately behind or north of Chapel Hall are **Kendall Hall** (1885; Withers) and the **Old Gymnasium** (1881; Withers).

## National Museum of Health and Medicine

6825 16th St N.W. ☎ 782-2200. Web: www.natmedmuse.afip.org. Open daily 10–5:30. Closed Christmas Day. Admission: free. Wheelchair accessible.

The National Museum of Health and Medicine (1954; Faulkner, Kingsbury and Stenhouse) has a unique and sometimes grisly collection of objects, specimens, photographs, and documents chronicling the history and practice of medicine over the centuries. The museum is affiliated with, and located in the building of, the Armed Forces Institute of Pathology (AFIP) at Walter Reed Army Medical Center. Quite naturally the museum's focus is on the history and practice of American medicine in general and military medicine in particular. Originally called the Army Medical Museum, it opened in 1863 in a red Victorian building on the corner of Independence Ave and 7th St S.W. The building was demolished in 1968 to make way for the Hirshhorn Museum and Sculpture Garden. Because of lack of space, the museum was closed for almost ten years and its collection dispersed. Since its reopening in 1974, the museum has spent many years rebuilding its collection, which now includes more than 5,000 skeletal remains and 10,000 preserved body organs.

The most popular collection for the nonsqueamish is the **Anatomical Collection,** made up of bones and body parts.

### Washington Notes

Among these are the bones of amputated legs shipped to Washington during the Civil War in barrels of whiskey. Some of the bones have the bullets that hit them attached. The most famous of these legs is probably that of

General Daniel Sickles, who shipped his appendage in an improvised coffin with his calling card attached.

There are bone fragments of President Abraham Lincoln's skull on display, as well as the bullet that was extracted from it.

There are also exhibits featuring X-ray machines, microscopes, surgical instruments, and an iron lung. The museum is located on the grounds of the Walter Reed Army Medical Center in a building (AFIP headquarters) constructed in the 1950s to be atomic bomb–proof. The building is windowless with steel and concrete walls six-ft thick, but the south wing (built in 1968), where the museum is located, has small slitlike windows, making it perhaps less safe from atomic bombs but more pleasant for visitors.

Over the years there has been talk of moving the museum to a Mall location, but currently that plan seems to be dormant.

## Rock Creek Cemetery

Rock Creek Church Rd and Webster St N.W. ☎ 829-0585. Open daily 7:30 A.M. until dusk.

Rock Creek Cemetery is the oldest cemetery in Washington. A free map of the cemetery is available from the **Administration Building,** which is located inside the main gate at Rock Creek Church Rd. Visitors are welcome.

Burials began here in 1719, and for those interested in old cemeteries, this is one of the most engaging, both for its natural beauty and its many impressive monuments. Probably the most famous of these is the shrouded figure created by Augustus Saint-Gaudens called *Grief* (1890–91), though its official name is *The Peace of God That Passeth Understanding.* (Stanford White designed the granite stele and the block upon which the sculpture sits.) This moving piece of sculpture was commissioned by Henry Adams to honor his wife, Marion Hooper Adams, known as Clover, who committed suicide in 1885. When Adams died in 1918, he was buried here with his wife.

Also buried here is a Washington legend, **Alexander Robey Shepherd** (1835–1902). Appointed executive director of the District's Board of Public Works in 1871, "Boss" Shepherd was known for his extravagant style of living and his high-handed political maneuvering. During his tenure, marked by overspending and questionable patronage, Shepherd paved hundreds of miles of capital streets, installed street lights and sidewalks, established the first city water and sewage systems, and planted thousands of trees. When his overspending left the District millions of dollars in debt, Shepherd was squeezed out by the Congress and, defeated and impoverished, moved to Mexico in 1879, where he discovered a mine of silver and gold and became a millionaire. When he died in 1902, his body was returned to Washington for burial.

## St. Paul's Episcopal Church, Rock Creek Parish

Rock Creek Church Rd and Webster St N.W. ☎ 726-2080. The oldest church in Washington, St. Paul's Episcopal Church (1775; architect unknown; 1922, Delos Smith) is owned and administered by Rock Creek Cemetery.

The parish was founded in 1712, and in 1719 Colonel John Bradford donated a quantity of tobacco and 100 acres of land to establish a site for a church building.

The present church was built in 1775, remodeled in 1864, and restored following a fire in 1921. Only the brick walls of the 1775 structure remained after the fire.

Delos Smith's restoration in 1922 was in a simple neo-Georgian style. The red brick colonial church has a square central tower, a white cupola with a surmounting cross, and tall round-arched windows.

## Rock Creek Park

Rock Creek has always been an integral part of this city's life, even before it was a city. Native Americans living along Rock Creek's banks mined soapstone to carve their cups and pipes. Today, city dwellers wander its banks, enjoying a respite from urban congestion. Many other residents only briefly admire the park's beauties as they speed through it on their way to work. Rock Creek Park starts at M St in Georgetown and continues through the northwest area of the city into Montgomery County, Maryland.

Established by an act of Congress in 1890, the park encompasses 2,000 acres of woodland, streams, rocky glens, valleys, meadows, 730 kinds of flowering plants, 140 varieties of birds, and 27 types of mammals.

> **Washington Notes**
> Among the park's creatures is the Hayes Spring scud, a quarter-inch invertebrate that is D.C.'s only endangered species.

The park also has 15 miles of trails, bike and bridle paths, picnic groves, playgrounds, a golf course, a mill, a log cabin, a Civil War fort, and a planetarium. For joggers, the most popular run is from Georgetown to the National Zoo and back, four miles round-trip. (Women joggers should not jog alone through the park.) For those who'd like to take advantage of other park activities, the best place to start is at the visitor center, called the **Rock Creek Nature Center and Planetarium** (5200 Glover Rd N.W.; ☎ 426-6829; Web: www.nps.gov). The center is open Wed–Sun 9–5. Planetarium programs are Wed at 4 (for children age 4–adult), Sat at 1 (for children age 4–adult) and 4 (for children age 7–adult). Admission: free. Tickets for the 75-seat capacity planetarium program are handed out 30 minutes before starting time. Maps and information about the park are available from National Park Service personnel.

**Fort DeRussy** (northeast of the intersection of Oregon Ave and Military Rd N.W.) can only be reached by foot—by hiking uphill from Oregon Ave about 200 yds and turning left where the path splits. Fort DeRussy is one of the best preserved of the 68 Civil War forts built around the city to protect it from Confederate troops. Fort DeRussy still has some earthenworks, the main drawbridge, and some artillery pieces.

The **log cabin** Joaquin Miller (1841–1913), Washington's "Poet of the Sierras," built and lived in on Meridian Hill (see Walk 15: "Adams Morgan") for a year during the 1880s now sits in Rock Creek Park. The cabin was moved to the park in 1912 and can be viewed from the outside at its location on Beach Dr just north of the intersection with Military Rd.

**Pierce Mill,** located at Tilden St and Beach Dr N.W., is an old gristmill established around 1820. It's open to visitors Wed–Sun, 10–4:30. Adjacent to the mill is the **Rock Creek Gallery** (2401 Tilden St N.W.; ☎ 244-2482) where local artists display their work. It's open Thurs–Sun, 11–4:30.

***Washington Notes***
Rock Creek Gallery, also known as the Art Barn, was originally Isaac Pierce's carriage house. Pierce, a Quaker from Pennsylvania, owned 150 acres stretching from where the National Zoo is today to Chevy Chase. Pierce's mill used Rock Creek's water power to grind grain for local farmers.

During the Cold War the Hungarian and the Czechoslovakian embassies were located on Tilden Street N.W. across from the Art Barn. A false wall in the Art Barn contained wires for listening devices and other gadgets. The Art Barn's director said they could always spot the CIA men "because they always wore sunglasses indoors, had real sharp creases in their pants, short haircuts and shiny shoes."

**Rock Creek Park Golf Course** is an 18-hole golf course (16th and Rittenhouse Sts N.W.; ☎ 882-7332; Web: www.golfdc.com). It is open daily, 6:30 A.M.–5:30 P.M., on a first-come, first-tee-off basis.

## Saint Sophia Greek Orthodox Cathedral
Massachusetts Ave and 36th St N.W. ☎ 333-4730. Web: www.saintsophia washington.org. Saint Sophia Greek Orthodox Cathedral (1956; Archie Protopapas; Demetrios Dukas, mosaics) is known for its exquisite mosaic work on the interior of the cathedral dome. Saint Sophia is the seat in Washington of the archbishop of the Greek Orthodox Archdiocese of North and South America (his principal base is in New York City). The cathedral is one of the largest Greek Orthodox churches in the U.S.

Saint Sophia's parish was founded in 1904 by a group of 35 newly arrived Greek immigrant families. The church is not named for a saint (the Greek Orthodox religion doesn't recognize canonization); the name, meaning "holy wisdom," refers to the embodiment of God's wisdom in the figure of Christ. The mosaic in the church's dome depicts the celestial hierarchy in which an enthroned Christ (thought to be the largest such figure in the Orthodox world) is surrounded by a host of seraphim. Each dome and gable on the exterior of the church is topped by a Greek cross. Above the rounded entrance portico is a representation of the two-headed eagle, symbolizing the church and the emperor sharing a common body, the emblem of allegiance to the patriarch of Constantinople as the heir to Byzantium.

## Washington Dolls' House and Toy Museum
5236 44th St N.W. ☎ 244-0024. Open Tues–Sat 10–5; Sun 12–5. Admission fee charged.

This is a small but intriguing museum for those interested in period dollhouses, dolls, and toys. The museum was founded in 1975 by Flora Gill Jacobs, who had been writing about dollhouses for more than 30 years when she decided to make her collection and expertise available to the public. On view are such rarities as a turn-of-the-century quintet of Baltimore row houses, a 1903 New Jersey seaside hotel, a tin tea party from Germany, and several hundred dolls, including five long-faced Jumeaus. There are dollhouses for sale and a **Consignment Corner** containing old dolls and toys. The museum is available for children's teas and parties.

# Additional Sites of Interest in Maryland

## Andrews Air Force Base

Andrews Air Force Base, ☎ (301) 981-1110, in Prince George's County, Maryland, is known primarily to the public as the home of Air Force One, the president's airborne White House. The base, under the command jurisdiction of the Air Mobility Command, serves a host of visitors. These range from the president to congressional delegations, foreign heads of state, and other visiting dignitaries. Andrews houses air force, army, navy and Marine Corps aircraft, and each May over Armed Forces Weekend, the base hosts one of the most extensive air shows in the world, attended by about 800,000 people.

The base is named in honor of General Frank M. Andrews, commanding general of the U.S. forces in the European Theater of Operations in World War II until his death in a 1943 aircraft accident in Iceland. Two buildings on the post have been designated as historic sites. **Chapel II** (1914; DL) is built on the site of the Forest Grove Church, a Methodist Episcopal Church established in 1868. The structure that replaced Forest Grove Church in 1880 was destroyed in a windstorm in 1914, and the present chapel, designated as the base's number two chapel, was built soon after, incorporating some of the stained glass from the 1880 church.

From 1696, when Prince George's County was established, until 1940 and the beginning of World War II, the land that is now Andrews Air Force Base was farmland. **Belle Chance** (1910; DL) is the name of farmland originally part of the Darcey family plantation and later owned by the Calvert family of Mount Airy, a branch of one of the most prominent of the early Maryland families. In the early 1900s, the land was purchased by Dr. William Stewart. When the home the Calvert family had lived in was destroyed by fire, Stewart built an all-concrete (and thus fireproof) house in the colonial revival and Spanish style, surrounded by a complex of landscaped gardens, lawns, and lakes. The house is now the residence of the assistant vice chief of staff of the air force and the site of special events.

Although there always seems to be a crowd of happy, waving people whenever the president exits Air Force One, they are there by invitation only. Andrews Air Force Base is closed to the public.

## Washington Temple of the Church of Jesus Christ of Latter-Day Saints

9900 Stoneybrook Dr. Kensington, MD. ☎ (301) 587-0144. Web: www.washingtonlds.org. Visitors Center open daily 10 A.M.–9 P.M. Grounds open 8 A.M.–9 P.M.

The Church of Jesus Christ of Latter-Day Saints Temple, or the Mormon Temple (1971–74; Keith Wilcox), as it is familiarly known by Washington-area residents, is an arresting sight, especially in the evening as seen from the Capital Beltway near Kensington. The golden statue of the Mormon angel Moroni, perched atop the highest of the white marble temple's six spires, is lit against the dark sky.

The Washington Temple is the center of faith of the area's 50,000 Mormons, as well as a center for Mormons in the East and the Midwest. Mormons come to the temple to worship and perform what the Mormons call sacred ordinances, such as marriage. Latter-Day Saint temples aren't places of regular worship; they are designed as a holy site for marriages and other religious services.

Non-Mormons are not allowed in the temple, but the **Visitors Center** offers information about the church's beliefs and has a short film about the temple. On weekend evenings, the center hosts a **Performing Arts Series,** where local musical groups perform sacred and classical music. The 57-acre temple grounds have won several national landscaping awards and include an arboretum and a garden. Surrounding the temple are more than 100 varieties of trees and shrubs, as well as many rhododendrons and azaleas.

## College Park Aviation Museum

1985 Corporal Frank Scott Dr, College Park, MD. ☎ (301) 864-6029. Open daily 10–5. Admission fee charged. Wheelchair accessible. World War I theme restaurant.

This 27,000-square-ft aviation museum, which opened in Sept 1998, has a large, open gallery for displaying full-size aircraft, such as the 1918 Curtiss Jenny. Four areas present historic planes or exhibits. There are some interactive displays, a hands-on and children's area, an outdoor patio area, and a hiking/bike trail.

Aviation enthusiasts are intrigued by the museum since it is located at the **College Park Airport,** the oldest continually operating airport in the world. The airport opened in 1909 when Wilbur Wright came here to teach the first military officers to fly the government's new "aeroplane."

The College Park Airport was the site of the first Army Aviation School (1911–13), the first machine gun fired from an airplane (1912), the first testing of a bomb-dropping device (1911), the first controlled helicopter flight (1924), as well as other firsts.

College Park Airport today is a general aviation airport, serving private pilot flight services. On display is a 1911 Wright B built by Ken Hyde of the Virginia Aeroplane and Machine Company. A library and archives is available by appointment, and there are special programs and exhibits throughout the year.

## University of Maryland

Rte. 1, College Park, MD. ☎ (301) 314-7777. Web: www.umd.edu. Visitor Center open Mon–Fri 8–5; Sat 9–3.

The University of Maryland, College Park, is the flagship institution of the University of Maryland system. The facility was founded as a land grant college in 1862 and now serves as the state's primary center for graduate study and research. Bachelor's, master's, and Ph.D.'s are awarded in arts and sciences, engineering, business, journalism, environmental sciences, public policy, and international studies. The school has an enrollment of more than 35,000, attracting students from the community and across the U.S. as well as international students. The university's basketball team is a big draw as well. Jim Henson, one of the school's most famous and fondly remembered graduates, created the Muppets.

## Glen Echo Park

7300 MacArthur Blvd, Glen Echo, MD. ☎ (301) 492-6229. Web: www. nps.gov/ glec. For recorded information about events, ☎ (301) 492-6282. Discovery Creek

Museum, ☎ (301) 364-3111. Adventure Theater, ☎ (301) 320-5331. Visitor Center open Mon–Fri 9–5.

Glen Echo Park began as a Chautauqua Assembly, then became the amusement park destination for Washington families, and is now a National Park Service arts and cultural center. The park, viewed by some as an artist colony nestled among the silent remains (bumper car rides and penny arcades) of the amusement park's heyday, seems to be always teetering on the verge of demolition, but then a miracle happens. Currently that miracle is coming in the form of $6.3 million from the Montgomery County Council for renovations scheduled to start sometime in 2000.

The park opened in 1891 as the National Chautauqua Assembly, the inspiration, or gimmick, of two brother developers, Edwin and Edward Baltzley, who thought having a chautauqua nearby would promote the sale of land and housing in the area. In the nearby town of Glen Echo are the Victorian houses the brothers built. The Chautauqua movement's purpose was to promote liberal and practical education among the masses. The Baltzley's chautauqua went out of business after one year, when an untrue rumor that a teacher had died of malaria greatly discouraged attendance.

From 1893 to 1898, the brothers rented the park to organizations presenting entertainments of various kinds, and then in 1899 they rented it to the Glen Echo Company, which turned the site into an amusement park. The handcarved Dentzel Carousel arrived in 1921, and soon afterward the Crystal Swimming Pool. The Spanish Ballroom was built in the 1930s. During World War II and into the 1950s, visitors to the park traveled by trolley from Union Station. The social and racial upheavals of the 1960s finally brought about the park's closing in 1968.

The park stood empty until 1971 when it was acquired by the federal government. The government decided to turn Glen Echo into an educational and cultural forum where artists, students, teachers, and visitors could mingle and learn from each other. Artists groups were invited to move into the buildings and repair and refurbish them in exchange for agreeing to open their facilities to the public, and for offering classes and free demonstrations or performances.

Artists exhibit their works in the **Old Stone Tower,** the only usable structure to survive from the Chautauqua Assembly. During the spring and summer, the **Dentzel Carousel** is in operation. Between March and Nov, there are dances and dance lessons on weekends in the **Spanish Ballroom.** Year-round there are theater performances for children in the **Adventure Theatre.** Adults can take classes and workshops in dance and the visual and performance arts. In Dec 1998, the park's newest attraction, the **Discovery Creek Children's Museum** opened, offering nature demonstrations and hands-on learning on the weekends. Workshops on changing topics are offered Sat at 10 (ages 3–5) and 11 (ages 3–11), and tours of changing exhibits are offered Sat at 1 and 2, and Sun at 12, 1, and 2.

## Clara Barton House

5801 Oxford Rd, Glen Echo, MD. ☎ (301) 492-6245. Web: www.nps.gov/clba. Open daily 10–4 by tour only; tours every hour. Admission: free.

Adjacent to the park is the Clara Barton House (late 1800s; Edwin and Edward Baltzley). This Victorian house was the final home of the founder of the Red Cross,

Clara Barton, and the property served as the Red Cross's first permanent headquarters from 1897 to 1904. The building has been preserved as authentically as possible, with many of Barton's original furnishings and period pieces.

## Goddard Space Flight Center Visitor Center

Baltimore-Washington Pkwy and Greenbelt Rd, Greenbelt, MD. ☎ (301) 286-8981. Web: www.gsfc.nasa.gov. Open daily 9–4. Guided tours Mon–Sat 11:30 and 2:30. Admission: free. Restrooms. Wheelchair accessible.

The National Aeronautics and Space Administration's (NASA) Goddard Space Flight Center was established in 1959, one year after NASA was founded, during the nascent period of America's space program. The center now encompasses 32 buildings on 1,270 acres, where its scientists and technicians create, build, test, launch, and operate satellite projects and monitor spaceships circling the Earth.

At the Visitor Center, spacecraft, articles from previous space flights, and exhibits about America's space program are on display, and guided tours of the facility are available. Visitors are shown the **Hubble Space Telescope Control Center** (and can see images coming back from the Hubble Telescope in deep space) and the **NASA Communications Center.** Model rockets by local enthusiasts are launched the first and third Sun of every month at 1 P.M. Launches (such as those from Cape Canaveral) can be seen on a viewing screen by the public at Goddard, but individuals have to be cleared through the Visitor Center prior to the day of the launch.

## National Weather Service Science and History Center Exhibit

1325 East-West Hwy, Silver Spring, MD. ☎ (301) 713-0622. Open Mon–Fri 8:30–5. Admission: free.

The National Weather Service Science and History Center Exhibit is for the true weather buff; others will be disappointed as the exhibit is a very small, one-room display of the tools used by the National Oceanic and Atmospheric Administration (NOAA) to provide weather reports and forecasts. On view are a remote data collector and TOTO (Totable Tornado Observatory), a robotlike device used to study tornadoes. An original U.S. Weather Bureau office, c. 1891, is also on display, with original furnishings and meteorological instruments.

## Paul E. Garber Preservation, Restoration, and Storage Facility

Old Silver Rd at St. Barnabas Rd in Suitland, MD. ☎ (301) 357-1400. Web: www.nasm.edu. Admission: free. Three-hour tours Mon–Fri at 10; Sat–Sun 10 and 1. Reservations must be made at least two weeks in advance, either by calling ☎ 357-1400 (the Smithsonian main number) or by writing to Smithsonian Institution, attn: Reservation Office, Educational Services Division, MRC-305, National Air and Space Museum, Washington, D.C. 20560. The tour is for those 14 and older. The facility is unheated in winter and not air-conditioned in summer.

This site is where the Smithsonian restores and stores aircraft, spacecraft, and other aviation artifacts. Although the facility has been in use since the early 1950s when the Smithsonian had to clear out its storage buildings at what is now O'Hare Airport in Chicago for use by the army during the Korean War, the current facility's low hangar-type metal buildings weren't opened to the public until 1977. The current tour includes a behind-the-scenes look at the workshop where all phases of restoration are handled. It takes from 2,000 to 30,000 work hours to restore an aircraft or spacecraft to its original condition. Visitors can see many of the 135 aircraft, spacecraft, engines, propellers, and models on site.

Among the historic aircraft on view are a Soviet MiG-15 and a Battle of Britain World War II Hawker Hurricane IIc. In 1980 the National Air and Space Museum (NASM) renamed this facility—originally known as the Silver Hill Restoration Facility—in honor of Paul E. Garber (1899–1992), head curator of the Aeronautics Division of the Smithsonian. A new NASM facility is scheduled to open at Washington Dulles International Airport in 2003, where visitors will be able to see many more aviation artifacts in addition to those currently on display at the Paul Garber Facility.

# Additional Sites of Interest in Virginia

## National Firearms Museum

11250 Waples Mill Rd, Fairfax, VA. Located on the first floor of the National Rifle Association (NRA) headquarters. ☎ (703) 267-1600. Web: www.nrahq.org. Open daily 10–4. Closed major holidays. Admission: free, but donations encouraged. Restrooms. Museum shop. Wheelchair accessible.

More than 2,000 firearms dating from 1350 to the present day are on permanent display in 13 galleries that simulate the history of eras such as the American colonial period, the American West, World War I, and Operation Desert Storm. Firearms brought to America on the *Mayflower* and those used by the Buffalo Soldiers in the West are exhibited. Also here are a restored Coney Island shooting gallery and a replica of a Civil War arms factory. Information about all the firearms on display is available from 14 interactive computer terminals located throughout the museum.

# 35 · Day Trips

Washington, D.C., is within easy reach of Baltimore and Annapolis, as well as many Civil War and historical sites.

## Civil War Sites

All of the following Civil War battle sites are administered by the National Park Service. Additional information is available from the park service Web site at www.nps.gov.

## Antietam National Battlefield

Sharpsburg, Maryland. ☎ (301) 432-5124. Park open daily summer 8:30–6; winter 8:30–5. Closed Thanksgiving, Christmas Day, and New Year's Day. Admission: entrance fee. Wheelchair accessible. Gift shop. Restrooms. Restaurants in town.

Directions: Take Rte. 270 north to Frederick, Maryland; from Frederick, take I-70 west to Hagerstown; at Hagerstown, take Rte. 65 south and follow the signs to the Antietam Visitor Center. Parking available at the center.

The Battle of Antietam, fought on Sept 17, 1862, was the bloodiest day of the Civil War, with over 23,000 casualties. Neither side could claim a decisive victory, but the fact that Union forces prevented General Lee's army from advancing into the North was seen as enough of a victory that President Lincoln could issue the Emancipation Proclamation four months later, on Jan 1, 1863. Antietam is one of the best-preserved Civil War battle sites. An audiocassette explaining the major engagements of the battle can be rented and used when you're driving or walking around the battlefield. The **Visitor Center** has an extensive display explaining the battle.

## Gettysburg National Military Park

Gettysburg, Pennsylvania. ☎ (717) 334-1124. Park open daily 6–10. Visitor Center open daily winter 8–5; summer 8–6. Closed Thanksgiving, Christmas Day, and New Year's Day. Admission: entrance fee. Wheelchair accessible. Gift shop. Restrooms. Restaurants in town.

Directions: Take Rte. 495 north to the 270 exit; take 270 north to Frederick, Maryland; at Frederick, take 15 north to Gettysburg; take the second exit (134) to the Visitor Center. Parking available at the center.

The Battle of Gettysburg, fought July 1–3, 1863, was the most decisive engagement of the American Civil War and the most famous. Millions of visitors from all over the world come to Gettysburg National Military Park to see the field across which Pickett's men made their fateful charge, or to visit the site of President Lincoln's Gettysburg Address in Gettysburg National Cemetery. The town, in effect, has become a large shopping and restaurant appendage to the park, although the outer area is still largely a farming community. Traffic is always heavy and attractions crowded, but for those interested in the American Civil War, this is the one to visit.

Auto-tape tours on audiocassette are available for rent, and guides will accompany visitors in their cars, explaining the battle in detail. Despite the comprehensive detail of these tours, it's always good to get out of the car. Walk along the trails or try a bicycle or horseback riding tour. The **Visitor Center** offers a 30-minute presentation using a lit board to explain exactly what happened in the three-day battle. The **Cyclorama Center** features a 360 ft long circular oil-on-canvas painting (completed in 1884) and a sound-and-light program depicting Pickett's Charge, as well as a film on the battle.

Shuttle buses depart from the Visitor Center to the **Eisenhower National Historic Site,** the farmhouse home of President and Mrs. Dwight Eisenhower during his retirement. For information about buses and tours, call ☎ (717) 338-9114.

## Fredericksburg and Spotsylvania National Military Park

Fredericksburg, Virginia. ☎ (540) 371-0802. Park open daily 9–7. Closed Thanksgiving, Christmas Day, and New Year's Day. Admission: entrance fee. Wheelchair accessible. Gift shop. Restrooms. Restaurants in town.

Directions: Take I-95 south to the Fredericksburg exit (130); from 130, take the Rte. 3 east exit; follow Rte. 3 to the seventh traffic light and turn left onto Lafayette Blvd; follow Lafayette Blvd. to the Fredericksburg Visitor Center. Parking is available at the center.

Because of a simple fact of geography—the city of Fredericksburg is the midpoint between the cities of Washington, D.C., and Richmond—four major battles were fought in this area between 1862 and 1864: Fredericksburg, Chancellorsville, Spotsylvania Court House, and the Wilderness. The National Military Park stretches for more than 7,800 acres. The drive within and between the four parks is about 75 miles.

The Battle of Fredericksburg took place Dec 11–15, 1862. The Fredericksburg Battlefield includes the Marye's Heights National Cemetery, the Lee Hill Exhibit Shelter, and the Old Salem Church. The **Chancellorsville Battlefield**, where fighting occurred April 27–May 6, 1863, was the site of strategic military maneuvers by Generals Robert E. Lee and Thomas J. "Stonewall" Jackson. Jackson died after being wounded by friendly fire at Chancellorsville. The Wilderness Church is on this battlefield. In the Wilderness Battle, fought May 5–6, 1864, Generals Ulysses S. Grant and Robert E. Lee confronted each other. The **Wilderness Battlefield** has a Wilderness Exhibit Shelter and the Wilderness Tavern. From May 8–21, 1864, Confederate and Union troops engaged in some of the most intense hand-to-hand fighting of the war on the **Spotsylvania Battlefield.** The battlefield includes the Spotsylvania Court House and the Spotsylvania Confederate Cemetery.

The town of Fredericksburg is also of interest for its colonial history. This was George Washington's boyhood home, and James Monroe practiced law here. For information about town attractions, call the Visitor Center, ☎ (703) 373-1776.

## Manassas (Bull Run) National Battlefield Park

Manassas, Virginia. ☎ (703) 361-1339. Park open daily 8:30–5. Closed Thanksgiving Day, Christmas Day, and New Year's Day. Admission: entrance fee. Wheelchair accessible. Gift shop. Restrooms. Restaurants in town.

Directions: Take I-66 to exit 47B onto Rte. 234 north; follow 234 to the Visitor Center. Parking is available at the center.

Two battles were fought here, a year apart. They were called Manassas by the Confederate forces and Bull Run by the Union forces. The first battle (July 21, 1861) was won decisively by the Confederacy and shocked the North, especially those picnickers from Washington who had driven from town to see the "fun." What they saw was a Confederate Army that refused to withdraw, led on by Brigadier General Thomas J. Jackson, who earned his nickname here when another commander exclaimed during battle, "There stands Jackson like a stonewall!"

The second battle (Aug 28–30, 1862) was less decisive but nevertheless also a Confederate victory, as Robert E. Lee defeated a larger and better equipped Union army. The same might be said of Manassas area residents who, during the 1990s, found themselves increasingly encroached upon by developers. It was during this decade that Manassas became, in effect, a bedroom community of Washington, D.C., but a small victory was won when a major shopping center was stopped in its tracks by community activists, including one grandmother who stepped in front of the bulldozers and declared that her grandchildren didn't need another shopping mall. Instead, it was better to preserve the ground upon which Union and Confederate soldiers had died.

There's always heavy traffic around Manassas, especially on the weekends.

# Annapolis, Maryland

**Visitor Center,** 160 Duke of Gloucester St, Annapolis, MD. ☎ (410) 263-7940.
Directions: Take Rte. 50 (New York Ave) to exit 24.

The word *charming* might have been invented to describe the town of Annapolis, although that is the last word that comes to mind when driving around and around on a Sat afternoon looking for a parking space. Known as the Sailboat Capital of the World, Annapolis is also the state capital of Maryland (a fact people usually forget) and the home of the U.S. Naval Academy (hard to forget with all the midshipmen wandering around town in their navy whites and blues). Annapolis also served as the capital of the fledgling United States of America from 1783 to 1784. It may be that the best reason to visit Annapolis is to sit at a restaurant by the water eating crab cakes and watching the parade of sailboats.

Other points of interest include:

**Maryland State House,** on State Circle; ☎ (410) 974-3400. The oldest state capitol in continual use and the one where the Treaty of Paris, which officially ended the Revolutionary War, was ratified. Free guided tours are available daily 11–3.

**U.S. Naval Academy.** Enter through Gate 1 at the junction of King George and Randall Sts. ☎ (410) 292-3363. Web: www.nadn.navy.mil. Visitor Center open Mar–Nov 9–5; Dec–Feb 9–4. Guided tours available. Museum open Mon–Sat 9–5; Sun 11–5.

# Baltimore, Maryland

**Visitors Center,** 451 Light St, Baltimore, MD. ☎ (410) 837-4636 or (800) 282-6632. Web: www.baltimore.org. Open 8:30–5.
Directions: Take I-95 north to I-395 and the downtown area.

Baltimore is one of the oldest and most historic cities in the United States, as well as being one of the country's largest seaports and the birthplace of the national anthem. Francis Scott Key wrote the lyrics to "The Star-Spangled Banner" while witnessing the British attack on Fort McHenry in 1814.

Baltimore's Inner Harbor draws millions of visitors a year to its **National Aquarium,** ☎ (410) 576-3800; the **Maryland Science Center,** ☎ (410) 685-5225; the **Baltimore Maritime Museum,** ☎ (410) 396-3854; **Port Discovery—the Children's Museum,** ☎ (410) 727-8120; and Harborplace, a shopping complex. Just 40 minutes from downtown Washington (on a good-traffic day), Baltimore also has art galleries, historic monuments, Edgar Allan Poe's grave, and the Baltimore Orioles.

Additional highlights include:

**Fort McHenry National Monument,** at the end of E. Fort Ave; ☎ (410) 962-4290. Web: www.nps.gov. Open daily 8–4:45. Closed Thanksgiving, Christmas Day, and New Year's Day.

**Walters Art Gallery,** 600 N. Charles St; ☎ (410) 547-9000. Open Tues–Sun 11–5. Admission fee. A collection that spans 5,000 years of art.

**B&O Railroad Museum,** 901 W. Pratt St; ☎ (410) 752-2464. Open daily 10–5. Admission fee. Over 120 train cars and engines.

**Edgar Allan Poe's Grave,** Westminster Churchyard at Fayette and Green Sts.

# Index

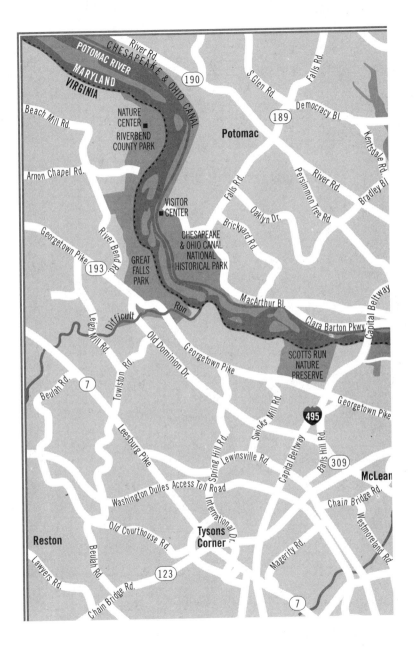

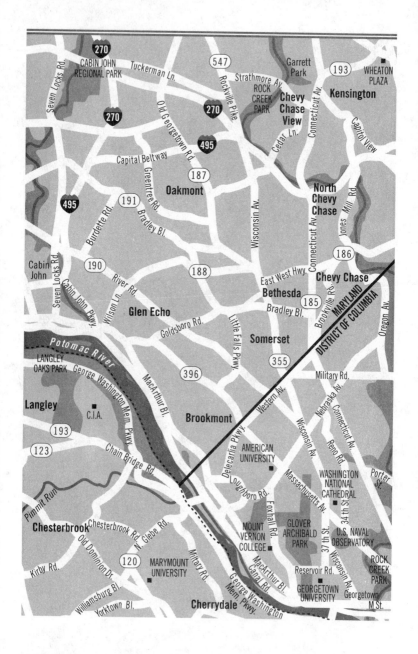

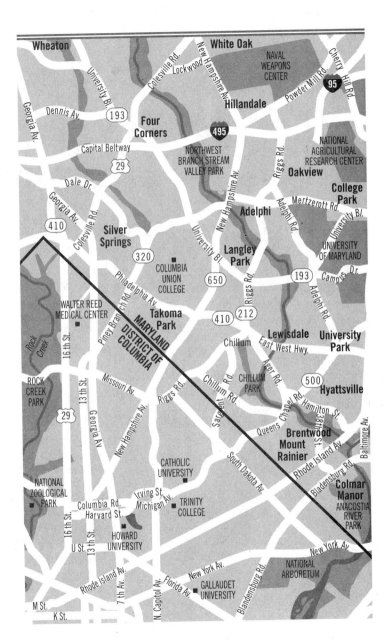

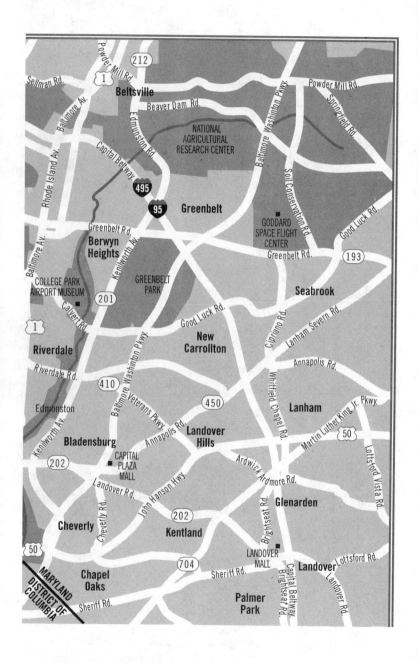

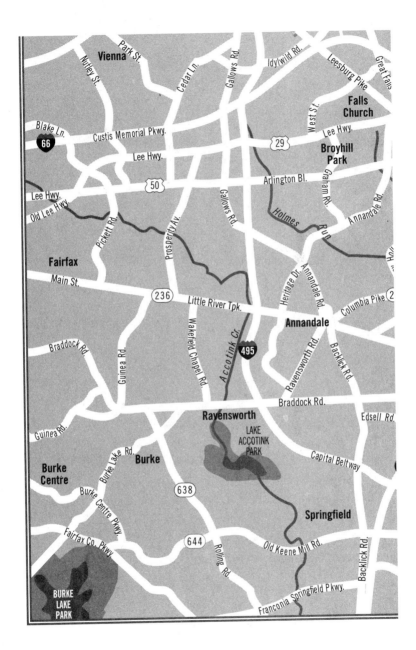

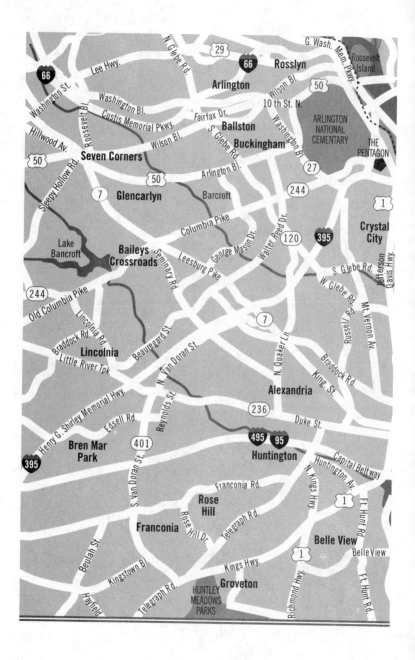

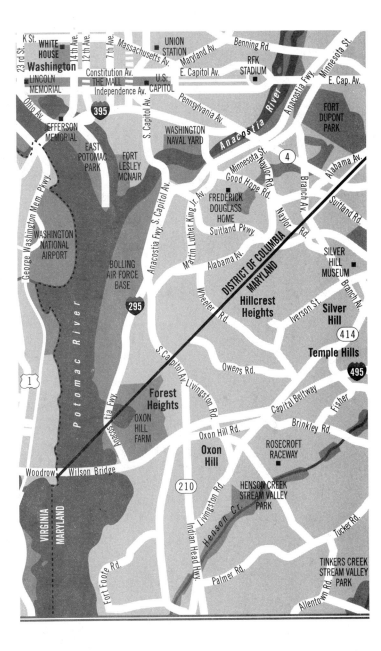

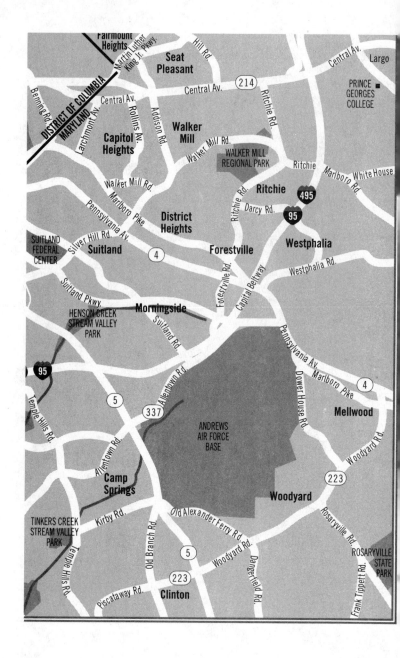

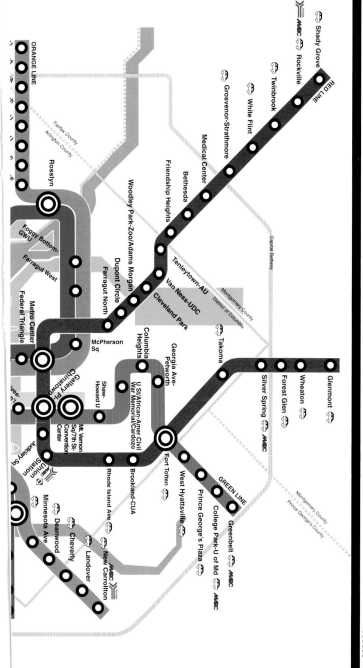

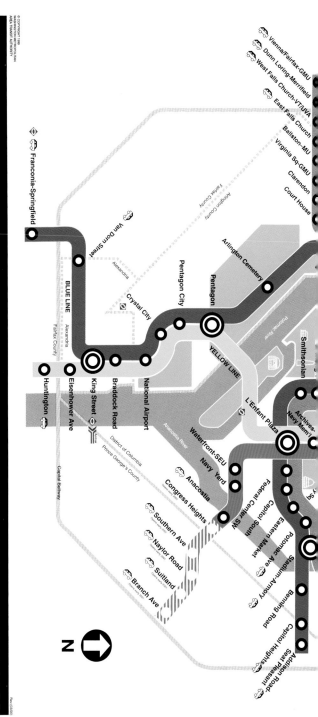

**No Smoking**

**No Food or Drinks**

**No Animals** (except service animals)

**No Audio or Video Devices** (without earphones)

**No Litter or Spitting**

**No Dangerous or Flammable Materials**

Map supplied courtesy of the Washington Metropolitan Area Transit Authority.

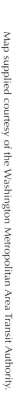